DRAMA
CRITICISM

Guide to Gale Literary Criticism Series

For criticism on	Consult these Gale series
Authors now living or who died after December 31, 1999	**CONTEMPORARY LITERARY CRITICISM (CLC)**
Authors who died between 1900 and 1999	**TWENTIETH-CENTURY LITERARY CRITICISM (TCLC)**
Authors who died between 1800 and 1899	**NINETEENTH-CENTURY LITERATURE CRITICISM (NCLC)**
Authors who died between 1400 and 1799	**LITERATURE CRITICISM FROM 1400 TO 1800 (LC)** **SHAKESPEAREAN CRITICISM (SC)**
Authors who died before 1400	**CLASSICAL AND MEDIEVAL LITERATURE CRITICISM (CMLC)**
Authors of books for children and young adults	**CHILDREN'S LITERATURE REVIEW (CLR)**
Dramatists	**DRAMA CRITICISM (DC)**
Poets	**POETRY CRITICISM (PC)**
Short story writers	**SHORT STORY CRITICISM (SSC)**
Literary topics and movements	**HARLEM RENAISSANCE: A GALE CRITICAL COMPANION (HR)** **THE BEAT GENERATION: A GALE CRITICAL COMPANION (BG)**
Asian American writers of the last two hundred years	**ASIAN AMERICAN LITERATURE (AAL)**
Black writers of the past two hundred years	**BLACK LITERATURE CRITICISM (BLC)** **BLACK LITERATURE CRITICISM SUPPLEMENT (BLCS)**
Hispanic writers of the late nineteenth and twentieth centuries	**HISPANIC LITERATURE CRITICISM (HLC)** **HISPANIC LITERATURE CRITICISM SUPPLEMENT (HLCS)**
Native North American writers and orators of the eighteenth, nineteenth, and twentieth centuries	**NATIVE NORTH AMERICAN LITERATURE (NNAL)**
Major authors from the Renaissance to the present	**WORLD LITERATURE CRITICISM, 1500 TO THE PRESENT (WLC)** **WORLD LITERATURE CRITICISM SUPPLEMENT (WLCS)**

ISSN 1056-4349

DRAMA
CRITICISM

Criticism of the Most Significant and Widely Studied
Dramatic Works from All the World's Literatures

VOLUME 21

Janet Witalec
Project Editor

GALE®

THOMSON
─────✳─────™
GALE

Detroit • New York • San Diego • San Francisco • Cleveland • New Haven, Conn. • Waterville, Maine • London • Munich

THOMSON
—★—
GALE

Drama Criticism, Vol. 21

Project Editor
Janet Witalec

Editorial
Tom Burns, Scott Darga, Kathy D. Darrow,
Rebecca Long, Lemma Shomali, Timothy J. Sisler

Research
Michelle Campbell, Tracie A. Richardson

Indexing Services
Synapse, the Knowledge Link Corporation

Permissions
Shalice Shah-Caldwell, Emma Hull

Imaging and Multimedia
Dean Dauphinais, Lezlie Light, Dan Newell,
Dave Oblender, Luke Rademacher

Composition and Electronic Capture
Carolyn Roney

Manufacturing
Stacy L. Melson

LIBRARY OF CONGRESS CATALOG CARD NUMBER 76-46132

ISBN 0-7876-6811-7
ISSN 1056-4349

Printed in the United States of America
10 9 8 7 6 5 4 3 2 1

Contents

Preface

Drama Criticism (*DC*) is principally intended for beginning students of literature and theater as well as the average playgoer. The series is therefore designed to introduce readers to the most frequently studied playwrights of all time periods and nationalities and to present discerning commentary on dramatic works of enduring interest. Furthermore, *DC* seeks to acquaint the reader with the uses and functions of criticism itself. Selected from a diverse body of commentary, the essays in *DC* offer insights into the authors and their works but do not require that the reader possess a wide background in literary studies. Where appropriate, reviews of important productions of the plays discussed are also included to give students a heightened awareness of drama as a dynamic art form, one that many claim is fully realized only in performance.

DC was created in response to suggestions by the staffs of high school, college, and public libraries. These librarians observed a need for a series that assembles critical commentary on the world's most renowned dramatists in the same manner as Gale's *Short Story Criticism* (*SSC*) and *Poetry Criticism* (*PC*), which present material on writers of short fiction and poetry. Although playwrights are covered in such Gale literary criticism series as *Contemporary Literary Criticism* (*CLC*), *Twentieth-Century Literary Criticism* (*TCLC*), *Nineteenth-Century Literature Criticism* (*NCLC*), *Literature Criticism from 1400 to 1800* (*LC*), and *Classical and Medieval Literature Criticism* (*CMLC*), *DC* directs more concentrated attention on individual dramatists than is possible in the broader, survey-oriented entries in these Gale series. Commentary on the works of William Shakespeare may be found in *Shakespearean Criticism* (*SC*).

Scope of the Series

By collecting and organizing commentary on dramatists, *DC* assists students in their efforts to gain insight into literature, achieve better understanding of the texts, and formulate ideas for papers and assignments. A variety of interpretations and assessments is offered, allowing students to pursue their own interests and promoting awareness that literature is dynamic and responsive to many different opinions.

Approximately five to ten authors are included in each volume, and each entry presents a historical survey of the critical response to that playwright's work. The length of an entry is intended to reflect the amount of critical attention the author has received from critics writing in English and from foreign critics in translation. Every attempt has been made to identify and include the most significant essays on each author's work. In order to provide these important critical pieces, the editors sometimes reprint essays that have appeared elsewhere in Gale's literary criticism series. Such duplication, however, never exceeds twenty percent of a *DC* volume.

Organization of the Book

A *DC* entry consists of the following elements:

- The **Author Heading** consists of the playwright's most commonly used name, followed by birth and death dates. If an author consistently wrote under a pseudonym, the pseudonym is listed in the author heading and the real name given in parentheses on the first line of the introduction. Also located at the beginning of the introduction are any name variations under which the dramatist wrote, including transliterated forms of the names of authors whose languages use nonroman alphabets.

- The **Introduction** contains background information that introduces the reader to the author and the critical debates surrounding his or her work.

- A **Portrait of the Author** is included when available.

- The list of **Principal Works** is divided into two sections. The first section contains the author's dramatic pieces and is organized chronologically by date of first performance. If this has not been conclusively determined, the composition or publication date is used. The second section provides information on the author's major works in other genres.

- Essays offering **overviews and general studies of the dramatist's entire literary career** give the student broad perspectives on the writer's artistic development, themes, and concerns that recur in several of his or her works, the author's place in literary history, and other wide-ranging topics.

- **Criticism** of individual plays offers the reader in-depth discussions of a select number of the author's most important works. In some cases, the criticism is divided into two sections, each arranged chronologically. When a significant performance of a play can be identified (typically, the premier of a twentieth-century work), the first section of criticism will feature **production reviews** of this staging. Most entries include sections devoted to **critical commentary** that assesses the literary merit of the selected plays. When necessary, essays are carefully excerpted to focus on the work under consideration; often, however, essays and reviews are reprinted in their entirety. Footnotes are reprinted at the end of each essay or excerpt. In the case of excerpted criticism, only those footnotes that pertain to the excerpted texts are included.

- Critical essays are prefaced by brief **Annotations** explicating each piece.

- A complete **Bibliographic Citation,** designed to help the interested reader locate the original essay or book, precedes each piece of criticism. Source citations in the Literary Criticism Series follow University of Chicago Press style, as outlined in *The Chicago Manual of Style,* 14th ed. (Chicago: The University of Chicago Press, 1993).

- An annotated bibliography of **Further Reading** appears at the end of each entry and suggests resources for additional study. In some cases, significant essays for which the editors could not obtain reprint rights are included here. Boxed material following the further reading list provides references to other biographical and critical sources on the author in series published by Gale.

Cumulative Indexes

A **Cumulative Author Index** lists all of the authors that appear in a wide variety of reference sources published by the Gale Group, including *DC*. A complete list of these sources is found facing the first page of the Author Index. The index also includes birth and death dates and cross references between pseudonyms and actual names.

A **Cumulative Nationality Index** lists all authors featured in *DC* by nationality, followed by the number of the *DC* volume in which their entry appears.

A **Cumulative Title Index** lists in alphabetical order the individual plays discussed in the criticism contained in *DC*. Each title is followed by the author's last name and corresponding volume and page numbers where commentary on the work is located. English-language translations of original foreign-language titles are cross-referenced to the foreign titles so that all references to discussion of a work are combined in one listing.

Citing *Drama Criticism*

When citing criticism reprinted in the Literary Criticism Series, students should provide complete bibliographic information so that the cited essay can be located in the original print or electronic source. Students who quote directly from reprinted criticism may use any accepted bibliographic format, such as University of Chicago Press style or Modern Language Association (MLA) style. Both the MLA and the University of Chicago formats are acceptable and recognized as being the current standards for citations. It is important, however, to choose one format for all citations; do not mix the two formats within a list of citations.

The examples below follow recommendations for preparing a bibliography set forth in *The Chicago Manual of Style,* 14th ed. (Chicago: The University of Chicago Press, 1993); the first example pertains to material drawn from periodicals, the second to material reprinted from books:

Morrison, Jago. "Narration and Unease in Ian McEwan's Later Fiction." *Critique* 42, no. 3 (spring 2001): 253-68. Reprinted in *Drama Criticism.* Vol. 19, edited by Janet Witalec, 212-20. Detroit: Gale, 2003.

Brossard, Nicole. "Poetic Politics." In *The Politics of Poetic Form: Poetry and Public Policy,* edited by Charles Bernstein, 73-82. New York: Roof Books, 1990. Reprinted in *Drama Criticism.* Vol. 19, edited by Janet Witalec, 3-8. Detroit: Gale, 2003.

The examples below follow recommendations for preparing a works cited list set forth in the *MLA Handbook for Writers of Research Papers,* 5th ed. (New York: The Modern Language Association of America, 1999); the first example pertains to material drawn from periodicals, the second to material reprinted from books:

Morrison, Jago. "Narration and Unease in Ian McEwan's Later Fiction." *Critique* 42.3 (spring 2001): 253-68. Reprinted in *Drama Criticism* Ed. Janet Witalec. Vol. 19. Detroit: Gale, 2003. 212-20.

Brossard, Nicole. "Poetic Politics." *The Politics of Poetic Form: Poetry and Public Policy.* Ed. Charles Bernstein. New York: Roof Books, 1990. 73-82. Reprinted in *Drama Criticism.* Ed. Janet Witalec.Vol. 19. Detroit: Gale, 2003. 3-8.

Suggestions are Welcome

Readers who wish to suggest new features, topics, or authors to appear in future volumes, or who have other suggestions or comments are cordially invited to call, write, or fax the Project Editor:

Project Editor, Literary Criticism Series
The Gale Group
27500 Drake Road
Farmington Hills, MI 48331-3535
1-800-347-4253 (GALE)
Fax: 248-699-8054

Acknowledgments

The editors wish to thank the copyright holders of the excerpted criticism included in this volume and the permissions managers of many book and magazine publishing companies for assisting us in securing reproduction rights. We are also grateful to the staffs of the Detroit Public Library, the Library of Congress, the University of Detroit Mercy Library, Wayne State University Purdy/Kresge Library Complex, and the University of Michigan Libraries for making their resources available to us. Following is a list of the copyright holders who have granted us permission to reproduce material in this volume of *DC*. Every effort has been made to trace copyright, but if omissions have been made, please let us know.

COPYRIGHTED MATERIAL IN *DC*, VOLUME 21, WAS REPRODUCED FROM THE FOLLOWING PERIODICALS:

Colloquia Germanica, v. 14, 1981 for "Hebbel and Georg Kaiser: Reflections of 'Judith' in 'Die Burger von Calais'" by George C. Tunstall. Copyright © 1981. Reproduced by permission of the author.—*The Commonweal,* February 12, 1954; December 23, 1955; November 8, 1963. Copyright © 1954, renewed 1982; copyright © 1955, renewed 1983; copyright © 1963, renewed 1991 by Commonweal Publishing Co., Inc. All reproduced by permission of Commonweal Foundation. For subscriptions, www.commonwealmagazine.org.—*Comparative Drama,* v. 8, Fall, 1974. Copyright © 1974 by the Editors of *Comparative Drama.* Reproduced by permission.—*Euphorion,* 1966. Copyright © 1966. Reproduced by permission.— *The French Review,* v. 55, December, 1981; v. 59, February, 1986; v. 63, October, 1989; v. 63, February, 1990; v. 67, March, 1994; v. 72, December, 1998. Copyright © 1981, 1986, 1989, 1990, 1994, 1998 by the American Association of Teachers of French. All reproduced by permission.—*French Studies,* v. 47, April, 1993. Copyright © 1993. Reproduced by permission.—*Hebbel-Jahrbuch 1969,* 1969. Copyright © 1969. Reproduced by permission.—*Hebbel-Jahrbuch 1977,* 1977. Copyright © 1977. Reproduced by permission.—*MLN,* v. 79, October, 1964; v. 87, October, 1972. Copyright © 1964, renewed 1992; copyright © 1972 by The Johns Hopkins University Press. Both reproduced by permission.—*Modern Drama,* v. 6, December, 1963; v. 8, December, 1965; v. 29, December, 1986. Copyright © 1963, 1965, 1986 by University of Toronto, Graduate Centre for Study of Drama. All reproduced by permission.—*Modern Language Review,* v. 77, July, 1982; v. 81, January, 1986. Copyright © 1982, 1986 by Modern Humanities Research Association. Both reproduced by permission of the publisher and the respective authors.—*The Nation, (New York),* May 27, 1961; October 5, 1964; October 8, 1973. Copyright © 1961, renewed 1989; copyright © 1964, renewed 1992; copyright © 1973 by The Nation magazine/ The Nation Company, Inc. Renewed 1989. All reproduced by permission.—*New German Studies,* v. 12, Summer, 1984. Copyright © 1984. Reproduced by permission.—*The New Republic,* January 25, 1954; December 5, 1955. Copyright © 1954, 1955, both renewed 1983 by The New Republic, Inc. Both reproduced by permission of *The New Republic.*—*Orbis Litterarum,* v. 28, 1973. Copyright © 1973 by Munksgaard International Publishers, Ltd. Reproduced by permission.— *Papers on French Seventeenth Century Literature,* v. 9, 1982; v. 10, 1983; v. 11, 1984; v. 15, 1988; v. 25, 1998. Copyright © 1982, 1983, 1984, 1988, 1998. All reproduced by permission.—*Romance Notes,* v. 22, Winter, 1981. Copyright © 1981. Reproduced by permission.—*South Atlantic Bulletin,* v. 33, May, 1968. Copyright © 1968. Reproduced by permission.—*Theatre Journal,* v. 34, October, 1982. Copyright © 1982 by University and College Theatre Association of the American Theatre Association. Reproduced by permission of The Johns Hopkins University Press.

COPYRIGHTED MATERIAL IN *DC*, VOLUME 21, WAS REPRODUCED FROM THE FOLLOWING BOOKS:

Amoia, Alba. From *Twentieth-Century European Drama.* Edited by Brian Docherty. St. Martin's Press, 1994. Copyright © 1994 by Brian Docherty, ed. All rights reserved. Reproduced by permission of Palgrave Macmillan.—Carlson, Marvin. From *The French Stage in the Nineteenth Century.* The Scarecrow Press, Inc., 1972. Copyright © 1972 by Marvin Carlson. All rights reserved. Reproduced by permission.—Carrington, Ildiko de Papp. From *The Rest of the Story: Critical Essays on Alice Munro.* Edited by Robert Thacker. ECW Press, 1999. Copyright © 1999 by ECW Press. All rights reserved. Reproduced by permission.—Greenberg, Mitchell. From *Corneille, Classicism and The Ruse of Symmetry.* Cambridge University Press, 1986. Copyright © 1986 by Cambridge University Press. All rights reserved. Reproduced by permission from Cambridge University Press and the author.—Harris, Brian. From *From the Bard to Broadway: The University of Florida Department of Classics Comparative Drama Conference Papers, Volume VII.* Edited by Karelisa V. Hartigan. University Press of America, 1987. Copyright © 1987 by University Press of America, Inc. All rights reserved. Reproduced by permission.—Hubert, Judd D. From *Convergences: Rhetoric and Poetic in Seventeenth-Century France, Essays for*

Hugh M. Davidson. Edited by David Lee Rubin and Mary B. McKinley. Ohio State University Press, 1989. Copyright © 1989 by Ohio State University Press. All rights reserved. Reproduced by permission.—Hubert, Judd D. From *Corneille's Performative Metaphors.* Rookwood Press, 1997. Copyright © 1997 by Rookwood Press, Inc. All rights reserved. Reproduced by permission.—Huneker, James. From *Iconoclasts: A Book of Dramatists.* Charles Scribner's Sons, 1922. Copyright © 1905 by Charles Scribner's Sons. All rights reserved. Reproduced by permission.—Knutsen, Harold C. From *Corneille Comique: Nine Studies of Pierre Corneille's Comedy with an Introduction and a Bibliography.* Edited by Milorad R. Margitic. Papers on French Literature, 1982. Copyright © 1982 by PFSCL. All rights reserved. Reproduced by permission.—Lob, Ladislaus. From *From Lessing to Hauptmann: Studies in German Drama.* University Tutorial Press, 1974. Copyright © 1974 by Ladislaus Lob. All rights reserved. Reproduced by permission.—McFarlane, Ian. From *The Equilibrium of Wit: Essays for Odette de Mourgues.* Edited by Peter Bayley and Dorothy Gabe Coleman. French Forum, 1982. Copyright © 1982 by French Forum, Publishers, Incorporated. All rights reserved. Reproduced by permission.— Purdie, Edna. From *Friedrich Hebbel: A Study of His Life and Work.* Oxford University Press, 1932. Reproduced by permission of Oxford University Press.—Schuler, Marilyn V. From *Myths and Realities of Contemporary French Theater: Comparative Views.* Edited by Patricia M. Hopkins and Wendell M. Aycock. Texas Tech Press, 1985. Copyright © 1985. Reproduced by permission.

PHOTOGRAPHS APPEARING IN *DC*, VOLUME 21, WERE RECEIVED FROM THE FOLLOWING SOURCES:

Anouilh, Jean, photograph. Copyright © by Bettmann/Corbis. Reproduced by permission.—Becque, Henri, engraving. Copyright © by The Art Archive/Musee Carnavalet Paris/Dagli Orti. Reproduced by permission.—Corneille, Pierre, photograph. Copyright © by The Art Archive/Bibliotheque des Arts Decoratifs Paris/Dagli Orti. Reproduced by permission.— Hebbel, Friedrich, engraving. Copyright © by Archive Photos, Inc. Reproduced by permission.

Literary Criticism Series Advisory Board

The members of the Gale Group Literary Criticism Series Advisory Board—reference librarians and subject specialists from public, academic, and school library systems—represent a cross-section of our customer base and offer a variety of informed perspectives on both the presentation and content of our literature criticism products. Advisory board members assess and define such quality issues as the relevance, currency, and usefulness of the author coverage, critical content, and literary topics included in our series; evaluate the layout, presentation, and general quality of our printed volumes; provide feedback on the criteria used for selecting authors and topics covered in our series; provide suggestions for potential enhancements to our series; identify any gaps in our coverage of authors or literary topics, recommending authors or topics for inclusion; analyze the appropriateness of our content and presentation for various user audiences, such as high school students, undergraduates, graduate students, librarians, and educators; and offer feedback on any proposed changes/enhancements to our series. We wish to thank the following advisors for their advice throughout the year.

Jean Anouilh
1910-1987

(Full name Jean Marie Lucien Pierre Anouilh) French playwright.

The following entry provides an overview of Anouilh's works from 1954 through 1999. For additional information on his career, see *DC*, Volume 8.

INTRODUCTION

One of France's foremost dramatists, Anouilh wrote more than forty plays in a wide variety of modes, including tragedy, farce, and romance. Central to his work is a skeptical, often bitter view of the human condition. Discovering and remaining true to one's self in a world of compromise is a theme that continually resurfaces in Anouilh's work. His protagonists typically strive to maintain their integrity in the face of pervasive corruption; however, success in this endeavor often requires existing in a fantasy world or dying for one's convictions.

BIOGRAPHICAL INFORMATION

Anouilh was born in Bordeaux on June 23, 1910. By the age of nine he was already writing plays in imitation of Edmond Rostand; at sixteen he completed his first long play. He briefly studied law at the Sorbonne in Paris, then became a copywriter in an advertising firm. During 1931 and 1932 Anouilh worked as the secretary to the Comédie des Champs-Élysées theatre company. *Le voyageur sans bagage* (1937; *Traveller without Luggage*) firmly established Anouilh in the theater, and for the next several decades his works were staged in Paris with great regularity, even during the German occupation of France during World War II. After the war many of his plays were produced in London and New York. During his career Anouilh won many awards, in both France and America. Several of his plays have been adapted for film and television. Anouilh died of a heart attack on October 3, 1987.

MAJOR WORKS

Anouilh rejected traditional classifications of his works as tragedies, farces, or romances; instead he categorized his plays as *pièces noires* (black plays), *nouvelles pièces noires* (new black plays), *pièces roses* (rosy plays),

pièces brillantes (brilliant plays), *pièces grinçantes* (grating plays), *pièces costumées* (costume plays), and *pièces baroques* (baroque plays). Anouilh's earliest plays were produced during the 1930s and generally fall in the categories of *pièces noires* and *pièces roses*. As the labels suggest, the former plays are dark in tone and explore evil and deception, while the latter include fantastical elements and convey a light-hearted mood. Among the major conflicts Anouilh addresses in both groups are those between wealth and poverty and the burden of the past as it relates to the present. Beginning in the 1940s Anouilh composed a number of plays, classified as *pièces noires,* that adapt Greek myth to modern settings. These include *Eurydice* (1941; *Point of Departure*), *Antigone* (1944), and *Médée* (1953; *Medea*). *Antigone* was the most popular of the three and remains one of Anouilh's most highly respected works.

Following World War II Anouilh's output was dominated by *pièces grinçantes* and *pièces brillantes*. The *pièces grinçantes* are marked by black humor, while the *pièces brillantes* convey a less bitter tone and employ witty dialogue. In these plays the conflict between good and evil is not as sharply defined as in Anouilh's early work. Among his later plays are *pièces costumées*, which are based on historical personages, and *pièces baroques*. When using history as a background for his drama, Anouilh drew upon figures of heroic dimension. For example, *L'alouette* (1953; *The Lark*) dramatizes the life of Joan of Arc, and *Becket; ou, l'honneur de Dieu* (1959; *Becket; or, The Honor of God*) concerns Thomas à Becket. The theatrical elements of Anouilh's work come to the forefront in his *pièces baroques*. For example, *Cher Antoine; ou, l'amour raté* (1969; *Dear Antoine; or, The Love that Failed*) the central character is a prominent playwright and the story unfolds as a play within a play. By stressing the artificiality of the theater, Anouilh probes the relationship between reality and illusion and works to create a dramatization of ideas rather than a representation of reality.

CRITICAL RECEPTION

Although Anouilh was among the most successful "boulevard" playwrights, having enjoyed many well-attended productions of his works in the Paris theater district, critics have debated his importance in contemporary drama. Some have faulted Anouilh for repetition of theme, for a lack of intellectualism, and for his reliance on theatricality. Others note, however, that Anouilh's strength as a playwright lay in his mastery of stagecraft, which makes his works entertaining, while they at the same time investigate serious themes. Commentators contend that Anouilh's work reflects the classical theater of Molière in its comic portrayal of human folly and misery and the experimental theater of Luigi Pirandello in its overt use of theatrical devices to explore the nature of reality and illusion.

PRINCIPAL WORKS

Plays

L'hermine [*The Ermine*] 1932
Y avait un prisonnier 1935
Le voyageur sans bagage [*Traveller without Luggage*] 1937
Le rendezvous de Senlis [*Dinner with the Family*] 1938
La sauvage [*Restless Heart*] 1938
Léocadia [*Time Remembered*] 1939
Eurydice [*Point of Departure*; also translated as *Legend of Lovers*] 1941

Antigone 1944
Jézabel 1945
Oreste 1945
Roméo et Jeannette 1946
L'invitation au château [*Ring around the Moon: A Charade with Music*] 1947
Ardèle; ou, la Marguerite [*Cry of the Peacock*] 1948
La répétition; ou, l'amour puni [*The Rehearsal*] 1950
Colombe [*Mademoiselle Colombe*] 1951
La valse des toréadors [*The Waltz of the Toreadors*] 1952
L'alouette [*The Lark*] 1953
Médée [*Medea*] 1953
Ornifle; ou, le courant d'air [*Ornifle*; also translated as *It's Later Than You Think*] 1955
Pauvre Bitos; ou, le dîner des têtes [*Poor Bitos*] 1956
Becket; ou, l'honneur de Dieu [*Becket; or, The Honor of God*] 1959
L'hurluberlu; ou, le réactionnaire amoureux [*The Fighting Cock*] 1959
La grotte [*The Cavern*] 1961
La foire d'empoigne 1962
Le boulanger, la boulangère, et le petit mitron 1968
Cher Antoine; ou, l'amour raté [*Dear Antoine; or, The Love that Failed*] 1969
Les poissons rouges ou mon père, ce héros 1970
La culotte 1978

GENERAL COMMENTARY

Alba Della Fazia (essay date December 1963)

SOURCE: Fazia, Alba Della. "Pirandello and His French Echo Anouilh." *Modern Drama* 6, no. 3 (December 1963): 346-67.

[*In the following essay, Fazia finds parallels between the plays of Anouilh and those of the Italian dramatist Luigi Pirandello.*]

"I can just hear a critic whispering into his neighbor's ear that he has already seen this in Pirandello,"[1] anticipates The Author in the opening scene of Jean Anouilh's recent play *La grotte*—a plotless play which has yet to be written and which depends largely on audience cooperation, according to Anouilh.

La grotte's point of departure is a *fait accompli*: the apparent murder of the cook. An investigation of the real cause of death ensues. The Author, a combination of Pirandello's Director in *Sei personaggi in cerca d'autore* and Hinkfuss of *Questa sera si recita a soggetto*, poses, before his audience, the problems of staging an "improvised" play. He wrangles with unruly characters and capricious stage technicians. He dramatizes the conflict between an author's illusory creation and his characters' living reality.

The Pirandello plays which may be considered as having no plot are those plays which present the problems of multiple personality (*Trovarsi, Quando si è qualcuno*, etc.) and those which present the relationships among life, art, and interpretation (*Sei personaggi in cerca d'autore, Questa sera si recita a soggetto, Ciascuno a suo modo*, etc.). These plays are developed through the actions and reactions of the characters and those with whom they come in contact, and through audience participation. A combination of these plotless Pirandello plays is what Anouilh has striven to achieve in **La grotte.**

In constructing their plays, both Pirandello and Anouilh generally use one of two methods. The first method is construction in true *commedia dell'arte* style, with much physical movement, popular joking, games, songs, and dances (*La giara, Liolà, L'Uomo, La bestia e la virtù,* **Le bal des voleurs, La valse des Toréadors, Léocadia**). The procedure is simple: the plot is exposed in direct language by the characters who exit and enter from one scene to the next either to add to the jocosity of events or to intensify the seriousness or mockseriousness of a scene. In *Liolà,* for example, the scenes in which Liolà appears or exits, singing and dancing with his three children, take the form of *commedia dell'arte lazzi* which delight the children and peasants who call for more songs and capers from Liolà, just as the *commedia* audiences demanded encores until poor Harlequin became quite exhausted.

The second method of play construction is the detective story style: deeds are committed prior to the opening of the play, the problem to be solved is posed at the outset and developed during the play like a psychiatric case history (*Sei personaggi, Così è* (*se vi pare*), *Ciascuno a suo modo, Questa sera si recita a soggetto, La morsa, Il dovere del medico,* **Y avait un prisonnier, Le voyageur sans bagage, La grotte, La foire d'empoigne**). The movement in these plays is mental rather than physical, the only lively scenes being those involving a crowd or group of personages whose movement is intended to contrast with the stability of the central character. The acts are linked by cerebral manipulations, as opposed to the *lazzi* of the first group; and the construction of the "detective" play is such that it progresses smoothly, though not outwardly serenely, towards a fixed destiny.

The better to complicate their plots, the better to play with their marionettes, the better to create theatrical kaleidoscopes, both Pirandello and Anouilh construct plays with a play within them. Pirandello employed the technique of the play within a play five times, Anouilh nine times. In some cases, the interpolated play is an actual or imaginary piece of literature; in other cases, it is improvised, directed, or evoked by the characters of the outer play. Of the first group, *Ciascuno a suo modo, Questa sera si recita a soggetto, I giganti della montagna,* **La répétition** and **Colombe** may be cited. *Ciascuno a suo modo* includes a Pirandello play within a Pirandello play. The construction of the drama is very unusual, and the dramatist himself declares at the beginning of the play that the number of acts cannot be specified in view of the unpleasant incidents that will arise during the course of the performance. The first act takes place in the ancient mansion of Donna Livia Palegari. A discussion is going on concerning her son Doro's defense of an actress' reputation against the attacks of his friend Francesco. The two friends, after each has reversed his opinions, challenge each other to a ridiculous duel. The actress in question, Delia Morello, comes to Doro's house to explain her situation and all seems to be progressing as a normal play should. But when the curtain falls at the end of the first act, it rises again immediately, and part of the theater lobby is visible on the stage. The spectators in the lobby are discussing the first act of the Pirandello play they have just witnessed. Some of the audience are irritated by the performance, others are thrilled. Among the spectators who have gone out to the lobby during intermission are Delia Moreno and Baron Nuti, who have recognized their story (which had appeared in the newspapers) being reenacted on the stage. In protest, Delia Moreno attempts to stop the performance, but before she can go backstage the second act of the play has begun on the stage that does not include the lobby, and she is forced to hear it through. By the end of this act, however, she is so upset by what she considers an insult to her private life that she runs to the stage entrange, slaps the Leading Lady, and creates such confusion that the play cannot go on, and thus ends *Ciascuno a suo modo.*

Questa sera si recita a soggetto is another unusually constructed play, having neither acts nor scenes, but containing a play within it. Again, the play being improvised by Hinkfuss and his company is based on "a Pirandello theme borrowed from one of his short stories." Doctor Hinkfuss first introduces individually and by name the actors and actresses who will play the roles in Pirandello's play: Signor Palmiro La Croce, his wife, their four daughters Mommina, Totina, Dorina, and Nenè, and five young officers who court the girls. Of these five, Rico Verri the Sicilian is the only serious, gloomy, and passionate one. At the end of the first act or tableau, the mother, her four daughters, and the aviation officers are on their way to the theater to see an opera: they come directly into the "real" audience, take their box seats unceremoniously, and, meanwhile, the stage has been transformed by means of screen projections and a phonograph into the opera stage, under

Hinkfuss' loud and conspicuous direction. When the curtain falls on the first act of the opera, the mother and her group go out to the lobby, and Doctor Hinkfuss appears on stage to invite the "real" audience to stay seated if they wish for there will be nothing of importance to see in the lobby, except the same people who have just left their boxes, and he assures the audience that the spectacle of set-changing before their eyes will be more entertaining. In effect (and this constitutes Act II), the "characters" in the lobby carry on very light and unimportant conversation, while Doctor Hinkfuss presents a number of bizarre scenes on the stage: an aviation field and other equally incredible creations. The audience meanwhile expresses its varying opinions of the imbroglio at every possible moment, for and against Pirandello. Act III brings the family back to their home, numerous tragic and comic events occur, and after the death scene of Palmiro La Croce a shout from Hinkfuss causes six days to elapse. At this point the actors and actresses, completely disgusted with Hinkfuss' direction, rebel and refuse to continue acting for they are tired of being marionettes. Having finally put him out of the house, they take up the story themselves. They play through to the tragic ending of the piece, and no one knows whether Mommina is really dead or not for the actress who plays her role lies motionless on the stage even after the play is over. And Hinkfuss, who had been with the electricians handling the lighting effects, returns to compliment his marionettes for their splendid tableau. Such is the unlimited fantasy of Pirandello's mind in constructing a play within a play.

In *I giganti della montagna,* the travelling theatrical company of Countess Ilsa have stopped at a weird villa to enact Pirandello's *La favola del figlio cambiato,* in an undetermined time and place, somewhere between fiction and reality.

In *La répétition,* Jean Anouilh's Count and Countess (stock marionettes in his theater) and their friends are rehearsing Marivaux's *La Double Inconstance* to be presented in the château during a banquet. It has been arranged for the diners to become players. The players will come to life like the Six Characters, and the spectators will be forced to hear them to the end.

The curtain rises on the fourth act of **Colombe** during the presentation of *La Maréchale d'Amour,* presumably written by Poète-Chéri in honor of Madame Alexandra. At the end of Madame Alexandra's and Du Bartas' performance of the play within the play, they take their curtain calls, and then resume their natural attitudes: Du Bartas removes his wig and reverts to his coarse, vulgar speech; Madame Alexandra limps away on her cane.

II

The second group of Pirandello and Anouilh plays are those which include an unwritten play within them. The

technique is obvious in *Enrico IV* and in *Sei personaggi.* The former play opens with a dramatic tableau of Enrico IV's throne room in the imperial palace, which the spectators would assume to be the setting for the play itself, were it not for certain parts of the dialogue. One actor, for example, listens to his comrades and looks around the room with amazement. Finally he bursts out in exasperation that during the entire two weeks he has been rehearsing, he thought he was to act in a play about Henry IV of France, and now he has discovered that the play is about Henry IV of Germany. Landolf, Ordulf, and Ariald feel that they are playing thankless roles in an unwritten play. Landolf, their spokesman, compares them to characters who have not found an author, actors who have not been given a play in which to perform. Throughout *Enrico IV,* the play within the play is resumed at frequent intervals, and its value and power are felt when the hero finally escapes into its sanctuary.

Sei personaggi in cerca d'autore is another drama of unusual construction that contains an unwritten play within it, on two different levels of reality and illusion. When the curtain rises on the first act, the Director, the actresses, and the actors are rehearsing Pirandello's *Il giuoco delle parti,* but this is not to be the play within the play. For shortly the Six Characters are to arrive and declare that they must play their "play in the making." The Father explains that the manuscript and the drama are within them, and that they are impatient to play it. That the drama of the Six Characters overwhelms and dissipates the "real" play is, of course, the classic example of the Pirandellian theme of illusion versus reality.

In **Le bal des voleurs,** Lady Hurf is the stage director for her comedy in which she will star together with the imaginary Duc de Miraflor and his Spanish nobles. She introduces her actors à la Hinkfuss and begs them to play their roles in the *commedia dell'arte* style in the marionette world of her illusion. In **Le rendezvous de Senlis,** the professional actors Madame de Montalembreuse and Philémon have been summoned to play the roles of Georges' ideal parents, and are thoroughly instructed in their roles by the young hero. Madame de Montalembreuse and Philémon have the extraordinary power that clowns have of masking their faces with tragedy or comedy at a moment's notice. For example, Philémon, having at first completely misunderstood Georges' concept of his ideal father, disguises himself as a wrinkled, bearded octogenarian, which permits Georges to explain, in a Pirandellian vein, that Philémon must mold his role around the concept in Isabelle's mind: a character who is already half alive, because someone *believes* he exists.

Léocadia is a series of acts within acts, as Amanda sometimes plays the role of Léocadia and sometimes reverts to her real self. Anouilh places the young milliner on the stage of Pont-au-Bronc, a park which is filled with people whose daily occupation is to don a costume and play a fixed role. Even the plants, the birds, and the rabbits seem to be playing their roles in the fantasy.

The plot of *L'invitation au château* is well-known: Horace has invited an insignificant dancer, Isabelle, to play the role of a dazzling young society woman at a ball in his wealthy aunt's home. His intention is simply to dissuade his twin brother, Frédéric, from his blind love for Diana Messerschmann, the beautiful but difficult daughter of a wealthy financier. After a number of episodes which are bound to occur when the poor meet the wealthy, the play ends with Isabelle and Frédéric falling in love, and Horace feeling free to claim for his wife Diana, who has become a pauper because her father has suddenly lost all his money in a crash. To make a happy ending even happier, Anouilh allows Messerschmann's money to come back to him, doubled in amount. The *deus ex machina* of this plot is the improvised presentation being planned by Horace. He tells Isabelle, his star, that he is the organizer of the comedy, but that he is depending on her ability to improvise during the performance. The *dénouement* of this play within the play, then, furnishes the appropriate ending for this "brilliant play."

Act II of *Ornifle* finds the characters dressed in seventeenth-century costume playing a scene *à la Molière*. Ornifle assumes the rôle of The Misanthrope, and his two private physicians, in black robes, ruffs, and pointed hats, are reminiscent of the doctors in *Le Malade imaginaire*. Anouilh intends the insertion of the "fête Molière" into the lives of his modern machines to be symbolic of escape from boredom, as is frequently the function of the play within a play.

The *diner de têtes* (the play's sub-title) in *Pauvre Bitos* is a performance in which players under the guise of Robespierre, Danton, Mirabeau, etc., relive the Reign of Terror. Bitos, as Robespierre, faints when he is "shot" and subsequently embodies an illusion similar to Henry IV's until, ultimately, as in *Sei personaggi,* the "real" Bitos fades, giving way to the character in the contained play.

In *La grotte*, The Seminarist, spokesman for the group of "invented" characters, as is The Father in *Sei personaggi,* explains in Pirandellian language that the "*pièce à faire*" must be played since it has already begun to be lived in the mind of the author. Once again, illusion triumphs over reality.

The play within a play, then, is an important technique for dramatists like Pirandello and Anouilh who belong to the school of the "the theater within the theater."

But comparisons between Anouilh's and Pirandello's theatrical techniques flag without the substantiating basis of similarity of themes. Adriano Tilgher, in his penetrating studies of Pirandello's theater,[2] enumerates at least twenty-two themes which appear and reappear in the plays and novels of the Sicilian dramatist. Of these, the themes which seem most obviously to be present in Jean Anouilh's plays may be limited to six: the impossibility of shedding one's past, evasion, the irreversibility of time, multiple personality, the relativity of truth, and illusion versus reality.

According to the two dramatists under discussion, everyone is escorted by his past, his family, his *milieu,* his education, and his habits, all of which superimpose deforming traits on the original being. If persons were alone, isolated, "naked," to use Pirandello's term, purity and love could exist, but in the world as we know it, antagonisms constantly arise between memories of past formation and present conditions.

The plot of Pirandello's play *Come tu mi vuoi* is well known: a Strange Lady has been living a bohemian life with a writer, Salter, and his daughter. The Lady is a dancer in a nightclub, and her friends are drunken, boisterous young men who spend their time between the nightclub and Salter's apartment. One day, the Strange Lady receives the visit of Boffi, a friend of Bruno Pieri, who informs the nightclub entertainer that Bruno has every reason to believe that she is Lucia Pieri, his beautiful, virtuous, and intelligent wife, who had been living happily with her husband until the invasion of Northern Italy during the World War. Lucia had been taken prisoner by the enemy, and nothing had been heard from her since. Hoping to escape her life of debauchery which she despises, the Strange Lady, who remembers nothing of her past or at least refuses to reveal anything of her former life, accepts Boffi's invitation to return to Bruno. She welcomes the opportunity of living a new life as the beloved wife of a respectable man. However, the Strange Lady finds that the world does not accept her new identity; Bruno's relatives hint to her that the recreation of Lucia Pieri was motivated by monetary reasons, and not by the real belief that the Strange Lady is Lucia; a diary found in the attic makes the Lady herself doubt that she could ever have been or will ever be able to be the noble Lucia; and Salter, refusing to recognize the transformation, brings from Vienna a demented woman who, he claims, is the real Lucia Pieri. The Strange Lady realizes that although she may want to shed her sordid past for a new life, those who know her will never accept the self-created being. Almost hysterical, she joins her enemies by offering proof (a birthmark) that the demented woman, and not she, is really Lucia, and leaves in despair with Salter to return to the personality that society chooses to give her and that she is unable to shed.

In 1937, when Pitoëff produced Anouilh's *Le voyageur sans bagage,* one might have thought that the characterization of the amnesia victim had been overdone on the stage. But Anouilh managed successfully to transpose Pirandello's play. Lucia Pieri has become Gaston, a soldier who is interned in an asylum because he is suffering from amnesia. Gaston has no "past baggage" to carry; he is perfectly happy as an amnesia victim. But presently society must interrupt this happiness, for a man with no past is frightening. Gaston is pushed into his supposed family by the philanthropic Duchess who believes that "our past is the best part of us" and by a lawyer who sees Gaston as the source of a fortune in the form of the government's pension to the family of a mutilated soldier. The stiff Madame Renaud accepts him simply because a mother could scarcely do otherwise, as does Gaston's supposed sister-in-law Valentine, whose husband knows that he had been deceived by his wife and brother. In the second tableau, we learn that the real son, Jacques Renaud, used to behave most despicably toward the cook, the chauffeur, the valet, and the maid. By this time, the indifferent Gaston begins to experience various emotions, and upon learning of Jacques Renaud's fight with his schoolmate, his sentiments toward the Renaud family are violent. The past that this supposed family recreates for him is so repulsive that Gaston refuses it and all its characters. But his refusal is treated as madness and he is told that no one can decline his past—that he must either "belong" or return to the asylum. The scene in which the identifying scar on Gaston's body is revealed, like the similar scene in *Come tu mi vuoi,* represents the decision of the hero. By his final act of leaving with the little English boy (to whom Gaston has confided the secret of the identifying scar), Gaston brings about the symbolic death of Jacques Renaud; he thus frees himself, if not from the vices of society, at least from a public malignity built around a man without a past and from the particularly sordid past being forced upon him.

The affinities between *Come tu mi vuoi* and *Le voyageur sans bagage* are obvious. Each play presents an amnesia victim whose past is a mystery and who is being claimed by a supposed relative for reintegration into an unfamiliar family. Both plays present the struggle of the heroes against petty manifestations of the so-called "truth" of the past—a truth which means for them the destruction of the happiness and tranquillity for which they are striving. Harassed by those who relentlessly try to force them into an undesirable past, the Strange Lady and Gaston wearily rebel. The Strange Lady's struggle ends in black defeat. She cannot shed her overwhelmingly insidious past. For Gaston, who is a little shrewder in evading his foes, the struggle ends in a form of escape, but the play remains pessimistic by the very nature of its theme.

Vestire gli ignudi is another of Pirandello's plays with the same theme of the impossibility of shedding one's past. Again, the characteristics of the play may be shown to have been reproduced by Anouilh. Ersilia Drei, governess of the child of the Italian consul to Smyrna, is a woman who, prior to the opening of the play, has led a life of successive moments of weakness. Expecting to become engaged, she had given herself to an Italian naval officer who subsequently left with his ship and later became engaged to another. Ersilia next turns to the Italian consul Grotti, but this illicit love is rudely shattered by the death of the consul's child in a fall from the balcony (due to the governess' carelessness) and the consequent discovery of the deception by the consul's wife, who dismisses Ersilia. The first act of the play introduces an Ersilia who has mustered sufficient courage to attempt suicide, but the poison has not been efficacious and Ersilia, in proportion as her body has weakened, has become stronger-minded. A noted writer has extended hospitality to the abandoned Ersilia, for, having read her story in the newspapers, he seems fortuitously to have found, in true Pirandellian fashion, "the seed of a short story." Through her contact with the writer (who has by this time formed an idea of his heroine), Ersilia becomes aware that in the eyes of those who know her, she wears an illusory dress which covers the ugly past within her. It is this dress which she struggles to keep wrapped around her, and she distorts her story to make the dress more beautiful. But the thin fabric of her "decent little dress" will not cover her past. At the end of the play, the presence of the consul and the naval officer forces Ersilia to recognize that she cannot shed her past for a new garment acceptable to society. This time the poison takes effect as Ersilia utters her last words: "I am dying naked. With nothing to cover me, scorned, crushed. . . . Let me die in silence, completely naked. . . . Go and announce that the woman who died . . . died . . . naked."[3]

Thérèse Tarde, "La Sauvage," is the French counterpart of Ersilia Drei. Thérèse is a member of a family of poor uncouth café musicians. The sordidness of her life, corresponding closely to Ersilia's life before her attempt at suicide, is described in detail by Anouilh. Thérèse is loved, however, by Florent, a wealthy and famous pianist. Florent wishes to marry Thérèse, and although she loves him, she foresees that she will never be happy in the new, respectable *milieu* that Florent offers her. After much hesitation, Thérèse agrees to marry Florent and submits to the fittings for her elaborate wedding gown, the symbol, as was Ersilia's "decent little dress," of a new life divorced from the past. But a few days spent with Florent's family convinces Thérèse that her past life is even stronger than her desire for happiness. Her vulgarity, her pathetic family, her past unhappiness will continue to haunt her, and she will be unable to forget hypocritically about them. So Thérèse leaves

Florent and advances determinedly toward her fixed destiny of unhappiness with her unsightly past and no garment to hide it.

Eurydice is another Ersilia Drei, combined with certain characteristics of the Strange Lady in *Come tu mi vuoi*. A member of a travelling stage troupe, Eurydice one day in a train station meets Orpheus, a wandering musician. The two fall immediately in love, and depart for Marseilles, leaving their respective families behind. After the first night at a dingy hotel, Eurydice begins to reveal to Orpheus how sordid her past life has been. She tells him of the numerous lovers she has had, how one committed suicide for her, and about Dulac, the jealous member of the troupe who will probably find her and snatch her away from Orpheus. As Eurydice relates these facts, she realizes that she must leave Orpheus and his pure love. Intending to return to her group, she boards a bus which is involved in an accident, fatal for Eurydice. Death provides the enveloping mantle, and suicide the purging force, against Orpheus' belief in Eurydice's sins.

The theme contained in Jeannette's fruitless struggle to free herself from her evil attachments and the solution by suicide in **Roméo et Jeannette** is almost identical with that of **La sauvage** and **Eurydice**. Frédéric and Julia are an engaged couple. One day, together with Frédéric's mother, they pay a visit to Julia's slovenly family, composed of a drunken father and a sister and brother (Jeannette and Lucien), both of whom have a large assortment of bewildering idiosyncrasies. Frédéric, however, falls in love almost immediately with Jeannette, who returns his love. Jeannette's sentiment is pure within her own soul, but, in the eyes of others, it is tainted with the sordidness of her past life and the continuing insistence of one of her distasteful, middle-aged, but wealthy lovers. Frédéric realizes he cannot marry the savage Jeannette who, completely unlike her sister Julia, is the finished product of a highly objectionable family and a vile *milieu*. He becomes increasingly aware that he must leave Jeannette when Julia, in her jealousy, attempts suicide by poison. The spurned Jeannette then angrily accepts the marriage proposal of her wealthy lover, and during the course of the celebration at his château, escapes in order to show her white gown to Frédéric. But she sees him and Julia going off together, so she begins walking out to the sea, so far out that the tide will have risen before she can return to safety. Frédéric spots her in her symbolic white dress, goes out to join her, and the two drown together. Once more a heroine has been unable to give herself a new identity to cover an ugly past.

In **La grotte,** Adèle, the kitchen-maid, has been asked to baptize the Countess' baby. The Countess feels she is performing a great act of charity in descending to the servants' quarters and bestowing such an honor on Adèle. But when Adèle sees the baby, she reacts hysterically, and in a long, frenzied tirade, in which she vividly describes her dung-covered dress, symbolic of her sordid past, she shows the vanity of trying to wring out the filth in the rains falling from the Countess' upstairs universe.

III

Pirandello and Anouilh have shown, with different situations but similar development, the tragic predicament of the person who visualizes for himself an identity that will make him beloved, but who instead is victimized by a society which smears his sacred countenance.

The impossibility of being truly oneself—"come io mi voglio"—and the conflict between an ideal and the sordidness of reality lead an unhypocritical character quite logically to a decision to escape the deforming influences of his past, family, and *milieu*. The antagonism between the purity of the individual and a perverted or criminal society ends, for Pirandello and Anouilh, either in actual death, in the symbolic death of an objective reality, or in insanity, as forms of evasion.

In *La vita che ti diedi, Il beretto a sonagli, **Y avait un prisonnier, L'Hermine, Antigone,** and **Ardèle,** escape is sought not from one's past but from an unbearable tragedy or an obnoxious society. In *La vita che ti diedi,* one of the plays in which Pirandello proclaims the necessity of the irrational as a means of escape, the theme of evasion is subordinate to that of illusion versus reality, but still manifest in the character and life of Donna Anna, who refuses to believe that her son is dead. *Il beretto a sonagli* is a deep and tragic expression of the possible solution of escape in insanity: Donna Beatrice suspects that her husband, Cavaliere Fiorica, is unfaithful to her and accuses the young wife of Ciampa, an employee of Fiorica. With the aid of the police, Fiorica is discovered with Ciampa's wife. Donna Beatrice feels free and relieved of her mental burden, but the affair has brought shame to her husband, to Ciampa, and to his wife. Moreover, Donna Beatrice is in an awkward situation herself, because the society of her day demands that she return to her husband's home and submit to his violence and wrath. In an effort to correct the situation in the eyes of the townspeople, Donna Beatrice accepts Ciampa's solution, which is to put on the cap and bells of madness and fling the truth into the faces of the people in the public square. For three months, Donna Beatrice plays the role of a madwoman. Her insanity negates the entire unpleasant incident and thus she escapes the condemning conventions of society.

Ludovic, of **Y avait un prisonnier,** Frantz, of **L'Hermine, Antigone,** and **Ardèle** are some of Anouilh's heroes who seek evasion from society. Ludovic, when he sees what his family has become, almost wishes he were still in jail (where he has spent almost one quarter of his life), and attempts to gain his freedom by swimming to shore from his family's yacht at sea. Frantz willingly gives himself up to the police after killing the wealthy Duchess, for he knows he will never escape society otherwise. Antigone and Ardèle willingly accept death to escape a concept of morality and duty that they cannot possibly understand.

The theme of evasion is, however, best illustrated in Pirandello's masterpiece *Enrico IV.* The play opens with the appearance of Henry IV's councilors and valets, in authentic costume, discussing events of the eleventh century, but soon we learn that the entire presentation is a fiction; that the man who pretends he is Henry IV has been insane for many years through the perfidious accident caused by a certain Baron Belcredi; that Henry's wealthy relative, out of pity, allows him to live in his imperial illusion, and that no one except Henry IV believes he is the German emperor. The Marquise Matilda Spina, whom Henry loved before his accident, her daughter Frida, Baron Belcredi (The Marquise's lover), and Doctor Genoni appear, with hopes of bringing Henry IV back to reality. The plan devised by the Doctor of confronting Henry with Matilda and her daughter Frida who greatly resembles her serves only to tax the strength of the hero, who rudely shocks the onlookers by revealing that his madness has been feigned for several years, and that he knows his true madness was caused by falling from his pageant horse that the jealous Belcredi had made rear by pricking it with his spur. In his anger, the pretending Henry IV stabs Belcredi to death, not so much because of the latter's wickedness as because Time has rendered the hero incapable of manifesting himself, his love, and his ideals. Henry then quickly re-escapes to his madness, the only dwelling where he may live free from society.

It is very possible that Anouilh had *Enrico IV* and other of Pirandello's plays in mind when he wrote *Léocadia* and *Le rendezvous de Senlis.* In *Léocadia,* it is a real prince, Albert Troubiscoï, around whom the theme of evasion is woven. The prince's beloved actress, Léocadia, has dramatically strangled herself to death two years prior to the opening of the play. His aunt, The Duchess, attempting to assuage the prince's sorrows, has stopped the clock of life at the Château so that things should remain exactly as they were at the time of the prince's happiness. Amanda, a young milliner who greatly resembles the dead Léocadia, is summoned to the Château to make the actress live again for the prince. But Amanda, like Frida in *Enrico IV,* plays her role poorly and is frightened by the strange surroundings at the Château. Finally the prince reveals that his unconsolable dream is feigned, that it is, perhaps, those who

surround him who are really mad and cause him to seek evasion. The play ends happily, for Amanda comes to love the prince, and it is not too late for him to return her love.

In *Le rendezvous de Senlis,* the same theme of evasion involves Georges, who is rebelling against an intolerable family and wife. To escape the oppressive reality of his life, he has concocted an ideal family and an ideal friend whom he will present to the young and virtuous Isabelle. The role of his parents will be played by hired actors (a Pirandellian situation). His friend Robert (who actually is his wife's lover) will remain invisible at the rendezvous to which Isabelle has been invited. The setting at Senlis is Georges' scene of escape, and Isabelle is the symbol of the realization of an unreal world.

Both Pirandello and Anouilh, then, have chosen the theme of evasion for several of their plays, and in some cases a similarity of development between the Italian and the French plays is evident.

IV

Closely linked with the two themes discussed thus far is that of the irreversibility of time. Between the past and the present there is a tremendous abyss, but sometimes it happens that by confronting the present with a situation contrary to what an individual expects, the present suddenly becomes thrown back into the past for that individual, though not for those who know him. Such was Henry IV's predicament when, having first recovered from his insanity, he realized that the ravaging effects of life and time had continued while he remained stationary, and that the only present for him was the illusion in which he had been living during the previous twelve years. Ferrante Morli in *La Signora Morli una e due* returned to his wife after a fifteen-year absence in America and found a situation that he could not recognize as "present." Such also was Ludovic's predicament when he was released from jail and found that his present was far removed from that of his family. These plays are a concentration of the vicissitudes of long years of life in the space of a few hours, and their plots are intended to show the ravaging effects of time.

In *Lumìe di Sicilia* is presented the same effect of a stationary past idea opposed to a scintillating present reality, the two of which can never be reconciled, no matter how intensely one strives to bring past symbols into the present. Micuccio, the peasant musician, had devoted his life's efforts to giving Sina Marnis, the peasant girl whom he loves, a singing career. After many years of separation from Sina, who has left her native village to seek her fortune, Micuccio goes to the city to claim Sina for his wife, but by this time she has become a successful *cantatrice* who has forgotten the relics of her past (symbolized by the Sicilian figs). Sina's old aunt Marta, who accompanies her niece on her singing tours, seems to have lost the power of measuring the time that has elapsed since she left her small village, of distinguishing true events from dreams. The peasant Micuccio, in the new, dazzling atmosphere, is rendered ridiculous by the city people who see time and events as fixed absolutes. Micuccio understands from their attitude that his present is Sina's past, and that she will never be able to partake again of Sicilian figs.

The situation is much the same in Anouilh's **Colombe,** Julien and Colombe, a former flower-vendor, are married. His mother, Madame Alexandra, is a famous actress. Madame Alexandra detests Julien and loves her other son Armand, because the latter flatters her and answers her every whim. Julien has come to the theater to plead with his mother: he needs money because he is going into the army and Colombe has to be provided for. Madame Alexandra offers to give Colombe a small part in her plays. Julien leaves for the army, and Colombe promptly falls in love with Armand and flirts with all the other men in the theater group. When Julien returns from war, he learns that his wife has deceived him. He renounces all, and the play ends as Julien reminisces about the first day he met Colombe (the roses in this scene are comparable to the symbol of the Sicilian figs) and how happy and pure their love was. Like Micuccio, Julien realizes that he cannot reverse the passage of time and its effects. Julien, towards the very end of the play says: "Now the story is beginning," as though he would like to turn back and start again. But Anouilh immediately reintroduces the figure of Colombe swearing her "eternal" love for Julien, a bitter reminder that time is only relative and not eternal for humans.

La morsa is another of Pirandello's plays based on the theme of the irreversibility of time. The drama is contained not in the dire results of uncontrollable Sicilian anger, but in the demonstration of how a horrible doubt in the present is the illusion of the past and the reality of the future. The love between Giulia and Antonio, who are deceiving the former's husband Andrea, is killed by their very suspicion that the husband knows even before this suspicion is verified.[4] Such is the time aspect of Pirandello's relativity. The speed of the formation and change of opinions, with relation to the truth of an individual, is much faster than the comparatively stationary truth. At the end of the play, having stupidly forced herself into the truth held fixed in Andrea's vise, Giulia kills herself.

Anouilh's Eurydice is somewhat similar to Giulia. Held in the vise of Orpheus' desire for truth, Eurydice cannot return to the past and liberates herself from the oppression of time by death. Only in the eternal life after death will her past and Orpheus' present be reconciled.

Finally, the theme of the irreversibility of time may be analyzed in *Tutto per bene* and compared with **La valse des Toréadors.** Martino Lori, in *Tutto per bene,* is a man whose entire life has been dominated by his worship of the memory of his dead wife, Silvia, and his paternal devotion to his daughter, Palma. Every day for sixteen years he has gone to the cemetery to place flowers on his wife's tomb. However, Lori abruptly discovers one day that Palma is not his own daughter, for Silvia had deceived him shortly after their marriage. The odious past is suddenly forced upon Lori with the vividness of the present. He seemingly has nothing left to live for, but he gratefully grasps at the straw of Palma's increased affection and resigns himself to the belief that all is for the best in a world where time cannot be recalled or reversed.

Old General Saint-Pé of **La valse des Toréadors** is another hero who must resign himself to changes in the present without attempting to revive the past. The General is a comical version of Henry IV. After having kept alive a platonic love for Mademoiselle de Sainte-Euverte for about twenty years, with the intention of marrying her after his wife's death, the General finally loses her to his young secretary, Gaston. Saint-Pé tries to convince himself that it is for the best and accepts his fate in much the same way as Martino Lori.

Antigone and *L'Alouette* (the drama of Jeanne d'Arc), by the very nature of their identities and by the special dramatic technique which Anouilh employs, demonstrate the theme of the irreversibility of time. In both plays simultaneously appear on the stage at the outset all the main characters in Antigone's and Jeanne's life, and the heroines themselves, each knowing full well that her death is imminent. Antigone and Jeanne see the past as the present and are unaware of the passage of time since the day they took the first step towards their doom. It is Créon and Ismène, Beaudricourt, King Charles, the Inquisitor, and Warwick who live and change with the times, and attempt to save the heroines, but Antigone and Jeanne turn a deaf ear to them in the knowledge that the hours destined for them to live will not run counterclockwise.

Pirandello and Anouilh, then, were both aware of the tremendous dramatic value of the theme of the irreversibility of time, and both playwrights developed the theme along similar lines.

V

The theme of multiple personality is a common one in Pirandello's and Anouilh's plays, and indeed in many classic and modern dramas. In 1926, Pirandello had written his novel *Uno, nessuno e centomila* in which the problem of multiple personality was set forth in detail. The hero, Vitangelo Moscarda, faced with the knowledge that his personality is multiple (depending on with whom he is in contact), maliciously decides to decompose these various personalities and bring forth his pure self. For those who have followed Vitangelo through Pirandello's eyes, the final true being is wholly acceptable. But for external society, the person who has thrown off the mask of Moscarda is insane and is greeted everywhere with bursts of laughter. From behind the discarded mask, a sorrowful visage appears that now no longer desires to identify itself with a name and therefore is a nonentity to the world.

A little of Vitangelo Moscarda exists in almost all of Pirandello's and Anouilh's characters. All the allusions to the discovery of one's multiple personality and the various reactions to this realization—sorrow, bewilderment, comprehension, shame, etc.—are too numerous to mention. A few examples will suffice to illustrate these reactions. A young lady in *Ciascuno a suo modo* is ashamed to see herself change:

> How am I? I don't know any more. . . . I feel only mobility and change in me. Nothing has weight any more. I turn one way and the other, I laugh, and then suddenly I hide in a corner and cry. What torment! What anguish! And I always want to hide my face from myself because I am so ashamed to see myself changing.[5]

D'Albis in *La ragione degli altri* is not the least startled when the heroine of the play reveals that she curiously feels she is not the same for herself as she is for others. D'Albis understands that the more inner lives we have, the less we realize how we look from the outside. Fulvia in *Come prima meglio di prima* is frightened by the realization that she is not "herself." She is one person as the mother of her first child, another as the mother of her second child. Martino Lori is faced with an image of himself that he does not recognize and is disgusted and horrified by that image. There are few Pirandellian plays without at least one character who keeps ever-present to the spectators the awareness of the multiplicity of our personalities, and who reminds us that we are one, no-one, and a hundred thousand.

One of the most striking multiple personality characters is Evelina Morli of *La Signora Morli una e due*. Evelina had married very young, and was gay and carefree like her husband Ferrante. After five years of marriage, however, her husband left her and their small son, and when the play opens Evelina is legally married to Lello Carpani, a serious and reserved lawyer. Evelina gives birth to a daughter, and gradually she becomes silent and subdued under Carpani's influence. After fourteen years, Ferrante returns from America to claim Evelina

and his son. At first furious upon seeing him, Evelina slowly revives her love for Ferrante and her former vivacious personality. She feels horror when she discovers two persons in herself and in her first husband. Ultimately, morality and society require that Evelina remain with her second husband and daughter, and by accepting these dictates Evelina assumes still another personality—that of a perfect mother.

Strongly resembling Evelina Morli is Amanda in the scene of *Léocadia* where the young milliner rebels against the contrary personality of an actress that she is forced to assume. Anouilh is obsessed by the problem of changing personality in *L'Invitation au château,* where the twin brothers Horace and Frédéric seem to be playing the game of split personality. André Bitos (of *Pauvre Bitos*) has the personalities of a studious schoolboy, a public prosecutor, and a Robespierre-like terrorist. During the play, Bitos is obliged to defend all three aspects of himself, and in the end he is unsure of who he really is.

But Anouilh's most memorable play on the theme of multiple personality is *Le bal des voleurs.* Lady Hurf and her two nieces are bored at their summer resort. Three thieves in the neighborhood lend some activity. They pretend, in order to enter Lady Hurf's quarters, that they are Spanish nobles. Lady Hurf plays their game. She entertains them lavishly, pretending to recognize them as her old friends. Her niece, Eva, who is being courted by the boring DuPont-DuFort *fils,* falls in love with one of the thieves, Hector, whom she had previously met in the park disguised as a young, honest chap. Hector, who must change his disguises in rapid succession in order to escape detection, finds that he does not please Eva in his present form but cannot remember under which disguise Eva loved him. He desperately changes his appearance several more times, only to incite Eva's mocking laughter. A ball to be held in town one evening (*Le Bal des Fleurs*) presents the opportunity for the thieves to raid the house while the others are at the dance. Lady Hurf has read the announcements erroneously. She thinks they will attend a *bal des voleurs*. All are dressed, therefore, as thieves: the Spanish nobles, Lady Hurf and her nieces, DuPont-DuFort *père* and *fils.* They are turned away from the ball because of their thieves' costumes. In the meanwhile, one of the thieves is stealing the valuables from Lady Hurf's house. Eva has escaped the group to be with the thief she loves and to help him steal. DuPont-DuFort *père,* having discovered that the Spanish nobles are frauds, denounces them to the police. But when the latter arrive, it is DuPont-DuFort *père* and *fils* who are arrested because they look most like thieves in their costumes and the real thieves are overlooked. *Schein ist sein.* The entire play is a series of masquerades which humorously stress the theme of changing personality. All the characters in *Le bal des voleurs* illustrate the theory exposed by Baldovino in *Il piacere dell'onestà*: we "make ourselves over" in accordance with the particular circumstances in which we find ourselves. Vividly illustrative of Baldovino's theory is Anouilh's **La foire d'empoigne** in which Napoleon and Louis XVIII, played by one and the same actor, politely alternate their entrances and exits, and Fouché, servant of two masters, shuttles obsequiously between monarch and Emperor.

Like Pirandello, Anouilh is deeply imbued with the idea of the multiplicity of human personalities and the realization that man cannot be reduced to a unity which will give him inner peace and happiness. Both dramatists are aware of the relativity of individuals' sentiments and emotions to society, to family and economic conditions, and of how these conflicts can cause the disturbing feeling of disunity. This explains why both Pirandello's and Anouilh's heroes are antisocial: they already have a sufficient number of individuals of both past and present within their one person which they must try to bring together, and consequently they cannot attempt to integrate themselves with family and society too.

VI

Così è (se vi pare) is such a well-known play and its message is so clear that no detailed analysis of the plot is necessary. It is enough to stress the theme of the relativity of truth that dominates the play, a theme which appears frequently in both Pirandello's and Anouilh's works. The curious people of a certain town require an explanation for the behavior, strange by their standards, of Mr. and Mrs. Ponza and Mrs. Frola, Ponza's mother-in-law. The villagers force interviews with the three heroes of the play, and their painstaking efforts to discover the secret of the strange family resolve into the Pirandellian question mark. The answer is that the truth is just what you would like it to be.

Anouilh may have been thinking of this play when he wrote **L'invitation au château,** for his purpose in confronting the high society of the château with the lowly Isabelle was to demonstrate that an insignificant dancer could appear to be the attractive niece of an "*homme du monde*" to those who wished to see her that way, nothing but a vulgar, earthy girl to others, and no one at all to herself. When Mrs. Frola, in the Italian play, was face to face with the Agazzi family and their friends, opinions leaned in one direction. When Mr. Ponza appeared after his mother-in-law's exits, opinions swayed in the opposite direction, and Lamberto Laudisi was always present to mock the pendulum-like nature of the people's opinions. Likewise, the truth about Isabelle's identity varied according to the persons with whom she was in contact, and Horace—the identical twin who must have observed on numerous occasions the fickleness of opinions in his double role—was in

Lamberto Laudisi's position to mock those who desired to know the "truth." For example, Horace says to Romainville, in words almost directly borrowed from Pirandello:

HORACE:

Who will believe you?

ROMAINVILLE:

Everyone, because it's the truth.

HORACE:

What does it matter that it's the truth, if it doesn't look true.

ROMAINVILLE:

Then, according to you, truth is nothing?

HORACE:

Nothing, my friend, without appearances.[6]

Another of Pirandello's plays in which the theme of the relativity of truth is predominant is *Ciascuno a suo modo*. The play opens with a discussion on the subject of the changing character of human opinions which consequently lead to illogical human behavior. A concrete example of this follows: Doro Palegari had defended, against the attacks of his friend, Francesco, a certain actress named Delia Morello who had caused the suicide of a promising young painter. The two friends uphold their views so staunchly that they finally challenge each other to a duel to defend their opinions. However, the intercession of Doro's mother and some reflection on the part of Francesco are sufficient for each of the two young men to change completely to the opposite point of view. The duel, then, is still inevitable. But a visit from Delia Morello in person again sways Doro who, returning to his original stand, is now to duel without knowing why. The two choral interludes and the second act of *Ciascuno a suo modo,* which mingle the reality of the Morello affair with an enactment of it on the stage (as has been described above), are additional opportunities for Pirandello to demonstrate the variety of human opinions. The "real" characters and the actors playing their roles all attempt to express the same truth and therefore come into conflict; the audience witnessing the play within the play disagree among themselves on the value of the presentation and of the author (Pirandello himself). Each person involved, then, is occupied with creating his own reality, *ciascuno a suo modo,* which inevitably leads to such discord that the third act of the play cannot be performed. Just as in life, the search for absolute truth cannot be concluded.

Perhaps the most powerful drama in which Jean Anouilh has illustrated the theme of the relativity of truth is **L'Alouette.** In the midst of the changing opinions of all who knew Jeanne d'Arc—her parents, the people of France, her executioners—Jeanne and her God remain a symbol of absolute truth. Antigone is a similar heroine, for whom changing opinions have no significance.

The theme of the relativity of truth cannot be limited to any particular number of plays of Pirandello and Anouilh. It seems to pervade in some degree almost all of the works of both authors. How similar to the townsfolk in *Così è (se vi pare)* are the villagers in *Pensaci, Giacomino!*, and the family of Ardèle, who are right in condemning old Professor Toti and Ardèle simply because they think they are right! And how similar to Isabelle of **L'Invitation au château** are the Strange Lady of *Come tu mi vuoi* and Eurydice who, faced with the problem of the relativity of truth, cries out: "Orpheus is telling the truth, but so is Dulac. It's too complicated!"[7]

VII

Beware of your reality, it is destined to become the illusion of tomorrow, warns the Father in *Sei personaggi in cerca d'autore*. The action of the play unfolds on the two different levels of reality and illusion. The Director, the actors, and the actresses rehearsing one of Pirandello's plays represent the plane of reality. The weird appearance of the Six Characters bathed in a greenish light represents the plane of illusion. Interrupting the rehearsal, the Six Characters partly relate, partly enact their tragic drama. The incomplete drama within them, which is gasping for expression, absorbs and overwhelms to such an extent the "real" actors who attempt to duplicate in their acting the drama of the Six, that the final scene, in which the little girl is drowned and the young man shoots himself, causes the plane of reality to disappear completely. Illusion versus reality. Illusion comes out victorious, the hero of the play. Anouilh's **La grotte** is likewise constructed on two planes—the universe of the upstairs and the downstairs kitchen—and the lighting forms an intrinsic part of the struggle between illusion and reality. In **Le rendezvous de Senlis** is found the same situation of actors creating an illusion which in the end triumphs over reality. Georges' ideal parents and friend, having taken spiritual form in Isabelle's mind, must be brought to life in their minutest detail by the group of hired actors. (In a Pirandellian vein, Georges tells the actors how necessary it is to give full life to these half-formed creatures. His words are almost a rewording of the Father's explanation of the actors' roles in *Sei personaggi*, and of Cotrone's words in *I giganti della montagna*.) During the course of the rehearsal for the meeting of Isabelle with his imaginary family, Georges is so completely taken up in the game of illusion that for a few moments he is able to savor the pleasure of living in a world of pure fantasy. But Isabelle, like the Six Characters, cannot take part in the game, for her reality is the unreal. When she learns of the deceit, she wonders in her bewilderment what can be true if the ideal friend is a lie. But captured by the spirit of Isabelle's fantastic illusion, Georges and the "real" friend snatch at the straw which allows them to escape the plane of reality and live in the happiness of an illusion.

Another of Pirandello's dramas based on the theme of illusion versus reality is *La vita che ti diedi*. In reality, Fulvio Luna is dead. He had wasted away his life by loving a woman who could never be his. For his mother, Donna Anna, Fulvio is not dead; she keeps him alive in the little world of her illusion and even succeeds in capturing within this world the woman her son loved. The entire play revolves around the necessity of constructing an illusion for oneself in order to bear mechanical reality.

The Prince and his entourage in **Léocadia** all live in an illusory world after the death of Léocadia Gardi, each for a different reason, but all so gripped by the power of that illusion that the reality of the outside world no longer exists for them.

The illusions of the various characters in Pirandello's and Anouilh's works are quite different for each play: for Henry IV it is the illusion of a king's power and of the cessation of time; for Martino Lori in *Tutto per bene* it is the self-imposed illusion that even after the collapse of his most beautiful hopes all is for the best in the best of worlds; and for Ersilia in *Vestire gli ignudi* it is the illusion of wearing a dress over the naked truth of her past. In almost all of Pirandello's plays there is an undercurrent of the theme of illusion versus reality. The presence of the theme is equally frequent in Anouilh's plays: Antigone scorns reality and lives with an illusory concept of her brother, Polynice—an illusion which gives her the strength to meet her death; the General and Mademoiselle de Sainte-Euverte of **La valse des Toréadors** fondle their illusion for almost twenty years and derive strength from it to endure their unattractive lives; and Anouilh hints that the closing scene of **Colombe** is the presentation of an illusion-in-the-making that will enable Julien to escape the horrible reality of the preceding parts of the play. The naïve General in **L'Hurluberlu** has two illusions: that a secret society of his creation will abolish the world's corruption, and that he can retain the love of his wife (twenty years younger than he) by secluding her in the country. But society snatches the General from his dreams. After the final shock of discovering a strange, horrible world of cynical amorality, the General's only recourse is to black pessimism and despair, but at the close of the play one somehow feels that Anouilh will accord the *hurluberlu* a return to his world of naïveté.

Further illustrations could be given, for the theme of illusion versus reality is almost inexhaustible. However, it is sufficient to have shown how this theme, as well as the preceding five themes, have been used by Pirandello and Anouilh in plays whose similarities are evident.

Since 1941, critics have been pointing out resemblances between the French dramatist's plays and Pirandellian drama, and even today the similarities remain noticeably strong. Jean Anouilh's work reveals Pirandellian influences to a greater extent than that of any other modern French dramatist. Neither Salacrou's, nor Beckett's, nor Achard's, nor Giraudoux's plays present Pirandello-like themes and dramatic techniques to the degree that Anouilh's plays do.

Notes

1. *La grotte* (Paris: La Table ronde, 1961), Act I, p. 11. All translations into English of this and subsequent non-English quotations are my own.

2. *Studi sul teatro contemporaneo* (Roma: Libreria di Scienze e lettere, 1923), and *La Scene e la vita, nuovi studî sul teatro contemporaneo* (Roma: Libreria di Scienze e lettere, 1925).

3. *Maschere nude* (Milano: A. Mondadori, 1938), IV, Act III, p. 262. Cf. George Bernard Shaw, *Too True to be Good* (New York: Dodd, Mead and Company, 1934), Act II, p. 132: "But how are we to bear this dreadful new nakedness: the nakedness of the souls who until now have always disguised themselves from one another in beautiful impossible idealisms to enable them to bear one another's company . . . Our souls go in rags now; and the young are spying through the holes and getting glimpses of the reality that was hidden."

4. Anouilh has treated this theme comically in *L'invitation au château* (Paris: La Table ronde, 1951), Act II, p. 64. Patrice Bombelles and Lady India attempt to hide their relationship from Messerschmann. Lady India: "Stand straight. Pretend we haven't seen him. Don't let him know yet whether we know that he knows." Bombelles: "Yes, but if he doesn't know yet, don't you think that by our showing too clearly that we know he knows, he may catch on that we know?"

5. *Maschere nude* (Milano: A. Mondadori, 1937), I, Act I, pp. 140-41.

6. Act I, p. 20, cf. *Così è (se vi pare)*, *Maschere nude* (Milano: A. Mondadori, 1937), V, Act I, sc. ii, p. 18, and *Ciascuno a suo modo, op. cit.*, Act I, pp. 137-38.

7. *Eurydice* (Paris: Calmann-Lévy, 1947), Act III, p. 388.

Alba Amoia (essay date 1994)

SOURCE: Amoia, Alba. "The Heroic World of Jean Anouilh." In *Twentieth-Century European Drama*, edited by Brian Docherty, pp. 109-23. New York: St. Martin's Press, 1994.

[*In the following essay, Amoia provides an overview of Anouilh's heroic heroines and contrasts these female characters with their unimpressive male counterparts.*]

Women are the dominant figures in the theatre of Jean Anouilh, around women rotates the axis of his world of heroism, and to women does the author ascribe the epithet, 'flowers in the midst of garbage'.

The cast of Anouilh's preeminent female characters ranges from the uncouth and sublime 'lark' (Joan of Arc) to the pure and untamed 'sauvage'; from the uncompromising Antigone to the adamant, hunchbacked 'daisy' (**Ardèle, ou la Marguerite**). Anouilh's intransigent heroines are willing to die in defence of a cherished principle; they refuse all happiness, love or romance that is not 'pure'; and they take an ethereal view of existence in their struggle against all forms of compromise and deceit. Often guided by compassion for the victimised and downtrodden, they fit into Joan of Arc's 'ordered world' of the poor, the ill, the aged, and the wounded. (Becket is perhaps the one male heroic exception in Anouilh's theatre, for he inspires the love of the downtrodden masses of Canterbury by championing them against the power of the Crown, the rich, and the Normans.)

Opposite in kind to the unyielding heroines, are the men in Anouilh's plays—distorted, depersonalised, degraded roués, who make a mockery of lofty goals, seek money and power, and are motivated by selfishness and baseness. Even historical giants such as Napoleon and Louis XVIII are doing nothing more, in **La Foire d'empoigne** (1962), than playing a petty game of grab, catching as catch can, unmindful of their unheroic demeanour. Male heroism for Anouilh? It is encapsulated in the ironic title of his 1970 play, **Les poissons rouges ou mon père, ce héros.** The 'hero's' highest form of self-expression as a child was urinating in the goldfish bowl. It is no wonder that, grown man and established author that he now is, he comes under attack from all sides, albeit by equally contemptible and ridiculous characters: his wife, mother-in-law, children, mistress, physician, and friend. The only figure in the play worthy of esteem is the pale little servant, Adele—a stock character in Anouilh's theatre, whose place is in the ranks of the downtrodden but who remains always generous and pure. The naive Adele is relentlessly ordered about by her mistress and made the victim of street urchins' pranks, but she is the only person in the household who refuses to be caught up in the accusations and insults cascading against the sorry hero, defending him even at the cost of rough banishment to the kitchen. Humble Adele, no less than Antigone, Eurydice, Medea, or Joan of Arc, attempts to modify the role she is destined to play during her life on earth. Unlike Gaston, for example, in *Le Voyageur sans bagage*, who can only weep when he discovers the role he is expected to play in the Renaud household, and seeks to escape moral responsibility for his horrendous past actions, Adele does not fear to defy society, face up to reality, and shoulder her own identity. Resistants rather than Collaborators, Anouilh's heroines champion realities and truths which reveal the hollowness and falseness of the male characters' compromises. Banishment or sentencing to death seems devastating to these heroines, but they walk steadily and undramatically off stage, while the anti-hero is left to decay morally in a corner from which he cannot escape nor even desire to escape. Anouilh's plays without heroes have acquired unforgettable heroines, who are ultimately vindicated and emerge triumphant in their implacable 'purity'.

Anouilh's 'pièces noires' and 'nouvelles pièces noires' are pessimistic, bitter, and permeated with gloom. They display most clearly his lack of faith in humanity and its institutions. His pessimism stems from the realisation that neither the so-called joys and comforts of life reserved for the happy few, nor the invitations to unsavoury adventures, promiscuity, and immorality extended to all, lead to real happiness. Concomitantly, resignation to abject poverty, rigid acceptance of one's role in life, strict morality, and punctilious observance of a code of honour, can lead only to tragedy or death. Purity and love cannot prevail on this earth, because of the intrinsic impurity of happiness. Anouilh's heroines, seeking a happiness known only to themselves, a 'purity' of self and an 'absolute' love, are faithful in their search even though they know that none is attainable in life. Heroines cannot be 'happy'. Because they reject 'le sale petit bonheur' reserved for the mediocre, they are condemned to a solitude that admits of neither love nor friendship. Their task of finding or creating the ambience in which their truth can thrive is limited to the realms of illusion and of death, where real love and purity do exist.

For Anouilh's heroines, offerings or worldly gain are meaningless. In their search for the realisation of an ideal far beyond the horizons of the masses, the temptations of the so-called good things in life do not sway them from their perpetual task of refusing mediocrity. Antigone's retort to her family's assurances that happiness awaits her because she is young, beautiful, and engaged to be married, is: 'You all disgust me with your happiness. With your life that has to be lived at any cost. And that daily ration of good fortune, which suffices as long as you're not too demanding.'[1] In words

that echo Joan of Arc's 'I don't want to have a happy ending . . . an ending that never ends',[2] she rejects Creon's image of a marriage that will permit her to live happily ever after. The heroine's rejection of a love that is less than perfect is incomprehensible to the mediocre masses, for whom 'love and marriage' are an integral part of life. Joan of Arc's disappearance from her father's farm to keep her divine appointment provokes her mother's prodding for explanations of the long absence, and her father's 'Ah! you're losing track of time now! I hope to God you haven't lost something else that you don't dare mention!' (*PC*, p. 26). It would be inconceivable for Joan to answer 'Saint Michael' to parents such as these. In *Antigone*, the uncomprehending Nurse immediately assumes that her charge's absence from the palace in the middle of the night can only be explained by a tryst with a common boy. Again, it would be absurd for Antigone to answer that she had gone to cover the body of her dead brother. Joan might avoid her father's violent thrashings and be 'happier' if only she would try to appear attractive to a village boy who will marry her, thereby easing her father's mind and his blows. She recognises her parent's right to destroy her physically, but maintains her spiritual rights: 'Beat me hard; you have the right to. But it's my right to continue to believe and to say no to you' (*PC*, p. 87). After an especially hard paternal drubbing, she refuses her mother's consolatory offer of an embroidered scarf: 'I don't want to look pretty, mommy . . . I don't want to get married' (p. 32). Later in the play, her words express even more clearly her renunciation of 'happiness' and her desire for nonconformity: 'I don't want things to turn out all right. . . . I don't want to live your time' (*PC*, p. 131).

Medea has already experienced marriage—that short, happy union which is soon followed by the inevitable period of noncommunication that eventually culminates in silence and hatred. Medea's Nurse tells her mistress that 'the earth is still full of good things: the sun on the bench at the resting-place, hot soup at noon, the coins you have earned in your hand, the drop of booze that warms your heart before you doze off'.[3] Medea, nauseated by the mediocrity of the Nurse's criteria, banishes her to unheroic realms: 'You have said too much, with your carcass, your drop of booze, and your sun shining on your rotten flesh. Get back to your dishes, your broom, your peelings, you and the rest of your [mediocre] race' (*NPN*, p. 367). Turning toward Corinth, where people are celebrating boisterously, Medea says: 'Something in me is stirring . . . and it says *no* to happiness' (*NPN*, p. 359). Her own children revolt her, for she already sees them as sly, deceitful adults who are, worst of all, anxious to 'live and be happy'. Jason predicts that there will never be other Medeas on this earth, that mothers will never name their daughters Medea, and that the Medea he knows will stand alone until the end of time. At the close of the play, as she and her children are being devoured by flames, she will proclaim: 'I am Medea, finally and forever.' A young woman of the lesser race who carries her head high, clenches her fists, scornfully spits on the ground, and stamps her feet in defiance, Medea is almost a stock character in Anouilh's plays. She survives through the ages in the dramatist's work as Antigone, Joan of Arc, 'la sauvage', Jeannette in *Roméo et Jeannette,* Adele (of *La Grotte*), and others—all of whom are atavisms of Medea.

Nowhere in Anouilh's plays does a heroine seek to satisfy a maternal instinct. Children are never portrayed as a delight or a comfort, but rather as tiring, vociferous mini-adults. In one play, *La Répétition* (1950), Anouilh is unsparing: his characters find deaf-mute children perhaps tolerable, but rose bushes preferable. The caricatural figure of the typical male child, Toto, who reappears in numerous plays, is a mixture of mime, prankster, and liar, who plays grotesque games of love to parody his parents. The female child is usually portrayed in her earliest teens, pregnant, pretentious, and possessed of some ridiculous name such as Camomilla.

Jason had formerly been the ideal for whom Medea had sacrificed all. After their marriage his love was lost and that love now repels her. When he tries to save her from the many enemies she has made because of him, she protests: 'What are you trying to save? This worn-out skin, this carcass Medea, good for nothing except to drag around in its boredom and its hatred? A little bread and a house somewhere, and she'll grow old in silence until nobody mentions her name any more, right?' (*NPN*, p. 359). The acceptance of 'happiness' means submersion in the eternal oblivion of conformity, which is the equivalent of vegetation. Electra, in Anouilh's *Oreste* (1945), describing Aegisthus's and Clytemnestra's marriage as a slow process of watching the approach of old age, the onset of coldness, lack of desire, and ultimately hatred, exclaims sardonically: 'Oh, the indissoluble sanctity of marriage!'[4] Electra pursues her vengeance by becoming a child of hate and destruction. She purposely makes herself ugly and dirty, tears her dresses, and rubs her skin against the lepers huddled at the walls of the palace of Argos. She has taken all mirrors out of her room because she knows and fears the self-created monster of destruction that will call Aegisthus and Clytemnestra out of the palace to die.

It is in his 'jarring' plays ('pièces grinçantes') that Anouilh expounds most discordantly upon the subjects of life and love, marriage and children. The plays end on a displeasing, disconcerting note, expressing total cynicism that love can exist between a man and a woman. Even the marriages of the wealthy, although based on the solid foundation of money, are not happy. The nefarious influence of money on love, which the poor heroines fear, is lived out each day by the rich: a routine of boredom, hostility, hatred, deception, hypocrisies and extravagances of all kinds. Anouilh's heroines, refusing orchids, champagne and furs, will request baser beverages and seek instead the warmth of a supportive hand in their revolt against society's hypocrisy. No truly happy couple is portrayed in any of the plays, and whatever pleasure might have existed in the premarital state is soon destroyed by marriage. Anouilh describes marriage as a chemical experiment in which 'a mixture at first bubbles and sparkles; then happiness volatilises, leaving in the retort nothing but a big grey lump of [marital] obligations.'[5] The stock figure of General Saint-Pé (in *Ardèle, La Valse des toréadors,* and *L'Hurluberlu*), as well as Antoine de Saint-Flour in *Les poissons rouges,* are symbolic of the pathetic, disillusioned, humiliated, and unheroic married man.

Anouilh's heroines are true to themselves, isolated in their contemporary world, persistent in their sincerity and fidelity, lacerated by the conflict between their ideal and the hypocrisy that underlies sordid reality. In the 'pièces noires', the antagonism between the 'pure' heroine and perverted society results in either actual or symbolic death, while, in the 'pièces roses' and 'brillantes', escape from the convulsed world takes the form of either the creation of an illusion that triumphs over reality, or a refuge in one's multiple personalities. The author is deeply concerned with this idea of the multiplicity and mutability of the human personality, and with the realisation that the human being cannot be reduced to a unity that will afford him inner peace and contentment. He is aware of the relativity of human sentiments and emotions to social, sociological and economic conditions, and of the disturbing feelings of disunity that result from the conflict between them. Perhaps the most forceful example the author has given us of a heroine for whom changing human opinions have no significance is Joan of Arc: in the face of the relative truths of her parents, the people of France, and her executioners, she remains a symbol of absolute truth.

Anouilh's distinction between the heroic and the mediocre is often explained in terms of the 'poor' and the 'rich' races. Of the two, it is the poor race that can father heroines—not the wealthy nor the nobility. The lower class produces remarkably courageous women, while the upper class spends its unheroic life taking futility seriously. By the very rottenness of family life among the wealthy, with its inaneness, its ménages à trois, or à quatre, its hypocrisy, and its debauchery, the growth of heroism in the 'rich' race is stunted. Within the poor race, Anouilh distinguishes between the happy and the unhappy, the mediocre and the heroic. He describes the former as 'an exploding, fertile race, a flabby mass of dough that eats its sausage, bears children, uses its tools, counts its *sous,* year after year, in spite of epidemics and wars, until old age catches up with it; people living life, everyday people, people it's hard to imagine as dead'. The latter he describes as 'the noble ones, the heroes. Those whom you can easily imagine stretched out dead, pale, with a bullet hole in the head—the cream of the crop'.[6] The 'flabby masses of dough' take the form of the Rouen mob awaiting the spectacle of the burning of Joan of Arc, or the spitting, stenching Thebes mob described in **Antigone,** with its thousand arms and its thousand faces, but only one indistinguishable expression of mockery and laughter.

The heroines look disdainfully on the mediocrity of those who inhabit the realms of superficiality, conformity, and weakness; this majority is analogous to the 'rich' race in that it masks truths and is afraid to face absolutes. Rather than daring to dream the impossible dream of something better, the mediocre take refuge in their petty maladies, their banalities, and their stomachs. The heroines, instead, seek answers to metaphysical questions and are eternally dissatisfied with themselves. Their conscience and concept of order, clearly conceived and stated, form the sharp dividing line between the rigorous demands of heroic honour and the mediocre satisfactions of the masses. Anouilh's heroines love honour not for honour's sake, but for the sake of an *idea of honour* which they have created for themselves. Whereas honour, for the author's anti-heroes, is something to be remembered or forgotten at will, to be bought and sold, soiled and washed, the heroine's idea of honour can be neither improvised nor defiled by compromise. The concept of an honour to be defended unto death is basic to the plays in which a heroine champions nonconformity, purity, and refusal to compromise. A truly sorry figure is King Charles of France, in **L'Alouette,** who has neither wealth, nor courage, nor anyone to defend his person, much less his title. For this pusillanimous king, the concept of honour is nonexistent, and it is Joan who will illustrate what the pursuit of honour is all about. Joan's duty is to remain loyal to her intransigent race and to her search for purity, regardless of how absurd or how grotesque her role may be. The sole commandment for Anouilh's 'insolent breed' of heroines is to do what has to be done, when it has to be done, and to do it wholeheartedly and completely, even though it is unpleasant and difficult. Cauchon, the Bishop of Beauvais, pleads with Joan to recant during her trial for heresy: 'Joan, try to understand that there is something absurd about your refusal' (*PC,* p. 112). Likewise, Antigone persistently tells Creon that she must return to her brother's grave to replace the earth that the guards have removed. Creon replies: 'You'll return to make such an absurd gesture again? . . . Even if you should succeed in covering the grave again, you know very well that we'll uncover the cadaver. So what are you accomplishing except dirtying your fingernails with blood and getting yourself hanged?' Antigone answers: 'Nothing but that, I know.

But at least I can do that. And everyone must do whatever he can' (*NPN,* p. 76). The 'insolent ones' are confident that God or the gods favour them and will grant them sufficient time in which to accomplish, with appropriate dignity, their absurd duty. Antigone will have time to perform the funeral rites for her dead brother with her tiny, rusty spade before she is hanged. Anouilh's heroines find lies repugnant, deception indecent, compromise inelegant. They insist on being aesthetically 'pure', on playing their role down to the last detail. The heroine is willing to adopt the commandment to do what has to be done, even though it may be absurd because she has been unable to find a solid truth in society on which she can base her definition of self and of her actions. The roots of her tragedy lie in the disjointed relations between herself and others: Antigone cannot accept Creon as her true authority; Medea could be happy in a world without Jason (who symbolises compromise), but she knows that the world contains both Jason and herself and, therefore, the seeds of conflict. She will have to oppose him unarmed in a losing battle, because he is of the 'rich' race. She cries out to him: 'Race of Abel, race of the just, race of the rich, how calmly you speak. It must be good to have the gods on your side, and the police, too' (*NPN,* p. 389). The serenity of the mediocre race is denied to the frenzied heroines who obstreperously reject the maxim that physical, political, or military might makes right. Antigone's position, vis-à-vis the king, who demands compromise, is identical to that of Medea. Antigone loves both life and her fiancé Haemon, but will nevertheless persist in performing the burial rites for her brother in the full knowledge that death will be her groom.

Rejecting all concepts of compromise and conformity, Anouilh's heroines starkly delineate and label their every action or sentiment of honour; nowhere do they see a grey area offering refuge, nor any opportunity to avoid justification of their acts. While the heroic figures refuse to accept the definition of happiness proffered by the mediocre, the mediocre, in turn, can understand neither what it is that the heroines are seeking, nor why, in their mental anorexia, they choose to absent themselves physically and spiritually from the routine of life's banquet.

The lifespan of the mediocre race is nothing but an endless and ugly vegetation. So powerful is the heroine's scorn for life's 'sale espoir' that, just as Joan of Arc is about to recant and Antigone is about to accede to her uncle's reasoning, the allusions to 'happiness' by Warwick and Creon, respectively, are enough for the women once again to prefer death to an act of compromise. The 'happiness' formula automatically antagonises the heroine; the picture of the 'petit bonheur' of the masses as a life of compromise and mediocrity, contrary to her demands for a state of perpetual happiness, shocks Antigone into reasserting her defiance. She thereupon taunts her uncle, the king, until he is forced to call in the guards. Only then does Creon understand her revolt. Polynices was merely a pretext; Antigone's *raison d'être* is to be put to death—to be a heroine. It is not difficult for Antigone to renounce even Haemon, because the idea that he will grow older and make compromises is unbearable: 'I love a young and hard Haemon, a Haemon demanding and faithful, like me. . . . But if the wear and tear of your life, your happiness, must change him in any way . . . then I no longer love Haemon' (*NPN*, p. 187). Antigone is reminiscent of Ibsen's uncompromising Brand, for whom 'the enemy' is personified as the spirit of compromise, the spirit of the *juste milieu*. Death, then, becomes a refuge and deliverance from this damnable existence. The vicarious experience of 'living' makes the heroines even more determined, at the crucial and decisive moment, to refuse to understand, to refuse to be 'reasonable'. 'Moi, je ne veux pas comprendre', is Antigone's rejoinder throughout the play, and it is echoed in other plays by heroines who refuse to be 'reasonable' by conforming to society's norms. Refusal to 'live', to 'grow up and understand', is a dominant theme in Anouilh's theatre, but the desire to remain childlike is not a form of desire for regression; it is, rather, a reasoned and deliberate decision not to conform when an ideal or a concept of honour is threatened.

Persons in power attempt unsuccessfully to dissuade extremists from their nonconformity by demonstrating the absurdity of their ideal. Creon tries to destroy Antigone's illusions by smearing the image in her mind of her brother Polynices and revealing that it may even be Eteocles' body that she has buried instead. Her sister Ismene tries to dissuade her from covering the body, arguing that he was not a good brother. Antigone, however, stands firm: 'What do I care for your politics, your necessities, your miserable stories. I can still say "no" . . . and I am sole judge' (*NPN*, p. 177). The concept of an absurd duty to be fulfilled can be judged only by a superior race of 'imbeciles'. Cauchon, in an attempt to destroy the will of the imprisoned Joan, tells her that all of her good soldiers have abandoned her and, weary of war, have fled Rouen. Even La Hire, her closest companion in battle, has hired himself out as a mercenary, she is told; but higher voices than Cauchon's also speak to Joan and those are the only ones she hears. Count Tigre, in *La Répétition,* is defamed by a debauched nobleman who attempts to disabuse the heroine, Lucile. Obstinately refusing to leave the château, for she cherishes the Count and her own illusions about him, Lucile persists in believing in the superiority of her ideal Tigre, despite most convincing evidence of his incorrigible flightiness.

Although Anouilh's heroines will accept death, if necessary, in order to fulfil their concept of duty, they nevertheless love life and cling to it humbly and sentimentally. Unabashedly seeking ways to lessen their fear, they are not at all like Corneille's classical feminine protagonists, who would die without openly expressing their innermost feelings. The Prologue in *Antigone* tells us that, as the heroine sits silently on the stage, she thinks about the fact that she is going to die, that she is young and would have liked to live, but that there is no changing the role that she must play. Later in the play, the following exchange takes place between Antigone and her sister: '(Ismene:) I don't want to die. (Antigone:) I too would have liked not to die . . . (Ismene:) I'm not very courageous, you know. (Antigone:) Neither am I. But what difference does it make?' (*NPN*, pp. 140,143). An almost identical scene is to be found in *Medea*: '(Nurse:) I am old, I don't want to die. (Medea:) I too . . . would have liked to live' (*NPN*, pp. 366-7). Joan, when asked by Cauchon whether she is afraid to die, admits that she is but that it makes no difference. Invariably, the heroines must bear their emotions and fears alone. They stand firm in the knowledge that they have been abandoned by all and that, in the end, society will destroy them. Antigone, after Ismene's renunciation of her part in the burial of Polynices, realises that it is up to her alone to defy Creon's edict. Creon, as the author of that edict, is also alone, but he can never reach the stature of the heroine, who has made no compromise with life. Electra had learned hatred and revenge all by herself and she, too, is the sole judge of her actions. Her mother's infidelity, and the assassination of her father, have given her an inflexible concept of duty and honour which will drive her unflinchingly to vengeance. Solitary, inaccessible heroines, abandoned by gods and by men, they all, like Joan, 'continue . . . with that curious mixture of humility and insolence, of grandeur and common sense, even up to the stake; . . . it is this solitude, in this silence of an absent God, in this deprivation and this bestial misery, that . . . [they are] great and alone' (*PC*, p. 56). Like Joan, they are 'little skylark[s] immobile against the sun, being shot at' (*PC*, p. 83)—an image that greatly disturbs those who have power but not glory. The Inquisitor in *L'Alouette,* for example, explains that the smaller, the frailer, the more tender, the *purer* the enemy, the more formidable he/she is. When Creon is told that it was a young girl who defied his orders, he muses over the dialogue that he anticipates between himself and the pale, intransigent rebel, knowing well that haughty contempt awaits him.

Describing George Bernard Shaw's Joan of Arc, Harold Clurman has written:

> She has to be stopped, done away with, because like all fanatically persistent moralists, she is a pest, a threat, unbearable to the ordinary. . . . Though she wins in history, she must lose in her person. She herself recognizes this, but cannot and does not wish to curb her force and fail her fate.[7]

Only when the fragile little 'enemies' of the Church or State are removed from the scene does stability again reign, but only temporarily, until the next heroine is conjured up. After each new heroine falls under the Inquisition or the gallows, silent calm descends upon the State, until the next gunshots are heard being fired at a skylark.

Anouilh gives the name of the shameless, dissolute and notorious wife of Ahab, King of Israel, to the anti-heroine of his play, *Jézabel* (1932), whose immorality and atrocious behaviour deny her son, Marc, the happiness he seeks. Opposed to Jézabel is Jacqueline, a paragon of purity, innocence and serenity, whom Marc loves and would like to bring into his home—but this is precluded by the fat, lazy, alcoholic, promiscuous, murderous woman that is his mother and for whom he feels responsible. In desperation, and clinging to the squalor that links him to his mother, Marc roughly expels Jacqueline from his life, refusing to understand her love, her gentleness, her pity, and the invitation to happiness that she extends to him. Once his beloved has left, however, Marc dashes out of his home, stricken with madness and suffering. The glimpse of purity provided by Jacqueline prevents him from remaining any longer with Jézabel. The reader must believe that Marc will overtake Jacqueline and achieve the purification that can be wrought through the heroine.

La Sauvage (1934) is in many ways similar to *Jézabel.* Thérèse Tarde, whose sordid life is evoked in relentless detail, is loved by the wealthy Florent, who offers her (as did Jacqueline to Marc) marriage, happiness, and forgetfulness of things past. Thérèse refuses the happiness Florent offers, convinced that suffering must be her vocation and her only hope for redemption, echoing Baudelaire's 'Je sais que la douleur est la noblesse unique'. The heroine is faced with the option of 'le sale petit bonheur' that money offers, and she derisively rejects it. Revolt stirs within her; she cries out that she simply does not want to understand certain things, that she will not be domesticated, and that she will not be tricked into looking only at the pleasant things in life. Thérèse envisions all the people of her sordid past as though banded together to receive her in their midst and thus prevent her from making any compromise with the rich. She can reach no comprehension of Florent and his 'race'; she can, however, understand that it is only through extreme violence or in supreme gestures that the 'poor' come a bit closer to the 'happiness' that is heroism or, vice versa, the heroism that constitutes true happiness.

Similarly, the heroine of *Roméo et Jeannette* (1945), reminiscent of the central character in Saul Bellow's *The Last Analysis,* is determined to undergo a baptism of filth and squalor in order to recover her true self. By shamelessly exposing her immorality to her Romeo, she

believes she will find the path of self-renewal. Jeannette, in the end, will drown herself in her symbolic white gown, taking the lead in the final tragedy in which the man she loves follows suit, both choosing sacrificial death for the sake of the 'pure' love denied to the mediocre.

La Grotte (1961) is one of the plays in which the stock character of the young servant, Adele, appears. Downstairs in the 'grotto' (the kitchen), she is trying desperately and with much physical pain to abort, after having been raped and become pregnant, by imbibing bitter brews. She is further martyrised by the Cook, who has discovered that her illegitimate son (the Seminarist) loves Adele; by the Seminarist, who insists that Adele remain 'pure'; by the despicable valet, who tries to 'sell' her to a café owner in Oran; and, finally, by the Author himself—a character in the play—who deafens her by shouting that her mentality is all wrong! Adele is miraculously 'a being who still remains pure and innocent in the filth in which she wallows'.[8] Up to a certain point in the play, Adele is a self-negating, timid creature, who submits whenever anyone raises a voice to her—a pathetic peasant girl without the mettle of Joan of Arc. But in the dramatic scene in which she finally rejects with scorn both the downstairs and the upstairs worlds that surround her, she shows herself to be of the ilk of a true Anouilh heroine. Her scathing contempt is directed against her father, who had made her a victim of his drunken desires; the coachman, who had seduced her in the filth of the stable; the Cook, who prepares concoctions to induce abortion and serves them with violent blows; the Count and the Countess 'upstairs'; the nuns who used to punish her in winter by forcing her to sit outdoors on a pail of cold water and ask for God's pardon; the Seminarist, whom she loves; and God, whom she does not love. Adele represents the innocence and purity of 'la sauvage' in the midst of corruption and abasement. The Author in the play says: 'It is for her, too—to render homage that she never would have received in her misery—that I wanted to write this play, and I wanted it to be a beautiful play' (*La Grotte,* p. 51).

If, in the 'pièces noires', society triumphs over the absolute ideal and compels the heroines to tragic escape, in the 'pièces roses', Anouilh's characters flee black reality through fantasy, illusion, and changing personality. It is as if the author felt that the world, with its fiendish problems, lacked and needed the sense of humour that he attempted to provide in 'rosy' situations, dexterously managed and manipulated by women, who give their audiences a sense of confidence and optimism. With sparkling humour, the English Lady Hurf (in *Le Bal des voleurs,* 1932), an old 'belle', bored in her sumptuous villa, plays out a comedy of errors, for her only escape from loneliness is into the realm of the illusion created on the evening of the thieves' ball. The aura of fantasy enveloping Lady Hurf and her entourage is carried over to Isabelle, in *Le Rendezvous de Senlis* (1937), in which Georges Delachaume, ashamed of the hypocrisy and avarice of his parents and harassed by the hysteria and jealousy of his wife, creates a world of dreams and fantasies into which he leads the naive young provincial girl, Isabelle, who symbolises detachment and purity, and with whose simplicity, happiness, radiance, and grandmothers, Georges falls fancifully in love.

Another of Anouilh's purely poetic fantasies is *Léocadia* (1939), in which the humble milliner, Amanda, succeeds miraculously in substituting for the dead dramatic actress Léocadia in the heart of the inconsolable Prince Albert Troubiscol. Amanda's magic is that she can render the repulsive attractive, the complicated simple, the unreal real, and the hypocritical sincere, just by being her honest and modest self.

Likewise, in the pleasantly jumbled fairy tale *L'Invitation au château* (1947), it is the poor, insignificant dancer, Isabelle, playing the role of a dazzling socialite, who is the heroine in the château and in the comedy. This young girl's indomitable pride bids her to refuse money: as useful as it is, it cannot replace her values, which are friendship and love. Similarly, Lucile, in *La Répétition,* emerges as the character possessed of the purest and most noble sentiments. Governess of the twelve orphans being raised in a wing of the château, the generous, self-giving Lucile holds herself apart from the sordid liaisons being played out in the aristocratic household. She has faith in higher values of romantic purity and true love. This 'pièce brillante' is delicately and scintillatingly fashioned around the tragic theme of the destruction of that love and Lucile's exile from the château, combined with the rosy theme of the jaded Count's love for the humble governess—a love that goes beyond time and circumstance, beyond good and evil.

Ardèle is the hunchbacked old maid, whose love for the hunchbacked tutor in the Saint-Pé household is genuine and sublime. A symbol of pure love, Ardèle is kept locked in her bedroom, whence she undertakes a protest hunger strike, remains invisible throughout the play, and is ultimately destroyed, for the night that her door is accidentally left unlocked, her lover slips into her room and the two commit suicide. Ardèle is the daisy whose petals wither and fall on too close contact with the grotesque loveless love scenes of the other couples in the play. What Anouilh has said about Joan of Arc applies also to Ardèle ou la Marguerite:

> 'You cannot explain Joan any more than you can explain the tiniest flower growing by the wayside. There it is—just a little living flower that has always known, ever since it was a microscopic seed, how many petals it would have and how big they would grow, exactly how blue its blue would be and how its delicate scent would be compounded.[9]

Anouilh's heroines are exceptional women united in a troubling, tragic destiny. In the story of their lives there is a dramatic constant—an enigmatic discomfort which modern psychiatry defines as 'mental anorexia'. Ardèle's refusal of food until the soul in her hump is recognised by those who will not see, Antigone's persistent defiance and refusal to obey edicts, indicate their indomitable perseverance in their search for self-annihilation. Anouilh's heroines are rebellious women with a will to self-sacrifice, in protest or on principle. Through the famous examples in his plays, Anouilh brings rich imagination to descriptions of adolescents, or mature and intelligent women, who refuse the food of life, choose to renounce 'happiness' and die, thereby giving expression to their hunger for something else—perhaps a hunger for 'nothingness'.

If the theatre of Jean Anouilh is destined to survive in future panoramas of French literature, his fame will unequivocally rest on those plays whose heroes are heroines.

Notes

1. Jean Anouilh, *Nouvelles pièces noires* (Paris: La Table ronde, 1958) p. 188. Subsequent page references are given in text as: '(*NPN*, p.)'.

2. Jean Anouilh, *Pièces costumées* (Paris: La Table ronde, 1960) p. 131. Subsequent page references are given in text as: '(*PC*, p.)'.

3. Anouilh, *Nouvelles pièces noires,* p. 366.

4. Jean Anouilh, *Oreste* (fragments), in Robert de Luppé, *Jean Anouilh, suive de fragments de la pièce de Jean Anouilh: Oreste* (Paris: Editions universitaires, 1959) p. 115.

5. Jean Anouilh, *Pièces brillantes,* (Paris: La Table ronde, 1951) p. 493.

6. Jean Anouilh, *Pièces noires* (Paris: Calmann-Lévy, 1945) p. 360.

7. Harold Clurman, *The Naked Image: Observations on the Modern Theatre* (New York: Macmillan, 1966) p. 142.

8. Jean Anouilh, *La Grotte* (Paris: La Table ronde, 1961) p. 141. Subsequent page references are given in text.

9. In the programme of the French production of *L'Alouette*; quoted in Christopher Fry's translation, *The Lark* (New York: Oxford University Press, 1956) p. ii.

LE VOYAGEUR SANS BAGAGE (*TRAVELLER WITHOUT LUGGAGE*)

PRODUCTION REVIEW

Harold Clurman (review date 5 October 1964)

SOURCE: Clurman, Harold. "Traveller without Luggage, The Committee." *Nation*, New York, N.Y., (5 October 1964): 202.

[*In the following unfavorable review of the 1964 New York production of* Traveller without Luggage, *Clurman argues that the play "shows some of the salient features of Anouilh's personality and an attitude which were to place him in the front rank of French playwrights between the late thirties and the fifties."*]

Since Jean Anouilh's *Traveller without Luggage* has suffered, as have many other French plays in the past, in being transferred from the boulevards to Broadway, I shall not dwell on its production at the Anta Theatre. The cast includes several talented actors—Ben Gazzara, Mildred Dunnock, Rae Allen, to name only three—and there are some well-played passages, notably in the second scene, but the right tone is never found. This is largely due to the very real difficulty that confronts American actors and directors who try to realize the exact nature of French behavior. They are removed from the cultural environment of such plays, and even their earnest efforts to suggest it therefore seem like affectation in moments of comedy, and the ungainly "emotionalism" in more dramatic exchanges.

The text itself is interesting in several respects. Written in 1937 when its author was 27, it was his first success. Though by no means his best play, *Traveller without Luggage* shows some of the salient features of Anouilh's personality and an attitude which were to place him in the front rank of French playwrights between the late thirties and the fifties.

Anouilh despises the world that bred him—the "wondrous time" before the First World War (1900-14), the last period of bourgeois security in France. The war was to explode many of the myths about the proverbial worth and refinement of its civilization. If there was truth in any of these myths, it could be substantiated after the war only by an acknowledgment of the moral and spiritual bankruptcy of the old bourgeoisie. And that class became the particular object of Anouilh's hatred.

The war-injured amnesiac of *Traveller without Luggage,* attempting to recall the conditions of life from which the shock of his wound cut him off, slowly discovers the rottenness of a life that contributed in no small measure to his own wretched character. He sees himself the product of a world that was mean, egotistic, snobbish, frivolous, cruel, sex-obsessed and loveless. Venomous scorn for the wealthy French middle class (as well as for the still lingering remnants of a well-heeled aristocracy) permeates most of Anouilh's work like an acid. The only redemption for a man born of that world is to reject it utterly. In *Traveller without Luggage,* anathematizing his past, Anouilh became a typical voice of a whole generation in a similar state of revulsion.

Anouilh—fortunately and unfortunately—has been unable to discard the luggage of the past. There is a good deal of a particular kind of French sentimentality in Anouilh's disillusionment; it has the taste of a rancid romanticism. There are also traces of a nobility whose antecedents are in an older (seventeenth-century) tradition mixed with a certain stored national experience. This produces a striking canniness (healthy in a Montaigne), which in Anouilh sometimes expresses itself as worldly wisdom and a peppery humor, and sometimes as a rather petty cynicism. All this is significant because the dramatist shares these traits with a very large segment of his compatriots.

Among the still serviceable things that Anouilh has inherited from the past is a sure sense of the stage. He is a consummate craftsman. Part of Anouilh's superb theatrical equipment is his ability to borrow and make new use of the staples of classic comedy—the oldest devices from Plautus through Molière to vaudeville. The surprise ending of *Traveller without Luggage*—in which the man who in horror wishes to escape his newly recovered family, and seizes upon a new family found by "poetic" license in a little boy—is a case in point. This is in itself a telling image and it turns an acrid and not very plausible tale into something beguiling.

The most genuine facet of Anouilh is his gift for artifice. All his plays are basically fables, contrivances of brilliantly imaginative showmanship, full of surprises and fascinating sleight-of-hand. Whatever his intentions, they often serve fundamentally serious ends.

The critical pendulum has swung from revering Anouilh as one of the "great" dramatists of our day to dismissing him as a highly skilled cheap-Jack (Anouilh has recently taken to disclaiming any exalted artistic aim). I myself veer from admiration to distrust. There is something meretricious in Anouilh's soulfulness and aching idealism. But, aside from his unmistakable adroitness, his adult shrewdness, independence, rebelliousness and corruption, mixed with the rich humanistic substance bequeathed by his country and which he seems to love with considerable resentment, make him representative of his time and place and give him an individual *face.* All this will finally be found to have value and will surely count when the overestimation of his excellence becomes as obsolete as are the too drastic denunciations of his defects.

CRITICAL COMMENTARY

Anca Vlasopolos (essay date December 1986)

SOURCE: Vlasopolos, Anca. "The Perils of Authorship in *Le voyageur sans bagage.*" *Modern Drama* 29, no. 4 (December 1986): 601-12.

[*In the following essay, Vlasopolos explores the reasons for the relative obscurity of* Traveler without Luggage.]

Despite its respectable history in performance, Anouilh's *Le voyageur sans bagage* has received little critical attention.[1] Regarded as Anouilh's first mature play, *Le voyageur sans bagage* is seen as heralding the existential themes of Anouilh's greater theater.[2] Perhaps critical neglect of the play has had to do with the historical position of this between-wars drama. Focused on the restless specter of the First World War, the 1937 *Voyageur sans bagage* appeared too late, too close to the outbreak of the Second World War, to be relevant in an immediate political sense. Anouilh's later productions, particularly ***Antigone,*** were a more satisfactory response to the overwhelming turmoil of Europe. Yet in a film like Renoir's *La grande illusion,* which was released at the same time as the first performance of *Le voyageur sans bagage,* World War I becomes an enduring and timely reflection on a past that presages, especially in the irony of the title, the greater horrors to come. Thus, it might seem odd that this play has not attracted more critical notice, even after a brief revival of performances and study during the sixties in the United States.[3]

Critics who describe the play as "family" drama provide a clue to its relative obscurity; instead of the epic, if not heroic, scope and the nearly all-male universe of *La grande illusion* and other war stories, *Le voyageur sans bagage* brings the war into the salon.[4] Without either glorifying the war or domesticating it, Anouilh makes it rage inside the nation, inside the very hearth. This subversive, dispiriting vision presents the Great War as a series of vicious, petty, family squabbles, which lead to the sacrifice of the young for the sake of socio-economic and political stability. A crisis of enormous proportions in European history appears in *Le voyageur sans bagage* as capable of being resolved only by yet another sacrifice of the essential being to a historically defined, contained entity.

As with other plays of any importance in the twentieth century, the most often-discussed aspect of *Le voyageur sans bagage* has been its genre, in particular its ending.

Anouilh seems to have attempted to obviate questions of genre by classifying his own theater according to the idiosyncratic categories of *pièces roses, pièces noires, pièces grinçantes, pièces brillantes,* etc. But this refusal of generic boundaries by the author has in no way hampered critics from applying traditional generic distinctions to his plays. There is general consensus that Anouilh writes tragicomedies that verge on the *rose* or on the *noir* without taking on completely the coloring ascribed to them by the author.[5] In this sense, at least, critics vie with the creator for the definition—a possession of sorts—of the text. Anouilh categorizes *Le voyageur sans bagage* as a *pièce noire,* and in my reading his color code goes unchallenged, despite the much-disputed ending, or rather because of it.

The ending, which for critics puts the play in the pink, has been variously labelled as prestidigitation, as self-conscious artificiality, and as self-reflexive play.[6] The pervasive critical approaches, classifications according to traditional genre, and exegeses focused on the hero of the play, only partially make room for a play like *Le voyageur sans bagage* in the canon of twentieth-century theater; explaining the problematic genre of a play by defining it as "play" or as self-conscious artificiality is a circular argument. Nor does the preoccupation with the main character's purity, identity, and motives confront the rivalry for authorship of the entity Gaston-Jacques in which every character participates and which leaves no character, including the main one, unsullied.[7]

Is it important that *Le voyageur sans bagage* undergo a revaluation? Because the play raises unresolved issues of genre, and because, as I shall argue, its plot suggests a sacrificial ritual, it merits consideration as representative twentieth-century theater. Moreover, the theme of *Le voyageur sans bagage,* the desire to lay to rest a war whose memory will not be contained, deserves our fullest attention.

Almost every character and certainly every group of characters wish to possess Gaston by giving him a habitation and a name. This convergence of mimetic desire on to Gaston produces the violent rivalries that seek kudos without acknowledging that in this case the kudos is a human being.[8] Why is the amnesiac the subject of such intense and dangerous desires? Both as Gaston and as Jacques Renaud, the man in question embodies the disquiet of a patriarchal order gone awry. Consequently, *Le voyageur sans bagage* displays a society anxious to recover its power and its authority over a history that has escaped its control. Gaston has never had the ahistorical existence of the "honest woman," one that is always inscribed by the male possessor, not by the woman herself. Despite his amnesia, he is not a blank to be written on, but rather a text washed over, even whitewashed, whose underlying message must be uncovered. Psychiatry in this play serves not to judge the veracity, hence the authority, of the self in telling its own story so much as to unearth and recover that which psychiatry in the service of society determines as lost.

As early as Act 1, Anouilh outlines in bold strokes a plot surrounding Gaston that can be characterized as sacrificial. Representative of war-torn Europe as well as isolated from it, Gaston as a left-over from the Great War must be disposed of so that the social order can be re-established. Although he survives the war, he remains its victim, and as such he becomes the focus of postwar distress. His individuality consists of contradictory, rival narratives, and his existence is an unfinished plot that characters in the play engage in bringing to an end. The plot hinges on the rivalry for possession that develops around Gaston. He is the kudos that the Duchess Dupont-Dufort and her nephew have wrested away from psychiatric and class rivals. He is to be bestowed at the Duchess's pleasure on the Renauds rather than on the other five families claiming him, whose proofs "sont sensiblement égales," because the Renauds are members of the *haute bourgeoisie,* the class closest to that of the Duchess herself.[9] As early as the first act, the Duchess sums up the reasons both for exalting and for defiling Gaston, reasons which dehumanize him and turn him into the singularity that can be sacrificed.

That the entity Gaston-Jacques, the yet-unread text, is separate in the Duchess's perception from the individual so called becomes clear in her worship of the entity, and defilement of the individual:

> Ainsi, vous êtes un des cas les plus troublants de la psychiatrie; une des énigmes les plus angoissantes de la Grande Guerre—et, si je traduis bien votre grossier langage, cela vous fait rire? Vous êtes, comme l'a dit très justement un journaliste de talent, le soldat inconnu vivant—et cela vous fait rire? Vous êtes donc incapable de respect, Gaston?
>
> (p. 13)

Lack of respect toward, as she puts it, what he personifies and what he represents is the least of the accusations levelled at Gaston. He is guilty of having a heart of stone, then of marble as "la pierre la plus dure," of being a child, and, worst of all crimes, of being an ingrate. Finally, after being chided for lacking respect for what he symbolizes, he is accused of growing conceited by taking the very same journalistic reports too seriously (p. 14). The absurdity of these accusations and of this misplaced worship gives the play its sardonic comedy, but it announces the more sinister accusations and worship that will attempt to capture Gaston and place him in a context that will obliterate his individuality.

Having intervened in Gaston's fate by bringing him first to the Renauds, the Duchess attempts to elevate her role to mythical stature. Her self-serving assertions contain ironic undertones: "J'ai l'impression d'entreprendre une lutte sans merci contre la fatalité, contre la mort, contre toutes les forces obscures du monde." In effect, she has allied herself to those forces by reducing Gaston to a trophy of internecine war, as her next remark suggests: "Je me suis vêtue de noir, j'ai pensé que c'était le plus indiqué" (p. 24). Just how much of a trophy Gaston is, how much symbolic value society has invested in him, and what strictly economic factors are at work become revealed with the entrance of the first contenders, the Renauds. Huspar, the attorney, reminds them and the audience that Gaston is one of four hundred thousand missing soldiers, the one who has been found, but not *placed.* He thus serves as a reminder of those who remain suspended in the no-man's-land of a plot without closure. The war cannot be over while so many are neither dead nor alive, while their families refuse "de renoncer à l'espoir" of recovering them. Apart from his symbolic value, Gaston represents a windfall to the claimants through his accumulated war pension, which as a resident of an asylum he has been forbidden to use.

Gaston himself would have been among the returning, were it not for the erasure of memory that severs him from the society eager to take him back. And there is unanimity in the desire to take him back, to his past, to his accumulated debts toward the society that he has managed to evade, even to his death on the battlefront. Both as Jacques Renaud and as Gaston, the traveller has so far escaped the rules and obligations of a strict and classbound patriarchy and thereby gained, if not our respect, our envy.

Whereas generic indeterminacy combined with a strong main character often results in an ambiguity of response to that character, Anouilh manages to create a protagonist who captures the sympathy of the audience. Supposedly pitted against the values of the society that he rejects, Gaston struggles to remain free of the others' conception and even remembrance of him. Anouilh thus successfully disguises Gaston's active participation in the recovery of the former self, his complicity in the struggle to wrest from his opponents the authorship of the entity Gaston-Jacques. More damning than Gaston's understandable desire to define his past according to his lights is his fashioning of a self around the very same bourgeois values he protests against. As Gaston joins the crowd claiming Gaston-Jacques as a prize in a contest, he provides the unanimity necessary for the sacrifice of that rediscovered being. Class, sex, and age go to war in an attempt to occupy the empty territory of Gaston's past existence. Gaston's presence at the Renauds is a show of power on the Duchess's part. She declares herself ready to lay down her life to defend the claims of the upper classes to the amnesiac: "n'ayez crainte, moi vivante on ne donnera pas Gaston à un lampiste!" (p. 28). Madame Renaud expresses surprise that others have so much as a right to be considered before the Renauds, particularly since the Duchess is in charge of the case. The Duchess, however, does not wish an empty victory; she attributes power to her opponents: "Nous vivons à une époque inouïe! Ces gens-là ont toutes les prétentions" (p. 28). Seeming alarmed by the arrival of the lower-class pretenders, she throws herself into the good fight with gusto. She announces, "Ces gens-là se croient frustrés. Ils vont faire un scandale, nous accuser de Dieu sait quoi" (p. 87). She sets up the strategy of combat by assessing her opponents' forces: "Ils sont autant qu'hier? C'est bien une idée de paysans de venir en groupe pour mieux se défendre" (p. 94). And not only the lower classes engage in the challenge to her might, but the whole "presse de gauche," against whom she employs her "espions" (p. 95), in the manner of world powers. Huspar's and Madame Renaud's responses to the Duchess's sounding the alarm show how specious her fears are. Huspar asserts, "Je suis sûr . . . que personne n'oserait vous suspecter" (p. 87), and Madame Renaud, exasperated, dismisses the danger of scandal. The Duchess herself, in the midst of preparing an offensive, is distracted from her urgent purpose by the sight of a stuffed squirrel, which makes her reflect on the possibility of making fur coats out of the creature. She is also quite sure of her position of unshakable strength, for she assures Madame Renaud that "L'épreuve a commencé par vous, il faudra, qu'ils le veuillent ou non, que nous la terminions régulièrement" (p. 95), despite the glaring irregularity of the beginning.

The aristocracy and the *haute bourgeoisie* can claim disinterestedness in their desire that the recovered Gaston be one of them, that they win in the fortunes of war. Whereas the dairy vendor and the infamous "lampiste," along with the other petty bourgeois and workers, can easily be seen as grasping for Gaston's two hundred and fifty thousand francs, surely the Renauds wish only to repossess their little Jacques. Madame Renaud puts the question in a way that brings out the difference in sensibility between classes: "Comment cette question d'argent peut-elle jouer dans une alternative aussi tragique?" (p. 29). The Duchess describes those near her class as "charmants" and "adorables" even before she has set eyes on them, through the class signature of their written communications (pp. 28, 94). While the lower-middle and working-class claimants are kept off stage, Anouilh creates a chorus of servants that comments on the doings of the masters. Thus, the class war is exposed in all its bitterness. With the exception of Juliette, young Jacques's mistress, the servants are united in their hatred of the returned master, whom they only imperfectly see, but whom they recognize, however indistinct he remains, as the enemy. In Act 2 a group of servants crowds before a keyhole: the chauffeur, looking at Gaston, recognizes the "sale gueule à ce petit salaud-là." Each adds his or her memory to an account

that sums up Jacques Renaud as an eighteen-year-old monster, whom all but Juliette would wish back in the grave.

The word "histoire" occurs with some regularity during Act 2, suggesting that the servants' comments have a choral function. Traditionally, the chorus's attempt to differentiate between heroic and ordinary life appears in the pious statements that try to sort out the story. Juliette says, "les morts, ils n'ont rien à voir avec les histoires des vivants," and the butler, after telling a damning story about young Jacques, says, "Les histoires des maîtres sont les histoires des maîtres" (p. 36, 39). And in the manner of a Sophoclean chorus, they all agree that they would rather retain their humble station than suffer the troubles of the great: "les vies commencées comme ça ne se terminent jamais bien"; "J'aime mieux être à ma place qu'à la sienne" (p. 42). Yet the stories that the servants tell and Juliette's romanticized remembrance of her affair with Jacques are precisely the elements of discourse that level class differences and attempt even to bridge the gap between the living and the dead. Since the conditions that generated the servants' injuries continue, the rather cowed *vue d'en bas* that the chorus usually gives on the doings of kings and gods takes on a martial tone in *Le voyageur sans bagage*. The servants, in effect, would end the plot by writing out yet another master: "Vous voulez que je vous dise le fin mot de l'histoire, moi? C'est pas à souhaiter pour nous ni pour personne que ce petit salaud-là, il soit pas mort" (p. 42).

The servants' projected ending fares as well, or as badly, as that of their masters and of the other French families claiming Gaston, and in that sense it gains a measure of equality. The family that with Gaston's complicity wins the coveted prize, the Madensales, figure as prominently in the economy of alternatives as the French families and their retinues. Their motives in seeking Gaston are mercenary; they do not desire the pension, but they need Gaston's person in order to settle an inheritance snag and to continue living in grand style, with the "très belle maison dans le Sussex avec des poneys superbes" (p. 119). Whereas in the Renaud family Gaston would resume his place in the small-scale war between masters and servants, in the Madensale household Gaston will actively perpetuate the power-through-wealth of the upper-middle class.

Although the class conflict seems the most intense, especially since it provides the necessary motivation for the plot, namely the choice of the Renauds as Gaston's most probable family, other equally fierce wars are being waged simultaneously, and in each case the same tactics of accusing and adoring the would-be Jacques are deployed. The sex war in *Le voyageur sans bagage* rages with a bitterness that matches Anouilh's misogynistic *La Valse des toréadors*. The women fare very badly. The sexually active Valentine and Juliette are narcissistic and utterly immoral. The mother figures are split between the cold and detestable Madame Renaud and the mostly comic Duchess, who as a completely desexualized older woman (she does not even have a child of her own) functions more as a politician securing his sphere of influence than as a woman in her relationship with Gaston. The men no less than the women make claims upon Gaston, but these are presented as reasonable in Huspar's case, and as affectionate and noble in the case of Georges. It seems that males ultimately win Gaston to a pre-female Eden, for all traces of the union that created the young "oncle Madensale" have been swallowed up by the sea. Gaston himself participates fully in this war on the male side, whereas he explicitly takes sides in the class war only in his final alliance with the Madensales. The sex division manifests itself most clearly in the methods for Gaston's recovery envisioned by men and women. The Duchess dreams of Gaston meeting his love at the Renauds' and recovering his memory by exchanging a kiss with her, "le premier au sortir de cette tombe" (p. 31). Valentine improves upon the Duchess by disclosing to Gaston that, disguised as a laundress, she seduced him at the asylum in the hope "qu'en me prenant vous retrouveriez la mémoire" (p. 83). Gaston, on the other hand, has a conflicting hope: "Je vous avouerai même que c'est de cet ami imaginaire que j'espérais recevoir la mémoire—comme un service tout naturel" (p. 50). For Gaston the male friendship displaces erotic love as the *natural* bond that would bring him to himself.

This hope becomes the casualty of precisely the kind of love Gaston has avoided. Juliette tells him in agonizing stages about the fight that Jacques had with his best friend over the servant girl they both liked. Gaston denies the power of sexuality and negates the female presence in his life by finding the story incomprehensible. He asks, "pour quelle étrange folie ils se sont battus aussi sauvagement?" She answers, "c'est pour moi." He asks twice, unbelieving, "C'est pour vous?" (pp. 61-2), attempting to reduce her significance and refuse her claim to his past. But whereas Juliette remains an episode of Jacques's youth, Valentine's claim to Gaston embraces his past, his present, and, she hopes, his future. Although Gaston never once wavers in his rejection of her, Valentine's claim and proof, like Juliette's, show Jacques as having betrayed another, even more potent, male bond—the fraternal one. This betrayal, of one male by another, over a woman who in the terms of orderly exchange belongs to the elder brother, becomes the most compelling reason for Gaston's rejection of the identity of Jacques.

Valentine serves as both the most effective mouthpiece for the social constraints that Gaston seeks to escape and the most easily defeated author of Gaston's story. She, as the agent of the recognition token, gives Gaston the irrefutable proof of his identity and at the same time the means of flight. What mars her authority over Gaston is that hers is a female discourse which can be stripped of power despite its knowledge. In his encounters with Valentine, the supposedly innocent Gaston seizes at once the prerogative of male discourse and uses it throughout to destroy Valentine's case without, however, being able to refute it. In claiming him, Valentine undermines the exchange of women on whose regularity patriarchal society depends. She uses the economy of this exchange for her own erotic gains. She explains:

> Vous étiez un enfant. J'étais orpheline, mineure sans un sou, avec une tante bienfaitrice qui m'avait déjà fait payer très cher les premiers partis refusés. Devais-je me vendre à un autre plutôt qu'à lui qui me rapprochait de vous?
>
> (p. 80)

Gaston's response dismisses the content of her claims to the surface form of an inferior discourse determined by gender: "Il y a une rubrique dans les magazines féminins où l'on répond à ce genre de questions" (p. 80).

The conflict between Valentine and Gaston escalates, but the power remains firmly within the province of male discourse. When Gaston declares to Valentine that regardless of proofs he has decided to reject his past, she asks, "Et si j'allais le crier, moi, partout, que je reconnais cette cicatrice?" Gaston's answer again demonstrates that despite his supposed isolation from the structures of power he not only knows of their workings but allies himself to the institutions that would dismiss the truth for the sake of social propriety:

> Au point de vue légal: vous êtes ma belle-soeur, vous vous prétendez ma maîtresse . . . Quel tribunal accepterait de prendre une décision aussi grave sur ce louche imbroglio d'alcôve dont vous seule pouvez parler?
>
> (p. 110)

Again, Valentine's proofs are reducible to the insignificant "parole" of a woman, and moreover of a tainted woman, which would not weigh in the "décision . . . grave" about a man's fate. Only in association with the order that she has been trying to subvert does Valentine regain power. Whereas her single voice does not signify, her voice as the "nous" of the Renauds and the *haute bourgeoisie,* as the "nous" of all of France, who desires to *place* Gaston and get the war over with, comes close to destroying him. But when she speaks for "toutes les femmes, tous les hommes" she is no longer a combatant in the sex war but a powerful representative of societal corruption, a corruption that Anouilh in this play ascribes in large part to the presence of women (pp. 113-4).

The rivalries that converge upon the entity Gaston-Jacques include the claims of age, this last yet another measure of degree, of power, in the patriarchal order. And once more Gaston allies himself with the trappings of power while seeming to struggle against them. Part of Jacques's monstrosity according to the servants' account had to do with his having raised his hand against his mother, threatening, but not committing, violence against her. Yet her position within the Renaud family relegates her to nothing more than titular rule. As an old *woman* she commands neither authority nor respect. As the surviving parent of Jacques, she stands condemned by both her sons as an incompetent head of the family. The patriarch has been absent, and this absence of the highest-ranking male typifies the havoc wrought on the social order by the Great War. It was, in fact, the absence of the next highest-ranking male, the eldest brother, that allowed Jacques's crimes of excess against society. Much of the play centers on Jacques's age—eighteen—at the time that his life as Jacques ended. The same teenager who is blamed as a monster by all but his two lovers is in part exculpated by both Georges and Gaston because of his age. The words "enfant" and "petit" recur in Georges's descriptions of Jacques, and the phrase "dix-huit ans" is charged with reproach in the exchange between Gaston and Madame Renaud; he concludes that to have let her young son go to war without having forgiven him renders her a detestable old woman.

Georges, whose claim to Gaston is the least articulated and the most ambiguous—after all, a recovered Jacques may renew his interest in Valentine—nevertheless comes closest to succeeding in winning Gaston for the Renauds. Unassuming and kindly, he is among the three most sympathetic characters in *Le voyageur sans bagage.* Yet he, too, speaks in the tones of a well-defined if somewhat shaky patriarchy that needs to repossess the prodigal son even at the cost of emasculating him. By reducing Jacques's potent destruction of social rules to the temper tantrums of a child, Georges attempts to annul the persistent memory of a society free from control, in which women, servants, and younger sons pleased themselves while the elders were at the front. In order to forgive Jacques, Georges needs to divide him from himself. He claims, "Cet orgueil, cette violence contre lesquels tu te débattais déjà à deux ans, c'étaient des monstres dont tu étais innocent et dont c'était à nous de te sauver" (p. 105). The monstrous Jacques is still there, but this time possessed by external forces about whose provenance Georges does not speculate. He concludes his reassessment of Jacques by reducing this figure of misrule to an impotent "pauvre petit" (p. 106). Gaston adopts precisely this prerogative of the mature male perspective to banish, even metaphorically to kill, the disturbing younger self. In his

dialogue with the uncomprehending butler, Gaston announces, "pour être libre, il vous faut laisser ce petit cadavre innocent derrière vous . . . C'est fait" (pp. 107-8).

As Gaston vies with the others in their attempt to inscribe and thus gain authority over Jacques's story, he must distance himself not only from the corrupting claims of erotic love but also from the alliance offered him by Georges. Georges presents himself as the friend of the orphaned little Jacques, but his confession about Jacques's demons indicates that he sees himself very much as a surrogate father. The privileges of age would to some extent emasculate Gaston, making him once more the much younger son. To a prescribed position of limited power within the family and society Gaston opposes his dream of original, absolute authorship: "Je suis un homme et je peux être, si je veux, aussi neuf qu'un enfant" (p. 109). But in *Le voyageur sans bagage* we have a wise child who knows his own father, as well as a child who is indeed father to the man. Gaston's escape confirms his move toward power, achieved through his *coup* against the other authors of his past and through his use of the privileges of class, sex, and age. Far from travelling light on his way to England, Gaston takes with him the burden of a patriarchy whose rules he has learned to manipulate for his own use, in order to secure for himself a position that from a traditional viewpoint certainly seems enviable. We see him reject the part of a younger son with a seemingly monstrous past. Less justifiably, he rejects the working- and lower-middle-class families claiming him, solely on the basis of Valentine's and his own assumptions about the "têtes de petits bourgeois et de paysans" and the "passés de calculs et d'avarice" that they would bring him (pp. 111-2). And, finally, Gaston rejects the asylum, the island of safety from social corruption that reduces him to a role similar to the one to which he and Georges have reduced the memory of Jacques: "un petit garçon impuissant" (p. 114).

Gaston breaks definitively with the Jacques-construct of the Renauds when he decides to rewrite the very inscription of erotic and illicit passion on his flesh as a signifier without a signified. The cicatrice from a wound given Jacques by Valentine in a moment of jealousy becomes the rigged token of recognition that allows the little Madensale and his lawyer to claim Gaston and remove him to England. The scar has no other significance in Gaston's textual revision than to carry him, along with his infantile *deus ex machina,* away from all the women and men, even the dead, of France (p. 113), who want to put him in his place. In accepting the Madensales, Gaston not only trades his painful discovery for economic ease, but for a universe in which he possesses the kudos, the absolute authorship and authority over himself and, significantly, over the only other two beings in his new life. Both the young uncle and the attorney, "Oncle Job," owe their economic security to Gaston. And Gaston becomes the surrogate father-older brother, which Georges threatened to become for him, for the little boy. The pastoral existence in the country house in Sussex excludes the erotic disturbances to bourgeois respectability that sexually active women represent.

The departures from sex, from the privileged Renaud family, and from the hierarchy of French society have almost unanimously been regarded as an assertion of purity on the part of Gaston. Even Anouilh regards his character's escape as a contrivance which maintains that purity.[10] The textual performance, however, indicates that a sacrifice has occurred and that Gaston has participated fully in the demise of the entity Gaston-Jacques. Gaston discusses the metaphorical killing of Jacques in terms that throw the butler, who does not perceive the distinction between reality and tropes, into a veritable panic. His second attempt to destroy the unwanted identity leads him to shatter the mirror containing his reflection, and by extension that of Jacques. *Le voyageur sans bagage* eschews the overt sacrifice of its main character on the altar of history for a more subtle, but no less devastating, exorcism: the specter of a historical crisis that will not stay in the common grave of a past everyone wishes to bury.

What becomes of the Gaston who had been dubbed "le soldat inconnu vivant"? Both the symbolic and the individual characters of Gaston disappear by the end of the play. Neither brutally amoral like the young lord of misrule Jacques, nor washed clean like the initial asylum inmate, the Gaston ready to wing his way to England has become an abysmal "honnête bourgeois." He has joined all those who had been trying to define and thus contain the disquieting past. He is the one who forever lays to rest the troublesome Jacques by relegating him to "une fosse commune en Allemagne" (p. 124). The "petit salaud" who broke the rules of bourgeois propriety and along with his uncensored peers threatened the fabric of the society that finally sent them to the front is ditched like unwanted luggage from the conscience of Gaston, of the Renauds, of war-bent Europe.

Because Anouilh installs Gaston into the ideal patriarchal dream of absolute control, *Le voyageur sans bagage* turns darkly against the issues it raises. The exacerbated rivalries for control, over relationships of class, sex, and age, over the plot of a story without closure, and finally over history, leads to households divided against themselves and ultimately to nations divided against each other. Anouilh brings up the unoriginal but telling point that in war killing means heroism while in peacetime it means murder (pp. 21-2),

but the play comes short of connecting the desire for absolute authority over the self, implicitly a denial of others' rights of access, to the desire for martial conquest.

The convergence of desire for absolute authority that results in war appears in displaced and miniaturized form in *Le voyageur sans bagage.* The consequence of war, a shift of questionable authoritarian control from the home to the front, and the attendant undirected freedom of those released from such control, does figure prominently in the play. But the final dark submersion of Gaston's life into the history that *Le voyageur sans bagage* shows to be violently unresolved eschews the very questions about history-makers that the play raises. Despite his critics' rose-colored view of the dénouement, Anouilh was justified in classifying *Le voyageur sans bagage* as a *pièce noire.*

Notes

1. Theater reviews aside, critics use *Le voyageur sans bagage* as the turning point in Anouilh's career from insignificant early plays to his characteristic theater, but the play has generated no sustained critical study.

2. Bernard Beugnot in the introduction (pp. 7-15) to *Les Critiques de notre temps et Anouilh* (Paris, 1977) sees *Le voyageur sans bagage* as the origin of artifice in Anouilh's theater; Paul Ginestier discusses the existential questions of being in *Anouilh* (Paris, 1969, pp. 27-36); in "Tendresse et cruauté dans le théâtre de Jean Anouilh" [*French Review,* 25 (1952), 337-347], Jacques Poujol points to the existentialism *avant la lettre* in *Le voyageur sans bagage.*

3. See Harold Clurman's "Jean Anouilh" in *The Naked Image: Observations on the Modern Theatre* (New York, 1958), pp. 25-36.

4. Philip Thody in *Anouilh* (Edinburgh and London, 1968) classifies *Le voyageur sans bagage* as "family drama" and notes that the 1937 theater reviewers referred to Gaston as a version of Oedipus (p. 20); Jacques Vier in *Le Théâtre de Jean Anouilh* (Paris, 1976), also labels the play "family drama" (p. 29).

5. While emphasizing Anouilh's taste for Pirandellian artifice, Beugnot calls genre "l'écorce de l'oeuvre" hiding the unity of themes (p. 11); in *Jean Anouilh* (New York, 1977), Lewis W. Falb asserts that Anouilh's color categories were improvised at the time of publication and that the best play of each group is "precisely the one that least conforms to the category" (p. 19); Ginestier thinks the color categories have "distinct disadvantages" (pp. 5-6); Pol Vandromme in *Un auteur et*

ses personnages (Paris, 1965) declares that nothing is either pink or black in Anouilh's theater, a pink play being one that finishes not happily but in time; Gabriel Marcel (quoted in Beugnot, 140-2) offers the same opinion that comedy in Anouilh's theater is strictly a matter of artificial solutions to insolubly tragic problems; both S. Benyon John in "Obsession and Technique in the Plays of Jean Anouilh" (*Modern Drama: Essays in Criticism,* eds. Travis Bogard and William I. Oliver [New York, 1965]) and H. G. McIntyre in *The Theatre of Jean Anouilh* (Totowa, 1981) analyze the melodramatic conventions in Anouilh's plays, which for John reveal the absurdity of the world (p. 37) and for McIntyre create "a comic and ironic framework between us and the action" (p. 35).

6. John Harvey in *Anouilh: A Study in Theatrics* (New Haven, 1964) describes the ending of *Le voyageur sans bagage* as "toying" and "pirouetting" away from truth (p. 174); John finds the ending "a perfectly gratuitous . . . fantasy" (p. 27); McIntyre asks that moral judgments be suspended since the play "is only a play" (p. 36); Falb refers to the ending as "obvious artificiality" (p. 30); in *Jean Anouilh: Poet of Pierrot and Pantaloon* (London, 1953) E. O. Marsh finds that the two verities of Anouilh's theater, innocence and experience, create a conflict resolved only by cheating (p. 81); Thody refers to the "artificiality of the ending" (p. 20); Vandromme writes that the play ends by prestidigitation (p. 56).

7. My view of Gaston differs from that of most critics, who apply the quest for purity of Anouilh's theater to Gaston's situation and who see Gaston as an embodiment of purity. For Gaston's purity, see John, pp. 20-21; Phillipe Jolivet, *Le Théâtre de Jean Anouilh* (Paris, 1963); p. 11; Harvey, p. 90; Hubert Gignoux, *Jean Anouilh* (Paris, 1946), p. 82; Marsh, p. 76; Poujol, p. 338. Two critics who dissent from the general reading of Gaston as pure are W. M. Gajewski (quoted in Beugnot, pp. 149-53) and Clurman, who respectively see Gaston's individuality as non-existent, having been appropriated by bourgeois society, and who condemn Anouilh's "rancid romanticism" (p. 32) as revealed in the opposition of individual and society.

8. For my analysis of *Le voyageur sans bagage* as ritual I depend on René Girard's *Violence and the Sacred,* trans. Patrick Gregory (Baltimore, 1977), and Victor Turner's *From Ritual to Theatre: The Human Seriousness of Play* (New York, 1982).

9. Jean Anouilh, *Le voyageur sans bagage* (Paris, 1958), p. 28. All further quotations of the play are from this edition.

10. See Anouilh about the ending of *Le voyageur sans bagage* as quoted in André François Rombout's *La Pureté dans le théâtre de Jean Anouilh* (Amsterdam, 1975), p. 283.

EURYDICE (*POINT OF DEPARTURE*)

CRITICAL COMMENTARY

Ildikó de Papp Carrington (essay date 1999)

SOURCE: Carrington, Ildikó de Papp. "Recasting the Orpheus Myth: Alice Munro's 'The Children Stay' and Jean Anouilh's *Eurydice*." In *The Rest of the Story: Critical Essays on Alice Munro,* edited by Robert Thacker, pp. 191-203. Toronto: ECW Press, 1999.

[*In the following essay, Carrington considers the role of Anouilh's play* Eurydice *in Alice Munro's short story "The Children Stay."*]

The classical myth of Orpheus and Eurydice tells the story of the young lovers' marriage, Eurydice's accidental death, and Orpheus's grief-stricken descent into the underworld to bring his beloved wife back into the world of the living. A poet and a musician, Orpheus sings so beautifully that he charms Hades into allowing him to take her back. But the Lord of the Dead imposes one condition: Orpheus must not look at her until they have completed their ascent to the upper world. Just as they reach it, however, he turns to see whether she is following him, and she is lost to him again and forever (Graves 111-12).

Alice Munro's first reference to this myth is a brief but climactic musical allusion to *Orfeo ed Euridice,* Christoph Gluck's eighteenth-century opera, in the title story of *Dance of the Happy Shades* (211-24), her first collection. When a handicapped girl, an unexpected performer in a children's piano recital, plays "The Dance of the Happy Shades," "something fragile, courtly and gay, that carries with it the freedom of a great unemotional happiness," the snobbish mothers in the audience do not know how to react to her indisputable talent (222). Although the piano teacher mentions the French title of the piece, *Danse des ombres heureuses,* nobody recognizes it as part of the opera based on the Orpheus myth (223). But through the contrast between the mothers' world and Gluck's otherworldly music, Munro emphasizes the unexpected effect of art on life.

In her second use of the Orpheus myth, Munro devotes an entire story to developing this powerful effect in an ironic intertextualization of Jean Anouilh's *Eurydice* (*Legend of Lovers*), a dramatic retelling of the Orpheus and Eurydice myth in modern France.[1] In "The Children Stay," one of Munro's revised *New Yorker* stories in *The Love of a Good Woman* (181-214), her latest collection, Pauline Keating is a disturbingly beautiful young mother rehearsing for the title role in an amateur Canadian production of Anouilh's play. With her husband, Brian, and his parents, Pauline discusses Anouilh's plot, quoting and paraphrasing the dialogue and analysing both the characters and the director's unexpected casting of the various roles. "What he sees in us is something only he can see," Pauline explains (196). But she carefully conceals the central fact: after the weekly Sunday rehearsal in downtown Victoria, British Columbia, she and the director, Jeffrey Toom, make love in the locked rehearsal room. When the Keatings' summer vacation on Vancouver Island in 1967 interrupts this exciting secret schedule, Jeffrey pursues Pauline out of the city, takes her to a motel in Campbell River, and forces her to phone Brian to announce that she and her lover are going to Washington State, where he has "a one-year appointment" in a college drama department (185). In response to this announcement, Brian imposes a condition: "The children stay" (212). Pauline's painfully reluctant acceptance of this condition not only gives Munro the title of her story but also structures her ironic intertextualization of Anouilh's drama.

In discussing Anouilh's use of the Orpheus myth in *Eurydice,* Leonard Cabell Pronko defines "[o]ne kind of aesthetic pleasure afforded . . . by any modern treatment of a well-known tale" as the process of "discovering the parallels that the author establishes with his sources" (199). Applied to Munro's use of Anouilh's play, this process of discovery not only reveals many parallels between his drama and her story but also, much more importantly, highlights the differences against the background of these parallels. In the original *New Yorker* version of the story, Pauline's comment on the director's casting, "What he sees in us is something different from the obvious," is Munro's clearly self-reflexive comment on her own casting (95). Munro thus indicates that she is using ironic intertextuality for the double purpose defined by Linda Hutcheon: to "mark . . . a *rupture* with, or at least a subversion or critique of, the [original] text" and, at the same time, to "establish . . . a community of discourse among readers and thus [to] mark . . . a kind of interpretive *continuity*" (96). The continuity results in "the elitist pleasure of irony," closely parallel to the aesthetic pleasure that Pronko defines, because both depend on recognizing the parallels (96), but the irony subverts the legend of the French lovers. By recasting the roles of the Anouilh characters, complicating, combining, and

multiplying them into "something different from the obvious," Munro makes these differences dramatically physical in order to define the multiple meanings of her title and to reject Anouilh's conception of love.

The lovers in *Eurydice* meet in a provincial railway-station restaurant, each accompanied by an embarrassing parent. Because both Orphée and Eurydice are very young, their love affair is part of their struggle to achieve individualization and disconnection by freeing themselves from their parents and their pasts. Orphée and his father are poor travelling musicians, but, unlike Orphée, his clingingly dependent and "rather ridiculous" old father plays so "abominably" that he would starve without his son (Anouilh 80, 58). Eurydice, her vain mother, and her mother's posturing lover are all members of a "tenth-rate [touring] company that plays in flea-pits" (79). Instantly falling in love and just as instantly agreeing that Eurydice's mother and her lover are "[h]orrible and stupid" (68), Orphée and Eurydice go off together to consummate their love in a dirty, badly furnished hotel room in Marseilles where, a waiter informs them, many other disgusting guests have done the same in the same bed, "All using their saliva to say 'our love'" (89). In contrast to these guests' repellent behaviour, the young couple's lovemaking is a confusing mixture of nervous fright, shame, and awkward tenderness.

Eurydice's shame is a reaction against her past, which contains not only a mother but also two recent lovers, Mathias, so desperately in love with Eurydice that he throws himself under a train as soon as she rejects him for Orphée, and Alfredo Dulac, the middle-aged impresario of the touring company. When Dulac, who for a year has been forcing Eurydice to submit to him, follows her and sends her a note at the hotel, she is so ashamed of her past that just before he arrives she runs away. Taking a bus out of the city, she dies when the bus crashes into a truck.

Orphée's attempt to get Eurydice back is engineered by a symbolic character, a young man who plays a double role in the drama. When Mathias commits suicide, the mysterious young man, in the background until this moment, calmly assures the appalled lovers that "It never hurts to die" (82). Then, just as Eurydice leaves the hotel, he reappears, introduces himself to Orphée as M. Henri, and makes a significant comment about the lovers' first meeting in the station: "These moments when we catch a glimpse of Fate laying her snares are very exciting, aren't they?" (95). After Eurydice's death, M. Henri returns a grief-stricken and completely disoriented Orphée to the same dreamlike station at night. When Orphée insists, "I want to know where we are," M. Henri identifies the place as "the doors of death" (101, 103). On the platform, a living Eurydice is "standing on the same spot where [Orphée] saw her

. . . for the first time" (104). Like Hades, M. Henri has the power to return Eurydice to Orphée but imposes the same condition: to keep her alive, Orphée must not look at her until dawn. This power, coupled with an excited awareness of the snares of fate, makes M. Henri not only the messenger of death but also the director of the play. "To a large extent, he is pulling the strings of the drama" (Pronko 189).

However, because Orphée has not actually entered "the doors of death" and because Eurydice is already alive again, his violation of M. Henri's condition shows that his youth makes him incapable of accepting reality. This inability is revealed by his obsession with male hands and their defiling touch. In the first act of *Eurydice,* when his questions force Eurydice to admit not only that she and Mathias have been lovers but also that she has had an earlier lover, Orphée replies, "I'll try never to think of . . . their hands touching you" (Anouilh 74). In the hotel room in the second act, he reveals the belief behind this obsession. Insisting that every experience, "good" or "evil," leaves a permanent mark on the remembering body, he convinces Eurydice, who has concealed her relationship with Dulac, that "all the hands that have ever touched you are still sticking to your flesh . . ." (86, 87). It is this conviction, confirmed by Dulac's note, that shames her into running away. When Dulac arrives at the hotel to tell Orphée that Eurydice, whom he calls "the child," has been his mistress for a year, Orphée accuses him of lying. Dulac's calmly patronizing reply, "You're a child, too, my boy," dismisses Orphée's insistence—"I love Eurydice and she loves me"—as irrelevant and immature (97). The man is talking about sex, the boy, about a young love that is frightened and disgusted by his beloved's sexuality. In the third act, when Eurydice is restored to Orphée and pleads, "Don't look at me. Let me live," he deliberately looks at her to force her to confess the truth: "Did he touch you with those hands all covered with rings?" (109). Begging forgiveness, she admits that he has, and Orphée recoils in horror: "I shall always see you with that man's hands on you" (111). Pronko emphasizes that, by altering the Greek myth, Anouilh

> changes the entire meaning of this crucial point in the myth. . . . Orphée's inability to see Eurydice is no longer a problem of ideality or a dream taking place in the underworld or the subconscious, lying in the realm of the eternal. It is reduced to a definite temporal reality, . . . on this side of death. And his breaking of the condition imposed upon him . . . is not so much an indication that Orphée could have lived with Eurydice had he not looked at her as it is a demonstration of Orphée's inability to make the compromise demanded by love on earth . . . [and by] the ugliness of life.
>
> (197-98)

When Eurydice is thus killed a second time, Orphée is left alone with M. Henri and his father, suddenly back and full of gratitude that his son has not deserted him. In their debate about life and death, they offer Orphée two sharply contrasted choices. In long, pompous, digressive speeches, his father keeps insisting on how wonderful life is, in spite of all that he has suffered, and how through "will power" one can accept life with all its imperfections (Anouilh 117). Cynically capitalizing on the bumbling banality with which this paternal advice is delivered, M. Henri offers Orphée the immaculate perfection of death. "You heard your father talking about life just now. It was grotesque, wasn't it, but that's what it is like" (116). In life Eurydice would be soiled, "covered with finger marks," but in death Orphée can possess the "Eurydice of [his] first meeting, eternally pure and young, eternally herself" (116). Because this untouched ideal is what Orphée wants, he decides to join Eurydice in death. Thus, he leaves his father twice, initially to consummate his love for Eurydice and finally to possess her forever. The child does not stay.

In Munro's "The Children Stay," Brian, commenting on Orphée's decision to die, recognizes his death as a rejection of both his father and his father's philosophy and admits, "Logically I can see killing yourself so you won't turn into your parents. . . . I just don't believe anybody would do it" (198). His comment is significant because, in contrast to the parent-child relationships in Anouilh's play, those in Munro's story are much more complicated: they involve not two generations but three. Pauline and Brian are the parents of two girls, a five year old and a toddler.

But even though Brian is a father, he cannot detach himself from his parents. Unlike Anouilh's Orphée, he wants to maintain intergenerational connection. An "only son" (193), he needs "to have his wife and his parents and his children bound together, . . . to involve Pauline in his life with his parents," and to connect her and their children "to his own childhood" (195). To satisfy this need, the younger Keatings and the senior Keatings always vacation together on Vancouver Island. Brian cannot "imagine a summer without this shared holiday," even though Pauline is unhappy because they cannot "do anything by themselves" (194). She is also unhappy when the principal of the school where Brian teaches refers to her husband as "[y]our boy" (194), a reference that echoes Dulac's patronizingly addressing Orphée as "my boy." Brian's physical appearance, his body "still almost as skinny as a teenager's," is another sign that in spite of fatherhood he is not so much a parent as a son (195).

As the difficulties of Brian's family roles demonstrate, another way in which Munro's casting complicates Anouilh's is that Munro assigns her characters multiple functions that combine the roles of the French characters. Jeffrey is a paradoxical combination of M. Henri and Orphée because his sexual power over Pauline permanently changes her life. Although she mentions M. Henri a few times, she never identifies his role in the play. But Brian, by teasingly referring to Jeffrey as "Monsieur le Directeur," establishes the parallel between the symbolic French director and the Canadian drama teacher (196). Like M. Henri, Jeffrey is powerful, both intellectually and physically. Intensely opinionated, he loves to argue and challenge opposition, and his sexual potency imbues him with an astonishing "live energy" (190). Even when he falls asleep after vigorous intercourse, "[c]onviction and contentiousness seem . . . to radiate" from his "warm" body (208). But like M. Henri's direction of the fated drama of Orphée and Eurydice, Jeffrey's role as the director of *Eurydice* is inseparable from the idea of death. His first name echoes that of Henri, and when Jeffrey and Pauline are introduced he jokes that his last name, Toom, is "Without the B" (184). The word *tomb* is initially associated with the "sordid" hotel where Jeffrey works as a summer night clerk: a prostitute has been murdered there, and guests "check . . . in to O. D. or bump themselves off" (184, 185). But the "dusty" rehearsal room in the old Victoria building in which Jeffrey and Pauline secretly make love also acquires tomblike qualities when he bolts the door before intercourse (188): "The sound of the bolt being pushed into place, the ominous or fatalistic sound of metal hitting metal, gave her a localized shock of capitulation" (190).

That Jeffrey's power is dangerous to Pauline emphasizes his second function: as her lover, Jeffrey also plays the role of Orphée. When they first meet, he looks "directly into Pauline's eyes—impertinently and searchingly" (185-86). Remembering this meeting, she rehearses her lines from the last act of *Eurydice*: "'Don't look at me. Don't look. Let me live'" (186). Her quoting Eurydice's plea at this point clearly labels his act as symbolic of the decision that he later forces on her. But, unlike Orphée, Jeffrey does not operate alone. Brian also compels Pauline to choose, not only between her lover and her husband but also between two kinds of living death.

Jeffrey, however, is hardly aware of the difficulty of her choice because, although he combines the roles of M. Henri as director and Orphée as lover, there is a crucial role that he does not play: he is not a parent. His total obliviousness to what being a parent means is initially indicated by his suggestion that Pauline bring Mara, her toddler, to his mother's house for an afternoon tryst. Seizing the opportunity presented by the absence of his mother for the day, Jeffrey phones Pauline with an invitation into his bed, but she refuses. When she explains that she has to take care of Mara, at first he does not even recognize her name, and then he suggests bringing her along. He sees his mother as a supervisor to get rid of, but Pauline cannot get rid of her maternal

responsibility to supervise her child. She fears not only the possibility of physical danger for Mara in a house that has not been toddler-proofed but also the potentiality of psychological trauma: "Mara might be storing up time bombs—memories of a strange house where she was strangely disregarded, of a closed door, noises on the other side of it" (201). Jeffrey's reply to Pauline's refusal, "I just wanted you in my bed," shows that in his "urgency" Jeffrey is thinking only of his own hands on her body (201, 202). Unlike Orphée, obsessed with the other hands sticking to Eurydice, he is almost totally unaware of the other hands clinging to Pauline.

She is covered, not by the symbolically defiling fingerprints of lustful men, but by the literally sticky, sandy handprints and footprints of two children playing on a saltwater beach. This difference is introduced by the name that Mara calls her, not Mommy, but Paw, Paw, for Pauline. Mara's childish mispronunciation suggests not only "Papa," with the implication that Pauline is more of an adult authority figure than the child's father, but also "paw," colloquial for "hand." The children's hands and feet and Pauline's own hands acquire increased significance when Jeffrey, who has pursued Pauline, telephones her again, just as oblivious to her situation as before, and she is summoned to the public phone in the hallway of the lodge at the beach. While she talks, she shifts the squirming, sand-caked toddler, who weighs "a ton," from one hip to another, but then Mara begins "bumping and scrambling against Pauline's side, anxious to get down" (203, 204). Simultaneously, five-year-old Caitlin goes into the lodge store, "leaving wet sandy footprints" (204). As Pauline tries to watch both children and to talk to Jeffrey, she reads the bulletin board signs beside the phone: "No Person Under Fourteen Years of Age Not Accompanied by Adult Allowed in Boats or Canoes," and an advertisement for palm reading, "Your Life is in Your Hands" (205). Because she has just been holding her child, the phone conversation that initiates the permanent change in her life and the lives of her children makes the metaphor painfully literal as well as figurative. The definition of children as persons under fourteen, however, is ironic: by being only literal and not figurative, it is insufficiently inclusive.

Munro structures the long penultimate section of her story to withhold the figurative and fully inclusive definition until the climax. The next morning, in a motel room where Pauline and Jeffrey have repeatedly made love, she recalls her second telephone conversation the day before, her announcement to Brian that she is leaving and the "impossible" condition that he imposes: "The children stay" (206, 212). Although Munro does not specify this condition the first time that Pauline recalls the second conversation, its psychological effect emerges from the subtle intertextualization of a scene in the last act of *Eurydice*.

In this intertextualization, Munro combines the roles of Orphée and Eurydice in Pauline. The disoriented Orphée does not know where M. Henri has taken him until he sees a living Eurydice "standing on the same spot where . . . [he] saw her . . . for the first time" (Anouilh 104). Similarly, in "The Children Stay," as Pauline speaks to Brian at the lodge, she can clearly hear that he is standing "where she stood not so long before, in the public hallway of the lodge," where she read the fateful sign about her life in her hands (205). As Pauline recalls standing there, she, like Orphée, is so shaken and disoriented that she hardly knows which phone she is calling from now: at the end of their strange and stunningly short conversation, she comes "out of the phone booth beside a row of gas pumps in Campbell River" (206), where Jeffrey has taken her to the motel. Her disorientation suggests that like Eurydice she has crossed some kind of boundary between life and death, but unlike Eurydice she has incurred a permanent pain, losing her children. Because she chooses to give up the life that she has literally held in her hands, it is not Jeffrey but Pauline who is Orphée.

But she experiences a terrible dilemma, a choice between her lover and her children. The motel room, in which she is painfully aware of where she is before opening her eyes the next morning, resembles the miserable hotel room in *Eurydice,* with junky, "broken" furniture, a "noisy air-conditioner," and a cheap, torn bedspread (206). "[H]ard-used between the legs," Pauline tells herself that her adultery is not so much a question of love as of sex (210). Although she reaches for romantic literary parallels in Anna Karenina and Emma Bovary, she tries to be totally honest: "None of this would happen if it wasn't for sex" (209). In sharp contrast to Orphée's disgust with Eurydice and Eurydice's own shame, Pauline argues earlier that Eurydice "probably . . . enjoyed" sex, even with Dulac, "because after a certain point she couldn't help enjoying it" (197). Based only on Dulac's conceited opinion, this argument emphasizes that Pauline fully enjoys her own sexuality. Although she is orgasmic with both her husband and her lover, "she believes" that it is only under Jeffrey's "weight . . . on her" that she is fortunate enough to experience "the inevitable flight, the feelings she doesn't have to strive for but only to give in to like breathing or dying" (210). Like Jeffrey's casting, however, what she sees in him is something that only she can see. Munro's repeated use of the word *believe* signals a characteristic passage of narratorial disparity, longer and more emphatic in the following revised version than in the original *New Yorker* version (102), in which Munro distances herself from her protagonist to qualify Pauline's conviction that Jeffrey is her fated lover.

> That was what Pauline must believe now—that there was this major difference in lives or in marriages or unions between people. That some of them had a neces-sity, a fatefulness, about them that others did not have. Of course she would have said the same thing a year ago. People did say that, they seemed to believe that, and to believe that their own cases were all of the first, the special kind, even when anybody could see that they were not and that these people did not know what they were talking about. Pauline would not have known what she was talking about.
>
> (*Love* 208)

But even though Pauline admits that "There's a lot she doesn't know" about her lover, including his widowed mother's "mysterious but important . . . role" in his life (210), she is convinced that, if she were to give Jeffrey up, she would suffocate: it "would be like tying a sack over her head" (209). Giving up her children, however, is also tantamount to dying.

When Pauline goes out into the motel parking lot, once again she recalls her phone conversation with her husband. In another subtle intertextualization of a scene in *Eurydice,* she alludes to Eurydice's death in the crash of the bus and the truck. As a truck on the highway comes toward Pauline, she thinks of "a large bleak fact coming at her," Brian's insistence that the children stay (211). After furiously asking "what about the kids?" (211), he answered his own question: "'The children,' he said, in [a] . . . shivering and vindictive voice. Changing the word 'kids' to 'children' was like slamming a board down on her—a heavy, formal, righteous threat. 'The children stay,' Brian said" (212).

This simile completes Munro's analepsis in two ways. First, it derives its fatal force from her perhaps unconsciously self-reflexive repetition of a scene at the end of "The Peace of Utrecht" (*Dance* 190-210), in which the narrator is told a terrible fact about her mother's last days. When her dying mother tried to escape from the hospital, she was brought back and coffined alive. To prevent another escape, "They nailed a board across her bed," thus literally nailing her into her deathbed as if into her coffin (208). Second, the sound of the figuratively slamming board echoes "[t]he sound of the bolt being pushed into place" when, near the beginning of "The Children Stay," Jeffrey locks the rehearsal room before he makes love to Pauline (190). By placing these sounds at the beginning and at the climax of her story and by making them so similar to each other, Munro combines the roles of Jeffrey and Brian in the triangle. Like Orphée, neither man will let Pauline live. But when they box her in by forcing her to choose, once again she becomes both of Anouilh's lovers at the same time. Unlike Eurydice, however, who is passive because she is simply killed a second time, Pauline is active because, like Orphée, she chooses to "die."

After an intensely traumatic conflict that transforms the philosophical debate between M. Henri and Orphée's father into counterpoised but contrasting pressures on her remembering body, Jeffrey's "weight . . . on her" hips and Mara's "weight . . . on her hip," Pauline chooses to give up her children (210, 212). But giving them up is an "acute pain" that she knows "will become chronic": "You won't get free of it, but you won't die of it," she tells herself, realizing that she must "carry [it] along and get used to [it] until it's only the past she's grieving for and not any possible present" because her children have grown up (213).

The first meaning of the story's title, therefore, is painfully and paradoxically double. Because the children stay with their father, they also stay with their mother: they are a permanent burden of guilt and grief for the parent who does not stay. The title's second meaning is the most obvious. Although all children grow up physically and most eventually leave their parents, some may nevertheless remain children emotionally and stay with their parents. This figurative definition of children excludes Pauline but includes both Jeffrey and Brian, who keeps "hang[ing] around" his parents (213). In the adulterous triangle, Pauline, unlike the "child" Eurydice, is the only grown-up because she makes her terrible compromise without blaming either her husband or her lover. She realizes that nobody will blame Brian because he tried to "make her see what she was doing" (212). Jeffrey, on the other hand, cannot see what he is doing to Pauline. After her phone conversation with Brian, which Jeffrey naïvely considers easier than Pauline expected, he clumsily articulates what she has been thinking, that perhaps Brian was "subconsciously" expecting her to leave him. When her silence begs Jeffrey "not to say any more," he apologizes (206). But just as he fails to see the impossibility of their making love when a toddler is in the next room, so too he is unable to comprehend the emotional price of her choice. Pauline realizes that "It isn't his fault. He's still an innocent or a savage, who doesn't know there's a pain so durable in the world" (213). The Anouilh *sauvage* is a character who is innocent, incorruptible, and intransigent, even though deeply scarred by pain and suffering (della Fazia 63, 49-52). Jeffrey is clearly not a savage in this sense. By making him a stranger to suffering, Munro argues that such innocence can come only from emotional inexperience. Although he shares this childishness with Orphée, he is not Orphée, because he does not have to die—that is, to give anything up to possess his Eurydice.

In the story's typical Munro epilogue in the present, Pauline's adult daughters, who neither "hate" nor "forgive" their mother, refer to her going "away with Orphée" (*Love* 213), but she repeatedly corrects them: "It wasn't Orphée" (214). Because their father has jokingly told them that their "mother ran away with Orphée," they confuse Jeffrey with the actor who played

Orphée (214). Pauline's corrections, however, are also a metafictional comment on Munro's subversive recasting of Anouilh's characters.

Because it is Pauline who actively chooses as both Orphée and Eurydice, her comments on Anouilh's lovers constitute Munro's self-reflexive analysis of her story and her rejection of Anouilh's conception of love. Comparing the lovers, Pauline argues that "Eurydice is more realistic" than Orphée and "loves him better in a way than he loves her" (197). Pauline is also more realistic than Jeffrey because, although she is only a year older than he is, she is an adult and he is still a naïve child, unaware of how much better she loves him. Both explicitly and implicitly, Anouilh's conception of an intransigent, pure, and fated love is also presented as childish for several reasons. Pauline tells Brian, "It's a beautiful play in one way but in another it is so silly," because its adolescent insistence on perfection and its refusal of compromise reject the tough decisions that facing reality daily demands (198).

In dramatizing the desperately disruptive force of Pauline's sexuality, Munro shows that Orphée's rejection of Eurydice's sexuality is also adolescent. In an unpublished interview with Barbara Martineau, Munro defined sex as "the big thing," not only the physical act itself but also "the whole thing of emotions that radiate out from good sex, which seems to me so central in adult life, and so irreplaceable" (qtd. in Ross 79). Caught up in these irreplaceable emotions, "her secret life disturb[ing] her like a radiant explosion," Pauline is a woman whose sexuality "shockingly" outweighs her sense of maternal responsibility (*Love* 200, 209). In two sentences added to the revised version of the story, Pauline, discussing the play with Brian, "dreamily" tells him that "Everybody has choices" (198), but, at the moment when she finally chooses to give up her daughters, a nightmarish reality solidifies around her. "A fluid choice, the choice of fantasy, is poured out on the ground and instantly hardens [into] . . . its undeniable shape" (213). This metaphor, like the bolt being pushed into place and the board slamming down on Pauline, emphasizes the consequences of her choice: now she has boxed *herself* in. Thus, another meaning of the title perhaps implies that women who fantasize about sex without recognizing the potentially dangerous power of their sexuality remain children ignorant of reality.

The final reason behind Munro's rejection of Anouilh's conception of love is thus paradoxical. In spite of all her analytical arguments, Pauline decides to join Jeffrey because she believes that their love, like that of Orphée and Eurydice, is fated. But the epilogue's retrospective recasting of roles shows the most fundamental reason why Jeffrey was not Orphée: he was not the fated lover that Pauline had once mistakenly believed him to be. "It wasn't Orphée," she tells her daughters, but "somebody else connected with the play," with whom she "lived . . . for a while" (213). When her daughters repeat, "Not Orphée," she insists, "No. Never him" (213). After thirty years, the disillusioned dissonance of "for a while" and "never" rejects Jeffrey as Orphée much more emphatically than does the original *New Yorker* ending: "It wasn't him" (103). Subverting her own argument, Pauline has miscast her lover and has finally been just as wrong about love as Anouilh. The shatteringly ironic contrast between "What we think is happening and what we understand later on . . ." is Munro's recurrent theme (Munro, "Interview" 90).

Note

1. For earlier examples of Munro's use of ironic intertextuality, see Carrington; and Munro, "Hired Girl" and "Wilderness Station."

Works Cited

Anouilh, Jean. *Eurydice (Legend of Lovers).* Trans. Kitty Black. *Five Plays.* New York: Hill, 1958. 55-120.

Carrington, Ildikó de Papp. "Double-Talking Devils: Alice Munro's 'A Wilderness Station.'" *Essays on Canadian Writing* 58 (1996): 71-92.

———. "Other Rooms, Other Texts, Other Selves: Alice Munro's 'Sunday Afternoon' and 'Hired Girl.'" *Journal of the Short Story in English* 30 (1998): 33-44.

della Fazia, Alba. *Jean Anouilh.* Twayne's World Author Series 76. New York: Twayne, 1969.

Graves, Robert. *The Greek Myths.* Vol. 1. Harmondsworth, Eng.: Penguin, 1964. 2 vols.

Hutcheon, Linda. *Splitting Images: Contemporary Canadian Ironies.* Toronto: Oxford UP, 1991.

Munro, Alice. "The Children Stay." *New Yorker* 22 and 29 Dec. 1997: 91-96, 98-100, 102-03.

———. "The Children Stay." *The Love of a Good Woman.* Toronto: McClelland, 1998. 181-214.

———. *Dance of the Happy Shades.* Toronto: McGraw-Hill, 1968.

———. "Hired Girl." *New Yorker* 11 Apr. 1994: 82-88.

———. "An Interview with Alice Munro." With Geoff Hancock. *Canadian Fiction Magazine* 43 (1982): 74-114. (Rpt. in *Canadian Writers at Work: Interviews with Geoff Hancock.* Toronto: Oxford UP, 1987. 187-224.)

———. Unpublished interview. With Barbara Martineau. 16 Feb. 1975. The Alice Munro Papers, Special Collections Division, U of Calgary, series 37.20.20.

———. "A Wilderness Station." *Open Secrets.* New York: Knopf, 1994. 190-225.

Pronko, Leonard Cabell. *The World of Jean Anouilh.* Berkeley: U of California P, 1968.

Ross, Catherine Sheldrick. *Alice Munro: A Double Life.* Canadian Biography Series. Toronto: ECW, 1992.

ANTIGONE

CRITICAL COMMENTARY

Michael Spingler (essay date fall 1974)

SOURCE: Spingler, Michael. "Anouilh's Little Antigone: Tragedy, Theatricalism, and the Romantic Self." *Comparative Drama* 8, no. 3 (fall 1974): 228-38.

[*In the following essay, Spingler asserts that Anouilh's use of the chorus in* Antigone *functions to "establish the play's essential theatricality" and reinforce his perception of romantic theatrical techniques.*]

The loss of a tragic sense in the theatre is a major concern of many modern dramatists and critics. In his *Antigone,* Jean Anouilh suggests that the reasons for this decline may be located within one of the fundamental developments of modern tragedy, that is, the replacement of action by character as the dramatic mainspring.[1] He sees the predominance of character as a fundamentally romantic development which leads to the emergence of a protagonist whose self-consciousness diminishes the tragic event. Anouilh's disenchantment with romantic posturing is expressed primarily in terms of a theatricalism which implies that tragedy based solely on character is really role-playing and self-dramatization. He does not see the role as a solution to the problem of writing a modern tragedy but as a reflection of the dilemma. In *Antigone,* the self-conscious role is inimical to the tragic spirit.[2]

There are three elements in the play which comprise the design Anouilh uses to dramatize his theme. At the heart of *Antigone* lies a persuasive denial of tragic vision put forward by Creon who, traditionally, should be the partner in the tragic action. In counterpoint to this, we find a highly sentimentalized and romantic rendering of Antigone which makes the play seem to be, at least superficially, a tragedy of character rather than of action. The unifying perspective through which we are invited to judge the conflict caused by a sentimental character replacing the moral structure of a tragic universe is provided by Anouilh's use of the chorus as a distancing device. Anouilh depends primarily upon the chorus to establish the play's essential theatricality.

Anouilh's chorus does not follow the Greek model of dancing and singing the transcendent vision of the tragedy. It is comprised instead of a single actor, a commentator whose observations invite the audience to assume a detached and critical perspective toward Antigone and her drama. A frame for the play and a creator of distance between it and the spectator, the chorus' presence on the stage recalls the Brechtian admonition not to mistake the staging of the event for the event itself.

This function of the chorus is clear from the first words of the play in which he introduces the characters as actors waiting to play a part: "Voilà. Ces personages vont vous jouer l'histoire d'Antigone."[3] The key word here is *jouer,* and the use of *histoire* rather than *tragédie* is also significant. He clarifies Antigone's position within the play by referring to her as a character who has not yet become fully realized: "Elle pense qu'elle va être Antigone toute à l'heure, qu'elle va surgir soudain de la maigre jeune fille noiraude et renfermée que personne ne prenait au sérieux dans la famille et se dresser seule en face du monde, seule en face de Créon, son oncle, qui est le roi. Elle pense qu'elle va mourir, qu'elle est jeune et qu'elle aussi, elle aurait bien aimé vivre" (p. 9). Initially, these words seem to be an introduction to the tragedy which is about to unfold, a preparation of the audience in order that it be familiar with the plot. Yet, if we consider these words more carefully and ask who, precisely, at this very moment, is thinking these thoughts, it becomes apparent that Antigone is an actress thinking about the characteristics and demands of her part just before going on.

This view of Antigone as both actress and character is essential to the play's theme. The chorus repeats it when she is led in by the guards: "Alors, voilà, cela commence. La petite Antigone est prise. La petite Antigone va pouvoir être elle-même pour la première fois" (p. 58). The sense of the importance of the role is very strong here, and the chorus has, in fact, pointed out the connection between Antigone's role and the element of fate within the play: ". . . et il n'y a rien à faire. Elle s'appelle Antigone et il va falloir qu'elle joue son rôle jusqua'au bout" (p. 10). Because of the chorus' insistence upon Antigone's dual nature as both character and player, we see her as tragic actress rather than tragic victim.

The chorus establishes a similar view towards the play itself. Because of his comments, we do not experience tragedy in the play as rhythm and structure but consider it at a distance as an abstract concept and problem. The chorus occasionally interrupts the action in order to explain the proceedings to the audience. His remarks before the confrontation between Antigone and Creon remind one of a public lecture on "The Theory of Tragedy." "Et voilà. Maintenant le ressort est bandé. Cela n'a plus qu'à se dérouler tout seule. C'est cela qui est commode dans la tragédie" (p. 56). The major theme of the chorus' comments is that tragedy is comforting because of its inevitability: ". . . on n'a plus qu'à se laisser faire. On est tranquille. Cela roule tout seule. . . . C'est propre, la tragédie. C'est reposant, c'est sûr . . . Et puis, surtout, c'est reposant, la tragédie, parce qu'on sait qu'il n'y a plus d'espoir . . ." (pp. 57-58). We may be tempted to consider this theory of tragedy an extremely dubious one, which is very possibly the reason for its inclusion in the play. We shall see that the notion that tragedy is restful because it is sure has its appeal for Antigone. Most important is the effect upon the audience of the intrusion, at a critical juncture, of any theory, doubtful or illuminating, which considers tragedy conceptually. A spectator cannot be expected to share in a tragic experience when he is being lectured about it by a man in evening dress.

The effect of the chorus is to create a climate of ambiguity much the same as the one described by Richard Coe concerning the theatre of Genet: "The drama is both true and not true simultaneously—it commands or should command, absolute belief, but only in a context of absolute unbelief; and the absolute belief (or suspension of disbelief) is only valid if it knows itself to exist in a context of unrealities—that is, if it is unceasingly aware of itself as illusion"[4] (p. 214). This self-conscious ambivalence is the essential mode within which the conflict between Antigone and Creon must be assessed. This conflict, as Anouilh presents it, is between a character who rebels against his tragic type-casting and a heroine who represents a romantic decaying of the tragic mold.

The principal set piece of the play in which Antigone faces Creon should contain the essence of the tragic issue. In Anouilh's version, instead of confronting a tragic antagonist who represents an opposing ethical view, Antigone faces a pragmatic and cynical man who refuses to enter into the tragic action with her. Creon's major argument is not that Antigone's act is wrong, merely that it is without significance. Moreover, his intent is not to justify his own moral position, but to convince Antigone that there is no longer an ethical base which would give her position the moral value of tragedy.[5] He begins his case by attacking the idea of tragedy associated with Antigone's father: "Et tuer votre père et coucher avec votre mère et apprendre cela après, mot par mot. Quel breuvage, hein, les mots qui vous condamnent? Et comme on les boit goulument quand on s'appelle Oedipe ou Antigone. Et le plus simple après, c'est encore de se crever les yeux et d'aller mendier avec ses enfants sur les routes" (p. 73). The direct reference to the events of *Oedipus Rex* is a device for self-conscious allusion: the character who looks from a distance at a dramatic tradition from which he springs. In this sense Creon's words and the chorus' complement each other. Both suggest an outside or alien view of tragedy and together they raise the question of the need, or lack of need, for tragedy in modern theatre.

Whereas the chorus' attitude toward tragedy is ambiguous, Creon's bias against it is clear. He looks upon Oedipus and his family as a pack of vain trouble makers, and he is intent upon banishing the tragedy they carry with them from his realm: "Thèbes a droit maintenant à un prince sans histoire. . . . J'ai résolu avec moins d'ambition que ton père de m'employer tout simplement à rendre l'ordre de ce monde moins absurde, si c'est possible" (p. 73). Creon, like the chorus, uses the word *histoire* to refer to the tragic material of the Oedipus myth. The king's use of the word has the sense of troublesome and annoying business, and he makes it clear that he has no intention of becoming involved in such an affair: "Et si demain un messager crasseux dévale du fond des montagnes pour m'annoncer qu'il n'est pas sûr de mon naissance, je le prierai tout simplement de s'en retourner d'où il vient" (p. 74). Creon is the protagonist who, when confronted with the tragic revelation, would simply turn his back on it and act as if nothing had happened. He refuses the tragic moment as being politically inexpedient.

The king's problem is to convince Antigone to refuse tragedy also. To do this, he attempts to discredit any external ethical support for the tragic act. He starts by questioning the religious values which are behind Antigone's deed, maintaining that there is no reason for Antigone to bury Polynices since the burial ritual is, in itself, meaningless: "Tu y crois donc vraiment, toi, à cet enterrement dans les règles? A cette ombre de ton père condamné à errer toujours si on ne jette pas sur le cadavre un peu de terre avec la formule du pretre? . . . Et tu risques la mort maintenant parce que j'ai refusé à ton frère ce passeport dérisoire, ce bredouillage en série sur sa dépouille, cette pantomine dont tu aurais été la première à avoir honte et mal si on l'avait jouée. C'est absurde" (pp. 76, 77). There is little that Antigone can reply to Creon's debunking of the burial rituals since she does not believe in them herself. She agrees that it is absurd to invoke them and admits that she has, in fact, thought of stopping the priests if they ever recited their prayers over someone she loved. Both Creon and Antigone reflect here a world in which skepticism weakens the sort of belief necessary to a tragic universe. The issue at the heart of the tragic necessity, Polynices unburied, is considered by both as based on nothing but a shabby hoax.

However, regardless of her attitude towards the burial ceremony, Antigone's loyalty to her brother remains the major external justification for her act. Polynices is the

last prop Creon pulls out from under her. He does so by revealing that her brothers were merely two thugs who plotted to murder their father and who were involved in a struggle with each other which resembled more a gangland war than a political revolt: "Nous avions à faire à deux larrons en foire qui se trompaient l'un l'autre en nous trompant et qui se sont égorgés comme deux petits voyous qu'ils étaient pour un pur règlement de comptes" (p. 95). Creon even claims that the bodies were so disfigured that he couldn't tell them apart, thus being obliged to choose arbitrarily one as the war hero and the other as the traitor. This final detail is certainly Anouilh's most imaginative twist to the classic myth, and, together with Creon's earlier remarks and the chorus' commentary, it completes the discrediting of the tragic universe associated with Antigone and her family.

At this point, any vestige of Greek tragic thought has been erased from the play. Without the moral basis for defying Creon, Antigone has no justification for continuing her tragic revolt. There is nothing for her to do but turn and go up to her room. Until this midpoint, Antigone's stand has been modeled after the Greek example; she defies Creon because of loyalty to Polynices. But Creon has very thoroughly discredited her tragic ideals and, now, she does not believe in the universal, ethical basis of tragedy any more than he does. The play must either stop or find a new direction. This new direction is based on Antigone's turning within herself to renew her tragic vocation.

Creon, himself, through a blunder, allows Antigone to find a justification for tragedy based on her sense of self which will replace the discredited moral universe. Like many cynical and ruthless men, the king has a sentimental streak which leads him to make a comparison between Antigone and a Creon of the past: "Je te comprends, j'aurais fait comme toi à vingt ans. C'est pour cela que je buvais tes paroles. J'écoutais du fonds du temps un petit Créon maigre et pâle comme toi et qui ne pensait qu'à tout donner lui aussi" (pp. 97-98). Creon then advises Antigone to be content with the simple things of life in which she may find some happiness. Her reply is one of the most telling of the play: "Quel sera-t-il mon bonheur? Quelle femme heureuse deviendra-t-elle la petite Antigone?" (p. 99) The term "un petit Créon" is a mistake which undoes all the king's previous argument because it causes Antigone to articulate her private sense of being. She responds with a term of her own, "la petite Antigone," which has already been used several times by the chorus. The definite rather than indefinite article suggests that she considers this definition of the self complete, permanent, and not to be compromised by Creon's picture of her future life. Antigone is now able to fill the void created by the disappearance of the tragic universe with an interior world whose major value is her fidelity to her self-conception. In dramatic terms, Antigone is clinging to her role which she sees in danger of being changed by Creon's view of the future. This is the turning point of the play. Antigone must abandon the Greek model and enter into the contemporary theatre of self-consciousness. Her sense of herself as a specific character is the third element in Anouilh's dramatic design. It complements the chorus' distancing commentary and Creon's rejection of a tragic universe, and, therefore, Anouilh establishes the character carefully in the opening scene of the play.

The scene between Antigone and her nurse is an invention of Anouilh and, from the first, it contains troubling inconsistencies with what one expects from tragedy. Its tone and mood are sentimental and domestic, the rough, loving, scold of a nurse contrasted with the sweet and fragile heroine.

Antigone's initial replies to the nurse are the most important indications of her character: *La nourrice*: D'où viens tu? *Antigone*: De me promener, nourrice. C'était beau. Tout était gris. Maintenant tu ne peux pas savoir, tout est déjà rose, jaune, vert. C'est devenu une carte postale. Il faut te lever plus tôt nourrice si tu veux voir un monde sans couleurs" (p. 14). These words may strike a strange note when one considers that they are spoken just after Antigone's burial of Polynices. The mood is lyrical and elated and seems inconsistent with the gravity of the situation. This is surely the point of the scene. The dialogue between Antigone and her nurse directs the spectator's attention away from Antigone's act and toward the personality and character of the girl herself. Her second reply to the nurse intensifies our impression of her: "Le jardin dormait encore. Je l'ai surpris nourrice. Je l'ai vu sans qu'il s'en doute. C'est beau un jardin qui ne pense pas encore aux hommes" (pp. 14-15). This Antigone will be quite familiar to a French audience. Her replies contain a preciosity which evokes the *poésie de banlieue* one might find in a Prévert scenario. When Antigone says, ". . . je me suis glissée dans la campagne sans qu'elle s'en aperçoive" (p. 15), we are reminded of the arabesques we expect from the lovely and eccentric girls who populate Giraudoux's theatre.

It is essential that we see Antigone in sentimental closeup because what counts finally is not what she does but how we see her and how she sees herself. It is a characteristic of self-conscious theatre that the two perceptions are very much the same. So, Anouilh provides a striking number of sentimental touches in the opening moments of the play. Antigone still uses her baby name for her nurse, "Nounou." The heroine has a little dog named "Douce" whose fate seems to be at least as important to her as the unfolding of the tragic action. Perhaps the best example of the sentimentality which eventually overshadows ethical considerations is

the revelation later that Antigone has buried Polynices with the toy shovel with which, as children, they built sand castles at the beach.

These details are extremely important to the play's design. The distance from tragedy established through the Chorus and Creon are all the more effective since Antigone is touching and convincing. One of the play's peculiar tensions is this combination of distance and intimacy; we are asked to judge at a distance a character with whom, in other circumstances, we might sympathize or identify. Having raised the problem of the place of tragedy in modern theatre, Anouilh asks whether a sentimental character can be the equal of a great tragic vision.

Antigone is clearly a type, suggesting a role, not of the Greek tragic heroine, but one defined by the lyricism of her first scene. She is the fresh, delicate ingenue caught up in her own image of youthful purity and sensitivity. She is a romantic who is enamoured of extravagant attitudes and gestures. What Antigone lacks in tragic stature she makes up for in touching character. Compared to her Greek counterpart, she is, indeed, the little Antigone. The very fragility of this role necessitates Antigone's protecting it with her life against the possibility of its corruption in time.

This concentration upon the self is the most important distinction the play suggests between Greek and modern tragedy. Whereas in Sophocles' play, Antigone's burial of Polynices is an act which cannot be undone, we have seen that, in Anouilh's version, that is precisely what happens when Creon undermines the tragic universe. Antigone does not claim that she owes it to a higher good to bury Polynices. In fact, her brother is never mentioned again. The reason for her defiance becomes her devotion to herself.[6] In answer to Creon's question of for whom she has done this deed, she replies, "Pour personne. Pour moi" (p. 78). Creon realizes too late that the only necessity for Antigone's death lies within herself: "Antigone était faite pour être morte. Elle-même ne le savait peut-être pas, mais Polynices n'était qu'un prétexte. Quand elle a dû y renoncer, elle a trouvé autre chose tout de suite. Ce qui importait pour elle c'était de refuser et de mourir" (p. 102). Death becomes the only way that Antigone can dramatize herself in a tragic role.

Antigone attempts to impose upon the world an interior mythology which pits a youth of intransigent purity and innocence against an old age of corrupting compromise. She sees the danger of "la petite Antigone" being transformed with the years into the equivalent of the corrupt and cynical king. So her stand becomes, essentially, a refusal to grow old in order to give her identity the lasting form of the role, removing it from the changing flow of life:[7] "Moi, je veux tout, tout de suite,—et que ce soit entier—ou alors je refuse! Je veux être sûre de tout aujourd'hui et que cela soit aussi beau que quand j'étais petite—ou mourir" (p. 97). Ironically, Antigone's position results from her acceptance of Creon's version of life, and she is left consequently with an extremely limited choice: either conform to the king's cynical view, or say no and die. Her stance recalls J. L. Styan's observation that sentimental plays often indulge a romantic impulse to accept or reject life.[8]

However, it is Anouilh's heroine, not his play, that is romantic. The play puts romantic attitudes in a perspective which reveals the flaws and pitfalls to which they can be prey. Rebellious postures such as Antigone's are essential to a romantic affirmation of the self which makes liberty synonymous with heroism and views heroism as a fundamentally solitary and self-fulfilling endeavor. When Ismene belatedly rushes in and offers to die with her sister, Antigone cries, "Ah! non. Pas maintenant. Pas toi! C'est moi, c'est moi seule. Tu ne te figures pas que tu vas venir mourir avec moi maintenant. Ce serait trop facile!" (p. 105) Antigone's infatuation with dying makes her resemble those modern heroes described by Victor Bromberg as fascinated by "the poetry of insurrection and the pathos of defeat."[9] Her fall is self-willed, and it reflects a romantic attempt to achieve tragic stature through attitude and gesture.

But it is not sufficient for Antigone to want to be tragic, for tragedy cannot be based solely on the self. As Lionel Abel observes, "We cannot urge the tragic sense on ourselves or on others. To try to attain it or recommend it is comical and self-refuting, tragedy being real only when unavoidable. There would be no such thing as tragedy if a tragic fate could be rationally chosen."[10] This is the fundamental problem explored in *Antigone.* There is a gap between the tragic spirit and the romantic desire for self-assertion, since tragedy takes place in the world whereas romantic affirmations such as Antigone's depend primarily upon a consciousness which has become uncertain as to what the world is.[11]

Antigone's enduring interest lies in the way it dramatizes the decline of tragic myth in the labyrinth of modern self-consciousness. The play itself seems to be earnestly seeking its own tradition. A discredited tragic universe has been replaced by sentimental character. The inadequacies and ultimate failure of this romantic substitute for tragedy are reflected in a theatricalism which questions the authenticity of the heroine. In a sense, Anouilh, through Creon and the chorus, has hollowed out the Greek myth, and the play's theatricalism is what is left when nostalgia for the tragic form's lost power to convey wisdom remains.

The play's theatricalism intersects with the idea of the impossibility of tragedy, and it is within this matrix that Antigone's fate looks, ultimately, absurd. This is the chorus' sour, final assessment of what has happened. As in all his remarks, he begins with a laconic and sardonic *voilà*: "Et voilà. Sans la petite Antigone, c'est vrai, ils auraient tous été tranquilles. Mais maintenant, c'est fini. Ils sont tout de même tranquilles. Tous ceux qui avaient à mourir sont morts. Ceux qui croyaient une chose, et puis ceux qui croyaient le contraire—même ceux qui ne croyaient rien et qui se sont trouvés pris dans l'histoire sans y rien comprendre. Morts pareils, tous, bien raides, bien inutiles, bien pourris. Et ceux qui vivent encore vont commencer tout doucement à les oublier et à confondre leurs noms. C'est fini. Antigone est calmée maintenant, nous ne saurons jamais de quelle fièvre" (p. 132). The suggestion of waste and futility conveyed by these words is the antithesis of the redemptive possibilities of tragedy.

The anti-tragic sense in *Antigone* is so strong that one is tempted to conclude that Anouilh has written the play to rid himself and his theatre of an exhausted dramatic tradition. His decided preference for the ambiguities of theatricalism over the affirmations of tragedy suggest that *Antigone* has much in common with his *pièces grincantes* and with contemporary dark comedy in general. The play shares with dark comedy the atmosphere of doubt brought on by the uneasy feeling that the myths which have given our civilization spiritual coherence are now without energy. In such plays commonly held affirmations give way to a climate of self-conscious anxiety. A world which Anouilh sees as containing more chance and play than structure and high purpose is epitomized in the card game which, fittingly, brings down the final curtain, suggesting that Antigone and her myth, at least for Anouilh, have finally been laid to rest.

Notes

1. Eric Bentley has described this development in his discussion of "bourgeois tragedy," in *The Playwright as Thinker* (New York: Meridian Books, 1946), pp. 23-47.

2. Anouilh has been criticized for his emphasis on character. John Harvey cites Hubert Gignoux's complaint that the hero's personality is more important than his tragic destiny. Mr. Harvey, however, sees the role as the key to Anouilh's writing a successful tragedy—*Anouilh, A Study in Theatrics* (New Haven and London: Yale Univ. Press, 1964), pp. 92, 100. My view is that the emphasis on personality is deliberate and that Anouilh uses the role as an anti-tragic element in the play.

3. Jean Anouilh, *Antigone* (Paris: La Table Ronde, 1971), p. 9. Further references to the play will be from this edition.

4. *The Vision of Jean Genet* (New York: Grove Press, 1968), p. 214.

5. Jacques Guicharnaud points out that Creon breaks down Antigone's "Greek" reasoning. He does not, however, discuss the implications of this breakdown in terms of role-playing and theatricalism—*Modern French Theatre from Giraudoux to Genet* (New Haven and London: Yale Univ. Press, 1967), p. 127.

6. It may be argued that Sophocles, also, is a dramatist of character. But, as H. D. F. Kitto observes, he is interested in the way character intertwines with a complex of events—*Greek Tragedy* (Garden City: Doubleday, 1954), p. 157. Anouilh's Antigone is not interested in events; she responds solely to her self-conception.

7. As befits a playwright who spent his formative years with the Pitoëff Company, Anouilh owes more to Chekov and Pirandello than to Sophocles. The influence of Pirandello on French theatre has been treated in Thomas Bishop's *Pirandello and the French Theatre* (New York: New York Univ. Press, 1960).

8. *The Elements of Drama* (Cambridge: Cambridge Univ. Press, 1967), p. 222.

9. *The Intellectual Hero, Studies in the French Novel, 1880-1955* (Chicago and London: Univ. of Chicago Press, 1964), p. 150.

10. "Is There a Tragic Sense of Life?" in *Moderns on Tragedy,* ed. Lionel Abel (Greenwich: Fawcett, 1967), p. 178.

11. *Moderns on Tragedy,* p. 183n. *Antigone* would fit Abel's definition of a metaplay. Abel asks the following significant question: "If Antigone were self-conscious enough to suspect her own motives in burying her brother Polynices, would her story be a tragic one?"—*Metatheatre* (New York: Hill and Wang, 1968), p. 77. Mr. Abel does not mention that Anouilh has devoted an entire play to answering the question.

W. D. Howarth (essay date 1983)

SOURCE: Howarth, W. D. "Anouilh's *Antigone*: An Analytical Commentary." In *Anouilh: Antigone*, pp. 22-47. London: Edward Arnold, 1983.

[In the following essay, Howarth provides a close reading of Antigone *and surveys critical and popular reaction to the play.]*

Though longer than Sophocles' original, Anouilh's is not a long play, and structurally the two works are very similar. Like the Greek tragedy, Anouilh's **Antigone** is not divided into acts, and is written for continuous play-

ing without interval. Moreover, it respects in large measure the Greek convention referred to above, according to which there were seldom more than two principal characters on stage together, and each scene, or episode, was normally a dialogue. Here, the only exceptions are brief linking scenes in which one or more of the Gardes, La Nourrice or Le Choeur, is temporarily present with two of the principal characters, and one isolated occasion on which Créon, Antigone, and Ismène together occupy the stage for no more than a page of dialogue—the counterpart of a similar *scène à trois* in Sophocles (lines 453-508). For the rest, the play is constructed on the Sophoclean pattern, with a succession of fairly short scenes bringing together either Antigone or Créon and one other character—and as a centrepiece the magnificent long scene between the two main characters themselves, which on its own constitutes well over a quarter of the whole play. Since there are no formal indications in the published text, it may be useful to begin by setting down a scheme of scene-divisions for easy reference. If we follow the established French practice of indicating a new scene with the entrance or exit of a character or characters, we arrive at the following picture[1]:

(i) pages 39-41 Prologue

(ii) 42-6 Antigone, La Nourrice

(iii) 46 Antigone, Ismène, La Nourrice

(iv) 46-51 Antigone, Ismène

(v) 51-3 Antigone, La Nourrice

(vi) 53-7 Antigone, Hémon

(vii) 57-8 Antigone, Ismène

(viii) 58-62 Créon, Le Garde

(ix) 62-3 Le Choeur

(x) 63-5 Antigone, Les Gardes

(xi) 65-8 Antigone, Créon, Les Gardes

(xii) 68-85 Antigone, Créon

(xiii) 85-6 Antigone, Créon, Ismène

(xiv) 86-7 Créon, Le Choeur

(xv) 87-9 Créon, Hémon, Le Choeur

(xvi) 89 Créon, Le Choeur

(xvii) 89 Créon, Antigone, Les Gardes, Le Choeur

(xviii) 90-5 Antigone, Le Garde

(xix) 95-6 Le Messager, Le Choeur

(xx) 96-7 Créon, Le Page, Le Choeur

(xxi) 97-8 Le Choeur

It will be seen that on one side of the central confrontation nearly all the scenes involve Antigone: she is indeed absent for only one scene, between Créon and

Le Garde; while on the other side Créon is on stage virtually the whole time, the only substantial exception being a scene between Le Garde and Antigone: evidence of a care for balanced composition which suggests a debt to the Sophoclean example.

The list of *Personnages,* if we compare it with the *dramatis personae* of the Greek play, hints straightaway both at the closeness of Anouilh's adaptation and at the nature of the changes he has introduced. The substitution of the Gardes (three speaking parts) for a single Sentry allows Anouilh to fill out, and embroider on, the dialogue reported in Sophocles (lines 219ff, 370ff); the Page de Créon is a functional character with a handful of lines, who exists purely as a recipient of the King's confidences, especially in the closing lines of the play. The principal characters—Créon, Antigone, Ismène, and Hémon, even Le Messager and Eurydice—are taken over (though Eurydice becomes a non-speaking part); and the only substantive changes appear to be that Tiresias is missing from the list, and that Antigone is provided with a *confidente* in the form of her old nurse. If the absence of the blind prophet suggests a 'désacralisation', or rationalization, of the mythical subject-matter, we can presume that the introduction of the Nourrice will act as a complement to this, and enable the French playwright to develop sympathy for his heroine on a more familiar domestic level.

There is one entry among the *dramatis personae* that is somewhat deceptive, however. 'Le Choeur' is by no means a simple equivalent of the Greek Chorus—which we may take, incidentally, to have been composed of the standard number of twelve or fifteen members, elders of the city of Thebes and therefore with a stake at first hand in the fortunes of its rulers. Anouilh's Choeur, or Prologue[2], on the other hand, is an individual, almost entirely detached from the action, and placed, as we shall see, in the unique position of privileged commentator, which suggests a loose comparison (inasmuch as he provides authorial comment) with the 'omniscient narrator' of prose fiction. In dramaturgical terms, the function of the Shakespearean Chorus (who speaks the Prologue to *Romeo and Juliet,* for instance, or the Prologue and Epilogue to *Henry V*) offers a closer analogy than the Chorus of Greek tragedy; though the role of Anouilh's Choeur is subtler and more idiosyncratic than this. In addition to his expository function (pp. 39-42, 62-3) and his function as Epilogue (pp. 97-8), this character does also on occasion assume the more traditional guise of confident and mentor to Créon (pp. 86-9), and even acts as a supplementary messenger (pp. 95-6). Far from being a conventional figure, Le Choeur represents Anouilh's principal innovation; and our attitude towards this feature will play a large part in determining our critical interpretation of the play.

About the staging of the play there is only this to say: that Anouilh seems deliberately to have left this unspeci-

fied, and himself to have envisaged a 'décor neutre', or purely functional space, with a minimum of embellishment. The ideal, as regards both set and costume, is surely that both should be as unobtrusive as possible, leaving the whole emphasis (possibly assisted by lighting effects) squarely on the characters themselves. Photographs of the early Paris productions show a set of this nature: plain drapes, three steps leading up to a semicircular rostrum, and a pair of simple stools; while the costume (the men wear either evening dress or dinner-jackets; the guards black raincoats; and the women long black dresses except for Ismène who wears white) is similarly intended to leave the greatest possible freedom to the actors[3]. The photograph of the New York production of 1946, on the other hand, looks wrong: Cedric Hardwicke (Créon) and Katherine Cornell (Antigone), although dressed in a similar manner to their French counterparts, suggest a scene from a drawing-room comedy because the furniture and drapes convey an atmosphere, not of functional austerity but of elegance and comfort. Anouilh obviously had in mind an indoor set, but that is about as far as the decor ought to go: the designer should aim at something with the same non-committal character, *mutatis mutandis,* as the open-air Greek stage.

(I) LE PROLOGUE (P. 39)

The curtain rises on the 'décor neutre', revealing all the characters on stage, who 'bavardent, tricotent, jouent aux cartes' during the long speech by the Prologue with which the play opens. The fact that they are all on stage to begin with, occupied in a variety of day-to-day activities, and that they get up and leave in turn towards the end of the Prologue's speech, to return only as and when the action requires their presence, brings convincing visual reinforcement to the idea implicit in what he says: that as well as being characters in Anouilh's play ('tous les *personnages . . .*'), these are members of a company of actors, waiting to assume the roles assigned to them in the forthcoming performance. In other words, Anouilh can be seen to be already suggesting an idea here that he will exploit more explicitly at the beginning of *L'Alouette* (1953), where the opening stage-direction reads in part:

> En entrant, les personnages décrochent leurs casques ou certains de leurs accessoires qui avaient été laissés sur scène à la fin de la précédente représentation, ils s'installent sur les bancs dont ils rectifient l'ordonnance . . .[4].

However, the Prologue does not say 'Ces acteurs vont vous jouer l'histoire d'Antigone', but 'Ces personnages . . .'. So that even when the actors have taken on their allotted parts within the play, they are still going to be performing, or acting out, a predetermined course of events: a notion that is at once given a most challenging illustration: 'Antigone . . .' (that is, not merely the actress playing the part, but the created character within the play) '. . . pense qu'elle va être Antigone tout à l'heure'. For the time being, she is 'la petite maigre . . . assise là-bas', 'la maigre jeune fille noiraude et renfermée . . .'; but her destiny, of which she is aware, is already calling her to make her stand against Créon, and to die for it. She is set apart from us, the spectators, 'qui sommes là bien tranquilles à la regarder, . . . qui n'avons pas à mourir ce soir'—set apart not only because as an actress she has stepped into the imaginary world on the other side of the footlights, but also because in her role as Antigone she is marked by a tragic destiny that does not concern itself with ordinary men and women.

It is easy to become over-familiar with a well known text, with the result that one may come to overlook its challenging or provocative character. This opening paragraph is a remarkable *tour de force,* presenting as it does with such economy of language the striking interplay of different levels of reality and illusion, and introducing the notion of life as the acting out of preordained roles, which will figure prominently in later scenes.

Ismène is contrasted throughout with Antigone, in every possible way. It is a contrast that could no doubt be said to be implicit in Sophocles, but from the beginning Anouilh makes it explicit: 'la blonde, la belle, l'heureuse Ismène' establishes her as the opposite of 'la maigre je-une fille noiraude et renfermée . . .' with her 'petit sourire triste'. The anecdotal account of the betrothal of Antigone and Hémon again develops suggestions that are perhaps latent in the Greek text, though in this case more of Anouilh's own gratuitous invention has gone into it. In particular, the effect of the anecdote is to present the relationship in anachronistic terms: though much less glaring than some of the examples that are to follow, the deliberate anachronism of 'un soir de bal où il n'avait dansé qu'avec Ismène', 'éblouissante dans sa nouvelle robe', 'L'orchestre attaquait une nouvelle danse', 'Ismène riait aux éclats . . . au milieu des au-tres garçons' is an attempt to close the gap between the mythological figures and the members of a twentieth-century audience. The last sentence of this paragraph: 'Il ne savait pas qu'il ne devait pas exister de mari d'Antigone . . .' reverts to the suggestive fatalism of the opening lines, and with 'ce titre princier . . .' the language takes on a more elevated tone; but the overall effect of the paragraph is to make the spectator feel: 'these are characters like ourselves'; they are no longer the remote heroes of a centuries-old tradition.

The thumbnail sketch of Créon looks forward to what will be the dominant traits of Anouilh's King: 'Il a des rides, il est fatigué. Il joue au jeu difficile de conduire les hommes'. Again, suggestive touches bridge the gap and help us to envisage Créon in twentieth-century

terms, not only as a man of culture and a patron of the arts: 'la musique, les belles reliures, les longues flâner-ies chez les petits antiquaires de Thèbes', but also as a man of conscience devoted to his duty: 'il a retroussé ses manches . . .', '. . . comme un ouvrier au seuil de sa journée'.

Eurydice, with her knitting, is an Anouilh stereotype: compare La Mère in *L'Alouette,* who similarly 'trico-tera pendant toute la pièce, sauf quand c'est à elle'; and so are the card-playing Gardes. 'Ils sentent l'ail, le cuir et le vin rouge . . .': here Anouilh is using his Prologue very much like an omniscient novelist, for 'Ils sen-tent . . .' is not something demonstrable, that specta-tors can test empirically; we have to take the author's word for it, as an 'objective correlative' of their mental limitations: '. . . et ils sont dépourvus de toute imagination'.

The Prologue's last paragraph discreetly fulfils a traditional expository function, with a brief summary of the antecedents of the plot: the events following on the exile of Oedipus and the curse laid on his sons. The events, indeed, of Racine's tragedy *La Thébaïde*; and Anouilh's phrase 'les deux frères ennemis sont morts . . .' reproduces, no doubt intentionally, the subtitle (*Les Frères ennemis*) of that play. At this point, the closing lines of the Prologue's speech bring us into the closest contact yet with Sophocles' text, where An-tigone says:

> Eteocles has been buried, they tell me, in state,
> With all honourable observances due to the dead.
> But Polynices, just as unhappily fallen—the order
> Says he is not to be buried, not to be mourned;
> To be left unburied, unwept, a feast of flesh
> For keen-eyed carrion birds.

(lines 20-5)

(II) ANTIGONE, LA NOURRICE (P. 42)

The dialogue begins with a passage of considerable charm, which owes nothing to the Greek original. Anti-gone's poetic evocation of the distinctive beauty of the hour before dawn, with its personification of the sleep-ing world of nature, has something in it of the imagina-tive quality of Giraudoux's prose-poetry ('Le jardin dormait encore. Je l'ai surpris, nourrice. Je l'ai vu sans qu'il s'en doute. C'est beau un jardin qui ne pense pas encore aux hommes . . . je me suis glissée dans la compagne sans qu'elle s'en aperçoive'), and one might be tempted to remember Anouilh's admiration for that writer. However, this is not 'fine writing' for its own sake: the poetic touches are entirely acceptable in their context, where they help to characterize Antigone as herself a child of nature, and there is none of the strain-ing after effect that sometimes marks Giraudoux's 'preciosity'.

At various points during this scene the dialogue almost takes on a comic tone, as Antigone and the Nourrice talk at cross purposes; not only does Antigone deliberately play on her old nurse's misunderstanding of the situation, but the Nourrice, alternately solicitous and scolding, acts on the familiar level of ordinary domestic considerations ('Il va falloir te laver les pieds avant de te remettre au lit . . . Je me lève pour voir si elle n'était pas découverte. Je trouve son lit froid . . .'), while Antigone on the other hand constantly invests the ordinary with a mysterious significance. The conversation between these two characters is of course a complete innovation, and indeed their invented relationship is one of the factors that contribute to the 'rounding' of Antigone's personality, and help to establish her close affinity with other early Anouilh heroines. Not that the whole scene is equally successful in this respect: the fragment of imaginary dialogue between the Nourrice and the dead Jocasta is somewhat laboured, and borders on the sentimental ('Voilà ce qu'elle me dira, ta mère, là-haut, quand j'y monterai, et moi j'aurai honte, honte à en mourir si je n'étais pas déjà morte, et je ne pourrai que baisser la tête et répondre: "Madame Jocaste, c'est vrai"'); but it is obviously introduced in order to prepare the way for Antigone's cryptic hint: 'Elle sait pourquoi je suis sortie ce matin'. More hints, in which the fate-motif is adumbrated ('. . . je n'aurai jamais d'autre amoureux . . .', 'il ne faut pas que je sois petite ce matin') bring the scene to a close, as Ismène enters and the Nourrice departs to prepare an anachronistic cup of coffee.

(III)-(IV) ANTIGONE, ISMÈNE, LA NOURRICE (P. 46)

From the beginning of this scene too, it is evident that the two speakers are not on the same 'wavelength'; but this time it is not so much a question of a 'sub-text'—mysterious hints that remain to be elucidated—as of an open and explicit difference of viewpoint. The subject of their disagreement is clear, since the Prologue has already informed us of Créon's edict; and throughout this scene we see disobedience, rebellion, contrasted with conformism and acceptance. Ismène's opposition to her sister is categorical: it is based on temperamental difference ('Tu es folle . . . Nous ne pouvons pas . . . Il nous ferait mourir . . . Je ne veux pas mourir'), and it is also backed up by rational argument: '. . . je comprends un peu notre oncle . . . Il est le roi, il faut qu'il donne l'exemple'. Antigone, for her part, is capable of expressing a wistful regret for what might have been ('Moi aussi j'aurais bien voulu ne pas mourir'); but she answers her sister in an equally categorical fashion, giving expression to the life-as-theatre metaphor which contributes so powerfully to the fatalistic theme of the play: 'A chacun son rôle. Lui, il doit nous faire mourir, et nous, nous devons aller enterrer notre frère. C'est comme cela que ç'a été distribué'.

On the other hand, it is clear from the beginning that Antigone's ready acceptance of this fate also depends on subjective, temperamental factors ('Moi je ne veux pas comprendre un peu . . . Je ne veux pas avoir raison . . .'). Her long speech: 'Comprendre . . . Vous n'avez que ce mot-là dans la bouche, tous, depuis que je suis toute petite . . .' may seem more suited, in some of its familiar detail ('Il fallait comprendre qu'on ne peut pas toucher à l'eau . . . Il fallait comprendre qu'on ne doit pas manger tout à la fois . . .'), to the situation of other Anouilh heroines than to that of a high-born daughter of the court of Thebes; but there can be no doubt that Anouilh's Antigone is presented as a consistent personality from the beginning, and the intransigent opposition to Créon is already being prepared in her stand against Ismène which, however arbitrary it may appear, unambiguously establishes her refusal to compromise: 'Comprendre. Toujours comprendre. Moi je ne veux pas comprendre. Je comprendrai quand je serai vieille . . . .'.

The scene with Ismène also gives expression to the important paradox that this character who seemingly arbitrarily renounces the possibility of life and happiness, does so in the name of a love of life more intense than that of her sister:

> Qui se levait la première, le matin, rien que pour sentir l'air froid sur sa peau nue? Qui se couchait la dernière seulement quand elle n'en pouvait plus de fatigue, pour vivre encore un peu de la nuit? Qui pleurait déjà toute petite, en pensant qu'il y avait tant de petites bêtes, tant de brins d'herbe dans le pré et qu'on ne pouvait pas tous les prendre?

This speech develops the 'child of nature' theme of the opening scene, and establishes a positive complement to her apparent death-wish.

W. M. Landers, commenting on this scene in his edition of the play, writes as follows:

> Ismène's attitude here is quite different from that of her namesake . . . The Ismene of Sophocles hangs back through fear of the consequences; she confesses to a sense of guilt at not helping her sister and entreats the dead to forgive her. Anouilh's Ismène is really on Créon's side, at least in the early part of the play . . .

and also cites the 'shift in the attitude of the populace', who, according to Ismène, here side with Créon, as evidence of a desire to 'equalize the moral forces opposed to each other in the central scene' (p. 101). It seems rather that these are subsidiary considerations, and that fundamentally the French Ismène, like her Greek counterpart, is motivated by lack of courage, so that when she says 'Je comprends un peu notre oncle' and 'ils pensent tous comme lui dans la ville', she is trying to rationalize what is essentially a question of temperament. Her final plea: 'C'est bon pour les hommes de croire aux idées et de mourir pour elles. Toi tu es une fille' is not only a close verbal echo of Sophocles' text at this point:

> O think, Antigone; we are women; it is not for us
> To fight against men . . .
>
> (lines 52-3)

but it also expresses what I take to be the essence of the character's psychological motivation in both plays.

(v) ANTIGONE, LA NOURRICE (P. 51)

The Nourrice's entry with coffee and *tartines* takes us away from Sophocles again; and in the theatre, this second scene of familiar dialogue on domestic matters has the effect of lowering the dramatic tension. The scene has been criticized for an excess of sentimentality: this is a matter of subjective taste, though it may well seem to most readers or spectators that Anouilh is taking something of a risk by placing such emphasis on the heroine's childlike relationship with her old nurse. The series of appellations 'mon pigeon', 'ma petite colombe', 'ma mésange', 'ma tourterelle' would not be out of place in a comedy; indeed, Anouilh uses a similar sequence elsewhere for comic effect.[5] On the other hand, Antigone's own affectionate appeal to the simple certainties of the past ('Mais fais-moi tout de même bien chaud comme lorsque j'étais malade . . .') is clearly meant to establish quite a different mood. But what might almost be seen as a kind of infantile regression on her part—suggested in the invocation of 'the wicked giant, the sandman, and the bogeyman who comes and steals little children away', together with the childlike rhythms of her speech at this point ('Alors je te le demande: ne la gronde pas. Promets que tu ne la gronderas pas. Je t'en prie, dis, je t'en prie, nounou . . . Et puis, promets-moi aussi que tu lui parleras, que tu lui parleras souvent') is surely rather overdone, and falls on the wrong side of the borderline between deeply-felt emotion and a more superficial sentiment. By the same token, the page devoted to the heroine's concern for the future of her dog, though it is no doubt intended to reinforce the feeling of foreboding that we by now share with Antigone, but which the Nourrice cannot share, runs the risk of producing the opposite effect by its build-up of homely detail, and of trivializing, rather than deepening, our relationship with the character.

(VI) ANTIGONE, HÉMON (P. 53)

The playwright is on surer ground in the scene between Antigone and Hémon: a scene that would have been out of place in Sophocles' version both for the structural reason discussed above, and also because his age took far less interest than we do in the literary possibilities of a romantic relationship between a pair of lovers. To have written a modern play on this subject, however, without taking the opportunity to bring the ill-starred lovers together, would have been virtually unthinkable; and as we have shown in our comments on the structure of Anouilh's play, above, the creation of this scene, which completes the triangular relationship between the principal characters, is one of the means by which the French dramatist produced a shift of emphasis, from the tragedy of Creon to a play whose focus is the conflict between Créon and Antigone. And while the subject-matter of the scene is of necessity just as new (and in fact may seem just as incongruous in relation to the Sophoclean material, for the notion of Antigone borrowing her sister's dress, perfume and lipstick in order to make herself attractive is another of the anachronisms that link her to characters like Thérèse and Jeannette), its effect is to heighten the emotional tension, and to increase our apprehension of impending catastrophe, rather than to dissipate them by means of irrelevance and triviality. Antigone's tender evocation of the child she and Hémon now will never have; her use of a conditional tense ('Le petit garçon que nous aurions eu . . . je l'aurais serré si fort . . . Il aurait eu une maman . . . plus sûre que toutes les mères . . . toi, tu aurais eu une vraie femme . . . j'aurais été très fière d'être ta femme . . .') that Hémon is unable to understand; her confession of an unsuccessful attempt to give herself to Hémon: all of these form part of a consistent build-up to the poignant climax of the scene, the elegiac ultimatum to her bewildered lover: '. . . jamais, jamais, je ne pourrai t'épouser' and the following speech, whose passionate intensity overcomes the threat of melodrama and carries complete conviction:

> Hémon, tu me l'as juré! Sors. Sors tout de suite sans rien dire. Si tu parles, si tu fais un seul pas vers moi, je me jette par cette fenêtre. Je te le jure, Hémon. Je te le jure sur la tête du petit garçon que nous avons eu tous les deux en rêve, du seul petit garçon que j'aurai jamais. Pars maintenant, pars vite. Tu sauras demain. Tu sauras tout à l'heure.

Hémon goes out at a high point of dramatic and emotional tension, all the more convincing because the scene has persuaded us of the couple's reciprocal affection. Hémon's is very much the more passive contribution, however, and it is Antigone who brings out the quality of their present relationship:

> Tu m'aimes, n'est-ce pas? Tu m'aimes comme une femme? Tes bras qui me serrent ne mentent pas . . . ? Tes grandes mains posées sur mon dos ne mentent pas, ni ton odeur, ni ce bon chaud, ni cette grande confiance qui m'inonde quand j'ai la tête au creux de ton cou?

as well as the impossibility of a shared future, with her superlatives and temporal adverbs which stress the finality of the step she is taking: 'C'est la dernière folie . . . jamais, jamais, je ne pourrai t'épouser . . . [le] seul petit garçon que j'aurai jamais . . . C'est tout ce que tu peux faire encore pour moi . . .'.

Much has been written about the quality of love in the early Anouilh plays, where it frequently tends to take the form of a tender, loyal comradeship whose overtly sexual character is much played down: what H. Gignoux calls, in a happy phrase that is not too wide of the mark, 'une sorte de camaraderie garçonnière, de scoutisme mixte' (p. 71). Elsewhere, the images 'petit soldat', 'petit frère', 'petit copain' recur; and although Anouilh does not draw on the same range of imagery to portray the relationship between Antigone and Hémon, nevertheless there are certain clear hints of an affinity in this respect with the system of values in force in *La Sauvage* and *Eurydice*. When Antigone says: 'Je suis noire et maigre. Ismène est rose et dorée comme un fruit'; when she says: 'j'avais fait tout cela pour être un peu plus comme les autres filles'—even when she compares herself to other women with 'leurs vraies poitrines'—she is implicitly defending a conception of her relationship with Hémon that is based not on conventional ideas of sexual attraction, but on a comradeship that is essentially asexual. It is true that she confesses to having tried to lead Hémon on so that he might want her to give herself to him; but the fact that her attempt was frustrated perhaps indicates that she had been acting out of character. This in no way detracts from the intimacy of the couple; and indeed I think it adds to the emotive power of the situation. For the reader or spectator who can relate Antigone in this way to other early heroines of similar temperamental make-up, her gauche and inexpert attempt to achieve sexual fulfilment before she goes to her death gives an extra poignancy to the scene.

(VII) ANTIGONE, ISMÈNE (P. 57)

This brief scene is of capital importance: if not in terms of plot or character, at least in terms of dramatic impact. Ismène's second appearance represents another innovation—in Sophocles we see Ismene twice only, and her second scene corresponds to the French character's third appearance—and its justification is that it rounds off the exposition, properly speaking, and leads up to the tremendously effective 'curtain-line' that marks Antigone's exit: 'C'est trop tard. Ce matin, quand tu m'as rencontrée, j'en venais'. Preliminaries are now over, and the 'coup de théâtre' of this announcement brings us fully up to date with past events; if Anouilh had followed a conventional division into acts, this would have been the end of Act I. As it is, it is the first occasion on which the stage has been left empty between episodes, without what in neo-classical dramaturgy is called 'liaison des scènes'; and in the theatre, the director may well decide to emphasize the fact by a slightly longer pause before the next sequence begins.

(VIII) CRÉON, LE GARDE (P. 58)

Compared with Sophocles' Sentry, Anouilh's Garde is much more obviously a representative of the rough common soldier (cf. the stage-direction 'C'est une brute');

and despite the closeness in certain details to the Sophoclean text, there is a degree of caricatural exaggeration which suggests that Anouilh's aim here is much nearer to Shakespeare's: that is the creation of 'comic relief' for its own sake, rather than (as in Sophocles, if one can accept Kitto's comment, quoted above) the establishing of a coherent scheme of things in which the divine purpose finds expression in the most diverse kinds of humanity.

To begin with, it is the closeness to Sophocles that strikes one: the elements are the same, assembled flexibly and with a certain amount of discreet expansion:

> —It's this, sir. The corpse . . . someone has just
>
> Buried it and gone. Dry dust over the body
>
> They scattered, in the manner of holy ritual.
>
> —What! Who dared to do it?
>
> —I don't know, sir.
>
> There was no sign of a pick, no scratch of a shovel . . .
>
> (lines 205-18)[6]

> —Le cadavre, chef. Quelqu'un l'avait recouvert. Oh! pas grand' chose. Ils n'avaient pas eu le temps avec nous autres à côté. Seulement un peu de terre . . . Mais assez tout de même pour le cacher aux vautours.
>
> —Tu es sûr que ce n'est pas une bête en grattant?
>
> —Non, chef. On a d'abord espéré ça, nous aussi. Mais la terre était jetée sur lui, selon les rites. C'est quelqu'un qui savait ce qu'il faisait.
>
> —Qui a osé? Qui a été assez fou pour braver ma loi? As-tu relevé des traces?
>
> —Rien, chef. Rien qu'un pas plus léger qu'un passage d'oiseau . . .

The Greek guards, like the French, have drawn lots to see who shall carry the unwelcome message to Creon; and although Sophocles' Sentry is perhaps less prone than Anouilh's Garde to insinuate that his colleagues are more to blame than himself: 'On n'a pas parlé, chef, je vous le jure! Mais moi, j'étais ici et peut-être que les autres, ils l'ont déjà dit à la relève . . .', there is a remarkable debt to the original, and this scene is in one sense one of the most closely copied in the whole play.

On the other hand, Anouilh's innovations and anachronisms are such as to give his Garde a distinct personality. With the mixture of servility and familiarity conveyed by the obtrusive 'chef' (which occurs no fewer than 21 times in this scene), the military jargon ('J'ai dix-sept ans de service. Je suis engagé volontaire, la médaille, deux citations. Je suis bien noté, chef. Moi je suis "service" . . .') and the popular expressions ('On est les trois du piquet de garde . . . Les autres c'est . . . Mes supérieurs ils disent . . .'), Garde Jonas, 'de la Deuxième Compagnie'[7], comes across as a coherent representation of a regular serving soldier in the modern idiom, as we know him from novels and films.

In Créon's case, the anachronisms are more discreet—'avec leur or bloqué dans Thèbes', for instance—so much so that it is possible to overlook even 'qui crachera devant mes fusils' at a first reading. But the whole of the long speech in which these phrases occur ('Un enfant . . . L'opposition brisée qui sourd et mine déjà partout . . .'), while not incompatible in general terms with the psychology of Sophocles' King, establishes Créon too as a sort of figure that is familiar to us in a modern context: a police chief or American state governor, perhaps—though 'les chefs de la plèbe puant l'ail' has a European rather than a transatlantic connotation. In this first meeting, Créon is presented as above all a realist. Not quite certain of the support of his people, suspicious of the role of the clergy, he is determined—unlike his Greek counterpart who insists on discovering the identity of the lawbreaker—to keep the matter quiet, so as not to provide a pretext for further unrest:

> . . . si tu parles, si le bruit court dans la ville qu'on a recouvert le cadavre de Polynice, vous mourrez tous les trois.

One of Anouilh's additions in this scene, unremarkable in itself, has a certain symbolic significance. This is the 'petite pelle d'enfant' (anachronistic in that we may assume that Oedipus and Jocasta were not in the habit of taking their young family for seaside holidays) which forms part of an important complex of references to childhood and the past—such as we have already commented on in the second scene with the Nourrice—by which the youth and the childlike qualities of Anouilh's heroine are established as a dominant motif. For the moment, the evidence of the spade serves to set Créon's suspicions on the wrong tack; but for the spectator who is already in the know, it symbolizes those values of incorruptible innocence and of obstinate determination to which Antigone has already given expression. And as Créon goes out, the words he speaks to the young Page:

> Tu mourrais, toi, pour moi? Tu crois que tu irais avec ta petite pelle? . . . Oui, bien sûr, tu irais tout de suite toi aussi . . .

not only have the effect of showing a more humane, understanding aspect of his character, but can also be related in the spectator's mind to the theme of obstinate dedication to a cause on the part of Antigone herself.

(IX) LE CHOEUR (P. 62)

The reflections on tragedy by Le Choeur constitute one of the most distinctive and one of the best-known scenes of Anouilh's play. The practice of putting a mouthpiece of the author's on stage to express, not a comment on the specific action of the individual play, but generalizations about fate, free will or similar philosophical preoccupations is of course an extension of the practice of Greek tragedy, where choric odes commonly also departed from the play's specific context in order to utter philosophical truths of more general application, as in this example from the *Antigone* itself:

> Happy are they who know not the taste of evil.
> From a house that heaven hath shaken
> The curse departs not
> But falls upon all of the blood,
> Like the restless surge of the sea when the dark storm
>   drives
> The black sand hurled from the deeps
> And the Thracian gales boom down
> On the echoing shore.
>
> (lines 509-16)

Among modern dramatists, Cocteau had most notably exploited the possibilities of this device. His own *Antigone* (1922) had virtually been an adaptation of Sophocles' text, somewhat abridged but little changed; but in a similar adaptation of Sophocles in *Oedipe-Roi* (1927) he had introduced a Prologue-chorus to comment on the cruelty of the gods in setting traps for men. This theme is developed, and given considerable prominence, in *La Machine infernale* seven years later; and Cocteau's dramaturgical invention here, as well as the specific image of the 'infernal machine' itself, must be considered as a major inspiration of the scene under consideration.

In Cocteau's play, the Prologue is used (as a disembodied Voice) not only to present the audience with a summary of the plot in advance, but also to comment on the action, which is described as follows:

> Regarde, spectateur, remonté à bloc, de telle sorte que le ressort se déroule avec lenteur tout le long d'une vie humaine, une des plus parfaites machines construites par les dieux infernaux pour l'anéantissement mathématique d'un mortel.

And at the beginning of each act, Cocteau uses La Voix to similar effect, in a manner more akin to that of the Shakespearean than of the Greek Chorus:

> La grande peste de Thèbes a l'air d'être le premier échec à cette fameuse chance d'Oedipe, car les dieux ont voulu, pour le fonctionnement de leur machine infernale, que toutes les malchances surgissent sous le déguisement de la chance . . .
>
> (Act IV)

From the beginning of this scene in Anouilh, the same metaphor recurs insistently ('Maintenant le ressort est bandé. Cela n'a plus qu'à se dérouler tout seul . . . on donne le petit coup de pouce pour que cela démarre

. . . on n'a plus qu'à laisser faire . . . Cela roule tout seul. C'est minutieux, bien huilé depuis toujours'). This sustained image, borrowed from Cocteau, presents a similar, though not an identical, view of the tragic action—the difference being that according to Anouilh's Choeur the human victim seems to be involved in a mechanistic process (there is no indication as to who winds up the clockwork mechanism), whereas for Cocteau the process implies the hostility of the gods: supernatural beings who in his scheme of things have their own superior destiny which they must obey: 'Le mystère a ses mystères. Les dieux possèdent leurs dieux' (*La Machine infernale,* Act II). In human terms, however, the view of tragedy is essentially the same: it is an inexorable, impersonal process that man is powerless to resist.

The plot of *La Machine infernale* is fully consistent with that proposition and with its corollary, that free will does not exist. For whenever Oedipe thinks he is making a free choice in order to frustrate the oracle's prediction, he is in fact playing into the hands of fate and making his 'anéantissement' the more certain. But the application to Antigone's case is a good deal more ambiguous. It is true that the image of the tragic 'machine' fits in well enough with the life-as-theatre metaphor, the notion of the heroine acting out a preordained destiny, which is expressed so challengingly in the opening lines spoken by Le Prologue; but as we shall see, this is not an interpretation to which we are necessarily led to subscribe by the main thrust of the action.

In the second paragraph of his soliloquy, Le Choeur sketches a contrast between tragedy and 'le drame' which prefigures, at least in its opening lines, the paragraph quoted above from Camus's 1955 lecture. 'Le drame' (that is to say, melodrama) is to do with the conflict between the wicked and the good ('ces traîtres'—the term always used of the 'villains' of melodrama—. . . ces méchants acharnés . . . cette innocence persécutée'), whereas in tragedy 'On est tous innocents en somme'. This can be taken either to mean that, as Camus was to say—and as conventional theories of tragedy ever since Aristotle had claimed—the tragic hero is neither wholly good nor wholly bad, but a character of 'middling virtue'; or else perhaps to show that Anouilh is offering, as Landers suggests, a 'typically Romantic' view of 'Man as the eternal victim of creation' (p. 103). In any case, Le Choeur continues, 'C'est une question de distribution': all are acting out their predestined roles. And it is for this reason, no doubt, that tragedy is 'propre', 'reposant', 'tranquille'. Chance, the accidental and avoidable, are excluded from tragedy; there is no reprieve, no hope. This view of the tragic process has a long and reputable ancestry in the history of European literature—Landers suggests a parallel with the stoicism of Vigny's 'La Mort du loup',

and there is also a clear affinity with the twentieth-century philosophy of the Absurd—but the resonance of 'le *sale* espoir' is peculiar to Anouilh, and to the very subjective scale of ethical values reflected in heroines like Thérèse and Antigone.

As Antigone enters, dragged in by the Gardes, Le Choeur's comment refers us back to the theme expressed in the opening lines of the play; while 'pour la première fois', together with 'pour la dernière fois' that we shall encounter later, provides a temporal framework for the unique tragic event, setting it apart from the accidental contingencies of ordinary everyday life.

(x) ANTIGONE, LES GARDES (P. 63)

This brief linking scene creates the opportunity to develop the homely, popular element contributed to the play by the Gardes: the sort of lifelike vignette that Anouilh does so well. With their naive assumption that they are about to become national heroes, and their self-absorbed argument about the relative merits of eating-places, these are the simple soldiers of any modern army; but they are also representatives of a more timeless humanity. If their dialogue is comic, it is because of its unconscious incongruity in the present context. This may be the tragedy of the house of Thebes, but it is essential to Anouilh's purpose (as, less obviously, it had been to Sophocles') that the heroine's preoccupation with death be juxtaposed with the obtrusive continuity of ordinary life.

(xi) ANTIGONE, CRÉON, LES GARDES (P. 65)

By contrast, the scene which follows returns us to Sophocles. The two supplementary guards now become non-speaking figures, and their spokesman is given a narrative that closely corresponds to the original. Anouilh does not retain the feature ('a storm of dust, like a plague from heaven', line 358) which has suggested to some commentators a supernatural intervention, hiding Antigone's reappearance from the guards; and some other details are the result of analogical transposition rather than of translation. And similarly, the circumstantial detail with which Antigone herself invests the episode of the 'petite pelle' is obviously also an invention of the modern dramatist. For the rest, the narrative is handled with the same economy as in Sophocles, and the scene leads into, rather than holds up, the confrontation between the two central characters.

(xii) ANTIGONE, CRÉON (P. 68)

Previous scenes have shown us that Créon is a realist, and that Antigone is pursuing some kind of ideal, or absolute; but the precise nature of their motives has not yet been revealed. It is the detailed unfolding of the characters' motivation, and the changing patterns of moral advantage—and therefore of sympathy in dramatic terms—that this produces, which provides the fascination of this justly celebrated scene. Not so much curiosity as to its outcome, for that we already know. We know Antigone is ordained to die, but not—in a play from which the gods are absent—how the moral forces, Camus's two 'forces légitimes', will be given dramatic expression.

Créon's first thought is to hush the matter up, and to prevent scandal ('tu vas rentrer chez toi . . . Je ferai disparaître ces trois hommes'); but Antigone firmly rejects this expedient, with the first of her reasons for disobeying Créon's order: 'Je le devais'. This moral imperative is expanded, drawing on the traditional interpretation of the action by Sophocles' heroine ('Ceux qu'on n'enterre pas errent éternellement . . .'), and expressing this in the form of an appeal to the notion of family—even the ill-fated family of Oedipus, whose members are now united in death: a passage whose simple imagery ('Polynice aujourd'hui a achevé sa chasse. Il rentre à la maison . . .') is both eloquent and moving.

There is no doubt that these opening exchanges generate a sympathetic feeling for Antigone, and that Créon's political expediency alienates our sympathy:

> —C'était un révolté et un traître, tu le savais.

> —C'était mon frère.

However, the next 'movement' of the scene[8] is introduced by Créon's acknowledgement that the rough justice of political expediency is not the answer, and that Antigone's motives require a different approach: in his long speech beginning 'L'orgueil d'Oedipe . . .' he changes from a threatening, hectoring approach to a more reflective, more reasonable manner. If his sarcasm at the expense of the 'orgueil d'Oedipe' and of the death-wish of father and daughter, shows his inability to comprehend Antigone's motivation, nevertheless his dignified exposition of his own attitude, his determination to be a 'prince sans histoire', is not lacking in humanity; and his touch of ironic humour in 'si demain un messager crasseux dévale du fond des montagnes . . .' also helps to redress somewhat the balance of sympathy.

The final paragraph of this long speech is still based on the same assumption: that Antigone has made her gesture, and that will be the end of the matter if it can be kept quiet; but Créon is now using a tone of friendly advice ('Tu vas rentrer chez toi . . .') rather than threatening her. The revelation that this second approach is no more effective than the first—represented with graphic economy when Antigone makes to go out of the door which leads back out of the palace, and by the pause that follows—introduces the next 'movement', which comes nearer to a genuine exchange of views, and to a real attempt on Créon's part to persuade, rather than to browbeat, his adversary.

The attempt at persuasion starts from Antigone's 'il faut faire ce que l'on peut': a confession of obstinate determination in face of absolute power. To argue her out of this attitude, Créon carries out a rational analysis of 'cet enterrement dans les règles': the ceremony is a 'pantomime', performed by mercenary priests, and is lacking in dignity and humanity. At each point Antigone gives way: 'Oui, je les ai vus . . . Si, je l'ai pensé . . . Oui, c'est absurde'—and this last term has at least some of the connotations it possesses in the vocabulary of twentieth-century philosophy. Antigone's defiance is an 'acte gratuit', devoid of rational meaning, and the exchange which follows is one of the most significant of the whole scene:

> —Pourquoi fais-tu ce geste, alors? Pour les autres, pour ceux qui y croient? Pour les dresser contre moi?

> —Non.

> —Ni pour les autres, ni pour ton frère? Pour qui alors?

> —Pour personne. Pour moi.

What had begun as a pious tribute to the dead is now acknowledged as a gratuitous death-wish; and Creon has to admit that although he might have saved Antigone from the penalty of his law, he is powerless to save her from herself. 'J'ai le mauvais rôle, c'est entendu, et tu as le bon': the distribution of sympathy he recognizes is a conventional one, though it is a 'distribution' (to use Le Choeur's term) that has a touch of the melodramatic about it, with its implication of a polarization into black and white. However, we are already aware that the relationship is not as simple as this: Antigone is apparently by no means a reluctant victim, just as Créon is not the conventional villain ('Si j'étais une bonne brute ordinaire de tyran . . .'). And the next 'movement' of the scene is devoted to a thoroughly plausible, and intellectually acceptable, exposition of the 'mauvais rôle' in which he has been cast. This section does not immediately get under way, though: the linking passage in which Créon tries a show of physical strength, while it fits well enough into the context as a demonstration of how a 'brute ordinaire de tyran' might behave, is really justified in theatrical terms as a visual distraction, breaking up this very long dialectical exchange. Similarly, the stage-direction 'Il la fait asseoir . . . Il enlève sa veste . . . en bras de chemise' invests the pause before the next 'movement' of the dialogue with a striking visual character. Créon has stripped off all pretence, as it were, in taking off his jacket, and he will now reveal to Antigone the secrets of his 'métier': a job that is 'ignoble', but which leaves him no choice. The choice that once faced him, as it now faces Antigone, was to say 'yes' or 'no':

> . . . je me suis senti tout d'un coup comme un ouvrier qui refusait un ouvrage. Cela ne m'a pas paru honnête. J'ai dit oui.

The essence of the confrontation between the two characters is the opposition between Créon's 'oui' and Antigone's 'non'—not only a refusal to obey Créon's edict, but a denial of a whole way of life, a rejection of life itself. And it is in this section of the scene that Créon's defence of an ordered, stable society begins to win our intellectual adherence:

> Le cadavre de ton frère qui pourrit sous mes fenêtres, c'est assez payé pour que l'ordre règne dans Thèbes. Mon fils t'aime. Ne m'oblige pas à payer avec toi encore. J'ai assez payé.

And perhaps even more than our intellectual adherence, for his speech beginning 'Mais, bon Dieu! Essaie de comprendre . . .', with its sustained image of the ship of state, forces our admiration for a decent man doing a necessary job of work, however unpalatable. But if Créon has won the spectator over at this point, he has made no impression so far on Antigone herself:

> Je ne veux pas comprendre. C'est bon pour vous. Moi je suis là pour autre chose que pour comprendre. Je suis là pour vous dire non et pour mourir.

We have moved a long way from the confrontation between an authoritarian ruler and a subject prepared to sacrifice her life for a noble cause: the opposition is now between a humane ruler working for his country's good and a rebel motivated by a totally anarchic individualism.

Since Antigone's is not a reasoned stance, but the product of intense emotive feeling, she will be won over, if at all, not by rational but by affective means. And in the next 'movement'—again preceded by a significant pause—what is conceived as a last despairing appeal to her reason ('c'est mon rôle et je vais te faire tuer. Seulement, avant, je veux que toi aussi tu sois bien sûre du tien') almost at once begins to operate on a different level, by reviving intimate recollections of the past, of that childhood which is so important as a nostalgic source of emotional strength to Antigone, and in respect of which she proves so vulnerable. In spite of himself, it seems, Créon's reference to the past hits exactly the right note, as Antigone spontaneously takes over from him with her childhood memories, defending her brother but also providing emotional justification for herself: 'Une fois . . . il était tout pâle, les yeux brillants et si beau dans son vêtement du soir! . . . Et il m'a donné une grande fleur de papier qu'il avait rapportée de sa nuit'. And his intuitive shot in the dark:

> Et tu l'as conservée, n'est-ce pas, cette fleur? Et hier, avant de t'en aller, tu as ouvert ton tiroir et tu l'as regardée, longtemps, pour te donner du courage?

finds the weak spot in her emotional armour:

ANTIGONE TRESSAILLE:

> Qui vous a dit cela?

She is now on the defensive: the 'fleur de cotillon' was the symbol, the 'objective correlative' of her emotional dependence on the past, and this is now to be systematically destroyed. As the graphic catalogue of her brother's moral turpitude and iniquity builds up, her repeated 'Ce n'est pas vrai!' tries to shut out the truth. Almost immediately, however, she is forced to capitulate, and long before the end of Créon's recital she is beaten—not by intellectual persuasion, but by a process of emotional humiliation.

Créon's victory is symbolized visually, after another of the pauses that mark off the stages in this crucial encounter, by Antigone making as if to leave by the other exit: the exit that represents submission, and the acceptance of life on Créon's terms. But it is a short-lived victory; and one of the most convincing touches in the scene is that it should be Créon's better nature—the measure of sympathetic humanity by which Anouilh's character distinguishes himself from his Greek counterpart—that brings about his undoing. His speech 'Rien d'autre ne compte . . .' is certainly motivated by relief that the argument is over: the past tenses ('tu allais le gaspiller . . . je buvais tes paroles. J'écoutais . . .') express this relief, and there is perhaps now also a reflection of the patronizing superiority of the older and wiser man to be seen in the repeated imperatives, the confident future tense of 'Tu verras . . . Tu l'apprendras toi aussi', and the sententious maxims ('Rien n'est vrai que ce qu'on ne dit pas . . . la vie ce n'est peut-être tout de même que le bonheur'). But it would be wrong, I think, to interpret Créon's conciliatory manner here ('j'aurais fait comme toi à vingt ans . . . J'écoutais du fond du temps un petit Créon maigre et pâle comme toi') and his frank confession of expediency ('Ne m'écoute pas quand je ferai mon prochain discours devant le tombeau d'Étéocle. Ce ne sera pas vrai . . .') as a cynical argumentative ploy. For the argument appears to be won; and Créon is inspired not so much by dialectical considerations—not even by the desire to press home his tactical advantage—as by a wholly human urge to make a genuine confession, and to show understanding and fellow-feeling.

And once again, it is not the faulty logic of an argument, but the emotive connotations of a single word, 'le bonheur', that allow Antigone's subjective imagination to take over and reassert her defiant stand. 'Le bonheur' revives Antigone's intransigent opposition to the normal order of things: she is once again recognizable as the blood-sister of those other Anouilh heroes and heroines who similarly reject all thought of compromise and conciliation. 'Quel sera-t-il mon bonheur? . . .': this speech could easily have been spoken by Thérèse in *La Sauvage*; while the notion of an ideal love, inexorable in its demands:

> . . . si Hémon ne doit plus pâlir quand je pâlis, s'il ne doit plus me croire morte quand je suis en retard de cinq minutes, s'il ne doit plus se sentir seul au monde et me détester quand je ris sans qu'il sache pourquoi . . .

is that to which Orphée subscribes in *Eurydice.* This is the poetic expression of an attitude that forms part of the psychology of all genuine sexual love; but if it is not tempered by other attributes such as tolerance and a sense of proportion, it is inimical to any permanent relationship in the real world. Antigone, however, has now moved out of the range of such common-sense considerations ('Je vous parle de trop loin maintenant, d'un royaume où vous ne pouvez plus entrer . . .'), and Créon's cause is lost for good.

The remainder of the scene is a 'dialogue de sourds'. On the one hand the man of reason, increasingly angry that his advantage has been lost; and on the other, the representative of an irrational anti-life force, exultant in her escape from his domination. It is in the speech already quoted above, which significantly begins with the phrase repeated from *La Sauvage*: 'Vous me dégoûtez tous avec votre bonheur! . . .' that Antigone comes nearest to a rational analysis of the difference that separates her from Créon. His idea of 'le bonheur' is rejected because it depends on a permanent compromise with the pettiness and the squalor of life: Créon and the other conformists and accepters of life are content to put up with 'cette petite chance, pour tous les jours si on n'est pas trop exigeant', whereas Antigone's own notion of 'le bonheur' is the intransigent ideal of an implacable Romantic:

> Moi, je veux tout, tout de suite,—et que ce soit entire,—ou alors je refuse! Je ne veux pas être modeste, moi, et me contenter d'un petit morceau si j'ai été bien sage. Je veux être sûre de tout aujourd'hui et que cela soit aussi beau que quand j'étais petite—ou mourir.

But the last page of the scene shows rational analysis giving way to insult and abuse, Créon threatening and using physical force, and Antigone taunting him with the repeated 'cuisinier', to end on a note of heightened dramatic tension.

(XIII) ANTIGONE, CRÉON, ISMÈNE (P. 85)

As in Sophocles, the central confrontation is brought to an end by the entrance of Ismène. Anouilh makes less of this scene between the sisters—in the Greek play

their argument is expressed in an effective passage of highly dramatic stichomythia—but essentially the purpose is the same: to allow the heroine to assert her independence. Sophocles' 'You chose; life was your choice, when mine was death' (line 481), corresponding to Anouilh's 'Tu as choisi la vie et moi la mort', reminds us once more of the close affinity in the attitude of the two heroines, however different Anouilh's interpretation of that attitude may be. Having rejected her sister's support, Antigone renews her taunting of Créon; and as the women go out, Anouilh brings Le Choeur in for a brief linking scene.

(XIV) CRÉON, LE CHOEUR (P. 86)

This considerably reduces the length of the corresponding scene in Sophocles, where a choric ode dwells on the perils lying in wait for those in a position of power: 'For mortals greatly to live is greatly to suffer' (line 531)—a cryptic warning to the wilful and unheeding Creon of the Greek play. Anouilh's Choeur is not so circumspect, with his 'Tu es fou, Créon. Qu'as-tu fait?'; but this direct challenge is met by Créon with a considered defence of his conduct which must carry conviction: 'C'est elle qui voulait mourir . . .'. What he says here—that Polynice's burial was a mere pretext, and that 'Ce qui importait pour elle, c'était de refuser et de mourir'—is surely entirely valid: no other explanation will account for Antigone's behaviour at the end of the scene with Créon, and this is certainly how we are meant to see her exit:

ANTIGONE:

> (*dans un grand cri soulagé*) Enfin, Créon!

It seems not unimportant, therefore, that Créon should be provided with the opportunity to justify himself in this way before the scene with Hémon.

(XV) CRÉON, HÉMON, LE CHOEUR (P. 87)

In the scene with Hémon itself, Créon's self-justification carries less weight, for now his intellectual persuasiveness is countered by the emotional appeal that Hémon makes to the spectator: a good deal less ambivalent than that made by the heroine, for his reaction to the threatened loss of his beloved has none of the arbitrary quality of her voluntary rejection of life. This is another scene that closely follows the inspiration of its Greek counterpart—though here too the French playwright has seen fit to reduce the length of the original, where both father and son speak in terms of measured debate before engaging in angry stichomythia. It is not clear why Anouilh should make Le Choeur intervene here as he does ('Est-ce qu'on ne peut pas imaginer quelque chose . . . Est-ce qu'on ne peut pas gagner du temps?'), except perhaps that the Greek Chorus also intervenes, though in a much less partisan spirit. In the French play as in the Greek, the scene mounts to a dramatic climax—a more affective climax in Anouilh's case, for Hémon, as Antigone has done, draws emotional reinforcement from the evocation of the past: 'Tu es encore puissant, toi, comme lorsque j'étais petit. Ah! je t'en supplie, père, que je t'admire, que je t'admire encore! Je suis trop seul et le monde est trop nu si je ne peux pas t'admirer'. The young man's emotional anguish is helpless against the resigned pragmatism of his father, however: 'Regarde-moi, c'est cela devenir un homme, voir le visage de son père en face un jour'. But where the Greek Haemon rushes out at the height of an angry explosion, and with Creon's vindictive threat ringing in his ears, Anouilh's character goes out in frustrated bewilderment to fulfil his tragic role.

(XVI) Créon, Le Choeur (p. 89)

And the only difference between the attitude of Créon and that of Le Choeur is that the latter, no omniscient commentator now, but a participant whose function is much nearer to that of the Greek Chorus, still hopes that some way may be found of averting the tragedy ('Créon, il faut faire quelque chose'). It is Créon, not le Choeur, who now seems to possess a compassionate insight into the tragic process.

(XVII) Créon, Antigone, Les Gardes, Le Choeur (p. 89)

As she does in Sophocles, Antigone makes a final reappearance before she goes to her death. But whereas the corresponding scene in the Greek play presents a moving exchange between the heroine and the Chorus:

> —But here is a sight beyond all bearing,
> At which my eyes cannot but weep;
> Antigone forth faring
> To her bridal-bower of endless sleep.
> —You see me, countrymen, on my last journey,
> Taking my last leave of the light of day;
> Going to my rest, where death shall take me
> Alive across the silent river . . .

> (lines 708-15)

Anouilh's purpose is to underline the pathos by other means; and after a brief linking scene, Antigone is left alone with Le Garde.

(XVIII) Antigone, Le Garde (p. 90)

As in the scenes with La Nourrice, the playwright has deliberately chosen at this point to adopt a tone at variance with what one traditionally expects of serious tragic drama; but here, the challenge of the familiar, colloquial style is a much more difficult one. For in the earlier scenes the nostalgic evocation of the heroine's childhood not only generates the sympathy that we feel for her in the initial stages of her clash with Créon, it also defines the vital emotional resources on which she

will draw in that encounter. In this closing scene, we may assume that the author's purpose is to reinforce the poignancy of Antigone's approaching death by juxtaposing it with the ordinary banalities of life; but if the lowering of the emotional tone, and the adoption of such a colloquial stylistic register, fails to strike the right note, it can easily lead to the dissipation of the spectator's sympathy. This is in an acute form the problem that faces every author of tragic drama in a domestic idiom.

The scene opens with the emotionally charged 'Mon dernier visage d'homme'; we may compare 'la dernière folie . . .' (p. 56), and two instances of 'pour la dernière fois' (pp. 78, 88), that fateful phrase which has such a powerful tragic resonance whenever it occurs as a half-line in Racine's verse: even in Anouilh's prose, it is impossible to mistake the emotional potential of the repeated 'dernier'. But at once the level of the dialogue drops to that of everyday conversation. It is not a case of intrinsically comic, or caricatural, characterization: the portrait of this very ordinary soldier, with his military slang, his self-importance, and his obsession with pay and perquisites, is thoroughly lifelike, and any comic effect derives from the incongruity between his very ordinariness and the high drama of the preceding scenes. The longer the exchanges go on, the greater will be the risk that the verbose, repetitive parade of trivia will neutralize the dramatic tension that has built up to its climax—or that the spectator will take refuge in laughter as a relief from that tension.

From Antigone's 'Je vais mourir tout à l'heure', the focus is no longer on Le Garde. For a moment she is unable to break through his self-absorption, but her question 'Comment vont-ils me faire mourir?' succeeds in reestablishing genuine communication. However, contact is abruptly broken again with her exclamation 'O tombeau! O lit nuptial! O ma demeure souterraine!'—a version of Sophocles'

> So to my grave,
> My bridal-bower, my everlasting prison,
> I go, to join those many of my kinsmen
> Who dwell in the mansions of Persephone.

> (lines 769-72)

The change to such a strikingly different mode of expression symbolizes her retreat into her own private sensibility. The beginning of Le Garde's next speech, with its mythological allusion ('Aux cavernes de Hadès . . .') is not too incongruous, but in no time at all he lapses into more of his trite observations on the military life.

The second half of this scene, which is taken up with Antigone's attempt to dictate a farewell letter to Hémon, is a masterly invention on Anouilh's part. The heroine's loss of the certainty and self-confidence she had shown when facing Créon ('je ne sais plus pour-quoi je meurs . . .'), the revelation of how near she came to being won over by him, can only be expressed in a confessional medium equivalent to the classical soliloquy; and in addition to the imaginative realization of such an equivalent, Anouilh has created a scene which offers the theatrically effective counterpoint between Antigone's intimate self-analysis ('Il vaut mieux que jamais personne ne sache. C'est comme s'ils devaient me voir nue et me toucher quand je serai morte') and the clumsy insensitivity of Le Garde ('C'est une drôle de lettre'). This is another scene which to the reader may perhaps seem to border on the facile and the over-sentimental; one can only say that it is capable of working successfully in the theatre, as a vehicle for genuinely-felt emotion.

(XIX) Le Messager, Le Choeur (p. 95)

The elimination of the scene with Tiresias, which oc-curs at this point in the Greek play, is quite the most significant change introduced by Anouilh. Not only does it go a long way towards abolishing the role of the gods, and depriving the myth of its metaphysical dimen-sion; it also has an important effect on the characteriza-tion of Créon. For the result of this scene is that Sophocles' King belatedly takes steps to undo what he has done, though of course he is too late to save Anti-gone. Anouilh's Créon undergoes no such change of heart: there is no mouthpiece of the gods to persuade him, and he remains unrepentant to the end.

From this point on in Anouilh's play, the final events happen even more rapidly than in Sophocles. Le Mes-sager is less prolix and sententious than his Greek counterpart, though the vital detail of his narrative is taken over unchanged:

> His son looked at him with one angry stare,
> Spat in his face, and then without a word
> Drew sword and struck out. But his father fled
> Unscathed. Whereon the poor demented boy
> Leaned on his sword and thrust it deeply home
> In his own side, and while his life ebbed out
> Embraced the maid in loose-enfolding arms,
> His spurting blood staining her pale cheeks red.
>
> (lines 1076-83)

> . . . Il regarde son père sans rien dire, une minute, et, tout à coup, il lui crache au visage, et tire son épée. Créon a bondi hors de portée. Alors Hémon le regarde avec ses yeux d'enfant, lourds de mépris, et Créon ne peut pas éviter ce regard comme la lame. Hémon re-garde ce vieil homme tremblant à l'autre bout de la caverne et, sans rien dire, il se plonge l'épée dans le ventre et il s'étend contre Antigone, l'embrassant dans une immense flaque rouge.

(XX) Créon, Le Page, Le Choeur (p. 96)

In what is presumably a deliberate change designed to produce a greater measure of sympathy for Créon at the end of the play, the closing lines spoken by Sophocles' Messenger, with their implication of Creon's guilt:

> Two bodies lie together, wedded in death,
> Their bridal sleep a witness to the world
> How great a calamity can come to man
> Through man's perversity
>
> (lines 1084-7)

are transferred to Créon himself:

> Je les ai fait coucher l'un près de l'autre, enfin! Ils sont lavés, maintenant, reposés. Ils sont seulement un peu pâles, mais si calmes. Deux amants. Ils ont fini, eux

—a passage in which it may not be too fanciful to see, as well as the transposition of Sophocles' text, an echo of the end of *Romeo and Juliet.*

Finally, le Choeur takes over for the narration of the death of Eurydice: one of the passages that stand out by their anachronistic detail, and a passage that can surely be criticized for its unwarranted trivialization of the original. A bourgeois Queen who does good works for the poor of Thebes, and who methodically finishes off her row of knitting before going away to commit suicide: is this successful modernization of the context, or a glaring lapse of taste? The same points apply as have been made in the commentary on scene xviii; this is, after all, the emotional climax of the play, and that it is not merely a question of old-fashioned, narrow standards of taste is suggested by Bergson's perceptive remark about laughter: 'Est comique tout incident qui appelle notre attention sur le physique d'une personne alors que le moral est en cause'.

(XXI) Le Choeur (p. 97)

The last section of this scene, together with the final scene in which Le Choeur appears on his own, are devoted to closing the 'frame' in which the death of Antigone has been presented, by re-establishing the continuum of ordinary life that had been disrupted by the violent events. 'La journée a été rude': the specta-tor, like the characters who have participated in the 'rude journée', has earned the right to rest. But for Créon, the active protagonist, there can be no rest ('devant l'ouvrage, on ne peut pourtant pas se croiser les bras . . .'); and he goes off to his council meeting. He has opted for life, he has a responsibility for others, and he must see it through to the end. This is more than just passive resignation to the continuity of things; and Créon's active acceptance of such a commitment can be seen as representing that reaffirmation of positive values after the destructive force of the tragic event has spent itself, that seems to be a necessary condition for the 'purging of the passions' traditionally associated with tragedy, and that can be clearly illustrated in such diverse examples as *Hamlet, King Lear, Phèdre* or *La*

Machine infernale. We do not feel emotional involvement with Créon at this point, any more than we do with Albany, Fortinbras, Racine's Thésée or Cocteau's Tirésias, who similarly 'close the frame', rounding-off the tragic process. We respect and (possibly) admire him, but our position is closer to that invoked by Le Choeur: the position of those for whom normal existence can resume (as it will for us as we leave the theatre), but whose life has, in spite of themselves, been marked by the impact of 'la petite Antigone':

> Sans la petite Antigone, c'est vrai, ils auraient tous été bien tranquilles. Mais maintenant, c'est fini. Ils sont tout de même tranquilles. . . .

For those who understood nothing, there is nothing to forget. Nothing has changed, and life will carry on as before: the Gardes 'continuent à jouer aux cartes'. Yet although this is the image that we are left with as the curtain falls, it does not determine our attitude as spectators, and we cannot identify with characters so incapable of reflection. Our affinity is with 'ceux qui vivent encore', who have come through the tragic anguish to a new serenity. With the passage of time we too may, as Le Choeur suggests, gradually begin 'à les oublier et à confondre leurs noms'; but for the time being 'Un grand apaisement triste tombe sur Thèbes'—and this is by no means an unsuccessful attempt to define the position of the spectator, whose 'tristesse' is also 'apaisée', but not yet eliminated, by the return to normality that forms an essential part of the cathartic process.

Notes

1. Page-references throughout are to the edition by W. M. Landers, London 1957.

2. Though Anouilh uses both terms, I take it as self-evident that the two roles are one and the same. This corresponds to stage practice in presenting the play in the theatre.

3. André Barsacq, who directed the 1944 production, comments as follows: 'L'*Antigone* m'a permis de réaliser ce rêve que je caressais depuis si longtemps: concevoir une mise en scène d'où tout pittoresque serait banni, faire se dérouler l'action dans un décor neutre, une sorte de scène idéale qui donnerait une impression de grandeur par la seule noblesse de ses lignes' ('Lois scéniques', *Revue Théâtrale*, 5, April-May 1947, pp. 157-8).

4. Cf the comment made by editors of *L'Alouette*: 'In *Antigone*, for instance, we are made to feel that what we are watching is a play and nothing else, moreover that we are participating in it. Similarly in *L'Alouette* . . .' (*L'Alouette*, ed. M. Thomas and S. Lee, London, 1956, p. 16).

5. In *Ardèle* (1948). Cf. *Pièces grinçantes*, Paris, 1956, p. 64.

6. See the continuation of this passage quoted above, p. 20.

7. The name 'Jonas' is a strange choice. It corresponds to the Old Testament 'Jonah', and is hardly plausible as a modern French *nom de famille*; Camus was to use it as the name of the central character of one of the stories in *L'Exil et le royaume* (1957), but this was apparently in order to fit in with an epigraph taken from the Book of Jonah. Here, it may perhaps carry the popular connotation 'one who brings ill-luck'.

8. I am using the term current in French dramaturgical analysis to denote identifiable sections of a long scene. Here, the 'movements' indicate shifts in the audience's relationship with the characters.

9. *Le Rire* (1899), Paris, 1946, p. 39.

W. D. Howarth (essay date 1983)

SOURCE: Howarth, W. D. "*Antigone* in 1944." In*Anouilh: Antigone*, pp. 47-52. London: Edward Arnold, 1983.

[*In the following essay, Howarth details the critical reception of* Antigone *in wartime France.*]

The study of the reception of Anouilh's play in 1944, and of its relationship to the political situation which existed, first under the German occupation and then after the liberation of Paris, has become much easier since the publication of an important monograph on the subject by Manfred Flügge[1]. Quite apart from the unusually broad range of Dr Flügge's enquiry, which sets **Antigone** in the general context of political attitudes current in France in the 1930s and 40s, he has accumulated an invaluable compendium of critical comment on the play from reviews and other ephemeral sources; moreover, he has had the rare good fortune (not vouchsafed to all who have written on Anouilh and his work, by any means) to elicit from the playwright himself a valuable commentary on the origins of the play.

From Anouilh's own indications—corrected by Flügge's research, where the dramatist's memory proved fallible—it now seems likely that the stimulus for the composition of **Antigone** (which, it was already known, existed in a complete state as early as 1942) came from the case of a young resistance fighter, Paul Collette, who in August 1942 fired on a group of collaborationist leaders at an anti-communist legionaries' rally at Versailles, severely wounding Marcel Déat and Pierre Laval. The connection appears all the more convincing if one considers the comment of a resistance journal:

Paul Collette s'estimait mandaté par sa conscience de Français. Il n'appartenait à aucun réseau. A aucun mouvement politique . . . Personne ni aucun mouvement ne pouvait, au regard de l'Histoire, expliquer le mobile de sa mission. Il s'agissait de l'acte gratuit dans toute la noblesse du terme. Ce jeune homme allait improviser un attentat.

(I, p. 234)

Completed in 1942, the play received the approval of the German censor; and the delay of two years before its first performance appears to have been due to André Barsacq, whose production of *Eurydice* had been only moderately successful, and who was unwilling to risk further financial liabilities. When production did go ahead, there was no need to seek further permission for a text which already bore the official stamp of approval; and the only difficulties raised during the first run of the play came from a report received in Berlin to the effect that *Antigone* was not suitable entertainment for the occupation troops. Barsacq was able to resist attempts to suspend performances, and the play ran without interruption from February until August.

'N'y allez pas, c'est une pièce nazie' was, it appears, a common reaction in resistance circles; and among those ordinary playgoers who did see *Antigone* in 1944 there must have been a large proportion who thought like this writer:

L'auteur, ai-je pensé, n'est pas sans amour ni pitié pour son Antigone, mais il est franchement du côté de Créon, et c'est à lui qu'il donne raison. J'ai même pensé, sommairement: 'Créon, c'est Laval'.

And even where the interpretation was less positive, there is abundant evidence that a great deal of the play's appeal lay in its highly provocative topicality:

Pour nous, le débat était dans l'opposition entre mystique et politique, surtout dans ce que cette opposition avait de brûlant à l'époque: en clair, Créon, pour nous, c'était Pétain, à qui se heurtait l'intransigeance de ceux qui n'admettaient pas le compromis et que représentait Antigone. Mais il nous semblait qu'Anouilh ne donnait pas entièrement tort à Créon. Il n'y a peut-être pas de pièce dont nous ayons autant discuté'.

(I, p. 268)

Looking back on this era, G. Hanoteau writes of a 'dialogue de sourds':

Les uns n'avaient entendu que Créon et l'antique légende se mettant au service . . . de la Collaboration, alors que leurs adversaires n'avaient retenu que les révoltes d'Antigone, première 'résistante' avec vingt-cinq siècles d'avance.

(I, p. 267)

When we come to the interpretations of *Antigone* published in the press of the period, we can see how Anouilh's play was regularly annexed by both pro-

German and resistance writers 'pour les besoins de la cause'. In such a highly-charged political atmosphere as that of occupied Paris, the favourable notices from reviewers of a known collaborationist tendency could be far more harmful than any adverse criticism. Indeed, a source of some of the most damaging accusations after the liberation of Paris was the extremely favourable reviews *Antigone* had received from Alain Laubreaux, a notable collaborator, who wrote no fewer than four laudatory pieces. While admiring the characterization of the heroine, this reviewer had seen in her 'la révolte de la pureté contre les mensonges des hommes, de l'âme contre la vie, une révolte insensée et magnifique, mais terriblement dangereuse pour l'espèce puisque dans la vie des sociétés elle aboutit au désordre et au chaos, et dans la vie des êtres elle aboutit au suicide' (*Je suis partout*); and in similar terms in another journal he wrote: 'Révolte condamnable puisqu'elle aboutit au chaos dans l'ordre social et au suicide dans l'ordre organique' (*Le Petit Parisien*) (II, pp. 49-50). Laubreaux' praise is repeated, and indeed amplified, by Charles Méré in *Aujourd'hui*, another journal with collaborationist sympathies:

. . . Dans la pièce de M. Jean Anouilh, le héros, c'est au contraire Créon, le roi juste, esclave de son devoir et qui doit aux intérêts de sa patrie sacrifier ses affections les plus chères. . . . En face de Créon, victime pitoyable de la tragédie, l'inintelligence d'Antigone fait figure de demi-folle, de dégénérée. . . . C'est la révoltée, l'anarchiste, génératrice de désordre, de désastre, de mort.

(II, p. 57)

It was not only interpretations of the play in a specific political sense that could be damaging, but the very fact of a favourable review in certain publications: for instance, the notice by J. de Féraudy in *Au Pilori*, a notoriously anti-semitic journal. And as disturbing as anything at this period must have been Anouilh's inclusion, in an article by L. Rebatet in *Je suis partout*, in a list of writers who, 's'ils ne font pas de politique, ne répugnent point pourtant à publier leurs oeuvres dans les journaux où on en fait beaucoup, et de plus énergiquement anti-gaulliste' (I, p. 308).

Until the liberation of Paris, the attack from the spokesmen of the resistance was confined to the organs of the clandestine press; and it was an article by Claude Roy of March 1944 that contained the most virulent denunciation of Anouilh as a playwright who had betrayed the resistance fighters by his travesty of the 'true' Antigone:

Sur les murs de Paris, le seul nom d'Antigone semble un appel, un camouflet à l'oppresseur de Vichy, au nazi qui passe devant l'affiche rouge et jaune de l'Atelier. Antigone ou la fidélité. Antigone proclame à la face du tyran qu'on peut mourir pour la justice, mourir pour la fidélité, mourir pour les valeurs qui donnent à la vie un prix, au destin un sens.

Antigone, lisons-nous. Au-delà d'Antigone, notre pensée déjà va vers tous ceux qui, chaque jour, meurent pour que vive leur honneur, leur vérité et leur patrie. Mais il s'agit de bien d'autre chose. Non de Sophocle, mais de Jean Anouilh. Et l'Antigone qu'on nous propose n'est pas *notre* Antigone, la seule, la vraie. Antigone-de-la-pureté.

For Anouilh's heroine, like Créon, 'méprise les hommes':

Parce qu'il les méprise, Créon les opprime et les mate. Le tyran glacé et la jeune exaltée étaient faits pour s'entendre. Si Antigone pouvait vivre, à force de dire 'Non' à la vie, elle dirait 'Oui' à tout. Sa mort n'est pas l'affirmation d'un héroïsme, mais un refus et un suicide. C'est moins un acte qu'un malentendu.

And the reason for such a portrayal is that Anouilh is one of those '. . . anciens loups qui ont accepté avec empressement le collier du chien, du chien policier':

Ce n'est pas un hasard qui les fait parfois, prudemment, s'enrôler sous le drapeau noir de la Waffen SS . . . Ce n'est pas un hasard qui fait de Jean Anouilh des *Pièces noires* un collaborateur occasionnel mais fervent de la feuille nazie, un admirateur naïf et femmelin du Führer et de son génie.

(II, pp. 70-1)

It is certain that Anouilh had to live through a most uncomfortable time during the period of 'l'épuration': the hasty and badly managed 'purge' of writers and other public figures whose record under the Occupation had not been untarnished, which under the guise of political justice allowed the settling of many an old score of a personal nature. Though his name never appeared on any known 'black list', there were certainly moves to discredit him at the time of the *reprise* of **Antigone** at the end of September 1944, and a letter was sent to Barsacq by the 'Commission pour l'épuration des théâtres', with the object of forcing him to withdraw from the direction of this revival. However, the play was in fact staged again, and Anouilh confesses in his letter to Flügge that it was at this point, not at the time of the first performances under the Occupation, that 'les vrais ennuis pour nous . . . ont commencé'. He describes the first performance of the revival as follows:

. . . Personne n'a osé applaudir à la fin jusqu'à ce que le Général Koenig [a Free French associate of de Gaulle, now military governor of Paris] se lève dans sa loge et crie: 'C'est admirable!' C'est ce qui m'a sauvé. Le reste n'a été qu'insinuations méchantes.

(II, p. 45)

From all this, it must be abundantly clear that it was extremely difficult, if not impossible, to approach **Antigone** in 1944 completely without political prejudice, and to judge it purely and simply as a work of art. Pol

Gaillard's verdict, published in the Communist *L'Humanité* in November of that year, is a good example of an aesthetic judgement determined by political and moral considerations:

Disons-le nettement puisqu'il reste encore des doutes, paraît-il: l'*Antigone* de Jean Anouilh n'est pas un chef-d'oeuvre, et elle ne peut que faire du mal aux Français. . . . Rien ne pouvait mieux servir les desseins nazis pendant l'occupation; rien ne peut davantage freiner le relèvement des Français par eux-mêmes aujourd'hui encore. . . . Malgré ses beautés, *Antigone* restera, dans l'oeuvre de M. Anouilh, non seulement un faux chef-d'oeuvre, mais une mauvaise action.

(I, p. 320)

And evidence of the effect of such tendentious criticism, as well as of the more balanced view that it was possible to adopt a mere three years later, is to be seen in this comment by Robert Kemp in 1947:

Quand fut représentée, en février 1944, l'*Antigone* de M. Jean Anouilh . . ., je n'ai eu ni l'occasion ni un désir vif de l'entendre. Des bruits, que je peux maintenant dire absurdes, me la faisaient croire trop conciliante pour mon goût. Or, c'est une oeuvre pure et dure, qui accepte sans doute avec plus d'indulgence que la tragédie de Sophocle le pragmatisme de Créon, mais sans qu'on y puisse découvrir le moindre esprit de complicité a l'égard de ce qui se passait alors dans notre personnel provisoirement dirigeant.

(I, p. 326)

What, finally, of Anouilh's own position at this period? It really does seem to be the case that, as Béatrice Dussane was to write, 'Anouilh est resté pendant toute l'Occupation confiné dans son travail d'écrivain, professant qu'il ignorait volontairement la politique' (I, p. 369). Difficult though this may be to accept as entirely valid, it certainly matches his own explanation in the letter to Flügge, where he says of his attitude at the time of the first performances of **Antigone**: 'à la création, dans ma naïveté un peu ahurie d'homme qui s'est toujours senti libre—je n'avais pas eu le sentiment de risquer quelque chose' (II, p. 45).

But a mere twelve months after the première of **Antigone,** Anouilh's naïve idealism came to an abrupt end. One of the victims of the 'épuration' was Robert Brasillach, a poet, critic and journalist, who had made himself enemies by his collaborationist activities during the Occupation, and who was tried and condemned to death. For Anouilh, who hardly knew Brasillach, this seems to have been a major turning-point in his life. He was moved to take a petition round to fellow men of letters, seeking signatures for the commutation of the death penalty: an act by no means lacking in courage, if one thinks of the playwright's own ambiguous situation at this very time. The petition was unsuccessful, and Brasillach was executed in February 1945:

En y réfléchissant depuis, rassis, sceptique, navré (au sens fort du terme) et étrangement allégé par l'âge, je me suis aperçu que le jeune homme que j'ai été et le jeune homme Brasillach sont morts le même jour et—toutes proportions gardées—de la même chose.

Tout cela est loin—et tout près. Le jeune homme Anouilh que j'étais resté, jusqu'en 1945, est parti un matin, mal assuré (il y avait de quoi en ces temps d'imposture), mais du pied gauche, pour aller recueillir les signatures de ses confrères pour Brasillach. Il a fait du porte à porte pendant huit jours et il est revenu vieux chez lui . . .[2]

Notes

1. *Verweigerung oder Neue Ordnung: Jean Anouilhs 'Antigone' im politischen und ideologischen Kontext der Besatzungszeit 1940-1944,* 2 vols., Rheinfelden, 1982. Except where otherwise indicated, page-references in this chapter are to Dr Flügge's book, to which I am considerably indebted.

2. Quoted in P. Vandromme, *Jean Anouilh, un auteur et ses personnages,* Paris, 1965, pp. 175-6.

Marilyn V. Schuler (essay date 1985)

SOURCE: Schuler, Marilyn V. "'Goddess' vs. 'Gyn/ Ecologist': A Comparative View of *Antigone* and *La folle de Chaillot.*" In *Myths and Realities of Contemporary French Theater: Comparative Views,* edited by Patricia M. Hopkins and Wendell M. Aycock, pp. 141-51. Lubbock: Texas Tech Press, 1985.

[*In the following essay, Schuler finds parallels between Anouilh's* Antigone *and Jean Giraudoux's* La Folle de Chaillot.]

Antigone and *La Folle de Chaillot,* both critical successes in France and the U.S. during the 1940s, are usually viewed as expressions of Resistance against Nazism and the Occupation of France during World War II.[1] The present paper proposes, however, a different basis for comparison. Anouilh's ***Antigone*** and Giraudoux's *Folle de Chaillot* will be examined here for their "representations of women" rather than as political protests during the Occupation.

Occupation and protest are present in both texts; but also in both, woman, by an interaction with the earth, is the agent who combats forces destructive to an ongoing society and to the future. Françoise d'Eaubonne and Mary Daly, among others, argue that the classical and traditional concept of woman as a symbolic and inspirational "other" which men follow to meet the challenges of human survival is not only contrary to fact but a manipulative means for allowing men to rationalize an unending preoccupation with conquest,

victory, and defeat. They posit a new, woman-centered strategy for human survival. Mary Daly has termed the strategy a "gyn/ecology."[2] These two attitudes toward women—the traditional on the one hand and the futuristic on the other—are the current foci of feminist critics on both sides of the Atlantic, and it is to them that we turn for a hermeneutics on which to base a new reading of the two plays. The contemporaneous texts by Anouilh and Giraudoux offer, I suggest, fertile possibilities for the elucidation of these two opposing "representations of women" as they appear here and throughout literature.

In Anouilh's play, there are two women who have the opportunity to save the civilization, but only Antigone will undertake the self-sacrifice necessary to overturn the spiritually barren world of Créon. Consigned to earth, Hémon dies in Antigone's arms in the manner of a Jungian subconscious return to the womb. Though Hémon gives no indication that he understands Antigone's spiritual purposes, he does manifest a feeling of being totally protected. In the classical mode, Antigone nourishes Hémon by her sacrifice and thus fulfills the noblest purpose of her life.

In Giraudoux's play, "la Folle" represents the critical importance of "feminine" characteristics: these characteristics are proposed as the foundation of healthy urban existence. The Madwoman supports socialization, young love, and street musicians. Her long life as woman is a progression of her growing suitability to save civilization. Her final consignment of the entrepreneur, the prospector, and the investor to the earth is undertaken only after consultation with her sister madwomen and with the consensus of the streetpeople of Paris. In a new mode, women honor women, and ecology and the primacy of life prevail over systematic destruction and exploitation.

Anouilh's Antigone epitomizes the view of woman as something outside the reality of men. His is the classical and patriarchal view of women based on Aristotle's philosophy of domination, which characterizes women as inferior to men, less rational than men, and consequently unfit for participation in the polis.[3] This exclusion of women from rational discourse has been sanctioned by its codification in myth. Mary Daly comments that Eliade has contributed to the perpetuation of this mind-set by his exclusion from the sacred sphere (and from reality) of what is done without a mythical model.[4] Eliade calls myths "paradigmatic models" and asserts that "what men do on their own initiative, what they do without a mythical model belongs to the sphere of the profane; hence it is a vain and illusory activity, and in the last analysis, unreal."[5] Anouilh's choice of myth as a dramatic vehicle is an indication that his theme, too, will be identified with the traditional view of woman as developed and articulated in several thousands of years of patriarchal history. This history can be defined succinctly in terms of a society where "masculism is the prevailing social and political value set," and of which "the driving principles are power, authority, discipline—maleness."[6]

The patriarchal concept of women in the context of Aristotelian categories was called into permanent question by the publication of Simone de Beauvoir's *Le Deuxième Sexe*. One of the primary objectives of the book was to demonstrate the inadequacies of all existing systems of thought when they addressed themselves to the woman question. De Beauvoir argued that all the systems were biased because they were limited, since from the beginning of history women had been left out. Since the publication of de Beauvoir's book (in 1949) and especially since 1968, feminists in France and the U.S. have undertaken new readings of existing systems of thought based on the argument that all were biased because they had been devised by men.[7] The reading proposed here for the two plays will take into account strategies posited by these feminist thinkers.

It is easy to make a case for Giraudoux's notion of the feminine as anti-war. He says that "[la femme] hait la guerre plus que l'homme" and that "par une antipathie profonde, aucune femme d'aucun pays ne tient à devenir dirigeante dans les problèmes de politique pure; sans doute qu'aucune femme ne veut être la première femme qui ait un jour à déclarer la guerre."[8] In *La Folle de Chaillot* Countess Aurélie espouses the anti-war stance. It is the threat of war at the hands of oil tycoons that sets in motion their destruction by the ingenious Aurélie. It is clear that Giraudoux intends "la Folle" to represent an anti-war stance.

Anouilh, prior to his satiric and off-handed treatment of the question in *La Culotte* (1978), does not articulate an overt stance vis-à-vis woman. His typical hero is nonetheless apt to be a woman and that woman, most frequently, "une jeune fille." One critic posits that the seeming fragility of the young woman provides Anouilh with the means of throwing into relief the grossness to which she is opposed. Her delicacy covers a hardness which is hardly "feminine," sweetness and femininity being reserved to those in his plays who represent powerlessness or impurity—virtuous hardness being opposed, in Anouilh's ethic, to what an unjust world offers in the way of the pliable and accommodating. Whether she be called Eurydice, Médée, Jeanne d'Arc or Antigone, the heroine of Anouilh will be "petite," "noire," "mal peignée."[9]

Antigone offers her sister the opportunity to share in the preservation of their dead brother's right to an assured passage to eternal life. Ismène ("la blonde, la belle, l'heureuse Ismène," p. 9), whose physical attributes as described by Anouilh have the effect of identifying her

with woman as the Aristotelian subordinate and inferior of man, sympathizes with Antigone's cause but refuses at a critical juncture to participate actively on the basis of attitudes and reasons which she, at various points early in the action, articulates. Anouilh's characterization of Ismène is pivotal in his decision to create in the person of Antigone the epitome and summary of opposition to Créon's order. (Conversely, Sophocles, in the original play, attributes to Ismene, Haemon, and Tiresias—as well as to Antigone—arguments of opposition to Creon.) Anouilh's Ismène delineates the following rationale for passive inactivity: (1) the irrationality of opposition to the patriarchy ("Tu [Antigone] es folle," p. 18); (2) incapacity to act ("Nous ne pouvons pas," p. 18); (3) the futility of opposition ("Il est plus fort que nous, Antigone. Il est le roi," p. 20); (4) fear of death ("Il nous ferait mourir," p. 18); (5) the inappropriateness of women's opposition to the *status quo* and, simultaneously, of women's theorizing in opposition to the male universal ("C'est bon pour les hommes de croire aux idées et de mourir pour elles. Toi tu es une fille," p. 22); (6) concern for Antigone's safety, and sisterly love ("Reste avec nous, ne va pas làbas cette nuit, je t'en supplie," p. 33, and . . . "Je ne veux pas vivre si tu meurs, je ne veux pas rester sans toi!" p. 68). Anouilh capitalizes on the dramatic effect inherent in Ismène's relationship with Antigone by transforming her into Antigone's supporter and having her return just before Antigone's demise, ready to die with her; Antigone, however, refuses her the right to do so. Anouilh thus achieves an innately destructive double effect: he sends Antigone (a woman who—justifiably—opposes the male order) to her death; he returns Ismène (a woman who—understandably—accepts the male order) to life within an order that is inherently inimical to her.

This dual destruction and denigration of women has the effect of reaffirming the inherent rightness of the patriarchal state. To the men in Antigone's environment the conservation of the state depends on their ability to lead by defeating the enemy within, which is the feminine instinct against war. Etéocle and Polynice, as well as Créon, annihilate a potential feminine consciousness in that they demonstrate no internal hesitation to wage war; Hémon's identification with Antigone underscores his unsuitability to live in a patriarchal society dominated by the expediency of war.

Anouilh clearly categorizes and polarizes masculine and feminine psychologies. Ismène will not use her feminine instincts for conservation of the society but she also will not wage war: these are the only choices of action that she is allowed in the play. She does not question the rightness of Antigone's thinking, but she feels that a woman is helpless in the face of brute force. In challenging the male order, however, Antigone epitomizes the male concept of the enemy within.[10]

Anouilh arouses keen interest in the decision and actions of his "conservative" heroine and, in fact, produces in the reader profound respect for her decision, finally, to sacrifice her life in defense of her stance, even though he denies Antigone the conscious formulation of her own motivation. Antigone describes her interment of her brother as "absurde" (p. 51) and her motivation as "Pour personne. Pour moi" (p. 52). She can defend her action only in personal terms: "Moi, je ne suis pas obligée de faire ce que je ne voudrais pas!" (p. 56). Her ultimate condemnation to death comes about almost casually and hinges on her rejection of Créon's advice to settle for "la consolation dérisoire de vieillir" (p. 64). Finally, in her farewell letter to Hémon, Antigone says, ". . . Je ne sais plus pourquoi je meurs" (p. 80). (In *L'Alouette,* Anouilh again denies his heroine the articulation of her essential being: he has Jeanne refuse to recant without apparently knowing the reasons for her own actions.)

The treatment of the earth in Anouilh's **Antigone** is conventional and classical. The earth is Mother Earth; it is the holy abode of the dead. It is the safe return to the womb of unending life, and protection. What Antigone has sought for her brothers, she wins for herself as well as for Hémon; the remaining society is cursed and denied this safe refuge.

Anouilh uses the occasion to present an extraordinary woman (as compared with the ordinary Ismène) and that woman's assessment of the tyrant, and her view of the essential importance of love and marriage to her own self-fulfillment as woman and to the preservation of the environment. On her way to the cave, Antigone says: "O tombeau! O lit nuptial! O ma demeure souterraine . . ." (p. 77).

Antigone's role is to provide a haven for the souls of men. Hémon follows her to the grave; it is his protection from annihilation. For him, Antigone's condemnation to death signals most importantly the end of his childhood and the end to a child's admiration for the father as all-powerful: "Ah! je t'en supplie, père, que je t'admire, que je t'admire encore! je suis trop seul et le monde est trop nu si je ne peux plus t'admirer" (p. 72). He now recognizes the inevitability of death and the need for Antigone to comfort him in that last aspect of life's journey. Antigone fulfills the duties and purposes of the classical goddess: she provides herself as the sacrifice.[11]

Anouilh's Antigone exhausts her salutary powers in the resolution of the play's conflict. There is no further service which remains within Antigone's capability. Antigone has powers specifically limited to the act of ultimate self-sacrifice. When Ismène says "Il est plus fort que nous, Antigone. Il est le roi. Et ils pensent tous comme lui dans la ville. Ils sont des milliers et des

milliers autour de nous, groillant dans toutes les rues de Thèbes" (p. 20), she is fortifying the fact that their only possible course of action is the act of self-immolation. Antigone's death returns integrity to the state. Créon is left to rule the empty palace and to await his own death.

Aurélie in *La Folle de Chaillot* is introduced as a woman of great spiritual clout. She is symbolic to the people in the sense that she is the epitome of positive healthy thinking. Contrary to the Président's desire that, in a world "vraiment moderne," human beings be indistinguishable one from the other, Aurélie is the triumphant expression of irrepressible individuality. Her actions are not symbolic gestures; they are efficacious procedures. Her plan to rid Paris of the destructive presence of the entrepreneur, the prospector, and the investor is a positive action that will promote the general welfare of the population. This is the most dramatically intense illustration of the distinction between the two women of the plays under consideration. Giraudoux intends that the Countess hear the problems of the Ragpicker and the others and that she then set upon the means for their positive resolution. Her instructions are comprehensive and are executed in minute detail. Her associates, Joséphine and Gabrielle, consider her the most competent and the Chief of Staff of the operation.

One of the most significant of Giraudoux's gyn/ecological theories is to be found in the Countess' treatment of the return to the earth. In the worldview of the Countess, the return to the bowels of the earth is the inevitable punishment for the anti-ecological. The despoilers, in being cast back into the earth, are being deprived of the evolutionary gains that have been made in the modern scientific civilization.

In the action of the play, the Countess sees life as interaction in the city, in the urban environment. She is free of the traditional and classical regard for the return to the earth as access to salvation. The Countess believes that evildoers who despoil the civilization are to be cast out of it and back into the earth's darkness. The literary value as well as the psychological importance of the return to the physical, primitive origins is effectively debunked in the work. Woman is no longer Earth Mother, and the affairs of civilization can no longer be conducted by profit-motivated men whose understanding of the true program of civilization is so limited. In *La Française et la France,* Giraudoux describes woman's task in the modern world as twofold: "une rénovation administrative du monde" and "une amélioration universelle de la morale ou de la vie sociale" (p. 198). There is a remarkable similarity between Giraudoux's mandate to French women (or to all women) in 1934 and recent statements by Françoise d'Eaubonne, who maintains that the fate of the human species and of the planet is at stake, and that no male-led "revolution" will counteract the horrors of overpopulation and destruction of natural resources.[12] D'Eaubonne coins the expression "éco-féminisme" to convey the importance in her ecological construct of a shift away from the historic egocentric, authoritarian, and destructive-of-women worldview associated with patriarchy. The Countess puts the same idea succinctly after having disposed of destructive elements: "Et voilà, l'affaire est finie. Vous voyez comme elle était simple. Il suffit d'une femme de sens pour que la folie du monde sur elle casse ses dents" (p. 191).

While the Countess does complete her duties and retire from the scene, she does not die. And she does not sacrifice self. In the Countess' return to her own peaceful quarters, there is a sense of temporary respite; Aurélie expects to be called upon again when needed: "La prochaine fois, n'attendez paz, chiffonnier. Dès que menacera une autre invasion de vos monstres, alertez-moi de suite" (p. 179). It should be noted here that Antigone's discourse on the road to death has the classical ring of the traditional prelude to the descent into Hades; the orientation of the Countess is to ongoing life.

While Antigone alone must undertake the salvation of the state in her capacity as a tragic heroine, the Countess freely calls on other women who willingly work as a cooperative group. In *Antigone,* Ismène reflects the classical and patriarchal position that women may not act as a body of power. The call for women to assent to a constructive teamwork is an extremely advanced and revolutionary notion, and one that Giraudoux had earlier advanced in *La Française et la France,* where he equates the concerted and decisive intervention of women's groups during the creation of the League of Nations with the dawn of a new era in human affairs: "Si les femmes n'ont pas assisté en tant que personnes à la création du monde, puisque Eve est née après Adam, ni à sa recréation par la machine, elles étaient de plain-pied pour la première fois avec lui pour cette nouvelle reconstruction . . ." (p. 201).

Remembering that *Antigone* and *La Folle de Chaillot* are contemporaneous dramatic creations, we recognize also that there is greater cultural acceptance of Antigone's mandate to act alone than there is of the Countess' teamwork approach. In order to justify women in a team effort not directed toward the service of a male enterprise, Giraudoux must make the Countess and her friends types of good witches. It has been noted that Antigone is described as mad; Giraudoux (as he does in many instances in his theater) likewise attaches the epithet "folle" to his heroine, who—as has been noted by a biographer—was inspired by a woman seen by Giraudoux in the same streets of Paris where he sets the play.[13] The word is put in proper perspective early in Act I, when Aurélie's bizarre apparition in the café offends the Président:

LE PRÉSIDENT:

   Garçon, faites circuler cette femme!

LE GARÇON:

   Je m'en garderai, Monsieur. Elle est ici chez elle.

LE PRÉSIDENT:

   C'est la gérante du café?

LE GARÇON:

   C'est la Folle de Chaillot, Monsieur.

LE PRÉSIDENT:

   Une Folle?

LE GARÇON:

   Pourquoi une folle? Pourquoi serait-elle folle?

LE PRÉSIDENT:

   C'est vous qui le dites, idiot!

LE GARÇON:

   Moi? Je dis comme on l'appelle. Pourquoi folle?
   Je ne vous permets pas de l'insulter. C'est la Folle
      de
   Chaillot.

[p. 102]

Giraudoux had spoken earlier in *La Française et la France* of "extravagance" and "les grandes extravagantes" in saying: "Le talent ou l'imagination chez la femme l'amène rapidement à l'extravagance" (p. 181) and he elaborates:

   . . . la diplomatie féminine mondiale doit, autant qu'à ses grandes sages, à celles qu'un de mes confrères appelle irrévérencieusement les grandes folles. Que ce soit par Mme de Staël, par Catherine II, par Mrs. Macpherson, ou par Isadora Duncan, des habitudes intellectuelles, physiques, morales ont souvent été données au monde entier par l'élan et l'ignorance de toute pudeur ou de tout ridicule avec lesquels certaines femmes, sous la pression de leur talent, se sont précipitées vers la conquête du monde.

[pp. 181-182]

It is the capacity for whimsy that enables the Countess to be the effective gyn/ecologist. This whimsy is sanity, and the ability to see the world as it is. Men bereft of whimsy assume that it is not an authentic quality. It becomes associated with woman's "irrationality," fancy, frivolous changeability, and penchant for the outlandish. Woman's whimsy is seen, at best, as the nature of the good witch and, at worst, as the bizarre behavior of a demented diabolism. In classical terms, these are the distinctions between the mermaids and the sirens and between the Muses and the Furies. In Hélène Cixous's words: "You only have to look at the Medusa straight on to see her. And she's not deadly. She's beautiful and she's laughing."[14]

Anouilh's view of woman is classical in the sense that, for him, woman is a reflector and extension of man. Her whimsy (which we have seen Giraudoux classify positively as "extravagance") impairs her ability for positive, objective action. For Anouilh, Antigone is a self-sacrificing example. Créon is the person who will or will not learn from her example; it is he who must correct society. Anouilh provides us with a classical goddess in an otherwise modern play touted for its hard-hitting realism, especially as conveyed in the modern idiom employed by the speakers of the play.

At first glance, the Countess and Antigone seem to be representatives of a unified France in a historically documented moment of dilemma shared by all the French. Certainly the critics, the popular press, and the public saw the plays as kindred in spirit. Anthologies in the late forties and early fifties included both plays, and there has been a longstanding association between the two in the U.S., for example, where both were presented in translation on the Broadway stage within a short time after their original production in Paris; both were later included in the "Best Plays" of their respective seasons. Both have been perennial choices by school, college, and amateur and professional theater groups in the U.S.

Close reading, however, reveals opposing representations of women that place the themes ultimately at opposite poles. The plays both concern themselves with their heroines' abilities to participate in the conservation of the civilization. In **Antigone,** women can only serve as symbol and example for man, who is the agent for constructive operation of the society. In *La Folle de Chaillot,* only woman can solve the problems of the civilization because only she has the understanding of and interaction with reality that are the qualities necessary to modern leaders in a thriving and forward-looking urban civilization.

Notes

1. *Antigone* opened in Paris February 4, 1944, and was presented for the first time in New York (in English) February 18, 1946. It appeared in Burns Mantle's *Best Plays of 1945-46. La Folle de Chaillot,* completed in 1943, was staged for the first time by Jouvet December 19, 1945. The English language version premiered in New York December 17, 1948. It is listed in *Best Plays of 1948-49* and won the Critics Circle Award for Best Foreign Play in 1949. Texts cited in the present paper are, for Jean Anouilh's *Antigone,* the Table Ronde edition published in 1947; for Jean Giraudoux's *La Folle de Chaillot,* Tome Quatrième of his *Théâtre,* the Bernard Grasset edition published in 1959, pp. 80-181.

2. Mary Daly, *Gyn/Ecology: The Metaethics of Radical Feminism* (Boston: Beacon Press, 1978), pp. 9-11 and passim.

3. For an exploration of the philosophical significance of sexual difference in Aristotle's philosophy, see Robin Schott's "Aristotle on Women," in *Kinesis,* XII, 2 (1982), pp. 69-84. I am grateful to the author, a colleague in philosophy at the University of Louisville, for sharing her research and her conclusions with me.

4. *Gyn/Ecology,* p. 44.

5. Mircea Eliade, *The Sacred and the Profane: The Nature of Religion,* trans. Willard R. Trask (New York: Harper Torchbooks, 1961), p. 96, as quoted in Daly, p. 44.

6. Sheila Ruth, "Sexism, Patriarchy, and Feminism," in *Women and Men: The Consequences of Power* (Cincinnati: Univ. of Cincinnati, Office of Women's Studies, 1977), p. 56.

7. Elaine Marks and Isabelle de Courtivron, eds., *New French Feminisms: An Anthology* (Amherst: Univ. of Massachusetts Press, 1980), p. 8. Marks and de Courtivron present, within a historical context, the creative and critical literary theories of twentieth-century French women.

8. Jean Giraudoux, *La Française et la France* (Paris: Gallimard, 1954), pp. 174 and 208. The texts cited in this paper were written and delivered at l'Université des Annales in 1934. Subsequent references are indicated in the present text by title and page number.

9. Anouilh's preoccupation with the dramatic possibilities inherent in the "jeune fille" has been alluded to in a number of critical studies. David Grossvogel, in his introduction to *Antigone* (Cambridge, Mass.: Integral Editions, 1959), pp. 9-10, provides especially valuable insights, which I gratefully acknowledge.

10. See Daly, pp. 354-365, for a discussion of woman as the object of patriarchal war.

11. Codification of the genealogy of the gods was first undertaken in the eighth century by Hesiod in *Theogony.* The attributes of the gods, their exploits, and their interaction with human beings are summarized in *Larousse Encyclopedia of Mythology,* trans. Richard Aldington and Delano Ames (London: Batchworth Press, 1959). Antigone belongs to the Royal House of Thebes through her father, Oedipus. Her genealogy and descent from Poseidon are illustrated in Michael Grant and John Hazel, *Gods and Mortals in Classical Mythology* (Springfield, Mass.: G. & C. Merriam, 1973), p. 439.

12. Françoise d'Eaubonne, *Le Féminisme ou la mort* (Paris: Femmes en Mouvement, 1974), pp. 213-252.

13. André Beucler, *Les Instants de Giraudoux et autres souvenirs* (Paris: Milieu du Monde, 1948), p. 14.

14. Hélène Cixous, "The Laugh of the Medusa," in *New French Feminisms,* p. 255. This is a revised version of "Le rire de la méduse," which appeared in *L'arc* (1975), pp. 39-54.

LA RÉPÉTITION; OU, L'AMOUR PUNI (THE REHEARSAL)

PRODUCTION REVIEW

Richard Gilman (review date 8 November 1963)

SOURCE: Gilman, Richard. "Versions of Dishonesty." *Commonweal* (8 November 1963): 194.

[*In the following negative review of the 1963 New York production of* The Rehearsal, *Gilman contends that "we are supposed to be left with a troubled but gratified sense of how the world really goes, but what we are actually left with is a sense of how to use the theater exquisitely for the purpose of simulating art."*]

Art, Picasso has remarked, is the lie that leads to truth. All theater "lies," the way all art does, pretending to be real in order to trap a hitherto unheard-of truth in the space between the pretense and reality itself. But in the commercial theater, where art is most often considered to be the province of stage designers and lighting experts (as in popular culture the interior decorator and the flower arranger are thought of as our most "artistic" types) the lies of the stage, its illusions and necessary deceptions, are practised for their own sakes; sterile reproductions of lies from outside the theater, from conventional fantasy or inherited sentiment, they result in nothing unheard of except an increment of ugliness. The difference is that between being unreal in order to be more than real and being unreal so as to be simply dishonest.

The forms of dishonesty that have exhibited themselves in this new season already constitute a map of deceit, a gazetteer of uninhabitable and impossible lands. And because mendacity in an institution inevitably infects everyone committed to its preservation, the biggest lie of all is that this is proving to be a superior season; on the contrary, it is precisely the "hits" which demonstrate how rapidly we are approaching a point where the true and the false will have become absolutely indistinguishable in our theaters.

I except *Chips with Everything,* the one new play on or off Broadway that deserves some of its honors, but I emphatically include *Luther,* a drama which grows steadily more unpleasant and unconvincing in the memory, and Jean Anouilh's **The Rehearsal,** which is an example of the obvious given a high sheen and the daunted masquerading as daring.

Anouilh has a reputation I have never been able to endorse, although I can understand how his command of theatrical procedures, his gloss and perfect though stringently limited taste, commend him to professionals and to that "upper-level" theater-goer for whom elegance is revelation and genteel cynicism is apocalypse. **The Rehearsal,** which was first performed in Paris in 1951, is central Anouilh, a play of considerable surface charm and faultless technique, whose vision is of the dark fate of love and innocence in a harsh, unprincipled world. "Bittersweet," has been, I think, the word most often employed to describe its prevailing quality.

Well, bittersweet is a word for dilettantes, for esthetic fence-sitters and moral hedgers, a word that makes experience palatable by jamming its contradictions together and thus robbing them of their terrors. In this play about the attempt of a notorious roué to regenerate himself through the love of a young innocent girl, Anouilh marches as though in the ranks of real fatality but is all the while preparing a denouement of breath-taking sentimentality and flaccid wisdom. A villain, who represents worldly inexorability and the hatred of the corrupted for the pure, sees to it that the effort is thwarted by convincing the girl that her lover has not changed and by seducing her himself, after which, mortally ashamed of himself—so that Anouilh may have it both ways, the "sweet" neutralizing the bitter—he arranges to get himself killed.

This is melodrama, but pretentious melodrama: it is to take the instruments and agencies of moral vision and make them the vision itself. Innocence corrupts *itself,* purity is inextricably involved with stigma, love carries the seeds of its own calamity: these are the truths which Anouilh continually and elaborately misses while he builds his fable of destruction from outside, of Iago without Othello and of ruin without choice. We are supposed to be left with a troubled but gratified sense of how the world really goes, but what we are actually left with is a sense of how to use the theater exquisitely for the purpose of simulating art.

COLOMBE (MADEMOISELLE COLUMBE)

PRODUCTION REVIEWS

Eric Bentley (review date 25 January 1954)

SOURCE: Bentley, Eric. "Good Play, Well Done." *New Republic* (25 January 1954): 20-1.

[*In the following review, Bentley praises the sets and acting in the 1954 New York production of* Colombe.]

Optimistic plays are very depressing. "Too bad reality is different," you say in the lobby. It takes a pessimistic play to cheer you up. When you say "Life isn't as bad as *that*" you are half way to declaring that everything in the garden is lovely. The great tonic of the Broadway season is *Mademoiselle Colombe* by Jean Anouilh, a tale of the futility of boy's meeting girl.

It is a production of many pleasures Boris Aronson's sets alone are worth the trip to the Longacre. This designer, whose reputation is for thoroughness and grandeur, shows himself, here as in *My Three Angels,* to have as light a touch as anyone in the profession; his joyous wit and controlled fantasy provide a desperately needed alternative to the lush decadence of, say, Oliver Messel or Lemuel Ayres. Aronson's principal exhibit in *Colombe* is a backstage scene in which Anouilh's peculiar blend of French reality with theatrical unreality is accurately translated into color and shape.

The play is also a showcase for some of our finest acting talent—by which I do not merely mean that some of our best actors are in it, nor yet that it enables them to show themselves off. Edna Best had a better chance to show herself off in *Ladies of the Corridor*; the authors gave her nothing else to show. Since Miss Best has one of the most charming selves in our theatre, it is pleasant to have her display it—but it is astonishing to have her dispense with charm altogether and get along quite as well without. Miss Best's part in *Colombe* is that of an aging actress, the boy's mother wholly shrewish and shrill. Miss Best wears a false nose, chalky make-up, and a red wig; struts, gesticulates wildly, and screams her head off; in fact, goes all out; all of which is remarkable at a time when she'd get higher marks for acting if she relaxed and was a bit of a bore. As it was, Miss Best showed the way to the rest of a cast which—except for two performers—Anouilh dresses up as caricatures, outrageous as Hogarth or the Keystone Cops: Sam Jaffe, Harry Bannister, Nehemiah Persoff, and others contribute notable cartoon-portraits. (Mikhail Rasumny is rather unintelligible.)

The exceptions are the boy and the girl through whom a more inward reality is explored. The girl is played by Julie Harris. If my delight over this actress is somewhat belated, I had better admit that I was in Europe when she came to prominence. Astonishing what can happen when one's back is turned! That Miss Harris has the special "offbeat personality" of the newer generation of actresses is the least of it and might well have set me against her. Her personality has the larger strangeness and even (potentially) the grander glamor that go to the making of a Garbo (different as Garbo is). Nor does the final impression come from mere color or timbre of personality. It comes, rather, from Miss Harris' gift, a gift not yet, to be sure, at its fullest development, but nonetheless unspoiled by any of the myriad forces which must have been trying to spoil it. One is afraid for her! She is like one of Anouilh's young women, all sensitive life, while round about is the wicked, insensitive world eager to hurt, not to mention the awful example of Misses X and Y, first ladies of our stage, fifty and forlorn.

Eli Wallach is a favorite actor of mine, but casting him as the hero of *Colombe* was an audacious bit of "offcasting" which has not succeeded. It is very well to ask a straight comedienne like Miss Best to do a character part, but to ask a character actor like Mr. Wallach to play a juvenile lead? The springy élan and homey vivacity that he has to offer he is compelled to save for one scene—the last. Before that we have to observe him grimly holding himself in or yet more grimly simulating qualities he cannot seem to possess like arrogance and intellectuality. The man who played the part in Paris was possibly a less accomplished actor; he didn't do very much with the part; but there was no complaint about him because he fell into place; it is one of those rather neutral roles. Mr. Wallach, though he works manfully, and always holds the attention (because he is an artist), is the Achilles' heel of the show; and the anti-European newspaper fraternity has aimed to kill.

Achilles is not all heel. Apart from one gamble that didn't come off, Harold Clurman, the director, has played an admirable game. Even the over-emphasis on the hero's badness can broaden one's notion of a play which—however you take it—is both witty and moving. I came away from the Paris production thinking Anouilh had but reiterated his standard theme of desecrated innocence, the only difference this time being that the innocent was a man. The Clurman production makes it clear that *Colombe* is—with *Antigone*—one of those more interesting plays of Anouilh in which there is some guilt on both sides of the conflict. The young woman is a very ordinary young woman (to make so ordinary a person so extraordinary on stage being a great joint achievement of Anouilh and Miss Harris), but the young man's superiority is pharasaical. In fact *Colombe* brings to mind a play that those who dislike Anouilh would dislike even more: *Le Misanthrope.*

Like Giraudoux, like Brecht, like Goethe, like Racine, like all foreign playwrights, Anouilh has been called untranslatable. So there sets in that process called Adaptation, which commonly means the conquest and destruction of an author by a jealous would-be rival. If the British version of *Colombe* was not quite that, it was nevertheless full of changes by which the Adaptor vainly sought to justify having his name in the same size type as Anouilh. It is a pleasure to report that the version used in New York—by Louis Kronenberger—is Hyperion to this satyr: more faithful to the original without being less amusing in itself. Following the British precedent, and presumably under instructions from his producers, Mr. Kronenberger did tone down the nausea and pessimism which are most conspicuous in the Edna Best role. In the French she says, "I'm constipated and I've 200 alexandrines to learn by tomorrow." In withholding this from the play, I can only hope Mr. Kronenberger is saving it for his next piece (in *Time*) on Miss X or Miss Y.

There were other small things to grumble about, such as an awkward transition to the last scene in which the PA system is ineffectively and indistinctly used. But by and large, it is a splendid evening, and you leave the theatre full of the hope that M. Anouilh's hopelessness inevitably engenders.

Richard Hayes (review date 12 February 1954)

SOURCE: Hayes, Richard. "The Stage." *Commonweal* (12 February 1954): 471-72.

[*In the following review, Hayes provides an unfavorable assessment of the 1954 New York production of* Colombe.]

Mlle Colombe, the fifth of Jean Anouilh's plays to achieve the condition of an American failure, has provoked a fresh rash of critical speculation on the international dissimilarities of theatrical taste. A small quantity of this analysis has been responsible and illuminating, but too much of it sententious and niggardly, designed to reinforce a heedless public in its indulgent prejudices. Myself, I suspect one need not go so far afield in determining the cause for this failure: the fault, dear Broadway, lies not in the French but in ourselves, and our curious impercipience to the particular weight and quality of M. Anouilh's world. We have had, since the war, productions of *Antigone, Legend of Lovers, Ring Round the Moon,* and *Cry of*

the Peacock, but each has been either understatement, overstatement or misstatement: closest to the mark was perhaps the rococo fantasy of Christopher Fry's version of *Ring Round the Moon.* Now, *Mlle Colombe,* which—even in Louis Kronenberger's fastidious translation—disappoints, but provocatively, so that we are constantly forced to reshape its raw material into an original image which has somehow become deformed and obscure.

Characteristically, Anouilh's plays are songs of innocence and experience. They proceed, and achieve their dramatic tension, by the juxtaposition of what Maurice Valency has called "the purity of the ideal and the degradation of the individual in the material world." The playwright's authentic and formidable distinction lies, however, in his talent for giving these two states a rich particularity, inexhaustibly vivacious and glittering, and redeemed at every juncture from banality or a casual cynicism. *Mlle Colombe,* to instance one case, is a cool and simple portrait of the vanity of love: it turns solely on the tragedy of an idealistic young man who loses his "dove" in a squalid, chattering, vivid nest of theatrical eagles, mistress of which is his mother, a truly grotesque old harridan embattled in age and craft and power: a kind of Madame DeFarge of the Boulevards, dropping slushy Alexandrines in a rich, plummy voice while she lops off the heads, hearts, hopes of all about her. Yet the "morality" of the slice-of-life to which M. Anouilh exposes us is so discreet, so embedded in the action, that every resource of intellect and sensibility must be sharpened to point up its bitter contrasts. The playwright is concerned with tragedy, not melodrama, and so he withholds comment: that task, as one critic has observed, he leaves to our consciences.

It is precisely in the realization of these nuances, echoes, that Harold Clurman's direction seems to me to falter. No American director is more sensitive to moral ambiguities and refractions than Mr. Clurman, yet he seems to have read *Mlle Colombe* as but another portrait of the romantic will discovering itself. To do so is to miss most of the play's bitter rue, the stain of sadness which deepens and spreads throughout it. Anouilh's humor, for example, cannot be merely grotesque: it must leave an aftertaste of disgust in the mouth, just as the fragrant charm of his heroines must visibly tarnish before our eyes.

Partly, too, the meanings of *Mlle Colombe* are blunted by crucial errors in casting. Eli Wallach, however distinguished his talents, simply cannot summon the style or finish necessary for a role of this sort. And Julie Harris, though never guilty of anything slovenly or common or inartistic, stays well within the range she so brilliantly defined in *I Am a Camera.* Her present performance represents no significant development of what is perhaps the most impressive young American talent on view. It falls to Edna Best to give Anouilh's creation the fullest realization, and her showy, strident domination of a difficult part delights the mind and the senses as thoroughly as it dismays the heart. No one will deny that the failure of **Mlle Colombe** still exceeds immeasurably the success of many a lesser play, but the present production has also the unfortunate effect of nurturing the illusion that Anouilh is a sauce too subtle and exotic for our robust, hearty and oh! so unexceptionable American taste.

LA VALSE DES TORÉADORS
(THE WALTZ OF THE TOREADORS)

PRODUCTION REVIEW

Harold Clurman (review date 8 October 1973)

SOURCE: Clurman, Harold. "Theatre." *Nation*, New York, N.Y. (8 October 1973): 349.

[*In the following review, Clurman gives a mixed assessment of the 1973 New York production of* The Waltz of the Toreadors, *deeming the drama "the play which reveals most of Anouilh's essential traits in perfect balance."*]

The Waltz of the Toreadors, produced in Paris in 1952 and a failure then, perhaps because it was not sufficiently cut and also because the author himself directed it, has since been successfully done in London and New York. It is, in my view, the play which reveals most of Anouilh's essential traits in perfect balance.

Anouilh is a romantic idealist whose idealism plagues him. He yearns for purity, nobility, moral courage, glory, but discerns little but pettiness, chicanery, deception and vice. Life riles him because it isn't consistent; he abhors the bulk of humanity because it professes virtues it doesn't practice. There is something comic in this and a great measure of "fun," but though he is able to laugh at it, it upsets his vitals. He is a sentimentalist become bitter because everything he beholds, everything that has happened to him since he first conceived of the loveliness of experience—especially in matters of love—has proved false and vain.

Oh, if it were only not so, Anouilh's plays seem to wail—beauty not despoiled, grandeur not debased, purity not debauched. But since it is so, we must make the best of it in humankind's shabby fashion, bedecking ourselves in social courtesies, official pomp and at best in common-sense compromise. Once in a long while some splendid gesture or leap of the soul, like a lark in the sky, momentarily redeems us.

This makes Anouilh both a conservative and a cynic. He will not budge from his safe position—"agin" everything except the Ideal. He endures life with a grimace of disgust, a salty chuckle, an ache of regret, and above all with sharp-edged *practical shrewdness*. The latter feature produces his formidable stage craftsmanship.

The Waltz of the Toreadors is an acidulous bonbon, a despondent farce. Within its coruscating invention, its delightful trickery, its rib-tickling skepticism, there also dwells something subtly tender, softly sighing. The colors of Vuillard and Bonnard surround it; a fragrance of old-time corruption, elegance and bourgeois crassness, decorum and dissoluteness emanates from it. An echo of sweet romance as the French from 1875 to 1900 dreamed of it—a kind of domestic or village romance—wafts through it.

You can still find some of this in the Circle in the Square production, but there is a Broadway alloy in it. It lacks a Gallic vista, that of genuine cultivation endowed with a sense of the past and of the distance which separates our crudities from the quaint and gentler gaucheries of a bygone day.

There is always something winning in Eli Wallach's performances, but the childlike aspirant who resides within the General he plays in **The Waltz** is not a jumpy boy but an imposing cavalry officer, a conspicuously masculine figure, "a gentleman of the old military academy," and in the weakness, contradictions, confusions and lostness of such a man is the cream of Anouilh's sorry jest. Wallach only approximates it.

Anne Jackson does many amusing things as the General's harridan wife. These diminish only when Brian Murray's direction falters in bite and snap to accommodate "psychological" nuances which are not in the play's proper vein.

Clarke Dunham's setting is handsome, but hardly characteristic of the period, province or condition. Practice in correct pronunciation of French names might lend a touch of authenticity to the atmosphere: for instance, the "s" in Ghislaine (the General's patient sweetheart) should be mute, as if it were spelled "Gheelen."

L'ALOUETTE (*THE LARK*)

PRODUCTION REVIEWS

Eric Bentley (review date 5 December 1955)

SOURCE: Bentley, Eric. "Theatre." *New Republic* (5 December 1955): 21.

[*In the following review, Bentley unfavorably compares Anouilh's portrayal of Joan of Arc in* The Lark *to George Bernard Shaw's conception of the Catholic heroine.*]

In 1890 Shaw complained of Bernhardt as Joan of Arc: "she intones her lines and poses like a saint." At the time, Joan was hovering uncomfortably between heaven and earth. Subsequently she was split in two: one half sent to heaven by the church and called, indeed, a saint, the other half brought rudely down to earth by our playwrights. It is this second Joan—named "natural man" by Miss Hellman's inquisitor—which Julie Harris has been called upon to play. Who is better qualified? She is the very idea of a modern actress. The *Times* recently published a photo to demonstrate that, on 42nd street, Miss Harris looks just like one of the crowd. Imagine what Sarah would say to that! But she would, at least partly, be wrong. In the first place, being the ordinary person has its advantages. No intoning, no posing like a saint. Julie Harris can convince you that this girl is indeed the daughter of the rustic couple of Domremy. In the second place, the ordinariness is only a mask. When Miss Harris takes it off, you see that she is beautiful, glamorous, and powerfully attractive. And she has learned to make subtle use of a wiry, expressive body and the stage-space surrounding it. Her performance as Joan [in *The Lark*] has many lovely and touching moments from the first tableau where she sits in despair with her head in her hands to the last where she stands erect and smiles her oval, homey, midwestern smile. Presumably with the help of her director, Joseph Anthony, than whom no one has a more daring sense of movement, she is able to say more with her body than one would have believed possible in so very verbal a play. No actress' Joan is likely to be complete. Under any director, speaking any script, Miss Harris' otherworldiness would always be more elfin than saintly, her belligerency rather that of Peter Pan than of a patriot and military strategist. But the greatest limitation—a lack of range, of variety—is imposed by the script.

Like Shaw, Anouilh has come to the life of Joan of Arc from a feeling that here was all that he had been trying to say in his previous plays. Shaw was right: the confrontation here of individual and society, intuition and philosophy, conscience and convention, vitality and system is Shavian theatre in a nutshell. And, prima facie, the Anouilh pattern also fits: here is another of those clear-eyed virgins whom a world of weary or wicked men takes and destroys. Well and good—provided that the playwright is interested in this kind of virgin and this kind of destroyer—is interested, that is to say, in religion and politics. Shaw fills Joan with his own religious sense, and interprets her career according to his own view of history: she was the first nationalist and the first protestant. Anouilh's lack of interest in such matters is total. He tells us that the Joan of history was a big, healthy girl but that he couldn't care less and his Joan is going to be weary, undernourished, and haggard. We are meant to understand, no doubt, that this author is after dramatic essences, not factual externals. But what is undramatic about a big raw-boned peasant lass? Is it not the weariness and emaciation that are unreal, the children, not of truth, but of Anouilh's philosophic system?

Admittedly, Shaw also gave us a highly personal view of Joan, which departs from the facts in at least one essential point, namely, in representing the trial as scrupulously fair. To this end, Shaw gave an inquisitor argument such as no inquisitor would ever (I think) have approved, let alone employed, and made Bishop Cauchon amiable and rational. Anouilh not only presents another highly personal interpretation, however, he also follows the Shavian version of the facts as if it were established history. Indeed, one of the New York reviewers excused his following in Shaw's footsteps on the grounds that it all really happened that way! At this point it is high time—if Catholic critics are too polite to speak out about Anouilh—that a Catholic dramatist should write a Joan play and remind the public, first, that the trial was as shameless and corrupt a frame-up as anything in Soviet annals and that, as for character, Bishop Cauchon was in all probability about as likeable, enlightened, and highminded as Senator McCarthy. We allow Shaw a certain license, partly because he came up with a fine play, partly because what he said has general application even if it is not specifically true of Joan. Anouilh can claim no such indulgence. Rather, one has the right to complain that in this the least imaginative of his dramas he also displays so little interest in the truth—the truth about Catholicism, for example. His inquisitor says: "love of man excludes the love of God"! It is true that a priest protests, but he is sent out of the room for his pains. It is true an attempt is made to make the inquisitor symbolize all who fanatically put an Idea before people. My points stand, *a fortiori,* that the play moves all the time away from concrete truth and towards abstract theory. And the theory is not very good theory. As a thinker, Anouilh has the narrow-mindedness we traditionally associate with the religious; only it's the fact that his mind contains *no* religion that makes him narrow. In vain that he tries in his play suddenly to be Positive and celebrate human goodness. The enthusiasm is *voulu* and unfelt. Real is only the old, comfortless, nauseated atheism. Despite his intentions, his Joan is a character *reduced* to his pattern, and (in the French original) dies chiefly to avoid the coming of old age.

This last was more than Miss Hellman could stomach. By a brief deletion, she desperately tries, in the last scene, to rescue Joan from Anouilh. She inserts a little speech of her own to guarantee that Joan, lost to sainthood à la Bernhardt, may be at least a good girl. She goes back into the body of the text and slashes the inquisitor's speeches so that our audiences will never find out what Anouilh meant to convey. Meanwhile, the producer has Leonard Bernstein turn on the phonograph at awkward moments (hark the metallic angels sing), otherwise chiefly relying on a director whose whole talent lies in what may be called dramatic choreography. Anouilh's conception was scenically very simple: his play is a discussion, and that's that. The New York production is a really grand show—visually much finer than *Tiger at the Gates,* for example—a show which, with Julie Harris in the midst of it, anyone interested in theatre will enjoy, especially those who are *not* interested in Joan of Arc, history in particular, or truth in general.

Richard Hayes (review date 23 December 1955)

SOURCE: Hayes, Richard. "The Stage: The Lark." *Commonweal* (23 December 1955): 304-05.

[*In the following review, Hayes elucidates the differences between the historical accounts of Joan of Arc and the dramatic representations of her in Anouilh's* The Lark *and George Bernard Shaw's* Saint Joan.]

"Some nights, when I am feeling depressed," Jean Anouilh has written of Joan of Arc, "I try to be rational and I say: the situation—social, political and military—was ripe for the phenomenon of Joan; a little shepherdess, one of the countless little shepherdesses who had seen the Virgin or heard voices, and who happened to be called Joan, came to fill a gap in the works, and then everything began turning." It is this image which dominates the play Miss Lillian Hellman has drawn from Anouilh's *L'Alouette,* and with which Miss Julie Harris has made so palpable a hit: the image, not of "the cornered animal caught at Rouen, but the lark singing in the open sky," brought down brokenly and in her flashing splendor by the malice of men. And it is as the lark that Joan takes her place in the company of Anouilh's celebrated heroines—young girls of a fantastic, lyrical purity and bloom—virgins all: doomed

to violation by the grossness of the world's body. (Virginity, here as elsewhere in Anouilh, is of the essence: "Being a virgin is a state of grace," Warwick says to Joan, in an explicit passage Miss Hellman has curiously chosen to mute.)

The Lark then: even the title suggests how Joan is held in Anouilh's imagination. To Shaw—who chiseled the moral image of Joan which has dominated us for three decades—she is not so much symbol as spiritual fact: the emphasis falls heavily on transcendent being: *Saint* Joan. It will be fruitful to consider shortly how closely these images correspond to the 'truth' of Joan—or reveal a reality beyond that truth—but for the moment, one might wonder at some elisions and alterations of mere fact which Anouilh and Shaw have so liberally imposed on the pattern of history. (The truth of poetry, of course, is not the truth of history, but the paradox of Joan is that she so bluntly demands justification in terms of both.) I must confess that I have not read the testimony of the original trial for condemnation, yet we are fortunate to have at hand Mme. Régine Pernoud's lately issued and absorbing account of the proceedings for Joan's rehabilitation: *The Retrial of Joan of Arc* (Harcourt). And after Mme. Pernoud's disinterested, irrefutable proof of Cauchon's venal and time-serving hypocrisy, are not Shaw's benignly politic cleric and Anouilh's anxious spiritual advisor inadmissible as versions of historical fact? (One may perhaps ignore the satiric treatment of Warwick: in both Shaw and Anouilh an 'official' personality, well-bred, *blasé*: in actuality, a moral terrorist and bully.) We may possibly concede some latitude to Shaw—in his calculated insolence to the twentieth century, he sought to illustrate that Joan had a fairer hearing in the Middle Ages than she would have had from us—yet there seems no justification for Anouilh.

Or consider the false abjuration (one witness tells us that Joan signed smiling in mockery); or the 'arranged' relapse (how, for instance, may an excommunicated heretic be permitted to receive Communion? detail not mentioned by Anouilh or Shaw); or Joan's constant appeals to have audience of the Pope (again omitted), or the squalid matter of the secular prison in which Joan was kept, the promiscuous sexual conditions of which forced her to resume the forbidden male attire. Shaw characteristically and with impertinent charm sees the issue of masculine dress as a triumph of rational good sense, and Anouilh extracts a genuine pathos out of the theme. But he also removes the sting of truth by obscuring from us the Bishop's awareness of Joan's intolerable situation: the horror lies in Cauchon's persistent denial of Joan's request for sanctuary in an ecclesiastical prison. Then again, the Inquisitor: Shaw's is mild by contrast with Anouilh's savage antagonist of "the natural man" (Miss Hellman's interpolation: the original reads 'man'), dedicated to the inexorable domination of the Idea, hunting down and extirpating "youth, generosity, human tenderness . . . the uncommendable, graceless, cloudy drink of the milk of human kindness." I perhaps need not comment on this after some centuries of Christian humanism, but there is still a small irony in the fact that it was Jean Bréhat, the Grand Inquisitor of France, who spent five years collating the testimony which would release Joan's name from its ignominy and disgrace.

Again, however, I would stress: the truths of poetry and history are distinct. Shaw gives us the first: his Joan—pert, defiant, feminist, "the born boss," protestant, nationalist—cuts across the attitudes with which the dramatist has invested her to stand in the lonely splendor of time, victim and symbol of the tragic political nature of reality. We may cavil at this feature, dispute that posture, but Joan is not diminished—with splendid grace, she bears the weight of ideality. The image of *The Lark* has, on the contrary, not only lacunae of truth, but less strength and resonance and poetic reality. There are many beautiful and suggestive passages in Anouilh's drama (I am speaking of Mr. Christopher Fry's cleanly sculptured translation, which is oddly being patronized as 'literal.' Should not one wish to know exactly what a playwright means to say? For all her sharp sense of 'good theater,' Miss Hellman seems to me to have reduced the play to a genteel muddle) yet ultimately too much is burked: Joan *insists*: she is hard and resistant, not part of the plastic reality out of which Anouilh has shaped his several masterpieces of contemporary drama. He may have seen in her another focus through which to explore what one critic has called his dominating theme—the quest for authenticity—yet Joan's authenticity ('the mystery of her charity' in Péguy's phrase) has its sanction beyond time and character and the exquisite charm of that moment of national *gloire* (the coronation at Rheims) which is, for Anouilh, the true end of the story, "a kind of joy."

Miss Julie Harris places Joan at the very center of this curious tapestry of medieval life: her performance—so delicate and touching and exact—is full of that special poetry of intensity which makes Miss Harris so unique and luminous a figure in our theater. This is not the visionary Joan of Claudel and Péguy, but it has something of the spendthrift audacity and vehemence of the wilful, enchanting creature we discern vaguely through the fine network of Mme. Pernoud's scholarship: the high-spirited girl who hotly matches her domestic skill against that of any housewife in Rouen; who gleefully threatens to pull the ears of the clerk who had erroneously transcribed one of her replies, and who potently flashes out at her judges: "Oh yes, you'll record anything against me all right, but you won't record anything *for* me." Yet for the first time in Miss Harris' career, I feel the absence of weight and variety in her playing: what her Joan lacks is the passionate echo of

the doomed girl tearing her hair in the cage of her prison, and calling on God to witness Cauchon's treachery. Beaudricourt is given an excellent reading by Mr. Theodore Bikel, and the Warwick of Mr. Christopher Plummer is masculine and adroit. As the Inquisitor, Mr. Joseph Wiseman gives his usual psychopathic performance. Mr. Joseph Anthony has animated the stage with fresh and ingenious movement, yet the production wants on the whole the fluid line of Anouilh's intention: in particular are the scenes of court life insufficiently stylized to enforce the playwright's dramatic point. Mr. Leonard Bernstein's celestial choirs rather dreadfully do not come off.

I would wish, in conclusion, to draw the attention of my readers to Mr. Eric Bentley's notice of *The Lark* in the *New Republic* of December 5: it is by far quite the most telling commentary the play has yet occasioned.

BECKET; OU, L'HONNEUR DE DIEU (BECKET; OR, THE HONOR OF GOD)

PRODUCTION REVIEW

Harold Clurman (review date 27 May 1961)

SOURCE: Clurman, Harold. "Theatre." *Nation*, New York, N.Y., (27 May 1961): 467-68.

[*In the following review, Clurman derides the acting in the 1961 New York production of* Becket *and asserts that the play is "intellectually (as well as historically) skimpy; of true religious sentiment there is barely a trace, and its morality is without real commitment."*]

Readers may have noticed that I frequently omit discussion or appraisal of actors from my notices. In view of my belief that acting is the crucial ingredient of the theatre as theatre, my failure to comment on the acting of many of the plays I see must seem peculiar.

The reason for this contradiction is that in most productions the acting is reasonably competent rather than creative. The actors—usually chosen because they physically approximate the characters the dramatist may have had in mind and because they have formerly proved some ability—illustrate the play acceptably, lend it body. In these circumstances the play presents the actors instead of the actors making the play.

It is not always the actors' fault that they commonly serve chiefly as attractive mouthpieces and models for the dramatist's text. The conditions of theatrical production on Broadway and in the commercial theatre generally are not conducive to creation. The director—even when he is an artist—also is burdened by limitations which make it difficult for him to lead the actor toward creative goals.

There can be little pleasure or gain to the reader of a review to be told that an actor is "O.K." or "will do"—which is how one feels about most performances. Nor does it serve any purpose to make the actor bear the brunt of sharp criticism when he is an actor of middling stamp, chosen for the wrong reasons, directed by a harassed gentleman who is required to deliver a "smash" within three and a half weeks for an audience with few considered standards.

We may learn something about acting, and the critic may usefully spend time discussing it, when the performance is very fine or when a splendid actor fails to act well. This latter is the case of Laurence Olivier as Henry II in Anouilh's *Becket* (Hudson Theatre).

In the first place, the return engagement of this play is something to be studied. Despite a generally enthusiastic press and more or less packed houses, the original (New York) production—with Anthony Quinn as Henry II and Olivier as Becket—lost an estimated $100,000. Olivier generously undertook to do the play on the road to help the producer recoup some of his losses. The actor would also have the opportunity to play Henry, the more colorful of the two leading roles. On the road the show did enormous business; Sir Laurence won great acclaim. The second batch of notices in New York have been ecstatic and the three-week engagement is a sell-out.

The first thing which must strike the most casual eye is that the production now seems shopworn: even the scenery looks shabby. The original director, Peter Glenville, could not have supervised the present proceedings—or if he did, he must have been listless or powerless. I suspect that a stage manager was nominally in charge while the star "arranged" his own interpretation.

Arrangement is the proper word, because Olivier's Henry is a congeries of characteristics or playing points rather than a unified portrayal. Leaving aside the harsh fact that Olivier may be too old for the role—the play is in some measure the story of two young comrades—Olivier has no conception of Henry as a person because he sees him only as a fat part, a series of acting opportunities. Because he is brilliantly endowed, because he speaks beautifully, moves beautifully and has a thorough command of the stage, Olivier enacts some of the part's "moments" with impressive power; but, for lack of direction or thought, he enacts them without much finesse. Here he is coy, there he is fierce, now he

is devilish, again he is hysterical. None of these turns are genuine (they are often transparent tricks) because they are not related to a center of meaning.

Anouilh's Henry is a naive, healthy, natural, instinctive "peasant" with the capacity to grow in understanding. He loves Becket in whom he beholds the perfection of his own best qualities—a high liver with the education and sophistication of an intelligent and disciplined worldling. Henry's personality is deeply rooted in what we think of as normal. He is innocently and savagely sensuous, he is trusting though wary, he is not at all stupid, he is curious and he is brave. He wants to rule and despite the impediments of his average selfishness he will become a man of considerable stature. There is no element of caricature in him, for all Anouilh's temptation in the direction of buffoonery, and when he cries out in anger, frustration or pain, his agony is never that of a neurotic.

From all this Olivier selects the elements of the most conventional comedy and outbursts of emotion (indicated through bold muscular violence and neurasthenic outcries copied from previously praised performances), all of them irrelevant to the composition and intent of the whole play. The result may make the groundlings applaud but must "make the judicious grieve."

I shall say little of Arthur Kennedy's Becket. He is a sensitive actor, but has had scant preparation (or careful guidance) for this part. His long soliloquy proves how little effect sincerity alone can have in such a play without careful training in simple dramatic *reading*.

As to the play itself, now that I have seen it three times (once in Paris), I cannot agree with those who maintain that it is one of Anouilh's best plays. It has many of Anouilh's virtues, as well as some of his worst faults: the Roman scene between Pope and Cardinal is atrociously vulgar.

Those who are respectful of the play on intellectual, moral or religious grounds are fooling themselves. It is intellectually (as well as historically) skimpy; of true religious sentiment there is barely a trace, and its morality is without real commitment. Instead of speaking of the "honor of God," Anouilh might more fittingly have spoken of the honor of one's job. Becket, as Chancellor, had defended Henry (that is what the head of a state is supposed to do); so, as Archbishop, Becket fights for the Church (or God) against the state, since that is what is demanded of a prince of the Church. If the play espouses a precept it is: stand for *some* principle. Perhaps even this is helpful at a time when no principles beyond success and self-interest seem to obtain.

CRITICAL COMMENTARY

Emil Roy (essay date December 1965)

SOURCE: Roy, Emil. "The Becket Plays: Eliot, Fry, and Anouilh." *Modern Drama* 8, no. 3 (December 1965): 268-76.

[*In the following essay, Roy underscores the differences between T. S. Eliot's* Murder in the Cathedral, *Christopher Fry's* Curtmantle, *and Anouilh's* Becket.]

Within the last three decades the martyrdom of Thomas Becket has furnished dramatic material for notable plays of T. S. Eliot, Christopher Fry, and Jean Anouilh.[1] *Murder in the Cathedral* (1935) and all of Fry's work including *Curtmantle* (1961) stem directly from Eliot's determination to have a poetic drama. Although Anouilh's play **Becket, or the Honor of God** (1961) owes little or nothing to Eliot or a theory of poetic drama, all three writers have dissociated themselves from modern realism. As Francis Fergusson has said in another context, they use the stage, the characters, and the story to demonstrate an idea which they take to be the undiscussible truth.[2] Eliot takes dramatic root in classical Greek and medieval morality plays, the Elizabethans and metaphysicals. Fry is distinctly Shavian, and Anouilh has singled out a performance of Pirandello's *Six Characters in Search of an Author* for its seminal impact on his work. Just as significant is the fact that although both *Murder* and *Curtmantle* are the culminations of a long and publicly debated process of theory and experimentation, they are apparently both dead-ends. Eliot never again used either a martyrdom or such a dazzling array of verse so prominently. Fry's play—which appeared after a "crisis of confidence" lasting nine years—may have ended his playwriting career. Anouilh's **Becket,** on the other hand, is still another illustration of human alienation from a sterile universe but one presenting a more mature, positive hero than had his earlier plays.

It could be said that Eliot's construction is focused and ritualistic, Fry's is panoramic and historical, and Anouilh's is musical and choreographic. This convenient scheme, which is useful if not applied too arbitrarily, would place *Murder* in a "theater of ideas," *Curtmantle* in a "theater of characters," and **Becket** in a "theater of situations." However, Eliot and Fry are both Christian. In agreeing to accept a being prior to existence, they seem less existentialist than Anouilh, Sartre, and their French contemporaries. Like Becket, Anouilh's protagonists refuse to accept any standards other than those they adopt for themselves. "I was a man without honor," Anouilh's Becket tells Henry. "And suddenly I found it . . . the honor of God. A frail, incomprehensible honor."

(114) But when Becket says in *Curtmantle*, "What a man is precedes experience" (40), he speaks for Fry who has attacked Sartre's existentialism in a recent letter: "In the main I find that kind as full of holes as a cullinder."[3] Even those of Fry's characters who have no insight into mystery are true children of life, differing from his heroes only in their lack of perception, O. Mandel points out.[4] Not nature but human nature is chaotic, splitting the reason away from the emotions. As Dynamene says in *A Phoenix Too Frequent,* "When the thoughts are alert for life, the instincts rage for destruction."[5] Man is responsible for accepting life, not for imposing his moral standards on it.

On the other hand Fry rejects Eliot's contention that human nature shares in the evil which befell all nature after the Fall, an idea stressed in *Murder* by the chorus:

> We are soiled by a filth that we cannot clean, united to
>   supernatural vermin
> It is not we alone, it is not the house, it is not the city that
>   is defiled,
> But the world that is wholly foul.
>
>   (214)

Fry sees evil as a consequence of man's consciousness that he must die and love for life the supreme good. "Dear Christ," Henry muses, "the day that any man would dread / Is when life goes separate from the man." (73) Thus he necessarily emphasizes vices and shortcomings rather than active evil in his protagonists. Eliot has made his position clear in his 1930 essay on Baudelaire. Striking out at the "Life-Forcers" for their failure to show much concern for the letter, he insists that the spirit is not enough. "A Christian martyrdom is no accident. . . . A martyr, a saint, is always made by the design of God" (199), Thomas preaches. Only a formal religion can provide a necessary moral and ethical order (although Eliot's orthodoxy mellowed later).

Their thematic differences also extend into character. In Fry's Henry the flaw is not a lack of heroism but too much of it, the king "not content to be one man, and not the human race." (13) A childish fascination with power obsesses Anouilh's Henry, balanced by the obsession with honor which dominates Becket. Although different from Eliot's, as J. Dierickx says, Anouilh's theater elevates characters "whose isolation is the result of some mysterious election, some disturbing vocation—for purity if not for sainthood."[6] The French existentialists usually set their heroes far above the inferior spiritual position of the placid, self-satisfied bourgeois. This pattern resembles the opposition of Understanding Hero-Blind Chorus which Dierickx sees as a familiar theme in Eliot's work. But in Eliot an implacable, nearly immobile fixation on the eternal is embodied in his saint who "no longer desires anything for himself, not even the glory of martyrdom." (199-200) While the title character in Anouilh's *Becket* (as in nearly all his plays) rejects the compromises of life in favor of an aesthetic ideal of purity, Fry's antagonists become embodiments of a historical dialectic. Eleanor tells Henry and Thomas,

> Together, we might have made a world of progress
> Between us, by our three variants of human nature,
> You and Becket and me, we could have been
> The complete reaching forward.

(47)

Eliot's Becket, however, moves and does not move—through a spiritual dialectic which resembles but is not part of the changes in the human soul, earthly governments, and the seasons.

If Eliot's play ends in the exaltation which the Chorus shares by its recognition and acceptance of the meaning of Becket's death and beatification, *Curtmantle* climaxes in the terror of the destruction of Henry's realm and family, pity for his tortured and defiled body, and tragic enlightenment. His retainer Marshal terms him "a man / Who had gone through life saving up all passion / To spend at last on his own downfall." (70) Anouilh's *Becket,* rather, ends with the ironic compromise, the final union of the king's and God's honor which renders both meaningless and worthless. "The honor of God," Henry cynically observes, "is a very good thing, and taken all in all, one gains by having it on one's side." (128) Unlike Anouilh, neither Fry nor Eliot is very interested in rationalizing Thomas's motives for resisting Henry. Near the beginnings of *Murder* and *Curtmantle,* both of them clarify the issues, though Eliot's concept of varieties of sin in conflict with good is replaced in Fry with a superhuman contest involving "the interplay of different laws" (ix), political and spiritual. Anouilh's Becket, however, carries on an incessant game of aspiration: "We must only do—absurdly—what we have been given to do—right to the end." (114) He frankly rejects any conception of an orderly spiritual structure within the universe and insists on an almost romantic testing of his consciousness on his pulses.

Turning to the plays in question, an idea or more precisely, an intuition prior to perception, dominates Eliot's play. *Murder* yokes the metaphysical concreteness of verse to an idealized Christian theology, setting forth the martyrdom of a saint for the spiritual refreshment of a saving remnant. With the deliberateness of ritual and the elegance of dance, Thomas Becket fulfills his destiny in terms of divine, human, and natural phases. The precise approaches of the four Tempters, each of them going a step beyond his predecessor, are formally duplicated by the frenzied, drunken accusa-tions, murder and self-defence of the four knights. Every speech reflects by intonation the kind of idea, class, level of intelligence, progress of the action and mounting danger to Thomas. Yet the play has more of the logically ordered *Symposium* in its movement than the *Bacchae* or any morality play. The very paucity of its literal, recognizable, concrete detail lifts the mind forcefully into interpretation while its insistence on reason above reason casts the mind back upon dumb faith: "They know and do not know, what it is to act or suffer." (182)

Anouilh's *Becket* is a study of good and bad faith, in which each of the situations demonstrates the acceptance or rejection of essences in favor of freedom to choose. Becket in turn is confidant, chancellor, archbishop, enemy, and victim of the King, but he never surrenders his drive for order in the name of honor. Although he comes to identify himself with a heroic desire for an impossible absolute, he clearly doubts the existence of any moral order shaping the universe. What looks like morality in him is only aesthetics, says Henry. Becket longs for an ethical code with the self-contained purity and completeness of an art object and finds his ideal only in death.

All the other characters sharpen the cutting edge of Becket's quest, for the situations rather than his character evolve. The comically inept Pope and his retainers graphically illustrate the corruption of wit by sterile function. If Becket's heroism is measured against the petty craftiness and intrigues of his peers, Henry is a caricature of Carlyle's great man: "I am prepared to forget a lot of things, but not that I am king." (112) He is a childish worshiper of power, a mean, despicable, and impulsive character. Henry is just wise enough to appreciate Becket's enormous abilities, and cunning enough to seek to make of him a servant. Only his self-pitying weaknesses, his passionate need for Beckett's love and his occasional frankness grant him a measure of sympathy. Gwendolyn's suicide supports the view that a perfect love between either men or man and woman cannot be maintained in this life, that death is preferable to compromise. Like his one-time mistress, Thomas chooses to die when all freedom to choose another course has been taken from him.

In *Curmantle* Becket has chosen to identify his life so completely with the Church that he is little more than an instrument, its "tongue" to be "used in argument" (21) between the State and the Church. Aside from minor idiosyncrasies, he closely resembles Eliot's figure. Fry's Henry, unlike Thomas is far more three dimensional. We become aware of his self-aggrandizement, his deep sense of family and personal loyalties, his furious temper, his passion for order, and his identification with simple absolutes. Dierickx notes that the Eliotic hero develops "towards renunciation, submission, acceptance, instead of violence and struggle; while Fry presents a man who is suddenly seized in a whirlwind of passion, after having however doubted his own capacities."[7] Fry is more interested in the man Henry than in the situations which inspire Anouilh or in Eliot's theological scheme, although his progression does have a certain abstract aptness.

From his first confrontation with Becket, Henry envisions a utopian embodiment for his personal dreams, a form of worldly immortality. By assuming godlike prerogatives he justifies his overconfident manipulations of wife, family, church, and kingdom. But Thomas prefers the more intellectualized perspective of innumerable alternatives to Henry's perfect conformity. The significance for him of choice or free will lies in the testing of character, not in any final resolution. Man's attempt to complete the victory of good over evil in this world would only cut off "the deep roots of disputation / Which dug in the dust, and formed Adam's body." (21)

Once Henry has committed his initial act of pride—naming Becket to fill the posts both of Chancellor and Archbishop, Becket is effectively deprived of meaningful choice. Henry finds himself trapped by the life-force no less than Thomas had. His ideal of English common law takes on a vitality of its own which bends Henry rather than stemming from him as he had wished.

Both Fry and Eliot fail to convincingly dramatize Becket's inner struggle between pride and acquiescence. But by stressing the theme of Law, Fry has found a useful equivalent for the "wheel" of fate which seems so abstract in *Murder.* For whether or not Becket "willed" his death, his martyrdom removed the church's opposition to the political supremacy of the secular government and affirmed the subordination of human to divine justice. Fry's denouement involves moral values but does not depend upon any final resolution of their conflicting claims. Thomas's spiritual ideal is ironically embodied in Henry's social instrument.

Poetic drama, as David E. Jones suggests in his book on Eliot, aims at organic unity, the crystallization of meaning in imagery, and a capacity for lifting the action onto a plane of universal significance.[8] Since only Eliot and Fry write in English verse often dense with imagery, only their plays could be compared fairly in this regard. Three years after *Murder* was produced in 1935, Fry used the same three-level scheme of character presentation in the short, primitivist *The Boy with a Cart.* His choral "People of South England" speak image-clogged blank verse while, like Eliot's murderers, minor characters often speak racier prose. The themes of martyrdom and church-building as in Eliot's earlier *The Rock* are used, and the sun-image becomes Fry's equivalent for the wheel Louis Martz has singled out as Eliot's presiding image.[9] But *Curtmantle* is separated both from *Murder* and Fry's own derivative early experiment by six mature plays. And in his final effort we find some of the spareness of verse toward which Eliot's own later plays moved. Both writers, it seems, have found it impossible either to be satisfied with a coterie audience or to use the whole range of lyric verse in a bourgeois theater of prose realism. Eliot has never been expansive. On the other hand, Fry's looseness has always plagued him with structural problems: after *Curtmantle*'s première he commented wryly to an interviewer from *Time*: "There are several plays here."[10] Despite Fry's early indebtedness to Eliot and his continued admiration of *Murder,* important differences emerge in their uses of poetry.

Recurrent images in the plays are similar: the Waste Land, seasons, beasts and birds, everyday tasks and the blood of redemption, an "under-pattern" Jones has traced through *Murder* in some detail. Fry had long since abandoned Eliot's stair-stepped characters on three levels of perception: the order of nature (represented by the chorus), the order of the mind (the priests, tempters and murderers) and finally the order of charity (Thomas). Yet both writers have conservative world-views. They assume that the universe has a Ptolemaic form and pressure. The bodies of man, the world and the cosmos are symbolically fitted within one another like concentric bowls or hoops. Their magnitudes may seem vastly different, it is true, but only to the unaided eye. To the awakened imagination, each is a microor macrocosm of the other. Many examples could be drawn from both Fry and Eliot:

> What is woven on the loom of fate,
> What is woven in the councils of princes
> Is woven also in our veins, our brains
>
>   (208)

say Eliot's chorus. When the witty uses of irony are added to this vast stock of comparisons, the possibilities for richness of texture and illumination are multiplied.

But while Fry's poetry confirms Henry's motivations as the action amplifies or distorts them, Eliot's is peculiarly abstract in reference; it often stands for the unseen or even the unknowable. *Curtmantle*'s imagery is man-in-society centered. Eliot's figures revolve about the theological paradoxes of acting and suffering. As Martz says, Becket's death is the still point of the world that turns within the play.[11]

Nearly all the images in *Murder* are literally circular or cyclical in a larger rhythmic sense. The unity of action and suffering within a single concept of God as Unmoved Mover are contained in the phrase, "the wheel may turn and still / Be forever still." (182) In Thomas's mind the wheel implies theological patterns of rise and fall: into grace from life, into heavenly glory from wordly disgrace, into divine vindication from earthly injustice. The alternating rise and fall of the seasons, empires and individual destinies are assimilated by Becket's wheel, visually formed at the end by the knights' swords with Thomas as the still point.

With few exceptions Thomas's images are banal, even embarrassingly flat: "the purple bullfinch in the lilac tree" (196) is unusual. Only for the priests, tempters and murderers who understand in terms of the reason does Thomas have the central position granted Henry by nearly all Fry's language. The priests see him as steersman, anvil to Henry's hammer, the firm rock in a sea of political strife. His stability at the wheel's center contrasts with the sinful waverings of mankind. In the minds of the tempters, however, Thomas fits into the cycle of hunter and hunted, eater and the eaten (with sacrificial and sacramental overtones reflecting Eliot's Dionysian and Christian sources). He is a cooked goose, an old stag circled by hounds, a morsel thrown to a thousand hungry appetites, or the unwary prey of hooks and traps. For the knights, in their sordid lust and anger, he has crept upon Henry's shirt like a blood-swollen louse.

Only in the language of the completely uncomprehending Women of Canterbury are the full potentialities of the similar, but discontinuous realms of body, earth and cosmos developed. Balanced opposites such as light and dark, cold and heat, high and low are complemented with progressions such as approach and withdrawal, ecstasy and indifference, pain and lassitude. Kenner rightly suspects that the incredible richness and allusiveness of the choral speeches must certainly be wasted on an audience as they tumble over and interact with one another.[12] One of the choral themes is fear of God's love more than of the violence of man. Balanced metaphors of emergence-from-withinness and impingement-from-withoutness suggest, respectively, their fears of inner demons and of outer violations. Innerness involves the heaving of a sick, laboring earth, cold in the groin, unskinning of onion-like brains, and bestial forms taking shape from thick air. From outside come the poking wind and tapping rain, corruption in the dish and incense in the latrine, root and shoot consuming eyes and ears: all death-bringers. Another overlapping theme is feeling in nullity: of eating and being eaten, of dissolving, of taking meaningless journeys. The chorus's perceptions are almost wholly kinetic, sensuous and visceral. So much of their imagery suggests both the unreality of what is perceived, along with the over-intensity of sensation and intuition. Becoming is the only reality to the chorus, while being is rarely glimpsed and then miraculously, "in a shaft of sunlight." (176)

What is incidental for Eliot becomes central for Fry. In *Curtmantle* the King focuses and complicates most of Fry's imagery. Henry figuratively appears as both steersman for the ship of state and as the ice, storms, and rocks which endanger it. He is both physician and disease for the body politic, blacksmith and metal for the country's disused framework, harrowing Christ and infernal labyrinth through which Englishmen wander. He is rationalist and priest, unifier and divider. The ironic complexity of his metonyms confirms the enormous gulf between his idealized goals and his ruthless methods, between his failure to provide an orderly transfer of power and the viability of the legal system he bequeaths his country. Thus Henry is England's sun and its darkness, its water and wasteland, both traveler and roadway.

While Eliot's still-turning wheel is dominant, in *Curtmantle* the cutting and revolving circle recurs compulsively at moments of crisis. Crowns, nests, rings, skulls and blood, a bull-fight arena and the Eliotic circle of swordsmen occur at various moments when Henry's security and authority are threatened. And the destructive splitting-apart of values, friends, and realm emerges in images of double and half-ness: double vision and two-ness of kingdoms, images and worlds. The effect is summed up wryly as "redemption by divine arithmetic." (19) Despite the orderliness and often striking relevance of Fry's imagery, it sometimes lacks the solidity and palpability so characteristic of Eliot, whose language penetrates to a core of archetype and ritual.

Given the dedicated, Christian commitment of his audience and the suspension of *Murder*'s time-scheme between 1170 and 1935, Eliot could make rigorous demands on both his auditors and his medium. His occasionally slashing attacks on tyranny are stated in often dense, ironic imagery within a pageant-like form close to litany. Its particular angle of perception rests upon *revealed* truth, a truth which in Fergusson's terms is at once reasoned and beyond reason.[13] If common sense and observation conflict with the lessons of martyrdom, that is one of Eliot's points. Fry's shift of emphasis from Thomas to Henry results from his attempt to dovetail the King's historical character with the more abstract theme of conflicting legal systems, civil, religious, moral, and divine. This entails a richer sweep of panoramic detail, more psychological depth and a looser kind of prosaic dialogue than either of his contemporaries use. Though willing to meet the demands of an easily-bored, unsophisticated audience, Fry has linked his brilliant, witty imagery to the whole play as carefully and artfully as Eliot has done. Anouilh is more secular, more radical and more existentialist than either of his English contemporaries. He has adopted a sparer, more theatricalist form to focus on a simpler loyalty-revenge relationship in a chaotic, impinging universe. Neither Fry nor Eliot are willing to find their worlds as disorderly and shapeless nor the conventions of their theater as acceptable as Anouilh. For the allusive, ironic resources of their—and perhaps most—verse depend rather heavily, it seems, upon the poet's acceptance of an ordered cosmos. Within this diverse design, allusive and ironic poetry can extend man's minutest perceptions at the same time it mirrors his incredible variety, as it has in *Murder in the Cathedral* and *Curtmantle*.

Notes

1. Texts cited in this study include Eliot's "Murder in the Cathedral," *The Complete Poems and Plays: 1909-1950* (New York, 1958), 173-221, Fry's *Curtmantle* (New York, 1961), and Anouilh's *Becket,* trans. Lucienne Hill (New York, 1964).

2. "Three Allegorists: Brecht, Wilder and Eliot," *The Human Image in Dramatic Literature* (Garden City, 1957), p. 41.

3. Letter of April 1, 1964.

4. "Theme in the Drama of Christopher Fry," *Etudes Anglaises,* X (October-December 1957), 337.

5. (London, 1946), p. 18.

6. "King and Archbishop: Henry II and Becket from Tennyson to Fry," *Revue des Langues Vivantes,* XXVIII (1961-62), p. 428.

7. P. 430.

8. *The Plays of T. S. Eliot* (London, 1960), p. 17.

9. "The Wheel and the Point: Aspects of Imagery and Theme in Eliot's Later Poetry," *Sewanee Review,* LV (Winter 1947), 126-147.

10. "Theatre Abroad: Return of the Phoenix," Vol. 77, no. 11 (March 11, 1961), p. 68.

11. P. 129.

12. *The Invisible Poet: T. S. Eliot* (Rahway, N. J., 1959), p. 284.

13. *The Idea of a Theatre* (Princeton, 1949), p. 220.

Jesse C. Gatlin Jr. (essay date December 1965)

SOURCE: Gatlin, Jesse C., Jr. "*Becket* and Honor: A Trim Reckoning." *Modern Drama* 8, no. 3 (December 1965): 277-83.

[*In the following essay, Gatlin investigates the role of honor in* Becket.]

> What is honor? A word. What is in that word honor? What is that honor? Air. A trim reckoning! . . . Honor is a mere scutcheon.
>
> —FALSTAFF in *Henry IV,* Part I

> Honor travels in a strait so narrow,
>
> Where one but goes abreast.
>
> —ULYSSES in *Troilus and Cressida*

Jean Anouilh uses the phrase "The Honor of God" as the sub-title of his play *Becket.* In the English translation of the play by Lucienne Hill,[1] the word "honor" appears more than twenty times, spoken by a variety of characters in a variety of situations.[2] It is as if Anouilh were determined to explore the meaning of the word by a sort of comprehensive dramatic demonstration of what is really essential to this abstraction which so many characters in the play use so glibly.

The term is first used in the opening scene of the play as King Henry, kneeling before the tomb of Becket to accept the lash as public penance for his part in Becket's murder, evokes in his mind the presence of the murdered man:

KING:

. . . Don't you think we'd have done better to understand each other?

BECKET:

Understand each other? It wasn't possible.

KING:

I said, "In all save the honor of the realm." It was you who taught me that slogan, after all.

BECKET:

I answered you, "In all save the honor of God." We were like two deaf men talking.

(pp. 11-12)

Here at the very start of the opening scene in the play, Anouilh defines the conflict which is to be explored, a conflict between two men's concepts of honor.

After this opening scene the next reference to "honor" occurs in a conversation in which Becket and Henry discuss Becket's background. Becket reveals that his father, a Saxon, had amassed "a considerable fortune" by collaborating dutifully with the Norman conquerors. Prodded by Henry, Becket admits his own reasons for collaborating:

BECKET:

. . . I adore hunting and only the Normans and their / proteges had the right to hunt. I adore luxury and luxury was Norman. I adore life and the Saxons' only birthright was slaughter. I'll add that I adore honor.

KING:

(*With faint surprise*) And was honor reconciled with collaboration too?

BECKET:

> (*Lightly*) I had the right to draw my sword against the first Norman nobleman who tried to lay hands on my sister. I killed him in single combat. It's a detail, but it has its points.

> (pp. 15-16)

Becket's "points" of honor here appear bluntly expedient, for he goes on to explain that, because of his honorable defense of her, his sister is now "respected" by the Norman barons. There is a hint here that she has perhaps been accepted as a mistress by one of the barons, rather than merely lusted after as an object of rape. Such are the wages of Becket's "honor" at this stage.

The next reference to honor occurs just after the drunken Henry needles Becket about his concept of morality. Henry has come to demand Becket's mistress, Gwendolyn, in return for having yielded to Becket a young Saxon peasant girl whom he, the King, had impulsively decided to bring to the palace as a concubine. Beckett had intended to leave the girl with her family, but after foreclosing his bargain by taking Gwendolyn, the King produces the Saxon girl to fulfill his part of the agreement.

KING:

> . . . What looks like morality in you is nothing more than esthetics. Is that true or isn't it?

BECKET:

> (*Meeting his eyes, says softly*) It's true, my Lord.

KING:

> I'm not cheating if I ask for her, am I? I said "favor for favor" and I asked you for your word of honor.

BECKET:

> (*Icily*) And I gave it to you.

> (p. 42)

Here Becket's "word of honor" is used as a weapon against him by the King, and we see a brutal unfolding of the irony that Becket's "honor" is merely a "word of honor." As he bids farewell to Gwendolyn, before she leaves with Henry to commit suicide in his litter, she says to Becket,

> You belong to a conquered race too. But through tasting too much of the honey of life, you've forgotten that even those who have been robbed of everything have one thing left to call their own.

> (p. 44)

Becket's reply leaves no doubt that he knows her meaning:

> Yes, I daresay, I had forgotten. There is a gap in me where honor ought to be. Go now.

> (p. 44)

She goes—and kills herself.

Perhaps his "honor" had saved his sister from rape by the lustful barons, but here it betrays his devoted mistress and makes a mockery of his professed concern for the women of the conquered race. Gwendolyn's action here becomes, within the structure of the play, both a foreshadowing and a pattern for the definition of honor that Becket himself is finally to reach. The nature of her love for Becket, unreciprocated though it is, is echoed later in Becket's love for what he calls the honor of God—a love which also may be unreciprocated. The point is that both Gwendolyn and Becket make a total commitment to an ideal which ultimately they are forced not only to live for but to die for—and both of them live and die for it unhesitatingly. Appropriately enough, the next reference to honor comes as Becket soliloquizes over the sleeping Henry, who has returned in fear to spend the night with Becket after Gwendolyn's suicide has unnerved him:

> . . . You can sleep peacefully though, my prince. So long as Becket is obliged to improvise his honor, he will serve you. And if one day, he meets it face to face. . . .

> (*A short pause*)

> But where is Becket's honor?

> (p. 47)

Here at the end of the first act we see that "honor," one of the "labels" Becket had referred to earlier as being necessary to give shape to the world in order that we can "know what we're doing" (p. 27), has become for him an enigmatic label indeed. No longer can he apply it indiscriminately to whatever act or notion it seems to identify; he is beginning to learn the truth that for him action plus its consequences, not merely impulsive action itself, are involved in the idea of honor.

In the second act of the play two brief references to "honor" serve to underscore the baffling multiplicity of meanings which the word can convey and to emphasize the degree to which, as Humpty Dumpty says in *Alice in Wonderland,* a word "means just what I want it to mean—neither more nor less." Becket is speaking to one of Henry's dunderheaded Norman barons:

1ST BARON:

> And a soldier's honor, my Lord Chancellor, what of that?

BECKET:

> (*Dryly*) A soldier's honor, Baron, is to win victories.

Then, a little later in the conversation:

1ST BARON:

> What about England's honor, then?

BECKET:

> (*Quietly*) England's honor, Baron, in the final reckoning, has always been to succeed.

(p. 52)

These words "England's honor . . . has always been to succeed," already echoed in Henry's reference to "the honor of the realm," are to echo again in the final line of the play, compounding the irony of Becket's murder and martyrdom and highlighting the truth that "honor," as Becket has existentially defined it, bears little real relation to "honor" as Henry continues to use it.

Becket's conversation with the barons shows that at this point he shares Henry's conception of "honor" as merely an expedient label for a public image. But in a confrontation of the two men a little later, their diverging interpretations become apparent. Grief stricken when Becket, whom he has now made Archbishop of Canterbury, returns to him the seal of the Lord Chancellor's post, Henry cries:

> You've sent me back the Three Lions of England, like a little boy who doesn't want to play with me any more. You think you have God's honor to defend now! I would have gone to war with all England's might behind me, and against England's interests, to defend you, little Saxon. I would have given the honor of the Kingdom laughingly . . . for you. . . . Only I loved you and you didn't love me . . . that's the difference.

(p. 79)

Here Henry sees and defines the crux of the conflict: Is honor a concept to be defined and defended at the sacrifice of personal feelings, or is it to be a "laughingly" yielded pawn in a game of image-making?

To emphasize the significance of Becket's newly developing concept, he confronts the corrupt Folliot, Bishop of London, with the reminder that "we are men of God and that we have an Honor [the capitalization is Anouilh's] to defend, which dates from all eternity" (p. 88), and then goes on to elaborate:

> . . . The Kingdom of God must be defended like any other Kingdom. Do you think that Right has only to show its handsome face for everything to drop in its lap? Without Might, its old enemy, Right counts for nothing.

(p. 89)

There is an echo here of Becket's statement to the barons that the honor of the soldier is to win victories and the honor of England is to succeed, but the cynicism of these earlier utterances is entirely absent. It becomes apparent that he is learning well that the word "honor" can be defined only as a result of commitments and the consequences of commitments. It is becoming for him more than a meaningless label.

There follows a series of scenes in which several confrontations—between King Louis of France and Bishop Folliot acting as Henry's ambassador, between the Pope and one of his Cardinals, and between King Louis and Becket himself—serve to reiterate the uses of "honor" as a merely expedient label and to demonstrate that in the world from which Becket is separating himself honor is still what it has always been: a public image to be sacrificed or salvaged as the occasion warrants. The sordid political maneuverings shown in these confrontations serve to remind us that Becket's soul-searching quest for the essence of honor is indeed a lonely one against overwhelming odds. He is like a man groping blindfolded for a virgin within a brothel where all the whores are named Honor and all the customers keep shouting the name of the one they prefer. It is a world that Becket has known only too well—and that Henry lives in continuously.

After a period of enforced exile in France, Becket finally resolves to end his banishment, and he petitions King Louis to help him return to England. As he says,

> I am a Primate of England. That is a rather showy label on my back. The honor of God and common sense, which for once coincide, dictate that instead of risking the knife thrust of some hired assassin, on the highway, I should go and have myself killed—if killed I must be—clad in my golden cope, with my miter on my head and my silver cross in my hand, among my flock in my own cathedral.

(p. 106)

King Louis, after remarking that "the honor of God is a very cumbersome thing," agrees to help and arranges the final climactic confrontation of Becket with Henry on the windy plain at La Forté-Bernard. In that scene, the conflict comes to a head and is defined with lucid finality. The word "honor" tolls like a bell throughout the scene:

BECKET:

> (*Quietly*) I'm waiting for the honor of God and the honor of the King to become one.

KING:

> You'll wait a long time then!

(p. 110)

. . . . .

BECKET:

> . . . I was a man without honor. And suddenly I found it—one I never imagined would ever become mine— the honor of God. A frail, incomprehensible honor, vulnerable as a boy-King fleeing from danger.

(p. 112)

(The allusion here recalls the scene when Henry had fled in terror to Becket's chamber after Gwendolyn's suicide in defense of her honor.)

. . . . .

BECKET:

> I shall agree to the nine other articles in a spirit of peace, and because I know that you must remain King—in all save the honor of God.
>
> (*A pause*)

KING:

> (*Coldly*) Very well. I will help you defend your God, since that is your new vocation, in memory of the companion you once were to me—in all save the honor of the Realm.
>
> (p. 113)

. . . . .

(*Suddenly*) You never loved me, did you, Becket?

BECKET:

> In so far as I was capable of love, yes, my prince, I did.

KING:

> Did you start to love God?
>
> (*He cries out:*)
>
> You mule! Can't you ever answer a simple question?

BECKET:

> (*Quietly*) I started to love the honor of God.
>
> (p. 114)

Note here the crucial qualification in Becket's reply. He loved not God, but the *honor* of God. This word, this scutcheon, this shaping label now is firmly defined within the heart of Thomas Becket, and it serves to show him the shape and the demands of the new world he has created for himself out of chaos.

Becket completes his definition of the word by his unresisting acceptance of death at the hands of Henry's barons. His last cry to God as he dies under their swords is, "Oh how difficult You make it all! And how heavy Your honor is to bear!" (p. 126)

The final scene completes the envelope within which the action of the play takes place. Henry absorbs his lashing and during it cries out, "Are you satisfied now, Becket? Does this settle our account? Has the honor of God been washed clean?" (p. 126) Then, the lashing completed, he addresses his barons "with a touch of hypocritical majesty beneath his slightly loutish manner":

The honor of God, gentlemen, is a very good thing, and taken all in all, one gains by having it on one's side.

(p. 127)

He goes on to decree that Becket shall be "honored and prayed to in this Kingdom as a saint" (p. 127); and after he appoints Becket's murderer to inquire into the murder, the play ends with his cynical statement that "no one will be in any doubt as to our Royal desire to defend the honor of God and the memory of our friend from this day forward." (p. 128) He walks out of the cathedral to the cheers of his Saxon subjects, whose services he needs to fight his wars and whose loyalty he has just cynically purchased at the cost of Becket's honor.

There is a disturbing ambiguity of effect at the end of the play. As he is portrayed, Becket has many of the attributes of a tragic hero: his noble death partakes of the tragic essence and evokes that sense of waste so prominent in our response to such deaths. Yet the framework scene that opens and closes the play is in the comic mode. Henry begins the play, and he ends it. He is still the successful king, so long as we accept his values as valid criteria for success. His use of Becket's honor—even of God's honor, and in the play the two are finally synonymous—for his own expedient advantage undercuts the tragedy of Becket and places the whole play in a context of irony.

But perhaps more pertinent to this discussion is the existential definition of the concept of honor. Looking back over the play, one sees that Anouilh has used the word as a dramatic demonstration of the existential notion that a man is the sum of his *acts* and that the essence of a concept must follow and not precede the acts themselves which define it. The word itself is, in truth, merely a label. To Becket the label comes to mean an ideal to serve, to live for, and ultimately to die for. But Becket's honor is achieved in solitude and defined in and by the actions to which he attaches the name; his definition is neither acceptable nor understandable to Henry nor to the world in which Henry has chosen to live. The label, however, is available to that world, and at the end of the play it is still as usefully expedient, as terrifyingly viable, as ironically impervious to abstract absolute definition as it has ever been. Anouilh hammers home the point that each man is effectively his own universe, condemned to strive, alone and unaided, wrestling his huge boulder up his chosen hill, and forced forever to find his justice and his reward not in the view from the hilltop nor in the satisfaction of reaching it, but in the lonely, never-ending task itself of labelling his burdens to suit his direst needs.

Notes

1. (New York, 1960). All page references are to this edition.

2. A comparison with the French text of the play reveals that in every instance except one, the word "honor" in the Hill translation is a literal rendering of the French *honneur.*

FURTHER READING

Criticism

Atkinson, Brooks. "Lark in London, Tells Life of the Martyr." *New York Times* (13 May 1955): 21-2.
    Unfavorably compares *The Lark* to George Bernard Shaw's *St. Joan.*

Gill, Brendan. "Enemy Country." *New Yorker* (1 October 1973): 59.
    Mixed review of the 1973 New York production of *The Waltz of the Toreadors.*

———. Review of *The Waltz of the Toreadors,* by Jean Anouilh. *New York Times* (17 January 1957): 17-18.
    Laudatory assessment of the 1957 New York production of *The Waltz of the Toreadors.*

Nichols, Lewis. Review of *Antigone,* by Jean Anouilh. *New York Times* (24 February 1946): 1.
    Calls the 1940 New York production of *Antigone* unfulfilling and disappointing.

Taubman, Howard. "Laurence Olivier Stars in Anouilh Version." *New York Times* (5 October 1960): 50-1.
    Mixed assessment of Anouilh's *Becket.*

Additional coverage of Anouilh's life and career is contained in the following sources published by the Gale Group: *Contemporary Authors,* **Vols. 17-20R;** *Contemporary Authors New Revision Series,* **Vol. 32;** *Contemporary Authors—Obituary,* **Vol. 123;** *Contemporary Literary Criticism,* **Vols. 1, 3, 8, 13, 40, 50;** *DISCovering Authors: Dramatists; Drama Criticism,* **Vol. 8;** *Drama for Students,* **Vols. 9, 10;** *Encyclopedia of World Literature in the 20th Century,* **Ed. 3;** *European Writers,* **Vol. 13;** *Guide to French Literature: 1789 to the Present; Literature Resource Center; Major 20th-Century Writers,* **Eds. 1, 2;** *Reference Guide to World Literature,* **Eds. 2, 3; and** *Twayne's World Authors.*

Henri Becque
1837-1899

(Full name Henri Francois Becque) French playwright.

The following entry presents criticism on Becque's life and works from 1913 through 1989.

INTRODUCTION

Through his plays, Becque introduced realism and naturalism to the French theater. He examined the French social classes from the nuclear bourgeois family in *Les Corbeaux* (1882; *The Vultures*) and addressed social issues of the time such as legalizing divorce in *L'Enlèvement* (1871; *The Abduction*). Becque's plays were at times considered controversial, especially *The Vultures* and *La Parisienne* (1885; *The Woman of Paris*). The controversy often made it difficult for Becque to get his work produced. In some instances, the audience would actually hiss through a performance as they did at the Theatre du Vaudeville during *The Abduction,* causing the play to only be performed five times. However, his literary work introduced the genre of *le comédie rosse*: bitter comedy. The naturalist style Becque presented in Paris and some of the most radical tendencies of his plays were explored by other writers outside of France including Henrik Ibsen, Anton Chekhov and Bertolt Brecht.

BIOGRAPHICAL INFORMATION

Becque was born April 18, 1837, to Alexandre-Louis and Jeanne Martin Becque in Paris. His father was a bookkeeper, which allowed Becque to consider his background as that of a petit bourgeois. He studied at the Lycée Bonaparte (Lycée Condorcet), but he did not attempt to pass the baccalaureate. In 1854 he held a job with the Chemins du fer du Nord (the Northern Railroad); other occupations Becque entertained included working as a stockbroker, a tutor and even a journalist. In 1865, Becque worked as a secretary for the Polish Count Potocki. His employment with the count provided an opportunity to participate in the Parisian theater where he met Victorin Joncieres, a young composer. Working with Joncieres, he wrote the libretto to the opera *Sardanapale* (1867). He followed

the opera with other plays, then entered the army to fight in the Franco-Prussian War. After the war, he returned to writing. Toward the end of his career, he began writing shorter plays to cater to theaters in Paris. Becque died homeless on May 12, 1899.

MAJOR WORKS

After working with Joncieres on *Sardanapale,* Becque wrote his first play, *L'Enfant prodigue* (1868; *The Prodigal Son,*), which tells the story of a young provincial who takes on a mistress, Clarisse, who in turn, is managing more than one affair. The characters in this first play, including a male character who becomes disillusioned, are typical of most of Becque's characters, which critics have considered to be one-dimensional. An impersonal reaction between social relations is a common theme and style carried through most of his plays.

The theme of a disillusioned young man is also found in Becque's next play, *Michel Pauper* (1870). This story revolves around a young man, Michel Pauper, and his demise because of his marriage. On his wedding night, Michel learns his bride is not a virgin, which leads him to destroy his diamond-manufacturing invention. Becque's play is considered a socialist play dealing with different levels of bourgeoisie effects on others. In the case of Michel Pauper, the petit bourgeois replaces the working class. Michel Pauper's character resembles many 19th-century European writers—such as Becque himself—because he is struggling and hoping for the life of those above his social status.

Becque examined another facet of French society when he wrote *The Abduction,* in which he argues for the legalization of divorce. The play details the relationship between Emma de Sainte-Croix and her husband, Raoul. After running away from her husband, another man declares his love for her. The other man is the husband of Emma's husband's mistress. By the end of the play, Becque rearranges the sexual relationships based on natural inclination. However, the play goes beyond sexual relationships and explores French society. Emma's unhappiness is due to her circumstances. She was married when she was young and had no knowledge of what marriage really was. As she matured, she became an intellectual woman her husband couldn't understand or bear. Emma begs Raoul for a separation, but he refuses, so eventually she leaves.

In *The Vultures,* Becque departs from flat, interchangeable characters. He changes his thematic focus from sex to money and its effect on a situation. *The Vultures* features two daughters, Marie and Blanche Vigneron, from an haute bourgeois family. In four acts, Becque takes the Vigneron family from their luxurious apartment to a shabby home. The family's money is stripped away by Teisser after the father dies. As Becque details their downfall, he adds humiliation when Blanche has to beg a woman to marry her son because of sexual relations and when Marie is forced to accept the marriage proposal of the man who helped destroy her family. *The Vultures* was not only a departure in style for Becque, but by providing a realistic look at society, it was also a departure from the conventional mid-to late-19th century theater.

Becque returned to a plot focusing on a woman managing multiple relationships in *The Woman of Paris.* In this play, his lead female character is a grande bourgeoisie. Again, like his earlier plays, the characters are accused of being interchangeable by critics.

CRITICAL RECEPTION

Critics have labeled Becque as the first French dramatist graduating from the naturalist school. Becque has also been classified as a realist who presents the play-going public a realistic look at society. Much of his work did not meet with popular approval, but Becque was unwilling to compromise and chose to produce his own plays. However, audiences found his work more curious than dramatically innovative and Becque withdrew from the theater for several years.

After completing *The Vultures,* it took Becque five years to get it produced. The first production proved a triumphant success and was acclaimed by a group of young playwrights. However, it was not until Andre Antoine founded the Theatre Libre, a theatrical group that rejected the banality and artificiality of contemporary French drama, that Becque's work found a sympathetic home.

In 1886, Becque was awarded the Legion of Honor. He later traveled to Italy where he was lionized as a brilliant dramatist, but at home, in France, he lived in poverty and solitude, receiving little income from his writing. Success came to Becque too late to inspire more works of the caliber of *The Vultures* and *The Woman of Paris.* Although his plays are rarely performed today, Becque holds a place of importance in the development of French drama.

PRINCIPAL WORKS

Plays

Sardanapale [with music by Victorin Joncieres] 1867
L'Enfant prodigue [*The Prodigal Son*] 1868
Michel Pauper 1870
L'Enlèvement [*The Abduction*] 1871
La Navette [*The Merry-Go-Round*] 1878
Les Honnêtes Femmes 1880
Les Corbeaux [*The Vultures*; *The Crows*] 1882
La Parisienne [*The Woman of Paris*] 1885
*Théâtre complet 2 vols. 1890
*Théâtre complet 3 vols. 1898
*Oeuvres complètes 7 vols. 1924-26

*These titles are collections of the complete dramatic works of Henry Becque.

GENERAL COMMENTARY

Freeman Tilden (essay date 1913)

SOURCE: Tilden, Freeman. "Introduction." In *The Vultures, The Woman of Paris, The Merry-Go-Round: Three Plays by Henry Becque,* pp. 7-8. New York: Mitchell Kennerley, 1913.

[In the following essay, Tilden provides an overview of Becque's produced plays, commenting that without the help of a few notable friends these productions would not have been possible.]

Henry Becque (1837-1899) was one of those men of letters to whom falls the ungrateful lot of giving the public what it does not want. In the very heyday of romanticism, Becque had the effrontery to hawk an entirely different line of wares in the Parisian theatrical markets. He boldly trespassed against the most sacred traditions built up and sustained under the guidance of Sardou. He flouted the "happy ending"; he questioned the infallibility of M. Sarcey; he even thought it possible to write a drama in five acts, when everybody knew that four acts must be the limit. Becque was a revolutionist.

Yet even revolutionists have friends and admirers. Becque had comparatively few, but those few were powerful enough to force the production of plays which, lacking this propulsion of friendship, could never have seen the light. One of these friends was Edouard Thierry, one-time director of the Comédie Française. Another, strange to say, was Sardou—that very Sardou against whose dramatic precepts Becque carried on a merciless warfare.

This man might have been popular. He was Parisian born. He had all the cleverness and knack and sophistication necessary to make him a brilliant transient on the stage of Paris. But he had a big dream, and the dream was to make the stage represent the marvellous dramatic commonplaces of every-day life. He saw that the sentimental nonsense with which the public was being regaled—high-class nonsense though some of it might be—represented a very small corner of Life, if it represented Life at all. The reaction of Becque's mind against the glorification of sentimental impossibilities was terrific. He conceived the idea of a "cruel theatre," in which truth should go defiantly bare; in which the characters should act like human beings instead of wire-worked puppets; in which the action should be the logical course of workday events, without the introduction of spurious material to keep the audience mystified or good-humored. In our day this is an old story. The tide turned against old-school romanticism long ago, and we

have our realism so refined that it often has less dramatic action than Life itself. If Becque had fallen into this trap—of being dull—that would have been the end of him. But he happened to be a master of stagecraft; and he knew how to manipulate the surprises of every-day existence, how to reproduce them with telling effect, how to tell a precise story so that the narration would be clear without being obvious. He had also an almost incredible persistence and faith in himself. He was a tireless worker. And he had some good friends. So he was permitted to drive the wedge that opened the way for realism. Becque's followers were many. More than one of them excelled the master in certain details, as was to be expected. They were not pioneering. They had a trail already blazed. It required a brutal strength like Becque's to knock over the idols of romance.

When Henry Becque first came knocking at the stage door, it was with an opera in three acts, *Sardanapale,* an avowed imitation of Lord Byron. With music by Victorin Joncières, a composer of merit, it was presented for the first time at the Théâtre Lyrique early in 1867. It enjoyed some success.

Following the opera came *L'Enfant Prodigue,* produced in 1868 at the Vaudeville. The freshness of this piece, with its unconventionality, its deliberately wicked and sometimes savage thrusts, combined with real wit and sprightliness, puzzled the critics a little. The dean of the profession, M. Sarcey, permitted himself to welcome the new dramatic author, and to praise him for his pleasant frivolity. M. Sarcey wrote rather gingerly, however. He evidently wanted to be in a position to beat a quick retreat. *The Prodigal Son* is certainly not great, but as a reading play it is good for the blues. And besides its wit, it contains at least one unexpectedly striking and powerful scene, that of the dinner of the *concierges.* In this scene *Clarisse* sings a curious street-girl song, "Les Pauvr's P'tit's Femmes," of exquisite humanness and pathos.

Following *The Prodigal Son,* it was to be expected that Becque, taking advantage of the foothold his vaudeville had given him, should come back with some joyous comedy. He appeared with a five-act drama, *Michel Pauper,* a play almost barbarous in its brutality. The wonder now is, not that it was not a success, but that it was ever presented at all. It must have seemed mad as a hatter in 1870. It does, indeed, at this distance, seem to have a touch of madness. It did demonstrate one thing, however: that Becque could construct a play. He used strange materials, he sounded uncanny depths, but he could write.

After the production of *L'Enlèvement* in 1871—a mordant comedy of provincial domesticity—Becque had nothing produced until *La Navette,* in 1878. This one-act comedy, translated in the present volume under the title **The Merry-Go-Round,** is light, malicious, even naughty on the surface. There is much under the surface. Becque's eyes were open in the seventies. He saw a lot of sham.

Les Honnêtes Femmes, another one-act comedy, was produced in 1880, and then Becque was at last engaged upon more enduring stuff. In the next five years were produced his two finished masterpieces, **Les Corbeaux** and **La Parisienne,** and a beginning was made of **Les Polichinelles,** unfortunately left undone at the dramatist's death.

Les Corbeaux (translated as **The Vultures** in this volume) was produced in 1882 at the Comédie Française. It was by mere chance that it was produced at all. Becque's difficulty was no longer that he was unknown; it was that the theatre-directors knew him only too well. He was a disturber of the peace of mind of quiet folks who wanted to "look on the bright side of things." He was the kind of author that puts out the lights at theatres in mid-season. Becque peddled **Les Corbeaux** from one theatre to another. It was rejected everywhere. Finally there was only one reputable theatre left, and that was the greatest of them all, the Comédie Française. Becque had not even considered the possibility of getting a hearing there. But M. Thierry read the play, and, though it staggered him a little, he recognized the genius in it. He was convinced that it should be put on. He was no longer at the head of the Comédie Française, but a request from him would, of course, be gracefully received by his successor, Émile Perrin. In this least promising of ways, **Les Corbeaux** had its first presentation at the famous theatre on September 14, 1882.

Les Corbeaux was not a play calculated to make its author a prime favorite among the run of play-goers. It hurt them. It assailed one of the darling institutions of the country, the notarial system. "You are attacking, offhand, the most respectable body of men I know of; you are bringing under suspicion the law itself," says *Bourdon,* the notary, in the second act of the play, in futile reply to the rude insinuations of the architect *Lefort.* That was just what Becque meant to do! He intended to reveal the possibilities of gross injustice, fraud and graft that lay within the hidebound, parochial and bureaucratic system which turned out *Bourdons,* and then, even against its will, felt bound to maintain them.

But worse even than his cold-blooded handling of tender subjects in particular, was Becque's general exaltation of the bourgeois viewpoint. "Exaltation" is a strong word, but it must have been a terrible blow, at a moment when the stage was dedicated to the depiction of chapters from the lives of the very nicest of people, to

find in **Les Corbeaux** that the only representatives of "an old family" were a vicious woman, dead broke and fortune-hunting, and her invertebrate son. Then, besides, Becque's stage settings were held to be too simple. The furnishings had been constantly growing more elaborate and expensive, and it seems that the arrangements of Becque might have come as a grateful relief to the theatre directors. It was not so. They didn't like it. It looked cheap.

Becque's social ideas were surprisingly "advanced." He sensed the wrongs of the little people, the underdogs in the struggle for existence. He voiced the protest of women against the prejudice that kept them from earning a decent livelihood and forced them, in one direction, to parasitism, and, in the other direction, to immorality.

Poor *Mrs. Vigneron!* So helplessly naïve and impractical was she that she could imagine herself at the head of her late husband's factory. *Bourdon,* the notary, disillusioned her on that point: "Would it look well for a woman to place herself at the head of a large establishment?"

La Parisienne, which had its first performance in 1885, was for other reasons a bitter pill to the public. Nobody questioned its wit. It was admitted that the diabolically clever dialogue of the first scene, leading up to the thunderbolt discovery of the audience that *Lafont* is not *Clotilde's* husband, but her lover, was alone worth the price of admission. But the critics, most of them, thought that Becque had slandered the Parisian woman. Someone said that the title of the play should be changed from **La Parisienne** to "Une Parisienne": but what the temper of the time could not forgive was the ruthlessness with which Henry Becque tore the veil of romance from illicit love—from adultery, if you please—and put it on the prosaic basis of every-day marriage. That was too much. However, as Mr. James Huneker remarks in his delightful essay on Becque, the conventional naughty triangle of the French theatre, after the presentation of **La Parisienne,** was done forever.

La Parisienne was Becque's last play. At the time of his death he was at work upon **Les Polichinelles,** a play even more militant in its social ideas than the others. But though there is reason for regret that Becque's work was cut short, it is certain that with his three volumes of plays he had performed his special mission. It is not too much to say that when Ibsen came upon the field with his great dramas, he had a decided advantage in his struggle from taking possession of the breastworks thrown up and manned by Henry Becque.

Nation (essay date 28 May 1914)

SOURCE: "The Stage of Henri Becque." *Nation* 98, no. 2552 (28 May 1914): 644.

[*In the following essay, the critic argues that Becque's writing skills were inferior to those of his rivals.*]

There was a time, thirty or forty years ago, when the name of Henri Becque occupied a very prominent place in the list of contemporary French playwrights, but his works seem hopelessly old-fashioned now, and it is not easy to divine the special reason which induced Mr. Edwin Björkman to include these pieces in his Modern Drama series. Still more difficult is it to acquiesce in the judgment of the translator, Mr. Freeman Tilden, who, in his preface, acclaims Becque as an epoch-making revolutionary, the discoverer of the drama of the commonplace, and a pioneer for Ibsen. Admirers of the famous Norwegian will not be pleased by the insinuation. Unquestionably, Becque, going to the masses for his subjects, was an innovator when compared with such writers as Augier, Feuillet, Sardou, and the younger Dumas, and was, in one sense, more of a realist than any of them. But he was essentially either a melodramatist or a *farceur,* and was inferior to his rivals in constructive skill, imagination, the composition of emotional climaxes, and polished dialogue. He had wit, a good sense of situation, an honest indignation against public abuses, and the courage of his convictions, but in his illustrations he was not much nearer to the truth of nature than the romanticists themselves.

This is the reason why *The Vultures* (*Les Corbeaux*), instead of being an effective satire upon an iniquitous system and professional rascality, becomes a diffuse and conventional melodrama of no particular significance. The subject—the opportunities afforded by then existing French regulations to greedy and unscrupulous practitioners to rob the widow and orphan under the cover of legal technicalities—is a good one, and it need not be doubted that, in selecting it, M. Becque was animated by sincere and philanthropic purpose. But he spoils a strong case by the extravagance and manifest artificiality of his premises and the complete theatricality of his personages. All the conditions of his story are prescribed, transparently, to insure a predestined issue, and would therefore be impotent as a demonstration, even if they could be regarded as fairly typical. His lewd and usurious old financier, his grasping and scoundrelly lawyer, his speculative architect, his dishonest tradesman, and the lesser vultures who batten upon the unfortunate Vigneron family, are one and all ancient puppets of the melodramatic stage. Madame Vigneron and her daughters, and the fortune-hunting Madame de Saint-Genis are almost equally destitute of originality or freshness. None of the characters, with the exception of the faithful old nurse, conveys the impression of an

actual living human being. For their inveterate loquacity, which constantly clogs the action, the responsibility, of course, rests upon the author, who has made them the mouthpieces of his explanations and protests; but the mixed literary quality of their discourse must be put to the credit of Mr. Tilden, who has employed all sorts of current American colloquialisms which seem strangely inconsistent with the supposed place and time, however ingenious they may be as English equivalents of French phrases.

The Woman of Paris (*La Parisienne*), which was vehemently denounced at the time of its first production as a gross libel upon the sex, is written with a certain cleverness and vivacity, but is no way brilliant either in form or in psychological analysis. It is a simple variation of a formula upon which hundreds of farcical comedies have been built. The fickle wife, who deceives an abominably complacent or phenomenally stupid husband, has, in this case, two lovers. There is a domestic quadrangle instead of the usual triangle. The construction is arbitrary rather than plausible or ingenious, and the use of prolonged soliloquies is excessive. Theatrically it is inferior, in sparkle, point, and essential veracity, to scores of pieces of a similar character, while as literature or drama it is of infinitesimal value. As for *The Merry-Go-Round* (*La Navette*), described as a comedy in one act, that is an ordinary French farce, in which an unprincipled little baggage plays at fast and loose with three of her lovers at once, the first of whom she dismisses, only to take up with him again after she has failed to make satisfactory terms with either of the other two. It is a cynical trifle which skilled French comedians doubtless could make fairly amusing, but why it should be thought worthy of translation into English as a choice example of modern drama, French or other, passes comprehension.

James Huneker (essay date 1922)

SOURCE: Huneker, James. "Henry Becque." In *Iconoclasts: A Book of Dramatists,* pp. 163-81. New York: Charles Scribner's Sons, 1922.

[*In the following essay, Huneker examines Becque's style through overviews of* The Vultures, The Prodigal Son, *and* The Woman of Paris.]

Emile Zola once wrote in his sweeping dictatorial manner, "Le théâtre sera naturaliste ou il ne sera pas"; but as Henry Becque said in his mordant style, Zola always convinced one in his pronunciamentos; it was only when he attempted to put his theories into action that they completely broke down. Alas! realism in the theatre after all the gong-sounding of café æstheticians, after the desperate campaigns of the one clairvoyant manager in the movement, Antoine, is as dead as the romanticism of Hernani. After the flamboyant, the drab—and now they are both relegated to the limbo of the tried-and-found-wanting.

When Zola sat down to pen his famous call to arms, Naturalism on the Stage, Antoine was still in the future, Dumas *fils* and Sardou ruled the Parisian theatre, Uncle Sarcey manufactured his diverting *feuilletons,* and Augier was become a classic. The author of L'Assommoir had like Alexander sighed for new worlds to subjugate. He had won a victory, thanks to Flaubert and the De Goncourts, in fiction; it remained for the theatre to provoke his ire It still clung obstinately to old-fashioned conventions and refused to be coerced either by Henrietta Maréchal or by the furious onslaught of Zola and his cohort of writing men.

In the essay referred to, Zola said that a piece of work will always be a corner of nature seen through a temperament. He told the truth when he declared that the "romantic movement was but a skirmish; romanticism, which corresponds to nothing durable, was simply a restless regret of the old world." Stendhal and Balzac had created the modern novel. The stage did not move with the other arts, though Diderot and Mercier "laid down squarely the basis of the naturalistic theatre." Victor Hugo gave the romantic drama its deathblow. Scribe was an ingenious cabinet-maker. Sardou "has no life—only movement." Dumas the younger was spoiled by cleverness—"a man of genius is not clever, and a man of genius is necessary to establish the naturalistic formula in a masterly fashion." Besides, Dumas preaches, always preaches. "Emile Augier is the real master of the French stage, the most sincere"; but he did not know how to disengage himself from conventions, from stereotyped ideas, from made-up ideas.

Who, then, was to be the saviour, according to Zola? And this writer did not underrate the difficulties of the task. He knew that "the dramatic author was enclosed in a rigid frame . . . that the solitary reader tolerates everything, goes where he is led, even when he is disgusted; while the spectators taken *en masse* are seized with prudishness, with frights, with sensibilities of which the author must take notice under pain of a certain fall. But everything marches forward! If the theatre will submit to Sardou's juggling, to the theories and witticisms of Dumas, to the sentimental characters of Augier, the theatre will be left in the onward movement of civilization"; and as Becque said in his Souvenirs of a Dramatic Author, the theatre has reached its end many times, yet somehow it continues to flourish despite the gloomy prophecies of the professors and critical malcontents. Every season, avowed Becque, that same cry rises to heaven,—"La fin du théâtre"; and the next season the curtain rises in the same old houses, on the same old plays.

However, Zola trumpeted forth his opinions. According to him the De Goncourt brothers were the first to put into motion realistic ideas. Henriette Maréchal, with its dialogue copied from the spoken conversation of contemporary life, with its various scenes copied boldly from reality, was a path breaker. And Becque again interrupts; Edmond de Goncourt posed for thirty years as a hissed author, "pour cette panade d'Henriette Maréchal." Away with the mechanism of the polished, dovetailed, machine-made play of Dumas. "I yearn for life with its shiver, its breath, and its strength; I long for life as it is," passionately declaimed the simple-minded bourgeois Zola, who then, in default of other naturalistic dramatists, turned his Thérèse Raquin into a play—and melodrama it was, not without its moments of power, but romantic and old-fashioned to a degree.

And this was Zola's fate: he contumaciously usurped the throne of realism, never realizing his life long that he was a romanticist of the deepest dye, a follower of Hugo, that melodramatic taleteller. All the while he fancied himself a lineal descendant of Balzac and Flaubert. Searching ceaselessly with his Diogenese lantern for a dramatist, he nevertheless overlooked not only a great one, but the true father of the latter-day movement in French dramatic literature—Henry Becque. What a paradox! Here was the unfortunate Becque walking the boulevards night and day with plays under his arm, plays up his sleeve, plays in his hat, plays at home—and always was he shown the door, only to reappear at the managerial window. Calm in his superiority, his temper untouched by his trials, Becque presented the picture of the true Parisian man of genius,—witty, ironical on the subject of his misfortunes, and absolutely undaunted by refusals. He persisted until he forced his way into the Comédie Française, despite the intriguing, the disappointments, the broken promises, and the open hostility of Sarcey, then the reigning pontiff of French dramatic criticism. Jules Clarétie pretended a sympathy that he did not feel, and it was only when pressure was brought by Edouard Thierry that his masterpiece, *Les Corbeaux,* was put on the stage after many disheartening delays; after it had been refused at the Vaudeville, the Gymnase, the Odéon, the Porte-Saint-Martin, the Gaîté, the Cluny, and the Ambigu. Such perseverance is positively heroic.

I know of few more diverting books than Becque's *Memoirs* and the record of his *Literary Quarrels.* If he was gay, careless, and unspoiled by his failures in his daily existence, he must have saved his bile for his books. They are vitriolic. The lashing he gives Sarcey and Clarétie is deadly. He had evidently put his revengeful feelings carefully away and only revived them when the time came, when his successes, his disciples, his election as the master of a powerful school, warranted his decanting the bitter vintage. How it sparkles, how it bites! He pours upon the head of Sarcey his choicest irony. After snubbing the young Becque, after pomp-ously telling him that he had no talent, that he should take Scribe for a model, Sarcey at the end, when he saw Becque as a possible strong figure in the dramatic world, calmly wrote: "Oh! Becque I have known a long time. He brought me his first piece. He owes it to me that his **The Prodigal Son** was played." To cap his attack, Becque prints this statement at the end of the miserable history of his efforts to secure a footing. It is almost too good to be true. Diabolically clever also is his imitation of a Sarcey *critique* on Molière, for Sarcey was no friend of character dramas.

In his preface to **The Ravens,** Becque announces that he is not a thinker, not a dreamer, not a psychologist, not a believer in heredity. As Jean Jullien truly said, the Becque plays prove nothing, are not photographic, are not deformations of life, but sincere life itself. The author relates that in composing—he had a large apartment on the rue de Matignon—he spent much time in front of a mirror searching for the exact gesture, for the exact glance of the eye, for the precise intonation. This fidelity to nature recalls a similar procedure of Flaubert, who chanted at the top of his formidable voice his phrases to hear if they would stand the test of breathing. Becque caught the just colour of every speech, and it is this preoccupation with essentials of his art that enabled him to set on their feet most solidly all his characters. They live, they have the breath of life in them; when they walk or talk, we believe in them. The peep he permits us to take into his workshop is of much value to the student.

He admired Antoine, naturally, and his opinion of Zola I have recorded. He rapped Brunetière sharply over the knuckles for assuming that criticism conserves the tradition of literature. Vain words, cries Becque; literature makes itself despite criticism, it is ever in advance of the critics. Only a sterile art is the result of academies. Curiously enough, Becque had a consuming admiration for Sardou. Him he proclaimed the real master, the man of imagination, observation, the masterly manipulator of the character of characters. This is rather disconcerting to those who admire in the Becque plays just those qualities in which Sardou is deficient. Perhaps the fact that Sardou absolutely forced the production of Becque's **L'Enfant Prodigue** may have accentuated his praise of that prestidigitator of Marly. Becque entertained a qualified opinion of Ibsen and an overwhelming feeling for Tolstoy as dramatist. The Russian's *Powers of Darkness* greatly affected the Frenchman. (Becque was born in 1837, died in 1900.)

And what is this naturalistic formula of Becque's that escaped the notice of the zealous Zola and set the pace for nearly all the younger men? Is it not the absence of a formula of the tricks of construction religiously handed down by the Scribe-Sardou school? As is gener-ally the case, the disciples have gone their master one better in their disdain of solid workmanship. The taint of the artificial, of the sawdust, is missing in Becque's masterpieces; yet with all their large rhythms, unconventional act-ends, and freedom from the *cliché*, there is no raggedness in detail; indeed, close study reveals the presence of a delicate, intricate mechanism, so shielded by the art of the dramatist as to illude us into believing that we are in the presence of unreasoned reality. Setting aside his pessimism, his harsh handling of character, his seeming want of sympathy,—a true objectivity, for he never takes sides with his characters,—Becque is as much a man of the theatre as Sardou. He saw the mad futility of the literary men who invaded the theatre full of arrogant belief in their formulas, in their newer conventions that would have supplanted older ones. A practical playwright, our author had no patience with those who attempted to dispense with the frame of the footlights, who would turn the playhouse into a literary farm through which would gambol all sorts of incompetents masquerading as original dramatic thinkers.

Becque's major quality is his gift of lifelike characterization. Character with him is of prime importance. He did not tear down the structure of the drama but merely removed much of the scaffolding which time had allowed to disfigure its façade. While Zola and the rest were devising methods for doing away with the formal drama, Becque sat reading Molière. Molière is his real master—Molière and life, as Augustin Filon truthfully says. In his endeavour to put before us his people in a simple, direct way he did smash several conventions. He usually lands his audience in the middle of the action, omitting the old-fashioned exposition act, careful preparation, and sometimes development, as we know it in the well-regulated drama. But search for his reasons and they are not long concealed. Logical he is, though it is not the cruel logic of Paul Hervieu, his most distinguished artistic descendant. The logic of Becque's events must retire before the logic of his characters, that is all. Humanity, then, is his chief concern. He cares little for literary style. He is not a stylist, though he has style—the stark, individual style of Henry Becque.

Complications, catastrophe, dénouement, all these are attenuated in the Becque plays. Atmosphere supplies the exposition, character painting, action. The impersonality of the dramatist is profound. If he had projected himself or his views upon the scene, then we would have been back with Dumas and his preachments. Are we returning to the Molière comedy of character? Movement in the accepted sense there is but little. Treatment and interpretation have been whittled away to a mere profile, so that in the Antoine repertory the anecdote bluntly expressed and dumped on the boards a slice of real life without comment—without skill, one is tempted to add.

Becque was nearer classic form than Hervieu, Donnay, De Curel, Georges Ancey, Leon Hennique, Emile Fabre, Maurice Donnay, Lemaître, Henri Lavedan, and the rest of the younger group that delighted in honouring him with the title of supreme master. After all, Becque's was a modified naturalism. He recognized the limitations of his material, and subdued his hand to them. M. Filon has pointed out that Becque and his followers tried to bring their work "into line with the philosophy of Taine," as Dumas and Augier's ideas corresponded with those of Victor Cousin, the eclectic philosopher. Positivism, rather than naked realism, is Becque's note. The cold-blooded pessimism that pervades so unpleasantly many of his comedies was the resultant of a temperament sorely tried by experience, and one steeped in the materialism of the Second Empire.

So we get from him the psychology of the crowd, instead of the hero ego of earlier dramatists. He contrives a dense atmosphere, into which he plunges his puppets, and often his people appear cold, heartless, cynical. He is a surgeon, more like Ibsen than he would ever acknowledge, in his calm exposure of social maladies. And what a storehouse have been his studies of character for the generation succeeding him! Becque forged the formula, the others but developed it.

The Becque plays! The last edition is in three volumes published by *La Plume* of Paris. It begins with an opera—fancy an opera by this antagonist of romance!—entitled **Sardanapale,** in three acts, "imitated" from Lord Byron. Victorin Joncières, a composer of respectable ability, furnished the music. The "machine" was represented for the first time at the Théâtre Lyrique, February 8, 1867. It need not detain us. **L'Enfant Prodigue,** a fouract vaudeville, saw the light, November 6, 1868, at the Théâtre Vaudeville. It is Becque at his wittiest, merriest best. In an unpremeditated manner it displays a mastery of intrigue that is amazing. For a man who despised mere technical display, this piece is a shining exemplar of virtuosity. Let those who would throw stones at Becque's nihilism in the matter of conventional craftsmanship read **The Prodigal Son** and marvel at its swiftness of action, its stripping the vessel of all unnecessary canvas, and scudding along under bare poles! The comedy is unfailing, the characterization rich in those cunning touches which are like salt applied to a smarting wound. The plot is slight, the adventures of several provincials who visit Paris and there become entangled in the toils of a shrewd adventuress. The underplot is woven skilfully into the main texture. Hypocrisy is scourged. A father and a son discover that they are trapped by the same woman. There is *genre* painting that is Dutch in its admirable minuteness and truth; a specimen is the scene at the *concierge's* dinner. Wicked in the quality called *l'esprit gaulois,* this farce is inimitable—and also a trifle old-fashioned.

In **Michel Pauper,**—given at the Porte-Saint-Martin, June, 1870,—Becque was feeling his way to simpler methods. The drama is in five acts and seven tableaux; and while it contains in solution all of Becque, it may be confessed that the outcome is rather an indigestible mess. The brutality of the opening scenes is undeniable. Michel is a clumsy fellow, who does not always retain our sympathy or respect. His courtship has all the delicacy of a peasant at pasture. But he is alive, his is a salient character. The suicide of De La Roseraye has been faithfully copied by Donnay in La Douloureuse, and by many others in Paris, London, and America. Hélène, poor girl, who is so rudely treated by Comte de Rivailler, would call forth a smile on the countenance of any one when she announces her misfortune in this stilted phraseology, "He asked of his own will what he could not obtain from mine." The ending has a suspicion of the "arranged," even of the violent melodramatic. And how shocking is the fall of Hélène! She is the first of the Becque cerebral female monsters, though she has at least more blood than some of his later creations. She loves the Count—the shadow of an excuse for her destruction of her noble-minded husband. However, one does not read **Michel Pauper** for amusement.

It is in **L'Enlèvement** that we find Becque managing with consummate address a genuine problem. It was produced at the Vaudeville, November 18, 1871. The three acts pass at a château in the provinces. Emma de Sainte-Croix, rather than endure the neglect and infidelities of her husband, lives in dignified retirement with her mother-in-law. She is a *femme savante,* though not of the odious bluestocking variety. She has a daily visitor in the person of a cultivated man who resides in the neighbourhood. At once we are submerged in a situation. De La Rouvre loves Emma. He, too, has been wretchedly mismated. His wife was a despicable voluptuary who cheated him with his domestics. He begs Emma to secure a divorce from her pleasure-loving husband. She refuses. She loathes the divorce courts. She loathes vulgar publicity. He proposes an elopement and is sharply brought to his senses by the woman. She loves the proprieties too much to indulge in romantic adventures, and has she not suffered enough through this love illusion? Her mother-in-law does not approve of the man's presence. Her son is always her son, and she hopes for reconciliation. If only Emma would be a little more lenient!

The prodigal husband returns. He is an admirable blackguard who respects neither his own honour nor that of his family. He flirts with his wife at his mother's instigation, but his heart is not in the game. Descends upon him one of his lady loves. She invades the château and is introduced to his wife as a supposedly casual passer-by. But she is detected as the worthless spouse of De La Rouvre. There is a scene. Later Raoul, the husband, forces his way into his wife's bedchamber and the episode on reading recalls Paul Hervieu's *Le Dédale*. The outcome, however, is different. Repulsed, the husband curses his wife, and she departs for India, elopes with her lover. Terse in dialogue, compact in construction, *L'Enlèvement* contains some of the best of Becque. Ibsen and Dumas are writ large in the general plan and dénouement, though the character drawing is wholly Becque's. Despite his economy of action and speech, he seldom gives one the feeling of abruptness in transitional passages. His scenes melt one into the other without a jar, and only after you have read or watched one of his plays do you realize the labour involved to produce such an illusion of life while disguising the controlling mechanism. All the familiar *points de repères,* the little tricks so dear to the average playmaker, are absent. Becque conceals his technical processes, and in that sense he has great art, though often seeming quite artless. And *L'Enlèvement* is more than a picture of manners; it is as definitely a problem play as *A Doll's House*. Only after being driven to it does Emma revolt. She is a *revoltée* of the cerebral type. The crowning insult is the attempt made upon her right to her person. Hervieu's heroine is passional, and it accounts for her lapse. We feel for her acutely. Emma's departure is logical.

With *La Parisienne,* Becque is once more on his own ground. Paris and its cynical view of the relations of the sexes is embodied in this diabolically adroit and disconcerting comedy—represented for the first time at the Comédie-Française, September 14, 1882, and reviewed at the Odéon, November 3, 1897. The play is full of a *blague* now slightly outmoded, but the types remain eternally true—those of the Parisian triangle. Only this three-cornered, even four-cornered, arrangement (for there are two "dear friends") is played with amazing variations.

Clotilde du Mesnil and Lafont are quarrelling over a letter when the curtain rises. He adjures her to resist temptation. "Resist, Clotilde; that is the only honourable course, and the only course worthy of you." She must remain dignified, honourable, the pride of her husband. Suddenly, in the midst of this ignoble squabble, she cries, "Prenez garde, voilà, mon mari!" Up to this moment the audience fancies that it has been witnessing a marital row. The shock is tremendous when the truth is learned. Nor are your feelings spared when later you hear Clotilde accuse Lafont of not being fond of *her* husband. The two wrangle over the accusation. In another speech she exclaims: "Vous êtes un libre penseur! Je crois que vous vous entendriez tres bien avec une maitresse qui n'aurait pas de religion, quelle horreur!" This extremely naïve statement reveals to us the land on the other side of good and evil in which dwell Becque's characters. Are they even cynical? Hardly, for there is no mockery, no parade of immorality, no speeches with equivocal meanings. The calm as-

sumption of external decency is merely a reversion to the baldest paganism. It is the modern over-cynicism. These people are so bad that, paradoxical as it may sound, they are good Certainly they are more refreshing and infinitely more moral than that wretched Camille, with her repentant whimperings and her nauseating speeches about soiled doves and their redemption.

And Lafont, stupid, loving, honest according to his lights, Lafont so marvellously presented by Antoine, is he not a being who lives! Clotilde as incarnated by Réjane is the worldling, neither stupid nor witty. She is simply a good-natured, vain woman, who deceives her husband and lover as naturally as she breathes.

Clotilde takes on a new *amant,* who treats her as badly as she treated Lafont. Deserted, she picks up the old thread and begins to live as before. As Mrs. Craigie says of this play: "There are critics who mistaking the situation for the philosophy have called this piece immoral. One would as soon call Georges Dandin or Tom Jones immoral. A true book, a true play, cannot be otherwise than moral. It is the false picture—no matter how pretty—which makes for immorality."

Throughout, these lovers quarrel like married folk. The social balance is upset, domestic virtues topsy-turvied. And yet the merciless stripping of the conventional romance,—the deluded husband, unhappy wife, and charming consoler of the afflicted,—these old properties of Gallic comedy are cast into the dust-bin. It is safe to say that since *La Parisienne* no French dramatic author has had the courage to revive the sentimental triangle as it was before this comedy was written. If he ventured to, he would be laughed off the stage. And for suppressing the sentimental married harlot let us be thankful to the memory of Becque.

Les Corbeaux is unique in modern comedy. Never played, to my knowledge, in English, its ideas, its characterization, its ground-plan, have been often ruthlessly appropriated. The verb "to steal" is never conjugated in theatreland. Yet this play's simplicity is appealing. A loving father of a family, a good-tempered bourgeois, dies suddenly. His affairs turn out badly. His widow and three daughters fall into the hands of the ravens, the partner of their father, his lawyer, his architect, and a motley crew of tradespeople. Ungrateful matter this for dramatic purposes. Scene by scene Becque exposes the outer and inner life of these defenceless women and their secret and malign persecutors. Every character is an elaborate portrait. Naturally, the family go to the dogs, and the wickedest villain of the lot catches in marriage the flower of the unhappy flock. His final speech is sublime, "My child, since your father's death you were hemmed in by a lot of designing scoundrels." And by inference he pats himself on the back, he, the worst scoundrel of all. If you tell me that the theme is not a pleasant or suitable one for the drama, I shall recommend you to the spirit of the late Henry Becque for answer. *Les Corbeaux* is the bible of the dramatic realists.

Remain seven small pieces, principally in one act. *La Navette* is wicked—and amusing. It aims at nothing else. *Les Honnêtes Femmes* might have been written by Dumas. It is a sugar-coated sermon extemporized by a young married woman for the benefit of a presumptive lover. She finds him a bride, and the curtain falls. *Le Départ* is of sterner metal. Here Becque beats Zola at his own game. The scene represents a working girl's atelier in a Parisian store. The various women are clearly outlined, so clearly that Huysmans in *Sœurs Vatard* is recalled. One girl is honest. She is honourable enough to refuse an offer of marriage made by the foolish young son of the proprietor, and for this wisdom receives insults from the father and is finally discharged for being too virtuous. She then incontinently goes to the devil. The devastating irony of the dramatist illuminates this little piece with sinister effect. And the moral is never far to seek in Becque—perhaps a twisted moral, yet not altogether a negligible one. In *Veuve* we find our old friend Clotilde of *La Parisienne,* now a widow. Her behaviour to her faithful admirer is a study of feminine malice, not only seen "through a temperament," but the outcome of unerring observation. Madeleine is a depressing sketch of a woman with a past who is educating her child at a convent It has poignant moments. The other two little affairs, *Le Domino à Quart* and *Une Exécution,* are exercises in pure humour of the volatile Parisian sort.

Becque's touch is light in comedy, rather clumsy in set drama. He is, as a rule, without charm, and he never indulges in mock pathos or cheap poetic flights. He excelled in depicting manners, and his dramatic method, as I have endeavoured to show, was direct and free from antique rhetoric and romantic turgidities. He has been superseded by a more comprehensive synthesis; France is become weary of the cynical sinners—yet that does not invalidate the high ranking of this man of genius. Whatever may be his deficiencies in the purely spiritual, Henry Becque will ever remain a commanding figure in the battalion of brilliant French dramatists.

Hugh Allison Smith (essay date 1925)

SOURCE: Smith, Hugh Allison. "Henri Becque and the Theatre Libre." In *Main Currents of Modern French Drama*, pp. 189-207. New York: Henry Holt & Company, 1925.

[*In the following essay, Smith compares the three main influences involved in the modification of Dumas and Augier's Social drama, including Becque and the Theatre Libre.*]

The significant work of Dumas and Augier was done by 1880, and with the weakening of their master hands, the chief faults of the form of drama they represented became apparent. The most fundamental of these was the artificial duality caused by combining the well-made play of Scribe, a comedy of intrigue complete in itself, with a social study, a character analysis, or the demonstration of a thesis. This inherent lack of singleness of purpose, difficult to conceal except for a master of dramatic art, and the further mingling in the same play of all forms of the serious and of the comic theatre, best exemplified in Sardou's pieces, were sure to bring about a strong reaction from the French, whose conception of art and of beauty lies so much in unity of aim and harmony of tone.

The inevitable revolt against these and other minor faults is perhaps coincident with the positive attempt of Naturalism to capture the stage, more than it is a result of this endeavor, but the two movements are inseparably united. They did not lead to the formation of a new school or genre—in fact, the attempt of the Naturalists to establish a school of drama failed quickly and decidedly—but they modified sufficiently the course of the theatre to make this an important date. The result was not only to overthrow the tyranny of the well-made play and simplify the genres, as well as to abolish minor conventions, but especially to win greater freedom in general; recent and contemporary drama has been free to follow various channels, and has been little hampered by any rules except those inherent in the theatre.

The three chief agencies in this attempt to modify the Social drama of Dumas and Augier are Henri Becque, the Naturalistic school of the novel headed by Zola, and the Théâtre Libre, founded by Antoine. The cooperation of all three might be thought of as the effort of extreme realism, or Naturalism, to establish itself on the stage.

Literary realism is a relative term, varying with the epoch; there is the realism of Molière, of Dumas fils, and of Becque or Zola. Moreover, it can not be taken simply as a truthful picture of life at any time, although that may be its professed ambition; there is frequently much in it that is quite conventional, perhaps even unrepresentative of life as a whole. The extreme realism of 1880 had as dominant characteristics its interest in the physical, sordid and ignoble sides of life, or at least in common, everyday life, and a pessimistic philosophy or point of view. Its methods professed to be inductive, and it secured its effects largely by an accumulation of detail, in the manner of the scientist who arrives at general laws through experiments and the collection of phenomena.

The general causes underlying Naturalism are for the most part those mentioned as explaining the realism of 1850, but some of them have been intensified and others can be added.

The pessimistic point of view of Naturalistic literature is the result of various influences. It is true that a strain of pessimism can always be found in the French drama, and, at times, it is quite marked with the writers of the Romantic school, who preceded the realists. But with the Romanticists it is more frequently a matter of mood and not a permanent point of view. With the realists, and particularly the Naturalists, it is erected into a philosophic system; indeed, it takes philosophy as its basis.

The current philosophy of this period, positivism and determinism, the philosophy of Comte, Taine and Renan, was frankly skeptical. If it did not entirely eliminate God, it largely took away the faith and consolation of the church and religion. We are not concerned here with the truth or falsity of such philosophy; the only question is that of its immediate effect, and it is certain that such skepticism, if it attacks seriously faith and religion, the hope, consolation and idealism which these give, makes for pessimism. However, a reasoned philosophy is more a matter for the educated few than for the masses, and there were other more general causes of pessimism.

Not the least of these general influences was the condition of French national or political life just at this time. It was the discouraging period following the French defeats of 1870, in the midst of the difficult struggle to reëstablish stable government. The generation writing from 1880 to 1890 had passed through this troubled epoch at its most impressionable age, and even the older generation was profoundly affected by it. We have seen the echoes in the theatre of Dumas and Augier. A more striking example could be found in Taine's comparison of the English and the French governments, often so pessimistic with regard to the latter.

The influence of science, democracy and commercialism has been mentioned in the chapter on the Realistic theatre, but it had become intensified in 1880. The materialism is especially to be noted. Old standards had fallen. The nobility, with its code of honor, *noblesse oblige,* had largely passed, and the clergy had lost much of its power and influence. Money was a greater force than ever before in French society, and in many ways a corrupting one. It was not surprising, then, that the moralist—and the French dramatist is frequently a moralist—should judge such society pessimistically.

But after all, realism, Naturalism, and pessimism were the natural stages in the inexorable progress of the logical French mind, starting with the Romantic principle that art should imitate nature and that all life is the proper field of drama. The Romanticists and the early realists combined the elevated and the common sides of life, but it was certain that the French artistic sense and love of unity would in the end revolt and tend, in a

single play, to devote itself to the one or the other. With a number of converging influences to aid, and above all through the attraction of a largely unworked vein, this meant for the prevailing Realistic School the field of common or sordid life, and in the end the exploitation of the ignoble character.

The process is gradual and is marked by the restriction of the sympathetic figures, to the point finally of substantial elimination. This in itself means pessimism, and its ultimate goal is the *comédie rosse,* where all the characters are too contemptible to merit the interest of a respectable audience. Such a play, whatever be its technique or ending, if it is taken seriously, is pessimistic.

These were the chief influences which before 1880 had already established Naturalism in the novel, where much more easily than in the theatre this mode of expression finds its place. Zola was at this time the high priest of the Naturalistic novel, and, as we know, he gave more than his blessing to this attempt to capture the stage. He himself wrote plays and dramatized some of his novels, as a rule quite unsuccessfully, and especially he proclaimed much of the theory in numerous articles on the stage. Other writers, such as Curel and Hervieu, also began with the novel.

It is particularly interesting to note in the articles of Zola that he is not aware that there are any inherent differences between the novel and the theatre—and this attitude is most frequent in attacks at this time on the various conventions of the stage. It is not surprising, then, that Zola, and other novelists who were unable to comprehend the stage, should fail in their attempts to give a new dramatic formula. They might supply the theatre with an atmosphere of extreme Naturalism and offer the stimulation of success in another field, but the examples of this new comedy must come from some one with dramatic talent. This was the work of Henri Becque.

Henri Becque (1837-1899)

Becque's dramas can hardly be called the models of the Naturalistic theatre, since he was so rare a combination of certain very decided qualities—with others wholly absent—that he is really inimitable; but he first successfully overthrew the chief barriers that the Naturalists were attacking and led them on the stage, where each comported himself according to his principles and particular character—in most cases very badly. When the most extreme were driven off by outraged taste and decency, the really worthy were able to carry forward French drama in a new atmosphere of freedom, but their work is decidedly different from that of Becque, and they hardly owe him more than the liberty to follow each his bent.

Henri Becque, who was born and lived at Paris, led a life of poverty and controversy. The latter, at least, would seem largely his own fault. He was a misanthrope to the point of abnormality, and rejoiced in the most cruel attacks on his colleagues and on humanity in general. His failure to succeed as a playwright, in any broad or popular sense, he attributed to the ill will, or persecution of theatrical managers, and to the stupidity of the public. He went so far as to bring suit against one manager for refusing a play, and he takes vengeance on the public in all of his pieces.

His dramatic output is small, consisting of only seven or eight plays, and of these only two are really important, *Les Corbeaux* in 1882 and *La Parisienne* in 1885.

The subject of *Les Corbeaux* is the despoiling of the Vigneron family. The mother, three daughters and a good-for-nothing son, on the sudden death of M. Vigneron, a well-to-do manufacturer, are left in the clutches of a dishonest partner and an unprincipled notary, as well as of a horde of other *corbeaux,* and are plucked of all their heritage. One of the daughters is finally forced to marry this partner, a sixty-year old Harpagon, to save the helpless family from abject poverty.

The action of the play is hardly more exciting than the *résumé* just given. Its style and composition are absolute in their simplicity and hard realism. There is not a sign of color, not a tirade, not a single theatrical *coup,* nothing but bitter irony to give life or flavor. There is no plot beyond that indicated, the inexorable closing in of the vultures about their helpless prey, and these victims are too weak to do more than flutter in an aimless way. It is in plot and technique the Naturalist's famous "bleeding slice of life."

Human nature is seen at its worst. The victims do not count; they are only food for the vultures. It is in the circling, the croaking and the satisfaction of these latter that we find whatever drama there is; and of them all, the partner, the notary, the music teacher, the architect, the furnisher, the fiancé and his mother, not one shows a spark of honesty or honor, nor a moment's impulse of compassion. One would expect them to appear inhuman monsters, therefore, and yet that is exactly what they resemble least, and it is here that we find the supreme art of the author. Their villainy is so natural and so unconscious that it seems proper, and, in listening to them, we have only one doubt: are they honest like ourselves or are we dishonest like them?

The picture is complete in its realism both of language and detail, and perfect in its observation. However, its value may be questioned. It has no conclusion except its unrelieved pessimism, and, natural as this seems, it is certainly a most narrow and one-sided view of life. A

family without a member or a friend sufficiently strong to defend its rights, in business contact with none but rascals, may be possible, but it is certainly rare. The author does not juggle the cards during the game in the way the Naturalists accused Dumas and Augier of doing, but he picks all the aces and kings before he begins. And the interest of this play, in any broad way, at least, is as questionable as its value as a picture of life. It is keen and strong, but somber and unentertaining; and the only serious reflection it invites is that we are all fundamentally dishonorable and egoistic—which is either an absurd bit of irony or a philosophic truth too remote to affect practical life.

La Parisienne is an even narrower "slice of life," the traditional little triangle, no broader or thicker than a tea sandwich. Clotilde is a perfect wife and a model mistress. As a lesson to her lover, and to secure an advantage to her husband, she dismisses this first lover and turns to another, but her sense of order and love of a serious, settled existence quickly reassert themselves and she returns to the first, and the perfect triangle is reestablished. The plot ends exactly where it began.

Its artistry is of the same sort as that of *Les Corbeaux* but even more flawless. The simple beauty of Clotilde's unconscious perversity would be almost touching if the author had not so rigidly excluded all sentiment from actions so natural and dignified. In fact, Becque has in this play arrived at such a perfect mastery of this genre that he occasionally allows his characters to give little moral lectures, without their seeming out of place. Take, for example, the one uttered by Clotilde's lover when he learns that she is on friendly terms with a frivolous and somewhat ultra-modern society lady.

> Think of me, Clotilde, and think of yourself. Consider that an imprudent act is quickly committed and can never be repaired. Don't let yourself yield to this inclination for risky adventures, which today makes so many victims. Resist, Clotilde, resist! In remaining faithful to me you remain worthy and honorable.[1]

But one should not infer from the above passage that Clotilde's virtue was really in danger. This is nothing but Lafont's jealousy. How strongly anchored her principles were in all matters we see throughout the play, and she even acknowledges that they are somewhat old-fashioned:

> You mean that I am old-fashioned! I haven't changed. Oh, as for that, yes, you are right; I am downright conservative. I love order, tranquillity and sound principles. I want to have the churches open when I care to go to them. . . . You are a free-thinker! I believe you would even get along with a mistress who had no religion. How horrible to think of it![2]

And all this appears entirely sincere and unconscious on Clotilde's part. As was said, she is a model wife and mistress. Her devotion to her husband and concern for his interests are unfaltering. Also, she wishes the best of relations and good feeling between the members of her *ménage à trois*. She even goes so far as to accuse Lafont of not caring enough for her husband—quite unjustly, for the two men are the best of friends:

CLOTILDE.

You don't like my husband!

LAFONT.

Why, yes, I do, I assure you.

CLOTILDE.

No, I warrant you that you don't. You don't care for Adolphe, I can see it in many ways. Perhaps it is because your characters don't agree, or possibly it is the situation that is responsible for it."[3]

The peculiar merit, then, of Becque is that he puts on the stage characters capable of any baseness and without the slightest moral consciousness, but who preserve the language, sentiments and outward appearances of the most honorable of people. This is the *comédie rosse*. **La Parisienne** is the first perfect example, perhaps, and certainly it is one of the most artistic. It is because of its artistic qualities that the French, even the serious critics, have so frequently admired the play. Except for this artistry, and for its constant irony, it is difficult to find anything of value in it. One can hardly accuse the author of confusing vice and virtue in his characters, since virtue is absent, but one can not help thinking how difficult it has been made for virtue to secure a certificate of good moral character when she does return. In any case, such pictures of life are almost discouraging to the maintenance of respectability, and if the author's point of view were general, one might hesitate to practice any virtues, in order to avoid the accusation of hypocrisy.

Becque has discarded the technique of the *pièce bien faite*. His plays do not come to an end. The curtain falls when the author has got all he can out of his situations and characters. The conclusion is left to the audience. The Naturalists' argument was that life does not begin or end, and all one can do is to give a cross-section of it. If this cross-section means something, all the better, but in any case they held that one must give it as it is, without intervention on the part of the author, and even without attempting to apply or explain it. They abolished the *raisonneur* and made the theatre purely objective. Especially, one should not touch up his pictures to make them more beautiful or agreeable. The public must learn to look life squarely in the face, however disagreeable that face may be.

This latter principle would have been more reasonable if the Naturalists had not chosen so regularly to visit life in her ugly moods. They objected to colored photography, but their own pictures were too constantly confined to the Rogue's Gallery. Human nature is seen only at its worst, and there is no relief of comedy, none of spirituality, nor of imagination, while the bitter irony practically destroys the possibility of sentiment. The tone is single and simple throughout, but it is also frequently somber and monotonous.

The chief merits of this theatre are its reliance on observation, and its power of character analysis, in which it places the main interest. These qualities, with the further freedom that had been won from the too narrow restraint of plot, form the new starting point of the modern theatre, the one from which most of contemporary French drama proceeds.

The immediate effect, however, of Becque's philosophy and characters was something very different. Unfortunately, his cynical views of life accorded too perfectly with the wave of pessimism that existed among the young writers of France in the last two decades of the nineteenth century, and for a time baseness became the theatrical fashion. While Becque should not be held responsible for all the excesses of his followers, there is no doubt that he first, in his *comédie rosse*, took away all virtue from comedy and gave it the taste of vice that started it on its famous Naturalistic orgy in the days of the Théâtre Libre, an orgy ended only when *delirium tremens* forced it to become sober.

THE THÉÂTRE LIBRE OF ANTOINE (1887-1894)

The Théâtre Libre, founded and controlled by Antoine from 1887 to 1894, is generally considered as the practical manifestation on the stage of the extreme realistic reforms typified by Zola and the Naturalistic novel and exemplified in the plays of Becque. Since it coincided with other influences and came at a period of natural reaction against certain features of the drama in vogue, it is not sure that it had all the importance in the development of the French theatre that is sometimes given to it. But whether it be simply the gnat buzzing on the yoke or really one of the oxen pulling the load up the hill, it offers in any case a suitable peg on which to hang the date of a partial reform in the modern French drama, and it illustrates in itself the limitations and failure of extreme realism, or Naturalism, on the stage.

André Antoine was a humble clerk in the Gas Company at Paris. He had had but slight education and little experience as an amateur actor when he founded the Théâtre Libre, but he was irresistibly attracted to the stage, and he soon developed remarkable qualities as an actor. In later years, through the originality and sheer force of his native genius, he became the outstanding theatrical manager of France.

He organized his theatre with the cooperation of a few amateur actors. They were absolutely without funds, and only on his monthly pay day was Antoine able to furnish the rent for the small hall they had hired; he even carried his letters of advertisement himself, to save postage. His first performance, in 1887, was a very doubtful success, and it required still greater courage and efforts to undertake another. However, this second performance brought valuable public notice, and he was encouraged to resign from the gas office and devote himself entirely to the project. The theatre flourished for four or five years and then declined, and Antoine resigned from it in 1894. Later he became a well-known actor, organized another theatre, and was for some years director of the National Theatre of the Odéon.

The avowed aim of the Théâtre Libre was to give opportunity to unknown authors, especially to those representing the Naturalistic ideas, and one of its greatest glories has been to bring before the public a number of new names which have since become famous in the French drama. Brieux and Curel are among those who were discovered by Antoine. Also the Théâtre Libre was one of the first theatres at Paris to represent any considerable number of foreign plays. Ibsen, Tolstoy, Hauptmann, and various other foreign dramatists found place on its programs, and along with the organization of the *Oeuvre* theatre, which has devoted itself particularly to this field, it inaugurated a much to be desired practice in France. The French have been exceptional, and on the whole quite unjustified, in the slight attention they have given to foreign plays, and notable progress has been made in correcting this attitude during the past thirty years.

It is probable, however, that the greatest service of the Théâtre Libre is to be found in its attack on French theatrical conventions, particularly on the style of acting and staging. The French have been unique in this respect. Conservative, and even given to routine by nature, and with all their drama first produced at Paris, in theatres subsidized in part by the government and aided by the National Conservatory, they have kept their theatrical traditions most intact.

No doubt, many of these are admirable, but they were largely formed in the Classic or, at latest, Romantic schools, in the elevated, heroic genres, and were strikingly out of keeping with the spirit of the realistic drama in the second half of the nineteenth century. Moreover, this incongruity is heightened by the natural French love of fine rhetoric, which is so foreign to Anglo-Saxons. The dramatic tirade, which by its oratory lifts a Frenchman out of his seat and makes an American wish to crawl under his, still persisted in the realistic prose drama at this time, where it was clearly not at home; it was perhaps even an anachronism in the temper of modern society.

Antoine attacked all these conventions and succeeded in transforming some of them. As in other things, his actors often went too far. They talked into the fire and

turned their backs too much to the audience, and sometimes did not make themselves understood, but in general their influence in changing theatrical conventions was salutary. It is only to be regretted that the strength of French tradition has prevented it from extending further. Antoine was one of the first in France, following the initiative of Sardou, to utilize fully the crowd on the stage, and his reforms in regard to realism and simplicity in staging were excellent.

If there were more revolutionists such as he to attack the abuses that still exist in the Paris theatres, due to routine and tradition, the really remarkable merit of the French theatre today would be more immediately apparent, at least to foreigners. It is true that many of these abuses are minor, relating to ticket-selling, seating, scenery and declamation, and the French may well point out that "the play's the thing," but this can hardly justify eighteenth century conditions in the theatre. In fact such conditions seem all the more regrettable, when they tend to mar the enjoyment of the perfect diction and admirable art of the actors to be found in the well-balanced performances given by the national, and by the other good theatres at Paris.

The Théâtre Libre was a subscription theatre. It was able thus to escape the censor, and to present plays that were forbidden on the other stages, but it also had the disadvantage of being confined to a restricted public. This was one of the causes of its decline. Encouraged by the applause of the partisans of Naturalism, and yielding also to his own preferences, Antoine, who had at first welcomed plays widely different in form and spirit, soon turned almost exclusively to the Naturalistic form, and even to a special type of it written for his theatre.

This type may be best comprehended as a deformation of Becque's *comédie rosse*. Becque's dramatic characters are despicable at heart but impeccable in manner and speech; in fact the essence of his art is in this contrast between their real character and their assumption of the complete guise of honorable people. The characters created by the extremists of the Théâtre Libre are not only despicable but delight in being so. They are base, ignoble creatures who rejoice in covering themselves with mud. The chief effort of these young authors seems to have been to scandalize the bourgeois—except when they delighted in puzzling him with disconnected scenes and plays without beginning or end.

In short, there are to be found all the disagreeable features of Naturalism: pessimism, coarseness and ugliness; and all of the anarchy in technique that was a protest against the well-made play. The public was soon disgusted. Extreme realism, such as is found in some of the novels of the Zola school, was clearly proven to be impossible on the stage. The Théâtre Libre failed as a purely Naturalistic genre.

Possibly the success of French Naturalism dealing with common and vulgar characters would have been greater on the stage, if it had been less cynical and contemptuous toward the life it so largely treats. In this respect, French realism seems to distinguish itself, in degree at least, from the realism of other countries. There is in Russian Naturalism, for example, a certain mysticism, doubtless a product of faith and religion, which gives it hope and some spirituality; and in English realism one finds a sentimental sympathy for the common characters, often even for those most ugly and sordid, which again keeps such literature from being so entirely cynical and depressing as that characteristically written by the French.

A complete explanation of the causes for the attitude of the French is perhaps difficult and too complex to be attempted here. However, one of the chief reasons is to be found in their conception of the artistic and beautiful, in their fondness for the perfect in line and form, and in their consequent contempt for the coarse and common clay with which they must work in this genre. In any case, the French rarely show the hearty enjoyment often found by the English in the common and vulgar scenes of life, and in the drama especially, where good humor, sympathy and emotion are such necessary appeals, the scientific hardness of French realism is a serious handicap.

The shortcomings and failures of the Naturalistic reforms treated here are obvious, but there are also important gains from this attempted revolution. No entirely new and important genres were set up. Authors continued to write plays of the same general character as before, often even the outright Social dramas of Dumas and Augier, but usually with modified forms and emphasis. Above all, the tyranny of the well-made play was overthrown and plot became less rigid and less important. Action was made dependent on the characters instead of having the characters controlled by the action, as was often the case before; and with this tyranny of plot broken down, both life and characters can be presented more fairly.

Most important of all, there has been a decided tendency away from drama dealing with specific problems and social questions, toward an analysis of character; there is less social and political science, and more psychology, philosophy and humanity.

This seems a decided gain. The only dramatic subject of perennial and universal interest is human nature, mankind. It is entirely proper, and perhaps even necessary, to study human nature in connection with its external manifestations, its reactions toward the life and problems of the day, but this study should emphasize man and not simply his actions. The French theatre, then, has returned far toward Molière. He too was a realist, a satirist and a philosopher, and he also was a writer of social drama, if the emphasis is placed on character as was just stated.

Furthermore, we find a complete restoration of the theatre of observation—with imagination again under restraint. It will be noted that this faculty of the mind is entirely absent in Becque. This subordination of imagination is the usual French tradition. And finally there is again, as in the Classic period, a decided tendency toward unity and harmony of tone, toward a separation of the kinds, or at least against such mingling as was found in the plays of Sardou. The separation of the genres is so much in conformance with the French ideas of order and beauty that it seems likely to reestablish itself, largely without any specific effort to this effect. All these tendencies will be noted in the contemporary authors who inherited from this reform.

Notes

1. Act I, scene I.

2. Act I, scene III.

3. Act III, scene VI.

Barrett H. Clark (essay date 1938)

SOURCE: Clark, Barrett H. "Henry Becque." In *A Study of Modern Drama: A Handbook for the Study and Appreciation of Typical Plays, European, English and American, of the Last Three-Quarters of a Century,* pp. 122-26. New York: D. Appleton-Century Company, 1938.

[In the following essay, Clark discusses Becque's life, career, and the plot of The Vultures.*]*

Henry Becque, the father of the modern French Naturalistic school, was born at Paris in 1837. His early works were produced in the sixties, but *The Parisian Woman* and *The Vultures,* his most important plays, were peddled about for years before they were performed. During the last years of his life, Becque was recognized as the master, the founder of one of the most important movements of modern times. He died in 1899.

The production of *The Vultures* in 1882 and *The Parisian Woman* in 1885 marked the beginning of the new school which, in 1887, under the leadership of André Antoine, had a theater of its own, the famous Free Theater.

Becque is termed a Naturalist because his characters were held to be living beings, because they give the illusion of reality, and because his technique is subordinate to and of less importance than his characterization. He writes because he wishes to present to us a "slice of life"; he has no lesson to teach, no sermon to pronounce, no thesis to prove. His plays, in the words of a French critic, "are life" itself. Huneker says, "Becque's major quality is his gift of lifelike characterization. Character with him is of prime importance. He did not tear down the structure of the drama, but merely removed much of the scaffolding which time had allowed to disfigure its façade."

Through the perspective of years we are now able to realize that the Naturalism of the 80's and 90's was only a phase, one of many methods of interpreting life. Becque, after all, came no closer to "reality" than many so-called Romantics. He was instrumental in bringing about a reaction against the clever artificialities of the facile technicians.

The Vultures

Play in 4 acts (1882). Texts: translation, as ***The Crows,*** by B. Papot (*Drama,* Chicago, 1912); by F. Tilden, in ***The Vultures, The Woman of Paris, The Merry-Go-Round*** (N. Y. 1913); reprint of the same in Moses' *Representative Continental Dramas* (Boston, 1924).

The Vultures was one of the numerous attempts made by the Naturalists to do for the drama what Zola and the Goncourts, Maupassant, and Daudet, were doing for the novel. The novelists all wrote plays; it was reserved for Becque to write ***The Vultures*** and ***The Woman of Paris,*** examples of the best that Naturalism had to offer. "It was Becque," says Dr. F. W. Chandler, "who in practice pointed the way to stage naturalism, achieving far more for that cause than did Zola."

1. The first act is given over almost altogether to exposition. With its long speeches, asides and soliloquies, we should to-day call it very old-fashioned. A glance at Pinero's *Thunderbolt* or Maugham's *Circle* will show the distance covered in the development of sheer technique since 1882. Yet in this play the French dramatist appears deliberately to avoid the facile expedients of his successful contemporaries: he will have none of the suave prattle of Sardou or Bisson; he prefers to attend to the chief business before him, which is the presentation of character—in huge slices, as it were.

Do you think that he was really unable to conduct his opening scenes as Sardou conducts, say, the opening scenes of *Divorçons* or *Patrie!?*

One important thing does happen in the first act: the death of Vigneron, announced just before the curtain falls, was hardly expected. The playwright of the "well-made" play school would call it "unprepared." So it is. It comes as a shock. But then the dramatist intended that it should shock. "This is life," he would say. "Don't people die suddenly in the midst of life, despite MM. Sardou and Bisson? Then why not show things in a play as they happen in life, which aims to reproduce, or at least to reflect, life?

This is also exposition, in that it prepares for the important business of the play, which has not yet begun; the play does not actually begin until the early part of the second act. As a matter of fact, the whole first act *could* be put into a page or two of exposition and placed at the beginning of what is now the second. But Becque, knowing what he was about, wished to prepare his background with all possible care. The home-life of the Vignerons, their ideas and tastes, their physical surroundings, are all elements in the picture.

2. There is one basic difference in treatment between this play and the usual French play of the present time. Such playwrights as Lavedan, Donnay, Capus, and above all Sacha Guitry, are "finished" writers, as to style and construction; Becque is brutal and direct, unpolished, and since the people he usually portrays are not "society," they are more "lifelike" than if they were.

The transition from scene to scene is abrupt, especially in the first act, too much so to give the illusion even of that rhythm which is so great an asset in all representations of life. Read pages 49 and 50 (*The Drama* edition); there are parts of three distinct episodes, and yet there are no modulation, no blending, no "bridging sections." More skilled, though perhaps less inspired dramatists, would have welded these incidents together, blended them into a harmonious whole.

3. The second act is typical of Becque's manner at its best; although it shows the influence of Molière, it has a savage note of satire, a brusque and peremptory movement. The three "vultures" scene is one of the most bitterly ironical in all modern drama. Here we have none of the suavity of a Capus, the brilliant charm of a Guitry; the dramatist seems almost to have forgotten that he was writing a play—for which we are grateful. His instinct has served him well.

4. It is in the third act that we find a good deal of the sort of material that was to be developed later by Hervieu and Brieux. Becque throws out a suggestion—the injustice of the law, for instance, a thesis which Hervieu was later to develop in *The Nippers*; or he shows the impossibility of an unmarried woman's making an honest living, which Brieux used in *Blanchette*

and *The Independent Woman.* François de Curel, Emile Fabre, Léon Hennique and a score of others, following the trail blazed by Becque, were quick to perceive the dramatic possibilities inherent in a play like *The Vultures,* which came to be regarded as the "Bible of the Naturalists."

5. The play has what is known as an unemphatic ending. Conventional plays of the school of Scribe and Sardou end almost invariably with what in America is called a "punch,"—a "big" scene. This is pointed, but the other method is no less so, often because of its very unobtrusiveness. The unemphatic ending contains a sting, a satirical touch that sums up the act, or, in some instances, illustrates the theme of the entire play. Galsworthy's *Strife,* for instance. Tench says to Harness, "D'you know, sir—these terms, they're the *very same* we drew up together, you and I, and put to both sides before the fight began? All this—all this—and—what for?" Harness then answers, "That's where the fun comes in!", and the curtain drops. In Louis N. Parker's *Disraeli,* the first act "curtain" is another example. This is, as we have already seen (p. 48), a common practice nowadays, and the reason for it is chiefly because it heightens illusion. In life, the exciting is mingled with the commonplace; one of the most interesting and dramatic things in life is the strange contrast between the sublime and the commonplace, the tragic and the comic. Therefore, instead of ending his act or play with a scene of great tension or high emotion, the dramatist seeks to reproduce a still more "lifelike" scene, placing one of these contrasted moments at the most critical point in his act, that is, in the last part of it. One of the quietest endings is in Wedekind's *Music.* "At the end, when Klara, after undergoing imprisonment, exile, poverty, public disgrace and the loss of her beloved child, finds herself bereft of even Reissner's regard, she is led away in a stupor from the miserable attic. It is then, in reply to a wish of the physician that she will suffer no lasting mental disturbance, that Lindekuh preludes the fall of the curtain by the caustic remark: 'She'll be able to sing a song.'"[1]

On the other hand, need it be said that not *all* of life is unemphatic? Is there not danger in overemphasizing the unemphatic? Galsworthy has been blamed for his cautious "curtains" on the grounds that life is seldom so tense and undramatic as he shows it.

Take, as an example of the emphatic ending, Echegaray's rather melodramatic play *Madman or Saint* (also translated as *Folly or Saintliness*). Is the strong scene with which this drama ends esthetically justifiable?

Note

1. From F. J. Ziegler's preface to his translation of Wedekind's "Awakening of Spring."

John Gassner (essay date 1954)

SOURCE: Gassner, John. "Henry Becque: The Mordant Virtuoso." In *The Theatre in Our Times: A Survey of the Men, Materials and Movements in the Modern Theatre,* pp. 114-22. New York: Crown Publishers, Inc., 1954.

[*In the following essay, Gassner takes a close look at Becque's two "masterpieces,"* The Vultures *and* The Woman of Paris.]

At a time when good writing for the theatre is at a low ebb in most countries, not excluding our own, it may be well to return to the fountain-springs of the modern drama, which are now so muddied by the demands of commerce. And in returning to the sources we could do worse than glance at the struggles of Henry Becque, the one founder of dramatic modernism who is least known in America although James Huneker acclaimed him, Ashley Dukes translated him, and his plays found a place in all the influential theatres of Europe. Today, when showmanly cleverness is still too often a substitute for true penetrativeness in the theatre, there is still more lip-service to his principles than actual observance of them. To remember Becque is to recall how difficult it has been and still is to maintain playwriting on the high level to which it was raised by him and others in the eighteen-eighties.

In remembering Becque, moreover, we are forced to give some thought to the entire question of salvation for the theatre through departures from realism. Blame for the pinchbeck nature of much dramatic writing is often placed on the triumph of the realistic technique, whereas Becque's plays, perhaps even more than Ibsen's and less only than Strindberg's, would expose the absurdity of the charge. It was precisely against meretricious theatricality that modern realism ranged its heaviest batteries, and the vacuity of much that passes for realistic drama here and abroad is the very antithesis of Becque's work as well as that of the pioneers who were his contemporaries. The proposal to discard realism so often voiced by faithhealers of the stage incorporates one fallacy: The imaginative or poetic style of drama with which they intend to displace realism can also play us false, and humbug is humbug no matter whether it wears the trappings of poetry or the sack-suit of prose, the homburg of fancy or the straw hat of suburban realism. When the play is dramaturgically unsound or unconvincing, the deception does not succeed for all the prestidigitation of fanciful and stylized playwriting.

Becque's battle for sound, objective theatre was won at the end of the nineteenth century and then lost in a flood of "Maeterlincked" sweetness without light, buried in Reinhardt spectacles, and distorted by expressionistic subjectivism that produced no results comparable in value to the objective workmanship we got in the best plays of Chekhov and O'Casey, for example. The theatre had just rounded out half a century since Becque died, and yet the victory he gained for objective revelation, without tasting more than thin slivers of its fruits himself, had to be won all over again in spite of the recent appearance of a few good plays by Tennessee Williams and Arthur Miller.

It was Henry Becque's ironic destiny to be neglected while he was laying the foundations of French dramatic realism and then to be unable to complete a single long play when the theatre finally caught up with his art. In the eighteen-seventies, Émile Zola was thundering precepts in prefaces and searching for saviors of the French stage. His eyes lighted readily enough on the de Goncourt brothers, the novelists who shared his credo of "naturalism" and authors of a wretched play, *Henriette Maréchal.* He even glanced appreciatively at himself, writing some half-dozen plays as exemplars of stage realism. Zola looked in every direction except that of Becque. When the dramatist later came to write his memoirs, he would, remembering Zola's indifference, remark glumly that "the dog barks and the caravan passes."

Upon graduation from the old Lycée Bonaparte, Henri-François Becque, the son of a lowly government clerk in Paris, first found employment in a railroad office. But influenced by a maternal uncle Martin Labize, who had collaborated with the famous Labiche on a comedy, the young man turned eagerly to the theatre. From clerking at the Chemins de Fer du Nord he moved to a small position in the chancellery of the Legion of Honor and then to the household of the Polish diplomat Count Potocski as tutor and private secretary. Here came his first opportunity to emerge as a writer, the Count having introduced him to a young composer Victorien Jonçieres, for whom Becque wrote the libretto to the forgotten opera *Sardanapale* in 1885. In the same year, Becque also became the drama critic of the newspaper *Le Peuple,* and in 1886 he had the additional good fortune of seeing a little farce produced successfully.

Encouraged by this first taste of success, the no longer so very young author resolved to rely solely on his literary labors for a livelihood, and the decision was to cost him nothing less than a lifetime of embittering experience with producers and critics. His zeal for the theatre carried him so far into recklessness that he produced his first full-length play, *Michel Pauper,* at his own expense in 1870. He was rewarded for his pains with a resounding failure, and his next attempt in 1871, *The Elopement,* fared no better. Twice defeated, the playwright returned to the chancellery of the Legion of Honor and, from there, graduated to a stockbroker's of-

fice, where he remained for several years. Some measure of success came to him in 1878 with the reproduction of a short play *The Shuttle,* and, in 1880, with *The Virtuous Women,* which ultimately found its way into the repertory of the Comédie Française. But neither play greatly improved his financial condition, and his temper was sorely tried by failure to obtain a production for his first masterpiece *The Vultures* (*Les Corbeaux*), written in 1877. It took him five years to win a hearing for the play, and its acceptance by the Comédie Française was only the prelude to a protracted struggle with the directors. Stubbornly rejecting all demands for changes in the text that would turn it into a "well-made play" of intrigue, Becque finally saw *The Vultures* on the stage in 1882 exactly as he had written it. But the disparity between his objective picture of middle-class life and the artificial style of stage production then in vogue gave him at best a qualified success. The hisses that greeted the play were as loud as the applause of the progressives in the auditorium, so that the premiere threatened to become another pitched battle like the "battle of 'Hernani'" half a century earlier, when romanticists had fought classicists on behalf of Hugo's romantic melodrama. Nor did Becque gain enough prestige at the time to be able to place his next play *The Parisian Woman* (*La Parisienne*) on the stage without first encountering humiliating rejections. The first production of this notable comedy in 1885 created a sensation without actually giving the author the success he deserved, and the Comédie Française, which condescended to present *La Parisienne* five years later, nearly turned a masterpiece into a fiasco with its inept staging methods.

When we look at the first of Becque's two masterpieces today, we are apt to find *The Vultures* almost as unique in our practical theatre as it was in the theatrical world between the years 1877 and 1882 when he tried to get his play produced. Although the theme seems familiar enough because we are accustomed to seeing business ethics criticized on the stage, we shall, if we are sailing in the weather of Broadway or West End theatrical production, consider Becque's dramaturgy altogether too simple, bare, and naïve. An American producer reading the play in innocence of its authorship would consider it the work of a promising young author who still "doesn't know his way around," for this is what the producer will find: He will read a first act that starts the play altogether too soon with a picture of the homelife of the middle-class Vignerons. The mother flutters about contentedly and the genial father dotes on his three daughters and makes them sing a *chanson* before he departs to keep an appointment. The pretty daughter Blanche looks forward to marrying a young man of good society; another daughter is absorbed in her study of music, and a third girl Marie is inconspicuously involved with nothing in particular. (When is the action to start, wonders the producer?) The house gradually fills with visitors, including Blanche's young man and the latter's aristocratic mother. They are just starting to celebrate Blanche's engagement, when a physician comes in to announce that Monsieur Vigneron has died of a heart-attack. And now it is really the turn of the producer to shake his head sadly. Why doesn't the inexperienced author manage it so that Vigneron will die on the stage—perhaps overexcite himself at the festivities and collapse in full sight of the audience? This is always good theatre, whereas the offstage death is untheatrical. The author would waste his breath if he explained that the first part of his act is a slice of life, and that he has no reason to turn Vigneron's death into a holiday for the boxoffice customers.

What follows is that Vigneron's business partner Teissier, his lawyer Bourdon, an architect, and a number of petty cheats proceed to pluck the helpless family. It is especially plain that the family's lawyer and the business partner are acting in collusion. Yet once the methods of the scoundrels are revealed, the playwright makes no effort to make a stage plot out of their rapacity, for the kind of plucking the Vignerons get is a routine matter that proceeds in a perfectly untheatrical, legalistic fashion. Instead of making an exciting thing of the business intrigue, then, the play turns to the personal complication of the impulsive Blanche, who gave herself to her fiancé only to learn that his mother refuses to countenance the marriage without a substantial dowry. And here, too, our hypothetical showman is bound to be disappointed. He would expect a pathetic scene between hero and heroine, but it is only the mother, who has gone from place to place to ascertain the Vigneron family's financial condition, who calmly tells Blanche that the marriage cannot take place. Becque, moreover, has no sooner held out the appetizing dish of an illegitimate pregnancy to the public than he austerely removes it from our sight. The girl's condition is quickly absorbed by the over-all dramatic development, which has in the meantime caught up with her sensible sister Marie, who has attracted her father's rascally partner Teissier.

The aged vulture proposes marriage and Marie, aware of her sister's condition and of the helplessness of the family, accepts him. Blanche's problem will no doubt be settled now one way or another, and the playwright does not even tell us this, because he is not interested in untying all the knots of his story simultaneously, as is so often the case in the theatre and so rarely the case in life. Teissier arranges the marriage through his lawyer Bourdon, and strangely enough it is this second swindler who most effectively protects Marie's interests by making her insist on a settlement of one half of Teissier's fortune. Becque has again disappointed the conventional showman by not writing a scene showing the reformation of the advocate. For Bourdon, according to his "realistic" view of life, it was absolutely right—a

Darwinist law of nature, so to speak—to rob the Vigneron nest when the father-bird was gone. Now it is equally right for Marie to pluck Teissier, for nature has placed an old man at the mercy of a young woman. *The Vultures* resolves itself as if Becque had dispassionately observed a law of nature working itself out in the decline and restoration of the Vignerons' fortunes. Yet nothing could be more ironic in tone and more devastatingly satiric than this exposé of how "social Darwinists" act and think. And the more indifferent Becque is to the amorality of his characters the more thoroughly he exposes them as the vultures they are.

Becque's virtuosity in refraining from virtuosity is even more remarkable in his second masterwork *La Parisienne*. This comedy does not even have a "resolution," for Clotilde Du Mesnil, who has been betraying her husband at the beginning of the play, simply continues to betray him at the end. Nor does *La Parisienne* actually possess a "crisis." There is never any question of Clotilde's being found out; the husband is a complacent individual who misses the lover's company more than the wife does. There is much comic conflict, it is true, in the first act, but it is between the woman and the lover, and it quickly disappears when Clotilde simply drops him, only to take him back toward the end of the play when she has herself been dropped by another lover. The blasé second lover, who has furthered her husband's political ambitions at her request, quietly informs her that he is leaving for the country. Neither for him nor for Clotilde has the breaking up of the relationship assumed any critical proportions. Recriminations are for people who feel intensely, whereas the point of Becque's comedy is precisely that nobody is capable of intense emotion in this Parisian *milieu*. Nobody, that is, except the first lover Lafont, and he is merely ridiculous, since he claims the proprietary rights of a husband to her fidelity. Without a real crisis and resolution, with hardly any exposition, and without inserting a single bout of wit or a single prurient line Becque managed to write one of the most brilliant—and amoral—comedies of all time.

La Parisienne is full of irony, unconscious in the case of the characters; but the most ironical thing about it is that Becque's aloof observation of life should make the play pass for one of the most cleverly written pieces of the theatre. When the late A. B. Walkley, a critic not given to unconsidered enthusiasms, saw Mme. Réjane play Clotilde in London in 1901, he marveled at "this whiff of sulphur combined with *odeur de femme*," and called the comedy "diabolically clever." "It purports to have been written by the late Mr. Henri Becque single-handed," he added, "but I suspect Old Nick to have been at his elbow, an unseen collaborator." Yet this effect was the result of nothing more than the author's pretense of acting as the part of life's amanuensis. The play begins, as Walkley noted, with "one of the most complex hoaxes ever devised by a playwright." We are led to believe that Clotilde is engaged in a lengthy conjugal brawl with a jealous husband, until she calls out *"Prenez garde, voila mon mari"* and we know that the man is her lover. But the hoax is life's trick on the characters, for the comic and realistic point of the illicit relationship is that usage has made it indistinguishable from the unromantic state of marriage. As a romance, prolonged adultery is a highly over-rated experience, and the jealousy of her lover proves as boring to Clotilde as would have been the jealousy of her husband. Becque's main achievement, however, was that his tenacious veracity should make Clotilde so monstrously immoral without turning her into a monster (she is patient, reasonable, considerate, and congenial), and so amusing without giving her an ounce of humor to flaunt before the public. Like Joyce's Molly Bloom, she is nature unadulterated by the sense of right and wrong.

Becque needed a theatre capable of giving life to his characters instead of dipping them into greasepaint and thrusting them out into the footlight area in order that they might hurl their lines into the auditorium. The entire point of the dramatic treatment in both *The Vultures* and *La Parisienne* was, after all, the revelation of moral turpitude in the society of his time through the natural conduct of his characters. They are drawn as people who consider their questionable morals above reproach, they regard their conduct and sentiments as norms of the social level on which they thrive. Both the humor and the indictment in Becque's two masterpieces arise entirely from the discrepancy between what his characters think of themselves and our judgment of them. The little foxes of *The Vultures* (and Lillian Hellman's *The Little Foxes* strongly recalls Becque's play) consider themselves merely realistic businessmen when they cheat a widow and three orphaned daughters of their inheritance. Clotilde in *La Parisienne* believes herself to be a devoted wife to her husband, for she wins him political advancement through her infidelity, and she considers herself so proper a person that she can seriously reprove her lover for his lack of religion. Unconscious irony can go no further than the conclusion of *The Vultures* when Teissier, the most ravenous of the rascals, proceeds to drive off the other vultures after winning Marie in marriage and remarks: "Since your father's death, my child, you have been surrounded by a pack of scoundrels."

To let the actor play up to the audience and address his remarks to it instead of to other characters, to push him out of the scenery that frames the room in which the action is supposed to take place, to allow him to declaim his lines with exaggerated gestures—these were the unpardonable sins that the conventional theatre committed against Becque and other realistic dramatists. A major upheaval was needed in theatrical art to make the revolution in playwriting effective. The revolution was

started by André Antoine when he founded the Théâtre Libre in 1887, and it is not surprising that Becque rallied to Antoine's support. It was this pioneering actor-manager who gave *La Parisienne* its first distinguished production in 1897, with Mme. Réjane playing Clotilde to his Lafont at the Théâtre Antoine, founded two years before Becque's death.

With the triumph of the new naturalistic stagecraft, Becque finally came into his own. But by then Becque was depleted of his creative energy. He wrote nothing of significance after 1885 except two short pieces, *The Start* (*Le Depart*) and *Widowed* (*Veuve*)—the former a sketch of a shopgirl's induction into vice by a respectable employer who discharges her for refusing to yield to his son, the latter a sequel to *La Parisienne* which shows us Clotilde widowed at last but otherwise unchanged. Three other one-acters written in the year 1877 were trifles, and *The Puppets,* an exposé of the world of finance started fifteen years earlier, was left unfinished at his death. Admitted to the Legion of Honor in 1886, lionized in society for his acrid wit, invited in 1893 to lecture in Italy where his plays had become popular, he nevertheless remained poor and lonely. His admirers racked their brains for ways of stimulating him to create more masterpieces, and Antoine even lured him to Brittany for a summer's vacation to induce him to write again. A fire that the solitary man started in his bedroom with a lighted cigar caused him a severe shock, and he had to be placed in a sanatorium by friends. He never recovered. His death on May 15, 1899, was a deep blow to the men of the theatre who honored his forthright struggle to modernize the French stage.

Writing in 1905 about Becque, James Huneker declared that *The Vultures* was "the bible of the dramatic realists." Yet, unlike Zola, Becque never propounded any formula of Naturalism for playwrights. He did not even evince any marked enthusiasm for Ibsen, and the only realist who affected him was Tolstoy, whose peasant tragedy *The Power of Darkness* impressed him greatly. With curious inconsistency, probably for personal reasons of gratitude, he maintained a life-long admiration for Victorien Sardou, whose theatrical contrivances Bernard Shaw once dismissed as "Sardoodledom." In writing a preface to *The Vultures,* Becque dissociated himself from the Naturalists' fondness for sordid drama and from their pet doctrine of heredity. He wrote: "I have never entertained a great liking for assassins, hysterical and alcoholic characters, or for the martyrs of heredity and victims of evolution." He distrusted any sort of legislation for dramatists, declaring, "there is no law and there are no rules; there are only plays which are so different that no generalization is applicable. . . ." Concerning his encounters with conservatism in the theatre, he maintained merely that there were no conventions that originality could not displace, that "the history of art is nothing but the history of struggles between original talents and routine-bound minds."

All that Becque intended to do was to set down reality without distorting it for the sake of theatrical expediency. In confining himself to a segment of life, he seemed to say, "Make what you will of it, this is how people behave in our time and place, this is how they think, and this is how they speak." He dispensed with tricks of the trade, such as artificially emotional or scintillating "big" scenes and act-endings that brought the curtain down with a bang at the expense of naturalness. Like Strindberg, when the Scandinavian playwright came to write his remarkably compact one-act dramas, *Miss Julie* and *The Creditors,* Becque pruned his plays of all inessentials at a time when witty conversations, *ex cathedra* preachments, and declamations were considered the indispensable machinery of any theatre that expected to attract an audience; against this kind of dramaturgy, Becque declared that drama was the art of elimination. He endeavored, moreover, to release a natural flow of action which would make it impossible for the parts of a play to be differentiated mechanically as "exposition," "climax," and "dénouement." In a play like *The Vultures,* which suffers from some prolixity, and in the more brilliantly executed, if more narrowly Parisian, comedy *La Parisienne,* it is Becque's sharp observation that stands foremost. Unlike Ibsen, he did not quite rid his work of occasional asides or soliloquies, but these do not materially detract from his realism. It is the integrity of the conception and the writing of both plays that has preserved them, and it is integrity, for which there has never been too much regard in the theatre, that explains the influence this dour playwright exerted on the formative modern drama. From the ideal that he set for dramatists, there have been, regrettably, more descents than ascents, and this is as good a reason as any for remembering him half a century after his death.

At this time, especially in the American theatre, there is, however, an equally good reason for giving some attention to his two masterpieces, and that reason must strike us as a paradox if we still adhere to a naïve view of realism as a mere transcription of life. Becque had the gift of making a transcript look like a travesty, or if you will, a travesty look like a transcript. The "naturalness" of his dramaturgy and writing, which made it possible for him to set down reality in such a matter-of-fact manner, was in his case an instrument of satiric comedy. To treat the behavior and thought-processes of his vultures and amoralists as perfectly "natural" was the most powerful method he could have adopted to outrage us and make us consider them monstrous. The result is travesty achieved by naturalness. That is, the logic or consistency of these characters makes them exaggerations or caricatures. Conversely, for Becque to

present such monsters of iniquity as perfectly natural specimens of the human species and of society is tantamount to directing his satire at the species and society. What, in other words, are we to think of the human race and of human society if Becque's amoralists are to be regarded as normal people!

It will be seen then that Becque used "realism," or "naturalism," far from naïvely. Unlike many later playwrights up to our own time, he was not the slave but the master of the realistic mode of playwriting coming into vogue in his day. He was a creator when he adopted the role of a transcriber, whereas many a playwright who succeeded him was a transcriber while adopting the role of a creator. Becque brought a distinctive, tart, and quizzical temperament and a nimble mind to the modern theatre. His astringent essays in *Souvenirs d'un Auteur Dramatique* and *Études d'Art Dramatique* also enforce this opinion. With these qualities he gave a unique comic style to naturalism, a style simultaneously "natural" and grotesque. One might call it a sort of expressionistic naturalism, without expressionistic fantasy and structure.

One can find this style, which is a quality of creativeness and urbane intellect, variously present in the work of European playwrights. It ferments in the plays of Carl Sternheim, barely known in America; in Hauptmann's *The Beaver Coat* and *The Conflagration (Der Rote Hahn)*; in Wedekind's *The Tenor*; in Granville-Barker's *The Voysey Inheritance*; in Pagnol's *Topaze,* Jules Romains' *Dr. Knock,* Crommelynck's *The Magnificent Cuckold,* and other French and Belgian pieces. In America, this kind of writing has not prevailed, unless we can ascribe it to *Tobacco Road,* where it is more salacious than tart, and to Edwin Justin Mayer's *The Children of Darkness,* where it is bespangled by romanticism. Other borderline cases may occur to us. But for the total charge of naturalistic irony and the full blast of boreal comedy, which American playgoers don't seem to be able to relish, we must go, first of all, to Henry Becque. We are, of course, under no particular obligation to like what we don't like. But the maturity of Becque's mind and the tempered steel of his spirit will remain a challenge to playwrights and a reminder that naturalistic playwriting can become a thoroughly creative act. Perhaps his denial of interest in Naturalism as propounded in France during his time, along with his favorable opinion of Sardou, will not seem egregious perversity or blindness on his part when we realize that he was not a simple purveyor of "slice of life" dramaturgy even while seeming to be just that. Becque, to conclude, was one of those pioneers of modern drama who, along with Ibsen, Strindberg, Shaw, and Chekhov, possessed true individuality and a rare power to shape reality while pretending to photograph it.

Marvin Carlson (essay date 1972)

SOURCE: Carlson, Marvin. "Realism & Symbolism (1870-1900)." In *The French Stage in the Nineteenth Century*, pp. 177-80. Metuchen, N.J.: Scarecrow Press, Inc., 1972.

[*In the following essay, Carlson proclaims Becque a major victim of the French theatre's prejudices towards new playwrights and the reintroduction of censorship in 1874.*]

In France, as elsewhere in Europe, the final decades of the nineteenth century provide the richest variety of theatre. Identifying the period with a single movement is therefore even more misleading here than identifying the 1830s and 1840s with the then-dominant romantic school. Nevertheless, there is considerable justice in the common association of the end of the century with realism. Realism, like romanticism, is subject to a wide range of interpretation, even if we restrict ourselves only to its manifestations in the theatre. It may suggest the literal reproduction of everyday life, a trend already present to some extent in such reformers as Montigny but carried much further in this period by Antoine. It may refer only to the use of contemporary as contrasted with classical or mythological subjects. Since Scribe and Augier had already studied the monied classes, this usually meant that the contemporary subjects of later realists were drawn from the lower classes. Realism may also involve a concern with historical accuracy (a concern it shares with romanticism). This may lead on the one hand to attempts to recreate the period of the play's action in the manner of Pixérécourt, Charles Kean, the Meininger, or the spectacles of Bernhardt and Sardou, or on the other to attempts to recreate the original conditions of production, as in the Poel Shakespearian stages or the Greek revivals done late in the century at the Odéon and Comédie. Each of these aspects of realism was involved in the experimentation undertaken by the Parisian theatre of this period.

This experimentation took many other forms as well, some rivaling realism in significance for the coming century, but in at least two respects realism's significance was unique. First, it was the realists who eventually achieved the shattering of the established and sterile forms that Zola so deplored, thereby opening the way to other experiments. Second, in this period so dominated socially and intellectually by the forces of positivist philosophy, materialism and scientism, the works of the realists struck a more responsive chord and thus won a wider and more lasting support than any of the subsequent movements the theatre offered.

The most important of these later alternatives to realism was the symbolist movement, appearing in the 1890s. It was in many respects a return to romanticism after the harsh and sometimes banal offerings of the realists. It emphasized the vague and the universal over the specific, emotion over reason, and, doubtless due to the influence of Wagner, a harmony of all elements in the work of art. The tradition of experimentation outside the established theatre was developed further by both realists and symbolists. The Porte-Saint-Martin, the Gymnase, and the Vaudeville had proven earlier in the century that established minor houses could challenge the national theatres. Antoine's Théâtre-Libre and Lugné-Poe's Théâtre de l'Oeuvre carried the process a step further, by mounting their challenge from entirely outside the existing theatre system. They thus established the pattern the avant-garde in the theatre has followed since. The Comédie eventually assimilated these new schools, or at least their most important products, but its major role had become that of repository of the established classics.

1. HENRY BECQUE AND ANDRÉ ANTOINE, 1881-1894

During the 1870s and early 1880s the French theatre experienced a rising sense of dissatisfaction, a growing suspicion that a plateau had been reached and that the existing system had become too rigid to allow new directors, new actors and, especially, new playwrights an opportunity to add vitality to the art. Young authors were discouraged by the preference of major theatres for Augier, Sardou, and the proven dramatists of the Second Empire. Censorship was reintroduced in 1874, but when Zola mounted a campaign against it in 1885 after the banning of *Germinal* he found most of the established dramatists in Paris united against him. He joined with other novelists such as Flaubert and Daudet to challenge the hold of these established authors on the theatre, but either their dramatic imagination or their determination proved insufficient, since all ended by allowing their works at last to be adapted by popular hacks such as Busnach or Belot, who had little concern for either experimentation or originality.

The major victim of this situation was Henry Becque, who complained frequently and bitterly of the commercialism and exclusiveness of the system which indeed denied him his rightful position as the major serious dramatist of France during this period:

> "About twenty-five authors," he observed, "share the theatres. The vogue of their works, almost always legitimate, but frequently somewhat excessive, and furthermore aided by outstanding interpretation, leads to runs of 200, 300, and even 500 nights. When these authors compete with each other and are often obliged to wait their turn even for guaranteed productions, how can unknowns hope to gain a turn?"

Becque, of course, persevered and triumphed, but his assertion that many other potential playwrights of his generation were stifled, while impossible to prove, seems unfortunately likely.

There was admittedly little in Becque's early work to indicate the development of a major talent. All of his first four plays were clear failures except a drama, **Michel Pauper** (1870), which Becque mounted at his own expense at the Porte-Saint-Martin. Thanks largely to the interpretation of Taillade, it achieved a favorable, if not enthusiastic, response. This was hardly enough to interest Parisian directors of the 1870s in a new author, and Becque tried in vain for five years to find a theatre to present his major work, **Les Corbeaux.** Neither Montigny nor his successor Koning was interested, neither Duquesnel nor his successor La Rounat at the Odéon, not Deslandes at the Vaudeville nor Ritt at the Porte-Saint-Martin. Even the less popular Gaîté, Ambigu, and Cluny refused him. At last, in 1881, despairing of ever seeing the play performed, Becque arranged for its publication. Then remarkably his publisher, Stock, praised the work to his friend Thierry, the former director of the Comédie, who arranged for a reading at the national theatre. Even more remarkable, the widely refused play was accepted by the Comédie for presentation by a vote of six to two.

All too soon, Becque found that this apparent triumph merely opened to him a new set of agonies. The actors of the Comédie, accustomed to the "realism" of Augier, Dumas *fils,* Feuillet, and Erckmann-Chatrian, were confused and irritated by this harsh and savage study of the destruction of a family by the former friends of its dead father. Like Hugo fifty years before, Becque found himself in constant quarrels with conservative actors over interpretation, indeed even over the language of his work. Just as Mlle Mars had refused to say Hugo's "*lion superbe et généreux,*" Coquelin now demanded that Becque's "*boustiffouller*" be replaced by "*se mettre à table.*" Got was clearly relieved to be withdrawn from the central role of Teissier in order to appear in a revival of *Le Roi s'amuse.* The opening was rather stormy, but far from another "battle of *Hernani.*" **Les Corbeaux** was generally associated in the public mind with Zola's new "naturalist" movement, but though opinion on the movement was sharply divided, little of the explosiveness of the early romantic period was now present. Reviews of the play were generally re-statements of the reviewers' previously expressed opinions on naturalism in general, so that conservatives spoke disparagingly of the "cynicism and salaciousness" of the work, while Zola's partisans praised its "realism and tough-mindedness." Neither the criticism nor the generally indifferent interpretation engaged the attention of the general public, and the run was a short one.

How far the battle for "naturalism in the theatre" was from being won by this single skirmish was made clear later, in 1882, when the Comédie refused by a vote of six to three to produce Becque's second major work, **La Parisienne.** Once again Becque made the rounds of Parisian theatres and once again found his work rejected in favor of such established figures as Sardou, Labiche, or Gondinet. In 1885 Becque wrote to Thierry, who had continued to give him encouragement, that he had been forced to entrust his work to the "inadequate artists and poverty-striken director" of the Renaissance.

Certainly, after acceptance at the Comédie, Becque had reason to complain of his fall to one of the capital's more obscure houses, but the little organization which presented his second work was not simply one among many indistinguishable ventures, and deserves more attention than theatre historians have given it. The director, Fernand Louveau (whose professional name was Samuel), began as the leader of an amateur dramatic society, the *Cercle des Arts Intimes,* which gave unproduced works by known authors. Louveau moved on to direct the Renaissance in 1884, but retained for several years his interest in experimentation, even in this commercial situation. Though **La Parisienne** was his only significant production, Louveau should be remembered as one who provided a model for the more influential André Antoine a few years later. The actors at the Renaissance had little training, of course, but for that very reason, as Antoine also later discovered, were in some ways better suited to the new approach in drama than the traditionally trained actors of the major houses. Mlle Antonine in particular, who played the original Clotilde, was generally considered superior to Suzanne Reichenberg in the 1890 revival at the Comédie **La Parisienne** was a far more successful work than the more bitter **Corbeaux,** and Becque had no difficulty in finding theatres willing to present the five lesser plays he wrote before his death in 1899. After 1885 he busied himself also with reviewing for several journals, defending his two major works, and organizing their revivals. The 1890 revival of **La Parisienne** at the Comédie was a failure, but Réjane at the Vaudeville gave the piece a triumphant vindication in 1893.

Despite Becque's eventual success, the difficulties he had in attaining it guaranteed that few of his contemporaries would follow his example. Slowly, the Parisian theatre began to evolve less difficult procedures for the discovery and encouragement of new talent. Louveau's productions made an important but limited contribution, since his authors were established even though the plays were unfamiliar. Another step was taken by a more prominent figure in the theatre world, Hilarion Ballande. In 1867 Ballande formed a *Société de patronage des auteurs dramatiques inconnus* which supported matinee performances of new playwrights. Unable to engage the interest of the public, Ballande changed two years later to "classic matinees" at the Gaîté and later at the Porte-Saint-Martin. These productions, like Louveau's, were of unusual works by known authors, though the Ballande matinees gained a far greater reputation because of his ability to attract to them most of the great names among established actors as well as the most promising new talents—Mélingue, Laferrière, Coquelin, Bernhardt, Desclée, Mounet-Sully, Taillade, Montaland, Reichenberg all were seen in Ballande productions. The matinees proved so successful that by 1880 almost every major theatre in Paris had established an experimental matinee program. Most followed Ballande's example in reviving minor classics, but some, most notably the Gymnase, produced even the more ephemeral comedies and *vaudevilles* of the early part of the century. In 1876 Ballande purchased the Déjazet, which he renamed the Troisième Théâtre-Français. Here again he attempted to introduce young authors, but his most important discovery was the distinctly minor Ernest Calonne, and his greatest successes continued to be revivals. Far more productive were the "*matinées in-édites*" which Tallien began giving at the Cluny in 1879 and which introduced Hennique, Brieux, and Salandri to the stage.

LA NAVETTE (THE MERRY-GO-ROUND)

PRODUCTION REVIEW

A. G. H. Spiers (review date 13 December 1917)

SOURCE: Spiers, A. G. H. "Reviews of Plays: Becque and Merimee at the Vieux Colombier." *Nation* 105, no. 2737 (13 December 1917): 674.

[*In the following review, Spiers remarks favorably on the production of Becque's* The Merry-Go-Round *at the Theatre du Vieux Colombier.*]

The second bill of the Théâtre du Vieux Colombier is a delight—a delight for the eyes as well as for the mind. I shall speak later of Copeau's stage-setting and costumes; our immediate attention is required by a question raised in the review of the preceding bill: can this company present with equal soundness and skill plays of very different types?

So far as can be judged from this second programme, the answer is an incontestable affirmative. Becque's *La Navette,* first given at the Gymnase in 1878, is a one-act play in which figure the five A's—Antonia, the woman; her three admirers, Alfred, Arthur, and Armand, and the maid Adèle. Like a shuttle (whence the name), Antonia weaves in and out among the men, giving up the first for the second, then listening to the advances of the third, only to return once more to the first. Nevertheless the play is neither hilarious nor sentimental. Clever

it certainly is, and moderately amusing; but its essential quality is not to be found in these external things. Within this framework one discerns a purpose, an ideal; for Henry Becque is one of those dramatists who have given a new direction to the development of the French drama. Four years after *La Navette,* he put on the stage *Les Corbeaux,* and three years later still, *La Parisienne.* In the first, the partner and the creditors of a dead man prey, without the slightest compunction, upon the wife and daughters he left behind; in the second, the characters of a *ménage à trois* are so moved by considerations of orderliness, of reciprocal obligations, and of what I might almost call family unity, that they reveal no sense of the immorality of their situation. Through these plays, Becque became the master whom succeeding dramatists have honored as the first to depict in their true sombreness situations and modes of life on which former writers had thrown a false glamour. And the little one-acter *La Navette* holds promise of these two more serious works.

Antonia is not witty, vivacious, nor alluring. Her admirers, though different from each other, are, with one possible exception, equally commonplace. Weak of purpose, incapable of disinterestedness even in their love, they consider only their petty rights, their purses, and their personal satisfaction. Of romance, they have not a trace. The excellence of the play lies in its sobriety and in the artistic treatment that makes us willing to consider the drabness of the situation. Boredom and the commonplace presented in such a way as to compel our attention, such is the definition of this little work; and as such the actors play it. They who have put so much dash into the "Fourberies de Scapin" are even bold enough to drag their acting here. It takes courage such as few possess today to interpret a play with such sincerity; but this courage is a proof of the highest appreciation of the actor's duty.

Flippant, rich in color, transporting us into an exotic atmosphere where only the commonplace is untrue and only the frivolous counts, the next play on the programme is very different from *La Navette.* This is Mérimée's *Le Carrosse du Saint Sacrement.* Don Andrès is Viceroy of Lima. Gouty, luxurious, quick-tempered, this *bon vivant* casts off his responsibilities with the nonchalance befitting the typical grandee of old, decadent Spain. He cares only for an actress, Périchole. He chortles over her pranks and he delights in her unconventionality, growing angry only when he suspects that he is not alone to possess her favors. How this arch beauty Périchole, appearing in all the loveliness of sumptuous apparel, weans him from his suspicion and obtains, besides, his gilded coach with which to outshine the contemptuous high-born ladies of the town, this is the story that Mérimée puts before us—this, and the fact that her beauty is not without its effect, either, upon the stately and gracious bishop to whose church she finally gives the coach.

Included in the second edition (1830) of the "Théâtre de Clara Gazul," this playlet seems a little gem of romantic levity. But much of our pleasure is undoubtedly due to Gournac's capital rendering of Don Andrès, to Mme. Bogaert's Périchole, and to the very beautiful setting and costumes.

For the third play of the evening, Copeau returns to Molière. The *Fourberies* of the last bill, especially the rôle of Scapin, was played in the manner of the most highly developed acting of the old *farceurs*. *La Jalousie du Barbouillé,* however, takes us back to a more rudimentary stage of their art. Based on an old tale, already used by Boccaccio, this farce is the first extant work of the French master. It is plebeian and coarse, with much of the boisterous fun of the mediæval populace. The characters are generalizations of the most elementary sort; and it is fitting, as well as historically correct, that they should be painted and dressed rather as puppets than as individuals. Le Barbouillé himself, as the name requires, is so coated with paint that his face is covered as with a mask. Noise, horse-play, and "go" are part and parcel of the play; and the actors give us all that. But they bring out, also, the broad lines of its caricature, the directness of its dialogue, and the remarkable speed and sureness with which Molière, even at this early date, develops an amusing situation. We laugh heartily and are not ashamed of our laughter; for the performance gives us an exhilarating sensation of health, energy, and animal spirits.

LES CORBEAUX (THE VULTURES)

CRITICAL COMMENTARY

Frank Wadleigh Chandler (essay date 1916)

SOURCE: Chandler, Frank Wadleigh. "Family Studies." In *Aspects of Modern Drama,* pp. 210-22. New York: Macmillan, 1916.

[*In the following essay, Chandler compares marital relationships in plays by Bjornson, Mirbeau and Barker to Becque's* The Vultures (*translated by Chandler as* The Ravens).]

I. The family study an outgrowth of the domestic drama. The family in relation to commercialism, as exhibited by Björnson, Becque, Mirbeau, and Barker: Björnson's

A Bankruptcy, a family which has forfeited the higher values of life growing regenerate through a business failure; Becque's **The Ravens,** a widow and her children becoming the prey of her husband's former business associates; Mirbeau's *Business Is Business* and Sowerby's *Rutherford and Son,* the blight of commercialism falling upon a family through the exclusive devotion to business of its head; Barker's *The Voysey Inheritance,* proposing a problem in practical ethics and answering it in the spirit of Ibsen and Shaw; Barker's *The Madras House,* a gallery of family portraits introduced in connection with a satire upon business and sex.

I

Marital relations are the principal subject of treatment in the domestic drama. But, with increasing frequency of late, this drama has utilized, also, relationships between parents and children, brothers and sisters, and the connection of the family as a whole with business and money, love and marriage. Moreover, special problems affecting the family circle have been proposed for solution. In plays where this is the case, emphasis is likely to fall upon the dramatist's thesis, the theory of conduct which he would advocate under certain conditions. With most of the family studies, however, the aim is pictorial—the representation of persons closely allied by blood or by marriage, their idiosyncrasies being thrown into prominence by some family crisis. For the most part, the crisis itself is less important than the characters it affects, and the family studies incline toward realism. They are realistic, not only in the minuteness of their observation of human nature, but also in their looseness of structure and matter-of-fact material.

The development of the dramatic family study is historically to be associated with the rise of naturalism. An early instance of such a study appears in what has been called the first naturalistic play—*The Selicke Family (Die Familie Selicke),* by Arno Holz and Johannes Schlaf. This piece, with its portrayal of a group of relatives suffering from poverty and from the dissipation of the family-head, a drunken bookseller, suggested to Hauptmann his *Before Sunrise,* which in turn prepared the way for his other family dramas—*The Festival of Peace, Lonely Lives,* and *Michael Kramer.* The fashion, once set, has spread until family studies now abound in the theatre. Not the least of these is *Milestones,* by Arnold Bennett and Edward Knoblauch, a work which extends the scope of the genre by tracing a domestic history through three generations, with a view to displaying in each the operation of the same law of individual growth from radicalism to old-fogeyism.

Of all such plays, one distinct group exhibits the family as affected by commercialism. Representative in this group are Björnson's *A Bankruptcy,* Becque's **The**

Ravens, Mirbeau's *Business Is Business,* and Barker's *The Voysey Inheritance.* In the first of these dramas, Björnson's *A Bankruptcy* (*En Fallit*), a family, which has forfeited all the higher values of life in scrambling for wealth, grows regenerate through a business failure. The seemingly prosperous Tjälde, whose devotion to commerce has led him to neglect wife and daughters, is steadily losing money. Yet he justifies his pretense of affluence as the only means for saving the sums confided to him by others. When his sharp practice excites suspicion, the bankers of Christiania send an agent to inspect his accounts. Tjälde endeavors to save himself by securing credit from a visiting magnate in whose honor he tenders a dinner. His efforts prove fruitless, and, being confronted by the agent, he declares that he will shoot the inquisitor or himself. But the agent is perfectly cool. He advises Tjälde to strip off the cloak of deceit which he has worn for so long, to confess himself a bankrupt, to begin life over. For years, his wife and daughters have struggled to keep up appearances; they will all be happier to start afresh in honest poverty.

The merchant yields to the agent's advice. Although his windows are stoned by irate workmen, his woes are lightened by the generosity of friends, and the members of his family are drawn together by their common affliction. The lieutenant, a pretender for the hand of Tjälde's younger daughter, takes French leave; but an awkward clerk, hitherto scorned by the elder daughter, rallies to the aid of the bankrupt and works wonders in assisting him to retrieve his fortunes. To cap the climax, the very agent who had forced the failure of Tjälde takes the place of the lieutenant as suitor of the younger daughter.

Obviously, this play is old-fashioned in its structure, characters, and perfunctory optimism. It is a dramatized *Vicar of Wakefield.* "Sweet are the uses of adversity" might be its motto. Like Björnson's *Geography and Love* and *When the New Wine Blooms,* it decries preoccupation with business and exalts the domestic virtues. With the misery of Tjälde and his family, when engaged in the race for wealth, is contrasted their happiness when returning to a life of simplicity.

Some years after the appearance of *A Bankruptcy,* Henri Becque produced his play of superior realism, **The Ravens** (**Les Corbeaux**). Here is presented still another aspect of the family in its relation to business,—the fate of a widow and her children who become the prey of her dead husband's unscrupulous associates. In the first act, the family of Vigneron, a well-to-do manufacturer, is celebrating the betrothal of his youngest daughter. Vigneron's crabbed old partner, his solicitor, his architect, and a music teacher unite in the festivities, which are suddenly interrupted by the death from apoplexy of Vigneron himself. The three acts that

remain exhibit the collapse of the family fortunes and the descent upon Mme. Vigneron and her children of these very guests—the 'ravens.' The youth who was to marry Blanche deserts her. The music teacher, who has assured Judith of her talents, now admits that her proposal to support the family by going on the stage is absurd. Vigneron's partner advises the widow to sell what is left of her real estate at a sacrifice, intending to purchase it himself in secret; and the architect, finding that the widow has no funds for more buildings, duns her for the fees already due him. The solicitor, hoping to line his own pockets, warns the widow against her husband's partner; and the latter, although past sixty, looks with greedy eyes upon the third daughter of Mme. Vigneron. When Marie scorns Teissier's dishonorable proposal, the old man, admiring what he takes to be merely her shrewdness, offers her marriage.

Although Marie detests Teissier, she feels that to take him is her only chance for saving her family. The solicitor assures her that at Teissier's death she will inherit half of his property. "You should know," says the man of the law, "that love does not exist. . . . There is nothing but business in the world, and marriage is a business transaction like any other. The opportunity which now presents itself to you, you will never find a second time." To her mother, Marie confesses her shame in yielding, yet she is spared the sense of guilt she would feel were she to refuse.

Old Teissier is satisfied with his bargain, but to test Marie, he supervises her meeting with a rascally creditor. When the fellow grows insolent, Teissier steps forth and sends him flying. Then he turns to the girl, exclaiming, "You are surrounded with rogues, my child, since the death of your father!" To Teissier it never occurs that he is the greatest rogue of the lot.

Something of the same satirical spirit animates a third drama dealing with the family as affected by lust for money. This is Octave Mirbeau's later piece, in three acts, *Business Is Business* (*Les Affaires sont les affaires*). Here the author's effort has been chiefly expended upon one character, the members of whose family are sketched but lightly. Isidore Lechat, a self-made man of affairs, turns all that he touches into gold, but, in the process, exploits friends and enemies alike. Those who think to get the better of him he invariably overthrows. He oppresses the poor, scandalizes the rich, and, without a qualm, offers up his family on the altar of Mammon. Lechat's wife cannot call her soul her own. Lechat's son turns to sport, quarrels with his father regarding the payment of his racing debts, and then, through the wild driving of his motor car, snuffs out his life. Lechat's daughter, the sensitive Germaine, revolting at her father's vulgarity, disappoints his plan of allying her with the son of a marquis by walking out of the house with a poor young chemist.

For a little, Lechat is unsteadied by such reverses. But he pulls himself together to retaliate upon two of his partners, contemptible rogues, who have thought to take advantage of his unnerved condition. The man of business, being assailed with cunning, rallies to reply in kind and crush these rivals, and upon his barren triumph falls the final curtain.

Although *Business Is Business* be overmoralized, its protagonist is a vital creation, reminiscent of Molière's best characters. Lechat is both a spender and a getter of money, but his spending is only a means to fresh getting. Gold is his god, and efficiency his demi-god. He patronizes the nobility, forcing the marquis, who comes to ask a loan of him, to consent to allying their families and to supporting his candidacy for the Chamber of Deputies. When the marquis complains that Lechat would buy him, that worthy replies: "I never buy; I merely exchange. Business is a matter of exchange. We exchange money, land, titles, votes, intelligence, social position, office, love, genius—whatever we have for whatever we lack. There is nothing more permissible, and, rest assured, nothing more honorable." To the poor young man who captures the affections of his daughter, Lechat responds with a compliment on the youth's acumen. Of course, the fellow has merely conceived a scheme for extorting money. "Say it squarely, make your price!" cries Lechat; "I will pay!"

Still another study of family life in relation to business is Githa Sowerby's *Rutherford and Son,* its protagonist a glassmaker in the north of England. This John Rutherford is a more tragic figure than Mirbeau's Lechat, an industrial fanatic who regards his work as his religion. By his Gradgrind theory and practice of life, he drives each of his three children from home, and is left at the end desolate, except for the daughter-in-law he has always despised and the grandchild that he hopes may succeed him. His daughter, who has sought relief from drudgery in an affair with her father's foreman, that father turns out of the house as disgraced, after having himself appropriated the foreman's invention and then cashiered him. One son he has early alienated, a youth who seeks refuge in the church. The other he ruins morally, for this weak but well-meaning fellow, defeated in his plan of profiting by the foreman's invention, breaks into his father's strong box, and becomes a fugitive from justice, the deserter of his wife and babe.

More subtle in its treatment of a family crisis induced by commercialism is Granville Barker's best play, *The Voysey Inheritance.* Here the attention centers upon Edward Voysey, who discovers that his father for long has maintained a crooked business which he, as the son, will inherit. What shall he do? Publish the truth, and ruin his father, the firm, and the creditors; or, keep silent, and struggle to pay back little by little the moneys that have been taken for secret speculation from the clients' accounts? This question, at first one of theory alone, becomes pressing and practical when Edward's father suddenly dies. The son, assembling his family, lays the case before them. By some, the truth has been known or guessed at; to others, it comes with a shock. But all are agreed in declining to use their own private means for righting the wrong. Edward, they argue, must continue the business in silence, sending the clients their interest, and striving to replace, as he can, the capital.

When Edward objects to cheating the firm back into credit, the woman he loves meets his scruples, and, inspired by her confidence, he accepts the 'Voysey inheritance.' Needless to say, his path is beset with dangers. He must refuse to a clerk the hush money paid him for years. He must face the wrath of his father's old friend, who comes to withdraw his account and learns that it exists for the most part on paper. When the secret leaks out and a general collapse seems imminent, Alice reassures her lover. The clients, she says, rather than suffer the losses of bankruptcy, will let him work out their salvation. If they put him in prison, she still will be proud of him since under this strain he has grown into manhood. "There was never any chance of my marrying you," says Alice, "when you were only a well-principled prig. I didn't want you . . . and I don't believe you really wanted me. Now you do, and you must always take what you want."

This statement echoes the doctrines of Ibsen and Shaw. Beware of mere formulas for conduct, says Barker. The rules of right and wrong must often be modified when applied in a concrete instance. Thus Edward Voysey, in accepting the burden imposed by his father's dishonesty is right pragmatically, although wrong ideally. On general principles, he ought to fling down that burden with pious aversion, proclaiming the crime of his father and accepting the consequences. Just that is what a moral idealist, like Ibsen's Gregers Werle, would do and then glory in the ruin he had wrought.

More important than the author's ethical theory, in *The Voysey Inheritance,* is his painting of character. For the parents of Edward, his brothers and sisters, and their connections by marriage compose an unforgettable family group. Most carefully drawn is the father, a deceiver of self as well as of others, half convinced of the truth of his own little fiction of having inherited the crooked business from his father, and now handing it on to Edward as a sacred trust. Yet, as Edward later discovers, the man who can talk so top-loftily has once got the affairs of the firm quite straight, only to return to swindling just for the zest of the game.

If the other members of the Voysey family are shown less completely, they are no less distinct. There is Edward's deaf, little mother, devoted to her husband, although aware of his trouble. There is Trenchard, her eldest son, keen, cold, cock-sure, estranged from his father, and noting in that father's fiction of inherited dishonesty a touch of the artist common to criminals. There are the other sons, booming Major Booth, who roars the family into subjection, and the gaily impractical Hugh. As for the daughters, Ethel is a spoiled darling, and Honor is 'mother's right hand,' a spinster resigned to her sad survival. Add to these folk Ethel's lover, and the wives of Hugh and the Major, with Colpus the vicar and the selfish old friend of the Voyseys, and you have a remarkable family group, described with a precision of detail unrivalled on the contemporary stage outside the theatre of Shaw.

It is the Shavian influence, more than any other, that permeates *The Voysey Inheritance.* Hugh and his wife and Alice and Voysey himself talk like the people of Shaw. Thus Voysey assumes that what he has selfishly done in his business has been all for the good of the clients—a pose dear to Shaw's heroes. Hugh, like the Shavian scoffers, sneers at the average Happy English Home and the tyranny of its ideals, above all "the middle-class ideal that you should respect your parents, live with them, think with them, grow like them." Hugh's wife, like the Shavian free-thinking young women, grows tired of his crying for what he can't get and proposes to leave him. And Alice, the heroine, speaks the language of Shaw in warning her Edward that he should no more neglect his happiness than he would neglect to wash his face, and in saying, "You have a religious nature. . . . Therefore you're not fond of creeds and ceremonies." Her guardian, whom she refers to as "a person of great character and no principles," has instructed her in the Shavian philosophy on the occasion of her inheriting a fortune. "You've no right to your money. You've not earned it or deserved it in any way. Therefore, don't be surprised or annoyed if any enterprising person tries to get it from you. He has at least as much right to it as you have . . . if he can use it better, he has more right."

It will be evident that Granville Barker, as a writer of intellectual drama, is not content with making mere family studies in the naturalistic fashion. Rather, he exhibits his family groups with a well defined purpose. And this purpose, in a play like *The Madras House,* becomes relatively more important than the individual portraiture. Yet that chaotic comedy does depict, in connection with its dominant satire upon sex and business, two branches of a curious family.

The Huxtables and the Madrases are products of the drapery trade, a commerce which depends upon tickling the vanity of women and the appetite of men. A philosophic promoter proposes to unite with others the drapery houses of old Mr. Huxtable and Constantine Madras—brothers-in-law and business rivals, who have

not spoken to each other for years. What happens in the play is of no consequence, but the satire it affords upon trade conditions and family life is amusing. The Huxtable group is composed of father, mother, and six maiden daughters, introduced as horrible examples of what our artificial civilization leads to. In the normal course of events these daughters should have been married; but now, falsely restricted from the society of men, they are miserable. Laura, the eldest, turns for relief to housekeeping. Minnie and Clara seek solace in missions. The brusque and business-like Emma, who might have succeeded in a profession, is enforced to idleness since it is not proper for a woman in her position to work; and Jane, the youngest, has had to decline two proposals, not only because her parents objected to the men as insufficiently wealthy, but also because her sisters disapproved, fearing that if the youngest were to marry, their chances would be minimized. So all have gone unwed. Jane, according to her mother, has displayed a wanton mind in squeezing consolation from a man's collar sent home from the laundry by error.

As for the Madras branch of the family, it consists of Constantine Madras, his wife, his son, and his daughter-in-law. Constantine has retired from active management of the Madras House, in order to practice, in Arabia, his peculiar theories in regard to women. Philip, his son, carries on the business in London, and for it neglects his own pretty wife, until one day he awakens to his folly. Then he resolves to turn from the foppery of decking out the vain and the vicious to something really useful. He rejects the handsome position offered him by the American promoter, and determines instead to court poverty and abuse by entering politics. "Why do I give up designing dresses and running a fashion shop to go on the London County Council?" he asks. "To save my soul alive!"

Carl W. Wooton (essay date May 1961)

SOURCE: Wooton, Carl W. "*The Vultures*: Becque's Realistic Comedy of Manners." *Modern Drama* 4, no. 1 (May 1961): 72-79.

[*In the following essay, Wooton discusses* The Vultures *and its importance in the early development of modern realism.*]

Henry Becque's **The Vultures,** although important in the early development of modern realism, seems to be, for the most part, a forgotten play, or at least one that has received little critical attention in America. Its inclusion in John Gassner's *A Treasury of the Theatre,* in an English translation by Freeman Tilden,[1] however, is likely to make it a familiar play, at least to undergraduate students. It is, perhaps, of value then to examine some of the assumptions made concerning the nature of the play and how well they fit the work as art. In an introduction to the play, Gassner writes of the characters as believing that, "their social conduct and sentiments are norms of the social level on which they live and thrive." He notes that although Becque has employed the slice-of-life technique of the realist, the play does not belong to the naturalistic school of Zola and his other contemporaries in the French theater. Indeed, as Gassner points out, Becque removed himself from Zola's brand of naturalism when he wrote in his own preface to *The Vultures*: "I have never entertained much liking for assassins, hysterical and alcoholic characters, or for the martyrs of heredity and victims of evolution." Becque's intent was to portray reality as he saw it, to be completely faithful to the nature of the language, the thoughts and the actions that the characters would exhibit if they could be seen operating within the real society Becque was mirroring on the stage.

An American critic, Samuel Montefiore Waxman, contends that *The Vultures* is excessively bitter. In his study, *Antoine and the Théâtre-Libre*, Waxman praises Becque's dialogue and characterization, but he says, "And the words of the ravens are cruel, sometimes needlessly cruel. They reflect Becque's black view of life." Waxman holds that this "black view" is a result of Becque's unfortunate financial experiences. He considers the play more as a comment on the defined vultures than as a revelation of the manners of all the characters within their world. By means of this point of view, he is able to find an element to offset Becque's natural pessimism: "The most beautiful sentiment of *Les Corbeaux* is the closeness with which the mother, daughters, and faithful servant cling to each other in their unequal battle with the ravens."[2]

The play is a slice-of-life, a realistic play. To stop with this analysis, however, is to fall short of the mark, short of Henry Becque's intent and artistry. *The Vultures* presents a group of characters who are both products and producers of their society. Becque examines their code and their manners by presenting them without commentary. Any condemnation of their behavior is implicit, inferred from the disparity between the characters' evaluation of themselves and their society and the audience's opinion of them. In addition to employing these realistic techniques, Becque indirectly assists the audience in forming its opinion by satirizing the characters' manners with a heavy irony and a grim humor, unlikely to provoke laughter. Becque thus seems to have created a realistic play, in which the techniques of the comedy of manners are used for moralizing purposes.

This blending is substantially intimated in James Huneker's, *Iconoclasts*. Huneker writes in one instance that "*Les Corbeaux* is unique in modern comedy," and, later, that "*Les Corbeaux* is the Bible of the dramatic realists." Huneker also argues, however, that "Molière is his [Becque's] real master," and he asks, "Are we returning to the Molière comedy of character?" Huneker's awareness of Molière's influence on Becque and his opinion that Becque's new realism was a modified, a subdued naturalism, makes him see the play as a blending of these two forms. Becque, he concludes, was "nearer classic form" than his contemporaries.[3] The Molière influence on Becque is seen in his plots, which are, as Adolphe Thalasso points out in *Le Théâtre Libre*, ". . . très simples, très simples aussi ses moyens d'exécution."[4] It is true that Becque's plots are very simple and his technique relatively free of complex symbols and mechanical conventions.

The plot of *The Vultures* is extremely simple, and Becque relies only once on a mechanical convention to unfold his drama. The action centers around the Vignerons, a middle-class family of means. Mr. Vigneron is a manufacturer in partnership with a Mr. Teissier. The curtain goes up on a seemingly ideal home as the Vigneron family is preparing a dinner party to celebrate the impending marriage of their youngest daughter, Blanche. Mr. Vigneron leaves as the guests begin to arrive. After the guests have been introduced, and while they are laughing at Gaston Vigneron's impersonation of his father, an unwelcome guest, a doctor, arrives to announce the sudden and unexpected death of Mr. Vigneron. The next two acts present a procession of "vultures" who attempt to take advantage of Mrs. Vigneron's inability to comprehend the problems of settling her husband's estate. The "vultures" preying on the family are many, but the most rapacious is Teissier, who, with the help of the lawyer, Bourdon, reduces the family to a state of penury. Blanche's wedding is canceled because of her inability to provide the contracted dowry; the family is forced to move to surroundings incongruous with their former social status. In Act IV, Blanche has drifted into insanity, Gaston has joined the army, and the eldest daughter, Judith, and Mrs. Vigneron cannot resolve their plight. The family is finally saved by Teissier, who develops an interest in the second Vigneron daughter, Marie. The solution of the Vignerons' difficulties is effected by an agreement between Teissier and Marie to form a union admittedly without love, a marriage that is in actuality a business contract. The death of the father brought the "vultures" into action, but it also revealed that in a society where money has superseded moral values, all must be "vultures" if they are to survive.

The first act opens with an idyllic scene of family singing and fun-making. Yet, the untenable basis of the Vigneron world and its moral code is immediately suggested by their concern with propriety and with the place and function of money. In the first conversation between Blanche and her mother, Becque intimates the tenuous source of the Vignerons' standards. Blanche questions whether the placing of a menu at each plate will add anything to the dinner. When Mrs. Vigneron replies that it will not detract from it, Blanche is immediately concerned with the question of its propriety, regardless of the effect. Mrs. Vigneron is "absolutely sure" it is the proper thing to do because she "saw it in the *Ladies' Home Companion.*" The satire is immediately aimed at society's subscription to an artificial code. Mrs. Vigneron further admits to being flattered by the prospect of having a "son-in-law from one of the oldest families." It is ironical that she should qualify her pride by adding, "But I wouldn't sacrifice one of my girls to mere vanity," when sacrificing one of her girls is just what she ultimately must do in order to salvage her world. The relative nature of the Vigneron morality is further revealed in the discussion about the witnesses for the wedding. Mr. Vigneron is impressed by his prospective son-in-law's witnesses, "a high government official and a general," because in the Vigneron world, the worth of the individual is determined by his relative position in the social scale.

Blanche is depicted as a romantic, and Becque uses her to expose the shortcomings of the Vigneron society's definition of sexual purity and of the nature of marriage. Her mother describes Blanche as "a child, as modest and innocent—the dear little girl—as can be." But Blanche's innocence is seen, after the economic collapse of the family, as ironic and, moreover, strangely dependent upon the family's social status. When the probability of her marriage to George de Saint-Genis becomes dubious, she admits to Marie that the marriage must take place because she has already granted her fiancé the privileges of marriage. Becque exposes the economic nature of marriage in a materialistic society in two interviews between Blanche and Mrs. de Saint-Genis, George's mother. Blanche admits her imprudence to Marie after Mrs. de Saint-Genis warns her that the marriage might not take place if the Vignerons' economic status is drastically altered. Blanche, the romantic, continues to believe in the certainty of her marriage to George de Saint-Genis until her second, and final, interview with Mrs. de Saint-Genis. When it becomes obvious that Mrs. de Saint-Genis is likely to succeed in her efforts to prevent the marriage, Blanche suffers the humiliation of admitting her mistake a second time. Her appearance of innocence and naïveté is disproved, but even with her purity negated, her guilt is a matter of question in the light of Mrs. de Saint-Genis' standards. The error of the young lovers offers Mrs. de Saint-Genis a socially acceptable reason for prohibiting the marriage. Yet, Becque makes it clear that, in the eyes of the world, Blanche's real guilt does not arise from her act of passion. The ambiguous relationship between Blanche's guilt and economic stability is established when Mrs. de Saint-Genis tells Blanche, "You see, I do not attach any undue importance

to the result of a moment of forgetfulness, justified by your youth, and all the surrounding circumstances. You ought to want your fault to remain a secret; my son is an honorable man who would never betray you. So much said, the next question is: *is it necessary for both of you to sacrifice your whole lives for the sake of a slip?*" (Italics mine.) Blanche's moral guilt is minimized, and the real danger to both of the lovers is the risk of making an economically unwise match. Mrs. de Saint-Genis, angered by Blanche's obstinacy, ends the interview by condemning Blanche as a "fallen woman." However, Blanche's guilt does not lie in her fall from virginity; her guilt is not a moral guilt. The crime of Blanche was to fall from her previous economic status; her guilt lies in the failure of her father to provide for his family in the event of his death and in her inability to fulfill the dowry agreement. Her ensuing breakdown results from her inability to recognize the dichotomy of the two types of guilt, one moral and the other social and amoral, and from her inability to cope with the problems posed by the change in her social position.

Mr. Vigneron defines the position and function of money in his family's world and emphasizes the importance of propriety. In his only reliance on a mechanical convention, Becque has Mrs. Vigneron tell the story of Mr. Vigneron's rise from struggling respectability to upper-middle-class properness. Mr. Vigneron praises Mrs. Vigneron as the ideal businessman's wife, standing by through all the lean years and helping him to enjoy the full ones. He admonishes his children to "measure up to her standard," because she is "a model woman." This creates the question, what are her standards? Ironically, they collapse with the loss of her economically determined position. Becque hints at the hypocrisy of bourgeois social values when he reveals Vigneron's ignorance of music. It is proper to listen to music, but it is not necessary to have a sound knowledge of the subject. The power and place of money in their lives is emphasized again when Vigneron speaks to his family of the future: "Just let the old man put in a few more years to ensure the future of this little family, and then he'll have earned the right to take a rest." In a society based on money, the future can be ensured only by economic gains, and the very "right" to rest is bought, not really earned. Vigneron has no opportunity to know that in the event of such an accident as his death, the same perverted emphasis on money that effected his family's rise will be the cause of his family's downfall.

The family's fall from status affects Judith and Gaston as much as it affects Blanche. Judith is a shy musician who has been led to believe by Merckens, her music teacher, that she possesses real talent. However, when she loses her social position, Merckens ceases flattering her and tells her brutally that her talent is insufficient for a career and that "there are no resources for a woman; or, at least, only one. . . . If you are good, people will respect you without doing anything for you; and if you're not, they'll do things for you without respecting you." Merckens' callousness and the collapse of her hopes to provide a living for her family force Judith to be the first to admit that the family can be saved only if Marie makes the "greatest sacrifice a woman can make" and marries Teissier. Gaston appears at first as a happy-go-lucky youth, bothered only with the problem of how best to entertain himself. He also cannot adjust to his new status and escapes by joining the army. Gaston and Judith, like Blanche, have not been prepared to cope with the reality of their society. Wealth permitted them to see only appearances, the lip service paid to traditional morals and sentimental values. Poverty forces them to realize that they possess neither charm, nor talent, nor position if they do not possess money.

The more obvious "vultures," Bourdon and Teissier, recognize the nature of their society, subscribe to its relative code and utilize the code to maintain their acquired position. To Bourdon, the Lawyers' Club is "meant to be a protection for us—not for the public." The club's standards must benefit those subscribing to them and protect the members in their pursuit of wealth. Standards are no longer established by comparison with an absolute scale of good and evil; utility alone validates them. Since the appearance of respectability is desirable, Bourdon is indignant when Lefort, the architect, suggests he is not trustworthy. He accuses Lefort of libeling "the most respectable body of men" he knows and of "bringing under suspicion the Law itself." Bourdon's flexibility enables him to operate at both the level of reality and the level of appearance.

Teissier needs to operate only at the level of reality. His wealth and position are secure enough to make respectability irrelevant. He does not see his parents anymore because they ask for money. "They are starving," he admits. When he sees Marie, he is attracted to her. He first wants to keep her as his mistress, and, when she refuses those terms, he offers her marriage. Marriage is the price she sets, and he is willing to pay it. People are justified by their usefulness in the same manner as codes and standards.

Since the Vigneron family is no longer useful to Marie, Teissier cannot understand why she is not willing to let her "family stay in the ditch and go out and do something" for her own account. Her refusal to be his mistress to escape poverty is motivated by her family loyalty, not by an absolute moral standard. Family loyalty is a human virtue, normally to be commended. However, in the perverted society of *The Vultures,* it is the instrument which brings Marie to sell herself. The standards she uses in judging her action are those accepted by society. She considers only the result, not the act.

Marie and Teissier both recognize the nature of his proposal. He considers it a practical arrangement and seeks in her the same qualities Harpagon, in Molière's *The Miser,* wanted in a wife. The girl Harpagon considers, likes neither "a well served table . . . nor splendid clothes, nor rich jewels, nor sumptuous furniture." Teissier wants a woman with "simple taste . . . who will conduct herself decently in . . . [his] house, and who won't steal everything in sight." Marie accepts the proposal, knowing that it will be a "dishonest, self-seeking marriage," but in the world they both accept, such is the nature of marriage. This marriage, as Blanche's was to have been, will be economically motivated. The Vignerons' former position allowed them to hide the economic basis of Blanche's proposed marriage, but their new condition prohibits a cloak of sentiment. Marie, knowing that Mrs. Vigneron and Judith might object, makes it clear that such a marriage is their only salvation, and she reminds them of their dependence upon a society of which they had once been a part and its relative standards and values. The Vigneron world, with its emphasis on reputation acquired by economic progress, in this respect, echoes the seventeenth-century world of the cynical wits. It is not difficult to envision Marie speaking to Judith and her mother in the words of Congreve's Mirabell: "Why do we daily commit disagreeable and dangerous actions? to save that idol, reputation." For all the difference in tone between the two plays, the world of *The Vultures* is still run by the rules of *The Way of the World.*

Becque's play employs such realistic techniques as realistic dialogue and settings. Its action is based upon a realistic concept, a slice-of-life, a series of accidents which affect the Vigneron family. However, Becque's approach is classical rather than realistic. He is not satisfied to represent life; he holds up vices for condemnation. But unlike his master, Molière, he offers no corrective. Molière's solution was temperance: learning is all right for women, in moderation; caring for one's health is all right, in moderation; frankness is all right, in moderation. Such a solution was possible for Molière because he lived in a stable, hierarchical society which recognized absolute moral values. Becque's society is flexible and dislocated; its code is utilitarian and relative. He does not reject the utilitarian code, but he dislikes it. His moralistic intent distinguishes him from the true realists.

His intent is to reveal a society composed entirely of "vultures." Some of the "vultures" are obvious, such as Bourdon and Teissier. Others, such as Marie, seem to become "vultures" in order to survive. When Teissier says to Marie, "Child, since your father died you've been surrounded by a lot of scoundrels," Marie seems to be victimized by the "vultures," while, in fact, she, by accepting Teissier's terms, has joined their ranks. In fact, Becque suggests that by being a part of this society she has always been a "vulture." The Vignerons owed their fortune to Teissier and his ruthless methods, as Vigneron acknowledges: "I reckon it's Teissier and his factory that have made me what I am." In a corrupt society, only those willing to accept the perverted standard and basis of that society can achieve success. In *The Vultures,* Becque reveals that what appeared in the beginning to be an ideal home, and later became a group of economic relationships, had actually never been anything but a group of economic relationships. In this exposition of society and manners, however, Becque has created a comedy of manners based upon a realistic concept; he has not presented "life as it is," the goal of the realistic playwright, but life as the satirist sees "it ought not to be"—the goal of the classical comic dramatist.

Notes

1. *A Treasury Of The Theatre,* ed. by John Gassner (New York, 1959). All references to the play are from this edition.

   I am indebted to Mrs. Mathe Allain for aid in translating critical material as well as for making an analytical comparison of certain passages from the French edition of *Les Corbeaux* with the English translation.

2. Samuel Montefiore Waxman, *Antoine and The Théâtre-Libre* (Cambridge, Mass., 1926), pp. 41-44.

3. James Huneker, *Iconoclasts* (New York, 1921), pp. 163-81.

4. Adolphe Thalasso, *Le Théâtre Libre* (Paris, 1909), p. 43.

Norman Araujo (essay date October 1989)

SOURCE: Araujo, Norman. "The Language of Business and the Business of Language in Becque's *Les Corbeaux*." *The French Review* 63, no. 1 (Oct 1989): 72-79.

[*In the following essay, Araujo delivers an in-depth discussion of* The Vultures, *which opened with mixed reviews.*]

Henry Becque's *Les Corbeaux* was presented for the first time on 14 September 1882, at the Comédie-Française. The work of a bookkeeper's son whose earlier plays had been little noticed, *Les Corbeaux* opened to mixed reviews, but would later be generally acclaimed as Becque's masterpiece and one of the finest and most original plays of the late nineteenth century.[1]

The plot, stark and simple, turns on the tragic vicissitudes of the Vigneron family, suddenly rendered vulnerable to the machinations of unscrupulous businessmen by the untimely death of Vigneron himself, a manufacturer. Act I begins with a description of the Vigneron family preparing for a dinner party to celebrate the forthcoming marriage of the youngest daughter, Blanche; it ends with the sudden death of her father and the lacerating grief of her mother. The following two acts detail the progressive psychological disarray and commercial decline of the family, as its business "friends," led by the deceased's partner, Teissier, conspire to ruin it financially: Blanche is thoroughly devastated by her aristocratic and opportunistic would-be mother-in-law's cancellation of her marriage because of her inability to provide the dowry agreed upon; her brother, Gaston, forsakes the family and joins the army; in their business transactions, the sorrowful and inexperienced Mme Vigneron and her two remaining daughters, Judith and Marie, prove no match for the double-dealing Teissier and his cohorts. Finally, in act IV, with Blanche lost to insanity, and absolute financial ruin threatening, the Vigneron family is seen resigning itself to the only possible solution to its plight: Marie's marriage of convenience to Teissier, who, having taken a fancy to her, guarantees that, as her husband, he will protect the family's monetary interests. Thus Becque's disillusioning commentary on the harsh realities of the bourgeois world of business comes to an end, surprisingly, not by means of a conventional *dénouement,* but through the quiet—though no less painful—resignation of the victims to their ironic fate.

Modern critical opinion has been somewhat divided as to whether *Les Corbeaux* is to be labeled a naturalistic drama or regarded as a technically unclassifiable work, closer in certain respects to Molière's classical treatment of character; but there has been fairly wide agreement to the effect that the play is realistic in its observation of bourgeois manners and morals under the Second Empire, and more than one critic has viewed it as a protest against the sentimental, economic, and intellectual oppression of women.[2]

A fresh analysis of *Les Corbeaux* suggests, however, that there is more to the work than social realism in the traditional sense and psychological insight based on classical paradigms. Indeed, possibly inspired by Balzacian imagery, the play's title, with its connotative resonance, invites the critic to explore other levels of meaning.[3] As the action unfolds, it quickly becomes obvious that the "vultures," or "ravens," or "crows" of the title are not birds in the literal sense but people, and that, however "realistic" his intended approach to his subject matter, Becque is concerned with the figurative use of language, and, as will be seen shortly, other uses as well.[4] Whatever lingering doubts there are about the figurative use of language in the title of *Les Corbeaux* are swept away when the faithful servant of the Vigneron household, Rosalie, declares in act IV, "Voyez-vous, quand les hommes d'affaires arrivent derrière un mort, on peut bien dire: v'là les corbeaux! Ils ne laissent que ce qu'ils ne peuvent pas emporter" (602).

But well before this elucidation of the title's meaning, it is clear that a central motif of **Les Corbeaux** has to do with language as such, with the problem of verbal communication as it arises between the Vigneron family and the vultures who exploit the weaknesses of the family. These weaknesses involve not only an ignorance of the law and of business practices, but also an ignorance of how language can be employed systematically to deceive; how, more fundamentally, meaning in language is relative, and reflective of the dominant social conventions rather than of any moral absolute.

The centrality of language itself to the fabric of the play's action is apparent from the very first scene, when Mme Vigneron and her daughter Blanche discuss the propriety of the expression *plus mauvais,* an expression that Mme Vigneron is convinced that she is using properly because she has seen it in the *Cuisinière bourgeoise* (565). The metalingual dimension implicit in this discussion will be developed later on in the play, as further commentary on language reveals both the Vignerons' inadequate grasp thereof and the hypocritical or destructive uses to which verbal expression is put by the materialistic false friend of the Vigneron family, Mme de Saint-Genis, and the vultures themselves.

A case in point is the conversation in act III between Mme de Saint-Genis and her would-be daughter-in-law, Blanche. As the conversation progresses, Mme de Saint-Genis explains that her son Georges will never go through with the marriage, given Blanche's changed financial status due to her father's sudden demise. Shaken by the thought that Georges would so easily give her up, it is Blanche who first broaches the question of sincerity in language, exclaiming, "Je saurai d'abord si votre fils a deux langages, l'un avec vous, l'autre avec moi" (600). Blanche makes this remark unaware, of course, that in the monologue of the preceding scene, Mme de Saint-Genis has acknowledged that Georges was indeed sincere in his love for her and agreed to abandon his marriage plans only when threatened with banishment from his mother's sight.

But Mme de Saint-Genis is not about to admit the sincerity of the sentimental language shared by Blanche and Georges. Rather, she counters with an attempt to equate that sincerity, at least as far as Blanche is concerned, with immorality. Thus when Blanche, confessing that she has been intimate with Georges, declares that she would willingly become his mistress rather than become the wife of another, Mme de Saint-Genis seizes the opportunity afforded her for a counter-

attack. First protesting that she has not called off her son's wedding for a mere "question d'intérêt" but because of Blanche's immoral attitude, she then proceeds to chastise Blanche for her licentious language: "Qu'est-ce que c'est que ce langage de fille perdue!" (601). The truth of the matter is that Mme de Saint-Genis's action was in fact prompted by the "question d'intérêt." But Blanche does not know that, nor is she capable of detecting that a major difference between her own language and that of Mme de Saint-Genis is the hypocritical content of the latter.

Blanche is not the only member of the Vigneron family to lose a costly battle of words. In her discussions with the lawyer Bourdon, one of the vultures, Mme Vigneron is similarly victimized, except that, in the case of Bourdon, language is at times both a vehicle for hypocritical expression and an instrument of obfuscation. Contrary to the manner of Mme de Saint-Genis, which is relatively uncomplicated in its hypocrisy—and, on occasion, even brutally frank—Bourdon's verbal technique is designed to overwhelm the unsuspecting, financially and legally unsophisticated Mme Vigneron with erudite and sonorous language. Seeking to convince her to sell her property, Bourdon refers to Roman history and Ciceronian oratory, warning Mme Vigneron that, while she hesitates, "Catilina est aux portes de Rome" (583). In a subsequent conversation that she has with her daughter Judith, Mme Vigneron indirectly reveals that she has not in the slightest understood Bourdon's stratagem. She complains of the considerable amount of "obscurité" in Bourdon's words, and asks Judith if she knows what he meant by the reference to Catiline (587); but what has escaped Mme Vigneron's attention is that Bourdon's allusion to Roman history—reminiscent of the obfuscatory practices of some of Molière's characters (Chardin 87)—is merely a learned cover for his scheme to conceal from her the true nature of her financial situation, which is less desperate than he claims.

Another encounter between these two characters confirms Mme Vigneron's verbal disadvantage when dealing with Bourdon and, in so doing, provides a key to a fuller understanding of the Vigneron family's inability to keep the vultures at bay. When, upset at Teissier's plan to sell the Vigneron factory, and unaware of this vulture's collusion with Bourdon, Mme Vigneron tells the latter that she is going to point out to Teissier that he is committing a "mauvaise action," she betrays the puritanical moral code that she is striving to apply in the Darwinian "survival of the fittest" atmosphere of financial conspiracies threatening her and her daughters (Hyslop 53). Bourdon's reaction to her words is equally revelatory: "Je doute fort, madame, qu'en tenant *ce langage* à votre adversaire, vous arriviez à l'émouvoir" (595; my italics). One critic has viewed this exchange as an illustration of the difference between the Vigneron family's naïvely idealistic language of "rights" and the vultures' cynically pragmatic language of "facts" (Chardin 84-85).

Whatever the validity of this distinction, further analysis of **Les Corbeaux** demonstrates that, beyond the question of the vultures' deceptive and cynical uses of language, the more basic issue involved is the very relativity of meaning itself, and how that relativity is linked to prevailing social customs. Two facts become obvious: one is that certain essential expressions of the language still employed by the Vigneron family and absolutely clear to it are no longer intelligible to most, if not all, of the vultures; the second is that other essential expressions have taken on new or more restrictive meanings, or have been altogether stripped of meaning in the vultures' lexicon.

An example of a term which, absolutely clear in meaning to the Vigneron family, has become unintelligible for the most part where the vultures are concerned is the adjective *honnête,* in its couplings with *homme* or *gens.* In the monologue that she delivers in act IV, Marie reflects on the temperament of her sisters and expresses particular concern about the vulnerability of Judith because the latter is "honnête" (608). Marie is talking about moral honesty, as is her father in act I, when he describes Mme de Saint-Genis as an "honnête femme" (567), or even, ironically, Mme de Saint-Genis herself when, cautioning Mme Vigneron against the pitfalls of her naïveté, she says to her, "Vous voyez des honnêtes gens partout" (578). The word *honnête* continues to retain its moral sense when Mme Vigneron wonders aloud, in the presence of Mme de Saint-Genis, whether her deceased husband is now "au ciel où vont les honnêtes gens comme lui," refusing, at the same time, to believe that he left any serious business problems behind because, as an "honnête homme," he did not have complicated financial transactions (577).

Unfortunately for the Vigneron family, the morality implicit in these uses of the word *honnête* is alien to the mentality and verbal code of the vultures. It is true that a vulture-come-lately, Dupuis, is not above employing the adjective *honnête* in a pseudomoralistic sense when he tries, in act IV, to collect from the grieving Vigneron family on a nonexistent debt. Attempting first to reassure Marie of his own honesty by praising that of her dead father, he recalls the supposedly congenial history of his dealings with the deceased, noting that "entre honnêtes gens, ça devrait toujours se passer ainsi" (609). A short time after this utterance, confronted by Teissier, he argues nervously that, as an "honnête homme," he would not be asking for the money if it were not due him (610). But the hollowness of Dupuis's hypocritical appropriation of the word *honnête* becomes apparent when, pressed menacingly by Teissier, he makes his wife the scapegoat, allowing the inference that she might have made an error of computation.

While it might be submitted that Dupuis is at least paying lip service to the meaning of *honnête* as understood by the Vigneron family, for Bourdon it appears that that meaning has ceased to exist. When, in view of her possible marriage to Teissier, Marie asks Bourdon whether her prospective husband is an "honnête homme," Bourdon's initial response is to ask Marie what she means by such a question (605). Then, without waiting for her clarification, he proceeds to interpret the question in the narrow framework of commercial law as related to Teissier's fidelity to his given word—on which fidelity Bourdon then casts doubt, advising Marie to have contractual agreements drawn up carefully stipulating her rights. Goaded on by an unsatisfied Marie, who is finally allowed to elaborate on her question, Bourdon now concedes that Teissier has probably not made his fortune honorably—but quickly adds, in a notable exemplification of the vultures' belief in the primacy of "fact" over "right," that the majority of fortunes in France have been made in the same way (605-606).

What is particularly significant in this exchange between Bourdon and Marie is that, in the course of Bourdon's reply, the notion of the *honnête homme* as a moral concept has been so eroded as to lose its referential consistency. Still struggling to exhaust, as he perceives them, the clarified implications of Marie's original question, by the end of his answer Bourdon is endeavoring to reassure her that, in his role as husband, Teissier will be more "honnête" than not; but the gist of his comments permits the inference that he takes "honnête" to mean "exercising sexual restraint" (606).

It is already demoralizing enough, from the standpoint of the members of the Vigneron family, to discover that, in the world of the vultures, a world dominating and absorbing their own, expressions such as *honnête homme* and *honnêtes gens* no longer have a definite meaning. More devastating still is the discovery that, in the language of the vultures, words like *affaire* have suffered a less readily apparent but more ominous fate: they continue to exist and to be employed, but the meaning ascribed to them has become exclusively commercial and self-servingly so. As in the case of *honnête,* the action of **Les Corbeaux** is designed in part to measure the moral distance separating what the word *affaire* means for the Vigneron family from what it means for the vultures.

At the beginning of the play, the word *affaire,* as used by the Vigneron family, continues to have two primary meanings, the general one of "matter" or "affair" and the commercially oriented one of "transaction" or "deal." Even when Mme Vigneron appears to intend the commercial sense of the word, that sense retains a benevolent neutrality. Hence she describes a joint business venture undertaken by her husband and Teissier in the following fashion: "M. Teisser et monsieur Vigneron ont fait une affaire ensemble; elle a été bonne pour tous les deux, partant quittes" (568). The intrinsic merit of this "affaire" was its balanced outcome: it was not consummated at the expense of one of the two associates.

On the lips of the vultures, however, the term not only loses its general meaning of "matter" or "affair" but has its commercial meaning circumscribed by the notion of a transaction or deal to be turned to the advantage of one person, or group of persons, at the expense of the designated victim, or victims. When, in a discussion with Mme Vigneron about the suitability of having Marie marry Teissier, Bourdon notes that such a union would not be a "mauvaise affaire" for Marie, he means that she would be the one to profit financially from it; and all his succeeding remarks on the subject only serve to embroider on this theme (595).

With the subsequent elaboration of his thought, the meaning of Bourdon's words penetrates even the naïveté of Mme Vigneron. Perceiving that he means "business deal" when he uses the word *affaire,* Mme Vigneron replies defiantly with a reiteration of her opposition to the selling of her factory and with the statement that she is not expecting anything from Teissier's fortune (595). But it is clear that she has not grasped the accent, the intensity of Bourdon's use of the word *affaire.* Nor will she do so in time to save her family from capitulation to the vultures. Her failure in this regard is foreshadowed in act I, when she offhandedly observes to Mme de Saint-Genis that the reason why Vigneron and Teissier do not fraternize more is that, once they have talked out their "affaires" at the factory, they have little more to say to each other (572). While Mme Vigneron does not indicate, at this early point, which of the two men pursued these business conversations with the greater ardor and single-mindedness, the evolution of the play's action and the emerging character portrayals will lend credence to the assumption that it was Teissier. Indirectly and unbeknownst to her, Mme Vigneron has touched here on the vultures' invasive conception of the *affaire*: an all-absorbing, intense activity devoted solely to the making of a profit. Indeed, one of *Les Corbeaux*'s tragic themes is the laggard development of Mme Vigernon's verbal awareness in this connection, tragic because that development is too little and too late.

The intensity with which the word *affaire* is charged for Bourdon, and by implication for Teissier, is again suggested to Mme Vigneron—and again with little effect—in another conversation with Bourdon, when the lawyer comes initially to announce that Teissier has made arrangements to sell the Vignerons' factory. Pretending indignantly to discern in Mme Vigneron's attitude a trace of suspicion directed against him, Bourdon criticizes in turn her passivity: "Pendant que vous

agitez sans rien conclure, attendant je ne sais quel événement qui ne se présentera pas, Teissier, lui, avec ses habitudes d'homme d'affaires, a marché de l'avant" (593). Whatever the duplicitous character of Bourdon's manner and presentation, his account of Teissier's action reflects the vultures' conviction that it is with relentless intensity that the successful "homme d'affaires" pursues his *affaire* to its profitable conclusion. Not, by the way, that Teissier himself has not already directly indicated to Mme Vigneron just how seriously he regards that phenomenon represented by the word *affaire.* The value that Teissier attaches to the business deal is rendered forcefully evident as early as act II, when he firmly prevents Mme Vigneron from intervening in a heated exchange between Bourdon and the architect Lefort, another vulture. Teissier justifies his preventive action by observing, sententiously, that one never interrupts a "conversation d'affaires" (586).

As much as an attestation of the fervor that Teissier brings to the upholding of the conventions in vogue among the vultures with respect to the conduct of business matters (this "fripon honnête" carries with him at all times the book of legal statutes in effect in French territory[5]), this scene provides a more accurate gauge of the distance separating Mme Vigneron's naïveté from the callousness of the vultures' ardent business practices. Not only is she incapable of determining the meaning that the vultures give to the word *affaire*; she is unable, in a broader context, to distinguish between a "mere disagreement" on business tactics and a truly violent altercation. Teissier, on the other hand, possesses the necessary sophistication to place such disagreements in perspective, the accomplishment of the successful—if morally condemnable—business deal being the very rationale for his existence.

Mme Vigneron's inability to grasp the practical ramifications of the ardor that Teissier brings to the promotion and defense of the "conversation d'affaires" is all the more detrimental to her family's material well-being since this ardor is the mark of a particular hierarchy of values for the vultures. It is not merely that, according to this hierarchy of values, the sole objective of the *affaire* is the generating of a profit; it is rather, and far more fundamentally, that generating a profit emerges as the only value of any true importance, the money question being the only question worth discussing at all. This truth becomes fully explicit when Bourdon, Mme Vigneron, and Marie are considering the latter's prospective marriage to Teissier. After rudely informing Mme Vigneron, in Darwinian terms, that she has simply experienced "la loi du plus fort," but now, through Marie's marriage to Teissier, has a chance to recoup financially, Bourdon comes back to Marie and to the nub of the issue at hand:

> Vous avez entendu, mademoiselle, ce que je viens de
> dire à votre mère. Faitesmoi autant de questions que

vous voudrez, mais, abordons, n'est-ce pas, *la seule qui soit véritablement importante, la question d'argent.* Je vous écoute.

(606; my italics)

The asserted primacy of the question of money is all the more striking in this context, it should be remembered, since Marie and Bourdon have just finished discussing Teissier's moral character.

But a more precise measure of the primacy of the question of money for the vultures is to be found in their manner of reacting to the very concepts of death, love, and marriage. Scholarly research has already shown how Becque utilizes the early death of Vigneron to unmask the vultures (Araujo 623-628). On the more specific level of the play's language, however, Vigneron's demise also serves to illuminate the fact that, for the vultures, the meaning of death has little to do with a sense of loss or grief but is purely relative—relative to the financial advantage to be derived therefrom, to the opportunity created for a lucrative *affaire*.

There is already more than a hint of this relativistic outlook in the approach that the materialistic Mme de Saint-Genis adopts in the face of Vigneron's death. To a Mme Vigneron in tears, Mme de Saint-Genis's attempt at consolation is hardly grounded in sentimental or spiritual sensitivity. She suggests, rather, that she herself was more to be pitied when she lost her own husband—because all he left her were debts and a fouryear-old child to raise (577). As revealing as is this effort to comfort Mme Vigneron monetarily, more revealing still is the verbal framework in which the effort is conveyed. Mme de Saint-Genis's lead-in statement is "Je sais ce que c'est que de perdre son mari," which, in the lexicon of the Vigneron family, would be the prelude to an expression of emotional communion in suffering. But, as is now evident, Mme de Saint-Genis intends a "communion" of a different sort.

As for the vultures themselves, their employment of a language even more impersonal in its final significance than that of Mme de Saint-Genis plainly demonstrates that for them death is absolutely devoid of any sentimental or spiritual meaning. Seeing Mme Vigneron for the first time after the death of her husband, Bourdon is completely closed to the propriety of condolences. He begins with a cold question designed to elicit financial information: "Dites-moi, madame, pendant que j'y pense: est-ce avec votre autorisation que madame de Saint-Genis s'est présentée chez moi pour connaître la situation que vous était faite par le décès de votre mari?" (583). Under similar circumstances, Teissier and Lefort behave in the same fashion, their queries differing only very slightly in form from Bourdon's (578, 586). In the particular case of Bourdon, not only does he fail to offer condolences to Mme Vign-

eron, but he has the effrontery to be shocked that she has not immediately inquired about her husband's financial arrangements. After all, he observes, giving his comments the form of a solemn truism, such inquiry is of the essence: "Quand on perd son mari, c'est la première chose dont on s'occupe" (583).

No different, basically, is the tenor of Teissier's remarks to Marie on the subject of selling her dead father's factory. The emphasis has merely shifted from the question of ordering one's material priorities when one's husband dies to the equally matter-of-fact question of how one best avails oneself of the death of a factory owner to promote a profitable *affaire*: "La mort de son directeur est une occasion excellente, qui ne se représentera pas, pour nous en défaire, profitons-en" (580). Once again, it is the impersonality of the allusion which is striking in the language of the vultures. Teissier elevates—or reduces—the matter of Vigneron's death to the level of a vague generality, as if Marie were not all all connected to this anonymous "directeur" whose demise has created an "occasion excellente." The qualification "excellente" is further evidence, as if such were needed, of Teissier's glacial indifference to Marie's bereavement.

Love and marriage fare no better than death in the code of the vultures. Given the foregoing analysis, it would not be illogical to assume that love and marriage would be of interest to the vultures only if related to a prospect of making money. But both concepts suffer even more cruel compression at their hands. Love is so compressed, in fact, that it disappears entirely; and marriage becomes only another form of "the only game in town"—the *affaire* or business transaction. Such are the profound conclusions to which Bourdon comes when conversing with Marie in act IV:

> Je parle, n'est-ce pas, à une jeune femme raisonnable, bien élevée, qui n'a pas de papillons dans la tête. Vous devez savoir que l'amour n'existe pas; je ne l'ai jamais rencontré pour ma part. Il n'y a que des affaires en ce monde; le mariage en est une comme toutes les autres. . . .

(607)

In what Bourdon imagines to be his reasonable perspective, "love" and "marriage" are now signifiers that have no signifieds: the former is nothing more than a myth; the latter has disappeared as an end in itself to become only a means toward the end of making money. It is not only Marie, however, who has failed to grasp these "truths." The whole Vigneron family shares in this failure, and, perhaps most ironically, Blanche. In act III, still naïvely expecting that her marriage to Georges will become a reality, Blanche vows to be more decisive in that marriage than her family has been in its business transactions (591). Not having been treated to Bourdon's "insights," what she cannot perceive is that there is no real distinction, in the world of the vultures, between *affaire* and *mariage*. Because of that absence of distinction, her marriage, now viewed by Mme de Saint-Genis as a *mauvaise affaire,* will not take place.

The vultures are not content to redefine or eliminate entirely essential concepts of the world of the Vigneron family, such as death, love, and marriage. Their code is designed to reflect a new "worldly wisdom" by the creation of maxims which dissipate the myths and illusions cultivated by the likes of the Vigneron family, myths and illusions predicated, in the vultures' opinions, on an irrelevant morality.[6] Dupuis, for example, takes philosophical note of the unpredictability of business: ". . . vous savez ce que sont les affaires, bonnes un jour, mauvaises le lendemain . . . (609). For Teissier, on the other hand, true to the tenor of his other remarks on the subject, what is to be stressed is that in business one comes quickly to the point: "On ne fait pas de cérémonies dans les affaires" (609).

Since for the vultures, as noted above, the *affaire* has necessarily to do, in the final analysis, with money, its acquisition and accumulation, it is not surprising that some of the maxims should address this paramount issue. Speaking of Vigneron, Teissier ventures a global definition of a man's worth in financial terms: "Un homme vaut davantage quand il possède quelque chose" (575). As far as Bourdon is concerned, if the love of money is the root of all evil, the lack of money is the root of spinsterhood. His words to Mme Vigneron on this matter are quite explicit: "C'est qu'en effet, madame, faute d'argent, les jeunes filles restent jeunes filles" (607). It is Bourdon again, finally, who utters the comprehensive proverbial expression that puts all the preceding maxims in context and provides a broad philosophical backdrop for them. Referring to what he takes to have been Vigneron's outlook on life, he assumes that the latter would have viewed with utmost concern the predicament of his wife and daughters, and advised the sacrificial gesture of Marie's marriage to Teissier: "Il connaissait la vie; il savait que tout se paye en ce monde . . ." (607). In Bourdon's world, then, the beginning of wisdom is not the fear of God but the realization that everything has a price—or, to try to match the intended literalness of Bourdon's expression—a price tag.

By its systematic exploration of the difference between the language spoken by the Vigneron family and that spoken by the vultures, with the attendant tragic consequences of this difference for the Vigneron family, *Les Corbeaux* points to a function of realistic literature consistent with Roland Barthes's reading of Balzac's *Sarrasine* and J. L. Austin's theory of speech acts. According to the conclusions reached by these writers, realism demonstrates not only how words become detached from their referential source in the process of social and economic change but also how, despite this detachment, language continues to enjoy representational authority. This authority stems from language's ability to continue to indicate, faithfully and effectively, that meaning is derived not from an "objective" reality but from social convention, from what society—in the case of *Les Corbeaux* that dominant segment of society comprising the vultures—chooses to accept as real.[7]

Against this onslaught of conventional meaning, the "truths" which constitute the moral predicate of the Vigneron family's verbal expression simply evaporate, having no independent means of support in the social context. That the evaporation of these "truths" is complete by the end of *Les Corbeaux* is powerfully underscored by the play's final verbal irony. Having intimidated and chased away Dupuis, Teissier feels duty-bound to alert Marie to the danger that Dupuis and others like him represent for her and her family now that her father is dead: "Vous êtes entourées de fripons, mon enfant, depuis la mort de votre père. Allons retrouver votre famille" (610). With his own *friponnerie*—as the Vignerons might have defined it—having become so second nature that he is not at all aware of it, Teissier literally gives new meaning here to the word *fripon*. It now simply designates anyone who poses a threat to his financial security and that, by "natural" extension, of his wife-to-be and her family.

Thus the ending of *Les Corbeaux* marks more than just the financial victory of the vultures. It also marks, in resounding as well as ironic terms, their definitive verbal victory. In the latter connection, the play's *dénouement* takes on a special significance: while one cannot directly trace back to Becque the twentieth-century French theater's concern with the problem of how meaning is created, it is evident that he anticipates that concern in *Les Corbeaux* and conveys it with unusual dramatic insight and artistry.

Notes

1. The circumstances surrounding the first presentation of *Les Corbeaux* are noted in Hyslop 5-6. Becque's earlier plays were *L'Enfant prodigue* (1868), *Michel Pauper* (1870), *L'Enlèvement* (1871), *La Navette* (1878), and *Les Honnêtes Femmes* (1880).

2. For the view that *Les Corbeaux* is essentially a naturalistic play, see Senart 189; Martino 178-181. For the view that *Les Corbeaux* is unclassifiable, and more in the Moliéresque tradition of character analysis, see Lindenberg 7-8; Hyslop 47, 81-83; Blanchart 49-50. For a discussion of realistic techniques in *Les Corbeaux,* see Hyslop 49, 81; Descotes 122; Wooton 72, 78; Martino 180-181. Interpretations of *Les Corbeaux* as a protest against the oppression of women are to be found in Chardin 82-83 and Arnaoutovitch 1: 426-429.

3. The idea of a Balzacian source for the title of Becque's play is advanced in Arnaoutovitch 2: 273-274.

4. For "vultures," "ravens," and "crows" as English translations of *corbeaux* in the title and body of Becque's play, see Wooton 72-73 and Becque 564. The author of the present article employs "vultures" throughout to designate *corbeaux*.

5. The expression *fripon honnête* is to be found, with reference to Teissier, in Senart 190.

6. According to Chardin, this new "worldly wisdom" reflects a historical shift from the ideology of the lower middle class to that of the world of finance and industry (82-83).

7. For a discussion of the ideas of Barthes and Austin regarding the opposition between constative meaning and referential truth in realistic prose, see Petrey 153-55, 161-62.

Works Cited

Araujo, Norman. "The Role of Death in Becque's *Les Corbeaux.*" *Revue des Langues Vivantes* 36 (1970): 621-631.

Arnaoutovitch, Alexandre. *Henry Becque.* 3 vols. Paris: PUF, 1927.

Austin, J. L. *How to Do Things with Words.* Cambridge: Harvard UP, 1975.

Barthes, Roland. *S/Z.* Paris: Seuil, 1970.

Becque, Henry. *Les Corbeaux. Nineteenth-Century French Plays.* Ed. Joseph L. Borgerhoff. New York: Appleton, 1931. 563-610.

Blanchard, Paul. *Henry Becque: son œuvre, portrait et autographe.* Paris: Nouvelle Revue Critique, 1930.

Chardin, Philippe. "Quelques problèmes idéologiques posés par *Les Corbeaux* d'Henry Becque." *Les Cahiers Naturalistes* 52 (1979): 81-92.

Descotes, Maurice. *Henry Becque et son théâtre.* Paris: Minard, 1962.

Hyslop, Lois Boe. *Henry Becque.* New York: Twayne, 1972.

Lindenberg, Daniel. "Un Dissident théâtral: les luttes d'Henry Becque (1817-1899)." *Comédie Française* May 1982: 7-12.

Martino, P. *Le Naturalisme français (1870-1895).* 2nd ed. Paris: Colin, 1930.

Petrey, Sandy. "Castration, Speech Acts, and the Realist Difference: *S/Z* versus *Sarrasine.*" *PMLA* 102 (1987): 153-65.

Senart, Philippe. "Henry Becque: *Les Corbeaux.*" *Nouvelle Revue des Deux Mondes,* Oct. 1982: 187-192.

Wooton, Carl W. "*The Vultures*: Becque's Realistic Comedy of Manners." *Modern Drama* 4.1 (1961): 72-79.

FURTHER READING

Criticism

Antoine, Andre. *Memories of the Theatre Libre.* Edited by H. D. Albright. Translated by Marvin A. Carlson. Coral Gables, Fla.: University of Miami Press, 1964, 239 p.

> Contains Andre Antoine's personal recollections of Becque's early productions.

Dimnet, Ernest. "Henry Becque's Posthumous Play." *Saturday Review* 110, no. 2871 (5 November 1910): 575-576.

> Dimnet gives a negative review of Becque's *Les Polichinelles.*

Additional coverage of Becque's life and career is contained in the following sources published by the Gale Group: *Dictionary of Literary Biography,* **Vol. 192;** *Guide to French Literature, 1789 to the Present; Literature Resource Center;* **and** *Nineteenth-Century Literature Criticism,* **Vol. 3.**

Pierre Corneille
1606-1684

French playwright.

The following entry presents criticism on Corneille's life and career from 1981 through 1998.

INTRODUCTION

Corneille was the first great tragic dramatist of France. Although many of his thirty-four plays are comedies or works of mixed type, he is particularly known for creating the genre of French classical tragedy with his innovative and controversial masterpiece, *Le Cid* (1637; *The Cid*). Though all of Corneille's plays are written in the verse format of his day, that of *vers alexadrin* (twelve-syllables per line), the playwright is well-known for deviating from the traditional format of neoclassical drama. Corneille's intense focus on human will, the will striving for freedom, and the fashioning of one's own destiny distinguishes his tragedies from classical Greek dramas, in which humans are depicted as helpless victims of fate. Although his theatrical career was marked by both triumphs and defeats, he was recognized in his lifetime as among his country's foremost dramatists and was commonly designated by the appellation "le grand Corneille."

BIOGRAPHICAL INFORMATION

Corneille was born into a middle-class family in Rouen and seems to have lived a quiet, retired, bourgeois life. He studied law but showed little aptitude for the profession. As a student he wrote poetry and won prizes for his Latin versification. In 1629 he offered his first play, the comedy *Mélite, ou Les fausses letters* (1630; *Mélite; or, The False Letters*), to a theatrical troupe led by the acclaimed actor Montdory during the group's stop in Rouen. The play was a great success when staged in Paris, and Corneille's theatrical career was effectively launched. Over the next several years, he wrote a number of successful comedies and tragedies. In 1636 Corneille first staged his innovative play, *The Cid,* which was a popular success but gave rise to a heated controversy known as "La Querelle du *Cid*" or "Quarrel of *Le Cid*." The play's numerous violations of the common neoclassical design for tragic drama prompted published attacks by Corneille's rivals as well as

defenses by Corneille and his supporters. *The Cid* was submitted to the newly formed Académie Française, then under the authority of Cardinal Richelieu, which issued a judgment siding with Corneille's opponents. Wounded and discouraged, he ceased writing plays for three years.

After his return to the theater in 1640, Corneille entered a very fertile period, producing at least three comedies and nine tragedies. The failure of his tragedy *Pertharite, roi des Lombards* (1652; *Pertharites, King of the Lombards*) led Corneille once again to leave the theater, this time for seven years. Although he attempted to regain his stature in 1659 with *Œdipe* (*Oedipus*), neither this tragedy nor the works that followed were nearly so successful as his former triumphs. Furthermore, the heroic mode of characterization that Corneille employed was giving way in public favor to the more firmly classical and Jansenist work of his younger rival, Jean Racine. Corneille retired from the theater in 1674 and died in obscurity ten years later.

MAJOR WORKS

The Cid is considered one of the masterpieces of French drama. The play concerns the growing French middle class and shrinking nobility, centralized government, and economic growth. It offers token regard to the neoclassical guidelines for the presentation and structure of tragedies, but the plot foreshadows the more elaborate plotting of the Elizabethan stage: within twenty-four hours the protagonist falls in love, fights a duel, kills his beloved's father, leads his outnumbered military force to a smashing victory over the Moors, and is vindicated in trial by combat, all the while alternately losing and then regaining favor with both his beloved and his nation's king. In his later plays, Corneille focused less on celebrating individual heroism and more on classical themes like conflicts between patriotic duty and love or the call for mercy contrasted with the need for disinterested justice. Among Corneille's later works, *Horace* (1640), *Polyeucte* (1643), and *Suréna* (1674) are often named as masterworks of French drama. In addition, Corneille's comedies, from his early *Mélite* through *Le Menteur* (1643; *The Liar*) are regarded as clever, well-crafted works.

CRITICAL RECEPTION

Critics have praised Corneille's plays for their great diversity, brilliant versification, and complexity of plot and situation. Scholars have also applauded his liberation of tragedy from the confinement and artificiality of neoclassical strictures. Much critical discussion of Corneille's work focuses on his relationship with his contemporary and rival, the playwright Jean Racine. Many scholars compare the objectives and accomplishments of Corneille with those of Racine, often to Racine's advantage. Although the decline of Corneille's reputation, begun in his own lifetime, continued throughout the eighteenth century, the next century saw a reappraisal of his place in literary history, and today he is situated in the front rank of French dramatists.

PRINCIPAL WORKS

Plays

Mélite, ou Les fausses lettres [*Mélite; or, The False Letters*] 1630
Clitandre 1631
La Veuve, ou Le Traître trahi [*The Widow; or, The Betrayer Betrayed*] 1632
La Suivante [*The Maidservant*] 1633

La Galerie du Palais, ou L'Amie rivalle [*The Palace Corridor; or, The Rival Friend*] 1633
La Place Royale, ou L'Amoureux extravagant [*Place Royale; or, The Extravagant Lover*] 1633
Médée 1635
L'Illusion comique [*The Comic Illusion*] 1635
Le Cid [*The Cid*] 1637
Horace 1640
Cinna, ou La Clémence d'Auguste [*Cinna; or, The Clemency of Augustus*] 1642
Polyeucte 1643
La Mort de Pompée [*The Death of Pompey*] 1643
Le Menteur [*The Liar*] 1643
La Suite du Menteur [*Sequel to The Liar*] 1644
Rodogune, Princesse des Parthes [*Rodogune, Princess of Parthia*] 1644
Théodore, vièrge et martyre [*Theodora, Virgin and Martyr*] 1645
Héraclius 1647
Andromède [*Andromeda*] 1650
Don Sanche d'Aragon [*Don Sancho of Aragon*] 1650
Nicomède 1651
Pertharite, roi des Lombards [*Pertharites, King of the Lombards*] 1652
Œdipe [*Oedipus*] 1659
La Toison d'Or [*The Golden Fleece*] 1660
Sertorius 1662
Sophonisbe [*Sophonisba*] 1663
Othon [*Otho*] 1664
Agésilas [*Agesilaus*] 1666
Attila 1667
Tite et Bérénice [*Titus and Bernice*] 1670
Pulchérie [*Pulcheria*] 1672
Suréna 1674
Œuvres complètes 3 vols. (dramas, poetry, prose) 1980-87

GENERAL COMMENTARY

G. J. Mallinson (essay date July 1982)

SOURCE: Mallinson, G. J. "The Variants of Corneille's Early Plays." *Modern Language Review* 77, no. 3 (July 1982): 547-57.

[*In the following essay, Mallinson examines Corneille's attitude toward his early comedies.*]

The first edition of Corneille's complete works, whatever its merits as financial speculation on the part of the publisher, was for the dramatist himself, seemingly, a cause of great concern. Comedies written a decade earlier were to be brought again to the public eye, plays which, according to the *avis* of 1644, would be better forgotten:

C'est contre mon inclination que mes libraires vous font ce présent, et j'aurais été plus aise de la suppression entière de la plus grande partie de ces poèmes, que d'en voir renouveler la mémoire par ce recueil.[1]

Corneille seemed no longer able to identify with this work of his youth, to view it with the same confidence and enthusiasm which characterized his early prefaces. He confessed to a general feeling of unease at the apparent frivolity and awkwardness of the work written in his literary apprenticeship. In this and in subsequent editions, he subjected his comedies to a series of emendations, altering, sometimes to a large extent, his original texts:

J'ai donc cru qu'il valait mieux, et pour votre contentement et pour ma réputation, y jeter un coup d'œil, non pas pour les corriger exactement (il eût été besoin de les refaire presque entiers), mais du moins pour en ôter ce qu'il y a de plus insupportable.

(pp. 182-83)

In their analyses of such changes, critics tend to stress the removal of certain unseemly allusions, archaic expressions, and general stylistic infelicities. Wiley speaks of the dramatist's move towards 'purification and condensation',[2] and Rivaille draws attention to his desire to tidy up numerous 'imperfections et faiblesses causées par l'inexpérience'.[3] In general, though, these emendations are considered to be a step away from artistic fluency, a move from the daring, spontaneous, and youthful to the more restrained, unadventurous, and dull. Buffum finds 'a great loss of picturesqueness and vitality',[4] and Tancock remarks on the liveliness of the early plays which is apparent 'before middle-aged respectability, abetted by his keen business instinct, led him to tone down his youthful verve and "improve" his later texts'.[5] Alterations are attributed to Corneille's sensitivity to the increasing refinement of literary taste, and they are seen to reflect a desperate attempt to give to his comedies a dignity consonant with his reputation as a master of tragedy.

For several reasons, however, such an interpretation of these *variantes* seems unsatisfactory. The general development of comedy in the 1640s and 1650s was far from being a simple movement towards greater polish and seemliness. Plays such as Gillet de la Tessonerie's *Francion,*[6] or L'Estoile's *L'Intrigue des Filous,*[7] make abundant use of daring innuendo, and the comic worlds of Scarron, d'Ouville, and Thomas Corneille devote a particular place to burlesque and farcical effects, to the ribaldries of servants, and to the ridiculing of the gullible and naive. If Corneille excises such moments from his own early comedies, therefore, it is not simply because they strike him as remnants of an outdated tradition.

Furthermore, at just the same time as he was writing his preface to the edition of 1644, he was also publishing his penultimate comedy, *Le Menteur,* an adaptation from a Spanish source in which he deliberately transforms Alarcón's essentially thrilling plot into a comic one. His preface to the play is characteristically confident, as he expresses pride in his own versatility:

J'ai fait **le Menteur** pour contenter les souhaits de beaucoup d'autres qui, suivant l'humeur des François, aiment le changement, et après tant de poèmes graves dont nos meilleures plumes ont enrichi la scène, m'ont demandé quelque chose de plus enjoué qui ne servît qu'à les divertir.[8]

The suggestion that he depart from tragedy is not seen as an insult to the established dramatist, but as a theatrical challenge which he is happy to accept. Significantly, this play remains largely unaltered in all subsequent editions of the *Œuvres complètes.* If Corneille is moved to make changes to his early works, it is clearly not just because he feels ashamed to have written comedies, and examination of his emendations reveals a complexity of attitude towards these particular plays which is far from being the simply dismissive one which his own pronouncements of 1644 would seem to suggest. It is the nature of this attitude which I propose to study more closely in the pages that follow.

Of the early texts, it is **Melite**[9] in particular which Corneille subjected to the most sustained revision, and here the dramatist's desire to remove certain farcical elements is at once apparent. Tirsis's ribald remark as he joins Cloris and Philandre in Act I, Scene 5:

Je pense ne pouvoir vous estre qu'importun, Vous feriés mieux un tiers, que d'en accepter un

(339-40)

is far more restrained in 1644:

De moins sorciers que moy pourroient bien deviner Qu'un troisiéme ne fait que vous importuner

and this same character's more daring observations about love are significantly altered. His forthright pronouncement of Act I, Scene 1:

La beauté, les attraits, le port, la bonne mine, Eschauffent bien les draps, mais non pas la cuisine

(117-18)

becomes in a later edition far more sober and refined as the references to physical attraction are attenuated:

La beauté, les attraits, l'esprit, la bonne mine, Eschauffent bien le cœur, mais non pas la cuisine.

In a similar way, Corneille consistently removes moments of less sophisticated comedy. He excises two monologues of Philandre, those of Act III, Scenes 6 and 8, in the original text, speeches which reveal particularly the comic ineptitude of a coward trying to appear brave.

Likewise, in Act II, Scene 1, he cuts out these lines from Eraste's speech of jealous anger, lines which stress not the despair but the foolishness of one who has inadvertently brought about his own downfall by introducing his mistress to a friend:

> Le perfide qu'il est me doit sa cognoissance,
> C'est moy qui l'ay conduit, et mis en sa puissance,
> C'est moy qui l'engageant à ce froid compliment
> Ay jetté de mes maux le premier fondement.
>
> (389-92)

At other moments, the older dramatist rewrites passages which uncover comic traits in his characters. In Act III, Scene 2, for instance, the foolish Philandre meets Tirsis, and they begin to argue over their rival claims to the heroine's affection. In the original version, Tirsis's rage is used to highlight Philandre's frantic struggle to justify his trepidation:

PHILANDRE:

> Quant à moy, ton trespas me cousteroit trop cher,
>   Il me faudroit apres par une prompte fuite
>   Esloigner trop long temps les beaux yeux
> de Melite.

TIRSIS:

> Ce discours de bouffon ne me satisfaict pas,
>   Nous sommes seuls icy, despeschons,
> pourpoint bas.

PHILANDRE:

> Vivons plustost amys, et parlons d'autre chose.
>
> (906-11)

The farcical nature of the exchange is underlined by the word *bouffon*; Philandre's role is to amuse, his cowardice a source of unambiguous comedy.

In 1660, however, this heavy irony is removed, and the stress shifts from the comic mechanisms of the plot, from the exchange of threat and excuse which underlines the coward's discomfiture. No longer simply a foil to Philandre's unconvincing casuistry, Tirsis reflects on the ignoble character of the wretch before him:

> Tant de raisonnement et si peu de courage
> Sont de tes lâchetez le digne témoignage.

Corneille does not suggest the ridiculousness of this lack of courage now, but the dishonour it implies, and in the comic confrontation is uncovered an issue of greater import. It is a change of emphasis which is apparent again at the end of the scene, when the two rivals separate.

In the original text, Philandre departs in haste, his awkward arguments scarcely concealing his overwhelming fear:

> Il est tout vray, je n'ose,
> Ny mon sang, ny ma vie en peril exposer;
> Ils ne sont plus à moy, je n'en puis disposer,
> Adieu, celle qui veut qu'à present je la serve
> Merite que pour elle ainsi je me conserve.
>
> (912-16)

In the revised version, however, the character is seen to abandon the role of *bouffon,* and leaves the stage in a much more positive way. His retreat is now less obviously the flight of a frightened coward, and suggests the dramatic response of the hero offended:

> Mon sang n'est plus à moy, je n'en puis disposer.
> Mais puisque ta douleur de mes raisons s'irrite,
> J'en prendray dés ce soir le congé de Melite.
> Adieu.

Corneille transforms an amusing scene into a more tense and thrilling encounter. Characters are no longer simply cogs in a comic mechanism, but are given the reactions of heroes.

This same dramatic dignity is given also to Eraste in subsequent versions. In Act I, Scene 2, the character of 1633 is ridiculous and deferent in the face of the heroine, self-consciously aware that he has failed to justify his love to the cynical Tirsis:

> Au peril de vous faire une Histoire importune
> Je viens vous raconter ma mauvaise fortune.
>
> (137-38)

In 1660, however, this suggestion of awkwardness and incompetence is replaced by the expression of greater self-assurance. From the earlier statement, in which the timid personality of Eraste is all-apparent, emerges the confident outlining of a problem, where the identity of the speaker has no role to play:

> De deux amis, Madame, appaisez la querelle,
> Un esclave d'Amour le defend d'un rebelle.

The changes analysed so far indicate clearly a tendency to remove certain comic elements from the presentation of characters, to replace comedy with drama, ridicule with dignity. Such emendations may suggest Corneille's repentance of the apparent frivolity of his youth, but their implications extend much further. Where, in the original texts, the roles and impact of characters are defined by the demands of a comic mechanism, Corneille's alterations suggest an increased emphasis on the characters themselves and on their reactions to events.

It is in this light that the removal of certain crude or farcical elements may be seen. In Act II, Scene 8, for instance, Melite and Tirsis become aware of and express their mutual love. In 1633, the hero is light-hearted and spontaneous; he can beg a kiss from his mistress quite unabashed:

Souffre donc qu'un baiser cueilly dessus ta bouche
M'asseure entierement que mon amour te touche

(759-60)

and his exchanges with Melite have a jovial and
unconcerned freshness about them. In a later edition,
Corneille may remove such talk of kissing for the sake
of propriety, but he does more than this; he adds a
further dimension which completely alters the impact of
the scene. The couplet quoted above is replaced in 1648
by a single line, at once less spontaneous and more
reflective:

Que d'amour et de joye un tel adveu me donne.

Delight, innuendo, and the conspicuous absence of wor-
ries about the social barriers which may separate them
are superseded in the emended text by talk of secrecy
and trust. There is no equivalent in 1633 of these lines,
spoken by the heroine:

Mais par là tu peux voir que mon affection
Prend confiance entiere en ta discretion.

Similarly, in 1633, the sonnet written by the hero is an
incidental element, the pretext for a moment of farcical
stage business. Tirsis's protestations:

Auparavant l'adieu reçoy de ma constance
Dedans ce peu de vers l'eternelle asseurance

(767-68)

are followed by this gesture to the heroine as she plans
to leave the stage: 'Il luy coule le Sonnet dans le sein
comme elle se desrobe.' Emphasis lies here on the
comic *jeu de scène*; the piece of paper is of more
importance than the feelings expressed in it. In 1648,
however, this sequence is transformed into an exchange
of sincerity and seriousness. Tirsis's protestations of
love are expanded:

Et si vous en voulez un serment par escrit,
Ce Sonnet que pour vous vient de tracer ma flame
Vous fera voir à nû jusqu'au fond de mon ame

and Melite's final acceptance of them is no longer the
pretext for unsophisticated comic effects, but becomes
an expression of the heroine's faith in her lover:

Je le prens toutefois comme un precieux gage
Du pouvoir que mes yeux ont pris sur ton courage.
Adieu, sois moy fidelle en despit du jaloux.

Emphasis shifts here from the concrete to the abstract,
from the piece of paper to the passion to which it testi-
fies. In a plot which depicts the waverings of trust in a
world of deception and misunderstanding, such emendations suggest more serious dramatic implications.

A similar change is made to the scene between Tirsis
and Cloris in Act III, Scene 4. The hero believes Melite
to have transferred her affections to Philandre, and his
sister tries to console him, urging him to forget one apparently so faithless. At the end of the encounter, the
hero of 1633 has these defiant lines as he rushes off in
despair:

Penses-tu m'amusant avecques des sottises
Par tes detractions rompre mes entreprises;
Non, non ces traits de langue espandus vainement
Ne m'arresteroient pas, encor un seul moment.

(1059-62)

The stress here lies on Tirsis's determination not to be
held back, on his defiance in the face of an obstacle. In
1660, however, this is not the case. At this time, Cloris's words of comfort represent not so much a barrier to
be overcome, but rather the source of more personal
confusion. His emended lines suggest now his painful
problem of distinguishing truth from falsehood, and
draw further attention to the suffering he undergoes at
the thought that his beloved may have deceived him:

Penses-tu m'arrester par ce torrent d'injures?
Que ce soient veritez, que ce soient impostures,
Tu redoubles mes maux au lieu de les guerir:
Adieu, rien que la mort ne peut me secourir.

This general shift of emphasis from the external to the
internal, from action to reaction, is seen again in certain
changes brought to the scenes of Eraste's madness and
to the role of Cliton. In Act IV, Scene 6 of the original
text, Corneille extracts comic effects from the fantasiz-
ing of his hero, having Cliton point out in astonishment
the discrepancy between the world he sees and the one
his master imagines:

Monsieur, que faites-vous? vostre raison s'esgare,
Voyez qu'il n'est icy de Styx, ny de Tenare,
Revenez à vous mesme.

(1483-85)

In 1660, however, the highlighting of this comic
contrast is replaced with words of more maturity and
understanding. The madness is not seen simply as a
subject for mirth, but is now conceived in terms of the
earlier suffering which lies behind it. Cliton's lines thus
become:

Monsieur que faites-vous, vostre raison troublée
Par l'effet des douleurs dont elle est accablée
Figure à vostre veuë . . .

The same tendency is apparent in Act V, Scene 2, when
Eraste is brought back to his senses. In 1633, the transition is seen to involve no pain; having learned that his
despair is unfounded, the hero feels his sanity return at
once:

Depuis ce que j'ay sceu de Melite et Tirsis,
Je sens que tout à coup mes regrets adoucis
Laissent en liberté les ressorts de mon ame.

(1717-19)

The move is mechanical, the recovery total, and as Eraste bids the nurse help him to visit Mélite, he refers to his madness as an event of the past:

> Nourrice, pren le soin d'un esprit esgaré,
> Qui s'est d'avecques moy si long temps separé.
>
> (1721-22)

In the text of 1660, however, Eraste no longer has this implied detachment from his folly. The earlier lines of mechanical transition are cut out, and the couplet of pleading becomes much more personal and committed. The *fact* of madness is not stressed now, but rather the suffering which caused it and the pity which it should arouse:

> Nourrice, prens pitié d'un esprit égaré,
> Qu'ont mes vives douleurs d'avec moy separé.

Such changes imply more than just the replacing of a comic focus, be it crude, farcical, or ridiculous, with one more obviously thrilling or heroic; they suggest also the increased sensitivity of characters to the events in which they are involved. Where, in the original version, mechanisms are of principal importance, Corneille is later seen to point out the possible suffering of his protagonists, either in the past or in the future.

It is such a tendency, apparent in the variants of *Melite,* which is reflected in certain changes made to the later plays. In *La Galerie du Palais,*[10] Act III, Scene 1, for instance, Aronte advises Lysandre to feign indifference to Célidée, as she had done to him. In the text of 1637, the emphasis rests on the effectiveness of such tactics:

> Puisque vous voulez feindre, il faut feindre à sa vue;
> Afin que votre feinte, aussitôt aperçue,
> Produise un prompt effet dans son esprit jaloux;
> Et pour en adresser plus sûrement les coups,
> Quand vous verrez quelque autre en discours avec elle,
> Feignez en sa présence une flamme nouvelle.
>
> (741-46 var.)

Such lines, in themselves, are neither particularly awkward nor do they suggest an inappropriately comic vision of events. Nevertheless, in 1660, Corneille changes them, and moves the stress from the plot itself to the effect which it has on the characters:

> Puisque vous voulez feindre, il faut feindre à sa vue;
> Qu'aussitôt votre feinte en puisse être aperçue,
> Qu'elle blesse les yeux de son esprit jaloux,
> Et porte jusqu'au cœur d'inévitables coups.
> Ce sera faire au vôtre un peu de violence;
> Mais tout le fruit consiste à feindre en sa présence.

The advice remains the same, but the possible suffering it implies is given greater emphasis: the extent of the heroine's discomfort is expanded, and Corneille introduces the suggestion that for the hero, too, such a *feinte* will be more than just a game.

It is in the context of such a movement that a particularly significant variant of *La Suivante*[11] is to be situated. In Act I, Scene 9, Amarante expresses her realization that Florame's love for her is only feigned, but she resolves to do all she can to upset the hero's suit of Daphnis, her mistress and rival. In the text of 1639, the monologue ends thus:

> Que m'importe de perdre une amitié si feinte?
> Dois-je pas m'ennuyer de son discours moqueur,
> Où sa langue jamais n'a l'aveu de son cœur?
> Non, je ne le sçaurois, et quoy qu'il m'en arrive,
> Je feray mes efforts afin qu'on ne m'en prive,
> Et j'y veux employer de si rusez destours,
> Qu'ils n'auront de long temps le fruit de leurs amours:
>
> (334-40)

In such lines, Amarante is presented simply as the villainess. She is determined to keep Florame for herself, and she focuses her attention on how she will bring this about. In 1660, however, Corneille completely alters the emphasis. In the emended version, it is not so much Amarante's resolve to keep the lover which is expressed as her particular reasons for wishing to do so:

> Que m'importe de perdre une amitié si feinte?
> Et que me peut servir un ridicule feu
> Ou jamais de son cœur sa bouche n'a l'adveu?
> Je m'en veux mal en vain; l'Amour a tant de force,
> Qu'il attache mes sens à cette fausse amorce,
> Et fera son possible à toûjours conserver
> Ce doux exterieur dont on me veut priver.

In 1639, Amarante is defined by her deeds as the schemer; her love for Florame is of importance less for itself than for the action it precipitates. In this change of 1660, however, a character once again emerges from a dramatic mechanism, and behind the role of villainess is suggested the identity of a girl in love, aware of the self-deception which she so happily exercises.

A similar movement is apparent also in one of the relatively few changes which Corneille makes to *La Place Royale.*[12] In the original text, Alidor's love for Angelique is quite evident, and this throws into relief his extravagance in constantly seeking to overcome it. In Act III, Scene 4, the hero recounts to Cleandre the great ordeal he has undergone by acting in a way so contrary to his personal inclinations:

> Quels efforts, cher amy, ne me suis je point faits?
> Me feindre tout de glace, & n'estre que de flame!
> La mépriser de bouche, & l'adorer dans l'ame!
>
> (724-26)

Stress lies here on the protagonist himself and on the absurdity of his behaviour. In 1660, however, Corneille alters this emphasis, looking now not so much at the comic paradox in Alidor's character as at the evident suffering of the one he deceives. In these emended lines, he intensifies the terms in which Alidor's ungallant actions are described, and it is these, rather than his feelings of love, which are given the important final emphasis:

> Malgré tout mon amour prendre un orgueil farouche,
> L'adorer dans le cœur, & l'outrager de bouche.

By the final scenes of the play, the despair of the heroine bursts through the comic framework and she retreats to a convent. Tensions which are latent in the original version are, in this later emendation, given greater dramatic emphasis.

In the denouements of the comedies, Corneille's changes follow a similar pattern. In *Melite*, Act v, Scene 4, for example, the hero and heroine are reunited after their trials. In 1633, the emphasis lies very obviously on the sensual aspects of the reunion; Tirsis recalls the 'adorables regards' of his beloved which he now longs to replace with something more solid and tangible:

> Je ne puis plus cherir vostre foible entretien
> Plus heureux je souspire apres un plus grand
>   bien. . . .
> Il faut un aliment plus solide à nos flames
> Par où nous unissions nos bouches et nos ames.

>   (1797-98, 1803-804)

In such lines, the hero commits himself to the pleasures of the present moment in all their delightful immediacy. In the emended version such allusions are removed, but in this change is implied a more reflective assessment of the joy which now opens out before the lovers. Instead of physical togetherness it is the idea of psychological liberation which is expressed, the joyful release from inner pressure and constraint. In 1660, Tirsis's lines become:

> Nous n'avons plus besoin de votre confidence,
> L'Amour en liberté peut dire ce qu'il pense.

Where formerly this expression of joy suggested the glorious culmination of a courtship, the move from a desired to a realized union, the hero's emended lines are seen to imply far more the effect of events on the protagonists' love, and their relief from the pressure of secrecy.

What is implied in this variant of *Melite* is seen more positively in changes which Corneille brings to the final scenes of *La Veuve*.[13] In Act v, Scene 1, for instance, Clarice expresses her desire to tell Philiste of her release from captivity. In the original text, her lines are quite straightforward:

> Tandis permettez moy de le faire advertir
> Qu'il luy faut en plaisirs ses douleurs convertir.

>   (1617-18)

The formula here is that of traditional comedy, which suggests the automatic transition from despair to joy; the mechanism, not the character, is important. In 1660, however, Corneille changes these lines. The essence of the formula remains the same, but the dramatist underlines more obviously the suffering which has taken place: an additional line emphasizes the degree of Philiste's anxiety, and to this is joined an indication of Clarice's own:

> Et souffrez cependant qu'on le puisse avertir
> Que nos maux en plaisirs se doivent convertir.
> La douleur trop long-temps regne sur son courage.

Where in the original text there are indications of formal smoothness, of characters slipping effortlessly from role to role, Corneille suggests now their greater sensitivity to the impact of events.

Particularly significant is the increased emphasis given to the possible suffering of Doris, helplessly caught between her mother and brother, each of whom tries to impose a different, but equally unsuitable partner on her. By Act v, Scene 9, however, she is betrothed to Celidan, a suitor she loves and who loves her. Earlier troubles are forgotten, and the heroine utters the traditional formula which harmonizes inclination and filial duty:

> Icy vostre merite est joint à leur puissance
> Et la raison s'accorde à mon obeissance.

>   (1991-92)

The process is mechanical, and attention is fixed on the joy of the present moment. In 1660, however, the tone is altered significantly as Corneille inserts six lines which stress quite explicitly the suffering which might have been. The threat to the character's happiness implicit in the plot is here brought to the forefront of attention:

> Reünir les esprits d'une mere et d'un frere,
> Du choix qu'ils m'avoient fait avoir sçeu me deffaire,
> M'arracher à Florange, et m'oster Alcidon,
> Et d'un cœur genereux me faire l'heureux don,
> C'est avoir sçeu me rendre un assez grand service
> Pour esperer beaucoup avec quelque justice.

In 1634, Doris loves Celidan for his traditional heroic qualities; in 1660, she loves him also for having saved her from misery. Once again, Corneille's alteration implies that characters do not simply discard one identity, one emotional state for another, and that the past has its role to play in the harmony of the present.

The general trend of these changes to the earlier plays is reflected again in certain emendations of the later ones. It is suggested, for instance, at the end of *La Galerie du Palais*, Act v, Scene 4. In 1637, Célidée's scene of reconciliation with Lysandre is characterized by subtly-implied self-deception on the part of the heroine. At the end of her confession, however, emphasis lies for a moment on the future happiness of the couple as they kiss and forget the past:

> Accepte un repentir accompagné de larmes,
> Ce baiser cependant punira ma rigueur,
> Et me fermant la bouche, il t'ouvrira mon cœur.

> (1614-16 var.)

In 1660, the first line is unchanged, but then Célidée continues:

> Et souffre que le tien nous fasse tour à tour
> Par ce petit divorce augmenter notre amour.

Corneille removes the allusion to kissing, but he does more than this in his emendation. Stress moves from the union of the present moment, enjoyable in its physical immediacy, and on to the consequences of the *feinte*. The altered lines imply further the suffering of Célidée, as she now recalls the earlier deception of her lover, and it is in terms of these former doubts and uncertainties that the reunion is to be appreciated. A change such as this underlines more strongly what is implicit in the original text: the suggestion that, at the end of the comedy, these characters do not simply revert to their initial roles as lovers, unaffected by their adventures, but that, in the course of the play, they have learned something about themselves and about each other.

A similar change is made at the end of *La Suivante.* In the final lines of Amarante's monologue of Act v, Scene 9, the servant curses the old man, whose passion for Florame's sister has thwarted her own designs. In the text of 1639, the curse is that of cuckoldry:

> Puisse enfin ta foiblesse et ton humeur jalouze
> Te frustrer desormais de tout contentement,
> Te remplir de soupçons, et cette jeune épouse
> Joindre à mille mespris le secours d'un amant!

> (1697-1700)

The vision is traditional and farcical; any implied suffering is subsumed beneath the stylization of the motif, which juxtaposes the lifelessness and gullibility of age with the energy and wiles of youth. In 1660, Corneille removes the allusion to adultery but, in doing so, he intensifies the suggestions of tension which exist already in the creation of order at the end of the play:

> Puisse le noir chagrin de ton humeur jalouse
> Me contraindre moy-mesme à déplorer ton sort,
> Te faire un long trépas, et cette jeune épouse
> User toute sa vie à souhaiter ta mort.

The fate of both husband and wife is now no longer viewed in terms of a conventional relationship of farce. Deep suffering is implied for both parties, as emphasis moves to the painful and slow passage of time extending beyond the traditionally happy ending.

Analysis of Corneille's variants reveals a desire to invest his early comedies with an increased dramatic seriousness which is fascinating in its implications. On one level it suggests a clear change in his attitude as to the nature of comedy and the effects it should seek, a change apparent also in his critical remarks on these same plays. Just as in the text themselves certain comic scenes are deliberately rendered more serious in their impact, so too in the *Examens* moments of undisputed comedy are either criticized as faulty or are given graver interpretations. In his *Examen* of *Melite,* the gullibility of Philandre is held to be *invraisemblable* (p. 80). The interview of Daphnis and Clarimond in *La Suivante,* Act III, Scene 2, where the heroine rejects the importunate pleas of a ridiculous suitor in a sequence of stychomythic exchanges, is seen to have 'une affectation assez dangereuse' (p. 91). Alidor's abortive attempt to have Angelique abducted in *La Place Royale,* Act IV, is conceived as an appropriate moral punishment for the heroine (pp. 95-96), and the vacillations of Alidor's character, which constitute his essence as a comic hero, are seen by the commentator of 1660 as a culpable dramatic weakness:

> . . . il semble ne commencer à l'aimer véritablement que quand il lui a donné sujet de le haïr. Cela fait une inégalité de moeurs qui est vicieuse.

> (p. 95)

Indeed, such is Corneille's desire to recast certain scenes in a more serious light that in his reference to Géronte's anger of *Le Menteur,* Act v, Scene 5, in the *Examen* to *L'Illusion comique,* he passes over his quite evident removal of the moral gravity in his source, and is led to argue that such dramatic outbursts, taken on their own terms, may be justified in comedy (p. 101).

This new conception of the genre is reflected also in *Don Sanche d'Aragon,* a play whose characters are high-born and whose tone is essentially noble, but which Corneille vigorously defends as a *comédie,* albeit a *comédie héroïque.* For the dramatist of 1650, it seems, irony and ridicule are not necessary adjuncts of comedy, a point which he emphasizes in his *Epître*:

> Cet agrément a été jusqu'ici tellement de la pratique de la comédie, que beaucoup ont cru qu'il était aussi de son essence, et je serais encore dans ce scrupule, si je n'en avais été guéri par votre Heinsius, de qui je viens d'apprendre heureusement que *movere risum non constituit comoediam, sed plebis aucupium, et abusus.*

> (p. 198)

It is thus particularly significant that it is at this stage in his career that he makes his often-quoted remark about the essential originality of *Melite,* namely, its absence of ridiculous characters:

> On n'avait jamais vu jusque-là que la comédie fît rire sans personnages ridicules, tels que les valets bouffons, les parasites, les capitans, les docteurs, etc.

> (p. 80)

The remark is apt, of course, in so far as it refers to his exclusion of the stock types of Plautine comedy. Corneille was certainly one of the first dramatists of the 1630s to move away from the stereotyped characters of farce in his search for more sophisticated comic effects. Yet, as the later variants suggest, his new understanding of comedy implies the rejection of all forms of the ridiculous, elements which had a manifestly important role to play in his earliest texts. Apparent here is a definite change of attitude, a curious denial of the achievements of the early works, particularly of their accomplished creation and exploitation of comic characters and situations.

However, this change in Corneille's conception of his early work is blended, paradoxically, with a certain continuity and consistency in his thought. The path which the emending dramatist has been seen to follow, the move from light-hearted comedy to suggestions of greater seriousness, is not totally new and unexpected, but is prefigured to a significant degree in the development of his comedies from **Melite** to **La Place Royale**, from the depiction of lovers who finally overcome all obstacles to their happiness to the depiction of those who do not. In his earliest plays, Corneille develops and refines comic techniques not simply in order to arouse unreflective laughter but also to create effects more subtle and suggestive. In his later plays particularly, tensions are felt beneath the mechanisms of comedy, and characters are seen to be unusually sensitive to the impact of events on them. In his emendations of **Melite** and **La Veuve,** the most heavily-altered of these plays, Corneille suggests a vision of the plots more obviously consonant with that of his later creations; in the changes to **La Galerie du Palais** and **La Suivante,** tensions already apparent in the texts are further underlined. It is significant, indeed, that no such radical changes are to be found in **La Place Royale**; already, in the original version, Corneille had taken his investigation as far as it could go. Seen in this light, the variants suggest not so much Corneille's rejection of his early interests but his rediscovery of them. Through these changes, he examines again and gives greater emphasis to the problem of suffering in comedy, a question which had fascinated him and several of his contemporaries in the 1630s, but which later writers, in their essentially burlesque conception of the genre, chose to ignore.

Notes

1. Pierre Corneille, *Writings on the Theatre,* edited by H. T. Barnwell (Oxford, 1965), p. 182. All subsequent quotations from Corneille's criticism are taken from this edition.

2. W. L. Wiley, 'Corneille's Refinement of his Early Plays', *Studies in Philology,* 59 (1962), p. 183.

3. Louis Rivaille, 'P. Corneille, correcteur de ses premières œuvres (1632-1644)' (thèse complémentaire pour le doctorat ès lettres, 1936), p. 55.

4. Imbrie Buffum, *Studies in the Baroque from Montaigne to Rotrou* (New Haven, 1957), p. 211.

5. L. W. Tancock, 'Work on Corneille since 1945', *Modern Languages,* 40 (1959), p. 111.

6. Gillet de la Tessonerie, *La Comédie de Francion* (Paris, 1642).

7. Claude de L'Estoile, *L'Intrigue des Filous* (Lyon, 1644).

8. *Œuvres de P. Corneille,* edited by C. Marty-Laveaux (Paris, 1862-68), IV, 130.

9. *Melite, ou Les Fausses Lettres,* pièce comique (1633), edited by M. Roques and M. Lièvre (Geneva, 1950).

10. *La Galerie du Palais, ou L'Amie Rivalle,* comédie (1637); in *Œuvres,* II, 1-112.

11. *La Suivante,* comédie (1637), edited by M. R. Margitic (Geneva, 1978).

12. *La Place Royale, ou L'Amoureux extravagant,* comédie (1637), edited by J.-C. Brunon (Paris, 1962).

13. *La Vefve, ou Le Traistre Trahy,* comédie (1634), edited by M. Roques and M. Lièvre (Geneva, 1954).

Harriet Stone (essay date October 1982)

SOURCE: Stone, Harriet. "Transformal Closures in *Le Cid, Horace, Cinna,* and *Polyeucte.*" *Theatre Journal* 34, no. 3 (October 1982): 302-21.

[*In the following essay, Stone scrutinizes the stylistic and thematic similarities of* The Cid, Horace, Cinna, *and* Polyeucte.]

Tragedy is the experience of loss—loss *of* or separation *from* an envisaged whole or state of fulfillment. That is, loss implies its logical corollary (totality); the one concept is defined through the other. So the enactment of tragedy involves the separation of the individual from his coveted possession, the transformation of an inclusive desire into an exclusive choice.

If tragedy lends itself particularly well to the theatre, it is because of the unique perspective afforded by the stage. The audience's view of the performing characters serves to concretize the abstract relation of part to whole, loss to fulfillment. Viewed against the artful backdrop of successive scenes and acts as these give structure to life's experience, the characters' physical presence on the stage conveys the larger dimensions of the whole of the drama, the theatre, and the world. The characters' suffering is created through the progressive and proportionate concentration of experience. Word, gesture, and silence gain significance as they are shown to reverberate within layers structuring the characters' enacted conflict.

French classical tragedy, with its concern for Aristotelian unities and symmetrical design, is a prime example of this tightened structure. As the following study of Corneille's *Le Cid, Horace, Cinna,* and *Polyeucte* reveals, the action produces tension through direct confrontation,[1] thereby exposing a unique reliance on boundary situations. Through the duel of *Le Cid,* the debate of *Horace,* the trial of *Cinna,* and the martyrdom of *Polyeucte,* Corneille extends the hero's dialogue within the limits of the dialectical form.

For if the classical model attempted to correct the excesses of the Renaissance, it profited greatly from the Renaissance sense of order. The Renaissance, as conceived by Poulet, perceived all experience, including the infinite, in terms of a circle, a closed geometric structure itself but one form of the divine order of creation.[2] This notion of absolute closure, in its implication of completeness reflected in the theatre, may be taken to account not only for the referential quality of classical language,[3] but might also help to explain how a tightening of rhetorical conventions in Corneille can be shown to parallel his thematic movement towards the infinite.

In *Corneille et la dialectique du héros*[4] Serge Doubrovsky uses the Hegelian model to discuss the hero's "projet de Maîtrise" in terms of a progression from the conquest of others in *Le Cid,* to the conquest of self in *Horace,* to the conquest of power in *Cinna,* to the conquest of God in *Polyeucte.* Underlying this kind of conflict, as it is exposed through the dialectical method, is what might be called a structural bipolarity that follows a corresponding development. By "bipolarity" I mean the juxtaposition of two mutually repellent forms. The notion comprises the physical space of Corneille's theatre, which tends to break down into halves. In the social perspective of the stage, the struggles of the aristocracy against the bourgeoisie suggest historic contradictions. These, Doubrovsky argues, are actually "transhistoric" because they expose an inalterable metaphysics, an "unchangeable" human dilemma.[5] Similarly, the bipolar model, indicating diametrical opposition, suggests a "transformal" closure or significance that extends the purely formal understanding of containment to an awareness of infinity. Yet where the dialectical method, through a process of refinement, points to a constant factor in human experience, formal analysis, measuring structural variations, is an expansive process

which reveals Corneille's own evolving aesthetic, his developing tragic vision. He extends the second or binding term of the opposition into progressively more elaborate systems of limits. Perceived in light of the expanding dimensions of the tragic form, Corneille's depiction of the hero's successive encounters with "the other," the self modeled after the Roman ideal, the power hierarchy, and God are understood to be stages of the individual's projection onto the infinite.

Specifically, antonymic relations in *Le Cid* are restructured in terms of paradigm in *Horace,* cycle in *Cinna,* and concentric orders in *Polyeucte.* Appreciable in terms of the operations of exclusion, incorporation, substitution, and superimposition respectively, the four tragedies depict the extension of the oppositional force into the vertical line, the full circle, and the circle within the circle. Corneille's ordering of the universe is thus systematically tightened or solidified. And the intensity of the hero's struggle is measurable in terms of the enclosing structure which grows literally around him.

The form that becomes a line that becomes a circle and a circle within a circle is not, of course, visually perceptible on the stage any more than in the text. Yet the spectator of the performed tragedy, like its reader, must have a sense of dimension, of mass bearing down upon the hero, if he is to comprehend the infinity in which the hero is enclosed.

Le Cid

The need to decide between disturbingly discordant alternatives constitutes the thematic interest of *Le Cid.* The exigencies of love and honor ("Réduit au triste choix ou de trahir ma flamme, / Ou de vivre en infâme"—"Reduced to the sad choice of either betraying my desire, / Or of living in infamy"[6]) are revealed to be incompatible for both Rodrigue and Chimène. Confronted, he after the fact, she before, with situations in which both must choose between realizing their passion and avenging their fathers' honor, the characters experience self-negation through exclusive possibilities.[7]

The language of the play is therefore structured on juxtapositions whose implied consequence seems to derive from the election of one or the other of its terms or postulates. Despite apparent semantic similarities, words are opposed in meaning, underscoring the inclusive demands of love in contrast with the limiting demands of duty. Consider, for example, Chimène's assessment of the conflict in Act V, where she confronts Rodrigue with the accusation: "Ton honneur t'est plus cher que je ne te suis chère, / Puisqu'il trempe tes mains dans le sang de mon père" (V,i,1509-10)—(Your honor is dearer to you than I am dear, / Since it dips your hands in the blood of my father). The repetition of "cher"/"chère" in the first line stresses at once the desire for unification and its impossibility. That the words, though parallel, are opposed is underscored by the difference in gender, which points to sexual opposition, denied union, despite shared passion.

A like exclusivity is apparent in Rodrigue's evaluation of his plight:

> Je dois à ma maîtresse aussi bien qu'à mon père:
> J'attire en me vengeant sa haine et sa colère;
> J'attire ses mépris en ne me vengeant pas.
> A mon plus doux espoir l'un me rend infidèle,
>   Et l'autre indigne d'elle.
>
> [I,vi,322-26]

I owe my mistress as well as my father: / In avenging myself I bring down her hatred and her anger; / I bring down her scorn in not avenging myself. / The one makes me unfaithful to my sweetest hope, / And the other unworthy of her.

The first line of this passage posits the two sides of the conflict, which the following two lines discuss in turn. The concluding lines subvert, however, any attempt at synthesis. For they incorporate the consequences of both courses of action, thereby defying the either/or proposition of the opening lines. The sense of impasse is furthered by the fact that only negative options are mentioned. Don Diègue's earlier ultimatum "Meurs ou tue" (I,v,275)—"Die or kill"—thus develops here into a paradigm of negative option. If Rodrigue does not avenge his father, he loses his honor, and if he loses his honor, he loses Chimène's respect. The juxtapositions are multiple, but the choices are consistently exclusive.

With Chimène the sense of exclusive choice is manifest in a negative doubling of the self. Inner conflict is perceived in terms of opposed selves:

> Silence, mon amour, laisse agir ma colère:
> S'il a vaincu deux rois, il a tué mon père;
> Ces tristes vêtements, où je lis mon malheur,
> Sont les premiers effets qu'ait produits sa valeur;
> Et quoi qu'on die ailleurs d'un coeur si magnanime,
> Ici tous les objets me parlent de son crime.
>
> [IV,i,1129-34]

Silence, my love, let my anger act: / If he vanquished two kings, he killed my father; / These sad garments, where I read my misfortune, / Are the first effects had by his valor; / And whatever one says elsewhere of such a magnanimous heart, / Here all objects speak to me of his crime.

This passage builds on the consistent opposition of "coeur"/"devoir"—passion/anger—established in the opening lines of Chimène's speech here: "On le vante, on le loue, et mon coeur y consent! / Mon honneur est muet, mon devoir impuissant!" (1127-28)—"He is exalted, he is praised, and my heart consents to this! / My honor is silent, and my duty overcome!" To the extent, however,

that one's admiration of Rodrigue's "coeur" is of its quality "magnanime," one is evaluating the passion of his act, i.e., his duty *as* passion. "Coeur" thus becomes the most comprehensive indication of conflict. Read in this light, these lines appear to be structured on the double meaning of "coeur" as the seat of both "amour" and "colère"—passion and violation—in the case of Chimène, and as the agent that paradoxically deprives through magnanimity—that both gives to and takes from—in the case of Rodrigue. The ellipsis of "coeur" in Chimène's reference to her opposed selves emphasizes their mutual exclusivity. Their simultaneous presence in a united "coeur" is denied by the necessity that the passionate self (in the restricted use of "coeur") be suppressed so that the angry self ("devoir") be heard. Chimène's characterization of Rodrigue's "coeur" as one that both defends ("magnanime") and offends ("crime"), that exists in a state of self-contradiction, thus characterizes her own "coeur" as well—though the surface of her language does not make a confrontation of these complications available to either character except in the resolving action.

This predominantly emotional argument is juxtaposed in the following lines with an equally exclusive opposition, seen instead in terms of an intellectual argument. The dilemma of the "coeur" here becomes the dilemma of the "esprit":

> Vous, qui rendez la force à mes ressentiments,
> Voiles, crêpes, habits, lugubres ornements,
> Pompe que me prescrit sa première victoire,
> Contre ma passion soutenez bien ma gloire;
> Et lorsque mon amour prendra trop de pouvoir,
> Parlez à mon esprit de mon triste devoir,
> Attaquez sans rien craindre une main triomphante.
>
> [IV,i,1135-41]

You, who restore strength to my resentments, / Veils, crapes, clothes, lugubrious ornaments, / Pompe that his first victory prescribes me, / Against my passion support my glory well; / And when my love will take too much power, / Speak to my mind of my sad duty, / Attack without fear a triumphant hand.

Rational and irrational selves are opposed in Chimène's attempt to suppress her passion through an appeal to her mourning dress, symbol of her duty to her father, to assert a rational control of her mind. Her clothes thus assume her internal dilemma, mediating between, or balancing, the opposed demands of honor and love. Chimène's inability to act on either choice is reinforced by the paradigm of mourning objects—objects of loss— which separate the rational and irrational demands of the psyche. The entire "Pompe" of "Voiles, crêpes, habits, lugubres ornements" stands as concrete testimony of dead resolution, failed action.

Thus the "coeur vs. esprit" dialectic is doubly presented as the conflict between the seats of the emotions and the intellect, respectively, and as the content of this conflict: "coeur" as passion vs. "esprit" as honor. The presence on both sides of the emotions vs. intellect debate of the conflict between passion and honor contributes to the sense of exclusive options, for they effectively cancel each other.

The depiction of ineluctable conflict is perhaps most poignantly explored in Chimène's despairing remark:

> La moitié de ma vie a mis l'autre au tombeau,
> Et m'oblige à venger, après ce coup funeste,
> Celle que je n'ai plus sur celle qui me reste.
>
> [III,iii,800-02]

> Half of my life put the other in the tomb, / And compels me to avenge, after this fatal blow, / The half that I have no longer against the half that I have still.

The specific reference to her mutually exclusive halves as self-negating underscores the rhetorical conventions apparent throughout the play. Balanced opposition denies both the extension through likeness and the expansion through substitution which the later works exploit.

HORACE

Significantly, while the conflict of the opening scenes of **Horace** resembles **Le Cid** in its opposition of love and honor, this tragedy emphasizes less the incompatibility of orders than their similarity. Sabine depicts the battle between Rome and Albe as that between new and old manifestations of the same existence:

> [Rome,] Ingrate, souviens-toi que du sang de ses rois
> Tu tiens ton nom, tes murs, et tes premières lois.
> Albe est ton origine: arrête, et considère
> Que tu portes le fer dans le sein de ta mère.
>
> [I,i,53-56]

> Ungrateful Rome, remember that from the blood of its kings / You hold your name, your walls, and your first laws. / Albe is your origin: stop and consider / That you are carrying the sword into your mother's breast.

War is thus portrayed as matricide, as the murder of one's origin and nurture, and, consequently, as the killing of oneself.

At another level, the battle is fought between brothers, further reducing the opposition to that of identical orders. Responding to the news that the leaders have pitted brother against brother, Curiace determines: "l'amitié, l'alliance et l'amour / Ne pourront empêcher que les trois Curiaces / Ne servent leur pays contre les trois Horaces" (II,ii,418-20)—("friendship, alliance, and love / Cannot prevent the three Curiaces / From serving their country against the three Horaces.") The symmetry of the last two lines is underscored by the triple bonds which the first line evokes. Linked in "amitié"

through respect for Horace, "alliance" through the latter's marriage to his sister Sabine, and "amour" through his love for Camille, Horace's sister, Curiace perceives the confrontation as that of "les trois" against "les trois"—of identical parts. He defines a self-negating relationship of self against the self, rather than self against other. Thus, where **Le Cid** has used juxtaposition to deny synthesis, **Horace** departs from a metaphorical construction of similarity, of like parts which must be joined for full meaning.

Horace's attitude towards the ensuing combat strengthens the notion of a unique Roman paradigm:

> Mais vouloir au public immoler ce qu'on aime,
> S'attacher au combat *contre un autre soi-même,*
> Attaquer un parti qui prend pour défenseur
> Le frère d'une femme et l'amant d'une soeur,
> Et rompant tous ces noeuds, s'armer pour la patrie
> Contre un sang qu'on voudroit racheter de sa vie,
> Une telle vertu n'appartenoit qu'à nous.
>
> [II,iii,443-49; emphasis mine]

> But to want to sacrifice for the public good what one loves, / To engage in combat against another self, / To attack a group that takes for its champion / A wife's brother and a sister's lover, / And breaking all these ties, to arm oneself for one's country / Against a blood that one would save with one's own life, / Such virtue belongs to us alone.

The matricide to which Sabine's lines refer and the fratricide stressed in Curiace's speech above are explicitly connected here to the notion of suicide.[8] Horace views the exceptional, or heroic, quality of his mission precisely in the opportunity it provides to negate the "other," to meet patriotic demands so as to deny the distinction of self-family-country-"vertu" (in both the political and religious codes), i.e., as an act of self-possession. Opposition thus serves to establish a paradigm of indivisible selves, to reveal what Doubrovsky terms "la nécessité tragique d'affirmer la supériorité dans l'identité."[9]

Unique identity is, however, undermined by Horace's murder of Camille. Insofar as this act repeats the murder of Curiace ("d'un autre soi-même" in the double sense of her being Curiace's lover and Horace's sister), it denies the completeness of the former by virtue of its duplicity. The perfect act is a consummation; it precludes completion in a second movement.[10]

No where is this more apparent than in Camille's own response. Her outrage culminates in her deliberate provocation of Horace to kill her: "Voir le dernier Romain à son dernier soupir, / Moi seule en être cause, et mourir de plaisir!" (IV,v,1317-18)—"See the last Roman breathe his last sigh, / I alone be the cause, and die with pleasure!" Distinguishing herself from Horace's eternal Rome, Camille denies the absolute quality of "patrie" as a final determinant:

Rome, l'unique objet de mon ressentiment!
Rome, à qui vient ton bras d'immoler mon amant!
Rome qui t'a vu naître, et que ton coeur adore!
Rome enfin que je hais parce qu'elle t'honore!

[IV,v,1301-04]

Rome, sole object of my resentment! / Rome, where
your arm comes to sacrifice my lover! / Rome, who
saw you born, and whom your heart adores! / Rome,
finally, whom I hate because she honors you!

The repetition of "Rome" in these lines rebuilds the
tension of juxtaposition, thereby suggesting alienation
rather than the desired recuperation of the self. Camille
doubly degrades Horace. For she negates the singularity
of the standard of perfection with which he identifies—
Rome as universal—and, through her own death,
precludes the sufficiency of his one act with regard to
this notion of "other."

CINNA

In **Cinna** the predominant opposition functions not as a
movement towards and away from the hero, or center,
but as a movement around him. Whereas juxtaposition
in **Horace** depicts the evolution of the self in terms of
Rome as an extended paradigm, here the self is
measured in terms of a cycle of shifting perceptions.
Horace describes the problem of the unification of the
self. In **Cinna** unification is denied by the very
multiplicity of the "other."

This concept is evident from the outset of the play,
where Emilie defends her plot to have Cinna murder
Auguste in terms of monetary exchange:

S'il [Cinna] veut me *posséder,* Auguste doit périr:
Sa tête est le seul *prix* dont il peut m'*acquérir.* . . .
Et des mêmes *présents* qu'il [Auguste] *verse* dans mes
   mains
J'*achète* contre lui les esprits des Romains; . . .
Pour qui venge son père il n'est point de *forfaits,*
Et c'est *vendre* son sang que se rendre aux bienfaits.

[I,ii,55-84; emphasis mine]

If he wants to possess me, Auguste must perish: / His
head is the only price for which he can acquire
me. . . . / And with the same presents that he [Au-
guste] deposits in my hands / I buy against him the
Romans' minds; . . . / For he who avenges his father
there is no price to pay [crime], / And to give oneself
over to benefits is to sell one's own blood.

The blackmail which determines the plot is thus affected through language which denotes substitution.
Moreover, the repeated juxtapositions (the murder of
Auguste is posited four times in these lines) suggest the
reinterpretation of the same event. Such elaboration is a
means of diffusing or diversifying a problem rather than
capturing its essence.

In terms of rhetorical conventions the principle of
exchange extends from metaphor, the continuity
between one object and another. The subversion of
paradigmatic forms into contiguous relations, i.e., the
extension of the metaphoric pattern to the metonymic,
creates a cycle of signifiers which reform rather than
synthesize experience. And this perpetual recycling, or
destabilization of perceptions, is at the root of Auguste's
frustration. Changes in the external situation prevent his
personal fulfillment. He must confront a world of shifting conditions; he is entrapped within an objective reality that continually redefines itself:

J'ai souhaité l'empire, et j'y suis parvenu;
Mais en le souhaitant, je ne l'ai pas connu:
Dans sa possession j'ai trouvé pour tous charmes
D'effroyables soucis, d'éternelles alarmes,
Mille ennemis secrets, la mort à tous propos,
Point de plaisir sans trouble, et jamais de repos.

[II,i,371-76]

I wished for the empire, and I have attained it; / But in
wishing for it, I knew not what it was: / In its possession I have found, for all its charms, / Frightening wor-
ries, endless alarms, / A thousand secret enemies, death
at every turn, / No pleasure without trouble, and never
rest.

The persistent flux of external circumstances produces
the necessity of continually reinterpreting the objective
world, thereby preventing "repos." Meanings substitute
for each other over time; truths continually change,
denying the self a firm grasp on the real.[11]

This flux manifests itself in Auguste's profound expression of frustration with the infidelity that surrounds
him:

Meurs, et dérobe-lui la gloire de ta chute;
Meurs: tu ferais pour vivre un lâche et vain ef-
   fort, . . .
Meurs, puisque c'est un mal que tu ne peux guérir;
Meurs enfin, puisqu'il faut ou tout perdre, ou
   mourir. . . .
Meurs; mais quitte du moins la vie avec éclat,

[IV,ii,1170-79]

Die, and rob him of the glory of your fall; / Die: you
would make only a cowardly and vain attempt to
live, . . . / Die, since it is an evil that you cannot cure;
/ Die finally, since it is necessary either to lose all or
die. . . . / Die; but at least leave life with a stir.

Every line represents an accurate account of the situation. Although each depicts a different rationale, the
consequence of the various logical forms is the
persistent "Meurs." These lines thus form a series of
interchangeable arguments which gain no greater
significance. They become no more absolute for being
considered together. Finding resolution only in death,
Auguste expresses the need to abandon the self for the
other in a final break with the hope of experiencing the
infinite in the real.

POLYEUCTE

André Stegmann discovers in Polyeucte a denial of juxtaposition in the "fusion intime (d'une intrigue amoureuse et d'un sacrifice sacré), l'amour jeune, noble, profond du couple Pauline-Polyeucte donnant l'enracinement charnel à la conversion éclatante du héros et à ses conséquences."[12] Consistent with what I regard as the more perceptive reading of Nadal[13] and Doubrovsky[14] which maintains that Corneille challenges the finality of the tragedy's Christian resolution, I submit, in contradistinction to Stegmann, that juxtaposition persists throughout the play as the superimposition of one order upon the other without fusion.

The argument for a Christian tragedy is not, however, to be dismissed entirely. Polyeucte's election of divine over earthly love, his fight to overcome his passion for Pauline in devotion to his God, is of profound significance: "Quittez cette chimère, et m'aimez. Je vous aime, / Beaucoup moins que mon Dieu, mais bien plus que moimême" (IV,iii,1279-80)—("Leave this chimera and love me. I love you, / Much less than my God, but much more than myself.") Similarly, Polyeucte's baptism, the martyrdom of Polyeucte and Néarque, and the conversions of Pauline and Félix mark the Christian intent of the playwright who wrote in his *Dédicace à la Reine Régente* (1643) that *Polyeucte* "l'entretiendra de Dieu."[15] Although the play is certainly Christian in its resolution, it is nevertheless more importantly secular in terms of the patterns it establishes. The forces of heroism and saintliness are both juxtaposed and fused. Where these forces are in conflict, one must choose between them; where heroism is attained through saintliness, one is asked to appreciate a final paradox.

The most striking stylistic difference between *Polyeucte* and the other plays examined in this article is the preponderance of "et" over "ou" constructions which it exhibits. Consider the following examples from the hero's speech:

> Pauline, sans raison dans la douleur plongée,
> Craint *et* croit déjà voir ma mort qu'elle a songée;
> Elle oppose ses pleurs au dessein que je fais,
> *Et* tâche à m'empêcher de sortir du palais.
> Je méprise sa crainte, *et* je cède à ses larmes;
>
> [I,i,13-17; emphasis mine]

Pauline, plunged without reason into sorrow, / Fears and already sees my death which she has imagined; / She challenges my design with her tears, / And tries to prevent me from leaving the palace. / I scorn her fear, and I yield to her tears;

> Je sens déjà mon coeur prêt à se révolter,
> *Et* ce n'est qu'en fuyant que j'y puis résister.
>
> [I,ii,123-24; emphasis mine]

I already feel my heart ready to rebel, / And it is only in fleeing that I can resist it.

That such connectives preclude fusion is, however, evident in the "mais"—"but"—implicit in these and other lines. In spite of the credence which Polyeucte places in the first clause, he proceeds with the second: "Je méprise sa crainte (mais) je cède à ses larmes." The conjunction thus merely disguises the sense of conflict, opposition.

Moreover, multiple relationships are perceived as limited for all their expansiveness. "Je vous aime," Polyeucte affirms to Pauline, "Le ciel m'en soit témoin, cent fois plus que moi-même; / Mais . . ." (I,ii,113-15)—"I do love you, / Heaven be my witness, a hundred times more than myself, / But. . . ." Love, though extending the self a hundred times over, is still seen to contrast with divine infinitude as the result of the conditional "Mais." Thus even the desired martyrdom is posited as but an exception to, or a restriction of, the absolute recuperation of the self: "Mais dans ce temple enfin la mort est assurée, / Mais dans le ciel déjà la palme est préparée (II,vi, 661-62)—("But in this temple death is finally assured, But in heaven the palm is already prepared.") These lines suggest a final opposition between self-serving and divine ends. As Doubrovsky so aptly states: "En mourant pour son Dieu, Polyeucte meurt donc exclusivement pour lui-même."[16]

Consistent with this juxtaposition, Polyeucte's attempt to unite Pauline with Sévère effects a final contrast of moral and divine interests, thus undermining the wholly sacrificial character of the hero's death:

> Mon amour, par pitié, cherche à vous soulager:
> Il voit quelle douleur dans l'âme vous possède,
> Et sait qu'un autre amour en est le seul remède.
>
> [V,iii,1586-88]

My love, out of pity, seeks to relieve you. / It sees what sadness in your mind possesses you, / And knows that another love is the sole remedy for it.

The mutual constancy of the love of Camille and Sévère is one of the outstanding "fusions" which the play offers. It is, however, to be realized only as a substitute proposition on the part of Polyeucte. It thus denies a sense of unity, opposes human and divine realms. Despite the conjunction "Et" and the adjective "autre," which are intended to connote an expansion of a unique order, Polyeucte's act is but a mere superimposition of one order on another. Division persists despite his attempts to confound separation. Rather than extend divinity into mortal existence, Polyeucte abandons the latter for the former. So the patronizing "pitié" indicates his conscious superiority in this regard. His plea to Pauline that she preserve his memory on earth reinforces not only the division between the human and the divine, but that between the saintly and the divine: "A la gloire. Chère Pauline, adieu: conservez ma mémoire"

(V,iii,1679-80)—("To glory. Dear Pauline, farewell: preserve my memory.") Polyeucte's concern here is with his own glory as much as with that of his Creator. His attempts to fuse the two are precluded by the bipolar structure which demands that his words be interpreted in light of the coexistent, but separate, orders of heroism and saintliness.

Reaching for God, Polyeucte would discover his soul in the omnipotent divine sphere; appealing for glory, he would have his name immortalized. Yet the tension of these two impulses is never fully resolved. Here, as in each of the tragedies under discussion, the movement to complete the form, to fuse the opposed terms of the dialectic, combines with the intended projection of this union over time. The bipolar structure, permitting both a vertical and a horizontal development, creates an interplay between synchronic and diachronic axes that is sustained through the concluding action.

Specifically, by defining one term through its association with another, bipolar opposition points to paradigms of meaning, or synchrony. Yet in establishing tension between two terms, bipolar relations shift from one term to the other, thereby designating diachronic movement. Thus juxtapositions in *Le Cid* affirm the potential for satisfying both love and honor (synchrony), while rooting the characters' sense of frustration in their need to choose between these demands (diachrony). Likewise, relations of similarity, substitution, and superimposition designate a synchronic, or paradigmatic, association of terms as well as a diachronic, or syntagmic, movement between terms. The extension of the metaphoric pattern in *Horace* to the metonymic in *Cinna* therefore represents a shift in focus from synchrony to diachrony, not a negation or suppression of either axis in either play. Similarly, superimposition in *Polyeucte* represents both the metaphoric emphasis of synchrony and the metonymic emphasis of successive options recurring over time. Each of the four dramas significantly concludes with arrested action that looks towards the future: synchronic development is maintained through repetition, memory, and other forms of doubling which pattern the diachronic development.

In Act V of *Le Cid* Rodrigue proposes to Chimène that he be killed. He justifies his position through a series of causal relations:

> Elle vouloit sa tête; et son cœur magnanime,
> S'il l'en eût refusée, eût pensé faire un crime.
> Pour venger son honneur il perdit son amour,
> Pour venger sa maîtresse il a quitté le jour,
>
> [V,i,1537-40]

> She wanted his head, and his magnanimous heart, / If he had refused her it, would have thought to have committed a crime. / To avenge his honor he lost his love, / To avenge his mistress he departed this life,

The election of one of the terms in the original exclusive relation (Rodrigue's honor vs. love) propels the action to a second (Chimène's honor vs. Rodrigue's life), whose resolution similarly involves a choice, moving Rodrigue to the final act of death. Yet the bipolar structure builds vertically at the same time. Rodrigue's "amour" is equated with "cœur," just as "a quitté le jour" is linked with "vouloit sa tête," thereby creating a paradigm of association which counters the contiguous movement from "cœur" to "tête." That is, these synecdoches are revealed through association with the second pair of lines to exist within a metaphorical framework. They are two parts of a paradoxical whole in which the act "venger" is inextricably linked to both Rodrigue's honor *and* his love. Rodrigue's honor could not withstand a disgrace to his mistress. Hence her honor is his honor, and his "cœur" the seat of his love as well as his duty.

Consistent with this, Don Fernand's ultimate resolution of the crisis rests on a stated belief in the potential for successive actions to reinterpret events, i.e., in a restructuring of perceptions over time: "Le temps assez souvent a rendu légitime / Ce qui sembloit d'abord ne se pouvoir sans crime" (V,vii,1813-14)—("Time has often enough rendered legitimate / That which at first seemed impossible without crime.") Thus Chimène's mourning period, whose duration emphasizes diachronic evolution, is to be marked by Rodrigue's "grands exploits"—"great exploits." These repeated triumphs pattern his activity, past as well as present, into a paradigm of love that is honor.

In *Horace* the concern is not with the capacity of an action to restructure perceptions, but to perpetuate itself over time. The emphasis turns from a reinterpretation of past events to a patterning of future events; change is precluded by the persistence of the act's significance. Distinguishing himself from those who valorize an action only for its momentary achievement, Horace views the heroic deed as one which secures an elevated status, sustained through memory:

> Le peuple, qui voit tout seulement par l'écorce,
> S'attache à son effet pour juger de sa force;
> Il veut que ses dehors gardent un même cours,
> Qu'ayant fait un miracle, elle en fasse toujours: . . .
> Il n'examine point si lors on pouvoit mieux,
> Ni que, s'il ne voit pas sans cesse une merveille,
> L'occasion est moindre, et la vertu pareille: . . .
>   Je ne vanterai point les exploits de mon bras;
> Votre Majesté, Sire, a vu mes trois combats:
> Il est bien malaisé qu'un pareil les seconde,
> Qu'une autre occasion à celle-ci réponde,
> Et que tout mon courage, après de si grands coups,
> Parvienne à des succès qui n'aillent au-dessous;
> Si bien que pour laisser une illustre mémoire,
> La mort seule aujourd'hui peut conserver ma
>   gloire: . . .

Permettez, ô grand Roi, que de ce bras vainqueur
Je m'immole à ma gloire, et non pas à ma soeur.

[V,ii,1559-94]

The people, who always see the exterior of everything, / Look to his action to judge his power; / They want his appearances to retain a unique course, / His power, having performed one miracle, to continue to perform them: . . . / They do not look to see if one could have done better then, / Nor, if they do not incessantly view a wonder, / That the occasion is less, and the virtue the same: . . . / I will not boast the exploits of my arm; / Your Majesty, Sire, saw my three battles: / It is difficult for a similar one to second them, / For another occasion to respond to this one, / And for all my courage, after such tremendous blows, / To attain successes that do not go beneath it; / So that to leave an illustrious memory / Only death can preserve my glory today: . . . / Permit me, o great King, with this victorious arm, / To sacrifice myself to my glory, and not to my sister.

While a syntagmic orientation registers a diminution of the single act over time, since subsequent circumstances are themselves less demanding, a synchronic orientation towards history measures greatness in terms of an irreversible hierarchy of achievement. It follows that while the act seen in terms of a diachronic progression has no bearing on subsequent acts, as each is believed to function independently, the synchronic progression points instead to the establishment of a paradigm of heroism that withstands the passage of time and fluctuations of circumstance. Hence successive acts are not less intense for their doubled quality. What is doubled is mastered, proficient, a "miracle" even if the success is less dramatic. Death arrests the heroic paradigm at a level where "gloire" is maintained through the consistent doubling of "mémoire" rather than the reductive doubling of syntagmic evolution.

Significantly, Tulle's clemency is based on the same paradigmatic evaluation:

Ce crime, quoique grand, énorme, inexcusable,
Vient de la même épée et part du même bras
Qui me fait aujourd'hui maître de deux Etats.

[V,iii,1740-42]

This crime, although great, enormous, inexcusable, / Comes from the same sword and escapes from the same arm / That today makes me master of two States.

He sees the heroic paradigm superimposed upon the diachronic passage of time, patterning it in such a way as to justify sparing Horace, and to make the heroism of his eventual death a certainty. Tulle thus both concurs with Horace's sense of glory as memory and adapts it to the future emphasis cited by the elder Horace:

C'est aux rois, c'est aux grands, c'est aux esprits bien faits,
A voir la vertu pleine en ses moindres effets;

C'est d'eux seuls qu'on reçoit la véritable gloire;
Eux seuls des vrais héros assurent la mémoire.

[V,iii,1719-20]

It is up to kings, it is up to great men, it is up to well fashioned minds, / To see virtue full in its least action; / It is from them alone that one receives true glory; / They alone assure the memory of real heroes.

Horace can "Vi[t] pour servir l'Etat" (V,iii,1763)—"Live to serve the State"—meeting its changing needs and strengthening its cumulative pride.

Consistent with the metonymic emphasis detailed above, the concluding action of **Cinna** interrupts the synchronic progression by which memory depicts coherent and consistent action. Arbitrarily imposing an "oubli magnanime" (V,iii,1733)—a "magnanimous forgetting"—Auguste seeks to introduce a syntagmic break with the past. To the degree, however, that it signals the conscious application of an artificial limit, Auguste's action reflects a profound sense of synchrony as well.

At the outset of Act V Auguste is incredulous before indications that an understanding of history should lead to conclusions so inconsistent with its meaning. He cannot conceive that Cinna's "mémoire" should culminate in an action so disruptive of synchronic significance:

Tu t'en souviens, Cinna: tant d'heur et tant de gloire
Ne peuvent pas sitôt sortir de ta mémoire;
Mais ce qu'on ne pourroit jamais s'imaginer,
Cinna, tu t'en souviens, et veut m'assassiner.

[V,i,1473-76]

You remember, Cinna: so much good fortune and so much glory / Cannot slip from your memory so soon; / But what one can never imagine, / Cinna, you remember, and want to assassinate me.

In much the same manner as Don Fernand, Livie in her wisdom attempts to compensate for the breakdown of the paradigmatic structure through movement on the diachronic axis. Subsequent events, she determines, reinterpret the past in a favorable light, patterning a coherent movement (synchrony) which extends into the future:

Tous ces crimes d'Etat qu'on fair pour la couronne,
Le ciel nous en absout alors qu'il nous la donne,
Et dans le sacré rang où sa faveur l'a mis,
Le passé devient juste et l'avenir permis.

[V,ii,1609-12]

All these State crimes that one committed for the crown, / Heaven absolves us of them in giving it to us. / And in the sacred rank where its favor put it, / The past becomes just and the future promised.

Livie implicitly reaffirms here the role of memory as a metaphorical device of association and identity. Extending this notion in much the manner of Horace, Auguste seeks the "miracle" of ineluctable achievement, i.e., definitive success perpetuated through memory:

Je suis maître de moi comme de l'univers;
Je le suis, je veux l'être. O siècles, ô mémoire,
Conservez à jamais ma dernière victoire!

[V,iii,1696-98]

I am master of myself as of the universe; / This I am,
and this I want to be. O centuries, o memory, / Preserve
forever my last victory!

But Auguste's link of "mémoire" with an "oubli magnanime" is a contradiction of terms which undercuts the establishment of an equilibrium and reinforces the sense of tragedy as rupture. Auguste rejects Cinna's assassination plot as a violation of synchronic order, yet his own plan to resolve the conflict through unconditional clemency demands a similar rejection of the past. Thus, while a departure from the past is valorized as the means to secure harmony, it is only in placing himself in the role of the supreme arbiter who "absout (des crimes) alors qu'il . . . (se) donne (la couronne)," of he who integrates past and future into a coherent whole, a "dernière victoire," that Auguste is able to justify the single act of rupture. The "immuable loi" (V,iii,1756)—"immutable law"—to which Livie refers must, then, be viewed as the "loi" of syntagmic progression seen in light of the fixity of paradigm. Auguste can only "tout oublier"—"forget everything"—after having "tout appris"—"learned everything"—(V,iii,1780); paradigms of meaning make possible the change he seeks.

Superimposition in **Polyeucte** culminates with the hero's attainment of the desired saintly martyrdom and the subsequent conversions of Pauline and Félix, acts which unite the play in a paradigm of Christian devotion. Yet the scenes preceding this resolution suggest that doubled action negates. The double conversions, themselves doubling Polyeucte's embrace of religion, deny rather than reinforce paradigm.

Consider Pauline's argument that her own death should follow Polyeucte's:

Ma mort suivra la mort de ce cher criminel;
Et les Dieux trouveront sa peine illégitime,
Puisqu'elle confondra l'innocence et le crime,
Et qu'elle changera, par ce redoublement,
En injuste rigueur un juste châtiment;

[V,iii,1622-26]

My death will follow the death of this dear criminal; /
And the Gods will find his pain illegitimate, / Since it
will confound innocence and crime, / And it will
change, by this doubling, / An unjust punishment into a
just severity;

Her death contradicts the necessity of Polyeucte's death; her faith precludes his ostracism. Doubling is thus a negative action whose product is "injustice," lack of connection between the meaning of the original act and successive acts.

Consistent with this denial of paradigmatic development, Polyeucte, too, regards successive actions as a series of battles to be fought: "Faut-il tant de fois vaincre avant que triompher?" (V,iii,1654)—("Is it necessary to vanquish so many times before triumphing?") Appropriately, he dies without knowledge of Pauline's and Félix' acceptance. Believing that his proselytizing has failed, he can be said to transcend the paradigm rather than complete it, to act in rejection of an ineluctable diachronic progression. Thus the paradigmatic order of God is permanently juxtaposed with the temporal inconsistencies of man.[17]

Viewed in the context of synchronic and diachronic development, bipolarity implies that doubling, no matter how parallel, precludes absolute cohesion. So the plays are tragic despite the return to order that occurs at the end of each of them. Resolution is clearly arbitrary, undermined by the juxtapositional emphasis which produces it; order stands in final contrast to the disorder which preceeded it. If, therefore, the study of structural opposition is justified, it is because Corneille calls attention to his art as elucidating conflict, as emphasizing the striving for the infinite rather than its realization.

Returning now to the classical conception of order with which this article began, it may be affirmed that the insistence on closed forms does not restrict the diversity of all that exists within the limits of these forms. Based on what Poulet terms the notion of "retour"—"return"—the Renaissance model assumed an ultimate order to appreciate the complexity of existence:

Le corps en retournant à la matière, l'âme en retournant à Dieu, accomplissent donc l'un et l'autre un cercle et un cycle. Mais le retour de l'âme à Dieu n'est pas seulement représentable sous la forme d'un mouvement périphérique. Dieu, cercle infini que l'âme envahit et parcourt est aussi Dieu, centre infini où elle s'enfonce. Le retour de l'âme est un retour au centre. Point de départ, le centre est aussi point d'aboutissement.[18]

The body, in returning to matter, and the soul, in returning to God, thus each completes a circle and a cycle. But the soul's return to God is not only representable in the form of a peripheral movement. God, infinite circle that the soul enters and overspreads, is also God, infinite center into which the soul is absorbed. The return of the soul is a return to the center. The starting point, the center is also the end point.

To the twentieth-century mind such structuring represents a valorization of the creation of signifiers within a closed system of referents.[19] For Corneille, as I have tried to show, the closed system is constantly redefined and tested. The enclosure of the theatrical space has been made coordinate with the theme it displays.

Notes

1. Cf. Albert Cook, *French Tragedy: The Power of Enactment* (Chicago: Swallow Press, 1981), p. 107: "For Corneille . . . the persons are always

fully public as well as private. The contradictions work out in the open of the tight stage, and no one who is willing to meet the demands of heroic virtue, as nearly all are in the tragedies through *Polyeucte,* goes under to the condition of being a fatal third, or lapses in the sorrow of unifying tenderness and firmness. The abstract balances between *amour* and *devoir,* or between *famille* and *patrie,* or between *Dieu* and *empire,* can constantly skeletalize the poetry because they have done so in the full equivalences of the action."

2. Georges Poulet, *Les metamorphoses du cercle* (Paris: Plon, 1961), p. xii notes how profoundly Leonardo da Vinci and Giordano Bruno were influenced by Meister Eckhart's doctrine defining God in each moment and in each place as constituting the center of all moments and of all places such that the maximum is realized in the minimum: "*In divinis quodlibet est in quodlibet, et maximum in minimo, et sic fructus in flore. Ratio, quia Deus, ut ait sapiens, est sphaera intellectualis infinita, cujas centrum est ubique, cum circumferentia nusquam, et cujas tot sunt circumferentiae, quot puncta. . . . Sic Deus est totus in qualibet creatura, in una, sicut in omnibus.*" I cite the full text from Denifle, *Archiv für Litteratur-und-Kirchengeschichte des Mittelalters,* v. II, 1886, p. 751, appearing in Poulet's notes, p. xxvii. In the *Paradiso,* XXX, 103-05, Dante writes of God: "E si distende in circular figura / In tanto, che la sua circonferenza / Sarebbe al sol troppo larga cintura." Du Bartas, *Oeuvres,* ed. U. T. Holmes, vol. II (Univ. of North Carolina Press, 1938), p. 104 describes God as a "cercle parfait / Dont le centre est partout et sur tout son rond trait." Traherne, *Centuries of Meditations,* ed. B. Dobell (London, 1908), p. 136, extends the circular symbolism to man as the center of an infinite universe: "My Soul is an infinite Sphere in a Centre." For a full discussion of the symbolism of the circle in the Renaissance see Poulet, pp. iii-21.

3. Roland Barthes, "L'Effet de Réel," *Communications,* 11 (1968), p. 89, distinguishes modern literature as that concerned with the need to "vider le signe et . . . reculer infiniment son objet jusqu'à mettre en cause, d'une façon radicale, l'esthétique séculaire de la 'représentation.'"— "empty the sign . . . and push back its object so far as to question, in a most fundamental manner, the secular aesthetic of 'representation.'" This and all other translations appearing in the article are my own.

4. Serge Doubrovsky, *Corneille et la dialectique du héros* (Paris: Gallimard, 1963).

5. Doubrovsky, p. 22; "Toute situation est historique; mais, inversement, toute histoire est transhis-

torique, parce qu'elle se produit sur le fond inchangeable de l'existence"—"Every situation is historic; but, conversely, all history is transhistoric because it is produced against the unchangeable backdrop of existence."

6. Corneille, *Oeuvres de P. Corneille,* v. 3 (Paris: Charles Marty-Laveaux, Hachette, 1922), I,vi,305-06. All references are to this edition.

7. Commenting on Corneille's 'static' quality which Cassirer and others have contrasted with Racine's 'dynamic' quality, Cook observes, p. 85; "Corneille . . . contains his recitative even more fully in the pattern he gloriously tautened. Corneille's speeches do confine, couplet by couplet, the plenum of emotion to the manifest recitation of its possible logical contrasts."

8. Cf. Doubrovsky, pp. 148-49: ". . . on s'atteint soi-même dans l'autre et le meurtre est, à la limite, suicide. L'originalité d'Horace, c'est d'avoir compris que la plus haute forme de l'héroïsme et le point où il atteint, en quelque sorte, la perfection, c'est le *fratricide conscient*"—". . . one realizes oneself in the other and murder is, in the extreme, suicide. Horace's originality is having understood that the highest form of heroism and the point at which it achieves, as it were, perfection, is the *conscious act of fratricide.*"

9. "the tragic necessity of affirming superiority in identity," Doubrovsky, p. 150.

10. I disagree here with Doubrovsky's assertion (p. 154) that ". . . Horace achèvera par le meurtre de Camille la mise à mort de Curiace. Il s'agit, en réalité, d'un seul mouvement, en deux temps"— ". . . through Camille's murder Horace will complete the killing of Curiace. Actually, it is a question of a single movement, in two steps." Not Horace's act here but his subsequent interpretation of it, achieves this integration. See my discussion p. 316.

11. Octave Nadal, *Le sentiment de l'amour dans l'oeuvre de Pierre Corneille* (Paris: Gallimard, 1948), pp. 197-98 argues: "[Auguste] ne semble plus faire corps avec ses actes; une rupture s'est faite . . . de ce qu'il désire à ce qu'il possède"— "[Auguste] no longer seems to be one with his acts; a gap has developed between what he desires and what he possesses." It must be observed, however, that the gap is itself the result of changing circumstances, of the continual production of events. The attainment of "L'Un à travers la multiplicité du Tout"—"One through the multiplicity of All"—is precluded precisely because the multiplicity is itself perpetually expanding.

12. "intimate fusion (of a love intrigue and a sacred sacrifice), the young, noble, and profound love of

the Pauline-Polyeucte couple providing a sensual base for the striking conversion of the hero and its consequences." André Stegmann, *L'Heroïsme cornélien,* v. II (Paris: Colin, 1968), p. 588.

13. Nadal, p. 275. Cited by Stegmann, loc. cit., et passim.

14. Doubrovsky, pp. 244-51. Cited by Stegmann, loc. cit., et passim.

15. "will speak to her of God." Citing these Christian elements, Doubrovsky observes (p. 227): ". . . on trouve, dans *Polyeucte,* une dogmatique d'une richesse et d'une exactitude incomparables, un catéchisme complet, au meilleur sens du terme"— ". . . in *Polyeucte* one finds a dogmatics of an incomparable richness and exactitude, a complete catechism, in the full sense of the term.

16. "In dying for his God, Polyeucte thus dies for himself alone." Doubrovsky, p. 251.

17. I thus find that Jean Rousset, *Forme et significa-tion: Essais sur les structures littéraires de Corneille à Claudel* (Paris: Corti, 1962, 1979), pp. 7-16, though he would deny the "excessive geometry" of his analysis, in fact offers a critical structure too rigid to account for the resonance of the play's final act. For Rousset concludes, p. 16: "Pauline et Polyeucte . . . se retrouvent . . . an cinquième acte, phase culminante de l'ascension, d'où ils s'élancent pour un dernier bond qui va les unir définitivement, au point suprême de liberté et de triomphe, en Dieu"—"Pauline et Polyeucte . . . meet again . . . in Act V, the culminating phase of their ascension, where they prepare for a final leap which will definitively unite them, in the supreme moment of liberty and triumph, in God."

18. Poulet, p. 15.

19. Particularly forceful in understanding Corneille is Jacques Lacan's notion of symbolic determina-tion. In "Le séminaire sur 'La Lettre volée,'" *Ecrits I* (Paris: Seuil, 1971), p. 40, Lacan subscribes to Freud's theory that the signifier functions in terms of "circular return": "le signifiant ne se maintient que dans un déplacement (rotatif) . . . ceci en rai-son de son fonctionnement alternant en principe, lequel exige qu'il quitte sa place, quitte à y faire retour circulairement"—"the signifier is main-tained only in a (rotary) shifting . . . this because of its functioning, in principle alternating, which requires that it leave its place only to circle back to it." The structure of existence is self-perpetuating due to the reciprocal relation of sig-nifier and experience. Signifiers, or what Lacan calls the symbolic, function to determine experi-ence, whose constituting element or cause is inseparable from, and hence reinforces, its func-

tioning. The "signifiant détermine le sujet"—"sig-nifier determines the subject"—in a self-contained, cyclical, ever-present pattern.

Harold C. Knutsen (essay date 1982)

SOURCE: Knutsen, Harold C. "Corneille's Early Comedies: Variations in Comic Form." In *Corneille Comique: Nine Studies of Pierre Corneille's Comedy with an Introduction and a Bibliography,* edited by Milorad R. Margitic, pp. 35-54. Paris: Papers on French Literature, 1982.

[*In the following essay, Knutsen views Corneille's early plays as "a series of variations in comic form."*]

It is difficult to avoid seeing Corneille's early comedies in a teleological perspective, as early stages in the inevitable progress of the dramatist and his heroes towards greatness.[1] But a few critics, beginning with Rivaille,[2] have sought to examine these plays on their own terms, either as part of the comic tradition of the time[3] or, more recently, as manifestations of the author's psychological make-up.[4] My purpose in the following remarks is to scrutinize Corneille's early comedies as a series of variations in comic form. As his Prefaces, *Discours* and *Examens* indicate, Corneille devoted some thought to comedy and its formal attributes, and we might do well to review briefly his significant com-ments on the matter before proceeding to the plays themselves.

Corneille's important remarks about comedy are contained in his *Discours . . . du poème dramatique,* published as a Preface to the first volume of the 1660 edition of his works. Unlike most critics of his time, Corneille proceeded boldly and imaginatively beyond Aristotle's sketchy discussion of comedy. Indeed, his summary of the typical comic plot—and particularly the denouement—startlingly anticipates the most modern views on the genre. Considering Aristotle's own com-ment upon the function of the comic ending as totally inadequate—"*rendre amis ceux qui étaient ennemis*"— Corneille proposes a more general purpose: "la récon-ciliation de toute sorte de mauvaise intelligence." This theme is usually embodied in one of two plot types:

. . . quand un fils rentre aux bonnes grâces d'un père qu'on a vu en colère contre lui pour ses débauches, ce qui est une fin assez ordinaire aux anciennes comédies.[5]

or

. . . [Quand] deux amants, séparés par quelque fourbe qu'on leur a faite, ou par quelque pouvoir dominant, se réunissent par l'éclaircissement de cette fourbe, ou par le consentement de ceux qui mettaient obstacle, ce qui arrive presque toujours dans les nôtres [comédies], qui n'ont que très rarement une autre fin que des mariages.[5]

The nucleus of the archetypal story is unmistakably here, especially in the "modern" plot: the primary boy-meets-girl motif; the obstacle figure—either the *senex iratus* of ancient comedy or the modern heavy father ("pouvoir dominant") that we find in Molière, for instance; the importance of trickery; and, most significantly, the way these various elements are fused together and resolved at the end: the "éclaircissement" of the deception practiced upon the lovers or the removal of the obstacle, and the multiple marriages in prospect as the curtain falls. That Corneille recognized as well the more general relevance of these plot features—the *dianoia* of comedy—is shown by his use of general and abstract terms like "réconciliation" and "mauvaise intelligence." For comedy tells of the restoration of an order threatened by disorder, the re-integration of a social unit sundered by discord.

Corneille takes issue with Aristotle on another point: far from being "une imitation de personnes basses et fourbes," as the *Poetics* would have it, comedy can embody "une . . . intrigue d'amour entre des rois" (p. 18). The *Examen* of **Mélite** expands upon this notion of a higher decorum. Corneille tells us that "la nouveauté de ce genre de comédie . . . et le style naïf qui faisait une peinture de la conversation des honnêtes gens" explain the success of his first venture into drama:

> On n'avait jamais vu jusque-là que la comédie fît rire sans personnages ridicules, tels que les valets bouffons, les parasites, les capitans, les docteurs, etc. Celle-ci faisait son effet par l'humeur enjouée de gens d'une condition du-dessus de ceux qu'on voit dans les comédies de Plaute et de Térence, qui n'étaient que des marchands.
>
> (p. 85)

Corneille distinguishes between a type of comedy drawing its effect from the ludicrous antics of the lower classes which the audience considers from the standpoint of its own superior standards of taste and conduct, and a form of comedy where those high ideals of refined demeanor constitute the substance of the play itself.

All of Corneille's early comedies, with the exception of *L'Illusion comique,* and its ludicrous Matamore, depict an upper-class world with no significant clashes in comic tone arising from social differences. We hear the refined banter of the well-bred, we see them move about fashionable Paris gathering places, we participate in their genteel games, especially the game of *galanterie.* Indeed, if the comedy of manners is a "form reflecting the life, thought and manners of upper-class society, faithful to its traditions and philosophy,"[6] Corneille can surely be considered a forerunner of this unique and enduring variant of the comic genre.

Corneille saw himself not only a practitioner of what became known as manners comedy but as an exponent of the "modern" comic plot. "Dans les comédies de ce premier volume," he writes in his *Discours . . . du poème dramatique,* "j'ai presque toujours établi deux amants en bonne intelligence; je les ai brouillés ensemble par quelque fourbe, et les ai réunis par l'éclaircissement de cette même fourbe qui les séparait" (p. 21). Even allowing, however, for a rather free interpretation of "presque toujours," we are puzzled that Corneille should make a generalization so readily subject to challenge. The highly unorthodox endings of *La Suivante* and *La Place Royale,* not to mention the whole structure of *L'Illusion comique,* suggest that Corneille was far more flexible in his creative use of comic features than in his after-the-fact formulation of precepts.[7] Corneille's theoretical pronouncements about comedy date from 1660, a quarter of a century after the last of the early comedies, *L'Illusion comique* (1635). No doubt the years of acrimony around "les règles" made Corneille sensitive, even myopic, about his early efforts. His *Examens* tend to be rather disappointingly focussed upon narrow aspects of dramatic theory—in particular, the three unities and their implications as regards verisimilitude. In the same *Examens,* however, he ingenously acknowledges flagrant departures from convention: he admits having concluded *La Place Royale* "bizarrement" (p. 476), and he seems genuinely bemused by that "galanterie extravagante" (p. 628) of his youth, *L'Illusion comique.*

This contradiction between a general view of comedy and particular exceptions to the rule is more apparent than real, however. The formal features of comedy cannot be divorced from the expectations that the audience has acquired in its experience of the genre. Spectators will recognize clues that anticipate such conventional devices as recognitions, and the skillful playwright will capitalize on this foreknowledge. But therein lies the secret of effective comic dramaturgy: a playwright who mechanically replicates all conventional elements will not only be tedious but will give an unpleasant impression of determination. One who breaks with all recurrent features will betray the very integrity of the form. Between these two extremes the comic playwright must tread carefully, fulfilling enough expectations to keep alive a general notion of the genre and departing from comic norms often enough to hold the spectator's attention by adroit use of the unexpected and to maintain an overall impression of spontaneity.

My contention is that Corneille, taking advantage perhaps of a more flexible notion of comedy in the 1630's, deliberately experimented in his early comedies with the conventions of the genre, and consciously sought to realize some expectations and deceive others. I argue, moreover, that there is a sequential logic to this enterprise. As Corneille moved from play to play he seems to have become increasingly aware of comic convention. He probes it more and more deeply and reaches, finally, a point where the unexpected comes with such force that the notion of comedy itself is threatened. This sense of quest, this powerful innovative drive, this pride in originality were to become hallmarks of his career; we should not be surprised to find them bulk large in his *période de gammes.*

In the light of this working hypothesis I shall consider in chronological order the first five comedies—*Mélite* (1629), *La Veuve* (1631), *La Galerie du Palais* (1632), *La Suivante* (1633) and *La Place Royale* (1633), all love-game comedies of the manners type. As the unconventional elements of *L'Illusion comique* (1635),[8] the last of these early comedies, have been extensively studied and are indeed so dominant as to make the play unique in the Corneille canon, this work will be left aside. The scope of this paper precludes a systematic exegesis, moreover; I shall thus confine myself chiefly to the early expository scenes, important as they are in fixing mood, anticipating events and setting character, and to the denouement, vital beyond any other moment in establishing the play's meaning and stabilizing its vision.

Mélite opens, as will many manners comedies from Congreve's *The Way of the World* to Wilde's *The Importance of being Ernest,* with a spirited discussion between two young blades. Eraste and Tircis evoke what will be the dominant polarities of all of Corneille's comedies to be considered here: fidelity/inconstancy, idealism/cynicism, permanence/transitoriness, high-mindedness/mercenary self-interest. Tircis, aptly described by Sweetser as "un jeune libertin affichant un cynisme à la mode,"[9] relentlessly demystifies the interrelationships of love, feminine beauty and marriage. A maxim like "bien qu'une beauté mérite qu'on l'adore, / Pour en perdre le goût, on n'a qu'à l'épouser" (vv. 82-83), reminds us of many a marriage-debunking epigram from Restoration comedy. With equal shamelessness, Tircis advances monetary gain as a prime motive for matrimony: however ugly Doris, for instance, may be, "Son revenu chez moi tiendrait lieu de mérite: / C'est comme il faut aimer" (vv. 114-15). Indeed, in one of the more ribald jests expunged by Corneille in later editions Tircis argues that "La beauté, les attraits, l'esprit, la bonne mine, / Echauffent bien les draps [later "le coeur"] mais non pas la cuisine" (vv. 117-18).

Eraste, the model courtly lover, professes contrary precepts of undying admiration of Mélite and fidelity to her, despite her "rigueur" towards him for a full two years. He rejects the "sale avarice" (v. 54) to which Tircis seems bound and comes back forcefully to the abiding, absolute singularity of his beloved: "Vénus, bien qu'immortelle, / Pensa mourir de honte en la voyant si belle" (vv. 73-74). We expect, then, Eraste to be rewarded at play's end and the opportunistic rake to receive some punishment for transgressing so openly the courtly code. But the tables are turned when Tircis,

upon seeing Mélite for the first time, falls irremediably in love and abandons his cynical credo.

The second couple, Philandre and Chloris, is introduced in sc. iv. This double plot combining "les premiers acteurs" and "personnages épisodiques," as Corneille called the two threads in the *Examen* of *La Place Royale* (v. 476), will characterize all five of our comedies, whatever their other divergences. The twofold love interest will often—though not always—take the form, as in *Mélite,* of a pair of ladies combined with three suitors. We might call this an odd-man-out pattern; it compels the spectator to speculate on who the loser will be, and for what reason he will be made to lose.

As Corneille has told us in his general plot summary, trickery is the main force which breaks up the initial harmony. "Bonne intelligence" is early achieved in this play: Mélite reciprocates Tircis' affection, while Philandre and Chloris seem on the verge of plighting their troth. Eraste, now the odd-man-out, creates a complex chain of confusing events by his false-letter stratagem. The most spectacular result will be his own madness, set off by the rumor of Mélite's death. Corneille uses Eraste's hallucinations to produce jarring effects that contribute further to the atmosphere of confusion and unreality: while his language is exalted and hyperbolical, his conduct is ludicrous. Thinking that Cliton is the infernal boatman Charon, he leaps on Cliton's back and is carried off-stage (IV,vi). His description of the aged *nourrice* is forcefully evocative, but he has nonetheless mistaken her for the beauteous Mélite (V,ii).

How to bring whom together? Eraste is cured of his madness upon learning that Mélite is alive, but will he become the permanent outsider because of his deceptions? Corneille does bring Tircis and Mélite together at the denouement as the fulfillment of the romantic premises of the play. But, unexpectedly, Philandre becomes the scapegoat. As a consequence of Eraste's scheme, he had foresaken Chloris for Mélite. This infidelity is punished by Chloris' scorn: "je te changerai pour le premier trouvé" (v. 1500); Philandre angrily leaves the stage threatening vengeance. In what will be a characteristic second-best arrangement in the group of minor lovers, Eraste gives up Mélite and will marry Chloris. Corneille gives us a final surprise by breaking the swelling mood of reconciliation and festivity with a throwback to farce. Tircis offers to constitute a third couple: "Nourrice," he instructs the wizened serving woman (played normally by a man), "va t'offrir pour maîtresse à Philandre" (v. 1808). And the nurse herself concludes the play with a direct, ludicrous address to the spectators.

While parental opposition—"le pouvoir dominant"—plays no significant role in *Mélite,* Corneille reminds us often of the family power structure and hints that it could become an obstacle. But Mélite succeeds in convincing her off-stage mother that she should marry Tircis, and Tircis himself, Chloris' brother standing in lieu of the absent father, authorizes marriage with Eraste.

The beginning of *La Veuve* replicates to a large degree that of *Mélite.* Philiste and Alcidon, two young gallants, debate a point of courtship. Like Eraste, Philiste shows steadfast and discreet loyalty to his mistress Clarice (the young widow of the title) and for the same period of two years (v. 5). Alcidon mocks this "ridicule effect de ta timidité" (v. 16). But we soon learn that Alcidon himself is a secret admirer of Clarice while feigning at the same time to court Doris, the second lady of the play. When a third gentleman, Céladon is mentioned as another of Clarice's suitors, we note again the pattern of two ladies and three *soupirants* and make the same conjectures as in *Mélite* as to the eventual pairings-off.

At this point, however, Corneille moves in a different direction. The off-stage mother of the previous play comes before us now as Chrysante, mother of Doris and Philiste. Family ties again are highlighted (as usually happens in comedy); but here the hierarchical authority relationship comes much more to the fore. Chrysante is a charming woman of the world, not unreminiscent of the indulgent mother of Molière's *La Princesse d'Elide.* But however easy her relations with her daughter, she does have in mind for Doris a rich but totally unsuitable marital prospect, Florange. The danger of a misalliance threatens, and we are reminded in these comedies for the first time of Molière, the exemplary practitioner of heavy-father comedy.

Although he never appears, Florange is a singular character in Corneille's comedies. Here is Doris' own account of his conduct at a ball:

> Mon baladin muet se retranche dans un coin,
> Pour faire mieux jouer la prunelle de loin;
> Après m'avoir de là longtemps considérée,
> Après m'avoir des yeux mille fois mesurée
> Il m'aborde en tremblant, avec ce compliment:
> "Vous m'attirez à vous ainsi que fait l'aimant."
> (Il pensait m'avoir dit le meilleur mot du monde.)
> Entendant ce haut style, aussitôt je seconde
> Et réponds brusquement, sans beaucoup m'émouvoir:
> "Vous êtes donc de fer, à ce que je puis voir."
> Ce grand mot étouffa tout ce qu'il voulait dire.
> Et pour toute réplique is se mit à sourire.

(vv. 195-206)

If I have cited this passage at length, it is because we have here for the first and only time in Corneille's early comedies a type that will prosper later, the "witwoud." Indeed, this kind of embodiment of social pretention and ineptitude will be the chief means by which natural breeding and true wit will be dramatically underscored

in the comedy of manners. Molière of course is no stranger to this technique, and Florange's awkwardness, his lame compliment, his ludicrous failure at repartee anticipate many a Molière misfit—Le Bourgeois gentilhomme, to name only one. Like Molière's doctors, moreover, Florange aspires to nourish social grace out of academic pedantry: "Il est nouveau venu des universités" (v. 220), notes Chrysante. The mother's concern, nonetheless, is the wealth he will bestow upon the family. Philiste is indignant at the fate awaiting his sister, but the mother coolly declares: "Le bien est en ce siècle une grande douceur: / Etant riche, on est tout" (vv. 1062-63). Corneille marks then a strong contrast between the romantic idealism of youth and the mercantilism of the parental generation, something Molière will develop in his own way in *L'Avare.*

In this play Corneille draws upon both the "pouvoir dominant" and the discord produced by trickery. If the happiness of the second lady, Doris, is threatened by her mother's mercenary ways, Clarice's eventual union with Philiste is menaced by Alcidon's unscrupulous and base scheming. Indeed, he goes so far as to kidnap Clarice in a scene of unusual and violent gestures.

As with the opening scenes, the denouement of *La Veuve* resembles that of the preceding comedy. Clarice is delivered through the good offices of Célidan, and she and Philiste will be wed. Célidan (like Eraste) will be given to the second lady, Doris, in another second-best arrangement. Chrysante, the mother, agrees to this match, recalling how she had loved Célidan's father, only to be forced into an unhappy marriage. This detail enhances the mood of optimism at the end of this play and reminds us of the undetermined nature of comedy in general. The ghosts of the past, far from imposing a repetition of misfortune as with Ibsen, are exorcised by comic providence.

Alcidon's conduct heightens this benign atmosphere further. Unlike the embittered Philandre of *Mélite,* he is repentant of his folly. But he still leaves the stage having deservedly lost in the love game, and has no place in the final society.

La Galerie du Palais marks a striking shift in comic shape and perspective. Parental figures become yet more important. Chrysante reappears as the mother of one of the gentlewomen, Hippolyte, while Pleirante comes on stage as the father of Célidée, the principal female role. The early scenes of the play tell us, moreover, that the two ladies are linked sentimentally with only two, not three men: Célidée is courted by Lysandre, while Dorimant, at first mockingly indifferent to love, becomes Hippolyte's suitor when he sees her in the *Galerie.* No rival then, no "outside agitator" as Abraham puts it.[10]

Nor are there in fact any parental obstacles, it turns out: Pleirante approves unreservedly of his daughter's affection for Lysandre, while Chrysante will have this time no rich misfit to impose on her daughter. On the contrary, as Pleirante tells Hippolyte in IV,ix:

> Votre mère sut hier à quel point il [Dorimant] vous aime,
> Et veut que ce soit vous qui vous donniez vous-même.

(vv. 1317-18)

Another new feature of the play concerns the auxiliaries. There were five domestic servants in *La Veuve,* but only the *nourrice,* a reminiscence of the farce tradition, stood out; the others had insignificant roles. In *La Galerie,* for the only time in Corneille's comedies, a discussion between two auxiliaries opens the play. Moreover each character save Célidée has a servant: Florice is Hippolyte's *suivante,* while Aronte and Cléante are *écuyers* to Lysandre and Dorimant respectively. Although the title *écuyer* suggests something above a valet, the two men function as servants and bear the signs of social subordination. They are always addressed by their superiors as "tu" and use only "vous" in return. Aronte, in addition, embodies some aspects of the tricky and resourceful valet type. It is he who advises (with disastrous results, it must be said) his master to counter disdain by disdain.

We are not far from a standard pattern of seventeenth-century comedy with its three divisions in the *dramatis personae*: lovers (symmetrically arranged in two pairs), parents, and auxiliaries. Indeed, we might now expect the normal dynamics associated with this schema: lovers achieving happiness over parental objections thanks to the machinations of servants. But we already know there will be no heavy fathers, so we anticipate a "fourbe"-type plot. But once again, Corneille moves in an unexpected direction: the disordering element will not be trickery but the arrogance of the heroine Célidée who, despite her lover's exemplary conduct, imposes a rather gratuitous ordeal on him. Her calculated indifference to test his fidelity sets off a chain reaction of confusion and complication. But, all is set right: Célidée and Lysandre, the "premiers acteurs," fulfill the romantic ideal, while Hippolyte, formerly in love with Lysandre, conveniently transfers her affection upon Dorimant.

For the first time, then, there are no losing lovers, no punishment or exclusion to break the mood of reconciliation. Indeed, even the scheming servant, Aronte, is forgiven by his irate master. On the other hand, the theme of escape from past bondage becomes again part of the denouement: Chrysante, in allowing her daughter a free choice, avoids perpetuating the forced marriage of which she herself was a victim in an earlier time.

The most extraordinary feature of the ending, however, is the reminder of comic convention within the action of the play. Florice, the *suivante,* half-mockingly

proposes that Chrysante and Pleirante, the parent figures, marry to complete the picture of hymeneal happiness. But Chrysante demurs: "Outre l'âge en tous deux un peu trop refroidie, / Cela sentirait trop sa fin de comédie" (vv. 1793-94).

This clever allusion to comic cliché heralds in a sense the three remaining comedies of Corneille's youth. After a four-square comedy so respectful of convention that the story can mock the form, Corneille can move only in the direction of ambiguity as in *La Suivante* and *La Place Royale* and toward, finally, the disintegration of the genre itself in *L'Illusion comique.*

For all of its "complexité mouvante," to use Margitić's phrase,[11] *La Suivante* begins rather predictably with an animated discussion between two gallants. Théante tells his friend Damon that he has decided, out of ambition, to abandon his courtship of the *suivante* Amarante in order to pursue her mistress Daphnis. We have learned to expect this kind of cynicism at the beginning of Corneille's comedies; we are not surprised, therefore, to hear it said of Florame, who will be paired with Théante in the love plot, that he is a duplicitous *coureur*:

> [Il] Fait par civilité toujours de feints hommages,
> Et sans avoir d'amour offrant partout des voeux
> Traite de peu d'esprit les véritables feux.

(vv. 34-36)

However, like Tircis in *Mélite* who falls in love irremediably after his professed contempt for marriage, Florame will successfully court Daphnis himself, and by II,v the only obstacle to fulfilment of their passion will be paternal benediction.

We have already met Daphnis' father at the beginning of Act II. While he is the only parental figure of *La Suivante,* his role has been momentously extended to encompass the "vieillard amoureux." He has engaged a neighbor to act as a go-between in his efforts to win—or, rather, to buy—the young beauty Florise, Florame's sister:

> Dis-lui que si l'amour d'un vieillard l'importune,
> Elle fait une planche à sa bonne fortune,
> Que l'excès de mes biens, à force de présents,
> Répare la vigueur qui manque à mes vieux ans.

(vv. 353-56)

We learn, with even more consternation, that Florame goes along with this mercenary bargain. Indeed, he turns it to his advantage by exacting, in return for his consent, the father's approval of his marriage with Daphnis. No wonder Bürger considers the dominant motif of this comedy "Die Bedeutung des Geldes" (pp. 197 ff.).[12]

When Corneille presents us with a third suitor for Daphnis' hand, Clarimond, we find the familiar two-ladies-three-gallants pattern already noted in *Mélite* and *La*

Veuve. But strange and disturbing elements appear as well: Théante is a fortune-hunting *inconstant;* a father figure threatens to impose two misalliances, his daughter's marriage and, worse yet, his own; and the second lady among "les personnages épisodiques" is a *suivante.* Amarante's role is in fact a main source of the play's troubling ambiguity. She functions as a servant, being obedient to Daphnis' beck and call. Yet her speech and demeanor betoken good breeding and high social level. Significantly, Daphnis does not use the "tu" form with her. Equal in rank to her mistress, unequal in function and wealth—such is her lot as she herself acknowledges (vv. 100-04). Money once again comes to the fore. The normal high-mindedness of romantic comedy has evaporated, leaving a sordid preoccupation with material gain as a base residue.

How will all these threads come together at play's end? Théante may become a faithful and magnanimous suitor. Comic convention suggests yet more plausibly that the threat of misalliance will be removed. It is customary after all that the young lady escape the ludicrous intentions of the greybeard—"vieillard amoureux" is an oximoron underlining an inherent absurdity—to find happiness in a more fitting romantic union. We may expect that Amarante will miraculously acquire the only thing she lacks to compete with Daphnis as an equal, a large estate, say, from a conveniently deceased uncle. But the play fulfills none of these expectations. The normal romantic union will take place only between Florame and Daphnis. Instead of the second-best marriage, we behold with astonishment the impending forced union between the father and Florise.

Along with this near-parody of the romantic denouement, Corneille presents us with three losers. Clarimond has not been seen since Act III; at the beginning of Act V Théante renounces Daphnis with no little acrimony. And Amarante, who has confessed the "fourberies" to which her frustrations had driven her, is not re-integrated; on the contrary, she delivers the bitter *stances* which conclude the play. Not only do we have a somber dispersal not unlike that of *Le Misanthrope,* for instance, but the final perspective is that of the humiliated outsider—as if Alceste should have had a final diatribe. Why, although high-born, should she lose Florame because she is impoverished? More perplexing yet, "fallait-il qu'un vieux fou fût épris de sa soeur?" (v. 1680)[13] She herself perceives not the triumph of "l'ordre commun" but, from her biased standpoint, its two-fold shattering: "Un jeune amant s'attache aux lois de l'avarice, / Et ce vieillard pour lui suit celles de l'amour" (vv. 1683-84). Words like "ciel," "destins," usually conveying an aura of providential happiness at the end of a comedy, become here an image of malevolent fate. And—perhaps Corneille's boldest stroke of all—in a genre described by Donatus as embracing life, the last word of *La Suivante* is "mort."

We now come to *La Place Royale,* the last play in our series. Until now, Corneille has begun his comedies typically with two gentlemen presenting contrasting views of love, courtship and marriage: Tircis and Eraste in *Mélite,* Philiste and Alcidon in *La Veuve,* Damon and Théante in *La Suivante.* In the first scene of *La Place Royale,* the playwright brings two ladies together—with the same effects of contrast we noted in the earlier plays. Angélique is now the apostle of absolute fidelity; Phylis appears as a witty young coquette whose apparent frivolity covers a keen realism and a clearly perceived need for self-protection. One may be faithful to one man, but will he be the parental choice? If not, one eventually is forced to accept a "maître" instead of "serviteur" (v. 50). On the other hand if one keeps all men at the same distance and regards them all with equal favor, any match imposed by parents will be acceptable: "Le moyen que de tant et de si différents / Quelqu'un n'ait assez d'heur pour plaire à mes parents?" (vv. 75-76).

Soon we meet the three gentlemen—Doraste, Cléandre and Alidor—who turn out to be suitors for Angélique. Remembering the development of *Mélite* and *La Veuve* we expect this odd-man-out arrangement to yield the usual result: the "premiers acteurs," ostensibly Angélique and Alidor, will constitute the couple united by a common romantic idealism, while the "personnages épisodiques" will settle down into second-best union— Phylis and one of the defeated suitors for Angélique. And one of the gentlemen will be an outright loser as are Philandre and Alcidon in earlier comedies. But in *La Place Royale* Corneille is bent upon deceiving our expectations with unprecedented audacity.

First of all, there is the "premier acteur" himself, the extraordinary Alidor, whose maxims eulogizing amorous *disponibilité* have so fascinated critics. As with Molière's *misanthrope,* Alidor's precepts carry a certain surface plausibility. Love is a form of possession that neutralizes the will and displaces the self. Indeed, Verhoeff goes so far as to endorse Doubrovsky's assertion (p. 70) that Corneille approves of Alidor's principles (pp. 46-47). Adduced as evidence is a passage from the *Epître dédicatoire* addressed directly to his secret benefactor: "C'est de vous que j'ai appris que l'amour d'un honnête homme doit être toujours volontaire: on ne doit jamais aimer en un point qu'on ne puisse n'aimer pas" (p. 475). Leaving aside the necessarily eulogistic nature of such writing, we need only read further to find that Corneille appears expressly to disapprove of Alidor: "ce n'est pas mon dessein de mériter par cette défense la haine de la plus belle moitié du monde, et qui domine si puissemment sur les volontés de l'autre" (loc. cit.). True, Doubrovsky dismisses this disclaimer as a mere *galant* concession to Corneille's feminine audience. But can Alidor's precepts be divorced from his callous and insolent conduct? Can this apparent fidelity to the self be seen, in comedy at least, as anything other than sterile narcissism? Couton comes closer to the mark in detecting "plus de caprice que de volonté véritable" (p. 474) in this character.

In any event, Alidor is a poetic creation fulfilling a dramatic function—to provide, I would argue, an opportunity for the playwright to examine critically certain aspects of comic convention. First, we witness an ironic contrast with the typical energy of comedy. Instead of seeking out Angélique, Alidor will flee her. Instead of respect and consideration, he will show impudence and contempt. Indeed, he will deliberately deceive Angélique into believing him unfaithful. The traditional false-letter stratagem, used conventionally in *Mélite,* functions here as a means of escaping, not recovering, the beloved. Finally, Alidor will drive home the stark contrast between time and eternity, between the happily-ever-after myth of permanence and his own vision, so persuasively expressed in vv. 227-36, of the evanescence of beauty and the erosion of human relationships.

More importantly, through Alidor, Corneille is able to carry off his astounding departure from the usual comic denouement. One of the signals for the happy ending is a downturn in the action—usually at the end of Act IV in a five-act play—where all appears lost for the lovers. The phrase "point of ritual death" is apt, for we usually find images of death—usually suicide—or of claustration—the heavy father's threat of sending a wilful daughter to a convent, or a girl's own choice in the face of marital misfortune. Thus in the last verse of Act IV Angélique, distraught by the deception and humiliation she has suffered from Alidor, vows to enter a "cloître." We expect the providential reversal that brings together in eternal bliss the "premiers acteurs." And as a matter of fact, a kind of final tableau is constituted in V,vii when almost all of the *dramatis personae* are present. Phylis and Cléandre plight their troth, just as Eliante and Philinte do in the second-best marriage of *Le Misanthrope.* But gone is the idealism—subdued as it is—of the Eliante-Philinte union. Phylis remains true to her principles, even if she agrees to wed Cléandre: "Sachez que mes désirs, toujours indifférents, / Iront sans résistance au gré de mes parents" (vv. 1248-49). Anxious to enjoy some precedence over other men, Cléandre wants assurance that he will be truly accepted by her. Her answer is a cryptic "Le monde vous croit riche, et mes parents sont vieux" (v. 1253)—a strong echo of the mercantile tone of *La Veuve.* The juxtaposition of the "personnages épisodiques" with "premiers acteurs" further underlines the sardonic nature of Corneille's denouement. As in *Le Misanthrope,* the main plot thread ends in defeat and dissolution. In fact, Corneille provides in *La Place Royale* a more telling critique of comic convention than Molière in his masterpiece. Angélique finally rejects the polite society which manners comedy imitates:

Un cloître désormais bornera mes desseins.
C'est là que je prendrai des mouvements plus sains;
C'est là que, loin du monde et de sa vaine pompe,
Je n'aurai qui tromper, non plus que qui me trompe.

(vv. 1452-55)

The world in a theological sense, transitory, deceiving, and corrupt, is evoked in this passage with all its echoes of homiletic *retraite* poetry. Phylis tries in vain to justify the pleasures of the social world. But all at once, four characters leave the stage together, and only Angélique and Alidor remain. The dramatic effect of this sudden dispersal Corneille underscores by the dark imagery and bitter tone of Angélique's ensuing farewell to worldly vanity. Her last words to Alidor: "pour jamais adieu" (v. 1489) are replete with a finality foreign to comedy and more appropriate, as Sweetser observes (p. 100), to Bérénice's tragic farewell.

Alidor's *stances,* like Amarante's, conclude the play. But instead of the bitterness evinced by the *suivante,* Alidor feels a kind of triumph: "Je vis dorénavant, puisque je vis à moi" (v. 1507). The danger of marriage is over, as the beloved is about to "se [donner] à Dieu." This allusion to a nun's mystical wedding is a final, telling comment upon the usual hymeneal celebration of comedy.

Corneille already seemed to have defied in *La Suivante* the integrity of the comic genre; in *La Place Royale* we can imagine no more startling a demystification of generic conventions. Yet, after *Médée* comes *L'Illusion comique,* Corneille's ultimate challenge to the comic form.

Notes

1. Both Bernard Dort, in his *Pierre Corneille dramaturge* (Paris: L'Arche, 1957), and Serge Doubrovsky, in his *Corneille et la dialectique du héros* (Paris: Gallimard, 1963), take this developmental approach.

2. Louis Rivaille, *Les Débuts de P. Corneille* (Paris: Boivin, 1936).

3. Peter Bürger, *Die frühen Komödien Pierre Corneilles und das französische Theater um 1630* (Frankfurt am Main: Athenäum Verlag, 1971).

4. Han Verhoeff, *Les Comédies de Corneille: une psycholecture* (Paris: Klincksieck, 1979).

5. Corneille, *Théâtre complet,* ed. G. Couton (Paris: Garnier Frères, 1971), vol. I, p. 20. All quotations from Corneille will be drawn from the first volume of this edition.

6. Newell Sawyer, *The Comedy of Manners from Sheridan to Maugham* (Philadelphia: n.p., 1931), p. 3.

7. Rivaille considers Corneille's generalization valid (p. 99). He allows only *La Place Royale* as an exception, and even then, were it not for the denouement, he argues, this play would fit Corneille's formula. Without challenging this rather casual attitude toward the comic ending, I should point out that Rivaille leaves aside entirely *L'Illusion comique,* a play which nonetheless was in the first volume of the 1660 edition and therefore to which Corneille's generalization should apply.

8. Couton's conjectured dates (pp. xx-xxi).

9. Marie-Odile Sweetser, *La Dramaturgie de Corneille* (Genève: Droz, 1977), p. 87.

10. Claude Abraham, *Corneille* (New York: Twayne, 1972), p. 40.

11. Introduction to *La Suivante,* ed. Milorad R. Margitić (Genève: Droz, 1978), p. xiv.

12. Far from being an *embourgeoisement* of comedy, however, *La Suivante* is, from my perspective, a sharp critique of mercantile values. Earlier comedies resolved the money question by the triumph of aristocratic liberalism in the denouement; here Corneille's mood becomes critical. But the comic vision still reflects the upper-class scorn of middle-class values.

13. Doubrovsky considers Géraste as representing positive values in the play: power and money (p. 58). His main evidence is Corneille's apparent defense of this "vieillard amoureux" in the *Examen.* But in the *Examen* of *La Place Royale* Corneille seems to justify Amarante's outburst at the end of *La Suivante* and to recognize the pathos of her situation. Thus the phrase "vieux fou" confirms, I would maintain, a standard comic judgment.

H. T. Barnwell (essay date January 1986)

SOURCE: Barnwell, H. T. "'They Have Their Exits and Their Entrances': Stage and Speech in Corneille's Drama." *The Modern Language Review* 81, no. 1 (January 1986): 51-63.

[*In the following essay, Barnwell considers "some of the ways in which Corneille orders and constructs the successive episodes of his plays and some of the connexions between that arrangement and speech."*]

1984 saw the commemoration of the tercentenary of the death of Pierre Corneille.[1] Since a glance through the titles of papers presented at the international colloquium held at Rouen in October would hardly suggest to the uninitiated that we were remembering a great playwright, it is perhaps timely to take one small step on his behalf in the direction which René Bray took for Molière some thirty years ago.[2] While often acknowledging that Corneille was a talented dramatist, critics tend to denigrate his pursuit of the dramatic on the grounds that it somehow obscures what they think of as the really interesting aspects of his work: his supposed ideology, his psychological insight, his rhetorical or (in the narrow sense) 'poetic' power, or the way in which his plays reflect the social, moral, and political preoccupations of his contemporaries. But why did that reticent, tongue-tied man, with his lawyer's training and official function, turn to writing for the theatre? In order to propound some ethical or political theory? If so, his earliest plays were a very odd beginning,[3] and the concept of a theatre of the imagination which emerges from *L'Illusion comique* a strange apologia.

I am simple-minded enough to assume—and the evidence of his own critical assessment of his work supports the assumption—that Corneille chose to write plays, not moral tracts or even novels, in order to interest and entertain his audiences, and that if those plays convey not a moral message but a vision of the moral universe, that vision is suggested through a particular dramatic form. It is the form that gives access to the vision. I take it for granted that no dramatist is great unless he is a complete master of his craft: what marks him out from the makers of well-made plays is his ability to suggest through it his perception, which may not even be conscious, of at least some abiding aspect of man's moral nature. Needing for present purposes strictly to circumscribe my subject, I shall confine myself to considering in a few examples some of the ways in which Corneille orders and constructs the successive episodes of his plays and some of the connexions between that arrangement and speech. I am aware that I am scratching the surface of a small area of a large, almost virgin field, though the substance of my remarks may seem all too obvious.

> All the world's a stage,
> And all the men and women merely players:
> They have their exits and their entrances;
> And one man in his time plays several parts,
> His acts being seven ages . . .
>
> (*As You Like It,* ii. 7)

In the present context, I take those lines to refer to the theatricalization of life on the stage. The parts the actors play involve exits and entrances and encounters with others. Entrance and exit also mean birth and death. In a sense, a dramatic character is born when he first appears on the stage, lives, while the play lasts, through a series of encounters theatrically manifested in his exits and entrances and expressed in speech, action, and gesture, and dies at his last exit.

Shakespeare's lines may be developed by reference to a passage in Oliver Taplin's book, *Greek Drama in Action* (London, 1978), where he is half-apologetic for the way in which he begins his study:

> It may seem odd to start with the moments when people are on the verge of absence, but a second glance sees that entrances and exits mark key junctures in a play— the beginnings and ends of acts, the engagement and disengagement of characters, the changes in the combination of the participants which alter the whole tone and direction of the drama. The timing; manner and direction of these comings and goings are fully in the control of the playwright, and his disposition of them may well signpost the way to our understanding of what he is about.
>
> (p. 31)

Another cue comes from Pierre Larthomas, whose book on *Le Langage dramatique* (Paris, 1972)[4] is based on the idea that dramatic language is generically distinct not only from the language of everyday life but from that of every other literary form. Dramatic language must fulfil specific functions: it must present convincingly to the audience characters caught up in certain situations which bring them together in particular relationships and, for the characters themselves, it must attempt to persuade others to act in certain ways, through deliberation, argument, and decision, a problem largely neglected in rhetorical studies. The text is written to be spoken, in conditions where speech is a form of action, action which must interest and excite the audience, as well as persuading the interlocutor, and must command the audience's sympathy (or repulsion), commiseration, awe, fear, and the like. But Aristotle long ago pointed out[5] that it is much more difficult to construct a play with the right 'combination of incidents', that is, in our terms, encounters effected by exits and entrances, than it is to write good verse or create satisfactory characters. Indeed, without the right 'combination of incidents', diction (or poetry in the ordinary sense) and characterization will achieve no dramatic effect, or emotional effect, in the theatre.

It is with the theatre and in the theatre that I begin my enquiry. While I do not wish merely to study technicalities, some aspects of theatrical conditions in the 1630s and 1640s, the years when Corneille was making his name as a dramatist, seem to me to be important, in ways not always recognized, for an understanding of the construction of his plays. It has been shown that during those years, in spite of the advent of the single set with its Serlian perspective, the multiple set with its compartments continued to be used, particularly at the Hôtel de Bourgogne.[6] At the same time, the convention, or rule, of the *liaison des scènes* was gradually being adopted. In the preface to the first edition of *La Suivante,* published in 1637, the year of *Le Cid,* Corneille himself first mentions it, regarding it as 'un embellisse-

ment et non pas un précepte', as he continued to do, at any rate up to about 1648.[7] The relationship between the single set and the *liaison des scènes* is clear enough. Before the first character appeared on the stage, the curtain went up and did not come down again until after the final exit: the set was exposed to view during the whole performance, including the intervals. An empty stage indicated the end of an act. Within each act, the individual scene was, as D'Aubignac put it, 'cette partie d'un acte qui apporte quelque changement au théâtre par le changement des acteurs', or, in Lamy's words: 'Une scène commence lorsqu'un acteur entre sur le théâtre, ou qu'il se retire.'[8] If the stage is not to be empty within an act, the action itself must be continuous through the successive linked encounters, each of which constitutes a scene. From this point of view a scene is not a more or less self-contained unit, but a phase in an uninterrupted development. Given the convention of the single set, D'Aubignac's detailed insistence on the *liaison des scènes* makes good enough sense, and Corneille does not deny it.

But the use of the multiple set is conducive to a different dramatic conception. Changes of place, and therefore a succession of scenes not linked by the continuing presence of one or more characters from one to the next, were common practice. In these conditions, the scene is less a phase in a continuous development than a distinct episode, one of a sequence in which incidents shown successively on the stage may not in fact be successive but simultaneous and occurring in different places. Such an arrangement depends for its cohesion less on a logical cause-and-effect development than on the presentation of interlocking aspects of a central theme.[9] It favours the creation of the more or less autonomous spectacular or rhetorical set-piece, the *scène à faire,* which generates pathos and alternates with scenes of action arousing suspense, curiosity, and excitement. But so long as no hiatus occurs between one character's exit and another's emergence from one of the compartments, the performance is in practice continuous enough to avoid giving the impression that the act has come to an end, even though no connexion is perceptible between exit and entrance. This was the kind of drama being produced by Corneille's most successful contemporaries (notably Rotrou, Mairet, Scudéry, and Tristan l'Hermite) when he was composing his first ten or twelve plays.

The nature of Corneille's output during the most crucial years of his development as a dramatist shows that he must have been very well aware of the implications of the two conventions of staging. In some respects, the evolution from **Médée** in 1635 to **Horace** in 1640 can be directly related to their coexistence in the Paris theatre of that period. **Médée** (a tragedy), **L'Illusion comique** (a comedy), and **Le Cid** (a tragicomedy), all written for a multiple set, satisfied that craving for spectacle alluded to by Rayssiguier in 1632.[10] Where spectacle was not actually staged, it was suggested in speeches of poetic evocation and description, often highly picturesque, of battles, duels, storms, and so on or, in pathetic fallacies, of a pastoral countryside. Such speeches, together with or resulting in lamentation or rejoicing, as the case may be, were the high points of many plays, and indeed, in tragedy, may often have constituted their real purpose, rhetorical rather than dramatic.

Médée, clearly that kind of play, resembles *Hercule mourant* (which had appeared a little earlier) both in subject-matter and Senecan sources and in dramatic conception: rhetorical set-pieces, monologues, altercations, imprecations, and laments, and scenes of visual spectacle, partly occasioned by the magical powers central to the theme of the plays. Many scenes are autonomous episodes, the *liaison* being frequently disregarded. The two inner plays of *L'Illusion comique* feature a sequence of episodes without logical connexion or *liaison,* alternating lamentation and action, the comic and the tragic. *Le Cid* likewise does not observe the unity of place or the *liaison des scènes.* A tragicomedy, though with a seriousness characteristic of tragedy,[11] it features spectacle and physical action. Clearly written for the single set, the scenes always linked, *Horace* on the other hand was the first tragedy to observe strict unity of place (*Pratique,* p. 111). Corneille's growing awareness of the rules and his readiness to write for the new stage contribute to the creation of this tragic masterpiece. The dynamism already evident in *Médée* (even Jason's final monologue is not purely passive lament, but a finally fruitless search for action, though it does turn out to be suicide) has, in *Horace,* found its proper vehicle, as I shall hope to show.

Once he has conceived of his subject and the general manner in which he intends to treat and order it, the playwright must decide how to make it begin. This certainly presented particular difficulties in the seventeenth-century theatre. The audience, as T. E. Lawrenson suggested,[12] without a 'collective purpose such as the mystery play possessed', constituted the first problem; it was also quite unlike the captive audiences of school or château for which so much earlier drama had been written. Then, of course, a number of spectators were on the stage itself.[13]

The problem was exacerbated by the undue depth of the stage: in order to be properly seen by candle-light and adequately heard, the actor must come right downstage before speaking. The texts of many plays by Corneille's predecessors and contemporaries, and indeed some of his own, testify to the difficulty;[14] it clearly persists through the seventeenth century, as witness Palmis, in *Suréna,* breaking off her conversation with Eurydice on seeing Pacorus approach. 'Le Prince vient, Mad-

ame . . .', she says, but it is only six lines later that he has reached the front of the stage, Palmis finally leaves, and Eurydice can greet him (ll. 1155-60).

Echoes of all this can be heard in the passage where, in his third *Discours* (pp. 69-70), Corneille discusses the proper motivation of exits and entrances with particular reference to the opening scene of *Cinna,* Emilie's monologue:

> L'auditeur attend l'acteur [at the beginning of the play, and after the curtain has gone up to reveal an empty stage]; et bien que le théâtre représente la chambre ou le cabinet de celui qui parle, il ne peut toutefois s'y montrer qu'il ne vienne de derrière la tapisserie [i.e., from backstage]. . . . Je n'ai vu personne se scandaliser de voir Emilie commencer *Cinna* sans dire pourquoi elle vient dans sa chambre [though the monologue suggests it is simply to seek solitude in order to come to terms with her overwrought emotions]. Elle est présumée y être avant que la pièce commence, et ce n'est que la nécessité de la représentation [the conditions of staging the play] qui la fait sortir de derrière le théâtre pour y venir.

All these practical difficulties made it necessary for the play to begin in such a way as to capture the audience's attention immediately. That depended on the actors' having a commanding presence and some arresting lines to speak. If the attention was to be held, the lines must be interesting, and begin at once to sow 'les semences de tout ce qui doit arriver', as Corneille expresses it (first *Discours,* p. 21), that is, to perform a strictly expository function, but also to establish some sympathy between the spectator and the character represented. The expository and emotional functions are, for Corneille, inseparable. As D'Aubignac saw (*Pratique,* pp. 279-81, 302), and as Larthomas points out (p. 58), purely informative exposition is dramatically inefficacious. Whenever possible, therefore, the expository scenes should directly involve, that is, bring onto the stage, one or more of the characters emotionally affected by the situation as it exists at the outset. Accordingly, in the 1660 revision of *Le Cid,* Corneille substituted for the original first scene, between Don Gomès and Elvire, a dialogue between Elvire and Chimène in which the heroine is in a state of great anxiety as to her father's choice of a husband for her. Part of that dialogue is a *récit,* as Elvire terms it (l. 23), performing the same function as the opening scene of 1637, and leaving the outcome of the council meeting uncertain and Chimène a prey to contrary emotions (l. 56).

Like Chimène, the Infante expresses highly-wrought emotions, but also determination to see the marriage through. Her exit makes no formal link with the encounter between the fathers which follows it, and whose movement (from controlled pride and anger, through stichomythic statement and retort, to the culmination of the 'soufflet', the mark of speech reduced to powerlessness) ends with the exit of Don Gomès. Don Diègue's monologue is, despite the opening line ('O rage, ô désespoir! ô vieillesse ennemie!'), far from being a passive lament: the injured pride, the sense of frustration, lead to an active determination to persuade Rodrigue, his love for Chimène notwithstanding, to avenge him. Immediately on Rodrigue's entry, that determination is put into effect: 'Meurs ou tue . . .', '. . . va, cours et nous venge.' The *stances* of Rodrigue's soliloquy, which follows, pass from despair and powerlessness ('Et malheureux objet d'une injuste rigueur,¦Je demeure immobile . . .') through inner conflict ('Que je sens de rudes combats!') to determination ('Courons à la vengeance'), raising the dramatic tension which Corneille deemed appropriate to the end of an act. The rhythmic development of Scenes 4 and 6 is parallel, from dismay to action, and it forms part of a pattern of alternating encounter and solitude (encounter with self), leading from the pathos of new, unexpected situations, not to lamentation—that may be its starting-point—but to action, all expressed in an expressive variety of rhetorical forms. It is notable, too, that once the action proper begins, with the encounter between the fathers, it is continuous and unrelenting.

That is the characteristic which Corneille develops, but now consistently, in *Horace,* the whole play conforming—as only *Polyeucte* and *Pompée* will do up to 1660 (see third *Discours,* pp. 76-79)—to the strict unity of place, and performed on the single set. Commenting favourably on Corneille's practice from *Horace* onwards, D'Aubignac was to say that '. . . il faut que les incidents soient préparés par des adresses ingénieuses, et que cela paraisse selon les rencontres dans la suite de l'action . . .' (*Pratique,* p. 125), encounters within the continuity of the action. As in the revised version of *Le Cid*—revised perhaps in the light of his experience in *Horace*—Corneille brings on first one of the two principal characters and her confidant. Why Sabine? As an invented character she needs to be immediately known within the web of relationships which makes the play. Unable to influence the course of the action, she is not merely its passive victim. At its emotional centre ('ma douleur', l. 1), she is immediately involved, not in pure lament, but in active conflict within herself—and with Julie, when Camille's situation is discussed, heralding the transition to Scene 2. The unity of place and the creation of a shared confidant enable Corneille to make a much tighter exit and entrance than in the revised version of *Le Cid,* and to maintain unbroken the impetus of the action already begun.

As in *Le Cid,* this second scene is parallel to the first but, thanks to the *liaison,* Sabine is seen to be integrated into the action in a way in which the Infante, in her *scène détachée,* is not. Following Sabine's inner conflict comes Camille's—the same sources, but different effect and expression. More impulsive, more impressionable, Camille launches into her long speech which is brought to an end only by the dramatic appearance of Curiace.

At this early stage in the play, a dramatic entrance—like that of Don Diègue and Don Gomès, but now formally integrated into what precedes it—changes and realigns the situation. The skilful and suspenseful handling of the dialogue is consistent not only with the passionate impatience of Camille, already established, but with the surprise occasioned by Curiace's entrance. The act still ends in uncertainty, Curiace, like Julie in Act III, Scene 6, having impulsively left the place of decision—made his stage entry—before its outcome was known. But the action is already realigned: shifted from the public to the private sphere, from the general to the particular, it will be concentrated in the lives of two families linked by bonds of love and marriage, the conflict paradoxically assuming a more universal significance.

It is precisely into this new situation that Corneille introduces Horace, after the interval between the acts. Although the Roman choice has already been made, the dramatist does not dissipate all the suspense at once, but withholds the Alban choice until Flavian's appearance (II, 2) interrupts the conversation between the two heroes. It is resumed on his departure, but the new realignment of the action is evident in their changed attitude to one another and in their tone. In the course of five scenes, then, two dramatic entrances have occurred, dramatic in themselves and in their immediate effects on the course of the action. They excite our interest in the characters' responses to them, expressed in both speech and action; they arouse curiosity.

In *Le Cid,* Corneille had actually staged the episode of the 'soufflet'. He does not, in *Horace,* stage even the meeting of the two opposing army commanders or the choosing of either set of champions: all that, like the combat itself, is reported to characters on the stage. The real, dramatic conflict is placed in their emotions, their suffering, their grappling with a changing situation occasioned by their comings and goings, by their encounters. Exploiting the 'limitations' of the single set, Corneille dramatizes not public events themselves but the responses to them of a close-knit group of individuals, active responses expressed in speech.

Parallel techniques are evident in *Cinna,* which is opened by another invented character. In her pursuit of Auguste, the spring of the action, Emilie can and does shape its course. As Corneille says (first *Discours,* p. 23), her inner conflict, expressed in a passionate soliloquy, occasions her allusive exposition of the initial situation. But the monologue itself, far from being passive lamentation, is a dramatization of her emotions in the form of a one-sided dialogue in which she addresses in turn those feelings, Cinna, her fears, and her love. Expressed in the rhetoric of antithetical exclamations and questions, not in reasoned argument, the inner conflict issues into a decision to pursue her vengeance (l. 48).

The testing of the decision, resulting from Fulvie's entrance, emphasizes its urgency (repetition of the word 'aujourd'hui' (ll. 138-39)). Like the choice of champions and the battle in **Horace,** the decisive action will not wait. The urgency, an essential feature of the dynamism expressed both in speech and in the successive developments and realignments effected by entrances and exits, is accentuated first by Cinna's arrival with his long account of the preparations for the assassination on the morrow, and then by Evandre's irruption and dramatically brief message (l. 280), whose uncertain significance makes the direction of the realignment ambiguous. As Corneille was later to point out (first *Discours,* pp. 22-23), these first scenes establish no direct logical link between the conspiracy and the summons, but their sequence establishes a (false) connexion in the minds of characters and spectators alike.

In the four great plays—for similar features characterize **Polyeucte**—the integration of passion, action, and speech is inseparable from the inner conflicts. But the same skill in opening with an appropriate sequence of scenes is discernible in the plays from **Pompée** onwards, where such conflicts are less important or virtually non-existent.

That tragedy opens with a deliberation which results in action: Ptolomée's decision to have Pompée killed in the hope of appeasing César. Far from being passionate, this scene provides a living demonstration of the young King's weakness in the presence of his Machiavellian counsellors. On the exit of Septime and Achillas to put the decision into effect, he is left alone with Photin, who stiffens his wavering resolve. It is immediately attacked when Cléopâtre enters, and has again to be encouraged when she makes her haughty exit. The sequence of the four scenes, Ptolomée and Photin being present and together throughout, on their own in two of them, provides encounters which express already the King's dependence on his evil genius, and, in speech, the battle for his mind.

All these examples of Corneille's techniques in effecting the exposition stand in marked contrast to those of his contemporaries who were still wedded to the *décor multiple,* presumably by their conception of tragedy. In Tristan's *Mariane,* for example, the first scene features Hérode's soliloquy on his awakening from his terrible dream: it creates a sense of foreboding and evokes pathos which together characterize the entire first act. The action, however, is not set in motion, and indeed it is not until the first scene of Act II, when Mariane recounts the background situation to Dina, that the exposition proper is effected: it is continued in the following scene and concludes only in Salomé's monologue at the end of it, the second part of which appears to be directly addressed to the audience. Not until after that can the action be said to commence. Tristan seems to deal with one aspect of his tragedy at a time, and perhaps the order adopted provides a clue to his priorities: an atmosphere of foreboding and pathos first, action itself last.

Whatever the actual form of the exposition in Corneille's plays, on the other hand, it is already action, present and urgent, expressed in and arising from encounters.[15] The occasion for making the informative exposition is almost always an encounter, even if of a character with himself, in a crisis which calls for decisive action. The search for a decision necessitates the weighing of the conflicting elements of the situation—in speech. Speech, however, performs other dramatic functions. For present purposes, I shall limit myself to the two least obviously dramatic forms, the *récit* and the monologue, in their relation to entrances and exits.

First, a general remark about the *récit.* In **Le Cid,** Rodrigue's account of the battle with the Moors (IV, 3)—eighty-four lines with one short interruption—delivered in the palace to the King and three of his nobles, occurs in a *scène détachée* following the one between Chimène and the Infante which takes place in the heroine's residence. A *morceau de bravoure* of the type found in tragedies and some tragicomedies of the 1630s and 1640s, the speech comprises a highly-detailed, concrete, picturesque account of the battle, rhetorical in concept and, at times, lyrical in execution. Athough, since it is not interrupted after the first ten lines, it obviously interests the listeners, it does not actually perform any dramatic function, and it is cut short by the arrival of Chimène, and is never completed. This *récit* is spoken by one who not only has directly participated in the action he describes but also is the hero of the play. What interests the audience, other than a good tale well told, is the pride and excitement of the speaker—not suspense, since the actual news of the victory has already been broken. As both Corneille (*Examen* of **Médée**) and D'Aubignac (*Pratique,* III, ii) agree, such long narratives require the listener on the stage to have sufficient interest and patience to hear them out. Now, after **Le Cid** (that is, after Corneille has begun to observe the unity of place, at least within each act,[16] and the *liaison des scènes*) this kind of autonomous *récit* disappears from his work. In the *Examen* of **Polyeucte** (pp. 120-21), he is able to say: 'Je n'ai point fait de narration de la mort de Polyeucte.' It was preferable to have it alluded to, through her emotional reaction to it, by Pauline. In later plays, **Sertorius, Sophonisbe,** and

Suréna, for example, the accounts of the deaths of the principal characters are laconic, to say the least, and in the second of these three tragedies, the battle lost by Syphax is not described at all. This is one of the many signs that Corneille moved gradually further away from the 'discours pathétiques' so much admired by D'Aubignac (*Pratique,* IV, vii) among others, and towards closer portrayal of the characters' hidden motives.

Usually, but not always, accounts of off-stage action are spoken by eye-witnesses to characters emotionally involved in its outcome. The *récit* acts upon them, and in so doing determines their own subsequent action. The spectator is also of course interested in the *récit* for its own sake—if nothing else, it satisfies his curiosity, not only about the actual events but also about the stage-listener's responses to them. Watching and hearing, he sees the off-stage action in his imagination, and the response to it before his eyes.

In the third and fourth acts of *Horace,* all this is very carefully contrived. The account of the combat is made to the three people directly concerned in its outcome: Sabine, Camille, and Le Vieil Horace. After Sabine's failure (II, 6) to dissuade the men from fighting, and Le Vieil Horace has rescued them from her, his son asks him to keep the women indoors. There, with him, they wait, after the young men have gone out to the battlefield, and while the gods are consulted: there, Sabine and Camille engage in their rather bitter exchange; there, Le Vieil Horace breaks in on them with the news that the combat is indeed going forward. His long, stoically patriotic speech is suddenly interrupted by the return of Julie with the incomplete account of the fight. Thanks to the interruptions and then to the fury of Le Vieil Horace, it consists of a mere seven discontinuous lines. What Corneille gives in this scene is not the conventional detailed *récit* but the reactions of the listeners. The old man storms out, intending to punish his surviving son, and the two women follow, attempting to restrain him. Act III ends on that uncertainty.

Le Vieil Horace returns at the beginning of Act IV, with Camille, who is still trying to reason with him when Valère bursts in with the completion of the story. With the certainty in his mind that his sons have been defeated, Le Vieil Horace keeps on breaking into the *récit,* if the interruptions allow it to be so called: twenty-nine lines are spoken before Valère can reveal the dramatic truth. For the old man, it is an occasion for rejoicing, in spite of the loss of two sons (l. 1141). Camille's reactions can all too easily be guessed at: she remains silent, even during her father's exhortation following the departure of Valère to inform the King of the old man's patriotic feelings.

Valère's interrupted *récit* is brief and active, verbs proliferating, picturesque details absent, a complete

contrast, in style and function, to the epic *récit* in *Le Cid.* As for Julie's narrative, whose incompleteness heightens the drama, Corneille's own comments testify to his skill: in order to cause Le Vieil Horace to show his anger, on false evidence, with his surviving son, 'il a été à propos . . . de se servir de l'impatience d'une femme qui suit brusquement sa première idée et présume le combat achevé, parce qu'elle a vu deux des Horaces par terre et le troisième en fuite' (*Examen* of *Horace,* p. 113). Corneille turns the *bienséances* and exigencies of stage conditions to advantage: the playwright, he says, 'doit choisir [les actions] qui lui sont les plus avantageuses à faire voir, soit par la beauté du spectacle, soit par l'éclat et la véhémence des passions qu'elles produisent . . .' (third *Discours,* p. 64). It is that vehemence, expressed in speech situated in encounter and in response to speech narrating off-stage events, which is the subject of these scenes.

Not all Corneille's *récits,* however, are of this kind. Those in *Pompée,* for example, are quite different. The second of them comes at the beginning of Act III, and very unusual it is. The speaker is Achorée, the listener Charmion, both minor characters and neither directly involved in the action. This account of Ptolomée's presentation of the head of the dead Pompée to César is made while Cléopâtre is in her own quarters awaiting, as she has put it (l. 640), his homage. Charmion listens attentively, not because of any personal concern but because she will need to recount to her mistress what Achorée has said. This is, like the earlier *récit* in Act II, Scene 2, a stately speech, though enlivened by Achorée's reactions to the shameful scene he has just witnessed. Few picturesque details are provided: Achorée concentrates on the demeanour of Ptolomée and, in particular, that of César—and this is the preparation for their interview in the following scene, when they make their entry together, with their followers. Achorée's *récit* foreshadows the dialogue which, in the very centre of the play, dramatically reveals the contrast in the moral statures of the two men, the heart of the action.

With regard to monologue, I have referred to the first scene of *Cinna* and to Corneille's comments on it. Although always passionate, monologues do not always express inner conflict: the four given to Cléopâtre in *Rodogune* consist of her reflections on action already taken and expression of determination for future action; in particular they are the means of conveying to the audience her true intentions behind the deceptions she is practising on others. In one sense, they eliminate suspense and surprise, but in another they enhance them, because, in Sophoclean manner, we are invited to watch the trap being set, and await in suspense the response of the victim. Cléopâtre's three monologues in Acts IV and V follow each other closely. Like the first, in Act II, their theme is hatred. Here, as the crisis heightens and

is precipitated by her actions against her sons and Rodogune, hatred and fury are intensified, first by the scene
of apparent reconciliation with Antiochus, then by the
open defiance of Séleucus. Between these scenes comes
another, in which Laonice, believing the reconciliation
to be genuine, expresses relief, and a second, when she
has gone out to summon Séleucus, in which Cléopâtre,
alone, rages against her other son (l. 1388), showing
that the apparent agreement is a trap. After Séleucus
has left her, she is again alone and, certain now that
neither son will avenge her on Rodogune, she despairs
and vows to kill all three (ll. 1480, 1491, 1495-96). On
that threatening note, Act IV ends. Cléopâtre reappears,
alone, to open Act v, gloating over the death of her first
victim, Séleucus, and plotting that of the others. When
Laonice appears to announce the completion of the wedding preparations, she dissimulates again (ll. 1537-38),
the better to commit the foul deeds which, however,
dramatically recoil upon her in the closing scenes. These
monologues are functional, so placed as to disclose the
speaker's true intentions and to prepare the action to
follow, and they arise out of action in encounters which
have immediately preceded them. Unlike most conventional monologues of their period, they are not passive
lamentations over a situation but active responses to it
and realignments of it, as the exits and entrances surrounding them clearly show. They are anything other
than 'discours pathétiques'.

Some monologues in Corneille's plays are such
speeches, but even they—Camille's and Auguste's, for
example—reveal other qualities and functions. I have
commented upon the sequence of scenes leading up to
Valère's *récit* and Camille's silence under her father's
exhortation. When he goes out to convey news of the
combat to Sabine, Camille is left alone and, no longer
surrounded by a family whose fierce patriotism she
does not share, she bursts into passionate speech, first
reversing the intention of her father's orders—she will
face her brother with her anger and grief—then uttering
a 'discours pathétique' in which she reviews all the
changes and chances of that fatal day—part lament,
part protest—and finally confirming her first resolve, to
challenge Horace (ll. 1243, 1247). The central 'discours
pathétique' is active: it reinforces her decision, brings
her emotion to fever-pitch just at the moment when the
warrior returns home, also highly-wrought with the ela-
tion of victory and the satisfaction of his 'gloire', bringing into the house his trophies, to him its visible
symbols, to Camille the relics of her lover and his brothers (see the irony of '. . . songe à mes trophées' (l.
1276)). Horace's entry brings the battle into the family.
His insensitive boasts and commands, a more brutal
repetition of the orders he had given Camille before the
combat (compare ll. 526, 1298), propel the altercation
to its fatal climax in Camille's rhetorical condemnation
of all that Horace has fought for (l. 1301) and in the
murder which inevitably follows it, and vindicates his

wife's and his victim's taunts of inhumanity and barbar-
ity (ll. 657, 1278). Set in the dramatic development, the
monologue is seen to be the consequence of action (the
father's exhortation, Horace's victory and return), action (as decision) in itself, and the cause of action (the
murder and all that ensues). Camille uses its pathos to
fan the flames of her passionate determination, not in a
conventional 'discours pathétique' but in an active
engagement characteristic of those 'grands sujets', as
Corneille calls them, which 'opposent l'impétuosité
[des passions] aux lois du devoir et aux tendresses du
sang' (first *Discours*, p. 2). Not only does the monologue, in its consequences, realign the action and bring
about the moral downfall of the hero: it enables us to
judge his motive as self-realization rather than public
duty—'Ma sœur, *voici* le bras qui venge nos deux frères
¦ . . . *voici* le bras ¦ Qui seul fait aujourd'hui le sort de
deux Etats ¦ . . . ces témoins de *ma* gloire ¦ . . .
l'heure de *ma* victoire' (ll. 1251-56), and that he is being tried in Act v as much for his 'gloire' as for the
actual murder.

Like Camille's monologue and the scene which follows
it, Auguste's soliloquy in **Cinna** is related to an earlier
episode, the big deliberation scene at the beginning of
Act II. The introduction to the soliloquy is as dramatic
as that to the earlier scene: Euphorbe's betrayal of
Cinna, which brings about the emperor's realization of
his solitude ('Quoi, mes plus chers amis! quoi, Cinna!
quoi, Maxime!' (l. 1081)) only a few hours after his
confidential discussion with his advisers (l. 1085). Like
Camille, he is in every sense left alone, to deliberate,
with a new urgency, on the same problem as before, but
in more personal terms. The rhetoric of argument and
counter-argument expresses his anxious, regretful,
retrospective view of his career. The emotional charge
makes the speech, like Camille's monologue, a 'discours pathétique', but the speaker is actively seeking a
solution to his problem. Livie's entrance, the arrangement of presences and absences having allowed Euphorbe to acquaint her with the situation, comes at the
point where Auguste's search reaches its most poignant
formulation (l. 1192). The importance of the dialogue
which follows lies not in the solution which it might
seem to offer but in the emperor's rejection of the arguments of political expediency in the name of others of
the same order. The encounter ends with suspense and
uncertainty, and it is not until Auguste has confronted
each of the conspirators in turn in the last act that he
comes to the realization that the way forward lies not in
political mastery and power but in the moral authority
of self-mastery. It is a curious paradox of the play that
only when, one by one, the conspirators have been
gathered round him again after their desertion and
absence does the inspired solution come to Auguste.

Such a solution is denied to Suréna, the hero of Corneille's last play, in which self-interrogation which

brings no answer gives way to interrogation which meets with stubborn resistance. That last play is built entirely around a succession of interrogations which tighten the web of tyranny, political and emotional—the first indeed used for the benefit of the second—around the hero and Eurydice. Orode and Pacorus in turn question them and their confidant, Suréna's sister, Palmis, in an endeavour to wrest from them the secret of their love. The number of encounters—eighteen scenes in all—is remarkably small; of the five main characters, never more than three appear together at one time, and in thirteen of the scenes, only two do so. The victims of the interrogations are picked off one by one, first by Pacorus, present throughout Act II (Suréna, Eurydice, Palmis), then by Orode in Act III (Suréna, Palmis), again by Pacorus in Act IV (Eurydice, Suréna), and finally by Orode in Act V (Eurydice). In the remaining scenes, the lovers confide in each other, resisting the advice of Palmis to acquiesce in the marriage demanded by the King. But Eurydice will not release Suréna, while he is both too loyal to defy the King openly and too devoted to his lady to contemplate marriage with anyone else. Locked into their love and their loyalty, the lovers are also locked into the inescapable spiral of the successive interrogations; but the interrogators, too, are prisoners: Orode of his fear of a rebellion led by Suréna, Pacorus of his jealousy of an unnamed rival. All are virtually imprisoned within the palace which no one enters from the outside world and from which no one departs, except ultimately Suréna, to his death, Eurydice having relented too late. In the same way, the lovers, when interrogated, are imprisoned in what has been called a double rhetoric:[17] explicit, to try to persuade the adversary; implicit, to dissimulate their real passions. The close-knit web of relationships, the cycle of interrogations, the necessity actively to dissimulate without actually lying, the power of the passions, the imprisoning palace, all combine to make this play, **Suréna, or The Impossible Exit,** a tragedy which, superficially, seems devoid of action, but one in which the last act still contains a greater number of scenes than the preceding four,[18] and in which soliloquy is rendered impossible.

Corneille's dramatic handling of *récit* and monologue and even of their absence complements his ideas about the maintenance of suspense and momentum right through the play, and particularly about withholding the dénouement until the last possible moment (first *Discours,* p. 26) and the precipitation of the action in the last act (third *Discours,* pp. 73-74). The removal of the short closing lament, spoken by Julie, at the end of the original version of **Horace** suggests that, having broken loose from the conventions of rhetorical tragedy, Corneille realized that the speech was inappropriate to his form of dynamic drama. Even in places where one might expect lamentation—Cornélie's apostrophe to the urn containing her husband's ashes, so different from

that of Alcmène in Rotrou's *Hercule mourant,* or the death of Sophonisbe or of Suréna—it does not occur. Instead of slowing the action down towards the end, Corneille speeds it up. I do not believe that his sole reason is the one that he gives, the impatience of the audience (first *Discours,* p. 26). A clue to something more fundamental lies in the remark that 'le combat des passions contre la nature, ou du devoir contre l'amour, occupe la meilleure partie du poème . . .' (second *Discours,* p. 41; compare p. 46). The emotion springs from those struggles. Once they were over and the consequences of decision worked out, Corneille had no interest in looking back, any more than his characters have. Suspense is aroused not only for its own sake but also in order to put them in situations in which they attract pity (second *Discours,* p. 46) and what he calls admiration (*Examen* of **Nicomède,** p. 152), situations represented in the encounters which provide the movement of the play.

It is also that dynamism which is revealed in the absence of lamentations. And even if we analyse the speeches of the Infante in **Le Cid,** a character unable to influence the course of the action, it is striking that they contain little actual self-pity. In Act I, Scene 3, for example, in a speech of thirty-nine lines, fifty-seven verbs occur, forty-six of them finite, but only eighteen adjectives. References to the past are expressed in the preterite tense: they denote things completed—there is no going back on them with regret; the speaker looks forward. The Infante is an extreme case, and serves to demonstrate that even before Corneille had come to adopt strict unity of place within the acts or the *liaison des scènes* his conception of drama was an essentially dynamic one. That conception was also already discernible in the energy and animated rhetoric displayed in **Médée,** and it found its proper vehicle in **Horace,** when the dramatist followed the new staging convention. Speech, occasioned by encounter, dynamically expresses dynamic action: 'Les actions sont l'âme de la tragédie', writes Corneille, 'où l'on ne doit parler qu'en agissant et pour agir' (first *Discours,* p. 19; compare *Examen* of **Le Cid,** p. 104, and *Pratique,* pp. 282-83). If speech is inseparable from action, so is pathos. The continuity of the action places the characters in perpetually changing crisis as they encounter one another, and the pathos, far from being expressed, as it were autonomously, in lamentation, lies in the inescapable need to act in ways which involve suffering, not in the inability to do so or in retrospective regret.

I conclude with a reflection prompted by a remark made by Ronald Peacock in his Presidential Address to the Modern Humanities Research Association in 1983:[19]

> In itself drama is very closely allied to the moral texture of life. As one kind of mimesis it is made up of those sequences of confrontation in which conflicts, actions,

decisions, and events are generated. The interest of these for serious drama is not simply their external physicality but their derivation from moral relationships.

The relentless forward thrust of the action from exposition to dénouement, the unbroken sequence of encounters in which passionately-held ethical values are brought into conflict, the dynamic nature of the language in which they are expressed, suggest in Corneille's plays a particular moral vision, the vision of a life which demands decision and action at every turn and unregretful acceptance of their consequences. If the phrase 'Cornelian heroism', so freely used, has a meaning, it seems to me to lie there, and it finds appropriate dramatic expression thanks to the playwright's discovery of a new dramatic form which exploited the possibilities of the apparently—but only apparently—restrictive *décor unique*.[20]

Notes

1. This article is a modified version of a paper read at the twenty-fifth annual conference of the Society for French Studies, held at Oxford in March 1984.

2. In *Molière, homme de théâtre* (Paris, 1954).

3. See, in this connexion, G. J. Mallinson's recent book, with its significant subtitle, *The Comedies of Corneille: Experiments in the Comic* (Manchester, 1984).

4. See, in particular, pp. 7-12, 25, 185-86.

5. *Poetics,* vi; see also ix: 'The poet must be more the poet of his stories or plots than of his verses.'

6. See, for example, W.-M. Deierkauf-Holsboer, *Histoire de la mise en scène française à Paris de 1600 à 1673* (Paris, 1960), p. 54; G. Védier, *Origine et évolution de la dramaturgie néoclassique. L'influence des arts plastiques en Italie et en France: le rideau, la mise en scène et les trois unités* (Paris, 1955), *passim*.

7. See, for example, the preface *Au Lecteur* of Corneille's *Œuvres (Seconde partie)* published in 1648, in my edition of his *Writings on the Theatre* (Oxford, 1965), p. 194, to which all page numbers hereafter refer. The passage from the preface to *La Suivante* is on page 179.

8. Abbé d'Aubignac, *La Pratique du théâtre,* edited by P. Martino (Algiers, 1927), p. 90 (hereafter *Pratique*); B. Lamy, *Nouvelles réflexions sur l'art poétique* (Paris, 1668), p. 160. See also J. Chapelain, *Discours de la poésie représentative,* in *Opuscules critiques,* edited by A. C. Hunter (Paris, 1936), p. 128.

9. See J. Morel, *Jean Rotrou, dramaturge de l'ambiguïté* (Paris, 1968), iii, i, *passim*.

10. *Aminte, Au Lecteur,* quoted in J. Scherer, *La Dramaturgie classique en France* (Paris, [1950]), p. 160.

11. R. C. Knight has studied the tragicomic origins of Corneille's concept of tragedy in 'Horace, première tragédie classique', in *Mélanges d'histoire littéraire (xvie-xviiie siècle) offerts à Raymond Lebègue* (Paris, 1969), pp. 195-200, an article to which the present one is complementary.

12. *The French Stage in the Seventeenth Century* (Manchester, 1957), p. 165.

13. See, among others, Chappuzeau, *Le Théâtre françois* (Lyons, 1674), p. 153. See also Mondory (quoted by Deierkauf-Holsboer, pp. 142-44), Abbé de Pure (quoted by P. Mélèse, *Le Théâtre et le public sous Louis XIV* (Paris, 1934), pp. 211-12, n. 4), Tallement des Réaux, *Historiettes* (Monmerqué et Paris edition. 1854-60), 9 vols, vii, 177.

14. Scherer cites this and others (p. 270) drawn from the early part of the seventeenth century.

15. Corneille produces no stereotyped pattern for the first act of his plays. The first scene of *Sertorius* is in some respects not unlike that of *Pompée*, but Perpenna has only one counsellor. The much-criticized first act of *Rodogune*, with its exposition in a dialogue between minor characters interrupted by the entrances of Antiochus and Séleucus and then resumed, is perhaps one of the least successful. It forms a marked contrast with *Nicomède*, which opens, unusually, for Corneille, with a dialogue between hero and heroine.

16. With the exception of *Cinna* (on which see Lawrenson's comments regarding staging arrangements, pp. 99-100), Corneille never, after *Le Cid*, effects a change of setting (or breaks the *liaison des scènes*) within any act of a play. This is true even of the machine-plays, *Andromède* and *La Toison d'or,* which are in some ways the successors of the spectacular vein of *L'Illusion comique* and *Médée* with the characteristics I have described.

17. See J. Morel, 'Rhétorique et tragédie aux dix-septième siècle', *XVIIe siècle,* 80-81 (1968), 94-95, 103-05).

18. On the construction of the play, see Bernard Croquette's interesting analysis in 'Structure de Suréna', *RSH [Revue des Sciences Humaines],* 38 (1973), 633-43.

19. 'Drama and the Moral Connexion', *MLR [Modern Language Review],* 78 (1963), xxiii-xxxii.

20. I do not, of course, mean to suggest that Corneille's superiority over his contemporaries is due solely to his adoption of the *décor unique* and the

concomitant 'rules', or that he was a better dramatist than, say, Shakespeare, whose practice was conditioned by stage conventions not dissimilar in their effects to those of the *décor multiple.* Neither do I imply that Corneille's plays are more dramatic than those of these other playwrights, but simply that they are more consistently dynamic, and that the dynamism expresses a particular view both of heroic action and its consequences and of the circumstances in which it must be taken.

Claire Carlin (essay date February 1986)

SOURCE: Carlin, Claire. "The Woman as Heavy: Female Villains in the Theater of Pierre Corneille." *French Review* 59, no. 3 (February 1986): 389-98.

[*In the following essay, Carlin discusses the innovative role of women in Corneille's comedies.*]

In the archetypal comic schema proposed by Northrop Frye,[1] a blocking character, usually a "heavy father" figure, tries to prevent the union of a pair of young lovers. The inappropriate desire of the older and often powerful man to possess the young woman for his own poses a potential threat to society as a whole, because societal renewal depends on the triumph of health and youth as represented by the young couple. Since the interests of the monomaniacal blocking character are directly opposed to those of society, the audience tends to punish the lustful elder with its laughter. If the monomaniac refuses to change his world view, he will be driven from the community, a scapegoat for all of the unhealthy impulses hitherto suppressed by the group. If, however, the potential scapegoat is willing to mend his ways, he will be reintegrated into society at the end of the play.

Pierre Corneille used the archetypal comic schema, but with some important variations that only serve to reinforce his claims to originality. In his first comedy, *Mélite,* which dates from 1629, Corneille created two blocking characters, both young men whose serious character flaws disqualify them from the role of principal comic hero. Neither gets the girl at the play's conclusion despite their efforts to disrupt the union of the relatively virtuous protagonists. An essential change has occurred in the nature of the blocking character: he is no longer an older man in a threatening position of authority. The implications of this shift become even more intriguing in two other Cornelian comedies, *La Galerie du palais* and *La Suivante,* for in these two plays the obsessed characters who threaten society are not only young, they are women.

Starting from a reversal in the archetypal comic blocking character, Corneille created a type of female role new to French theater. This is not to suggest that strong, mischievous, or evil women had not previously appeared in French, Greek or Roman drama. Nonetheless, the woman as initiator of the play's action was an innovation in Corneille's time. Since, from all the evidence, the playwright valued originality as the foundation of his work, one excellent way to achieve it was to assign essential dramatic functions to a new type of character. During *La Querelle du Cid* which lasted from 1637 to approximately 1640, he was attacked by many critics, including the newly born French Academy, for Chimène's scandalous behavior in deigning to speak with her fiancé after he had killed her father in a duel.[2] Again in 1663, he was assailed by one critic in particular, the Abbé d'Aubignac, for his portrayal of unbecomingly willful women in three different plays.[3] In spite of what these criticisms might imply, Corneille always made his women (as well as his male heroes) subservient to authoritarian structures. The female blocking characters attempt, in both his comedies and his tragedies, to usurp traditionally male prerogatives with more vigor and greater success than Corneille's queens or virtuous wives and fiancées, but all of his heroines are, in the end, only the result of his desire to bring new twists to his basic comic schema. Corneille envisaged no social impact from his creations; they were not designed to solicit more freedom for the women of seventeenth-century France. Nevertheless, he introduced to the French stage feminine "movers and shakers" who refuse to accept passively the male-dominated world they inhabit.

Corneille began his career as a playwright at a crucial moment in the history of feminism. Ian Maclean cites 1630 as the date after which important works by a new school of enlightened moralists began to explore the social and political condition of women from a perspective that, for the first time since the Middle Ages, departed from the traditional rhetoric employed by the writers involved in the *Querelle des femmes.*[4] Although anti-feminist tracts were still being written, the *femme forte* was emerging as a distinctive social and literary figure. The strong woman differed from the virtuous woman praised by writers of the Renaissance and before in that she possessed masculine qualities such as bravery, fortitude, and forcefulness which, when combined with ideal feminine traits, made her not man's equal, but his moral, physical, and intellectual superior. Corneille's female heavies, on the other hand, combine male aggressivity with negative characteristics commonly associated with women since Biblical times: lubricity, avarice, and all-consuming ambition.[5] Nonetheless, we should recall that the idea of ambition adopts positive connotations in the Cornelian canon. His distinction between tragedy and comedy focuses on the sort of political ambition to which the villains considered here subscribe: "La dignité de la tragédie demande quelque grand intérêt d'Etat, ou quelque passion plus noble et plus mâle que l'amour, telles que sont l'ambition ou la vengeance.''[6]

The ambiguity of ambition, as both fault and virtue, is illustrated in male as well as female characters throughout Corneille's theater. However, ambition is rewarded only when the character's goals coincide with those of the community. The only difference between the famous Cornelian concept of *gloire* nobly sought by Rodrigue in *Le Cid* and the lust for power of the female villains is their source of validation. Rodrigue looks to the group for approval, while monomaniacs of both sexes use others as pawns in an exclusive game meant only for one, a game they will inevitably lose because their obsessive vision does not fit into Corneille's fundamentally comic perspective. Corneille permits his anti-heroines to hold center stage only to make their defeat more resounding.

The first example of a female villain in the corpus comes in Corneille's second play, the tragicomedy *Clitandre* (1630). Evil Dorise takes her innocent rival into the forest at dawn in order to murder her. Like the blocking characters of all the plays to follow, Dorise has a sense of the theatrical. In an imaginary play-within-a-play scenario, she describes to the naïve Caliste how they will witness her lover's unfaithfulness. However, the *mise en scène* Dorise actually has in mind consists of Caliste's death by a blow to the stomach with a sword, an act she envisages with delight (I.iii.149-56).[7]

Only the accidental passing of duelling gentlemen saves Caliste from the dramatic death Dorise has devised. Since no harm is ultimately done to the innocent, Dorise is permitted, as is often the case in both comedy and tragicomedy, to be reintroduced into the society of youthful lovers. The violence of the genre c. 1630 is attenuated by a happy ending. The hybrid nature of tragicomedy is well illustrated in the character of Dorise: in Cornelian tragedy, female villains who commit acts of violence are not welcomed back into the group, while we shall see that in his comedies physical violence is not part of the woman's arsenal at all. Nevertheless, the male monomaniacs in Corneille's second comedy, *La Veuve* (1631) and in *La Place royale* (1633) both enact kidnappings (and both are rejected from reintegration into society). The comic villainess needs to be all the more creative since she cannot manipulate others by force.

Corneille's two comedies with female blocking characters present, as in *Clitandre,* competition between two women for the affections of a man. In *La Galerie du palais ou l'amie rivale* (first performed in 1632), Hippolyte convinces her friend Célidée that the loyalty of Célidée's fiancé needs to be tested. Célidée should, ac-cording to Hippolyte, feign indifference to Lysandre's attentions despite their recent engagement. Hippolyte's motivation in suggesting this ruse is not difficult to determine: she is ready to do whatever is necessary in order to win Lysandre for herself. When, to her dismay, Lysandre does not abandon Célidée in spite of the latter's offensive behavior, Hippolyte is forced to draw upon her talent as a creator of illusion once again. She must reassert her power over Célidée who wishes to end the charade now that Lysandre has proven himself. Hippolyte directs a masterful scene during which her companion, Florice, exclaims that Lysandre has not suffered nearly enough to prove eternal love. Of course, Célidée takes the bait once more. She must prove that Lysandre is totally devoted to her no matter how severe the test, and Hippolyte goads her on: "Ce sera trop longtemps lui paraître cruelle" (III. iv.849). Célidée is sure of herself, however: "Tu connaîtras par là combien il m'est fidèle" (III.iv.850).

It appears as though Hippolyte's scheming is about to bear fruit. She arranges for Lysandre to observe Célidée's enthusiastic reception of a rival, Dorimant. Having finally reached the limit of his patience, Lysandre does look to Hippolyte, but not for solace as she had expected. His only desire is to make Célidée jealous in her turn. Lysandre must act in his own performance in order to defeat Hippolyte's negative illusion and set the stage for final reconcilation.

In an elaboration on Frye's theory of the archetypal comic schema, the comic hero (Lysandre) and the blocking character (Hippolyte) may be seen principally as purveyors of an illusion which may be characterized as either positive or negative. Hippolyte's active striving to impose her vision on others can be effectively expressed in theatrical terms precisely because she acts as a conjurer of illusion. She is a competent dramatist, director, and actress at various moments. Her remarkable gifts make her destructive goal all the more attainable and threatening. Lysandre, on the other hand, acts only briefly and less masterfully than does Hippolyte. Nevertheless, he is eventually victorious because the entire life-force of comedy is behind him. The preservation of social order requires that he and Célidée triumph over the negative, disruptive impulse represented by Hippolyte, just as Caliste and Rosidor overcome the obstacles posed by Dorise in *Clitandre.*

The ideal couple may possess minor flaws in character, as shown in their weakness and credulity when faced with Hippolyte's staging of their separation, but because they are united by a mutual love whose annihilation the positive illusion will not permit, they serve as the principal standard bearers of societal rebirth. Thus, the play will end with their reunion: "amour jamais ne fut égal au nôtre" proclaims Célidée (V.vii.1758), sealing a promise of future stability in the relationship.

Yet, Hippolyte is not excluded from the happy future. At the urging of benevolent parents, she and her admirer Dorimant agree to wed. Their marriage will be founded on Dorimant's sincere love for Hippolyte and on her willingness to form this secondary couple in spite of lukewarm feelings for her future husband. As in *Clitandre,* Corneille does not detract from the positive atmosphere of the comic by ending with the formation of a less than ideal pair. Rather, the playwright reinforces the optimistic effect of Lysandre and Célidée's wedding by making it serve as an example to others. It is the strength of their union, ironically enough reaffirmed by the trial Hippolyte has put them through, that inspires Hippolyte to accept reintegration into the group.

The female blocking character of *La Suivante* (1633) does not fare as well. In spite of a birth and upbringing which make her potentially the social equal of the family she serves, Amarante is dependent on them because of her poverty. She must compete at a great disadvantage with her mistress, Daphnis, for the attentions of the many suitors who frequent their home. Amarante has taken a particular fancy to Florame, who, unfortunately, has his eye on Daphnis's fortune. Realizing that she is once again being used as a stepping stone to Daphnis's heart and wealth, Amarante plans her revenge with a desire enhanced by years of bitter resentment: "Et j'y veux employer de si rusés détours, / Qu'ils n'auront de longtemps le fruit de leurs amours" (I.ix.339-40).

Like Hippolyte, Amarante is a talented actress and director. In a clever *mise en scène,* Amarante is able to convince Daphnis's father that his daughter loves Clarimond, an insufferably persistent young man whose vanity is matched only by his awkwardness. Since parents tend to be benevolent in Corneille's comedies and since Clarimond's financial status is fairly impressive, it is not surprising that Géraste is quite willing to tell his daughter that the one she loves has been granted her hand in marriage. The plot then revolves around this *quiproquo,* a case of mistaken identity carefully protected by Amarante.

Daphnis and Florame are blissfully happy until Géraste inexplicably changes his mind (having actually opted for Florame because he wishes to marry Florame's younger sister himself). The result of Amarante's ruse is simply a gradual realization of her impotence, which almost turns to folly until finally she is unmasked as the author of everyone's problems. Her negative illusion is dispelled when confronted by the lovers' luck: the positive comic illusion wins again over the monomaniac's egotistical vision.

The ultimate resolution finds—as is usual in Corneille's comedies—two couples united. The main couple of Daphnis and Florame is seconded, as in *La Galerie,* by a less than ideal pair, consisting of old Géraste and Florise, Florame's sister. The last word is given to Amarante, however, who comments on the mercenary nature of both forthcoming marriages. Florame, in Amarante's view, wants Daphnis only for her money, while Géraste has in effect purchased his young bride. It is as if the laws of nature had been reversed: "Puisqu'un jeune amant suit les lois de l'avarice, / Il faut bien qu'un vieillard suive celles de l'amour" (V.ix.1683-84). Amarante concludes the play by cursing Géraste's unhealthy desires which have cost her the man she loves:

> Vieillard, qui de ta fille achètes une femme
> Dont peut-être aussitôt tu seras mécontent,
> Puisse le Ciel aux soins qui te vont ronger l'âme
> Dénier le repos du tombeau qui t'attend!
> Puisse enfin ta faiblesse et ton humeur jalouse
> Te frustrer désormais de tout contentement,
> Te remplir de soupçons, et cette jeune épouse
> Joindre à mille mépris le secours d'un amant!
>
> (V.ix.1693-1700)

This strikingly uncomical ending suggests that the image of a model society usually portrayed in the final scene of a classical comedy has been radically devalorized. Neither the possible flaw in the ideal couple nor the triumph of infirmity in the character of Géraste seem very promising for the future. The refusal to reintegrate the blocking character signals particularly severe consequences since as a young, attractive woman *she* should be part of the community rather than Géraste. However, Daphnis and Florame truly love each other and share the desire to be married. Amarante works from within the community of youth to hinder by devious means the formation of an appropriate couple. Her plot must be frustrated in order for the collectivity to profit from the union of a strong young couple. Amarante cannot follow the example of Hippolyte at the play's conclusion since Théante, her second choice, has left for Italy rather than face a life of poverty with her. Money plays a key role in *La Suivante.* This somber reality leads Amarante in her final tirade to proclaim that she sees herself as henceforth excluded from the pool of potential young lovers: "Si je prends quelque peine, un autre en a les fruits, / Qu'au misérable état où je me vois réduite / J'aurai bien à passer encor de tristes nuits!" (V.ix.1690-92). Amarante experiences a more lasting ostracism than the moment of public humiliation suffered by Hippolyte: thus her bitterness deepens. She appears ready in her defeat to renounce the creative role of trouble-maker which has so far failed to be productive. Neither Amarante nor Hippolyte can control her situation despite aggressive behavior. Hippolyte's mother has the final say over her daughter's actions just as Amarante's poverty governs her existence. In spite of the disadvantages they experience in terms of effective social and economic power, both young women nevertheless pose a threat to society which surpasses that of the traditional comic blocking character: they threaten to undermine the cohesion of the very group responsible for society's rebirth. Amarante is not reintegrated because she menaces her peers not only through her scheming but also because of the poverty which labels her an outcast from the utopian world comedy strives to form. Corneille does not allow these female characters to escape social convention, yet he does give them the role of instigator of the play's action, a role rare for female characters in French classical theater.

Three fundamental reversals have occurred in the Cornelian depiction of the blocking character. Youth has taken the place of age, while apparent weakness has replaced the strength represented by the traditional elderly male monomaniac. A paradox is already in place, even before the introduction of the feminine: the negative illusion produced by supposedly powerless youth requires a larger dose of the comic life force to defeat it than does the scheming of a character located outside the healthy young community that comic order should establish. When the blocking character becomes a woman, the menace to society grows. The ideal comic heroine as depicted in Corneille's other early comedies (*Mélite, La Veuve,* and *La Place royale*) is spirited, yet nurturing and non-aggressive. The same may be said of Celidée in *La Galerie du palais* and Daphnis in *La Suivante,* although the latter is rather hard on Amarante because of her servant status. These heroines are also less inventive than Hippolyte and Amarante, creators of negative comic illusion whose destructive dramas propose the elimination of the double marriage happy ending the collectivity has chosen as being in its best interest. The villainesses put forth a scenario pleasing only to themselves—thus their downfall is inevitable.

With this total reversal in the age, social position, and sex of the comic blocking character, Corneille created an original type that could not be forgotten once he began to write the tragedies that make up most of his corpus. Jacques Scherer has clearly demonstrated that seventeenth-century comedy and tragedy are quite similar in dramatic structure; Corneille, in fact, serves as the basis for his conclusion.[8] Corneille himself defines the fundamental difference between the two genres by the introduction of politics in tragedy (v. note 6). It should also be noted that in Cornelian tragedy, the hero plays a more active role than in the comedies, where the comic life force may triumph without much help from the hero. Generally, however, the basic outline of his tragedies resembles that of his comedies, in that the tragic hero is intent upon the renewal of a society menaced by internal pressures rather than by the heavy hand of fate imposing itself from the outside. Social ills are sometimes the work of several characters, but the malady the hero must cure often manifests itself, as in Cornelian comedy, in the form of a single blocking character, a *monomane* whose selfish vision of what

society should be would prove detrimental to the group were he to be permitted to impose it. As in the comedies, Corneille, in some plays, allows women to serve as villains.

Analyses of Corneille's female characters have led critics to some rather startling generalizations. Corneille has been described both as a seventeenth-century promoter of feminism and as a misogynist with an unconscious fear of strong-willed women.[9] It is evident that forceful female characters exist in abundance in his tragedies. Some strive for the same inner mastery of emotion that the male hero displays simply in order to be worthy of him or, at times, to enhance their own sense of self-worth. In either case, their outward dependence on men is apparent. Their fiancés and husbands may act, in duel, in battle, or in the political arena, while the women must await the outcome of male action. This is certainly true of the heroines of Corneille's best-known tragedies: Chimène in *Le Cid,* Sabine and Camille in *Horace,* Emilie in *Cinna,* and Pauline in *Polyeucte.*

However, when Corneille depicts a queen, heroic *virtus* assumes greater prominence. Corneille's female monarchs prefer political power and royal obligations to the love of a man.[10] His very first tragic heroine, Médée, is remarkable for her sense of self-fulfillment in the face of humiliation and punishment. When asked what is left to her now that she has lost her home and family, Médée replies proudly, "Moi, moi, dis-je, et c'est assez" (I.iv.317). Her infanticide announces the "monstrous mothers," an exceptional group of women who appear in three plays. These regal characters are of central interest here, since they are the inheritors of the legacy of Amarante and Hippolyte. The negative illusion created by the female blocking characters in Cornelian comedy has its direct counterpart in the tragedies, although the stakes are higher and the destructive potential more evident in the latter.

These three evil women are responsible for the tragic movement that menaces the hero, who is either their son or step-son; they are motivated solely by the retention of political power. Cléopâtre in *Rodogune* (1644) tries to have her sons killed in order to avoid stepping down from the throne, and she succeeds in having one of them murdered. Marcelle in *Théodore, vièrge et martyre* (1645) ruthlessly plots the demise of her step-son. Arsinoé in *Nicomède* also plans the assassination of her heroic step-son, who miraculously survives the traps she lays for him. The goals and the victims of their ruses are different from those of the comic female "heavies." Instead of wanting to snare a man in order to win social security, the monstruous mothers prefer to destroy men in order to usurp their role. Yet, the woman as a primary source of disruption within a microcosm of society functions in much the same way both in the

Cornelian comedies previously discussed and in these three tragedies, with very little variation.

Just as Amarante and Hippolyte played on the credulity of others, the monstrous mothers manage to deceive those who might serve as the instruments of their assassination plans. Unsuspecting observers are pulled into the play-within-a-play which the women stage; caught up in the illusion, the other characters are swept along without realizing that the role of accomplice has been forced upon them. In the cases of Arsinoé and Marcelle, it is their elderly husbands who unwittingly aid their second wives in attempting to murder royal offspring. Cléopâtre, although not the famous Egyptian queen, is equally devious: she cleverly pits her twin sons one against the other. She alone knows the order of their birth, and this is the key to the illusion Cléopâtre produces, as she explains to her lady in waiting:

> Apprends, ma confidante, apprends à me connaître.
> Si je cache en quel rang le ciel les a fait naître,
> Vois, vois que, tant que l'ordre en demeure douteux,
> Aucun des deux ne règne, et je règne pour eux.

(II.ii.443-46)

The queen takes delight in hiding her scheme from those she manipulates, but she nonetheless requires an appreciative audience for her elaborate invention. Thus her *confidante* is awarded the role of official spectator. Marcelle and Arsinoé also feel the need to expose their plots to a subordinate, just as in *La Galerie du palais* Hippolyte confided in Florice. (Amarante, being a *suivante* herself, is deprived of this pleasure, which is yet another source of her resentment.)

Unlike the female villains of the comedies, all three of these criminals manipulate men with ease, yet as will be demonstrated, they are wary of other women. All three must compete with the spector of another wife, a problem intensified in Cléopâtre's case by the fact that she is the older, divorced first wife of her recently deceased husband. To complicate matters, both her sons are in love with their new step-mother, Rodogune, the young woman who succeeded Cléopâtre.

This convergence of the second wife and the son's lover in *Rodogune* brings us to the second layer of feminine competition. The female blocking characters in the comedies are friend/sister figures in relation to the virtuous heroine of the play, whereas in these tragedies they are mature women, perverted mother figures whose victims include both their son and his potential mate. Marcelle hopes to be able to control her step-son by eliminating Théodore, the woman he loves: "L'amour va rarement jusque dans un tombeau / S'unir au reste affreux de l'objet le plus beau" (I.iii.261-62). Marcelle intends to stay in power by offering her own daughter as a more appropriate fiancée, but when this manoeuvre fails, the death of the menacing couple becomes her only alternative.

Arsinoé also uses her natural child, a son, as bait to lure the fiancée of her step-son into her camp. The princess Laodice holds a great deal of territory which Arsinoé would like to keep on her side of the family. When her scheme fails, however, murder is the only alternative that occurs to her. Arsinoé encourages her son to do the dirty work: "Venge-toi d'une ingrate, et quitte une cruelle, / A present que le sort t'a mis au-dessus d'elle" (V.i.1487-88).

Cléopâtre differs from Marcelle and Arsinoé in that she does not plan to spare even her natural children, but like the other two monstrous mothers, the initial object of her vengeance is a threatening woman. Cléopâtre turns her wrath on Rodogune, whose political clout makes her even more of an impediment to power than are the princes. Cléopâtre cries out to the crown she seems about to lose:

> L'amour que j'ai pour toi tourne en haine pour elle:
> Autant que l'un fut grand, l'autre sera cruelle;
> Et puisqu'en te perdant j'ai sur qui m'en venger,
> Ma perte est supportable, et mon mal est léger.

(II.ii.479-82)

For Cléopâtre, the thought of revenge makes her impending loss almost pleasurable. In fact, she poisons herself in the hope that her son and Rodogune will drink from her cup. Rodogune refuses; Cléopâtre dies having failed to destroy her rival, but she manages a final, impressive *coup de théâtre*.

Marcelle ends *Théodore* with a flourish as well. She simultaneously stabs both Théodore and the young woman's suitor in the chest, mortally wounding them. Marcelle's step-son observes this brutality, and faints at the gory sight, only to be greeted when he regains consciousness by the spectacle of Marcelle's suicide, a last scene played out expressly for his benefit. The sadistic impulses exhibited by Cléopâtre and Marcelle are a function of their taste for theatricality, which in turn represents the very essence of their role as blocking character. Their vision of the world involves complete power, and their penchant for producing playlets is an attempt to convince others to participate in their negative illusion. When the illusion begins to fade definitively, both Marcelle and Cléopâtre succumb to their theatrical nature, dying in a moment of unforgettable drama.

Since Cléopâtre and Marcelle are villainesses of tragedy, they are accorded the privilege of spectacular suicides, an opportunity denied their comic forebear, Amarante. Nevertheless, Amarante is the spiritual sister of Cléopâtre and Marcelle for, like them, she is not reintegrated into society in the play's final scene, but rather wrenches herself away from the group in as violently dramatic a manner as possible. These women make themselves outcasts, a role they choose to play when their preferred role is unavailable. Conversely, Arsinoé in **Nicomède,** like Hippolyte in **La Galerie du palais** and Dorise in **Clitandre,** sees the wisdom of compromise with the norms of the collectivity which willingly welcomes them back into society once they abandon their obsession with imposing their personal version of societal organization upon others. Both the comic and tragic female heavies are in competition with a virtuous woman to whom they lose out. In all cases their attempt to separate a young couple ends in defeat, precisely because the good of the group always triumphs over individual obsession in Cornelian drama, whether the play be labelled tragedy, comedy, or tragicomedy.

Indeed, the blocking characters described here illustrate an essential truth about Corneille's theater: its perspective is consistently comic, if we accept Charles Mauron's definition of comedy as facilitating spectator identification with the group rather than with the individual protagonist.[11] Violence from women or men, whether it be physical or simply verbal, will find itself dissipated when it is aimed against the welfare of society. In depicting his female heavies, Corneille demonstrated that the monomaniac and his or her threat could take on any form and still finish the play defeated. The evil version of the *femme forte* could not be triumphant, but Corneille's comic world view in its fantasy of group victory allowed her to experiment with power.

Notes

1. *Anatomy of Criticism: Four Essays* (Princeton: Princeton Univ. Press, 1957), pp. 44-50.

2. All of the documents pertaining to *La Querelle* have been collected in *La Querelle du Cid, pièces et pamphlets publiés d'après les originaux,* ed. A. Gasté (Paris, 1898; rpt. Genève: Slatkine, 1970).

3. The Abbé d'Aubignac was particularly offended by the unfeminine behavior of Corneille's heroines in *Sophonisbe, Sertorius,* and *Œdipe.* Inspired by these three plays, Aubignac wrote three vitriolic *Dissertations concernant le poème dramatique* which are reproduced in the *Recueil de dissertations sur plusieurs tragédies de Corneille et Racine,* ed. F. Granet (Paris, 1740; rpt. Hildesheim: Georg Olms Verlag, 1975), I, 134-53; 212-92; II, 1-69.

4. *Woman Triumphant: Feminism in French Literature 1610-1652* (Oxford: Clarendon Press, 1977), pp. 62-63.

5. Maclean, pp. 246-47.

6. *Discours de l'utilité et des parties du poème dramatique* in *Pierre Corneille: Writings on the Theatre,* ed. H. T. Barnwell (Oxford: Blackwell, 1965), p. 8.

7. The recent Pléiade edition of the *Œuvres complètes,* two of whose three volumes have appeared, will be used here. Ed. G. Couton (Paris: Gallimard, 1984).

8. *La Dramaturgie classique en France* (Paris: Nizet, 1950), pp. 11-12.

9. Han Verhoeff in *Les Comédies de Corneille: une psycholecture* (Paris: Klincksieck, 1979) and again in *Les Grandes Tragédies de Corneille: une psycholecture* (Paris: Minard, 1982) interprets the whole of Corneille's theater as an unconscious reaction against aggressive women. Harriet Allentuch in "Reflexions on Women in the Theater of Corneille" (*Kentucky Romance Quarterly,* 21 [1974], 97-111), speaks of Corneille's female "heroes" who "strive to shape their own destinies by the exercise of will" (p. 97). Allentuch qualifies her remarks about female aggressiveness in Corneille's theater by admitting that the womanly heroic enterprise fails in practical social terms, but she shows that this failure does not alter the character traits of these determined female heroes. Allentuch has come under attack for her feminist perspective, especially by Mary M. Rowan in "Corneille's Orphaned Heroines: Their Fathers and Their Kings" (*French Review,* 52 [March 1979], 594-603). Rowan stresses female subservience to male authority; she is critical of Allentuch's global characterization of Corneille's women as capable of appropriating male (chivalric) values (p. 602, n. 19).

10. These formidable queens include Cléopâtre in *Pompée* (first performed in 1642), Viriate in *Sertorius* (1662), Sophonisbe in the play of that name (1663), Bérénice in *Tite et Bérénice* (1670), and *Pulchérie* (1672).

11. *Psychocritique du genre comique* (Paris: Corti, 1964), pp. 8-15; 26-27. Even in relation to the heroes of Cornelian tragedy, the audience reacts as judge rather than as fellow sufferer.

Judd D. Hubert (essay date 1997)

SOURCE: Hubert, Judd D. "Two Crowned Feminist." In *Corneille's Performative Metaphors,* pp. 154-64. Charlottesville, VA: Rookwood Press, 1997.

[*In the following essay, Hubert discusses the defining characteristics of* Titus and Bernice *and* Pulcheria.]

Tite et Bérénice

Admiration and sublimity, as Marie-Odile Sweetser has shown, reach a climax at the dénouement of **Tite et Bérénice** even though the name characters, with the possible exception of Bérénice, remain at a further remove from plenitude than Othon and Plautine.[1] Like **Don Sanche d'Aragon,** this play richly deserves its classification as a *comédie héroïque*; and its lack of success, dating all the way back to its first run, may have resulted from reluctance on the part of audiences and readers to recognize its humorous and satirical aspects. If he had indeed wished to compete with Racine, Corneille might have served his cause far better by composing a drama eliciting tears rather than snickers. Unlike his alleged rival, he may have felt that a work completely devoid of violence or even physical danger lacked the indispensable ingredients to qualify as a tragedy or a tragicomedy. In fact, until the present century, even admiring critics mistakenly defined **Bérénice** as an elegy rather than as a truly tragic play.[2]

With the exception of Bérénice, all the principals teeter at times on the very brink of ridicule. Better still, a minor character, Albin, arrogates the function of chief dramatist, not only by manipulating his master, Domitian, but by engineering without the imperial family's knowledge or consent the queen's clandestine return to Rome.[3] Like Molière's Scapin, Albin shows far more intelligence and initiative than his master or, for that matter, Tite himself. Thus, Corneille has pushed even further the reversal of roles that marks the relationship between Galba and *les dépositaires,* because in **Tite et Bérénice** power inversion undermines not only Domitian and the emperor, but Rome itself. Albin enhances his theatrical maneuvers by literally functioning as the play's designated theoretician, in which capacity he undermines the behavior of his superiors. Having profitably studied La Rochefoucauld's *Maximes,* he shows his master how self-love can determine his and Domitie's every move.[4] Albin thus reduces them to the state of puppets who unknowingly conceal within themselves a purposeful actant who pulls all the strings. Thus, an imp of the perverse substitutes for the more dignified variety of fate featured in traditional tragedy.

Tite fares hardly better than his brother or his future sister-in-law, for he can never make up his mind. Moreover, his counselor, Flavian, who, like Albin, shows far greater reliability than his chief, must constantly remind Tite of his imperial duties. Finally, Tite makes himself ridiculous by becoming, like the frustrated lover in *Les Fâcheux,* the target of officious bores who insist on bringing him the latest news about the eruption of Mount Vesuvius and relief efforts to help the homeless. The implied false analogy between the emperor's unrequited ardor and the volcano's fiery displays should make any sophisticated audience titter, at least if the director allows the humor of the situation to shine through in performance.[5] Tite for once gives a direct order, but only after the Senate has finished its deliberation, thus providing another instance of his habitual belatedness:

> Allez dire au sénat, Flavian, qu'il se lève;
> Quoi qu'il ait commencé, je défends qu'il achève.
> Soit qu'il parle à présent du Vésuve ou de moi,
> Qu'il cesse, et que chacun se retire chez soi,
>
> (V.v.1659-62)

In addition, Corneille may even have taken advantage of the similarity of the names, Domitian and Domitie, which, though historically correct, might encourage an audience to look for a comic rapport between the two characters. Indeed, the *dépits amoureux* and political maneuvering which mark and mar their relationship hardly belong to tragedy.

Domitie stands out as by far the most comic character in this mock-heroic play. She makes herself look silly by naïvely reasserting on every occasion her overweening ambition, which operates like an irrepressible jack-in-the-box eager to spring forth without warning, for instance: "Et Néron, des mortels et l'horreur et l'effroi, / M'eût paru grand héros, s'il m'eût offert sa foi" (I.i.85-86). The antithetical and chiastic structure of these two lines verbally retraces the unwelcome outbursts of that predictable toy. Paradoxically, Domitie makes inordinate use of the language of totality and plenitude while obstinately personifying her glory, her heart, her love, her duty, or any other abstraction capable of enhancing her image. Thus, she displays her inner fragmentation in the very act of building herself up as a complete entity and reduces plenitude to a cliché by pointlessly reasserting it on every occasion. Fixing her sights on Tite, she shamelessly tells Domitian: "Tout mon cœur vous préfère à cet heureux rival: / Pour m'avoir toute à vous, devenez son égal" (I.ii.233-34). By thus separating her heart from the rest of her person, she reduces totality to fragmentation. Moreover, she believes that if Domitian truly appreciated her, he would readily sacrifice his own passionate interests and do his utmost to make her empress. She considers unselfishness a sacred duty for lovers, but certainly not for herself, for she can envision only the glorious role that will keep her forever in the limelight. By repeated recourse to the vocabulary of totality, she attempts to impose, at least to her own satisfaction, a full-blown image consisting of a collage of heterogeneous elements masquerading as perfections. And the more she strives to attain the completeness that corresponds to imperial power, the more she distances herself from plenitude. When she offers "tout mon cœur"—which she does on more than one occasion—she must unavoidably benefit from the transaction insofar as she exchanges a void for a title. Her resemblance to a contraption emerges in the opening lines of the play, where she personifies her sorrow: "Laisse-moi mon chagrin, tout injuste qu'il est: / Je le chasse, il revient; je l'étouffe, il renaît" (I.i.1-2).

Ensconced in the supreme position Domitie aspires to share, enjoying uncontested omnipotence, unable to imagine further titles to conquer, and thus finding himself in the enviable situation of Auguste at the conclusion of *Cinna,* Tite bitterly parodies his predecessor's triumphant declaration: "Maître de l'univers sans l'être de moi-même, / Je suis le seul rebelle à ce pouvoir suprême" (II.i.407-8). Vespasian had discouraged Tite's marriage to a queen. At present, Tite unconvincingly adopts his father's role, at least for his brother's benefit:

> Son trépas a changé toutes choses de face,
> J'ai pris ses sentiments lorsque j'ai pris sa place,
> Je m'impose à mon tour les lois qu'il m'imposait,
> Et me dis après lui tout ce qu'il me disait.
> J'ai des yeux d'empereur, et n'ai plus ceux de Tite,
>
> (II.ii.491-95)

In spite of his imperial casting, Tite's stage presence remains that of a forlorn but diffident lover. Vespasian's echo manages to prevail only because Bérénice has so far refrained from making her voice heard. Indeed, the emperor believes that his beloved has not even left Judea. Tite's speech to Domitian shows his acceptance of a part dictated by another while suggesting his inability to perform it. Before Bérénice's arrival, Tite had frequently switched between the roles of emperor and lover while trying to delay his dreaded marriage to Domitie. Needless to say, he doubly fails as an actor while showing his incapacity to produce a compelling scenario. Not surprisingly, he practices elusion far more than the other characters.

Despite total mastery on the political level, Tite lacks the will, if not the power, to impose his desires on his subjects and on the senate, which will predictably take a decision in his and Bérénice's favor. Far from attaining a reciprocated plenitude in love, Tite discovers that two totalities can hardly occupy the same theatrical space and indeed must exclude one another like sumo wrestlers. Passionately in love with Bérénice, but aware of Domitie's ostentatious merits, he conditionally concludes: "Elle aurait tout mon cœur, s'il était tout à moi" (II.i.386). In terms of Cornelian generosity, he must ironically make a total gift of his fragmented heart, posited as indivisible. Although the heart often expresses itself in terms of possession and power, it has absolutely no use for the exchanges that prevail in politics. Racine agrees in this respect with Corneille, for in *Bérénice,* power in the political sense and power in the amorous sense exclude one another.[6] In any case Tite cannot reconcile the totality of power with the plenitude of love, perhaps because the former precludes sharing, whereas the latter thrives on it. Since he has no other recourse than to take his imperial power as a point of departure, his project must end in a failure made manifest by his inability to play simultaneously two incompatible roles or to choose one rather than the other. Praising the queen because she loves "Tite et non pas l'Empereur," he invites Domitie's retort: "La personne et le rang ne se séparent point" (V.ii.1534).

Choosing love instead of power as her point of departure, the queen makes her move toward performative plenitude in a most spectacular fashion, for, to the onstage audience's unbounded admiration, she rejects for the sake of love a happy ending. Checkmated and upstaged in every respect, Tite has no other recourse than to concede:

> Tout est à vous: l'amour, l'honneur, Rome l'ordonne.
> Un si noble refus n'enrichira personne.
> J'en jure par l'espoir qui nous fut le plus doux:
> Tout est à vous, Madame, et ne sera qu'à vous,
> Et ce que mon amour doit à l'excès du vôtre
> Ne deviendra jamais le partage d'une autre.
>
> (V.iv.1743-48)

Having won the enthusiastic approval of Rome and the Senate, Bérénice attains a precarious kind of plenitude by substituting glory and universal approval for love:

> Ma gloire ne peut croître, et peut se démentir.
> Elle passe aujourd'hui celle du plus grand homme,
> Puisque je triomphe et dans Rome et de Rome.
>
> (V.v.1718-20)

Indeed, Bérénice ostentatiously proclaims her glory and applauds her own performance. She even prides herself, as a good actress and directress should, on her timing. She feels that she has reached the apex of her glory and that the future might spoil her performance, as well as that of Corneille, if she prolonged the show. It remains for the despairing Tite to ask a question, all the more futile in that it remains hopelessly rhetorical: "L'amour peut-il se faire une si dure loi?" (V.v.1725). The play ends when, concretized by performance, two totalities, the first relevant to love, the second to politics, face one another at the very moment when they must separate forever. The poetic deprivation attendant upon sacrifice arouses the admiration of the spectators—at least of those who remain on stage—and approximates sublimity. As Bérénice herself admits, she cannot go any further without overreaching herself. But what if the spectators at the end of the play still remember Albin's—and La Rochefoucauld's—deconstructions? What if they apply his theories, not only to Domitian's passion and to Domitie's blatant ambition, but to the abnegation so beautifully displayed by the queen? Her renunciation of a happy outcome may result from a special kind of self-love far more subtle than that of the other principals and which happens to coincide with the triumph of theatricality. In the eyes of Bérénice, love, by reversal, assumes the characteristics of political power and possession: "Votre cœur est à moi, j'y règne; c'est assez" (1714). We may wonder how the sublime, even though it relies on staging, can form an alliance with self-love, whose camouflaged appearance threatens to undermine it. Self-love suffers indeed from a disadvantage insofar as it becomes visible only as an aftermath by means of dispassionate analysis. In the meantime, the audience can continue to enjoy illusion at least until the curtain falls. Corneille could even rely on the blinding self-love lurking in the vast majority of his spectators to prolong the effect of Bérénice's generosity long after the show. Prigent often refers, no doubt with good reason, to a "dégradation de l'univers cornélien" in this and other late plays (473).[7] I feel that, at least in *Tite et Bérénice,* Corneille has deliberately deconstructed this so-called universe—a universe which inevitably includes the audience.

PULCHÉRIE

In *Pulchérie,* Corneille has once again distorted, but perhaps even more subtly than in previous plays, his historical sources, for he needed to transform a famous empress venerated as a saint into an amorous heroine, cast in the same mold as Emilie, Laodice, and especially Bérénice, who had recently taken full advantage of a similar predicament. Although the adjective *héroïque* suits both the plot and the characters, *comédie,* at least in the modern sense of the term, hardly applies since, unlike Domitie, Domitian, and Tite, the principals do not display ridiculous traits or lend themselves to satirical comments. Indeed, this work imaginatively recounts edifying events that had unfolded during the thirtieth year of Pulchérie's reign. Corneille reduced this number by half so as to rejuvenate his protagonist who, in the name of her younger brother, had ably ruled, since the age of fifteen, the Byzantine empire. By the same token, Corneille increased the difference in age between Pulchérie and her future husband, Martian, historically her senior by no more than nine years.[8] We can interpret the empress's decision to preserve her virginity—a feature to which she owes in part her saintliness—both as a sacrificial homage to the man she loves and as a means of retaining power: "Martian reçoit et ma main et ma foi / Pour me conserver toute, et tout l'empire à moi" (V.vi.1671-72). Marriage to Martian makes her renunciation all the easier, for this elder statesman can offer her nothing more tangible than his edifying submissiveness and his unrequitable passion.[9] Thus, once again Corneille has subordinated history to thematic and generic requirements. After all, he had to derive spectacular roles and interesting peripeteia from a pious narrative minimally conducive to theatrical display. Nevertheless, from this unpromising material he did indeed educe situations and performances quite exceptional in his theater. I do not mean to imply that Pulchérie and Martian stand out as unique in Corneille's repertory, for in *Sertorius* the playwright had already dramatized the loves of an elderly leader and in *Rodogune* the predicament of an ambitious queen prevented by law from ruling in her own name. But the originality of *Pulchérie* lies not so much in content or even casting than in novel relationships between performative requirements and rhetorical byplay, neither of them having much to do with historical events.

From a rhetorical standpoint, personification once again predominates, though not as ostentatiously as in the famous soliloquy where Cléopâtre fills the scene with invisible actants. In *Pulchérie,* personification arises from inner divisions or contradictions that the characters had so far repressed, hidden, or disguised, but that must presently manifest themselves as spectacle. In an ambivalent declaration to Léon, the protagonist envisions a paradoxical and perhaps aporic alliance between love and power:

> Ma passion pour vous, généreuse et solide,
> A la vertu pour âme, et la raison pour guide,
> La gloire pour objet, et veut sous votre loi
> Mettre en ce jour illustre et l'univers et moi.

(I.i.9-12)

In a camouflaged attempt to reconcile two incompatible projects, Pulchérie's so-called passion replaces, by means of ennobling personifications, the expected vocabulary of love with emblems of glory and power. Her linguistic displacement and reversal serve only to subordinate love to a rigorous order which Léon, himself an accomplished rhetorician, equates with tyranny:

> Et que peut cet amour dont vous êtes maîtresse,
> Cet amour dont le trône a toute la tendresse,
> Esclave ambitieux du suprême degré,
> D'un titre qui l'allume et l'éteint à son gré?

(I.i.61-64)

He has understood the unsuitability and indeed the falsity of Pulchérie's attempt to recreate her passion in the image of an ethereal and idealized political enterprise ironically modeled on platonic love.[10] In thus substituting for its opposite, politics somehow detaches itself from history, which alone can give it meaning.

Pulchérie and Léon frequently push personification quite far in the direction of metonymy as though they felt the need to lend greater concreteness to vague abstractions, whether cerebral or emotional. Léon complains of his beloved's ambivalence: "Et si son cœur encor lui parle en ma faveur, / Son trône me dédaigne en dépit de son cœur" (II.iv.667-68). Thus materialized, the emblems of love and power abandon any chance of reaching an accord. Moreover, by substituting the part for the whole, this trope ironically favors separation and fragmentation over plenitude or even totality. This kind of metonymic displacement inevitably leads to severance and amputation, all the more so because throughout the play terms indicative of separation and cleavage alternate with words referring to union. Some of these expressions, notably "attacher" and, more seldom, "partager," can ironically designate division while continuing to evoke togetherness. Moreover, unreliable comparisons among the various characters frequently recur because of the need to evaluate the respective merits of each of the candidates seeking imperial power. Because of his youth, Léon becomes the innocent victim of invidious comparisons with his more experienced, but less dashing, rivals.[11] This need to measure the accomplishments of political adversaries tends to invade the private domain, as evidenced in Léon's remark concerning Pulchérie's ambivalence: "Plus elle m'assurait de son affection, / Plus je me faisais peur de son ambition" (II. iii. 663-64). Unstable relationships between public life and personal feelings appear everywhere, for instance in Martian's theatrical and somewhat cynical analysis of Justine's role playing:

> Pour l'intérêt public rarement on soupire,
> Si quelque ennui secret n'y mêle son martyre:
> L'un se cache sous l'autre, et fait un faux éclat;
> Et jamais à ton âge, on ne plaignit l'Etat.
>
> (II.i.393-96)

Martian's deconstruction of his daughter's motives could hardly apply to her future spouse, Léon, who, concerned only with Pulchérie's metonymic heart, confines himself to a role quite devoid of ambivalence.

The young hero's successful but counterproductive project consists in persuading the Senate to appoint Pulchérie empress in her own right instead of the expected male head of state. Though predictable and indeed programmed from the very beginning, the protagonist's reaction upon hearing these good tidings verges nevertheless on paradox, for she bitterly complains about her lover's exemplary, but self-defeating, manipulations:

> M'avoir fait obtenir plus qu'il ne m'était dû,
> C'est ce qui m'a perdue, et qui vous a perdu.
> Si vous m'aimiez, Seigneur, vous me deviez mieux
>   croire,
> Ne pas intéresser mon devoir et ma gloire:
> Ce sont deux ennemis que vous nous avez faits,
> Et que tout notre amour n'apaisera jamais.
>
> (III.ii.907-12)

Pulchérie's ungrateful retort provides a *mise en abyme* of the entire play, both from the standpoint of casting and rhetoric. The personification of abstractions becomes so intense that the conflicting sides of Pulchérie's role, both of them reacting willfully and aggressively, combine to persecute and separate forever this aporic couple. Previously, she had treated her love—as distant from herself as her glory and her duty—in the manner of an obedient subject (III.i.755-60). Moreover, her complaint features a rather surprising comparison: "plus qu'il ne m'était dû," revealing that the senators have overwhelmed her with their choice. It thus appears that the multiplication of comparisons so characteristic of this heroic comedy merely renews the system of exchange that had failed so miserably in *Cinna* and

subsequent tragedies. In maneuvering the Senate, Léon had done his best to elude an unfavorable comparison between himself and his rivals concerning power and merit. Instead of letting the state do the casting so as to preserve at least a slim chance for their reciprocated love, his action squarely places the burden on Pulchérie, henceforth a prisoner, without any possibility of reprieve, of her imperial role. By asserting on two occasions, even before her confrontation with Léon: "Je suis impératrice, et j'étais Pulchérie" (III.i.754 and 794), she considers herself reduced to wearing the unremovable mask of power, all of which gives rise to a series of chiastic oxymora fraught with paradox:

> Sexe, ton sort en moi ne peut se démentir:
> Pour être souveraine il faut m'assujettir,
> En montant sur le trône entrer dans l'esclavage,
> Et recevoir des lois de qui me rend hommage.
>
> (V.ii.1475-78)

A few lines later, her rhetorical bent moves her to sarcasm: "Il vaut mieux, pour essai de ma toute-puissance, / Montrer un digne effet de pleine obéissance" (1485-86). In her superseded role as woman, she continues to obey, whereas in playing the part of empress she enjoys absolute power at the expense of her feelings. She goes so far as to subordinate power to role playing, as her allusion to the legendary Semiramis so clearly reveals:

> Elle usurpa le nom et l'habit de son fils,
> Et sous l'obscurité d'une longue tutelle,
> Cet habit et ce nom régnaient tous deux plus qu'elle.
>
> (V.i.1452-54)

At the dénouement, stability and harmony of an exclusively political nature prevail thanks to fragmentation and unbalance on the personal level. Unfortunately, division and lack of balance prevail, for all the rhetoric—from Pulchérie's first speeches until her final rejoinders—repeats the same displacing structure, apparent also in the characters and the unfolding of events. And one can blame this personal unbalance on an excruciating chronological curtailment:

> Vos hauts faits à grands pas nous portaient à l'empire;
> J'avais réduit mon frère à ne m'en point dédire:
> Il vous y donnait part, et j'étais toute à vous;
> Mais ce malheureux prince est mort trop tôt pour nous.
>
> (I.i.21-24)

Only death could prevent the lamented Théodose from uttering the well rehearsed lines that Pulchérie had taught him. Like Cléopâtre before her, she fails as dramatist because of her inability to protect herself against chance by imposing complete mastery over time. For this reason, the future Léon Ier le Grand suffers from a chronological unbalance in respect to his own career. He could apply to himself Sévère's bitter words:

J'impute à mon malheur toute la trahison;
Un peu moins de fortune, et plus tôt arrivée
Eût gagné l'un par l'autre, et me l'eût conservée;
Trop heureux, mais trop tard, je n'ai pu l'acquérir.

(II.i.448-51)

Unlike Sévère, Léon, who has to contend with another kind of saintliness, may owe his belatedness not only to his youth, but to Pulchérie's maneuvers. And Léon's unhappy situation contrasts with that of Rodrigue, whose youthful valor had sufficed to silence all opposition. As Michel Prigent has shown, Corneille in his later years refrained from giving youth the upper hand over experience, for he had acquired by then an acute sense of political reality.[12] But the inexperienced hero's defeat in spite of his rapid military progress appears less striking than that of the practiced empress, who seemed to hold all the trumps. Pulchérie finally consents to place politics on a higher level than love only because of her failure to conciliate and combine the roles of sovereign and gratified spouse. Unlike Rodrigue, Léon does not have to make a difficult decision or face a dangerous conflict. Because he cannot decently refuse to marry Martian's daughter, Justine, he has no other recourse than to forsake his somewhat passive role as a banal précieux, not to say pastoral lover, in favor of a far more spectacular future as emperor. Since he will take his place in history only many years after the dénouement, it would seem, from the standpoint of the hero's incipient but already eventful career, that the play must come to an end before it can really begin. Pulchérie's final declaration, which actually confirms the implications of her earlier protestations of love, definitively removes him from the part he had so earnestly performed while placing within his grasp, thanks to his marriage with Justine, the imperial role that will make him famous:

Aimez-moi, j'y consens: je dis plus, je le veux,
Mais comme impératrice, et non pas comme amante;
Que la passion cesse, et que le zèle augmente.
Justine, qui m'écoute, agréera bien, Seigneur,
Que je conserve ainsi ma part en votre cœur.

(V.vi.1716-20)

Pulchérie has succeeded in adding a corresponding cleavage—that of Léon's heart—to her own division between empress and lover. Indicative of separation rather than sharing, the term "part" confines Léon to a reduced and narrow role, that of subject, in which capacity he must downgrade, or perhaps elevate, his passion to a patriotic love suitable to his subordinate position in a hierarchy. This change does not prevent Pulchérie and Léon from showing the highest esteem for one another. But esteem, the usual of love in Corneille's theater, must in this particular instance operate in reverse and thus lead to regression and not to transgression.

Actually, her previous declarations had suffered, if I may use an architectural term, from overhang, from *porte-à-faux,* insofar as they invariably showed a discrepancy, mainly because each one had proposed its own denial, tantamount to elusion. Discrepancy of one sort or another affects not only Pulchérie, but practically all the other characters, notably Léon and Martian, who, for different reasons, could readily apply to themselves Hamlet's remark: "The time is out of joint" (I.v.188). The former cannot overcome tardiness in rank; the latter the far greater disparity of age. Strangely enough, the inevitable separation between Léon and Pulchérie had preceded the opening of the play. Her brother's death had created an insuperable cleavage, for it had prevented him from naming her fiancé his legitimate successor. Because of this misfortune, Léon must momentarily perform in suspended time, no longer a suitable lover and not yet a glorious emperor, but burdened nonetheless with both of these roles. Unfolding in an imaginary space and in suspended time, the events finally reduce the principals to a kind of dignified immobility where they seem to pose for one of those hieratic and spectacular mosaics that attract so many art lovers to Ravenna. Politics appears to triumph in both the mosaics and the play. But in the latter, Léon, who considers his future casting as emperor as no more than a makeshift part, reduces political power to an inferior employment; and history itself becomes unhinged in its attempt to catch up with theatricalized events.

Notes

1. See also Sweetser's recent article "Amour et renoncement: renouvellement de l'art cornélien dans la dernière période."

2. In his *La Bérénice de Racine,* Michaut reversed the trend by defining the play as a proper tragedy. In 1764, Prémontval, in his manuscript commentary on the play, had revealed its tragic qualities. See Hubert, "Une Appréciation inédite de Racine en 1764."

3. See in this connection André Stegmann's comments, 1283ff. See also Doubrovsky's discussion of the *comédie héroïque,* 392-414.

4. In connection with Domitie, Prigent aptly quotes La Rochefoucauld's Maxime 490: "On passe souvent de l'amour à l'ambition, mais on ne revient guère de l'ambition à l'amour." In many respects, this play could readily fit into the chapter entitled "La Démolition du héros" in Bénichou's *Les Morales du grand siècle,* 97-111.

5. Professor Claude Francis, an actress as well as a scholar, attracted my attention to the hilarious aspects of the play.

6. For "empire" in *Bérénice,* see Hubert, *Essai d'exégèse racinienne,* 120.

7. Instead of dwelling on political degradation, Mallinson in his "Du Jeu de l'amour et de la politique" has provided a subtle and, to a certain extent, metadramatic analysis of motives. As in the early comedies, "les amants cherchent refuge derrière un masque, essayent de s'approprier une identité et un langage stables et cohérents pour se défendre de sentiments qu'ils ne comprennent et ne maîtrisent qu'à peine." As a result, Corneille "crée un effet de théâtre dans le théâtre, une pièce qui se cache derrière une autre" (95). In short, Corneille has written a proper comedy.

8. For a discussion, initiated by Stegmann, concerning the age of the name character, see Sweetser, 236ff.

9. The heroine's virginity has given rise to interesting commentaries. Prigent states "Pulchérie conquiert son identité par l'affirmation de la virginité et de la stérilité: la nature est une impasse absolue" (492). Sweetser has insisted on the name character's suffering rather than on her political ambition (236ff).

10. In both the political and amorous pronouncements of Pulchérie, her Platonism shows a strong tinge of preciosity, deliberately antithetical to the forceful role she plays throughout. In an interesting comparison between this play and *Bérénice,* Zimmermann states: "Admirons plutôt que Corneille ait pu donner à une femme le rôle de Titus, qu'il ait créé une femme qui n'est pas condamnée à attendre qu'un homme dispose d'elle et n'a de choix, comme Camille, Emilie et tant d'autres grandes révoltées de ce théâtre, qu'entre la soumission et la mort" (105). Alice Rathé proposes a quite different approach in "Distribution des rôles dans *Pulchérie,*" where she describes the play as "le prélude, les préparatifs d'un spectacle, les délibérations et les affres qui accompagnent le choix des acteurs et la mise au point de l'intrigue" (98). Moreover, she emphasizes its comic aspects: "Ces multiples noces, improvisées tant bien que mal et accompagnées d'un clin d'œil complice à l'adresse du public, offrent un dénouement digne de la meilleure tradition comique classique, comme en font foi *La Trinuzia* de Firenzuola au XVIe siècle et *Le Mariage de Figaro* à la fin du XVIIIe siècle" (99). This sprightly commentary shows, by implication, that many "serious" scholars forget that Corneille's theater pertains primarily to showbusiness and entertainment.

11. Doubrovsky, 417, considers Léon's youth a weakness, whereas Prigent, 485, regards the hero's failure as inevitable because in this late work experience must triumph over nature, irresistible in an early play such as *Le Cid.*

12. Prigent repeatedly shows that political realities have become more and more dominant in the late works.

Russell J. Goulbourne (essay date 1998)

SOURCE: Goulbourne, Russell J. "Visual Effects and the Theatrical Illusion in Pierre Corneille's Early Plays." *Papers on French Seventeenth Century Literature* 25, no. 49 (1998): 531-44.

[*In the following essay, Goulbourne explores the visual aspects of Corneille's early plays.*]

"Il faut voir représenter Corneille pour en sentir tout l'effet." With these words, Louis-Sébastien Mercier alerts the reader of his *Nouvel essai sur l'art dramatique* (1773) to Corneille's theatricality and particularly to his exploitation of the visual resources of the stage.[1] For a long time, however, Mercier's was a lone voice. Seventeenth-century French drama, especially serious drama, has often been seen primarily as verbal and lacking in visual interest. Commentators of Corneille have privileged ideas and psychology over theatrical pleasure.[2] In recent years some critics have begun to explore the importance of the visual in the serious plays of the period. A central book has been David Maskell's study of the theatricality of Racine which places special emphasis on the visual dimension of his theatre.[3] Corneille, however, is still usually praised for the excitement generated by his characters' tirades or for his psychological analysis.[4] Critics have not yet properly attended to the visual qualities of his plays. That is the purpose of this article. Its evidence will be Corneille's use of all those devices (décor, exits and entrances, movements and gestures, stage properties, and costume) that Maskell finds used effectively and significantly by Racine. Corneille's use of these devices is varied, but I shall relate them here to his well-known thematic preoccupation with self-conscious theatricality. Given all the recognition that critics have accorded this theme in Corneille's work, it is surprising that it has always been approached from a verbal point of view.[5] I shall show how Corneille's insistent deployment of visual effects underpins three forms of self-conscious theatricality in the plays: role-playing, the activities of theatrical director-figures, and the playful treatment of dramatic conventions. My evidence will be drawn from the sixteen plays up to and including ***Rodogune*** and will thus embrace comedies, tragicomedies, and tragedies.[6]

ROLE-PLAYING

The representation of characters playing a role to manipulate other characters on stage is suggestive of the relationship between actor and audience. This emphasis on deceit and trickery runs through Corneille's early plays, both comic and serious.[7] A number of characters reveal themselves as convincing actors who are able to persuade their on-stage audience.

Two characters in the comedies stand out as convincing role-players: Alidor (*La Place Royale*) and Dorante (*Le Menteur*).[8] Afraid of love, Alidor seeks to wear the mask of the *esprit fort* and convince both his onstage audience and himself that he loves none of the women he courts. Alidor's role-playing is expressed not only by what he says, but also by what he visibly does.[9]

Alidor makes two main attempts to rid himself of Angélique and pass her on to his friend Cléandre. His first attempt involves the use of a stage property, a false letter, in which he declares his love for "Clarine" and which one of his servants conveniently passes on to Angélique in Act II, Scene 1. Alidor's subsequent visit to Angélique (II.2) offers further visual evidence of his role-playing. He plays the role of the unfaithful lover, graceless, indifferent, contemptuous. The audience sees Alidor reading the letter which Angélique holds in her hands (Stage Direction, 358); while Angélique loses her temper, Alidor reacts with cool contempt: "il rit quand je soupire" (382). His response to her tearing up the letter (SD, 385) involves the use of another stage property. He holds up Angélique's mirror in front of her face to show her how ugly she is (SD, 394). His play-acting works, and Angélique dismisses him. A consummate actor, Alidor uses words, actions, and stage properties to appear convincing.

Alidor's first scheme, however, is not entirely successful: thanks to Phylis's scheming Angélique is to marry, not Cléandre, but Doraste (III.2). So Alidor launches his second scheme (III.4). He realises that he now has to play the role of repentant lover in order to win back Angélique from Doraste so as to be able to pass her on to Cléandre. Another role means another performance. This performance occurs in Act III, Scene 6, and, as before, Alidor deploys appropriate gestures to support his verbal trickery. He enters Angélique's *cabinet* (SD, 776) and promptly kneels before her: "Tu te mets à genoux" (785) is Angélique's observation. Angélique has to address him because he does not speak: "Quoi? Tu ne me dis mot?" (797); he is in tears ("muettes larmes" (802)). Angélique is intially reproachful, but she acknowledges that Alidor's physical appearance is affecting her: "Demande le pardon que tes regards m'arrachent" (805). Alidor's role-playing is emphatically visual: posture, tears, and facial expression all help to convince Angélique that he is sorry. Realising her weakness she tries to leave, but Alidor stops her (SD, 810): the action of preventing her exit is another visual effect used to support Alidor's persuasion. He admits to deceiving her in the past, and asks her either

to flee with him or let him kill himself. This mock-heroic verbal gesture of self-sacrifice is reinforced by further visual effects implicit in the written text. He draws his sword and presents it to Angélique ("Mais voici . . ." (843)). He makes as if to kill himself with it ("Ma mort . . ." (863)), but Angélique stops him ("Retiens ce coup fatal" (865)), thereby signalling her renewed trust in him and her consent to his plan to leave together that night. She has clearly been persuaded by his words and, significantly, by his actions. As soon as he is alone, however, Alidor delights in the success of his role-playing: "Que ne peut l'artifice et le fard du langage!" (906). His words and actions have created a convincing theatrical performance. Angélique is taken in, but the theatre audience can see through Alidor's parody of conventional gestures.

Dorante is perhaps the most accomplished of role-players in a play the very title of which, *Le Menteur,* alerts us to its world of deceit and trickery. He is anxious to create a socially advantageous persona by way of self-promotion. He does this by lying. As well as trying to impress the ladies by the use of military language (I.6.322-44), he makes notable use of costume and gesture to give credibility to his lies.[10]

He draws attention to his costume in the very first line of the play: "A la fin j'ai quitté la robe pour l'épée" (1). As "robe" was the common metonymy for the judicial nobility and "épée" for the military nobility, Dorante is pointing figuratively to his change of status. More literally, however, he is highlighting that he no longer wears the clothes of a law student; he now carries the sword of an *homme de guerre*. For Dorante the sword is an essential part of the accoutrements necessary for him to look the part: "Dis-moi, me trouves-tu bien fait en cavalier?" (7).

Gesture is also part of Dorante's language of deceit and trickery. In Act II, Scene 5 Dorante plays a role in front of his father. Géronte wants him to marry Clarice, and Dorante, not knowing that this is actually the lady he spoke to in the Tuileries, launches into a complex account of his marriage to a woman in Poitiers. Dorante reinforces his verbal pleading by kneeling before his father: "Souffrez qu'aux yeux de tous / Pour obtenir pardon, j'embrasse vos genoux" (591-92); he is clearly conscious of performing in front of an audience ("aux yeux de tous"). His comic parody of this gesture of supplication is momentary, however, as his father quickly bids him stand up (593). But the visual game-play does not end there. Lines 649ff strongly suggest movement and gestures ("je me faisais passage," "je recule," "elle pousse," "nous entassons"). The result of Dorante's verbal and visual display is that Géronte believes him and decides to cancel the arrangement with Clarice's father. Alone with Cliton (II.6), Dorante delights in the "artifice" (686) with which he has played his role.

Although critics more readily associate role-playing, deceit, and trickery with comedy than with serious plays, Corneille's serious plays too depict characters who are convincing role-players: Chimène (*Le Cid*), Sabine and Camille (*Horace*). Chimène plays the role of dutiful daughter, determined to restore her late father's honour by seeking Don Rodrigue's death, though she is actually in love with him.[11] This conflict is first stated explicitly to Elvire in Act III, Scene 3. It is revealed to the other characters in three theatrical situations. In the first, Chimène's inner conflict is discovered by Don Rodrigue (III.1-4): it is a carefully stage-managed situation. In Act III, Scene 1 Elvire makes Don Rodrigue hide as Chimène approaches (782). He hides behind a curtain and so becomes, for the theatre audience, an on-stage spectator of Chimène's emotions. In Act III, Scene 3 Chimène's revelation that she is playing a role is heard by her hidden audience, Don Rodrigue.

The second theatrical situation in which Chimène's mask momentarily slips is when the truth is extracted from her by the King who tricks her into believing that Don Rodrigue is dead (IV.5). Chimène faints, which Don Diègue, like a judicial orator, rightly seizes on as evidence of her love for Don Rodrigue: "Mais voyez qu'elle pâme, et d'un amour parfait / Dans cette pâmoison, Sire, admirez l'effet" (1353-54). The King reveals the truth to Chimène (1357-59), whereupon she tries to extricate herself from this awkward situation, suggesting that she fainted for joy (1360).

Chimène lets her mask slip again in Act V, Scene 5 when Don Sanche enters and places a blood-stained sword at her feet: "Madame, à vos genoux j'apporte cette épée" (1715). Chimène jumps to the wrong conclusion: she assumes that Don Rodrigue is dead and declares her love for him. Only in the following scene does the truth emerge when the King reveals that Don Rodrigue is alive and that Don Sanche "a fait un faux rapport" (1770). Chimène's role-playing, although for a long time convincing to the other characters, has now broken down and her true feelings have become clear: her reaction to the sword opens the way towards her enforced reconciliation with Don Rodrigue.

All the principal characters in *Horace* engage in role-playing that, particularly in the cases of Sabine and Camille, is made vivid and all the more convincing by the use of visual devices.[12] In Act II, Scene 6 Sabine plays the role of the suffering martyr, offering herself as a victim in order to provide some justification for the duel that Horace and Curiace are about to fight. Her role-playing has a strong visual element. She stands between the two men ("ce corps au milieu" (660)), and dares one of them to draw his sword and kill her. The effectiveness of Sabine's performance is suggested by the men's response. This is largely non-verbal. They are

stunned and do not move, as Sabine's repeated calls to them suggest (635, 640, 647, 657, 661). They sigh, their faces go pale, they are visibly gripped by fear: "Vous poussez des soupirs, vos visages pâlissent! / Quelle peur vous saisit?" (664-65). Sabine holds the stage for most of the scene (613-62) before Horace eventually manages to reassert duty over love and dismiss his wife (675).

In Act IV, Scene 3 Le Vieil Horace urges Camille to put on a show of sisterly love for Horace: "Faites-vous voir sa sœur" (1193). Camille responds to this theatrical challenge in equally theatrical terms. In the following Scene she resolves to show Horace where her true love lies: "je lui ferai voir . . ." (1195). The emphasis is on the visual impact of a confrontation. Moments before Horace arrives, Camille is seen, like an actress, preparing herself for performance: "préparons-nous à montrer . . ." (1249). Her performance is designed not to follow her father's instructions, but to play quite a different role. It is meant to incense Horace, which it certainly does (IV.5). Fanatically obsessed with his own *gloire,* Horace assumes the role of Rome herself as a mask for his own dubious motives, and responds violently to Camille's verbal attacks on the city. He is Camille's audience and is manipulated by her theatrical role-playing into a violent reaction: he draws his sword and chases her off stage to kill her (SD, 1320).

Not all Corneille's role-playing characters play their parts so successfully. But even the unsuccessful role-players of course contribute significantly to foregrounding the relationship between actor and audience in the theatre. A good example of such a character is Matamore (*L'Illusion comique*).

He engages in some of Corneille's most happily contrived and ineffectual role-playing: the gap between his intentions and his actions is so great as to shatter any illusion of reality. He seeks to create the illusion of heroism, and critics commonly point out the verbal displays with which he tries to do so.[13] He presents himself as a noble hero and great lover (II.2), a man of power and true valour (II.4), a fearless warrior (III.3). This verbal role-playing, however, is subject to repeated, comic deflation, emphasised by visual effects.

A series of three exits (II.2; III.4; III.11) gives visual expression to the comic deflation of Matamore's verbal role-playing. Actions speak louder than words and betray his cowardly character.[14] In Act II, Scene 2 he plays the role of the noble hero and great lover, boasting about his string of female admirers (291-308). However, when he sees his mistress, Isabelle, approaching, accompanied by Adraste, his rival (333-4), he leaves quickly, claiming that he does not want to be aggressive in front of Isabelle. Matamore's true cowardice is expressed visually by his hasty exit.

Matamore's actions betray his words again in Act III, Scene 4. In the previous scene Géronte tells Matamore that he cannot marry Isabelle, and then exits (734), utterly contemptuous of the ridiculous captain. Matamore gives vent to his anger only when his opponent has gone, and even then only by hurling empty insults at him. Clindor, however, urges his master to fight back: he points to Matamore's sword (746). In contrast to Act II, Scene 2, where Matamore's hasty exist revealed the cowardice behind his role-playing, here it is Matamore's refusal to exit which has the same effect. Desperate to explain why he should not leave to fight, Matamore launches into a verbal *tour de force* warning Clindor of what could happen if he drew his sword (747-58). Matamore's refusal to exit or even to draw his sword speaks eloquently of his cowardice, as does his subsequent hasty exit. As soon as he sees the door to Géronte's house opening, he flees: "Adieu, je vois ouvrir la porte" (761). Ironically it is Lyse, a mere servant-girl, who emerges.

The third of Matamore's comic exits occurs in Act III, Scene 11. Having quickly given way to Clindor's threats, Matamore has sanctioned the betrothal of Isabelle to his assistant (III.9). The two men are joined by Isabelle in Act III, Scene 10, and Matamore tries to play the role of father-figure and overseer of the betrothal. His self-importance is shot down by visual means in the following Scene when he suddenly finds himself in the middle of an attack on Clindor by Adraste and his men. Instantly, together with Isabelle and Lyse, Matamore flees inside the house: "Cette porte est ouverte, allons gagner le haut" (968). There he remains, not emerging until the following act. Trembling with fear, as Lyse observes ("Vous tremblez" (IV.4.1173)), he tries to explain to Isabelle and Lyse why he has been in their house for the past four days. The visual spectacle of Matamore's hasty exit and his being gripped by fear days after the attack offers a comic, and, in part visually engineered, puncturing of his high-flown words.

THEATRICAL DIRECTORS

Another type of Cornelian character suggestive of the art of theatre is the *meneur de jeu,* who might, in more modern theatrical terms, be seen as a director-figure. Such characters manipulate others and set up theatrical scenarios and on-stage illusions. In depicting his director-figures and their activities, Corneille draws extensively on visual effects.

The dominant and most elaborate illusion in *Clitandre* is that engineered by Pymante to rid himself of Rosidor and incriminate Clitandre. Like an actor, he plays a role, but, significantly, like a theatrical director, he directs the roles of others. In Act I, Scene 4 we learn that he has made Géronte, Clitandre's *écuyer,* send a letter, forged in the name of Clitandre, to Rosidor, challenging him to a duel. We also see him, Géronte, and Lycaste, another of Clitandre's servants, disguised as peasants (SD, 156; SD, 181). Pymante, the director, is preparing his actors for their performance: the attack on Rosidor. Costume plays an important part. Like actors, the characters have masked their own identities and are ready to go out on stage. The performance takes place in Act I, Scene 7 when Rosidor and the three "peasants" burst onto the stage fighting. Although the performance does not strictly follow its script (Rosidor is only injured, and Géronte and Lycaste are killed), the desired effect is still created: Rosidor unmasks the dead men and, recognising them as Clitandre's servants, is convinced of Clitandre's treachery. Pymante's illusion, however, crumbles in Act IV, Scene 4, when, still dressed as a peasant, he attacks Dorise, dressed as a nobleman, and is overpowered by the Prince. Ironically it is the very costume that helped Pymante initially to give a convincing performance and hide his own identity that brings about his downfall. The truth emerges in Act IV, Scene 7, when Pymante is tied up and led away by the Prince's men: a visual sign of his failure to maintain his illusion.

A character's attempt to create an on-stage illusion is spectacularly undermined in *Rodogune,* a play which is centrally about characters manipulating each other.[15] The key role is that of Cléopâtre, Queen of Syria, mother of Séleucus and Antiochus. She is a skilled illusion-maker: her power and influence rest largely on her ability to trick and deceive, to play roles and direct the roles of others. But despite her skill, Cléopâtre loses control of her theatrical scenario and ultimately fails to achieve her aim.

Her overriding aim is to retain political power at all costs. In order to achieve this aim she exploits the power of illusion, deviously promising Antiochus that he can marry Rodogune (IV.3). When she is alone (IV.5), her references to the wedding resound with the language of theatrical illusion: "éblouir" (1390), "apparence" (1392), "déguisement" (1394). While the other characters prepare for the wedding ceremony, the audience knows that what it is about to witness is an elaborate on-stage theatrical performance. It is a performance that has a significantly visual dimension.

Cléopâtre has poisoned Séleucus, and plans to poison Antiochus and Rodogune during the wedding ceremony (V.3).[16] The hand of Cléopâtre, the theatrical director, is clearly visible behind the staging of the mock wedding ceremony. There is an on-stage audience of Parthians and Syrians. The seating arrangement, indicated by Corneille's lengthy stage direction (SD, 1572), emphasises the theatrical nature of the occasion. Cléopâtre arranges her actors for the performance. Antiochus is seated on a *fauteuil,* the seat of honour, and Rodogune is at his right-hand side. Cléopâtre feigns humility by sitting beneath them. The stage is literally set for a ceremony: for the unknowing participants it has the illusion of reality. Cléopâtre has the cup brought on (SD, 1586), and presents it to the couple as a visual sign of her love for them (1591-94). This stage property now becomes the focus of the audience's attention. It contains the poison by which Cléopâtre hopes to achieve her aim, so she is eager that her victims drink from it. Corneille exploits the dramatic excitement of seeing the cup pass from one person to another. Antiochus takes the cup (SD, 1594) and is about to drink (1604) when Timagène bursts in, confused and out of breath (V.4). This surprise entrance, unwelcome for Cléopâtre, signals the intrusion of outer reality on her carefully prepared illusion. Timagène brings the news of Séleucus's death; gradually Cléopâtre's world of artifice begins to crumble. She failed to tie up all the loose ends, and her son's death was witnessed by his *gouverneur.* Séleucus's dying words ("Une main qui nous fut bien chère" (1643)), reported by Timagène, turn the focus on Cléopâtre and Rodogune. Eager to maintain her illusion, the Queen modifies her script and defends herself strongly, shedding tears to support her case (1704-06). Eventually Antiochus decides to go ahead with the wedding regardless: the illusion appears to be intact. Rodogune, however, is suspicious about the wine, and twice she restrains Antiochus from drinking it (SD, 1781; 1782). Determined that her plot should not falter, Cléopâtre tries to prove the wine is harmless by drinking some herself (SD, 1792). Her action appears to have the desired effect: Antiochus takes the cup to drink the wine (SD, 1795; 1805). For a second time, however, and this time decisively, reality intrudes on the world of make-believe: the effects of the poison manifest themselves sooner than Cléopâtre had anticipated. Her changed physical appearance (1805-8) shatters her illusion once and for all.[17] Antiochus does not drink, and a faltering Cléopâtre exists to die (SD, 1830), calling down curses on the couple. A wide range of visual effects (décor, physical action, a stage property, entrances and exits) underlines how Cléopâtre plays with illusion and reality and ultimately loses control of, and falls victim to, her own theatricality.

Not all the director-figures in Corneille's plays fail, however. In *Le Cid* the King sets up a theatrical scenario in an attempt to discover Chimène's true feelings for Don Rodrigue. In Act IV, Scene 4 the King sets himself up as a director-actor and decides to play a trick on Chimène. Director-like, he gives the other characters their roles: "Contrefaites le triste" (1347). When Chimène enters in the following Scene, the King, like the actor, now has his on-stage audience. Chimène's response to the King's fiction, the announcement that Don Rodrigue has died in battle, is a visual one: she

faints. Like the dramatist, the King has managed to trick his audience and elicit an emotional response: as a creator of illusion he has been a success.

Another character who meets with success as a theatrical director is Alcandre in *L'Illusion comique.* Pridamant's search for his son Clindor leads him to the magician Alcandre. In Acts II-IV Alcandre conjures up three series of images in which spirits perform stories from Clindor's life. The tragic action of Act V (Clindor and Isabelle are actually performing a tragedy on a Parisian stage) is seen by both Pridamant and the theatre audience as if it were a continuation of the illusions of reality conjured up in the previous three acts. Costume is important for the success of Alcandre's illusion. The clothes that Clindor wears in the last act were shown in Act I, Scene 2 to the spectators, who assumed them to be his own clothes rather than theatrical costume. So we believe in the catastrophic ending suffered by the young lovers as we had believed in the dramatic action in Acts II-IV. It is only when Alcandre reveals the actors sharing out the takings that we realise that we have been taken in. Alcandre the magician becomes a symbol of the power of the dramatist, creating an on-stage illusion of reality and destroying it at will. Whereas most of the other director-figures in Corneille's plays find their theatrical scenarios being undermined by the intrusion of outer reality, Alcandre holds all the strings together until he is ready triumphantly to dismantle his creation.

PLAYING WITH CONVENTIONS

Corneille's interest in the question of illusion and reality and in the relation between the so-called rules and actual performance is shown by the playful or semiplayful treatment of these issues in certain plays: *Clitandre* and *Médée* both draw attention to the notion of *vraisemblance;* a number of plays contain ironic references to themselves as plays taking place in a theatre; and *L'Illusion comique* plays most overtly with the conventions whereby an illusion of reality is supposed to be created. It is true that some of these effects rely more on the characters' words, but many are created by specifically visual means.

Michael Hawcroft has shown the self-conscious play of theatricality in *Clitandre.*[18] The play's conspicuous references to time, the relentless speed with which a large number of incidents succeed each other, the use of the vocabulary of illusion, the scenes which enact or suggest the operations of illusionist theatre, and Corneille's own criticism in the *Examen* all positively invite the reader to approach the play as one in which the dramatist plays with the notion of *vraisemblance.* Corneille suggests his sceptical attitude to the theory of *vraisemblance* emerging in the 1630s by writing a play charged with *invraisemblance.*

Médée, like *Clitandre,* takes *invraisemblance* as its keynote, but in a different way. It is not so much the speed with which incidents occur as the nature of the incidents themselves that makes the dramatic action *invraisemblable.* What the audience sees flouts the laws of nature completely, but paradoxically the theatre gives credibility to this *invraisemblance* in opposition to dramatic theory.[19]

Médée, a magician like Alcandre, pits her world of illusion against the real world of Jason, Créon, and Créuse. She displays her magic powers on four important occasions: she frees Aegée from prison (IV.5); she immobilises Theudas in order to obtain information from him (V.1); she infuses her gown with a selective poison that consumes Créon and Créuse, but not Jason (IV.1; V.2-4); she escapes in an airborne chariot pulled by dragons (V.5). These feats of magic are different from Alcandre's conjuring-up of illusions. Whereas Alcandre lulls his audience into believing in his illusions of apparent reality, Médée's tricks fly in the face of reality: they are strikingly lacking in *vraisemblance.*

Aegée's release (IV.5) is given bold visual expression by virtue of the fact that we see him actually inside his prison cell, bound in chains.[20] But with a tap of her wand (1231-32), Médée grants Aegée freedom. The power of magic overcomes the reality of a prison cell and chains. Similarly, the visual impact of seeing Médée immobilise Theudas as he crosses the stage (V.1.1311) underlines the *invraisemblance* of these actions. The audience sees things happen on the stage which it knows cannot happen in real life, but the theatre somehow sanctions them.

This blatant flouting of reality finds further visual expression in Médée's dress. In Act IV, Scene 1 Médée, like a theatrical director, carefully orchestrates the role the dress is to play. The audience witnesses the exciting spectacle of Médée concocting her magic potion inside her den. The dress performs its role as planned, before the eyes of the audience, in Act V, Scenes 2-3. Créon and Créuse, the latter still wearing the dress, are consumed by an intense heat which makes their clothes stick to them and burn their skin. The dress, initially an ordinary inanimate object, here assumes an active role in singling out father and daughter for pain and suffering. Any sense of reality or *vraisemblance* is visibly shattered by Médée's magic.

The *invraisemblance* culminates in Act V, Scene 5 where Médée takes flight from her balcony in her chariot drawn by winged dragons (1600-4): a spectacular ending to a spectacular play. Through Médée's four displays of magic Corneille underscores the reality of illusion at the expense of the illusion of reality, dramatic excitement at the expense of allegiance to dramatic theory, *invraisemblance* at the expense of *vraisemblance.*

Another self-consciously playful way of treating the theme of illusion and reality is the use of self-reference, in particular ironic references to the physical décor. As early as *Mélite* there is an allusion to the stage set. In Act V, Scene 2, when Eraste is gripped by madness at the news of Mélite's death and believes himself to be descending into hell, the Nurse alerts him to the houses and walls in an attempt to bring him back to reality (1711-14):

> Mais voyez si l'Enfer ressemble à cette place,
> Ces murs, ces bâtiments ont-ils de la même face?
> Le logis de Mélite et celui de Cliton
> Ont-ils quelque rapport à celui de Pluton?

Eraste is brought back to reality by the theatrical décor, itself an attempted illusion of reality. The device occurs again in *La Galerie du Palais* when Dorimant alerts Aronte that he is "en ce Marais" (IV.2.1101). Such references draw the audience's attention to the fact that they are not watching real life, but a play being performed in a theatre, thus undermining the theatrical illusion.

The most sustained instance of the visual being used to underpin Corneille's game with theatrical illusion is the use of décor in *L'Illusion comique.* The play's complex structure is based on three levels of reality: the frame-play (Pridamant and Alcandre), the play-within-the-play (scenes from Clindor's life in Acts II-IV), and the play-within-the-play-within-the-play (tragic action of Act V). The décor supports this tripartite structure and so helps to foreground the shifting relationship between illusion and reality.[21]

The first level is represented visually by Alcandre's cave, to which there are numerous references in the first scene (e.g. 2, 5, 7, 9). It remains visible throughout the play, and it is from there that Pridamant and Alcandre observe the "fantômes vains" (218), Alcandre warning Pridamant not to venture out without him (216-17). Thus, Alcandre and Pridamant are also visible on stage throughout the play, and they comment on the action at the end of each of Acts II-V. They are an on-stage audience watching the dramatic action just like a theatre audience.[22]

The second level of reality is represented visually by Géronte's house and a prison. It is in this setting that the "visions" of Acts II-IV appear. If Alcandre's cave can be interpreted as a metaphor for the auditorium, these sets are the stage for the main dramatic action. This spatial relationship emphasies visually the first two levels of the play's structure. Alcandre, the magician-dramatist, conjures up spirits to perform before his captive audience, Pridamant.

Similar visual emphasis is given to the third level of the structure, the inner illusion of Act V, which is seen as if it were a continuation of the second level of reality. The stage-set (a garden) lies behind a curtain which is dropped at the end of Scene 5 (SD, 1724). When this curtain is raised again in the following scene (SD, 1746), the mechanics of the theatrical illusion begin to be dismantled. When the characters are shown counting money, it is clear that they are actors in a Parisian theatre. The exploration of the theatrical illusion through the three-tier structure of the play is thus given visual emphasis by the décor.[23]

I draw two main conclusions from my analysis. The first is that critical attention to visual effects reveals much about Corneille's preoccupations. It is odd that critics should for so long have relied on primarily verbal features of performance for their discussion of Corneille's constant preoccupation with the theme of illusion and reality and the art of theatre. Corneille foregrounds this theme as much by visual as by verbal devices. And given that theatre is first and foremost a *spectator* art, it seems highly appropriate that scenery, entrances and exits, gestures and movements, costumes and stage properties should be used to highlight the theatrical themes of Corneille's plays. The visual is not an incidental part of the dramatist's theatrical language, even though it may appear so on the page. Another insight offered by this analysis of visual effects is the similarity between Corneille's comic and serious plays, exploiting similarly theatrical themes and using similar visual techniques. It is a similarity which has previously been noticed only from a verbal point of view.[24] A second conclusion relates to David Maskell's book on Racine. To support his view that Racine is exceptional in his time for incorporating visual effects in exciting and symbolic ways into his tragedies, he makes some comparison with dramatists writing in the period 1659-1664. He concludes: "The French tragedies of the Corneille brothers between 1659 and 1664 are not totally devoid of visual effects, but the visual dimension lacks coherence" (p. 184). Whilst the evidence of this article has related Corneille's visual effects in his early career to only one theme, that of self-conscious theatricality, the weight of evidence might well suggest that Corneille was keener on exploiting the visual language of the theatre when he was younger than when he returned to the theatre in later life. This observation might help to account for the more lasting success of some of his earlier plays compared with those of his later years where his youthful, vibrant and playful theatricality will be sought in vain.[25]

Notes

1. Quoted by G. Couton in *Corneille et la tragédie politique* (Paris: Presses Universitaires de France, 1984), p. 124.

2. Notable and lasting examples are: O. Nadal, *Le Sentiment de l'amour dans l'œuvre de Pierre Corneille* (Paris: Gallimard, 1948); S. Doubrovsky, *Corneille et la dialectique du héros* (Paris: Gallimard, 1963); and A. Stegmann, *L'Héroïsme cornélien: Genèse et signification,* 2 vols (Paris: Armand Colin, 1969). Exceptions to this trend, however, include H. T. Barnwell, *The Tragic Drama of Corneille and Racine: An Old Parallel Revisited* (Oxford University Press, 1982), which emphasises plot construction, and his "'They have their exits and entrances': Stage and Speech in Corneille's Drama", *Modern Language Review,* 81 (1986), 51-63.

3. *Racine: A Theatrical Reading* (Oxford University Press, 1991).

4. Madame de Sévigné famously admired the "tirades de Corneille qui font frissonner" (*Correspondance,* ed. R. Duchêne, 3 vols., Paris: Gallimard, 1972-78, vol. 1, p. 459). G. J. Mallinson praises Corneille's comedies for the "particular acuteness in his analysis of human feelings" (*The Comedies of Corneille: Experiments in the Comic* (Manchester University Press, 1984), p. 218).

5. See, for example, R. J. Nelson, *Play within a Play: The Dramatist's Conception of his Art* (New Haven, Conn.: Yale University Press, 1958); T. J. Reiss, *Toward Dramatic Illusion: Theatrical Technique from Hardy to* Horace (New Haven, Conn.: Yale University Press, 1971); G. Forestier, *Le Théâtre dans le théâtre sur la scène française du XVIIᵉ siècle* (Geneva: Droz, 1981) and "Illusion comique et illusion mimétique", *Papers on French Seventeenth Century Literature,* 21 (1984), 377-91; and F. Lasserre, "La Réflexion sur le théâtre dans les comédies de Corneille", *Papers on French Seventeenth Century Literature,* 24 (1986), 283-312. The more recent study by M. J. Muratore, *Cornelian Theatre: The Metadramatic Dimension* (Birmingham, Alabama: Summa Publications Inc., 1990) has the advantage of extending the study of self-conscious theatricality to the serious plays (the tetralogy together with *Médée* and *Rodogune*).

6. All references to Corneille's plays will be to his *Œuvres complètes,* ed. G. Couton, 3 vols (Paris: Gallimard, 1980-87).

7. In his "Cornelian Illusion", *Symposium,* 14 (1960), 85-99, P. Koch points out that "intellectual illusion is quite common in Corneille's plays, where many characters are guilty of miscalculation or lying" (p. 88).

8. In his "Le Joueur de rôles: Un Personnage typique des comédies de Corneille", *Revue Romane,* 2 (1967), 136-48, J. Pedersen examines "la manie qu'ont les personnages de paraître autres qu'ils ne sont" (p. 138) and sees Alidor and Dorante as the most important role-players in the comedies (p. 139).

9. See G. J. Mallinson, pp. 136-47 and 157-62, for an analysis of Alidor's verbal role-playing.

10. See G. J. Mallinson, pp. 198-209, for an analysis of Dorante's verbal trickery.

11. See M. J. Muratore, pp. 24-5, for a discussion of Chimène's role-playing.

12. See M. J. Muratore, pp. 33-42, for a discussion of the characters' role-playing, but without specific reference to visual effects.

13. See G. J. Mallinson, pp. 164-70 and 186-7, for an analysis of Matamore's verbal role-playing.

14. In relation to Matamore, J. Pedersen notes, significantly, that "sa couardise *saute aux yeux*"(p. 146, my emphasis).

15. M. J. Muratore describes the play as "a factory of illusion" (p. 63).

16. In his "Visual Imagery and Christian Humanism in *Rodogune*", *French Review,* 63 (1989-90), 464-74, G. E. Reed describes this scene as a "tableau" (p. 470).

17. This visual climax is represented in the illustrations accompanying the play in both the 1660 and the 1764 editions of Corneille's works.

18. "Corneille's *Clitandre* and the Theatrical Illusion", *French Studies,* 47 (1993), 142-55.

19. See M. Fumaroli, "De *Médée* à *Phèdre*: Naissance et mise à mort de la tragédie cornélienne", in his *Héros et Orateurs: Rhétorique et dramaturgie cornéliennes* (Geneva: Droz, 1990), pp. 493-518, and M. J. Muratore, pp. 9-18. In contrast to my analysis, which interprets Médée's actions as blantantly implausible, these critics discuss them in terms of a shifting relationship between illusion and reality similar to that found in *L'Illusion comique.*

20. La Mesnardière suggests that it was normal practice for such prison scenes to be played within the compartment: "Il faut que l'endroit de la scène qui représente les cachots soit fermé par des clôtures qui puissent vraisemblablement arrêter les prisonniers. Jamais la personne captive ne doit sortir en parlant hors des bornes de la prison pour se jeter de ce lieu-là sur le devant du théâtre" (*La Poétique,* Geneva: Slatkine Reprints, 1972, p. 413).

21. See J. Golder, "The Stage Settings of Corneille's Early Plays", *Seventeenth-Century French Studies,* 7 (1985), 184-97.

22. See C. Cherpack, "The Captive Audience in *L'Illusion comique*", *Modern Language Notes,* 81 (1966), 342-44.

23. See M. Alcover, "Les Lieux et les temps dans *L'Illusion comique*", *French Studies,* 30 (1976), 393-404, who, in contrast, suggests that the whole stage represents the cave and that everything happens inside the cave.

24. See P. J. Yarrow, *Corneille* (London: Macmillan, 1963), pp. 145-77, and G. J. Mallinson, "'Le même génie': Corneille, from Comedy to Tragedy", *Seventeenth-Century French Studies,* 7 (1985), 4-16, for a discussion of the links between the comedies and the tragedies in terms of characters, dialogue and situation. P. J. Yarrow notes that "the theme of the falseness of appearances occurs over and over again" (p. 150). G. J. Mallinson draws attention to the large number of characters who "take refuge behind a mask, using a variety of tricks and subterfuges played on others and themselves" (p. 15).

25. I would like to thank David Maskell and Michael Hawcroft for their help and encouragement during the preparation of this article.

CLITANDRE

CRITICAL COMMENTARY

Michael Hawcroft (essay date April 1993)

SOURCE: Hawcroft, Michael. "Corneille's *Clitandre* and the Theatrical Illusion." *French Studies* 47, no. 2 (April 1993): 142-55.

[*In the following essay, Hawcroft asserts that it is possible to view* Clitandre *as "an attempt to engage metaphorically with the theoretical debates around 1630, dominated as they were by the twenty-four hour rule and the concept of theatrical illusion."*]

The tragicomedy **Clitandre** is Corneille's second play, first performed in the theatrical season 1630-31, and first published in 1632.[1] It is far from being one of Corneille's best-remembered plays. Modern critics can be scathing about it. Lancaster complains that 'the plot is amateurish and the interest is not centered in any one person or couple' and he thinks it is 'inferior in construction to most of the tragicomedies of the day'.[2] Geoffrey Brereton writes about 'its feeble and chaotic structure' and is unhappy that 'one does not know who the principal characters are or with whom to sympathize'.[3] To be fair to these critics, it must be said that they are only following avenues of assessment that Corneille himself opened up: the 1632 preface warns of the play's near-unintelligibility in performance;[4] the *Discours* simply ignore *Clitandre*—it is perhaps the only pre-1660 play of Corneille's not to be mentioned there; the *Examen* treats the play as a joke. He agrees with his modern critics about the lack of structure and the problem of knowing who the main characters are: 'Pour la constitution, elle est si désordonnée, que vous avez de la peine à deviner qui sont les premiers acteurs'.[5]

Some more recent critics, however, admire the play. Their admiration is part of the trend which seeks to embrace the whole of Corneille's work in its diversity rather than to concentrate on a small number of similar serious plays which conveniently illustrate well-worn critical themes. It is also part of the trend which seeks to reassess works of the period in terms of a baroque aesthetic. For the sympathetic critics, disorder becomes diversity, confusion becomes vivacity, and excess becomes exuberance.

Couton reassures us that 'on ne perdra pas son temps et on ne s'ennuiera pas en lisant cette pièce luxuriante'. He promises 'une prodigieuse vitalité'.[6] Larthomas is another great defender of the play's vitality: 'il y a dans ce "poème" une fantaisie, une vivacité, une sensualité que l'on ne trouve guère ensuite dans la tragédie ou le drame français'.[7] And Roger Guichemerre combines criticism and admiration for *Clitandre*: 'Cette tragicomédie mal composée [. . .] valait surtout par l'expressionnisme baroque d'un style cherchant à frapper la sensibilité du spectateur'.[8]

I want to propose a different approach to the play. The very qualities which lead some to dismiss it as chaotic and others to praise its baroque exuberance can be interpreted as the basis of a dialogue which the play maintains at least implicitly with the so-called rules of drama. In other words I want to read the play as one in which the dramatist self-consciously plays with the notion of illusionist theatre.

CORNEILLE ON *CLITANDRE*

This approach is not pure fantasy. Corneille in his critical writings positively invites readers to approach the play in this way. In the 1632 preface he implies that *Clitandre* was written as a response to the critics of *Mélite.* He says it is very different from *Mélite.* Some criticized his comedy for having 'peu d'effets' (p. 95); in contrast, he says, *Clitandre* is packed full of intrigues. It appears too that some criticized *Mélite* for not following the unity of time ('la règle d'un jour' (p. 95)). Accordingly Corneille has made *Clitandre* obey the unity of time. His preface evokes the debate that was being conducted around 1630 concerning the so-called twenty-four hour rule and suggests Corneille's own independent position in the debate:

> Si j'ai renfermé cette pièce dans la règle d'un jour, ce n'est pas que je me repente de n'y avoir point mis *Mélite,* ou que je me sois résolu à m'y attacher dorénavant. Aujourd'hui, quelques-uns adorent cette règle; beaucoup la méprisent; pour moi, j'ai voulu seulement montrer que si je m'en éloigne, ce n'est pas faute de la connaître.

> (p. 95)

Some, like Chapelain, support the rule; others, like Ogier, have argued against it; but Corneille will follow it or not, as it pleases him. And in *Clitandre* he has chosen to follow it in order to show the critics of *Mélite* that he is capable of doing so.

In fact, these comments simplify Corneille's attitude to the twenty-four hour rule in *Clitandre.* For what he goes on to say implicitly in the preface, and what he says explicitly in the 1660 *Examen,* is that he envisages a more complex and playful approach to the rule in the play.

In the preface he recognizes that there is a discrepancy between his intention to follow the rule and the spirit in which he has executed his intention. The ancients follow the rule and contract the action of their plays into twenty-four hours by making events take place off stage and by introducing messengers to report them. Corneille on the other hand has put everything on stage ('j'ai mis les accidents mêmes sur la scène' (p. 95)), with the consequent risk of there appearing to be too many things happening in the twenty-four hour period. In adopting this course, Corneille implies that he is not simply toeing the regular line in *Clitandre*: 'je me donne ici quelque sorte de liberté de choquer les anciens, d'autant qu'ils ne sont plus en état de me répondre' (p. 95). Corneille is following the rule, but in a subversive way.

In the 1660 *Examen* this spirit of playful defiance is made more explicit. Corneille remembers coming to Paris thirty years earlier to see how *Mélite* was being received. He heard that it was being criticized for the 'peu d'effets' and for too familiar a style. This is how he recalls his reaction to this criticism:

> Pour la justifier [*Mélite*] contre cette censure par une espèce de bravade, et montrer que ce genre de pièces avait les vraies beautés de théâtre, j'entrepris d'en faire une régulière (c'est-à-dire dans ces vingt et quatre heures), pleine d'incidents, et d'un style plus élevé, mais qui ne vaudrait rien du tout; en quoi je réussis parfaitement.

> (pp. 101-02)

In other words, in 1660 Corneille presented the 1632 *Clitandre* as a play constructed to defend *Mélite*'s irregularity and to show that following the rules does not necessarily lead to good drama. The underlying subject of *Clitandre,* then, would be 'how to follow the rules and write a worthless play'.

Modern critics do not believe what Corneille says in the *Examen* about his original aims in writing the play. Robert J. Nelson claims that 'the early preface is far too self-indulgent and self-congratulatory for Corneille's motivation to be so negative'.[9] On the other hand, the 1632 preface does dwell on the play's near-incomprehensibility for spectators. Corneille's verbal games in the *Examens*—his humour, irony, self-depreciation, and self-praise—do not allow us to penetrate his intentions in writing *Clitandre*. But, whatever his intentions, we can at least say that in both 1632 and 1660 the play is presented as being a product of Corneille's reflections on dramatic theory. As François Lasserre says, '*Clitandre* est le fruit d'une vive réaction au premier heurt avec la dictature des règles, et le sens de la pièce, son agencement, l'importance qu'il faut lui reconnaître dans l'œuvre cornélien resteront en relation avec cette donnée essentielle'.[10] I shall argue that, in its themes and techniques, the play sometimes metaphorically, but sometimes more explicitly, enacts a sceptical attitude to the dramatic theory that was emerging around 1630.

DRAMATIC THEORY

What did this theory consist of? Corneille, in both the preface and the *Examen,* is slightly misleading. He implies that the only critical issue in the air around 1630 was the twenty-four hour rule: 'C'était l'unique règle que l'on connût en ce temps-là' (*Examen*, p. 101). It is true that in 1630 what was orthodox neo-classical dramatic theory in Italy was not yet orthodox in France and it certainly lacked the complex infrastructure that it had acquired by 1660; it is also true that in 1630 the focus of discussion was the twenty-four hour rule.[11] But everybody knew that the main issue was not whether the dramatic action was supposed to evolve in twenty-four hours or not; the big issue for which the twenty-four hour rule was merely a pretext was whether and why dramatists should try to create the illusion of reality on stage. The main text was Chapelain's *Lettre sur la règle des vingt-quatre heures* of 1630, not published, but certainly circulated.[12] Chapelain thought that the dramatist should construct plays so as to create the illusion of reality ('pour rendre la feinte pareille à la vérité même', p. 115): his text rings with the words 'vraisemblance' (p. 116), 'tromper' (p. 117), and 'fausseté' (p. 117). The reason for the illusion was to involve the spectator emotionally and certainly pleasurably so that he would be receptive to the dramatist's moral lesson ('pour le purger de ses passions déréglées', p. 115). Corneille was never to agree that the dramatist should have a primarily moral aim. As regards the illusion of reality, the fifth act of *L'Illusion comique* is certainly a striking representation of the mechanics of the dramatic illusion, but in his theoretical writing Corneille never discussed his work in terms of creating an illusion, as Barnwell points out.[13] Barnwell sums up

Corneille's later position as follows: 'if the playwright succeeds in exciting emotion and curiosity, the audience will not be in the least concerned about the illusionist *vraisemblance* of the passage of time' (p. 303). Barnwell speculates that Corneille may have written the preface to *Clitandre* as a reply to Chapelain's *Lettre* (p. 305). The usual interpretation of the preface is that Corneille is seeking to show that, though independent-minded, he can follow the rules when he wishes to do so. But taken together with the play itself, the preface shows us a young Corneille sceptically questioning the new-fangled rules. *Clitandre* foregrounds playfully the whole notion of *vraisemblance* in general and the twenty-four hour rule in particular.

TIME

A dramatist who, around 1630, wished to nail his colours to the new, regular mast could do nothing better than write a play whose action evolved within twenty-four hours. To take the credit for their achievement in regularity, dramatists would make their characters refer to the time of day so that audiences could not miss the fact that the rule was being followed.

Mairet was the first to combine explicit theoretical allegiance to regularity with dramatic practice in his *tragi-comédie pastorale, La Silvanire,* first performed in 1630 and published with its important preface in 1631.[14] Mairet begins *La Silvanire* at dawn. Nobody who hears the first speech can be in any doubt about this. The shepherd Hylas addresses his friend Aglante and says that the dawn is so splendid as to give promise of an excellent day:

> Nous voyons cependant contre toute espérance
> D'une belle journée une belle apparence;
> Les trônes de nos rois ont-ils rien de pareil
> Au vif éclat de feu du berceau du soleil?
> Et quelque vanité qu'on donne à leur puissance
> Ont-ils cette splendeur qui luit à sa naissance?
>
> (ll. 7-12)

What Mairet has done is to make a functional reference to the dawn an occasion for poetic elaboration. There are two further references to time passing later in the play. In Act II, Scene I, at the end of a long monologue, Silvanire prepares to go to sleep with the words:

> Donc en laissant passer l'excessive chaleur,
> Rêvons sur le sujet de mon prochain malheur.
>
> (ll. 556-58)

This is an unobtrusive reference to midday. Finally in Act V, Scene 2 Alciron finds the tomb of Silvanire with the help of the dawn:

> Mais déjà les couleurs de la prochaine aurore
> Annoncent le retour du soleil qui la suit;

A la confusion des flambeaux de la nuit,
J'aperçois le sépulcre où je sais qu'on l'a mise.

(ll. 2032-36)

This reference certainly alerts the audience to the completion of the play between one dawn and the next, but it has its dramatic justification in explaining Alciron's discovery of Silvanire's tomb.[15]

Corneille's references to time in **Clitandre** are far more frequent and obtrusive. The characters refer to periods of time and so remind the audience that time is passing in hours rather than days, months, or years. Rosidor asks to be left alone, but takes the trouble to specify how long he wants to be alone:

Laisse-moi seul, Lysarque, une heure en ma puissance.

(l. 66)

Lysarque reports the time limit to Clitandre's reprieve from execution, four hours to be precise:

[. . .] l'on n'a su gagner qu'avec un grand effort
Quatre heures qu'il lui donne à songer à la mort.

(ll. 1095-96)

Clitandre's imprisonment and possible execution that very day provide the opportunity for some suspenseful references to time. The king decrees ominously: 'Ce jour que nous voyons lui sera le dernier' (l. 836). Cléon lets the prince hope that Clitandre might be saved before the deadline:

Hâtant un peu de pas, quelque espoir me demeure
Que vous arriverez auparavant qu'il meure.

(ll. 1469-70)

Characters refer to events earlier in the play with reminders that they took place on the same day. Caliste explains in Act III, Scene 2 that she must excuse her failure to attend on the queen because of Dorise's plot:

Il me lui faut conter comme l'on m'a surprise,
Excuser mon absence en accusant Dorise,
Et l'informer comment par un cruel destin
Mon devoir auprès d'elle a manqué ce matin.

(l. 869)

Indeed sometimes the dialogue seems to be constructed precisely to highlight the fact that the day remains the same. In Act II, Scene 2 Lysarque approaches Pymante, who is dressed as a peasant, and asks him if he has seen anything suspicious in the wood. Pymante replies evasively: 'Attendez, il y peut avoir quelque huit jours [. . .]' (l. 475). This reference allows Lysarque to jump in and make the correction: 'Je parle d'aujourd'hui' (l. 476).

Act I has a couple of reminders that the play has begun in the early morning. Géronte:

[. . .] sans doute bientôt le jour qui vient de naître
Amène Rosidor séduit d'un faux cartel.

(ll. 158-59)

And Caliste:

Ma sœur, l'heure s'avance, et nous serons à peine
Si nous ne retournons, au lever de la Reine.

(ll. 221-22)

But anybody who has heard Caliste's opening sixty-two-line monologue is unlikely to need these reminders. The speech is densely woven out of references to night, sleep, waking, and dawn:

Tout le monde au château plongé dans le sommeil,
Loin de savoir ma fuite ignore mon réveil.

(ll. 3-4)

D'elle j'ai su les lieux où l'amour qui les joint
Ce matin doit passer jusques au dernier point.

(ll. 11-12)

Elle doit m'y conduire
Sitôt que le Soleil commencera de luire.

(ll. 13-14)

La dormeuse m'oublie et ne se peut lever.

(l. 16)

La nuit qui dure encor fit que rien ne la presse.

(l. 18)

Ma jalouse fureur, mon dépit, mon amour
Ont troublé mon repos avant le point du jour.

(ll. 19-20)

Eveille-toi, brigand.

(l. 24)

Le jour s'en va paraître.

(l. 28)

An apostrophe to the sun reveals that dawn is just about to break:

Et toi, père du jour, dont le flambeau naissant
Va chasser mon erreur avecque le croissant,
S'il est vrai que Téthys te reçoit dans sa couche,
Prends, Soleil, prends encor deux baisers sur sa bouche.

(ll. 47-50)

The sun does not listen to her plea and day dawns:

et l'aube de ses rais
A déjà reblanchi le haut de ces forêts.

(ll. 55-56)

The references come so thick and fast in the speech as to make one question their purpose. No other play of the early 1630s to my knowledge makes such extensive and obtrusive reference to time and none drives home so relentlessly the time of day in the opening speech. It could be that Corneille is so keen to show that he can follow the twenty-four hour rule that he goes much further than anyone else did elsewhere to advertise the regularity. Alternatively, these references might invite a criticism of the new illusionist theory by highlighting the implausibility of having so many things happen in such a short space of time. And a lot does happen in *Clitandre*. Dorise executes an unsuccessful plot to kill Caliste. Pymante tries to kill Rosidor. Clitandre and the prince go hunting. Clitandre is sent to prison. The prince is stranded in the forest when his horse is struck down by a thunderbolt. Pymante tries to rape Dorise. Search parties are sent first for the attackers of Rosidor, then for the prince. By multiplying the references to the short space of time, Corneille advertises the implausibility of the illusion.

Jacques Truchet sees some thematic parody in *Clitandre.* He wonders if the restoration of order at the end of the play does not contain 'quelque chose de parodique':[16] the king appears to put things right, but it is in fact only chance that prevents his peremptory judgement and the criminals' wiles from prevailing. If there is a hint of thematic parody in the ending, there is certainly a hint of parody in Corneille's technical construction of his play. His adherence to the twenty-four hour rule is so overstated that it suggests a parody of other dramatists like Mairet who deploy the technique in the hope of creating illusionist drama. It is not clear that Corneille meant to be parodic in his treatment of this rule, but the text certainly lends itself to such an interpretation.

ILLUSIONS

The view that Corneille implements the twenty-four hour rule in a self-consciously playful and experimental, rather than a wholly serious, way is supported by the way in which the text implicitly tackles the larger question of *vraisemblance*. The play foregrounds the theme of the theatrical illusion by exploiting the same vocabulary that the theorists used: *feinte* (e.g. l. 229), *vérité* (e.g. l. 1716), *vraisemblance* (e.g. l. 1916), *tromper* (e.g. l. 494)—and by depicting scenes which enact or suggest the operations of illusionist theatre.

There is a brief example of this in Act IV, Scene 4. Dorise and Pymante are still in the disguises which they donned earlier in the play: Dorise is dressed as a nobleman and Pymante as a peasant. The last time the audience has seen them is when Dorise stabbed Pymante in the eye and fled with her victim in furious pursuit (Act IV, Scenes 1-2). In Act IV, Scene 3 the Prince is on stage alone when he hears a noise which he wrongly takes to

signal the arrival of his men. It is important to visualize the stage picture at this point. Pymante and Dorise enter hurriedly; Pymante catches Dorise and knocks her to the floor ('terrassant Dorise'). This happens without their realising that the Prince is present. It is like a play, at which the Prince is a spectator. The comment that he makes from the sidelines 'ô l'indigne spectacle' (l. 1309) is an expression of outrage, but the word 'spectacle' also suggests the theatrical nature of the situation. The Prince tries to interfere and change the course of events: he calls out to Pymante 'Arrête, scélérat!' and he tries to rescue Dorise. This moment is comparable to that in Act V of *L'Illusion comique* when, in the performance of the tragedy, Éraste stabs Clindor. Pridamant, who, like the prince, is watching from the sidelines, thinks that he is witnessing the murder of his son rather than the feigned death of his son performing on stage: 'On l'assassine, ô Dieux! daignez le secourir' (l. 1563). There is an important difference between these two moments in the plays. In *L'Illusion comique* the audience has been taken in like Pridamant and is disillusioned at the same time as he is; moreover the treatment is related explicitly to the theatrical illusion. In *Clitandre* the spectators' appreciation of the scene as one suggestive of the theatrical illusion depends upon the dramatic irony whereby *they* know that the fighters are Pymante and Dorise, but the prince thinks he is seeing a mere peasant attack a nobleman. When the prince eventually sees the reality of the scene in front of him, he expresses astonishment: 'Tu me montres vraiment de merveilleux effets' (l. 1343); and Dorise comments on his delusion and disillusionment:

> Quelques étonnements qu'une telle surprise
> Jette dans votre esprit que vos yeux ont déçu,
> D'autres le saisiront quand vous aurez tout su.

(ll. 1350-53)

The prince's astonishment and surprise are of the same degree as Pridamant's when he is shown that the scene he has been watching is not quite what it had seemed: 'Que vois-je? chez les morts compte-t-on de l'argent?' (l. 1747). For both characters the illusion has been so convincing that its dismantling requires some adjustment which leads them to present the experience in terms of a miracle. The theatrical implications of these scenes are explicit in *L'Illusion* and implicit in *Clitandre.*

Unlike this illusion involving Pymante and Dorise, most of the illusions in the play are presented as only partially convincing: *vraisemblance* is subverted. The play's most elaborate and dominant illusion concerns Pymante's attempt to rid himself of his rival Rosidor and to inculpate his other rival Clitandre. In devising and executing this scheme Pymante can be perceived metaphorically as a dramatist-actor-director: he engineers a plot, he plays a role himself, and directs the roles of others, and he tries to make his audience, primarily the king, believe that the play is real.

In Act I, Scene 2 Rosidor explains that he has received a challenge to a duel written in Clitandre's hand: the two of them are to meet that day in the forest to decide who will win Caliste. All this is an illusion by which Rosidor, and initially the audience, are taken in. The challenge is part of Pymante's scheme to kill Rosidor and to make it look as if it was Clitandre's crime. The audience realizes this in the course of Act I, Scene 4 when they see Pymante in the role of theatrical director and his actors preparing their roles: Pymante and Clitandre's servants, Géronte and Lycaste, are disguised as peasants: Géronte explains that he wrote the challenge and counterfeited his master's signature. They prepare to despatch Rosidor, taking their masks, swords, and carrying their real clothes ready for their escape. Like actors, they wear clothes that mask their own identity. For the illusion of reality to work everything must corroborate it: the peasants' clothes and the counterfeit signature do just that. When the 'play' has been performed, the 'actors' intend once again to don their real clothes and resume their true identity.

But, as if to point out the difficulty of controlling all the elements that might corroborate the illusion, Corneille follows this scene with one in which Cléon tells Rosidor's equerry, Lysarque, that there can be no substance in the challenge. He has just seen Clitandre going hunting with the prince, so it is most unlikely that Clitandre intends to meet Rosidor for a duel in the forest. Cléon suspects that the challenge is a false one, invented by Rosidor to tease Lysarque. This scene of amusing dramatic irony has implications for Corneille's presentation of theatrical *vraisemblance*. Corneille has first taken in the audience, Rosidor, and his equerry with Pymante's illusion. But he destroys the illusion for the audience in Act I, Scene 4, and then shows Cléon attempting to destroy it for the equerry in Act I, Scene 5. Cléon's subversion of the illusion in particular suggests to the theatre audience that *vraisemblance* is created by a series of flimsy corroborations, which are easily dismantled by his chance sighting of Clitandre. To some of the characters the illusion remains *vraisemblable*; to Cléon and to the audience it is *invraisemblable*. The important suggestion from Corneille's point of view is that the degree of *vraisemblance* is arbitrarily dependent upon individual spectators.

The planned performance takes place in Act I, Scene 7. It does not follow the scenario exactly, but it does create the desired illusion. The men do not succeed in killing Rosidor, only in wounding him. Pymante flees and Rosidor kills Géronte and Lycaste. Rosidor unmasks the dead and on recognizing Clitandre's men takes this as further evidence that it is Clitandre's doing: 'Le seul

Clitandre arma contre moi ces voleurs' (l. 29) and he couples this with the equally illusory written evidence to secure Clitandre's conviction:

> Je te rends convaincu de ta seule écriture,
> Sitôt que j'aurai pu faire ma plainte au Roi.
>
> (ll. 270-71)

The audience sees Rosidor taken in by what appears to him to be plausible (namely the artifices of Pymante, actor-director), even though the audience itself has been invited to judge these very artifices as flimsy.

Pymante has to continue his performance until he is well away from the scene of the crime. Act II, Scene 2 shows him playing the peasant with Lysarque, who has come in search of Rosidor and Clitandre. Pymante, alone, congratulates himself on his illusionist skills. He makes two points. First, he is safe as long as he can pass for a peasant, which he has just successfully done. 'J'ai leur crédulité sous ces habits trompée' (l. 494), he says: this is exactly what an actor does. Clothes will be every bit as deceptive in *L'Illusion comique*. When Pridamant sees his son's wardrobe in Act I, he thinks the clothes are Clindor's personal ones. So when he sees him wearing those very clothes in Act V and being killed, the clothes are taken to corroborate the illusion of reality whereby it is Clindor himself who is dying. The other point on which Pymante congratulates himself in advance is that Lysarque will find the dead bodies of Géronte and Lycaste and will jump to the conclusion that Clitandre is guilty (ll. 494-500). He needs to take account of just one further point to prevent the illusion from being destroyed: he must retrieve his own clothes which were left by the tree.

The next scene (Act II, Scene 3) shows Lysarque making precisely the same mistake that Pymante had hoped he would make. The bodies of Géronte and Lycaste are taken to corroborate the guilt of Clitandre. And later, although Pymante is not there to enjoy it, Act III, Scene 1 shows the king, with Rosidor, deluded by the dead bodies of Clitandre's men and by the handwriting of the challenge. Such is the power of the illusion that the king has already had Clitandre arrested and thrown into prison.

The disillusionment of the characters, their realization that Clitandre did not write the challenge and send men to attack Rosidor happens in stages. First, Clitandre, alone in prison, realizes that somebody must have dreamt up a scheme to betray him (ll. 1433-38). His comments dwell on the *invraisemblance* of the illusion in terms appropriate to the theatre ('déguisement', 'masque'):

> Mais leur déguisement d'autre côté m'étonne,
> Jamais un bon dessein ne déguise personne,
> Leur masque les condamne.
>
> (ll. 1433-35)

Once again, the audience is implicitly invited to consider the *invraisemblance* of the theatrical illusion. Later, Pymante and Dorise admit the truth to the prince, who in any case had never been taken in by the performance because he had been out hunting (Act IV, Scene 7). And finally, in Act V, Scenes 4 and 5, the king and Rosidor are disillusioned and for Pymante the show is over. The illusion is well and truly broken.

The prince thinks he sees a fight between a peasant and a nobleman; Rosidor and the king (among others) think that Clitandre has arranged the murder of Rosidor. These are the main illusions, but there are others. Caliste thinks that Rosidor is having an affair with Hippolyte; Dorise thinks that Pymante is a peasant and Pymante that Dorise is Géronte; Rosidor thinks that Caliste is dead and Caliste that Rosidor is an assassin. The repeated creation and dismantling of illusions may well link ***Clitandre*** to the so-called baroque aesthetic of which the theme of appearance and reality is supposed to be a feature. They certainly create an exciting play about trickery and deceit. Is there any need, therefore, to associate Corneille's insistence on illusion in ***Clitandre*** with self-conscious theatricality? The illusions are not explicitly theatrical illusions like that in the last act of *L'Illusion comique*; none of them functions explicitly as a play-within-a-play. But what characterizes ***Clitandre*** is the relentless force with which the illusions succeed each other. ***Clitandre*** also has its plot-makers. Just as Alcandre can be seen as a dramatist-figure in *L'Illusion comique,* Dorise and Pymante both take charge of their illusions which they prepare carefully to ensure that their on-stage audience is taken in by them. The self-conscious theatricality of these dramatist-characters is more convincing when they are compared to some of Racine's characters. M. Edwards calls Créon in *La Thébaïde* an 'homme de théâtre',[17] T. Cave calls Joad in *Athalie* a 'masterplotter',[18] and D. Maskell calls Acomat in *Bajazet* an 'impresario'.[19] All these characters have something of the dramatist about them in the way they try to arrange events so that the plot might turn out as they wish. But in none of these cases do the characters direct and engage in an on-stage performance which, in its deliberate falseness, aims to deceive an on-stage audience. It is true that this same criterion would make *Tartuffe* a play about the theatrical illusion, but in *Tartuffe* there is only the one illusion and the number of references to religious behaviour forestall this illusionist reading; whereas in ***Clitandre*** the torrential sequence of often fragile illusions and the vocabulary with which the characters refer to them irresistibly recall the theories of illusionist theatre emerging in the early 1630s.

THE VOCABULARY OF ILLUSION

'[Le spectateur] voit ici les choses comme si véritablement elles arrivaient devant lui', says Mairet in his preface to *La Silvanire*.[20] The dramatist must do everything 'pour rendre la feinte pareille à la vérité même', urges Chapelain in the *Lettre sur la règle des vingt-quatre heures*.[21] The spectator's pleasure 'consiste principalement en la vraisemblance'.[22] The new theorists clamour for credible illusions to be put on stage. Against their remarks set this one: 'Combien la vraisemblance a peu de vérité'. It might be the remark of a sceptical theorist pointing out that what happens on stage can never be like real life. But the remark is made by the king in ***Clitandre*** as he draws a lesson from his experience in the play. He has been taken in by an illusion and explains that what appears to be the truth rarely is the truth. He elaborates the point at some length:

> Que souvent notre esprit trompé de l'apparence
> Règle ses mouvements avec peu d'assurance!
> Qu'il est peu de lumière en nos entendements,
> Et que d'incertitude en nos raisonnements!
> Qui voudra désormais se fie aux impostures
> Qu'en notre jugement forment les conjectures,
> Tu [Clitandre] suffis pour apprendre à la postérité
> Combien la vraisemblance a peu de vérité.
>
> (ll. 1709-16)

Of course this appeal to distinguish between appearance and reality, plausibility and truth fits very well the trickery of which the king has been a victim in the course of the play. But the last two lines of the quotation hold up Clitandre as an exemplary figure and might also suggest once again that Corneille is cocking a snook at the *vraisemblance* supposedly achieved by adherence to the new rules: *vraisemblance* is an irrelevant theatrical aim, because the illusion is so fragile and because a play like ***Clitandre,*** which teems with implausible incidents, can also be exciting theatrically. This is the 'espèce de bravade' of which Corneille wrote in the *Examen*: he has written a play which deliberately mocks the new theory, but which can still grip an audience.

Not only the king, but Clitandre too uses the language of theatrical illusion when he is in prison. In this case, however, the problem is that he cannot believe the reality of his being there:

> Peu s'en faut dans l'excès de ma confusion
> Que je ne prenne tout pour une illusion.
>
> (ll. 883-84)

What he thinks of as reality (his innocence) does not tally with what he sees: 'Non, cela ne se peut, vous vous trompez, mes yeux.' (l. 896) Clitandre decides that his guilt and imprisonment must be just illusory even though they seem so real and tangible. In the immediately preceding scene Rosidor had, from a different perspective, warned the king that what appears to be real is not always so:

L'apparence déçoit, et souvent on a vu
Sortir la vérité d'un moyen impourvu,
Bien que la conjecture y fût encor plus forte.

(ll. 843-45)

All these statements find their justification within the fictional world of the play, but to the reader or spectator of the early 1630s conversant with dramatic theory, and certainly to the reader who has Corneille's preface in mind, they have a metaphorical significance, which is to imply scepticism towards the whole notion of illusionist theory.

There is another feature of Corneille's mockery of the rules. Chapelain argued that the point of the illusion was to enable the play to make a moral impact on the audience:

> Je pose donc pour fondement que l'imitation en tous poèmes doit être si parfaite qu'il ne paraisse aucune différence entre la chose imitée et celle qui imite, car le principal effet de celle-ci consiste à proposer à l'esprit, pour le purger de ses passions déréglées, les objets comme vrais et comme présents.[23]

Those characters, however, who succumb to the illusions in *Clitandre* derive no moral benefit from them at all. Caliste is nearly murdered by believing in Dorise's illusion; the prince becomes involved in a fight when he mistakes the characters' identities; and the king, taken in by Pymante's illusion, throws an innocent man into prison. It is only when the illusions are shown to be criminal schemes and not reality, in short when the illusions are dismantled, that the on-stage characters can lead safe and morally acceptable lives. If interpreted as theatrical metaphors, these illusions respond negatively to Chapelain's claims for the moral impact and cathartic effect of illusionist theatre. Corneille will express the same negative views explicitly in his later theoretical writings.[24]

DRAMA ABOUT DRAMA

It is not necessary to read *Clitandre* as a metaphorical exploration of dramatic theory; indeed, such a reading would be very partial. *Clitandre* is above all an exciting play in which scheming, evil characters try to outdo the innocent and the good; it has, according to Larthomas, the potential to become 'un bon roman de la série noire';[25] It is a daring mixture of tragedy, tragicomedy, comedy, and pastoral, a feast for the eyes as well as for the ears. But it would also be a partial reading which did not recognize the hints of subversion in the play. Corneille's references to theory in the preface and the *Examen*, his arguably parodic treatment of the twenty-four hour rule in the play itself, the extensive foregrounding of the theme of illusion, and the highlighting of the *vraisemblance* of many of the characters' schemes justify a reading of *Clitandre* as theatre reflect-

ing upon itself, and make of the play an even bolder theatrical experiment than it is usually agreed to be and an ancestor of *L'Illusion comique*. Whereas Barnwell speculates that the preface to the play might be a reply to Chapelain's *Lettre sur la règle des vingt-quatre heures*, it is possible to see the whole play as an attempt to engage metaphorically with the theoretical debates around 1630, dominated as they were by the twenty-four hour rule and the concept of theatrical illusion.

In an article on *Médée* and *Phèdre*,[26] Marc Fumaroli opens up an interesting new perspective on evaluating seventeenth-century plays: 'je crois que cette *réflexivité sur soi* du texte dramatique est un trait structurel de tous les chefs-d'œuvres du théâtre du XVIIe siècle: c'est probablement à la présence de ce trait que se reconnaît le chef-d'œuvre, par opposition à l'œuvre "plate"'. If Fumaroli were right, the Cornelian canon would have to be reviewed, and *Clitandre* would earn a central and distinguished place.[27]

Notes

1. By 1682, when Corneille published the last edition of his complete plays before his death, the play was considerably shorter and less exuberant. I refer throughout to the 1632 state of the text as reproduced in vol. 1 of his *Œuvres complètes*, 3 vols (Paris, Gallimard, 1980-87).

2. H. C. Lancaster, *A History of French Dramatic Literature in the Seventeenth Century*, 5 parts in 9 vols (Baltimore, Johns Hopkins University Press, 1929-42), 1, 521, 524.

3. G. Brereton, *French Tragic Drama in the Sixteenth and Seventeenth Centuries* (London, Methuen, 1973), pp. 128, 124.

4. 'Le moindre défaut ou d'attention du spectateur, ou de mémoire de l'acteur, laisse une obscurité perpétuelle en la suite, et ôte presque l'entière intelligence de ces grands mouvements dont les pensées ne s'égarent point du fait' (*Œuvres complètes*, I, 95).

5. *Œuvres complètes*, I, 102.

6. *Œuvres complètes*, I, 1200, 1197.

7. P. Larthomas, 'Le Premier *Clitandre*: Note sur la dramaturgie et le style de Corneille', in *Form and Meaning: Aesthetic Coherence in Seventeenth-Century French Drama*, eds W. D. Howarth and others (Avebury, Avebury Publishing Co., 1982), 41-50, p. 49.

8. R. Guichemerre, *La Tragi-comédie* (Paris, Presses Universitaires de France, 1981), p. 34.

9. R. J. Nelson, *Corneille: His Heroes and their World* (Philadelphia, University of Pennsylvania Press, 1963), p. 37.

10. F. Lasserre, 'Avant *L'Illusion . . . Clitandre*', *Papers in French Seventeenth-Century Literature,* 26-27 (1987), p. 705. Lasserre's starting-point is the same as mine, but thereafter our analyses diverge. He studies illusion as a baroque theme, and for him the king and prince are dramatist-figures, while Clitandre is a spectator. It is difficult to accept this reading of the roles of the king and prince, given that they are essentially passive rather than active characters.

11. The abbé d'Aubignac claims that it was the twenty-four hour rule that caused most debate. Everybody talked about it: 'il n'y a point de Ruelles de lict où les femmes n'entreprennent d'en faire des leçons'. See *La Pratique du théâtre,* ed. P. Martino (Algiers, Carbonel, 1927), p. 113.

12. J. Chapelain, *Opuscules critiques,* ed. A. C. Hunter (Paris, Droz, 1936).

13. H. T. Barnwell, 'Some Reflections on Corneille's Theory of *Vraisemblance* as Formulated in the *Discours*', *Forum for Modern Language Studies,* I (1965), 295-310, p. 302.

14. Included in *Théâtre du XVIIe siècle* vol. 1, ed. J. Scherer (Paris, Gallimard, 1975), from which my quotations are taken.

15. On reference to time in plays, see J. Scherer, *La Dramaturgie classique en France* (Paris, Nizet, [1950]), pp. 110-24.

16. J. Truchet, 'A propos de *Clitandre*', in *Héroïsme et création littéraire sous les règnes d'Henri IV et de Louis XIII (colloque de Strasbourg),* eds N. Hepp and G. Livet (Paris, Klincksieck, 1974), 251-59, p. 259.

17. M. Edwards, 'Créon: Homme de théâtre', *Jeunesse de Racine,* 1963, 67-81.

18. T. Cave, *Recognitions: A Study in Poetics* (Oxford, Clarendon Press, 1988), p. 363.

19. D. Maskell, *Racine: A Theatrical Reading* (Oxford, Clarendon Press, 1991), p. 89, n. 12.

20. *Théâtre du XVIIe siècle,* I, 484.

21. *Opuscules critiques,* 115.

22. J. Mairet in *Théâtre du XVIIe siècle,* I, 485.

23. *Lettre sur la règle des vingt-quatre heures* in *Opuscules critiques,* 115.

24. E.g. in the epistle introducing *La Suite du Menteur:* 'pour moi, qui tiens avec Aristote et Horace que notre art n'a pour but que le divertissement' (*Œuvres complètes,* II, 95). See also his detailed discussions in the first and second *Discours.*

25. 'Le Premier *Clitandre*', p. 42.

26. M. Fumaroli, 'De *Médée* à *Phèdre*: Naissance et mise à mort de la tragédie "cornélienne"' in *Héros et orateurs: Rhétorique et dramaturgie cornéliennes* (Geneva, Droz, 1990), 493-518, p. 507, n. 10.

27. There might be a place for *Clitandre* in the 'tradition of those plays written in the 1630s whose principal preoccupation is not the changing fortunes of lovers, but the theatre', a tradition into which G. J. Mallinson fits '*L'Hospital des fous* of Charles Beys: The Madman and the Actor' (*French Studies,* 36 (1982), 12-25, pp. 23-24).

LA VEUVE (THE WIDOW)

CRITICAL COMMENTARY

Ian McFarlane (essay date 1982)

SOURCE: McFarlane, Ian. "A Reading of *La Veuve.*" In *The Equilibrium of Wit: Essays for Odette de Mourgues,* edited by Peter Bayley and Dorothy Gabe Coleman, pp. 135-49. Lexington, KY: French Forum, 1982.

[*In the following essay, McFarlane explores stylistic aspects of* The Widow, *particularly Corneille's use of language, action, and characterization.*]

In the Letter-preface to *La Suivante,* Corneille quotes from Montaigne (I, 37): "Qu'on me donne l'action la plus excellente et pure, je m'en vais y fournir vraisemblablement cinquante vicieuses intentions." This points to a persistent fascination with the relations between state of mind and outer gesture and with the difficulties that face us when we try to find out what people are really about: one of the factors in play is language, curiously inadequate as a vehicle of communication, concealing as much as it reveals, and working according to some strange principle of refraction. Corneille no doubt found plenty in the *Essais* to confirm him in his views; and his plays often bear on the interplay between intelligence, feeling and language. This is certainly the case with *La Veuve,* though criticism has more often interested itself in its links with *Mélite,* of which it is in part a parodistic variation; in its treatment of the problem of social inequality—a hare too enthusiastically chased; or in a certain realism, a feature which is less obvious to the modern reader accustomed to the text of the later editions. All this is attempting to make the best of a bad job—and unnecessarily so, since *La*

Veuve has plenty to catch our eye without appeals to its significance in the development of the dramatist or of contemporary theater. Here we can see the young Corneille on the way to forging a style that can reproduce faithfully the interplay of wit, feeling and the discrepancies between *paraître* and *être*. This is brought about not only by Corneille's growing linguistic maturity but by the way in which certain effects, hitherto left to essentially dramatic effects, are incorporated in the language itself.

As in so many of Corneille's plays, the action is essentially a movement from obscurity towards the manifest, both in the action and in the psychology.[1] Such imagery as occurs often belongs to the domains of darkness and light, as well as of sight. Here, we can detect various sources of obscurity: Alcidon, in his sinister mendacity, and the Nourrice, his agent, who in more coarse-grained fashion muddies the waters and blurs further the margins separating truth and falsehood. Then there is the interference of friendship which is seen to be an obstacle to common sense and decency; it blinds the intelligence of Philiste and Célidan. Moreover, the reticence of the two "personnages sympathiques," Philiste and Clarice, delays the manifestation of true feeling. There are, however, two other factors of a more general nature which complicate the picture: on the one hand, the murkiness of language, with its potential for misunderstanding, manipulation and partial communication; and on the other, the inconsistencies and discontinuities of the human character. The problem of language will engage our attention presently; for the time being, we shall look at the way the characters behave.

I

So far from being simple characters cast in a rigid mold, Corneille's men and women can be highly inconsistent; volte-faces have been defined in terms of dramatic necessity,[2] and there is more than a grain of truth in this explanation; but the reader of Montaigne knew that the contrariness of human nature had deeper roots, that we are patchwork quilts, that virtue and vice are so intermingled that ordinary ethical norms are difficult to apply. And when we are in a world of *feinte* such as is conjured up in **La Veuve,** we can easily lose our way: it seems that everybody is, to a greater or lesser extent, prone to dissimulation. Philiste and Clarice are not exempt, and Célidan outdoes Alcidon on his own ground; useful, indeed good arguments will be found in the mouths of unprincipled persons (as Montaigne had noticed fifty years before), whether it be Alcidon or the Nourrice; Philiste is quite happy "Si d'un mauvais dessein il tire un bon effet" (l. 574), and one would have no trouble in finding other instances. We are in a world of paradox, but the play is not just a *jeu d'esprit*; this is the world as Corneille sees it, the result of hu-

man nature with all its warts, twists and obscurities. It cannot be painted in black and white: the characters do not so much divide into convenient ethical camps as illustrate different degrees of dissimulation; but there is a difference in intention and motivation among the characters. Alcidon may be at the other end of the spectrum from Philiste, but one might well ask how it comes about that these two men are bound to each other by ties of friendship.

If there is any looseness in the structure of the action—a point that may be overdone[3]—the conception of human nature gives a unity of its own to the play; and this is reflected in the large space given by Corneille to devices of repetition and echo. Certain traits will be repeated from character to character, a theme developed à propos of one person will reappear in a totally separate context or in the mouth of a character possessed of very different values; major leitmotifs tend to occur in at least two figures: friendship (Philiste and Célidan), money (Chrysante and Géron), family pressures (Chrysante and Doris). One of the features of **La Veuve** is precisely the way in which technical devices are made to harmonize with the values and characters involved.

In fact, the structure of his play is worked out quite satisfactorily; it centers on the theme of feeling, true and false. The "sympathique" couple, Philiste and Clarice, do not contribute actively to the plot: their basic relationship remains unchanged throughout, though the problem of its expression is more difficult to resolve. Philiste's sense of friendship towards Alcidon prevents him from taking any action likely to run counter to his loyalty, which remains unimpaired until the final scene. Clarice is less well defined than Philiste: there are certain inhibitions that prevent her at first from making her feelings explicit, and she is perhaps not much more than the embodiment of love gradually revealed. Philiste has more pronounced features: though at first he appears as rather sly (I, sc. 1) and though one wonders why his reticence has lasted already for two years—the psychoanalytical explanation offered by Verhoeff (hidden fear of women) does not really help here[4]—the rest of his behavior is actuated by feelings very willing to manifest themselves. He is essentially an emotive, perhaps a choleric. His blind friendship for Alcidon, his bouts of *fureur,* his irascibility in his dealings with his mother, or the Nourrice, show him to be related to various dramatic traditions and may give him a slightly comic nuance; but some of this is set off against his silences in his conversations with Clarice. These two have a thematic rather than a dramatic value, for they stand for genuine emotions, and thus provide a backcloth against which the other characters can be assessed.

The action and awareness of the issues involved must therefore come primarily from elsewhere. So far as the action is concerned, the source is Alcidon. He is obviously clever—he is the only character who prides himself on his intelligence and condemns others for their stupidity—and he has an evident pleasure in the sheer mechanics of dissimulation. He has another characteristic which will recur in later plays of Corneille: he works entirely through intermediaries. He tries to use Philiste, Célidan, the Nourrice and Doris to secure his ends; and it is noteworthy that he does not have any dialogue scene with the professed object of his love, Clarice; indeed he sees her for the first time in the unmasking scene at the end of Act V, and even then his reply to Clarice is more in the nature of a private meditation. In the long run, he will be outwitted at his own game, but one must also allow for a certain vanity, which not only makes him look a trifle fatuous, but by clouding his intelligence with an affective element, accounts in some measure for his ultimate downfall. The high-watermark of his success is when Clarice is kidnapped at night; this is a well-known device, but it is symbolic that Alcidon's stratagems should be associated with the dark and that he is unmasked in the fullness of daylight.

His plans are much facilitated by the way in which friendship works to his advantage, though there comes a moment when he is fearful of the consequences of overzealous loyalty; it is indeed a principle which seems to override any other ethical consideration. As long as Philiste and Célidan are blinded by ties of loyalty, he can prosper. However, Alcidon's discomfiture is initiated by the way he overplays his hand. This is foreshadowed in his dealings with Doris, with whom he is allegedly in love. Doris may be thought to have few distinguishing features: she is fairly passive, she has no strong feelings about marriage, she appears obedient to her mother's wishes, though there are later signs of restiveness on that score. On the other hand, the fact that she is *not* emotionally involved allows her intelligence to work unhampered; and right from the outset she has no illusions about Alcidon's professed love: he is simply a "conteur à gages" (l. 178); later she takes over his phrase "le fard de mon langage" at his expense (l. 1715). Admittedly, in view of the psychological "données" of the cast, there is no "reliable witness" among the characters; but Doris is the only one to approximate to this, insofar as she and the audience come to terms. She is the means of puncturing some of the bubbles created by Alcidon, and she is thus the source of comic effect by creating a contrast between Alcidon caught up in his own web of words and deceits, and her own straightforward incisiveness. She helps to reveal the vanity in his make-up, for he continues to imagine fondly that she is in love with him; and more broadly she becomes a source of the dramatic irony which is such a feature of this play. So that, structurally, she is much more important than her character would lead us to think, and this may have been recognized in 1660 by Corneille, who gives her a speech in the final scene of the play which in previous versions was at this point fragmented so that various characters could say their short piece; as a result, her final appearance sticks more in the memory than was previously the case.

However, Doris does not actively take much part in Alcidon's unmasking; this role is assigned to Célidan, who first appears in Act III and whose friendship for Alcidon, at first working in his favor, is undermined by a growing awareness of his duplicity. Célidan seems, in a sense, a bit of a *ficelle*; without a further character, there is no reason why Alcidon should not attain his ends, for none of the others has the wit, the vigor or the opportunity to initiate countermeasures. It is also true that Célidan's metamorphosis from the blind, slightly bovine friend to the alert and active schemer is a trifle sudden and schematic. Though there is substance in this, it is fair to point out that Célidan is a man actuated by his feelings: so long as friendship lasts, he preserves a dog-like fidelity which makes him uninteresting and predictable; but when the scales fall from his eyes, his intelligence is fired and sharpened by the injury done to his pride and sense of values, so that the incisiveness and tempo of his language is accordingly quickened. He puts into practice what, in the 1644 text, is placed into the mouth of Chrysante: "Il faut jouer au fin contre un esprit si double" (p. 40); and he wins through by a combination of stratagems borrowed from Alcidon and the play of his own "franchise." He is indeed able to improvise the action of duplicity as he goes along, and he seems to take some slight pleasure in this.

Of Chrysante, there is little to be said: her ancestry in the theater is well known. She stands for the unsympathetic parent, but also for money, something which is not looked on with favor in the play: Clarice after all is not inhibited from marrying Philiste by his own impecunious position. In her volte-face, Chrysante emerges as an example of a woman whose feelings were ignored at the time of her marriage; but her attitudes seem rather forced and improbable, and the cynic might well add that her "conversion" occurs after she becomes aware of Célidan's financial and social position. On the other hand, she is useful as a *repoussoir* for characters (notably Philiste) who can give vent to their feelings.

The structure of the play is thus built round these characters who stand for certain values, but are all capable of dissimulation in varying degree, and whose relationships are further bedevilled by the unreliable nature of language.

II

So far, we have considered the interplay of emotion true and false; but language brings its own problems, since it seems to stand in the way of genuine emotion, and at the same time not only to allow for misunderstanding, but positively to aid and abet the schemes of dissimulation. In this respect, **La Veuve** resembles **Cinna** to the extent that the action marks the progress towards a narrowing of the gap between language and true feeling. That Corneille was fully aware of this emerges from both his comments on various plays and from what the characters themselves have to say in **La Veuve.** In the "Au Lecteur," deleted from 1644 onwards, he draws attention to the "naïveté du stile" to be found in the play (p. 5). What he means is that he wants to avoid linguistic pomp and circumstance or "l'esclat des vers" that would be a superimposed decoration and to ensure that a style commensurate with the action, tone and themes would be brought into play (cf. "La perfection des portraicts consiste en la ressemblance"). He was particularly pleased with the way the characters talked "en équivoques, et en propositions dont ils te laissent les conséquences à tirer," but this equivocity was after all no more than the linguistic correlative of psychological duplicity, so that he was finding his way towards a linguistic instrument that was capable of expressing a more sophisticated text than earlier comedy had provided. For this reason among others, we find him rejecting various stylistic and dramatic elements that had so far found favor. In the *Examen* he pointed to the "aversion naturelle que j'ay tousjours euë pour les *Aparte*" (p. 144). By *aparte* he means the type which is meant to reach the audience, not another character on stage or listening off stage; this latter category is legitimate in his view, and is in fact practiced in **La Veuve.** This is all the more interesting as the action might well, in principle, have called for extensive use of the *aparte* (p. 145). In avoiding it, Corneille was obliged to make much more use of dramatic irony and to sharpen his dialogue in such a way that the audience would obtain the information it needed from conversation of a more natural, but also more sophisticated nature. The elimination of such a dramatic device encourages the development of dialogue of finer precision and art. He also rejects the use of *pointes,* which he regarded as "fausses lumieres": compared with **Mélite,** he considered it "plus net et dégagé des pointes dont l'autre est semée" (p. 146). The reason for this is, as he suggests, that *pointes* are the expression of wit, certainly, but of an external wit, not that which stems from the conversation of characters. Here he may also be reacting against a feature of the Petrarchan idiom to which he was increasingly unsympathetic; but the important thing is that wit must derive from psychology and not remain purely decorative.

Here no doubt is one of the reasons why Corneille indulges in some satire of the Petrarchan idiom. This appears through the off-stage character Florange, ostensibly in love with Doris. He expresses himself in a series of clichés which Doris has little difficulty in deflating.[5] He talks like a book, having little experience of life—he has recently come down from the University; he imagines that to speak like a Petrarchan swain is to give proof of amatory sentiment, and if he goes off on another tack, it is to introduce trivial chitchat into his conversation—a theme incidentally that is echoed in Alcidon's comments on the local "salon." Corneille may be satirizing fashion, but he is also drawing attention to an exaggerated, possibly outworn idiom that has driven a wedge between the self and the communication of feeling. Such clichés are tantamount to a lack of sentiment, or, in a different context, to the presence of concealment. It may therefore be that Corneille's use of a certain linguistic "realism" is the reverse of this same medal. The dramatist is having to tread a middle path which allows him to remain within a language that certainly had precious features but does not attract caricature, and at the same time remains sufficiently supple and sharp to express sophisticated feeling and intelligence. Corneille is concentrating his attention on creating a linguistic vehicle that will not only correspond to the psychology of the characters—so that there will be no *pointes,* rhetoric or extraneous sources of comic such as the *aparte*—but will also fill the space left by the absence of elements of farce.

However, this problem is complicated by the fact that language seems to raise barriers between the self and other people; and the problem is doubly compounded when we are dealing with manifestations of hypocrisy, to which all the characters in greater or lesser degree are prone. The matter is raised by all the main characters: Alcidon, Philiste, Clarice and Célidan. The first scene introduces it as a major theme of the play: Philiste and Alcidon discuss to what extent love should be openly declared. Philiste tells his friend that he is afraid to speak his feelings unambiguously to Clarice, for he believes that such an overt expression would provoke an unwelcome response—of course, this is a theme that gained currency in part through the vogue of Petrarchism. To give verbal shape to a sentiment is possibly to kill it; in I, sc. I, Philiste goes so far as to suggest that signs may be more useful than words. And so he holds his peace (as did Florange on occasion to Doris—once again the echo technique is at work). It may be that Philiste is deeply suspicious of a certain love idiom (such as Petrarchism), but his critique goes further than this. Alcidon, on the other hand, defends the contrary point of view: frankness in such matters is more wholesome and will lead to a happy outcome. Of course, in the event neither man is being entirely honest: Alcidon, who agrees secretly with part of what Philiste tells him, wants him to declare his love, so that he, Alcidon, will benefit from the lady's expected response. Philiste, for his part, believes that his view, which is really tactical, will lure the lady into a receptive state of mind and thus attain his goal. So here Corneille is linking two questions, the unpredictable, harmful or ineffectual consequences of language, and the various motives that lie behind.

Alcidon marks, one may think, a halfway house between Eraste (*Mélite*) and Dorante (*Le Menteur*). Language is the means whereby he manipulates others—indeed, language more often than not works in the register of *avoir* and not of *être*. He has not reached the stage where language (the form of his duplicity) begins to take on a life of its own so that he is, as it were, carried off into a private world created by the hot air of his rhetoric. He thus does not take on the comic characteristics of Matamore (*Illusion*) or Dorante, but he is not far related: his feelings for Clarice do not seem to be at all that deep, witness his reactions at the end of the play; and his vanity suggests that his self-engrossed cleverness is more important in his eyes. I do not think that he develops such a measure of linguistic dynamism as Dorante and other characters in whom rhetoric is the yardstick of their hypocrisy or mythomania; but he does illustrate the manner in which language can become a means of betrayal, and of removal from the mainsprings of life.

Célidan and Clarice echo in their different ways the themes developed by Alcidon and Philiste: Clarice wishes for a greater outspokenness on the part of her lover, and Célidan duplicates Philiste to the extent that he puts himself at a disadvantage in his relations with Alcidon because he is silent about his love for Doris, though the reasons for his silence are naturally different. Silence is ultimately condemned, for it prevents the beloved from understanding what is going on, and it may create situations which unscrupulous persons can turn to their own advantage.

So, for Corneille, a major dramatic problem is how he is going to bring out into the open the latent feelings of the true lovers. Nor is it simply a technical matter: if the genuine feelings are not given their full ventilation, the gyrations of Alcidon and the Nourrice will seem to be working in a void.

III

One obvious, traditional means is the monologue. At that period, monologues still enjoy considerable popularity; they are an ideal way of communicating to the audience feelings that the characters are unable or unwilling to express to one another. Interestingly, the device is reduced to the bare minimum where Alcidon is concerned: he needs other persons to develop himself. But Philiste and Clarice each have a solo scene couched in lyrical *stances*: this medium of heightened feeling introduces an important tonal quality into the play as a whole, though it may also be exploited for dramatic effect, when Clarice is abducted immediately after her

stances. It will be recalled that Act I opened in a tone of less than total sincerity, even on the part of Philiste, so that a curtain where genuine emotion has broken through restores a badly needed balance. Philiste's *stances* in the opening scene of Act II (originally addressed to his feelings, whereas in 1660 they are discussed in the third person) rely much on an antithetical presentation for their effect and have more than a trace of preciosity ("Secrets tyrans de ma pensée," "plein de grace et de feu," "mon âme dans cet esclavage," etc.), but he does not come to grips with the difficulties raised by his silence. Clarice, in a metrical scheme that is perhaps more subtle, knows from Philiste's eyes rather than from his language ("propos mystérieux") that his love is real; but she senses that there is no gap between feeling and language ("L'amour est maintenant le maistre de nos bouches / Ainsi que de nos cœurs," ll. 1145-46). Philiste's monologue in Act IV, sc. 2, after Clarice's kidnapping, allows him to give vent to his feelings—love, but mingled with despair, *rage,* suffering. Here the more exalted alexandrine is pressed into service. The *fureur* scenes (especially Act IV, sc. I) may belong to a tradition of burlesque, inherited from tragi-comedy or tragedy, and popular enough at the time; but Corneille is using the tradition in its essential spirit, so that the tone of the play is deepened. Once again, consecrated or popular elements that were dramatically effective in their own right are employed only because they reflect the feelings of the characters and are seen as a valid means of their expression.

The most important, and most difficult, manifestation of feeling is to be found in the scenes between Philiste and Clarice; here we see feeling and wit mingling to suggest, often in oblique fashion, the love that exists between Philiste and Clarice. We have seen that Philiste is a man of strong feelings; only in his dealings with Clarice is he tongue-tied.[6] Clarice is a more sedate person but her love is inhibited in its expression of sentiment, perhaps a trace of *amour-propre.* So in the two scenes between Philiste and Clarice (Act I, sc. 5 and Act II, sc. 5) Corneille's problem is to find ways and means of transmitting to the audience (as well as to the two characters) their underlying emotions. Philiste resorts to such oblique reference (by means of the local salon) that Clarice wonders whether he is not in love with one of its denizens. The first scene is mostly an exercise in imperfect communication, and Philiste's expatiating on his theory of love and silence does nothing to help matters. The second scene still shows him on the defensive, though he had previously had doubts about the wisdom of his silent tactics:

> Pourquoy m'imaginer qu'un discours amoureux,
> Par un contraire effet change un amour en haine,
> Et malgré mon bon-heur me rende malheureux?

> (II, sc. I, ll. 448-50)

His language verges on the precious; he indulges in *sententiae* which generalize his experience; he sketches, with a flourish of oblique rhetoric, a theory of love that Dagoucin himself would have rejected. Then when Clarice is impelled to take the initiative, he is unable to believe his ears, partly perhaps he is hoist with the petard of his own theories, for he accuses Clarice of an *accorte feinte* herself. So that the stratagem of the catcher caught is to be found at a variety of levels in the play. In Act V, sc. 7, where the two meet on their own before the dénouement, the salon theme is reintroduced into their dialogue, partly for dramatic symmetry, partly because their playfulness is an oblique expression of feeling reciprocated; and in the final scene, from 1660 Corneille removes the trace of a dialogue that was exchanged between them; paradoxically, silence is in order, now that true feelings are uninhibited.

The third device is the juxtaposition of the scenes enacted between Philiste and Clarice, and those between Alcidon and Doris, so that the genuine and the bogus are thrown into evident contrast. Corneille pointed to the link himself when he wrote (in the *Examen*) about painting

> un amour reciproque, qui parust dans les entretiens de deux personnes qui ne parlent point d'amour ensemble, et de mettre des complimens d'amour suivis entre deux gens qui n'en ont point du tout l'un pour l'autre.
>
> (p. 145)

Thus the scenes between Alcidon and Doris form a sort of descant on those involving the true lovers. Alcidon, as we know, is using Doris as a means of access to Clarice, and Doris goes through the gestures and language of love simply because her brother had asked her to do so; but she is more clear-sighted than Alcidon for all his cleverness. He, ironically, uses the language of love, because on his own theory love must always be openly expressed, but also because he fondly imagines that Doris is in love with him. But Corneille may be using amatory language ironically here: for instance, *braise* is used to describe Alcidon's passion; it disappears in 1660, probably because it was no longer acceptable to good taste. But perhaps it was already overprecious when the play was performed and therefore telling in Alcidon's mouth.[7] He even suggests that his incompetent language is due to the force of his feelings, "En peux tu recevoir de l'entretien d'un homme / Qui t'explique si mal le feu qui le consomme?" (ll. 671-72), and he goes on to complain that words fail to correspond to the feelings within. Later on, he amplifies this in a scene with Philiste (whom he is duping) in a remark that has wider application:

> . . . Qu'à grand peine deux mots se peuvent eschapper
> Sans quelque double sens afin de nous tromper,

> Et que souvent de bouche un dessein se propose
> Ce pendant que l'esprit songe à tout autre chose.
>
> (ll. 913-16)

All this allows for a display of contrasted styles between Doris and Alcidon, the latter becoming more and more devious and involved, she more forthright and in a position to use dramatic irony, a device on which the play relies for a great deal of its effect. Interestingly, in Act III, sc. 3, Doris uses monetary imagery to expose Alcidon's linguistic duplicity; and we know from other scenes, notably those where Chrysante appears, exactly what the more sympathetic characters think of money as the measure of all things. But the fun of the scenes lies in the fact, pointed out by Doris, that they resemble one another to the extent that their feelings are not expressed by their language. She also observes that Alcidon knows nothing about love; so that in practice Alcidon confirms, against his own statements, the gap between language and feeling of which Philiste talks so much.

IV

The psychological "données" of the action make it difficult for the lovers to mingle "wit" and feeling in one and the same scene; only occasionally does the combination peep through the veils and filters. But Corneille goes to evident pains to see that true emotion is adequately shown on the stage. The rest of the play should be apprehended with the help of this touchstone. This does not mean that wit is absent from other characters or situations, on the contrary. It arises in the main through two mechanisms: either the contrast of false and genuine sentiment (e.g., Alcidon-Doris), or from an intelligence, usually sharpened by emotion, in conflict with one that is more sluggish through routine, unawareness or vanity. The devices used form a fairly tight cluster and by systematic exploitation they serve to confer a sense of unity of the play: echo techniques, repetition of various kinds, dramatic irony, the working out of themes, situations and stratagems in such a way that they are not confined to one character. All this not only produces a thematic unity, but expresses less cynicism than a Montaignian awareness of the complexity of human nature and its motivation, and of the relations between language and feelings.

This last matter is a major theme, and one may speculate whether the writing of the play, in addition to stemming from Corneille's concern with the problem, did not increase his understanding. Stylistically, this shows in his rejection of effects that were in some measure dissociated from the psychology of the characters: *pointes* (though traces remain, for instance, in the endings of Philiste's *stances*), lines that would impress by literary merit ("vers . . . puissants et majestueux," "Au Lecteur," p. 5), eccentricities of Petrarchan origin and so forth. When figures of traditional rhetoric are pressed into service, they suit situation and pychology. Thus stichomythia occurs more often than not in scenes where different sets of values are contrasted (Philiste and Chrysante) or where a character is being unmasked by another now wise to the situation (Philiste, Nourrice). It does not appear as a means of heightened emotion expressed between major characters at a moment of crisis. *Sententiae* are infrequent: they will be found when the Nourrice is speaking, or when Alcidon tries to reinforce his (bogus) attitude to friendship, or when Philiste converts his personal feelings into generalized experience. Corneille does not as a rule exploit wordplay, though the double-entendre, the inevitable concomitant of dramatic irony, naturally comes into play, as for example when Célidan says to Alcidon "Une subtilité si dextrement tissuë / Ne peut jamais avoir qu'une admirable issuë" (ll. 1683-84). However, when Corneille makes Célidan, who has pierced Alcidon's devious plans, say "C'est ainsi que tu veux m'obliger doublement" (l. 138), one may think that *doublement* should be taken in two ways.

On the other hand, Corneille is concerned to forge a linguistic instrument which is able, not only to show the duplicity of language, but to take advantage of this state of affairs. What he is in the process of creating in **La Veuve** is an instrument that is shorn of literary cliché and traditions, but is not simply a more "realistic" phenomenon. The realistic elements of language are fairly superficial; what is more important is that Corneille is creating a language that is certainly literary (note over the years his concessions to the evolution of taste) but acquires strength partly because it is closer to the sources of motive and conduct, but also because it carries within itself the seeds of its own comic. By rejecting the registers of farce, of Petrarchism, and certain rhetorical elements, he has narrowed the linguistic range within which he must work, but he has explored in greater depth the possibilities it contained. Of course, it could be said that some of the techniques of farce have become verbalized and incorporated into a higher form of comedy. With the passage of time there comes not only a certain *épuration* of the vocabulary, but a refinement of other elements. Roques and Lièvre in their introduction note that **La Veuve** was less altered in subsequent editions than **Mélite,** but they add "les variantes portent surtout sur la qualité du vocabulaire et du style et la bienséance des manières" (p. xxxvii), an observation that confirms our view of Corneille's linguistic sensitivity in this play, reflecting both his own development and the changes in contemporary taste. Of course, there are minor alterations that show Corneille looking for a more precise epithet or changing its position in the line; sometimes a variant indicates a different attitude to a character, as in l. 1910 where "Ce colere Alcidon" becomes "Ce bizarre Alcidon," Elsewhere, stylistic considerations are in play: in l. 69,

"Ses soupirs et les miens" becomes "Mes soupirs et les siens," probably to avoid the repetition of *Ses* at the beginning of the line. But other variants are more fundamental: there is an undoubted reduction of staccato effects and broken lines, in favor of more sustained rhythms. Thus ll. 31-32, "Ouy j'en doute et l'exces de ma beatitude / Est le seul fondement de mon incertitude," become "Ouy, j'en doute, et l'exces du bonheur qui m'accable / Me surprend, me confond, me paroist incroyable," where an increased dynamism is imparted to the lines, brought about by both the triadic movement and the cluster of more active verbs. Elsewhere, rapid exchanges are removed: ll. 1669-73 are a good illustration of this, and in ll. 1910-14, Alcidon's interruption of Philiste is excised in 1660.

Particularly noteworthy is the reduction of a vocabulary that, originally heard as frank and perhaps familiar, may offend the ears of a later generation. Words and phrases such as *lourdaut* or *toucher la grosse corde* (l. 53) make way for more refined language. Even a phrase like *C'est bien le mot pour rire* (l. 202) disappears in later editions; as do such words as *gourmand* (l. 44), *brasser* (ll. 134 and 653), *baiser* (ll. 72, 729, etc.), and *œillade,* which becomes *prunelle* in l. 204. It is perhaps for reasons of decorum that the Nourrice's resemblance to a witch is toned down: thus ll. 528-31

PHILISTE:

   . . . Vien ça que je t'estrangle.

LA NOURRICE:

   Ah, ah.

PHILISTE:

            Crache, parjure,
   Ton ame abominable, et que l'enfer attend,

LA NOURRICE:

   De grace quatre mots, et tu seras content.

PHILISTE:

   Et je seray content! qui te fait si hardie . . .

disappear from 1660 on; the forthrightness of the language may well have jarred by then. But even an image as anodyne as "un ver de jalousie" (l. 947) makes way for the colorless "un peu de jalousie." Alternations are much in evidence in the language of love: here two different considerations are at work. On the other hand, the amatory vocabulary of the 1630's has taken on a shop-soiled air: *feux* disappears, as does *braise,* and ll. 81-83,

   Et que le peu souvent que ce bon-heur arrive
   Picquant nostre appetit tend sa pointe plus vive,
   Nostre flamme irritée en croist de jour en jour,

become

> Et mille autres douceurs aux seuls amants connuës
> Nous font voir chaque jour nos amies toutes nuës,
> Nous sont de bons garands d'un feu qui chaque
>   jour. . . .

These lines are spoken by Philiste and they raise the other problem that was probably in Corneille's mind. Earlier, I mentioned that the dramatist had poked fun at the Petrarchan love idiom through the invisible character Florange. For readers of today the distinction between an outworn Petrarchan idiom and an acceptable precious language may not always be clear cut, and no doubt Corneille had to tread a cautious middle path which kept him clear of obvious pitfalls. However, with the passage of time, the distinctions would be blurred even for the public of 1660, and Corneille would be faced with the problem of Philiste using a language of love that must not be exposed to the irony with which he had treated Petrarchism in his younger days. It is therefore not surprising that Philiste's opening scene with Alcidon contains considerable corrections along these lines. Ll. 21-23,

> Sans te mettre en soucy du feu qui me consomme
> Appren comment l'amour se traicte en honneste
>   homme
> Aussi tost qu'une Dame en ses retz nous a pris,

become in 1660

> Sans te mettre en soucy quelle en sera la suite
> Appren comment l'amour doit regler sa conduite,
> Aussitost qu'une Dame a charmé nos esprits.

The evolution of public taste no doubt deprived Corneille to some extent of one of his linguistic tools intended to ward off the dangers of language; his "realism" in this domain was alas whittled away as the century drew on. But if his sensitivity to developing taste brought some disadvantage in its train, there were compensations, for his language acquired gradually more finesse, it becomes more capable of refined irony, and it is less dependent on dramatic devices that he had earlier used for certain effects. One illustration may be taken from l. 1298. Originally it read "Quoy? ta poltronnerie a changé bien soudain." In 1660 it became "J'admire avec plaisir ce changement soudain," where the interrogative had disappeared and a more elegant balance of the hemistiches has been created.

Obviously, more could be said on this score; but *La Veuve,* probably underestimated these days, is an excellent example of the way Corneille is working towards a solution of the linguistic problems posed, on the one hand, by his view of human nature, and on the other, by his wish to avoid certain well-worn dramatic devices for which he had lost his taste. What is emerging is a

linguistic tool that conveys admirably his awareness of the different layers of behavior, the relations between *paraître* and *être,* and the balance between feeling and intelligence. And the variants, over the years, show that though he is highly sensitive to the vagaries of taste, such is his mastery of language that the need to sacrifice something of a relative linguistic "realism" helps him, in the long run, to evolve a more sophisticated style.

Notes

1. I use the edition prepared by Mario Roques and Marion Liève for the *TLF*: Pierre Corneille, *La Veuve,* comédie, texte de la première édition (1634) publié avec les variantes (Geneva-Lille, 1954).

2. J. Boorsch, "Remarques sur la technique dramatique de Corneille," in *Studies by Members of the French Department of Yale University,* ed. A. Feuillerat, Yale Romance Studies, 18 (1941), pp. 101-62.

3. The older Corneille showed concern about aspects of Act V (*Examen*).

4. Hans Verhoeff, *Les Comédies de Corneille. Une psycholecture* (Paris, 1979).

5. These views are echoed by Géron.

6. Peter Bürger, *Die frühen Komödien Pierre Corneilles und das französische Theater von 1630* (Frankfurt-am-Main), esp. pp. 174-82.

7. On the language of preciosity see Roger Lathuillère, *La Préciosité. Etude historique et linguistique,* I (Geneva, 1966).

LA SUIVANTE (THE MAIDSERVANT)

CRITICAL COMMENTARY

James F. Gaines (essay date 1988)

SOURCE: Gaines, James F. "Usurpation and Heroic Lies: A Baroque Dilemma in *La Suivante.*" *Papers on French Seventeenth Century Literature* 15, no. 29 (1988): 451-62.

[*In the following essay, Gaines contends that the usurpation of social rank plays a prominent role in* The Maidservant.]

It is not astonishing that usurpation of social rank, the manipulation of appearances in order to lay claim to an unauthorized essential identity, should play a prominent role in the evolution of baroque social comedy, especially in France, where mobility was slower and more strictly regulated than in most other European lands. But one is perhaps surprised to find the topic making its debut in the early works of Pierre Corneille, who has been classified not infrequently as the ultimate vicarious spokesman for nobiliary *gloire* and qualitative heroism.[1] A deeper look, particularly at the dramatist's "middle period" dispels this impression. From *La Mort de Pompée* to *Pertharite,* from *Agésilas* to *Nicomède,* his tragedies reveal an ongoing preoccupation with usurpation in its more customary royal aspect, a trend that parallels the comic instances because it is based on the same principles—merit versus birth, material expediency versus abstract law.[2]

In *La Suivante,* which dates from about 1634, Corneille presents the problems of a would-be usurper in the mundane light of courtship. Though banal, this background is also fundamentally important, for Serge Doubrovsky has shown that the gilded youth of Cornelian comedy use amorous adventures as a substitute for the alienated domain of military combat, a proving ground for identity and power.[3] Jean-Marie Apostolidès sees most of seventeenth-century drama as a displaced form of ritual that "masks" the primitive aristocratic sacrifice of blood on the battlefield.[4] In *La Suivante,* it is clear that courtship is the key to affiliation, to the future, to fate itself. Like the resplendent warriors of *Le Cid* or *Horace,* the usurpers attempt to dazzle those around them who will testify to the apotheosis of their merit or the ignominy of their humiliation. Usurpation is a lie, but as André Rousseaux pointed out, it is a lie that purports to be heroic, an effort to impose pure will on the unchanging, and yet ever-changing, shape of the universe.[5]

The title of *La Suivante* designates a new class of serving-woman who had only recently emerged in French society and on the stage. In the author's previous comedy, *La Galerie du Palais,* a minor character first appeared with that label, replacing the stereotypical nurse or *duenna* inherited from Latin, Spanish, and Italian theater. The *suivante* was essentially a lady's companion rather than simply a maid. Though not exactly a peer of the woman she served, the *suivante* was entitled to a higher degree of respect than other servants, largely because she often came from a bourgeois background and may have known a loftier way of life before some financial misfortune forced her to enter service. Her language, her manner of dress, and her habits distinguished her from the downtrodden scullery girls and *bonnes de chambre* who occupied the lowest rungs of the domestic hierarchy. Corneille in fact depicts the mistress addressing her *suivante* with the

honorific pronoun *vous* instead of the condescending *tu* prescribed for humble folk. Paradoxically, the creation of the *suivante* was due to a usurping tendency within the households of the bourgeoisie, who sought to ape the fashions of the court, where titled ladies served as *dames suivantes* to the female members of the royal family.

However, Corneille's protagonist, Amarante, is not content with her ambiguous station and wishes to astound her employers by marrying out of servitude, into the aristocracy. A century before the irrepressible maids of Marivaux and Richardson fling open the doors of the domestic prison, Amarante calls upon her innate qualities to restore her to dignity, under the rallying cry "Le mérite y fait tout" (223).[6] If love is the yardstick of status, she will become the rival of her own mistress Daphnis and compete for the attentions and commitment of two noble suitors, Théante and Florame, who frequent old Géraste's mansion.

The fact that Amarante not only catches the eye of these gallants but elicits some expression of love on their part is an almost unheard of coup for someone of her station. The conquests make her bold enough to boast of her superior charms and to use a sophisticated, even heroic vocabulary to describe her influence over the young men: "La difficulte d'une telle victoire / M'en augmente l'ardeur comme elle en croît la gloire" (197-98). When Florame complains of the difficulty of reconciling his attraction to Amarante with his friendship for Théante, the *suivante* replies with lofty lines that echo many tragic kings: "Je ne prendrai jamais pour un manque de foi / D'oublier un ami pour se donner à moi" (207-08). She pointedly calls the gentlemen her "servants" and uses their "hommage" to contradict the cruel reality of her dependency in Géraste's household.

Since Amarante's supposed control of the hearts of noble suitors entails a stunning testimony to her surpassing personal merit, this amatory victory over her mistress offers moral and tangible consolation for the misfortunes that have reduced her to domestic servitude. While she enjoys the flattering ministrations of fashionable *beaux* like Théante and Florame, Daphnis must content herself with the admiration of Clarimond, a vapid and undesirable creature. Although it soon becomes obvious that Théante is planning to shift his attention to Daphnis and has introduced Florame into the household only to distract Amarante during this maneuver, she finds a pat explanation for this defection in the motives of greed: "Il voudrait pour m'aimer que j'eusse d'autres charmes, / Que l'éclat de mon sang, mieux soutenu de biens, / Ne fût point ravalé par le rang que je tiens" (302-04). She is absolutely correct in this analysis, for Théante crassly abandons himself to the pursuit of a hefty dowry without ever being able to completely stifle the tender emotions he feels for the serving lady. And if she fails to conquer the heart of Florame, it is only because this Machiavelli of the boudoir is quite indifferent to any fine sentiments and, like the consummate actor of Diderot's *Paradoxe sur le comédien,* succeeds best in projecting what he can never feel. According to the codes of tenderness, Amarante deserves the credit she has gained and more besides. She does not belong alongside the imaginary coquettes who are mocked in the comedies of Desmarets de Saint-Sorlin and Molière.[7]

But what precisely is the value of the inborn quality that Amarante expresses in the phrase "l'éclat de mon sang?" The term *sang* usually denotes in this context some hereditary dignity that could scarcely be claimed by anyone below the more comfortable levels of the bourgeoisie. Having been raised in such circumstances, was she obliged to forsake a decent marriage because elder sisters exhausted the family's dowry funds—a not uncommon occurrence? Or was she the victim of some sudden disaster that left her without parents or protectors and forced her to seek service in the households of her former neighbors and equals? The case was frequent enough to be described by La Bruyère in "Des Biens de fortune," no. 6.[8] If, before succumbing to financial difficulty, Amarante's father had followed the bourgeois practice of designating himself "noble homme" in his contracts and of owning a country property that could pass for an estate, the young lady could well maintain an illusion of dignity, a pride in lineage that would survive collapse or bankruptcy. But the social theorists of Louis XIII's reign were categorical in their denial of such aspirations: any person unable to maintain the lifestyle suitable to his or her hierarchical position, whether of ancient or recent nobility, royal officer or bourgeois "living nobly" from rents, loses the right to that dignity. This point was all the more poignantly obvious to the public in an age when the threat of *recherches de noblesse,* or royal inquests into nobiliary claims, was becoming more and more pressing. Amarante's poverty nullifies her right to her self-professed status.[9]

Thus, the *suivante*'s pretensions are both fully heroic and fully equivocal. By trying to behave like an aristocratic object of love, she is seeking to escape from a network of monetary contingencies that controls not only her fate, but that of her masters as well. It is a leap to independence, however imaginary, that, as Bernard Dort has pointed out, exercised an ongoing fascination for Corneille.[10] While Géraste and his clan remain frankly reliant on their strongboxes full of wealth, Amarante intends to bypass the stage of identity through quantifiable possession to attain an identity based absolutely on the perfect union of objective appearance and innate worth. But Géraste warns his servant in the third act that her hypergamous dreams risk a rude awakening, for hers is not the only lie at work: "Où les

conditions n'ont point d'égalité, / L'amour ne se fait guère avec sincérité" (835-36).

Amarante's equivocation may be the most striking in the play, but by the same token it is the least effective. Daphnis continually sends her servant off on false errands to facilitate her rendezvous with her lovers, and beguiles her with promises of non-intervention. Théante attempts to trick Amarante by foisting her off on his friend Florame so that he can try his hand at capturing Daphnis' dowry. His confidant, "faithful Damis," betrays every one of his secrets to anyone who will listen. In reality, the only one Théante succeeds in tricking is himself, since Florame no sooner enters the house than he begins to negotiate with both daughter and father more successfully than Théante had done. The shameless friend has an unanticipated trump to play, inasmuch as he is willing to give his sister to Géraste in exchange for Daphnis.

Géraste's lust for this sister Florise, who never appears on stage, is more than simply a flight of sexagenarian fancy, since it is connected closely to the old man's ideology of financial exchange. Neither noble nor common blood has any worth other than that which is granted by money. It goes to follow that there should be nothing strange about a mismatch between a poor noblewoman and a rich bourgeois, as long as her consent can be bought with cash. Géraste bids the pandering Célie, "Dis-lui que si l'amour d'un vieillard l'importune, / Elle fait une planche à sa bonne fortune, / Que l'excès de mes biens, à force de présents, / Répare la vigueur qui manque à mes vieux ans" (353-57). Although Géraste is willing to sanction this prostitution beneath the façade of marriage, there is nothing conventional about it. The noblewoman would not only be degraded by marriage with a commoner, but also effectively sterilized in his icy clutches. Yet there is no question of her consent, since she is under the control of her brother, already reified and assimilated, like everyone else in the play, by the determinism of surplus wealth, which has been identified by Knutson and Bürger.[11] Both for Florame and for her father, Daphnis is reduced by the fourth act to a mere *prix.* The transports of love, described in **La Galerie du Palais** as a mixture of "attraction, sweet swooning, delightful dalliance and wild abandon," are here reduced to *contentement,* the measured satisfaction of desires both sexual and financial.

At the end of the second act, the fundamental exchange between Florame and Géraste is all but concluded, and the compliance of the girls assured. While Théante seeks to resuscitate his heroic lie by luring Florame into a duel with Clarimond, Amarante confronts her mistress directly with a bitter protest. "Il faudrait vous céder," she complains, "C'est ainsi qu'avec vous je ne puis rien garder" (539-40). The manner in which Corneille portrays the servant's impotence and humiliation blocks any growth of sympathy on the part of the spectator. But on the other hand, one is forced to acknowledge the point that she drives home in mock-tragic fashion, namely that her pretensions spring from the sacrosanct bourgeois principles of liberty and property.

Clarimond is the key to the secondary lies that Amarante and Théante generate in the "tourbillon de mensonges" that occupies the latter half of the play.[12] On the one hand, Théante's forged challenge is designed to provoke a bloody showdown between Clarimond and Florame which will lead to the death, imprisonment, or exile of the latter, thus leaving Théante free to woo Daphnis. At the same time, Amarante, hoping that confusion will stall and embroil matters so that she may rescue one suitor from the affair, falsely announces that Daphnis has named Clarimond as her choice for husband. When Géraste sees his deal with Florame obstructed, and assumes that his daughter is resisting his authority, perhaps he may react rashly enough to remove her, at least temporarily, as a rival for the affections of the young men. Both plots present considerable opportunity for Clarimond, provided that he is able to take on the trappings of a pre-existing, traditional order that successfully offers an alternative to the cynical, superficial codes of financial reification.

It is not to be, for now that Amarante's attempt to cheat fate has become contingent on the actions of male "champions," the heroic lie can only collapse into a harmless, conventional *feinte.* Just when the men in the play are on the point of ceasing to treat the women as appraisable "goods" and when they profess their readiness to "win Daphnis at the point of the sword," Théante's basic bad faith comes into play. Florame, informed of the intrigue by the ever-treacherous Damis, names Théante as his second. Even though Clarimond is reputed to be a mediocre fencer, Théante is uncomfortable in this exposed position, especially since "La valeur aux duels fait moins que la fortune" (1226). Unwilling to contain his fear or to shoulder the responsibility for violence, Théante interrupts the combat as it is about to begin and effects a reconciliation between Florame and Clarimond, without confessing to his deception. From that point on, his entire course of behavior during the denouement involves both a denial of his intrigues and a denial of self, for any admission of emotional dependency on either Daphnis or her underling would make manifest his hierarchical submission to Florame. Amarante must be sacrificed: "Bien que ses yeux encor règnent sur mon courage, / Le bonheur de Florame à la quitter m'engage" (1413-14). He fears that by allowing any disparity of success to develop between himself and Florame, he would sink from his rival to be his follower, and vows henceforth to indulge only in emotions that will make him greater than the competition. Though framed in mock-heroic

terms, this discourse is merely a smoke screen for retreat: rather than continuing to vie with Florame in the salons of Paris, Théante withdraws to exile in Italy. His abandonment of the heroic lie illustrates a maxim of La Rochefoucauld: "One often passes from love to ambition, but almost never from ambition to love" (n. 490, p. 110).

Amarante's initiative meets with no more success than Théante's, for although she is able to stir up a family quarrel, the mutual interests of father and daughter are too obvious to remain hidden for long. The *suivante* finally acknowledges defeat: "Daphnis me le ravit, non par son beau visage, / Non par son bel esprit ou ses doux entretiens, / Non que sur moi sa race ait aucun avantage, / Mais par le seul éclat qui sort d'un peu de biens" (1669-72). Her anger focuses on her employer, who is strolling in the garden, awaiting the delivery of the bride who symbolizes the troubling fusion of noble status and bourgeois wealth, and whose absence throughout the action coincides with an erotic void. In place of the traditional shivaree accorded to a May-December marriage, she casts a curse on the new social order that has excluded her, and hopes that Géronte will soon be haunted in his tomb by chagrin and remorse, as his young mate rejoices over his death.

If Amarante is, in Marie-Odile Sweetser's words, "malicious," or in those of Roger Guichemerre, "perfidious," it is a symptom of a more widespread social malignancy in Corneille's theater, and her renunciation of that universe recalls the final consciousness of previous characters, such as Philandre, the deceived lover in **Mélite,** or Angélique, the reified lady in **La Place Royale** who finally exclaims "Je me veux exempter de ce honteux commerce."[13] In a world of disintegrating values and ephemeral promises, plagued by an enormous crisis of degree, Amarante is the heroine of a fairy tale in reverse, a Cendrillon whose fourflushing prince charming smashes the glass slipper and happily moves in with the affluent step-sister. Instead of fulfilling her merit, the degrading spell of money transforms her into a malevolent witch, whose sorcery falls on the wizened *magister ludi* of financial exchange. This comedy reveals a transitional state of social consciousness, which recognizes neither the bourgeoisie nor the aristocracy as an institutional embodiment or legitimate prescriber of ideal order. Fully informed of the flaws in the social hierarchy, Corneille nevertheless depicts Paris as an amoral "capitale de la métamorphose," where idealized codes of heroism and supremacy are exposed to unremitting counterfeiting. The phrase comes from **Le Menteur,** which inherits and develops the usurpation theme to attain a new level of virtuosity, while buffering the social shock effect of a protagonist who is rich, male, *haut bourgeois,* and protected by indulgent relatives and friends.[14]

The chivalric nostalgia that Bénichou sees at work in the author's tragedies is progressively exorcised in **La Suivante,** as the usurper, within the parameters of merit as she construes it, strives to outperform her "legitimate" counterpart, only to be subjugated by a financial determinism that belies the basis of any hereditary scale of value. Amarante's heroic lies appear justified to the extent that they demonstrate an ambition to seek a reasonable place for manifest merit in the face of an equivocal society. But their failure reminds one that they are far from any kind of critical confrontation between sets of collective values, such as one finds in Diderot, or even in the contemporary comedy of Pierre Du Ryer, whose *Vendanges de Suresne* present a moralistic polarization between a bourgeoisie proud of its progress and a rapacious bogey-man of an aristocracy. If usurpation is undercut, it is by an essential element of contingency, for any attempt to master the realm of appearances in spite of the logic of capital is doomed to failure. And here lies the truly troubling, subversive idea for the bourgeoisie of both the seventeenth century and today: that the concept of a completely noncontingent haven at the summit of a financially operative hierarchy may be no more than a liar's dream.

Notes

1. See for example Paul Bénichou, *Morales du grand siècle.* Second ed. (Paris: Gallimard, 1967), pp. 80-84, 92-93; and Serge Doubrovsky, *Corneille et la dialectique du héros* (Paris: Gallimard, 1963), pp. 35-37, 55-59. Pierre Goubert, in *L'Ancien Régime* (Paris: Armand Colin, 1973), points out that the crisis of this troubled nobility sought outlets not only through revolt or acquiescence, but also through various types of "liberal" reform (II, 69-71).

2. Tragic usurpers are in fact often brought closer to their comic counterparts by the epithets cast upon them by the spokesman of legitimacy; consider for example the way Cléopâtre in *La Mort de Pompée* attributes her brother's coup to the influence of his low-born advisors Photin, Achillas, and Septime, "Ces âmes que le ciel ne forma que de boue" (I, 3, 265).

3. Doubrovsky, pp. 76-83.

4. Jean-Marie Apostolidès, *Le Prince sacrifié* (Paris: Editions de Minuit, 1985), pp. 11-24.

5. Rousseaux is referring mainly to Dorante, the hero of *Le Menteur,* whom he sees as the ultimate defender of magic, secular values, love, and progress—in brief, of all human existence. See "Corneille ou le mensonge héroïque," in *Le Monde classique* (Paris: A. Michel, 1944), pp. 37-68.

6. All quotes come from André Stegmann's edition: Pierre Corneille, *Oeuvres complètes* (Paris: Seuil, 1963).

7. The two most notable of these hallucinating sweethearts are Hortense of Desmarets' *Visionnaires* and Bélise of *Les Femmes savantes.*

8. "Deux marchands étaient voisins et faisaient le même commerce, qui ont eu dans la suite une fortune toute différente. Ils avaient chacun une fille unique; elles ont été nourries ensemble, et ont vécu dans cette familiarité que donnent un même âge et une même condition: l'une des deux, pour se tirer d'une extrême misère, cherche à se placer; elle entre au service d'une fort grande dame et l'une des premières de la cour, chez sa compagne." La Bruyère, *Oeuvres complètes,* ed. Julian Benda (Paris: Gallimard, 1951), p. 177.

9. See my discussion of the codes of *dérogeance* that apply to the bourgeoisie as well as to the aristocrats in *Social Structures in Molière's Theater* (Columbus, Ohio: Ohio State University Press, 1984), pp. 176-77, 192-93. On the anxiety caused by the *recherches de noblesse,* see Roland Mousnier, *Les Hiérchies sociales de 1450 à nos jours* (Paris: PUF, 1969), pp. 61-85; and Goubert, *L'Ancien Régime,* I, 128-203.

10. Dort's analysis tends to stress the stodgy, bourgeois elements in Corneille's background, his role as an *officier,* his roots in Rouen, and his attachment to the Church; see *Corneille* (Paris: L'Arche, 1957), pp. 8-18, 31-35. This middle-class conservatism does much to explain his subsequent loyalty during the Fronde revolt and his refusal to relocate to Paris, which was part of the reason for his rejection by the Académie in 1646, when Maynard's chair was accorded instead to his old Parisian rival Du Ryer. Another predominantly bourgeois interpretation of Corneille's theater is to be found in Valdemar Vedel's *Deux classiques français vus par un étranger,* trans. E. Cornet (Paris: Champion, 1935), pp. 11-25, 71-77.

11. Harold Knutson, "Corneille's Early Comedies: Variations in Comic Form," in *Corneille comique,* ed. Milorad Margitic, *Biblio 17,* n. 4 (Paris, Seattle, and Tübingen: *PFSCL,* 1982), pp. 44-49; Peter Bürger, *Die frühen Komödien Pierre Corneilles und das französischen Theater um 1630* (Frankfurt-am-Main: Suhrkamp, 1971), pp. 191ff.

12. The whirlwind imagery comes from Octave Nadal, *Le Sentiment de l'amour dans l'oeuvre de Pierre Corneille* (Paris: Gallimard, 1948), p. 105.

13. Linking Amarante with Dorante and other noncomic figures such as Cléopâtre in *Rodogune,* Marie-Odile Sweetser observes that the unhappy end of the protagonist, which fails to elicit the sympathy of the audience, nevertheless contains in its grotesque spectacle the seeds of tragic catastro-

phe; see *La Dramaturgie de Corneille* (Geneva: Droz, 1977), pp. 94-98. See also Roger Guichemerre, "Le Personnage du rival perfide dans les premières comédies de Pierre Corneille," in *Corneille comique*, pp. 63-66. Milorad Margitic specifies that Corneille's characters give rise to laughter to the extent that their pretensions fail to match with interior or exterior reality and their ostensible ego thus appears more or less false or absurd (Corneille, *La Suivante,* ed., M. Margitic (Geneva: Droz, 1978), pp. xxxviii-xlii). But Amarante, whose demythification is completed by the end of the second act, is somewhat of an exception to this general rule. Humor, in the Freudian sense of a liberation of the ego from material contingency, is rare in this work, where the subject, stuck in the gears of an insuperable universe even more mechanical than Bergson's model, feels and expresses all the horror and despair of her situation.

14. For more on usurpation in *Le Menteur,* see my article, "*Le Menteur* and *Don Juan*: A Case of Theatrical and Literary Adaptation," *Kentucky Romance Quarterly,* 32 (1985), 245-54.

MÉDÉE

CRITICAL COMMENTARY

Mitchell Greenberg (essay date 1986)

SOURCE: Greenberg, Mitchell. "Mythifying Matrix: Corneille's *Médée* and the Birth of Tragedy." In *Corneille, Classicism and the Ruses of Symmetry*, pp. 16-36. Cambridge: Cambridge University Press, 1986.

[*In the following essay, Greenberg offers a thematic and stylistic analysis of* Médée.]

'. . . que peut faire une femme?'

Corneille enters the tragic universe through the door of myth. By choosing to stage, as his first tragedy, Medea's infanticide, Corneille both affirms a belief in (literary) genealogy, of his own place in progression (Euripides, Seneca, Corneille), and plunges back into a universe that pre-exists history. C. Lévi-Strauss has taught us that one of the essential attributes of myth is its 'eternal' quality, a quality which negates 'time' and ignores 'progress':

Un mythe se rapporte toujours à des événements passés: 'avant la création du monde', ou pendant les premiers âges, en tout cas, 'il y a longtemps'. Mais la valeur intrinsèque attribuée au mythe provient de ce que les événements censés se dérouler à un moment du temps forment aussi une structure permanente. Celle-ci se rapporte au passé, au présent, au futur.

('Structure du mythe', p. 231)[1]

Situated at an eternal moment of conflict before the imposition of the Law, before the radical separation of the universe into the domains of nature and culture, and co-terminous with the scission of the sexes, myth traces the shifting parameters of these undefined borders. At its most extreme the mythic universe defies all order and seeks refuge in the illogical mode of the magical and the sacred.[2] It is a world whose outlines come into focus in brief flashes of narration only to be engulfed, once again, in the vast expanses of the unrepresentable.

Perhaps the fascination for myth, especially in those cultures that have already passed into 'history', passed beyond, that is, that horrifying moment which marks the instauration of the Law, is precisely the power that the myth retains to transcend those barriers that enclose culture. The projection of myth as spectacle (tragedy) fascinates because it plays out for us, over and over again, excessive desires that culture has only, with great effort, contained. These desires remain, however, vital and aggressive in the unconscious—both in the collective unconscious of the audience and, to a different degree, in the individual psyche of each spectator who participates in this mythic 'speculation'.[3]

For a limited time this 'speculation' allows those desires and fears that have been harnessed by culture to resurface within the minds and bodies of the spectators, to stand as their mirror, their Other—the negative determinant—the unrepresentable force that informs, in its negation, their being in the world:

Par le dédoublement de la représentation: représentation le mythe, représentation de la représentation: la tragédie, par cette incarnation qui donne à la fable une seconde vie (comme le rêve rend la vie aux pensées qu'il met en scène), le mythe qui était dans l'épos un discours proposé à la représentation se mue dans la tragédie en discours imposé par la représentation. Il devient discours de l'Autre.[4]

The staging of desire is the articulation of the silent discourse of the Other. As spectacle, however, myth must function within the parameters of paradox: it supposes the established presence of the interdiction that founds desire—the interdiction of incest—and must project itself as 'mimesis' of a moment before this interdiction. Perhaps for this reason it finds its most fertile ground in the mise-en-scène of familial binding. The origins of family, its constitution and disintegration as recounted in myth, provide the most compelling of tragic scenarios because it is here, in this vortex of con-flictual passions, that the desiring subject is most radi-cally affected in those sexual, political and economic structures in which s/he is most invested. It is here that the subject becomes the object of the most violent threat to his own dispersion:

> La famille est (donc) l'espace tragique par excellence. Sans doute parce que les noeuds d'amour, donc de haine, sont en elle les tous premiers en date et en importance. . . . L'espace tragique est l'espace du dévoilement et de la révélation sur les relations origi-naires de la parenté.[5]

These 'original' relations are never simple. They force the spectator out of time, and make him stand in his own pre-history, at a moment before repression, before s/he entered into a state of 'difference', of sexual differ-ence, within the sphere of signification. On one es-sential level myth is always the attempt to explain (sacrifice) an initial indeterminacy, an inherent (poly-)sexuality, of the constitution of the subject as a sexed, that is a masculine or feminine, being, and to explain why this difference is essential to cultural order. The evolution from indifference to difference is a violent one, implying a threat of death, of mutilation and of chaos, where the subject constantly is being dispersed along the axes of its own fragmentation. It is for this reason that 'myth' stages, in its narration, the conflict between the most elementary of oppositions (male—female) and their own mediation in enunciation. In this scenario the sexual opposition metaphorizes a more es-sential metaphysical coupling, the opposition between materiality and ideality.[6] These metaphorized conflicts are constant and, ultimately, remain unresolvable, but it is the myth's function to offer itself as their possible mediation.

This mediation is progressive. It is never terminable, never complete, yet it mirrors and repeats the social-izing role of the family. As a unit the family mediates the demands of society and individuality. It becomes the model of all cultural investments that conflict with individual libidinal investments. For this reason the family as myth and the myth of family enter the space of representation as the 'already there' of the tragic, the 'already there' of the violence of sexual desire and the passion of this desire pushed to its limits, to the destruc-tion of those limits, to the end of the 'self'.

Violence, of course, is at the very heart of *Médée*. In choosing to center his first tragedy around the fury of betrayed love, Corneille reveals a penchant for a particular type of the tragic he will later, in his 'great' plays, eschew. In the *Discours,* written almost thirty years after *Médée,* Corneille specifically states that politics, not love, must be the motivating force of tragedy. Tragedy's true nature demands a plot in which major questions of State—the end of a dynasty, the death of a great king, the destruction of an empire—are hanging in the balance. Love can only be allowed into the tragic universe as incidental to these events. It must take an ancillary role and leave the main spotlight to political concerns.[7]

Quite clearly *Médée* does not do this. Although we are aware of a political undercurrent in its plot, an undercur-rent to which I will return, the crux of this tragedy is sexual desire, jealousy and revenge. It is a tragedy of excess, a play of unbridled emotions. It is probably not for nothing that in this, his first tragedy, Corneille chooses as his subject the passions, fears and murder-ous powers of a woman scorned. This first venture into the tragic universe presents us with an 'original' drama, a prototypical 'family romance' in which the conflicting tensions are so great, the resolution so utterly traumatic to the political universe, that its violence will cast a long shadow over the tragedies to come.

As the author most associated with the elaboration of the Classical edifice, an edifice which reflects while representing the Law, Corneille poses as the first stone of this edifice a tragedy that refuses this Law. By plac-ing at the entrance of his own tragic universe a work, a myth, that portrays the reign and victory of excess, Cor-neille institutes that excess as the desire/fear his great tragedies must mask. It is with the troubling conundrum of *Médée* that the subsequent tragedies must struggle as they elaborate the strictures of symmetry and order that are attained only through repression—the repressions of *Médée,* of Medea.

It would betray the essential paradox of myth if we were to look only at the *story* of Jason and Medea, to look at Jason and Medea as simple allegorical incarna-tions of the struggle between nature and culture along the lines of sexual division. These characters are situ-ated at an ambiguous moment that predates the imposi-tion of sexual difference. The mythic time exists before the imposition of the Law of sexual distinction, and also it is co-terminous with this imposition.[8] What this implies is that the myth on one level affirms 'sexual indifference', affirms an inchoate world of desire, a state of (bi-)sexuality, that has not as yet been chan-nelled into a masculine/feminine split. At the same time, it also denies this ambivalence: characters are repre-sented as already 'recognizable' sexed human beings structuring the world as a symmetrical, sexual division. This is the logical aporia where myth (as narration) leads us. We are compelled, in a fetishizing gesture, both to deny and to affirm sexual differences, both to affirm and to deny any initial moment of poly-sexuality and its immediate sundering into the sexual (that is, cultural) roles, in order to make some order.[9] What this means for our understanding of the myth-tragedy of Medea and Jason is that we must always bear in mind that Medea and Jason do represent 'Mother' and

'Father', that they are female and male in the universe that the myth delineates, but also that this dichotomy is set into larger opposing camps, into the camps of nature and of culture. In these camps the natural is associated with a 'feminine' essence, whose history in metaphysics is identified with 'matter', and in which 'culture' is associated with the masculine, a concept, in turn, essentialized as 'form' or 'ideal'. The conflict in **Médée** is posed as the struggle between matter and form, between materiality and ideality.[10]

The universe of **Médée** in which this struggle takes place is structured by a legal code which is a guarantor of Patriarchy. It is a code that vouchsafes a system of exchange—the devolution of property/power—among males, and guarantees genealogy as a 'metaphoric' investment that both affirms and denies death (castration) as the basis of Law. In order for this denial to be constantly veiled, in order in other words for its 'mauvaise foi' never to be brought to consciousness, males invest their libido in an economy of reproduction, a reproduction of a constant chain of new males that guarantees their primacy. It is this obsessive desire for reproduction, or the re-presentation of their own image, that haunts both Créon and Jason, those representatives of legality in **Médée**. It enables them self-assuredly to appropriate their descendance to themselves in order to guarantee their continuity. Genealogy—the transference of power—can be read as an essential step in the formulation of culture because it assures the predominance of metaphor (masculine idealization) over the dispersion of metonymy (female materiality) in the reduplication, through the male child, of the 'Same'.[11] It is in order to assure his reduplication, and thus his 'immortality', that Créon (without male descent) desires and agrees to the divorce of Jason and Médée. He wants Jason to marry his own daughter and assure him a progeny to whom, as he says, he can

> laisser ma couronne à mon unique race,
> Et cet espoir si doux, qui m'a toujours flatté,
> De revivre à jamais en sa postérité.
>
> (v, iv, 1406-08)[12]

Créon is in a particularly difficult situation for a Greek (and, one assumes, a seventeenth-century French) male. He has no male heir. His only child is a daughter, Créuse. No one assures, therefore, the continuation of Créon. Without male descent Créon himself is a defective, incomplete man. Greek legal codes foresaw such a predicament and rose to the challenge male-less inheritance posed to Greek society: in these aberrant cases Solon's law on the 'epikleroi' allowed the father to substitute a surrogate for himself. This surrogate, marrying the heiress, assures the father's continuity while avoiding the scandal of incest: 'On sait en quoi consiste l'épiclérat: un père privé de descendance mâle peut suppléer à cette carence en devenant nominalement le

père de l'enfant que sa fille pourra avoir' (Green, *Un oeil en trop,* pp. 244-5).[13] Créon must have a surrogate, a 'self-son' substitute. In earliest times this task was usually entrusted to the closest male relative of the father (perhaps to the father himself) but in less remote moments this role devolves upon a stranger (Jason): 'Au lieu d'épouser le plus proche parent du père, c'est dans les contes, à un aventurier de naissance royale mais sans patrimoine que la fille s'unit. Celui-ci est le plus souvent banni de son pays en raison d'un meurtre' (Green, p. 245). Jason, the noble 'outcast', alienated from his own community, arrives at the gates of Corinth 'unattached'. He becomes the perfect surrogate, the conduit that guarantees Créon's survival.

This initial and essential desire for posterity motivates masculine rivalry and competition for power: Créon wants to have his line continued; Jason wants the power of a throne ('Un sceptre est l'objet seul qui fait ton nouveau choix'). It also forms the basis of the legal code that is so vehemently destroyed in **Médée.**

The play opens with a questioning of the investments of this legal code. Médée is presented and presents herself as a victim of injustice. By repudiating her, Jason is breaking a judicial vow:

> Souverains protecteurs des lois de l'hyménée,
> Dieux garants de la foi que Jason m'a donnée,
> Vous qu'il prit à témoins d'une immortelle ardeur
> Quand par un faux serment il vainquit ma pudeur,
> Voyez de quel mépris vous traite son parjure,
> Et m'aidez à venger cette commune injure.
>
> (i, iv, 201-06)

Rhetorically Médée's entrance is a plea for justice; she has been wronged and her initial reaction is to pose her demand for reparations in terms of the legal code inside whose parameter she has moved. Médée shows both the confusion and the rage of the woman who has been 'had' by a system based on her alienation and appropriation. Jason's repudiation of her is doubly significant: not only is Médée rejected sexually—Jason prefers another (younger) woman—but Jason's divorce casts Médée out of the 'polis'. She is deprived of her place within the community and becomes, by this ostracism, an outcast. Outside this community her humanity is denied, her demonic 'natural' legacy enhanced; Médée, dehumanized, becomes a monster:

> Où me renvoyez-vous, si vous me bannissez?
> Irai-je sur le Phase, où j'ai trahi mon père,
> Apaiser de mon sang les mânes de mon frère?
> Irai-je en Thessalie, où le meurtre d'un roi
> Pour victime aujourd'hui ne demande que moi?
> Il n'est point de climat dont mon amour fatale
> N'ait acquis à mon nom la haine générale;
> Et ce qu'ont fait pour vous mon savoir et ma main
> M'a fait un ennemi de tout le genre humain.
>
> (iii, iii, 776-84)

In the system of exchange that the play articulates, Médée, suffering the ingratitude of her husband, also suffers the alienation of her identity. Having renounced for Jason her father/Law, she becomes a 'nonperson'. Now with neither father nor husband she is condemned to wander family-less in a 'no-man's' land of the unknown.

The conflict in the play, its tragic center, will involve the question of guilt and innocence within this system of exchange. It is a question that necessarily involves the very foundation of culture as it emerges from nature. It also, and co-terminously, involves questions of sexual identity and subjectivity as products of Law rather than as givens in nature. By so doing, it brings into question the metaphysics of sexuality and power that this tragedy-myth articulates.

Médée has been accepted into the 'polis' (culture) upon the sacrifice of her 'nature'. She has abandoned her difference to participate in a system of exchange that assures male prerogative. Médée's position is charged with the ambiguities of a legal code that functions as a sexual investment of power. Her situation is paradoxical because she suffers as a wife-woman in a system which she has accepted to the detriment of her own force. Médée is scorned by a culture that has imposed impotence upon her in return for a certain idealized role—maternity—within community. She has been allowed into the 'polis' only after agreeing to leave her powers at its borders. In exchange she assumes the role of Mother. Médée has been allowed into Corinth on the condition that she be a 'woman'—that is, that she accept the 'lack' masculinity needs in a woman and its supplementation in maternity.[14] In her defense, Médée claims to have been scrupulous in maintaining her role in this exchange. 'Votre simplicité,' she tells Créon, 'n'a point été déçue.'

> Quand votre coeur, sensible à la compassion
> Malgré tous mes forfaits, prit ma protection
> Si l'on me peut depuis imputer quelque crime,
> C'est trop peu de l'exil, ma mort est légitime:
> Si non, à quel propos me traitez-vous ainsi?
> Je suis coupable ailleurs, mais innocente ici.
>
> (II, ii, 483-88)

At the play's opening, she is brought face to face with this system's sham, and her own loss. Confronted by Créon, the representative of this Law, Médée reacts by refusing to submit further to it. Reassuming her nature, Médée affirms her power. This affirmation denies the illusion of any original lack, any weakness, and threatens the self-deluding foundation upon which male culture is based.

In order to give the lie to the bonds of a community based on interdiction and renouncement Médée reaffirms the role that she has temporarily abandoned at

Corinth. In her fury, Médée's rhetoric transforms her into a monster/witch whose unnatural power hauntingly conjures up the frightening image of the 'phallic' woman, the uncastrated 'mother', an object of both fear and desire.[15] Médée represents the fantasy of unbridled, threatening power that recognizes no Law:

> Ce corps n'enferme pas une âme si commune;
> Je n'ai jamais aceepté qu'elle me fît la loi,
> Et toujours ma fortune a dépendu de moi.
>
> (III, iii, 882-84)

Médée declares herself to be beyond (or before) the Law. Her anarchical stance is inimical to any ideal of 'community' based on privation. Médée does not, cannot, curb her desire. It is this rampant passion that has led her to overthrow the nascent order of a cultural system by bringing her into constant conflict with its symbolic head. Médée has deposed the Father (both her own, Pélie, and Créon) and is cast in the role of eternal parricide/regicide. She becomes the outside limit of any order of culture. Her passion (her excess) is her crime, and this crime, as Créon tells her, is her ostracism:

> Repasse tes forfaits, repasse tes erreurs,
> Et de tant de pays nomme quelque contrée
> Dont tes méchancetés te permettent l'entrée.
> Toute la Thessalie en armes te poursuit;
> Ton père te déteste et l'univers te fuit.
>
> (II, ii, 388-92)

Médée, object of the Father's opprobrium, is an external exile from the human community. That community cannot exist without the renunciation of individual (feminine) desire and without this renunciation being immediately idealized as Law. This 'legality' becomes a standard of exchange that joins together those who have accepted repression. Community, the myths tell us, is the imposition of form on matter, a political construct which is sexualized or a sexual construct that is immediately politicized by the association, ancient and seemingly universal, of the female to matter and the male to form. It is this double gesture that *Médée* stages and undoes for us.

Médée represses a power greater than any man's. When Jason refuses to flee with her from Corinth, arguing that they could never escape the combined forces of two kings, her response, 'Bornes-tu mon pouvoir à celui des humains?', uncovers his weakness, his lack of faith, and her force. Jason, of course, should know better. He has been the principal beneficiary of Médée's talents. Rather than being controlled by men, Médée holds them in her sway. It is she rather than any of the men in the play who is the epitome of potency, but this potency, so frightening, cannot be 'real' (human). Médée is potent because she is unreal, a sorceress, an 'unnatural' combination of the temptress and the Fury: Corneille has her describe herself as the eternal image of the succubus:

Moi-même (en les cueillant) je fis pâlir la lune,
Quand, les cheveux flottants, le bras et le pied nu,
J'en dépouillai jadis un climat inconnu.

(IV, i, 982-84)

Her floating hair, silhouetted against the pale moon, signals her as a new Medusa. Like Medusa she is a symbol of both life and death, flaccidity and virility. Hers is the power that men fear and desire, the power and call of indeterminacy, of a return to a state of pre-subjectivity, to a state before difference.[16]

It is precisely in her role as an essential ambivalence that Médée both kills and creates, both devours men and empowers them with her own potency. Médée uses her gift of sorcery both to destroy and to occasion culture. She is situated as a primal force—'nature'—but nature as the symbolic inscription of femininity. Médée is unpredictable, she is pure 'matter', and both desires and repels 'form'.

In the first exchange between Jason and Pollux, Corneille underlines the fact that Médée's fame was initially acquired by her ability to restore potency and reverse the normal decline of the male:

JASON:

Mon père, tout caduc, émouvant ma pitié
Je conjurai Médée, au nom de l'amitié . . .

POLLUX:

J'ai su comme son art, forçant les destinées
Lui rendit la vigueur des ses jeunes années.

(I, i, 51-4)

What Médée effects for Jason's father, physically, she effects metaphorically for Aegée. He, too, is an old, declining monarch who is fettered by the real chains of his prison. Though he is powerless and at the door of death, Médée restores his 'courage':

Ni grilles ni verrous ne tiennent contre moi.
Cessez, indignes fers, de captiver un roi;
Est-ce à vous à presser le bras d'un tel monarque?
Et vous, reconnaissez Médée à cette marque,
Et fuyez un tyran dont le forcement
Joindroit votre supplice à mon bannissement;
Avec la liberté reprenez le courage.

(IV, v, 1218-24)

It is not only the old men whom Médée stimulates. The young heroes, too, the Argonauts, are entirely indebted to her for the successful conclusion of their quest. It was Médée, not any force of superior skill or cunning of theirs, who was responsible for the rape of the Golden Fleece:

seule, j'ai par mes charmes
Mis au joug les taureaux et défait les gensdarmes.

Si lors à mon devoir mon désir limité
Eût conservé ma gloire et me fidélité,
Si j'eusse eu de l'horreur de tant d'énormes fautes,
Que devenoit Jason, et tous vos Argonautes?
Sans moi, ce vaillant chef, que vous m'avez ravi,
Fût péri le premier, et tous l'auroient suivi.
Je ne me repens point d'avoir, par mon adresse
Sauvé le sang des Dieux et la fleur de la Grèce:
. . . . .
Tous vos héros enfin tiennent de moi la vie.[17]

(II, ii, 429-38, 441)

With her superhuman powers Médée is a threat to all systems of hierarchy devised by culture. She triumphs by reversing, or ignoring, the order the world has defined as 'natural'. As sorceress, Médée is an 'unnatural' presence—a negative, destructive force. She restores the father, but she can also eliminate him. She betrays her own father, and uses her sorcery to reverse the 'natural' order of filial piety, encouraging the daughters of Pelias to their most unfilial of tasks:

A force de pitié ces filles inhumaines
De leur père endormi vont épuiser les veines:
Leur tendresse crédule, à grands coups de couteau,
Prodigue ce vieux sang, et fait place au nouveau;
Le coup le plus mortel s'impute à grand service;
On nomme piété ce cruel sacrifice;
Et l'amour paternel qui fait agir leurs bras
Croiroit commettre un crime à n'en commettre pas.
Médée est éloquente à leur donner courage.

(I, i, 81-9)

The concept of 'natural' or 'unnatural' for Médée is of course spurious. Médée is a metaphor for the primary ingredients of life, the four elements, earth, fire, air and water:

Sa vengeance à la main, elle n'a qu'à résoudre,
Un mot du haut des cieux fait descendre la foudre,
Les mers, pour noyer tout n'attendent que sa loi;
La terre offre à s'ouvrir sous le palais des Rois;
L'air tient les vents tous prêts à suivre la colère,
Toute la nature esclave . . .

(III, i, 701-06)

tu vois en moi seule et le fer et la flamme,
Et la terre et le mer et l'enfer et les cieux.

(I, v, 322-23)

She can either concentrate these elements into a single force, giving life, the creation of an individual (Jason's father), or disperse them into the original chaos of nothing. As such, like Dionysus, she is an ambivalent 'matrix', origin and end of all suffering, all tragedy.[18]

Although she controls the elements, the single element that is most closely associated with her throughout the play, her birthright as granddaughter of the Sun, is fire:

Mais, pour exécuter tout ce que j'entreprends,
Quels Dieux me fournissent des services assez grands?

Ce n'est plus vous, enfers, qu'ici je sollicite;
Vos feux sont impuissants pour ce que je médite.
Auteur de ma naissance, aussi bien que du jour,
Qu'à regret tu dépars à ce fatal séjour,
Soleil, qui vois l'affront qu'on va faire à ta race,
Donne-moi tes chevaux à conduire à ta place:
Accorde cette grâce à mon désir bouillant.
Je veux choir sur Corinthe avec un char brûlant;
Mais ne crains pas de cette chute à l'univers funeste;
Corinthe consumé garantira le reste;
De mon juste courroux les implacables voeux
Dans ses odieux murs arrêteront tes feux.
Créon en est le prince, et prend Jason pour gendre:
C'est assez mériter d'être réduit en cendre.

(I, v, 255-70)

Her look burns. When Créon gazes into Médée's eyes and sees the fire that is blazing there he must turn away:

Voyez comme elle s'enfle et d'orgueil et d'audace!
Ses yeux ne sont que feux, ses regards que menace!

(II, ii, 377-78)

She emits an all-consuming fire that embraces both Créon and Créuse. Both are consumed. In the blaze of Médée's passionate revenge their bodies become their own pyre:

elle sent aussitôt une ardeur qui la tue:
Un feu subtil s'allume, et ses brandons épars
Sur votre don fatal courent de toutes parts;
Et Jason et le Roi s'y jettent pour l'éteindre;
Mais (ô nouveau sujet de pleurer et de plaindre!)
Ce feu saisit le Roi: ce prince en un moment
Se trouve enveloppé du même embrasement.

(v, i, 1306-12)

We can only explain the hold Jason has on Médée if we do see their burning passion as an essential mediation of forces that preexist representation (forces of matter) but that representation (the myth as narration, the narration as a tragedy) presents to us embodied in a 'love' story. Any reader familiar with the literary antecedents of Corneille's **Médée** must be aware that one of the major differences between Corneille and his models is the larger role Corneille attributes to Jason. Compared with his predecessors, Corneille allows Jason to participate more fully in his own downfall.[19] By expanding Jason's role Corneille elaborates a far greater symmetry between his male and female protagonists than had existed in his literary antecedents. This attempt restructures the myth, and demands our attention because it is here, in the creation of this character, that we see for the first time the desire of a particular period and of a particular author invested in the insistence upon a 'symmetrical' sexual coupling.

It would be difficult to understand the tragic-passionate crux of the myth as Corneille portrays it if we could not look behind what is so obviously the rather one-dimensional character of Jason. On the level of representation (Jason as 'role') the character appears to be essentially a 'matamore', a self-involved, self-obsessed braggart who is, in every way, inferior to his wife. Not only is Jason inferior to her, he is entirely indebted to her. As we have already noted, all of the heroic exploits of Jason and his Argonauts are attributed to Médée. It is she, rather than they, who is the 'hero'. What the play leaves to Jason, therefore, is his braggadocio, his swaggering self-assurance which projects a certain sexual power that is the reflection of a particularly obvious form of narcissism.

In a (strange) reversal of roles Jason's narcissism, as it is here represented by Corneille, corresponds closely to Freud's analysis of the same phenomenon in beautiful women. It is a narcissism that reflects the subject's complete enclosure upon itself. It is this tantalizing image of a perfect, self-sufficient whole that becomes the universal object of desire. In a sense, therefore, Jason's narcissism is 'feminine' and it is this 'femininity' that makes him attractive to women. There is a strange chassé-croisé here in which the bisexual nature of males and females, a nature that is not admitted into culture, resurfaces in the subtext of representation.[20]

Jason's only force in the play, his only interest, is this narcissism that impels his enormous sexual power. Jason attracts women, attracts Médée, because he, unlike them, represents sexuality as a promise of plenitude: Jason's narcissism functions as the projection of a sexual image, an image which paradoxically is a containment, an imposition of form. It is this closure (a representation of ideality) that the women (unformed matter) desire. Jason's chief claim to fame does not lie in his heroism but in his attraction. From the very beginning of the play, Jason is presented as a priapic force. He, too, like Médée, is a force of nature. Unlike Médée's, however, Jason's sexuality is essentially channeled into a political scheme. It is always a force that inspires desire, but it also sublimates this desire to political ends. Jason always seduces to advance his career in the world. It is through his sexual power that Jason creates an image of hero/master that he projects out into the world and which is affirmed by the desire he inspires in others. Jason's real (and only) heroism is his subjugation of female desire to his desire for power. In the context of **Médée** the representation of Jason situates his sexuality within the realm of a history that figures the progress of Law over nature. Jason is, as the male, both weaker and stronger than the females: he is weaker in his overall power, but stronger in directing and controlling the power he has as repression. Through his sexuality Jason creates politics:

Aussi je ne suis pas de ces amants vulgaires;
J'accommode ma flamme au bien de mes affaires;
Et sous quelque climat que me jette le sort,

Par maxime d'état je me fais cet effort.
Nous voulant à Lemnos rafraîchir dans la ville,
Qu'eûssions nous fait, Pollux, sans l'amour
    d'Hypsipyle?
Et depuis à Colchos, que fit votre Jason,
Que cajoler Médée, et gagner la toison?
Alors, sans mon amour, qu'eût fait votre vaillance?
Eût-elle du dragon trompé la vigilance?
Le peuple que la terre enfantoit tout armé,
Qui de vous l'eût défait, si Jason n'eût aimé?
Maintenant qu'un exil m'interdit ma patrie,
Créuse est le sujet de mon idolâtrie;
Et j'ai trouvé l'adresse, en lui faisant la cour
De relever mon sort sur les ailes d'Amour.

(I, i, 29-44)

The attraction of Jason's narcissism coupled with a reputation for amorous conquest makes of him a symbol of fecundity, a new Priapus. Jason is a 'hero' because he dompts monsters: he masters and subjugates the 'monster' that is female sexuality, that uncontrollable, chaotic force of unformed matter. He domesticates this force and implants on it his own mark. He is the male principle that molds matter into culture. Despite his failings, Jason represents the superiority of ideality over materiality, of reason over passion, of men over women. Women, because they desire him, subjugate themselves to him. It is their sexual submission to Jason that makes of him the 'standard' of communal life. His virility, his sexual prowess, captures and subjugates matter and channels its excess into the repression of culture. In this way Jason's exploitation of his potency makes of him a true 'hero of culture', a 'Sovereign'.[21]

Jason exists and has value as the object of universal desire, a desire Médée shares. Her attraction/desire for Jason (and of this desire there can be no doubt; Médée's relation to Jason is totally passional, while his for her is completely political) has led her to accept a form of self-imposed servitude. For him she has come from the far outlands of the world, from barbarous Scythia, and established herself within the confines of civilization. This geographic shift from 'Barbary' to Corinth corresponds to a primary metaphysical change. Coming into culture (history), Médée submits to the rule of the male, submits to his Law, and for a time being, the time of sexual fulfilment, is content with the inferior role that is assigned to her.

Once in Corinth, however, both Créuse and Créon also desire Jason.

Que vous dirai-je plus? Mon bonheur ordinaire
M'acquiert les volontés de la fille et du père;
Si bien que de tous deux également chéri;
L'un me veut pour gendre et l'autre pour mari.

(I, i, 109-12)

Jason joins the sexual to the political, making them inseparable. He yokes the masculine and the feminine within the sphere of his own sexual potency. As the representative of this 'order', of the sovereignty of form over matter, Jason needs the confirmation of its reproduction as his own validation. Jason needs his children because paternity is the verification of the power of metaphor, the hold of reason over matter. His children are the proof of Jason's political power, his ability to re-produce form to maintain his sovereignty as this re-presentation.[22] Jason needs these 'testicular'[23] witnesses of his own 'triumph' which, imposed diachronically, validates paternity as genealogy, genealogy as the basis of culture, and culture as the order, the declension of the same, a proof of his eternity.[24]

For this reason Jason insists on keeping *his* children. By demanding that they remain with him in Corinth, that they do not accompany their mother into exile, he is effectively denying their (and his) link to the female, denying their connection to matter and situating them solely within the masculine domain. They are his investment in order, in legality. Instead of leaving them as the mediating union between the male and the female (but is this mediation ever possible?) Jason attempts to eradicate them as in-difference, and to use them as proof of his own sovereignty. This is, of course, tantamount to the suppression of Médée. It is this suppression that will prove intolerable (the myth will not be sacrificed to 'history'), that will return, in its fury, to give the lie to the pretension of Law, to any system of exchange that would exclude 'dépense', to the very existence of culture itself.

All the characters in the play who are situated within the polis and whose investments reside within culture can retain their status only by imposing on an other the guilt they all share. Although Médée and Jason bear equal responsibility for their fate, and although Créon also becomes their accomplice when he admits them into his kingdom and grants them asylum, it is Médée who is made to bear the burden of their past. In the realm of (masculine) political expedience the female, the mere receptacle of the male, is expendable. She is easily replaced. Médée must be sacrificed to the rule of the Father in order for Jason to advance his own interests, the interests of culture.

It is obvious that the legal system which serves as the standard of culture in the universe of the play is designed to function for Patriarchy. The Law of the Father which is articulated by Créon operates on the exclusion of the feminine, an exclusion which in *Médée* takes the form of ritual banishment. In order to prepare for his ascension to royal power, Jason must be cleansed of guilt. The only way to do this is to make of Médée the 'pharmakos', the sacrificial victim who carries evil out of the city. All the characters who are defined within Patriarchy are joined by their commitment to legality. They all have recourse to the Law, to repression, to excuse their sacrifice of Médée. For each of them she is made to bear the entire responsibility of those events from which Jason profited. He, however, is exonerated of all blame:

MÉDÉE:

> O d'un injuste affront les coups les plus cruels!
> Vous faîtes différence entre deux criminels!
> Vous voulez qu'on l'honore, et que de deux complices
> L'un ait votre couronne, et l'autre des supplices!

CRÉON:

> Cesse de plus mêler ton intérêt au sien.
> Ton Jason, pris à part est trop homme de bien.
> . . . . .
> Le séparant de toi sa défense est facile;
> Jamais il n'a trahi son père ni sa ville;
> Jamais sang innocent n'a fait rougir ses mains;
> Jamais il n'a prêté son bras à tes desseins.

(II, ii, 455-64)

CRÉUSE:

> Laissez agir, grand roi, la raison sur votre âme,
> Et ne le chargez point des crimes de sa femme,
> J'épouse un malheureux, et mon père y consent,
> Mais prince, mais vaillant, et surtout innocent.

(II, v, 625-28)

JASON:

> Il manque encor ce point à mon sort déplorable,
> Que de tes cruautés on me fasse coupable.

(III, iii, 857-58)

It is obvious that the three witnesses in Médée's trial are prejudiced representatives of a system of desire as Law that can perpetuate itself only by the communal suppression of an intrusive, alien other. Médée is cast out of community, she is made to bear the burden of her refusal to accept an 'original lack', that women should acknowledge, of her own subjugation to Jason and to culture. Despite her own claims to innocence (or at least to the innocence of her motive, passion; she acts only out of Love), Médée, by the same gesture that disculpates Jason, is univocally condemned as evil.

This condemnation is, in the context of this tragedy, a form of hubris and it is this hubris that brings about Jason's and culture's downfall. It is Jason's error to attempt to suppress as alien, to banish beyond the confines of the city, what is actually also an integral part of itself/himself. Médée, as 'nature', inheres in Jason, but it is this unacknowledged fact, too fearsome to contemplate, that must undergo repression. This point of 'hubris', the instance of repression, situates the passage of myth and history, the interaction of legality and nature, in the narration of *Médée.* At this juncture, the mythic sub-text of the narration becomes co-terminous

with the historical/legal dimension of the narrative (that is the role of myth as mediation—to be both at once) and attempts to reassert its irrepressible ambiguity.

As 'myth', neither Jason nor Médée is reducible to essential antitheses, neither male nor female. Each partakes in 'essential' attributes of both sexes, as defined in culture—both are sexual forces that are complementary and interconnected. They represent impulses in which difference, sexual difference, overlaps. It is this space of overlapping, of indeterminacy, that representation (narration, history) attempts to deny in favor of difference (that is, in favor of the Law). Only as they enter culture (as objects of narration) are Médée and Jason representable as separate essences, essences which are immediately sexualized and politicized. In culture, their inherent ambivalence, the way they both partake of a primary bisexuality, is denied. The tragedy, the representation of myth, stresses this conflict, which is the conflict of culture—which might even be the definition of culture—that is the denial of an inchoate sexuality and its separation into 'sexuality', a separation which cannot be accomplished without the violent repression of desire in scission.

The conflict of differentiation (the questioning of the ambiguous space of mediation) is accused most radically when each partner attempts to claim as his/her own the metaphors of their mediation, the children. Both Médée and Jason want to keep the children, but for different reasons, different libidinal investments. For Médée the children reflect Jason; they are the mirror in which Médée can gaze and see not herself, but Jason:

> Souffre que mes enfants accompagnent ma fuite;
> Que je t'admire encore en chacun de leurs traits,
> Que je t'aime et te baise en ces petits portraits;
> Et que de leur cher objet, entretenant ma flamme,
> Te présente à mes yeux aussi bien qu'à mon âme.

(III, iii, 918-22)

Médée loves her children because they are an image of Jason. They represent him to her and thus we might say that they stand in for Jason, and more particularly for Médée's own subjugation to Jason. The children are Jason's male prerogative. They represent what she desires in him and what is denied her—his ability to reproduce himself, to form, impose order on matter. The children are indeed Médée's 'fetish'; they point to Médée (in Law) as self-imposed castration. In her worshipping of them as portraits of Jason (= same) they become the symbol of her (matter's) subjugation to him (ideality). And they also deny this subjugation: they also stand for the 'phallus' (power, integrity) that Médée has relinquished by becoming (their) 'mother', accepting her place with Jason in culture. The children are both the sign of her castration and its refusal. Médée, the 'phallic' woman, had accepted castration, had abandoned her power to the Law, but the Law has returned it to her (mastered) in her maternity.

For Jason, too, as we have already seen, the children function as a fetish. Representing his own ability to reproduce himself, they deny his own lack of power in nature. This lack of power is, of course, sublimated in the children as substitutes of himself. They are guarantors of his continuity within the Law. They are proof of his position as progenitor of history.

The children are the most highly invested of a series of mediating objects (the Golden Fleece, Médée's dress) that both deny and affirm nature and culture, myth and history. They are the most vulnerable of objects, the objects in which the battle between nature and culture (between male and female) will be most effectively played out.

We should not forget that Corneille's text underlines the children's role as mediators: they are made to go back and forth between Médée and Créuse, between Médée and Jason, between Jason and Créon. They are the shuttle going back and forth between exile and polis. It is precisely because of their role as mediators that each parent thinks of their destruction as a way of destroying his/her other without destroying himself/herself. In Corneille, both parents contemplate the murder of the children, Jason as well as Médée:

JASON:

> Instruments des fureurs d'une mère insensée,
> Indignes rejetons de mon amour passée,
> Quel malheureux destin vous avoit réservés
> A porter le trépas à qui vous avoit sauvés?
> C'est vous, petits ingrats, que malgré la nature,
> Il me faut immoler dessus leur sepulture.
> Que la sorcière en vous commence de souffrir:
> Que son premier torment soit de vous voir mourir.
> Toutefous qu'ont-ils fait qu'obéir à leur mère?

(v, v, 1529-37)

In his rage, Jason wants to sacrifice his children in order to punish Médée—but Médée the 'sorceress', Médée denizen of nature, the force that mocks him. He contemplates their murder as a way of negating, or at least affecting, the power that escapes his control and therefore continually risks giving the lie to the Law.

Médée, on the other hand, comes to contemplate destroying her children as a final attack on Jason inside the Law:

> Il aime ses enfants, ce courage inflexible:
> Son foible est découvert, par eux il est sensible;

> Par eux mon bras, armé d'une juste rigueur,
> Va trouver des chemins à lui percer le coeur.

(IV, v, 945-48)

and again:

> Que n'a-t-elle déjà des enfants de Jason,
> Sur qui plus pleinement venger sa trahison!
> Suppléons-y les miens; immolons avec joie
> Ceux qu'à me dire adieu Créuse me renvoie.
> Nature, je le puis sans violer ta loi:
> Ils viennent de sa part, et ne sont plus à moi.
> Mais ils sont innocents; . . .
> Il sont trop criminels d'avoir Jason pour père;
> Il faut que leur trépas redouble son tourment;
> Il faut qu'il souffre en père aussi bien qu'en amant.

(v, ii, 1331-40)

By destroying the children Médée effectively attacks the foundation of Jason's hold on politics, on repression, on the Law. Médée correctly identifies the children as the symbol of her alienation in culture. In both instances ('ses enfants'; 'Ils viennent de sa part et ne sont plus à moi') she disassociates herself from her children because they are the integral link to Jason's position in the polis, and to her condemnation by it. By deciding to destroy them, Médée relinquishes her role as 'mother', the imposition on her, by the order of Patriarchy, of her 'maternal' nature—the brand of her castration. By one spectacular act of destruction Médée not only kills her children, but also effectively destroys the fetters of the Law, and the base upon which rests the culture of the (play's) universe.

Médée begins her attack on the Law by destroying Créon and Créuse. Corneille gives this destruction to us as a blazing spectacle of Médée's nature/power. This spectacle which is offered to our gaze is meant to galvanize us, to point out the immense disparity that exists between the victim (culture) and the executioner (nature-matter).[25] Médée goes on to demonstrate this 'disequilibrium' fully by the final eradication of all Law. As long as the children remain alive there is always a chance for Jason (the Father) to recoup his power, assured by the continuation of his image. Their destruction, however, removes all hope, all idea of continuity, and reduces him to a state of utter impotence. In the last scene we see Jason who, in his grief over the death of Créuse and deprived of those symbols that reflect his own self-sufficiency back to him, is bereft of all the exterior 'forms' that represent him. He no longer has an image, no longer has a self. He has been undone by Médée's power. The hypocrisy that subtends his role in society has been revealed. Faced with the undeniable superiority of Médée, Jason is left defenseless, unable to take any revenge:[26]

> Mais que me servira cette vaine poursuite,
> Si l'air est un chemin toujours libre à ta fuite,

Si toujours tes dragons sont prêts à t'enlever,
Si toujours tes forfaits ont de quoi me braver?

(v, vii, 1593-96)

Deprived of the illusion of his political base, deprived of his narcissistic reflection of himself, deprived of his progeny, Jason can only turn his impotent rage against his vacant self. By his suicide Jason surrenders the last vestiges of resistance to Médée. He destroys those limits that (his) culture has so laboriously erected, and, breaking them, returns to the limitless, selfless, indifferent embrace of Death.

Corneille's **Médée** ends on an ominous note for Patriarchy, for order and for control. The last act plays out for us the utter destruction of the Law: Créon and Créuse, symbols of history, of the polis and of the small sphere of culture, have been destroyed. Jason in his melancholic despair, a despair that is the most narcissistic of sufferings, in an ultimate act of desperation does away with himself. This suicide is another new twist Corneille brings to the myth. More important, the children, metaphors of mediation, symbolic terms of the acceptance of castration, of the structuring of desire around the Father, imitation and proof of the triumph of ideality over chaotic matter, of culture over nature, have been obliterated. In her last liberating act Médée has freed herself from the bonds of Law to which she had submitted herself. Nothing remains. All semblance of 'human' community, of the organization inherent in community, has been destroyed in the bloodbath released by Médée.

In the end, only Médée remains, or rather only the image of Médée as we last see her in the penultimate scene of the tragedy. There, she is no longer the wife, no longer the mother, but she becomes again a mythic, supernatural force, who assumes in her being a power that defies difference, that denies sexuality's symmetrical divisions in which she, as woman, is lost. Coming back into her own, Médée 'supernatural' leaves the scene of representation transported through the air by her dragon-drawn chariot.

Médée leaves this world of representation, and yet remains, by her absence, an effective threat that always lurks in the shadows, in the folds of the Cornelian universe. Perhaps we can see **Médée,** Medea, as both the transhistorical fear of all Patriarchy (**Médée** as myth), and at the same time (**Médée** as tragedy) as the pointed reminder of the dread of dissolution that was particularly poignant, as I have suggested, in French society at the beginning of the seventeenth century. Free and uncontainable, Médée becomes the original object of desire and fear whose repression will constitute the political and sexual tension of the great tragedies to come. These tragedies, reflecting the structures of Classical Patriarchy, always show these structures to be

teetering on the brink of an abyss. This abyss, Patriarchy's attraction-repulsion of the feminine, can, as we have seen, undermine the entire edifice of the Father and bring it tumbling down in ruin around him.[27]

Notes

1. C. Lévi-Strauss, 'Structure du mythe', in *Anthropologie structurale* (Paris: Plon, 1958).

2. *Ibid.,* p. 229: 'Tout peut arriver dans un mythe: il semble que la succession des événements n'y soit subordonée à aucune règle de logique ou de continuité. Tout sujet peut avoir un quelconque prédicat, toute relation concevable est possible.'

3. The following works, which all deal with the mutual involvement and investment of theater as spectacle and the audience—collective and individual—have guided my thinking: Green, *Un oeil en trop*; Mannoni, 'L'illusion théâtrale', in *Clefs pour l'imaginaire*; Ubersfeld, *Lire le théâtre,* esp. chaps. 1, 'Texte et représentation' and 6, 'Le discours théâtral'.

4. Green, *Un oeil en trop,* p. 96.

5. *Ibid,* p. 18.

6. See J.—J. Goux, 'Différence de sexes et périple de l'histoire', in *Les Iconoclastes* (Paris: Seuil, 1978), p. 191: 'C'est en questionnant la division mythique des apports du mâle et de la femelle dans la procréation qu'il est possible . . . de reconstituer l'archéologie de l'idéalisme. L'idéalisme est d'abord *une conception de la conception.* L'homme dans la procréation apporte la *forme* de la progéniture, la femme apporte la *matière.* C'est ce que disent tous les discours mythiques sur la procréation.'

7. Corneille, *Discours de l'utilité et des partis du poème dramatique,* p. 13: '[la] dignité [de la tragédie] demande quelque grand intérêt d'Etat, ou quelque passion plus noble et plus mâle que l'amour . . . il faut qu'il [l'amour] se contente du second rang dans le poème, et laisse [à la politique] le premier'.

8. See A. Artaud, *Le Théâtre et son double* (Paris: N.R.F., 1964), p. 38: 'Et c'est ainsi que tous les grands Mythes sont noirs et qu'on ne peut imaginer hors d'une atmosphère de carnage, de torture, de sang versé toutes les magnifiques Fables qui racontent aux foules *le premier partage sexuel* et le premier carnage d'essence qui apparaissent dans la création.'

9. The characters, on one level, function as allegories of impulses. Impulses, as Freud talked about them, are marked by their ability to revert into their opposite (manifestations). See 'Instincts and their Vicissitudes' (*Standard Edition,* XIV).

10. See Goux, 'Différence de sexes', p. 191: 'Or, les métaphores d'Aristote et de Platon attestent que l'opposition philosophique entre la matière et l'idée puise directement à cette archéologie mythique de la conception avec la dimension du désir qu'elle implique. Aristote dit clairement "la matière désire la forme comme la femelle désire l'homme".'

11. Irigaray, *Speculum,* p. 89.

12. All references to *Médée* are to the edition by A. de Leyssac (Geneva: Droz, 1978).

13. Also for the definition of 'epiclery' in Greek law one could consult W. K. Lacey, *The Family in Classical Greece* (Ithaca: Cornell University Press, 1968).

14. For an analysis of the role of marriage and maternity and the exchange value of women within the ideological parameters of Patriarchy, and particularly the slippage from femininity to maternity, see Irigaray, *Speculum,* esp. pp. 97-129.

15. A. Green, 'Sur la mère phallique', *Revue française de psychanalyse,* jan.-fév., 1968, p. 2.

16. See Freud's brief essay on Medusa (*Standard Edition,* XVIII).

17. It is interesting to note that in his *La Toison d'or,* written in 1660, Corneille insists on the fact that although Jason accomplishes (with Médée's help) the preliminary tasks allowing him to reach the Golden Fleece, it is Médée who actually takes it and brings it to the Greeks:

MÉDÉE:

Ne laissons pas ainsi la victoire imparfaite:

Par le milieu des airs, courons à leur defaite;

Et nous-mêmes portons à leur témérité

Jusqu'à dans ce vaisseau ce qu'elle a mérité . . .

(v, v, 2100-03)

18. See F. Nietzsche, *The Birth of Tragedy.*

19. See W. Goode, 'Medea and Jason: Hero and Non-Hero in Corneille's *Médée*', in *French Review* (51, May 1978) and also de Leyssac's introduction to his edition of *Médée.*

20. Freud, 'On Narcissism: an Introduction' (*Standard Edition,* XIV).

21. At least in G. Dumézil's definition: 'Souveraineté et fécondité sont des puissances solidaires et comme deux aspects de la Puissance.' Quoted in Green, *Un oeil en trop,* p. 24.

22. See Irigaray, *Speculum,* p. 63: 'Or, pour que ce moi soit valeureux il faut bien qu'un "miroir" le rassure, réassure sur sa validité. La femme étayera

ce redoublement spéculaire renvoyant à l'homme "son image", le répétant comme "même . . . La femme donc sera le même à une inversion près . . . comme, *en tant que mère,* elle permettra la répétition de même."'

23. Irigaray, *Speculum,* p. 98.

24. See Goux, 'Différence de sexes', p. 200: 'En tant qu'il est le garant de la permanence du "même" dans la reproduction, c'est le père et non la mère qui a à rèpondre de la vie et de la tendresse essentielles du vivant. Il sera le représentation de la reproduction, le signifiant de la perpétuation vitale, voire donc aussi, par un pas de plus, le garant de l'éternité.'

25. 'L'exécution de la peine est faite pour donner non pas le spectacle de la mesure, mais du *déséquilibre et de l'excès.* Il doit y avoir dans cette liturgie de la peine une affirmation emphatique du pouvoir et de sa *suprématie intrinsèque.*' Foucault, *Surveiller et punir,* p. 12.

26. *Ibid.,* p. 39: 'Dans les *excès* des supplices toute une économie du pouvoir est investie.'

27. For a reading of the Medea myth that stresses its socio-political implications, corroborating my own interpretation, see C. Alvaro, *La lunga notte di Medea* (Milan: Bompiani, 1949). For a more anthropologico-psychoanalytical reading see G. Carboni and D. Nobili, *La Mauvaise Mère* (trans. R. Myjori, Paris: Petite Bibliothèque Payot, 1977). See also B. d'Astorg's 'Médée, mère, meurtrière', in his *Les Noces orientales* (Paris: Seuil, 1980).

LE CID (THE CID)

CRITICAL COMMENTARY

Helen L. Harrison (essay date December 1998)

SOURCE: Harrison, Helen L. "*Payer* or *Récompenser*: Royal Gratitude in *Le Cid.*" *French Review* 72, no. 2 (December 1998): 238-49.

[*In the following essay, Harrison addresses the issue of royal gratitude as portrayed in* The Cid.]

When the Académie Française delivered its judgment on *Le Cid,* Don Fernand's support for the marriage of Rodrigue and Chimène met with condemnation. The

Academicians ruled that a marriage between a woman and her father's killer would have been immoral. At the same time, the Académie criticized the Castillean king as an abusive tyrant who lightly gave away property—namely Chimène herself—which did not belong to him (Académie 388-89). By questioning the appropriateness of the king's gift to Rodrigue, the Académie directs our attention to the problem of royal gratitude.

For a seventeenth-century audience, a king who has received extraordinary services from a subject is in a delicate position. The monarch's own interests dictate that he reward such services.[1] In so doing, he practices the liberality expected of all nobles. He inspires his subjects to work and to fight for him. On the other hand, service to the crown must remain a duty, not a venture motivated by self-interest alone. A king must never allow those beneath him to view his gifts merely as their due. Should reward and recognition become obvious payment, the bond between a king and his subjects would become a contractual one rather than a divinely ordained relationship. While a noble who has received a favor from a peer finds himself in the uncomfortable and inferior position of being *obligé*, no subject can gain such an advantage over a monarch.[2] The final scene of **Le Cid** is the culmination of a series of tests having to do with royal gratitude in this play. Not only the major characters but also the members of Corneille's public reveal their attitude toward monarchy as they assess the king's gifts and his method of bestowing them.[3]

The first discussion of royal gratitude privileges deferred rewards over immediate payment for services. As Don Diègue and the Comte leave the royal council, they disagree as to whether the king has been just in making Don Diègue tutor to the prince:

DON DIÈGUE

> Cette marque d'honneur qu'il met dans ma famille
> Montre à tous qu'il est juste, et fait connaître assez
> Qu'il sait récompenser les services passés.

LE COMTE

> Pour grands que soient les Rois, il sont ce que nous
>   sommes
> Ils peuvent se tromper comme les autres hommes,
> Et ce choix sert de preuve à tous les Courtisans
> Qu'ils savent mal payer les services présents.

                                             (I.iv.148-54)

The two warriors share the assumption that services to the sovereign should receive compensation. The parallelism of verses 150 and 154 could be read as symptomatic of similar attitudes toward the relations between subject and monarch. On closer examination, however, these verses already reveal different stances toward the king and toward gratitude. The conflict between the two

men is not simply a matter of whether or not the king has made a good decision, but a question of how all such decisions should be interpreted and of who has the right to judge the monarch.

For Diègue, the king's decision results from royal justice. Don Fernand has remembered the deeds of his old champion and has decided to reward them. The verb used by Don Diègue for the monarch's action is "récompenser," which means, etymologically, to reestablish a balance, to weigh one thing with another (Wartburg, *recompensare*).[4] Finding an appropriate recompense thus entails exercising judgment. The giver rather than the receiver decides in this context what the reward should be. In praising his monarch's decision, Don Diègue depicts the king as a unique being who displays his virtue to a global and undifferentiated audience, "tous."

The Comte, in contrast, places the king on the same level with his nobles by destroying this uniqueness. He speaks not of "le roi" but of "les rois." Monarchs become one class of beings who must prove themselves to another, potentially adversarial group, "les Courtisans."[5] Rather than seeing the political structure in terms of king and subjects, the current champion of Castille posits kings who need the goodwill of their vassals. In saying that kings "savent mal payer les services présents," the Comte makes his sovereign little more than the employer of mercenary troops. His complaint hints that Fernand's poor example might discourage other nobles from serving him well. Nothing in his speech glosses over the immediate exchange which Chimène's father expects between the king and those who protect his realm.

The choice between Don Diègue and the Comte has thus served to expose differing views of kings and to make plain the sovereign's determination to place himself outside the bonds of obligation which would govern him were he only the first among equals. The king eschews using the coveted appointment for the purpose of retaining the military support he currently needs. He rewards good servants, but he does so in his own time and his own way. By selecting Diègue rather than Gomès, Don Fernand shows that temporal distance does not diminish the value of works which support the monarchy. The lapse of time between the older man's service and this particular reward obfuscates any resemblance which the appointment has to mercenary payment and also makes the example of royal gratitude more striking than a favor bestowed on Chimène's father would be. If pride and interest did not blind Don Gomès, he could read in the king's decision the message that the sovereign would remember and consider distinguished military service even after a warrior had lost his strength.

The ability to transcend the present and to remain above temporal constraints is a distinguishing feature of royal gratitude, and it is a feature which recalcitrant nobles such as the Comte cannot accept. As Chimène's father rages over the preference accorded past rather than present services, he reveals that his allegiance lies chiefly with the old, feudal order rather than with the absolutist regime which Don Fernand strives to create. Several critics have remarked upon the conflict between Gomès and Diègue as a tension between these two conceptions of society, but it is necessary to emphasize that the transition from feudalism to absolutism is underway before the play begins.[6] Even Don Gomès has a foot in both camps. Hence he accepts, as does Don Diègue, a second defining feature of royal gratitude, namely that the reward for services to the crown should be an opportunity to perform more services. The two men want to teach the prince. Both the past and present champion sense that their prestige and identity depend upn the sovereign's favor.

The two great nobles want the king's *reconnaissance* in both senses of the word. Gratitude for their services constitutes recognition of their identities. The chance to serve as the prince's tutor can confirm the king's belief in a warrior's valor and merit. Such an expression of gratitude would demonstrate that the king and all his realm see Gomès as he wishes to be seen, as the incomparable champion of Castille.[7] Hence the sharpness of the barb when Don Diègue, after a speech which at first seems conciliatory, adds "Un Monarque entre nous met de la différence" (I.iv.208). Gomès is enough of a modern courtier to feel that his worth has been denied if the king does not recognize him, yet not enough of a courtier to see that he must accept the sovereign's choices without murmuring. The apparent slight to his honor corrodes the Comte's allegiance to the new order, just as it saps his goodwill and admiration toward Diègue and his son.

As the initial dispute over the king's gratitude separates the adherents of a new absolutism from poorly adapted feudal lords, the scene between the fathers lays the groundwork for Don Arias's words on the king's superiority to debt: "Quoiqu'on fasse d'illustre et de considérable / Jamais à son sujet un Roi n'est redevable" (II.i.371-72). Despite his military service, Gomès has neither the right to expect special protection for his offenses, nor the right to demand payment for his acts of valor. No subject ever has such rights. In Don Fernand's first scene with Rodrigue, however, the monarch apparently belies Don Arias's words.

After Rodrigue defeats the invading Moors, the king finds himself in a position which offers him little hope of providing a suitable recompense to his champion. Everyone now knows that Don Fernand owes Rodrigue his kingdom. Monarch or no, Don Fernand appears as

redevable. The challenge to him is to turn his indebtedness to his own ends, to make his expressions of gratitude enhance rather than diminish his prestige, despite the inadequacy of any tangible rewards which he can bestow on his champion.

In these circumstances, the king declares the debt openly and acknowledges his inability to repay it:

> Pour te récompenser ma force est trop petite,
> Et j'ai moins de pouvoir que tu n'as de mérite.
> Le pays délivré d'un si rude ennemi,
> Mon sceptre dans ma main par la tienne affermi,
> Et les Mores défaits avant qu'en ces alarmes
> J'eusse pu donner ordre à repousser leurs armes,
> Ne sont point des exploits qui laissent à ton Roi
> Le moyen ni l'espoir de s'acquitter vers toi.
>
> (IV.iii.1223-30)

This speech, while denying that the hero will receive more than words of praise from his king, already constitutes a type of reward for the young courtier. The king himself recognizes Rodrigue's prowess. At the same time, this apparent declaration of royal bankruptcy works to lessen expectations that any further reward will be forthcoming. This heightens the effect of the benefits bestowed in the second part of the king's speech:

> Mais deux Rois, tes captifs, feront ta récompense,
> Ils t'ont nommé tous deux leur Cid en ma présence,
> . . . . .
> Sois désormais le Cid, qu'à ce grand nom tout cède,
> Qu'il devienne l'effroi de Grenade et Tolède,
> Et qu'il marque à tous ceux qui vivent sous mes lois
> Et ce que tu me vaux et ce que je te dois.
>
> (IV.iii.1231-32;1235-38)

On the one hand, the king protects himself and his new champion from any accusation of entering into a contractual, mercenary exchange. The king specifically says that he is still Rodrigue's debtor and that the *récompense* comes from the Moorish kings. Yet, in contrast to the Spanish source, no Moorish king is present to give the hero his new name (Castro y Bellvis 50). The king himself makes it public and thus creates for Rodrigue a new identity. In doing so, the monarch both shows his power to transform an individual and attributes prophetic powers to himself. He promises the Cid a future.

Once again, we see in this passage the ability of the king to transcend time as he displays his gratitude. All of what Rodrigue will do and be henceforth comes to read as the king's gift. Future services to the Crown become the reward bestowed for past services. And, in what is perhaps the most surprising move of all, the king's debt becomes a sign of his generosity.

Rather than negate his debt, the king memorializes it. By coopting the word Cid and making it a mark of the value he attaches to Rodrigue and the debt he owes him, Don Fernand links himself to the young hero, Rodrigue's fame to his. The personal pronouns in line 1238—*tu, me, je, te*—reinforce this association. Rodrigue's title becomes a monument not only to the young warrior but also to his sovereign.

The king's thanks to Rodrigue serve another strategic purpose. The speech provokes Rodrigue to restate the principle of a subject's endless indebtedness and to recognize his master's freedom from a system of payment:

> Que votre Majesté, Sire, épargne ma honte,
> D'un si foible service elle fait trop de compte,
> Et me force à rougir devant un si grand Roi
> De mériter si peu l'honneur que j'en reçois.
> Je sais trop que je dois au bien de votre Empire
> Et le sang qui m'anime et l'air que je respire,
> Et quand je les perdrai pour un si digne objet,
> Je ferai seulement le devoir d'un sujet.
>
> (IV.iii.1239-46)

While the king's own words had at first seemed to echo the ideas of the Comte, Rodrigue's clearly recall the precepts recited by Don Arias. This exchange thus demonstrates that while Rodrigue replaces Chimène's father as military champion, he will not become Don Gomès. The modesty with which Rodrigue belittles his own heroic actions contrasts favorably with the Comte's overweening pride. Rodrigue will continue to see himself as the king's ever-obligated subject.

This second example of royal gratitude functions, as did the first, as a test. The king's gratitude toward Don Diègue tested Gomès's ability to serve the emerging order, the absolutism which the king envisions but which he cannot yet completely practice. The second example requires Rodrigue to prove his loyalty to the new regime. The scene with Rodrigue cannot disguise that the monarchy of Castille needs heroic defenders and will fall without them. Nonetheless, just as the king designates Rodrigue as a hero who will win lasting glory, Rodrigue affirms his lord's status as indisputable sovereign of the realm. Royal *reconnaissance* incites the subject's *reconnaissance*. Both men benefit from this mutual recognition, but it establishes a hierarchy in which the military hero, however glorious, remains subordinate to his monarch. In recognizing an insurmountable distance between his deserts and the monarch's generosity, Rodrigue presents an example for the spectators within Fernand's court and within the Paris theater to follow.

The third scene I have chosen presents, as we shall soon see, a test to Corneille's audience as well as to the members of Don Fernand's court. Don Fernand has allowed Chimène's champion to challenge Rodrigue to a duel, but has decreed that Chimène must accept the victor of this combat as her husband.[8] This decree is not explicitly formulated as an expression of gratitude to Rodrigue, yet the king's words suggest that he views Chimène as an additional recompense for his new champion:

> Et le combat fini, m'amenez le vainqueur.
> Quel qu'il soit, même prix est acquis à sa peine,
> Je le veux de ma main présenter à Chimène,
> Et que pour récompense il reçoive sa foi.
>
> (IV.v.1466-69)

Once Rodrigue has won the duel, Chimène's usefulness as royal recompense becomes even more apparent, though not unproblematic. Chimène has undergone a series of trials which prove both her love for Rodrigue and her loyalty to her father, and she now balks at a marriage which would place one above the other. The king grants her a delay of one year and enjoins Rodrigue to spend this time fighting the Moors in their own lands. Further service to the king will win Rodrigue additional glory and, according to Don Fernand, Chimène's hand. The king will collaborate with Rodrigue's valor to obtain the desired end: "Pour vaincre un point d'honneur qui combat contre toi, / Laisse faire le temps, ta vaillance, et ton Roi" (V.vii.1865-66).

Whether or not one believes that the marriage between Rodrigue and Chimène will occur depends upon whether one accepts the claims for royal gift-giving which earlier scenes supported. The king makes explicit in this scene the superiority to time which the text has already attributed to him. He has shown that he gives the future as well as the present. His decree is law, whether fulfilled immediately or in a year: "Cet Hymen différé ne rompt pas une loi / Qui sans marquer de temps lui destine ta foi" (V.vii.1845-46). This confidence functions as a sign of the king's power. Rather than make his rewards less real or less valuable, delay can in fact make his gift more palatable to Chimène and will incite Rodrigue to perform more feats for the good of the realm.[9] Don Fernand's past generosity and his determination to establish himself as absolute should lead the audience to conclude that the marriage, which is after all historical, will take place.

Here I seem to be in the uncomfortable position of disagreeing not only with such perspicacious critics as Mitchell Greenberg but also with Corneille himself. The 1660 *examen* answers the critics of **Le Cid** who maintained that Chimène shows herself to be *impudique* in agreeing to marry the man who killed her father by asserting that the heroine never gives her consent to the marriage. Her response to the monarch's decree is silence, and Corneille warns against interpreting silence as consent in this case:

> Je sais bien que le silence passe d'ordinaire
> pour une marque de consentement; mais quand

les Rois parlent, c'en est une de
contradiction: on ne manque jamais à leur
applaudir quand on entre dans leurs
sentiments; et le seul moyen de leur
contredire avec le respect qui leur est dû,
c'est de se taire.

(Corneille, 1:701)

The remarks on universal eagerness to flatter kings seem
more appropriate to the post-Fronde monarchy of 1660
than to either the France of 1637 or the Castille of the
play. Louis XIII still faced insubordination from the
grands and from his own family. As to Don Fernand,
he is a king establishing an absolute monarchy, not yet
the unquestioned center of an adoring and submissive
court. Chimène's silence indeed protects her from having to give an unequivocal answer to the king's decree,
but in the heat of the Querelle du Cid, neither Corneille
nor his defenders explained her silence as dissent. As
Couton notes, this passage from the *examen* has more
to do with answering old objections to this tragi-comedy
than with how Corneille or his contemporaries read the
play in 1637 (*Réalisme* 102).

Greenberg views Chimène as a scandalous figure who
clings to the old regressive order represented by her
father and indefinitely defers marriage with Rodrigue
(63-65). I would argue instead that the deferral of the
marriage is a royal decision which places this example
of royal gratitude in line with the two earlier ones. By
demanding that Rodrigue place his hope in time and the
king, Don Fernand reminds the audience that the Crown
will not forget its servants. *Le Cid* depicts a world
which has undergone radical change, and the king's
increased power comes with that change. Yet, the king's
insistence on his own memory and foresight makes him
the conveyor of continuity. The scenes involving royal
gratitude thus contain the reassurance that the new order
still respects the virtues of the old one. Those who feel
troubled by a world in which absolutism is conquering
a feudal past should respond not by rebelling but by
turning their faith and service to the monarch.

Royal gratitude does not necessarily exhaust state cof-
fers, for it may, in concrete terms, be cheap. One can
argue that Don Fernand gives nothing but promises and
demands. Nonetheless, he makes his subjects and the
audience believe in the worth of these promises and
demands. By rewarding worthy subjects with opportunities for further service and by refusing to privilege the
present over the past or the future, Don Fernand
transforms his gratitude from a possible sign of weakness to a means of increasing his own glory and power.

As evidence of royal power and prerogatives, Don
Fernand's gifts to his subjects and his demands upon
them should have won the approval of all who wished
the strength of the French crown to continue to grow.

The extremely successful play had almost all theater-
goers, including the *nobles d'épée,* admiring a triumph
of absolutism over feudalism as they applauded the
love and eventual marriage of Rodrigue and Chimène.
The play both urged service to the monarchy and reaffirmed that the king, although a unique being, shared
the values of his nobility. The two performances of *Le
Cid* at the Palais-Cardinal, the dedication of the
published text to Mme. de Combalet, Richelieu's niece,
and the gift of nobility to Corneille's father all suggest
that Richelieu recognized the merits, and perhaps the
usefulness, of this tragicomedy when he first saw it.[10]
Yet, the Cardinal and his protégés turned against the
Cid soon after its publication. What do the attacks
launched against *Le Cid* tell us about the degree to
which Corneille's treatment of gratitude conformed or
failed to conform to the ideologies of his time?

First of all, the critical minority agreed that the insolent
response to royal gifts exemplified by the Comte
deserved censure. Scudéry and the members of the Académie viewed the Comte as a *fanfaron* (*Observations*
84-85, Académie 376-77). The Académie specifically
related "l'insupportable audace avec laquelle il [Gomès]
parle du Roy son Maistre" to the Comte's attitude
toward payment for services to the Crown. Gomès, according to the Académie, fits the secondary definition
of *fanfaron*: "homme de cœur, mais qui ne fait de
bonnes actions que pour en tirer avantage, et qui me-
sprise chacun, et n'estime que soy-mesme" (377). These
words, though not intended as praise of Corneille, suggest that he had succeeded in making the Comte's
expectations of immediate royal payment appear to his
contemporaries as outmoded and reprehensible.

Parallels between the Comte's ambition and the attitudes of the *grands* of the 1630s may partly account
for Scudéry's disapproval of this character. Georges de
Scudéry prided himself on being noble and on being
both a poet and a warrior. His *Observations* are replete
with reminders that he knows how the nobles who
defend a country speak while Corneille knows only
how to "parler de la guerre en bon bourgeois qui va à la
garde" (102). Scudéry and his allies in the quarrel
repeatedly remind the reader of Corneille's bourgeois
origins.[11] Especially if we remember that Scudéry had
close ties with the house of Condé, it seems quite credible that he would have resented the extent to which
Don Gomès made the power and presumption of the
grands and the ostentation of the old nobility look
anachronistic.[12] Despite the Cardinal's patronage, Scudéry was not ready for complete acceptance of absolutism, as his loyalty to Condé during the Fronde showed.
At least in later years, he believed that the Crown could
indeed be "redevable" to its *grands*.

As for the final scene involving royal gratitude, the
criticisms of the Académie suggest that Corneille, in the
eyes of his judges and their patron, had gone both too

far and not far enough in delineating the powers of the king. On the one hand, the Académie implicitly recognized that time could not diminish the effects of royal gratitude. Instead of reading the one-year delay as introducing the possibility that the marriage would never take place at all, the Academicians rebuked Corneille for letting his king abuse power. Don Fernand allows his gratitude to one subject to make him unjust towards another. Seen in this light, Don Fernand violates the restrictions which even absolutist theoreticians like Bodin place on sovereigns, for he confiscates property without sufficient cause or compensation.[13] His liberality comes to resemble theft. There is so little doubt about the king's ability to keep his word to Rodrigue, whatever Chimène's intentions, that he may be viewed not merely as an absolute monarch but as a tyrant.

The remarks of the Académie also suggest that Corneille has not gone far enough in differentiating royal *récompense* from contractual exchange. As we have seen, the critique regards Chimène as the king's payment to Rodrigue. Thus, Corneille's efforts to glorify royal gratitude by showing the greatness of the gift—the Cid's future and his bride—and by using remoteness in time to decrease the resemblance between the gift and payment would appear less than wholly successful, at least according to the poet's rivals. Corneille had made his audience assume Don Fernand's power to fulfill his promises, but this success had attenuated the effect of the deferral of the marriage. Time no longer obfuscates the reward's resemblance to payment. An institution whose patron favored clearly didactic drama could still find that Don Fernand acted like Rodrigue's debtor.[14]

The 1660 edition of the play confirms how easily the king's superiority to obligation could be undermined and reminds us how much the ideological function of the play depended on the time of its reception. In this version, Chimène herself echoes the Académie's objections to Don Fernand's use of her: "Si Rodrigue à l'Etat devient si nécessaire, / De ce qu'il fait pour vous dois-je être le salaire?" (1: 1508). This verse appears to derive from the Académie's suggestion that the poet could have made Chimène's marriage more acceptable by positing it as necessary for the state. Yet, the change threatens the claims for royal rewards made earlier in the play. The word *salaire* underscores Chimène's commodification and makes the king's gift into a calculated payment to a powerful subject. Such calculation is at odds both with noble liberality and with the king's superiority to obligation.

The change in the final scene suggests, as do some of Corneille's critical observations in the 1660 *Œuvres,* that he no longer considered Don Fernand a worthy representative of emerging absolutism.[15] His assumptions concerning the relative power of sovereign and

nobles had changed in the course of thirty-three years, in part because the monarchical ideology of *Le Cid* had gained grounds. Shedding a favorable light on the origins of absolutism had become less pertinent. By 1660, Don Fernand had lost his potential importance as a promising precursor to modern monarchs. The differences between his Castille and modern France had grown far more evident than any similarity between his moves toward absolutism and the progress of the French state. Richelieu and Mazarin had triumphed. From the perspective of 1660, *Le Cid* could appear as a story from a distant feudal past rather than as an enactment of the demise of feudalism.

Yet, depiction of royal gratitude had not become irrelevant for Corneille. The first version of *Le Cid* had, after all, offered standards of gratitude which the Crown had never met. Disappointment in royal patronage, the strengthening of central power after the Fronde, and lingering bitterness over the treatment of *Le Cid* could have decreased the poet's faith in a monarchy that would surpass the liberality of the *noblesse* and honor past services as well as present ones. The use of royal ingratitude in *Nicomède,* first performed in 1651, suggests increasing doubt that sovereigns could be both unfettered by debt and generous toward deserving subjects. Such plays as *Othon, Agesilas,* and *Suréna* reflect Corneille's continued concern with the vicissitudes of royal gratitude.

The response to *Le Cid* as well as Corneille's revisions underscore the difficulties of creating a convincing monarch who rewards services not because he must but because he chooses to do so. Any later doubts about the generosity of kings notwithstanding, Corneille bolsters absolutist ideology in the 1637 *Cid* as he makes his public applaud royal gifts and forces his rivals to denigrate noble bravado. As the text privileges royal *récompense* over common payment, the play urges allegiance to the new order and challenges those in power to make absolutism's myths of royal gratitude a reality.

Notes

1. Machiavelli states that a prince who is blatantly ungrateful towards a subject risks lasting infamy. While Machiavelli justifies ingratitude if it derives from suspicion, fear of an overly powerful subject can make a monarch seem weak and untrustworthy (1: 277-78). Corneille would have known Machiavelli's discourses, but as Couton observes, the French poet's treatment of gratitude is far from Machiavellian. See Couton's "Notice" to *Nicomède* (Corneille 2: 1461-71).

2. For discussions of noble *libéralité,* see among others Apostolidès, *Le Roi-machine* 21-22, and Bénichou 182. On obligation and power over one's *obligé,* see Gross 41-42. The competition

involved in noble expenditure resembles the *pot-latch* discussed in Mauss 29-57.

3. In examining the king's gifts, I am obviously looking at only one aspect of exchange in this play. A more exhaustive study of exchange in *Le Cid* would of course treat the Infante's insistence that Rodrigue is her gift to Chimène as well as the vendetta system which the king abrogates.

4. In addition to Wartburg, Furetière's dictionary is enlightening as to differences of register between *récompenser* and *payer*. Examples of usage given under *récompense* and *récompenser* speak of heavenly recompenses and of "Dieu qui récompense." No such examples occur under *paier*.

5. For a similar interpretation, see Mittag 158.

6. See Apostolidès, *Le Prince sacrifié* 60-61, Couton, *Réalisme de Corneille* 72, and Lyons 9. Lyons notes that the transition between orders has already begun and views the real change in this play as one in the system of justice.

7. Mittag notes Gomès's need for recognition and views his hyperbolic discourse as compensation for the king's failure to recognize him (157).

8. In the Spanish play, the king makes no such decree. Instead, Chimène offers her hand in exchange for Rodrigue's head. Since she omits to say the head must be detached from the shoulders, Rodrigue declares that he himself fulfills her demand. The king agrees but does not bring about the marriage himself (Castro y Bellvis 67).

9. As Apostolidès observes, those feats take place outside the king's own realm. This gift has the practical advantage of removing a hero who could compete with royal power (*Prince sacrifié* 62). I would argue that the terms of the gift also protect the king from competition by affirming his uniqueness and supremacy.

10. Differing views of the relationship between Richelieu and Corneille and of Richelieu's response to *Le Cid* may be found in Battifol, Howarth, Maurens, and Stegmann 69-80.

11. See, for example, Claveret 308 and Mairet and Scarron, *Apologie pour M. Mairet* 332.

12. For a very different view of Gomès's nobility, see Bareau.

13. On the king's duty to observe natural and divine law and to respect property rights, see Bodin 1: 140, 273.

14. For examples of Richelieu's theatrical taste, see Hall 162-99, especially 193-99.

15. See the "Examen" of *Clitandre* (Corneille 1: 103) and the "Examen" of *Le Cid* (1: 703).

Works Cited

Académie française. *Les Sentiments de L'Académie françoise sur la tragi-comedie du Cid.* Gasté 355-417.

Apostolidès, Jean-Marie. *Le Prince sacrifié: théâtre et politique au temps de Louis XIV.* Paris: Minuit, 1985.

———. *Le Roi-machine: spectacle et politique au temps de Louis XIV.* Paris: Minuit, 1981.

Bareau, Michel. "Au nom de père et du fils: de la tragédie nobiliare dans le *Cid.*" Ed. Michel Bareau. *Pierre Corneille: ambiguïtés.* Edmonton: Alta, 1989. 19-40.

Batiffol, Louis. *Richelieu et Corneille: la légende de la persécution de l'auteur du Cid.* Paris: Calman-Lévy, 1936.

Bénichou, Paul. *Morales du Grand Siècle.* Paris: Gallimard, 1948.

Bodin, Jean. *Les Six Livres de la république.* Genève, 1629. 2 vols.

Castro y Bellvis, Guillen de. *"Les Exploits de Jeunesse du Cid" de Guillen de Castro et "Le Cid" de Pierre Corneille.* Ed. J. Larochette. Bruxelles: J. Lebègue et cie., 1945.

Corneille, Pierre. *Le Cid. Œuvres complètes.* 1: 691-777.

———. *Œuvres complètes.* Ed. Georges Couton. 3 vols. Bibliothèque de la Pléiade. Paris: Gallimard, 1980-87.

Couton, Georges. *Réalisme de Corneille, deux études: La Clef de Mélite, Réalités dans le Cid.* Paris: Les Belles Lettres, 1953.

Furetière, Antoine. *Dictionnaire universel, contenant generalement tous les Mots français tant vieux que modernes, & les Termes de toutes les Sciences et des Arts.* 1690. Hildesheim and New York: Georg Olms Verlag, 1972. 4 vols.

Gasté, Armand. *La Querelle du Cid: pièces et pamphlets publiés d'après les originaux.* Paris: Welter, 1898.

Greenberg, Mitchell. *Corneille, Classicism, and the Ruses of Symmetry.* Cambridge: Cambridge UP, 1986.

Gross, Nathan. *From Gesture to Idea: Esthetics and Ethics in Molière's Comedy.* New York: Columbia UP, 1982.

Hall, H. Gaston. *Richelieu's Desmarets and the Century of Louis XIV.* Oxford: Clarendon Press, 1990.

Howarth, W. D. "Mécénat et raison d'état: Richelieu, Corneille et la tragédie politique." *L'Age d'or du mécénat (1598-1661).* Actes du colloque international CNRS (mars 1983). Eds. Jean Mesnard and Roland Mousnier. 59-68.

Lyons, John D. *The Tragedy of Origins: Pierre Corneille and Historical Perspective.* Stanford, CA: Stanford UP, 1996.

Machiavelli, Niccolo. *The Discourses of Machiavelli.* Trans. Leslie. J. Walker. Boston: Routledge and K. Paul, 1975. 2 vols.

Mairet, Jean, and Paul Scarron. "Apologie pour Monsieur Mairet contre les calomnies du sieur Corneille de Rouen." Gasté 328-47.

Maurens, Jacques. *La Tragédie sans tragique: le néo-stoïcisme dans l'œuvre de Pierre Corneille.* Paris: Armand Colin, 1966.

Mauss, Marcel. "L'Essai sur le don." *Cohésion sociale et dimensions de la sociologie.* Vol. 3. of *Œuvres.* 3 vols. Paris: Minuit, 1969, 29-57.

Mittag, Wolfgang. *Individuum und Staat im dramatischen Werk Pierre Corneilles.* Inaugural dissertation. Westfälische Wilhelms-Universität zu Münster, 1976.

Scudéry, Georges de. "Observations sur *Le Cid.*" Gasté 71-111.

Stegmann, André. *L'Héroïsme cornélien: genèse et signification.* 2 vols. Paris: A. Colin, 1968.

Wartburg, Walther von. *Französiches etymologisches Wörterbuch: eine Darstellung des galloromanischen Sprachschatzes.* Bonn: F. Klepp, 1928-68. 20 vols.

HORACE

CRITICAL COMMENTARY

Susan Tiefenbrun (essay date 1983)

SOURCE: Tiefenbrun, Susan. "Blood and Water in *Horace*: A Feminist Reading." *Papers on French Seventeenth Century Literature* 10, no. 19 (1983): 617-34.

[*In the following essay, Tiefenbrun investigates the function of the blood and water motif in* Horace.]

> Woman is the lesser man, and all thy
>   passions matched with mine,
> Are as moonlight unto sunlight, and
>   as water unto wine.
>
> —(Alfred Lord Tennyson)
>
> She was as false as water.
>
> (*Othello*, V, 2, 132)

The analysis of two scenes from *Horace,* Act III, 1 and Act IV, 5, which were carefully selected for their representational value, will, in the hands of a text-oriented reader, reveal the stylistic function of formality[1] and the geometric symmetry of French classical tragedy. When the grid of a particular metaphoric system is placed like a filter over these same passages, a kind of reading results which corroborates the first, substantiates the expansive power of literary language, and extends the function of words from sign to symbol. The purpose of this study is to show the degree to which the metaphoric system of Blood and Water (1) generates the language of Corneille's play (2) facilitates the perception of Sabine and Camille as symbols in the passages selected for analysis, and (3) constitutes the source of a gender-related idiolect.

All words are signs whose graphic form represents something real, a referent. We know from Saussure that the relationship between the sign and the referent is arbitrary. A sign can, within the idiolect of a text, take on the function of a symbol representing an idea or an ideology. If, in the course of the reading process, the reader perceives a high frequency of association between the word and the thing that the word is supposed to symbolize, and if the association between the two elements is motivated either by resemblance or contiguity, symbolization and its poetic effects can be shown to function effectively in the text.[2] Implicit in this symbolic process is the extension of meaning from the concrete to the abstract level, which results in the expansion of possibilities for interpretation. Sabine and Camille, for example, are symbols, actantial representations of the two sides of the Cornelian ethic, which are otherwise represented throughout the play by a number of variants, e.g. the Horatii vs the Curiatii, Horace vs Camille, Rome vs Albe, Father vs Mother, Male vs Female, Blood vs Water. The blood and water motif plays a special role in establishing the symbolic function of Sabine and Camille who, like metonyms, take on in their speech and actions the partial properties of their respective symbol. Within the semiotic webbing[3] of the text, each of these variants works harmoniously with the others on a paradigm to produce in the reader's mind the impression of a tightly constructed classical whole. The interrelatedness of these structures produces a unique kind of contemplative pleasure for the attentive reader who, sensing the cohesiveness of the whole, perceives the geometry of tragedy, and participates actively but patiently in the deconstruction of the literary creation.

Before we begin a detailed investigation of the blood/water motif in *Horace,* it will be necessary to determine (1) the precise nature of the motivation inherent in the symbolic association, (2) the frequency of the association throughout the play, and (3) the extent to which this metaphoric system is overdetermined and thereby participates in the linguistic production ot the text. Finally, a more detailed study of the elaboration of the blood/water motif will be undertaken in a close reading of Sabine's monolog (III, 1) as well as the famous scene (IV,5) in which Horace kills his sister, Camille, for her love of the enemy. In this way we hope to compare and contrast the two female characters who represent not only the elements of the metaphoric system but the evolution of the Cornelian ethic.

I. BLOOD AND WATER MOTIF

Water, which is the first of the two elements to appear in **Horace,** continues throughout the first act as a major thematic structure in contrast to Act II which is characterized by a predominance of blood imagery. The structural arrangement of Act I is binary. The women of the play, Sabine and Camille, appear first and are followed by Curiace, the weaker of the two male leaders. The association of women, water, and weakness is thus established structurally from the outset in Act I. By its property of flow and its association with creation, water can evoke positive images of life and love. One of the most common baroque metaphors for the expression of inconstancy, recurrence, emotion, and sexuality is water, whose thinness and transparency can elicit negative connotations. In **Horace** womanly tears signifying weakness and uncontrolled sentimentality are contrasted to the intellectual restraint of the male hero who hides emotion. In a striking attempt at the creation of a real female identity, Sabine states that the women in her sphere of influence refuse such artifice:

> L'usage d'un tel art, nous le laissons aux hommes,
> Et ne voulons passer que pour ce que nous sommes.
>
> (III,5,943)

And, yet, in her own actions Sabine displays a special kind of "male" strength early in the play by her ability to command her own tears:

> Commander à ses *pleurs* en cette extrémité,
> C'est montrer pour le sexe assez de fermeté.
>
> (I,1,13-14)

In contrast to Sabine's male strength, Camille's effusiveness is expressed through the metaphors of flowing streams and tears whose unifying base is water:

> Et combien de *ruisseaux coulèrent* de mes yeux!
>
> (I,2,181)

> Et quels *pleurs* j'ai *versés* à chaque événement.
>
> (I,2,185)

Curiace, whose structural function in Act I is to represent a relatively strong figure in contrast to the women, will in Act II,1 display his weakness before

Horace. Here Curiace's thoughts turn to friendship and love, and the literary expression of his emotional bent appears in the form of water metaphors similar to those of Sabine and Camille: *De tous les côtes j'ai des* pleurs *à répandre* (II,1,396).

While Act I is characterized by a predominance of water metaphors that mirror the weakness of the characters presented, Act II, structured on a ternary model, represents the dynamics of the male Cornelian ethic by means of blood metaphors. Blood, like water, is a polyvalent symbol having both positive and negative connotations. Its redness links it to heat, passion, fire, and love (*flammes, rougir, feux*). Blood is thicker than water and also more substantial on the scale of Cornelian values. Blood flows like wine and is associated with battle, violence, pain, sacrifice, martyrdom, and death. Blood is also the life source that nourishes, and the symbol of origin and identity.

Marriage is the basis of all kinship relations in society. When the link between bloods is too close, incest prohibition is broken. The universality of this rule substantiates man's natural tendency to avoid blood. It is through marriage that the Self/Other split is enhanced and the tendency toward pernicious endogamy is avoided. Corneille provokes his readers with the conflicts that exist between marriage and the establishment of personal as well as gender-related identity. Marriage involves a familial separation and the concomitant abandonment of one's identity for another. National or social similarity can ease the alterity inherent in the marriage covenant which traditionally brings together people of different bloods.[4] Valère represents a factor of similarity for Camille whose imminent marriage to Curiace threatens her Roman identity.

In **Horace** blood is the symbol for man, who is twice represented as a blood-thirsty tiger (*tigre altéré de sang*), eager for combat and death. The constancy, reason, and strength required of the male hero bring honor and glory to his name. What can weaken the firm grip on an ethic built upon self-sacrifice are empathetic relationships demanding a dissolution of the self and an acceptance of the other: friendship, marriage, and love, expressed through water metaphors. When the love of blood (represented by combat, honor, conquest and victory) is carried to the extreme, a philosophy is born in which might makes right and ends justify means; barbarism and brutality result: *Quand la brutalité fait la haute vertu* (1242). Despite the profusion and interaction of variants on both paradigms of blood and water, it is clear that on the scale of Cornelian values duty takes precedence over blood relations. That is the significance of Horace's famous pronouncement about his allegedly cowardly son: *Qu'il mourût!* (1021)

Act II undergoes its own small evolution as a result of the *coup de théâtre* in scene 2. Horace continues to speak the language of blood in scene 1,[5] while Curiace weeps.[6] In scene 3, in the face of duty and the call of the hunt, Curiace now adopts blood metaphors[7] to express his shock at the barbaric strength and inhuman "joie"[8] felt by Rome's chosen leader. In the development Of Act II Curiace and Camille together represent emotional love through water metaphors,[9] whereas Sabine's brotherly love for Curiace is logically identified with blood metaphors.[10] Both women offer opposite forms of defense against the Cornelian ethic of violence and death. Unlike Camille who chooses the path of sentimentality, Sabine displays a false but effective form of her own violence. When Camille cries in Act II, her tears act as a powerful weapon designed to dissuade Curiace from spilling his blood: *Il faut bien que je pleure* (II,5,571). Curiace understands the semiotic significance of tears, which he identifies as a language as powerful as blood and conquest:

> Que les *pleurs* d'une amante ont de puissants dis-
> cours,
> Et qu'un bel oeil est fort avec un tel secours.
>
> (II,5,577-578)

The stylistic force of associating water (tears) with power is derived from the reversal of the reader's expectation. Given the traditional associations of blood with violence and water with weakness—an association which is corroborated in the idiolect of **Horace**—the shocking identity of tears and power can here be construed as a signal for the evolution of the Cornelian ethic. Corneille shows that tears transform heroes into humans:

> Et laissez-moi sauver ma vertu de vos *pleurs*.
> Je sens qu'elle chancelle, et défend mal la place.
>
> (II,5,582-3)

Like love, tears destroy the essence of man's identity:

> Plus je suis votre amant, moins je suis Curiace.
>
> (II,5,584)

> Allez, ne m'aimez plus, ne versez plus de *larmes*.
>
> (II,5,587)

Sabine's best trick is to step out of the role of a woman in Act II,6 in order to speak like a man, not in terms of water and tears like her sister-in-law Camille, but in the metaphoric code of blood. Sabine's play acting, which is nothing less than an extended use of verbal irony, achieves a transformation so threatening and creates a character so blood thirsty that Horace is moved to remind his wife of her subordinate position in the family structure: *Aime assez ton mari pour n'en triompher point* (II,6,674). It is here, just before the very end of Act II, that old man Horace makes his appearance as the symbol of Cornelian heroism. His unshakeable posi-

tion reaffirms the association of women, weakness and water, summarizes man's role in the world through the metaphor of spilled blood, and openly reveals his hostility toward women and their tears:

> Qu'est ceci, mes enfants? écoutes-vous vos flammes,
> Et perdez-vous encore le temps avec des femmes?
> Prêts à verser du *sang*, regardez-vous des *pleurs*?
>
> (II,6,679-81)

This revulsion for sentiment is shared by his son, Horace, who is horrified at the thought of a man weeping. He exclaims to Curiace: *Quoi! vous me pleureriez mourant pour mon pays!* (398), and he substitutes the concept of pleasure for the pain of death in a memorable oxymoron: *charmes/larmes*:

> Pour un coeur généreux ce trepas a des charmes;
> La gloire qui le suit ne souffre point de *larmes*.
>
> (399-400)

II. SABINE'S MONOLOG AND THE METAPHORIC SYSTEM OF BLOOD/WATER

Although Sabine's monolog does nothing more than delay action and describe incompatible states of mind, the speech is remarkable in its high degree of stylization and effect of geometric symmetry. Architecturally, the monolog is organized on a carefully sustained binary model in which the first part of the speech (711-738) offers hope and the second part (739-764) despair. The *sang/rang* couplet is the key to the connection between the two halves of the speech as well as the mirror of its dialectic.

> Et sans considérer aux dépens de quel sang
> Leur vertu les élève en cet illustre rang.
>
> (729-30)

Moreover, the reprise of the rhyming *sang/rang* pair (753-754) establishes the thematic importance and symbolic function of the blood and water motif appearing throughout the play in masked forms. For example, very early in the monolog, nature or blood relations are contrasted to the concept of love which is expressed elsewhere in the play by semes of water: *La nature ou l'amour parle pour chacun d'eux* (717). In this verse the opposition of nature and love, variants of blood and water, mirrors Sabine's ambivalent feelings which are reflected grammatically in the striking use of *ou*.

The first half of the monolog (719-735) permeated with the Cornelian ethic of self-sacrifice and glory is characterized by the unterrating of blood relations. The order of nouns is significant in the determination of this valuative judgment: *femme/soeur* (712) *époux/frère* (716); *femme/soeur* (720); *femme/fille* (732). The literalization of the underrating of blood ties occurs at the end of this first segment in the collocation of the rhyming *sans/sang: Et, sans considérer aux dépens de quel sang* (729). Sabine identifies the stance of stoic self-sacrifice as peculiar to men (*Et l'esprit le plus mâle* (I,1,5); *Mon esprit en conçoit une mâle assurance,* (II,1,379), and her husband reinforces the gender differentation. The male-dominated point of view provides the security of plurality (reflected grammatically by pluralization) and the rewards of conformity (cf. clusters of plural imperatives): *leur honneur, leur constance; songeons, faisons.* The female-dominated position, which is symbolized by water and expressed poetically in the form of tears, emotion, love, and life, contains only latent power and requires the risky negation of an accepted order: *Non, non, mon frère, non, je ne viens en ce lieu / Que pour vous embrasser et pour vous dire adieu* (613-614). The separation from society suggested in the female revolt can result in the attainment of individuality, which is mirrored grammatically in the systematic substitution in the second half of the monolog of the plural imperatives and pronouns by the singular subject (je): *Songeons pour quelle cause* vs *je songe par quel bras,* etc.

When the second half of the monolog reverses the affirmations of the first, and the paradigms of visual deception and temporal evanescence are firmly established in remarkable symmetry (739-746) (*flatteuse illusion, erreur, vain, impuissante lumière, faux brillant / éblouir, peu durer, tôt t'évanouir, charmais, ce moment*), the reader is instantly reminded of a similar reversal effect that took place in Sabine's speech in Act II,6. Fraught with irony and linguistic manipulations designed to imitate male speech patterns and create a sense of strength, Sabine's speech in Act II seems to contradict the weakness she had demonstrated openly in her initial speech in Act I,1 (*Approuvez ma faiblesse et souffrez ma douleur*). Sabine's language in Act II,6 is a sham designed to stop the spilling of blood between families. Put another way, Sabine chooses to fight fire with fire. This technique does not work, and Sabine's language will change as she, herself, transforms gradually from false male to true female. In the course of Sabine's transformation and search for identity as a woman (*Et ne voulons passer que pour ce que nous sommes.* 943), the reader can observe a concomitant preference for water metaphors in contrast to previously selected blood metaphors. Camille's speech in Act IV,5 will constitute a similar show, for in it we see nothing more than a calculated display of the power of love designed to threaten her brother. In a court of law her threats could be construed as reason enough for Horace to claim self-defense:

> Et prenez, s'il se peut, plaisir à lui deplaire.
> Il vient: préparons-nous à *montrer* constamment
> Ce que doit une amante à la mort d'un amant.
>
> (1248-50)

Earlier in Act II, Camille chose to adopt water (tears) to fight the fire in an attempt to dissuade Curiace from his duty. Her offense is as impressive as Sabine's, and both women are incarcerated as a result of their dangerous influence on the men.

In the second half of Sabine's monolog a sudden reversal of the value of kinship relations is manifested by word order change. Blood-ties are overrated: *frère/epoux* (750); *fille/femme* (756). In the corresponding verse which literalizes this re-evaluation of priorities (formally noted as the *sans/sang* collocation), the words *pour* and *sang* are brought together in an unprecedented series of parallelisms:

> Et ne vois les vainqueurs en leur illustre rang
> Que *pour* considérer aux dépens de quel *sang.*
>
> (753-754)

And like the Cid, who in an analogous moment of indecision is *percé jusqu'au fond du coeur,* Sabine describes her mental state in terms not of tears but rather of blood: *Je sens mon triste coeur percé de tous les coups* (749). The emergence of the self (*La maison des vaincus touche seule mon âme*) issues forth from Sabine's adoption of a powerful ethic of humanity characterized by tears rather than blood and dominated by the love of life rather than death. Camille will complete the picture of this new ethic in Act IV,5 by affirming the power of love.

III. ACT IV, 5 CAMILLE VS HORACE

Prior to Camille's confrontation with her brother, old man Horace crystallizes the dialectics of heroism in familiar metaphors of blood and water. The cliché of washing hands in water is reconstructed ironically in terms of blood:

> Vos *pleurs* en sa faveur sont de faibles défenses:
> J'atteste des grands dieux les suprêmes puissances.
> Qu'avant ce jour fini, ces mains, ces propres mains
> *Laveront* dans son *sang* la honte des Romains.
>
> (III,6,1047-50)

This same collocation and superposition of codes will occur in Camille's scene, Act IV,5, in which she refers to her brother as a blood-thirsty tiger: *Tigre altéré de sang, qui me défends les larmes.* (1287), a reconstruction of the cliché based on thirst for water. In this celebrated verse the internal rhyme *sang/défends* links Horace, Camille's blood brother, with the notion of prohibition of personal desire. The next line containing the verb *vouloir* (*Qui veux que dans sa mort je trouve encore des charmes*) (1288) continues the seme of desire, corroborates the association of Horace with his restrictive if not perverted desire, and prepares us for Horace's atrocity. Sabine also refers to men as tigers in Act II,7,694; in this verse which contrasts men with women, Sabine suddenly associates women with death in a curious role reversal indicative of her state of identity crisis: *Tigres, allez combattre, et nous, allons mourir.*

An unexpected linguistic reversal occurs in scene 2 just before Camille's confrontation with Horace. In a moment of exaltation and surprise after learning the truth about his brave son, old man Horace, incarnation of blood itself, speaks the language of tears and love by means of an extended water metaphor:

> O mon fils! ô ma joie! ô l'honneur de nos jours!
> . . . . .
> Quand pourra mon amour *baigner* avec tendresse
> Ton front victorieux de *larmes* d'allégresse?
>
> (IV,2,1141,1147-48)

This codal reversal prepares Act IV,5 and the elaboration of a new ethic of love encoded in a profusion of water metaphors.

Act IV,5 is a succinct replay of Act II in which a dual defense system against Cornelian heroism is attempted first by Camille's sentimentality and then by Sabine's display of force. Through the metonymies of the arm and the sword, Horace draws attention to the underlying symbols of blood which caused the tragic sequence of events in Camille's life: *Ma soeur, voici le bras qui venge nos deux frères* (1251); *Vois ces marques d'honneur, ces témoins de ma gloire* (1225). Horace is painfully insensitive to Camille's personal loss as he renders abstract (*gloire, victoire*) the death of a loved one. Through metonymic associations he transforms her loss into his property (swords), and he engages in a disconcerting materialization of the spiritual: *ma gloire, ma victoire, mes trophées*. Camille's response to Horace comes in her own idiolect, the language of tears: *Recevez donc mes pleurs, c'est ce que je lui dois* (1257). Horace speaks the language of blood and scorns sentimentality: *Et nos deux frères morts dans le malheur des armes / Sont trop payés de sang pour exiger des larmes* (1260). Horace, like his father, is the actantial metaphor of blood itself, and his blushing is in perfect conformity with this linguistic codal system. Semes of redness shared by both blood and embarrassment motivate the association: *Ne me fais plus rougir d'entendre tes soupirs* (1274).

Codal intersection occurs in the word *flammes* whose seme of redness attaches it equally to blood and to love, a variant of the water code: *Tes flammes désormais doivent être étouffées* (1276). Horace's metaphor for Camille takes the shape of a fiery monster. She symbolizes temptation, the curse, evil itself: *Et ce souhait impie encore qu'impuissant / Est un monstre qu'il faut étouffer en naissant* (1334). Camille and her insurgent desires must be stifled if the Cornelian ethic is to

survive. Horace sees to it that she is ultimately condemned to Hades: *Va dedans les enfers, plaindre ton Curiace* (1320).

At the dramatic point of codal intersection, Camille undergoes a subtle transformation expressed by a spatial metaphor of displacement: *Ne cherche plus ta soeur où tu l'avais laissée* (1283). Camille adopts an unprecedented posture of power, and her language is characterized by signifieds of combat, violence and death. Her signifying system remains constant, however, for she continues to utilize the code of water to convey power (*courroux du ciel, pleuvoir, déluge de feux*). A threat to her brother, the blood-thirsty tiger, Camille is depicted as *une furie, attaché à tes pas* (1285). In this analogy Horace is identified with blood and the prohibition of personal desire (*sang/défends*) and Camille with water (*larmes*). Her new found aggressivity and desire to prove the power of love set up a relationship of similarity between brother and sister which was prepared earlier in scene 4 by her threatening tone: *Qu'un véritable amour brave la main des Parques* (1195-96). In Act IV,5 her threats take the linguistic form of two hortatory subjunctives (*Puissent tant de malheurs / Que tu tombes* 1290-91) which are expanded later into a whole series. She inflicts on Horace a universal curse tantamount to treason and the total destruction of Rome (1305-1318). Camille's particular form of destruction reflects her own style and signifying practice of water. Hers is a reign not of terror in which the streets of Rome flow with wine but a reign of water, a literal "rain" (*pleuvoir*), a *déluge de feux*:

> Que le courroux du ciel allumé par mes voeux
> Fasse *pleuvoir* sur elle un *déluge* de feux!
>
> (1313-14)

Tears are the tenor of yet another metaphor of violence whose vehicle is a thunderbolt (*foudre*). Water and love (*coup de foudre*) are linked to the ethic of power and destruction: *Puissé-je de mes yeux y voir tomber ce foudre* (1315).

Camille's transformation from feminine weakness to strength is achieved linguistically by the collocation of water/blood semes in the poetic form *pleure/mort: Je l'adorais vivant, et je le pleure mort* (1282). Her association of water and death (*pleure/mort*) prepares Horace's blood-chilling oxymoron linking love (water code) and death: *Aime, aime cette mort qui fait notre bonheur* (1298). By affiliation with the dead lover, and by the force of her threatening language, Camille herself becomes associated with death. Hers is not a death of glory, however but one of personal pleasure: *Moi seule en être cause, et mourir de plaisir!* (1218). A woman alone, single and singular, Camille has said "no" to authority and has earned the right to be (*être*). The last word, *plaisir*, totally anathema to the Cornelian ethic of sacrifice in the name of a cause greater than the self, evokes the wrath of Horace and results in Camille's murder and public condemnation. To Horace, Camille represents nothing more than a water-logged philosophy (*pleurer*)! His is a hard ethic (*châtiment*) characterized by immediacy of action (*soudain*), repression against revolt (*oser*), and insistence on total obedience (*quiconque*) to a greater cause (*romain*):

> Ainsi recoive un châtiment soudain
> Quiconque ose *pleurer* un ennemi romain.

> (1322-23)

Like Sabine, who was literally repulsed by her own emotional tendencies in Act I, Camille continues to conceive of herself as a lowly female inclined to tears and ready to adopt an ethic of humanity. She evokes this lowered self-image ironically in order to proclaim what must be the ultimate curse on man—envy of a woman: *Que tu tombes au point de me porter envie* (1292).

Camille's complete separation and individuation are realized in this scene during her eloquent and anaphoric attack on Rome, the metaphoric equivalent of the father. Rome is the symbol of accepted authority, the blood ethic, the father whom Camille must kill in order to be a woman. By a subtle manipulation and alternation of pronouns, Rome is identified with Horace, the brother, who is nothing less in stature or morality than his father, the old Horace:

> Rome, qui t'a vu naître, et que ton coeur adore!
> Rome enfin que je hais parce qu'elle t'honore!

> (1303-04)

Rome is as much the father as Albe represents the mother, the fused self, man's first love:

> Albe où je commence de respirer le jour
> Albe, mon cher pays et mon premier amour.

> (I,1,28-30)

> Albe est ton origine: arrête et considère
> Que tu portes le fer dans le sein de ta *mère*.

> (I,1,55-56)

There is no doubt that Camille makes a courageous attempt to recreate her own identity as a woman. Nevertheless, Act IV ends not on a note of triumph but on one of reproach. Horace scorns Sabine's tears and feminine inferiority:

> Sèche tes *pleurs*, Sabine, ou les cache à ma vue.

> (1348)

> C'est à toi d'*élever* tes sentiments aux miens.

> (1343)

The best advice Horace can give to Sabine, who is in search of her female identity, is to imitate her husband!

> Sois plus femme que soeur, et, te réglant sur *moi*,
> Fais-toi de *mon exemple* une immuable loi.

> (1361-62)

Male hostility to females continues in Act V when old man Horace displays total indifference toward his daughter, Camille, who has been brutally murdered. This parricide, which is ultimately pardoned in the face of Horace's greater glory, illustrates the pernicious effect of fanaticism and the perversion of justice. With the shocking exoneration of this atrocity, which must have set Corneille's own legal mind on edge, the reader is drawn back to the text to re-read and reconsider the wisdom of Sabine's deliberations in a more sympathetic light.

Whether or not it was the intention of the author to shed light on the plight of the woman in the classical age, there is no doubt that Corneille has created, through a highly selective poetic language and an interrelated system of symbols, a gender-differentiated idiolect which mirrors the behavior and philosophical points of view of his characters. Close textual analysis and a study of a specific network of metaphors underlying the symbolic structure of the play have made it possible to determine the particular nature of these gender-differentiated idiolects in **Horace** and the degree to which they function in the literary language of classical tragedy.

Notes

1. This paper constitutes the product of research and discussion generated at the MLA session entitled The Function of Formality in French Classical Drama held in New York in December, 1981.

2. Tzvetan Todorov has traced the history and development of the sign/symbol differentiation in his book *Théories du symbole* (Paris: Seuil, 1977). A brief overview of the issues are found in Ducrot and Todorov. *Dictionnaire encyclonédique des sciences du language* (Paris: Seuil, 1972), 131-138.

3. cf. Thomas Sebeok, "The Semiotic Web: A Chronicle of Prejudices", *Bulletin of Literary Semiotics,* 2 (1975), 1-65.

4. cf. Claude Lévi-strauss, *Elementary Structures of Kinship* trans., Bell and Sturmer (Boston: Beacon Press, 1969): "Incest is a phenomenon which has the distinctive characteristics of both nature and of its theoretical contradiction, culture. The prohibition of incest has the universality of bent and instinct, and the coercive character of law and institution." (p. 10).

5. cf. II, 1, 385: Qui veut *mourir* ou vaincre est vaincu rarement;

II, 1, 399- Pour un coeur généreux *ce trépas* a des charmes;

400: La gloire qui le suit ne souffre point de *larmes,*

II, 3, 477- Et, rompant tous ces noeuds, s'armer pour la patrie

449: Contre *un sang* qu'on voudrait racheter de sa vie, Une telle vertu n'appartenait qu'à nous;

6. II, 1, 396- De tous les deux côtés, j'ai des pleurs à répandre:

397: De tous les deux côtés mes désirs sont trahis.

7. II, 3, 468- J'ai le coeur aussi bon, mais enfin je suis homme.

469: Je vois que votre honneur demande tout *mon sang.*

8. II, 3, 492: J'accepte aveuglément cette gloire avec *joie,*

cf. II, 3, 499- Avec *une allégresse* aussi pleine et sincere

500: Que j'épousai la soeur, je combattrai le frère;

9. cf. II,5,571: Vous en *pleurez,* Camille.

II,5,582: Et laissez-moi sauvez ma vertu de vos *pleurs;*

II,5,587: Allez, ne *m'aimez* plus, ne versez plus de *larmes,*

II,6,611: El laissant à ses *pleurs* vaincre ce grand courage,

10. Votre *sang* est trop bon, n'en craignez rien de lâche,

(II,6,615)

Commencez par sa soeur à répandre *son sang.*

Commencez par sa femme à lui *percer* le flanc.

(II,6,641-642)

Je verrai les lauriers d'un frère ou d'un mari

Fumer encor d'un *sang* que j'aurai tant chéri?

(II,6,649-650)

CINNA

CRITICAL COMMENTARY

Judd D. Hubert (essay date 1989)

SOURCE: Hubert, Judd D. "A Theatrical Reading of *Cinna.*" In *Convergences: Rhetoric and Poetic in Seventeenth-Century France, Essays for High M. Davidson,* edited by David Lee Rubin and Mary B. McKinley, pp. 101-09. Columbus: Ohio State University Press, 1989.

[*In the following essay, Hubert provides a metadramatic interpretation of* Cinna.]

In interpreting **Cinna,** not only do I favor a metadramatic approach, but I go so far as to postulate that a given character's so-called tragic flaw coincides with performative failure, or sometimes self-defeating success, as dramatist, director, actor, spectator.

Auguste, in substituting Cinna and Maxime for Maecenas and Agrippa, has hardly shown skill in casting. He has picked as advisers the leaders of a conspiracy against his life; he has substituted for his wayward daughter a firebrand eager to destroy him. Grown weary of the imperial role he himself had imposed, he wishes to abdicate and thus cease altogether to function as dramatist.

Emilie fares no better, for her part as lover constantly interferes with her star role as avenger. Inevitably, she lapses into a state of confusion, akin to the bewilderment of her beloved Cinna, that reluctant assassin who would gladly accept his casting as chief counselor in the imperial establishment. In Maxime, we find a character repeatedly upstaged and outperformed by every one, including his own confidant Euphorbe whose trite plotting generically belongs to comedy. Paradoxically, Corneille's remarkable success as playwright depends on these performative shortcomings of his dramatis personae—but naturally not on inadequacies on the part of his actors and actresses.

Metaphorically, exchange, as Jacques Ehrmann has shown,[1] dominates the play; while dramatically the big switch, as Susan Tiefenbrun has proved, operates throughout, even to the point of turning the political world upside down.[2] Finally, the often repeated motif of sacrifice relates equally to exchanging and switching; by reason of ambiguity, it contains within itself all the dynamics of reversal.

Cinna plans to kill the emperor during the religious ceremony, thereby conveniently substituting one sacrificial victim for another. The emperor's punishment would thus fit his numerous and well-documented crimes against the citizens of Rome. Cinna, Emilie, and even Auguste frequently describe the proscriptions and massacres of the civil war in terms of sacrificial immolations, a metaphorical switch conducive to dramatic reversal. The entire play lends itself to a Girardian interpretation; indeed, Corneille has dramatized a sacrificial crisis similar to those described in *La Violence et le sacré.*[3] One might even claim that the denoument of *Cinna* shows how Auguste puts an end to this crisis, not by a sacrifice but by the imposition of a new order based on law, relegating violence and religion to an inoperative past. But from a theatrical standpoint, Auguste has assumed a new role and assigned specific parts to his subordinates who must henceforth perform according to his script. Instead of rewriting chronicles, they face with equanimity a rigorously programmed future. Corneille, a thoroughly modern dramatist, not to say legal mind, dispenses altogether with scapegoats—not only here but even in his *Oedipe.* The emperor's achievement at the denouement may provide a *mis-een-abyme* of Cornelian drama, for he succeeds in imposing a workable order on the world, an order reflecting the efficacy expected of a well-made and professionally staged play. Auguste's historical triumph, which ends the tragedy, appears to arise from and reflect on Corneille's theatrical mastery.

The play opens with Emilie's dramatically complex soliloquy. She generates a plurality of voices pertaining to two conflicting personifications or, if you prefer, actants, each one striving for domination: revenge and love. Reversal operates from the beginning, for revenge, clearly defined as duty, arrogates the vocabulary of Eros: *désire, séduite, ardents transports* as well as such metonymies as *enfants* and *naissance.* Conversely, love, deprived in part of its usual terminology and forced to fall back on the vocabulary of duty, uses terms indicative of subordination or morality such as *sers, céder, honte, gloire, généreux.* Emilie reaches paradoxical heights in stating:

> Au milieu toutefois d'une fureur si juste,
> J'aime encore plus Cinna que je ne hais Auguste,
> Et je sens refroidir ce bouillant mouvement
> Quand il faut, pour le suivre, exposer mon amant.

[17-20]

Coldness pertains to love; boiling and fury to the self-imposed duty of avenging her father. As she no longer knows what role to perform or what play to write, she exhorts the warring factions within her to exchange their parts. In other words, she requires an impossible performance that would reflect not only her own predicament but also the proneness to reversal so characteristic of the play as well as the sacrificial crisis that undermines all action.

Stylistically, Emilie keeps at a distance the competing and alienating personifications she has herself set in motion. By thus combining displacement with presence, elusion with illusion, she automatically condemns herself to failure in everything she undertakes. Her own statements, in so far as we can distinguish them from the voices she puts into play, involve the related themes of evaluation and exchange, which we can also consider as metaphorical equivalents of her initial displacement

and elusion. Exchange and evaluation, however, have very little in common with love or with the kind of generosity which, at the end, will impose an acceptable order. Indeed, they can only lead to blackmail and a perpetuation of the sacrificial crisis: ". . . des mêmes présents qu'il verse dans mes mains / J'achète contre lui les esprits des Romains" (79-80). Auguste's material generosity will, by reversal, lead to his own undoing. But Emilie here and elsewhere advocates a moral switch, similar to the exchange of terminology between love and revenge: "Pour qui venge son père il n'est point de forfaits, / Et c'est vendre son sang que se rendre aux bienfaits" (83-84), and later: "Je fais gloire, pour moi, de cette ignominie" (973). Duty, through this reversal, assumes all the verbal characteristics of crime.

Unlike the secretive Emilie, Cinna, according to the narrative of his meeting with his co-conspirators, knows how to manipulate an audience:

> Au seul nom de César, d'Auguste, et d'empereur
> Vous eussiez vu leurs yeux s'enflammer de fureur,
> Et dans un même instant, par un effet contraire,
> Leur front pâlir d'horreur et rougir de colère.

[159-62]

Cinna's imaginary audience, by thus achieving a physionomical impossibility in responding to an identity, leaves far behind Corneille's real audience which, at that moment, can hardly feel hatred against an emperor who gave his name to a century. Moreover, this imaginary audience serves as a magnifying mirror for both Cinna's and Emilie's postures:

> Tous s'y montrent portés avec tant d'allégresse
> Qu'ils semblent comme moi servir une maîtresse;
> Et tous font éclater un si puissant courroux,
> Qu'ils semblent tous venger un père, comme vous.

[149-52]

In this manner, Cinna, even before he addresses them, has transformed the conspirators into performative extensions of himself and Emilie. Their behavior as audience leads from the beginning to an impossibility, as the models he provides for avenging a father and serving a mistress would seem to exclude one another no less than joy and wrath. Perhaps the behavior of the conspirators reflects the contradictions inherent in both Cinna and Emilie. Moreover, Cinna, in order to spellbind his audience, merely narrates the past; and the conspiracy against the emperor's life, by adding just another sacrifice and immolation, will do no more than repeat what has happened so frequently in the recent history of Rome.

Although Corneille may not have entrusted Cinna with his own superlative intelligence and imagination as dramatist, he has given him a keen sense of the spectacular and a remarkable understanding of his various audiences—the conspirators, Emilie, and the emperor. Like Emilie, he shows a weakness for personified abstractions:

> Ma vertu pour le moins ne me trahira pas:
> Vous la verrez, brillante au bord des précipices,
> Se couronner de gloire en bravant les supplices,
> Rendre Auguste jaloux du sang qu'il répandra,
> Et le faire trembler alors qu'il me perdra.
>
> [312-16]

Unlike Emilie, he makes his abstraction act in a spectacular and heroic manner. His narrative, written in the future tense, brings about another dramatic reversal, for it shows Auguste behaving like a craven victim and Cinna like an intrepid hero. The conspirator resembles La Fontaine's milkmaid Perette, even though he pitches his rhetoric on a somewhat higher plane. But recourse to rhetoric, particularly in the future tense, makes one suspect that Cinna does not exactly coincide with the heroic posture he intended for Emilie. In a sense, he sorely needs to limit himself to *vertu*, Roman of course, in the same way that Emilie has to exclude all but filial revenge. Both of them personify abstractions, perhaps because neither one has discovered a valid part to play or a suitable drama in which to perform.

Cinna achieves his greatest theatrical triumph in convincing Auguste to change his mind and continue to perform as emperor. Auguste had spoken of his political power in the vocabulary of personal, almost erotic, gratification, using such terms as *aimer, beautés, jouit, déplaît, assouvie, charmes, plaisirs, désir, possession.* He has thus operated a lexical reversal not unlike Emilie's, between personal and collective values. To convince Auguste of his error, Cinna reinstates the emperor's public image and the idea of glory or, in theatrical terms, his spectacular role in the universe as opposed to his private identity. Cinna's strategy consists, so to speak, in reasserting the positive values and attitudes prevalent in practically every serious play Corneille ever wrote. Although Cinna expresses opinions at variance with those he had advocated in his fiery statements to the conspirators, he nonetheless reasserts the compelling influence of the past, whereby he differs from the emperor who sees only the present. Theatrically, these two opposed standpoints express the relationship between immediacy and historical representation, between presence and fable. Cinna paradoxically reaffirms the historical perspective of the audience off-stage against the very statesman who had shaped the historical events! These events appear in three different perspectives: Auguste views them from the vantage point of personal gratification; Cinna, in his speech to the conspirators, as a pure unfolding; and, in his advice to Auguste, from the perspective of an admiring historian—after the fact and with an eye to the results:

> Si le pouvoir suprême est blâmé par Auguste,
> César fut un tyran, et son trépas fut juste,
> Et vous devez aux Dieux compte de tout le sang
> Dont vous l'avez vengé pour monter à son rang.
>
> [429-32]

According to this advice, only a positive political attitude toward power can give meaning to the past. Corneille's Cinna, a prize pupil of the Jesuits, justifies the emperor in terms of an implicit declaration of intentions. He himself had merely redirected his own intentions in moving from one audience to the next. In both instances, he provides his listeners with precisely the ideas they wish and expect to hear. Although he knows how to appeal to any audience, he does so in the manner of a catalyst rather than a dramatist. Worse still, he falls under the spell his own words have cast.

In attempting to counter Cinna's argument, Maxime also invokes the judgment of posterity, but in terms of personal transcendence rather than history:

> Votre gloire redouble à mépriser l'empire;
> Et vous serez fameux chez la postérité
> Moins pour l'avoir conquis que pour l'avoir quitté.
> Le bonheur peut conduire à la grandeur suprême;
> Mais pour y renoncer il faut la vertu même.
>
> [474-78]

By following Maxime's advice, Auguste would admire his own transcendent image in a sort of self-perpetuating immediacy. Maxime fails because the emperor must situate his role historically and perform actively rather than contemplatively in front of a vast and changing audience. Nonetheless, both Cinna and Maxime advocate complementary aspects of Cornelian drama: historical representation and heroic admiration, here given as antithetical, but that Auguste will reconcile and combine in the final scene.

In clinching the argument, Cinna associates two apparently antithetical concepts: finance and, surprisingly, pity, an inconspicuous commodity in Octave's rise to power:

> Que l'amour du pays, que la pitié vous touche;
> Votre Rome à genoux vous parle par ma bouche.
> Considérez le prix que vous avez coûté.
>
> [605-07]

How can Auguste possibly resist the touching spectacle of himself as leading man in a historical love duet with suppliant Rome? By comparison, Maxime's abstract images of virtue and generosity would hardly hold the stage.

Cinna, both in his address to the conspirators and his counsel to the emperor, merely catalyzes a mixture already present. He does not even possess a theatrical presence that he can claim as his own. His role in the imperial establishment derives from the emperor's miscasting, and his part in the conspiracy from Emilie's dramatization of past events. In both these contradictory capacities, he functions as a deputy, as an extension of competing playwrights, Auguste and Emilie.

Torn between the two of them, he has recourse to a reversal, to a lexical switch, whereby the beloved Emilie assumes all the characteristics of a tyrant, while Auguste, because of his appreciation of Cinna, deserves only love and service. In a sense, his advice to the emperor, based, or so he tells Maxime and Emilie, on deception, untruth and illusion, has convinced him as much as it has Auguste. He thus becomes an admirer, so to speak, of his own discourse, which happens to coincide with political truth, circa 1640. Through his mediation, the emperor has at last understood the value of historically motivated performance.

Caught between his newly discovered monarchical zeal and his oath to Emilie, or, if you prefer, two mutually exclusive scripts, Cinna once again falls back on a narrative written in the future tense:

> Vous le voulez, j'y cours, ma parole est donnée;
> Mais ma main, aussitôt contre mon sein tournée,
> Aux mânes d'un tel prince immolant votre amant,
> A mon crime forcé joindra mon châtiment,
> Et par cette action dans l'autre confondue
> Recouvrera ma gloire aussitôt que perdue.
>
> [1061-66]

The two irreconcilable texts will coincide, thanks to Cinna's imagination, in a spectacularly sacrificial display, hardly acceptable to Emilie or even the emperor. And like Auguste, Cinna combines, by means of illusion, the roles of sacrificer and victim.

Once he has discovered the conspiracy, Auguste, like Emilie and Cinna before him, hesitates between incompatible roles of revenge and clemency, but finally combines the part of victim with that of executioner in a spectacular narrative where Rome's sacrificial crisis reaches a climax:

> Meurs; mais quitte du moins la vie avec éclat;
> Eteins en le flambeau dans le sang de l'ingrat;
> A toi-même en mourant immole ce perfide;
> Contentant ses désirs, punis son parricide;
> Fais un tourment pour lui de ton propre trépas,
> En faisant qu'il le voie et n'en jouisse pas.
> Mais jouissons plutôt nous-même de sa peine,
> Et si Rome nous hait, triomphons de sa haine.
>
> [1179-86]

Auguste's narrative provides the same spectacular features as Cinna's, but stresses erotic, not to say sadomasochistic, gratification rather than heroic gesture and

replaces the future tense by the imperative, in keeping with the speaker's rank. Moreover, Auguste reverts to the private world from which Cinna's counsels had momentarily dislodged him, for once again he views power, punishment and sacrifice in terms of personal reaction. Clearly, he has not yet succeeded in putting his role, his act, and his play together. He too compounds elusion, for he describes himself as a "Coeur irrésolu / Qui fuit en même temps tout ce qu'il se propose!" (1188-89).

Another kind of discrepancy or displacement resulting from personal feelings occurs in Emilie: "D'où me vient cette joie? et que mal à propos / Mon esprit malgré moi goûte un entier repos!" (1288-89). And she adds: "A chaque occasion le ciel y fait descendre / Un sentiment contraire à celui qu'il doit prendre" (1292-93). It would seem that no character in the play can maintain any kind of unity of focus. A civil war rages within every one of them, leading to betrayal and self-betrayal.

Emilie's use of the word "descendre" may provide a clue to these discrepancies. Ascent and descent throughout the play appear equally favorable or unfavorable. Emilie cannot accept Cinna as a gift from the emperor, for this downward movement would bring shame and servitude, while an upward thrust on the part of Cinna, by immolating Auguste, would win her hand. However, Octave's usurpation of power, with its accompaniment of proscriptions, had certainly followed an upward movement, as the emperor himself suggests in a famous line: "Et monté sur le faîte, il aspire à descendre" (370). Perhaps the trouble derives from the inevitability of displacement and from the tendency to confuse identity with position or role.

Despite these contradictory feelings and movements, Auguste will nevertheless discover a solution acceptable to all, but only after he has uncovered the full extent of everybody's betrayal, proof of his descent into hell. Indeed, the downward movement must reach rock bottom before the resulting upward thrust can take over. Auguste exclaims:

> Je suis maître de moi comme de l'univers;
> Je le suis, je veux l'être. O siècles, ô mémoire,
> Conservez à jamais ma dernière victoire!
> Je triomphe aujourd'hui du plus juste courroux
> De qui le souvenir puisse aller jusqu'à vous.
>
> [1696-1700]

The emperor, speaking authoritatively in the present tense, finally puts his personal reactions and the world on precisely the same footing, with the full knowledge that he must impose his will both inside and outside. He realizes that these personal reactions had mattered even more, perhaps because they could do more damage, than all the conspiracies arrayed against him.

Indeed, he insists on his triumph over his wrath, without even mentioning his victory over the conspirators. He has laid the past to rest and takes charge of posterity. History, finally made meaningful, or suitable for representation, fills the stage at the moment the curtain drops.

Notes

1. Jacques, Ehrmann. "Les Structures de l'échange dans *Cinna*," *Les Temps Modernes,* 246, November 1966, pp. 929-60.

2. Susan Tiefenbrun, *Signs of the Hidden* (Amsterdam: Rodopi), pp. 181-208.

3. René Girard, *La Violence et le sacré* (Paris: Grasset, 1972).

POLYEUCTE

CRITICAL COMMENTARY

John Cairncross (essay date 1982)

SOURCE: Cairncross, John. "*Polyeucte*: A Flawed Masterpiece." *Papers on French Seventeenth Century Literature* 9, no. 17 (1982): 571-90.

[*In the following essay, Cairncross underscores the flaws in* Polyeucte *and traces the critical reaction to the play throughout the years.*]

For the last forty years, critics have placed **Polyeucte** (? 1642) on a pinnacle. The wave of enthusiasm can be traced back to Péguy's famous essay, *Victor-Marie, comte Hugo* (1910). But the groundswell of enthusiasm starts, significantly, just before the Second World War with Brasillach's *Corneille* (1938), where he defines the work as the greatest sacred drama of France, "the one in which all virtues, human or divine, are blended. Truly, the whole of Christianity is here." Monseigneur Calvet, whose commentary on the play comes four years later, is unremittingly dithyrambic. In 1949, Francis Ambrière has no hesitation in assuring his readers that it is "the greatest religious play *in the world*" (in English). Since then, apart from a few dissenting voices such as Schlumberger (a Protestant) and Adam (who can be roughly defined as anti-clerical), there has been almost complete unanimity on the subject. Pierre Michel, in his edition of the play (1972), lays it down that, in the current age, **Polyeucte** is regarded "not only as the summit of Corneille's art, but as his most living play".

Yet, strangely enough, until about 1935, critics were at one in showing considerable reservations about the work. As Petit de Julleville notes in the Hachette edition (p.32), "No illustrious voice was raised among the contemporaries to praise this tragedy highly." Boileau, the uncrowned king of literary circles, never mentions it, nor does Racine allude to it when welcoming the playwright's younger brother to the French Academy. The "learned" were unanimous in condemning it. Such success as it did achieve was among the groundlings, and was attributable to the touching idyll between Pauline (before her conversion) and her pagan suitor, Sévère. The "Christian" section, on the contrary, was condemned on all hands. We are told that, in the opinion of the influential Hôtel de Rambouillet, "the Christian element in particular had jarred very badly"—for reasons which will be dealt with below. This dichotomy in the play was stressed by almost all critics at the time.

Thus, the prince de Conti, a former patron of Molière and later a vigorous campaigner for purer morals, asks: "Is there anything dryer and more unattractive than the sacred half of the play? Is there anyone who is not a thousand times more deeply touched by the grief of Sévère when he finds that Pauline is married than by the martyrdom of Polyeucte?" Saint Evremond, a freethinker, is of much the same opinion. "What would have made a fine sermon would make a wretched tragedy were it not that the dialogue between Pauline and Sévère, animated by other feelings and passions, saved the author's reputation which the Christian virtues of our martyrs would have deprived him of." According to Voltaire, the classical scholar, Dacier, at a slightly later date, also attributed the success of the play to the scene between the former sweethearts. And Voltaire goes on to say: "This opinion is fairly general."

Voltaire's own view, apart from its frequently irreverent tone, is very much in line with these reactions. He admits that there are many fine traits in **Polyeucte** and that it needed a great genius to handle such a difficult subject. But his main contention is that the hero-martyr and his pious verse would long ago have been forgotten but for his wife's attraction to the handsome pagan. In the same spirit, he notes that "the undying success of the play is due to the extreme beauty of Sévère's role and to the *piquant* situation of Pauline".

Even in the nineteenth century, attitudes changed little. Talma, the famous actor, would have none of the martyr's role, but plumped unhesitatingly for that of Sévère whom he regarded as the main character. Sainte-Beuve is of much the same opinion. Petit de Julleville, as usual, sums up the position neatly when he says: "For two hundred years, everyone seems to have sided against Polyeucte; he is the obstacle in the way of the happiness of Pauline and Sévère; he is the disastrous accident which brings out the nobility of Sévère and the virtuousness of Pauline" (*op. cit.,* p.35). Such an interpretation, the critic continues, is completely wrong. In other words, the public has consistently misunderstood the playwright's intentions, and it is only through the superior insight of modern critics that we can get the play into perspective.

This is surely a somewhat naive approach and confuses intentions with effectiveness. No doubt Corneille *meant* Polyeucte to be the central figure in the drama, but one cannot simply excuse the writer for failing to translate his plans into effect by putting all the blame on the perversity of the audience who applauds at the wrong points.

In fact, there is a much simpler explanation. This is that the public were perfectly right in their preference—on literary and to some extent also on "ideological" grounds; it usually *is* in the right. Both the ethos and aesthetics of Corneille's other dramas correspond exactly to the aristocratic and this-wordly code set out in the pagan romance in **Polyeucte.** But this code is utterly at odds with the values of asceticism and contempt for the things of the world defended by the martyr. Corneille is thus operating on alien ground in the latter episodes. Moreover, the other-worldly precepts preached by the hero never really took deep roots in France, even at the height of the Counter-Reformation. And the two halves simply do not blend.

What is perhaps more serious is that, in an age when absolute subservience to the state was current, Corneille had to represent his main character as a hot-headed and fanatical rebel, and at the same time contend that the Christians were faithful soldiers of the Emperor in order to justify the final triumph of Christianity. Then, persecution would give way (under the same monarch) to tolerance going as far as the appointment of a Christian provincial governor. Such a reassuring *dénouement* was inevitable in a play dealing with martyrdom, or indeed in baroque "tragi-comedies" in general. Lastly, the attempt to cram such a rich tale into the tight framework of the classical tragedy was bound to fail, especially in the exposition, the more so as Corneille observed the three unities more scrupulously in this work than in **Le Cid** and even than in **Cinna.**

On the success of Corneille's stagecraft, characterization and verse in the Sévère-Pauline idyll there is no need to dwell. Critics of the most varying schools are in agreement on this point, while sometimes deploring its beauty and power. Adam is surely right when he describes the meeting of the two former sweethearts as "one of the summits of the literature of all time".

Similarly, Sévère's moral grandeur, which makes him cousin to so many others of Corneille's heroes, provides another example of that nobility of soul so vigorously applauded in his plays.

But, when we turn to Polyeucte, the picture changes. In the exposition, the problem is largely a technical one. Even the most resourceful genius could hardly develop a subject which presupposes the marriage and conversion and covers the baptism of the hero in the space of twenty-four hours (or less). The subject—a baroque one if there ever was—imposed an impossible strain on the classical framework. The perceptive Schlumberger rightly defines the tragedy as "the most hazardous undertaking on which Corneille had ever ventured".

Yet, in chalking out his plan, Corneille started with the substantial advantage of having invented almost all the details. No other tragedy of his owes so little to his sources. But such freedom availed him little. The setting out of the facts is both inadequate and unenlightening. All we can glean from the play is that the hero has been married for two weeks, but the courtship seems to have lasted a somewhat longer period. Presumably, the conversion came after the marriage. It can hardly be supposed that Polyeucte, who seems to have plunged into action against paganism without worrying about the complications for his wife, married her without telling her of the momentous change in his faith. Moreover, he never appears to have posed the question of being remarried by a Christian rite, and defines his marriage as realizing "un juste et sainte amour". (51).

The essential point is that he is a young man deeply in love, and the whole tone of the first few scenes vis-à-vis his wife is one of *galanterie* and high comedy (especially when he takes flight in order to be baptized). He puts the fear of offending his wife (in the case of "men like me") above fear of death. And his amorous attitude extends (though not always very tactfully) up to the point immediately preceding his conversion (621-6). So much so, that Michel (*op. cit.,* p. 59, n. 6) asks: "How could one ever suspect that grace is about to take possession of [the hero] and make him give up the woman he loves?" How indeed?

The contrast between Néarque's severity and Polyeucte's light-hearted approach clearly emerges. To the bachelor mentor, he replies that his marriage justifies a little delay, and that, if he is called upon to face torture, God will give him strength. One has the impression, notes Schlumberger, that the change of faith for the hero is a somewhat superficial affair. He "does not seem to suspect that conversion means a reversal of all feelings and that a man does not hasten to baptism between two rounds of billing and cooing during his honeymoon" (*Plaisir à Corneille,* p. 90).

Ideally what was needed was a much wider time horizon, in which we would have been shown Polyeucte revelling in his married bliss, *then* the conversion, and gradually the realization of what such a profound change entails and of the fearful conflict which it may raise (or *will,* in Néarque's view) between earthly and heavenly love.

As it is, the evolution is such as to leave the spectator unconvinced, and nowhere as much as when the hero experiences the inrush of grace. Up till line 636, as has often been pointed out, Polyeucte has behaved perfectly "normally". When he takes leave of Pauline to attend the pagan ceremony, he promises her that he will be correct towards Sévère.

> Nous ne nous combattrons que de civilité.
>
> (636)

But four lines later we guess and, three lines after that, we know, that he means to commit an outrage on the established faith. This is the crucial development in the play, since it paves the way for his martyrdom.

The switch from day-to-day behaviour to religious fervour is so abrupt as to be inexplicable. Naturally, we know that the change is to be attributed to grace. And the new-found ardour can be explained theologically, and faithfully reflects the doctrines—especially those on grace—which Corneille imbibed from his Jesuit mentors. But *Polyeucte* is a play, and not an exposition of doctrine. In all the rest of Corneille's dramatic works, sudden changes (such as those of Auguste and Emilie in *Cinna*) have been carefully led up to—as is essential if the spectator's assent is to be won. This particular episode is totally at odds with Corneille's usual stagecraft, or, we might add, with that of any other accomplished playwright.

The problem raised by the hero's conduct after his conversion is of much the same nature. It is that of a clash between the ethos of martyrdom and the values which he consistently expounded in his other plays. In short, when trying to cast some of his material in a Counter-Reformation mould, he was imposing a serious constraint on his creative genius.

The values which he was propounding in the Christian part of *Polyeucte* are explicitly formulated. A convert must, we learn (talking of God),

> Négliger, pour lui plaire, frère, enfants, mère et femme,
>
> (75)

a precept at the antipodes of a code which glorifies rank, and the corresponding ambition and privileges.

The maxim in the line just quoted is, as the Bordas edition observes, in line with the teaching of the Gospels. But it is not usually practised. And it required no great skill on Molière's part to hold this attitude up to ridicule in *Tartuffe* when he makes Orgon confess:

> Et je verrais mourir frère, enfants, mère et femme
> Que je m'en soucierais autant que de cela.
>
> (278-79)

Little wonder that, ever since the première, the audience's sympathies have usually been all with Pauline who is sacrificed, "without a qualm", on the altar of the convert's convictions. What is more, when she urges him desperately to allow himself to be saved from execution, she finds her devotion contemptuously rejected as "Honteux attachements de la chair et du monde" (1107) and as "ruses de l'enfer". (1653).

Polyeucte's conduct has been defended by an English editor who writes: "In an age of tranquillity, it is easy to dismiss his actions as fanatical and inhuman. Recent events have shown us that anyone may find himself face to face with similar problems." But the fact is that Polyeucte does not "find himself" in a debacle. He plunges into it, committing in the process "both treason and sacrilege" (925). He is not, like anti-Nazis or Soviet dissidents, willing to risk death or imprisonment for his beliefs. He is heaven-bent on martyrdom, regardless of the consequences (for his wife, among others). He sees his friend, Néarque, go to death "with envious eyes" (958). Earlier in the play, when the same Néarque tries to dissuade Polyeucte from committing his rash gesture of overthrowing the idols, he replies that he knows he is risking his life, but that he will be certain of salvation.

> Mes crimes, en vivant, me la pourraient ôter.
> Quand elle ouvre le Ciel, peut-elle sembler dure?
>
> (664-66)

In fact, the totalitarian spirit in the play is represented by the martyr, and not by the tolerant Roman pagan régime.

Similarly, he has a masochistic desire for suffering. For Christians

> Les supplices . . . sont ce qu'à nous les plaisirs,
>
> (951)

i.e. for pagans, says Pauline. And her husband amply confirms this view.

> [La félicité] d'un vrai chrétien n'est que dans les souf-
>   frances;
> Les plus cruels tourments lui sont des récompensees.
> Dieu, qui rend le centuple aux bonnes actions,
> Pour comble donne encor les persécutions.
>
> (1535-38)

Lines 89-90 express the same concept.

If we look for a true parallel with such a delight in the morbid, we have not far to seek. *The Martyrdom of Saint Bartholomew* by Ribera, in the Prado, echoes the mood to perfection. Ribera, it may be recalled, was a Spanish artist who spent a great part of his life in Naples (then the capital of the Spanish dominions in Italy), and used his Caravaggesque technique to emphasize the harrowing mental and physical sufferings of martyred saints and penitents. The picture is generally dated 1639, or just before *Polyeucte* was first performed.

The clash between the martyr's profession of faith and the ethos prevailing in France at that time is particularly visible in the relation of the Christians in the play to established authority. We have already seen the negative reaction of the Hôtel de Rambouillet to the work because of the Christian element. The nature of this opposition is spelt out in an account by Voltaire. According to this writer, the whole of the Hôtel de Rambouillet, and particularly Godeau, the Bishop of Vence, was loud in its demunciation of the hero's iconoclastic zeal. "People said that this [gesture] was imprudent, that several bishops and synods [of the early church] had expressly forbidden the attacks on law and order; and that Christians were even refused communion if, by such foolhardly attacks, they exposed the church to persecution."

The all-powerful Cardinal de Richelieu also frowned on the play, allegedly on the grounds that nobody was put up to refute the slanders on the early Christians put into the mouth of Stratonice (780-83). This is not impossible, but it overlooks the fact that the main charge against the Christians was that they were rebels, and that Polyeucte behaves as a rebel in the play. It seems much more probable that the prince of the church who, like most of the men of his age, glorified "la raison d'état" was more concerned with a Christian defying the state and revelling in his defiance. It should be remembered that France had just emerged from bloody wars of religion and that most Frenchmen were profoundly disturbed at any threat to the new-found equilibrium and order. The hero's reckless attack on the official cult and his unbridled militancy filled the average Frenchman with horror.

The probability of such an interpretation being correct is borne out by a similar view, expressed by Madame de Maintenon, the power behind Louis XIV at the time of the Revocation of the Edict of Nantes (which had guaranteed tolerance to French Protestants). Writing in 1688 (three years after the Revocation), she said: "One ought above all to forbid performances which convey the idea of martyrdom, nothing being more dangerous for the New Catholics *[as the forcible converts were called]* and for the old ones."

It need only be added that the average theatre-goer of the time was much better read in ecclesiastical history than his modern equivalent, and was well aware of the ban on the provocation of the authorities by the early church—a point which is skated over gracefully by many modern writers.

In the play, the Christians are constantly stamped (by the pagans) as rebels. And Polyeucte, by his gesture, amply justifies this charge. It will be remembered that, in ancient Rome, civic and religious rites were inextricably interwoven. Even such a liberal emperor as Marcus Aurelius was determined, notes Michel (*op. cit.,* p. 36, n. 7), to stamp out Christianity as representing a threat to social order.

The subversiveness of Polyeucte's outrage is, if anything, underlined by him in subsequent declarations. He denounces Decius, the Emperor, as "tigre altéré de sang," (1125), an anti-Christ who has destroyed God's saints and who will soon be called upon to pay for his sins. (He was in fact killed the following year.)

In the face of these statements, it is difficult to take very seriously his announcement that

> Je dois ma vie au peuple, au prince, à sa couronne.
>
> (1211)

It is a strange way of serving his king to profane a ceremony of which the king was an integral part.

Nor does he show the slightest sign of retracting or of apologizing for his deeds. On the contrary. He would repeat the gesture

> Même aux yeux de Félix, même aux yeux de sévère,
> Même aux yeux du Sénat, aux yeux de l'Empereur.
>
> (1672-73)

Given such defiance, it is hardly to be wondered at that Decius is represented as taking a firm line with the new religion.

The conversion of Pauline suffers from the same flaws as that of her husband—and for the same reasons. Partly it takes place with such speed and lack of motivation that the spectator is left unconvinced, and partly it is manifestly inserted in the play in order to show the blood of the martyr working wonders from on high and preparing the final triumph of the church. Both aesthetics and substance combine to weaken this episode.

Throughout Act IV and most of Act V she is rejected by her husband, and his lack of response to her devotion has certainly not endeared him to her. Thus, in line 1580, she cries to Félix and Polyeucte:

> . . . Qui de vous deux m'aujourd'hui m'assassine?

Five lines later on, she cries to her husband:

> Tigre! Assassine-moi du moins sans m'outrager.

Just before she is led off to die, she exclaims:

> Ne désespère pas une âme qui t'adore.

(1607)

In the spirit of conjugal fidelity, she swears that she will follow him to the grave (1681). When she next appears on the stage (1719), she tells us that

> Mon époux, en mourant, m'a laissé ses lumieres.

(1724)

And she cries,

> Je vois, je sais, je crois, je suis désabusée.

(1727)

It is not clear what she sees, and the only psychological explanation of her sudden change is that she has decided to adopt Polyeucte's faith in order to preserve her links with him. The real answer is that the *dénouement* called for her conversion.

Another line of approach is that Pauline has all the virtues needed for conversion and has been consistently sympathetic to her husband's new creed. Neither contention will hold water. Many of Corneille's pagan heroines are similarly virtuous, but it has never been suggested that they should turn Christian. Pauline is in fact typical of the playwright's "généreux" ethos, as is the whole of the pagan section of the play. And her comments on the Christians are consistently hostile. Her first reference is unambiguous: ". . . des chrétiens une impie assemblée." (234). When Pauline tells her attendant to stop talking about the sectarians (265), it is not because she dislikes the girl's strictures, but because she does not want the delicate subject to be discussed in her father's hearing (especially after the nightmare, with its various threats and its mention of the impious sect).

Her later statements are on the same lines. In line 254, she refers to ". . . des chrétiens les complots et les charmes." When Polyeucte's outrage is denounced, she agrees that the Christians have all the defects and vices. Polyeucte is

> Un méchant, un infâme, un rebelle, un perfide.

(781)

Again, when she stresses the Christians' resistance to torture (934-6), she is not defending them, but persuading Félix that it is useless to expect his son-in-law to recant under pressure. In the key scene between husband and wife, Pauline sweeps aside Polyeucte's arguments in defence of his conduct with the withering comment:

> Voilà de vos chrétiens les ridicules songes;
> Voilà jusqu'à quel point vous charment leurs mensonges.

(1199-1200)

When, a little later, Polyeucte urges her to adopt his creed, she is profoundly shocked:

> Que dis-tu, malheureux? Qu'oses-tu souhaiter?

(1273)

And, in a final plea to her father, she admits that the prisoner's crime is "à peine pardonnable," (1615) and terms the offender "mad". In short, she is always and unvaryingly hostile to Christianity.

The conversion of Félix is even more astonishing. If we are to adopt virtue as the explanation of conversion, what are we to say in this case? Again, the real reason for his sudden and unforeseeable switch is to pave the way for the *Laus dei* at the end.

But it is not only his unmotivated illumination that mare this part of the play. It is also the sharp contradiction between his role of villain (heavily underscored by Corneille) and his clarity as regards the happenings in the tragedy. True, he is hardly a lovable character, especially when he daydreams that, once Polyeucte is out of the way, Sévère, the Emperor's favourite, will be free to marry his daughter. He is utterly mistaken, too, when, with his cheap Machiavellianism, he imagines that Sévère is merely trying to trap him by pleading in favour of the prisoner's life.

However, the constant attacks on his decision to execute his son-in-law are completely unjustified (1747-50). Félix rightly emphasizes that Polyeucte's crime is treason, and he has gone to great lengths in trying to save the offender. He should by rights, and in observance of the Emperor's instructions, have dispatched him at once. In such circumstances,

> Le sang ni l'amitié n'ont plus de privilège.

(926)

When Félix's confidant, Albin, joins the pressure group to have Polyeucte pardoned, Félix replies coolly that such an act would mean forfeiting his own post and probably his life. Sévère may indulge in the belief that he is strong enough at court to sway the Emperor, but Félix, with every show of reason, replies

> Je connais mieux que lui la haine de Décie.

(1484)

In short, the idea that Félix is merely being hard-hearted in sticking to the law is a carefully fostered *trompe-l'oeil*. Corneille needed to generate sympathy for Polyeucte and hate for Félix. But, as the Governor constantly repeats, if Polyeucte goes to his death, this is because he is determined on it and refuses to grasp any of the lifebuoys offered him.

Neither Sévère's please for mercy (misinterpreted) nor the curious rising (1067-72) of the mob (which had at first been horrified 833 at the attack on its idols) affects the main issue. They may have hastened the prisoner's death (1752 and 1080). They have not influenced what was, short of a miracle, an inevitable execution. Like Félix's manoeuvre, they create suspense and also the illusion that Polyeucte *might* have escaped.

Lastly, there is the question of the *dénouement*. Petit de Julleville suggested (*op. cit.,* p. 178, n. 4) that the play could with advantage have ended on line 1762, that is, before Félix's conversion. But such a course, though more dramatically satisfying, would have deprived the playwright of the very effects which were essential for him. Nevertheless, that critic was right in feeling that there was an odd incongruity between the play and its end. It is not just that Félix's change of heart strikes one as bizarre, especially when he refers to the previous events (including the chopping off of his son-in-law's head) as "notre heureuse aventure". (1811) It is rather that the *dénouement* and the premises of the play do not correspond.

The contradictions are particularly patent in the words and deeds of Sévère. The evolution of this character is worth following. Up to line 1394 (i.e. almost to the end of Act IV), he is the great-hearted pagan gentleman who is deeply in love with Pauline and ready to intervene at her request in favour of Polyeucte. His confidant warns him that this is an impossible venture, since Decius regards the Christians as rebels and traitors. The favorite will therefore run the risk of forfeiting his standing at court should he persist in his quixotic gesture of trying to rescue a sectarian accused of a serious crime against the state. Nevertheless, Sévère goes so far as to threaten Félix with disgrace unless he pardons the offender. Here we are in an unreal world, for it is unthinkable that Decius should remove or downgrade a trusted functionary merely because he has faithfully carried out orders (as indeed Félix had done in the past) (256).

But this curious conduct (with its underlying misunderstandings or illusions) is simply the forerunner of a curious transmogrification of Sévère's role. All of a sudden, the Roman knight launches out into a lengthy tirade which reveals him as a sympathizer with the new creed (1411-43). A kind of Christian fellow-traveller, he affirms that he is unaware of the reasons for their persecution (1413). But all the other pagan characters in the play could, and in some cases do, enlighten him on this matter. And he has seen for himself Polyeucte's "treasonable" act in toppling the idols.

Leaving aside the positive reasons for his sympathy with them (such as their blameless morals), we may concentrate on the two heads of accusation stressed in the play. One is that they are sorcerers. Sévère does not deal very convincingly with this charge, but sidesteps it deftly, and comments that other religions . . . "ont leurs secrets comme eux". (1420). Hence, he suggests, discrimination against them on that score is unjustified.

But the crux of the problem is elsewhere. It lies in the charge of disloyalty to the Emperor and his cult. Sévère delivers a certificate of good conduct to them on the field of battle (1439-42). But, as Couton points out (*Corneille,* p. 79), the Christians cannot possibly render unto Caesar what is Caesar's if that involves bowing the knee to what they regard as false gods. Which it does. Hence, Sévère is simply being naive or disingenuous or both, when he puts serving God and the Emperor on the same plane and in the same line (1804)—unless of course he is deceiving himself into thinking that the new religion has already become the established one.

In fact, Sévère's acts imply that the new régime is already here, or at least is imminent. He not only confirms the Christian convert, Félix, in his office as Governor of the province, but also promises an end to persecution—both of which are utterly improbable in the circumstances. (In fact, the change came over fifty years later.) His optimism is based on his naive conviction that he can win round the Christian-eater, Decius. He comments somewhat airily that the Emperor and he see eye to eye on everything except on this one point (the persecution of the Christians), on which the official policy seems unjust (1414), much as if this were a minor detail which need merely be brought to the Emperor's attention for it to be immediately corrected.

These illusions are only explicable by the fact that he, too, is virtually a convert, and goes so far as to say of the Christians:

> J'ai trop de pitié d'eux pour ne pas les défendre.
>
> (1443)

This change of heart and the illusory hopes which it inspires (illusory not just in terms of history, but of the dramatic presuppositions of the action), are needed to complete the picture of harmony and of the triumph of the faith—a kind of baroque "glory", suffusing the end of the play in a rich reassuring glow.

The ending thus devised is miraculous. As Polyeucte points out:

> Mais ces secrets pour vous sont fâcheux à comprendre.
>
> (1539)

Such a form of art is poles apart from the Jansenist approach exemplified in Racine's *Athalie* or *Phèdre* where miracles are portrayed as being plausible, and hence distinguishable as such only to the elect (as was the case of the ageing queen's tenderness for the youthful Joas). The gain to verisimilitude in art in such a conception is clear. This probably explains why most critics, regardless of belief, are agreed in regarding *Athalie* as the supreme religious tragedy in French literature.

Polyeucte, however, is a masterpiece, too, though a flawed one, and for slightly different reasons than those usually advanced. Hence, if readers do not pitch their expectations too high, they can only derive pleasure from such an unusual and remarkable play.[1]

Note

1. This article is reproduced, with slight alterations, from the *Preface* to my translation of *Polyeucte* published in a Penguin volume of plays by Corneille (pp. 23-37) by kind permission of Penguin Books Ltd.

LE MENTEUR (THE LIAR)

CRITICAL COMMENTARY

Elaine R. Hopkins (essay date winter 1981)

SOURCE: Hopkins, Elaine R. "Comedy and Parody in *Le Menteur.*" *Romance Notes* 22, no. 2 (winter 1981): 192-96.

[*In the following essay, Hopkins elucidates the elements of classical tragedy which are parodied in* The Liar.]

Histories of the theatre show that tragedy came first, and that comedy developed later as a new reflection upon well-known themes. In *Tragedy and Comedy,* Walter Kerr states that the Greek tragic trilogies almost always were followed by a fourth play, a comic treatment of the same material covered in the tragedies. This was the "satyr play," from which our word *satire* got its original meaning of a comic imitation. Kerr states further that

> The earliest comic fragments to have survived are parodies of serious passages from the *Iliad* and the *Odyssey,* and the very first playwright who can be identified as a comic playwright, Epicharmus, seems to have specialized in burlesquing heroic legend.[1]

At its origin comedy was essentially mimetic, and parody was the technique used to express the comic message.

Edouard Morot-Sir has suggested in his article "La dynamique de théâtre et Molière" that parody would not be comic without an element of gaiety, but would rather be "grimaçante, grinçante, et vite insupportable." By the same token, "sans parodie la gaieté de la fête tomberait vite dans l'ennui et ne réussirait pas à créer le miracle théâtral."[2] Morot-Sir and Kerr both affirm the idea that comedy is a parody of tragedy.[3] In the 17th century tragedy was considered the superior genre, and the spectators defined comedy by contrast with tragedy. A large part of the magic of Molière's comedy consists of the parodic treatment of tragedy, particularly of the tragic style. This enabled him to compete with Corneille's popularity while helping to establish comedy's reputation and respectability.

Kerr writes, "Comedy, it seems, is never the gaiety of things, it is the groan made gay."[4] This touches the essence of comedy, and justifies the widespread use of parody in comedy. A tragic plot generally consists of an unfortunate fate befalling an innocent victim: this is the "groan." In order to parody themes and structures of tragedy, one may simply set up a potentially tragic situation which through wit and accident has a happy ending. This is precisely what Corneille, as the reigning tragedian of his time, was in a perfect position to do. ***Le Menteur*** is adapted from *La Verdad Sospechosa* of Juan de Alarcón, to whom Corneille owes the plot; the style and the ending are his own. The problem of authorship is unimportant here. It is important that Corneille chose to adapt a comedy at a time when he was producing some of his greatest tragedies. The play contains evidence of parody.

There are four elements of classical tragedy which are parodied in ***Le Menteur***: 1) the situation, 2) the *dénouement,* 3) the hero, and 4) the style.

The situation in which we find Dorante, the hero, is a parody of that of many comedies before and since ***Le Menteur,*** and also of tragedy: two young lovers thwarted by an odious parent. In traditional comedy the parent always gives in or is tricked, and the lovers get married in the end. The tragic version of this plot results in a play like *Romeo and Juliet.* There is no sacrifice in comedy, but tragedy requires it. Géronte is a caricature of the unyielding father of tragedy and of traditional comedy. He only wants Dorante to be happy and shows himself to be very indulgent toward his son even when he thinks that Dorante has gotten married without his consent and is about to have a child. His only concern is that Dorante get married and provide him with grandchildren. As a consequence of the confusion of the names of Clarice and Laucrèce, Dorante refuses to accept the hand of the woman his father wants him to marry, who is precisely the one he loves. But, as if by chance, Dorante finds that the woman he will be forced to marry in the end is as worthy of his affection as the other; a potentially tragic ending is thus averted, and no sacrifice is required.

The second parodic element of **Le Menteur** is the *dénouement,* and more particularly the moral which follows. The *dénouement* in this case is a parody of the cathartic effect of tragedy and of comedy as well which has as its intention to teach a moral lesson. Tartuffe receives his just punishment, Agnès tricks Arnolphe, and so on. Dorante is a master *fourbe,* but he triumphs in the end. The last verses, pronounced by Cliton, indicate that Corneille took Dorante's side against society and admired his cleverness and wit. The "moral" of the play parodies all traditional morals: Corneille celebrates rather than discourages men of wit, even if it is in deceit that they excel:

> Comme en sa propre fourbe un menteur s'embarrasse
> Peu sauraient comme lui s'en tirer avec grâce.
> Vous autres qui doutiez s'il en pourrait sortir,
> Par un si rare exemple apprenez à mentir.[5]

Dorante can be identified immediately as a comic rather than a tragic hero by his very name, and as soon as he utters his first speech he reveals his bourgeois background. He details for Cliton his changes in plans: he had gone to school to study law, but gave it up to become a soldier. He is fresh from school, but has put on a new uniform to hide his inexperience and to appear *à la mode.* As soon as the ladies appear on the scene, the flow of lies begins, so fast and so outrageous throughout the play that even Cliton cannot say when Dorante is lying and when he is telling the truth. There is no conflict between honor and duty in this hero's mind, and the gratification of passion is sought through any available means. The tragic possibilities are numerous, not for Dorante but for his victims. However, the entire atmosphere is one of light-hearted recklessness, and we are not concerned with who may get hurt by Dorante's lies. At several moments he is on the verge of betraying himself, but he always catches himself in time, and we applaud him.

Tragic style is parodied through two different types of discourse, the first of which is amorous. Dorante sees Clarice and falls in love immediately. They use the traditional *précieux* vocabulary of love which is found in classical tragedy, indeed in Corneille's own tragedies: *feu, flamme, s'embrase, étincelle, brûler,* etc. This vocabulary is here used in a much different context: for Dorante, love is a word game based on the illusion that he wants to create. The "love" he experiences is closer to lust, and its direction changes *au besoin.* Clarice is betrothed to Alcippe, but attracted to Dorante. She would willingly abandon Alcippe for Dorante, but she is a *chevalière d'industrie,* and wants to be sure that Dorante will marry her. Love for Clarice is a social convention based on inclination and curiosity.

Heroic discourse, the verbal preoccupation of tragic heroes (Corneille's own in particular) with *honneur* and *devoir,* is parodied in **Le Menteur.** At the beginning of the fifth scene of the first act of **Le Cid,** the dishonored Don Diègue asks his son, "Rodrigue, as-tu du cœur?" (p. 768). There are in this line so many potentially comic elements that a slightly ironic delivery would cause the audience to dissolve in laughter. Corneille played up the ironic aspect of this line, and he parodied his own tragic style by inserting essentially the same line into an incongruous context, thereby creating a comic effect. Géronte comes onstage saying to Dorante, "Etes-vous gentilhomme?" (p. 1181). These are not nobles, but *bourgeois gentilshommes,* and the serious tone of Geronte's worrying about his honor is comical when read with a consciousness of the parody.[6] Géronte uses the same vocabulary as Don Diègue—*honneur, naissance, vertu, rang, sang, gloire,* etc. Géronte's last line in this scene—"Et que ton sang indigne à mes pieds répandu / Rendra prompte justice à mon honneur perdu." (p. 1185)—would have an hilarious effect upon the spectator reacting to the contrast between these words and the character of Géronte, especially as compared with that of Don Diègue.

The last scene of the play also includes a direct quote from one of Corneille's own tragedies, written just before **Le Menteur.** Both marriages will take place, to everyone's great satisfaction, and each party offers a comment on the subject. All the parents involved are in agreement with their children, and Lucrèce borrows a line from Camille (**Horace**) and affirms, "Le devoir d'une fille est dans l'obéissance" (p. 1196). If one remembers the circumstances which sollicited this comment in the tragedy, Lucrèce's use of the same line is all the more comic. Duty here is a pleasure, because it requires that she marry the man she loves, whereas for Camille duty had meant a real sacrifice.

In the past comedy and tragedy were two separate genres, each with its own rules and conventions. Throughout history comedy has been tragedy's inferior rival, skillfully using parody to gain acceptance as a legitimate brother. Tragedy as an art form represents the expression of a certain type of deep human emotion. This form of expression dominated the theatre in ancient Greece, in Elizabethan England, and in 17th-century France. Parody is a form of expression also generated by a deep human need. In contemporary theatre it is parody which dominates. Authors such as Ionesco, Beckett, Genet, Adamov, and Ghelderode use parody not just as a technique, but as a *mode,* one which suits the modern audience's experience better than pure comedy or pure tragedy.

Notes

1. Walter Kerr, *Tragedy and Comedy,* (New York: Simon and Schuster, 1967), p. 23.

2. Edouard Morot-Sir, "La dynamique de théâtre et Molière", in *Romance Notes,* Volume XV, Supplement No. 1 (1973), p. 47.

3. I consider parody to be a *mode,* expressing a world-view, a manner of reacting to the world. The parodic mode uses techniques of imitation (including travesty and burlesque) with comic and/or derisive intent. The possible objects of parody in literature (although this is not its exclusive domain) include texts, styles, genres, conventions, and other systems of signification.

4. *Tragedy and Comedy,* p. 19.

5. *Théâtre Complet,* Editions de la Pléiade, (Paris: Gallimard, 1950), p. 1197. All subsequent references to Corneille's plays will be to this edition.

6. This particular technique of treating a common subject in noble style is called travesty, and it is a subset of the general category of parody.

RODOGUNE, PRINCESSE DES PARTHES (*RODUGNE, PRINCESS OF PARTHES*)

CRITICAL COMMENTARY

Gervais E. Reed (essay date February 1990)

SOURCE: Reed, Gervais E. "Visual Imagery and Christian Humanism in *Rodogune*." *French Review* 63, no. 3 (February 1990): 464-74.

[*In the following essay, Reed considers Corneille's emphasis on visual imagery and Christian theology in* Rodogune.]

Nearly 350 years after its first run in Paris, Pierre Corneille's *Rodogune* still stimulates critical discussion.[1] For example, Jacques Scherer (xx) has argued that *Rodogune* represents Corneille's desire to return to the excitement of depicting horrible crimes like those of *Médée,* his first tragedy. Couton (II, 1283) echoes this judgment in his new edition of the playwright's complete works. Because the tragedy of ideas had run its course, Couton says, Corneille depoliticized this play as well as *Théodore* and *Héraclius,* and he did

with all three tragedies what journalists do when news runs dry: he put crime on the front page. According to Serge Doubrovsky (292), violation of human nature became a new motif in Corneille's production when he created monstrous female figures like Cléopâtre. Unlike August, Horace, or Polyeucte, these heroines do not dominate the currents and counter-currents of their human nature; rather, they subordinate everything to politics. Robert J. Nelson (166) hears in *Rodogune* a discordant note in the Cornelian canon, while, more recently, Mitchell Greenberg (150-53) has followed this line of reasoning to say that Cornelian tragedy fell into a metaphysical quagmire, exemplified by the pessimistic conclusion to *Rodogune.* On the other hand, André Stegmann chides Doubrovsky for not seeing the source of Cléopâtre's evil actions in her unrestrained human nature. According to Stegmann, Corneille depicts the same heroic effort and the same personal virtues that we find in earlier plays, but now they threaten to lead to impure ends. Although the young heroes Antiochus and Séleucus behave passively, their inaction leads unexpectedly to a happy ending. Like Stegmann, Marie-Odile Sweetser (145-60) proposes that Corneille resolved—not without difficulty, especially concerning Séleucus' death—a Manichaean struggle to show the triumph of love and a providential action. Finally, Marc Fumaroli argues for historical continuity in all of Corneille's work. The playwright's theoretical essays serve as evidence, he says, that Corneille writing as a critic in 1660 felt perfectly comfortable with what he had written as a poet almost twenty years earlier. *Rodogune,* Fumaroli says, has a double meaning. The play depicts a pagan world in which natural reason cooperates unwittingly with Providence; because of this cooperation, natural reason is saved for eventual expansion in evangelical revelation.

These varying critical arguments encourage us to look closely for ourselves beneath the swags and swirls of Corneille's baroque plot. The very language of the tragedy—notably the language of sight—invites our scrutiny, for under appearances, Corneille suggests, we may well find the revelation of truth. A man of the theatre, he exploited the language of vision in order to heighten drama and to create suspense (Couton II, 1277). Then in a final moment of tragic irony, he created spectacle—a word to be taken here in its etymological sense—to express his Christian view that God intervenes in human history in order to ensure that order and justice prevail.

The language of *Rodogune* resembles the vocabulary of earlier plays like *Cinna* and *Polyeucte* as well as that of *L'Imitation de Jésus-Christ,* the long devotional poem that Corneille completed within a decade of the première of *Rodogune.* The characters of *Cinna* grasp meaning where they can find it and act according to views that are, until the final tableau, constantly belied.

More often than not, Corneille expresses the conflict in terms of perceptual error that is resolved when the characters find the one source of true lucidity that illumines all dimensions of human experience. Knowledge of self, Emilie suggests as she submits to Auguste, emanates miraculously from a divine source:

> Et je me rends, Seigneur, à ces hautes bontés;
> Je recouvre la vue auprès de leurs clartés;
> Je connais mon forfait, qui me semblait justice.
> . . . . .
> Le ciel a résolu votre grandeur suprême,
> Et pour preuve, Seigneur, je n'en veux que moi-même.

> (v. 1715-17, 1721-22)

Emilie's words complement a line that the Emperor himself has thrown away in a moment of conjugal irritation: "Le ciel m'inspirera ce qu'ici je dois faire" (v. 1258; Stegmann II, 584). With **Polyeucte,** Corneille sets human love against divine love, an opposition that finds resolution in Polyeucte's martyrdom and Pauline's vision:

> Mon époux en mourant m'a laissé ses lumières,
> Son sang, dont tes bourreaux viennent de me couvrir,
> M'a dessillé les yeux, et me les vient d'ouvrir.
> Je vois, je sais, je crois, je suis désabusée. . . .

> (v. 1724-27)

Corneille's visual vocabulary remains constant, even at mid-career when he stopped writing plays in order to devote himself to a translation or, more precisely, paraphrase in verse of *De Imitatione Christi.* In this meditation, Thomas à Kempis calls upon the Christian to see Christ as an image worthy of emulation. The concrete imagery of *L'Imitation de Jésus-Christ* invites the Christian to compose his meditations visually. Like the Latin text, Corneille's verse stimulates the visual imagination of the believer who is urged to see in his mind's eye the example of the saints:

> Tu vois en tous les saints de merveilleux exemples,
> C'est la pure religion,
> C'est l'entière perfection
> Qu'en ces grands miroirs tu contemples.
> . . . . .
> Regarde les martyrs, les vierges, les apôtres,
> Et tous ceux de qui la ferveur
> Sur les sacrés pas du Sauveur
> A frayé des chemins aux nôtres.

> (I, 18)

With such concrete imagery the poet attempts to bring what is ineffable within range of human understanding; visual language is the means by which Corneille appeals to the believer's visual imagination in order to compose an image for meditation (Reed, *passim*).

For a Latinist like Corneille, the notion of image is inseparable from the concept of imitation. Both denote the Greek idea of likeness. Throughout his career and in any number of essays—prefaces, dedications, critical pieces—Corneille conceived of theatre as mimetic, and he characteristically expressed the idea in the language of sight. In the preface to **La Veuve,** he wrote that comedy is a portrait of human action and thought (76); he dedicated **Cinna** to Montauron as a picture of one of Octavian's finest acts (268); and when, nearly thirty years after **La Veuve,** he wrote **Œdipe,** he told Fouquet in the dedication that he still felt the vigor of youth and the ability to sketch great historical figures: "Et je me trouve encor la main qui crayonna / L'âme du grand Pompée et l'esprit de Cinna" (566). However typical of his writing this visual language may be, none of it is unique to Corneille. In fact, his rhetoric reflects the thought of an epoch, and the language of vision reflects a way of thinking in seventeenth century France. Descartes felt the need to take reason beyond the limit of what he saw, but he often cites as analogies visual phenomena in order to corroborate his philosophical propositions: "Les idées sont en moi comme des tableaux, ou des images" (287). Literature cannot be separated from philosophy, nor, moreover, can philosophy be separated from theology. The Church entered every corner of life during the century of Louis XIII and Louis XIV. Descartes and Pascal came to grips with religious institutions, as did Racine, Molière, and La Rochefoucauld. Corneille's thought was shaped in large measure by his Jesuit education in Rouen where he was introduced not only to the Jesuits' pedagogical use of plays but also to their rules for meditation. Since the founding of the order in the mid-sixteenth century, the Society of Jesus had deliberately developed a manner of meditation that structured thought and passion, theological abstraction and concrete imagery, in an effort to know and to feel the Incarnation with every human faculty (Martz, 83). In fact, the Jesuits celebrated their centenary in 1640 with an elegant folio of poems, dissertations, and devices. The visual illustrations and the variety of genres attest to the Jesuits' effort to reach a wide audience. It would be an oversimplification to say that Jesuit education or meditation is the only source of Corneille's theatre; but it might not be an exaggeration to see some elements of the Jesuit tradition in Corneille's thought, among them the idea of theatre as visual image or likeness.

Corneille thought of his plays as imitations of justice and peace, concepts that ultimately derive from divine authority. Reading chronologically, we expect to see examples of certain heroic virtues, for beginning with **Le Cid,** Corneille dramatized courage, loyalty, constancy, and submission to a superior order, all qualities that are familiar to Cornelian scholars as what Stegmann has called the heroic equation (II, 599). But Corneille may have reached an impasse in his development around 1643-44. Donald Sellstrom argues (*passim*) that the characters in **La Mort de Pompée** seem unable to enjoy the providential support of earlier heroes. He traces this difference to two sources. On the one hand, the historical framework that Corneille borrowed from Lucan may suggest the limited possibilities of a world before the Redemption; on the other hand, Christian elements that Corneille borrowed from Tasso may imply redemptive possibilities about to be realized. Like *La Mort de Pompée, Rodogune* depicts pagan figures, but unlike the earlier play, it reiterates perhaps more overtly themes and imagery of Corneille's earlier work and prefigures his later work, including devotional poetry. Like these works, *Rodogune* is informed by Corneille's providential view of history. From the first lines of the tragedy, Corneille directs our attention to the aspiration for civil order. A long period of war and political turmoil will soon end in a marriage. Corneille exploits our expectations, for he has resolved earlier conflicts—*Le Cid, Cinna, Polyeucte*—in the harmonious and sometimes miraculous union of heroic lovers. Corneille offered in *Rodogune,* however, a surprise that originates in his logic as we have come to know it. The promise of a marriage will lead—at least temporarily—to results engineered by Cléopâtre, an astonishingly malevolent queen. With his consummate sense of theatre, Corneille allows us to gape briefly at the catastrophe brought on by her vicious machinations; then abruptly he turns our attention to a last dazzling moment in which evil is expelled and justice and order are re-established.

Corneille's dramatic effects derive in large measure from the visual imagery of his poetry and from exploitation of the theatre as spectacle. The confidante of the Queen of Syria introduces the idea of the play as visual image. Laonice uses the word "jour" four times in the first seven lines, then develops the idea of "jour" as both day and light by using the verb "luire" and creating contrast with the noun "nuit." In this first moment of the play, Corneille insists on the visual imagery and on the unity of time. Day breaks to reveal the play both as history and as action to be played within the sight of all:

> Ce grand jour est venu, mon frère, où notre reine,
> Cessant de plus tenir la couronne incertaine,
> Doit rompre aux yeux de tous son silence obstiné,
> De deux princes gémeaux nous déclarer l'aîné.
>
> (v. 7-10)

These opening lines, like the overture to an opera, introduce the principal themes of revelation, obfuscation, and disguise. Reduced to its simplest form, the intricate plot turns on the ambitions of Cléopâtre who will today reveal the secret of the birth of her twin sons by designating one the elder and therefore the heir to the throne. Her successor will not only reign over Syria but also marry Rodogune, sister of the king of Parthia. The baroque convolution of political ambitions, declarations of love, jealousies and rumors interests the audience in watching the Syrian queen as she attempts to

retain her place in a patrilineal monarchy. Her Machiavellian strategy involves duping one of her sons into murdering Rodogune, thus removing a threat to her own authority and assuring her political power. The queen's confidante describes the tortuous situation, and as she does so, she invites us to look and, moreover, to "admire" what we see:

> Mais n'admirez-vous point que cette même reine
> Le [l'aîné] donne pour époux à l'objet de sa haine,
> Et n'en doit faire un roi qu'afin de couronner
> Celle que dans les fers elle aimait à gêner?
>
> (v. 15-18)

One needs only to think of "admirer" in its Latin sense of viewing with wonder in order to understand that Laonice's lines are addressed as much to the spectators as to her brother Timagène.

The text invites the audience to look beneath the surface of events. Well-intentioned but dim-sighted, Laonice misleads the spectators because she judges events according to appearances. Reproaching her confidante for her dull perception, the queen distinguishes two manners of seeing. Courtiers see into the princes they serve, says Cléopâtre; commoners too must learn to penetrate appearances:

> Pour un esprit de cour, et nourri chez les grands,
> Tes yeux dans leurs secrets sont bien peu pénétrants.
> . . . . .
> N'apprendras-tu jamais, âme basse et grossière,
> A voir par d'autres yeux que les yeux du vulgaire?
>
> (v. 441-42, 487-88)

Cléopâtre's aristocratic rebuke summons us as spectators to sharpen our visual sense, to perceive the truth beneath appearance, to participate, as it were, in the tragedy that will be played before our eyes. Cléopâtre teaches by precept, and, in addition, Rodogune demonstrates by example her sensitivity as a Cornelian heroine. A princess sees what a commoner cannot. When Laonice assures her that the queen is no longer jealous, the more discerning Rodogune proceeds cautiously. She distinguishes the offender from the offended. She and Cléopâtre may be reconciled in appearance, she says, but reconciliation is no more than illusion:

> Et quoiqu'en apparence on les réconcilie,
> Il le craint, il le hait, et jamais ne s'y fie,
> Et toujours alarmé de cette illusion,
> Sitôt qu'il peut le perdre il prend l'occasion.
> Telle est pour moi la Reine.
>
> (v. 323-27)

Corneille's language of illusion draws the audience into the essential drama. What, in fact, are Cléopâtre's motives in bringing Rodogune out of prison and her sons out of exile? Which twin will, as the elder, succeed to the throne and receive the Parthian princess in marriage? These are questions that Rodogune expresses in explicitly visual language:

> L'hymen semble à mes yeux cacher quelque supplice,
> Le trône sous mes pas creuser un précipice,
> Je vois de nouveaux fers après les miens brisés,
> Et je prends tous ces biens pour des maux déguisés.

> (v. 307-10)

The spectator recognizes Rodogune's foresight as one quality of a Cornelian heroine. The vocabulary of seeming, seeing, and disguise summons the audience to witness events attentively.

In this play that centers on the idea of looking for truth beneath appearances, the notion of disguise becomes increasingly important. After Laonice introduces the theme of seeing, Timagène develops it with two variations, the ideas of disguise and of darkness (v. 42). The nouns "déguisement" and "obscurité" recur throughout the play, heightening with each repetition the visual metaphor. While Rodogune sees her release from imprisonment as evil disguised as good, Cléopâtre removes her disguise at her first appearance:

> Serments fallacieux, salutaire contrainte,
> Que m'imposa la force et qu'accepta ma crainte,
> Heureux déguisements d'un immortel courroux,
> Vains fantômes d'Etat, évanouissez-vous!

> (v. 395-98)

The honesty of Cléopâtre's confession startles us in a *coup de théâtre* as disarming as Auguste's entrance at the beginning of Act II of *Cinna.* Her excessive political ambition horrifies us, but her honesty wins our interest if not our sympathy. Her confession also establishes her immediately as a highly theatrical personage. The vocabulary of disguise and feint varies the theme of vision, for Cléopâtre confesses that she is performing the rôle of benevolent queen mother in order to dupe Rodogune whom she considers "imprudente" (v. 419). This adjective construed in its Latin sense as "unforeseeing" serves as a clue to the dangerous game that Cléopâtre is playing against Rodogune. In the scene following her monologue, Corneille sustains the language of sight. As if she were on stage—which, of course, she is— Cléopâtre invites her confidante to take a place and to watch what becomes a frankly theatrical performance. In this play within the play, Cléopâtre wears three masks. She converses with the twins in the guise of loving mother, generous queen, and deceived wife. She performs superbly, enchants her sons and, momentarily, wins their sympathy. But she miscalculates her power to charm. When she asks them to avenge their father's death, Séleucus sees the mask and removes it:

> De ses pleurs tant vantés je découvre le fard,
> Nous avons en son cœur, vous et moi, peu de part,
> . . . . .
> Et quoi que nous étale un langage si doux,
> Elle a tout fait pour elle, et n'a rien fait pour nous.

> (v. 733-34, 737-38)

Cléopâtre repeats her performance in Act IV. Accusing her sons of rebellion, she trembles and even weeps. Her performance fools Laonice, and Antiochus's good faith leads him temporarily into credulity. But again Séleucus sets his clarity of vision against his mother's play-acting: he sees more than Cléopâtre thinks that he sees, he tells her, and more than he wants to see; then he adds that neither his sight nor his courage will falter, and he swears affection for his brother and loyalty to him as king (v. 1469-74).

Corneille's text suggests repeatedly how eyes reveal truth, anticipating the visual gesture of Racine's plays that Starobinski (69-89) has appropriately labeled "la poétique du regard." Séleucus sees the queen's machinations; courtiers see the twins' affection for each other and their love for Rodogune; she hesitates to see them, for fear of letting her preference be seen; Cléopâtre sees her sons' reactions. Corneille works stage directions into the spoken text as Cléopâtre notices their astonishment: "Quoi, vous montrez tous deux un visage étonné!" (v. 646) Virtually the same scene is repeated in the next act. When Rodogune requests as a condition of marriage the murder of Cléopâtre, she sees the twins' shock and hesitation: "Quoi? cette ardeur s'éteint! l'un et l'autre soupire! / J'avais su le prévoir, j'avais su le prédire" (v. 1039-40). In both scenes, visual language calls attention to the importance of visible gesture.

Stage directions become more and more explicit in *Rodogune,* for Corneille expanded the imagery of the text to make the dénouement symbolic on the stage. Although extensive stage directions are rarely found in French classical tragedy, Corneille choreographed the wedding scene in Act V in order to create an image of the succession. This tableau possesses an irony as piercing as any speech. Cléopâtre resumes the rôle of queen mother; she also plays chief of protocol for the ceremony. She invites Antiochus to take the rank appropriate to the heir apparent, seating him at stage center as imperiously as Racine's Agrippine telling Néron to take his place. Cléopâtre assigns Rodogune to a place on his left. With feigned humility, she herself takes a place below Antiochus but on his right, the significance of which Corneille explains: "mais en rang inférieur, et qui marque quelque inégalité" (V, 3). Characteristically, Cléopâtre performs well, and she succeeds in convincing her credulous son of her maternal benevolence. Writing stage directions into the text, Corneille calls attention to the blocking and to the theatricality of Cléopâtre's speech and gestures:

Oronte, vous voyez avec quelle franchise
Je leur rends ce pouvoir dont je me suis démise:
Prêtez les yeux au reste, et voyez les effets
Suivre de point en point les traités de la paix.

(v. 1583-86)

Oronte understands the visual symbolism of the scene. He answers with flattery and with the irony of a skilled diplomat: "Votre sincérité s'y fait assez paraître, / Madame, et j'en ferai récit au Roi mon maître" (v. 1587-88). When Laonice appears carrying the poisoned nuptial cup, stage movement underscores the irony of the spoken word. We see the lethal cup, and we suspect that Cléopâtre will never relinquish her power. The visual quality of word and gesture creates one of the most dramatic moments in Corneille's theatre.

All of the visual imagery comes together in the final act. Corneille has revealed visually the queen's duplicitous nature as well as the twins' honest esteem and affection for Rodogune. Light and darkness become symbolic as Timagène dispels the obscurity surrounding the death of Séleucus who has refused to collaborate with his mother. Timagène tells Antiochus how he has found the boy lying in a dark corner of the palace gardens: "Je l'ai trouvé, Seigneur, au bout de cette allée, / Où la clarté du ciel semble toujours voilée" (v. 1611-12). Timagène describes how, quite literally, the eyes admit light to the mind and how at death light is extinguished; then he quotes Séleucus's final words that Antiochus finds obscure in a figurative sense: "Oh! de ses derniers mots fatale obscurité!" (v. 1657) While Antiochus wavers, deliberates, but sees only his own misfortune, Cléopâtre perseveres in her plan to murder Rodogune by tricking her into drinking from the poisoned nuptial cup. The strategem fails, however, when the bride sees the danger. Cléopâtre insists on her integrity, and to prove it, she tests the cup. Rodogune calls attention to the visible effects of the poison on Cléopâtre. To the realistic details—her rolling eyes, frightful perspiration, and heaving chest—Cléopâtre herself lends figurative value as she strips her mask in a final gesture that reveals her hatred and her political ambitions: "[Ma haine] a paru trop tôt pour te perdre avec moi" (v. 1813). Cléopâtre curses her son's marriage to Rodogune and their children, then Laonice leads her off stage to die, while the young couple and the courtiers remain to contemplate the disorder caused by the queen's passions. The tone of the scene changes abruptly. The older, experienced ambassador explains in measured rhythm to the young, innocent king that divine justice has been done. The gods have punished vice and rewarded virtue, he says, for Antiochus has been saved from death and from a more grievous danger, loss of reputation. Stunned by the tragic disarray he looks upon, Antiochus ponders, then in one of those rapid, even miraculous transformations that take place in Corneille's world, Antiochus quickly takes charge of the kingdom.

Using the inclusive royal first person, he gives the order to prepare the temple for a funeral, then he speaks the final words of the play. A last couplet, which Corneille constructed of visual language, delivers all of Syria to a future that in the context of Oronte's reassurances we may take as one offering to Antiochus and his subjects hope for redemption: "Et nous verrons après, par d'autres sacrifices, / Si les Dieux voudront être à nous vœux plus propices" (v. 1843-44).

In this final speech Corneille reiterates the language of vision with which he created a visual representation of the succession to the throne of Syria. He actualizes the history of Cleopatra Thea that he has drawn from ancient historians, Appian of Alexandria, Flavius Josephus, Justin, and the Book of the Maccabees. He presents to his spectators in the theatre a visual likeness of history that he intends to be as real as the mental images by which his characters live. Heroines like Rodogune and Emilie in *Cinna* see life in the mind's eye. Rodogune visualizes Cléopâtre's murder of Nicanor, an act that she has witnessed and that she continues to imagine. In an apostrophe addressed to her hatred and anger, she calls on these emotions to sustain the memory of Nicanor's bloody end:

Rapportez à mes yeux son image sanglante,
D'amour et de fureur encore étincelante,
Telle que je le vis, quand tout percé de coups,
Il me cria: "Vengeance! Adieu: je meurs pour vous!"

(v. 859-62)

The bloody image serves as an emblem that is as inspiring to her as the image of the assassinated Toranius that motivates Emilie to join Cinna's conspiracy. Rodogune carries in the present the image of her past; she sees Cléopâtre's murderous hand wanting to complete its crime (v. 875-82). Rodogune not only transports her passionate desire for revenge into the present moment, but also transforms it into the visual, symbolic presence of one of the twins in whom she sees the "living portrait" of their father (v. 884). In Corneille's poetic world, such visual images are as real as the pennon carried by the avant-garde of a medieval army. They motivate his characters, and they embody his heroes' concepts. When Rodogune challenges Cléopâtre to test the nuptial cup as visible proof of her trustworthiness, and when she persuades Antiochus to see the disorder in his dying mother's eyes, she acts in conformity with the image of Nicanor that she has articulated in Act III and that she reiterates to Antiochus in Act IV:

Lorsque j'ai soupiré, ce n'était pas pour vous,
J'ai donné ces soupirs aux mânes d'un époux,
Et ce sont les effets du souvenir fidèle
Que sa mort à toute heure en mon âme rappelle.

(v. 1153-56)

The repetition of the image of Nicanor motivates Rodogune emblematically to avenge his murder; it also emphasizes the larger visual metaphor of which Rodogune is part. Early in the play Laonice compares Rodogune to a rising sun: "Rodogune a paru, sortant de sa prison, / Comme un soleil levant dessus notre horizon" (v. 281-82). Rodogune threatens Cléopâtre's political security, but in a wider, symbolic sense she represents the defeat of evil forces by good and the dispelling of darkness by light. Neither she nor Cléopâtre can understand the full import of their struggle. Nor can Antiochus comprehend the meaning of events until they are played out. For the time being, he and Cléopâtre confront each other's opposing points of view. In this test of wills and perceptions, Cléopâtre flatters herself that she can see the dénouement:

> Périssez, périssez: votre rébellion
> Mérite plus d'horreur que de compassion.
> Mes yeux sauront le voir sans verser une larme,
> Sans regarder en vous que l'objet qui vous charme,
> Et je triompherai, voyant périr mes fils,
> De ses adorateurs et de mes ennemis.
>
> (v. 1333-38)

Cléopâtre's language informs the catastrophe with such precision that the final act might be understood as an expression of the idea that life conforms to one's perception of it. But such an interpretation would miss the irony. As a matter of fact, Corneille does not end the tragedy with destruction by the forces of evil. Oronte and Antiochus lead the audience to believe that despite the evil queen's unwavering resolution and awesome courage, events do not coincide with her vision. The incongruity between her expectations—as well as ours—and what actually happens makes of *Rodogune* one of Corneille's most suspenseful dramas. Cléopâtre believes that she can master the future of Syria and control her own destiny; but events turn against her. Corneille's dénouement shows the audience that if a human being can control events to such an extent, then Providence determines history even more. Thus the very theatricality of the final scene carries significance, for the play's imagery persuades us that forces greater than individual will are working in events. Corneille created words and gestures that coincide in visual metaphor to suggest that history conforms to humankind's perception of it only if we know how to discern its ironies. The final lines of *Rodogune* derive from the Christian humanist's concept that when men and women look discerningly beneath appearances, they will see Providence working in history.

Although Corneille chose a pagan subject for *Rodogune,* the tragedy dramatizes his Christian humanism. Preparing a collected edition of his plays for publication in 1660, Corneille wrote in his "Discours de la tragédie" that Cléopâtre is not punished by human vengeance but by divine justice (836). As he reflected on his plays during the decades following their composi-

tion, *Rodogune* did not strike Corneille as a departure from anything else that he had written. On the contrary, he compared it in his famous *examen* to *Cinna* and *Le Cid,* both of which enjoyed great popular success; but *Rodogune* seemed to him even more characteristic of what he wanted to accomplish. Corneille listed among its qualities facility of language and poetic strength (417). For Corneille, idea and language meld in *Rodogune.* For us, the reiteration of a word or words in a literary text may seem coincidental and may not today always seem significant. In seventeenth century France, however, Corneille's insistent repetition of a certain vocabulary expresses his dramatic vision. The visual rhetoric of plays like *Cinna* and *Polyeucte* or of a devotional poem like *L'Imitation de Jésus-Christ* emanates from the same imagination that informs *Rodogune.* Whether writing plays for the secular stage or spiritual exercises for the devout, Corneille wrote often with the language of sight to express his Christian humanism. Visual imagery serves, therefore, as one more indication of the remarkable unity of Pierre Corneille's thought and poetic vision.

Note

1. A shorter version of this essay was read at a symposium, "The Western Tradition: The Christian Perspective," at Marquette University, 24-26 March 1983.

Works Cited

Corneille, Pierre. *Œuvres complètes.* Ed. André Stegmann. Paris: Seuil, 1963. All quotations are taken from this edition.

Couton, Georges, ed. Pierre Corneille, *Œuvres complètes.* Paris: Gallimard, 1980-87.

Descartes, René. *Œuvres et lettres.* Ed. André Bridoux. Paris: Gallimard, 1953.

Doubrovsky, Serge. *Corneille et la dialectique du héros.* Paris: Gallimard, 1963.

Fumaroli, Marc. "Tragique païen et tragique chrétien dans *Rodogune,*" RSH [*Revue des Sciences Humaines*] 38 (1973): 599-631.

Greenberg, Mitchell. *Corneille, Classicism and the Ruses of Symmetry.* New York: Cambridge UP, 1986.

Martz, Louis L. *The Poetry of Meditation, A Study in English Religious Literature of the Seventeenth Century.* New Haven: Yale UP, 1954.

Nelson, Robert J. *Corneille: His Heroes and Their Worlds.* Philadelphia: U of Pennsylvania P, 1963.

Reed, Gervais E. "Stylistic and Thematic Parallels in Corneille's Theatre and his *Imitation de Jésus-Christ,*" *Symposium* 33 (1979): 263-87.

Scherer, Jacques, ed. *Rodogune*. Geneva: Droz, 1946.

Sellstrom, A. Donald. "*La Mort de Pompée*: Roman History and Tasso's Theory of Christian Epic," *PMLA* [*Publications of the Modern Language Association of America*] 97 (1982): 830-43.

Starobinski, Jean. *L'Œil vivant.* Paris: Gallimard, 1961.

Stegmann, André. *L'Héroïsme cornélien: genèse et signification,* 2 vols. Paris: Colin, 1968.

Sweetser, Marie-Odile. *La Dramaturgie de Corneille.* Genève: Droz, 1977.

ŒDIPE (OEDIPUS)

CRITICAL COMMENTARY

Harriet Ray Allentuch (essay date March 1994)

SOURCE: Allentuch, Harriet Ray. "Is Corneille's *Œdipe* Œdipal?" *French Review* 67, no. 4 (March 1994): 571-79.

[*In the following essay, Allentuch regards* Oedipus *as representative of Corneille's subconscious dramatic concerns.*]

Corneille's now forgotten *Œdipe* (1659) was one of the triumphs of his long dramatic career. It pleased his new patron, Fouquet, and enthralled audiences at court and at the Hôtel de Bourgogne. With *Œdipe* Corneille reemerged as the premier French tragic dramatist of his day: the play ended his seven-year retirement from the stage and its success removed the sting of failure associated with *Pertharite* (1652). For several years *Œdipe* continued to enjoy an audience; the Comédie Française presented it ninety-four times between 1680 and 1729.[1] But since the eighteenth century no one has seen a performance of the work, and among critics and Corneille scholars, none urges a revival. Most of them view Corneille's play as, at best, a strange medley and, at worst, a betrayal of the ancient myth so hauntingly dramatized by Sophocles. Judd Hubert condemns it as no "Œdipe" at all but an "anti-Œdipe" (47).

In the present study there is no attempt to reverse this judgment, but rather to read the play for what it suggests about some of the recurrent patterns of Corneille's imagination. There is no denying that the additions and changes Corneille made to bring the classical myth to the French stage tend to distance it from us and to deepen the shadow cast upon his achievement by Sophocles. However, there is much to be learned about Corneille's habits as a working dramatist and as an imaginative mind from his response to Œdipus, the ultimate tragic subject. The Freudian psychocritic, Charles Mauron, who sees an idiosyncratic œdipal myth as an organizing, whispered subtext in Corneille's theater, presents views which merit consideration. Mauron's reading of Corneille's unconscious personal myth is based on a study of the best-known plays from *La Place royale* through *Polyeucte*. Yet, how does his reading stand up when confronted with Corneille's treatment of the actual, inherited œdipal material?

The problem of locating subconscious patterns idiosyncratic to Corneille is complicated by the diverse demands and attitudes of the audience Corneille sought to please. On the one hand, *Œdipus Rex* enjoyed high prestige in the seventeenth century; it was widely known that Aristotle judged the play a paradigm for tragedy. It was, in Terence Cave's terms, a "seductive masterplot" ("Recognitions" 322). To write a successful French *Œdipe* was for Corneille to reassert his status as the master French dramatist. On the other hand, the rules of propriety were incompatible with the sympathetic portrayal of a parricidal and incestuous hero. Furthermore, imaginative material rich in prophecies and coincidences and dependent upon the prolonged ignorance of the hero did not lend itself to plotting according to the strictures of dramatic coherence and *vraisemblance*. A further problem, or so Corneille wrote, was the lack of a love plot in *Œdipus Rex*. He thought that his audience would be unwilling to applaud a play in which women played so small a part.[2]

Radical revisions in accordance with the tastes and taboos of his audience were therefore incumbent upon the dramatist, whatever his own attitudes. But Corneille had a further problem with the Sophoclean text. He could make no sense of Œdipus's guilt. "[Il] me semble ne faire aucune faute." (*Œuvres complètes* III, 145). Since Œdipus committed incest unwittingly, killed his father without recognizing him and only after being attacked, he was innocent of any crime. The Greek vision of an abyss at the heart of things seems to have made neither logical nor imaginative sense to the French dramatist.

The principal means Corneille adopted for accommodating the Sophoclean tragedy to his times was the addition of an "heureux" episode involving the passions of Thésée and Dircé, presented by Corneille as Jocasta's daughter from her union with Laius. This means that in place of the singular plot and viewpoint characterizing the Sophoclean tragedy, its action a gradual unveiling of the past to a hero long morally blind, Corneille substitutes divided sympathies and a double plot. The first half of the play centers on the conflicts and dilemmas of Dircé and Thésée and alludes only sporadically to the legendary material, which is largely obscured from view until the middle of Act III. Corneille introduces Sophocles's principal *données* mainly in the last two acts of *Œdipe.*

The "heureux" episode is an exalted love story, full of pathos and the kind of romantic fantasies that crowd popular seventeenth-century French novels such as those of La Calprenède and Madeleine de Scudéry. Dircé and Thésée are sublime lovers, true *généreux.* They vie with each other in self-sacrifice, opening the play with a love scene meant to stir the audience to tears. Although the plague has reduced Thésée's royal entourage to a single man, he refuses to leave Thebes. Better death than separation from Dircé, he insists. She too thinks only of Thésée and is in anguish at the thought that he may die because of her. Just as Corneille enchants his audience by juxtaposing the passion and pathos of Sévère and Pauline against the martyrdom of Polyeucte, so with the ardent devotion of Thésée and Dircé he brings relief from the horrors of Œdipus and Thebes.

Dircé has another role in the first half of the play. She is Œdipe's antagonist. Royal princess, daughter of Laïus, she is the rightful heir to the throne. Like the militant Emilie, in Corneille's *Cinna,* whom she recalls despite her monarchist faith, Dircé opens and closes the play. Like Emilie too, she is turned toward the past, haunted by the loss of her father and a sense of terrible injustice in the state. She challenges Œdipe as a usurper, imposed by the Sphinx. "Vous régnez en ma place," she tells him in a bitter confrontation (II, 1, 468). The major tension driving the first half of the play, however, arises from Œdipe's opposition to Dircé's marriage to Thésée. In his initial appearances Œdipe is a "standard Cornelian tyrant" (Cave, "Corneille" 90). Because Dircé has blood rights to the throne, he imagines that once united to Thésée, she will plot to reclaim the Theban throne. So he promises her to the feckless Hémon and is ready to use force to make his will prevail. By such turns of events Corneille finds a plot device for endowing his protagonist with the onus of tangible guilt lacking in the ancient myth.

Throughout this love-cum-politics portion of the plot, Œdipe plays the oppressor and Dircé the heroic rebel, attached to legitimacy and the memory of Laïus. Defiant, ambitious herself for glory, Dircé recalls not only Emilie but many of Corneille's heroines who, lacking the freedom of action of men, resist their tyrant and are prepared to die rather than yield. "Qui ne craint point la mort ne craint point les Tyrans," she cries out to Œdipe in a stoic maxim characteristic of Cornelian heroes and heroines (II, 1, 500). She treats his threats with regal contempt and when he demands obedience, tells him that although the Theban populace paid for his services

with a throne, *she* is not for sale. Powerless as a woman to challenge Œdipe physically, Dircé takes her stand, as do many Cornelian heroines, in her refusal to be an object of disposal and in her incoercible will. To his imperative: "Je suis Roi, je puis tout," she retorts: "Je puis fort peu de chose, / Mais enfin de mon cœur moi seule je dispose" (II, 1, 493-94).[3]

The drama of such scenes makes clear that Corneille's use of the double plot does not, by itself, explain the play's failure to survive. Nor is a double action, in the abstract, unworkable. Sophocles's *Œdipus at Colonus* sustains a dual action: Œdipus overcomes a series of obstacles and wins a final resting place outside Athens in a first series of scenes; his death is willed and managed by the gods in a second sequence. By general consensus, Corneille himself succeeds with a two-part plot in *Horace,* although the fifth-act trial of the hero is clearly separable from the hero's exploits in the rest of the play.[4]

In *Œdipe* the existence of two actions is not, in itself, the aesthetic problem; but their discordance is. As Georges Couton indicates, the two plots overlap; they never mesh.[5] Moreover, to move from one to the other, Corneille invents a series of bizarre complications in the spirit of romantic imbroglio drama with its confusion about identities and a brother-sister incest motif. This is a vein Corneille exploits in *Don Sanche* and *Héraclius;* here it is out of place. He also borrows the ghost of Laïus from Seneca's version of the Œdipus myth. Whereas Seneca's ghost names Œdipus as his murderer, Corneille's ghost speaks ambiguously: the dead king insists that the plague will end only when he has been avenged by "the blood of my race." Both Dircé and Thésée (who claims for a time to be Laïus's lost son) become candidates for the role of *bouc émissaire.* There is much sentimental anguish in a scene between the lovers, now separated by putative blood ties. Ultimately Œdipe begins to ask the questions that doom him, and in his own fashion, Corneille rejoins the ancient myth.

The discordance that mars Corneille's dramaturgy after the mid-point of Act III means more than a confusion of genres. It means a new dramatic psychology. Corneille radically changes his hero in mid-stream. Suddenly Œdipe is a different man. The usurper-tyrant and persecutor of the lovers now appears greater than they, noble and generous. As if to make the transition, he himself expresses bewilderment at his change: "J'admire un changement si confus que le mien . . . Moi-même en cet état je ne puis me comprendre" (III, 4, 1048 and 1058). In the middle of the play, without knowing why, Œdipe feels an urgent need to see Dircé and Thésée married. He abandons the *raison d'etat* and all interest in obstructing the lovers (III, 4, 1049-52).

Whereas Sophocles provides a reversal arising from sudden knowledge—the hunter recognizing himself as the prey he is hunting—Corneille works a miracle. Nevertheless, in a rationalist theater miracles are best obscured. Sophocles keeps Œdipus on stage demanding answers that unravel the mystery of his identity; Corneille removes the hero to the wings. For an entire act (from III, 4 to IV, 4) Œdipe is invisible and Jocaste leads the fateful investigation. Questioning Thésée, she fails to hear the call of the blood; he is not her son. She also interrogates a witness of both the king's murder and the rescue of the royal infant exposed on the mountainside. Gradually the full truth emerges.

After Œdipe reappears, the miraculous transformation is completed. No Cornelian hero gains more glory. The calculating tyrant of earlier scenes is endowed with a heroic past never mentioned before this moment: he remembers countless "exploits généreux" (1820), monsters slain, laws upheld, injustices punished. He faces his tragedy with stoic calm. Noble, solicitous, concerned above all to spare Jocaste, he even trusts Thésée, toward whom he has shown so much suspicion: "Thésée a trop de cœur pour une trahison" (V, i, 1651). The new Œdipe meets a new Dircé who rewrites their old encounters: she has never hated him, she maintains, and has called him tyrant only with immense effort and the anguish of remorse:

> Ah, Seigneur, pour Hémon j'ai su mal obéir,
> Mais je n'ai point été jusques à vous haïr
>
> Pour vous nommer Tyran il fallait cent efforts
> Ce mot ne m'a jamais échappé sans remords.
>   (V, 5, 1799-1800 and 1807-08)

In the end it is Dircé who validates Œdipe's kingship, extols him as "le plus grand de nos rois" (1852), even demands to die in his place. It is Dircé, his former accuser, who now calls him innocent: "Quel crime avez-vous fait que d'être malheureux?" (1819). The transformed Œdipe insists, however, upon suffering alone. Like so many earlier Cornelian heroes, he embraces his fate as "un trépas glorieux," an opportunity to sacrifice himself for the welfare of Thebes. His self-blinding, recounted rather than staged because of the *bienséances,* is deliberately willed, chosen over death as an act of personal fortitude and moral outrage. In blinding himself he seeks revenge against unjust gods, whose light he refuses to look upon, and survives to become an immemorial example of divine cruelty:

> Prévenons, a-t-il dit, l'injustice des Dieux,
> Commençons à mourir, avant qu'ils nous l'ordonnent.
> Qu'ainsi que mes forfaits, mes supplices étonnent.
> Ne voyons plus le Ciel après sa cruauté,
> Pour nous venger de lui, dédaignons sa clarté,
> Refusons-lui nos yeux, et gardons quelque vie
> Qui montre encore à tous quelle est sa tyrannie.
>   (V, 9, 1988-94)

No sooner does his blood reach the ground than three men rise up from the dead and the Theban plague comes to an end in a new miracle unmentioned in the Greek text. Where the Greek playwright shows the "best of men" undone by fate, Corneille transforms a tyrant into a redeemer.

As incongruous as this *dénouement* appears to modern sensibilities, it conforms with the resolution of many of Corneille's tragedies and with what Charles Mauron has deciphered as Corneille's unconscious subtext or private variant of the Œdipus myth in the Freudian sense of the term. Mauron reveals this subtext by superimposing the four best-known tragedies (*Le Cid, Horace, Cinna, Polyeucte*) to uncover obsessive similarities.[6] Though Mauron never mentions *Œdipe,* he describes a two-part action as distinctively Cornelian: violence against a father or paternal representative separated from revenge of the father, solidarity with him and exculpation of the son—who ultimately ascends to glory. To make the point he contrasts Corneille and Shakespeare. In *Hamlet,* the hero is simultaneously a parricide and his father's avenger when he kills Claudius; the Cornelian hero is successively one and then the other. It is often the role of the Cornelian heroine, as it is Dircé's role in *Œdipe,* to suffer because of the hero's violence, become his accuser, yet at the *dénouement,* support his cause and herald his greatness.[7]

According to Mauron, Corneille normally represents the hero's parricide on the manifest level by doubling the father or paternal representative. This means that the heroine's father or brother, not the hero's own father, becomes the object of œdipal violence occurring either before the curtain's rise or in the course of the drama. Thus Rodrigue kills Chimène's father after the exposition, Horace slays Sabine's brother during the thick of the action, and Polyeucte strikes down Pauline's gods and attacks her father's authority at the close of the second act. In contrast, Auguste in *Cinna* has killed the heroine's father some time prior to the opening of the play. Like Auguste, Œdipe, who unknowingly shares a father with Dircé, has killed Laïus long ago. Whenever the violence occurs, it always belongs to the first half of the double action which ultimately leads to accusations against the hero, although he views his violence as justified. On the manifest level, Corneille's Œdipe recalls the murder he committed long ago on the road to Thebes, but he sees his behavior as righteous because he is persuaded that the man he killed must have been Laïus's murderer. Nevertheless, Œdipe's exercise of power in the early scenes with Dircé has been characterized as a violent usurpation—as if to suggest, before the formal discovery of the truth and the full disclosure of his guilt, the latent filial dread: "On ne peut remplacer le père, dans la vie, sans le pousser hors de la vie" (Mauron 261). If the first half of the double action does not portray the hero as guilty of parricide, by various means it whispers a parricidal accusation.

The purpose of the second half of the action, in Mauron's view, is to assuage the anxiety provoked by such whispered thoughts, and reaffirming the son's solidarity with the father and the father's values, win him exoneration and acclaim. Thus the conclusion of Corneille's four best-known tragedies shows the son's exculpation and ascension to glory. As René Bray observed long ago: "Les dénouements chez Corneille ne sont pas des catastrophes mais des apothéoses" (33). In *Le Cid* and *Horace,* the protagonists become national heroes at the closing, and despite their violence, kings declare them above the law. In *Cinna* and *Polyeucte,* Auguste and the martyred Polyeucte win all hearts. Dircé and Thésée conclude *Œdipe* attesting to the hero's sublimity.

> Il ne s'emporte point contre un sort si barbare,
> La surprenante horreur de cet accablement
> Ne coûte à sa grande âme aucun égarement,
> Et sa haute vertu toujours inébranlable
> Le soutient au-dessus de tout ce qui l'accable.
>
> (1882-86)

The gods confirm his greatness: Thebes is saved.

In sum, if Mauron is right, *Œdipe*'s double action arises not only from Corneille's conscious efforts to suit the play to his audience—with elements ranging from speeches on free will, scenes worthy of courtly romance, and discourses on monarchical politics—but also from the dictates of his unconscious personal myth, which ultimately requires submission to the father and to superego values. Still, what distinguishes *Œdipe* from several more enduringly successful Cornelian plays is that here the subtext is poorly embedded in the dramatic scheme. Where, for example, the two actions fuse in Corneille's four best-known tragedies, here they do not. The discordance is unmistakable; it obtrudes in a mixture of genres and conflicting character portrayals. Even in *Horace,* where critics commonly perceive and debate the double action, we are never jarred by two disparate images of the hero. The text of *Cinna* does suggest a split within Auguste and the presence of a murderous repudiated self, whom the emperor addresses in a monologue as Octave. But we see no violent Octave on stage. If there is a transformation, making Auguste's ultimate apotheosis credible, its inception precedes the curtain's rise. When Œdipe the tyrant becomes Œdipe the savior, he bewilders us. Perhaps Corneille's choice of a seductive masterplot in which the doubling of the father cannot be used as a device to attenuate the son's guilt helps to explain the French poet's difficulties. It may also explain the enormity of the hero's transformation. Corneille attempts to obscure and compensate for an undisguisable œdipal trangression by abruptly transforming the transgressor into a sacred king the shedding of whose blood resurrects the dead and obliterates his crimes. Although, as Jacques Scherer asserts, Corneille's audience was used to thinking of kings as the Lord's anointed, endowed with healing powers (167), this extraordinary *dénouement* has no organic relation to the preceding drama.

Paradoxically, whatever Corneille's failure to synthesize successfully conscious and unconscious thinking, to perform the full secondary revision the play requires, in some ways, he rejoins Sophocles at the *dénouement,* not only the Sophocles of *Œdipus at Colonus* who sanctifies his hero, but the Sophocles of *Œdipus Rex.* When Œdipus blinds himself, the chorus tells of "terrible things, and none done blindly now, all done with a will" (1359-60). Œdipus too, recognizing that he has fulfilled the prophecy he has striven to avoid, insists on his autonomy:

> Apollo, friends, Apollo—
> He ordained my agonies—these, my pains on pains!
> But the hand that struck my eyes was mine,
> mine alone—no one else—
> I did it all myself!
>
> (1467-71)

This assumption of responsibility and Œdipus's extraordinary courage, in the face of a fate that crushes him, prevents what is sometimes called a tragedy of destiny from ending on an unequivocal note of despair. Corneille's *Œdipe* describes his self-blinding similarly, in a series of resolute imperatives that underscore his will to master and transcend his plight ("Prévenons," "Commençons," "Ne voyons plus," "dédaignons," "Refusons," "gardons" 1988-94). Both playwrights move toward an ultimate impression of human grandeur in the midst of an implacable order of things.

Corneille goes much further in resisting despair and here Mauron's reading casts particular light. Where Œdipus submits to the gods' verdict, Œdipe insists upon their injustice. Guilty in the first half of the play, usurper, violent man, he is completely innocent in the second. No tyrant now, he calls the gods tyrants. Moreover at the very moment that he recognizes himself as Laïus's son and punishes Laïus's assassin—his own former self—he wins acceptance from his father. As the curtain falls, Thésée insists that the dead King is now satisfied: "Le sang de Laïus a rempli son devoir, / Son Ombre est satisfaite" (V, 9, 2004-05). Having avenged himself, the son finds his way back to the father and is heralded both as his rightful successor and as Thebes's redeemer. According to Mauron's reading of the four best-known plays, identification with the father and withdrawal into sublimity is the principal Cornelian defense against the anxiety provoked by unconscious œdipal fantasies. On the manifest level, the marvels that accompany Œdipe's self-blinding and make him Thebes's savior bring the play to a close on a note of exaltation.

In a recent probing analysis of *Œdipe,* Terence Cave has argued that the duality of the plot with its romance episode and œdipal episode, ending in miracles and sublimity, were Corneille's principal means for obscuring the scandal of his themes for his audience and for "averting his gaze" ("Corneille" 85) from "dark desires and monstrous acts" (88). Cave argues that the inerasable "unease" that the text creates (because of its glaring dualities, mixed genres, mania for motivation and plausibility), the way it draws attention to its own techniques for rendering unacceptable material readable or visible, arises from audience and author anxiety about recognition plots, particularly when they touch on monstrous transgressions. That may well be. Cave does not explain, however, the recurrence in Corneille's theater of the same manner of accommodating taboo material—the split in the action, the antagonist-vindicator role of the heroine, the working out of a father-son solidarity at the *dénouement* with the son exonerated for his violence and rendered sublime. Moreover, Corneille did succeed in making the ancient myth stageworthy, if not for us, at least for his own time, and he did so without altogether erasing Œdipus's transgressions.[8] With *Œdipe,* the seventeenth-century theater kept the ancient story alive in a form it found permissible. Perhaps Corneille's manner of "correcting" his model and defending against too direct exposure to fascinating but dangerously suggestive material coincided with the defenses of many members of his audience. Whatever the play's disappointments now, *Œdipe* apparently was no anti-Œdipe in its own age.

Notes

1. For more on the original performances of the play and its reception in the seventeenth and eighteenth centuries, see Lancaster II, 431-38 and Couton 1.

2. "J'ai reconnu . . . qu'enfin l'amour n'ayant point de part dans ce sujet, ni les femmes d'emploi, il était dénué des principaux ornements qui nous gagnent d'ordinaire la voix publique" ("Œuvres" III, 18-19).

3. Cf. Emilie: "Il peut faire trembler la terre sous ses pas, / . . . Mais le cœur d'Emilie est hors de son pouvoir" (III, 4, 939-43). See also Allentuch, "Reflections".

4. See especially the luminous study by Harvey.

5. "Ainsi s'imbriquent plutôt que ne se fondent les éléments de l'ancienne légende avec une intrigue matrimoniale qui s'étale pendant les deux premiers actes pour devenir ensuite moins envahissante" (65).

6. For a fuller discussion see Allentuch, "Mauron".

7. Verhoeff, a disciple of Mauron, has particularly underscored the role of the heroine as an antagonist and threat to the hero who nevertheless validates him before the curtain falls.

8. This is also the opinion of Christian Delmas, but his approach differs from mine. He describes Thésée and Dircé as "doublons d'Œdipe" (161) and sees the œdipal problems as expressed through them and in this way kept before the public during the first two acts.

Works Cited

Allentuch, Harriet R. "Mauron, Corneille, and the Unconscious." *French Forum* 4 (January 1979): 55-68.

————. "Reflections on Women in the Theater of Corneille." *Kentucky Romance Quarterly* 21 (1974): 97-111.

Bray, René. "Un Essai de définition du génie cornélien." *La Nef* 27 (février 1947): 26-34.

Cave, Terence. "Corneille, Œdipus, Racine." *Convergences: Rhetoric and Poetic in Seventeenth-Century France.* Eds. David Lee Rubin and Mary B. McKinley. Columbus: Ohio State UP, 1989. 82-100.

————. *Recognitions: A Study in Poetics.* Oxford: Clarendon Press, 1988.

Corneille, Pierre. *Œuvres complètes.* Ed. Georges Couton. 3 vols. La Pléiade. Paris: Gallimard, 1980-87.

Couton, Georges. *La Vieillesse de Corneille.* Paris: Librairie Maloine, 1949.

Delmas, Christian. "Corneille et le mythe: le cas d'Œdipe." *Mythologie et mythe dans le théâtre français (1650-76).* Droz: Genève, 1985.

Harvey, Lawrence E. "Corneille's *Horace*: A Study in Tragic and Artistic Ambivalence." *Studies in Seventeenth-Century French Literature.* Ed. Jean-Jacques Demorest. Ithaca: Cornell UP, 1962. 65-95.

Hubert, Judd. "L'Anti-Œdipe de Corneille." *17e siècle* 146 (1985): 47-56.

Lancaster, H. C. *A History of French Dramatic Literature in the Seventeenth Century, 1652-72.* Vol. 2. Baltimore: Johns Hopkins UP, 1966.

Mauron, Charles. *Des Métaphores obsédantes au mythe personnel.* Paris: Corti, 1964. 243-69.

Scherer, Jacques. *Dramaturgies d'Œdipe.* Paris: PU de France, 1987.

Sophocles. *Œdipus the King* in *The Three Theban Plays.* Trans. Robert Fagles. New York: Penguin, 1984.

Verhoeff, Han. *Les Grandes tragédies de Corneille: une psycholecture.* Paris: Archives des Lettres Modernes, 1982.

SOPHONSIBE (SOPHINISBA)

CRITICAL COMMENTARY

H. T. Barnwell (essay date 1984)

SOURCE: Barnwell, H. T. "Corneille in 1663: The Tragedy of *Sophonisbe*." *Papers on French Seventeenth Century Literature* 11, no. 21 (1984): 575-92.

[*In the following essay, Barnwell provides an interpretation of* Sophonisba *in light of Saint-Evremond's critical comments on Corneille and his play.*]

Of Corneille's tragedies, *Sophonisbe* is one of the least esteemed both by his contemporaries and by the critics who have followed them over the past three hundred years. Yet the dramatist himself thought it one of his best plays. Was he mistaken? Or, at least, does this tragedy deserve its poor reputation? With few exceptions (e.g. Serge Doubrovsky: "cette pièce méconnue et, à bien des égards, très belle, un des chefs-d'oeuvre de Corneille"; and Marie-Odile Sweetser makes a detailed analysis), most modern critics either virtually pass over it (André Stegmann devotes two pages to it after the dozen accorded to *Sertorius,* and R. J. Nelson gives it scarcely a page after the ten on *Sertorius* and as many as seventeen on *Oedipe*), or regard it—Lanson and Lancaster no less than the first (and only) spectators and D'Aubignac—as a failure. Indeed most modern critics seem to follow the author of the *Dissertations* in considering the characters of *Sophonisbe* unsympathetic, *vraisemblance, bienséance* and unities disregarded, the plot too complex: they tend, like him, to fault Corneille on matters of detail and technique without considering their significance in the development of the dramatic action as a whole. After René Bray's account of the quarrel of 1663, to which little can be added and which viewed the play as a last defiance of classical orthodoxy, we have been offered the idea of a Corneille reflecting less the aesthetic preoccupations of his day than contemporary events, personalities, political and moral thought, or expressing an ideology (often anachronistic), or writing successive chapters of his spiritual or sentimental autobiography. Moreover, when, like D'Aubignac, modern critics compare Corneille's tragedy with Mairet's, it is almost always to the advantage of the latter[1].

In these few pages, I do not propose either to comment in detail on the remarks of these critics or to situate *Sophonisbe* in its context, literary or historical. Some of the opinions expressed by the poet's contemporaries in the course of the quarrel or its prolongations are, however, enlightening, whether we think them valid or not. Among them are the views of the first real critic of the dramatist: he was not involved in the polemics of 1663 but entertained prejudices quite the contrary of those of the hostile theorist who was D'Aubignac. Although they did not appear until later and were not primarily concerned with *Sophonisbe,* some of the writings of the then exiled Saint-Evremond constitute a spirited defence of the ageing Corneille and of this tragedy in particular. It is in the light of a few of Saint-Evremond's remarks that I shall attempt an interpretation of *Sophonisbe.* The most significant of these are in the following passage, which is situated in a discussion of "les femmes illustres"[2]:

> . . . Il faut considérer Sophonisbe, dont le caractère eût pu être envié des Romains même. Il faut la voir sacrifier le jeune Massinisse au vieux Syphax pour le bien de sa patrie; il faut la voir écouter aussi peu les scrupules du devoir en quittant Syphax qu'elle avait fait les sentiments de son amour en se détachant de Massinisse; il faut la voir qui soumet toutes sortes d'attachements, ce qui nous lie, ce qui nous unit, les plus fortes chaînes, les plus douces passions, à son amour pour Carthage et à sa haine pour Rome. Il faut la voir enfin, quand tout l'abandonne, ne pas se manquer à elle-même, et dans l'inutilité des coeurs qu'elle avait gagnés pour sauver son pays, tirer du sien un dernier secours pour sauver sa gloire et sa liberté[3].

In spite of obvious lacunae and simplification of plot and passions, Saint-Evremond grasps with remarkable perspicacity the unity and consistency of the heroine and, at the same time, the essential articulation of the action. An analysis of some aspects of the action in the form of an elaboration of Saint-Evremond's comments will, I hope, result in an appreciation both of the aesthetic unity of the play and of its tragic import.

Corneille himself asserts in his preface that he has not imitated Mairet: in his own defence he advances arguments in which historical truth looms large. In some important details he certainly returns more closely than his predecessor to Livy's account, but the invention of the character of Eryxe is, as most critics agree, of capital importance for an understanding of the play. M. Stegmann, for example, states: "L'intrigue de la curieuse tragédie de Sophonisbe, apparemment dévouée au culte de la patrie et de la liberté, repose en fait sur une vengeance de jalousie"[4]. Indeed, early in the play, the heroine speaks to Herminie, her confidant, of her former love for Massinisse and of the political reasons for her marriage to Syphax:

> J'immolai ma tendresse au bien de ma patrie:
> Pour lui gagner Syphax j'eusse immolé ma vie.

Syphax's victory in the battle against Massinisse had added the latter's kingdom to Carthage and enhanced Sophonisbe's greatness: the glory of her city is inseparable from her own:

Aussi contre Carthage et contre ma grandeur
Tu me vis n'écouter ni ma foi ni mon coeur.

(ll. 43-4, 53-4)

The war undertaken by Syphax against Eryxe on the orders of Sophonisbe was an attempt by the Carthaginian heroine to avenge Massinisse's refusal to marry Syphax's sister rather than Eryxe whose suitor he became on the marriage of Sophonisbe to Syphax. Eryxe has been defeated and captured, but when, at the beginning of the play, Syphax appears to be on the point of bringing to a conclusion a second war, with the Romans and their new ally, Massinisse, it is clear that one of the conditions would be the liberation of Eryxe and her marriage to the same Massinisse. It is in order to prevent that love-match that the jealous Sophonisbe wishes the peace negotiations to fail, and that in spite of the favourable terms Syphax seems likely to secure for Carthage as well as for himself[5].

The exposition of these facts in Act I, scene 2[6], is followed by the episode in which Sophonisbe's suspicions about the love of Eryxe and Massinisse are confirmed. It is in this context that the encounter takes place between Sophonisbe and Syphax in which the latter reluctantly agrees to continue the war. Sophonisbe's arguments are purely political and moral: she despises the passionate love which impels her husband towards an armistice, contrasting it with the patriotism which drove her to abandon her passionate love for Massinisse. While it is undeniable that where for Syphax his political alliance with Carthage had been decided by his passion for Sophonisbe (ll. 265-70), the same alliance had been concluded on her side despite her love for Massinisse and cemented by her marriage to Syphax, it is deeply ironical that, whatever the reasons put forward in Act I, scene 4, her real and immediate motive for continuing the war is personal pride and passionate jealousy. Her devotion to Carthage and to her own *gloire* both as Syphax's queen and as Hasdrubal's daughter are certainly genuine, but as soon as the imminent peace raises the possibility of union between her rival and Massinisse, political and military action are undertaken on the impulse of passionate jealousy. The ensuing defeat, reported at the beginning of Act II, is a catastrophe for Sophonisbe not only from the military and political standpoint, but because her *gloire* is also imperilled both by captivity and the threat of a Roman triumph, and by the removal of the obstacle to the dreaded marriage. All aspects of her *gloire* are inseparably linked, and it is out of that that Corneille has made the unity of his play. Sophonisbe will later admit (ll. 1542-60) that the military and political disaster has been provoked by her pride and her jealousy of Eryxe. Passion has deprived her of political prudence.

Early in the play, therefore, that passion, while being inextricable from it, diminishes both the purity and the achievements of heroic patriotism. And the royal and personal *gloire* of which Sophonisbe speaks (l. 53), although inseparable from patriotism, will in part be loosed from it and assume a different aspect when the consequences of the Roman victory become clear. Carthage isolated and Syphax defeated, Sophonisbe's situation in relation to Eryxe is turned upside down: the captive queen is freed, while the one who believed herself free is a captive, humiliated before the woman she herself had taken delight in humbling (ll. 228, 393-8, 575-6); and, as Eryxe (ll. 393-4) and Massinisse (l. 562) see, to this humiliation is added that of the impending "opprobre du triomphe". It is no longer for Sophonisbe a matter of enhancing the glory of Carthage or her own by positive action, but rather of avoiding personal shame and the humiliation of her regal status. Her *gloire* itself is not abandoned, but its object is diminished and the reasons for action are negative. When Massinisse, the victor, offers to marry her (in his turn forsaking Eryxe) in an endeavour to spare her the Roman triumph, she accepts, not for the love with which she still loves him but from a desire to save what remains of her *gloire*. In her devotion to it, she still thinks wishfully of Carthage: the shame of captivity could be avoided by death, but marriage and alliance with Massinisse seem to offer the possibility of a Carthaginian renewal (ll. 599-600, 708-30). That may be a dream for future realisation, which is why she now prefers life to suicide; but more immediately marriage may also release her from shameful captivity—though it is to death that she must eventually resort even for that—and it allows her to triumph again over Eryxe, a victory to compensate for military defeat.

From the crucial discussion (II, 4) between Sophonisbe and Massinisse about the possibility of marriage, it is evident that the driving force behind her ideal of *gloire*, patriotic, regal or jealous, is an overwhelming desire for independence which she has not sacrificed in marrying Syphax and will not sacrifice in marrying Massinisse (ll. 696-8). The concomitant of this desire is her hatred for Rome whether as the enemy of Carthage or as her captor. The same desire extends to her willingness to forgo love and to her scorn for those who are enslaved to it (Syphax, Massinisse), and to her ambition to order alliances, marriages and wars for the good of Carthage and its freedom, an ambition which for her justifies faithlessness and moral perjury (ll. 607ff.). Even having made the fatal, jealousy-inspired error in Act I, and having begun to feel its consequences in Act II, Sophonisbe is still proclaiming her desire for independence and freedom of action.

Yet she had, before the action of the play ever begins, become dependent, for the defence of Carthage, on Syphax, and then, in Act I, is dependent on him for the continuation of the war. He fails her, both because he is defeated and because he has not the courage to die rather than be taken prisoner (ll. 1081-96). Now, while still expressing her will to independence, she is in fact again dependent, this time on Massinisse, who will also fail her, first in his inability to have his marriage approved by the Romans and in his useless pleas to Scipion, in which she will not stoop to join, and finally in his unwillingness to show himself worthy of the heroine by dying rather than remain ignominiously in the service of the allies who are his masters. But she will not be dependent on Massinisse for her death: for that, the only remaining means of preserving her dignity, her *gloire,* her freedom, her independence, she has made her own provision. It is of course ironical, too, that in making his offer of marriage to Sophonisbe Massinisse himself has been dependent on Eryxe's willingness to release him from his promise to her, and that he is now dependent on the approval of the Romans. It is also a measure of the diminishment of Sophonisbe's ideals that, when Massinisse obtains Eryxe's consent, the greatest satisfaction of her *gloire* arises not out of possible release from captivity and humiliation, but out of her jealous triumph over her rival (ll. 708-14, 729-34): jealousy is a form of offended *gloire.* When Sophonisbe warns first Herminie (ll. 750ff.) and then Massinisse (ll. 944ff.) of Eryxe's hidden jealousy, she is in fact commenting (unconsciously?) on the power of her own.

It is within the framework of the rivalry and jealousy that the development of the plot with its *péripéties* is worked out. The main articulations are to be seen in the sequence Act I, scene 3 - Act II, scene 3 - Act III, scene 3 - Act V, scene 4. Each of these four episodes takes the form of a dialogue between the two queens. In the first, Sophonsibe is confident of victory over the Romans and, therefore, of being able to prevent Eryxe's marriage to Massinisse: it is in that confidence and with that aim that she urges Syphax to refuse the Romans' peace terms. The second episode results from the defeat of Sophonisbe's and Syphax's forces: Eryxe is freed and can marry Massinisse. "Tout a changé de face, / Madame", she says to Sophonisbe, "et les destins vous ont mise en ma place" (ll. 575-6). It is out of that humiliation and the threat of a Roman triumph (see the following scene) that the plan for marriage with Massinisse emerges. When the plan is realised—except for the crucial approval of the Romans—Sophonisbe's jealousy is in the ascendancy once more, and again Eryxe comments: "Une seconde fois tout a changé de face, / Madame, et c'est à moi de vous quitter la place" (ll. 917-8). From that point onwards, the plot itself concerns Massinisse's vain attempt to persuade the Romans to give his marriage their approval. When that fails and Sophonisbe has no means of escape but suicide, her jealousy of Eryxe demands a final meeting with her which forms the last of our four episodes. This time it is Sophonisbe who opens the dialogue, ironically echoing her rival's words: "Une troisième fois mon sort change de face, / Madame, et c'est mon tour de vous quitter la place" (ll. 1643-4). The verbal parallels and the identity of the rhymes accentuate the *péripéties* and draw attention to the importance of the episodes in the developing dramatic action. Now Sophonisbe hands Massinisse back to her rival, but she attempts to save her own *gloire* by making Eryxe's victory a hollow one: either she will marry Massinisse although he has proved himself unworthy, and so dishonour herself, or she will refuse him because he is dishonoured. In either event Sophonisbe scores a moral victory: she frees herself from jealousy—her passion for liberty again—and from dependence on her rival as she will immediately afterwards free herself from captivity and shame.

It is significant that the action of the whole play is framed between the first and last of these episodes, the first providing the impulse for the continuation of the war and its disastrous result, the last rescuing all that can be saved as much from defeat in love as from defeat in war. Whatever else may be lost, Sophonisbe will not, at the end any more than at the beginning, concede victory to her rival. Early in Act V (ll. 1545-60), when the Romans prove to be unrelenting—because of their fear of a dangerous new alliance between Sophonisbe and Massinisse, who would be safer married to Eryxe—, the captive queen admits that all her troubles have arisen out of her jealousy and pride; and it is that pride which demands to be satisfied in a last interview (her final appearance) with her rival. A deep irony lies in the fact that the Sophonisbe who scorns the passionate behaviour of the two men who love her (see especially III, 4 and 6) brings total disaster upon herself thanks to her own jealous love for one of them. Out of this, her *hubris* ("Tout mon *orgueil* disait à mon âme *jalouse* / Qu'une heure de remise en eût fait son épouse . . ."—ll. 1553-4), arises the fatal *hamartia* ("La présence d'Eryxe aujourd'hui m'a perdue; / Je me serais sans elle un peu mieux défendue; / J'aurais su mieux choisir et les temps et les lieux . . ." - ll. 1550-2). Yet to read many of the commentaries on the play is to remain unaware of the "importune tendresse" (l. 1529) to which the heroine admits and which lies at its very heart. Clearly, when he invented Eryxe, "qui pourrait . . . passer en quelque sorte pour inutile", as he says in the preface, Corneille was not only not mistaken but was, as he also claims, providing essential motives for the other characters' activities; but he was also giving to his play an important ironic and tragic dimension and endowing it with a vital unity[7].

To emphasise thus the importance of the jealousy theme is not of course to deny the reality of the other motives which dictate Sophonisbe's behaviour. It is, however, in the coherence of the plot and action the most powerful unifying factor. An aspect of the heroine's *gloire,* it is the origin of the descending movement from aspiration to Carthaginian victory at the beginning, through hope of avoiding captivity, to becoming simply a means of souring, if not of preventing, the marriage of Eryxe to Massinisse: it is at the root of the diminishment of Sophonisbe's idealism. By the time we reach the central scenes of the play (especially III, 4) her sole preoccupation is to avoid the dishonour of a Roman triumph and her fear is that Massinisse will fail to save her from it. In the rashness of his passion (his *hubris*) he is over-confident of success, as he admits when Eryxe doubts his ability to rescue Sophonisbe (ll. 559-60), who herself is tempted to believe in it, so potent is her dread of the ignominy of a triumph (ll. 997-8, 1015-6, 1023-4, 1449-50). Yet she still claims to be independent in the defence of her *gloire* ("Je . . . / . . . prends pour seul objet ma gloire à satisfaire"—ll. 993-4).

Reduced as it is in its objectives, Sophonisbe's *gloire* is still contrasted, in her last encounters with Syphax and Massinisse (III, 6; IV, 5), with her perception, and their own, of their values. Syphax deludes himself into believing that Sophonisbe still loves him despite his defeat and dishonourable survival, and into thinking that she is willing to share his captivity. For him, her *gloire* resides in that marital fidelity (ll. 1001-2), fidelity even in sharing his ignominy in order to reveal her love for him. His repetition of the word *gloire* (l. 1013) brings the devastating riposte which opens the abyss between them ("Ma gloire est d'éviter les fers que vous portez, / D'éviter le triomphe où vous vous soumettez"—ll. 1015-6) and the announcement that she has married Massinisse precisely in order to satisfy that *gloire*, negatively ("éviter") though it is now expressed. Syphax has placed all his *gloire*, now betrayed (l. 1030), in faithfully loving Sophonisbe as her husband: for her he has betrayed both his and her *gloire* as monarchs in spite of his promise (l. 1041: cf. l. 386), while she still lives for hers and, unlike him, is ready to die for it (l. 1045: cf. ll. 383-43; ll. 1039-40, 1091-2, 1098). Her resounding repudiation of Syphax's shameful cowardice ("Je vis pour vous punir de trop aimer à vivre"—l. 1094) culminates in a new proclamation of her independence ("Toute ma passion est pour ma liberté"—l. 1107), even if it is coupled with its negative counterpart which is now her obsessive concern ("Et toute mon horreur pour la captivité"—l. 1108), culminates, too, in a scornful challenge: she will abandon Massinisse again and return to Syphax if he can save her from dishonour and—the recurring wishful thought of patriotic glory—restore her to Carthage (ll. 1109-1112)[8].

But again, unknown to her, *hubris* has overtaken her: in her passionate denunciation of Syphax she is swept along by a misplaced faith in Roman recognition of her new marriage. Stung by scorn and, ironically enough, by jealousy of Massinisse (ll. 1217-20), Syphax will warn the Romans (III, 7; IV, 2) of the danger of a marriage and an alliance between Massinisse and the "Fury" (l. 1213) who will stop at nothing to defeat them and rescue Carthage ("Ce vainqueur avec elle épousera

Carthage"—l. 1222). Sophonisbe has overstepped the mark again, as she did in persuading Syphax to continue the war, and her own boast will prove to be only too prophetic: "Quand il en sera temps, je mourrai pour ma gloire" (l. 1098); but that *gloire* will be equated with escape from the Roman triumph. Meanwhile Syphax, impelled by his own jealousy of Massinisse and anger at Sophonisbe's boasts over her hasty marriage to him, turns informer, saving his own skin for the second time and proving that he prefers life too much.

Massinisse, too, fails Sophonisbe. Immediately after Syphax has admitted to Lélius that it was her power over him which led to his break with Rome, and that Massinisse could be wrested from his alliance in the same way, the interview between the Roman and Numidian commanders takes place (IV, 3). Contrasted with Lélius's cool *Realpolitik,* Massinisse's ardently passionate pleas serve only to confirm Syphax's assessment of the situation and to incur the Roman's disdain ("Vous parlez tant d'amour, qu'il faut que je confesse / Que j'ai honte pour vous de voir tant de faiblesse", etc.—ll. 1361ff.). Sophonisbe's fate is taken out of the hands of Lélius by the arrival of Scipion (IV, 4), with whom Massinisse must now deal directly, but not before he is allowed what turns out to be a final interview with his bride (IV, 5).

Massinisse's pleas to Lélius are a kind of love-song for the absent Sophonisbe. Faced with her in person, he continues in the same vein, pleading with her, now, to accompany him to Scipion's camp in order to plead with him. And just as Lélius had upbraided him for his passionate weakness, so now does Sophonisbe ("Le trouble de vos sens, dont vous n'êtes plus maître, / Vous a fait oublier, Seigneur, à me connaître"—ll. 1433-3: see also later (ll. 1578-9): ". . . Je sais qu'il est Numide. / Toute sa nation est sujette à l'amour . . ."). Although Sophonisbe admits her love, even now, for Massinisse (ll. 1455, 1471-2, 1503-8), she still places it after her *gloire* ("Ma gloire est encor maîtresse"—l. 1506) whose objective remains freedom from captivity (". . . Je ne veux qu'éviter l'aspect du Capitole . . ."—l. 1450; cf. ll. 1471-2). It is to that end, and not for love, that she has married Massinisse (ll. 1455-6) and, although she will not stoop to the shame and dishonour (l. 1437) of pleading with Scipion, she presses her husband, as his ally, to do so on her behalf. He needs the support of her love (ll. 1497-8), and when she has laconically reassured him, he goes. In this remarkable scene, in which the *glorieuse* is dramatically contrasted with the *passionné*[9] Sophonisbe clings to regal and patriotic pride and to her liberty (ll. 1435-40, 1467-72): the second predominates, but not to the exclusion of the first. This scene is of course the counterpart of her final interview with Syphax, but in a lower key: the hope of a Carthaginian recovery has receded and, unlike Syphax, Massinisse does not so much as utter the word *gloire* and has not fought, even reluctantly, for Sophonisbe. His pleading, like Syphax's battle, fails, as she fears (V, 1) and, like Syphax, he fails to fulfil the demands of both honour and love after his fruitless mission (V, 2). Sophonisbe, however, unlike her husbands, does not fail in courage: she saves her *gloire,* "quand tout l'abandonne", as Saint-Evremond says, and rejects the means of doing so provided by the "slave" of the Romans (ll. 1599-1614).

But Massinisse's survival means his probable marriage to Eryxe, which Sophonisbe would see as further dishonour for herself. She is tempted in her turn to survive, as she admits in confidence to Herminie. The hard, fanatical, pitiless, single-minded heroine seen in Sophonisbe by critics from D'Aubignac to Antoine Adam seems elusive. Although determined in the last resort to escape in death from dishonour, her love for Massinisse (and her jealousy of Eryxe) are strong enough to tempt her, if only momentarily:

> Cependant de mon feu l'importune tendresse
> Aussi bien que la gloire en mon sort s'intéresse,
> Veut régner en mon coeur comme ma liberté,
> Et n'ose l'avouer de toute sa fierté.

(ll. 1529-32)

The struggle between *gloire* and Carthage on the one hand (l. 1533) and the "bassesse" of passion on the other (l. 1534) is real, but the thought of Massinisse's failure suffices for *gloire* to prevail: ultimately, both *gloire* and passionate love are satisfied, brought together in the jealousy which inspires her last interview with Eryxe. Even on this diminished scale, Sophonisbe preserves her liberty to act (this last conversation, the suicide and its nature), a liberty which she contrasts with the slavery (ll. 1601, 1608) of Massinisse and his unwillingness to act by dying as she will die (l. 1600). Throughout the descent represented by military defeat, captivity, loss of kingdom and of native city, threat of Roman triumph, loss of truly-loved husband to apparently victorious rival, Sophonisbe does not finally fail to follow the injunction made to Massinisse:

> Tant que vous serez roi, souffrez que je sois reine,
> Avec la liberté d'aimer et de hair,
> Et sans nécessité de craindre ou d'obéir.

(ll. 692-94)

She even threatens Massinisse with her own survival and submission to a triumph so as to shame him with sight of "la femme du vainqueur à côté du vaincu" (l. 1634). But, survived by both her ineffectual husbands, she prefers in the end to die and to punish their cowardice (l. 1787) and to be true to herself and to Carthage (ll. 1790-4).

Neither of the survivors reappears: no traditional funeral oration is pronounced; no emotional *récit* of the death scene is spoken; no rhetorical lament or final suicide

(contrast Mairet's play) takes place. In spite of D'Aubignac's criticisms, all this is entirely appropriate[10]. The laconic closing exchanges between Lépide, Lélius and Eryxe do not, however, fail to point to the forces which have guided the heroine's actions: *gloire* in the form of pride (*orgueil,* ll. 1765, 1798; *pompe,* l. 1801; *fierté,* ll. 1804, 1812; *grand coeur,* l. 1808) and of hatred of Rome (*haine,* ll. 1766, 1799, 1811; *triomphe de nous,* l. 1802). It is of course tragically ironic that these last tributes, whose sincerity cannot be doubted, come, not from husband or friend, but from the objects of hatred and implacable jealousy, the Roman officers and Eryxe, none of whom has played any active part in the development of the drama. It is also appropriate, in this context, that the final decision, which seals the heroine's fate, should be taken by one who is absent and invisible throughout, and that Sophonisbe's solitude should symbolise her desertion by those who, in Saint-Evremond's words, have proved "l'inutilité des coeurs qu'elle avait gagnés pour sauver son pays". At the end, although the sphere of her activity has been, as we have seen, progressively restricted, Sophonisbe's *gloire,* both regal and patriotic, is reasserted, and captivity, slavery and ignominy are avoided—but at the cost of her life—while the shame of the kings survives in their subservience. For this devotion—unscrupulous on Sophonisbe's own admission—to an ideal, diminished though it becomes, we can feel that awe, that *admiration* of which Corneille speaks in connexion with Nicomède, likewise devoted to independence, patriotism and royal dignity; in her peril we can fear for her; in the error of judgement which arises out of her jealousy and of which she becomes the victim we can pity her. It is the nature of that jealousy and its source in her "tendresse" for Massinisse that makes her human[11]. In all that, as in her recognition of her error[12], the play is a true tragedy, punctuated as it is by references to the mutability of men and of destiny (ll. 548, 575-6, 917, 926-30, 1058). It is a tragedy, too, in that Sophonisbe has, in the nature of things, to depend on the kings her husbands—both of them turncoats—for effective action, and that they fail her, while the source of her own fatal error lies in the presence of a character reduced by captivity and dependence to total inactivity. Moreover, the peripety (in the Aristotelian sense) which overtakes her arises out of her passionate devotion to the freedom of Carthage: Syphax's battle results in her captivity, but it is itself caused by her slavery to her passionate jealousy of Eryxe. *Sophonisbe* is as much a tragedy—I do not say as moving or as poetic—as *Horace*: if the set-piece *récits* of battles and the like and the lyrical laments and passionate altercations are gone, this is because—Saint Evremond clearly saw it[13]—as Corneille grew older he became more interested in uncovering the secret motives of his characters than in their "poetic" expression. If D'Aubignac regretted it—and his *Dissertations* are largely made up of regrets for the passing of the playwright's earlier manner—it is because his own expectations were still those of the generation which had applauded Mairet's play and Corneille's early masterpieces[14]. Corneille had moved on in his perpetual search for novelty and originality, not so much in the direction of the *tragédie galante* characteristic of the early 1660s, as in that of a more cerebral and austere tragedy[15]. His remarks, in his preface, about Mairet's *Sophonisbe* and his own, contain nothing less than the truth.

Instead of Mairet's tragedy of pathos occasioned by great sensual passion in adversity and passively experienced, and of the lyrical rhetoric which expresses it, Corneille in 1663 constructs an even more authentic tragedy in which the heroine is involved in an action of which she is both cause (her *hamartia*) and victim, an action which brings about her downfall ("from great prosperity", in Aristotle's phrase) through the *hubris* of pride and jealousy. Yet it is also a heroic tragedy in that Sophonisbe's "grandeur d'âme" remains unimpaired: her willingness to die keeps it untarnished, even if its objectives are tragically diminished as the action progresses. Provided that we study the play from the inside, and are prepared to follow its heroine, not only in her almost superhuman attachment to her *gloire,* but also in the decline of its objectives, we can see in **Sophonisbe** a very remarkable play, rich in paradox and irony. We shall not then fall into the error of D'Aubignac who came to it with preconceptions of what Corneille's tragedies should be, and was disappointed, or of those modern critics who approach it also from the outside, with fixed ideas derived from evidence extraneous to the play, about the moral and political values he is presumed to illustrate or even advocate. Instead, we shall see that **Sophonisbe** shows that in 1663 Corneille was as vital, original, independent and unpredictable a tragic playwright as he had been in 1640 and as he would still be in 1674.

Notes

1. In addition to those named, many modern critics of Corneille devote some discussion to *Sophonisbe.* In the present context a bibliography is unnecessary.

2. It is probable that Corneille's portrayal of Sophonisbe's heroism is indebted to such writers as Le Moyne, Scudéry, Du Bosc, Grenaille and others.

3. *Dissertation sur le Grand Alexandre* (1668), in *Oeuvres en prose* (ed. R. Ternois, Paris, 4 vols, 1962-69), II, 84-102. (The passage quoted is on pp. 99-100.) See also the two letters to Mme Bourneau (ibid., 76-83), *Sur les tragédies* (III, 27), *Sur les caractères des tragédies* (III, 336), *A un auteur qui me demandait mon sentiment d'une pièce ou l'héroïne ne faisait que se lamenter* (III, 340-3), *Défense de quelques pièces de M. Corneille* (IV, 423-31).

4. *L'héroïsme cornélien. Genèse et signification* (Paris, 2 vols, 1968), II, 527. This aspect of the play is neglected by S. Doubrovsky and G. Couton, for example, who see in Sophonisbe an exclusive passion for the throne and for Carthage: *Corneille et la dialectique du héros* (Paris, 1963), 353; *La Vieillesse de Corneille* (Paris, 1949), 83. The jealousy theme is ignored by D'Aubignac.

5. Yet D'Aubignac (*Dissertation sur Sophonisbe,* in Granet, *Recueil de dissertations sur plusiers tragédies de Corneille et de Racine* (Paris, 2 vols, 1740), I, 136-7 claims that the political speeches "étouffent tous les sentiments de tendresse, de jalousie et des autres passions".

6. This is, as J. Scherer (*La Dramaturgie classique en France,* Paris, 1950, 46) points out, the real exposition scene.

7. D'Aubignac (*Dissertation,* 147, 151) sees in Eryxe "une actrice inutilement introduite sur la scène". H. C. Lancaster (*A History of French Dramatic Literature . . . ,* Baltimore, 5 pts in 9 vols, 1929-42, III, ii, 479-80) thinks that the part was created for the sake of the actress, La Beauchâteau, G. May (*Tragédie cornélienne, tragédie racinienne,* Urbana, 1948, 49-50) that it was part of an attempt to reproduce the situation of *Pertharite.* The anonymous author of the *Lettre sur les remarques qu'on a faites sur la Sophonisbe de M. Corneille* (in Granet, I, 212) sees her role as essential, because she "précipite le mariage de Massinisse avec Sophonisbe et donne lieu à tous les événements qui le suivent".

8. Timante, in Villier's *Entretien sur les tragédies de ce temps* (Granet, I, 25) maintains that Sophonisbe dies only "parce qu'elle aime la gloire et qu'elle ne veut pas survivre à la perte de sa liberté". One notes the juxtaposition of "gloire" and "liberté".

9. Cf. R. J. Nelson, *Corneille. His Heroes and their Worlds,* Philadelphia, 1963, 230.

10. As the "later" Donneau de Visé (*Défense de Sophonisbe,* Granet, I, 179) clearly saw: ". . . cette solitude de la scène a quelque chose de triste et de grand tout ensemble, qui fait mieux connaître le revers de la fortune". He was attacking the criticisms of D'Aubignac (*Dissertation,* 146-51), based on the return of Massinisse and his final lament in Mairet's play. Cf. Saint-Evremond (*A un auteur . . . ,* 342) on the vanity of "de longues lamentations" at the end of tragedies, with which D'Aubignac, oddly enough, had seemed earlier to agree (*La Pratique du théâtre,* ed. P. Martino, Algiers, 1927, 140). See also S. Doubrovsky, op. cit., 355.

11. As against A. Stegmann, who finds only Syphax and Eryxe sympathetic (op. cit., II, 374), M.-O.

Sweetser draws attention to the genuine sacrifice of Sophonisbe's real love for Massinisse (*La Dramaturgie de Corneille,* Geneva, 1977, 207-8); cf., more generally, her article, "Place de l'amour dans la hiérarchie des valeurs cornéliennes" in *Travaux de Linguistique et de Littérature,* X, 2, 63-77.

12. Act V, sc. 1 is not, however, in the Aristotelian sense a scene of "discovery" (*anagnorisis*): Sophonisbe is never unaware of what she is doing or why.

13. *A un auteur . . . ,* 340.

14. Apart from the continual comparisons of Corneille's play with Mairet's in his first *Dissertation,* see also, for example, the second, on *Sertorius* (Granet, I, 238-9) and *La Pratique du théâtre,* 278.

15. Cf. the remarks of L. Herland in "Les qualités requises du personnage de tragédie et les sources de la pitié tragique, d'après la querelle de *Sophonisbe* (1663)", *Mélanges de la Société toulousaine d'études classiques,* I, (1948), 205-22, especially pp. 207, 221.

OTHON (OTHO)

CRITICAL COMMENTARY

Elizabeth Ellington Gunter (essay date December 1981)

SOURCE: Gunter, Elizabeth Ellington. "The Function of Vinius in *Othon.*" *French Review* 55, no. 2 (December 1981): 188-92.

[*In the following essay, Gunter investigates the character of Vinius in* Otho, *maintaining that he can be viewed "as a mock hero whose main function is to serve as a dramatic and psychological foil for Othon."*]

Critics have claimed that the imperial advisors in Corneille's **Othon** come close to dominating the action of the play. Among these advisors, Lacus and the ex-slave Martian are obviously self-interested, ambitious villains who possess no redeeming qualities. Vinius, on the other hand, appears more complex and so has elicited more comment. Nevertheless, Claude Abraham condemns him as "a double-dealing mediocrity,"[1] and Marie-Odile Sweetser adds that his "bassesse" and "mal-

honnêteté"[2] make him unworthy of any sympathy. André Stegmann, however, declares that he is "moins coupable, contraint qu'il est, comme tous, d'essayer d'éviter le pire, en usant des armes impures de l'adversaire."[3] And Helen Bates McDermott even sees some positive traits in his personality: for her, he is the "prime theoretician and pedagogue to Othon," the most successful practitioner of the "amoral *savoir*" that is the "eminent political value"[4] in the play. Indeed, Vinius can be seen as a mock hero whose main function is to serve as a dramatic and psychological foil for Othon. By serving as a foil, Vinius shows that the "old" heroism of Corneille's earlier plays, in which the virtuous hero confidently pursues his *gloire,* is no longer possible and helps to define what the more realistic "new" heroism is.

In this somber play about the disastrous consequences of allowing advisors (especially those who have no sense of identity with the best interests of the state) too much power, Vinius is not just another corrupt politician. In the first place, though Vinius is ambitious, he has a sense of pride. He warns Othon and Plautine that if Othon does not marry Emperor Galba's niece Camille and thereby become emperor himself, he will commit suicide rather than be condemned to death by the other advisors:

> Je ne crains point la mort, mais je hais l'infamie
> D'en recevoir la loi d'une main ennemie;
> Et je saurai verser tout mon sang en Romain,
> Si le choix que j'attends ne me retient la main.[5]

Furthermore, from the beginning of the play when Othon explains his need for a protector to the last act when Othon weeps over Vinius as he dies, Vinius appears to dominate Othon totally. Not only is Othon forced to ally himself with "ce consul, qui ravage, qui pille, / Qui peut tout . . . auprès de l'Empereur" (I.i. 10-11) in order to survive, but he also fears him, as his refusal to desert Vinius' daughter Plautine shows: "Surtout de Vinius le sensible courage / Feroit tout pour me perdre après un tel outrage" (I.i. 89-90). Indeed, in this opening conversation between Othon and his friend Albin, great emphasis is given to Vinius. Corneille carefully builds up interest in him and leads the audience to anticipate his arrival. Yet when he does arrive, he does not appear as a powerful man in control of those around him, but rather it is he who seeks Othon's support against the other advisors. Ironically, he orders Othon (who has just finished protesting to Albin that Vinius would destroy him if he were to desert Plautine) to stop loving Plautine and court Camille. An astute politician, Vinius has quickly evaluated Galba's recent decision to choose as next emperor whomever Camille marries, and he has seen that Othon must be that choice if he, his daughter, and Othon are to survive. Having seized the first opportunity, Vinius has already suggested Othon as a possible husband to Camille and has judged her involuntary reaction to be favorable. Here he wastes no time informing Othon of these new circumstances, as he commands him to court Camille. In this ensuing discussion, Vinius appears strong and assertive, Othon weak and indecisive. Vinius has no hesitancy about what needs to be done. Not one to let virtue stand in the way of success, he responds sarcastically to Othon's declaration of fidelity to Plautine:

> De tant de fermeté j'aurois l'âme ravie,
> Si cet excès d'amour nous assuroit la vie;
> Mais il nous faut le trône, ou renoncer au jour;
> Et quand nous périrons, que servira l'amour?
>
> (I.ii.225-28)

Vinius becomes even more the man to be reckoned with when Othon suggests that they appeal to Othon's rival Pison, who, Othon believes, will allow them to live. Of course, Vinius knows better: "Seigneur, quand pour l'empire on s'est vu désigner, / Il faut, quoi qu'il arrive, ou périr ou régner" (I.ii.235-36). Since Othon still refuses to place anything above his love for Plautine, Vinius leaves him with her to decide what he will do. Typically, Othon soon agrees to follow Vinius' scheme. When Vinius reappears on stage (IV.ii), he again enters suddenly to announce another change of events and to propose another plan of action to Othon. The army's displeasure over the choice of Pison as emperor has been relayed to him by several of its most zealous members, who have also assured him that the troops and the Empire will be Othon's if he will but show himself. Othon barely has time to utter a feeble protest or two before Vinius sends him on his way. Again, it is Vinius who is assertive and strong, Othon passive and weak.

Vinius is a formidable personage to others besides Othon. Though physically absent from the second and third acts, he remains present in everyone's mind. Obviously his daughter Plautine thinks of him when she declares her willingness to sacrifice her happiness to save his life. Martian compares himself favorably with him in his attempt to win Plautine's hand. Lacus sees him as a dangerous threat; for, if Othon becomes emperor,

> Vinius en aura lui seul tout l'avantage;
> Comme il l'a proposé, ce sera son ouvrage;
> Et la mort, ou l'exil, ou les abaissements,
> Seront pour vous et moi ses vrais remercîments.
>
> (II.iv.661-64)

Even Camille refers to Vinius' power (II.v). Moreover, Vinius gives a demonstration of his considerable political skills in the fifth act of this play, which is "plus purement politique encore que *Sertorius* ou *Sophonisbe*,"[6] when he opposes Lacus' suggestions to Galba regarding the rebellion. Throughout this confrontation with Lacus, Vinius exhibits a shrewd knowledge of both the political situation around him and human psychology as he calmly lies and molds the truth to fit his own purposes. McDermott believes that this craftiness can be seen to make him "on the political level . . . the actual hero of *Othon*."[7] Also, since politics so dominates the action of this play, Vinius' political "heroism" is much more significant than similar political "heroism" is in most of Corneille's other plays. Since he is the hero on a political level, he is all the more a mock hero on the metaphysical level.

Finally, it is Vinius who dies a hero's death when Lacus stabs him in a fit of anger upon seeing Othon triumphant. His death is heroic insofar as it occurs while Vinius is helping the titular hero achieve power and because that hero treats it as such. He runs to Vinius' aid in the street, weeps over him as he dies, and embraces his corpse after his death. By ironic contrast, the passive Othon, who has frequently spoken of suicide, lives, although his last appearance in the play is hardly forceful or heroic. He seems more the lovesick suitor than the triumphant new emperor as he first tells Plautine that he is "plus mort" than her father and will die unless her love restores him to life, and next tells Albin that he must go after Plautine to seek her orders before going to the Capitol to receive the Senate's oaths of loyalty.

Yet despite Vinius' forcefulness, his political knowledge, his influence over others, especially Othon, and his heroic death, he is obviously not the hero of the play. To begin with, he seems too much the buffoon, "souvent proche d'Arnolphe."[8] For example, his first words to Othon strike the spectator as nothing short of comic:

VINIUS:

> Il en faut une preuve, et non pas seulement
> Qui consiste aux devoirs dont s'empresse un amant:
> Il la faut plus solide, il la faut d'un grand homme,
> D'un cœur digne en effet de commander à Rome.
> Il faut ne plus l'aimer.

OTHO:

>   Quoi! pour
> preuve d'amour . . .

VINIUS:

> Il faut faire encor plus, Seigneur, en ce grand jour:
> Il faut aimer ailleurs.

OTHO:

>   Ah! que m'osez-
> vous dire?
>
> (I.ii.119-25)

Likewise, his subsequent entrance (IV.ii) seems comic in that his words to Othon parody those of Don Diègue to Rodrigue in *Le Cid*: "Seigneur, / Vous empêcherez tous, si vous avez du cœur" (IV.ii.1247-48). In addition, Vinius treats his daughter Plautine in an exceptionally shabby manner, promising her in any marriage (even to a lascivious ex-slave) that will help him politically, taking no account of her feelings, urging her to expedient self-interest rather than honor. Furthermore, Vinius uses deception and violence to attain his ends. Morally corrupt according to traditional heroic standards, he places expediency and power above truth, honor, constancy, and any other traditional virtue one can name except a certain type of pride. Above all, he uses people—they exist only as pawns in his game.

With these non-heroic attributes, the reader may wonder why Vinius appears as anything other than a villain. The answer lies in his willingness to act. Of all the characters in the play, Vinius comes closest to being a protagonist in that he makes things happen. Of all the masculine roles in the play, his is the most dramatic. It is ironic that he dies while the weak Othon becomes emperor. Yet the failure of Vinius' more positive attributes to save him reflects Corneille's realization that, in a topsy-turvy Machiavellian world where corrupt advisors manipulate the ruler and ex-slaves depose kings and marry queens, such attributes are no longer guarantees of success. Political advancement and even the choice of a marriage partner are determined by chance. Traditional virtues, such as honor and attention to duty, merely limit a character's options and make him even more vulnerable. In short, virtuous action becomes a liability, a weakness, a subject of sarcasm in the eyes of persons such as these three advisors; and would-be heroes, such as Othon, find themselves obliged to practice vices in courts, such as Néron's, in order to stay alive. Even if a character like Othon were to prefer death to dishonor, he would not be able to exercise the traditional heroism seen in *Le Cid* or *Horace*. That heroism requires an audience to admire the character's actions; such an audience is lacking in Othon's world. Only Plautine would begin to understand and appreciate the traditional heroism of Corneille's earlier plays in which duty and passion are forged together by the heroic character's sense of integrity, his magnanimity, and his confidence in both himself and the values he and his society share. Except for Plautine and Othon, the characters in *Othon* would not only fail to appreciate such heroism, but they probably would not even recognize it for what it was and would therefore eliminate the possibility of such a heroic character's achieving *gloire* and the self-fulfillment that comes from reputation.

Othon understands this; he sees that his actions in Galba's world are quite limited. He practices the only hero-ism that is possible in such a world; he faces up to reality, tries to survive while living as virtuously as possible—in Lusitania, "il s'y montra grand prince" (II.iv.610)—and he attempts to find self-fulfillment in his private life, in his love for the virtuous Plautine. He knows he must compromise his values; he must participate in corruption to some extent merely in order to live. This "new" heroism is relative and pessimistic. Surrounded by persons who have no sense of the traditional heroic values and who justify anything in the name of power and success, Othon knows that his chances for lasting personal happiness, as well as his world's chances for lasting order, are very slim indeed. The active Vinius, by serving as a foil for the passive Othon, gives a concrete example of the futility of resourcefulness, knowledge, and willingness to act in such a world. His role as corrupt advisor/mock hero, unique in Corneille's theater, is central to Corneille's most extreme portrait of the impossibility of heroism in such a political world. Although we see the problem of political marriage in Corneille's other plays of this period such as *Sophonisbe* and *Agésilas,* and the degeneration of heroism in Sertorius' indecision, in Sophonisbe's self-interest, and in Massinisse's weakness, nowhere else are such an advisor and such a hero paired together. In no other play does Corneille offer such arguments against Machiavellian politics or such a somber picture of political reality. *Othon* is, in André Stegmann's words, "un cas limite";[9] and Vinius, far from being just another corrupt advisor, is in regard to heroism as important to the meaning of the play as Othon.

Notes

1. *Pierre Corneille* (New York: Twayne, 1972), p. 127.

2. *La Dramaturgie de Corneille* (Geneva: Droz, 1977), p. 218.

3. *L'Héroïsme cornélien: Genèse et signification* (Paris: Armand Colin, 1968), II, 628.

4. "Uses of Irony in *Othon,*" *French Review,* 51 (1978), 651.

5. Pierre Corneille, *Œuvres de P. Corneille,* ed. Ch. Marty-Laveaux (Paris: Hachette, 1862), VI, 587. All quotations from *Othon* are taken from this edition.

6. André Stegmann, "Notice sur *Othon,*" in *Œuvres complètes* (Paris: Seuil, 1963), p. 664.

7. McDermott, p. 651.

8. Stegmann, *L'Héroïsme cornélien,* I, 191-92.

9. Stegmann, "Notice," p. 664, n. 2.

FURTHER READING

Criticism

Baker, Susan Read. "An 'I' for an Eye: Corneille's *Clitandre*." *Papers on French Seventeenth Century Literature* 13, no. 24 (1986): 87-101.

Considers *Clitandre*'s place within Corneille's oeuvre.

————. "Strategies of Seduction in *Cinna*." In *Homage to Paul Bénichou*, edited by Sylvie Romanowski and Monique Bilezikian, pp. 75-91. Birmingham, AL: Summa Publications, 1994.

Contends that "seduction as a sexual, political, and textual practice dominates the economy of *Cinna*."

Bornedal, Peter. "The Law of the Name: The Imaginary Recipient in Corneille's *Le Cid*." *Orbis Litterarum* 52, no. 3 (1997): 157-77.

Investigates the function of the "imaginary recipient" in *The Cid*.

Glynn, Marie. "Some Performative Aspects of the Expression 'Deux Mots' in *Le Cid*." *Romance Notes* 32, no. 2 (winter 1991): 163-68.

Discusses the role of rhetoric in *The Cid*.

Kowsar, Mohammad. "In Defense of Desire: Chimène's Role in *Le Cid* Reconsidered." *Theatre Journal* 34, no. 3 (October 1982): 289-301.

Reappraises Chimène's role in *The Cid*.

Lalande, Roxanne Decker. "Corneille's Liar: The Counterfeiter as Creative Artist." *Papers on French Seventeenth Century Literature* 12, no. 22 (1985): 131-50.

Examines "how Corneille deflects his audience's attention away from ethical concerns and focuses it instead on his hero's fascinating tactics" in *The Liar*.

Lyons, John D. "Corneille and the Triumph of Pleasure, or The Four Axioms of Tragic Pleasure." *Papers on French Seventeenth Century Literature* 19, no. 37 (1992): 329-36.

Elucidates Corneille's dramatic theory.

Margitić, Milorad R. *Corneille Comique: Nine Studies of Pierre Corneille's Comedy with an Introduction and a Bibliography*. Paris: Papers on French Literature, 1982, 222 p.

Collection of critical essays on Corneille's comedies.

Mourgues, Odette de. "Coherence and Incoherence in *Cinna*." In *Form and Meaning: Aesthetic Coherence in Seventeenth-Century French Drama*, edited by William D. Howarth, Ian McFarlane, and Margaret McGowan, pp. 51-74. Amersham, England: Avebury Publishing Co., 1982.

Probes inconsistencies in *Cinna*.

Muratore, M. J. "Corneille's *Polyeucte* the Divine Comedy." *Symposium* 40, no. 2 (summer 1986): 107-16.

Contends that *Polyeucte*'s "ostentatious repudiation of paganism not only has a taint of performance about it but embodies the very essence of dramatic illusion: transforming old realities into new ones."

Newman, Karen. "Corneille's City Comedy: Courtship and Consumption in Early Modern Paris." *Renaissance Drama* 27 (1996): 105-22.

Survey's Corneille's early city comedies.

Reed, Gervais E. "The Unity of Thought, Feeling and Expression in Corneille's *Cinna*." *Symposium* 44, no. 3 (fall 1990): 206-21.

Stylistic and thematic analysis of *Cinna*.

Tucker, Holly. "Corneille's *Médée*: Gifts of Vengeance." *French Review* 69, no. 1 (October 1995): 1-12.

Investigates the role of gift-giving in *Médée*.

Woshinsky, Barbara R. "Rhetorical Vision in Corneille." In *Signs of Certainty: The Linguistic Imperative in French Classical Literature*, pp. 15-52. Saratoga, CA: ANMA Libra, 1991.

Provides an analysis of Corneille's use of rhetoric in his plays.

Additional coverage of Corneille's life and career is contained in the following sources published by Gale Group: *Dictionary of Literary Biography,* **Vol. 268;** *DISCovering Authors: British Edition;* *DISCovering Authors Modules: Most-studied Authors; European Writers,* **Vol. 3;** *Guide to French Literature: Beginnings to 1789; Literature Criticism from 1400 to 1800,* **Vol. 28;** *Literature Resource Center; Reference Guide to World Literature* **Eds. 2, 3; and** *Twayne's World Authors.*

Friedrich Hebbel
1813-1863

(Full name Christian Friedrich Hebbel) German playwright and poet.

The following entry presents criticism on Hebbel's life and works from 1927 through 1987.

INTRODUCTION

Hebbel is considered an important transitional figure in European drama. Scholars maintain that his works reflect both the Romantic idealism of Johann Wolfgang Goethe and Friedrich Schiller and the psychological realism of Carl Hauptmann and Henrik Ibsen. Hebbel viewed the dramatic process as a conflict between the individual searching for identity and meaning and the seemingly intransigent world-historical Idea propounded by philosopher G. W. F. Hegel, who believed that an omnipresent, unstoppable moral force determines the course of history.

BIOGRAPHICAL INFORMATION

Hebbel was born in the small town of Wesselburen in the Holstein district of what is now Germany. His father was an impoverished mason who died when Hebbel was fourteen, leaving him and his brother to be raised by their mother, who was employed as a domestic. In order to continue his education, Hebbel worked as an errand boy and clerk for the local magistrate, studying during his free time. In 1932 he sent some poetry and short stories to the popular novelist Amalie Schoppe, who published several of the pieces in two Hamburg periodicals she edited. Schoppe invited Hebbel to Hamburg to prepare for admission to the university; however, he failed to pass the necessary entrance examinations. He left Hamburg in 1836 to attend jurisprudence lectures at the University of Heidelberg, and eventually traveled to Munich where he worked as a reporter. Unable to support himself, however, Hebbel returned to Hamburg early in 1839, accepting a position as a correspondent for the *Telegraph für Deutschland*. Later that year he began writing his first drama, *Judith: Eine Tragödie in fünf Acten* (*Judith: A Tragedy in Five Acts*) which was completed in January 1840 and first produced in 1841. A stipend from the king of Denmark allowed Hebbel to complete his second drama, *Gen-*

oveva: Tragödie in fünf Acten (1843). In 1863 Hebbel won the first Schiller Prize in German literature for his trilogy, *Die Nibelungen: Ein deutsches Trauerspiel in drei Abtheilungen* (1862; *The Nibelungs: A Tragedy in Three Acts*). He died after contracting pneumonia that same year.

MAJOR WORKS

Nearly all of Hebbel's plays are tragedies, the notable exceptions being the comedies *Der Diamant: Eine Komödie in fünf Acten* (1847) and *Der Rubin: Ein Märchen-Lustspiel in drei Acten* (1851), which critics have described as black comedies. His best-known works are distinguished by the presence of a remarkable individual who struggles against the world-historical Idea. To heighten the drama of this struggle and highlight the problems that have historically fostered such encounters, Hebbel set his plays during turning points of world history. For example, *Judith* relates the attempted extermination of Jews by the Assyrians; *Herodes und Mariamne: Eine Tragödie in fünf Acten* (1850; *Herod and Mariamne*), events immediately preceding the birth of Jesus; *Agnes Bernauer: Ein deutsches Trauerspiel in fünf Aufzügen* (1852; *Agnes Bernauer: A German Tragedy in Five Acts*), the beginnings of the breakdown of fifteenth-century feudalism; and *The Nibelungs,* the twilight of German paganism. In another drama, *Maria Magdalen: Ein bürgerliches Trauerspiel in drei Acten, nebst einem Vorwort* (1844; *Maria Magdalena*), Hebbel emphasizes more personal aspects of tragedy, using non-historical characters to depict the universality of an individual's plight. Critics have also noted the important role that women play in Hebbel's work. With the exception of his autobiographical drama *Michel Angelo: Ein Drama in zwei Akten* (1851) and his unfinished *Demetrius: Eine Tragödie* (1864), women are central to the dramatic conflict in each of his tragedies.

CRITICAL RECEPTION

Although reception of his work was initially lukewarm, Hebbel eventually became recognized as a leading dramatist in his time. His plays were staged throughout Europe, and he was invited to conduct performances at the courts of both Weimar and Munich. Critical interest in Hebbel dissipated shortly after his death; however, a state-sponsored Hebbel resurgence was initiated during the German National Socialist movement. While such attention restored the dramatist to the forefront of German literature, the misguided "Nazification" of Hebbel's work stigmatized him in the post-war world. However, new interpretations of his dramas have emerged and newer productions have been staged. *Judith, Maria Magdalena,* and *Gyges und sein Ring: Eine Tragödie in fünf Acten* (1856; *Gyges and His Ring*) have remained fixtures in the repertoire of many German theatres.

PRINCIPAL WORKS

Plays

Judith: Eine Tragödie in fünf Acten [*Judith: A Tragedy in Five Acts*] 1841
Genoveva: Tragödie in fünf Acten 1843
Maria Magdalen: Ein bürgerliches Trauerspiel in drei Acten, nebst einem Vorwort [*Maria Magdalena*] (essay and drama) 1844
Der Diamant: Eine Komödie in fünf Acten 1847

Ein Trauerspiel in Sizilien: Tragicomödie in einem Act, nebst einem Sendschreiben an H. T. Rötscher (drama and letter) 1847
Herodes und Mariamne: Eine Tragödie in fünf Acten [*Herod and Mariamne*] 1850
Der Rubin: Ein Märchen-Lustspiel in drei Acten 1851
Michel Angelo: Ein Drama in zwei Acten 1851
Agnes Bernauer: Ein deutsches Trauerspiel in fünf Aufzügen [*Agnes Bernauer: A German Tragedy in Five Acts*] 1852
Gyges und sein Ring: Eine Tragödie in fünf Acten [*Gyges and His Ring*] 1856
Die Nibelungen: Ein deutsches Trauerspiel in drei Abtheilungen [*The Nibelungs: A Tragedy in Three Acts*] 2 vols. 1862
Demetrius: Eine Tragödie (unfinished drama) 1864

Other Major Works

Gedichte (poetry) 1842
Neue Gedichte (poetry) 1848
Erzählungen und Novellen (novellas) 1855
Mutter und Kind: Ein Gedicht in sieben Gesängen (poetry) 1859
Sämtliche Werke 12 vols. (dramas, essays, poetry, letters, and novellas) 1865-67
Tagebücher 2 vols. (diaries) 1885-87
Sämtliche Werke: Historisch-Kritische Ausgabe 24 vols. (dramas, essays, diaries, poetry, letters, and novellas) 1901-07
Friedrich Hebbel: Sämtliche Werke nebst Tagebüchern und einer Auswahl der Briefe 6 vols. (dramas, essays, diaries, poetry, letters, and novellas) 1911-25
Werke 5 vols. (dramas, essays, diaries, poetry, letters, and novellas) 1963-67

GENERAL COMMENTARY

Edna Purdie (essay date 1932)

SOURCE: Purdie, Edna. "Dramatic Technique" and "Conception of Tragedy." In *Friedrich Hebbel: A Study of His Life and Work,* pp. 235-69. London: Oxford University Press, 1932.

[*In the following essay, Purdie discusses Hebbel's dramatic theory and technique.*]

DRAMATIC TECHNIQUE

Any detailed analysis of Hebbel's plays must in great measure demonstrate the poet's sense of dramatic effect and his mastery of dramatic means. Moreover, it is impossible to draw a rigid line of demarcation between dramatic technique and the substance of a drama, since the very substance is to some extent the outcome of the form. But Hebbel's actual methods are worthy of some general consideration. They illuminate his individual aims, and in certain ways their influence may be traced in subsequent dramatic history.

Dramatic technique must comprehend all the means used by the dramatic artist to attain his ends—the sum of the practical methods by which he expresses his meaning in dramatic form. With Hebbel, who was before all else a tragic dramatist, the chief end to be attained is a revelation of the underlying necessity for tragic development. Thus his methods of showing the interaction of character and circumstance must be stressed in any study of his technical achievement as a dramatist; the revelation of character is the key to his whole dramatic technique, from the structure of the action down to the brief stage directions.

Few readers or spectators of Hebbel's tragedies could fail to be struck by their architectural quality. Clarity of outline, ordered progress of the action, characterize them all, from *Judith* to *Demetrius*; but perhaps *Maria Magdalena* stands out amongst them as an example of austere compression and swift, relentless movement. The tragic necessity becomes more plainly visible with every scene—a process later generalized by Hebbel in his diary:

> 1ste Stufe künstlerischer Wirkung: es kann so seyn!
>
> 2te Stufe künstlerischer Wirkung: es ist!
>
> 3te Stufe künstlerischer Wirkung: es muss so seyn![1]

This entry may be compared with an earlier one made while he was still at work on *Maria Magdalena,* describing dramatic structure in a visual image: '. . . die Idee [muss] im ersten Act als zuckendes Licht, im zweiten als Stern, der mit Nebeln kämpft, im dritten als dämmernder Mond, im vierten als stralende Sonne, die Keiner mehr verläugnen kann, und im fünften als verzehrender und zerstörender Komet hervortreten. . . .'[2]

The opening acts of Hebbel's tragedies themselves illuminate this image. A gleam of light is often thrown upon a vital contrast. 'Dein Hochzeits-Kleid?' are Klara's first words to her mother in *Maria Magdalena,* dimly foreshadowing the tragic theme; and through this, the swiftest of all Hebbel's opening acts, the situation rapidly develops, till the mother's wedding-dress becomes her shroud and Klara's own marriage fatally impossible. So also do Kandaules' first words to Gyges:

> Heut sollst Du seh'n, was Lydien vermag!

suggest that pride of possession which leads him into tragic guilt, and Hagen's initial question in *Der gehörnte Siegfried*:

> Nun, keine Jagd?

draws an answer stressing the central contrast in the tragic theme:

> Es ist ja heil'ger Tag!

The main facts of the situation emerge clearly from the opening act in Hebbel's dramas, preparing the mind for a decision or event essential to the tragic sequence. Thus in the first act of *Herodes und Mariamne,* Herodes is shown in his contrasting relations with Mariamne and the outside world; the mind of Mariamne is revealed in her interview with the king, and her refusal to comply with his demand provides the occasion for his fatal decision to treat her life as one of his possessions. 'Nun lebt sie unter'm Schwert!'—he exclaims: the act closes with this decisive step. A similar development may be traced in the first act of *Gyges und sein Ring.* The central characteristics of Kandaules on the one hand, of Rhodope on the other, are indicated in two successive scenes; the ring of Gyges, offered to Kandaules in the opening dialogue between them, occasions the king's resolve, in the last scene of the act, to satisfy his pride of possession by a secret injury to Rhodope. Here, too, the first act ends with a decision that involves the tragic outcome.

In *Kriemhilds Rache,* the resolve of Kriemhild to marry Etzel, which concludes the opening act, stands in a different relation to the action of the play; it is rather a condition of the tragic situation than a decision that invites the tragic issue. Nevertheless, the dramatic effect of Kriemhild's consent resembles that of the action taken by Herodes or Kandaules: it is a portent, the lightning flash before the coming storm.

In the whole drama of *Die Nibelungen,* the 'Vorspiel'— *Der gehörnte Siegfried*—may be said to fulfil the functions of an opening act. The situation is swiftly indicated, the characters outlined; and the Prologue concludes with the momentous bargain that is the origin of *Siegfrieds Tod* and *Kriemhilds Rache.* (Hebbel adopted a similar expedient in *Demetrius,* where the Prologue ends with the acceptance and proclamation of the new Tsar).

Where two parallel actions are involved, the first and second acts may be considered as a unit. In *Judith,* Act I is devoted to the Holofernes action and ends with the general's decision to assail Bethulia and destroy the Hebrews; Act II, which draws the contrasting picture of Judith's state of mind, closes on her challenge to Ephraim to kill Holofernes and her incipient resolve to justify the challenge when he refuses to accept it. Similarly, the first act of *Siegfrieds Tod* deals with the situation of Brunhild and her relations with Siegfried, while the second act—though mainly concerned with Siegfried and Kriemhild—ends with Siegfried's reluctant decision to fulfil his bargain with Gunther to the uttermost.

The opening act of *Agnes Bernauer,* on the other hand, offers a picture of both sides of the situation, and thus constitutes an unusually lengthy piece of exposition. In the first half, Agnes is shown in her relations with her environment—her father, her suitor, her contemporaries; in the second, Albrecht's sudden passion is portrayed, and his determination to woo her in earnest is foreshadowed in the final scene. The first act of *Genoveva* is almost equally static. In a sense, however, the decision taken by Golo at the end contributes actively to the catastrophe—intended as a test of Providence, the breakneck climb, successfully achieved, only intensifies temptation by offering a subtle argument to Golo's mind.

Hebbel's general dislike of a purely preparatory opening act is matched by his aversion to the normal 'ritardando' of the fourth act in a five-act drama. Nothing in his picture of the development of a dramatic theme is more striking than the statement that by the fourth act, the central idea must appear 'als stralende Sonne, die Keiner mehr verläugnen kann'. Instead of envisaging a retarding moment between the crisis of the third act and the catastrophe in the fifth, he sees the progress of the action rather as a continuous movement, quickening in speed as it nears the appointed end. Only in *Siegfrieds Tod* and *Kriemhilds Rache* (where the poet's close reliance on his source must not be overlooked) do we find something like the normal retardation of the action.

In *Judith,* while Act III is devoted to Judith's resolve and the great crowd scene in Bethulia, Act IV brings the chief antagonists face to face for the first time; and the spiritual conflict here evident leads directly to the ultimate conflict and catastrophe. A striking form of this progression is to be found in *Herodes und Mariamne*: the fourth act contains Mariamne's discovery of Herodes' second betrayal of her person—the climax of her spiritual tragedy; this is followed by her festival, and by the final clash between herself and Herodes on the king's return. Each of the two heroines thus plays a deliberate part at the end of the fourth act, leaving the unmasking to the fifth; but as Mariamne's inner tragedy is greater than that of Judith, so too is its issue more compelling.

In *Gyges und sein Ring* the fourth act is entirely occupied by the decisive dialogue between Gyges and the queen. The climax of the inner action is the resolve of Gyges to accept Rhodope's terms; it is preceded by the gradual unfolding of the truth, through the statement of Kandaules and the consequent explanation offered by Gyges to the queen, and is followed by a clear indication of the catastrophe:

RHODOPE:

> Nun Brautgewand und Todtenhemd, herbei!
>
> . . . . .
>
> (*To Lesbia*) Du wirst mir wohl nicht danken, armes Kind!
> Und doch! Zuletzt! Ja, Lesbia, zuletzt!

The fourth act of *Demetrius* provides an interesting parallel to this. Here also the discovery of the truth marks the spiritual crisis, and Demetrius is faced with a choice that is decisive for the tragic issue; and similarly, the last words of the act prepare us for that issue.

The momentous decision of Herzog Ernst is taken in the fourth act. 'Agnes Bernauer, fahr' hin!' are the final words of the first half, before the scene changes to Straubing, where the warrant is executed. The turning-point in the drama of Herzog Ernst is here; the arrest of Agnes which follows constitutes a moment of suspense in hers—suspense that is deepened by the final words of Preising which afford a gleam of hope:

> Gott gebe, dass sie jetzt auf mich höre! Noch kann ich sie vom Tode retten und ich will's.
>
> (IV. 12)

This suggestion of a possible way of escape (which yet does not command belief) is rare in Hebbel's tragedies. The appearance of Drago's spirit at the end of the fourth act of *Genoveva* is too little related to the immediate action to be taken as a parallel—though actually it does suggest the solution which later formed the *Epilogue to Genoveva.* A more direct comparison might be made with a fleeting hope in Klara's desperate soliloquy at the end of Act II in *Maria Magdalena* (the equivalent moment in a three-act drama): 'Ich bettle ja nicht um mein Glück, ich bettle um mein Elend, um mein tiefstes Elend—mein Elend wirst Du mir geben!' (II. 6); but even this is immediately followed by such an indication of the tragic issue as occurs in *Gyges* or *Demetrius*: 'Drei Brunnen triffst Du auf dem Weg zu ihm—Dass Du mir an Keinem stehen bleibst! Noch hast Du nicht das Recht dazu!'

Retarding moments are not found at any fixed point in Hebbel's tragedies. Where they occur, their object is to make the outcome appear the more inevitable. Such is the moment between the two tests in *Herodes und Mariamne* (Act III, Sc. 6) where the outward action is suspended, but the inner conflict between Herodes and the queen grows more acute; so too in the fifth act of this drama, the explanation offered to Titus by Mariamne—while it retards the course of events—increases the force of the blow dealt to Herodes, and thus heightens the effect of the catastrophe. The most obviously retarding moment in *Maria Magdalena*—the third scene of the second act, where the merchant Wolfram arrives at Meister Anton's house and tells Klara of her brother's innocence—serves partly to explain the previous action, but mainly to deepen the tragic irony of her own situation. It is thus matched by the scene in the last act between Karl and his sister, where through an apparently slow-moving dialogue the force of Klara's determination rapidly increases till she finds in Karl's trivial request excuse for action.

Thus consideration of the structure of his plays shows that both outward events and the pause between events are used by Hebbel to further that revelation of character which forms the true action of the tragedies. This close connexion is for him the principle of dramatic exposition: the revelation of events entirely subserves the presentation of character. By this, perhaps more clearly than by any other single trait, he proves himself a major dramatist.

Every dramatic author has to evolve a satisfactory mode of linking the present with the past. The problems offered by dramatic themes are variously solved, not only by different writers, but in different ages; and Hebbel's methods of exposing essential facts are of interest to the observer of modern drama.

In *Maria Magdalena* and in *Herodes und Mariamne* an event which contains tragic possibilities has already taken place before the opening of the drama, and is disclosed in the course of the action. Klara's surrender to Leonhard's demand is the key to her tragic situation; the state of affairs between them is first revealed with consummate skill in the fourth scene of Act I. The point of view of each is indicated here, to be later expanded in Klara's conversation with the Secretary (Act II, Scene 5) and in Leonhard's short monologue at the beginning of Act III. The exposition of this fact is thus only completed in the last act, when its consequences have already assumed tragic proportions, and only in the final scene is the fact placed by the Secretary in its true relation to those consequences. Meanwhile, four separate standpoints from which Klara's action may be judged have been disclosed; and in their differences we have learnt to know the essential characteristics of Klara herself, Leonhard, the Secretary, and Meister Anton.

The death of Aristobolus, compassed by Herodes before the drama opens, fulfils a similar function in *Herodes und Mariamne*. It is mainly important for its bearing on Herodes' relations with the queen, but it has at the same time a further dramatic value: Joab, Joseph, and Alexandra react in characteristic ways to the king's despotic violence, and thus the purely subjective view of Herodes' action which would ensue from its revelation by a single person is avoided. This was a method which Hebbel had tried in the second act of *Genoveva*, though with less success; there four different judgements are passed on Golo's venturesome exploit in four successive scenes—an arrangement, however, which

only emphasizes the effect of epic narrative characteristic of this play. In *Herodes und Mariamne* allusions to the death of Aristobolus recur like a refrain throughout the drama from the first scene to the last. Skilfully interwoven with Joab's account of his reception by Octavian, the first hint of Herodes' responsibility for the death of Mariamne's brother elicits the king's immediate answer:

> Dank, Alexandra, Dank!
>
> (I. 1.)

and his suspicion of the part played by Alexandra receives confirmation in the second act, where she is shown plotting for revenge. It is she who in her triumphant exclamation

> Ha, Aristobolus!
> Du bist gerächt, mein Sohn, und ich in Dir!
>
> (V. 8.)

evokes Herodes' final assertion of despotic power, just as, by her intrigues and hatred, she helped to lead him to the initial act of violence. The effect upon Mariamne is more complex. The very conflict in her feelings betrays her love for Herodes, and the contrast between her allusions to her brother's death in conversation with him and with Alexandra (Act I, Scene 3, and Act II, Scene 3) throws a flood of light upon her state of mind. Still more illuminating is her admission in Act III, when she reproaches Herodes for his injurious order:

> Dem Brudermord
> Hast Du das Siegel der Nothwendigkeit,
> Dem man sich beugen muss, wie man auch schaudert,
> Zwar aufgedrückt, doch es gelingt Dir nie,
> Mit diesem Siegel auch den Mord an mir
> Zu stempeln, der wird bleiben, was er ist,
> Ein Frevel, den man höchstens wiederholen,
> Doch nun und nimmer überbieten kann.
>
> (III. 3.)

But she ultimately recognizes the significance of the king's act:

> Du kannst der Schwester nicht mehr trau'n, seit Du
> Den Bruder tödtetest . . .
>
> (V. 6.)

and in her final words she relates her own death to that of Aristobolus:

> Du, Aristobolus, sei mir gegrüsst!
> Gleich bin ich bei Dir in der ew'gen Nacht!
>
> (V. 6.)

So here too the initial fact, accomplished before the drama opens, and indicating tragic possibilities, gradually acquires its full significance through the course of the action, and in the final act is related to the tragic issue.

This method, by which the gradual growth in significance of a given fact is shown, is matched in Hebbel's plays by the way in which minor facts that have some bearing on the action are revealed. In *Maria Magdalena* the cause of the bailiff's grudge against Meister Anton—issuing in the over-hasty arrest of Karl and, as a consequence, his mother's death—is explained only in the second act (Act II, Scene 3); and the incident there related emphasizes precisely that unbending rigour in Meister Anton which brings about Klara's resolve and the ensuing catastrophe. So too in *Herodes und Mariamne* the story of Herodes' youthful defiance in front of the Sanhedrim, related by Sameas in Act II, Scene 1, crowns the previous narrative of Alexandra, and reinforces effectually that quality in Herodes' character which has already led him to a fatal step, soon to be revealed to Mariamne. The jealousy of Salome, indicated at the end of the second act and more fully in the third, is explained in the fifth act, at the moment when it acquires an added importance from Salome's impassioned account of Mariamne's behaviour at her festival; the fact disclosed thus gains a further interest by its close relation to the feelings of the narrator. This method is also used effectively by Hebbel to lend vividness to a long dramatic narrative. When Judith tells Mirza the story of her marriage (in Act II, Scene 1) the facts are already partly familiar to her hearer; it is essential that we should become aware of them, but Mirza's attention must be held as well as ours. The poet solves this problem by endowing Judith's tale with a new subjective interest. Mirza, hitherto aware only of a set of facts, now learns their inner meaning and the psychological effect on Judith of her strange experience. The retrospective narrative thus gains immensely in vividness and interest: Mirza's reaction to the story as we listen to it increases its significance.

A similar mode of lending immediate importance to a dramatic narrative is found in the first act of *Siegfrieds Tod*. Frigga's relation of Brunhild's mysterious history, with its indication of the latter's supernormal powers, is linked with an insistent entreaty to her to avoid approaching danger by offering sacrifice to the ancient gods. The effect of the story on Brunhild—who shows, like Mirza, a partial acquaintance with the facts—is to intensify her own belief and to sharpen her challenge to the approaching combatants; thus the entry of the Burgundians which immediately succeeds the narrative of Frigga gains in dramatic force. In the same way, Etzel's willing obedience to Kriemhild's wishes for the reception of the Nibelungen is grounded on his satisfaction that she has borne him an heir—this, the essential fact revealed in Etzel's speech (*Kriemhilds Rache*, Act III, Scene 2) suggests to Kriemhild the powerful motive needed to incite the king to break the peace he is determined to preserve. So Etzel's retrospective account

of their marriage is skilfully interwoven with Kriemhild's present problem, and offers her a mode of solving it which contributes in a direct way to the catastrophe.

Another method of increasing the effect of a dramatic narrative is to give it an unexpected issue. Whereas the speaker may intend only a partial statement of the facts, the whole situation may be unwittingly laid bare. Genoveva's discovery, from the letter brought by Tristan, that Siegfried has been wounded is a minor example of this reversal of intention; it leads to a long narrative, not in itself conspicuously interesting, but important by reason of its effect on Genoveva and, through her, on Golo. A much more subtle use of similar means occurs in *Herodes und Mariamne*. Joseph's betrayal of Herodes' orders is unintentional; he is enmeshed by his own statements, unable to extricate himself from Mariamne's questions. In this drama Hebbel was faced with the added difficulty of a repeated situation. He solved it by a sharp differentiation between the characters of Joseph and Soemus, and by an ironic reversal in the position of Mariamne. The two men act from differing motives, but arrive at the same end; neither intends to reveal the whole situation, but whereas Joseph merely becomes involved in a difficulty he has not foreseen, Soemus deliberately takes his decision in the course of his dialogue with Mariamne. She, on the other hand, is conscious of the dread possibility in the second instance as she cannot be in the first; and in her very efforts to banish it from her mind, to behave with complete loyalty, as if it did not exist, she provokes Soemus to disclose the truth. Thus the two dialogues have an issue not wholly expected by the speakers; but the audience shares the knowledge of such a possibility with one or both of the actors.

Partial acquaintance with the facts of a given situation may also be expanded in another way: an action may be reported by the characters as they follow it with the interest of spectators. This favourite dramatic device is used by Hebbel with extraordinary power in *Der gehörnte Siegfried* and in *Kriemhilds Rache*. Siegfried's prowess in a contest of strength with Hagen, Gunther, and his brothers is an important fact in the Prelude to the Nibelungen drama, where the tragic guilt of Siegfried and of Gunther is incurred by means of the former's matchless powers. Hebbel conveys this knowledge indirectly. The joint report of Ute and Kriemhild, as they watch the contest from a window, states the facts, but this statement becomes dramatically vivid for two reasons: the issue is not expected by either of the women, and as the facts emerge, Ute skilfully relates them to the feelings of Kriemhild. Thus the scene serves not only to emphasize an essential factor in the situation but also to reveal Kriemhild's growing interest in the stranger, and to give significant indications of her character. In the final act of *Kriemhilds Rache* (Scenes

1-13) the method of dramatic report is used with still greater effect, at the highest point of conflict; the last desperate stand of the Nibelungen is reported at intervals to Kriemhild, and the growing terror of the action is reflected in the heightened passion of the tragic heroine.

The reports of Alexandra, Salome, and Titus on Mariamne's behaviour at her festival portray in a similar way a tense dramatic moment. Here a mask conceals the passion in the heart of Mariamne, and the gradually increasing horror of the spectators alone reflects the real action. Their incomprehension deepens the effect on us of Mariamne's choice—while the dramatic spectators are unaware of the essential fact, the audience shares her tragic knowledge.

It is plain that in Hebbel's dramas the exposition of fact cannot be separated from the exposition of character; he never forgot the difference between the historical and the dramatic value of events. But he was also a master in the art of revealing character by other means, direct and indirect. When Hagen speaks of Siegfried in Acts IV and V of *Siegfrieds Tod,* his words not only show a certain side of Siegfried's character but, more strongly, illuminate his own.

> Ja, hätt' er Strich gehalten, wär' er sicher,
> Doch wusst' ich wohl, es werde nicht gescheh'n.
> Wenn man durchsichtig ist, wie ein Insect,
> Das roth und grün erscheint, wie seine Speise,
> So muss man sich vor Heimlichkeiten hüten,
> Denn schon das Eingeweide schwatzt sie aus!
>
> (*Siegfrieds Tod,* IV. 7.)

Hagen says of him, when he plans the murder; and when it is accomplished, he counters Siegfried's words with

> Jetzt schweigt er. Aber jetzt ist's kein Verdienst!
>
> (V. 2.)

So, too, when Klara and Karl refer to Meister Anton, their comments reveal fully as much of themselves as of their father. Klara's perception of his real feelings, so carefully concealed, is characteristic of her own tender nature; Karl's impatient parody of Meister Anton's rigid discipline betrays his instability:

> Hobeln, Sägen, Hämmern, dazwischen Essen, Trinken und Schlafen, damit wir immer fort hobeln, sägen und hämmern können, Sonntags ein Kniefall obendrein: ich danke Dir, Herr, dass ich hobeln, sägen und hämmern darf!
>
> (III. 8.)

Modern as he is in many of his methods, Hebbel still believed in the older convention of the monologue as a means of revealing character. But he considered it appropriate only in certain conditions. 'Monologe: laute Athemzüge der Seele,' he wrote in 1861;[3] their function was to express dual forces in the character.[4] After *Judith* and *Genoveva* he makes more sparing use of the soliloquy, until in the last tragedies it is short and tense, occurring only at a crucial moment of preparation or decision. In *Judith* three monologues are spoken by Holofernes, one by Judith, one by Mirza; but their length, together with the general character of the dialogue, creates the impression of a more extensive use. In *Genoveva* the monologue is dominant; passionately interested in the intricacies of Golo's mind, Hebbel yielded, for the only time, to the fascination of revealing a character absorbed in self-analysis. *Maria Magdalena* marks the beginning of a change. It is true that the actual number of soliloquies is greater than in *Judith*; yet they are more compressed, and the tempo is more rapid. Klara, unbearably constrained, discloses at intervals the gradually increasing pressure that drives her to her doom—but this relief of her overburdened heart appears essential to the emotional progression of the play. Leonhard's monologues heighten the contrast between the two characters: entirely concerned with the weighing of alternatives, they emphasize his insensibility as fully as Klara's reveal her dependence upon feeling. Of the five monologues spoken by Herodes, two only belong to the older, longer type. Both these express the king's doubts of Mariamne: one (I. 4) precedes the first decision, the second (III. 6) follows the important conversation before the second test. At each of these moments, Herodes is subject to conflicting impulses; in each case, his soliloquy ends in a momentous decision. The other three express, in a short, swift summary, the momentary situation; they show the result of action, not the preparation for it. The two types of monologue are plainly to be distinguished; and from now onwards Hebbel makes increasing use of the second, shorter kind. The deliberative monologue is used by Alexandra in this play (II. 2), by Herzog Ernst and Preisinger in *Agnes Bernauer* (III. 1 and 3; IV. 1 and 3), by Rhodope in *Gyges und sein Ring* (III and IV), and by Schuiskoi in *Demetrius* (II. 13); but it is the swift exposition of a frame of mind that emerges from the soliloquies of Agnes Bernauer (V. 1), of Gyges (II) and of Kriemhild in *Kriemhilds Rache* (I. 3 and 7; III. 2; and IV. 15). In *Die Nibelungen* indeed, the short soliloquy alone is found—three times in *Siegfrieds Tod* (II. 4; IV. 7, IV. 16), and seven times in *Kriemhilds Rache* (I. 3, I. 7; II. 6; III. 2, III. 5; IV. 10, IV. 15), where often it occupies a scene of four or five lines, and except for the empty stage has almost the effect of an aside.

The dramatic convention of the monologue was obviously suited to the type of character which most frequently attracted Hebbel. He uses it fully to disclose the inner mind. Where the tempo of the play requires it, he intensifies the passion and compresses the content of soliloquy—Kriemhild only once exceeds the limit of five lines in **Kriemhilds Rache.** And neither Meister Anton, in his rigid economy of emotion, nor Mariamne, in her intense reserve, uses this form of self-expression; Hebbel did not adapt his characters to the convention.

He was inclined, however, to a less sparing use of asides—a possible substitute for the dramatic soliloquy. Here he makes considerable—occasionally excessive—demands upon the skill of the actor and the quickness of the audience. The great scene between Herodes and Mariamne depends for its effect upon the success with which both actors convey to the audience the feelings which must not be betrayed to each other. In particular, Mariamne's words

Die Probe
Ist keine, wenn er ahnt, was Dich bewegt!

and

Lenk, Ewiger, sein Herz!
. . . . .
. . . so vergess' ich, was gescheh'n;

are vital to the comprehension of her problem; but it is no less vital that Herodes—deaf with grief and indignation—should not hear them. Judith's final aside to Mirza in Act IV is important for the undertaking of the part that she is playing; here, however, in a triangular grouping, it is easier to ensure that Holofernes does not hear her explanation. In **Genoveva,** on the other hand, there is the same exaggerated use of asides as of soliloquy; in particular, the scene between Golo and Genoveva in Act II (Sc. 4) is difficult to render credible. Golo's long speeches to himself, while Genoveva stands by uncomprehending, would strain the technical powers of any actors, and not even Genoveva's words

Ihr redet, Golo, warum nicht mit mir?
Ich sah Euch niemals so, Ihr seid wohl krank

avail much to ease the difficult situation.[5]

But again it may be noted that Hebbel's later tragedies show less use of this device than do the earlier ones. In **Gyges und sein Ring** the swift comment of Kandaules in his conversation with Rhodope (Act III) can be conveyed with ease; in **Die Nibelungen** the short soliloquy virtually replaces murmured comment in a dialogue. Hebbel was more inclined in this drama than in any other to free the stage, for a fleeting moment, of all the characters but one, and thus create a sense of movement in the action.

He had indeed a keen sense for this kind of stage effect, and fully realized the value alike of the static and the moving group. The picture of Holofernes or Herodes at the opening of the drama is complete: dominant among a dependent company, they create an immediate sense of power and isolation. Such a static picture, but without the central figure, is also presented in the first scene of

Kriemhilds Rache. Her absence throws the emphasis on Hagen, and on the grouping of the Nibelungen kindred, and the elaborate scenes lend double significance to the three-lined soliloquy (I. 3) that shows the tragic heroine for the first time on the stage.

But the group picture is only used by Hebbel to open these three plays, where it achieves a special end. More frequently the curtain rises on one or two characters, who prepare the way for the gradual filling of the stage. The conversation between Klara and her mother at the opening of **Maria Magdalena** leads to the passage of Karl in the second scene, and this is followed by two further dialogues, between Klara and Leonhard and between Leonhard and Meister Anton. In the fourth and fifth scenes the entry of one character is balanced by the exit of another; but in the last two scenes of the act the stage gradually fills, until the curtain falls upon Meister Anton's exit from a group stricken by sudden disaster into immobility. This gradual widening of the picture in the opening act may be seen, with slight differences of form, in **Genoveva** (Siegfried—Golo—Genoveva—Drago), in **Der gehörnte Siegfried** (Hagen, Gunther, Volker—Siegfried—Ute, Kriemhild), in **Siegfrieds Tod** (Brunhild, Frigga—Siegfried, Gunther, Hagen), and in the *Prologue to Demetrius* (Odowalsky, Poniatowsky—Gregory—Maschinka—Demetrius—Marina); but it is found in its most symmetrical form in **Agnes Bernauer.** Here Theobald, Agnes, Knippeldollinger, Barbara, and Caspar Bernauer make successive appearances upon the stage, while short dialogues between Agnes and Theobald punctuate their entrances and exits. Until the ninth scene the stage gradually fills; in the three succeeding ones it empties, leaving Caspar Bernauer alone for a short soliloquy before the scene completely changes.

Hebbel is equally skilful in creating an effective moment at the end of an act. Here, too, the close may be leisurely or swift. On the one hand, the stage may gradually be cleared, leaving one character whose final words are vital to the psychological action. Such a close is to be found in the third act of **Judith,** where the crowd melts away, and Delia is left to express the inner significance of its behaviour: 'Weiter haben sie keinen Trost für mich, als dass sie sagen: Er, den ich liebte, sei ein Sünder gewesen'. Or, on the other hand, the curtain may fall upon a moment of surprise or of dismay—here the emphasis is on the situation. Rhodope's revelation to Lesbia of the proof of Gyges' love is an instance of this form:

Rhodope:

Und wenn mich Gyges sah: wann sah er mich?

Lesbia:

(*legt sich die Hand vor die Augen*)

RHODOPE:

> Nun sprich als Mädchen, ob er sterben muss!
>
>   (III.)

The two methods are both used in **Herodes und Mariamne,** with an interesting contrast in effect. At the end of the second act, the arrival of Herodes strikes an excited group to silence:

ALEXANDRA:

> (*stürzt herein*) Der König!

JOSEPH:

>   In der Stadt?

ALEXANDRA:

>   Schon in der
> Burg!

The curtain descends on a motionless company—to rise in the next act on the entry of the king. Interest is entirely concentrated in this final scene on the momentous event; the portrayal of its effect upon the inner action is reserved for the succeeding act. A different result is obtained by the second method in Act IV. Here the stage becomes empty gradually, and Herodes, left with Titus, draws a poignant contrast:

> Zu der hab' ich einmal gesprochen:
> Zwei Menschen, die sich lieben, wie sie sollen,
> Können einander gar nicht überleben,
>   . . . . .
> Titus, verlach' mich nicht! So ist's! So ist's!
> Allein die Menschen lieben sich nicht so!
>
>   (IV. 8.)

Attention is thus riveted on the dominant motive of Herodes' action: the impression of Mariamne's exit is subservient to its effect upon the king. In this way the opening of the fifth act is prepared, and Herodes' determination foreshadowed.

Such linking of one act to another is a remarkable characteristic of **Kriemhilds Rache.** Each curtain falls upon an anticipatory phrase. The first act closes with a general indication of the future:

> Mein treuer Eckewart hat mich gewiegt,
> Und ob auch alle Andern mich verlassen,
> Er fehlt gewiss nicht hinter meinem Sarg.

—words which (immediately following on Kriemhild's consent to a second marriage) clearly point towards the tragic end. Act II concludes with Gunther's acceptance of Hagen's gloomy prophecy:

>   Und Du
> Bist unser Tod, wenn's drunten wirklich steht,
> Wie Du's uns prophezeist. Doch—
>   (*Er schlägt Hagen auf die Schulter*)
>   Komm nur, Tod!
>   (*folgen den Andern.*)

And this anticipation seems immediately confirmed by Kriemhild's opening words in the next act. Hagen's defiance ends Act III:

>   Nein, das vom Todtenschiff!
> Das Letzte, wie der Freund den Freund erstiht,
> Und dann die Fackel—Das geht Morgen los,

and Act IV virtually continues the scene after an interval of a few moments. And this fourth act closes with Etzel's ominous warning:

>   was den Heunenkönig
> Auf dieser Erde einst so furchtbar machte,
> Das sollt Ihr seh'n in seinem engen Raum!

words which find an echo in Hildebrant's initial question in Act V:

> Wie lange soll der Jammer denn noch dauern?

Hebbel had a vivid sense not only for architectural, but also for pictorial and musical effects. It is true that his plays—with the possible exception of **Maria Magdalena,** where the background is almost a part of the action—are little dependent on their actual stage-setting. But there are pictures, such as the dance at Augsburg in **Agnes Bernauer,** or the night scenes in Moscow in **Demetrius,** that are remarkably full of life and rich in colour. Above all, he can create a sense of movement. The grouping of the dance scene and the Regensburg tourney in **Agnes Bernauer,** the movement of the crowd in the foreground against the background of a solemn procession in the third act of **Demetrius** reveal the master-playwright. And that this skill was intuitive is amply proved by the grouping of the crowd scenes in his first play (**Judith,** Acts III and V). In **Kriemhilds Rache,** the double action of the last act depends upon a more complex use of the back of the stage than in any other of Hebbel's dramas; a wonderful pictorial effect is achieved by the contrast between the moving struggle in the background and Kriemhild's relentless immobility in the foreground of the scene. A musical effect adds sharpness to this contrast: on Dietrich's tale of the slain—matching in its accumulating detail the movement of the battle—fall the hammer-strokes of Kriemhild's refrain, 'Und Hagen lebt'. Elsewhere, too, Hebbel uses a 'Leitmotiv' in the same way to give point to a dramatic moment. The scene between Frigga and Brunhild after the discovery of the secret conveys the impression of an impending fate through echo and repetition:

BRUNHILD:

> Frigga, mein Leben oder auch das seine!

FRIGGA:

> Das seine, Kind!

BRUNHILD:

> Ich ward nicht bloss verschmäht,
> Ich ward verschenkt, ich ward wohl gar verhandelt!

FRIGGA:

> Verhandelt, Kind!

BRUNHILD:

> Ihm selbst zum Weib zu schlecht, War ich der Pfen-
> ning, der ihm eins verschaffte!

FRIGGA:

> Der Pfenning, Kind!

BRUNHILD:

> Das ist noch mehr, als Mord, Und dafür will ich
> Rache! Rache, Rache!

> (*Siegfrieds Tod,* III. 11.)

Subtler repetitions, ironic in effect, occur in the first act of **Herodes und Mariamne**—the word 'Perlen' forms an irregular refrain throughout the first half of the king's interview with Mariamne in Act I, and the clash of wills at the end of the scene is stressed by echoed words. Ironic repetition is indeed characteristic of this play.

With all his sense for such constructive detail, Hebbel did not approve of prescribing detail for the interpretation of his characters. Rather he believed that the one rendered the other unnecessary, and he was accordingly sparing in his use of stage directions. 'Ich selbst schreibe dem Schauspieler in meinen dramatischen Arbeiten ungern etwas vor', he wrote to Kühne in 1847, 'und bestrebe mich, nach Art der Alten, ihm durch kleine Fingerzeige im Dialog selbst die Geberden, die ich zur Begleitung wünsche, leise anzudeuten. Das geht so weit, dass ich nicht einmal des Vorhangs gern erwähne . . .'[6] An important gesture may be indicated, as well as exits, entrances, and on occasion relative positions on the stage; but beyond these and the marking of asides there is little detail for actor and producer. Nor do the scenic indications state any but the salient features of the setting—a throne, the time of day, a vista of landscape in the distance (once, in **Kriemhilds Rache,** Act V, the essential structure in the background is described). Relations of time and place were emphasized in the substance of the plays, and so the poet—in contrast to the majority of modern dramatists—left the details of production alone. In this, perhaps, he was not so far wrong. At least it is clear that he demanded—and perhaps therefore obtains—the fullest collaboration of the actors; having looked after his own business, he expected them to look after theirs. It may be that Christine Hebbel's interpretations contributed something to this attitude. It is certain that his passion-ate interest in character, evident in almost every aspect of his own technique as a dramatist, gave him the true measure for the actor's art.

CONCEPTION OF TRAGEDY

For the majority of critics, the central problem presented by Hebbel's dramatic art has been the problem of his self-consciousness as an artist. The relation of his dramatic theory to his dramas, the question of priority, has perhaps been over-emphasized, from the very fact that such a wealth of material exists to provide evidence for his mental processes. It is easy to let the diary and the correspondence weigh down the scales, more difficult to isolate the impressions that result from the dramas themselves. The idea of Hebbel as a speculative thinker, embodying metaphysical conceptions in dramatic form, frequently recurs, sometimes turning discussions of his plays into philosophic arguments. Even where this point is not reached, Hebbel's characters are often enough considered less for their dramatic value than as exponents of a view which they are held to represent. The poet's own statements, there is no doubt, often tend to create an impression of a calculated intellectual basis to his dramas, of a reflective process that conditions their development. But in estimating the value of these statements, two facts must not be overlooked. The entries concerning a given drama are in general subsequent to—or at most, contemporaneous with—the actual composition of the drama; rarely do we find (except as criticism of previous versions of a theme) reflections that precede the initial stages of dramatic creation. And, secondly, against the speculative reflections of a philosophic mind, there must be weighed other statements that Hebbel makes on the creative process. 'Dichten und Denken sind verschiedene Processe, einer schliesst den anderen aus, wie ich mehr und mehr erkenne',[7] he wrote to Elise in 1843; and five years later, on an occasion when the creative mood had been disturbed, he recorded in the diary: 'Man sollte vorsichtig werden; die Stimmung des Dichters hat zu viel vom Nachtwandeln, sie wird eben so leicht gestört, wie der Traum-Zustand, worin diess geschieht. Sonderbar ist es, dass ich in einer solchen Stimmung immer Melodieen höre, und das, was ich schreibe, darnach absinge. . . .'[8] A similar statement is made in a letter to Kolbenheyer in 1854: 'Denn das dramatische Produciren ist nun einmal ein Traum- und Nachtwandeln, welches sich von allem anderen Wandeln und Wandern dadurch unterscheidet, dass man einen und denselben Weg nicht zwei Mal machen kann';[9] while to his friend Uechtritz he explained the alternation in himself of creative activity and rest: '. . . bei mir [folgt] auf eine Zeit der Production immer eine andere der grössten Abspannung, in der es mir absolut unmöglich ist, aus mir selbst heraus zu gehen. Das war bei mir von Jugend auf der Fall; ich kenne nur Springfluten oder vollständige Ebben.'[10]

Hebbel well knew the difference between a philosophy of life and dramatic creation. Only fools, he wrote in 1842, would banish metaphysics from the drama: 'Aber es ist ein grosser Unterschied, ob sich die Metaphysik aus dem Leben entwickelt, oder ob umgekehrt sich das Leben aus der Metaphysik entwickeln soll'.[11] 'Die Poesie ist Leben, nicht Denken, Umkleiden, nicht Skalpiren . . .',[12] he writes on another occasion; and in a letter to Engländer of 1863, he proclaims once again his poetic independence:

> 'Sie wissen, dass ich zu dem Stück [*Gyges und sein Ring*] kam, wie der Knabe zum Vogel; er fängt ihn, weil er gerade da sitzt, und sieht sich ihn erst näher an, wenn er ihn in der Hand hat, um zu erfahren, was es für ein Kerl ist. Sie wissen aber nicht, dass es mit allen meinen Stücken so ging und werden mir diess jetzt auf mein ehrliches Wort wohl glauben. Der Maria Magdalena z. B. . . . liegt ein Vorfall zu Grunde, den ich in München selbst erlebte. . . . Da wurde der dramatische "Fehde-Handschuh" gesponnen, wenn auch nicht gleich gewoben, den ich nach Hermann Hettner der ganzen Europäischen Gesellschaft hingeworfen haben soll. . . .'[13]

Thus, if Hebbel's own statements are to count, his reiterated emphasis on the unconscious nature of the creative process cannot be disregarded; we must conclude that he was well aware, in himself, of the separation between reflective thought and imaginative realization.

But if, as Hebbel maintained—and his dramas bear out the statement if they are examined with an open mind—he first conceived individual characters in individual situations, he was irresistibly impelled to reflect upon them afterwards. He recognized, as they developed, further evidence of many conclusions he had come to about life, about the relations of men to their environment. Hailing fresh proofs as he perceived them, he would note with ardour the ideas on man and man's destiny that they reinforced; seizing on that which could most easily be embodied in logical form, he was perpetually endeavouring to formulate, from his poetic intuitions, an ordered statement of man's relation to the cosmos. So a 'theory of tragedy' may be constructed from his critical essays, and (above all) from the entries in the journal; but Hebbel's tragedies are not rightly to be judged thereby. The dramatic theory should rather be tested by the dramas, than the dramas be measured by the critical reflections of their author. Theory and practice may, and often do, coincide; but their identity must not be assumed. Hebbel was, after all, a poet and a dramatist, and it is in the light of his more important achievement as an artist that his theory of art should be considered.[14] He had a naturally inquiring mind, and the whole trend of his age was towards observation and analysis; these two facts serve to explain the wealth of comment and criticism in his personal papers and in his correspondence.[15]

The centre of Hebbel's critical reflections is his conviction that human life is fundamentally tragic. While his dramas present the fate of the individual, proof and illustration of this intense personal conviction, his dramatic theory consists in the attempt to present the world drama as a whole. He was constantly endeavouring to relate the tragic experience of the human soul to a larger process, which should illumine and justify such experience. His 'theory of tragedy' is thus a series of conclusions drawn from observation of the reactions of men to the world in which they live. By temperament and circumstance combined, Hebbel was peculiarly open to tragic experience, and its necessity was his abiding conviction; for him, tragic art illuminated and transformed the isolated suffering of the individual by revealing this underlying necessity. The persistent sense of warring forces, irreconcilable and ever-present, governed Hebbel's picture of the world and human life: he knew them in his own person, as experience that could not be evaded. He saw life as a conflict of the individual against surrounding circumstance, and visualized in varying images the battle of which he was so keenly conscious. 'Alles Leben ist Kampf des Individuellen mit dem Universum'.[16] 'Das Leben ist der grosse Strom, die Individualitäten sind Tropfen, die tragischen aber Eisstücke, die wieder zerschmolzen werden müssen und sich, damit dies möglich sey, an einander abreissen und zerstossen'.[17] 'Leben ist Verharren im Angemessenen', he writes to Emil Rousseau. 'Ein Theil des Lebens ist *Ufer* (Gott und Natur) ein anderer (Mensch und Menschheit) ist *Strom*. Wo und wie spiegeln sie sich, tränken und durchdringen sie sich gegenseitig? Dies scheint mir die grosse Frage von Anbeginn, die dem Dichter der Genius vorlegt'.[18] And in a letter to Rousseau's sister in 1843, he indicates the function of tragic art: 'Das Leben ist eine furchtbare Nothwendigkeit, die auf Treu und Glauben angenommen werden muss, die aber Keiner begreift, und die tragische Kunst, die, indem sie das individuelle Leben der Idee gegenüber vernichtet, sich zugleich darüber erhebt, ist der leuchtendste Blitz des menschlichen Bewusstseyns, der aber freilich Nichts erhellen kann, was er nicht zugleich verzehrte'.[19]

The individual, in Hebbel's conception of the world-drama, is irresistibly driven to assert those qualities which make him individual. But this emphasis, this self-assertion, is incompatible with the preservation of a general balance; and herein lies the necessity for tragedy. The stronger the character, the more inevitably must the conflict between the two interests arise; the higher the differentiation of the individual, the more certain is his defeat. 'Die Helden stürzen, weil sie sich überheben'.[20] 'Maasslosigkeit' is the inevitable guilt incurred by the tragic individual in his relation to the whole;[21] and the universe is necessarily victor in the involuntary contest.

This belief was not held without a struggle. 'Wozu dieser Fluch der Kraft?' Hebbel, himself a strong man, cries in 1842.[22] 'Was ist das? Sobald der Mensch sich fühlt und sich aufrichtet, empfindet er etwas, wie einen Druck von oben, und doch lebt er nur so weit, als er sich fühlt. Es ist, als ob er sich aus einem Abgrund erhöbe und von unbekannter Hand immer wieder hinein gestossen würde.'[23] But the temperamental conviction was reinforced by observation and experience. On the one hand, the poet—child of a century whose main discoveries were the fruit of close and dispassionate scrutiny of facts—examined the selective processes of the natural world and saw their issue: 'Das Gute selbst kann Feind des Guten seyn, die Rose kann die Lilie verdrängen wollen, Beide sind existenzberechtigt, aber nur Eins hat Existenz.'[24] The processes of Nature continue, while the single existence is submerged. Like autumn leaves that early fall and wither, but fertilize the products of a new year, so the life of the individual contributes to that of the universe; and as the leaf that falls is of little account in the total sum, so too is the man who suffers: 'der Baum hat der Blätter im Ueberfluss und die Welt der Menschen'.[25] In such an image Hebbel saw the general relation of individual effort to the whole. And his own experience, both in conflict with circumstances and in a tragic sex-relationship, revealed to him a mode of individual self-assertion. A temperamental inability to compromise, a continuous early struggle for existence, and Hebbel's relation with Elise Lensing, formed the basis of experience from which sprang his conception of tragedy.

It is in the relations of the individual effort to the world-process, and in those of individual men and women to each other, that the tragic conflict manifests itself in Hebbel's dramas. In either case, the tragic guilt of the individual is the same. Judith and Holofernes, Mariamne and Herodes, Golo and Kandaules, transgress their limitations and incur the penalty. All these, in varying degree, are guilty of a tragic self-assertion. But such characters as Genoveva, Agnes Bernauer, Klara, or Rhodope, do not actively provoke their fate. In placing these as central figures in their dramas, Hebbel widens the range of tragic character and tragic conflict. Their tragic guilt consists in their outstanding quality; by virtue of this alone they invite their destiny. Genoveva's charity, Agnes Bernauer's beauty, are as abnormal as Holofernes' strength or Golo's passion; and all incur a tragic fate. Thus not only the fight against outward circumstance, not only the battle of good and evil in the human soul, but the conflict of good with good, the sacrifice and downfall of the innocent, are Hebbel's tragic themes. Tragic guilt and ethical guilt need not be identical. Such a figure as that of Agnes Bernauer is an extreme type of the innocent victim, whose only flaw is an excess of quality; the very characteristics of beauty and integrity that raise her above the average human level render her death more inevitable in the given situation.

Such tragic themes as that of *Herodes und Mariamne*— the conflict of two dominant natures—strike us perhaps as more familiar than those of this second type, where the central figure contributes less actively to the catastrophe. There is little doubt that the spectacle of such passive suffering as that of Agnes, Klara, or Genoveva corresponds to those problems of undeserved misfortune and innocent sacrifice which proclaim themselves insistently in human life. But in their effort to present the picture of an ordered universe, the poet and the dramatist have for the most part chosen characters in situations where the connexion between action and catastrophe is closer—the very term 'poetic justice' bears witness to such a connexion.

It is here that Hebbel's vision of the world is most clearly conditioned by the age in which he lived. Much has been said of the relation between his conception of the world-order and contemporary philosophic thought.[26] But it is at least equally close to the scientific thought of the mid-nineteenth century, when scientist and social historian alike were emphasizing the relations of man to his environment and the influence of that environment upon his personal life. In both fields of observation there is a common spectacle: highly differentiated individuals, while they may ultimately contribute to the advancement of the type, or of the community, may themselves be compelled, by their very individual quality, to succumb before the pressure of the average. Thus the individual unit that is far in advance of the normal type may be doomed to immediate failure, though its ultimate value may be great, apart from individual failure or success. Development, in fact, proceeds by the preservation of 'balance in Nature': the continuance of any living organism depends upon the maintenance of a delicate equilibrium.[27]

Hebbel's dramas, presenting a stern vision of humanity at grips with a relentless process, imply a similar picture of balance in the cosmos. He was little concerned with the average individual, who by compromise and caution leads a sheltered life—little interested in spiritual safety. He was, on the contrary, passionately concerned with those who walk dangerously, who disturb the balance and incur the penalty. Excess, of whatever kind, brings retribution. Herodes, dominant in virtue of his spacious conceptions and his strength, is immoderate in his disregard of the personality of others. Agnes, equally dominant in virtue of her qualities, also oversets the balance, and pays toll with her life for being what she is. Her relation to her age and type determine her doom; guiltless in any ethical sense, she is a source of danger to the whole. The idea of guilt that is not sin, of flaw that is not fault, is one familiar to the later conception of evolution; it also issues naturally, and almost unavoidably, from Hebbel's picture of balance in the cosmic process. Thus tragic guilt implies that the individual stands in a relation to his environment that renders compromise impossible. This relation may involve widely varying degrees of personal ethical responsibility: the essential factor is that it should admit of no alternative. 'Nothwendigkeit', as Hebbel terms it, is identical with tragic guilt. In the moment when an individual disturbs or deviates from the normal order by an assertion of supernormal character, a reaction is necessitated, an opposing force must restore the balance: 'die auf die Uebertretung der . . . Gränzen folgende Zerstöhrung eines Individuums geschieht immer durch diese entgegengesetzte Veränderung.'[28]

If Hebbel's conception of tragic fate resembles the conclusions of a scientific observer, watching the selective processes of the natural world, the answer that he suggests to our demand for justice, or compensation, offers a further parallel. He points away from the individual to the general process. The majority of his characters do not attain to inner harmony. Holofernes is murdered in his power, and Judith remains, with her problem unsolved. Klara sacrifices herself to save her father, but she gropes in the dark for any other justification of her doom: 'Wär's um mich allein—ich wollt's ja tragen, ich wollt's geduldig hinnehmen, als verdiente Strafe für, *ich weiss nicht was,* wenn die Welt mich in meinem Elend mit Füssen träte, statt mir beizustehen. . . . Aber ich bin's nicht allein, und leichter find' ich am jüngsten Tag noch eine Antwort auf des Richters Frage: warum hast Du Dich selbst umgebracht? als auf die: warum hast Du Deinen Vater so weit getrieben?' (III. 2). Herodes, unchanged by tragic experience, clings but the more firmly to that despotic power which betrayed him into dealing a mortal injury to Mariamne. Agnes Bernauer, choosing death rather than the renunciation of Albrecht's love, questions in her last words the justice of her sentence: 'Thut mir, wie Ihr müsst und dürft, ich will's leiden. Bald weiss ich, ob's mit Recht geschah! (V. 3). These figures, considered by themselves, suggest no sense of harmony.

Mariamne, on the other hand, chooses death deliberately, seeing in it both vengeance and the solution of her own problem. By following this deep instinct of her being, by leaving to Herodes a legacy of remorse to avenge her injured spirit, she may perhaps be said to attain a kind of harmony within herself, as she meets death with stoic pride. In the logic of her action she finally asserts the value of her personality. In a different manner, Golo, too, arrives at a solution, when he chooses death as an atonement for his crime against Genoveva.

But such a measure of self-harmony is not generally portrayed in Hebbel's tragic characters. Only in one drama—*Gyges und sein Ring*—do we find all the chief actors arriving at a solution of their problem. Hebbel was indeed convinced that harmony, or 'Versöhnung' was to be sought elsewhere than in the individual character. Beyond and above the individual case, in the unity and continuity of the whole process, he sees the reconciliation of the tragic dissonance. 'Die Versöhnung im Tragischen geschieht im Interesse der *Gesammtheit,* nicht in dem des *Einzelnen,* des Helden . . .'[29] he wrote in 1843; and fifteen months later: 'Dass in der dramatischen Kunst die Versöhnung immer über den Kreis des speciellen Dramas hinaus fällt, werden Wenige begreifen.'[30] For a rhetorical glossing over of the tragic catastrophe he had no use; early in 1843 he wrote of Oehlenschläger: 'Er will Versöhnung im Drama—wer will sie nicht? Ich kann sie nur darin nicht finden, dass der Held, oder der Dichter für ihn, seine gefalteten Hände über die Wunde legt und sie dadurch verdeckt!'[31]—a characteristically uncompromising utterance. 'Es ist thörigt', he wrote a little later, 'von dem Dichter das zu verlangen, was Gott selbst nicht darbietet, Versöhnung und Ausgleichung der Dissonanzen. Aber allerdings kann man fodern, dass er die Dissonanzen selbst gebe und nicht in der Mitte zwischen dem Zufälligen und dem Nothwendigen stehen bleibe. So darf er jeden Character zu Grunde gehen lassen, aber er muss uns zugleich zeigen, dass der Untergang unvermeidlich, dass er, wie der Tod, mit der Geburt selbst gesetzt ist'.[32]

By temperament and conviction, Hebbel saw the life of the individual as an essentially tragic phenomenon. By its force, the single unit contributes to the forward movement of the whole, but is itself submerged. There *is* a balance that gives meaning to the cosmic process; but only in the contemplation of the whole can the tragedy of the individual be seen in a perspective which reveals its purpose and significance. The wound, Hebbel writes, can only be healed 'durch den Nachweis, dass sie für die erhöhte Gesundheit nothwendig war'.[33]

> 'Diejenigen, die vom Tragödien-Dichter verlangen, dass er nicht bloss die sittliche Idee retten, sondern zugleich auch den Helden vor dem Untergang bewahren soll, fordern eigentlich etwas eben so Unvernünftiges, als wenn sie vom Arzt verlangten, dass er den Organismus nicht bloss von einer Krankheit befreien, sondern die Krankheit selbst auch, als eine individuelle Modification des allgemeinen Lebensprocesses, respectiren und also am Leben erhalten solle.'[34]

The mood of the scientific observer is here plainly to be recognized.

Thus, though Judith and Holofernes are both in their different ways defeated, Bethulia, the Hebrew city, is saved. Though Genoveva's tragic suffering continues and Golo dies in torment, his deliberate choice of death suggests the vindication of fundamental human values. If Klara's actual sacrifice was vain, the motive force of love inspiring it is vital to the world, and 'Maria Magdalena' indicates its meaning. Though neither Mariamne nor Herodes solves the problem presented by their relationship, the pageant-like passing of the Kings of Orient heralds a new world to which Herodes, with all his tenacious grasp of power, must yield. And when Siegfried and Brunhild, in their abnormal strength and courage, have wrought each other's doom, and Kriemhild, transformed into a destroying Fury, has been herself destroyed, Dietrich survives to usher in a new order, and suggests the victory of the world-process as it fulfils itself.

It has often been asserted that in this final suggestion of the relation between individual suffering and the larger process Hebbel was superimposing on the dramatic situation a metaphysical idea. But the implied reproach can hardly be maintained in face of the profound dramatic effect produced by the concluding scenes of *Herodes und Mariamne* and *Die Nibelungen*. The poet here was far from being led astray by the speculative critic: on the contrary, he triumphantly justifies, in these swift, suggestive scenes, his own imaginative power.

Two of Hebbel's major dramas suggest the solution of the dramatic problem in a different way. In *Agnes Bernauer* a logical reconciliation is offered at the end; in *Gyges und sein Ring* the tragic characters themselves attain to inner harmony through sacrifice. There is a striking contrast in the effect of the two plays. Both solutions rest on the recognition of tragic guilt; but whereas Albrecht yields to a logical argument after the death of Agnes—the innocent sacrifice—Rhodope, Gyges, and Kandaules all come to recognize before the end that their personal desires must be surrendered. Kandaules acknowledges his fault and atones for it with his life; Gyges expiates his half-unwitting crime by obedience to Rhodope's will; Rhodope herself fulfils the sacrifice by choosing death when atonement has been made. In Hebbel's other great dramas, the balance is restored by the cosmic process, overpowering or disregarding the wills of men: it is the world-process that inevitably conquers, though in the strength of the individual opposing it lies the basic value of human life. But in *Gyges und sein Ring* the spirit of man, transcending its limitation of one-sidedness, aids the restoration of harmony by an active recognition of governing necessity. Herein lies man's essential freedom—to acquiesce voluntarily in the laws that condition the world-process. By this acquiescence the tragic individual can arrive at the inner solution of his problem; the human mind can attain, through tragic experience, a serene and perfect poise.

It is not insignificant that *Gyges und sein Ring* is the first of Hebbel's dramas to create this impression of at-

tained serenity. With that unswerving honesty which was the native characteristic of his mind, he refused to suggest a solution until he had experienced it. 'Ich weiss nicht, ob ich mich irre', he wrote in 1847, 'aber mir däucht es eine Sünde wider den heiligen Geist der Wahrheit, wenn der Dichter seinem Kunstwerk eine Versöhnung mit der menschlichen Situation und den Weltzuständen überhaupt, einzuhauchen sucht, von der er selbst noch fern ist. Mir scheint, dass das Kunstwerk dann jeden Werth verliert.'[35] By 1854, the year of Elise Lensing's death, the tragic relation which had filled his early years as a dramatist had also reached solution. The mark of that relation is plainly visible in Hebbel's earlier dramas. The individual conflict is felt in terms of sex; here the poet himself knew, in its acutest form, the will to power, the encroachment of one personality upon another, the assertion of the individual right to be. The expiation (if expiation were appropriate) of Hebbel's relations with Elise Lensing might well be found in the stern conception of tragedy which possessed his mind—and were it so, she might rest satisfied with such a monument.

But there is a distinct progression in the line of Hebbel's heroines. Judith in her active transgression of a woman's sphere, Genoveva and Klara in their feminine role of passive sufferers, arouse less interest and admiration than does the commanding figure of Mariamne, who both acts and suffers. Agnes, even more completely a passive heroine than Klara, is yet a more absorbing personality. In Rhodope, her immediate successor, Hebbel's ideal of womanhood seems to be expressed; and if the poet's experience with Elise Lensing is of paramount importance for his choice of tragic themes, his marriage to Christine Enghaus would equally seem to have had no small influence on his portrayal of feminine character. Rhodope presents, more fully than any other of his heroines, Hebbel's conception of purely feminine qualities. Her weapons are not found in any other armoury; her logic does not belong to any system of philosophy. Her intuition is certain, her knowledge innate; and she convinces by the very absence of all argument. In no way does she transgress her limitations as a woman and as an individual: and it is by following her own deep feeling that she brings both Gyges and Kandaules to appreciate it, and obey her will.

Kriemhild in *Die Nibelungen* is a militant character in the fullest sense. But her activity, violating all bounds of sex and nature, belonged to the data provided by the *Nibelungenlied,* and Hebbel had less freedom here than in the creation of any other female character. Thus she belongs to the group of active combatants; but the dramatist shows her developing, under the most cruel stress, from a gentle woman into a being of abnormal stature and gigantic will, possessed of only one idea. By this excessive development of the individual will, Kriemhild too invites her fate; she is struck down by the hand of a vassal, crudely stirred to action by her un-natural deeds of vengeance. By a kind of inversion, she represents Hebbel's deep conviction: 'Durch Dulden Thun: Idee des Weibes'.[36] 'Im Gemüth', he wrote later, 'wurzelt die Kraft des [weiblichen] Geschlechts'.[37]

Thus from Judith to Rhodope, the heroines of Hebbel's major dramas emphasize ethical values. In **Demetrius,** for the first time, the women characters are of less moment than the hero. The problem of Demetrius must be solved by him alone; Marina does not, Marfa cannot, aid him in his inner conflict. It is at least conceivable that **Gyges und sein Ring** marked the close of Hebbel's long preoccupation with feminine character and the dualism of sex; that in the sympathy that is finally attained, in their several relations, between Gyges, Kandaules, and Rhodope, the poet too found peace.

'Die Ideen sind im Drama dasselbe, was der Contra-Punct in der Musik; Nichts an sich, aber Grundbedingung für Alles.'[38] Hebbel could hardly have summed up more exactly than in this observation the characteristic of his dramatic work—the relation of the conscious to the unconscious artist. In the fascinating pursuit of observing his subtle mind assimilating and converting its experience, we may be tempted to forget that the second process of the two took place in the depths, where it could not be recorded. But the tragedies, if they are allowed to speak in their own tongue, will vindicate the dramatic poet. Through character and situation Hebbel offers us a vision of humanity at odds with fate—the picture of the universe as he saw it with a poet's eyes. That he was primarily attracted by the abnormal character and the unusual situation is undeniable; but by virtue of his own experience and a profound imaginative mind, he endowed them with a wider significance, suggesting the universal in the individual instance. '. . . Der dramatische Dichter', he wrote '[muss] sich in demselben Sinn auf jede Species menschlicher Charactere einlassen, wie der Naturforscher auf jede Thier- und Pflanzengattung, gleichviel, ob sie schön oder hässlich, giftig oder heilsam ist, indem er die Totalität darzustellen hat!'[39] The characters of his tragedies, from Judith to Demetrius, go far to substantiate this claim.

The universal process, as Hebbel sees it, is stern and unrelenting; the individual life is of little moment in the course of Nature and of human history. The Dithmarschen mason's poet son knew that the world was no forcing-house for tender plants; but he arrived, after great travail, at a belief in the abiding value of effort. 'Wir müssen nicht klagen, dass Alles vergänglich sey. Das Vergänglichste, wenn es uns wahrhaft berührt, weckt in uns ein Unvergängliches'.[40] An intuitive certainty rather than a logical conclusion, this early belief was the mainspring of Hebbel's personal life; in his life's work its justification may be found.

Notes

1. *Tagebücher,* ed. cit., vol. iii. 4791, 1 Jan. 1851.

2. *Tagebücher,* ed. cit., vol. ii. 2897, 25 Nov. 1843.

3. *Tagebücher,* ed. cit., vol. iv. 5907, 3 May 1861.

4. *Tagebücher,* ed. cit., vol. ii. 2971, 27 Dec. 1843.

5. In the theatre version this scene was cut considerably, and Genoveva's words are corrected to

   Ihr meidet meinen Blick und redet doch?

   in an obvious effort to ease the actor's task (v. *Werke,* ed. cit., vol. i, p. 438. Lesarten und Anmerkungen to *Genoveva*).

6. *Tagebücher,* ed. cit., vol. iii. 3943, 30 Jan. 1847, and Letter to Gustav Kühne, 28 Jan. 1847, *Briefe,* ed. cit., vol. iv, p. 5.

7. Letter to Elise Lensing, 4 Apr. 1843, *Briefe,* ed. cit., vol. ii, p. 253.

8. *Tagebücher,* ed. cit., vol. iii. 4435, 22 Aug. 1848.

9. Letter to Moritz Kolbenheyer, 13 June 1854, *Briefe,* ed. cit., vol. v, p. 164.

10. Letter to Friedrich von Uechtritz, 19 Mar. 1855, *Briefe,* ed. cit., vol. v, p. 219. Cp. also a previous letter to Uechtritz, 14 Dec. 1854, *Briefe,* ed. cit., vol. v, p. 203.

11. *Tagebücher,* ed. cit., vol. ii. 2605, 7 Oct. 1842.

12. Ibid. 2947, 19 Dec. 1843.

13. Letter to Sigmund Englander, 23 Feb. 1863, *Briefe,* ed. cit., vol. vii, pp. 302-3.

14. It may seem superfluous to insist upon an argument so elementary. But the tide of Hebbel criticism has set so strongly in a metaphysical direction that emphasis upon his dramatic view of life seems necessary. Such statements as the following would appear to assume the paramount importance of Hebbel's philosophical ideas: 'Hebbels System, der Pantragismus, ist eine einseiting auf das Drama zugeschnittene Welt- und Kunstanschauung' (A. Scheunert, *Der Pantragismus als System der Weltanschauung und Ästhetik Friedrich Hebbels,* Hamburg u. Leipzig, 1903, p. 10); 'Dass [Hebbels] poetische Schöpfungen als höchst wichtige, aufklärende Beispiele für die von ihm aufgestellten Lehren zu verwerten sind, ist selbstverständlich' (op. cit., p. 17); 'Das Ziel der vorliegenden Untersuchung war es . . . zu zeigen, wie das gesamte Hebbelsche Gedankensystem von einer alles befruchtenden Grundidee ausgehend, unabhängig von fremden Einflüssen, sich organisch aus sich selbst entwickelt, um schliesslich in einem neuen Dramatypus dem Ganzen den

krönenden Abschluss zu geben (F. Zinkernagel, *Die Grundlagen der Hebbelschen Tragödie,* Berlin, 1904, p. v).

15. It may here be noted that Hebbel's critical essays embody ideas which are, for the most part, expressed more clearly in the *Tagebücher,* where he wrote naturally and freely; entries in the diary are therefore chosen for quotation, wherever possible, in preference to the more involved and elaborate statements in the formal essays.

16. *Tagebücher,* ed. cit., vol. ii. 2129, 13 Sept. 1840.

17. Ibid. 2664, 6 Mar. 1843.

18. Letter to Emil Rousseau, 30 Dec. 1836, *Briefe,* ed. cit., vol. i, p. 140.

19. Letter to Charlotte Rousseau, 7 July 1843, *Briefe,* ed. cit., vol. ii, p. 272, and *Tagebücher,* ed. cit., vol. ii. 2721.

20. Ibid. 2578, 29 July 1842.

21. Ibid. 3158, 13 June 1844.

22. Ibid. 2578, 29 July 1842.

23. Ibid. 2078, 13 Aug. 1840.

24. *Tagebücher,* ed. cit., vol. i. 1823, 7 Dec. 1839.

25. *Tagebücher,* ed. cit., vol. ii. 2881, 21 Nov. 1843.

26. In the diary for 1844, Hebbel noted his discovery that Hegel's conception of tragic guilt was like his own. 'Hätt' ich's gewusst', he adds, 'als ich gegen Herrn Heiberg schrieb!' (*Tagebücher,* ed. cit., vol. ii. 3088 (and *Anmerkung*), 25 Mar. 1844). He had already written *Genoveva* and *Maria Magdalena* when this entry was made.

27. In this connexion two passages may be quoted from an early nineteenth-century biologist, which suggest an interesting, though probably a fortuitous parallel: 'Bewegung ist Stöhrung des Gleichgewichts entgegengesetzter Kräfte. Diese Stöhrung aber ist nur dadurch möglich, dass die eine der letztern wächst, indem die andere abnimmt' (G. R. Treviranus, *Biologie,* vol. i, pp. 28-9, Göttingen, 1802). Applying this to a general conception of development, the author continues: 'Hat die Zufälligkeit der äussern Einwirkungen, bey welchen die eigenthümliche Thätigkeit der lebenden Organismen unverändert fortdauert, Gränzen, und zieht jede Uebertretung dieser Gränzen die Zerstöhrung jener Organismen nach sich, so ist zwar keine *fortdauernde* Stöhrung des allgemeinen Organismus von Seiten eines lebenden Individuums möglich. Allein schon die *erste* Uebertretung dieser Gränzen wird Unordnungen in dem erstern nach sich ziehen. . . . Wir müssen annehmen,

dass jede Abweichung eines lebenden Individuums von der zur Erhaltung des allgemeinen Organismus nöthigen Thätigkeit eine entgegengesetzte Veränderung desselben nach sich zieht, und dass die auf die Uebertretung der erwähnten Gränzen folgende Zerstöhrung eines Individuums immer durch diese entgegengesetzte Veränderung geschieht. Ein Uebermass von Thätigkeit muss durch ein Minus, ein Minus durch ein Plus, und *eine* anomalische Abweichung derselben durch eine andere, nach entgegengesetzter Richtung gehende anomalische Abweichung wieder gut gemacht werden' (*op. cit.,* vol. i, pp. 67-8). This work of Treviranus was published in parts between 1802 and 1822.

28. G. R. Treviranus, loc. cit.

29. *Tagebücher,* ed. cit., vol. ii. 2664, 6 Mar. 1843.

30. Ibid. 3168, 25 June 1844.

31. Ibid. 2635, 5 Jan. 1843.

32. *Tagebücher,* ed. cit., vol. ii, 2776, 29 Aug. 1843.

33. Ibid. 2845, 11 Nov. 1843.

34. *Tagebücher,* ed. cit., vol. iii, 3892, 10 Jan. 1847.

35. *Tagebücher,* ed. cit., vol. iii. 4150, 19 Apr. 1847.

36. *Tagebucher,* ed. cit., vol. i. 1516, 24 Feb. 1839.

37. *Tagebücher,* ed. cit., vol. iii. 3635, 30 June 1846.

38. *Tagebücher,* ed. cit., vol. iv. 5695, 1 Apr. 1859.

39. *Tagebücher,* ed. cit., vol. iii. 4908, 27 June 1851.

40. *Tagebücher,* ed. cit., vol. i. 585, 17 Jan. 1837.

Edith J. R. Isaacs (essay date December 1938)

SOURCE: Isaacs, Edith J. R. "Concerning the Author of Herod and Mariamne." *Theatre Arts Monthly* (December 1938): 886-90.

[*In the following essay, Isaacs considers the appeal of Hebbel's drama.*]

Twenty-five years ago every important theatre in Germany included some of Friedrich Hebbel's tragedies in its repertory, with **Herod and Mariamne** a prime favorite wherever there was an actress beautiful, majestic and magnetic enough to master the leading part. There were fine roles for actors in Hebbel's plays, but as material for the art of the actress such characters as Mariamne, Agnes Bernauer, Judith, and the noble Rhodope in **Gyges and His Ring** were unsurpassed. The plays themselves, whether in prose or verse, were mighty works.

Hebbel enjoyed conspicuous success during his lifetime; then for more than a generation his plays were neglected. There seemed to be little reason for the change and as little for Hebbel's sudden return to popularity early this century. Yet today again the tides have turned, and as Katharine Cornell brings back the drama of which Hebbel wrote, 'I shall write a play that will be played everywhere,' the author is hardly more than a name.

A closer study brings some logic into these shifts of fortune. During his lifetime Hebbel's plays were enjoyed for their powerful situations and melodramatic action, and he himself was admired as a great dramatic poet. When realism became a theatre fashion, Hebbel was outmoded. It was only when that fashion passed, in turn, that he was recognized as the first great 'modern', the first psychological. dramatist, the man who—a generation before Ibsen—had preached the right of women to develop and to defend their own personality.

Someone who, many years ago, discovered with keen personal pleasure the wealth of Hebbel's dramatic gifts of story, character and style, wrote of him:

> We needed somebody first to teach us, as Ibsen did, in terms that we could understand, what psychological drama was. We did not understand Nora, nor *The Master Builder,* nor *Ghosts,* when they came to us, any better than Mariamne or Maria, nor did we like them as much. But they were not too large, only too strange, for us to grasp. When we studied them we found that we could better understand ourselves through them, and then—studying ourselves again—we learned to know them. We did not like them even then, but we needed them, our social organism craved them, they were a part of the spirit of the age, the Zeitgeist; and so, in spite of our dislike and our rebellion, our society accepted them.
>
> *Judith,* which was the first of Hebbel's great tragedies, was published in 1841; *Gyges and His Ring* in 1856; and between these two came all of Hebbel's important work except the *Nibelungen Trilogy* (1862). *A Doll's House* appeared in 1879, almost a generation later, and yet no doubt we shall always continue to speak of Hebbel as if he had followed Ibsen, because that is the way he came to us, because that is the way he must, in the nature of things, have come. Ibsen's people are concrete and human and within our ken; Hebbel's are magnificently conceived and universal; Ibsen's tragic figures are human sinners; Hebbel's—no less human, only grander—are the sins themselves.

Perhaps if the world had learned to read Hebbel's own theories of what the artist is, and of what the drama should be, his plays might have been understood more readily, for no man helps his readers more; no critic or philosopher has understood the needs of the theatre more surely; no poet, except perhaps Goethe, worked more directly from reason to creation, knew more exactly what he meant to do before he did it. In his critical writings Hebbel has given so clearly his account of the workings of the artist mind, of the artist's responsibility toward his material and toward society, that the shortest road to an appreciation of his work is perhaps not through a lengthening of biographical detail but through translating sentences and paragraphs like the following—a few only, which may encourage the reading of more:

> The child sees in the most profound verse of the Bible only those good old friends of his, the six-and-twenty letters of the alphabet through which it is expressed.

> Nature should never create any poets who are not Goethes, for therein lurks the devil. Every talent tyrannically demands a life for its unfolding and completion, and the smallest talent presses the hardest. Is the reward worth the struggle? The answer to that question can drive you mad.'

> In what does simplicity in art consist? Is it really a condition of complete dullness, in which an artist knows nothing of himself, or of his own activities? That is impossible, for if he does not know or feel 'this impulse is strong,' 'this thought is beautiful,' why does he delineate the one, why hold the other fast?

> I must quarrel with the widespread obsession that a poet has anything to give except himself, except his own life process. He can do nothing else and it is not necessary that he should, for if he really lives, if he is not mean and vain and does not crawl into his own demanding ego but allows himself to be permeated by the unseen forces always in flux about him, ready to create new forms and ideas, he can follow the lead of his spirit contentedly and can be sure that in his needs he presents the needs of the world, creates in his own fantasies a picture of the future. It is not necessary that he should mix personally in fights that are taking place in the streets at the moment.

> Art is concerned with both the inner and the outer life. You might even say that it presents both in their purest aspects and their fullest capacity. The highest forms of art and its principles are the result of the variety of elements which it draws forth out of life and re-creates. But life itself always appears in a dual form—as Being and as Becoming—and that art solves its problem most completely that holds the two most carefully in the balance. Only so does it guarantee to itself a future as well as a present, both of which are important; only so can it become what it should become, life within life. For a situation that is complete stifles the creative breath without which it cannot thrive, and one which is still restlessly embryonic bars out the finished form.

> Drama is a presentation of the life process itself, not only in the sense that it shows life in its entire breadth, which epic poetry also does, but in that it shows a crisis, in which a free individual . . . stands opposed to the whole of mankind, of which he remains a part in spite of his great freedom.

> The material of drama is made up of stories and characters. . . . The handling of characters is of the greatest importance. They must under no circumstances appear as complete, as men who have only to play out certain situations for whatever external happiness or unhappiness may be in them but who cannot win or lose in their essential nature and capacity. This is death

to the drama, death before birth. Drama achieves life only as it shows us how the individual struggles between his personal will and the universal will that modifies and changes action—which is the expression of personal freedom—through situation—which is the expression of necessity. The most perfect drama is achieved when the struggle between Fate and the protagonist is duplicated between the protagonist and the characters opposed to him, and when every relationship in the play, down to the last, unfolds itself in a similar way.

The material of life is unending but the medium of art has fixed limits. Life knows no finality. The thread on which it spins out its happenings extends into the infinite. Art, however, must break the thread; somehow or other it must be tied and knotted, and this is the point that Goethe must have had in mind when he said that all forms of art carry something of untruth with them.

You ask, in what relationship does drama stand to history, and how far must it be historic? I think only so far as it is this by nature, and as art may be considered the highest form of historical writing, since it cannot present the most magnificent and important life processes without recreating as well the historic crises which called them forth or created them.

The process of dramatic individualization is best illustrated by water. Water is water everywhere, and man is man, but just as water takes on a certain mysterious taste from every subsoil through which it flows or trickles, so does a man's history and fate take on something peculiar to each time and nation.

History is for the poet a vehicle for the personification of his principles and ideas, not, conversely, the poet the angel of resurrection for history.

Life is like the ocean; individuals are drops of water, but the tragic figures are icebergs that must be thawed into the whole again, and that tear and rend each other to make this possible. Tragic reconciliation always occurs in the interest of the race, not of the individual.

A man does not think to completion everything he thinks, or feel to the full all that he feels. Life's expressions have a way of crossing and of canceling one another. And this above all must the dramatic form accomplish: it must in every case express the whole of a situation, all the cross-currents of its various elements, and the turmoil which this brings in its wake. From this it follows that the simplicity of dialogue which is so highly regarded is often a fault, and complexity a duty. It is easy to recognize in the waters that raise the fewest bubbles the ones in which least fishes swim.'

Paul G. Graham (essay date December 1940)

SOURCE: Graham, Paul G. "The Principle of Necessity in Hebbel's Theory of Tragedy." *Germanic Review* 15, no. 4 (December 1940): 258-62.

[In the following essay, Graham regards the principle of necessity as an integral aspect of Hebbel's dramatic theory.]

In Hebel's theory of tragedy no single aspect is of greater fundamental significance than the principle of necessity. Hebbel scholars such as Scheunert, Walzel, Schnyder, Frenkel, Seidmann, Purdie, and Rees refer to the importance of the principle of necessity without giving a clear and satisfying account of it. Hebbel employs the terms "notwending" and "Notwendigkeit" for at least three kinds of necessity. First: necessity in the popular sense of compulsion as applied to those acts, conditions and relations of everyday life which are unavoidable. Second, and of greater importance than the first, although also not of immediate concern here, is the application of the term to logical motivation, as illustrated by his statement that dramatic action and the interrelations of characters and situations must arise with necessity from the nature of the characters and circumstances. Likewise, he describes *Herodes und Mariamne* as a tragedy of unqualified necessity, believing that he had, after exerting great effort, succeeded in the flawless motivation of Joseph's disclosure to Mariamne of the secret order to kill her. Third: necessity as descriptive of the inevitable nature of the conflict between the individual and the Whole. This essential quality of the tragic conflict must be examined as an integral part of Hebbel's theory of tragedy.

Very briefly, the highest ideal of the dramatist, according to Hebbel, is to reveal the "Grundverhältnisse, innerhalb derer alles vereinzelte Dasein entsteht und vergeht."[1] Dualism is the fundamental basis of his philosophy. Individual activity, whether the motive be good or evil, indeed even mere existence of the individual, tends to endanger the unified and harmonious character of the Whole, and according to the principle of self-correction—to use Hebbel's own term—the individual is destroyed. Life, says Hebbel, is a frightful necessity, and tragic art should demonstrate that individual life conflicts with the Idea and is finally crushed. Life is a form of guilt which is inevitably punished. Death is a sacrifice which every human being must make for the sake of the Idea.

We may now ask what position necessity occupies in this metaphysical structure. Fundamentally there is only one kind of necessity, that is, the world must have continuing existence. By dividing itself into numberless individual variations the Whole achieves its own consciousness and development, but must eventually restore its own harmony and guarantee its own perpetuation. It is inconceivable that there can be life without struggle and tragic conflict. One is immediately impressed by the striking similarity of these ideas to those of Hegel's theory of tragedy. The question of influence is not of immediate concern here; but it may be recalled that in general such comparative studies have indicated that Hebbel was indebted to Hegel only insofar as ideas which the dramatist arrived at independently were later confirmed and often clarified by his subsequent study of the philosopher. Hegel speaks of the destruction of the individuals who disturb the moral substance and of the ultimate reconciliation through the reestablishment and preservation of the harmonious and unified morality. Unlike Hegel, Hebbel considered this process to be the sole formative principle in the history of the world. Thus he was able to argue that morality and necessity are identical. But this conception of necessity has two aspects, a twofold form of realization. First, the Idea must relentlessly achieve self-preservation, and second, individual existence inevitably implies self-assertion. This is designated by Scheunert as the "dualism of necessity."[2] The resulting opposition is the essence of tragedy. "So darf er [der Dichter] jeden Character zu Grunde gehen lassen, aber er muß uns zugleich zeigen, daß der Untergang unvermeidlich, daß er, wie der Tod, mit der Geburt selbst gesetzt ist."[3] Again Hebbel writes: "Das Wesen der Darstellung besteht in der Veranschaulichung der Notwendigkeit."[4]

At the height of his career as a dramatist he set down the following formula:

> 1ste Stufe künstlerischer Wirkung: es kann so seyn!
>
> 2te Stufe künstlerischer Wirkung: es ist!
>
> 3te Stufe künstlerischer Wirkung: es muß so seyn![5]

The tragedy of human existence derives not from the nature of man's actions but from the nature of man himself. This principle of determinism, which is a basic metaphysical truth for Hebbel, denies the free-will of man except in a very special, ironical sense. "Der Mensch hat freien Willen—d.h. er kann einwilligen in's Notwendige!"[6] The individual, believing in his possession of free-will, clashes ultimately with the forces of the Whole. "Was nur dem Meister der Kunst begreiflich ist: die Notwendigkeit, das Wesentlichste oft ganz beiläufig zu sagen, um den schönen Schein der Freiheit nicht aufzuheben!"[7] Man does not comprehend that his will is but a part of the infinite will. "In der Maßlosigkeit liegt die Schuld. . . . Diese Schuld ist eine uranfängliche, von dem Begriff des Menschen nicht zu trennende und kaum in sein Bewußtsein fallende, sie ist mit dem Leben selbst gesetzt."[8] Life is a necessity which no one comprehends, and the highest ideal of tragic art is the portrayal of the destruction of individual life in its conflict with the Idea. It is this concept of necessity in which even the final and difficult question of reconciliation is rooted, for if the drama can depict that which is necessary and unalterable it will then enable men to reconcile themselves with their destiny.

> Wenn der Mensch sein individuelles Verhältniß zum Universum in seiner Notwendigkeit begreift, so hat er seine Bildung vollendet und eigentlich auch schon aufgehört, ein Individuum zu sein, denn der Begriff dieser Notwendigkeit, die Fähigkeit, sich bis zu ihm durch zu arbeiten und die Kraft, ihn festzuhalten, ist eben das Universelle im Individuellen, löscht allen unberechtigten Egoismus aus und befreit den Geist vom Tode, indem er diesen im Wesentlichen anticipirt.[9]

Once the individual recognizes the fundamental necessity, the limitations on his freedom, then all possibility of a desire to defy these will have disappeared.

Hebbel repeatedly asserted that reconciliation of any other kind than this was absurd, for life itself offered reconciliation only at this level. Using a favorite term, Hebbel declared that the poet must present the dissonance of life itself and not stop halfway between that which is accidental and that which is necessary. Occasionally the individual recognizes that his own destruction is necessary, even valuable, for the Whole. In any case, if the poet could demonstrate this necessity, then one could speak of reconciliation. Hebbel's definition is as follows: "Versöhnung im Drama: Heilung der Wunde durch den Nachweis, daß sie für die erhöhte Gesundheit notwending war.[10] Because his own dramas were so frequently criticized for their lack of reconciliation, Hebbel defended his own procedure vehemently, indeed often with bitterness of tone.

> Diejenigen, die vom Tragödien-Dichter verlangen, daß er nicht bloß die sittliche Idee retten, sondern zugleich auch den Helden vor dem Untergang bewahren soll, fordern eigentlich etwas eben so Unvernünftiges, als wenn sie vom Arzt verlangten, daß er den Organismus nicht bloß von einer Krankheit befreien, sondern die Krankheit selbst auch, als eine individuelle Modifikation des allgemeinen Lebensprocesses, respectiren und also am Leben erhalten solle.[11]

When *Maria Magdalene* was performed in Vienna in 1848, he wrote to Rötscher that the only thing which the majority of the audience could not swallow was the lack of reconciliation from a trivial, narrow point of view. For them, he said, insight into the necessity of the tragedy did not represent reconciliation because they had been spoiled by sentimental trash.[12]

This conception, then, of the principle of necessity holds that the freedom of the great organism of which the individual is a part is only possible through the limitations imposed on individual existence and that reconciliation can only be derived from a recognition of the unalterable nature of this relationship. The importance of this principle for Hebbel is to be deduced, not only from his theoretical statements, but also from the dramas themselves, from the choice of materials, from the significant changes he made in the latter, and from the recurring emphasis on this principle in the various characters and conflicts which he portrayed. A detailed analysis of the fate of the chief characters in Hebbel's tragedies is not possible within the limits of this article. Nor is it perhaps necessary, for if time permitted recalling merely the main outlines of the major dramas, it would be apparent, I believe, that whether we chose characters such as Judith, Holofernes, Mariamne, Herodes, Golo, and Kandaules, who through active self-assertion evoke their tragic destiny, or leading characters such as Genoveva, Klara, Agnes Bernauer, and Rhodope, who because of their own fundamental nature or some outstanding quality rather than because of their actions suffer a tragic fate—it would, then, be apparent that Hebbel in every case sought to demonstrate and emphasize the compelling basis of the relationship of the individual and the Idea, that is, necessity. That he was relatively more successful in the later dramas in the formulation and expression of this metaphysical pattern is likewise evident. Herzog Ernst calls Agnes Bernauer "das reinste Opfer, das der Notwendigkeit im Lauf aller Jahrhunderte gefallen ist."[13] Mariamne accuses Herodes in the words: "Solch einen Frevel verdammt das Schicksal, das ihn zwar beginnen, doch nicht gelingen ließ!"[14] In the same drama Titus explains his failure to reveal Mariamne's innocence with the significant words: "Mich hielt mein Wort zurück und mehr als das: die unerbittliche Notwendigkeit."[15]

It was this concept, then, that Hebbel sought to express in both theory and practice, a concept which was an integral part of the principles of dualism and reconciliation. This was for Hebbel the ideal of all art, but above all else of tragedy. "Der Notwendigkeit ist die Menschheit untergeordnet."[16] It is the task of poetry to represent that which is necessary and immutable—the fundamental conditions of all individual existence in their unalterability—to represent these in the most beautiful forms in the hope that mankind might be reconciled with its destiny.

Notes

1. R. M. Werner, *Friedrich Hebbel, Sämtliche Werke* (I-XII; *Tagebücher*, I-IV; *Briefe*, I-VIII. Berlin-Steglitz: B. Behr's Verlag, 1900-1907. Hereafter referred to as *Werke, Tagebücher, Briefe*), *Briefe* II, 272.

2. A. Scheunert, *Der Pantragismus als System der Weltanschauung und Ästhetik Friedrich Hebbels* (Hamburg und Leipzig: Verlag von Leopold Voss, 1903), p. 32.

3. *Tagebücher,* II, 269.

4. *Tagebücher,* III, 303.

5. *Tagebücher,* III, 375.

6. *Tagebücher,* II, 155.

7. *Tagebücher,* III, 128.

8. *Werke,* XI, 29.

9. *Tagebücher,* III, 269-270.

10. *Tagebücher,* II, 295.

11. *Tagebücher,* III, 162.

12. *Briefe,* IV, 106.

13. *Werke,* III, 234 (Act V, Sc. 10).

14. *Werke,* II, 282 (Act III, Sc. 3).

15. *Werke,* II, 360 (Act V, Sc. 8).

16. *Briefe,* I, 131.

Edna Purdie (essay date 1966)

SOURCE: Purdie, Edna. "Hebbel: Some Aspects of Research and Criticism in the Decade, 1953-1963." *Euphorion* (1966): 110-24.

[*In the following essay, Purdie surveys the major trends in the critical analysis of Hebbel's work from 1953-1963.*]

In any survey, however incomplete, of scholarly work concerning Hebbel during the decade preceding the centenary of 1963, at least two trends can be discerned. On the one hand, a new impulse to investigation of his relations with predecessors and contemporaries, greatly stimulated by Wolfgang Liepe's researches into further sources of Hebbel's thought and imagery, and powerfully supported by publications sponsored by the Hebbel-Gesellschaft and the University of Kiel; on the other, a healthy revival of activity in the critical editing of Hebbel's writings, whether in collected form or as individual works. These trends, as will at once be seen, are not mutually exclusive; Liepe has suggested enlargement of the corpus of Hebbel's work, and many editors have made notable contributions to its evaluation. If in the attempt to give some account of what has been achieved I turn first to the very substantial evidence of the editorial approach, this is because I believe that Hebbel as an artist has suffered in the past from the emphasis laid by his critics on abstract notions, and therefore fresh consideration of what he actually wrote is the more welcome. There is no lack of variety in editorial achievements, and much unobtrusive scholarly work is embodied in them.

It is natural that the critical editions of collected works should have appeared mainly in Germany, whereas those of individual works are more widely distributed. Among the fairly numerous recent collected editions[1] special mention may be made of *Werke,* edited by G. Fricke, W. Keller, and K. Pörnbacher, to be issued in five volumes, of which two have already appeared[2]. This edition contains in each case the text (which corresponds to that in R. M. Werner's Historisch-kritische Ausgabe) and notes which give concise information concerning sources, details of publication (and performance in respect of plays), a few relevant observations by Hebbel himself, and some carefully selected annotations of the text. All the dramas and dramatic fragments are contained in the first two volumes; in the remaining volumes the non-dramatic poetic works, the tales, the theoretical and autobiographical writings, the diaries and letters are to appear. This edition when completed will be a valuable addition to the material easily available for students of Hebbel's work.

Nothing comparable to these larger undertakings can be recorded from abroad. On the other hand interesting and scholarly work has been done in the editing of single works. Here a notable revival of interest in *Agnes Bernauer* can be observed; critical editions, with substantial introductions and annotations, have appeared in Britain[3] and Italy[4] as well as in Germany[5]. It is clear from the individual editions that certain aspects have claimed attention in differing measure: the historical sources, the problem of guilt, the question of style.

Both English editions reveal an empirical approach. Hebbel's treatment of his material is elucidated by reference to his sources; dramatic structure and dramatic dialogue are analysed with specific examples. Mary Wiesener-Garland is in the main concerned with the connection of the two central themes, with the development of the action and analysis of the characters; she also briefly indicates stylistic relations with verse tragedy and later realist drama. Gillian Rodger discusses the problem of sins committed in the name of justice, and emphasises the change in Hebbel's conception of tragedy shown by the interlocking of the separate tragedies of Agnes and Herzog Ernst; she analyses the formal means of presenting reconciliation through poetic symbolism, balanced structure and rhythmical prose.

In contrast to the sympathetic and predominantly empirical approach of both these editors, the strongly marked theoretical standpoint of Hermann Glaser is conspicuous. Adhering to the general notion of Hebbel's "Pantragismus", he gives a highly unfavourable verdict on *Agnes Bernauer,* and condemns most of its interpreters. The central point of his work (indicated in the subtitle *Dichtung und Wirklichkeit*) is the *Agnes Bernauer* theme rather than Hebbel's tragedy; but the latter is the only complete play printed in the volume. Selected extracts from other versions of the story are preceded by a brief survey—in which the editor states his own definite preference for the dialect play with music by Carl Orff (*Die Bernauerin.* In: *Bairisches Welttheater,* Wiesbaden, 1957), of which he prints two scenes. In the earlier sections of the "Dokumentation", extracts from historical sources illustrate an account of the complicated situation in Bavaria; the final section contains two of Hebbel's theoretical essays (*Mein Wort über das Drama* and the Preface to *Maria Magdalena*), together with a few relevant passages from diary and correspondence.

This editor's personal and political convictions are plainly visible in the section devoted to "die literarhistorische Betrachtung", and colour his judgments on

every aspect of Hebbel's drama, including its language; his crude account of this stands in marked contrast to the perceptive observations of Gillian Rodger on its particular variety of poetic realism. A bibliography and a chronological table of versions of the theme are appended to this edition, which would have been a more useful one if the editor had been less uncompromisingly antagonistic to Hebbel's play.

Differences in the editorial approach to *Agnes Bernauer* are no doubt in some measure connected with the reasons for revival of interest in this play. It has appeared to some critics—whether justifiably or not—to suggest immediate connections with the preoccupations of our day, and is regarded as material evidence for Hebbel's political and social views. The recent emphasis on this aspect will be seen more clearly in the consideration of the controversial issues discussed in articles relating to this tragedy[6].

While other dramas by Hebbel have been reprinted during this period in popular form (*Judith, Maria Magdalena, Herodes und Mariamne, Gyges und sein Ring, Die Nibelungen*), and have of course received attention in the critical editions of his collected works, no other single play seems to have so much attracted individual editors[7].

Critical editions of *Maria Magdalena* and *Herodes und Mariamne* had already appeared in England during the previous decade in a well-known series (*Blackwell's German Texts*); to these were now added in the same series a representative selection of Hebbel's poems (selected and edited with Introduction and Notes by Edna Purdie, Oxford 1953) and one of his theoretical writings (*Selected Essays,* edited with Introduction and Notes by Derrick Barlow, Oxford 1962). A revised edition of a selection of poems with notes and commentary by Kurt Esselbrügge appeared in Germany (*Riesenhaft fühle ich's weben . . . Eine Auswahl aus der Lyrik.* Stuttgart, Riederer (2nd revised ed.) 1959).

During this same period much attention has been paid to autobiographical material. A critical edition of Hebbel's fragment *Meine Kindheit* (edited with Introduction and Notes by Dorothy Knight, London and Edinburgh, Thomas Nelson and Sons, 1956) made this fragment easily accessible to English readers; a German edition of the autobiographical material appeared in a popular form[8]. *Meine Kindheit* had already been included, together with a selection of extracts from Hebbel's diaries and correspondence, in *Friedrich Hebbel. Der Mensch und der Dichter in Selbstzeugnissen.* (Hrsg. von Gerhard Helbig, Leipzig: Koehler & Amelung, 1958.) Hebbel's autobiographical fragment and the *Selbstbiographie* which be wrote for F. A. Brockhaus in 1852 are the only complete items in this collection; the rest of the book consists of passages selected with a definite purpose: the material is limited, we are told, to that which "noch heute als Kulturerbe gelten kann" (p. 240). In the light of this statement it is interesting to note the paucity of extracts concerning Hebbel's poetic and dramatic work; indeed the editor expressly states that the thinker and the man are probably more interesting to us than his work (p. 235), though he does recognise on occasion that Hebbel is always a poet (p. 232). This arbitrary exclusion of much that is of fundamental importance in the *Tagebücher,* and the complete dominance of social and sociological theory in the process of selection, deprives this book of any claim to impartial presentation of evidence. The generally unsympathetic tone of the "Nachwort" will not surprise the informed reader who has already observed the procedure adopted by the editor. The fact that the diary entries, although dated, do not bear the numbers attached to them in Werner's Historisch-kritische Ausgabe renders it more difficult for other readers to realise how small a portion of the available material is presented.

A welcome contrast in attitude and method is to be found in the wide selection by Anni Meetz printed in Reclams Universal-Bibliothek (8247-52). The editor's own work on Hebbel makes her fully aware of the equal reflection of the man and the artist in his diaries, and in a concise Nachwort she puts them in perspective. The entries bear the numbers given in Werner's edition, in order that comparison and citation may be easy.

An important addition to the biographical material available to scholars is this same editor's collection of hitherto unpublished letters[9]. This volume, together with a collection of Wolfgang Liepe's essays, likewise emanating from Kiel, formed an important contribution to the centenary celebrations of 1963. Almost all the letters belong to the later period of Hebbel's life, after he had settled in Vienna; they are divided into two sections—family letters, and correspondence with contemporaries connected with literature and the theatre. The edition has been compiled with sympathy and scrupulous care. The first section has a special interest, since it fills a hitherto unfilled gap: it contains the letters written by his wife to Hebbel on his various journeys from 1851 onwards, which were carefully kept by Hebbel himself and subsequently by Christine Hebbel till her death. (Hebbel's own letters to her are contained in Werner's edition of the *Briefe* and are not reprinted in this volume). If there had ever been a shadow of doubt as to the depth and integrity of the relation between these two persons of differing artistic gifts, this correspondence which can now be seen as a whole would dispel it. The second section of the volume throws additional light on Hebbel's personality and on a number of the situations that confronted him as a dramatist[10]. Anni Meetz's brief but well-informed and well-constructed account of Hebbel and his work issued in

the Sammlung Metzler (*Realienbücher für Germanisten.* Stuttgart 1962) contains also a useful list of published documents, as well as a short survey of Hebbel criticism since the late nineteenth century.

The picture of Hebbel and his work has thus undoubtedly been filled out and revivified by the very considerable activity of scholars in editing and commenting on his writings. There has been an equal if not a greater degree of activity in the form of critical essays and articles, a large number of which have appeared in Germany. These again fall into two categories: essays of a general character, and interpretations of individual works. Two important publications which marked the centenary both contain studies of each kind. The volume of essays by Wolfgang Liepe issued as a memorial to him in 1963[11] contains ten on different aspects of Hebbel's work, and the collection *Hebbel in neuer Sicht* (Ed. Helmut Kreuzer. Stuttgart, W. Kohlhammer Verlag 1963) consists of sixteen articles on specific themes, of which eight deal with particular dramas. Both these collections include some articles reprinted (or revised) from earlier publications, and are thus to a considerable degree representative of trends of criticism during the whole decade under review.

A bridge between the two forms of expressing the revival of interest in Hebbel may be discerned in the work of Wolfgang Liepe, whose influence on it from the Chair he occupied at the University of Kiel until his death in 1962 was profound. Three of Liepe's essays are concerned with some poems and prose works which he attributes to Hebbel, and which, if the attribution is accepted, considerably enlarge and deepen our knowledge of his early development as a writer. The three poems, which appeared anonymously in the Ditmarser und Eiderstedter Bote in 1828 and 1829, are reprinted here; of the six *unbekannte und unerkannte Frühprosen* four (also anonymous) are printed as an appendix to the article concerning them, while the tale *Die einsamen Kinder* is the subject of a third essay. The principle of the attribution to Hebbel of the anonymous writings is that of comparison. This has a wide range, covering not only the acknowledged early tales and poems, but also the work of writers whose influence on Hebbel in his youth is the subject of investigation in other articles—notably the philosophers Gotthilf Heinrich Schubert and Ludwig Feuerbach—or is discussed in various connections with reference to Hebbel's early experiences of literature, particularly in relation to the *Urania* of C. A. Tiedge[12].

Liepe's deep and extensive knowledge of the works of these writers and of Hebbel's own works enables him to adduce a formidable series of parallels as evidence for his argument. Themes and treatment in the prose tales are set in striking juxtaposition with one another and with the ideas expressed in the mystic-philosophic writings which he regards as primary sources available to Hebbel in the early Wesselburen period. A similar analysis of some early poems, in particular *Proteus,* had already led to a similar conclusion; and Schubert is presented as the long-sought link between Hebbel and Schelling (*Der Schlüssel zum Weltbild Hebbels,* originally published in 1951); in a further article Ludwig Feuerbach is added as another link, and a third essay deals with the relation between the ideas of Hebbel and Schelling. There is a welcome recognition in the second and third of these articles that originality of thought has little to do with the artistic value of a work of art; and a plain statement that the reason for investigation is to analyse the part played by assimilation of the ideas of others in the expression of the poet's own experience by poetic means. This important distinction has not always been clear to critics of Hebbel in this and other decades. Liepe's firm grasp of it is evidenced in the perceptive textual analysis of *Nachtlied* (first published in *Die deutsche Lyrik. Interpretationen.* Ed. B. von Wiese, Düsseldorf, A. Bagel, II, 1956), and the suggestive comparisons of several lyrics in the article on Hebbel and Schelling. The statement that the poet was fascinated by Schelling's poetic diction rests on the critic's own keen ear for rhythm and cadence. But while the results of the comparative method are in the main convincing, there is perhaps too little recognition of the possibility of a common source for some of the similarities of diction. (The imagistic use of *Tropfen* and *Quell* can be paralleled in Klopstock's poetry as well as in Feuerbach's early writings, as can the similar use of *Tau* as a symbol of the merging of individual and universal life. And while it is the comparison with Tiedge's *Urania* that is emphasised in the attribution to Hebbel of *Der Greis,* there is also much in this poem that echoes the sound of Schiller's verse).

Two important conclusions are drawn from the detailed investigation of similarities in form and content between Hebbel and the two philosophical writers. One is a categorical denial of the notion that during his youth in Wesselburen he was isolated from the general stream of thought and culture. On the contrary, it is persuasively argued (though the absence of external evidence is a regrettable factor in the situation), he was in direct connection with the intellectual movement of his time "deren innere Spannung ihm die Spannung des eigenen Wesens deutete" (p. 297). Insistence on the basic character and importance of the ideas assimilated in Wesselburen recurs as a refrain through these articles; it is supported by many perceptive references to various aspects of Hebbel's mature works (such as the continuing significance of the notion of a decisive moment, first emphasised in *Die einsamen Kinder,* in the later portrayal of tragic characters).

The second conclusion is one which also emerges from the more general essays *Weltbild und Dichtung* and *Zum Problem der Schuld bei Hebbel,* and is of vital importance. Liepe rejects decisively the view of some recent critics who see in Hebbel an example of the metaphysical despair of nihilism and assert his interpretation of Necessity to be deterministic. He points to the clear distinction between the presentation of tragic collision in the dramas and the notion of cosmic unity which pervades the lyrics, thus restoring a balance of which the poet himself was conscious. This vivid realisation of polarity in Hebbel's outlook, of the "hell-dunkle Tönung" of his whole work (the poet's predilection for the word-group of *dämmern* might be cited in support of this description) gives a breadth and depth to this collection of essays which make them uniquely important as scholarly contributions to modern Hebbel criticism.

Interesting parallels and differences of view can be observed in an essay on Hebbel's apprenticeship to poetry by the Italian scholar Carlo Grünanger (reprinted in *Scritti minori di letteratura tedesca,* Brescia, 1962), more particularly in the comments on the relation of some early lyrics to *Proteus* and *Nachtlied.* Perceptive observations—such as that on Hebbel's gift of isolating something in space and time and of concentrating in a single point the tragic vision of the whole, or the description of *Herakles' Tod* (1830) as a far-off anticipation of *Der Bramine*—cast light not only on the early poems but also on his lyric poetry in general. So too the end of *Die einsamen Kinder,* which is considered as a "human document", is seen as pointing forward to the same late poem, which is regarded as the true expression of the poet's own nature. This conviction of Hebbel's essential faith underlies the essay *Federico Hebbel e la Poesia del Numinoso* printed in Studi Germanici (N.S., 1964, II, 1)—the unrevised text of a lecture written just before Grünanger's death, which was intended for the centenary celebrations in Rome. Grünanger sees the true theme of Hebbel's work, not as the conflict of the sexes, the sacrifice of the individual to the "Idea", or the nihilistic surrender to inescapable destiny, but as the solitude and agony of the individual seeking complete love; *arcanus terror* characterises the highest moments of the tragic dramas, while many of the lyrical poems reveal a cosmic intuition. ***Maria Magdalena,*** seen primarily as a drama of suffering, is for him a *chef-d'oeuvre; Nachtlied* and *Der Bramine* bear witness to the poet's apprehension of an ultimate reality. This approach is a valuable counterpoise to the determinist view, but likewise results in a somewhat over-simplified picture.

The opposite extreme—of great complexity—may be observed in the comprehensive analysis attempted by Joachim Müller in: *Das Weltbild Friedrich Hebbels* (Halle, VEB Max Niemeyer Verlag, 1955). The plan of this work makes it difficult for the reader to gain a coherent view of it, and renders repetition and overlapping inevitable. The eight chapters which form the main part of the book deal with different elements in the composite picture, ranging from Hebbel's view of pain and his symbolic use of the *motifs* of sleep and dream, through his concept of the relation between individual and universe and of the divine principle in the world, to his attitude towards art in general and drama in particular, and towards the state, society and history. That such elements are of necessity interwoven in almost any literary and philosophical analysis of Hebbel's work is plain; but this thematic arrangement involves author and reader in a continuous process of recollection and anticipation which does not favour clarity of view. There is moreover considerable disparity in critical approach, according to the differing themes. Whereas the analysis of Hebbel's use of symbols and *motifs,* or of his belief in poetry as the main mode of revealing the inner threads of the texture of the universe, is firmly based on concrete evidence, in other sections—and notably in the final one—tendentious interpretations are interspersed without any comparable basis. Oscillation of this kind is indeed a feature of the book, and can be observed in the initial and concluding sections as well as in the treatment of separate themes. There is a salutary rejection of the assumption that Hebbel's theoretical statements should be taken as explanations or criteria of his artistic achievement; the term "Gestaltdenker" is used to emphasise the interdependence of thought and the creative process (the distinction between which Hebbel himself emphatically maintained). There is an equal emphasis on the dualist basis of the poet's outlook. In the final estimate of Hebbel's place in the sweep of his century, Müller sees him as at once the culminating figure of the epoch beginning with Lessing and Herder and the first exponent of a new movement of thought ("geschichtsphilosophischer Realismus") pointing forward to dialectical materialism.

There is in this work a curious mixture of perceptive criticism and a priori argument which creates an impression of dissonance; in his final sentence however the writer lays due emphasis on the importance of the poet's creative role.

An essay *Friedrich Hebbel und sein Zeitalter* which was appended by Gerhard Fricke to his edition of Hebbel's works in this same year (1955)[13] presents some interesting points of comparison and contrast. Rejecting the process of postulating a system of thought as guide to the poet's creative work, Fricke formulates the basic tragic concept (illustrated by reference to *Judith, Genoveva, Maria Magdalena, Herodes und Mariamne,* and *Agnes Bernauer*) as being man's incapacity to seize and hold an absolute, in whatever form, combined with his irresistible urge to achieve this. It is this interpreta-

tion of universally conflicting forces which constitutes for him Hebbel's individual contribution to the evolution of "high tragedy"; the metaphysical basis, in his view, marks it as the final stage of this form. But he sees the dramatist as also belonging to our present age, fearlessly examining a reality without concepts of divinity, and thus offers his own interpretation of Hebbel's dual role in 19th-century drama. Fricke's analysis is in general cogent and persuasive. But the absence of any consideration of *Gyges und sein Ring,* with its varying emphasis and different outcome, may be regretted; surely this drama gives an individual turn to the concept of Necessity.

The work of Helga Frisch, *Symbolik und Tragik in Hebbels Dramen* (Bonn, H. Bouvier und Co. Verlag, 1960, 2nd ed. 1963) is characterised by abstract analysis, supported by citation of Hebbel's own theoretical statements and applied to his tragic dramas. A detailed exposition of the structure of dramatic symbolism in *Judith* indicates the main argument concerning the relationship between symbol ("Zeichen") and action—the function of the first being to point forward to the second. This kind of symbol is contrasted with the oracle of Greek tragedy; they are seen as revealing two different interpretations of the individual's relation to that which is outside him, two opposed concepts of fate. Whereas the oracle isolates the hero from universal life and throws him back on himself, the symbol expresses the subordination of the person to the surrounding universe; it stands for "ein Außen schlechthin" by which the individual is unwittingly governed (p. 30).

The application of this principle to *Judith* results in an analysis which shows a keen ear for anticipatory notes and duly emphasises the important factors in the tragedy. But the subsequent attempt to evaluate all Hebbel's major dramas by reference to the theory of foreshadowing and actuality, action and reaction, leads to a very restricted view of *Genoveva,* where other tragic factors are disregarded, and to a limited conception of the tragic action in *Maria Magdalena.* Under the heading "Freiheit und Notwendigkeit" the symbolical aspects of *Agnes Bernauer* and *Herodes und Mariamne* are examined, notably in respect of the relationship between life and death; this relationship also forms the basis of a concluding chapter, in which death is presented as the completion and solution of tragic experience: man's guilt is expiated and his innocence restored, if he offers himself as a sacrifice to death.

The general ideas in this work are not unassailable, and the language in which they are expressed is highly abstract; this in turn conditions the way in which the analysis of individual plays or passages is formulated. While these analyses are liable to contain an element of special pleading, they are often acute and stimulating.

The reader must not however expect a comprehensive examination of symbols in Hebbel's dramas; only that which supports the particular relation formulated at the outset between symbolism and the concept of tragedy comes under scrutiny. Within this restricted area some interesting suggestions are put forward.

In an interesting study of a single aspect of Hebbel's dramatic technique[14], Sten G. Flygt suggests that there is a basic pattern in his use of discovery as a vital element in the tragic action. Analysis of the modes of revelation—most successful perhaps in respect of *Judith, Herodes und Mariamne, Gyges und sein Ring* and *Demetrius*—leads to the conclusion that a "hostile principle" lodged within the character attains its purpose through a fatal disclosure, and that we thereby become aware of the life-milieu as a trap or net, whose meshes are "drawn tighter by every movement made in the struggle to get out". It is emphasised that such a function of disclosure is separate from any consideration of it as an element in the "analytic technique" of exposition, and that its distinctive form is being considered as an individual feature of Hebbel's art.

The centenary volume *Hebbel in neuer Sicht* contains four articles which made their first appearance in the *Hebbel-Jahrbuch,* and a scrutiny of the contents of this collection and of the volume of Liepe's essays already discussed will show how great has been the practical value of the Jahrbuch to scholarly research. Indeed throughout the decade under consideration, its articles offer a varied and stimulating contribution to the appreciation of Hebbel as a writer and as a human being. Apart from papers on more general themes, such a detailed study as Walther Vontin's examination of the extant fragments of Hebbel's projected revision of *Judith*[15] serves to remind us once again of the value of scrupulous textual analysis, while the bibliographies by Peter Michelsen from 1953 to 1956, by Walter A. Reichart (dealing specifically with America and England) in 1961, and by Hayo Matthiesen in 1963 are interesting and extremely useful aids to scholarship. In the present survey it is not possible to give an account of the contents of successive issues, but a mere list of them would suffice to prove the importance of the *Jahrbuch.* The centenary number contains several substantial articles, of which one, by Benno von Wiese, gives a general survey of Hebbel's tragic outlook (*Der Tragiker Friedrich Hebbel*), and another deals with an important aspect of it (Ilse Brugger: *Die "Mensch-Ding" Problematik bei Hebbel*). The first of these (a *Festvortrag* held in Wesselburen) is largely concerned with an analysis of the basic elements in Hebbel's presentation of life, and an assessment of their relation to the thought and feeling of later generations. It is perhaps natural that on such an occasion the aim should be to emphasise the point of kinship to the modern age; von Wiese finds this in the daring concept of the tragic interdependence of God and man, in the combination of a "dialectical metaphysic" and a psychological probing into human isolation. He maintains that this aspect of Hebbel—his analysis and revelation of the incongruities of life—has hitherte been little recognised, and briefly reviews the dramas from this standpoint.

Ilse Brugge concentrates on a theme which she regards as central in any consideration of Hebbel's outlook: the tragic consequence of degrading a person into a means, or an object, and thus violating an essential right of human personality. This aspect of Hebbel's tragedies—especially in relation to *Herodes und Mariamne* and *Gyges und sein Ring*—has of course been treated by many critics. A great virtue of this essay is the wide scope of reference; dramas, lyrics and epigrams, diaries and letters are all sources from which the writer draws her evidence. At the same time she is aware (as some are not) that dates may be important in the assessment of such evidence; a comment on the differing implications of *Die Kuh* and *Mutter und Kind* brings out this point, and may also serve to exemplify the range of illustration. The interpretation offered of *Herodes und Mariamne* follows a line of thought suggested by Kurt May[16] (to whom reference is made), stressing the deterioration induced in Mariamne by Herodes' treatment of her as a "thing"; that of *Gyges und sein Ring* contains a welcome recognition that in this drama there is a positive side to the tragic expiation. Similarly a positive value is seen in the transformation of the love between Agnes and Albrecht in *Agnes Bernauer,* and in the underlying thought of *Der Rubin*[17].

The studies in the collection *Hebbel in neuer Sicht* are varied in character and content. In addition to the four articles reprinted from the *Jahrbuch,* there are six others which are enlarged or revised versions of previous essays; the remainder were written for this volume, which is appropriately dedicated to the memory of Wolfgang Liepe and Kurt May. General themes are treated by Klaus Ziegler (*Wandlungen des Tragischen*), Benno von Wiese (*Die Religion Büchners und Hebbels*), Wolfgang Liepe (*Zum Problem der Schuld bei Hebbel*) and Marie Luise Gansberg (*Zur Sprache in Hebbels Dramen*); the *Tagebücher* are discussed, from differing angles, by Peter Michelsen and Joachim Müller, and Hebbel's achievement in lyrical poetry and prose tale is assessed by Fritz Martini and Ingrid Kreuzer respectively. The remaining eight essays are devoted to individual dramas, from *Judith* to *Die Nibelungen*.

There is no less variation in the standpoints of the writers. Whether directly or by implication, all of them offer an estimate of Hebbel's metaphysical position—Ziegler in connection with the depreciatory verdict of Karl Jaspers on the tragic essence of his dramas, Benno von Wiese by means of a comparison between Büchner's reaction to life's contradictions and Hebbel's

"Pantragismus . . . hinter dem noch eine besondere Art von religiöser Mystik steckt" (p. 28), Liepe through an analysis of Hebbel's dramatic presentation of the nature of tragic experience. This critic recognises the central problem of Hebbelian drama to be ethical in kind: the violation of the human rights of another person, the immoderate claim of self-assertion. And in the definite statement that Hebbel shows in his tragedies that it is human beings who fail, and not, as they believe, the world order that is at fault (p. 49), Liepe is refuting the argument of ambivalence as well as that of nihilism.

A concluding estimate of ambivalence, or ambiguity, or irreconcilable contradictoriness, emerges from several of the studies. Peter Michelsen sees paradox as fundamental in Hebbel's thought[18], Wolfgang Wittkowski discerns in *Judith* a basic dualism, a deep and unresolvable discord in the deity itself and between God and Nature, but combats the theory that Hebbel believed in nothing by emphasising his adherence to the "ewige Ordnung der Natur" as a permanent value, and his conviction of the inescapable tragic consequence of disturbing it. The same critic, in a somewhat unsympathetic but sometimes acute analysis of *Genoveva,* expresses general agreement with the views of Liepe and Helmut Kreuzer, while rejecting the former's assertion that Golo's final decision constitutes a triumph of conscience. The essays by Lawrence Ryan on *Herodes und Mariamne* and Helmut Kreuzer on *Agnes Bernauer* both deal, from different angles, with Hebbel's view of history. Ryan sees in *Herodes und Mariamne* an attempt to bind "die hohe Tragödie" to history without surrendering it in the process, and to preserve this form of drama even in the absence of the absolute metaphysical assumptions underlying classical tragedy. Noting the formidable body of opinion in recent times that regards Hebbel's attempt to combine a historical interpretation with an individual tragedy of love as unsuccessful, he puts forward an interpretation of the final scenes as linking the universal element in the historical moment to the tragic failure of the individual urge to immoderate self-assertion; but at the same time he emphasises the difficulties inherent in the attempt to show that which is universal in that which is historically conditioned. The detailed analysis of the two main characters which leads to this conclusion contains acute individual observations on the nature of their relationship to one another (betraying more sympathy for Herodes than for Mariamne); but in common with many other critics of this play Ryan appears frequently insensitive to its dramatic power.

Contrasts of view in respect of *Herodes und Mariamne* are well illustrated by two articles published in previous years. Rainer Gruenter[19] considers the central characters to be worked out with precision from Hebbel's theory of tragic necessity, and condemns them as human beings. Mariamne in particular attracts this unfavourable verdict, and there is little consideration of the many side-lights on her personality. Nihilism of feeling and thinking in characters who are totally destructive ("alles verzehren") is for him the hall mark of this drama. Some interesting observations on the cuts made by Hebbel himself occur in the course of the argument. Derrick Barlow[20], on the other hand, sets out a full analysis of the motives underlying Mariamne's behaviour, and with a close scrutiny of the text offers an individual interpretation of her point of view. He combats the notion that her action is a form of revenge for an outrage against her personality; he also rejects the view that it proceeds from a desire for justice. The drama is for him a tragedy of marriage because Mariamne's love for Herodes is of a quality to which the latter shows himself unable to respond, although he is offered several chances. Mariamne's final hope of giving Herodes a true picture of her, Barlow argues, is in death. Even this fails, for Herodes shows himself unworthy of her self-sacrificing love, as Meister Anton proved unworthy of Klara's; but this quality of love is symbolically represented in the scene of the passage of the Magi.

Helmut Kreuzer's study of *Agnes Bernauer* (partially incorporating his essay on this play as Hebbel's "moderne Antigone" in the *Hebbel-Jahrbuch* 1961) deals with a number of the controversial issues raised in recent criticism of it. He combats the view of the heroine's moral inferiority to Herzog Ernst (stated for example by Wittkowski, in *Menschenbild und Tragik in Hebbels Agnes Bernauer.* Germanisch-Romanische Monatsschrift N.F. VIII [1958]); he also denies central importance to the notion of a "Tragödie der Schönheit"—while recognising the poetic value of the opening scenes where it prevails, and perceiving the dominant influence on Albrecht of Agnes's beauty as the expression of an inner perfection. In a suggestive analysis of Hebbel's dramatic technique in this play Kreuzer points out the appropriateness of its structure to the diametrical opposition between Agnes and Herzog Ernst, and briefly indicates a further reflection of contrasts in the language and imagery[21]; the dramatic importance of biblical elements here is rightly emphasised. This critic formulates the central theme of the drama as the conflict between two realms: the external world of historical order, forming the bulwark of humanity against chaos, and the world of inner values, testifying to its spiritual essence. In this kind of conflict the antagonists are compelled by conscience to become murderers or victims; thus, he contends, Hebbel presented a metaphysical basis of tragedy. He was not offering a nihilistic interpretation, nor was he tied to any specific concept of the state, but was convinced of an absolute law which shows itself absolute even to the cleavage of its own substance. The analysis of *Agnes Bernauer* is followed by brief observations on some treatments of the Antigone theme in ancient and modern times which reveal different implications from those of Hebbel's drama.

This approach to **Agnes Bernauer** has something in common with the standpoint of Gerhard Fricke's essay in the *Hebbel-Jahrbuch* of 1951[22] with its insistence on the tragic nature of the opposition between absolute and relative values ("die Tragödie des unbedingten Daseins inmitten einer durch und durch bedingten Welt", *Studien,* p. 348). And it is this latter critic who offers a possible explanation of the revival of interest in **Agnes Bernauer,** when he concludes that acceptance of the necessity to renounce any hope of the absolute in this world of imperfection and limitation is "der zugleich tragische und fromme Sinn" of this tragedy, and that it is this meaning which makes it the most positive of Hebbel's works, and the one which has the most profound message for our day.

A study of this same play by Paul Gerhard Klussmann[23] reveals a more empirical approach. This writer sets out from a detailed analysis of the dramatic structure, and considers the implications of the balance which Hebbel achieved by this means. In particular he emphasises the two-sidedness of both the forces governing the tragic action-love (beauty) and the state (community)—and discerns in the limitation of their opposition to one another a basis for understanding, and thus the recognition of a possible unity. It is in this sense that the final words of Agnes are interpreted.

While **Agnes Bernauer** has thus been the centre of divergent views on metaphysical implications, it has also called forth, as has been seen, differing verdicts on its style and language. In this respect, again, the drama occupies a special position among the later works, and presents interesting material for stylistic analysis. Other plays have also been considered from this point of view. *Hebbel in neuer Sicht* contains a study by Martin Stern of the central symbol in **Maria Magdalena** which offers an interesting and detailed analysis of the dominant metaphors and images in this play, relating them both to the inner action and to Hebbel's own spiritual experience[24], and reaching the conclusion that in their totality they reveal antithesis as the true form of this experience. Another study of Hebbel's language in this collection attempts a general synthesis (Marie Luise Gansberg's *Zur Sprache in Hebbels Dramen*), relating the variations in his style to the complex historical situation in the fourth decade of the century and citing relevant entries in the *Tagebücher*. The writer sees Hebbel as confronted with the stylistic dilemma of iambic verse drama in the mid-century, and seeking to resolve it by a compromise between the classical tradition and the realist trend—a compromise which in her view succeeds to a considerable extent in **Herodes und Mariamne** and **Die Nibelungen.** The analysis of individual passages

and the suggested stylistic comparisons with other dramatists contain many perceptive observations, but the governing thesis of adjustment to the contemporary situation results in an unsympathetic attitude towards the remarkable style and verse patterns of **Gyges und sein Ring,** and some lack of appreciation of the dramatic effect of syntactical idiosyncrasies. The suggestion—based on a comparison of a passage from **Die Nibelungen** with one from *Wallensteins Tod*—that Hebbel's imagery, in contrast to that of Schiller, is better suited to the study than the stage leads to the further suggestion that it is more appropriate to lyric than to drama. In this connection reference may be made to an English investigation of Hebbel's poetic language as an organic whole[25], which attempts an analysis of him as a creative linguistic artist, and compares his own lyrical expression of living in a shifting world with the expression of duality of experience by his dramatic characters.

The revival of interest in Hebbel's lyrical poetry is reflected in *Hebbel in neuer Sicht,* in the form of a study by Fritz Martini entitled *Der Lyriker Hebbel. Theorie und Gedicht.* Here too we find an estimate of the poet in relation to the contemporary situation—seen in this instance as a state of contradiction between established form and type and the changed outlook of the time. Martini's view is a reflection of the general picture offered in his work *Deutsche Literatur im bürgerlichen Realismus 1842-1848* (Stuttgart 1962) from which this essay is derived in substance. He sees Hebbel's particular achievement as being the recreating of inherited forms and language in a new objectivity, and finds the essence of his lyric poetry in its intertwining of opposites. Much of the essay is devoted to this kind of theoretical analysis; but there are also many acute and perceptive comments on the distinctive features of the poet's practice, such as the sense for plasticity of language, rhythmic structure and concentrated form. Only a small proportion of Hebbel's total output takes high rank in this critic's estimation. It includes neither the ballads nor any of the other narrative poems, all of which he regards as governed by contemporary taste and style, and consists almost entirely of those lyrics in which the feeling self, experiencing a concrete situation, apprehends the infinite. At the same time there is unquestioning recognition of the whole body of lyric poetry as vital evidence in any view of Hebbel that is not to be one-sided.

For Martini, Hebbel's productive period as a lyric poet is from 1836 to 1848; an earlier study had selected a still shorter one, the four years from 1836 to 1840—with a possible extension to 1843. The essay *Hebbel als Lyriker* by Ivo Braak, which appeared in the *Hebbel-Jahrbuch* for 1954, contained a striking description of the distinctive features of *Nachtlied* (which is quoted by Martini). The theme of this essay is formulated in an initial question: was Hebbel a true lyric poet? The answer, reached after delicate analysis of a few poems chosen for their characteristic aspects, is an affirmative; in these poems, all "in diesem, ihm allein eigenen Ton", the poet, Braak avers, achieved a perfect whole.

A wider view of Hebbel's development as a lyrist is given by Heinz Stolte in an essay entitled *Ahne das Wunder der Form!*—a quotation from the distich *Die Form*—which appeared in the *Hebbel-Jahrbuch* for 1961. The sub-title of this essay is *Zur lyrischen Biographie Friedrich Hebbels,* and the writer, while recognising differences of achievement in different periods, is more concerned to show the basic features which constantly recur, and to describe the individual structure of the poet's experience of the world, the "inner form" of his lyrical poetry. Dualism, or the tension of opposites, is seen as its basis; ambivalence—here explained as the alternation of negative and positive interpretation of the conflict between the individual and the cosmos—as its characteristic mode. Perceptive analyses of individual poems support Stolte's exposition of the phases of Hebbel's development as a lyric poet; and he shows himself aware that some of the late poems can well stand beside those of the earlier years whose quality is more generally acknowledged. In some acute comparisons he traces successive stages in the treatment of a basic theme, and thereby illuminates Hebbel's outlook and his development alike.

Appreciation of the importance of the evidence afforded by Hebbel's lyric poetry about his view of life may thus be seen to have increased in Germany in recent years. The poet's recording of "the swift movements of apprehension which convince him of his participation in a continuing process and a larger world"[26] may well have come to seem more than ever important by contrast with the nihilist view.

The temptation to consider Hebbel's prose tales and his early comedy **Der Diamant** as evidence for a complete pessimism is resisted in two essays published in *Hebbel in neuer Sicht*[27]. Though each of the writers recognises the fundamental elements of unsolved paradox and of grim realism, neither considers these works entirely in isolation, but rather as forming the reverse of the coin of tragedy. Ingrid Kreuzer views the tales as representing an early and important stage in the development of Hebbel's outlook on the world, citing his own confession that he turned to comedy for the relief of an overcharged spirit, and found it in the portrayal of the senseless absurdity of men and things[28]. With a sharp eye for difference as well as similarity, she distinguishes between the tales based on unexpected situation and those based on fixed character, and notes the consequent variations in structure and *tempo* of the narrative; attributing the general disapproval of the tales in part to their merciless objectivity, she suggests interesting links with the short story and other similar forms in the

twentieth century. Wolfgang Hecht draws attention to the early date of Hebbel's preoccupation with comedies and comic tales, and examines **Der Diamant** as a stage in his development towards the goal of tragedy. Emphasis is laid on its intimate association with Hebbel's theory of comedy, and on the significance of the two-fold setting in two contrasted worlds. The reflection of this duality in the structure of the play is duly pointed out—a parallel with **Judith** might well be drawn in this respect, even to the filling of the fourth act by the collision of opposites—and the contrast in dimension of the two sets of figures is seen in relation to Hebbel's concept of reality. In attempting an answer to the fundamental question of values raised by the comedy, this critic affirms that both a nihilistic and an optimistic trend can be discerned. His argument rests largely on a subtle analysis of the characters of the Prince and the Princess, and their function in the drama. For each of them the experience of love has metaphysical implications, and their response to it has ethical value; the Prince in particular thus offers a counterweight to the "Nichtigkeit der Welt" presented through the action of the comedy. At the same time, both are potentially tragic figures; and Hecht sees **Der Diamant** as a mixed form of drama, representing at least in some respects a development towards tragi-comedy[29].

To this latter aspect of Hebbel's work a study by Horst Oppel had already drawn attention[30]. Without embarking on rehabilitation of a play unfavourably regarded by the majority of critics, the writer attempts to analyse its features and to relate them to the later development of tragi-comedy as an essential means of expressing social criticism. He insists that it was Hebbel's intention to prove that the grim incident of the play was not an isolated one, but represented the general course of things; that the play was a deliberate attempt to reproduce actual life, unalloyed, in its senseless absurdity[31]. As a corollary, he affirms that the figures are types elucidating sociological or psychological positions. Greater interest perhaps attaches to the analysis of the technique of the play: the conventions of the "Maskenspiel" and the procedure of cross-examination are seen as the basic elements in a classical structure, within which marionette-like figures have severely restricted possibilities of movement. The contrast with **Herodes und Mariamne** is emphasised; from the petty purposes and mean intentions of the *Trauerspiel in Sizilien,* Hebbel passed to the driving forces and elemental passions, and thus regained his own true sphere.

Essays on Hebbel's latest finished dramas complete the collection *Hebbel in neuer Sicht: Hebbels "Gyges und sein Ring" (im Rahmen der Stoffgeschichte)* by Helmut Kreuzer, partly based on his earlier article on the unity of conception in this play (*Hebbel-Jahrbuch* 1958,) and *Hebbels Nibelungen—ein deutsches Trauerspiel* by Jost Hermand. Kreuzer's perceptive analysis of the characters and their problems—especially in respect of Kandaules many subtle points are noted—leads him to a conclusion which is at variance with some recent interpretations. He rejects the suggestion that Rhodope feels love for Gyges and that this supplies an additional motive for her death[32]; equally he combats the view that Kandaules arrives at any true understanding in the end. In his own earlier essay Kreuzer had already argued against some general interpretations of the play: the opposition of progressive and reactionary, the contrast of sin and ideal standard (or the combination of these two interpretations into an insoluble contradiction). He had set out the governing factors as polarity and rhythm— the relation of the sexes, the notions of time, the concepts of government and community forming a whole, in which no individual figure has a true understanding of connections. The later article enlarges the argument considerably, and points to the unfolding of beauty and nobility in human relations and the positive ethical aspects of the characters as being the form of "tragic reconciliation" offered in this drama.

Kreuzer's view differs from that of Heinz Stolte in more than the interpretation of Rhodope's relation to Gyges. Stolte's emphasis is on progress as the core of the drama and, through the death of Kandaules and of Rhodope, the attainment of a new stage of development as its conclusion. He sees the symbol of the ring as relating also to a prefound problem of humanity today, arguing that in its completeness of control over all private hidden life it represents the outstanding danger of our present culture.

Gyges und sein Ring is the key illustration to a lengthy article by Bert Nagel in the *Hebbel-Jahrbuch* of 1962[33]. Analysis of the play occupies approximately one third of the whole, and in company with the other major dramas *Gyges* also serves at intervals to support the general assessment of Hebbel's presentation of the tragic individual. Nagel agrees with Liepe in recognising a religious stamp in Hebbel's work, and in regarding polarity as its characteristic feature. He also stresses the basic importance of the theme "Achtung vor dem Menschenbild". *Gyges und sein Ring* appears to him to make the central themes of Hebbel's work completely clear: the destructive power of ideologies, or fixity of tragic characters (particular instances are Meister Anton, Mariamne, Rhodope); the balance of responsibility between a pair of partners (and the alternation of sympathy thereby aroused); the choice of unusual incident, persons, and conjunction of circumstances. He points to the element of monologue—even in scenes cast in the form of dialogue—and relates it to the isolation, or self-imprisonment, of the tragic characters. Nagel does not accept the argument for unity of conception in relation to *Gyges und sein Ring,* and contends that there is here, as elsewhere in Hebbel's tragedies, a change of standpoint—citing the poet's own statement

(in a letter of 14 Dec. 1854 to Friedrich von Uechtritz) that it was only on completion of the work that the notion of all-compelling "Sitte" arose in his mind, as an island rises out of the ocean. The tragic aspect of Gyges' fate is recognised, and it is argued that in this play there is an open end, since Rhodope's death can be variously interpreted.

Nagel quotes extensively from other critics, both on the general theme and on the particular instance, and it is not always easy to separate the track of his own argument. But in his insistence that Hebbel here presented order as the basis of existence, and in his advocacy of an unprejudiced and close examination of the drama itself he makes two important points; and he gives an interesting analysis of the characters and their motives.

Jost Hermand sets Hebbel's *Nibelungen* tragedy in relation to other treatments of the theme (by Fouqué, Raupach[34], Wagner) and to his own political development after 1848. Whether the connection with his political thinking does very much to explain Hebbel's abiding interest in the subject and his immense labour on the trilogy may perhaps be doubted; but the discussion of characters and technique is acute and stimulating, as is the recognition that Hebbel's particular contribution of psychological interpretation constitutes both the strength and the weakness of the drama. A concise survey of the changing attitudes of critics towards *Die Nibelungen* leads to Jost Hermand's own conclusion, that the positive values, the concept of something absolute above the self which can be apprehended, convincingly refute the nihilist interpretation favoured by some noted modern critics.

It is evident that in this last decade a greater emphasis has been laid on the interpretation of individual works; in this respect criticism of Hebbel has conformed to a general tendency. Specific discussions of the plays, above all of *Judith, Herodes und Mariamne, Agnes Bernauer* and *Gyges und sein Ring* (each of which has been the subject of at least four, in some cases five or six separate and substantial articles) have taken their place beside studies of more general themes; a similar situation, though in a minor way, exists in respect of lyric and prose tales. Perhaps too it may be said that with the noticeable movement against the extreme pessimist view, German and earlier English criticism are more in accord than was the case some thirty years ago[35]. But the nihilist view is still represented, and indeed forms a ground with some critics for regarding Hebbel as a fore-runner of our age, in presenting life as an insoluble contradiction, destructive of any illusion of harmony. Between the two positions lies a considerable stretch of no-man's-land. Ambivalence or ambiguity is seen as the distinctive feature of Hebbel's outlook—a view which can easily be supported by conflicting entries in his diary or statements in his letters, if there is inadequate recognition of the fact that changing circumstances or successive moods are liable to be reflected in a differing emphasis on differing aspects of the artist's world. A more radical view of these discrepancies is stated by Benno von Wiese, who regards them as the expression of a dialectic process which seeks the unity of opposites in all the variables of life, "also noch mitten im Widersprüchlichen" (*Der Tragiker Friedrich Hebbel. Hebbel-Jahrbuch* 1963). It is in the paradox of the unity of opposites that this critic sees the essence of Hebbel's tragic presentation of the individual in relation to history; adding, with reference to **Herodes und Mariamne,** that the dramatist here gives us "einen dichterischen Einblick in das Beunruhigende aller Geschichte" and embodies the idea that "gerade die hohen Werte den Untergang des Menschen herausfordern"[36].

The effort to fit Hebbel's picture of the world to the present uncertainties and dissolving views has been a conspicuous feature of the criticism of this decade. It has led to a re-examination of the biographical documents as well as of his individual works, and the process has produced much stimulating commentary. But it has in some measure led to an over-emphasis on ambiguity of outlook, matching an earlier over-emphasis on a theory of tragedy. It may perhaps be permissible to hope that in the next decade attention will again be focussed—as it has been in a few of the major contributions of this one—on the art of the poet and the power of his imagination. While Hebbel, as we are now able to see, gave a characteristic and historically important turn to the presentation of the inner self—the semiconscious actor in the drama of existence—the force of his greater works still lies in the portrayal of remarkable persons in crucial situations. In his ability to make them live, on the stage and in the mind and memory, he can bear comparison with all but the greatest of those who have served the tragic Muse.

Notes

1. Such as *Werke,* ed. W. Vontin, 2 vols., Hamburg, Hoffmann und Campe Verlag, 1958; *Werke,* ed. H. L. Geiger, 2 vols., Berlin and Darmstadt, Tempel, 1961; *Werke* (Jubiläumsausgabe), ed. H. Stolte, 2 vols., Hamburg, Standard-Verlag, 1963; *Gesammelte Werke,* with Introduction by Anni Meetz, 2 vols., Gütersloh, Bertelsmann [1963].

2. I: München, Carl Hanser Verlag, 1963; II: 1964.

3. *Agnes Bernauer.* Ed. with Introduction by Mary Wiesener-Garland and Notes by M. B. Evans. London: Harrap 1953; *Agnes Bernauer.* Ed. with Introduction and Notes by Gillian Rodger, London and Edinburgh: Thomas Nelson and Sons 1961.

4. *Agnes Bernauer.* Con Introduzione e commenti da Ida Barbiere. Firenze 1955.

5. *Agnes Bernauer.* Mit einem Essay von Hermann Glaser. Frankfurt/Main-Berlin, Verlag Ullstein, 1964 [= *Ullstein Buch* Nr. 5020.]

6. See below, pp. 118 f.

7. Translations of Hebbel's works are a separate subject. For interesting indications of their unusual spread see the bibliographical material set out by Ludwig Koopmann in the *Hebbel-Jahrbuch* for 1957.

8. *Aufzeichnungen aus meinem Leben.* Mit Anmerkungen und einem Nachwort versehen von W. Schiller. Reclams Universal-Bibliothek, Nr. 48, 1961.

9. *Neue Hebbel-Briefe.* Neumünster, Karl Wachholtz Verlag, 1963 = *Kieler Studien zur deutschen Literaturgeschichte* 1.

10. A brief extension of the *Neue Hebbel-Briefe* is to be found in an article by Anni Meetz, in Nordelbingen: *Hebbel und Prinzess Marie von Sayn-Wittgenstein.* Heide, Boyens und Co. 1964 = *Beiträge zur Heimatforschung in Schleswig-Holstein, Hamburg und Lübeck* 33.

11. *Beiträge zur Literatur- und Geistesgeschichte.* Neumünster: Karl Wachholtz Verlag 1963 = *Kieler Studien zur deutschen Literaturgeschichte* 2.

12. Although two of these articles appeared somewhat earlier (1951 and 1952) they are so closely connected with the later ones that they cannot be disregarded here.

13. Reprinted in *Studien und Interpretationen.* Frankfurt/Main: Hans F. Menck Verlag 1956, as is also the essay *Gedanken zu Hebbels Judith,* first published in the *Hebbel-Jahrbuch* 1953. For Fricke's analysis of *Agnes Bernauer* in this volume see below, p. 119.

14. *Revelation-scenes in the plays of Friedrich Hebbel.* In: The Germanic Review 28,1 (1953). This writer's study *Friedrich Hebbel's Conception of Movement in the Absolute and in History* had appeared in 1952.

15. *Judith: Götze aus Erz und Ton* (1960).

16. *Hebbels "Herodes und Mariamne"* (originally published in the *Hebbel-Jahrbuch* 1949/50) in: *Form und Bedeutung.* Stuttgart: Ernst Klett Verlag 1957.

17. The Spanish version of this essay appeared in a substantial centenary volume issued under the aegis of Ilse Brugge by the University of La Plata: *Friedrich Hebbel 1813-1863.* Homenaje del Instituto de Literatura Alemana, La Plata 1963, which also contains a version of Benno von Wiese's *Fes-*

tvortrag and a number of other essays (translated or original), a brief survey of some critical works on Hebbel, and a chronological table.

18. *Das Paradoxe als Grundstruktur Hebbelschen Denkens* (originally published in the *Hebbel-Jahrbuch*1952).

19. *Herodes und Mariamne.* In: *Das deutsche Drama vom Barock bis zur Gegenwart. Interpretationen.* Ed. B. von Wiese. II, Düsseldorf 1958 (2nd ed. 1960).

20. *Mariamne's Motives in Hebbel's Herodes und Mariamne.* In: Modern Language Review 55,2 (1960).

21. Interesting parallels can be found in the Introduction to the edition by Gillian Rodger. See above, p. 111.

22. *Hebbels "Agnes Bernauer",* reprinted in *Studien und Interpretationen,* ed. cit.

23. In *Das deutsche Drama vom Barock bis zur Gegenwart. Interpretationen.* II, ed. cit.

24. The aspect of personal experience is stressed by Kurt May in an essay *Hebbels Maria Magdalene* (In: *Form und Bedeutung,* ed. cit.).

25. Patricia M. Boswell: *A Study of Friedrich Hebbel's poetic language with special reference to the use of imagery and symbols.* M. A. thesis, London 1963.

26. *Poems.* Selected and edited by Edna Purdie, ed. cit., Introduction, p. xviii.

27. Ingrid Kreuzer, *Hebbel als Novellist*; Wolfgang Hecht, *Hebbels "Diamant".*

28. An essay by Kurt Esselbrügge, *Hebbel und der Humor (Hebbel-Jahrbuch* 1955) gives a comprehensive sketch of the different forms of Hebbel's expression of the comic.

29. A highly abstract analysis of the effort to present the contradictoriness of existence in this comedy is the basis of an article by Karlheinz Schulz-Streeck: *Friedrich Hebbels "Der Diamant" als metaphysische Komödie. Hebbel-Jahrbuch* 1957). This critic considers that Hebbel created a new kind of comedy, giving symbolic form to that which cannot be logically understood—"der Sinn des Seins".

30. *Hebbels Tragikomödie "Ein Trauerspiel in Sizilien".* In: *Gedenkschrift für F. J. Schneider.* Weimar: Hermann Böhlaus Nachfolger 1956.

31. Karl S. Guthke, on the other hand *(Hebbels "Trauerspiel in Sizilien". (Zur Frage der Gattung), Hebbel-Jahrbuch* 1957) sets out from an analysis of principles governing this *genre,* and discusses both Hebbel's own theoretical statements and his play in the light of them. His analysis leads to the conclusion that Hebbel was on the way to tragicomedy as an art-form, achieving in some respects the double perspective characteristic of this form, but that his characters do not adequately show the mixture of comic and tragic elements within themselves. For this critic *Ein Trauerspiel in Sizilien* belongs to the category of satire, which he regards as the form of mixture most congenial to Hebbel.

32. Among those maintaining this view is Heinz Stolte in: *Hebbels "Gyges und sein Ring" im Lichte historischer Erfahrungen (Hebbel-Jahrbuch* 1959).

33. *Die Tragik des Menschen in Hebbels Dichtung. Zum Verständnis der Tragödie "Gyges und sein Ring"*

34. A comparison of the dramas by Raupach and Hebbel is made in an article by Jean M. Leaver: *The first performances of Hebbel's Genoveva and Nibelungen dramas, and their connection with Ernst Raupach's dramas on the same subjects.* In: Modern Language Review 55 (1960). Carlo Grünanger traces the theme in modern times in *La Poesia dei Nibelunghi* (Acme V,1 (1952); reprinted in *Scritti minori di letteratura tedesca,* ed. cit.).

35. The present writer's own conclusion that Hebbel "arrived, after great travail, at a belief in the abiding value of effort" (E. Purdie: *Friedrich Hebbel. A Study of his Life and Work.* Oxford University Press, London, 1932, p. 269) is not very far removed from that of Wolfgang Liepe: "In allen Stadien seiner dichterischen Entwicklung hat die Idee des Daseins als sittlicher Aufgabe das dramatische Werk Hebbels davor bewahrt, in die Tragödie des Nihilismus abzugleiten" (*Beiträge,* ed. cit., p. 381).

36. That the notion thus couched in ethical and metaphysical terms may have a close parallel in scientific thought in the early nineteenth century is a suggestion that I have made elsewhere (*Friedrich Hebbel,* ed. cit., pp. 261f.).

Von Günter E. Salter (essay date 1969)

SOURCE: Salter, Von Günter E. "Friedrich Hebbel's Conception of God." *Hebbel-Jahrbuch 1969* (1969): 122-43.

[*In the following essay, Salter elucidates Hebbel's conception of God as evinced in his work.*]

The main difficulty in developing an understanding of Friedrich Hebbel's conception of God is not a lack of pertinent remarks by the poet, but it rather lies in the apparent inconsistency and contradiction of the many aphorisms and thoughts relative to the subject matter which abound in his diary and letters. A rather cursory examination of these writings would tend to lend credence to the verdict of some critics who in searching for a philosophical system expounded in the diary find the aphorisms to be without coherence, indicative of a thought process whose momentary effusions coexist in desultory isolation. Peter Michelsen who embraces this for the poet somewhat less than flattering view attempts to substantiate his judgement with the following anecdote in which he simultaneously takes issue with the naive interpretation of the incident by its narrator, Erich Kulke. In his "Erinnerungen an Friedrich Hebbel" Kulke reports on what seemed to him the poet's loss of memory:

> Thus he wanted to cite to me once a passage from his poem '*Auf dem Meer*' and quoted: 'There is no universal dying' (es gibt kein allgemeines Sterben), while the passage in question asserted the exact opposite: 'Man does not die an individual death' (man kann nicht einzeln sterben)[1].

This incident does not by any means suggest to Michelsen a lapse in memory which possibly could explain a less than accurate rendition of the original formulation; but the complete reversal of sense which turns a once held conviction in such a central question into its very antithesis indicates a weakness in Hebbel's thought process and affirms to this critic the belief that the aphorisms are indeed unconnected mental issues which do not follow a recognizable pattern nor do they formulate a consistent philosophy. Other critics hold that Hebbel's conception of God as expressed in the diary and letters is free of contradiction, and that his aphorisms present a uniform, lucid, compatible idea of a Supreme Being. The truth, as so often is the case, lies somewhere between these two extreme viewpoints.

It must be stated at the outset that here we are faced with a unique conception of God. Unless one succumbs to the temptation of forcing Hebbel's aphorisms onto Procrustes' bed, any attempt to fit his thoughts to the traditional concept of a Judaic, Christian, Pantheistic, Deistic, or Pagan God must, of necessity, end in failure and contradiction and lead to an apparently justified charge of incoherence and inconsistency. An objective examination of Hebbel's philosophy, however, will reveal that his God exhibits traits which are characteristic of all of these Gods; yet he is none of these entirely or exclusively. Once this point has been understood, a major obstacle in comprehending Hebbel's beliefs has been overcome, although there still remains a good deal of obscurity and ambiguity. Hebbel appears to be talking about different entities when he mentions God and the Divine (Gott und das Göttliche). Bearing this in mind, it can be asserted with a certain degree of assurance that Hebbel's religious thoughts are entirely consistent when they refer to the Divine as the supreme cosmic power and the ultimate objective value of the world; they appear contradictory when the poet speaks of God[2].

It shall be the objective of this paper, based on Hebbel's diary and letters, to develop his conception of God, trace traditional concepts in his aphorisms, explore any original Hebbelian thought, point out and—if possible—explain apparent contradictions, and finally conclude whether Hebbel's God is the "Hausvater" who decrees, guides, and directs, meting out deserved rewards and punishment according to his absolute will and power, limiting man's free will and freedom of choice, and reserving to himself the right of divine, direct, and universal intervention.

There can be no doubt that Friedrich Hebbel was a religious, pious, and devout man, although not in a traditional ecclesiastical sense. Until he reached the age of fourteen years he received a strict religious education. Nightly prayers and Bible reading were a matter of habit in the family and left their imprint upon Hebbel throughout his life. How lasting an impression his childhood prayers made, taught by a Christian mother who endeavored to instill into young Friedrich a feeling of reverence toward and dependence upon a God who supervises man's every activity, becomes evident when such relatively insignificant experiences of years gone by force their way, seemingly unprovoked, into his consciousness:

> When I was still a little child and my mother put a clean shirt on me, I was always asked on such an occasion to say this little prayer: 'Das walte Gott, Vater, Sohn und heiliger Geist!' Tonight when I tired of reading Macbeth, this suddenly came to my mind[3].

Hebbel's knowledge of the Scripture, both in scope and accuracy, is astounding for a layman, revealing the thorough and frequent instructions he did receive in Bible study during the time of his youth. Although given to exaggeration, he obviously stated a fact when in his correspondence with Pfarrer Luck in response to the cleric's exhortation to read the Bible he offered the reply that not only had he memorized half the Scripture since he was a child, but that most of the Protestant and Catholic legends of importance were also known to him[4]. In spite of the concentrated efforts of his mentors, Hebbel preserved his independence of thought; and while still almost a child, fourteen years of age, he turned his back on church dogma and could imagine God only as a poet whose creations gladden the hearts of men[5]. Of course, he did not forget his childhood Scripture lessons nor Biblical parlance in which he occasionally liked to indulge, exhibiting inspired touches of oblique humor. Thus he wrote to Elise Lensing:

> I do not know how everything will come out; however, permit me to parody a Bible verse: God who clothes the lilies of the field (Lewald and his innocent clique)

and who feeds the sparrows under the heavens (Gutzkow and Wienbarg), he will, of this I am sure, not forget to take care of me[6].

To arrive at a clear conception of God which satisfies both his intellect and feeling is a problem which occupied Hebbel all of his life as even a superficial study of his diary and letters will indicate. These writings contain about 225 direct references to God and the Divine in addition to more than 1100 instances of mentioning various other religious terms and concepts. Yet nowhere does God emerge as a clearly defined entity, nor do the aphorisms indicate an increasing clarity of concept as Hebbel grows older. The groping attempts at precise formulation are apparent in the earlier years as they are in the later ones; and they are, at times, contradictory. In order to be fair to Hebbel and to answer his severe critics, it must be stated that one cannot make the same demands on a diary of this nature as could be made on a scientific, scholarly thesis where inconsistency and contradiction are not to be tolerated. The diary served Hebbel as a sounding-board for his ideas; it was necessary for him as a medium of discussion not only between human beings, but also between him and God with whom he wrestled without ceasing[7]. Thus we find in his diary a multitude of aspects and characteristics of the great Absolute which cannot be fathomed by the limited human comprehension in its entirety; and that is the reason why Hebbel, although rejecting Christian belief, leaves room for faith. He scoffs at those who would not accept anything unless substantiated by incontrovertible proof: "Proof! Who is able to prove everything! It is for this very reason that the faith of man has enthroned a God to reign over the world, not an attorney-at-law[8]."

Notwithstanding some rather caustic remarks bordering on irreverence and blasphemy which shall be discussed in a later paragraph, Hebbel is sincere in assuring Pfarrer Luck that his relationship to religion is not a hostile one[9]. Indeed, time and again Hebbel has called upon a personal God in moments of distress, in critical situations, in hours of despair, or in instants of happiness and confidence, choosing the Christian form of prayer which repeatedly has been recorded verbatim in his diary:

> God, thou seest my heart; thou knowest that it hides no vain wishes; that I only desire those things which I must desire, if I am to remain man among men; thou further knowest that I have often wrangled with thee about my lot simply because of the uncertain future which faces me; do assist me[10]!

Upon receipt of the notification that the King of Denmark has granted him a travel stipend, Hebbel commits the following prayer to paper:

> Now, Eternal Father in Heaven, who hast not regarded the impotent anger of this foolish, sick man, but instead in thy grace hast built for me a bridge into the future

and given me a pledge of success, I feel the magnitude of thy grace and the extent of my responsibility; I shall strive earnestly[11].

And a week later when the grant was officially confirmed by the appropriate agency, he prays:

> Thanks be to thee, my Heavenly Father, that thou hast poured out the abundance of thy grace upon the undeserving one; this gives me confidence that even I shall reach my goal[12].

While working on *Genoveva* with good success he notes:

> I do not deserve it, but God is infinitely gracious to me . . . Thanks, deepest thanks to the Eternal One[13].

Many more diary entries such as: ". . . to depend on God in everything"[14], ". . . if God only directs my path"[15], ". . . the grace of God is visibly about me"[16], bear testimony of the poet's intuitively felt dependence upon a God whom he addresses in traditional Christian terms and manner. The fervor of his prayer, the almost palpable sincerity, the profundity of unfeigned emotion precludes any suspicion that Hebbel engaged in mere formality through habit and training.

Were our examination to stop at this point, Friedrich Hebbel would appear to be a steadfast Christian in the tradition of his friends Pfarrer Luck or Fritz Uechtritz. Such a deduction is of course contrary to the facts. But it is true that Hebbel had an innate piety which to him was the basic emotion governing the relationship of the individual to the Absolute, a conviction which he expressed in his drama *Moloch* by identifying piety toward the Highest Powers as the root of the world. That this piety should be lacking in any individual seemed inconceivable to him; only its expression would differ from timid hope to confident assurance[17]. We have seen how Hebbel engaged in prayers of supplication and thanksgiving for the realization of particular gifts he had hoped for. Yet it is his piety which often manifests itself spontaneously in feelings of contentment and gratitude. After a visit with two friends Hebbel relives a moment of spontaneous piety and recollects:

> Heute mit Herrn Radeker und Hauer auf dem Petriturm. Himmlischer Frühlingsmittag. Die Stadt, sich herausschälend aus dem Rauch. Das Glockenspiel: Wachet auf, ruft uns die Stimme! Christliche Empfindungen. "Werdet nur alle gut—dacht' ich—dadurch zwingt ihr Gott, euch glücklich zu machen[18]."

The completion of his first drama *Judith* fills Hebbel with a feeling of gratitude for God's assistance in this venture. He recalls the many instants of anger and rebellion and promises not to be ungrateful anymore toward the "Eternal One"[19]. In moments of tenderness and cognizance of the material and spiritual comforts he possessed in Elise Lensing, Hebbel confesses his lack of appreciation of God's goodness, tells of thanksgiving on bended knee and resolves henceforth to accord more gratefulness to the Highest Power[20].

If the image of God emerging from the foregoing remarks is hard to reconcile with Hebbel's anti-Christian statement and anti-anthropomorphous concept of God, his reference to heaven and hell is entirely inconsistent with his conception of the universe. He states:

> The hell of the unbelievers will be easy to endure, as it will offer them proof of heaven and God whose existence they once doubted[21].

Yet according to Hebbel, the individual form—man—has become separated from the Whole; and it is its ultimate and highest destiny to be reunited through submergence with the Absolute[22]. In this "Weltbild" there is no room for a heaven or a hell, places of metaphysical reward or punishment.

While it can be stated unequivocally that Friedrich Hebbel was a religious man, it can be asserted with equal assurance that he was decidedly a Non-Christian. According to the *Eckermann Gespräche,* Goethe once said of himself: "Ich bin kein Unchrist, auch kein Antichrist, aber entschiedener Nichtchrist." The same applies to Hebbel. He definitely believes in a God, however vague and nebulous his conception of him might be; but in Christ he only sees the historic personality, one religion founder among many, a wise man and teacher of highest ethical and moral principles to be sure, but no Savior whose vicarious atonement accomplished the reconciliation between God and man to heal the rift occasioned by original sin. Hebbel rejected the idea of a mediator as unnecessary and superfluous. He believed that the idea of God is necessarily inherent in man. Every man knows of God, experiences God. Consequently, the belief in God is possible on a direct, immediate basis; and the intermediary faith which leans on the authority of Christ is a substitute. Thus Hebbel calls Christianity as such a substitute[23]. What Hebbel fails to realize in this argument is that his conclusion was no point of contention to begin with. The Christian does not need Christ to believe in God—according to the Bible even the devils believe on him—but to secure his salvation, an issue which Hebbel completely overlooked. In his effort to deny the deity of Christ, Hebbel makes the following statement:

> Was alles zugleich ist oder doch seyn soll, kann nicht dargestellt werden, darum kein Christus[24].

The conclusion is not a valid one, because the premise is fallacious. According to Christian belief, Christ divested himself of his deity while in the flesh and became man among men, however without sin. Since Hebbel claimed a thorough knowledge of the Scripture, it is hard to understand that he should have overlooked so important a point that Christ was not "zugleich" God and man. And while intellectually he rejected Christianity as an illogical concept which could not stand the test of reason, emotionally he yearned for the comfort and reassurance that such a belief could offer:

> O könnt' ich mit euch allen, die ihr begraben seid und in eurer Höhle von Staub einem fröhlichen Erwachen entgegenschlaft, könnte ich mit euch im Glauben an einen Erlöser Jesus Christus Brüderschaft machen[25].

The Christian conception of God appeared to Hebbel too simplified and lacking in intellectual stimulation. He questions the possibility of returning to doctrinal faith once a real confrontation has occurred between the Absolute and man. An individual will not ineluctably become an evangelist or Christ himself upon initially perceiving a breath of the Deity; neither will he endeavor to find additional revelation and fulfilment in the catechism or the Golden Calf[26]. To accept church dogma unquestioningly instead of searching for ultimate truths on an individual basis smacks of intellectual cowardice and inertia: Cowardice, because many an individual believes in God, in immortality, for the simple reason that he dares not oppose such colossal ideas[27]; inertia, as man gains a conception of God more readily than of himself (Der Mensch denkt sich leichter einen Gott als sich selbst)[28]. Hebbel cannot accept an established religion offering him a God of clearly outlined properties and characteristics, cast in a role of a performer with specified rules of conduct and predictable actions. God is too immense an entity to be corseted by human imagination; that is why all existing religions are merely a product of man's gullability and refusal to wrestle with the momentous problem of recognizing God. Hebbel formulates this thought as follows:

> For millenia the unknown artist attempts to sculpture a God. The instant a quaint chip of marble falls under his chisel we pursue it exclaiming: there He is! How will we feel when on that day in the future THE GOD will stand before us in all his splendor[29]?

The diary and letters make it unmistakably clear that Hebbel does not lay claim to infallibility in his conception of God; he only asserts his prerogative to develop this conception independently and impute as much truth and power to the endresult of his efforts as defenders of ecclesiastical doctrine and dogma do to their particular conceptions; perfect knowledge is an impossibility. The whole Cosmos proclaims, that man will not see the heart of the world (das Herz der Welt) just as he can never see his own heart, and that he possesses the most sacred right to interpret in his own way the omnipotent heartbeat which he perceives[30]. Hebbel is not concerned that individual interpretation, as in his own case, may contain contradiction and error. God is not to be under-stood by intellect alone, nor comprehended solely by the spirit, nor fathomed exclusively through emotions. He must be perceived by the total personality in a combined process of rational and mystical experience, for truth exists at that point where knowledge and faith intersect. Religion is man's capability not to resolve contradictions, but to deny them[31].

Hebbel was not willing to extend the tolerance which he demanded for his own views to those of other people. It was a source of constant irritation to him to meet God the "Hausvater" in Elise Lensing's letters, as this oversimplified conception of the great Absolute insulted his intelligence. He believed in an almighty Being, but not a good "Hausvater" above the stars lacking the power to protect his children from injury, but ready to offer remedies for wounds sustained[32]. The zeal with which he protests against Elise's childlike faith is noth-ing less than amusing:

> Dann schreibe du mir, damit ich erfahre, wie es steht, füge aber, ich bitte Dich zum zweiten Mal, keine Beru-fungen auf den lieben Gott usw., von denen Dein letz-ter Brief wieder wimmelt, hinzu. Der liebe Gott ist, wie die Luft; wir leben und weben in ihr, aber wir können keine Würste und keinen Speck herausschneiden[33].

Toward the end of his letter he warns again against the mentioning of God or presentiments, as his hand subconsciously reaches out in order to crumple letters containing similar references.

The idea that a finite book—the Bible—contains the revelation of the infinite God is also refuted by Hebbel; in fact, God's revelation in the Bible does not even fol-low from Christian concepts. Had it been his wish to reveal himself, God, by virtue of his love which does not permit him to mislead mankind, and by virtue of his omnipotence which enables him to do the following, would have been obliged to deliver a book exalted beyond misinterpretation, ready to be universally comprehended. Obviously, in Hebbel's view, the Bible does not meet these qualifications, but Nature does where God has made manifest his existence in a man-ner which can be understood by everyone. This argu-ment ends in a rhetorical question: "If Christ desired the gospels, why did he not write himself[34]?"

Except for scattered attempts at extremely bold formula-tions of the interdependence of God and the world in which Hebbel speculates on an at least conceivable pos-sibility that the world created God[35] and that, if there is no colossal Individual in the beginning, there might be one at the end[36], he accepted the basic God-world relationship as one of creator and creature. While the Bible teaches the same relationship, any agreement with Hebbel's conception is purely incidental. The Judaic God Jehova of the Old Testament who, save for his

revelation through the Messiah, is identical with the Christian God created the world by whim and caprice and sustains it for no other reason than that it pleases him to do so. There was no necessary creation for the self-realization of the Absolute through individuation; and as a result the creature does not serve a cosmic purpose, but lives in utter subjection to and complete dependence on God. Hebbel rejects this conception as not being consistent with man's dignity and self respect:

> Die Bibel kann schon darum nicht von Gott sein, weil er darin gar zu viel Gutes von sich selbst und gar zu viel Schlimmes von den Menschen sagt. Oder gleicht der Umstand, daß er diese gemacht hat, alles aus[37]?

A God, muses Hebbel, must indeed be a very sorry God, if man, his creature, would have constant need of him[38]. This train of thought is entirely in agreement with Hebbel's prayers, as it only negates the concept of a helpless, stumbling individual whom God must lead every step of the way; but it does not deny a dignified relationship in which the creature in all self respect can approach the Absolute in search for guidance and as-sistance. None of his prayers recorded in the diary or the letters evokes an image of the prostrate suppliant, none indicates surrender, none includes the meek Christian adjunct: Thy will be done! Hebbel wants to preserve his existence before God, while the humble Christian surrenders it:

> God, thou knowest me: I ask not for trifles, not for honor and glory . . . only for continuation of my inward and outward existence (Fortdauer der inneren und äußeren Existenz) . . . and for your blessings upon my spiritual life. Therefore I will believe that thou wilt grant my request[39].

He asks for continuation of his own existence; there is no humble surrender. The "I will believe that thou wilt grant my request" exudes a quiet atmosphere of crea-turely pride and removes itself far from contrition and subjection. Hebbel does expect to be heard when he ap-proaches the Highest Power claiming his due:

> To each prayer one ought to add: Give me what I request now, not at some future date when it has lost its value to me, handing to the mature man the rattle which as a child he so keenly desired[40].

A letter to Gustav Kühne articulates the belief that even God operates under inexorable limitations after the mysterious moment of creation has passed. God cannot correct his own failure such as straightening the hunchback whom he has made; all he can do, by virtue of the refining impulse (Läuterungstrieb) implanted in man, is to induce him to trim his nails and cut his hair[41]. We read in the diary: "God places man into the world without printing a table of contents of his essence upon his forehead[42]." These remarks, taken out of context, are suggestive of a deistic theology surmising a complete withdrawal of the Deity once the world had been created and set in motion. But other related remarks make it plain that Hebbel sees definite interaction between the Creator and the creature on a sustained scale; and in this regard the above mentioned thoughts are compatible with his belief in the dignity of man. It appears, as if a cosmic contest is taking place; a challenge is hurled by the Absolute to test man's self-confidence and determination:

> Gott schickt ein Unglück dir in's Haus:
> Mach du dir selbst ein Glück daraus[43]!

This aphorism affirms the continuing connection of God with the affairs of the world; and in almost Promethean self-assertion it confirms the classical conviction of man's power to steer his own fate. The Deity is confronted with opposing forces which negate its claim to absoluteness. Any Christian humility or Biedermeier resignation[44] is proudly rejected in reliance upon inherent creative powers. The concept of grace (Gnade) appears absurd to Hebbel, because he exalts consequential morality to the status of the highest principle which demands precise consistency and excludes any capricious deviation or unfounded manner of action[45]. Thus the Judaic-Christian God is denied; and a principle is established which binds both God and man, and places man in dignity, if not in power, on par with the Deity.

With the one exception found in the gospel of St. John, 4:24[46], the Bible portrays a personal God, beginning with the first book, Genesis, which proclaims man's creation in the image of God, through the last book, Revelation, where God sits enthroned to receive homage from all the peoples and all the nations of the earth[47]. In spite of genuine piety, Hebbel had no anthropomorphous conception of the Deity. Although—in the language of the Bible—he lives in him as in an all-pervasive atmosphere, God is not simply a magnified human being to him. "I cannot conceive of a God who speaks[48]" or "God cannot be painted[49]" are but a few attempts to discredit the Biblical image of the Almighty. The attributes of a personal God who creates the world at his whim and impulse are, among others, despotism and unlimited freedom. Hebbel ascribes neither to his God, as was shown in the preceding paragraph; therefore: No personal God! He cannot offer a precise counter formulation to the Christian idea, but he does not consider it necessary and tells Pfarrer Luck:

> Auf Ihrem Standpunkt sind Sie des persönlichen Gottes und des unsterblichen Menschen gewiß; auf dem meinigen ist alles Geheimnis und jeder Versuch, das Welträtsel zu lösen, ein Gedankentrauerspiel, nicht . . . bloßes Drama und noch weniger Hymnus[50].

Hebbel's campaign against the Christian conception of God did not confine itself to rational discourse or logical argument but was waged, on occasion, with frivol-ity, irreverence, and blasphemy. We find juxtaposition of the sublime and the ordinary: "Filth is almost as ubiquitous as God[51];" there is defilement by association: "People, filled with God's breath like an inflated intestine[52];" biting sarcasm speaks from the tape-worm's prayer praising God that in his goodness he has created man so that the worm might feed[53]; ridicule is evident in the spoof on a Catholic sacrament: "A mass costs but one guilder! Only God permits himself to be devoured for such a trifling sum[54]." Whether it was Hebbel's intention to shake his contemporaries out of their comfortable lethargy with such provocative remarks in order that they might re-evaluate religious beliefs and habits passed down from generation to generation, is at least a possibility which each reader of the aphorisms has to decide for himself. But that Hebbel should actually utter a statement denying the existence of God is totally unexpected and stands in irreconcilable opposition to his religion, as will be seen in the following paragraphs. Yet there is such a statement:

> Man kann sich über die Eigenschaften eines Objects, welches gar nicht existiert, wohl nicht füglich vereinigen. Dieß ist der letzte Grund aller deistischen Religionen und ihrer Zerspaltung in Secten[55].

It will be noted that this though represents one of the very last entries in Hebbel's diary, which is somewhat ironic and gives rise to the speculation that after a lifetime of sometimes groping, sometimes painstaking attemps at formulating a precise conception of God, this aphorism expresses a final conviction.

Up to this point the negative aspects of Hebbel's religion have been stressed, giving emphasis to his polemics against established conceptions of God, notably the Christian one; it does now seem advisable to consider the poet's formulations of his own conception. He has pondered continually over the nature of a Supreme Being; and if contradiction does occur, it is to be excepted, since God, as Joachim Müller points out, is primal contradiction as well as primal consistency (der Urwiderspruch wie das Uridentische)[56]. Basically, Hebbel conceives of God as the life-giving and life-sustaining principle, the eternal cohesion of all existence, world principle and world substance, in short: the "idea", the cosmic order which manifests itself in causal necessity, not in arbitrariness. Nature aspires to a pinnacle; since man feels that he himself is not this pinnacle, there must exist a corresponding higher being as both the focal point and origin of the universe. This being is God. Hebbel abstracts Him from his own inadequacy and the consistency (Konsequenz) of nature[57]. Compatible with this conception is the apophthegm: "Man conceived his own opposite and he had his God[58]," an aphorism which, in isolation, does not suggest any clarity of perception. Viewed in context, however, it does ascribe infinity, ubiquity, immortality, and omnipotence to God, properties which finite man does not possess. God is the embodiment of all power, physical as well as psychic power, which implies that He is also subject to sensual desires[59]; and with this thought Hebbel once again invites criticism for an implied contradiction as he moves God into the realm of possible arbitrary actions to satisfy these desires.

With his theory that life is merely a reflection of eternal and immutable concepts, Hebbel approximates Goethe who embraced a similar conviction. Reminiscent of Faust's opening monologue in *Faust II* where the arrival of the morning sun so overwhelms him that he is compelled to turn his back and view her splendor only in the iridescence of the cataract, a symbolic act which so demonstrates man's insufficiency that Faust exclaims in resignation: "Am farbigen Abglanz haben wir das Leben!", Hebbel sees life as an everlasting reflection and a series of graduated mirror images: God is reflected in the world, the world in man, man in the arts[60]. All things individual and finite are but a manifestation of an iridescence which is inseparably fused with the One and Everlasting[61]. This abstractly identified entity, the One and Everlasting, is also named Nature in the aphorisms; at times Hebbel calls it the Deity or God, both concepts functioning as synonyms. How Hebbel reconciles this abstraction with the "Eternal Father in Heaven" of his personal prayers is a rather esoteric matter at best and supports once again the assertion that his religious thoughts are consistent when he talks about the Deity or the Divine, but they become contradictory when he talks about God.

Hebbel recognizes in God the undifferentiated Absolute, the final cosmic unity, the great all embracing Whole. God can only be sought in totality, not in detail as the materialists are attempting to do. This shoud be self-evident, since matter only unfolds its beauty in a state of cohesion. Thus, the total human being is beautiful, not the individual part which is merely functional; there is no transition from the duodenum of the Venus de Milo to her face or her eyes[62]. Spirit and nature rest in the universality of the Absolute[63] which attains consciousness in the human mind. At this point Ludwig Feuerbach's influence becomes obvious; and the 20-year old Hebbel articulates an affirmation of the universality of the Absolute and a rejection of any Christian conception in his poem *Die Toten*:

> Wir liegen hier unten
> In kühliger Nacht,
> Auf ruhigem Lager,
> Für ewig gemacht,
> Wir schlummern so lieblich
> Und träumen so süß,
> Nicht brauchend den Himmel,
> Den Gott uns verhieß[64].

"A thread of eternal wisdom extends through the universe[65]." With this aphorism Hebbel acknowledges a rational cosmic cause of all existence. By the principle of individuation necessary for its self-realization, the great Whole has created the infinite number of individual forms representing the universe. God's act of creation is accomplished through thought process; men are in God what individual thoughts are in man[66]. As a thousand brainwaves whir about our ego, millions of shapes surround God[67]. Hebbel calls "man a frost in God[68]" seeing the divine thought caught up at the very instant of emanation in a frost which is the human body. He carries this image of the frozen individual to a logical conclusion. The frozen thought of God embodies an inner ardor, the Divine breath, which contests with the frost encompassing the individual as its body. Man cannot survive this contest: The divine glow will either melt the frost or suffer extinction; man dies in either case[69].

The God of Hebbel's conception does not withdraw from the world upon completion of the creative act, but maintains a continued interest in it as its sustainer and keeper, even engaging in acts of direct intervention in human affairs to satisfy an eternal purpose. He is all-pervasive and ever present. Repeatedly Hebbel illustrates this conception by equating the relationship between the air and man's physical body with the one existing between God and the human spirit. Every thought, each sensation is a breath of God[70]. Attempts to sever this relationship are vain and foolish. Any voluntary interruption of the breathing process in the physical life can be of only relatively short duration; the air will eventually force its way into the lungs. This analogy applies to man's spiritual life. Hebbel indicates here a complete dependence of the human upon the Absolute: To renunciate life is to renunciate God[71]. Compatible with the foregoing remarks is Hebbel's statement that while God is the creator and sustainer of the world, He is not aware of the human being on an individualized, personal basis. Man knows of the blood coursing through his veins, but he has no awareness or cognizance of the individual drops. What these drops are in man, the individuals are in God[72]. Once again the glaring inconsistency must be pointed out between this conception of God and the one apparent from Hebbel's prayers. The contradiction cannot be explained by a chronological span separating the various aphorisms, because the just cited statements fall into approximately the period of his most fervent prayers. Instead of a progressively clearer and more coherent formulation of Hebbel's conception of God, we find an oscillation ranging from the good "Hausvater" to bold abstraction.

God's will and necessary action are identical. He has not only the right but also the duty to ensure the undisturbed course of events toward fulfilment of eternal laws established by himself as the Absolute Power: "Gottes Wille ist Funktion des Weltvollzugs. Gottes Wille ist Wirken wie sein Tun Wollen ist[73]." In a letter to Mme. Stich, Hebbel expresses this function of the Deity which he has affirmed in a number of his dramas:

> My entire tragedy (*Judith*) is founded on the premise that in times of extraordinary situations the Deity intervenes directly in the course of events and causes man to execute enormous deeds which he would not have accomplished through own impulse and desire[74].

If so far the dependence of the individual on God has been shown, it must also be explained that God has need of the individual: There exists a mutual dependence, an interdependence. The Infinite Being needs individual forms for its own existence, as a creation without them is unthinkable. God recognizes Himself only in His creation which becomes a necessary unending process. Through a ceaseless flow of individual forms God Himself remains in a state of constant generation. The creation brings self-realization as well as liberation to the Deity[75]. The process of creation, however, is also a tragic one, as God must sacrifice His own unity. "The world is God's falling into sin[76]," or "the world is the great wound of God[77]," are two of Hebbel's favorite metaphors. Man's longing for immortality is the persistent pain of the wound which was inflicted when individuation occurred[78]. It becomes plain that a dualism is introduced here consisting in the desire of the Absolute for individuation and the incapacity of the individual to assert its independence. The dualism for the individual manifests itself in the fact that it is, at the same time, individual as well as part of the Whole. It is limited by the general postulate of nature and cannot live according to its impulse, as its so-called freedom is nothing but ignorance of the extent to which it depends on universally applicable laws[79]. Individual death is the sacrifice which man must offer to the idea. Because of the individual separation, death is a medium which God has introduced to fashion anew the golden thread of life which has become soiled at the moment of sin, the tearing away from the Whole[80].

Hebbel the poet joins Hebbel the philosopher in conveying the process of creation:

> Ein Königssohn, verlassen,
> Irrt in der Fremde allein.
> Was möchte er dort umfassen?
> Er will beim Vater sein.
> Der Vater, voll Verlangen,
> Sieht längst schon nach ihm aus;
> Er möchte ihn gern empfangen
> Im reichgeschmückten Haus[81].

The three stages of God's self-realization are thus symbolically paraphrased. The prince, the spirit, originates with God, the king of creation. God, the father, reveals Himself in the creation in order to recognize Himself, to find Himself. Creator and creature, father and son, await longingly the time of reunification in the final realization of identity, in the

lavishly decorated mansion. Man, imbued with this spirit, perceives emotionally and intuitively his own kinship with the Absolute, while the intellectual penetration of the deep mystery is an impossibility:

> Doch ach, er weiß es nimmer,
> Wer und von wann er sei;
> Und dennoch fühlt er sich immer
> So königlich stolz und frei[81].

Hebbel's concept of the interdependence between individual and Absolute has additional aspects. Man, through his mental powers, is able to inspire God to further acts of creation. He envisions an ideal which will spark in God the thought to create it[82]. The exceptional human being, the poet, has even the capacity to improve the Deity's handiwork. It is through the poet alone that God receives a bonus on His creation, as the poet returns the world to the Deity in a beauty greater than the one it originally possessed[83].

"Essence and existence, idea and manifestation are one in God[84]." This is one of several of Hebbel's statements revealing a pantheistic conception. Another one is: "God is cause and consequence; He pervades and contains everything that lives[85]," or "God is everything, because He is nothing, nothing finite[86]." Hebbel talks about the eternal order of nature which even the Deity may not disturb unpunished[87]. Such aphorisms are very inviting to classify Hebbel as a pantheist as some critics have done. It must, however, be taken into consideration that Hebbel really does not equate God with Nature or the universe, but rather sees God as the focal point of the cosmos, who concentrates Himself in the world to the extent in which He is abstracted from man and nature. This does not agree with the traditional concept of pantheism[88]. Where Hebbel conceives of God as the Idea conscious of itself, he differs with Spinoza. Spinoza's God is without consciousness, as He is selfless; with Hebbel, God is the conscience of nature, and this presupposes self-consciousness[89]. Furthermore, Hebbel perceives God not only on the intellectual level but on the intuitional level as well; for that reason, his pantheism is mystical in nature, whereas in Spinoza the intellect is decisive.

As stated in the introduction, Hebbel's conception of God does not fit any traditional pattern but is unique. Disregarding the one diary entry mentioned earlier in this paper, it is quite evident that Hebbel never entertained any doubts about the existence of God, only about the nature of the Supreme Being. He writes to Pfarrer Luck:

> Übrigens verstehen sich Demuth und Bescheidenheit sowie unbedingte Unterordnung und Unterwürfigkeit unter das große Ganze überall von selbst[90].

It is further evident, numerous attempts notwithstanding to convert Elise Lensing's childlike and rather primitive faith to a religious conviction that would reflect some of his own enlightened views which he so freely communicated to her, that Hebbel acknowledged the availability of many ways on which man could enter into a meaningful relationship with God. Any religious conviction, however, which did not emanate from the profound depths of the individual human soul, he rejected. Personal experience, individual feeling, emotion, intuition, and perception lead to God, not dogma and tradition of whatever origin. That is why Hebbel so vehemently attacks the Bible and its claim to be the only revelation of God: "An die Bibel glauben, wie an die Algebra, von der man Nichts versteht, und die man doch nicht bestreitet[91]." As the Alpha and Omega of all religious perception and expression, God hears the prayer of the Christian, the pagan, and the pantheist alike. When the world of classical antiquity prayed to Jupiter, Hebbel states, our God was obliged to grant its requests[92]. Or he asks: "Was there really such a difference between idolatry and modern worship service? Was the idol not merely an imperfect example of God[93]?"

The God of Hebbel does not conform to the concept of a "Hausvater" who takes a personal interest in the welfare of his charges, demands proper behavioral conduct, and corrects violations of established rules through the withholding of privileges or the inflicting of punishment. As has been shown before, God is too immense an entity to have a cognizance of every individual being in its own personal existence. He guides the universe by eternal, inexorable laws which even He cannot suspend; and in this capacity as World Principle (Weltprinzip) He does not resemble the "Hausvater" who deems arbitrary actions his prerogative.

There now seems to remain the task to attempt a reconciliation of the two obviously conflicting conceptions: The God of Hebbel's prayers, and the God as He appears from the majority of Hebbel's aphorisms. But this reconciliation is not necessary nor is it possible; neither would it be justified simply to accuse Hebbel of general inconsistency and incoherence, although some instances of definite contradiction have been pointed out, especially when Hebbel wants to prove certain issues on the intellectual level which do not belong on this level at all. The apparent inconsistency, rather, must be understood in the light of this aphorism:

> Gott theilt sich nur dem Gefühl, nicht dem Verstand mit; dieser ist sein Widersacher, weil er ihn nicht erfassen kann. Das weist dem Verstande den Rang an[94].

Feeling, emotion, intuition vary and change; they defy rational, logical development and conclusion. If Hebbel, in the exaltation and exuberance of the moment, did choose the Christian form of prayer to address the Absolute, he makes no apology for it. He conceived of God as the World Principle; God is not only existence but also essence which man can and shall worship in spirit and in truth[95].

Notes

Für Zitate nach Werner vgl. Vorbemerkung nach dem Inhaltsverzeichnis.

1. Peter Michelsen, *Friedrich Hebbels Tagebücher. Eine Analyse.* Vandenhoeck u. Ruprecht, 1966. page 20.

2. Joachim Müller, *Das Weltbild Friedrich Hebbels.* Max Niemeyer Verlag, Halle/Saale, 1955, p. 118.

3. Werner, *Tagebücher.* II, 2468.

4. T. IV, 5847.

5. Joachim Frenkel, *Friedrich Hebbels Verhältnis zur Religion.* In: Hebbelforschungen Nr. II, herausgegeben v. R. M. Werner u. Bloch-Wunschmann, B. Behrs Verlag, Berlin 1907, p. 2

6. Br. I, 90 f.

7. Carl Augstein, *Hebbel als Denker.* Verlag: Minerva-Verlag, Berlin 1947, p. 19.

8. T. III, 4264.

9. T. IV, 5847.

10. T. II, 2545.

11. T. II, 2671.

12. T. II, 2672.

13. T. II, 2143.

14. T. II, 2154.

15. T. II, 2585.

16. T. II, 2586.

17. Br. V, 205.

18. T. II, 1910.

19. Br. II, 79.

20. T. II, 2459; T. II, 2467; T. II, 2808.

21. T. III, 3628.

22. S. G. Flygt, *Friedrich Hebbel's Conception of Movement in the Absolute and in History.* (Chapel Hill, N. C. USA. 1952), p. 75.

23. Müller (Nr. 2) p. 139.

24. T. III, 3420.

25. T. I, 228.

26. T. I, 641.

27. T. I, 716.

28. T. III, 4048.

29. T. II, 2061.

30. Frenkel (Nr. 5), p. 36.

31. T. I, 1853.

32. Müller (Nr. 2), p. 120.

33. Br. III, 212.

34. T. I, 72.

35. T. II, 1971.

36. T. III, 3739.

37. T. III, 3303.

38. T. I, 660.

39. T. II, 2416.

40. T. II, 2726.

41. Br. IV, 343.

42. T. II, 3066.

43. T. I, 1667.

44. Compare Mörikes poem *Gebet*: Herr, schicke, was du willst, / Ein Liebes oder Leides, / Ich bin vergnügt, daß beides / Aus deinen Händen quillt.

45. Frenkel (Nr. 5), p. 42.

46. God is a spirit: and they that worship him must worship him in spirit and in truth.

47. Other references to the personal God: God walked in the garden of Eden, walked with Moses on Mt. Sinai, confronted Satan in the book of Job, several accounts Revelation, etc.

48. T. I, 66.

49. T. I, 1810.

50. Br. VII, 8.

51. T. III, 3590.

52. T. III, 3734.

53. T. III, 3764.

54. T. III, 4917.

55. T. IV, 6343.

56. Müller (Nr. 2) p. 129.

57. Br. I, 163.

58. T. II, 1883.

59. T. I, 77.

60. T. III, 4024.

61. T. II, 2731.

62. T. IV, 5919.

63. Wolfgang Liepe, *Beiträge zur Literatur- und Geistesgeschichte,* herausgegeben v. Eberhard Schulz. Verlag Karl Wachholtz, Neumünster 1963. p. 186.

64. Liepe (Nr. 63) p. 175.

65. Frenkel (Nr. 5) p. 3.

66. T. III, 3988.

67. T. III, 3446.

68. T. III, 3696.

69. T. II, 2633.

70. T. II, 2531.

71. T. I, 1140.

72. T. II, 2274.

73. Müller (Nr. 2) p. 127.

74. Br. II, 35.

75. Frenkel (Nr. 5) p. 21.

76. T. II, 3031.

77. T. II, 2663.

78. T. III, 3736.

79. T. III, 4969.

80. Frenkel (Nr. 5) p. 12 f.

81. Liepe (Nr. 63) p. 221.

82. T. I, 96.

83. T. II, 2024

84. Frenkel (Nr. 5) p. 7.

85. Frenkel (Nr. 5) p. 8.

86. T. II, 2784.

87. T. I, 1011.

88. Müller (Nr. 2) p. 122.

89. Frenkel (Nr. 5) p. 9.

90. T. IV, 5847.

91. T. II, 1970.

92. T. II, 1874.

93. T. II, 2250.

94. T. I, 1268.

95. Müller (Nr. 2) p. 123.

Ladislaus Löb (essay date 1974)

SOURCE: Löb, Ladislaus. "Hebbel." In *From Lessing to Hauptmann: Studies in German Drama,* pp. 239-87. London: University Tutorial Press, 1974.

[*In the following essay, Löb provides a thematic and stylistic overview of Hebbel's dramatic theory and his major dramatic works.*]

LIFE AND SIGNIFICANCE

Among Germany's outstanding dramatists Hebbel is one of the most debatable claimants to greatness. At their worst his plays abound in hysterical atmospheres, extravagant characters, hair-splitting arguments and contrived situations. At their best they rise to powerful tragic conflicts reflecting the perplexities of an unusual individual living at a time of social and intellectual upheaval. Even more than Büchner, Hebbel is caught between a new Realistic outlook and a longing for the lost idealistic age. He is a Realist in his presentation of the deterministic interaction of psychological and environmental forces within a framework of historical change, and in his frequent use of colloquial language. He is a would-be idealist in his dramatisation of metaphysical concepts through plots which proceed in a near-Classical manner from exposition through climax to catastrophe, involving momentous events and larger-than-life protagonists given to grand rhetoric often in blank verse. Aspiring to transcendental absolutes he is troubled by the relativity of human experience, and it has been convincingly argued that the basic tensions in his work derive from the dichotomy of his intellectual search for a belief and his intuitive denial of any certainty or meaning.

Christian Friedrich Hebbel was born on 18 March 1813 in Wesselburen, a village in the Dithmarschen district of Schleswig-Holstein. After attending the local primary school he became an assistant to the parish clerk J. J. Mohr when his father, an impoverished stonemason, died in 1827. In 1835 Amalie Schoppe, the novelist and editor, impressed by his early poems and stories, set up a fund enabling him to move to Hamburg; there he unsuccessfully studied for the "Abitur" and began to live with Elise Lensing, a teacher turned sempstress nine years his senior. In 1836 he went to Heidelberg and thence to Munich where, meagrely supported by Elise, he attended university lectures and continued writing. In 1837 he had an affair with Beppi Schwarz, daughter of a joiner in whose house he was lodging. In 1838 his mother and his friend Emil Rousseau died. In 1839 he walked back to Hamburg; after recovering from pneumonia, he started contributing to Karl Gutzkow's journal *Telegraph für Deutschland*. In 1840 Elise gave birth to his first son Max, while he fell in love with Emma Schröder, a Senator's daughter; his first play, ***Judith,*** was performed in Berlin in the same year. In 1842 in Copenhagen the poet Adam Oehlenschläger helped him obtain from King Christian VIII a travel grant which took him to Paris in 1843 and to Rome in 1844; meanwhile in Hamburg Max died in 1843 and Elise's second son Ernst was born in 1844. In 1844 he was awarded a doctorate of philosophy by the university of Erlangen for a version of his essay *Mein Wort über das Drama*. In 1845 he found himself in Vienna, lionised by the aristocratic brothers von Zerboni and by Christine

Enghaus, the Burgtheater actress, whom he married in 1846. 1847 saw the death of Ariel, his first son by Christine, and the birth of a daughter called Tine or Titi; in 1847 too Ernst died in Hamburg and on Christine's insistence Elise joined their ménage in Vienna for more than a year. In 1848 he narrowly missed election for the Frankfurt parliament as a liberal-conservative member. A well-known journalist by then, he worked from 1849 to 1850 as literary editor of the *Österreichische Tageszeitung*. His reputation as a dramatist was growing, and on journeys to Munich, Hamburg, Weimar, Paris, London and elsewhere he met many celebrities of the time. In 1854, the year following the death of Elise, he bought a house in Orth near Gmunden, where he subsequently spent part of every summer. In 1863 he received the Schiller prize for ***Die Nibelungen*** which, first performed in 1861, was his one genuinely popular success. On 13 December 1863 he died in Vienna as a result of his earlier deprivations.

A brief sketch based on Hebbel's diaries and letters may give some insight into his personality. In his childhood he was oppressed by poverty and by his father's harshness. In his teens he underwent real and imagined humiliations by Mohr and felt frustrated by the provinciality of Wesselburen. During his early twenties some tactlessness in Amalie Schoppe's Hamburg circle aggravated his resentment at being financially dependent on people to whom he was intellectually superior. Munich in his middle twenties and Paris in his early thirties represented the nadir of his fortunes. Poised on the brink of starvation, he despaired of ever earning a living: like Kleist, he refused to adopt a humdrum profession, although the delay of recognition and the characteristic recurrence of fallow periods after bouts of creativity made him doubt his artistic talent. In his eighteen Vienna years the improvement of his circumstances led to a mood of comparative peace but he never completely overcame his long-ingrained bitterness.

His most painful experiences arose from his relations with Elise. As a penniless and lonely youth he readily accepted her love and her slender means, and although he soon recognised their incompatibility he let the affair drag on for ten years. His sense of obligation was mixed with revulsion from the narrow existence she offered and the claims she made on him. Repeatedly he promised to marry her and then dashed her hopes by declaring that he did not love her, that he could never keep a family, and that his genius needed freedom. He believed his own general arguments against marriage as well as his over-estimation, induced by guilt feelings, of Elise's goodness; but his self-deceit may be measured by the speed with which he ditched her and married when he saw the promise of material comfort and genuine companionship in Christine.

If the world treated Hebbel unkindly, he too could be unkind. His use of Elise demonstrates his weakness and his callousness. His quarrels with Mohr, Amalie Schoppe, his friend Emil Kuh, the author and theatre manager Heinrich Laube and such writers and critics as Gutzkow, J. L. Heiberg or Julian Schmidt show his capacity for ingratitude, vindictiveness and tyranny. Fanatical, uncompromising, touchy but inconsiderate, depressive yet arrogantly self-assertive, devoid of humour, bristling with the tenseness of the self-made and self-taught, wrapped in abstruse speculation and driven by sado-masochistic paranoia, Hebbel was not an attractive character. Nevertheless, his egotism was the reverse side of his single-minded devotion to a calling in which he eventually succeeded against daunting physical, mental and social odds. However one evaluates his plays, they certainly owe a unique quality to the tragic complexities of his impressive personality.

Hebbel was born in the same year as Büchner. Although he lived considerably longer, both belong to the same period of German literature. For background information the reader may wish to consult the section entitled "Realismus" in the preceding chapter.

Dramatic Theory

For many decades Hebbel's plays were interpreted in accordance with his theoretical statements. In the 1930s critics began to analyse them as independent entities. Recent scholarship assumes that his theories make a limited but indispensable contribution to an understanding of his practice. Although he denies direct influences, he seems to have arrived at his views, which recall Schelling's and Hegel's, by first reading their respective followers, the Romantic spiritualist Gotthilf Heinrich Schubert and the atheist Ludwig Feuerbach; some gnostic and pantheist elements further mingle with hints of the emergent materialism, nihilism and existentialism of his epoch. But he is an artist, not a thinker. The observations he scatters over his diaries, letters and essays are fragmentary, aphoristic, often bizarre, occasionally self-contradictory. They do not add up to a philosophical system or to a chronological progression but they indicate his lasting preoccupations.

Many of Hebbel's aesthetic pronouncements reflect the Poetic Realist's desire to reproduce actuality and at the same time to reveal a meaning. Thus he demands that drama should present life in its concrete immediacy but should nevertheless suggest an all-embracing rationale behind the seemingly arbitrary variety of appearances:

> Das Drama . . . hat . . . die Aufgabe, das Leben in seiner Unmittelbarkeit zur Anschauung zu bringen, und den alles umfassenden Verstand, der ihm im ganzen zugrunde liegen muß, im einzelnen hinter anscheinender Willkür zu verstecken . . .[1]

The dramatist's task is to show the ideal not as something remote from, but as a higher dimension of, the real; he should not lay bare, but should nevertheless suggest, a general law governing the specific phenomena of the world:

> Den dramatischen Dichter macht . . . die Kunst . . . *Allgemeines* und *Besonderes* so ineinander zu mischen, daß . . . das Gesetz, dem alles Lebendige gehorcht, . . . niemals *nackt zum Vorschein kommt* und niemals . . . *völlig vermißt wird.*[2]

The portrayal of the real consists, as Hebbel's own plays are meant to demonstrate, above all in the observation of psychological truth:

> . . . so setze ich den Realismus hier und überall ausschließlich in das psychologische Moment . . .[3]

Psychological truth involves a near-scientific understanding of how men are formed by historical circumstances:

> Wie jede Kristallisation von gewissen physikalischen Bedingungen abhängt, so jede Individualisierung des menschlichen Wesens von der Beschaffenheit der Geschichtsepoche, in die es fällt.[4]

Psychological truth excludes both artificial idealisation and a concern with accidentals; it rests on the recognition of what is essentially human:

> . . . der dramatische Dichter soll freilich keineswegs idealisieren, aber er soll doch auch nur das echt Menschliche, nicht das rein Zufällige . . . wiedergeben . . .[5]

The essentially human cannot, however, be separated from the superhuman. Characters must appear unfinished because the great forces outside man express themselves through their effect on his development:

> Der Mensch darf uns daher nicht abgeschlossen vorgeführt werden . . . die großen Kräfte und Mächte außer ihm, verkörpern sich, indem sie Einfluß auf ihn üben . . .[6]

Unlike the supernatural fate of ancient drama, destiny as conceived by modern dramatists derives from the perennial aspects of human nature but is nevertheless a manifestation of an incomprehensible God:

> . . . wir Neueren suchen die Menschen-Natur . . . auf gewisse ewige und unveränderliche Grundzüge zurückzuführen . . . das moderne *Schicksal* ist die Silhouette Gottes, des Unbegreiflichen und Unerfaßbaren.[7]

Every genuine work of art thus proves to be a mysterious and complex symbol, which can neither be made nor fathomed by the intellect:

> Jedes echte Kunstwerk ist ein geheimnisvolles, vieldeutiges, in gewissem Sinn unergründliches Symbol. Je mehr nun eine Dichtung aus dem bloßen Gedanken hervorging, je weniger ist sie dies . . .[8]

Proper—or Poetic—Realism is created by the artist's imagination which plumbs such depths of the world as are inaccessible to the other human faculties and which, instead of taking the empirical surface for the whole of reality, intuitively encompasses the truth beneath it:

> . . . meine Anschauungs-Weise setzt demnach an die Stelle eines falschen Realismus, der den Teil für das Ganze nimmt, nur den wahren, der auch das mit umfaßt, was nicht auf der Oberfläche liegt.[9]

Time and again Hebbel tries to formulate that truth. The highest form of art, he declares, begging various questions, is tragedy since the laws of drama are those of the world itself and since history assumes tragic qualities in every crisis:

> Denn das Drama ist nur darum die höchste Form der Kunst und die Tragödie wieder die höchste Form des Dramas, weil das Gesetz des Dramas dem Weltlauf selbst zugrunde liegt und weil die Geschichte sich in allen großen Krisen immer zur Tragödie zuspitzt.[10]

Tragedy arises from the fact that all life is a struggle between the individual and the universe:

> Alles Leben ist Kampf des Individuellen mit dem Universum.[11]

The very existence of the individual is a defiant bid by a part to tear itself away from the whole:

> *Leben* ist der Versuch des trotzig-widerspenstigen *Teils*, sich vom Ganzen loszureißen . . .[12]

Since the only necessity is that the universal should survive, individuals—whose own concerns are irrelevant—must be punished for thus threatening the universal:

> Es gibt nur eine Notwendigkeit, die, daß die Welt besteht; wie es den Individuen aber in der Welt ergeht, ist gleichgültig. Das Böse, das sie verüben, muß, indem es die Existenz der Welt gefährdet, bestraft werden . . .[13]

At the same time the universal is an abstract concept which can only be actualised in concrete individuals:

> Das Universum kommt nur durch Individualisierung zum Selbstgenuß . . .[14]

The life of the individual which, through constant evolution, continues the original act of creation prevents the world from stagnating:

> Der Mensch ist die Kontinuation des Schöpfungsakts, eine ewig werdende, nie fertige Schöpfung, die den Abschluß der Welt, ihre Erstarrung und Verstockung, verhindert.[15]

And the individual is born to die after a spell of apparent independence, so that the world may safely enjoy his contribution, as a tree is fertilised by its falling leaves:

> *Geburt* ist derselbe Prozeß, der das Blatt vom Baum abreißt, damit es sich anscheinend-selbständig einen Augenblick im Spiel der Winde drehe und dann zu Boden falle, um dort zu faulen und den Baum neu mit düngen zu helfen.[16]

The terrible necessity of a life in which the individual is bound to perish for the benefit of the universe ("eine furchtbare Notwendigkeit") is the theme of tragedy, which is the most illuminating product of the human mind ("der leuchtendste Blitz des menschlichen Bewußtseins").[17] Tragic guilt is not a transgression in a moral or religious sense. It arises from a basic discrepancy between the ideal and the phenomenal and it consists in the self-preservation and self-assertion of the individual, which is natural but which nevertheless represents an immoderate stand against the "Idea", that is, the abstract essence of the universal. This immoderation is an integral existential part of all individual phenomena; it can therefore only be obliterated through the destruction of the phenomena themselves. As the destruction occurs, the Idea, which was forced to assume the imperfect shape of the individual, becomes free again and the tragedy ends in reconciliation:

> . . . wie der Begriff der tragischen *Schuld* nur aus dem Leben selbst, aus der ursprünglichen Inkongruenz zwischen Idee und Erscheinung, die sich in der letzteren eben als Maßlosigkeit, der natürlichen Folge des Selbst-Erhaltungs- und Behauptungstriebes, des ersten und berechtigtsten von allen, äußert, entwickelt werden darf, . . . so ist auch der Begriff der tragischen Versöhnung nur aus der Maßlosigkeit, die, da sie sich in der Erscheinung nicht aufheben kann, diese selbst aufhebt, indem sie sie zerstört und so die Idee wieder von ihrer mangelhaften Form befreit, zu entwickeln.[18]

The tragic process, aiming at the reconciliation of the universal rather than the individual, is strikingly illustrated by a conceit which combines psychology and metaphysics in the spirit of Hebbel's Poetic Realism. The drops of water in the river of life are those commonplace men who passively constitute the body of the universal. The pieces of ice are tragic individuals who, by assuming an identity, disturb the flow of the whole; as they break against one another they succumb to human conflicts, but as they melt swelling the flood they prove to serve the superhuman cause of the universal of which they have remained parts despite their recalcitrance:

> Die Versöhnung im Tragischen geschieht im Interesse der *Gesamtheit,* nicht in dem des *Einzelnen* . . . Das Leben ist der große Strom, die Individualitäten sind Tropfen, die tragischen aber Eisstücke, die wieder zerschmolzen werden müssen und sich, damit dies möglich sei, aneinander abreißen und zerstoßen.[19]

Hebbel's positive interpretation of tragedy, however, is often contradicted by sceptical statements. His conclusions about the inconstant, subjective and arbitrary quality of all human judgments characterises his own views:

Die einzige Wahrheit, die das Leben mich gelehrt hat, ist die, daß der Mensch über nichts zu einer unveränderlichen Überzeugung kommt und daß alle seine Urteile nichts, als Entschlüsse sind . . .[20]

Thus he may define death as a sacrifice of the individual to the Idea ("Der Tod ist ein Opfer, das jeder Mensch der Idee bringt"[21]). But he may invalidate this idealistic notion by suggesting in the existentialist manner that there is no higher value than life itself ("Gibt es denn wirklich ein Gut, das höheren Wert hat, als das Leben selbst?"[22]). And he may revoke his assertion of tragic reconciliation in his despair at realising that heroes fall simply because they overreach themselves and that the purpose of universal progress is less certain than the individual suffering which is its price:

Es gibt keine Versöhnung. Die Helden stürzen, weil sie sich überheben . . . Warum diese aufsteigende Linie, die jeden höheren Grad mit so unsäglichen Schmerzen erkaufen muß?[23]

Such doubts lead him to advocate—and attempt—a new kind of drama whose dialectic will reveal even the universal as subject to change and relativity by including conflicts of different universal forces as well as of individuals, or by debating, as he says, not only man's relationship to the Idea but the justification of the Idea itself:

. . . daß also nicht bloß das Verhältnis des Menschen zu der Idee, sondern die Berechtigung der Idee selbst debattiert werden wird.[24]

Hebbel's questionings have a clearly religious dimension. He rejects all positive religions but finds the secular humanism of his time wanting. Nature, he believes, is consistent in its striving for a perfect being, which must be God since man is inadequate:

Die Natur strebt nach einem Gipfel . . . Dies Wesen ist Gott. Ich abstrahiere ihn aus meiner eigenen Unzulänglichkeit und aus der Konsequenz der Natur.[25]

He cannot accept a transcendental personal deity, but in the self-preservation of life as a whole—or of the Idea—he sees an eternal wisdom which seems divine:

Ich glaube nicht an einen guten Hausvater über den Sternen . . . , aber allerdings zieht sich ein Faden ewiger Weisheit (der ja eben nur die *Äußerung* der *Selbst-Erhaltung* im *Ganzen* ist) durch die Welt . . .[26]

If God is identical with the universal Idea He can only become a living reality by dissolving into individual men ("Gott: größtes Individuum . . . mehr und mehr sich selbst in Individuen auflösend"[27]). God thus becomes limited by the imperfections of the individual, so that the world may be described in bizarre or near-blasphemous images as His corset ("Die Schöpfung ist die Schnürbrust der Gottheit"[28]) or as His fall ("Die

Welt ist Gottes Sündenfall"[29]). God may further be imagined not as the creative origin but as a supreme individual at the culmination, of the dialectical development of the world ("Wenn nicht ein ungeheueres Individuum am Anfang, warum nicht am Ende?"[30]). Finally, the notion that at a given time the Son was bound to issue from the Father indicates a dualism in God, who may therefore be responsible for the world's contradictions:

Die Schellingsche Idee, daß zu einer bestimmten Zeit aus Gott dem Vater Gott der Sohn hervortreten mußte, führt den Dualismus in die Gottheit selbst hinüber . . . und macht Gott zur Wurzel der Welt-Entzweiung.[31]

Hebbel's sporadic religious speculations show the deity to be problematic, relative, split within itself. He cannot believe in a harmonious, omnipotent, other-worldly providence, and his basic experience is that of suffering humanity. This is in evidence when, characteristically mixing intellectual sophistry with tragic emotion, he suggests, in analogy to a definition of physical pain, that each human individual may be a pain felt by God, the universal:

Wenn in uns das Einzelgefühl des Teils das Gemein-Gefühl des Organismus überragt, entsteht Schmerz. Könnten wir nicht in diesem Sinne Schmerzen Gottes sein?[32]

Hebbel's philosophical and psychological interests leave little scope for politics. His sparse political comments show tendencies towards the Right. Like most of his contemporaries, he is a nationalist. Unlike Büchner and various other writers, but like the majority of the German middle and upper classes of the period, he is a conservative although he has some liberal sympathies. His attitude is succinctly explained with reference to the 1848 revolution, which confirmed him in his conservatism; since the revolutionaries threatened to deliver all civilisation to chaos in the uncertain hope of a new world, he decided to support the old régime, even at the risk of a return to the absolutist abuses, as the lesser evil:

Von nun an schien mir nur die Wahl zu bleiben, ob man, unter Aufopferung der gesamten Zivilisation das Chaos, dem dereinst eine neue Welt entsteigen könne, mit heraufbeschwören helfen oder die paralysierten früheren Gewalten auf die Gefahr hin, sie noch einmal nach wieder erlangter Kräftigung schnöde gemißbraucht zu sehen, bis zu einem gewissen Grade unterstützen wolle. Ich hielt die letztere Gefahr für geringer . . . und handelte demgemäß.[33]

Despite his reservations he believes that the conservative state offers a better chance of survival and a closer approximation to the divine order than the anarchy he associates with democracy. Thus he concludes, with a resigned awareness of the relativity of earthly values, that the moral law must, at least temporarily, speak through a monstrous political system:

Aber ich fürchte, das sittliche Gesetz wird noch einige Zeit durch den Mund eines Moloch sprechen müssen.[34]

Two isolated entries in Hebbel's diaries provide significant insights into his dramatic practice. The paradoxical definition of essential femininity as doing through suffering foreshadows his many female characters who either achieve greatness through passive submission or cause havoc through what he considers, in nineteenth-century fashion, as unfeminine activity:

Durch Dulden Tun: Idee des Weibes.[35]

The Kantian maxim that the worst sin is to use a human being as a means to one's own ends anticipates the way many of his male characters degrade others—mostly women—to objects of possession or enjoyment:

Einen Menschen zum bloßen Mittel herabzuwürdigen: ärgste Sünde.[36]

Hebbel's most coherent discussion of drama occurs in the treatise *Mein Wort über das Drama* (1843) and in the preface *Vorwort zur Maria Magdalene* (1844), which reiterate many suggestions of the diaries, letters and minor essays.

Mein Wort über das Drama combines an earlier article called *Ein Wort über das Drama* with a later polemic against the Danish critic Heiberg. The subject of drama, Hebbel repeats, is the basic process of life, which signifies the conflict arising from the paradoxical fact that the individual becomes detached from and opposed to, but still remains part of, the universal:

Das Drama stellt den Lebensprozeß an sich dar . . . in dem Sinne, daß es uns das bedenkliche Verhältnis vergegenwärtigt, worin das aus dem ursprünglichen Nexus entlassene Individuum dem Ganzen, dessen Teil es trotz seiner unbegreiflichen Freiheit noch immer geblieben ist, gegenübersteht.[37]

Drama must reveal both "being", or the eternal and universal, and "becoming", or the temporal and individual—the former by stressing the perennial truth that all individuality contains an essential ingredient of guilt since it is bound to be immoderate in its opposition to the universal; the latter by clothing the constants of human nature and destiny in the changing phenomena of history:

Das Drama ist demnach . . . ans Seiende, wie ans Werdende verwiesen: ans Seiende, indem es nicht müde werden darf, die ewige Wahrheit zu wiederholen, daß das Leben als Vereinzelung, die nicht Maß zu halten weiß, die Schuld nicht bloß zufällig erzeugt, sondern sie notwendig und wesentlich mit einschließt und bedingt; ans Werdende, indem es an immer neuen Stoffen, wie die wandelnde Zeit und ihr Niederschlag, die Geschichte, sie ihm entgegenbringt, darzutun hat, daß der

Mensch, wie die Dinge um ihn her sich auch verändern mögen, seiner Natur und seinem Geschick nach ewig derselbe bleibt.[38]

The individual cannot help asserting a will of his own, although by doing so he must upset the balance of the universal which abhors extremes. Consequently dramatic guilt has existential rather than moral connotations; recalling Kleist's and Büchner's fatalism rather than Lessing's or Schiller's Aristotelean notion of the tragic flaw, it stems from the sheer fact of human volition, so that for the dramatist it is immaterial whether the hero falls through good or bad intentions:

Hiebei ist nicht zu übersehen, daß die dramatische Schuld . . . unmittelbar aus dem Willen selbst, aus der starren eigenmächtigen Ausdehnung des Ichs, hervorgeht, und daß es daher dramatisch völlig gleichgültig ist, ob der Held an einer vortrefflichen oder einer verwerflichen Bestrebung scheitert.[39]

Indeed the effect is more tragic if the hero falls through goodness:

. . . es ist, wenn das erschütterndste Bild zustande kommen soll, notwendig, daß jenes, nicht dieses, geschieht.[40]

Of the two chief elements of drama, character seems more important to Hebbel than plot. Drama is only alive when it demonstrates how the individual develops in the conflict of his own will and the will of the world. By modifying human deeds, or freedom, through events, or necessity, drama shows how the individual's attempts to act out his inner urges provoke the opposition of outside forces designed to restore the balance of the whole—that is, it accommodates Hebbel's concern with psychology as well as his dialectical philosophy:

Nur dadurch, daß es uns veranschaulicht, wie das Individuum im Kampf zwischen seinem persönlichen und dem allgemeinen Weltwillen, der die Tat, den Ausdruck der Freiheit, immer durch die Begebenheit, den Ausdruck der Notwendigkeit, modifiziert und umgestaltet, seine Form und seinen Schwerpunkt gewinnt, und daß es uns so die Natur alles menschlichen Handelns klar macht, das beständig, sowie es ein inneres Motiv zu manifestieren sucht, zugleich ein widerstrebendes, auf Herstellung des Gleichgewichts berechnetes äußeres entbindet—nur dadurch wird das Drama lebendig.[41]

Hebbel distinguishes three kinds of drama. Social drama, he believes, is too mundane to convey timeless truths. Historical drama can reproduce eternal processes together with the circumstances of a specific period; the period may be that in which the play is set or that in which it is written, but in either case the dramatist must—as Hebbel maintains, echoing Lessing and Schiller but contradicting Büchner—express his own views through historical topics:

Die Geschichte ist für den Dichter ein Vehikel zur Verkörperung seiner Anschauungen und Ideen, nicht aber ist umgekehrt der Dichter der Auferstehungsengel der Geschichte . . .[42]

Philosophical drama should embody metaphysical concepts in authentic pictures of life rather than falsify life by metaphysical preconceptions:

> Auch *philosophische* Dramen liegen vor. Bei diesen kommt alles darauf an, ob die Metaphysik aus dem Leben hervorgeht, oder ob das Leben aus der Metaphysik hervorgehen soll.[43]

Hebbel himself strives for a combination of the three, which—by demonstrating how the philosophical ideas underlying the religions begin to affect some individuals and provoke dialectical clashes—would symbolise the most profound social and historical developments over centuries. It is debatable how new such a drama is and how far Hebbel succeeds in practising it. Nevertheless, the argument illuminates his habit of setting his plays at historical turning-points and of giving the personal problems of his characters a metaphysical meaning:

> . . . es ist ein Drama möglich, das den Strom der Geschichte bis in seine geheimnisvollsten Quellen, die positiven Religionen, hinein verfolgt und das, weil es in dialektischer Form alle Konsequenzen der diesen zugrunde liegenden innersten Ideen an den zuerst bewußt oder unbewußt davon ergriffenen Individuen veranschaulicht, ein Symbolum der gesamten historischen und gesellschaftlichen Zustände, die sich im Lauf der Jahrhunderte daraus entwickeln mußten, aufstellt . . .[44]

Both drama and philosophy deal with the universal. Philosophy, which is concerned directly with the abstract Idea, has not yet fulfilled its task for it has not explained why individuation must occur. Drama, on the other hand, has long met its obligations by showing how in the world of concrete phenomena the individual destroys himself through his own immoderation, thus ridding the Idea of an irksome opponent and of an imperfect temporal manifestation:

> Die Philosophie hat ihrem Teil der gemeinschaftlichen Aufgabe noch nicht genügt . . . , denn die *Vereinzelung* ist noch nicht auf ihre innere *Notwendigkeit* zurückgeführt. Die Kunst dagegen hat ihr Geschäft bei Alten und Neuern noch stets zur rechten Zeit vollbracht, sie hat die Vereinzelung durch die ihr eingepflanzte Maßlosigkeit selbst immer wieder aufzulösen und die Idee von ihrer mangelhaften Form zu befreien gewußt.[45]

Immoderate self-assertion is the existential guilt of the individual. But it is also the source of reconciliation since it serves to end the individual's flawed life:

> In der Maßlosigkeit liegt die Schuld, zugleich aber auch, da das Vereinzelte nur darum maßlos ist, weil es, als unvollkommen, keinen Anspruch auf Dauer hat und deshalb auf seine eigene *Zerstörung* hinarbeiten muß, die Versöhnung . . . Diese Schuld ist . . . mit dem Leben selbst gesetzt.[46]

Thus tragedy yields satisfaction, but it is the Idea that is satisfied through the destruction of its individual opponent, not the individual. The satisfaction is incomplete if the individual goes down defiant; it is complete if he departs in peace having understood his universal obligation. But in both cases the necessity of the split remains unexplained and the search for meaning founders on a mystery which drama shares with the world itself:

> Doch dies ist die Seite, wo das Drama sich mit dem Weltmysterium in eine und dieselbe Nacht verliert. Das Höchste, was es erreicht, ist die Satisfaktion, die es der Idee durch den Untergang des ihr durch sein Handeln oder durch sein Dasein selbst widerstrebenden Individuums verschafft, eine Satisfaktion, die bald unvollständig ist, indem das Individuum trotzig und in sich verbissen untergeht . . . , bald vollständig, indem das Individuum im Untergang selbst eine geläuterte Anschauung seines Verhältnisses zum Ganzen gewinnt und in Frieden abtritt. Doch dies genügt auch im zweiten Fall nur halb, denn wenn der Riß sich auch wieder schließt, warum mußte der Riß geschehen?[47]

This ultimate uncertainty, however, is no obstacle to artistic success. For drama must present not the speculative metaphysical aspects of the Idea but its living manifestation through the interaction of human nature and human destiny—or through the methods of Poetic Realism:

> Eben aber mit der unmittelbar im Leben selbst aufgehenden . . . , nimmermehr jedoch mit der eigentlich *spekulativen* Seite der Idee hat es die dramatische Kunst zu tun. Menschen-Natur und Menschen-Geschick, wie sie sich wechselseitig bedingen, soll sie erforschen und darstellen, nicht aber . . . in die unergründlichen Tiefen der Metaphysik hinabsteigen.[48]

The discussion continues in the general sections of *Vorwort zur Maria Magdalene*. Hebbel repeats that drama, the highest art, should portray the relationship of temporal conditions and the universal Idea:

> Das Drama, als die Spitze aller Kunst, soll den jedesmaligen *Welt-* und *Menschen-Zustand* in seinem *Verhältnis zur Idee* . . . veranschaulichen.[49]

True drama is written when these conditions are undergoing a decisive change:

> . . . das Drama ist nur dann *möglich*, wenn in diesem Zustand eine entscheidende *Veränderung* vor sich geht . . .[50]

In the first great period the tragedy of fate emerged when reflection ousted naivety in Greece. In the second the Shakespearean tragedy of character arose from a similar crisis in Christianity induced by Protestantism. The third began when Goethe sought to show dialectical contradictions in the central Idea itself. For all their dubious relevance to drama in general, these statements betray Hebbel's sense of an all-embracing relativity; this sense of relativity lies behind his habit of splitting the universal into conflicting epochs, represented by conflicting characters, in such a manner that one character may overreach himself either in serving the age he represents or in fighting the age represented by another character, who in his turn may be guilty of over-assertion either in support of his own age or in opposition to that of the first character. Thus the comment on Goethe illuminates Hebbel's own tragedies:

> . . . er hat die Dialektik unmittelbar in die Idee selbst hineingeworfen, er hat den Widerspruch . . . in dem Zentrum . . . aufzuzeigen . . . gesucht.[51]

Hebbel believes that in his day history is changing again. Conservative as he is, he sees the change in the growing demand for a better foundation of existing institutions. Drama must contribute to this process by metaphysically justifying the world as it is. To do that, the dramatist must not idealise reality but must foreshadow the transition to the ideal by emphasising the evils of individual life and implying his awareness of the Idea whose supremacy will restore universal unity when the individual falls:

> Nur wo . . . euch das Leben in seiner Gebrochenheit entgegentritt und zugleich in eurem Geist . . . das Moment der Idee, in dem es die verlorne Einheit wieder findet, da ergreift es . . .[52]

The universal Idea, then, should not be pictured allegorically or discussed philosophically; it should be suggested dialectically as the metaphysical consequence of the human conflicts of the characters:

> . . . daß man hier nicht an ein allegorisches Herausputzen der Idee, überhaupt nicht an die philosophische, sondern an die unmittelbar ins Leben selbst verlegte Dialektik denken muß . . .[53]

The poetic imagination, whose first conceptions are subconscious and often rooted in childhood, is concrete rather than speculative, as Hebbel argues, forgetting his own proneness to speculation; in a successful drama therefore the spirit will assume a body, the dualistic ideas will materialise in characters, and the inner action will appear in an external plot capable of arousing interest according to certain laws of theatrical precipitation:

> . . . daß der echte dramatische Darstellungs-Prozeß . . . alles Geistige verleiblichen, daß er die dualistischen Ideen-Faktoren . . . zu Charakteren verdichten, daß er das innere Ereignis . . . in einer äußeren Geschichte . . . dem Steigerungs-Gesetz der Form gemäß . . . spannend und Interesse erweckend gestalten . . . wird.[54]

Such a concrete presentation is nevertheless symbolic of abstract truth. Resuming his discussion of drama and philosophy, Hebbel urges the latter to merge into the former since art is philosophy realised, as the world itself—in an idealistic view—is the Idea embodied in reality:

> Aber die Kunst ist . . . die realisierte Philosophie, wie die Welt die realisierte Idee . . .[55]

And resuming his discussion of drama and history he repeats that art is the supreme form of historiography for it conveys the abstract general content of history through the concrete life of a particular period:

> . . . daß die Kunst . . . den allgemeinen . . . Gehalt der Geschichte in der Schale der speziellen Perioden . . . darbieten kann.[56]

Hebbel's specific comments on **Maria Magdalene** will be considered later. A summary of his dramatic theory may therefore conclude this section. He pleads for a Poetic Realism which would combine the modern positivist observation of actuality with a metaphysical symbolism reminiscent of Classical and Romantic approaches, and which would convey a tragic outlook. Life is a perennial struggle between the individual and the universal. The individual must assert himself against the universal and yet remain a part of it. In order to fulfil himself—and indeed to prevent the universal from stagnating—he must carry his one-sided qualities to extremes. This immoderation may be morally good or bad but it is existentially unavoidable and it is always guilty in that it threatens the balance of the universal; moreover it restricts the universal, which has had to assume the individual's imperfect shape to manifest itself. Consequently the individual must be destroyed. The destruction is caused by human conflict but it frees the universal from both the threat and the imperfection of the individual—the individual suffers but the universal Idea is reconciled. At times Hebbel finds comfort in this notion of reconciliation; at other times he feels troubled by the impossibility of understanding why the individual must be exposed to such pain. Similarly he is torn between a sense of the universal as a divine absolute and a fear that even the universal or divine is subject to relativity and self-contradiction. In short, his longing for an idealistic belief is under constant attack from scepticism.

Hebbel's theories are dogmatic, narrow, question-begging, clumsily expressed. His theatrical practice often invalidates or exceeds them. Nevertheless, with all their limitations, they are essential for an appreciation of his plays.

THE MAJOR PLAYS

Hebbel is above all a dramatist. His poems and stories never equal the power of his plays. But even his plays vary in quality. This study will therefore concentrate on the five major ones, ignoring such minor pieces as **Der Diamant** (completed in 1841), **Julia** and **Ein Trauerspiel in Sizilien** (both completed in 1847), **Der Rubin** (1849), or **Michel Angelo** (1850), as well as the immature though psychologically interesting *Genoveva* (1841), the once renowned but jejune *Die Nibelungen* (1860) and the unfinished *Demetrius* (begun in 1858).

JUDITH

Hebbel's first play, **Judith** (written in 1839-40, first performed in 1840, published in 1841), is based on the apocryphal *Book of Judith* and bears echoes of Schiller's *Die Jungfrau von Orleans*. Holofernes, the Assyrian general, is besieging the Hebrew town of Bethulia. Judith, a young Hebrew widow, visits him in his camp and after letting him make love to her kills him, whereupon her fellow-countrymen slaughter the Assyrians. Realising that she has killed Holofernes out of personal anger rather than in fulfilment of a divine mission, Judith resolves to die if she should prove to be pregnant by him. As is his habit, Hebbel repeatedly comments on his own work. The present discussion will try to incorporate and to transcend his self-interpretation, which is chiefly found in his diaries and in a preface.[57]

The play is largely about Judith, but Holofernes is worth some attention. Modelled in part on Napoleon, he has affinities with Baroque and "Sturm und Drang" heroes and with Nietzsche's Superman. His insatiable ambition, his demented urge to destroy what he respects, and his extreme mixture of lust and hate make him a monster. Nevertheless, there is an interesting metaphysical dimension to his ravings. As he commits his atrocities he feels impelled to annihilate the stale old world, so that something better may take its place. He longs for a force which could overcome him because he is weary of knowing no being greater than himself. He has visions of manifesting his superhuman will by serenely submitting to unspeakable tortures, in order to frighten puny humanity into worshipping him as a god, before he dies in secret. His hybris, expressed with frenzied bombast and sado-masochistic spite, is a perverted demonstration of his unsatisfied need for the divine. Hebbel interprets him as a great individual in whom the pagan age overreaches itself to make way for universal progress through Judaism towards Christianity; but he also reflects the boredom, frustration, religious doubt, existential fear and irrational vitalism contained in the darker moods of the nineteenth century:

HOLOFERNES:

> . . . die Welt kommt mir jämmerlich vor, mir deucht, ich bin geboren, sie zu zerstören, damit was Besseres kommen kann . . . Er komme, der sich mir entgegen stellt, der mich darnieder wirft . . . Es ist öde, nichts ehren können, als sich selbst . . . Und wenn sie das Ärgste mir getan zu haben glauben . . . und ich sie, trotz all meiner Pein, in Tod und Wahnsinn hinein lächle: dann donnre ich ihnen zu: Kniet nieder, denn ich bin euer Gott, und schließe Lippen und Augen und sterbe still und geheim.

(V, p. 60-1.)[58]

The perplexities of Judith, Hebbel suggests, show that human beings, however devoted to a divine calling, cannot help being partially impure in their motivation; and that the divinity cannot prevent its own human instruments from being crushed in the universal process it has directed through them. But the play itself seems even more sceptical. Judith remembers a dream in which her anguished cry for God is answered from an abyss; as she throws herself down she feels enfolded in soft arms but, proving too heavy, sinks deeper and deeper. The image may indicate the earthly impurity of mankind and the inability of the divine to save its human instruments; but it is not certain that the voice in the abyss—with its erotic lure—is really divine:

JUDITH:

> . . . Gott! rief ich in meiner Angst,—hie bin ich! tönte es aus dem Abgrund herauf, freundlich, süß; ich sprang, weiche Arme fingen mich auf . . . , aber ich war zu schwer, er konnte mich nicht halten, ich sank, sank . . .

(II, p. 19.)

In a more explicit passage Judith compares her prayers to suicide; whether interpreted as a nihilist's escape or as an existentialist's leap into the unknown, the repeated image of a self-induced fall indicates despair rather than belief:

JUDITH:

> . . . Mein Gebet ist dann ein Untertauchen in Gott . . . , ich springe in den Ewigen hinein, wie Verzweifelnde in ein tiefes Wasser—

(II, p. 22.)

In fact Judith's religious struggles arise from sexual frustration. Hebbel makes her a widow whose marriage was never consummated, and he comments that this invention enables her to assume a role inaccessible to ordinary women while her eventual defloration reflects the mingling of pure divine dedication with human impurity. When she urges her suitor Ephraim to kill Holofernes according to the will of God and of the universe ("Denn du willst, was alles will; worüber die Gottheit brütet", II, p. 26) she speaks in religious terms, voicing Hebbel's theory that the destruction of one outstanding individual by another serves the progress and consolidation of the world. But when Ephraim and the other Hebrew men prove so cowardly that she feels justified in attempting the manly deed, her divine motives are mixed, as Hebbel himself explains, with vanity:

JUDITH:

> . . . Und ist deine Feigheit die deines ganzen Geschlechts, . . . dann hat ein Weib das Recht erlangt auf eine große Tat . . .

(II, p. 27.)

What Hebbel does not explain is that Judith's tantalising position of being both widow and virgin intensifies her sexual desire. When Ephraim reports Holofernes' crimes she is made, clumsily but clearly, to betray her semi-conscious fascination:

JUDITH:

> Ich mögt ihn sehen! (*Für sich*). Was sagt ich da!

> (II, p. 24.)

Later, yearning for a sign from God, she is only aware of darkness. Her vacillation suggests that, even when she decides that her plan to sin with Holofernes in order to exterminate him is inspired by God, she is attracted by the sin itself; her weakness is further revealed by her fear of seeing good qualities in the tyrant. Hebbel wants her to lapse from her divine mission through human frailty, but actually she appears to be rationalising erotic urges by means of religious notions which may be totally imaginary:

JUDITH:

> . . . Gott! Gott! . . . ich harre mit Angst eines Winkes von dir, . . . aber in mir und außer mir bleibts dunkel. Nur ein Gedanke kam mir, . . . doch, der kam nicht von dir. Oder kam er von dir? . . . Der Weg zu meiner Tat geht durch die Sünde! . . . schütze mich, daß ich nichts Gutes von ihm sehe!

> (III, p. 28-9.)

As she sees Holofernes' power both in cruelty and magnanimity, she cannot help admiring him. After letting him kiss her according to her plan, she realises with horror that she is responding as a woman to his virility:

JUDITH:

> (*für sich*). O, warum bin ich Weib!

> (V, p. 58.)

When, having scornfully pardoned Ephraim's underhand murder bid, he displays the full extent of his sombre greatness, she feels in utter confusion that she is about to worship him instead of God:

JUDITH:

> . . . Mensch, entsetzlicher, du drängst dich zwischen mich und meinen Gott!

> (V, p. 61.)

She seems ready to abandon her mission and live for Holofernes. But he, instead of loving her, merely uses her—as she puts it in a rhetorical second-person account—to titillate himself, with some difficulty, into concluding an alcoholic intoxication by a sexual one before falling into a drunken stupor. Consequently, as

Hebbel himself argues, she kills him not in order to do her duty but to avenge her physical and emotional humiliation. At the same time she punishes her own sexuality, indicated by her confession that her own senses were aroused despite her disgust. Thus Hebbel transcends his theory in presenting a psychological problem with a candour and complexity remarkable for his time:

JUDITH:

> . . . wo du an Leib und Seel ausgekeltert wirst, um an die Stelle des gemißbrauchten Weins zu treten und einen gemeinen Rausch mit einem noch gemeineren schließen zu helfen,—wo die einschlafende Begier von deinen eigenen Lippen so viel Feuer borgt, als sie braucht, um an deinem Heiligsten den Mord zu vollziehen,—wo deine Sinne selbst . . . gegen dich aufstehen . . .

> (V, p. 65.)

She is momentarily reassured by the thought that she has served her people, but as she remembers that she in fact obeyed her own desires she feels unbearably alone with her conscience; this would confirm Hebbel's interpretation that although she has furthered the progress of the universal she must suffer for the over-assertion of her individual impurity:

JUDITH:

> . . . Das Elend meines Volks peitschte mich hierher . . . Nein, . . . nichts trieb mich, als der Gedanke an mich selbst . . . Mein Volk ist erlöst, doch . . . jetzt muß ich meine Tat allein tragen, und sie zermalmt mich!

> (V, p. 67-8.)

Another aspect of her guilt is that by killing a man she has transgressed against a woman's vocation of motherhood and passivity:

MIRZA:

> . . . Ein Weib soll Männer gebären, nimmermehr soll sie Männer töten!

> (V, p. 64.)

And the association of her beauty with poison—besides alluding to the Romantic figure of the femme fatale—reflects Hebbel's view that individuality is pernicious even in its most attractive extreme:

JUDITH:

> . . . Meine Schönheit ist die der Tollkirsche; ihr Genuß bringt Wahnsinn und Tod!

> (II, p. 23.)

All these circumstances may have been meant to contribute to Judith's tragedy. The action, however, points to the sexual motivation. Thus perhaps the ultimate cause of her despair is not her betrayal of God but the fact, on which Hebbel himself only comments in passing, that she has killed the one man she could have loved:

JUDITH:

> Ja, ich habe den ersten und letzten Mann der Erde getötet . . .
>
> (V, p. 73.)

Hebbel's far-fetched explanation of her wish that she may not have conceived Holofernes' child is that, in thus sparing her the need to prevent the birth of a potential matricide by making the Hebrews kill her, God would demonstrate the divine value of her deed; but while the references to prayer could show her intended return to faith, the open ending again suggests questions rather than answers:

JUDITH:

> . . . Bete zu Gott, daß mein Schoß unfruchtbar sei. Vielleicht ist er mir gnädig!
>
> (V, p. 75.)

A similar ambivalence occurs in Hebbel's treatment of the Hebrews. He writes that their monotheism represents a moral advance on the paganism of the Assyrians. One of Holofernes' officers, who apprehends the supreme power of the Jewish God from the start, formally acknowledges it after the rescue of the Hebrews:

ACHIOR:

> . . . Groß bist du, Gott Israels, und es ist kein Gott, außer dir!
>
> (V, p. 73.)

The mute Daniel's sudden ability to speak, forestalling the Hebrews' surrender and driving one defeatist to suicide, is accepted as a divine miracle, and his killing of another defeatist is considered a further proof of his divine message and protection:

DER PRIESTER:

> Der Herr hat ihn gesandt, der Herr wird ihn schützen.
>
> (III, p. 45.)

On the other hand the Hebrews—terrified by Holofernes, quarrelling among themselves, contemplating not only surrender but the consumption of sacred wine and human flesh—seem unworthy of such a distinction. They are neither holy nor pure, as Judith urges them to be, and their final triumph over the Assyrians proves them butchers rather than inspired heroes; although Hebbel might argue that this presentation of a nation

under stress shows how the divine spirit is adulterated when it assumes human shape, their divine motivation, like Judith's, appears altogether doubtful:

JUDITH:

> . . . Werdet heilig und rein . . . Das ist Schlächter-Mut!
>
> (V, p. 74.)

To summarise in terms of Hebbel's theories, Holofernes is destroyed because of the boundless assertion of individuality in his self-deification, while Judith's suffering is due to individual immoderation shown by the preponderance of her personal passion over her divine mission. The confusion of Judith's motives may suggest that the universal, or divine, Idea can only embody itself in imperfect human individuals but is served by both the guilt and the atonement of the individual. In keeping with Hebbel's hints about the dialectic within the Idea, Judith's and the Hebrews' victory over Holofernes and heathendom may represent a victory of the progressive side of the universal over its reactionary side; alternatively, such a dialectic may be implied in the inability of the divinity to save its human tool from destruction.

Theory apart, *Judith* provides the first example of the recurrent Hebbelian love-hate involving a male character's ruthless desire for domination and the equally violent reaction of a female one; Holofernes' sado-masochism and Judith's attempts to rationalise, as well as to satisfy and to avenge, her frustrated sexuality demonstrate Hebbel's Realistic insight into psychopathology. On the religious level Holofernes' blasphemies seem to issue from a hopeless longing for God, while Judith seems intent not on preserving but on finding a belief, and her divine aspirations could be fantasies induced by unsatisfied erotic instinct; thus the text shows not the reassuring if paradoxical contribution of individual frailty to the universal order but the sceptical notion that the existence of an absolute metaphysical power may be an illusion. The play is melodramatic, hysterical, obscured by unintegrated themes; nevertheless, it dramatises Hebbel's perplexities with considerable originality.

MARIA MAGDALENE

Maria Magdalene (written in 1843, published in 1844, first performed in 1846) is Hebbel's most Realistic tragedy, set in nineteenth-century provincial Germany. Meister Anton, a joiner, has a son, Karl, and a daughter, Klara. When Karl is arrested for alleged theft his mother dies of shock and Meister Anton threatens to commit suicide if Klara also proved a disgrace. Klara is in fact pregnant by Leonhard, a subaltern civil servant, to whom she became engaged when the Secretary whom she loved left town to study. Leonhard, planning a more profitable match, breaks off the engagement. The Secretary returns and declares his love but, discovering Klara's pregnancy, decides to fight Leonhard instead of reassuring her of his loyalty. Karl is released and goes to sea, while Klara, after entreating Leonhard in vain to marry her, drowns herself. The Secretary kills Leonhard and is fatally wounded. Meister Anton remains behind in confusion.

The play is partly autobiographical. The lower middle-class setting is modelled on Hebbel's background; Meister Anton's dourness on that of Hebbel's father; Klara's love affairs and Karl's arrest on Hebbel's experiences in the Schwarz family in Munich; and the men's treatment of Klara on Hebbel's own cruelty to Elise Lensing.

As usual, Hebbel comments freely on his work. In *Vorwort zur Maria Magdalene* he explains that he has written a new kind of domestic tragedy[59]. In the old kind, he says, the catastrophe derived from class distinctions which could have been remedied by social means and therefore represented no unavoidable tragic necessity, whereas in his play it results from the inescapably one-sided views of characters who all belong to the short-sighted bourgeoisie; conventional domestic tragedy, he further objects, tended to ennoble or belittle its protagonists by using stilted or sentimental language, whereas his dialogue is appropriate to the characters' own class and interests. In his letters and diaries he emphasises that he has taken care to omit all abstract speculations of which his characters would be incapable; and to bring about the tragedy through the clash of attitudes which are equally justified in that the characters cannot help obeying the forces of personality and environment[60]. One may wonder whether class distinctions are less tragic than the outlook of characters conditioned by one class. But it is true that in this least theory-ridden of his plays Hebbel fulfils his own demand for Poetic Realism.

Leonhard, to some extent, combines the traditional roles of seducer and intriguer in domestic tragedy. He becomes town treasurer by making his rival drunk. When he learns that Klara has no dowry, he uses Karl's arrest as an excuse for ending the engagement; when she urges him to marry her he pretends an obligation to the mayor's niece, whom he courts for his own advancement. His horror of a duel with the Secretary shows him up as a physical coward, his relief at the prospect of Klara's suicide as a moral one. Nevertheless, he is not a melodramatic villain. With his shabby ambition, his calculating greed and his unctuous hypocrisy, he is a plausible exponent of nineteenth-century bourgeois society. If there is a hint of metaphysical evil about him it is acceptably conveyed by such subjective responses as Klara's sense of glimpsing hell through him:

KLARA:

> . . . mir ist, als hätt ich durch deine Brust bis in den Abgrund der Hölle hinuntergesehen . . .

> (III, iv, p. 371.)[61]

The Secretary is akin to the weak young lover of conventional domestic tragedy. Unlike the other men, he can appreciate Klara's goodness, but he is a slave to prejudice; that is why he involuntarily precipitates her death by declaring that he cannot get over the idea of her pregnancy and by leaving her in order to challenge Leonhard whom he despises but whose ridicule he fears:

SEKRETÄR:

> Darüber kann kein Mann weg! Vor dem Kerl, dem man ins Gesicht spucken mögte, die Augen niederschlagen müssen?

> (II, v, p. 366.)

Only when Klara is dead and he is dying does he realise that, if Meister Anton actually drove her to suicide, he himself did nothing to stop her. Together they have destroyed Klara—and themselves—by paying attention to the whispers and sneers of worse men, that is, by adopting the code of a corrupt society:

SEKRETÄR:

> . . . Er hat sie auf den Weg des Todes hinausgewiesen, ich, ich bin schuld, daß sie nicht wieder umgekehrt ist. Er dachte . . . an die *Zungen,* die hinter ihm herzischeln würden, aber nicht an die *Nichtswürdigkeit* der *Schlangen,* denen sie angehören, . . . ich . . . dachte an den Buben, der dazu ein Gesicht ziehen könnte, und . . . der *schlechter* war, als ich . . .

> (III, xi, p. 381.)

Meister Anton joins the blustering fathers of domestic tragedy but he is also the play's most interesting Realistic character. He reveals much of himself when he describes his approach to religion. He cannot feel elevated in the open but only in church where he is separated from the world by heavy doors and where high walls close in on him with small windows dimly filtering the light of day but showing the morgue with the skull; the gloomy and oppressive quality of the images—repeated throughout the dialogue—expresses his severe conventionality, his unnatural joylessness, his hostility to life itself:

MEISTER ANTON:

> . . . wenn ich mein Herz erhoben fühlen soll, so muß ich erst die schweren eisernen Kirchtüren hinter mir zuschlagen hören, und mir einbilden, es seien die Tore der Welt gewesen, die düstern hohen Mauern mit den schmalen Fenstern, die das helle freche Welt-Licht nur verdunkelt durchlassen, als ob sie es sichteten, müßten sich um mich zusammendrängen, und in der Ferne muß ich das Beinhaus mit dem eingemauerten Totenkopf sehen können.

> (I, v, p. 343.)

His ponderous inflexibility is aptly suggested by the metaphor of the millstone he wears for a collar:

MEISTER ANTON:

> Ich trage einen *Mühlstein* wohl zuweilen als *Halskrause* . . .
>
> (I, v, p. 344.)

A contrived but telling image may illustrate how his inner development was determined by poverty, which killed his parents and embittered him from childhood. He was at first as tender as a hedgehog whose spikes point inward so that every pressure gives it acute pain—the pressures come from a cruel society, but the spikes suggest masochism; when he turns his skin inside out he pricks others in self-defence, but with a touch of sadism:

MEISTER ANTON:

> . . . Ich bin so wenig, wie Er, als ein borstiger Igel zur Welt gekommen, aber ich bin nach und nach einer geworden. Erst waren all die Stacheln bei mir nach innen gerichtet, da kniffen und drückten sie alle zu ihrem Spaß auf meiner nachgiebigen glatten Haut herum . . . ich kehrte meine Haut um, nun fuhren ihnen die Borsten in die Finger, und ich hatte Frieden.
>
> (I, v, p. 345.)

The world has done him wrong; unfortunately in protecting himself he cannot help doing wrong to his fellow-men:

MEISTER ANTON:

> . . . ich hab so groß Unrecht erlitten, daß ich Unrecht tun muß, um nicht zu erliegen . . .
>
> (II, i, p. 356.)

He wrongs Karl by believing him capable of crime. He wrongs the bailiff by snobbishly refusing to drink with him, and he thus becomes the indirect cause of Karl's arrest and his wife's death. Above all he wrongs Klara by driving her to suicide instead of understanding and helping her in her distress. His explanation of his attitude is that he cannot bear being either pitied or despised—in short, like the Secretary, he bows to the false judgments of public opinion:

MEISTER ANTON:

> . . . Ich kanns in einer Welt nicht aushalten, wo die Leute mitleidig sein müßten, wenn sie nicht vor mir ausspucken sollen.
>
> (II, i, p. 355.)

At the end of the play he is confused but, unlike the Secretary, he fails to recognise his share of the guilt:

MEISTER ANTON:

> Ich verstehe die Welt nicht mehr!
>
> (III, xi, p. 382.)

Meister Anton, then, is a character whose sensitivity in a harsh world has grown into a self-centred sado-masochism; whose righteousness has degenerated into self-righteousness; whose lack of genuine morality has resulted in a submission to hypocritical conventions; in whom serenity and warmth of heart have been ousted by a sour quest for respectability; to whom the purpose of life seems to be drudgery; and who even turns religion into a mechanical routine. Karl's caustic description of the twenty commandments, in which rules of petty propriety mix with divine imperatives, and of the toil, which is only interrupted by food, drink, sleep and prayer followed by more toil, indicts both Meister Anton and the dreary society of which he is a product as well as an agent:

KARL:

> . . . Der Hut gehört auf den dritten Nagel, nicht auf den vierten! Um halb zehn muß man müde sein! . . . Das steht in einer Reihe mit: Du sollst Gott fürchten und lieben! . . . Hobeln, sägen, hämmern, dazwischen essen, trinken und schlafen, damit wir immerfort hobeln, sägen und hämmern können, sonntags ein Kniefall obendrein: ich danke dir, Herr, daß ich hobeln, sägen und hämmern darf!
>
> (III, vii-viii, p. 374-6.)

The only character to escape from such an existence is Karl. Significantly, the images associated with him convey not claustrophobia but movement, light and openness; and while Klara dies by water, his rebellion succeeds by water, as is underlined by his cheerful song about a ship's departure before he becomes a sailor:

KARL:

> (*singt*) Dort bläht ein Schiff die Segel,
> Frisch saust hinein der Wind! . . .
> Der Anker wird gelichtet,
> Das Steuer flugs gerichtet,
>   Nun fliegts hinaus geschwind!
>
> (III, viii, p. 377.)

Unlike the active Judith, Klara is a passive victim of Leonhard's treachery, the Secretary's pusillanimity and Meister Anton's tyranny. Her bondage is emphasised by the fact that she is already pregnant when the play begins. Her most painful thought on recognising Leonhard's baseness is that she is tied to him:

KLARA:

> O mein Gott, an diesen Menschen bin ich gekettet!
>
> (I, iv, p. 340.)

When the Secretary left for college it was people's mockery and her own anger at being jilted, as well as her mother's exhortations to keep to her class, that made her yield to Leonhard:

KLARA:

> . . . Spott und Hohn von allen Seiten, als du auf die Akademie gezogen warst . . . Und dann die Mutter! Halte dich zu deinesgleichen! . . . Dazu mein eignes Herz. Hat er dich vergessen, zeig ihm, daß auch du—o Gott!

> (II, v, p. 365.)

When she implores Leonhard to marry her she has no real choice since the other alternative, to her mind, is death:

KLARA:

> . . . Er oder der Tod! Wunderts wen, daß ich ihn wähle?

> (II, p. 364.)

Thus Klara too respects the prejudices of society. Nevertheless, she is not altogether conventional, for she wants to save not her own but her father's reputation, and she would accept illegitimate motherhood as a punishment for she knows not what, if she would not hurt him by doing so:

KLARA:

> . . . Wärs um mich allein—ich wollts ja tragen, ich wollts geduldig hinnehmen, als verdiente Strafe für, ich weiß nicht was . . . Aber ich bins nicht allein . . .

> (III, ii, p. 369.)

Her frequent guilt feelings may indicate that she judges herself by society's standards, but they also have religious connotations, as do other sections of the dialogue. While the Secretary repeatedly uses biblical imagery and Leonhard's and Meister Anton's behaviour denies spiritual as well as ethical values, she relates her conduct to religion. When in her anguish she cannot finish the Lord's Prayer but forgives Leonhard and asks God to forgive her for committing suicide in place of her father, she proves her ability to obey not the letter but the spirit of Christianity:

KLARA:

> . . . Vater unser, der du bist im Himmel—. . . Gott, mein armer Kopf—ich kann nicht einmal beten—. . . Vergib uns unsere Schuld . . . Ja! ich vergeb ihm gewiß . . . O Gott, ich komme nur, weil sonst mein Vater käme! Vergib mir, wie ich—

> (III, viii, p. 378-9.)

Encouraged by the New-Testament allusion of the title, some critics consider Klara's death, with its element of self-sacrifice, as an act of spiritual deliverance. But although she does in a sense sin and repent, she is hardly redeemed as was Mary Magdalene, and her destruction is accompanied by a mood of unrelieved determinism.

In terms of Hebbel's theories Klara's defiance of sexual conventions might represent the fatal self-assertion of the individual against the universal; the three men accept these conventions but even they act as individuals and must consequently suffer. In the light of a dialectic within the Idea, Hebbel may be pleading for a genuinely moral society by exposing its evil antithesis; or he may be hinting at universal progress as the old world begins to crumble with Meister Anton's final bewilderment while Klara's nobility foreshadows a better future.

Such explanations are not, however, confirmed by the text. The abuse of a female protagonist by ruthless male ones, together with a similarly recurrent Hebbelian conflict of male characters over a female, contains a demand for humanity and Christian charity. But there is no positive solution, and Hebbel's success derives from the very absence of metaphysical argument. Classical in its simple plot, its economical use of actors and its approximation to the Unities, Realistic in its stylised but authentic colloquialism and its socio-psychological motivation, *Maria Magdalene* urgently conveys the agony of human beings caught between their own limitations and the compulsions of their narrow-minded class. Some of the problems may seem as dated today as do parts of the stagecraft and rhetoric, but the play is still powerful in its social criticism and its tragic portrayal of an existence without freedom or meaning.

HERODES UND MARIAMNE

Herodes und Mariamne (written in 1847-48, first performed in 1849, published in 1850) is considered by many critics as Hebbel's masterpiece. The action takes place in Jerusalem. In self-defence against the ambitious intrigues of Alexandra, his mother-in-law, Herodes, the Jewish king, had her son Aristobolus drowned. Summoned to Mark Antony, he fears that the Roman overlord might decide to get rid of him in order to seize his wife Mariamne. When Mariamne refuses his request for a promise of suicide, he orders his relative Joseph to kill her if he should fail to return. He returns but is called away again to fight Octavian, Antony's political rival, and he gives the same order to his follower Soemus. When he returns once more Mariamne, outraged by her discovery of the orders, arranges a feast feigning an adulteress's joy at her husband's death, and he has her duly executed. When the three Magi announce the birth of Jesus he decrees the Slaughter of the Innocents.

The play is based on Flavius Josephus' *Antiquities of the Jews* and his *History of the Jewish Wars*; it is also influenced by J. L. Deinhardstein's *Ludovico,* which is an adaptation of P. Massinger's *The Duke of Milan*. Hebbel's chief additions are Mariamne's feast and the arrival of the Magi. On the whole he tries to make the psychology more convincing and more complex—his Joseph reveals Herodes' orders under duress, not in order to prove Herodes' love, and his Mariamne, unlike Josephus', loves Herodes. His own comments, which will be discussed with the relevant points in the text, are found mainly in a review entitled *Ludovico* and in various letters.[62]

Hebbel's statement that Herodes' violent actions are conditioned by the explosive historical situation is confirmed by the play. He is threatened by Alexandra's machinations and by uprisings such as that of the Pharisees under Sameas; by the despotism and quarrels of Antony and Octavian; and finally by the arrival of Jesus. His image of a man encircled by predatory animals describes his circumstances with a characteristic Hebbelian mixture of power and artificiality:

HERODES:

> . . . Ich gleiche
> Dem Mann der Fabel, den der Löwe vorn,
> Der Tiger hinten packte, dem die Geier
> Mit Schnäbeln und mit Klaun von oben drohten,
> Und der auf einem Schlangenklumpen stand.

> (I, ii, l. 254-8.)[63]

It is, as Hebbel explains, his loneliness in his desperate plight which makes him unable to fight unless he is assured of Mariamne's love:

HERODES:

> . . . Du mußt es ja empfinden, daß ich jetzt
> Nicht für mich kämpfen kann, wenn du mir nicht
> Versicherst, daß dein Herz noch für mich schlägt!

> (I, iii, l. 395-7.)

The worst aspect of his love is his jealousy. He wants Mariamne to be killed if he died, because he cannot bear—or even utter—the notion that she might ever belong to another man:

HERODES:

> . . . Gradaus, ich kanns
> Nicht tragen, daß sie einem andern jemals—
> Das wär mir bittrer, als—

> (I, v, l. 619-21.)

This jealousy seems rooted in a sexual inferiority complex, unconscious to Herodes and to Hebbel the self-interpreter, but suggested by Hebbel the dramatist when Mariamne blames Herodes' distrust of her constancy on his disbelief in his manly appeal compared with Mark Antony's:

MARIAMNE:

> . . . Daß du verzagst, in deines Weibes Herzen
> Durch deines Männer-Wertes Vollgehalt
> Ihn aufzuwägen . . .

> (III, ii, l. 1621-3.)

Herodes' distrust of Mariamne, which may express a more general disorientation, is linked with his violence. Thus, when he sentences her to death not because he is convinced of her infidelity but because he can no longer bear the uncertainty whether her stubborn silence hides innocence or guilt, Hebbel's familiar themes of doubt and pathological love-hate are both evident:

HERODES:

> . . . ich will
> Nicht Tag für Tag mich mit dem Rätsel quälen
> . . . ich will mich aus dem Wirbel
> Von Haß und Liebe, eh er mich erstickt,
> Erretten, kost es, was kosten es mag!

> (V, v, l. 2900-6.)

Even when he realises his error he continues to act in character. Having lost his wife, he will fight to keep the crown and resist fate although he knows that it will defeat him through Jesus—the Slaughter of Bethlehem once more confirms his defiance, his possessiveness and his unreasonable but impressive refusal to yield to necessity:

HERODES:

> . . . Darum bleib ich noch
> Und halte fest, was ich noch hab . . .
> Doch, Schicksal, du verrechnetest dich sehr . . .
> Ich bin Soldat, ich kämpfe selbst mit dir,
> Und beiß dich noch im Liegen in die Ferse!

> (V, viii, l. 3290-302.)

The play's chief interest lies in the interaction of Herodes' and Mariamne's responses. Hebbel's comment that Herodes' love-hate is matched by Mariamne's is confirmed by the events and by the dialogue:

ALEXANDRA:

> . . . sie haßt und liebt ihn jetzt zugleich!

> (II, iii, l. 940.)

She understands that he had to kill her brother as a result of her mother's schemes. Nevertheless, with the shadow of Aristobolus between them, her treatment of him has lost its intuitive rightness:

MARIAMNE:

> . . . Obgleich wir nie jetzt mehr zu zweien sind,
> Und mir der dritte so den Sinn verstört,
> Daß ich verstumme, wenn ich reden sollte,
> Und daß ich rede, wenn zu schweigen wär . . .

> (II, iii, l. 1076-9.)

Her hostility grows when he asks for her promise to commit suicide if he failed to return from his first visit to Antony; she could kill herself voluntarily but not on his demand:

MARIAMNE:

> . . . Das kann man tun, erleiden kann mans nicht!

(I, iii, l. 428.)

While he feels that her refusal robs him of all assurance, she wants him to trust his knowledge of her personality and not an enforced oath:

HERODES:

> Du hältst das Wort zurück,
> Das schlichte Wort, wo ich auf einen Schwur
> Von dir gehofft: worauf noch soll ich baun?

MARIAMNE:

> Und leistete ich den, was bürgte dir,
> Daß ich ihn hielte? Immer nur ich selbst,
> Mein Wesen, wie dus kennst.

(I, iii, l. 476-82.)

That is why, ironically, it is only when he has left that she swears of her own free will to die if he died:

MARIAMNE:

> . . . Den Schwur, den ich zurückhielt, als er scheidend
> Ihn forderte, den leist ich jetzt: Ich sterbe,
> Wenn er stirbt.

(II, iii, l. 1986-8.)

When he leaves for the second time she is delighted because the repetition—theatrically clumsy despite its historical truth—may show that his order to Joseph revealed a momentary passion rather than his basic character. As she wants to test him she must conceal her motives:

MARIAMNE:

> . . . Halt an dich, Herz! Verrat dich nicht! Die Probe
> Ist keine, wenn er ahnt, was dich bewegt!

(III, vi, l. 1823-4.)

But her pleasure at his departure and her unwillingness to answer his charges of adultery are bound to worsen his suspicions:

HERODES:

> Wer schweigt, wie du,
> Weckt den Verdacht, daß er die Wahrheit nicht
> Zu sagen wagt . . .

(III, vi, l. 1892-4.)

As Hebbel comments, Herodes' distrust was provoked by his own sense of guilt about killing Aristobolus and was deepened by Mariamne's consequent change of attitude towards him. Now that she knows about his order to Joseph and apparently refuses to forgive him, he is driven to repeat the order to Soemus since he fears that if she has not been unfaithful out of fickleness she might become unfaithful for revenge:

HERODES:

> . . . seltsam hat sie, seit ihr Bruder starb,
> Sich gegen mich verändert . . .
> Drum kann ich ihr nicht mehr vertraun, wie sonst! . . .
> Jetzt muß ich weiter gehn! Denn, nun sies weiß,
> Nun muß ich das von ihrer Rache fürchten,
> Was ich von ihrer Wankelmütigkeit
> Vielleicht mit Unrecht fürchtete . . .

(III, vi, l. 1923-54.)

When Mariamne discovers his new order she feels that her life has become utterly meaningless:

MARIAMNE:

> So ist das Ende da! . . .
> Ich hatte nichts, ich habe nichts, ich werde
> Nichts haben!

(IV, iii, l. 2139-44.)

She gave him the benefit of the doubt after the first order, but when the second order proves his distorted view of her she cannot bear the disappointment:

MARIAMNE:

> . . . Als ich mir sagen mußte: eher gleicht
> Dein Schatten dir, als das verzerrte Bild,
> Das er im tiefsten Innern von dir trägt!
> Das hielt ich nicht mehr aus . . .

(V, vi, l. 3033-6.)

That is why, after momentarily contemplating suicide, she induces him to sentence her as a supposed adulteress, by arranging the feast, by declining to defend herself in court, and by ensuring that her innocence remains a secret till she is dead:

MARIAMNE:

> . . . Du sollst das Weib, das du erblicktest, töten
> Und erst im Tod mich sehen, wie ich bin!

(V, vi, l. 3041-2.)

She presents her conduct as necessary and logical, but it is really an expression of senseless fury. One is even aware of a morbid erotic thrill as she associates death at the hand of Herodes with caresses:

MARIAMNE:

> . . . Du bist der Tod!
> Der Tod umarmt und küßt mit Schwert und Gift!

> (IV, viii, l. 2530-1.)

The action, then, shows how the incompatibility of two lovers comes to a head under political stress. They both consider love as the supreme value but seek fulfilment in diametrically opposed ways. He demands external proofs of her fidelity while she needs to be trusted without proofs. The more he wants, the less she can give; the less she gives, the more he wants. His suspicions, aggravated by her conduct, provoke her intransigence; her intransigence drives him to outrageous measures; his measures cause her, in her despair, to make him destroy her physically and himself emotionally. Thus they are caught in a vicious circle of attraction and repulsion, involuntary error and deliberate deception. Self-centred, unable to appreciate each other's point of view, profoundly irrational beneath their rationalisations, they cannot even understand themselves, for Herodes is unaware of the inferiority complex underlying his jealousy, while Mariamne's motives in testing and punishing him are more confused than she realises.

Hebbel himself would like to go beyond the personal framework. The play is meant to demonstrate, through the birth of Jesus, how Christianity overcomes the old world of both Jews and Romans:

JOAB:

> . . . ein Kind,
> Das Throne stürzen, Tote wecken, Sterne
> Vom Himmel reißen und von Ewigkeit
> Zu Ewigkeit die Welt regieren werde.

> (V, iv, l. 2780-3.)

When Mariamne learns about Herodes' first order she accuses him of violating all mankind in her:

MARIAMNE:

> . . . Du hast in mir die Menschheit
> Geschändet . . .

> (III, iii, l. 1684-5.)

When she discovers his second order she tells Soemus that by using them both as mere objects Herodes has transgressed against sacred values:

MARIAMNE:

> . . . Du bist, wie ich, in deinem Heiligsten
> Gekränkt, wie ich, zum Ding herabgesetzt!

> (IV, iii, l. 2202-3.)

Accordingly it has been stated that Herodes is a representative of the dying spirit of barbarism, who gives the Idea an incomplete satisfaction by going down defiant as a result of his individual self-assertion against universal progress, while Mariamne is a representative of the new Christian concept of human dignity, who satisfies the Idea completely by sacrificing her individual survival to promote the progress of the universal. This interpretation is hardly tenable. Mariamne is another Hebbelian heroine destroyed by a ruthless hero, but—active like Judith rather than passive like Klara—her vindictiveness seems no more Christian than the tyranny of Herodes; if he sins against her right to self-determination, she offends against his claim to charity. It might therefore be more appropriate to argue that the chief protagonists together form the doomed barbaric thesis to the triumphant antithesis of Christianity. But even this interpretation is vitiated by the fact that the religious hints in the dialogue seem unorganic and that the arrival of the Magi, the outstanding symbol of historical progress, has the quality of a mere afterthought.

A more convincing interpretation is that Herodes' attempts to enforce Mariamne's fidelity by grossly tangible methods reflect a vain aspiration to the essential through empirical appearances, whereas Mariamne's demands for Herodes' unconditional trust reflect an equally vain denial of all appearances in the pursuit of the essential. An idealist might solve the problem by destroying his protagonists physically while exalting the victory of some immortal value. Hebbel is not such an idealist. If the advent of Christianity is intended to be a superhuman solution, it is presented unconvincingly in theatrical terms. If, on the other hand, love is the absolute, the failure of the marriage indicates that man's quest for a meaning is thwarted by his own irrational limitations. The internal evidence thus supports those critics who see the play as the dramatisation of a sceptically relativist outlook. Hebbel succeeds where this outlook expresses itself through the investigation of neurotic relationships between the sexes such as are foreshadowed in Kleist and become prominent in much of modern European drama. He fails where he contradicts his own comment that the characters' conduct is natural by carrying them to grotesque extremes of rage, inflexibility and sophistry; and where he gives way to metaphysico-historical speculation which runs counter to the Realistic views behind the action and dialogue. Taken as a whole, *Herodes und Mariamne,* despite its absurdities, is an impressive example of Hebbel's ability to convey psychopathological insights through the ironic conflicts of a relentless tragic plot.

AGNES BERNAUER

Hebbel's most political play is **Agnes Bernauer** (written in 1851, first performed and published in 1852). The action is set in South Germany in the 1420s. Albrecht, son of Ernst Duke of Bavaria, secretly marries Agnes Bernauer, an Augsburg barber's daughter, while his father plans a match between him and the heiress of Brunswick. Ernst disinherits Albrecht, appointing his nephew Adolf as his successor. When Adolf dies he foresees a war of succession; as Agnes refuses to renounce her misalliance with Albrecht he has her drowned in the Danube. Albrecht captures Ernst, who persuades him to assume the ducal duties and retires to a monastery. Hebbel's chief alteration to the story—which he took from chronicles and history books[64] as well as from earlier literary versions such as J. A. von. Törring's tragedy *Agnes Bernauerin*—is that his Ernst is not a villain but a responsible statesman.

The medieval castles, battles, secret tribunals, pure love and pernicious intrigue hark back to the Romantic drama of chivalry, the political assassination of an innocent to the Baroque drama of state and martyrdom. The psychological and social motivation, the sceptical outlook and the prose dialogue are characteristic of nineteenth-century Realism. The clash between the marriage of a simple but admirable daughter of the people to an idealistic aristocrat and the demands of class and court recall domestic tragedy of a more traditional kind than **Maria Magdalene.** The explanations given by Hebbel in his diaries and letters will be considered, as before, with the text.[65]

Although the play forms a unity, the first half concentrates on Agnes' love and the second on Ernst's political problems. There is evidence to support Hebbel's statement that Agnes' destiny demonstrates how extreme beauty must cause its own tragic downfall. At the start her angelic quality, suggested by her nickname, is linked with elements of destructiveness as she upsets half the town by involuntarily attracting the men's desire and the girls' jealousy:

TÖRRING:

Der Engel von Augsburg?

NOTHHAFFT VON WERNBERG:

So nennt man hier eine Baderstochter Agnes Bernauer, deren Schönheit die halbe Stadt verrückt machen soll.

(I, xiv, p. 692.)[66]

As soon as Albrecht sees her he is in love but his admiration is mixed with a sense of strangeness and danger:

ALBRECHT:

. . . fremd und wunderbar . . . die sieht keiner, ohne die höchste Gefahr!

(I, xvii, p. 695.)

The union of Agnes and Albrecht is repeatedly shown to be spiritually right but nevertheless fatal. Thus Agnes' father accepts it as a decree of the stars and at the same time foresees disaster:

KASPAR BERNAUER:

. . . Wer kann gegen die Sterne! Aber mich graust, Agnes, wenn ich an deine Zukunft denke . . .

(II, v, p. 704.)

And Albrecht identifies it with the divine meaning underlying the whole world, ignoring the social and political obstacles:

ALBRECHT:

. . . Worauf sollte Gott die Welt gebaut haben, wenn nicht auf das Gefühl, was mich zu dir zieht und dich zu mir?

(II, ix, p. 711.)

After the wedding—which is symbolically sanctioned through the discovery of his deceased mother's jewelry in her prayer-stool—Albrecht declares that his love of God can only be an extension of his love of Agnes; while he invokes an ecstasy which, merging human lust with divine happiness, imperceptibly transports man to Paradise, she feels ready to die at the height of her fulfilment. The scene has mystical overtones but mainly reflects Hebbel's Romantic association of erotic bliss and extinction as well as his tragic conception of extreme beauty:

ALBRECHT:

. . . Ja, Agnes, wenn ich bei Gott aufhören soll, muß ich bei *dir* anfangen . . .

AGNES:

Und käme jetzt der Tod, ich dürfte nicht mehr sagen: Du kommst zu früh!

ALBRECHT:

. . . All unsre Wollust mündet in Gott . . . Und zuweilen stößt er die Welle zurück, dann überströmt sie den Menschen, und er ist auf einmal dahin, wandelt im Paradiese und spürt keine Veränderung!

(III, ix, p. 724.)

When Agnes' sentence is about to be signed the text explicitly states that she must die because she is beautiful and virtuous:

PREISING:

Aber es ist doch auch entsetzlich, daß sie sterben soll, bloß weil sie schön und sittsam war!

(IV, iv, p. 736.)

She is innocent in a moral sense, but her positive qualities have, ironically, created a situation in which morality is replaced by causality and in which the order of the world—based on harmony between father and son, ruler and subjects—is dangerously disturbed:

AGNES:

> Und was hab ich verbrochen?

PREISING:

> . . . Die Ordnung der Welt gestört, Vater und Sohn
> entzweit, dem Volk seinen Fürsten entfremdet, einen
> Zustand herbeigeführt, in dem nicht mehr nach Schuld
> und Unschuld, nur noch nach Ursach und Wirkung ge-
> fragt werden kann!
>
> (V, ii, p. 751.)

As she refuses to save her life at the cost of her purity
by declaring her marriage sinful and taking the veil,
Hebbel for once grants a character the spiritual solace
of an acceptance which is akin to Christian martyrdom
and stoic sublimity. But he still betrays his uncertainty
by indicating that Agnes may only know after death
whether her self-sacrifice was justified:

AGNES:

> . . . Rein war mein erster Hauch, rein soll auch mein
> letzter sein! Tut mir, wie Ihr müßt und dürft, ich wills
> leiden! Bald weiß ich, obs mit Recht geschah!
>
> (V, iii, p. 754.)

Nevertheless, Agnes' nobility and dignity turn her
physical defeat into a moral victory. This is even
acknowledged by Ernst who, having rejected her as Albrecht's wife, honours her as—to repeat his curiously
inverted use of the word—Albrecht's widow; the
gesture may seem gratuitous but is meant to emphasise
that Agnes has fallen victim to a cruel necessity despite,
or indeed because of, her purity:

ERNST:

> . . . Deine Gemahlin konnte ich nicht anerkennen,
> deine Witwe will ich selbst bestatten . . . damit das re-
> inste Opfer, das der Notwendigkeit im Lauf aller Jahr-
> hunderte gefallen ist, nie im Andenken der Menschen
> erlösche!
>
> (V, x, p. 764.)

The political theme, which centres on Ernst, becomes
prominent in the second half of the play. Bavaria is
split into warring factions and threatened by the greed
of the Emperor. Ernst, troubled by his country's decline,
has long toiled to restore at least its status of Electorate;
he is motivated by dynastic ambition as well as by
patriotism:

ERNST:

> . . . Das war Baiern einst, und das ist Baiern jetzt! . . .
> ich stückle und flicke ja auch schon ein Leben lang, ob
> ich nicht wenigstens den alten Kurfürsten-Mantel
> wieder zusammen bringe . . .
>
> (III, i, p. 713.)

Similarly, it is his despotism as well as his dedication
that mislead him into taking for granted Albrecht's assent to the political marriage he has arranged:

PREISING:

> Und Albrecht! Wird er einverstanden sein?

ERNST:

> . . . das, denk ich, versteht sich von selbst!
>
> (III, vi, p. 717.)

When he procures false proofs from corrupt lawyers
that Agnes may be executed in any expedient manner to
prevent disaster, for all the legal jargon it is clear that
his eventual signing of her sentence is a crime:

PREISING:

> . . . "Rechtlicher Beweis . . . , daß die Agnes Ber-
> nauer . . . zur Abwendung schweren Unheils, auf
> welche Weise es immer sei, vom Leben zum Tode ge-
> bracht werden dürfe!" . . . Mich graust!
>
> (IV, iii, p. 734.)

Nevertheless, Ernst is no tyrant. When Albrecht claims
a man's right to choose his own wife, the Chancellor
reminds him of his obligations as a ruler:

PREISING:

> Ihr seid ein Fürst, Ihr sollt über Millionen herrschen
> . . . , einmal müßt Ihr auch ihnen ein Opfer bringen
> . . .
>
> (III, x, p. 726.)

His refusal to marry the Brunswick heiress might have
revived the dormant enmity between their houses:

PREISING:

> . . . Hier nicht mit beiden Händen zugreifen . . . heißt
> auch die endlich eingeschlafene Feindschaft zwischen
> Welf und Wittelsbach wieder aufwecken . . .
>
> (III, x, p. 726.)

And his marriage to Agnes, a commoner, threatens to
cause a civil war by confusing the issue of succession
in Bavaria itself:

PREISING:

> . . . wenn die Erbfolge gestört wird oder auch nur
> zweifelhaft bleibt, so bricht früher oder später der
> Bürgerkrieg mit allen seinen Schrecken herein . . .
>
> (IV, iv, p. 736.)

It is to avert this situation that Ernst, albeit reluctantly,
first names his nephew his successor instead of his son
and then has the innocent Agnes killed to save a
multitude of others:

ERNST:

> . . . Es ist ein Unglück für sie und kein Glück für mich, aber im Namen der Witwen und Waisen, die der Krieg machen würde . . . : Agnes Bernauer, fahr hin!
>
> (IV, iv, p. 738.)

One wonders whether a civil war resulting from Agnes' survival would have been as inevitable as, or more dangerous than, Albrecht's revolt following her death. Ernst himself, however, is convinced of his rightness, which seems confirmed by his success in pacifying Albrecht. When Albrecht interprets his capture of Ernst as God's repudiation of the murder, Ernst trusts that in doing his duty he was carrying out God's will:

ERNST:

> . . . Ich habe meine Pflicht getan . . .

ALBRECHT:

> Eure Pflicht! Gott hat Euch in meine Hand gegeben! Zeugt er so für den, der seine Pflicht tat?

ERNST:

> Gott will dich versuchen! . . . Ich mußte tun, was ich tat . . .
>
> (V, ix, p. 759.)

Hebbel in fact shows two opposed views of God. Ernst believes that by upholding the human order at whatever cost to himself he is upholding the divine order, and he accuses Albrecht of rebelling against both:

ERNST:

> . . . wenn du dich wider göttliche und menschliche Ordnung empörst: ich bin gesetzt, sie aufrecht zu erhalten, und darf nicht fragen, was es mich kostet!
>
> (V, ix, p. 760.)

Albrecht sees the divine order in the creation of Agnes, while he cannot even find words to denounce the human order which destroyed her:

ALBRECHT:

> . . . die göttliche Ordnung rief sie ins Leben . . . Die menschliche—. . . Die menschliche—
>
> (V, ix, p. 760.)

Albrecht considers the Emperor's and the Pope's threats to outlaw and excommunicate him as violence; Ernst demands submission to the Empire as a power hallowed by law and tradition:

ERNST:

> . . . so ist es eine Gewalt, die alle deine Väter dir antun, . . . die Gewalt des Rechts! . . . bin ichs, der zu dir redet, ists nicht das ganze Deutsche Reich?
>
> (V, x, p. 762-3.)

To Ernst a prince is merely human but stands for a higher purpose, like a flag which is bound to decay but which is nevertheless an inspiring national symbol; men living in time are separated from the divine and must imprint a pretended value on what is worthless, raising some above others in a social hierarchy—in other words, while Albrecht aspired to a divine fulfilment on earth through love, Ernst holds that humanity can at best imitate the eternal order of God by building an earthly order out of such relative entities as state and ruler:

ERNST:

> . . . Wir Menschen in unsrer Bedürftigkeit . . . müssen das an sich Wertlose stempeln und ihm einen Wert beilegen, wir müssen den Staub über den Staub erhöhen, bis wir wieder vor dem stehen, der nicht Könige und Bettler, nur Gute und Böse kennt . . .
>
> (V, x, p. 764.)

Ernst's arguments eventually dissuade Albrecht from both revenge and suicide. When he offers to surrender his arms he reaffirms his respect for the Emperor:

ALBRECHT:

> . . . Kaiserlicher Majestät meinen Respekt! . . . Euch, mein Herr und Vater—(Er will ihm das Schwert überreichen).
>
> (V, x, p. 764.)

When Ernst leaves for a monastery to await his judgment, he accepts the office of acting Duke, but his homage is paid explicitly to his father and not to the state—Ernst's example has led him to recognise both the connexion and the difference between the practical need to serve the political structure and the moral greatness of self-denial:

ALBRECHT:

> (will niederknien). Vater, nicht vor Kaiser und Reich, aber vor dir!
>
> (V, x, p. 765.)

In the light of Hebbel's theories, the play dramatises the tragic relationship of the individual and the universal. Agnes is destroyed because her excessive individual beauty, although passive and pure, endangers the balance of society as a whole; her death gives the Idea an incomplete satisfaction since she considers it unjust. Albrecht and Ernst completely satisfy the Idea: Albrecht suffers for his active individual resistance before he submits to society; Ernst, recalling the notion that the universal may abandon its own human instrument, never swerves from his duty to society but must nevertheless face the painful consequences of his individual actions. In keeping with Hebbel's views on historical progress it has been suggested that Ernst stands for obsolescent feudalism while Agnes embodies new liberal demands, and that Albrecht's rule promises a more humane synthesis of the two systems; according to the text, however, the progress, if there is any, could well be meant to consist in the consolidation of the state's power over the subject. Incidentally, the Hebbelian destruction of a female character by male ones, together with the quarrel of male characters provoked by the female, is again a central theme.

As always, Hebbel asks religious questions. Ernst reluctantly decides to sacrifice Agnes and then to abdicate in atonement; Agnes chooses to die rather than desecrate her purity; Albrecht overcomes his passion by accepting Ernst's view of necessity. Thus Hebbel departs from his usual practice by hinting at a near-Schillerian spiritual freedom. But again he proclaims no idealistic convictions. Critics have argued that the conflict arises from the incompatibility of the absolute or divine and the relative or human. Agnes and Albrecht feel, rightly, that their love is divine; Ernst believes, and Albrecht eventually agrees, that the state is not divine but must, to prevent chaos, be treated as if it were divine. Both cases are tragic: if the divine assumes human shape, as it does in love, it endangers the human world as seen in the state, and must be destroyed by means of the human vulnerability it has acquired; but if the human world is thus saved it loses its divine quality. Moreover, if it is man's divine duty to uphold the human order by destroying the direct manifestation of the divine in it, then the divine itself appears to be split by a tragic dialectic. Once more Hebbel's search for certainty ends in scepticism.

The play mainly succeeds on the Realistic level of characters tragically caught between humane feeling and politics. Far from relying on deliberate villainy, Hebbel shows, as his own comments emphasise, a situation in which all the protagonists are right from their own point of view but in which the positive claims of love clash irreconcilably with the positive claims of the state. One sympathises with the lovers who are destroyed, for once, not by neuroses but by circumstances. One also sympathises, however, with the statesman who sincerely obeys his notion of duty by doing what he knows is wrong, to avert what he fears would be worse. One has reservations not because Agnes is destroyed out of a real or imagined political necessity but because Hebbel himself, through Ernst's arguments and Albrecht's acquiescence, gives murder a moral justification, underlined by his praise of Ernst in his self-interpretations; and because the old German Empire, which he avowedly intended to exalt, is hard to accept as the nearest human approach to the divine order. The play is an impressive piece of political realism in drama. It provides important insights into the spiritual questionings of its author and his time as well as into the mood of German conservatism after 1848.

Nevertheless, its message—again unequivocally stated in Hebbel's comments—that the individual must always bow to the state, brings the tragedy close to totalitarian propaganda.

GYGES UND SEIN RING

Hebbel's last major play is **Gyges und sein Ring** (written in 1853-54, published in 1856, first performed in 1889). Its relative adherence to the Unities, its simple and balanced plot, its small number of idealised characters and its fairly harmonious blank verse approach Classicism; its themes, however, are as Hebbelian as ever.

The action is set in mythical pre-history. Kandaules, king of Lydia, urges Rhodope, his Graeco-Indian wife, to show herself in public. Goaded by her refusal, he persuades Gyges, a Greek visitor, to make himself invisible with a magic ring and watch her unveil her beauty in her bedroom. Discovering the deceit, Rhodope induces Gyges, who has fallen in love with her, to fight a duel with Kandaules. Kandaules dies, and Rhodope marries Gyges but commits suicide before the consummation. In Herodotus' *History* and Plato's *Republic*[67] which, together with A. Holtzmann's *Indische Sagen,* provided the sources, the motivation is crude ambition, lust and revenge, and Gyges rules happily with Rhodope after murdering Kandaules; Hebbel aims at greater psychological complexity and metaphysico-historical implications. His self-interpretations are scantier than usual.[68]

On the psychological level, Kandaules suffers from a kind of exhibitionism. In trying to show off Rhodope, he asks for reassurance that he owns the most beautiful of all women. Like Meister Anton, then, he judges by the standards of others; like Herodes, he seems unsure of his masculine worth; and like most of Hebbel's male protagonists, he considers a woman as a possession:

KANDAULES:

> . . . Sie ist
> Der Frauen Königin, doch ich besitze
> Sie, wie das Meer die Perlen, keiner ahnt,
> Wie reich ich bin . . .
>
> (I, l. 531-45.)[69]

Gyges, on the other hand, recognises the wrongness of Kandaules' wish and of his own assent soon after eavesdropping on Rhodope:

GYGES:

> Und jetzt noch schauerts durch die Seele mir,
> Als hätt ich eine Missetat begangen . . .
>
> (II, l. 631-2.)

He rages more and more against himself for committing an unparalleled offence which he describes, in one of many images, as the inadvertent destruction of the world's most precious jewel:

GYGES:

> . . . So hab ich auch das Kleinod dieser Welt
> Zerstört und ahnte nicht, daß ich es tat.

> (IV, l. 1423-4.)

His recurrent wish to die has an element of atonement but also of erotic desire. Like many Hebbelian characters, he would experience fulfilment in expiring at the feet of the woman he loves:

GYGES:

> . . . zu ihren Füßen . . .
> Verhaucht ich meines Odems letzten Rest!

> (II, l. 718-22.)

At the same time he wants to end a life which does not seem worth living since she belongs to another man:

GYGES:

> . . . Ich wurde reif zum Tode, denn ich sah,
> Daß alles, was das Leben bieten kann,
> Vergeben war . . .

> (IV, l. 1492-4.)

Gyges' moral sentiments are badly integrated with his longing for a love-death. Nevertheless, Hebbel tries to make both him and Kandaules thoroughly noble. When Gyges confesses his love for Rhodope, Kandaules rejects his offer to die and proposes to let him leave as a friend. When Rhodope demands the killing of Gyges, whom she first believes to be the only culprit, Kandaules' pleas for him reveal loyalty together with a sense of guilt. Later Kandaules is ready to exonerate Gyges by telling Rhodope the truth, while Gyges finds excuses for Kandaules and refuses to murder him although he could hope to possess Rhodope as a result. Gyges' goodness is summed up by the servant:

THOAS:

> . . . er ist wirklich brav und treu . . .

> (V, l. 1697.)

Kandaules' goodness is summed up by Gyges:

GYGES:

> So edel war er stets!

> (V, l. 1727.)

Once more, then, Hebbel strives to derive the tragedy not from villainy but from necessity. The friends cannot help fighting each other because Kandaules believes that he must prove his love to Rhodope while Gyges believes that only his victory can prevent her threatened suicide:

KANDAULES:

> Ich muß ihr zeigen, daß ich so viel Schönheit Nicht leicht verliere . . .

GYGES:

> Sie lebt und stirbt mit mir! Ich muß!

> (V, l. 1866-8.)

Rhodope's motivation is even harder to accept than the men's. When she learns that Gyges has seen her unveiled she feels utterly polluted:

RHODOPE:

> . . . Ich bin befleckt, wie niemals noch ein Weib!

> (III, l. 902.)

When Kandaules dies and her marriage to Gyges ensures that she has only been seen by her lawful husbands, she feels purified but kills herself:

RHODOPE:

> . . . Ich bin entsühnt . . .
> Jetzt aber scheide ich mich
> (*Sie durchsticht sich*)
> so von dir!

> (V, l. 1973-5.)

Hebbel tries to make her conduct psychologically plausible by suggesting that her reserve, embodied in her veil, has become an integral part of her personality owing to her exotic upbringing:

KANDAULES:

> . . . dein Vater thront,
> Wo indische und griechsche Art sich mischen,
> Dein Schleier ist ein Teil von deinem Selbst.

> (III, l. 989-91.)

Thus her own inclinations confirm her country's law whereby a person who is defiled as she has been must not survive:

RHODOPE:

> . . . Sie kann nicht leben, und sie wills auch nicht!

> (IV, l. 1273.)

Nevertheless, her reaction is out of all human proportion with the insult. Nor is she more convincing as an alleged instrument of the gods' revenge for the loss of the purity she represented:

RHODOPE:

> . . . Jetzt rufe ich nach Blut, jetzt ist von mir
> Nur so viel übrig, als die Götter brauchen,
> Um das zu rächen, was ich einmal war!

> (III, l. 1197-9.)

To some extent her calls for Kandaules' death and her own suicide might express the despair of a highly-strung woman hurt by the man she loves; her exaggerated modesty and the absurd sophistry of her marriage to Gyges might be just acceptable as symptoms of emotional imbalance; and her sense of divine obligation might pass as a rationalisation of neurosis. Unfortunately Hebbel wants her frenzy to seem morally and spiritually right. As Gyges puts it in mythological images, the injury done to a pure female soul disturbs both the natural and the supernatural world to such a degree that their harmony can only be restored through the destruction of the offender:

GYGES:

> Wenn den kastalschen Quell
> Aus dem die Lieblinge der Götter trinken . . . ,
> Ein Steinwurf trübt, so fängt er an, zu tosen
> Und steigt in wilden Wirbeln himmelan . . .
> Und eher kehrt die Harmonie nicht wieder,
> Bis ein ergrimmter Strom den frechen Schleudrer
> Hinunter knirscht in seinen dunklen Schoß . . .

> (IV, l. 1426-39.)

And Kandaules' willingness to atone should prove, as Hebbel comments, not only his own nobility but also the value of the purity he has soiled:

KANDAULES:

> Wer frevelte,
> Muß Buße tun, und wer nicht lächelnd opfert,
> Der opfert nicht!

> (V, l. 1748-50.)

The personal and spiritual problems are linked with the familiar dialectic of two ages. Kandaules is first seen replacing the old giant symbols of royalty with a new crown and sword of more human size:

KANDAULES:

> So ist es recht!
> (*Er setzt das Diadem auf*).
> Das sitzt! . . .
> (*Er gürtet sich das Schwert um*).
> Dies Schwert ist etwas leichter, wie das alte . . .

> (I, l. 61-76.)

His request that Rhodope should appear in public is another sign of his desire to promote, in his own metaphor, the wind of change:

KANDAULES:

> . . . Bläst auch der frische Wind an allen Orten
> Die Schleier weg: du hältst den deinen fest.

> (I, l. 442-3.)

The people's revulsion from his attempts to abolish the sacred practice of five centuries manifests the resistance of the old-established to reform:

THOAS:

> . . . als du es das letzte Mal versuchtest,
> Die alten Heiligtümer zu verdrängen,
> Da stand das Volk entsetzt und staunend da
> Und murrte, wie noch nie!

> (I, l. 16-9.)

Rhodope's refusal to show herself at the games, conditioned by the old customs of her country, is another example of traditionalism:

RHODOPE:

> . . . Bei uns ist das nicht Sitte . . .

> (I, l. 334.)

In a sense, then, the struggle between Rhodope and Kandaules is one between conservatism and innovation, and for once the man stands for the new and the woman for the old. Eventually Kandaules realises why he deserves his downfall. Rhodope's veil and the country's royal insignia are in themselves worthless but they have a symbolic meaning; although one day everybody will share his outlook, at the moment the world holds on to traditions which were once newly won but have since come to be taken for granted, and which are justified by men's need for them if not by their intrinsic value:

KANDAULES:

> . . . Man soll nicht immer fragen:
> Was ist ein Ding? Zuweilen auch: was gilts?
> Ich weiß gewiß, die Zeit wird einmal kommen,
> Wo alles denkt, wie ich; was steckt denn auch
> In Schleiern, Kronen oder rostgen Schwertern,
> Das ewig wäre? Doch die müde Welt
> Ist über diesen Dingen eingeschlafen,
> Die sie in ihrem letzten Kampf errang,
> Und hält sie fest.

> (V, l. 1807-15.)

The reformer, who wakes the world from the sleep of tradition, must be able to overcome its resistance and to replace what he takes away from it by something better; Kandaules, unlike his mythical ancestor, lacked this ability:

KANDAULES:

> . . . Wer sie ihr nehmen will,
> Der weckt sie auf. Drum prüf er sich vorher,
> Ob er auch stark genug ist, sie zu binden,
> Wenn sie, halb wachgerüttelt, um sich schlägt,
> Und reich genug, ihr Höheres zu bieten,
> Wenn sie den Tand unwillig fahren läßt.
> Herakles war der Mann, ich bin es nicht . . .

> (V, l. 1815-21.)

It is with his own failure in mind that he warns Gyges never to disturb the existing order:

KANDAULES:

> . . . Nur rühre nimmer an den Schlaf der Welt!
>
> (V, l. 1855.)

If Kandaules stands for innovation and Rhodope for tradition, Gyges may offer a synthesis of these opposites. His accession to the throne seems intended to mark the beginning of an age in which energy is united with, rather than pitted against, refinement, as is foreshadowed when earlier on he wins both the athletic and musical contests:

GYGES:

> . . . daß man Knochen haben kann,
> Und Mark in diesen Knochen, wenn man auch
> Die Saiten einer Zither nicht zerreißt . . .
>
> (II, l. 579-81.)

And Kandaules' compliment—a post-Classical homage to Hellenism—hints that Gyges, the self-effacing representative of Greece, could embody a more balanced world about to dawn:

GYGES:

> Herr, ich kämpfte heut
> Als Grieche, nicht als Gyges.

KANDAULES:

> Um so schlimmer
> Für uns, wenn du die neue Regel bist!
>
> (I, l. 462-5.)

The magic ring is significant in the same context. Rhodope sees it as one of those objects which gods and men exchanged as love tokens in the legendary past, but which might now bring the gods' revenge upon the man who usurps their power—that is, as a symbol of ancient hybris and nemesis modified by Hebbel's modern notion of the gulf separating the human from the divine and of the dangers inherent in individual self-assertion:

RHODOPE:

> . . . Sie stammen aus der Zeit,
> Wo Gott und Mensch noch miteinander gingen
> Und Liebespfänder tauschten.
> . . . Graust dich nicht,
> Dir ihre dunkle Gabe anzueignen
> Und ihre Rache auf dein Haupt zu ziehn?
>
> (I, l. 423-30.)

When Kandaules relates the world's destiny to the ring—also wishing in retrospect that it had remained unused—the theme of tragic individuality links with that of historical progress:

KANDAULES:

> . . . er wäre besser
> In seiner Gruft geblieben!
> . . . es hängt
> Vielleicht an ihm das ganze Weltgeschick.
>
> (V, l. 1778-84.)

Hebbel's last major play is typical of his entire work. Rhodope, whose passive dignity turns into active vindictiveness, unites the two chief attitudes found separately or jointly in most of Hebbel's heroines; Kandaules shares his ruthless possessiveness with most of Hebbel's heroes, while his fight with Gyges repeats the familiar clash of male characters over a female; and again a woman is destroyed by men in a vicious circle of sadomasochistic love-hate and incompatible aspirations. In terms of Hebbel's theories, Rhodope and Kandaules continue the line of those individuals who unintentionally threaten the balance of the universe—Rhodope, like earlier heroines, through her extreme beauty; Kandaules, like earlier heroes, through his extreme obstinacy and inconsiderateness. While Rhodope falls as another supporter of tradition and opponent of innovation, Kandaules falls as another representative of a new outlook and rebel against the old. The Idea, in Hebbel's terminology, is given full satisfaction as both assent to their destruction, and universal history may progress as the dialectical conflict of the two individuals and their respective worlds ends in Gyges' possibly more harmonious rule.

This interpretation is borne out by hints in the dialogue and in Hebbel's comments but, as so often, the intended message forms no unity with the play as a whole. The schematic structure just outlined becomes more complex as Rhodope's defence of tradition degenerates into a rigid obscurantism, and as Kandaules' humanist reforms mingle with sexual confusions and, ironically, ignore the human needs of his wife and his subjects. Such realistic ambiguities, however interesting, seem at variance with the metaphysico-historical roles apparently allocated to Rhodope and Kandaules, while the synthesis of Gyges is not sufficiently developed in the action.

Perhaps the chief cause of one's misgivings is that yet again there is a contradiction between Hebbel's realism and his idealism. This contradiction grows most tangible when he tries to prove, despite his doubts, that psychological and political relativities can be given an absolute moral or spiritual meaning. In **Maria Magdalene,** perhaps his masterpiece, he denounces middle-class conventions without imposing a positive message on his portrayal of life. In **Judith,** however, the ambiguity of a divine mission which may be a mere rationalisation of frustrated sexuality is confusing; in **Herodes und Mariamne** the advent of Christianity is attached as an afterthought to the tragedy of distrust between lovers; in **Agnes Bernauer** the tragic collision of love and the state is impressive, but the justification of murder as moral duty is dubious. A similar weakness is evident in **Gyges und sein Ring.** On the political level Hebbel's tone indicates sympathy for Kandaules' reforms while his overt statements support Rhodope's traditionalism which, incidentally, reflects his own somewhat reluctant conservatism. On the metaphysico-historical level Rhodope's conviction—echoed by Kandaules, Gyges and Hebbel's self-comments—that her revenge for her defilement is the gods' retribution for the disruption of the divine order of the world is belied by the absurdity of her frenzy and by the suggestion that that order will be superseded by a different one in the future.

The contradictions of **Gyges und sein Ring,** then, are characteristic of those running through the whole of Hebbel's work. On the one hand he is painfully aware as a Realist of the relative, subjective, indeed illusory nature of transcendental aspiration; on the other hand he longs back to the absolute certainties of an idealistic faith. When he dramatises the perplexities of a disenchanted Realist he can be most impressive; when he tries to make the real appear as ideal, the relative as absolute, the irrational as part of a higher rationality, he provokes disbelief and at times distaste. The expression of his intuitive scepticism through acute psychological insights and tragic conflicts is often marred by intellectual speculations designed to elicit a meaning from an existence which he feels to be meaningless. Even so, his major plays, with all their flaws, are more powerful than the smoother products of many lesser dramatists.

Notes

Unless otherwise stated the edition referred to is Friedrich Hebbel, *Werke,* herausgegeben von Werner Keller und Karl Pörnbacher, München 1963-67, 5 vols.

1. *Über den Stil des Dramas,* vol. 3, p. 582.

2. *Schiller und Körner, Hebbels Werke in vier Bänden,* herausgegeben von Friedrich Brandes, Leipzig 1921, vol. 4, p. 384.

3. *Tagebücher 2,* 23 Feb. 1863, no. 6085, vol. 5, p. 351.

4. *Tagebücher 1,* Dec. 1846, no. 3865, vol. 4, p. 806.

5. *Über Theodor Körner und Heinrich von Kleist, Hebbels Werke,* ed. Brandes, vol. 4, p. 262.

6. *Tagebücher 1,* Feb. 1839, no. 1471, vol. 4, p. 271.

7. ibid. March 1838, no. 1034, p. 196-7.

8. ibid. Feb. 1841, no. 2265, p. 427.

9. To S. Engländer, 1 May 1863, vol. 5, p. 842.

10. *Gervinus' Geschichte des neunzehnten Jahrhunderts, Hebbels Werke,* ed. Brandes, vol. 4, p. 560.

11. *Tagebücher 1,* Sep. 1840, no. 2129, vol. 4, p. 403.

12. ibid. Feb. 1841, no. 2262, p. 426.

13. ibid. Nov. 1843, no. 2828, p. 574.

14. ibid. March 1847, no. 4039, p. 860.

15. ibid. Nov. 1838, no. 1364, p. 253

16. ibid. Feb. 1841, no. 2261, p. 426.

17. ibid. July 1843, no. 2721, p. 551.

18. ibid. June 1844, no. 3158, p. 666-7.

19. ibid. March 1843, no. 2664, p. 539.

20. ibid. 3 Oct. 1846, no. 3713, p. 780-1.

21. ibid. Oct. (?) 1847, no. 4324, p. 913.

22. ibid. Oct. 1839, no. 1686 a, p. 315.

23. ibid. July (?) 1842, no. 2578, p. 505.

24. ibid. Nov. 1843, no. 2864, p. 583

25. To Elise Lensing, 12 Feb. 1837, vol. 5, p. 485-6.

26. *Tagebücher 1,* 5 Dec. 1843, no. 2932, vol. 4, p. 607.

27. ibid. July 1841, no. 2359, p. 444.

28. ibid. Oct. (?) 1839, no. 1744, p. 326.

29. ibid. Jan. (?) 1844, no. 3031, p. 643.

30. ibid. Oct. 1846, no. 3739, p. 783.

31. ibid. Apr. 1839, no. 1546, p. 293.

32. ibid. Apr. (?) 1845, no. 3457, p. 738.

33. To A. Ruge, 15 Sep. 1852, vol. 5, p. 741.

34. To Amalie Schoppe, 1 May 1848, p. 662.

35. *Tagebücher 1,* Feb. (?) 1839, no. 1516, vol. 4, p. 286.

36. ibid. May (?) 1839, no. 1611, p. 304.

37. Vol. 3, p. 545.

38. ibid. p. 545-6.

39. ibid. p. 546.

40. ibid. p. 568.

41. ibid. p. 546.

42. ibid. p. 550.

43. ibid. p. 550.

44. ibid. p. 560.

45. ibid. p. 567.

46. ibid. p. 467-8.

47. ibid. p. 569-70.

48. ibid. p. 571-2.

49. Vol. 1, p. 307.

50. ibid. p. 307.

51. ibid. p. 308.

52. ibid. p. 312.

53. ibid. p. 313.

54. ibid. p. 320.

55. ibid. p. 321.

56. ibid. p. 323.

57. *Tagebücher 1,* March 1838, Nov. 1839, 3 Jan. and 3 Apr. 1840, nos. 1011, 1012, 1802, 1872, 1958, vol. 4, p. 191-2, 336, 354, 372-3, *Vorwort,* vol. 1, p. 8-9.

58. The play is quoted from vol. 1. There is no consistent division into numbered scenes.

59. Vol. 1, p. 325-8.

60. Above all *Tagebücher 1,* 4 and 8 Dec. 1843, nos. 2910, 2926, vol. 4, p. 601-2, 604-5. To Auguste Stich-Crelinger, 11 Dec. 1843, vol. 5, p. 585-6.

61. The play is quoted from vol. 1.

62. *Hebbels Werke,* ed. Brandes, vol. 4, p. 438-49. To A. R. E. Janinski, 14 Aug. 1848; to G. Kühne, 19 March 1850; to R. Zimmermann, 22 May 1850; to A. Ruge, 15 Sep. 1852; to G. von Cotta, 10 Nov. 1857: vol. 5, p. 672, 684, 686, 744, 789.

63. The play is quoted from vol. 1.

64. Notably C. Mannert, *Geschichte Bayerns aus den Quellen*; J. H. von Falckenstein, *Vollständige Geschichte des großen Herzogtums und ehemaligen Königreichs Bayern*; F. J. Lipowsky, *Agnes Bernauerin historisch geschildert.*

65. *Tagebücher 2,* 30 Sep., 24 Dec. 1851, nos. 4941, 4982, vol. 5, p. 97, 103. To F. von Dingelstedt, 12 Dec. 1851, 26 Jan. 1852; to K. Werner, 16 Feb. 1852; to G. Gervinus, 11 Dec. 1852; to A. Pichler, 10 Feb. 1853; to F. Uechtritz, 14 Dec. 1854; to G. Cotta, 10 Nov. 1857; to S. Engländer, 27 Jan. 1863: vol. 5, p. 707-9, 746-7, 760-1, 789, 837.

66. The play is quoted from vol. 1.

67. As quoted in H. A. Pierer's *Universal-Lexikon.*

68. To F. Uechtritz, 14 Dec. 1854; to K. Werner, 16 May 1856: vol. 5, p. 759-60, 773.

69. The play is quoted from vol. 2. There is no consistent division into numbered scenes.

JUDITH

CRITICAL COMMENTARY

George C. Tunstall (essay date 1981)

SOURCE: Tunstall, George C. "Hebbel and Georg Kaiser: Reflections of Judith in *Die Bürger von Calais.*" *Colloquia Germanica* 14, no. 2 (1981): 130-41.

[*In the following essay, Tunstall determines Hebbel's influence on the playwright Georg Kaiser.*]

Der Weg zu meiner That geht durch die Sünde! . . .

Ist nicht meine That so viel werth, als sie mich kostet?

—Hebbel, *Judith*[1]

Although the critical literature on the Expressionist playwright Georg Kaiser contains occasional mention of the possibility that he was influenced by Friedrich Hebbel, very little cogent or concrete evidence has been offered to substantiate such a claim.[2] Wilhelm Steffens was the most recent critic to stress Hebbel's significance for Kaiser, but his statements are based almost exclusively on Wolfgang Paulsen's comments in his monograph on the dramatist from 1960.[3] There Paulsen had maintained: "Kaisers eigentliche dramatische Ansätze aber liegen doch, nach Überwindung der ersten Anregungen aus der Welt Hofmannsthals und Georges, . . . in der Nähe Hebbels und nicht Schillers, wie überhaupt wohl die Auseinandersetzung mit Hebbel für die junge Dramatiker-Generation, die durch den Expressionismus hindurchzugehen hatte, fruchtbarer gewesen ist, als unsere Literaturgeschichten wahrhaben wollen."[4] Paulsen has made by far the most important contribution to the theme of Hebbel-Kaiser, and anyone who deals with the topic must begin by weighing carefully his perceptive observations.

The issue of Hebbel's influence on Kaiser has been clouded somewhat by the circumstances surrounding the first play that the dramatist published, *Die jüdische Witwe: Biblische Komödie.*[5] Opinions have varied on the question of whether in this work Kaiser wrote a travesty of Hebbel's *Judith* (1840), of the biblical story from the apocrypha, or of both. Paulsen appeared to opt for a parody of Hebbel's drama when he wrote: "Gerade am Hebbel-Stoff der 'Jüdischen Witwe' hatte er sie [die ihm so eigene Formsprache] sich ja erarbeitet . . ." (p. 100), whereas Eric A. Fivian earlier claimed: "Aus Hebbels Drama übernimmt er [Kaiser] nur das Motiv der 'jungfräulichen Witwe', alles andere tritt als unwichtig zurück."[6] Ernst Schürer states unequivocally: "Kaiser's comedy is a parody of the biblical version of the story, not of Hebbel's play."[7]

The fact of the matter is that, although Kaiser did spin out one of the possibilities inherent in the motivational problem that Hebbel had introduced in *Judith,* i. e. whether the heroine murdered Holofernes purely out of divine inspiration or whether in the final analysis she did it in order to vindicate her humiliated womanhood, he nevertheless did not really parody Hebbel's text itself. Kaiser's Judith is a young nymphomaniac whose family marries her off to the doddering and impotent voyeur, Manasse. In order to unterscore the sexual side of his "heroine", Kaiser infused the stage designs and the text of his comedy with such features as Freudian sexual symbolism and parody—not of the apocryphal text, however, but instead of the sexual imagery from "The Song of Solomon".[8]

How Kaiser is believed to have treated Hebbel in *Die jüdische Witwe* has had a bearing upon the interpretation of his relationship in general to this nineteenth-century predecessor. It has led in some instances to what I consider to be the false conclusion that with this comedy Kaiser rejected Hebbel's *Judith* for good—and with it, for the most part at least, the playwright himself. Paulsen wrote, for example: "Der junge Dichter stößt sich von Hebbel gleichsam ab, indem er ihn zu überbieten trachtet . . ." (pp. 99-100). But Paulsen does concede a formalistic influence:"Vorbildlich wurde Hebbel für ihn aber doch durch etwas ganz anderes: die Grundtendenz seines Dramas nämlich, den Stoff jeweils von der Form her zu erfassen und zu beleben" (p. 100). In the footnote (no. 80, p. 123) to the sentence that immediately precedes the first one quoted above, Paulsen refers to Eberhard Lämmert's statement: "Mit dem Zarathustra-Wort 'Oh meine Brüder, zerbrecht, zerbrecht mir die alten Tafeln' hatte Kaiser 1908 seiner 'Jüdischen Witwe' den polemischen Akzent gegen die biblische Überlieferung wie gegen Hebbels 'Judith' aufgeprägt . . .".[9] This brings up another problematical side of *Die jüdische Witwe*: Kaiser's attitude at this time toward Friedrich Nietzsche, which is, I believe, analogous to his view of Hebbel.

What Lämmert failed to take into account in his reference to the citation from *Also sprach Zarathustra* that graces the published version of the play as motto is that in the fourth act of *Die jüdische Witwe* Kaiser parodies the style of Nietzsche's work from which the motto stems. Herbert W. Reichert pointed this out in 1964—albeit without placing the same emphasis upon the phenomenon that I would like to here. Reichert cites the example: "Siehe mit deiner Sternenseele den Mond an, wenn der blasse in's blaue Tuch der Nacht gezeichnet steht—also spricht Zarathustra" (*Die jüdische Witwe*, p. 100).[10] There is a strong element of ambivalence involved in this comedy. Whereas Kaiser's use of the motto from *Zarathustra* is usually interpreted as the dramatist's homage to his philosophical mentor,[11] it could just as well have been meant in the ironical—and

more typically Kaiserian—sense that even the master himself was not immune to his own weapon.

The point is that during this artistically formative period in Kaiser's career as a writer he was wont to first reject and then later to accept just as wholeheartedly literary forerunners. In the two years that followed the completion of the fourth and final version of *Die jüdische Witwe* (1909-1910), for example, the dramatist's negative attitude toward most of previous literary tradition changed noticeably. Whereas as late as *Die Versuchung* (finished in 1910) Kaiser still parodied Nietzsche, in subsequent works that were written during the transitional period that lasted from 1910 to 1912 he borrowed in a now straightforward (i. e. not parodistic) way from *Also sprach Zarathustra*. As I have shown elsewhere, such works by Kaiser as *König Hahnrei* (1910), *Von morgens bis mitternachts* (1912), and *Die Bürger von Calais* (1912-13) owe a tremendous debt to Friedrich Nietzsche.[12]

Hebbel, I believe, fared in a similar way with Kaiser during these years. Although in his first published work the dramatist appeared to reject Hebbel's position in *Judith,* he was nevertheless later to borrow from that same drama. Support for such an interpretation can be garnered through making a minor revision in the following statement by Paulsen regarding Hebbel's influence on Kaiser: "Was Hebbel für Kaiser bedeutet hat, erhellt . . . aus den 'Bürgern von Calais' unmittelbarer als aus der 'Jüdischen Witwe': der zum Ritus gesteigerte Prozeß der Handlungswiederholung und thematischen Korrespondenzen, auf denen das Stück strukturell aufgebaut ist, geht sicher (in der Brechung durch die Hofmannsthal-Welt) auf 'Herodes und Mariamne' zurück, und ganz ähnlich verhält es sich mit dem anderen Neugewinn Kaisers in den 'Bürgern von Calais': der ihm so eigenen Formsprache" (p. 100). The reference to Hebbel's impact being more directly apparent in *Die Bürger von Calais* than in *Die jüdische Witwe* is an astute observation, but Paulsen fails to explain precisely why he singled out *Herodes und Mariamne* as being especially influential; there is, for example, no indication in Kaiser's writings that he was intimately familiar with the work. Only of *Judith* can one be certain that the playwright had more than mere passing knowledge.

My purpose in this paper is, then, to trace on a number of different levels what I consider to be reflections of Hebbel's *Judith* in *Die Bürger von Calais*. A comparison of the general situations dealt with, of structural features, such plot details as characterization of the masses, a few parallel characters, certain stylistic similarities, and the corresponding conclusions in the two dramas will, I believe, demonstrate to what extent Hebbel's work played a role in the shaping of the play upon which Kaiser's public career as a dramatist was founded.

To begin with, the two dramas *Judith* and *Die Bürger von Calais* resemble each other in a number of general ways. Most obvious, of course, is the similarity between the situations in both of them: in each a city is faced with certain and apparently inescapable destruction at the hand of a powerful enemy. Whereas in Hebbel's *Judith* Bethulien faces annihilation by the Assyrian army under the leadership of the infamous *Übermensch* Holofernes, in Kaiser's play, which is based upon an episode from the Hundred Years' War that occurred in 1346, the port city of Calais has been under siege by the English forces for a year. In each instance a sacrifice of some sort is required in order to stem the tide of fate; and that sacrifice, once it is brought, succeeds at least to a certain extent in achieving its goal. In the two works, however, there remains a residuum of doubt concerning the outcome: in Hebbel's drama the doubt is engendered in the heroine herself concerning her actual motivation in beheading Holofernes; in Kaiser's by the question of the efficacy of Eustache de Saint-Pierre's taking his own life in order to resolve the dilemma of the seventh volunteer. Any apparent discrepancies in the two "heroic" acts are dispelled, though, when viewed from the perspective of the absolute ideal after which each character has striven. In both cases the welfare of the masses appears to be the motivating force, but in the actual execution of the sacrifice personal concerns tend to eclipse the idealistic point of departure. Judith, whose goal it was to carry out a divine mission, becomes emotionally involved with the superhuman object of her mission and will undoubtedly—in accordance with Hebbel's pantragic plan—have to atone for her tragic error with death; in Eustache's case, the original goal of protecting the harbor from destruction becomes subjugated to the less circumspect aim of purifying the motivation of the other six volunteers as they prepare to make the supreme sacrifice.

Beyond these general characteristics that both dramas have in common, there are a few structural features which suggest a possible closer link between the two works. One of these is the revue technique that Kaiser employs at the beginning of Act II in which he has each of the volunteers appear with a loved one or business associate: the fifth citizen with his confidant, the third with his mother, the fourth with wife and child, etc. Hebbel employed a similar—although not identical—dramatic technique in the second half of his third act, in which Judith and Mirza go out into the streets of Bethulien. The scene is divided into numerous brief episodes that take place among various inhabitants of the city. These segments in both dramas fulfill similar functions: in Kaiser's case the audience learns through the short encounters how painfully the uncertainty concerning the outcome affects each of the volunteers and their friends and families. Although yet willing to offer the sacrifice, each volunteer nevertheless still clings to life and hopes that he might be the lucky

seventh and go free. In Hebbel's play the episodic technique offers the audience a cross section of the population in Bethulien and how it es reacting to the threat of siege and facing the shortages of food and water. Most striking in this portion of the work is the rampant lack of faith in God and of confidence that he will deliver them from their suffering.

This revue technique is precisely the kind of formalistic possibility that particularly fascinated Kaiser, as is evident from his skillful use of it in the parallelly structured first and fifth acts of *Die jüdische Witwe*. The source for it there was obviously Hebbel's *Judith*. I would go so far as to say that the opening portion of Act II in *Die Bürger von Calais* is modelled—with minor modifications—after the second half of Hebbel's third act. *Die jüdische Witwe*, in which Kaiser copied Hebbel's technique more faithfully, represents the first stage in the playwright's treatment of this dramaturgical device which then attained perfection in *Die Bürger von Calais*.

For additional reasons, though, there seems to be a connection between this particular section of Hebbel's drama and various parts of Kaiser's *Die Bürger von Calais*. The masses in both dramas are most certainly portrayed in a similar fashion. Under the duress of waiting for a decision to be made or for something to happen that will change the circumstances, the *Volk* of Hebbel's drama and the *Bürgervolk* of Kaiser's react in much the same way: with impatience and a tendency toward desperation and resultant violence. When Josua, for example, points out that the inhabitants of Bethulien apparently sealed their fate by not opening the gates immediately to the Assyrians, he raises the question of who it was that seduced them into not capitulating. The response from the *Volk* is simply: "Wer anders, als Priester und Aelteste?" (*Judith,* p. 37). On the next page he incites the masses to drive the elders and priests out of the city: "Wißt Ihr was? Wir wollen Aelteste und Priester aus der Stadt heraustreiben . . ." In Act III of Kaiser's play a similar scene occurs when the citizens believe that Eustache has deceived them; there various citizens shout their calls for violent action against Eustache: "Wir stoßen Eustache de Saint-Pierre vor uns auf den Markt!" (p. 100)[13]—"Eustache de Saint-Pierre soll den Schlüssel [der Stadt] auf seinen Knien hinausschleppen!"—"Eustache de Saint-Pierre soll auf dem offenen Markte geschändet werden!" (both *Bürger,* p. 101). The masses in both works demonstrate doubt, distrust, and the desire for revenge at the slightest provocation.

Somewhat more concrete evidence for a relationship between Hebbel's *Judith* and Kaiser's *Die Bürger von Calais* than the general characteristics, the structural feature, and the treatment of the masses consists in a series of parallel characters in the dramas. All of them in Hebbel's play also happen to appear in the second part of Act III. The first of these is Achior who is introduced already in Act I, in which he explains to Holofernes the mysterious nature of the Hebrew God. Annoyed by such information, Holofernes banishes Achior into Bethulien where he is to await his certain death as soon as the Assyrian army overruns the city. Then in Act III Achior serves the converse function of describing to the inhabitants of the city what Holofernes is like. In Kaiser's play the captive French officer, who explains to the assembly how the English forces treacherously routed the French army, plays a similar role. When he has finished his description of the ambush, the English envoy releases him into the city, explaining: "Du bist frei in der Stadt—du wirst in den Straßen deutlich sprechen, wo du dich zeigst" (*Bürger,* p. 24). Whereas the French officer is to instill fear in the citizens of Calais in order to get them to accept more readily the terms of surrender, in Hebbel's work Judith perceives an ulterior motive in Achior's frightening revelations about Holofernes, as she reports to the latter: "Er [Achior] dankt es Dir [Holofernes] dadurch, daß er Dein Bild in Blut malt und Dir jedes Herz abwendig macht" (*Judith,* p. 52).

Other characters in Kaiser's play who have parallels in Hebbel's include Jean d'Aire who is described in the stage notes to *Die Bürger von Calais* as "einen hohen Siebziger" (p. 15) and appears to be modelled after *Der Aelteste* in Hebbel's play, who at one point in Act III explains to the inhabitants of Bethulien who seek his help: "Ich bin heute gerade drei und siebzig Jahr alt geworden, und mögte wohl zu den Vätern eingehen; auf ein Paar Athemzüge mehr oder weniger kommt's nicht an" (*Judith,* p. 38). In Act II of *Die Bürger von Calais* Jean d'Aire explains to the other volunteers that he is old and close to death, so that the sacrifice does not have the same sting for him as for them; he is going to die soon anyway: "Ich gehe weite Wege nicht mehr. Jeder Weg ist kurz—das Ziel ist nah. Ich sehe es so dicht vor mir . . . Meine Zeit ist ausgeschenkt . . ." (*Bürger,* p. 67).

Even more striking is the correspondence between the figure of Samuel in Act III of Hebbel's play and Eustache's father at the end of Kaiser's work. Hebbel's stage direction describing Samuel reads: "*Samuel, ein uralter Greis, von seinem Enkel geführt, tritt auf*" (*Judith,* p. 31). Note the stage direction in the middle of Samuel's long speech on the same page: "Er faßt seinen Bart." Kaiser's stage note near the end of Act III describes Eustache's father as follows: "In kleinem Abstande folgt der Vater Eustache de Saint-Pierres—hagerer überalter Greis, kahlhäuptig; ein dünner Bart zittert um das Gesicht, das er aufwärts richtet nach Blinder Art . . . Ein schlanker Knabe führt ihn um die Hüfte" (*Bürger,* p. 102). The parallels between "ein uralter Greis" and "überalter Greis", the youth leading

both, and the beard (no other beard is mentioned in Kaiser's text) seem to be more than mere coincidence. The father's blindness, by the way, he shares with another character from the same part of Hebbel's play, namely Daniel. Whereas Daniel, who until this scene was unable to speak but suddenly does so, Eustache's father all of a sudden begins to "see" metaphorically despite his physical blindness. Eustache's father becomes the prophet of the New Man through his "enlightenment" and Daniel in Hebbel's play is proclaimed by the *Volk*: "Ein Prophet, ein Prophet!" (*Judith,* p. 35).

The matter of style and stylistic influence is much more complex and more difficult to deal with than the similarities treated thus far in this study. This is because it is so seldom that they exist in as clear-cut a one-to-one relationship as some of the points touched upon above. But the topic must nevertheless be broached at this point in order to offer as complete a picture as possible of certain important linguistic links that exist between *Judith* and *Die Bürger von Calais.* Although such superficial similarities as the mention of *Gnade, Trotz, zögern,* etc. in the following lines from both works:

MESOPOTAMISCHE GESANDTE:

. . . Mesopotamien unterwirft sich unter jeder Bedingung, es hofft bloß auf Gnade.

HOLOGERNES:

Ich weiß nicht, ob ich diese Hoffnung erfüllen darf. Ihr habt lange gezögert.

(*Judith,* p. 11)

DER ENGLISCHE OFFIZIER:

. . . Mit gerechter Strafe züchtigt der König von England den Trotz, der vor ihm die Stadt verschloß . . . Der König von England will Gnade üben.

(*Bürger,* p. 25)

are of little avail because they are a bit too coincidental and circumstantial, other aspects of Kaiser's language and style seem to indicate that the dramatist may well have schooled his language in *Die Bürger von Calais* on Hebbel's style in portions of *Judith.* A few examples will point out the kind of influence that I believe was involved here.

In dealing with influences on Kaiser's style it is of the utmost importance to concentrate upon the types of motifs, themes, turns of phrase, etc. that impressed the dramatist most—and not just during the early period, but throughout his literary career. In the present case they seem to fall into the following categories: 1) graphically visual expressions, especially those having to do with visual perception; 2) certain words with a moral tinge, particularly those that tend to elicit an intensely emotional or irrational response from the beholder; these are often closely related to the first group; and 3) verbs of a markedly dynamic nature. There are abundant examples of these types of words throughout Hebbel's entire *oeuvre,* but they are noticeably denser in his first play, ***Judith.*** A few juxtapositions will show, I believe, how strongly Kaiser seems to have reacted to some of them.

Among expressions dealing with visual portrayal and visual perception in general, the dichotomy of light and darkness plays a key role in both ***Judith*** and *Die Bürger von Calais.*[14] Such images are used most frequently by both dramatists in an epistemological context. In attempting to ascertain what she must do, for example, Judith first perceives her position in terms of darkness: ". . . aber in mir und außer mir bleibt's dunkel"; but as soon as she realizes what her mission is to be, she comments: "Du [Herr] machst mein Auge hell" (both ***Judith,*** p. 26). Compare her words with those of Jean d'Aire, as he explains to the other volunteers how different the sacrifice is for him than for them: "Es ist hell um mich—das Dunkel ist gewichen . . ." (*Bürger,* p. 67).

Related to the realm of visual perception in both dramas is the phenomenon of *blenden* or "blinding". Whereas Holofernes uses the verb in its literal sense in his comment: "Nur die Blinden sind elend! Ich schwör's, ich will nie wieder Jemand blenden lassen" (***Judith,*** p. 50), the English officer in *Die Bürger von Calais* uses the term in both a literal and a figurative sense simultaneously when he describes how his army set up decoy armor to deceive the citizens of Calais into thinking that the English were still camped there so that they could slip away in order to ambush the unsuspecting French army: "Im Sande vor Calais liegen Helme—Lanzen, wie Lanzen—Helme still liegen—wenn ein Kind sie nicht wegräumt.—Die Sonne spiegelt darauf—das blendet!" (*Bürger,* p. 21).

The verb *verblenden,* which means to blind (i. e. deceive) through words or actions, plays an especially important role in both dramas, as, for example, in the words of Duguesclins in his reply to the English officer's claim that the French king was falsely enthroned: "Der König von England schilt uns blind—so erhält er das Maß für unsere Verblendung . . ." (*Bürger,* p. 20). The similarity in the uses of *verblendet* in the following citations from the two plays seems to me to be more than coincidental. The first occurs in Judith's words to Holofernes: "Auf meinen Knieen bitt' ich Dich wegen dieser Beleidigung meines verblendeten Volks um Vergebung" (***Judith,*** p. 52); this, on the other hand, is part of the English officer's reply to Duguesclins' allegation that the former is lying: "Der freche Dieb versteckte sich . . . und täuschte das verblendete Volk von Frankreich . . ." (*Bürger,* p. 19).

The verbs *täuschen, verraten, lügen* (and their corresponding substantive forms) with their moral implications are likewise used along similar lines to those of *verblenden* in the two works under consideration. The brief exchange between Mirza and Judith at the end of Act IV combines these various contexts. To Mirza's outraged question: "Verfluchte, so bist du gekommen, Dein Volk zu verrathen?" Judith answers by beginning to cry; when asked why she is crying, she explains: "Freudenthränen darüber, daß ich Dich täuschte. Ich schaudere vor der Kraft der Lüge in meinem Munde" (***Judith,*** p. 56). A parallel to such deceptive appearances is found in the crowd's reaction to the absence of Eustache on the morning on which the sacrifice is to be made: "Täuschte er nicht dreist mit den Kugeln—und log plump mit den Losen?" (*Bürger,* p. 97), "Eustache de Saint-Pierre hat uns alle verraten!" (*Bürger,* p. 100), etc. Note also Duguesclins' repeated use of the word *Lüge* (*Bürger,* pp. 19-20) in his tirade against the English officer.

Another echo from ***Judith*** occurs in Eustache's use of the word *Frevel* in relationship to the *Tat,* i. e. the sacrifice. Judith referred to Holofernes' sleep after their lovemaking as "der ärgste Frevel" (***Judith,*** p. 70) and in her agonizing about what has happened she says to Mirza: "Nicht wahr, Mirza, wenn's ein Gräuel wäre, wenn ich wirklich gefrevelt hätte, Du würdest mich das ja nicht fühlen lassen; Du würdest ja, und wollt' ich selbst über mich zu Gericht sitzen und mich verdammen, freundlich zu mir sagen: Du thust Dir Unrecht, es war eine Heldenthat!" (***Judith,*** p. 71). Compare Eustache's warning about the motivation behind the volunteers' willingness to offer their lives to save the city: "Seid ihr würdig, ihn [diesen Weg] zu gehen? . . . Diese Tat zu tun—die ein Frevel ist—ohne verwandelte Täter?"; and later in the same speech: "Ein halbes ist die Tat—ein halbes der Täter—eins zerstört ohne das andere—sind wir nur Frevler?" (*Bürger,* p. 78). In my opinion there are clear parallels between these contexts.

Examples of strikingly dynamic verbs that merit mention include in particular the uncommon expressions *peitschen* and *Sturm laufen* that occur in both works. Compare Judith's utterance: "Das Elend meines Volks peitschte mich hierher . . ." (***Judith,*** p. 72) with the description near the beginning of Kaiser's text: "So peitscht kein Sturm . . ." (*Bürger,* p. 17). Likewise Judith's words: "Du glaubst, sie [Holofernes' Kraft] sei da, um gegen die Welt Sturm zu laufen . . ." (***Judith,*** p. 65) with the threat that the English officer repeats: ". . . so läßt der König von England in derselben Stunde den Sturm laufen und die Stadt in den Hafen stürzen!" (*Bürger,* p. 25). As isolated examples they would hardly be convincing; but in combination with the other points made in this study, they seem to fit a pattern.

The style of Kaiser's drama in general bears marked similarities to that in the speeches of Hebbel's heroine. Certain of Judith's lines, for example, could easily be mistaken for lines from Kaiser's drama, as in her question: "Wollt Ihr es jetzt dulden, daß man Euer tiefstes Gefühl der Lüge zeiht?" (***Judith,*** p. 36) that suggests Eustache's line: "Euer größtes Werk wird eure tiefste Pflicht" (*Bürger,* p. 30). Other motifs that sound a familiar note include that of the *Weg,* especially in connection with *wandeln,* in Judith's words: "Willst Du dem Herrn den Weg vorschreiben, den er wandeln soll? Reinigt er nicht jeden Weg dadurch, daß er ihn wandelt?" (***Judith,*** p. 36) that have the same majestic ring and pathos as many of the speeches in *Die Bürger von Calais.* The motto to the present paper likewise offers a good example that further underscores similarities in language and plot in the works, as does also Judith's question to the priests and elders at the end of ***Judith:*** "Wenn's nicht heilige Pflicht war, wenn ich's lassen durfte, ist's dann nicht Hochmut und Frevel?" (***Judith,*** p. 80).

Before concluding I would like to make one more point that has to do with the strangely anticlimatic conclusions of both works. Each play ends with what seems to be an unnecessary addendum that tends to rob each work of its full potential effectiveness by leaving a bit too much food for thought. The parallels are obvious: Hebbel's play actually culminates in the death of Holofernes and Kaiser's in Eustache's suicide. Death, it might be noted, is projected in both cases beyond the parameters of the dramas themselves: in ***Judith*** through the heroine's request of the priests that they kill her should she bear a child from Holofernes; in Kaiser's play through the revelation at its conclusion that the world of the New Man lies in a realm transcendent of life, as Lämmert has aptly pointed out.[15]

Two separate and unrelated statements form Hebbel's drama seem in a strange way to anticipate what happens at the end of Kaiser's play. The first comes from the second half of Act III, in which Samaja asks: "Und warum thut er [der Herr] nicht ein Wunder im Herzen des Holofernes und bewegt ihn zum Abzug?" (***Judith,*** p. 36). The birth of a son to the English king in the camp before Calais in Kaiser's play with the king's subsequent decision to free the volunteers from their sacrifice ist almost tantamount to the type of miracle that Samaja suggests. The other statement comes from Holofernes and has to do with two themes that especially fascinate him: death and suicide. In his conversation with Judith in Act V the Assyrian leader states: "Ja, ja, die Kraft ist zum Selbstmord berufen, so spricht die Weisheit, die keine Kraft ist" (***Judith,*** p. 65). Holofernes' death itself almost borders on suicide because it seems practically self-willed, particularly in view of the fact that he actually urges—perhaps challenges would be more appropriate—Judith to carry out the act. These

words have a further parallel in Holofernes' earlier comment from Act IV: "Freilich, der Gedanke ist der Dieb am Leben . . ." (***Judith,*** p. 48). Such a sentiment reflects surprisingly accurately Kaiser's outlook during the early years, as it is manifest, for example, in the *Geist—Leben* dualism that informs so many works of that period, especially *Die jüdische Witwe. Die Bürger von Calais* represents the culmination or limit in the opposite direction from that of the earlier comedy in which everything was centered on the *Leben* side of the antithesis, for in this play the spirit reigns supreme and is willing to uphold the idea(l) at any cost—even that of self-destruction.

The evidence presented in this paper should suffice to establish that Kaiser was indeed influenced in a positive way by Hebbel's ***Judith*** and apparently during the most crucial period in his literary development, namely the years in which he composed *Die Bürger von Calais.* In contrast to Wolfgang Paulsen who some twenty years ago wrote concerning Kaiser and Hebbel: "Wichtig ist uns lediglich die Feststellung, daß die großen Leistungen der Vergangenheit nicht spurlos an ihm vorübergegangen sind, oder er an ihnen—daß sie ihn vielmehr auf eine eindrücklichere Weise gebildet haben, als das irgendeine direkte Entlehnung zu tun vermocht hätte" (p. 103), I believe that, at least in this one instance, some direct borrowing did take place; but the material taken over from Hebbel was synthesized so successfully into the new work of art that only close textual study could identify and disclose its point of origin.

Notes

1. Hebbel's *Judith* is cited according to the following edition: Friedrich Hebbel, *Sämtliche Werke, Historisch-kritische Ausgabe,* hrsg. von Richard Maria Werner, I. Abt., 1. Band: *Dramen I (1841-1847)* (Berlin: Behrs, 1904). Page references to the drama that appears on pp. 1-81 in this volume will be given parenthetically in the text preceded by *Judith.* The motto quotation is from p. 26.

2. See Max Freyhan, *Georg Kaisers Werk* (Berlin: Die Schmiede, 1926), pp. 112-13; Ludwig Lewin, *Die Jagd nach dem Erlebnis: Ein Buch über Georg Kaiser* (Berlin: Die Schmiede, 1926), p. 67; Eric Albert Fivian, *Georg Kaiser und seine Stellung im Expressionismus* (München: Desch, 1947), pp. 16-17; Adolf Schütz, *Georg Kaisers Nachlaß: Eine Untersuchung über die Entwicklungslinien im Lebenswerk des Dichters,* Diss. Bern 1949 (Basel: Frobenius, 1951), pp. 150-54. Klaus Ziegler's otherwise informative article "Georg Kaiser und das moderne Drama", *Hebbel-Jahrbuch,* 1952, 44-68, does not go into the subject of Hebbel and Kaiser.

3. Wilhelm Steffens, *Georg Kaiser,* Friedrichs Dramatiker des Welttheaters, No. 58 (Velber bei Hannover: Friedrich, 1969), pp. 66-67 and 71.

4. Wolfgang Paulsen, *Georg Kaiser: Die Perspektiven seines Werkes* (Tübingen: Niemeyer, 1960), p. 99. See also pp. 24, 26, 35-36, 41, 49, 80, 92, 95, 99-100, 103, and footnote 80 on p. 123.

5. Georg Kaiser, *Die jüdische Witwe: Biblische Komödie* (Berlin: S. Fischer, 1911). Any quotations from the play are taken from this original edition; page references will be included parenthetically in the text.

6. Eric Albert Fivian, *Georg Kaiser und seine Stellung im Expressionismus*, p. 17.

7. Ernst Schürer, *Georg Kaiser*, Twayne's World Authors Series, No. 196 (New York: Twayne, 1971), p. 72. He bases his statement on the motto from Nietzsche's *Also sprach Zarathustra* which I discuss below.

8. Acts I and V take place in the temple and parallel each other. The first act, in which Judith is dragged up the stairs to her wedding with Manasse, is dominated by a huge pilaster that suggests a phallic symbol: "Ein Absatz, nach dem aus der Tiefe, links von dem riesigen Mittelpfeiler, die breite Treppe kommt" (p. 9); and the fifth, in which Judith finally finds gratification with the handsome young high priest, Jojakim, in the Holy of Holies, opens with what suggests a vaginal symbol: "Die Wand zieht im Halbrund - die Mitte hat eine breite, weit geschwungene Öffnung, die ein hoher Teppich füllt" (p. 133). The parody of "Das Hohelied Salomos" occurs in Rebekka's description of her sister's beauty: "Judith, . . . du bist jung und so schön . . . Wie scharlachrote Wolle blühen die Spitzen deiner Wangen—und deine Füße laufen ebenso spitz wie Mandelkerne aus'" and somewhat later: "Unsere Judith ist ein Reh" (p. 33). The allusions here are to the fourth chapter of "Das Hohelied" which bears the title "Vorzüge der Freundin" and begins: "Siehe, meine Freundin, du bist schön! siehe, schön bist du!" Kaiser's curious "wie scharlachrote Wolle" and "Spitzen deiner Wangen" are composites derived from verses 2 and 3 of that chapter which read: "Deine Zähne sind wie eine Herde Schafe mit beschnittener Wolle, die aus der Schwemme kommen . . ." and "Deine Lippen sind wie eine scharlachfarbene Schnur . . . Deine Wangen sind wie der Ritz [cf. Kaiser's *Spitzen*] am Granatapfel zwischen deinen Zöpfen." The *Reh*-motif is found in verse 5: "Deine zwei Brüste sind wie zwei junge Rehzwillinge, die unter den Rosen weiden."

9. Eberhard Lämmert, "Kaiser: *Die Bürger von Calais*", in *Das deutsche Drama vom Barock bis zur Gegenwart,* ed. Benno von Wiese (Düsseldorf: Bagel, 1958), Vol. II: *Vom Realismus bis zur Gegenwart* (pp. 305-24); the quotation is from p. 306.

10. Herbert W. Reichert, "Nietzsche and Georg Kaiser", *Studies in Philology,* 61 (1964), 85-108; I refer to p. 100.

11. Wolfgang Fix writes, for example, in his article "'Es ist nichts so, wie es ist': Das dramatische Werk Georg Kaisers," *Deutsche Rundschau,* 76 (1950), 474-78: "Dies [das Nietzsche-Motto] ist Kaisers erste öffentliche Huldigung an Nietzsche" (p. 475).

12. See the present writer's forthcoming contribution entitled "The Turning Point in Georg Kaiser's Attitude toward Friedrich Nietzsche" in Vol. 11 (1982) of *Nietzsche-Studien: Internationales Jahrbuch für die Nietzsche-Forschung.*

13. I cite Kaiser's work according to the first printed version: Georg Kaiser, *Die Bürger von Calais: Bühnenspiel in drei Akten* (Berlin: S. Fischer, 1914). Page references will be included in parentheses in the text of this study preceded by *Bürger.*

14. For a detailed discussion of light symbolism, including such related phenomena as fire imagery and seeing/blindness, in Kaiser's play, see the present writer's article "Light Symbolism in Georg Kaiser's *Die Bürger von Calais*" in the *JEGP,* 78 (1979), 178-92.

15. Lämmert writes in his interpretation of *Die Bürger von Calais* that was cited above (footnote 9): "Zu seinem Geheimnis gehört es, daß der neue Mensch nur im Tode verwirklicht wird" (p. 318).

G. A. Wells (essay date summer 1984)

SOURCE: Wells, G. A. "Ethical Absolutism, Hebbel and *Judith*." *New German Studies* 12, no. 2 (summer 1984): 95-106.

[In the following essay, Wells discusses ethical issues in Judith.*]*

What is meant by saying that moral rules are either absolute or relative? An illustration will help. Suppose that a man has sought refuge in my house knowing that the police are seeking to arrest him on a capital charge. Suppose further that I know he is innocent, yet that circumstantial evidence is likely to lead to his conviction and execution if he is arrested. If a policeman then calls, and asks me whether I know where the man is, my reply may depend on the relative weighting I give to three obvious moral rules, the first two of which conflict with the third:

1) That maximum cooperation must be given to the authorities who enforce the law.

2) That the truth must be told.

3) That a fellow human being in danger must be assisted.

When one or other of these rules is said to be absolute, what is meant is that it must always, in these or any other circumstances, be given priority over others which conflict with it. On the other hand, when all ethical rules are said to be relative, the meaning is that there is no moral rule which can invariably be given this priority.

Insistence on absolute standards is often defended by appeal to Kant, who wrote contemptuously of the kind of grocer who merely on prudential grounds does not cheat children, instead of being honest without regard to any consequences. But Kant is in fact in no better position than this grocer. Kant argues that, to act ethically, we must be able to will that the rule we are acting on should be followed by all other people. If, for instance, a man makes it a rule to seek revenge for every injury, he yet cannot—so Kant says—will that everyone else should do so. But why not? Only because that would mean that others would always be taking revenge on each other and on him. When he pays his debts he can, however, says Kant, will that everyone else should follow this course. Now this is plainly an explanation of moral law in terms of utility; and Schopenhauer was able to quote a number of passages where Kant in effect concedes this: e.g. 'that I cannot will that there should be a universal law permitting lying, because people would then no longer believe me or would pay me back with the same coin'.[1]

Kant pretends to dispense with utility, and argues that a homicidal maniac must be told the truth, even if this guides him to one of his chosen victims, because the principle 'Thou shalt not lie' is an absolute that must be upheld irrespective of consequences.[2] Close study of real human situations has made some less prone to such rigorism. Macaulay, for instance, said, apropos of the situation in England in 1687:

> A nation may be placed in such a situation that the majority must either impose disabilities or submit to them, and that what would, under ordinary circumstances, be justly condemned as persecution, may fall within the bounds of legitimate self defence.[3]

I take this to mean that political measures draw their virtue or viciousness from the circumstances of the time, and that to say that tolerance is always and in every circumstance a good, and intolerance an evil, is to base political justice on an unconditional imperative as elusive as that on which Kant professed to base individual morality.

How difficult those questions are can be seen not merely from Kant's adherence to utility while professing to repudiate it, but also from the absolutism which

sometimes informs the arguments of professed utilitarians. They know that it is vain to tell men that they must calculate the future effects, throughout all eternity, of their actions; and so they would fain show that certain simple maxims may be relied on always to produce desirable effects. Thus J. S. Mill, in his *On Liberty,* would like to show that licence to express any views is always ultimately beneficial. This he could not show, even if he made it plausible. But because he wants a general rule that can be applied without continual reference to the fundamental utilitarian principle, a rule of action that need not involve laborious investigation of probable consequences, he tries to prove too much. All he is really entitled to say is that, on the whole, or on the average, freedom of expression is more helpful to society than hurtful.

Fundamental questions concerning ethical behaviour are raised in Hebbel's ***Judith.*** He believed—according to his preface to ***Maria Magdalena***—that it is the function of drama to show the relation of individuals and societies to 'die Idee', by which he here means 'das alles bedingende sittliche Zentrum, das wir im Weltorganismus schon seiner Selbsterhaltung wegen annehmen müssen'. If, he says in *Mein Wort über das Drama,* an individual transgresses against this 'Idee', against these ethical principles which are to be accepted as absolutes, then the 'Idee' will 'take satisfaction' in his destruction. His Judith voices a similar view, saying, when she learns that Holofernes tramples down all others: 'Die Natur . . . wird den zweiten Mann nicht erschaffen, oder nur darum, damit er den ersten vertilge' (Act Two).

Not only Holofernes, lacking in any sense of duty to God or man, but also the deeply religious Judith offends, in Hebbel's conception, against 'die Idee'. In his diary he wrote that she finally realizes 'daß sie über die Grenzen hinausgegangen ist' (Tgb. 1872: 3.1.40). Although, as K. Ziegler has noted,[4] she is not so much as mentioned in Act One of the play, none of the characters there having even heard of her, the two independent worlds which clash in this tragedy have it in common that both offend against ethical absolutes.

Judith's first words recount a dream in which she went to the Deity in response to his summons, only to find that 'ich war zu schwer, er konnte mich nicht halten'. She regards this as an intimation of what her position vis-à-vis the Deity will be; for dreams, she says, signal 'die Dinge, die kommen sollen'. She believes, then, that some god-inspired work will divorce her from God presumably by sullying her in some way. There follows her narrative of her unconsummated marriage. We gather from this account that her husband regarded her with a mixture of reverence, sympathy and horror (even loathing), and so had some intimation that she was (or was to become) both holy and horrible. This must reinforce the impression that she has gained from her dream; and both are meant as motivation for her realizing in Act Three that, if God is commanding her to kill Holofernes and so save His chosen people, she will have to sin in the process: 'Der Weg zu meiner Tat geht durch die Sünde'. Fulfilling even this divinely appointed mission will nevertheless involve what she regards as an ethical transgression. Her early disgust that Ephraim 'gehört zu denen, die sogar dann sündigen, wenn sie etwas Gutes tun wollen' (Act Three) is calculated to draw attention to her own predicament.

Many commentators, noting how frustrating an unconsummated marriage must be—particularly for one who believes, as Judith does, that a woman's function in life is to bear children—have taken her account of her six months of marriage merely as an indication that she strongly desires the sexual experience she has hitherto been denied. And they have understood this as an additional motive which impels her towards Holofernes. M. Durzak goes so far as to say that the religious motive which she alleges is merely an unreal rationalization of her real (sexual) motive.[5] Such interpretation ignores the fact that in so many of his plays Hebbel deliberately attributes a given action to multiple motives in order to avoid what he called simplifying human behaviour to the level of clockwork.[6] Judith certainly feels attracted to Holofernes as a man of exceptional strength and valour, as is stressed elsewhere in the play. But the behaviour of her late husband and his whole attitude to her is narrated not so much because it suggests to us that she desires sexual fulfilment as because it suggests to her that there is something fundamentally amiss with her, that her beauty will kill the man who does finally enjoy it: 'Meine Schönheit ist die der Tollkirsche; ihr Genuß bringt Wahnsinn und Tod' (Act Two). This idea counts for as much in driving her to the enemy of her people as any attraction she, in spite of herself, feels for him.

In a well-known diary entry Hebbel reiterates the idea that, even when using a particular person as an instrument for achieving some purpose, the Deity is powerless to save that person from destruction if what he does at the Deity's behest offends against 'die ewige Ordnung der Natur' (Tgb. 1011, 7.3.38). W. Wittkowski has pointed out that what is meant by this 'ewige Ordnung' is 'das Gefüge aller Werte und Gesetzlichkeiten. Gut und Böse stehen als unabhängig von Gott fest, objektiv und absolut'.[7] One purpose of the crowd scene (III, 2) is to illustrate this idea that God cannot sustain someone who sins in serving Him. The dumb Daniel suddenly acquires the power of speech and apparently with the voice of God commands the people to stone his brother for counselling action contrary to God's will; but then relapses into his former dumbness, burdened by the guilt of fratricide.

It is in Act Five of the play that ethical absolutism is unambiguously obtruded. Judith has earlier said, in the spirit of her patriarchal society, that woman's natural function is to bear children. And in III, 2 murder—the reference is to the killing of his brother ordered by Daniel—was said to be 'gegen die Natur' and hence 'gegen Gott'. In V, 1 Mirza brings these two points together in criticism of the deed she sees Judith about to perpetrate: 'Ein Weib soll Männer gebären, nimmermehr soll sie Männer töten'. Mirza is thus made the spokesman of an ethical precept which she considers binding even in the Jews' present desperate situation, and the infringement of which under any circumstances constitutes (in the phrase Hebbel used in his diary) 'über die Grenzen hinausgehen'. Hence, when Judith has done the deed and appeals to Mirza to say that her act is no 'Greul', that she has not 'gefrevelt', Mirza keeps a hostile silence; whereupon Judith answers her own question by claiming that her deed is no crime but a 'Heldentat'. But she has to admit that what drove her to it was not the desire to serve God—a motive which she had lost from sight—but burning indignation at Holofernes' outrage of her.

Wittkowski argues that Judith feels remorse because she has committed murder at all, not because she murdered in order to avenge a personal injury instead of in order to serve God: 'Judith leidet unter der Tat, nicht unter den Motiven'. He admits, however, that Hebbel had to represent her as impelled to the deed by motives other than service to God so as to make her final sense of annihilation plausible. Had she done the deed purely because God ordered her to it, she might have felt tainted as a murderess, but could hardly have felt this taint as so crushing a burden that it outweighed the merit of her obedience to God's command.[8] As things are, having confessed to impurity of motive, having admitted that she was not thinking of 'das Elend meines Volks' and that 'nichts trieb mich, als der Gedanke an mich selbst', she adds: 'Jetzt'—i.e. because she acted on an impure motive—'muß ich meine Tat allein tragen, und sie zermalmt mich'. The 'allein' implies that, had her motive been disinterested service to God and to her people, then she could have shared the burden of guilt with them. This in turn implies that, even had her motives been thus impeccable, she would nevertheless have felt some guilt at infringing the ethical absolute 'Thou shalt not kill'.

That she should feel such scruples—scruples that are independent of her motives—in murdering a ruthless murderer whose declared intention is to annihilate the whole nation to which she belongs is not altogether implausible. Westermarck has given a great deal of evidence to show that moral ideas are based on instinctive tendencies to approve or disapprove certain acts,[9] and it is surely this emotional origin which gives many moral maxims a paramountcy and inspires the feeling that they must be obeyed even when obedience to them is inconvenient or painful. It is recognition of such paramountcy, acceptance of the moral maxim as a *categorical* imperative, that makes the moral absolutist reject utilitarianism.

One must, however, admit that, as Hebbel's Holofernes is an egoist to the point of caricature, the utilitarian grounds—not to mention the religious ones—which Judith has for disposing of him are so strong and so obvious that her scruples on absolutist grounds are somewhat unexpected. In fact the principal weakness of this play lies—as Hebbel later readily conceded[10]—in the grotesque exaggeration of everything about Holofernes. Even his redeeming characteristic of fearlessness is indicated in the manner of a boy's adventure magazine. It is reported that, on riding up to a precipice from which his companion recoiled in fright, he 'wagt den grausamen Sprung' across—not because their path lay in that direction, but merely because he thought he saw water on the other side. When he found that there was in fact none, he leaped back with the laconic comment: 'Verschlafen wir den Durst' and was asleep within seconds (III, 2). One can see why F. T. Vischer called him 'ein aufgeblasener Frosch'.[11] Again, Holofernes declares: 'Jäger haben mich als einen derben Buben in der Löwenhöhle aufgelesen, eine Löwin hat mich gesäugt' (Act Four). Hebbel presumably means this to indicate that Holofernes—unlike Judith, who owes ideas important for her behaviour to the Jewish society in which she has grown up—is unconditioned by any human background. When Nestroy's Holofernes declares: 'da is in ganz Wien, will ich sagen in ganz Assyrien, keiner, der mir's Wasser reicht', this particular piece of 'Verwienerung'[12] cannot but remind us that the character here parodied is in no way specifically Assyrian; whereas Judith's belief that she is, or may be, the Deity's chosen vessel is a reflection of what her fellow-citizens are shown to believe in III, 2. This distinction between the two principals is an important one; but Hebbel's method of indicating it is, in the case of Holofernes, grotesque. Furthermore, as Holofernes is reluctant to accept any ideas except his own, his character has to be drawn largely by monologues, none of which includes anything as interesting as deliberation—he is never sufficiently hesitant to have to weigh alternatives—but which merely illustrate his self-confidence and self-assertiveness at length. When in Act One he is on stage with others, his will to power is shown by the way he dominates the conversation. Yet towards the end of the Act, Hebbel has to make him fall silent so that he (and we) can be told facts essential to the exposition about the Jews who are opposing him. In the first Act of *Herodes und Mariamne* Hebbel likewise has both to draw the character of an egoist and also convey details of the situation facing him. But

there he succeeds in doing both simultaneously and does not represent his hero as at first all talk and then all silence.

Judith could not expect her people to sympathize with her scruples over murdering someone who was determined to kill them all. And so she puts it to them that her guilt consists in having killed a man of exceptional greatness in order that they, little folk as they are, may survive:

> Ich habe den ersten und letzten Mann der Erde getötet, damit du (zu dem einen) in Frieden deine Schafe weiden, du (zu einem zweiten) deinen Kohl pflanzen . . . kannst . . . Mich trieb's die Tat zu tun, an euch ist's, sie zu rechtfertigen! Werdet heilig und rein, dann kann ich sie verantworten!

This is no hypocrisy, as she did feel admiration for Holofernes, as well as hatred for his crimes, and had seen in him a man she could respect, even love. So her sense of guilt seems to be compound: she has done wrong in committing murder at all; she has done especial wrong in killing an outstanding individual; and thirdly she has done wrong because she was impelled to the deed by the motive of personal revenge. The first of these three elements is, as I have tried to show, not what one would expect from Judith in her circumstances, and so has been overlooked by most commentators, except Wittkowski, who stresses it to the exclusion of all other factors. L. Lütkehaus, commenting on his work, gives a juster summary: 'Nur die Verbindung von Tat- und Motivschuldthese wird der Frage nach der Schuld Judiths gerecht'.[13] He notes that Hebbel himself hinted as much when he added to the diary entry where he declared her deed an infringement of an inflexible ethical principle ('sie ist über die Grenzen hinausgegangen'): 'Sie hat mindestens das Rechte aus unrechten Gründen getan'.

Judith is finally determined not to bear Holofernes a son, not to carry, as Hebbel put it, 'die Nemesis in ihrem eigenen Schoß' (*Mein Wort über das Drama*)—a son, then, whose duty it would be to avenge the murder of his father, who would accept 'das alte Diktum: Auge um Auge, Zahn um Zahn, Blut um Blut' (ibid.) as an absolute, and who in doing so would fail in his like duty to observe the principle 'Thou shalt not kill'. Judith's decision to die rather than give birth to Holofernes' son constitutes an abandonment of ethical absolutism, an awareness that two maxims which are both felt to be unconditionally compelling may conflict with each other. This awareness does not, however, amount to a rejection of all her religious beliefs, as some commentators have supposed.[14] Her final words, to Mirza, are: 'Bete zu Gott, daß mein Schoß unfruchtbar sei! Vielleicht ist er mir gnädig'. She would hardly thus instigate prayers to a deity in whom she has ceased to believe. Hebbel has, it is true, left the idealism of Weimar classicism far behind, but he was no atheist or nihilist,[15] and it was not his intention to end his first play in such a way as to suggest such views.

It is of interest to note that the view that certain inflexible principles suffice to indicate what one ought to do in any situation is put in a very negative light in some of Hebbel's later plays. Meister Anton brings about the tragic catastrophe in **Maria Magdalena** by having a ready rule of thumb to distinguish right from wrong in any given case and by forcing on Klara the decisions he has reached from such premisses. Hebbel himself affirmed that the tragic outcome here depends on the inadequacy of such simple rules as guides in complex human situations: 'Hier ist das Tragische . . . ganz einfach aus der bürgerlichen Welt selbst abgeleitet, aus ihrem zähen . . . Beharren auf den überlieferten patriarchalischen Anschauungen und ihrer Unfähigkeit, sich in verwickelten Lagen zu helfen'.[16] In Hebbel's very last composition, **Demetrius,** the characters are not uninfluential bourgeoisie, but statesmen whose actions affect the lives of all their subjects. And the realist Mniczek points out that such persons cannot rely on ten inflexible commandments or on a catechism which allows only one answer to any question. He says to Demetrius:

> Mein Fürst und Czar,
> Gott Vater war Regent im Paradies
> Und hatte einen einz'gen Untertan,
> Und dennoch kam er mit dem Katechismus
> Nicht aus . . .
> . . . . .
> Denkst du die deinen durch die zehn Gebote
> Zu zügeln? Hoff' es nicht! Du hoffst umsonst.[17]

Demetrius believes that, even as Czar, he can follow simple maxims, such as absolute truthfulness, at whatever sacrifice to himself. Mniczek has to tell him that he can thus satisfy his own conscience only by contravening 'größere Pflichten' (l.1277); that he has no right to sacrifice himself if this entails the ruin of those who have honestly and conscientiously made themselves dependent on him:

> Hast du den Mut, bloß um dich rein zu halten
> Vom kleinsten Hauch, der Seelen trüben kann,
> Die große Wechselrechnung durchzustreichen,
> Die uns verknüpft, und Lieb' und Treu zu opfern,
> Und glaubst du, daß du rein bleibst, wenn du's
> tust?
> Der Himmel selbst ruht auf gespaltnen Kräften,
> Die ganze Welt auf Stoß und Gegenstoß;
> Denkst du, der Mensch ist davon ausgenommen?
> Pflicht gegen Pflicht, das ist auch sein Gesetz!

(IV, 10; lines 2985-93)

Demetrius finds this unanswerable (lines 3057-59). As at the end of **Judith,** it is irreconcilable conflict between supposedly absolute duties that leads to abandonment of the absolutist standpoint.

Notes

1. Quoted in Schopenhauer's *Preisschrift über die Grundlage der Moral,* paragraph 7.

2. See Kant's *Über ein vermeintes Recht aus Menschenliebe zu lügen.*

3. *History of England* (5 vol. edition), London, 1905, II, pp. 209-10.

4. *Judith,* in *Das deutsche Drama. Interpretationen,* ed. B. von Wiese, Düsseldorf, 1958, II, p. 106.

5. 'Hebbels *Judith.* Deutungsprobleme und Deutung', *Hebbel Jahrbuch,* 1971/2, p. 55.

6. On this, see my paper 'Psychological Realism in Hebbel's *Gyges und sein Ring',* *German Life and Letters,* vol. 38, no. 1 (October 1984).

7. 'Hebbels *Judith',* in *Hebbel in neuer Sicht,* ed. H. Kreuzer, 2nd ed., Stuttgart, 1969, p. 165.

8. ibid., p. 167.

9. *The Origin and Development of the Moral Ideas,* 2nd ed., London, 1912.

10. See Hebbel's letter to F. Bamberg of 6.3.49, in *Hebbels Briefwechsel,* edited by F. Bamberg, vol. 1, Berlin, 1890, p. 318.

11. *Altes und Neues,* Stuttgart, 1889, p. 5.

12. cf. J. R. P. McKenzie, 'The Technique of *Verwienerung* in Nestroy's *Judith und Holofernes',* *New German Studies,* 1 (1973), 119-32.

13. 'Verdinglichung. Zu Hebbels *Judith',* *Hebbel Jahrbuch,* 1970, p. 93.

14. e.g. Ziegler, *art.cit.,* p. 118.

15. Hebbel wrote, while he was working on *Judith,* that he would retain his belief in God until he found a tree writing a poem or a dog painting a Madonna (Tgb. 1937). The evolutionist would reply that, however great the difference between man and other animals appears to be, it is possible to find in them forms of behaviour which, under certain conditions, might develop into human culture, and to show that such conditions may plausibly be supposed to have existed.

16. Letter to August Stich-Crelinger, 11.12.43, in *Hebbels Briefwechsel, vol.cit.,* in note 10 above, p. 159.

17. *Demetrius,* IV, 1, lines 2304-11 in R. M. Werner's standard edition of the play (Hebbel, *Sämtliche Werke,* 1. Abteilung, 6. Bd., Berlin, 1904). Further line references will be to the lines as there numbered.

MARIA MAGDALEN (MARIA MAGDALENA)

CRITICAL COMMENTARY

Rolf K. Högel (essay date October 1972)

SOURCE: Högel, Rolf K. "'Ort: Eine Mittlere Stadt': The Setting of Hebbel's *Maria Magdalene*." *MLN* 87, no. 5 (October 1972): 763-68.

[*In the following essay, Högel discusses the ambiguity of the setting of* Maria Magdalena.]

Below the list of the dramatis personae of his *Maria Magdalene* (1844) Hebbel briefly states the setting of this bourgeois tragedy: "eine mittlere Stadt." The geographical location of this town is not indicated.

In relating these facts to the text of the drama itself two questions may occur to the attentive reader and spectator as well as to the stage director engaged in performing this play: (1) Does Meister Anton's family really live in a town fitting into the category of what could be termed a German "mittlere Stadt' at the time Hebbel was working on *Maria Magdalene*? (2) In what geographical area of Germany is Meister Anton's home town to be localized?

Pertinent contributions of literary criticism reflect diverse views held on either question. E. Kuh, for example, takes a "small North German town" to be the setting of *Maria Magdalene*,[1] and he believes that Hebbel incorporated into his drama the spirit of the people living between the Eider river and the North Sea.[2] F. Mehring, on the other hand, seems to consider as the scene of action the München of Hebbel's youth which he characterizes as one of the most backward and illiberal cities in Germany.[3] L. Brun, like E. Kuh, regards a "small North German town" as the setting.[4] F. Bielfeldt, in support of the racial theories of the Third Reich, glorifies the play's characters as ideal representatives of Dithmarschen's middle class.[5] In more recent contributions K. May obviously assumes a small town in Lower Germany to be the drama's setting,[6] while A. Meetz describes it as a composition of North and South German traits, with those of the North prevailing.[7] S. G. Flygt expresses a similar view.[8]

Of German stage directors, R. Noelte, in his television version of *Maria Magdalene* of 1963, selected for the setting a small place in Dithmarschen, encompassed by an unmistakably North German landscape.[9]

Finally, there are at least four independent translations of *Maria Magdalene* into Low German, each of which is necessarily based on the assumption that the drama is set in Northern Germany, preferably in Dithmarschen.[10]

Hebbel himself, in a letter to S. Engländer of 1863, designates the landlord of one of his Munich abodes (1838-39), Anton Schwarz, the model of his Meister Anton, recalling, on this occasion, the terrifying effect the arrest of the son made on the members of that family.[11] R. M. Werner stresses the importance of that event for the composition of *Maria Magdalene,* and, in evaluating some of Hebbel's unpublished diary entries, he links Beppi Schwarz's confessions of her own seduction and defilement with Klara's predicament in the drama.[12] We should, however, bear in mind that both Hebbel's and Werner's statements are related more closely to the creation and the development of the plot than to the present problem of elucidating the drama's setting.

In order to determine the category of a German "mittlere Stadt" of the middle of the nineteenth century, let us look at the total population of some cities and towns of that time:

Berlin had 419,000 inhabitants (in 1850),[13] Hamburg 155,000 (in 1840),[14] Köln 101,000 (in 1852),[15] München 94,400 (in 1852),[16] Bremen 49,636 (in 1840),[17] Stuttgart 42,217 (in 1840),[18] Kassel 31,686 (in 1841),[19] Regensburg 20,678 (in 1843),[20] Hildesheim 14,700 (in 1848),[21] Osnabrück 11,718 (in 1842),[22] Fulda 9,199 (in 1844),[23] Landshut 8,343 (in 1835),[24] Detmold 4,716 (in 1841).[25]

Wesselburen in Dithmarschen, Hebbel's place of birth, had 1,312 inhabitants (in 1841).[26]

Starting from these numbers as a basis, it seems adequate to define the category of the German middle-sized town of the 1840's and early 1850's as holding between 10,000 and 60,000 inhabitants.

Does Meister Anton's family dwell in a town fitting into this category? The text of the drama indicates that in Meister Anton's home town most of the families live in single homes, not in rows of houses. Behind those homes extend gardens (III, 6) in which rose bushes grow and, here and there, arbors and benches are put up for a rest (I, 4). A wood is located within walking distance (III, 6). There is a marketplace in the center of the town (III, 10). The supply of drinking water is provided by a number of wells scattered in the residential district (II, 6). The burying ground and the church building are so close to Meister Anton's home that from there Klara is able to watch her mother talking to the sexton and see her enter the church (I, 3).

For the appraisal of the size and the extension of the place some further details are informative. In his inquiry of Karl's carousing debt Meister Anton is able to talk to all local innkeepers on a walk of the town (II, 1). A native of the place himself, he seems to know every fellow inhabitant intimately, pockmarked Fritz (II, 1) and bailiff Adam (II, 3) as well as the druggist (I, 5) and the pastor (II, 1). Conversely everybody here knows Meister Anton for his exceeding honesty (I, 7) The secretary, on his return from the academy, immediately remembers Leonhard from their common boyhood days (III, 6). News has no long way to go to reach everyone in this community: Leonhard's appointment as town clerk is soon learnt by Meister Anton while out at work at the mourning house of the Müller family (I, 5), and the tidings of merchant Wolfram's misfortune, his wife's insanity, rapidly spread over the place (II, 3). There is every reason to surmise that in this community lives only one druggist (I, 5), only one master joiner and coffin maker, only one Lutheran pastor (II, 1) and that there is only one Lutheran church where one can publish and hear the latest banns of marriage (I, 4). Examinations for the vacant position of the town clerk are held and letters of appointment expedited by the mayor himself who seems to represent in his person both the town council (if there is any) and the municipal administration (I, 4).

The ways of life and thinking characteristic of the members of this community are strictly conservative, dominated by the conception of a static hierarchically structured society and by the traditional sets of religious and moral values which at no time are seriously exposed to doubt or criticism.

Meister Anton's place of residence—this is the conclusion to be drawn from the particulars above—is a small remote town or major village, of a few thousand inhabitants at best, in a rural, partly wooded environment. It definitely does not fit into the category of a middle-sized German town of the mid-nineteenth century, represented by such towns as Bremen, Stuttgart, Kassel, and Osnabrück. Hebbel's initial statement must, hence, appear as imprecise and misleading.

Let us hereupon turn to the second question of this investigation: In what region of Germany is Meister Anton's place of residence, regardless of its size and rank, to be localized?

Several of the observers quoted above tend to assume Northern Germany to be the setting of the drama, in all likelihood with Wesselburen in Dithmarschen in mind. What indications in the text support this assumption? There is, at first, the Lutheran creed predominating among the residents of Meister Anton's place, and, secondly, the proximity of the open sea offering Karl an easy escape from his father's mastery (III, 7, 8, 9, 10). And there is the genuine small town atmosphere which might well accord with that of Hebbel's birthplace.

Beyond these indications, however, no further evidence suggesting a setting in Wesselburen or in some other

small town in Northern Germany can be established from the text. The marketplace, most prominent point in Karl's running the gauntlet through the town (III, 6), lacks its proper equivalent in Wesselburen's layout, and the forest, scene of the secretary's and Leonhard's duel (III, 6), can scarcely have existed on the surrounding marshes. Meister Anton once mentions having visited the fair in Nürnberg (II, 1), and after Karl's shameful arrest he informs Klara of his decision to go to a deaf old timber merchant in the mountains from where he presumes to return late the same evening (II, 1). Wesselburen, however, is about 170 miles from the nearest wooded mountains, the Harz. Finally, the currency valid in Hebbel's setting is the "Gulden" and the "Thaler," which in the late 1830's and in the 1840's were current within the territories belonging to the German Customs Union and in Austria, whereas in Schleswig and Holstein, including Dithmarschen, the legal currency was the Danish "Krone."

As has become evident, a definite location of Meister Anton's town cannot be determined from the text; any attempt at locating it in a definite area is fruitless. All that can be ascertained is that the setting of *Maria Magdalene* is a small lower middle class community in some imaginary part of Germany. This would seem clear as well from the language of the characters, which is standard High German.

The reasons for Hebbel's choice of a neutral setting for his *Maria Magdalene* must be seen in his primary and almost exclusive concern with the demonstration of his philosophical and dramatic principles. "I intended to regenerate the bourgeois tragedy," he comments, retrospectively, "and I intended to show that also within the most limited circle a crushing tragedy may occur, provided you know how to deduce it from the proper elements, i. e. from those belonging to that of the circle itself" (Diary entry of December 4, 1843).

What has especially given rise to the impression that Hebbel meant to portray a particular German lower middle class family living at a particular place is that the characters seems to have been taken from real life. They were indeed modelled after individuals whom Hebbel himself had known in Wesselburen, Hamburg, and München. This peculiarity of Hebbel's characters and the tendency of many spectators or readers to identify, if only partly, with them have made them seem more real than they are.

The neutrality of the setting and the characters in *Maria Magdalene* is ample evidence that Hebbel can by no means be classified as a naturalist or be placed in the vicinity of naturalism, as has been attempted on several occasions in the past.[27] Hebbel's procedure of not copying presisely and exactly some particular individuals and conditions existing at a particular place at a particular time indicates his resolve to impart universality and timelessness to his drama.

Notes

1. Emil Kuh, *Biographie Friedrich Hebbel's,* Vol. 2 (Wien, 1877), p. 79.

2. *Ibid.,* p. 105.

3. Franz Mehring, *Zur Literaturgeschichte von Hebbel bis Gorki* (Berlin, 1929), p. 36.

4. Louis Brun, *Hebbel* (Leipzig, 1922), p. 1123.

5. Franz Bielfeldt, *Hebbels Menschengestaltung als dichterischer Ausdruck nordisch-deutschen Wesens* (Berlin, 1939), p. 35.

6. Kurt May, *Form und Bedeutung—Interpretationen deutscher Dichtung des 18. und 19. Jahrhunderts,* 2nd ed. (Stuttgart, 1963), p. 283.

7. Anni Meetz, *Friedrich Hebbel* (Stuttgart, 1962), p. 38.

8. Sten G. Flygt, *Friedrich Hebbel* (New York, 1968), p. 155.

9. Erika Sterz, "Hebbel als Dramatiker für das Fernsehspiel," *Hebbel-Jahrbuch 1967* (Heide in Holstein, 1967), pp. 81, 99.

10. Detlev Cölln, "Zur Geschichte der Hebbel-Gesellschaft," Part III, *Hebbel-Jahrbuch 1958* (Heide in Holstein, no date), p. 131.

11. Hebbel, Letter to Sigmund Engländer of February 23, 1863, *Friedrich Hebbel, Sämtliche Werke,* ed. R. M. Werner (Berlin, 1901-1907), Vol. 7, No. 847.

12. Richard Maria Werner, "Einleitung des Herausgebers," *ibid.,* Vol. 2, p. xv.

13. *Brockhaus Enzyklopädie* (Wiesbaden, 1967), Vol. 2, p. 570.

14. *Der Grosse Brockhaus* (Wiesbaden, 1954), Vol. 5, p. 219.

15. *Brockhaus Enzyklopädie* (Wiesbaden, 1970), Vol. 10, p. 360.

16. *Der Grosse Brockhaus* (Wiesbaden, 1955), vol. 8, p. 189.

17. Statistisches Landesamt Bremen, *Die Bevölkerung des Landes Bremen von 1812 bis 1958* (Bremen, 1958).

18. Statistisches Amt der Stadt Stuttgart, *Statistisches Handbuch der Stadt Stuttgart* (Stuttgart, 1960).

19. *Adreßbuch der Stadt Cassel 1844* (Cassel, no date).

20. Statistische Abteilung der Stadt Regensburg, *Bevölkerungsentwicklung der Stadt Regensburg* (Regensburg, 1971)

21. Stadt Hildesheim, *Statistisches Jahrbuch der Stadt Hildesheim 1962/63* (Hildesheim, no date).

22. Walter Drönewolf, "Stadterweiterung und Wohnhausbau in Osnabrück 1843-1913," *Osnabrücker Mitteilungen 40* (Osnabrück, 1917), pp. 1-152, table x.

23. Stadtarchiv Fulda, *Volkszählung—xxvi 8, Fasc. 5.*

24. *Adreßbuch der Stadt Landshut 1969* (Landshut, 1969), p. vii.

25. *Lippesches Magazin,* Vol. 8 (Lemgo und Detmold, 1843), p. 10.

26. Johannes von Schröder, *Topographie des Herzogthums Holstein, des Fürstenthums Lübeck und der freien und Hansestädte Hamburg und Lübeck* (Oldenburg in Holstein, 1841), II, p. 457.

27. See, e. g., Warren R. Maurer, "Hebbel im Urteil der Naturalisten," *Hebbel-Jahrbuch 1967,* pp. 114-115; Otfried Büthe, "Berühmte Hebbel-Inszenierungen," *Hebbel-Jahrbuch 1968* (Heide in Holstein, 1968), p. 80.

Edward McInnes (essay date 1973)

SOURCE: McInnes, Edward. "Maria Magdalena and the Bürgerliches Trauerspiel." *Orbis Litterarum* 28 (1973): 46-67.

[*In the following essay, McInnes examines the place of* Maria Magdalena *within the development of German drama.*]

Despite the sustained critical attention which Hebbel's **Maria Magdalena** has received over the years, its place in the development of German drama remains strangely ill-defined. Literary histories have certainly not been slow to claim that the play marks a turning-point in the growth of domestic tragedy, and several attempts have been made to define its specific historical position.[1] Yet such assessments have seldom ventured beyond the confines of received assumption. Perhaps here alone in the whole field of Hebbel criticism are the claims of the dramatist himself still allowed an unavowed authority over basic critical presuppositions. Even to this day the understanding of the historical significance of this work, of its relation to earlier conceptions of the bürgerliches Trauerspiel, and of its possible links with later developments in drama, is still generally governed by Hebbel's own explicit theoretical statements. We can go no further till we qualify the dramatist's estimate of the comprehensive originality of *Maria Magdalena,* of its essential independence of earlier preoccupations in the field of social drama. Our first task must be to question that vague but widely held conviction, stated for instance by Elise Dosenheimer, that it was Hebbel who first grasped the contingency of social experience as the governing centre of tragic exploration and who in so doing introduced a new form of domestic tragedy.[2] To say this is to uphold Hebbel's own somewhat casual denigration of what has since come to be recognised as a significant development in the realm of drama. It is to disregard a shaping imaginative tendency common to the experimental drama of the Sturm und Drang, to the ambitious, if less creative, drama of Young Germany and to many minor works which found wide acceptance in the theatre of the time.[3] The growth of a vital, although subsidiary, tradition of social drama throughout the previous decades had been in fact primarily controlled by a consistent artistic drive to confront an experience of the exposure of the individual to non-personal influence both within and without the self. Works like Lenz's *Der Hofmeister* or *Die Soldaten* or, in Hebbel's own day, Gutzkow's *Richard Savage,* were born of a like concern to diagnose the serious self-estrangement of individuals trapped in accepted prejudice and illusion. And even in plays like Wagner's *Die Kindermörderin* or *Kabale und Liebe* the intrusion of aristocratic power upon the middle-class world is not, as Hebbel claimed, dissociated from the analysis of the moral character of this world. It is seen rather as impinging upon characters bound by their inability to respond to another order of life and to the threat it represents.[4] Underlying the sense of destructive social division in all these plays there is an awareness of a severe alienation between parent and child which has its root in a shared dependence upon communally enforced standards and desires. Here already that constriction of the habituated mind which Hebbel defines in his Foreword, is variously apprehended as a hidden, ominous source of tragic disorder.[5]

If we are to see the position of *Maria Magdalena* in the development of the bürgerliches Trauerspiel we must fully accept this initial continuity of preoccupation. The attempts of von Wiese or Purdie to sever the conception of the work completely from the influence of the Sturm und Drang, or of May and Dosenheimer from that of the Young German drama, reveal a markedly limited interest in those plays which seem to suggest comparison with Hebbel's major achievement and serve in the end only to hide something of importance.[6] For the originality of the dramatist's creative purpose is to be sought less in the character of its social-psychological presuppositions or insights, than in the attempt to effect a new relationship between empirical concern and dramatic consciousness. What distinguishes the conception of *Maria Magdalena* from that of earlier domestic dramas is the intensity of Hebbel's quest to make the dramatic form fully responsive to deterministic perception, to create a tragic structure which was aesthetically valid because socially significant. Here, in assessing Hebbel's artistic intention, the Foreword is of unique importance. His deliberations in the important final section are informed by a truly prophetic sense of a discrepancy between the impetus of analytical insight, on the one hand, and the constraints of dramatic form as currently understood, on the other. Earlier attempts to apprehend the determinate life had been thwarted in his view by a consistent failure to conceive the action as necessarily grounded in the socially conditioned situation which was the essential dramatic premise.[7] The given social reality, in other words, was made amenable to the dramatic vision only by the introduction of extraneous, complicating factors through which the characters acquired an agency and fate unrelated to the social. The unsparing sharpness with which this critical insight is worked out, indicates the force of Hebbel's own artistic ambition. His aim was above all to realise an organic, analytical structure in which the energies of the dramatic form would derive solely from the environmentally controlled responses of the characters and in which therefore tragic necessity would be symbolic of actual social entrapment. The implications of this astringent undertaking are immense and demand the closest critical attention. Indeed the attempt to define the place of *Maria Magdalena* in the development of German drama is above all an attempt to elucidate the artistic means by which the dramatist sought to negotiate this artistic aim and then to assess critically the imaginative possibilities which this involves. This, however, is a much harder task than may at first appear.

Almost all Hebbel critics have acknowledged the primary success of the dramatist in translating positivistic insight into coherent dramatic process. Yet in saying this they have been by no means agreed as to the specific nature of this creative achievement. This is the supreme irony overshadowing the history of the critical reception of the work: that commentators who have agreed in praising the clarity of its empirical assumptions, the logic of its inward development, should have come to such opposed conclusions about its final imaginative significance. But although there is such a striking gap between the unanimity of the initial findings of criticism and the diversity of its ultimate evaluations, no one (to my knowledge) has recognised that a fundamental problem is involved. Divergent interpretations have been put forward and impressively sustained, but in no case have their controlling presuppositions been subjected to systematic investigation.

If we examine the various critical responses to *Maria Magdalena,* it is clear that the basic disagreement has arisen in the attempt to define the nature of the relationship between exposition and evolving action, between the analysis of foregoing developments and the progressive movement in the dramatic present. To the extent that the understanding of the dramatic figures is dependent upon direct expository statement, their controlling motives have generally appeared transparent to clear discursive insight.[8] But the more the characters—and in particular the figure of the heroine—have emerged from the sphere of diagnostic report into the immediacy of the dramatic present, the less their relationships have proved consistently susceptible of certain interpretation. This is something worth considering. It is only in the painstaking elucidation of past experience that critics have unanimously perceived a complete harmony between the working of the dramatist's creative imagination and the impetus of his severe analytical purpose. But here at least they have found compelling clarity. Commentators from Vischer to Ziegler, from Rötscher to May have consistently seen the delineation of those attitudes which have drawn the dramatic figures into confrontation as fully articulating Hebbel's theoretical view of the shared bondage of imprisoned lives.[9] He has succeeded in the general consensus in revealing in the fall of Klara and in the feelings towards her of her father and fiancé, the subjection of the characters to one sole process of determination. The responses of the individual figures, which seem at first sight mutually incompatible, are shown to be impelled by a common force of subliminal constraint which effectively controls the conscious mind. In each case the apparent drive towards self-assertion (it is agreed) is successfully diagnosed as an impulse of recoil from a world which seems continually to threaten the security of the individual's existence. The history of the play's critical reception shows, in short, that the tragic dilemma has been almost invariably understood in terms fully compatible with the determinist scheme outlined by Hebbel in his Foreword: as the point at which the separate lives, each in its own blind constriction, come into unwilled, uncomprehended conflict.[10]

But if the critical apprehension of the central dramatic dilemma has been strikingly uniform, the interpretations of its final resolution have differed vastly and irreconcilably. On the one hand, some commentators invoking with varying emphasis the authority of the dramatist's own theoretical pronouncements, have regarded the evolving action in the dramatic present as the simple consummation of the determining process which has brought the crisis into being. Some of the most compelling readings of **Maria Magdalena,** like those of Tibal, Wagner and Dosenheimer, have asserted a direct continuity between the seduction of the heroine and her eventual suicide. No one has put this more incisively than Ziegler:

> Was am Ende des Dramas mit Klaras Selbstmord als Tatsache und Wirklichkeit aktuell gegeben und vollendet ist, ist mit ihrer Verführung und ihrer damit dro-

> hend beschworenen Verurteilung und Ausstoßung durch die Gesellschaft potentiell, als Wesensverhalt und Möglichkeit, schon von allem Anfang an da.[12]

The conception of the drama in this view is totally expository. The development in the dramatic present is to be understood as a progressive analysis of the existent situation of entrapment—a logical revelation of the futility of the heroine's hopes of eventual escape. There is in this supposition no development in the essential relations of the dramatic figures; they all remain (with the partial exception of the Sekretär) the victims of uncomprehended compulsions, each deprived of releasing knowledge of himself or of those to whom he is bound.

But although this interpretation soon gained an orthodox standing through its conformity with Hebbel's own explicit comments, it has never ruled unchallenged. One of the dramatist's most sympathetic early critics, Emil Kuh, and more recently two such influential scholars as Purdie and von Wiese, showed some dissatisfaction with accepted interpretations by cautiously proposing the subjective experience of the heroine as a distinctive centre of moral value.[13] In so doing they inevitably assumed that this experience was in some way independent of environmental constraint, that it embodied a mode of awareness qualitatively separate from that of the figures by whom she is surrounded. None of them, however, was prepared to assert the full implications of this assumption: to accept this view of the heroine as a basis for questioning the inherited estimate of the dramatic action as the unfolding of nonpersonal processes beyond the scope of personal control. On the contrary, they all in their various ways seem to have attempted to incorporate this potentially transforming insight into an interpretation which leaves the total deterministic framework untouched.[14] Whatever the force of this crucial perception, it did not lead to a reassessment of the final tragic experience. This hesitancy between conflicting imaginative suggestions, although charactertistic of many responses to the drama, reveals a critical confusion which has not been fully acknowledged.[15] It was clearly a recognition of this that stimulated May's revolutionary attempt in 1943 to confront the issues involved and to offer a systematic re-interpretation of the work.

May's first aim was to place the figure of the heroine at the very centre of the tragic experience. To see Klara as the helpless victim of external forces was to ignore a direct imaginative impression of a vital, maturing personality. It was in his view a blatant misreading of the text to suggest that her suicide was the simple consequence of her seduction. Between the two events an immense process of inward change has taken place:

> Klara geht aber wissend und wollend in ihren eigenen Tod. Sie entschließt sich zum Sterben als ihrer eigenen Tat. Über den letzten Augenblick ihres armen irdischen

Lebens wird mit Betonung (im Text mit Sperrdruck) gesagt, sie sei nicht hinein*gestürzt,* sondern hinein*gesprungen* . . . Klara entflieht nicht wie ein gehetztes Wild; sie geht und bringt sich dar.[16]

The failure of the orthodox interpretation stems in May's view from an unconsidered willingness on the part of critics to accept Hebbel's own assumption of a direct continuity of motive between Anton's threat of suicide and Klara's submission to this threat. These, he claims, can in no sense be regarded as stages in one causal development; they represent, in fact, modes of aspiration and purpose which are in total contradiction and which disclose a challenging moral discrepany at the very heart of the tragic motivation. The sacrificial death of Klara, as May sees it, far from being determined by this environmental process, utterly transcends it. It reveals a sphere of ultimate value which is foreign to the debased vision of this society and in terms of which this society is finally judged and condemned.[17]

It is hard to overestimate the historical importance of this interpretation of May's. It seemed to open up whole new possibilities of insight and evaluation. This redirective influence has recently been acknowledged by scholars like Müller and Kreuzer, whose studies of various aspects of the drama have been among the most valuable in post-war criticism.[18] The liberating authority of May's reading derived, I believe, from the fact that it powerfully endorsed an intuitive sense of the innate moral significance of the tragic action which had at best been only hesitantly acknowledged in earlier interpretations. Here for the first time tendencies of imaginative feeling, which seemed incompatible with determinist presuppositions, were fully affirmed and accorded a decisive place in the understanding of the work as a whole.

The achievement of May's interpretation in calling in question many of the one-sided assumptions which had governed attitudes to the drama, is beyond dispute. Yet it does not in the last analysis resolve the fundamental critical dilemma it seeks to confront; it merely succeeds in revealing this dilemma in another, more baffling, light. The very fact that this interpretation, which so lucidly refutes the apparent logic of the positivist exegesis, should have gained such wide acceptance without really replacing more traditional readings, is in itself highly perplexing.[19] This indeed would seem to throw into doubt the validity of existing critical strategies. It would seem to point to some imaginative depth in the dramatic statement which is responsive to opposing modes of insight but which in the end does not yield fully to either; to some energy of suggestion which is basically resistent to the pragmatic confidence of critical exposition. May's reading, like those it seeks to supersede, has not, I believe, fully acknowledged those evocative tensions which force themselves elusively and often bewilderingly upon the engaged imagination. Like them it does not sound the confusing, abrasive disorder of direct imaginative response, but seeks to subdue it to a clear pattern of rational significance which is at odds with the vitality of direct imaginative experience.

This sense of a severe discrepancy between interpretative analysis and immediate response should not be lightly dismissed. It should be accepted rather as a valid starting-point from which to probe the assumptions controlling the various types of critical investigation to which the drama has been subjected. If taken seriously it can, I think, force us to contemplate problems which are critically very relevant but which have never really been asked. It can prompt us to question the sensitivity of existing critical methods to the specific artistic form in which the dramatic vision is expressed in *Maria Magdalena.* It can impel us to assess their relative capacities to respond to the imaginative medium in which this specific tragic process is embodied, to evaluate the effects and possibilities peculiar to this dramatic mode. The question which is to direct our investigation must be this: to what extent are these different critical approaches responsive to the implications inherent in Hebbel's use of the analytical form—in his quest for a new quality of dramatic realism?

When looked at from this point of view the confrontations of critics with this uniquely challenging play seem somewhat rigid and insensitive. Their various approaches to *Maria Magdalena* have been largely governed by assumptions concerning Hebbel's work as a whole. The sense of the specific imaginative character of this drama has been largely annulled by an employment of techniques which have been evolved in the study of his other plays; the need for a decisive shift of imaginative focus has been generally overlooked. Nowhere is this rigidity of approach more obvious than in the severely deterministic interpretations of commentators like Tibal, Ziegler and Dosenheimer. Here the force of an abstractive concern is so powerful as to consistently suppress a consciousness of the unique formal character of the drama.

This is particularly evident in their discussion of the figure of the heroine. None of these scholars allows sufficiently for the fact that the dramatic analysis of Klara's subjective consciousness is necessarily dependent upon her own ability to comprehend and interpret her own evolving experience.[20] In their concern to dissect her self-awareness as the object of converging social influences they have consistently tended to ignore the crucial fact that it is she herself as discriminating subject who gives us fullest access to this inward world. It is above all through her own unsparing self-diagnosis that the circumstances of her seduction are dramatically revealed and, more importantly, morally evaluated. First in her opening conversation with Leonhard (I, 4) and then in her extensive confession to Friedrich (II, 5) Klara shows that she has come through suffering to a new understanding of her own inner frailty—an understanding so clear and so free of self-indulgence as to disclose a significant development in her moral consciousness. The live, maturing personality who sits in judgement on past failure cannot be simply identified with the being who incurred that failure. There is in this figure some principle of growth which cannot be accommodated to the radically positivistic assessment. This character—and of this there can be not doubt—imposes itself upon the imagination as one that has achieved some measure of freedom from the constraints in which it had been blindly caught up, as one that is in some sense renewed.

But here we must proceed with caution. Here again we must pay due attention to a characteristic tension between the overt significance of the specific dramatic statement and the implications of its dramatic context. We cannot (as May's exposition constantly presupposes) have a full, indubitable knowledge of the change which takes place in the heroine. All we can surely know is the way in which this change impresses itself on her tortured, questing consciousness. There is no doubt that Klara herself, in her concern to avert the danger which threatens her father, sees her whole life as finally released from the pressures of communally accepted attitude. In her awareness of her father's suffering she acknowledges a sense of ultimate purpose which is completely new in her life and which annuls all uncertainty or self-concern. All her thinking, in anguish, in hope or in strictest self-restraint, is controlled by a sole awareness of the suffering which threatens her father.[21] In this she acknowledges an imperative which annuls all worldly consideration. In her final confrontation with Leonhard she declares this sense of the freedom of her purpose from the pressures of communal expectation:

> Wär's um mich allein—ich wollt's ja tragen, ich wollt's geduldig hinnehmen als verdiente Strafe für, ich weiß nicht was, wenn die Welt mich in meinem Elend mit Füßen träte. . . .
>
>   (III, 2)

The conscious mind of Klara—and this much is certain—is fired by a sense of sacrificial aim which is impatient of all social sanction. In acknowledging this ultimate command she sees herself as rejecting all relative ties and responsibilities. Faced by this absolute claim upon her, even her own life and that of her unborn child lose their importance:

> Aber ich bin's nicht allein und leichter find' ich am jüngsten Tag noch eine Antwort auf des Richters Frage: Warum hast du dich selbst umgebracht? als auf die: Warum hast du deinen Vater so weit getrieben?
>
>   (III, 2)

The recognition of the depth and singleness of Klara's will to self-immolation necessarily permeates and conditions our whole response to the drama. At times the force of this impression is indeed such that it seems to guarantee the sense of a value which is completely independent of the barren world in which the drama is set. But it is, I believe, characteristic of the artistic character of *Maria Magdalena* that this feeling of unmixed acknowledgement cannot persist for long—that it is recurrently beset by a confusing doubt. The awareness of the consuming force of the heroine's design coexists with the perplexing uncertainty about the capacity of her mind to come to terms with the immensity of this inward change which has come upon her. In acknowledging the finality of the affective process, we are forced to recognise the frailty and restriction of the mind which is its only register. To regard Klara's subjective self-understanding (like May) as the source of a final imaginative certainty in terms of which the value of conflicting suggestions can be assessed, is to separate it from the total imaginative framework in which alone it acquires aesthetic meaning. No, the apprehension of the inward development of the heroine, however great its momentary power over the receptive mind, is encompassed throughout by a qualifying awareness of her continuing (if indefinable) susceptibility to the pressures of this destructive milieu.

This ambiguity is inescapably given in the character of the dramatic language. Whatever the reality of Klara's experience of regeneration, it can only be understood and endorsed by her reflective mind in terms of categories and images which have shaped her spiritual development from infancy. Her experience of an inward freedom from society thus necessarily finds expression in formulae which reveal some degree of continuing dependence upon it. This brings us to the very heart of the problem of interpretation. In her situation of ultimate dilemma those religious certainties which have governed her growing awareness of life clearly acquire for Klara a new transforming significance; but they none the less still entail those values and invoke those sanctions which she has been taught from the first to observe. They still, that is, uphold the same world-view through which her unquestioning sense of personal servitude has been socially enforced. The heroine's will to total self-surrender thus appears as essentially opaque. The awareness of purpose in which it issues may be seen as arising out of a total dependence upon socially imposed constraint, or it may be seen as the consequence of a supremely free commitment of the moral self. Between these alternatives, the death accepted in defeat and that embraced in the sense of a final responsibility, there is clearly an absolute ethical distinction and upon this the interpretation of the tragedy will in the end largely depend. Yet in the outward behaviour of Klara before her suicide there is no conclusive revelation of the will from which it derives, no binding disclosure of the motive by which alone its moral character can be determined. The sacrificial impulse which from one point of view seems to deny all links with this narrow world, seems from another to be enclosed by all manner of equivocal parallels. For this act of self-immolation, whatever its inward character, is born in response to the same religious vision which upholds the fearful life-denying asceticism of her parents. In what sense then can it be called unique? Is it merely to be seen as a climatic revelation of a compulsive, blinding subservience to a religion which rejects the values of life and aspires only to a fulfilment in the world beyond? Does the impetus of her sacrificial desire stem from an unavowed desire to be delivered from an alien, meaningless world? Or does this directing sense of purpose reveal, as we are impelled at times to believe, an energy of will utterly disjoined from the sterile resignation of her parents and the assertive egotism of the younger generation? To these decisive questions we are driven again and again to return, but we can have no final answer. The act of Klara which seems at one moment to contradict the whole corrupting bias of life in this community, seems at others to have its roots in this life so deeply overshadowed by the pervasive reality of death.[22]

What does at least seem certain, however, is that it is here alone in the apprehension of the heroine, that we are assailed by such fundamental doubt. While the religious outlook of Anton and his wife, like the secular aspirations of Karl and Leonhard, appears as fully explicable in terms of environmental dependence, the experience of Klara seems to resist any such clear, reductive definition. It seems at times to touch areas of imaginative feeling inaccessible to discursive insight, yet at others to fall like other aspects of the dramatic statement within the scope of the sceptical intelligence. It is, I believe, in this tense, suggestive counterpointing of imaginative implications that Hebbel moves most significantly beyond the established methods of the mid-century bürgerliches Trauerspiel and explores new possibilities of dramatic evocation. This can be seen if we compare the conception of the figure of Klara with that of figures in other works to whom she bears a clear outward resemblance. The reactions of the heroine in *Der Hofmeister* or *Die Kindermörderin,* in Raupach's *Der Müller und sein Kind* or Gutzkow's *Liesli* remain in the situation of total breakdown consistently understandable within the terms of a controlling deterministic premise.[23] In all these works a progressive enquiry into the nature of the conditioned consciousness finds its fulfilment in the diagnosis of psychic disintegration. Here the revelation of the inward exposure of the heroine reaches its climax in the enactment of a situation whose moral-social implications are obvious and emphatic. Such clarity of procedure and effect is quite alien to **Maria Magdalena.** Although the initial analysis of the inward weakness of the heroine is

in some ways strikingly similar to that in these other plays, it issues not in the manifestation of overt inward disorder but in the disclosure of an apparently coherent moral experience in which the energies of the individual seem heightened and transformed. Here alone the awareness of supreme crisis does not lead to a paralysis of the will but to its seeming regeneration.

This disorientating uncertainty about the hidden reality of the heroine's death is matched, moreover, by a similar doubt about its final social significance. The only thing which is indisputably obvious is that it does not fulfil its explicit saving purpose. The fact that her will to die has been observed and made public, means that Klara's death cannot protect her father from disgrace; it can only expose him to a greater, more threatening ignominy. Nor is it as if this revelation of her desperate intention makes it possible for her death to influence her father's life in an unforeseen but genuinely creative way. Her sacrifice does not release the springs of his deepest suppressed feelings, it does not awaken any sense of anguished responsibility and failure. It contrives only to heighten that compulsive drive to self-vindication which has increasingly isolated Anton from all around and warped his deepest capacity for emotion.[24]

But this obvious failure of Klara's death to fulfil its immediate objective, some have claimed, is more than offset by its wider creative impact on the life of the younger generation. In the self-indictment of Friedrich and in his ensuing condemnation of Anton (it is said) the hidden power of her act to inspire a more sensitive, personal mode of moral awareness is symbolically announced.[25] Yet despite the dramatist's clear concern to endow this regenerate insight of Friedrich's with a high representative significance, the manner of its artistic embodiment is such as to preclude any simple sense of its direct social effectiveness. For this renewal of spirit is consummated on the very edges of the tragic action, in the contemplation of disaster (III, 11). It is born of the crushing awareness that he has failed to save the life of Klara and that this life, like his own, is spent in vain. The imaginative authority of this insight is thus inevitably qualified by the irony of its situation in the total dramatic development. The fact that this growth of understanding takes place under such abnormal pressures and so far from the conditions of average social experience, that it is impelled by a sense of despairing futility—this all seems calculated to undermine the certainty of its effective impact upon the life of society at large and thus inevitably to throw the hope of corporate renewal into doubt.

Nor can the figure of Karl be seen to fulfil a clear symbolic function.[26] Here again there is a telling discrepancy between the apparent simplicity of Hebbel's theoretical concern and the complex workings of his creative imagination. We are, I believe, unable to assess the impact of Klara's death upon her brother's life because we can have no final certainty about the innermost potentialities of the character as such. Are we to see this death as helping to free him from a destructiveness which has its sole roots in adverse experience, or as ultimately confirming a tendency to brutality which is inherent in his essential nature? It may well be that this disaster will strengthen his determination to create a new life in freedom and that he will, as he has claimed, return one day in triumph (III, 8). But it is equally possible that his understanding of the events leading up to his sister's suicide will only heighten his stated desire to murder the man who in wrongfully arresting him helped to precipitate this unexpected horror. His eventual return may indeed reveal the triumphant renewal of his family's existence; but it may equally well mark its final disintegration.

But the uncertainty does not end here. Even if the creative suggestion embodied in these two figures is fully accepted, the nature of its final influence upon the life of society remains profoundly in doubt. For our awareness of this potential effect is contained within a wider recognition of the innate tendency of existence in this community to resist change. Whatever the power of this influence, how can its impact be measured against the force of those constraints which bind the individual mind to the authority of the collective? These questions are forced inescapably upon us by the fact that the only *unquestionable* triumph in this catastrophe is that of the vigilant, judging community. The fact that Klara's act of self-destruction is seen, seems to reveal yet again the final obeissance of individual initiative to collective attitude. It seems to emphasise with a harsh, climactic irony the subjection of personal aspiration and intent to established modes of evaluation—the assimilation of the exceptional and potentially creative event to the compelling force of a corporate will which ruthlessly enforces one single standard and so suppresses all impetus of growth. How is this implication of sterility so closely associated with the central dramatic analysis, to be related to the conflicting suggestion of development? Can such evocative intimations claim some imaginative priority over the sense of empirical probabilities? Or must all references to another order of significance be in the end strictly subordinated to the authority of discursive methods of explanation? This is a question which we are forced to confront but to which we can find no certain answer. It involves a conflict between different modes of imaginative assertion which both have their basis in the given structures of the dramatic statement, but which imply totally contradictory possibilities of final understanding.

To apprehend the tragic action in *Maria Magdalena* is to remain fundamentally and consistently open to discordant tendencies of imaginative insight. The at-tempt to resolve this tension, I have suggested, involves a disregard of some aspect of the densely organised fabric of divergent suggestions. The dramatic statement is inherently ambivalent. I am aware that this judgement goes against the consensus of critical opinion which, although in very different ways, has attributed to the work a full cathartic effect in the classical sense. It is my belief, however, that the responding mind is here denied all final experience of tragic resolution; that it can gain no certain knowledge of the moral character and effect of the central dramatic development and thus about the world in which the action is set. The culminating impression is not that of harmonious certainty but of disconcerting enigma; contradictory indications are not finally subsumed in one cohering perception but remain in sharp, abrasive discordance. The spectacle of Klara's death plunges us, in fact, into the contemplation of a dilemma of the deepest moral significance. Is this death to be seen as vindicating man's hidden capacities for self-renewal which precede and finally transcend his subjection to environmental influence? or as revealing a bondage of spirit so severe that it destroys the very possibility of rational self-understanding? Does the catastrophe intimate the power of the purified vision to penetrate collective life or does it merely demonstrate the final subservience of the spiritual to non-personal process? To be true to direct imaginative awareness we must, I believe, confront and hold in suspension these contradictory possibilities; we must respond to a mode of understanding which is enforced and authorised by analytical methods, while at the same time admitting an ulterior suggestion of creative forces in man's mind and thus in human life which elude empirical definition. The drama, it seems to me, sets in tension two irreconcilable estimates of man's stature as a moral being and of his position in the world in which he lives. It advances two opposed possibilities of dramatic causation, which in turn entail two contradictory systems of value. But it offers no final synthesis. There is here no tendency of imaginative affirmation which is not beset by alienating doubt, no feeling of detached scepticism which is not challenged by the will to sympathetic engagement.

Maria Magdalena cannot therefore, in my view, be accommodated to neo-classical definitions of the tragic. It must be seen rather as a work of tragic exploration in a peculiarly modern sense—as a sounding of incongruous possibilities of tragic feeling. The seminal tragic intuition which Hebbel was seeking to negotiate seems to have been outlined in those laconic but impenetrable words in his diary: "Durch Dulden tun: Idee des Weibes."[27] This vision of the mysterious creative force of self-forgetting endurance clearly embraced a whole range of impulses and insights—emotional, moral, intellectual—which were so severely dissociated that they could not be fully confronted in ratiocinative terms. The ability to embody this inward tension in coherent imaginative form represents a decisive stage in Hebbel's artistic development.[28] It was above all an achievement of artistic comprehension, of a complex co-relating of divergent orders of imaginative sensibility. At one level this preoccupation entailed an engagement with an impelling awareness of historical process, of severe tensions in contemporary social existence which seemed to demand elucidation by means of discursive methods of observation and analysis; at another it inspired a creative confrontation with imaginative impulses which were not fully accessible to conscious understanding: with profound mythic implications which could only be expressed in opposition to the determining impetus of analytical insight.[29] It is, I believe, this collision of imaginative insights which finds intense poetic embodiment in **Maria Magdalena**. In pursuing a pragmatic investigation of the causes of Klara's seduction and death the dramatist, it would seem, was driven to question and consciously reject an archetypal tragic image of redemptive suffering; so great was the authority of the tragic archetype over his creative consciousness, however, that it seems to have dislocated the comprehensive certainty of his expository intention. The peculiarly elusive effect of the drama stems from the fact that it touches the springs of mythic association while ostensibly exploiting the reductive means of positivistic analysis, and that in the end it validates neither frame of imaginative reference. The source of the play's creative life is to be sought finally, I believe, in the strength of its inner organisation—in the power with which the balance of conflicting suggestions is enforced and contained within one unified imaginative structure.

If we can accept that the dramatic statement in **Maria Magdalena** is, as I have claimed, essentially exploratory, then its position in the development of the German drama must be reconsidered. No other drama of the time was born of such a radical, if largely unconscious, impulse to realise imaginative effects which were completely at odds with accepted notions of the function and potentiality of the drama. The concern to investigate the conditioned consciousness in mid-century plays did give rise to widespread and often far-reaching technical experimentation, but this was consistently controlled by a compelling artistic dependence upon inherited estimates of the drama as an autonomous, self-sufficient form. The conception of the domestic dramas of Gutzkow and Freytag, of Bauernfeld and Ludwig, can be seen to have been governed by a basic concern to assimilate a strong relativising drive towards analytical scrutiny, to an ultimate reconciling vision of experience. In plays like Gutzkow's *Werner* or Freytag's *Die Valentine,* as also in Ludwig's more powerfully original *Der Erbförster,* expository concern is strangely linked with an underlying sense of the synthesising power of artistic insight.[30] Here, as in many minor works of the time, a process of enquiry is increasingly subordinated to the disclosure of a final interpretative insight. The individual assertions of the dramatic figures are here persistently (although with varying degrees of explicitness) 'placed' and evaluated through their relation to a controlling perception of a transcendent order of being.

This drive to accommodate the analytical is most obtrusively apparent in a conventional and often incongruous use of choric figures who are seen as independent of the confining pressures of the dramatic world, as enunciating standards of moral value in terms of which this world can be judged.[31] The same impulse is also, although less conspicuously, evident in a regulative or 'epic' use of theatrical devices like aside and stage-direction. This is most noticeable in works like *Der Erbförster* or *Der Meineidbauer* in which the diagnostic impetus of the creative imagination is particularly strong. Here the stage-direction in particular acquires a decisive importance as the means of conveying an authoritative insight into areas of the hero's affective existence which elude his conscious insight and find expression only in involuntary physical reactions. Although this technique, especially in Ludwig's work, stems from a sensitive, realistic concern to acknowledge the limitations of personal self-knowledge and articulateness, it can be seen in the end to subserve an ulterior dramatic need to assert a final moral-psychological evaluation of character by means of which its universal destiny can be understood.[32] In *Der Erbförster,* as in so many plays of the time, a profound crisis in dramatic apprehension is manifest in the confused attempt to relate the interrogatory impetus of analytical insight to an inherited conception of the drama as a symbolic form in which an absolute vision of life is expressed. In **Maria Magdalena,** it seems to me, Hebbel moves beyond this epochal dichotomy. Here the processes of exploration are not accommodated to an ultimate, harmonising interpretation. Here there is no figure whose vision indubitably transcends the enclosing constriction. Here the stage-direction which reveals discontinuities in subjective awareness does not offer the corrective elucidations of an unseen author, does not assuringly supplement the inadequacies of the spoken word; it serves rather to reinforce a fundamental uncertainty about the capacity of the rational being to come to terms with his own radically fragmented experience.

In developing this so-called 'retrospective method' as an instrument of social investigation Hebbel went further than he or his contemporaries realised. He was taking the drama, I believe, into a decisive new phase of development, the implications of which could not be foreseen. In this analytical form the artistic statement was dependent to an unprecedented degree upon the powers of the isolated individual to recall and interpret experience. It entailed, however, not only an awareness of the mutual disconnection of the single figures but also of a severe dissociation within the consciousness of the experiencing subject itself, of a radical divorce between the questing intelligence and the determining energies of the affective life. In interiorising the essential dramatic process Hebbel was thus placing it largely beyond the scope of inter-personal discussion; he was locating it in a sphere of subjective awareness only partially accessible to the introspective mind and almost completely out of reach of authoritative outside comment. In this new realistic form ambiguity is not an accidental consequence but an essential condition of imaginative effect.[33]

If we can see *Maria Magdalena* from this point of view there are, it seems to me, possibilities of finding new links between the impetus of Hebbel's creative vision and that of Büchner and Grabbe—possibilities which have been obscured by the undue dependence of critics upon the sense of a basic opposition between 'closed' and 'open' drama.[34] It would also seem to necessitate another look at the relations between *Maria Magdalena* and the work of Ibsen. If we do accept the strong relativistic impulse of Hebbel's dramatic conception, then we must probe possible connections between this and the conception not primarily of the earlier polemic dramas which has generally been stressed, but of the later, more elusive works like *The Wild Duck* and *Hedda Gabbler*. But this new assessment of Hebbel's play would seem to me above all to open up possibilities of revealing a hidden continuity between mid-century drama and that of Naturalism, and in particular of Hauptmann's work. In the plays of his late-naturalist period, I believe, Hauptmann has exploited and uniquely refined imaginative possibilities first seriously negotiated in *Maria Magdalena*. Here with a supreme mimetic sensitivity he evolved a form in which the whole dramatic substance is presented as the aggregate of the specific assertions of single individuals, each isolated by the force of his own limiting experience, each apparently denied the possibility of transcending insight.[35] The peculiar imaginative vitality of works like *Rose Bernd* and *Gabriel Schillings Flucht* stems from the power with which these individual perspectives are differentiated and set in mutual confrontation. This sense of the relative validity of the competing insights informs the apprehension of the whole dramatic world and it culminates in the awareness of a crucial area of uncertainty: that of the relationship between the experiencing mind of the stricken protagonist and the situation in which he is caught up. We are drawn increasingly to question the ostensible connection between our general awareness of causal process and our imaginative recognition of the subjective experience of the hero. On the one hand, we are impelled to postulate (on the basis of seemingly coherent indications) a conflict between the protagonist and the other dramatic figures which is without final significance and devoid of real tragic implication. At the same time,

however, we are driven by the sheer intensity of the hero's subjective vision to embrace (temporally at least) other categories of connection and purpose which are implicit in his own understanding of his own experience. In so doing we are drawn into admitting an awareness of significances which, although not ultimately incompatible with our acknowledgement of causal process, are by no means inherent in it and which in the end in fact demand its total re-assessment. Whether, as in *Fuhrmann Henschel* or in *Rose Bernd,* we are drawn by the force of the protagonist's own compelling certainty to accept an ulterior sense of a supernatural agency at work in human affairs, or, as in *Michael Kramer* and *Gabriel Schillings Flucht,* of a religious order of being within which suffering gains an ultimate, redemptive significance, we are in every case affirming an imaginative dimension within which the specific dramatic action moves beyond the merely contingent and the hero acquires a transcendent destiny.[36] But in these works, as in *Maria Magdalena,* this provisional acceptance of higher significance, which derives from a coercive involvement with the subjective experience of the central figure, is not finally insusceptible to the pressures of the sceptical intelligence. Here too the individual figure, which is the source of the transforming insight, is isolated from genuine understanding and thus from possible assessment on the part of other characters; here too the pretension to ultimate insight is implicitly called in question by the sheer depths of the suffering from which it springs. In these plays of Hauptmann, as in Hebbel's drama, doubt is an intrinsic, shaping element in the dramatic experience. It is a factor which criticism has generally failed to acknowledge or to evaluate.

The concern to understand the position of *Maria Magdalena* in the development of the bürgerliches Trauenspiel is not, I believe, something of local or specialist interest alone. To attempt to redefine its relation to the plays of the Sturm und Drang, to the artistic tendencies of contemporary works, and to the basic initiatives of the Naturalist drama, is to try to grasp anew the evolving aspirations and achievements of realism in the German drama. But in this there is still a long, long way to go.

Notes

1. O. Walzel: "Das bürgerliche Drama" (1914). In: *Vom Geistesleben alter und neuer Zeit.* 1922, pp. 142-231.

   P. Fechter: *Das europäische Drama.* Vol. I, 1956, p. 358.

2. E. Dosenheimer: *Das soziale Drama von Lessing bis Sternheim.* 1949, p. 82 and p. 90. E. Purdie: *Friedrich Hebbel.* 1932, pp. 120 ff.

3. There has been an immense advance in the understanding of the drama of the Sturm und

Drang in the past few years. The following studies seem to me to be of particular importance: W. Schaer: *Die Gesellschaft im deutschen bürgerlichen Drama des 18.* Jahrhunderts. 1963; R. Götte: *"Die Tochter im Familiendrama des 18. Jahrhunderts."* Phil. Diss. Bonn. 1964; H. Arntzen: *Die ernste Komödie.* 1968. There are also signs of a revival of interest in the artistic ideas and initiatives of Young Germany. Of special relevance to the present discussion are: J. Hermand: *Das junge Deutschland. Texte und Dokumente.* 1966; E. W. Dobert: *Karl Gutzkow und seine Zeit.* 1968. H. Koopmann: *Das junge Deutschland; Analyse seines Selbstverständnisses.* 1970.

4. I have looked at this in detail in: "The Sturm und Drang and the Development of Social Drama." *DVJS.* 1972, 1, pp. 61-81.

5. In his famous discussion in the 12th part of his Foreword, Hebbel described the failure of domestic tragedy in Germany as stemming from the fact that "man es nicht aus seinen inneren, ihm allein eigenen Elementen, aus der schroffen Geschlossenheit, womit die aller Dialektik unfähigen Individuen sich in dem beschränktesten Kreis gegenüberstehen, und aus dem hieraus entspringenden schrecklichen Gebundenheit des Lebens in der Einseitigkeit aufgebaut". Cf. F. Hebbel: *Sämtliche Werke.* Historisch-kritische Ausgabe, ed. R. M. Werner, 1901 ff. 1te. Abteilung, Vol. XI. See also his letter to Auguste Stich-Crelinger, 11th December 1843, *Werke,* 11te Abteilung, Vol. XI, p. 348.

6. B. von Wiese: *Die deutsche Tragödie von Lessing bis Hebbel.* 3rd ed. 1955, p. 608.

E. Purdie: *Friedrich Hebbel.* p. 122.

K. May: "Maria Magdalene im Zusammenhang der jüngsten Hebbelforschung." *Dichtung und Volkstum.* 1943, pp. 32-61. See especially p. 60.

E. Dosenheimer: *Das soziale Drama,* p. 90.

7. O. Walzel: *Das bürgerliche Drama,* pp. 212 ff.

E. Dosenheimer: *Das soziale Drama,* pp. 88 ff.

8. There were, on the other hand, frequent *moral* objections to Hebbel's conception of Klara's seduction. In early critiques of the play it was a common complaint that the motivation of her fall, however understandable as a psychological phenomenon, lacked a general, aesthetic significance. See e.g. J. Schmidt in: *Die Grenzboten,* 1847, pp. 501-513; F. Kühne in: *Europa,* 1848, pp. 291-297, characteristically complained of "dies ganz rationell geklügelte Selbstopfer" and stated the widely accepted principle: "Wo uns das Böse weder durch die Schrecken der Naturgewalt erfaßt, noch komisch reizt, da steht es bloß als Widerwärtigkeit da und hat als solche weder dichterische Macht, noch dichterisches Recht."

9. H. T. Rötscher in: *Jahrbücher für dramatische Kunst und Literatur.* 1848, II, pp. 145-154.

A. M. Wagner: *Das Drama Friedrich Hebbels.* 1911, pp. 32 and 236.

K. Ziegler: *Mensch und Welt in der Tragödie Friedrich Hebbels.* 2nd ed. 1966, pp. 103 ff.

K. May: *Maria Magdalene,* pp. 37-40.

E. Dosenheimer: *Das soziale Drama,* pp. 83 ff. The author characteristically emphasizes the fact that even the apparently accidental influences upon the tragic situation (the loss of Klara's dowry [I, 6], the impetuousness of the bailiff [II, 3]) are closely bound up with the assertive character of Anton.

10. F. Bamberg in: *Jahrbücher für dramatische Kunst und Literatur.* 1848, I, pp. 135-150.

11. A. Tibal: *Hebbel, sa vie et ses oeuvres. De 1813 à 1845.* 1911, pp. 537-574.

A. M. Wagner: *Das Drama Friedrich Hebbels,* pp. 237 ff.

E. Dosenheimer: *Das soziale Drama,* p. 84, writes: "Sie handelt nicht, an ihr wird gehandelt, sie geht nicht aus der Welt, sie wird aus ihr gedrängt."

12. K. Ziegler: *Mensch und Welt in der Tragödie Friedrich Hebbels,* p. 103.

13. E. Kuh: *Biographie Friedrich Hebbels.* 3rd ed. 1912. Vol. II, pp. 57-74.

E. Purdie: *Friedrich Hebbel,* p. 114.

B. von Wiese: *Die deutsche Tragödie,* p. 614.

14. E. Purdie, in *Friedrich Hebbel,* speaks of Klara as becoming "active through suffering" (p. 114), yet also describes her as being "almost equally in bond to her environment" as her father (p. 121). Her final assessment of the plays rests upon the traditional assumption that the milieu "constitutes the tragic necessity" (p. 120).

B. von Wiese, in *Die deutsche Tragödie,* claims that in the figure of Klara "eine höhere Sittlichkeit des Duldens" is embodied and sees the character in fact as achieving "etwas von dem Adel reiner Menschlichkeit" (p. 615). Yet he also attempts to see the total tragic process as demonstrating how "ein hilfloser und seiner gesellschaftlichen Umgebung wehrlos ausgelieferter Mensch, "aus der Welt herausgedrängt wird" (p. 609). This last quotation shows a substantial acceptance of Hebbel's own theoretical comments on the play.

15. W. Fischer: *Hebbel. Maria Magdalena,* 2nd ed., 1963, pp. 30-36, sets side by side quotations from the interpretations of Ziegler and May without acknowledging in any way that these interpretations rest on contradictory assumptions.

16. K. May: *Maria Magdalene,* pp. 39-40.

17. K. May: *Maria Magdalene,* pp. 41-42. Klara's act represents in May's view a transforming force of reconciliation at the heart of the tragic action: "In Klaras Opfer hat Hebbel die Lösung, die Erlösung für die Welt Meister Antons gedichtet" (p. 54).

18. M. Stern: "Das zentrale Symbol in Hebbels 'Maria Magdalena'." In: *Hebbel in neuer Sicht,* ed. H. Kreuzer, 1963, pp. 228-246.

J. Müller: "Zur motivischen und dramaturgischen Struktur von Hebbels 'Maria Magdalena'." In: *Hebbel Jahrbuch,* 1968 ed. L. Koopmann, pp. 45-76.

19. W. Fischer's *Maria Magdalena* exemplifies this with peculiar clarity.

20. K. Ziegler: *Mensch und Welt in der Tragödie Friedrich Hebbels,* pp. 103 ff. E. Dosenheimer: *Das soziale Drama,* p. 84.

21. See particularly II, 2; II, 5; III, 2 and III, 8.

22. M. Stern: *Das zentrale Symbol,* pp. 230 and 237.

23. J. M. R. Lenz: *Der Hofmeister,* IV, 2 and 4.

H. L. Wagner: *Die Kindermörderin,* VI, pp. 509 ff.

References to these plays are to: *Sturm und Drang. Dramatische Schriften.* ed. E. Loewenthal and L. Schneider (undated).

Raupach: *Der Müller und sein Kind. Dramatische Werke ernster Gattung.* 1835. Vol. III. II, 5; IV, 2.

K. Gutskow: *Liesli. In Dramatische Werke.* 4. Gesamtausgabe. 1881. Vol. 4. See especially III, 6 and 7.

It is only the figure of Luise in Schiller's *Kabale und Liebe* who could be seen as a valid anticipation of Hebbel's conception of Klara. But despite the ambiguities of the heroine's behaviour, she is here clearly seen as responding to two separate, objective spheres of value—that imposed by her contingent social identity and that embodied in her creative love of Ferdinand. See E. McInnes: "The Sturm und Drang and the Development of Social Drama." *DVJS,* 1972. I. pp. 68 ff.

24. At the moment of deepest disaster Anton's concern is not with the cause of her death but with its appearance in the eyes of the community. This is revealed in his spontaneous attempt to refute the report of the girl who claimed to see the act of suicide: "Die soll sich's überlegen, eh' sie spricht. Es ist nicht hell genug, daß sie das mit Bestimmtheit hat unterscheiden können." (III, 11).

25. Cf. e.g. F. Bamberg in: *Jahrbücher für dramatische Kunst und Literatur.* 1848. I. pp. 45-50.

26. A. M. Wagner: *Das Drama Friedrich Hebbels.* p. 237.

H. Sievers: *Maria Magdalena auf der Bühne.* 1933. p. 10.

27. F. Hebbel: *Tagebücher,* I. 1516, 24th February 1839.

28. Rees shows clearly in his fine Introduction to his 1944 edition of *Maria Magdalena* (pp. xxvii-xxxii) that preoccupations with sexual attachment and morality apparent throughout Hebbel's work in the previous years are here brought to a point of final crystallisation.

29. A clear, if negative, indication of the complexity of Hebbel's apprehension of Klara is his violent dismissal of the figure of Marie in Lenz's *Die Soldaten.* His argument that such sexual vulnerability could not be made the basis of a significant moral destiny seems equally to call in question the potentially tragic status of his own heroine as this is defined in his analytical scheme. F. Hebbel: *Tagebuch 1471,* 2nd February 1839.

30. I have looked at this in detail in an article: "Strategies of Inwardness. Gutzkow's domestic Plays and the liberal Drama in the 1840's", which is to appear shortly in *Maske und Kothurn.*

31. The Pastor for example has an overtly choric function in *Der Erbförster.* In: O. Ludwig: *Werke,* ed. A. Bartels (undated). Vol. II. Cf. II, 8 and V, 8.

Similar in conception are the figures of Dr. Fels in *Werner* (K. Gutzkow: *Dramatische Werke,* Vol. I, cf. II, 3 and 5; V, 6) and that of Hiller in *Graf Waldemar* (in G. Freytag: *Gesammelte Werke* [Hirzel], undated. Vol. VI, cf. II, 2; III, 1; IV, 2.).

32. There are particularly obvious examples of such interpretative use of stage-directions in *Der Erbförster.* In: O. Ludwig: *Werke,* Vol. II, I, 4. Here the hero's advice to his future son-in-law to treat Marie with severity is followed by the qualifying stage-direction: "Er wendet sich um, seine Weichheit zu verbergen, mit Gebärden seinen Zorn ausdrückend, daß er sie nicht bezwingen kann." See also the detailed directions appended to the speeches of Stein in I, 7.

In *Der Meineidbauer* a similar descriptive tendency in the use of stage-directions is even more obviously apparent. In: L. Anzengruber: *Sämtliche Werke,* ed. R. Latzke and O. Rommel, 1921, Vol. III, II, 10 and III, 2.

The final indication of sunrise is a direct attempt to endorse symbolically the last words of the play spoken by Vroni: "Da sein neue Leut und die Welt fangt erst an!" and thus to set the whole dramatic action in an optimistic, evolutionary perspective.

33. There are interesting possibilities of relating this to the fact of the withdrawal of the authorising, directing presence of the narrator in the 19th century novel, which has been so incisively analysed by R. Brinkmann in *Wirklichkeit und Illusion* (1957). In a recent study of Storm (clearly stimulated and guided by Brinkmann's analysis), T. J. Rogers has already tentatively and briefly suggested some interesting affinities of method between novel and drama. In: T. J. Rogers: *Techniques of Solipsism,* 1970, pp. 117-118.

34. V. Klotz: *Geschlossene und offene Form im Drama,* 3rd ed, 1968. Klotz has done much for the understanding of formal developments in the drama since the Sturm und Drang. But his account needs some important qualification. In his concern to propose an 'open form' as a dialectical counterpart to the 'closed', classical structure he is forced largely to ignore the central development of realism in drama in the 19th century. This was shaped in the work of Hebbel and Ludwig, Ibsen and Hauptmann by a consistent will to assimilate the pressures of empirical insight to inherited modes of dramatic structure. Their common concern was to extend and renew existent patterns of formal awareness in drama, to make them responsive to analytical insight. *Maria Magdalena* is a prime example of such a synthesising impulse.

35. The first study really to face up to the problem of ambiguity in Hauptmann's work is that of J. Osborne in *The Naturalist Drama in Germany,* 1971. See especially pp. 148-156; 164-170. At the same time I must confess that I find his own attempts at interpretation often one-sided and only partly persuasive. Nonetheless his study has the merit of confronting a difficulty sharply and intelligently which has been almost totally ignored.

36. G. Hauptmann: *Sämtliche Werke* (Centenar Ausgabe), ed. H.-E. Hass. 1962—. Cf. *Fuhrmann Henschel,* Vol. I, pp. 989-1001; *Michael Kramer,* Vol. I, pp. 1168-1179; *Rose Bernd,* Vol. II, pp. 252-259; *Gabriel Schilling's Flucht,* Vol. II, pp. 447, 450. Cf. also pp. 474 ff.

HERODES UND MARIAMNE (HEROD AND MARIAMNE)

CRITICAL COMMENTARY

Claude Abraham (essay date May 1968)

SOURCE: Abraham, Claude. "Tristan and Hebbel: Mariane and Mariamne." *South Atlantic Bulletin* 33, no. 3 (May 1968): 1-4.

[*In the following essay, Abraham finds parallels between Hebbel's* Herod and Mariamne *and Tristan L'Hermite's* La Mariane.]

The story of Herod and Mariamne has been dramatized again and again. Marcus Landau counted some thirty versions,[1] and Maurice Valency added, "without any difficulty, thirteen others."[2] Yet, only two versions—one by a Frenchman of the Baroque period, the other by a German realist—have survived. While these plays seem to have little but the topic in common, it is our purpose here to show that underneath the obvious differences lurk basic similarities, and that it is undoubtedly because of these similarities that the works of Tristan L'Hermite and of Hebbel have survived.

Tristan's *La Mariane* was first performed early in 1636 and published in 1637. Its immediate success rivaled that of Corneille's *Le Cid.* It appeared in ten different editions during the author's lifetime and in no less than twenty-three before the end of the following century. Neglected during the nineteenth century, it is currently enjoying a modest cult not only among scholars but also in print and on the stage. In 1660, Corneille, who was always jealous of his rivals, praised Tristan's "grand effort d'esprit," and modern reviewers, even severe critics such as Lemarchand and Salacrou, have praised recent performances, the latter calling *La Mariane* "un chef-d'oeuvre de la littérature française."[3]

Hebbel's *Herodes und Mariamne,* like *La Mariane,* gained but a few friends during the nineteenth century. Hebbel called the play "ohne Zweifel mein Bestes."[4] This feeling was shared by the "zwei oder drei Kunstrichter, deren Deutschland sich rühmen kann,"[5] but when it appeared in 1849 it was not a total success, and only in this century has Hebbel's faith been vindicated and his genius recognized.

Outwardly, the plays have little in common. Using a "décor à compartiments," Tristan is fairly obedient to the three unities and follows Josephus quite closely.

The Paris audience of 1637 often thought more of the poetic garb than of the dramatic content of a play. As a result, Tristan, superior poet but mediocre dramatist, allowed many long declamatory tirades to abound in a play which many modern viewers consider somewhat static. To obey the unity of time, Tristan's play begins very near the crisis: Herod is already the murderer of the last of the Hasmoneans. Mariane has already found out that he meant to have her killed too, and thus, as the play opens, we are confronted by a conscience-stricken tyrant on the verge of madness, and his unforgiving and unyielding wife.

Because the German theater audience of 1850 had quite different tastes, **Herodes und Mariamne** has no really long tirades. Its language is quite realistic—imagine a *précieuse's* reaction to "pfui, ich sprech' ja, wie mein Vater!" (1. 917)—and the poetry, while lofty, cannot be compared with Tristan's lyricism. The play was conceived to center around both characters, "aber natürlich das ganze Leben de Herodes umfassend."[6]

Yet, in spite of these, and other outward dissimilarities too numerous and obvious to be mentioned here, the plays have much in common. In spite of the authors' protestations, the plays focus not just on either or both of the main protagonists, but on the irreconcilable positions of the two. Lacy Lockert, in his analysis of Tristan's play, suggests that "Herod and not its titular heroine is the central character in [Tristan's] *Mariamne* [sic]. The entire play is built around him."[7] As I have pointed out in a previous study, Hérode and Mariane cannot exist one without the other and the tragedy resides precisely in that Mariane, failing to realize that Hérode is as necessary to her hatred as she is to his love, rejects all his overtures and makes all communication impossible.[8] More and more, as work on the play progresses, Hebbel stresses the importance of psychological realism. "In this respect, he sought to develop individuals whose actions and destinies were the only possible results of such characters."[9] So, while one critic suggests that "obviously, the slaughter of the Innocents has no proper business in a Mariamne play, and cannot be motivated in any usual version of the plot," and questions "whether Hebbel has improved much on Tirso with respect to the motivation of the massacre,"[10] it is obvious that this final proof of Herodes' madness is as natural to Hebbel's character as Hérode's fitful tirade is to Tristan's creation, both lapses resulting directly from what D. Dalla Valle calls the "zona di solitudine e ostentazione, di sofferta incomunicabilitá,"[11] a solitude sought and enforced in both plays by a wrathful wife.

From the very beginning, Tristan presents a guilty Hérode whose conscience will not let him rest, yet one whose bravado allows him to regain the upper hand. His victory, however, is hollow, for only Mariane means anything to him, and her hatred is implacable from the start.

While Tristan's Hérode is alone on stage at the start, Hebbel's Herodes is surrounded by his court. Yet he too feels alone in a court where fear reigns (11. 52-54), but it is a loneliness which he does not care to end. On the contrary, while Hérode calls his court to his side (1. 15), Herodes sends his away, for he feels that everyone is against him (11. 254-58). Thus, in spite of outward differences, the stage is set in both plays for the entrance of the wife whose murderous husband tries to hide feelings of guilt and insecurity behind a mask of belligerence. However, with her entrance, we are made immediately aware of one basic difference: Tristan's play opens shortly before the death of Mariane; Hérode has returned from his one and only trip; Mariane is already aware, not only of his role as murderer of her family, but also of his wish to have her killed should he not return. This wish, which was made in a fit of jealous fear, is misinterpreted by Mariane, in whose mind it becomes the final proof of her husband's lack of love for her. Hebbel's play opens earlier in the history of the tragic couple. Herodes is about to take the fateful trip to Anthony's court and Mariamne, while unforgiving as the sister of Aristobolus, is still the dutiful wife, though sensing her love slowly slipping away. "Ich kenne meine Pflicht" (1. 273), says the wife who would gladly set back the hands of time: "O, dass er nicht die blut'gen Hände hätte!" (1. 299). Mariane, too, once loved Hérode, and without her, he would have lost "à la fois, et le sceptre, et le jour" (1. 286), but that love is quite dead by the time the play starts. Not so in Hebbel's play. Mariamne still loves her husband and would willingly die if he should not return. Hebbel, unlike Tristan, carefully allows Herodes to present this possibility to his wife as "ein Übermass von Liebe" (1. 420). As a result, there is no misunderstanding, only a further disappointment: the murderer of her brother does not trust her. Earlier she had asked the big question: how could he "Die Schwester lieben und den Bruder töten?" (1. 355). Now she murmurs her own answer:

> Ja, um so eher tät ich das, je
>   sich'rer
> Ich selbst, wenn dich der Tod
>   von hinnen riefe,
> In meinem Schmerz zum Dolche
>   greifen könnte:
> Das kann man tun, erleiden
>   kann man's nicht!
>
> (ll. 425-428)

When Herodes points to the example of a wife who died beside her dead husband, Mariamne leaves no doubt:

> Sie liess ja nicht zum Opfertier
> sich machen,
> Sie hat sich selbst geopfert, das
> beweist,
> Dass ihr der Tote mehr war, als
> die Welt!
>
> (ll. 433-435)

At this stage, we still have a Mariamne who, as Alexandra puts it, "hasst und liebt ihn jetzt zugleich" (l. 940), while Tristan's Mariane, with her opening lines, shows that she sees in her husband only

> un monstre abominable,
> Qui du trépas des miens me
> parait tout sanglant.
>
> (ll. 348-349)

There is no doubt as to her feelings: she is a queen, and Hérode is the foe:

> Si mon corps est captif, mon
> âme ne l'est pas:
>   . . . . .
> Qu'Hérode m'importune, ou
> d'amour ou de haine,
> On me verra toujours vivre et
> mourir en reine.
>
> (ll. 362-368)

Whenever Hérode seeks Mariane, he will find only the specter of the murdered Hasmoneans. Mariamne fails to satisfy her mother in this respect:

> Hättest du
> Dem blut'gen Schatten deines
> Bruders auch
> Das schwesterliche Opfer eine
> Rache
> Herzlos entziehen können . . .
>   . . . . .
> Er selbst, der Mörder, hätte
> nicht gewagt,
> Sich dir zu nähern. . . .
>
> (ll. 951-960)

During Hebbel's second act, Mariamne reminds us less of Mariane than of Corneille's Pauline. She constantly defends her husband's deeds, not because of her love for him but out of a sense of duty. She did not choose this mate, but when this destiny was visited upon her by Alexandra, she decided to be true to it:

> Ich zog es vor, dem Mann ein
> Weib zu sein,
> Dem du mich zugeführt, und
> über ihn

> Die Makkabäerin so zu verges-
> sen,
> Wie er den König über mich
> vergass.
>
> (ll. 1004-7)

The murder of Aristobolus, as she constantly reminds her mother (ll. 1036-39, 1049-88, etc.), is as much the doing of Alexandra's ambitious plotting as it is Herodes' desire to safeguard his crown. As Hardy, in creating the prototype of a Herod *parvenu,* put it, "Les appas d'un royaume autorisent le crime."[12] Thus, in Mariamne's mind, if the safeguarding of a crown is the legitimate concern of a ruler, then the murder of Aristobolus is a direct result of Alexandra's plotting. However, while Pauline's sense of duty undergoes a steady metamorphosis and turns into love, Mariamne's love dies before our very eyes until only its shell—a duty to a now dead ideal—remains.

Tristan wisely decided to combine Herod's two trips—and consequently the two threats to Mariane's life—into one and to begin the play after the return. Hebbel uses these two trips to show in detail how they affected the relationship between the protagonists. Throughout the second act, during which Herodes is on his first trip, Mariamne is of one mind: "ich sterbe, / wenn er stribt" (ll. 1087-88). But it soon dawns on her that this resolution is gratuitous. Herodes has already settled the issue by making of her an "Opfertier," appointing Joseph the "Opferpriester" in the event of his own death (l. 1324). While Mariamne deplores the coldness of their parting (ll. 1291-95), Herodes has left the order for her death

> Als ein Beweis, dass er dich
> liebt, wie nie
> Ein Mann sein Weib noch liebte.
>
> (ll. 1340-41)

This revelation shatters Mariamne's dream:

> Von jetzt erst fängt mein Leben
> an,
> Bis heute träumt ich!
>
> (ll. 1359-60)

She realized at this point that, like Artaxerxes, the human clock, she is but a thing, a toy, to Herod:

> Ich war ihm nur ein Ding und
> weiter nichts!
>
> (l. 1382)

With the opening of Act III, Herodes, having returned from his first trip, seeks his wife who now avoids him. Here, the first true parallel between the two plays becomes obvious. Salome, the proud sister, quickly seizes the occasion to point out Mariamne's reluctance, hoping to widen the breach:

Sie ging, als sie vernahm,
Dass du dich näthertest.

(ll. 1507-8)

Her resentment stems in large from the fact that, as her counterpart in Tristan's play had put it, the proud princess "parle de nous comme de ses valets" (1. 298) and demonstrates an insufferable pride:

War der Stolz,
Womit sie mir und deiner Mutter immer
Begegnete, war er ein Grund
zur Liebe?

(ll. 2628-30)

Herodes, however, like Hérode, will not hear of it. As Salome begins her accusations, he interrupts violently:

Ich sag' dir eins! Wär an dem
Tag,
An dem ich sie zum erstenmal
erblickte,
Ein Kläger aufgestanden wider
sie,
Er hätt' nicht leicht Gehör bei
mir gefunden,
Doch leichter noch, wie heut!
Das werne dich!

(ll. 1528-32)

Hérode, mindful of his debt, had excused her by siding with her:

Et puis, il est bien juste, à dire
vérité,
Qu'elle garde entre vous un peu
de majesté.
Mille rois glorieux sont ses
dignes ancêtres,
Et l'on peut la nommer la fille
de nos maitres.

(ll. 293-296)

Thus, while Herodes closes the matter with a warning and a brief statement that leaves no doubt as to his will (ll. 1533-34), Hérode implies rather an equivocal stand that betrays a certain dissatisfaction of his own.

Now, for the first time, as Herodes seeks Mariamne, the slain Aristobolus confronts him and separates them:

Sie hätt' mich küssen müssen
Der Allgewalt des Augenblicks
erliegend,
Und dann die Lippen sich zer-
beissen mögen,
Wenn das Gespenst denn noch
nicht von ihr wich!

(ll. 1555-58)

In Tristan's play, this ghost is all-important. Mariane cannot forget her murdered relatives:

Soit lors que je repose, ou soit
lors que je veille,
Leur plainte à tous moments
vient frapper mon oreille;
. . . . .
Et puis qu'après cela je flatte
l'inhumain
Qui ne vient que d'ôter la vie
à mon germain?
Plutôt le feu me brûle, ou
l'onde son contraire
Rende mon corps pareil à celui
de mon frère.

(ll. 383-428)

It is a proud princess, conscious of her essence, that rejects a husband who, by his recent order to kill her, has completed an odious self-portrait. With Hebbel, it is a different matter entirely. Mariamne is, first and foremost, a wife who now fully realizes that her husband did not trust ser (ll. 1604-7). She resents the fact that he doubts that she still has

. . . in meinem Busen
Noch ein Gefühl von Pflicht, ein
Rtst von Stolz.

(ll. 1611-12)

Herodes, like Hérode, further insults his wife when he suggests the price she must have paid for such a disclosure (ll. 1626-27), and threatens her, but Mari-amne, in anger, explodes.

Dem Brudermord
Hast du das Siegel der Not-
wendigkeit,
Dem man sich beugen muss,
wie man auch schaudert,
Zwar aufgedrückt, doch es ge-
lingt dir nie,
Mit diesem Siegel auch den
Mord an mir
Zu stempeln, der wird bleiben,
was er ist,
Ein Frevel, den man höchstens
wiederholen,
Doch nun und nimmer über-
bieten kann!

(ll. 1640-47)

His defense is meaningless:

Du sprichst umsonst! Du hast
in mir die Menschheit
Geschändet. . . .

(ll. 1684-85)

With the announcement of Herodes' second trip, the misunderstanding grows. Mariamne, clinging to hope, sees in this new departure a second chance for saving a foundering marriage. Unable to control her emotions, she betrays her joy and Herodes is quick to misinterpret:

> Dein Angesicht
> Hat sich erheitert! Aber hoffe
> nicht
> Zu viel!

(ll. 1807-9)

The argument that ensues merely widens the rift and culminates in Mariamne's cry "Jetzt bin ich stumm!" (l. 1855), recalling the outburst of Tristan's heroine who, unwilling to believe in a love that infringed upon a solitude so essential to her position, decides to be a stranger at her own trial: "Crois tout ce que tu dis, et tout ce que tu penses" (l. 980).

Henceforth, both plays move on the same plane, both authors exploiting a rift they have developed in such diverse ways. Goaded by Mariane, Hérode blurts out words of hatred—a hatred he does not feel, but one which can be understood and believed by Mariane who welcomes his outburst:

> Poursuis, poursuis barbare, et
> sois inexorable,
> Tu me rends un devoir qui m'est
> fort agréable,
> Et ta haine obstinée à me priver
> du jour,
> M'oblige beaucoup plus que n'a
> fait ton amour.

(ll. 855-858)

Here is the Hérode she understands. When, attempting to correct the impression, he speaks of love, he merely causes the impenetrable wall of misunderstanding to reappear:

> On connait à ce style, et doux,
> et décevant,
> Comme en l'art de trahir ton
> esprit est savant;
> C'est avec trop de soin m'ouvrir
> la sépulture:
> Pour me perdre il suffit d'une
> seule imposture.

(ll. 917-920)

Hebbel reverses the roles, but without changing the basic problem. Mariamne's last warning (ll. 1875-86) is completely misunderstood, for Herodes, pursued by feelings of guilt, now wants to believe that she no longer loves him:

> Wenn sie mich liebte! Hat sie
> mich geliebt?
> Ich glaub' es. Aber jetz—Wie
> sich der Tote
> Im Grabe noch zu rächen weiss!

> Ich Schaffte
> Ihn fort, um meine Krone mir
> zu sichern,
> Er nahm, was mehr wog, mit
> hinweg: ihr Herz!

(ll. 1918-22)

He has lost faith in a love which, according to his values, no longer makes sense, and now clings to the belief in a hatred that does not exist. This hatred and distrust, created in his own mind, become a reality that supersedes any other. Mariamne is well aware of this, and Soemus' revelation of Herodes' second order for her death (ll. 2131-38) is anticipated and anticlimactic. She sees herself, once again, "zum Ding herabgesetzt" (l. 2203), and decides to accept Herodes' judgment. Henceforth, she will *be* what she *seemed* to be to Herodes. The transformation is complete: in Herodes' world, the *paraitre* has become the *être*. Echoing the already quoted lines of her French counterpart—"Crois tout ce que tu dis, et tout ce que tu penses"—she revels in the picture of wantonness that she has created:

> Wie ich beim Scheiden stand
> vor seinem Geist,
> So hat er mich beim Wiedersehn
> gefunden.

(ll. 2849-50)

Herodes, like Hérode, does indeed think the worst from the moment he returns,[13] but Mariamne, recalling the lines of Tristan's heroine, refuses even to speak to her husband and merely tells the soldiers "so führt mich ab!" (l. 2602)

Both Mariamne and Mariane are strangers at their trials. Both refuse to defend themselves and merely allow the breach to widen. After the trial, neither queen deigns to speak to her husband and Mariamne, for once as proud as Tristan's heroine, merely tells Joab to lead her to her death:

> Ich bin bereit, sobald du selbst
> es bist,
> Und Königinnen, weisst du,
> warten nicht!

(ll. 2957-58)

Mariane, having turned her eyes to the next world, rejects all those around her. At peace with herself, she is, for the first time, truly self-sufficient. She rejects the pity of the soldier who leads her to her death, and considers her mother's sorrow equally superfluous (ll. 1359-60). When Alexandra, to save her own life, disowns her daughter and accuses her publicly, Mariane, without anger, simply replies, "Vous vivrez innocente, et je mourrai coupable" (l. 1932. The divorce is complete. Perfect stranger, she no longer needs anything or anyone, not even vindication or vengeance, not even Meursault's desired "cris de haine."

Mariamne is of a different fiber. To the ghost that was present at her trial she declared "du sollst mit mir zufrieden sein!" (l. 2832). It is again this need to justify herself—and her death—which leads her to seek out Titus, the disinterested Roman, to bear witness to her innocence, but only after her death. Her very death will thus open Herodes' eyes, as her silent oath attests:

> Du willst im Tode meinen
>   Henker machen?
> Du sollst das Weib, das du erb-
>   licktest, töten
> Und erst im Tod mich sehen
>   wie ich bin!

(ll. 3039-42)

Thus, Herodes will consider himself her murderer, even though, by refusing to defend herself, she is, in fact, committing suicide, a fact that does not escape her: "ich werf' das Leben weg!" (l. 3062)

Mariane dies gladly, reaching for a new life. Mariamne, not believing in an afterlife (ll. 2979-80), merely puts down a burden that has become unbearable (ll. 3087-89). Were Herodes to reform, to reach out, she would welcome him back (ll. 3094-3101), but she realizes that this cannot be, and with a sorrowful "Herodes, lebe wohl!" (l. 3113), she joins Aristobolus "in der ew'gen Nacht" (l. 3115).

Both Mariane and Mariamne are proud vestiges of a noble line. Both suffer without joy their union to one they consider a *parvenu*. But while Mariamne is willing to perform her wifely duties, Mariane is not. From the start, Tristan presents a proud princess at odds with the world around her. Her very essence prevents her from communicating with this alien world. Tristan's entire play centers around a single crisis: Hérode's futile attempts to breach a wall that Mariane has erected. Hebbel, on the other hand, has chosen to base his play on what might be considered a more existential plane: the building of that wall. However, if both plays have remained in the public eye, if their dramatic and tragic impact can still be felt today, it is because both authors were able to capture the feeling of unbearable solitude, the futile yearning to be understood which still plagues us today.

Notes

1. "Die Dramen von Herodes und Mariamne," ZVL, N.S. 8 (1895), p. 175.

2. *The Tragedies of Herod and Mariamne* (N.Y.; 1940), p. vii.

3. *France-Soir* (22 December, 1958).

4. *Sämtliche Werke*, ed. R. M. Werner (Berlin, 1901), XX, 196.

5. *Ibid.*, p. 178

6. *Werke*, XV, 135.

7. *Studies in French Classical Tragedy* (Nashville, 1958), p. 119.

8. *The Strangers: The Tragic World of Tristan L'Hermite* (Gainesville, 1966), Ch. II.

9. Paul G. Graham. *The Relation of History to Drama in the Works of Friedrich Hebbel.* Smith College Studies in Modern Languages, XV, 1-2 (Northhampton, 1933), p. 41.

10. Valency, p. 42.

11. *Il teatro di Tristan L'Hermite* (Torino, 1965), 228.

12. *Mariamne*, II, 1.

13. Cf., ll. 2593, 2697-99, 2721, etc.

MICHEL ANGELO

CRITICIAL COMMENTARY

Brian Harris (essay date 1987)

SOURCE: Harris, Brian. "The Michelangelo Dramas of Friedrich Hebbel and Hugo Ball: From Historicism toward Expressionism." In *From the Bard to Broadway: The University of Florida Department of Classics Comparative Drama Conference Papers, Vol. VII*, edited by Karelisa V. Hartigan, pp. 96-106. Lanham, Md.: University Press of America, 1987.

[*In the following essay, Harris asserts that Ball wrote his tragicomic* Michelangelo's Nose *in "direct critical response" to Hebbel's* Michel Angelo *and "to the nineteenth-century traditions from which it emerges."*]

Hugo Ball (1886-1927) had left student life at the university in Munich in 1910 to pursue a career in the theatre. Back in Munich in 1912, after a year at the Reinhardt theatre school in Berlin, then a year as stage manager and sometime director with the municipal theatre in Plauen, Ball was drawn into orbit around Vassily Kandinsky and other members of the Blaue Reiter group. But Ball's emergence after late 1913 as an Expressionist in Munich theatrical circles was cut short by the outbreak of World War I. Instead, his artistic and theatrical career reached its climax in 1916 in his Dada magic bishop sound poems and in his emergence as a cofounder and the theoretician of Zurich Dada (1916-

17). For, following his brief immersion into the "lavish ambiguities" of the "creative anarchy" and "destructive nihilism" of Dada, Ball broke decisively in 1917 with artistic matters and turned his attention instead toward radical politics, cultural criticism, and religion.[1] However, two influences had coalesced in Ball's thinking during his university career in Munich (1906-10) to propel him toward theatrical life. They are the ideas of Friedrich Nietzsche and the writing of the nineteenth-century German dramatist Friedrich Hebbel.

Ball left Munich in 1910 without submitting his doctoral dissertation "Nietzsche in Basel: A Polemic."[2] The writings of Nietzsche had set out the philosophical and psychological premises of a new age of human freedom. And Ball's treatise shows clearly that he had by 1910 become magnetized by the creative potential of Nietzschean dionysian irrationality and the promise it seemed to hold for theatrical innovations and, hence, for the reshaping of human values and culture into an esthetic cosmodicy that celebrated individual liberty. By this time too Ball had concluded that he was likely destined to reform German theatre to a level of perfection beyond Hebbel's art.[3] In fact, in 1908 Ball wrote a tragicomedy, *Michelangelo's Nose* [Die Nase des Michelangelo], which is a direct critical response to Hebbel's two-act drama *Michel Angelo* (1855) and to the nineteenth-century traditions from which it emerges.[4]

Even in his youth Hugo Ball had been preoccupied with the life and works of Friedrich Hebbel.[5] And as a young playwright Ball would have learned much from them. For Hebbel's works crystallize the major crises of nineteenth-century German theatre.[6] He was linked by the works of Goethe and Schiller to the Renaissance tradition of universality in drama; yet he also laid the foundation for the social theatre of Ibsen and opened channels to psychological realism and to naturalism. His works were thus caught between the need to satisfy a tradition that dictated using historical subjects having universal implications and the need to refer directly to the world in which he lived. In the broader context of European theatre, Hebbel's writings reflect four major themes of the intellectual crisis that was coming to a head during the last half of the nineteenth century. These are: (1) the dissonance between idea and reality; (2) a crisis in the ideal of humanity and the resultant crisis in the concept of the dramatic hero; (3) the dissolution of Christian values and beliefs and the emergence of pessimism as a cultural phenomenon; and (4) the dual significance of history in the age of expanding historicism (Wiese, 1955, 292). In effect Hebbel's drama reveals that tragedy as theodicy was no longer possible; that tragedy was giving way to nihilism; and that new theatrical forms might well be needed to penetrate what Benno von Wiese has described as the new direction in European sensibility toward the "foundation and origin of the ego and, hence, of everything" (1955, 297). And

this was the same new terrain of human internality that Nietzsche's works were mapping out for Hugo Ball in philosophical terms.

It is easy to see, then, why Hugo Ball in 1908 should have been drawn to Hebbel's drama *Michel Angelo.* For it underscores the significance of art in the evolution of human culture and in the formation of human values, and, at the same time, it would have put into sharp relief the conflicts which Ball then was experiencing in his own intellectual and artistic life.

Hebbel completed his two-act drama *Michel Angelo* in 1851. It presents the reconciliation of Michelangelo with himself, with traditional art—symbolized by the painter Raphael—and with the higher human goals of Renaissance society and culture—symbolized by the Pope (Hebbel, 1963, I, 651-78). Michelangelo has been frustrated in his attempts to achieve greatness and fame. At odds with public opinion and the tastes of his age, he is jealous of Raphael, whose fame intensifies his own frustration. The conflict between Michelangelo and Raphael symbolizes two ideals of art in the Renaissance: the established, classical ideal (personified by Raphael) and a new personal expressiveness (represented by Michelangelo). The Pope reconciles the conflict by redirecting the creative energies of both artists toward the greater goals of Renaissance civilization. The resulting harmony guarantees personal fulfillment and moral progress that in turn promises to elevate the human spirit.

The play *Michel Angelo* was of great personal and artistic significance to Hebbel. He had been compared to Michelangelo in 1850. And his Michelangelo character represents a problem he knew only too well: "the self-assurance of the creative individual and the settling of accounts with a world that fails to appreciate the creative individual" (Fricke, 1963, I, 803). In the tension between Michelangelo and Raphael, and in the subordination of this conflict to higher ethical goals, Hebbel presents the "'mutual validation and acknowledgement'" of great personalities and energies which only a higher force can mediate.[7] Hebbel worried that the play might be seen only as a drama about artists and the jealousies between them; he had hoped to present a universal ethical process "which is repeated in every human life and emerges somewhat more sharply in the artist's existence."[8] In dramatizing the reconciliation of conflicts between individual artists Hebbel was reaffirming a dynamic moral-esthetic structure that ensured personal freedom and fulfillment, and engendered cultural progress toward a higher state of humanity.

With indirect symbolic reference to himself and to his own age and its attitudes, Friedrich Hebbel presents in *Michel Angelo* his nineteenth-century vision of the

Renaissance ideal of art and culture. His play is a work of art about the "work" of art, and it affirms Renaissance ideals while adapting those ideals to his own artistry and epoch. Moreover, the play touches upon issues of historical consciousness and the evolution of historical attitudes. Finally, the play restates Hebbel's basic view of the integration of creativity, art, and individuality into society, and asserts this integration as an essential force in moral and cultural evolution. However, Hugo Ball's tragicomedy *Michelangelo's Nose* raises serious questions about the cultural vision of the Renaissance, about Hebbel's view of Renaissance values, and about the dramatic vehicle of Hebbel's views, the historical drama.

In Ball's play, Pietro Torrigiano, who has disfigured Michelangelo by breaking his nose, returns to Rome from England. He has been hounded for his deed and forced to live in exile. He has come home, hoping to be reconciled with Michelangelo.

Michelangelo is a bitter man. The sculptor Torrigiano has become a symbol of his failing artistic powers. When the two men meet, their hatred breaks out anew. But Michelangelo is overcome by compassion for his enemy. He realizes his own part in the inhuman persecution of Torrigiano and resolves to help him regain his position as artist and member of society. Michelangelo's decision also promises to regenerate his own waning powers. However, Michelangelo's personal conflict is complicated by his youthful friend and supporter Cellini, who hates Torrigiano for what he did to Michelangelo and who, through his hold over public opinion, has ruthlessly followed Michelangelo's lead in persecuting him. Michelangelo's change of heart sets him against Cellini, who demands Torrigiano's execution. Cellini manipulates public sentiment to force the Pope to reject Michelangelo's pleas for mercy. In attempting to remain true to his past, Michelangelo is compelled to acknowledge Cellini's claim. Yet in his awakened humanity for Torrigiano, Michelangelo must reject Cellini and public opinion. The conflict is irreconcilable.

Michelangelo petitions the Pope to forgive Torrigiano. Cellini incites the populace in order to force the Pope to side with him against Torrigiano. Above all, the Pope is a politician, a manager of affairs of state, a Machiavellian figure, as is Cellini. Torrigiano, the outsider, the rebel, is driven to commit suicide, and Michelangelo can only stand helplessly as the alliance between public opinion and a politicized religious institution takes its toll. The moral structure represented by the union of art, state, and Church emerges as a disguise of special interests. Both Michelangelo and Torrigiano, whose reconciliation would embody the true spirit of Renaissance humanity, are pushed aside by a relentless and politically opportunistic theocracy. Michelangelo, the Renaissance ideal, cannot achieve the personal equilibrium needed to regenerate his life, his moral idealism, or his art.

But Ball's character Michelangelo does more than reflect Renaissance ideals. One speech in the first act of Ball's drama reveals that Michelangelo is also an early twentieth-century hero. It is early in the action. Michelangelo is offering his friendship and protection in a burst of charitable understanding and repentance that gives an insight into the ethical and moral principles which he represents:

> Mankind continues to be mankind.
> Do not touch Ixion's wheel! No one can slow it!
> That is the last dance in the carnival farce of
>   life
> In which I was to play some humorless, witless
>   fool!
> Yet I myself can no longer crush this man, even
>   if
> He should escape the butchering knives of the
>   zealous mob
> That waits for him beyond these walls. No, then
>   let
> Him be as safe and sound as once he was, but
>   now,
> Here in Rome in the midst of those fanatics.
> It is never too late. Oh, seeds that years ago
>   had fallen
> Upon these stoney cliffs, send forth once more
>   your growth![9]

It has been noted that Michelangelo's speech voices the affirmation of humanity to be found in Expressionist thought (Steinke, 1967, 71). But, in addition, Ball has taken the image complex of seeds and sowing directly from Hebbel's *Michel Angelo.*

Hebbel's play had concluded with Michelangelo and Raphael being reconciled to the greater moral goals of art in Renaissance society, and with Michelangelo being commissioned to work on the Sistine Chapel. At the end of Hebbel's drama the Pope recites a parable teaching of the conflict between good and evil and of the ultimate victory of good. The controlling image in his speech is that of sowing and abundant harvest and growth in spite of and because of weeds planted by the Devil.[10] In the passage cited above, Ball's Michelangelo has invoked that image from the perspective of the Pope in Hebbel's drama. But late in the fourth act of Ball's play Torrigiano bitterly characterizes his persecution: "They tore me from the world as if I were some weed" (1911, 63). His words bitingly expose the hypocrisy and failure of the productive ideal of culture expounded in Hebbel's drama.

Ball here has done more than borrow an image. His Michelangelo character faces the crisis of his own personal and artistic failure, and a deeper conflict than

Hebbel's Michelangelo. For Ball, any reconciliation between Michelangelo and Raphael is only an initial step toward the resolution of a conflict which transcends Hebbel's drama. Ball's play concludes that Michelangelo and Torrigiano must be reconciled in order to save both artists from repressive bondage and to affirm the spiritual ideal of intrinsic human value. At the end of the first act Ball's Michelangelo promises Torrigiano "You shall stand then / At my side when the Sistine Chapel is unveiled" (1911, 20). But in the end, Torrigiano commits suicide, and Michelangelo is crushed by irreconcilable conflicts.

It has been observed that Ball's Torrigiano is a "tortured, suffering tragic victim of inhuman persecution, of terrible misfortune, and of fantastic miscarriage of justice," and that the figure is a "champion of the dignity and freedom of the individual" (Steinke, 1967, 33). However, it is equally clear that Michelangelo is a correlative hero. In Ball's play both Michelangelo and Torrigiano admit that the world is insane, that they are out of phase with the institutions around them. And both characters fall victim to an autonomous religious structure that is ruled by secular forces in a world where demagoguery substitutes for truth and charity. Torrigiano's suicide is heroic because he wills it. But Michelangelo is the measure of Torrigiano's fate; for he is the artist who lives and works on, knowing that the conditions of his own survival contradict the essential humanity upon which his art and his life are based. In Ball's play the rebellious human spirit seeks to be reconciled with a higher cultural ideal, but the rebel is maliciously destroyed. And the ideal itself is exposed as a pathetic sham.

There is yet additional significance in the relationship between Michelangelo and Torrigiano that must be taken into account. Does Michelangelo represent Hebbel, does Torrigiano represent Ball? This seems so. In adapting Hebbel's strategy of indirect symbolism that refers to himself and his own age to a criticism of Hebbel's use of that device, Ball has further emphasized the failure of a dramatic tradition that attempts to reconcile historical significance with individuality. For Ball, traditional individuality itself is an empty concept; in effect, Ball's Torrigiano constitutes an intellectual perception of the Hebbel/Michelangelo complex. Ball's play has, thus, accepted no traditional values. And this pervasive historical cynicism and critical irony finds its correlative in a style of dislocation which provides the final sign that Ball viewed Hebbel's dramatic vision and the traditions upon which it rests as useless to his own age.

Hebbel's works also marked, among other emergencies, a nineteenth-century crisis in the use of poetry in the theatre. He was the last dramatic poet after Schiller, and the first to show a subject matter connected with nineteenth-century social thought and treated in prose (Peacock, 1960a, 72). Hebbel's attempts to continue the Weimau poetic tradition in the theatre communicate, in the words of Ronald Peacock, the "sense of a forced poetic effort, of versifying to fulfill a laudable literary intention" (1960a, 73-74). Ball draws attention to Hebbel's lack of poetic sensibility and to the demise of poetic theatre in a most effective way—by using unrhymed iambic hexameter as the metrical form in his drama. The traditional dignity of this form, coupled with the critical, satirical aspects of the play, gives Ball's piece a sharply polemic character.[11] But this anti-heroic heroic verse form also constitutes a stylistic commentary on the use of poetic expression in Hebbel's dramas. Ball's language punctures Hebbel's heavy, pompous poetry. This, in turn, helps reveal a major function of the comic elements in Ball's play, namely, to register in dramatic and poetic form the widening gap between Hebbel's intention and the possibility of realizing that intention in Ball's own age.

For Ball, comicality—"Komik"—measures the human comprehension of the disparity between the ideal and the real (1946, 85-86).[12] In numerous speeches affirming the basic and sacred dignity of humanity, Ball's character Michelangelo echoes an intellectual perception reminiscent of Hebbel—that is, the traditional ideal of humanity and historical process. By contrast, Ball's Torrigiano directly displays the brutal political realities of social existence. The irreconcilability of Michelangelo and Torrigiano, if ideal and reality, is, thus, precisely the focus of Ball's drama. And the disjunction between style and content, the tension between heroic verse form and satirical action, comprises Ball's dramatic-poetic figuration of a cultural crisis that was first sensed by Hebbel, and of the theatrical emergency inherited from Hebbel's attempts to resolve that crisis through traditional forms. Ball's tragicomedy has taken the shape that comedy and tragedy must take in a world where absolute values are revealed to be masks of relative interests. For only if there is underlying faith in "progress . . . toward finer civilization" as Ronald Peacock has asserted, can comedy and tragedy function as complementary, yet distinct expressions (1960b, 158).[13] The tensions between themes, action, and style in Ball's drama thus constitute his perception of moral relativism and expose the historical cynicism and the nihilism of his own epoch.

Hugo Ball's tragicomedy *Michelangelo's Nose* moved beyond the Renaissance ideals which Friedrich Hebbel in his drama **Michel Angelo** sought to adapt to the nineteenth century, and beyond the moral historicism which underlies the traditional relationship between tragic and comic visions. Ball's play opened to him tentative prospects toward the new theatre of archetypes and the subconscious which he began to develop as an Expressionist in Munich in 1914, and which he later brought to an extreme formulation in his Zurich Dada magic bishop sound poems of 1916, when he compressed dramatic expression to archetypal, if not mythical, subjectivity in the phonic incantations of a wing-flapping Cubist shaman. And because Ball's Michelangelo drama was so directly responsive in 1908 to the legacy that Hebbel had left to the twentieth century, it helps elucidate the complex transition in German theatre from historicism to Expressionism.

Notes

1. For this characterization of Dada, see Middleton (1978, 39). The essay that follows is a revised version of the first chapter of my dissertation (Harris 1979). In November 1985 I read an earlier form of this paper at the Southeast Modern Language Association meeting in Atlanta, Georgia.

2. Ball's dissertation has now been published. See Ball (1978). All quotations in English that have been drawn from German-language sources are my translations.

3. Ball-Hennings (1931, 24), quoting from a letter written to her by August Hofmann, Ball's cousin, who lived in Munich and knew Ball well.

4. To date I am the only one to have pointed out the relationship between Hebbel's play and Ball's play. Bähr (1982) and Mann (1983), the two most recent accounts of Ball's theatrical activities, do not refer to Hebbel's *Michel Angelo*. Nor do they make reference to my dissertation, where I first make this comparison and which sheds much new light on Ball's career.

5. See Ball-Hennings (1946, xi). In a letter to Käthe Brodnitz written sometime between January and late March 1916, Ball recalls and acknowledges his early devotion to Hebbel's works (1972, XVI, 52).

6. See Peacock (1960a, 64-76); and Wiese (1955), especially chs. twenty-three and twenty-four, and the final chapter, German Tragedy between Theodicy and Nihilism.

7. Fricke (1963, I: 803), quoting from Hebbel's letter of 14 August 1848 to E. Janinski.

8. Fricke (1963, I: 804), quoting from Hebbel's letter of 22 June 1855 to Wilhelm Jordan. Hebbel had written to Friedrich Uechtritz on 19 March 1855 that *Michel Angelo* was particularly important to him "because it presents not merely specific artistic conflict, but those universal human conflicts that recur in any realm where noble and genuine striving seeks to assert itself" (Fricke, 1963, I, 804).

9. Ball's German text (1911, 17) reads as follows:

   Mensch bleibt Mensch.
   Die Hand weg vom Ixionsrade! Keiner hemmts!
   Das ist der Kehraus zu dem Fastnachtsstück
     von Leben,
   In dem ich Narr sein sollt und keinen Spass
     verstand!
   Doch kann ich selbst den Mann nicht mehr
     zerschmettern, soll
   Er auch von der Zelotenschar, die draussen
     passt
   Auf ihn, nicht abgeschlachtet werden. Nein,
     dann sei
   Er auch befestigt wieder wie ers war, und
     zwar:
   In Rom hier mitten unter den Fanatikern.
   Zu spät ists nie. Geht Same, der auf Felsen
     fiel,
   Doch nach Jahrzehnten noch mit grünem
     Ausschlag auf!

10. See Hebel (1963, I, 676-77, lines 673-708). Matt. 13: 3-8 is the biblical source of this imagery (the parable of the sower of the seed).

11. Steinke believes that Ball's play is "a piece of polemical writing dressed up in the form of a drama" (1967, 44). However, I do not take the socio-polemic aspects of Ball's play as ends in themselves. In my view Ball's target is both Renaissance idealism and Hebbel's nineteenth-century vision of it.

12. Ball's discussion of "Komik" dates from April 1916, when he was in the initial stages of his Dada period. However, I believe that the concept is highly relevant to his *Michelangelo* and reveals the continuity of his thinking on the theatre between 1908 and 1916.

13. Peacock's essay in general delineates the relationship between the moral-ethical structure underlying tragedy and comedy and the "communal sense of civilization" (158). Moral relativism thus constitutes a sign of the "failure of civilized consciousness" (159).

Works Cited

Joachim Bähr, Hans. "Hugo Ball und das Theater: Die Jahre 1910-14," *Hugo Ball Almanach* VI 75-131.

Ball, Hugo. *Die Nase des Michelangelo: Traikomödie* (Leipzig: Rowohlt).

———. *Die Flucht aus der Zeit* (Lucerne: Josef Stocker).

———. "Hugo Ball and Käthe Brodnitz: Bisher univeröffentlichte Briefe und Kurzmitteilungen asu den 'Dada'-Jahren," ed. Richard W. Sheppard, *Jahrbuch der Deutschen Schillergesellschaft* XVI 37-70.

———. "Nietzsche in Basel: Eine Streitschrift," ed. Richard W. Sheppard and Annemarie Schütt-Hennings *Hugo Ball Almanach 1978* (Pirmasens: Stadt Pirmasens). 2-65.

Ball-Hennings, Emmy. *Hugo Ball's Weg zu Gott: Ein Buch der Erinnerung* (Munich: Kösel and Pustet).

———. Foreword. *Die Fluch aus der Zeit,* by Hugo Ball (Lucerne: Josef Stocker) viixxix.

Fricke, Gerhard. ed., Commentary on *Michel Angelo* by Friedrich Hebbel. In Vol. I of *Werke.* 5 vols. (Munich: Hanser). I 803-06.

Harris, Brain L. *Hugo Ball's Critique of the German Mind: A Translation with Introduction and Notes to Hugo Ball's Zur Kritik der deutschen Intelligenz.* Diss. U. Texas at Austin, 1979 (Ann Arbor: UMI, 7920126).

Hebbel, Friedrich. *Michel Angelo.* In Vol. I of *Werke,* ed. Gerhard Fricke, Werner Keller, and Karl Pörnbacher. 5 vols. (Munich: Hanser) I 651-78.

Mann, Philip. "Hugo Ball's Expressionist Theatre" *Literaturwissenschaftliches Jahrbuch* XXIV 175-208.

Middleton, Christopher. "'Bolshevism in Art'" Dada and Politics," *Bolshevism in Art and Other Expository Writings* (Manchester: Carcanet New Press) 38-61.

Peacock, Ronald. "Hebbel," *The Poet in the Theatre.* Dramabook, (New York: Hill and Wang) 64-76.

———. "Tragedy, Comedy and Civilization," *The Poet in the Theatre.* Dramabook (New York: Hill and Wang) 151-59.

Steinke, Gerhard E. *The Life and Works of Hugh Ball, Founder of Dadaism.* Studies in German Literature 11 (The Hague: Mouton).

von Wiese, Benno. *Die deutsche Tragödie von Lessing bis Hebbel.* 3rd ed. (Hamburg: Hoffmann and Campe).

AGNES BERNAUER

CRITICAL COMMENTARY

Harvey W. Hewett-Thayer (essay date 1927)

SOURCE: Hewett-Thayer, Harvey W. "Ludwig Tieck and Hebbel's Tragedy of Beauty." *Germanic Review* 2I (1927): 16-25.

[*In the following essay, Hewett-Thayer investigates the origins of Hebbel's play* Agnes Bernauer, *contending that it can be traced back to Ludwig Tieck's novel* Vittoria Accorombona.]

The genesis of Hebbel's *Agnes Bernauer* and his treatment of its underlying themes have been the subject of considerable discussion. Hebbel began his *Agnes* in late September 1851 and finished it in the last days of December. In her essay on "The Sources of Hebbel's *Agnes Bernauer,*"[1] Agnes Löwenstein suggests that Hebbel may have become acquainted with the Agnes Bernauer story during his residence in Munich (September 1836-March 1839), a conjecture based on the historical relationship of the subject to that locality. After his own play was finished, Hebbel stated that he was already acquainted with Törring's *Agnes Bernauer* (1780) and thought well of it.[2] It is not apparent when he read this early play on the story of the Augsburg heroine. Karl Schultze-Jahde remarks,[3] without giving evidence however, "vermutlich erst 1851." Törring's play was a fairly conspicuous example of the Ritterdrama, in the following of Goethe's *Götz,* and it is possible that Hebbel had long been acquainted with it.

Hebbel's first reference to the conception of the play in his mind is familiar, an entry in his diary under the date September 30, 1851: "Längst hatte ich die Idee, auch die Schönheit einmal von der tragischen, den Untergang durch sich selbst bedingenden Seite dar zu stellen, und die Agnes Bernauer ist dazu wie gefunden."[4] This note was written after Hebbel had completed the first act of his play. It is important but difficult to assign a definite time value to the word "längst" in this quotation. Despite the self-analysis and self-betrayal in his letters and diaries, Hebbel frequently kept his own counsel, but one is justified in inferring from the above that the purpose of writing a play illustrating the tragic side of beauty was present with him for some time as an abstract idea before he began to incorporate it in definite figures. Two entries in his diary as early as 1845 have been connected with this plan. The first is without exact date but is from the beginning of January 1845:

> Idee zu einer Tragödie. Ein wunderschönes Mädchen, noch unbekannt mit der Gewalt ihrer Reize, tritt in's Leben ein aus klösterlicher Abgeschiedenheit. Alles schaart sich um sie zusammen. Brüder entzweien sich auf Tod und Leben, Freundschafts-Bande zerreißen, ihre eigenen Freundinnen, neidisch oder durch Untreue ihrer Anbeter verletzt, verlassen sie. Sie liebt Einen, dessen Bruder seinem Leben nachzustellen anfängt, da schaudert sie vor sich selbst und tritt in's Kloster zurück.[5]

The second entry is in the form of an anecdote which Hebbel relates, but it is obvious that he thought of it as material for a drama; it is under the date January 8, 1845.

> In Hannover. Ein schönes Mädchen tritt, von ihrer Mutter dazu genöthigt, in den Dienst. Aber das Bewußtseyn ihrer Schönheit macht es ihr unmöglich, zu dienen. Sie

glaubt, ihre Schönheit müsse ihr Glück machen, auch erblickt sie Keiner, der nicht davon geblendet wird, doch die Anträge, die man ihr macht, deuten alle auf's Hurenhaus, keiner auf ein gräfliches Schloß. Sie wird erbittert, kann es in den Verhältnissen (vielleicht auch noch durch den Neid häßlicher Weiber im Hause gequält) nicht länger aushalten, und kehrt zu ihrer Mutter zurück. Aber auch bei dieser will sie keine niedrigen Arbeiten mehr verrichten, wenn sie in den Stall gehen und melken soll, sagt sie, sie sey dazu da, eine Gräfin zu werden, nicht aber, die Kühe zu melken. Die Mutter, aufgebracht, mißhandelt sie, sie geht fort und stürzt sich in einen Brunnen.

(Scene: sie soll waschen, und das Wasser zeigt ihr ihr Bild!)[6]

Hebbel's early play *Genoveva* has elements which might seem to illustrate the idea of beauty in its tragic aspects; this interpretation gathers some force from Hebbel's own conception of the dramatic situation in the Genoveva story, as recorded in his diary under February 2, 1839.[7]

Genovevas Schicksal muß erfüllt werden, damit Golos Hölle ganz werde; kann er nicht ganz selig seyn, so will er doch ganz verdammt seyn. Er läßt sie ermorden und ist nun als Verbrecher, was er ehemals als Mensch und Mann war, denn dahin drängt ein ewiges Gesetz der Natur, nur fallende Engel wurden Teufel, nicht der fallende Mensch. Dies sind die Hauptmomente: eine ungeheure Blutthat, die aus einem holden Lächeln, einem falsch ausgelegten gütigen Blick entspringt; himmlische Schönheit, die durch sich selbst, durch ihren eigenen Glanz, ihren göttlichen Adel, in Marter und Tod stürzt.

Hebbel's interest, however, centers almost entirely in Golo; Genoveva is hardly more than an accessory and necessary figure in the development of the destiny of Golo. The fate of Genoveva, despite the title, is incidental and traditional. Hebbel plainly did not associate this drama with the conception of the "Tragik des Schönen," as exemplified later in *Agnes Bernauer*; his own words, quoted above, with reference to the later play indicate this unmistakably.

It seems possible, as a conjecture at any rate, to associate the inception of Hebbel's plan directly or indirectly with Tieck's novel *Vittoria Accorombona*. Ludwig Tieck, the ageing survivor of the romantic epoch, was one of Hebbel's older contemporaries whom he most respected.[8] This has ample evidence despite the petulant passage in a letter to Charlotte Rousseau, February 14, 1843.[9] Here he quotes a remark which he made to Oehlenschläger, "Die Könige lieben die Kronprinzen nicht, aber sie werden dadurch nicht unsterblich, daß sie diese todt schlagen," and then adds, "Tieck lobt und protegirt, wie ehemals Goethe, nur das Mittelmäßige." And it was unquestionably with an interest in Tieck's judgment, not merely with a view to the practical, one might

almost say, commercial aspect of the matter, that in August 1838 he sent to Tieck the manuscript of his humorous story *Schnock,* accompanied by *Anna* and *Der Rubin.*[10] He wished a critical estimate as well as a recommendation to a publisher. Hebbel's disappointment at Tieck's delay in acknowledging the receipt of the manuscripts,—neither humility nor patience was a conspicuous virtue with Hebbel,—and Tieck's apologies and cordial commendation are familiar.[11] Tieck's letter is dated June 23, 1839.[12] Doubtless encouraged by Tieck's sincere recognition of his talent, Hebbel almost immediately submitted another work for his approval, his first tragedy, *Judith,* the letter accompanying it being dated February 17, 1840.[13]

The references to Tieck's work in Hebbel's *Briefe* and *Tagebücher* are fairly numerous, and his admiration for Tieck's *Novellen* is well attested. For example, he comments on the general style of the Novellen,[14] mentions individual stories, as *Des Lebens Überfluß,*[15] agrees and disagrees with Rahel's criticism of Tieck's *Dichterleben,*[16] and he particularly recommends to Elise Lensing the reading of Tieck's latest story.[17] One is unquestionably correct in assuming that Hebbel was eager to read any new work by Tieck and was interested in its reception by the critics.[18] In the early spring of 1851 Hebbel visited Berlin with a view to securing an engagement for his wife as "Gast" at the Court Theatre. On this occasion Hebbel called on Tieck. In midsummer he came again to the Prussian capital, primarily to attend the performances for which he had arranged at the former visit. This time he was a frequent visitor at Tieck's home in the Friedrichstraße. We have good evidence of their mutual enjoyment in discussing literature together. Tieck's opinion of Hebbel's personality is a fine tribute to the insight of the aged romanticist, and from these visits Hebbel provides us with one of the most impressive pictures which we possess of Tieck in his last years.[19] It may not be entirely without significance that Hebbel began work on *Agnes Bernauer* almost directly after his return to Vienna from this second visit to Berlin.

Tieck's novel *Vittoria Accorombona* was begun in 1836, completed in July 1840,[20] and was issued the same year by Max and Company in Breslau, practically simultaneously with the publication of his last Novelle, *Waldeinsamkeit,* which appeared in the *Urania* for 1841. Initial stimulus for *Vittoria Accorombona* was supplied by Webster's play *The White Devil, or Vittoria Accorombona* (1612).[21] Tieck's novel is a brilliant, colorful picture of Italy in the sixteenth century, with exuberant passions, intrigue, murder, bandits, and illicit love, with a multitude of characters and a succession of stirring scenes. But, despite the variety of its content, the novelist has known how to secure unity, through the personality of the heroine; Vittoria Accorombona dominates the tale, largely through qualities which set her aside from and above her environment, and chief among these qualities is her overwhelming beauty.

It was inevitable that the importance of Tieck's new work should be at once recognized, though obviously no one foresaw that with it Tieck had completed his career as a man of letters. *Vittoria Accorombona* was reviewed by the chief journals of literary criticism, and for the most part with a real recognition of its outstanding merits.[22] The chief faults of the novel in the eyes of the reviewers were its unblushing depiction of sensuality, however natural the inclusion of such matters might be in a story of the period, and Tieck's seeming championship of the "free woman"; in the latter point Tieck seemed to have gone quite over to the enemy's camp and to have joined hands with the Young Germans.

In the present connection, however, attention is particularly directed to the reviews in the *Blätter für literarische Unterhaltung* (1840, pp. 1121-22, 1465-67, 1469-72, and 1473-74, respectively October 4, December 28, 29, and 30, 1840). The first review, that of October 4, is unsigned except for the figure "95," the other articles are signed by "Richard Morning," the pen-name of Adolf Zeising; the first is further confessedly in the nature of an announcement, and the editor in a footnote promises a more extended consideration of Tieck's story; from the content it seems probable, but is by no means certain, that Zeising was also the author of the preliminary notice. The reviewer, Adolf Zeising, born in 1810, was at this time a young teacher in Bernburg, at the Gymnasium and the Höhere Töchterschule; later he was a professor in Leipsic and Munich. His works are varied, but his chief contributions were in the field of esthetics; he has been called the "founder of mathematical esthetics," and he wrote several novels which were intended to illustrate his esthetic and philosophical views. Zeising was early an admirer of Tieck; an essay on "Parallele zwischen Tieck und Goethe" had brought him into personal relationship to Tieck while the latter was still a resident of Dresden. After Tieck's death, Zeising wrote a Novelle, *Meister Tiecks Heimgang,* in which he imitated Tieck's style with considerable success.[23]

The review of October 4 begins with a general analysis of the function of criticism, and an account of the chief contemporary tendencies in German literature. The reviewer expresses disapproval both of youthful radicals and old-fashioned conservatives; the former present the discontent, the disruption, the unhealthiness, of the generation; their favorite characters are criminals and rascals. The opposite party, offended at these abominations, think to cure literature (Poesie) by homeopathic doses of more literature, and depict virtue as a flat, sugary mediocrity; their favorite characters are "tote Vet-

tern und Muhmen, und Basen." This statement of the contending parties in German literature prepares the way for the introduction of Tieck, whom, despite contemporary cavil, the reviewer regards as superior to both tendencies.

In the beginning of his long review, Zeising states that his aim is to get at the "Lebensprinzip" of Tieck's story, the indwelling idea, and at the outset he declares that this kernel of the tale is the "Tragik des Schönen." Zeising's analysis of *Vittoria Accorombona* from this point of view corresponds nearly identically with the idea of the "tragedy of beauty" as Hebbel conceived it and incorporated it in **Agnes Bernauer**: with slight variations, due to difference of plot, the critic's reasoning could be applied accurately to Hebbel's play.

> Es ist dieser Roman ein gewaltiges und seiner Idee nach bis jetzt einziges Kunstwerk. Wie schön das Tragische sei, das haben wol mit gleicher Kunst und gleichem Effect auch andere Tragödien zur Anschauung gebracht; aber wie tragisch das Schöne sei—das ist noch nie von einem Dichter so wahr und so poetisch, so ergreifend und so versöhnend dargestellt, ja es ist wol noch nie zum eigentlichen Grundgedanken einer so großartigen Dichtung gemacht worden. Andere werden über die Grundidee dieses Werkes anders denken; man wird dem herrlichen Gedichte bald diese, bald jene Tendenz unterlegen, wie es gerade den Ansichten und Gesinnungen des Einen oder des Andern genehm und bequem ist; mir aber will es scheinen, als ob es überall nur die Tragik des Schönen sei, was dem Dichter als begeisternde und leitende Uranschauung vor Augen geschwebt habe, wenn sich ihm dieselbe auch nicht in so abstracter und begriffsmäßiger Form, als in welcher wir es hier aussprechen müssen, sondern von vornherein in concretem, lebensvollem Bilde dargestellt hat. Es ist ein neuer, origineller und höchst genialer Griff, den Tieck hiermit in das Reich der tragischen Ideen gethan. Sämmtliche tragische Charaktere, die bis dahin von Dichtern erschaffen oder nur behandelt sind, finden ihren Untergang, weil sie sich selbst übernehmend aus dem Kreise des Schönen heraustreten, das Maß überschreiten, übermütig die Grenzen und Schranken, innerhalb welcher allein ein Glück für ein beschränktes Wesen möglich ist, niederreißen und so sich selbst dem Allgemeinen, dem Absoluten in die vernichtenden Arme liefern. Vittoria dagegen, der tragische Hauptcharakter dieses Romans, geht unter, eben weil sie durchweg schön ist, weil sie, wie groß und herrlich sie auch dasteht, doch nie sich selbst vergißt, im Glücke nie stolz und übermüthig, im Unglücke nie trotzig und ungeduldig wird, sondern stets sich in den schönen Grenzen des Ebenmaßes erhält. . . .

Zeising then seeks to substantiate the opinion of Vittoria's character expressed in the last sentence, and he concludes that she is,

> ein Bild der reinsten, makellosesten Schönheit, der geistigen wie der körperlichen, daß sie nie einen Schritt über die Linie der Anmuth und Würde hinausgethan,

sich immer in den Schranken des Ebenmaßes und der Harmonie behauptet habe, und daß daher von einer Schuld im gewöhnlichen Sinne des Wortes, um derentwillen sie ihr tragisches Schicksal habe erdulden müssen, gar nicht die Rede sein könne.

Objections might then be made that the catastrophe seems an utterly unjust and cruel deed of violence on the part of a blind and envious destiny. Zeising goes on to say:

Es wären dies alles ganz gerechte Einwendungen und Vorwürfe, wenn nicht der Dichter, wie wir oben bereits angedeutet, einen neuen Blick in die tragische Welt eröffnet und auch die im Rein-Schönen liegende Tragik aufgedeckt hätte. Denn wenn einerseits der tragische Keim in alle Dem liegt, was übermüthig über die Schranken hinausgeht und sich selbst als das Unbedingte und Absolute setzen möchte, so muß er, wie wir, der Sache tiefer nachdenkend, nothwendig annehmen müssen, umgekehrt auch in Dem versteckt sein, was sich gänzlich von jenem Übermuthe, jenem Sichselbstvergessen frei erhält, weil es eben durch seine Selbstbegrenzung, durch seine Abgeschlossenheit in sich selbst eine Selbstgenügsamkeit ausdrückt, die ebenfalls nur dem Absoluten zukommt und daher an jedem Einzelwesen nur eine in sich haltlose Usurpation sein kann. Daher die Vergänglichkeit und Hinfälligkeit aller schönen Erscheinungen, daher die kurze Dauer jedes harmonischen vollkommene Befriedung gewährenden Zustandes. Die einzelne Erscheinung kann sich einmal nicht dauernd mit dem All, mit dem Absoluten im Einklang erhalten; ja, daß sie als Einzelnes, wenn auch nur vorübergehend, das Absolute zu repräsentiren, sich selbst als solches zu setzen sucht, muß dem Absoluten als eine Anmaßung erscheinen, gegen welche es nothwendig reagiren muß. So entsteht zwischen dem Schönen und dem Absoluten ein Kampf, ein Conflict, der nicht anders als mit einer Auflösung des Schönen in das Absolute, mit einem Untergang der schönen Erscheinung als Erscheinung endigen kann.

It may be emphasized that *Vittoria Accorombona* came out during a period when Hebbel was particularly interested in Tieck and eagerly desirous of gaining Tieck's approval of his own work. Without explicit reference to it, one may yet be warranted in assuming that Hebbel read *Vittoria Accorombona* soon after its publication.[24] That Hebbel read Zeising's review is incapable of proof, but the probabilities are entirely on that side. He was an avid reader of the critical press, and especially so in the years of his literary apprenticeship. He was offering material for publication in several of the critical journals, and in this way was trying both to turn a penny and to gain a foothold in the literary world. To Brockhaus, the publisher of the *Blätter für literarische Unterhaltung,* he had offered his *Schnock* for publication; he comments on Alexis's review of his *Gedichte* and on a review of his **Genoveva** which he attributes to Alexis, both issued in that journal.[25] That Hebbel makes no mention of the review is in his case

no evidence that he was unacquainted with it. Hebbel was not infrequently very reticent about his sources, preferring to foster the impression that an idea had germinated entirely within himself. The evidence which is here gathered would seem to point to the likelihood that Tieck's story and Zeising's review gave Hebbel his definite conception of the "tragedy of beauty."

Notes

1. *Modern Language Review,* 4, 302-22 (April, 1909), and VII, 330-50 (July 1912).

2. Friedrich Hebbel, *Sämtliche Werke, Historisch-Kritische Ausgabe,* besorgt von Richard Maria Werner, Berlin, Erste Abteilung, *Werke,* Vols. I-XV, 1901; Zweite Abteilung, *Tagebücher,* Vols. I-IV, 1903; Dritte Abteilung, *Briefe,* Vols. I-VIII, 1904-1907. Cf. letter to Gutzkow, *Tagebücher,* III, 443-44, and *Briefe,* V, 123. In the following pages, references to Hebbel's works are to this edition, unless otherwise specified.

3. Karl Schultze-Jahde, "Hebbels Agnes Bernauer," *Preußische Jahrbücher,* 198, 163-84, 1924.

4. *Tagebücher,* III, 406.

5. *Tagebücher,* III, 2-3.

6. *Tagebücher,* III, 4-5. Agnes Löwenstein quotes both of these passages.

7. *Tagebücher,* I, 319-23.

8. Cf. F. Kuh, *Biographie Friedrich Hebbels,* I, 245: "Unter den neueren Autoren, die ihm während des Jahres 1838 den größten Anteil eingeflößt hatten, stand Tieck obenan."

9. *Briefe,* II, 209.

10. In a letter to Regierungsrat Rousseau, October 25, 1828, Hebbel states that the manuscripts were sent "Anfang des Augustmonats" (*Briefe,* I, 345), and in a letter to Elise Lensing, November 18, 1838, he gives the exact date, "unterm 3. August" (*Briefe,* I, 356), but in writing to Tieck some months later, April 21, 1839, he says that they were sent in July (*Briefe,* II, 1). Cf. also *Briefe,* I, 366-67, letter to E. Lensing, December 12, 1838, and I, 392-93, letter to the same, February 19, 1839; further, *Briefe,* II, 6, 14.

11. Cf. references above and *Briefe,* I, 379; II, 365-66.

12. Bamberg dates this letter erroneously January 23, 1839 (*Briefwechsel,* I, 143-44) which supplies an inconsistent chronology for the correspondence; this incorrect date is incorporated in so late a work as Louis Brun's *Hebbel* (1922), p. 1022, though a few pages later (p. 1026) the correct date is given as the date when Hebbel received the letter.

13. *Briefe,* II, 26-27. Cf. also letter of April 26, 1840, *Briefe,* II, 36-37. He sent a printed copy of the drama "als Manuscript gedruckt"; there were apparently fifty copies printed; cf. *Briefe,* II, 8 (February 7, 1840), and *Briefe,* II, 42.

14. *Tagebücher,* I, 212 (February, 1838), and 230-31; also *Briefe,* I, 281, letter to Rousseau, April 3, 1838.

15. *Tagebücher,* I, 333, February 16, 1839.

16. *Tagebücher,* I, 286-87, November 24, 1838.

17. *Briefe,* I, 379, January 12, 1839.

18. Kuh also asserts that Tieck's works were "unstreitig" the model for Hebbel's *Der Diamant,* and suggests that Klaus, the madman in Hebbel's *Genoveva,* was derived from the idiot youth in Tieck's *Der fünfzehnte November: Biographie,* I, 387 and 378. For further significant references to Tieck in Hebbel's work, cf. *Werke,* VI, 350, and VII, 227-28, Hebbel's epigrams on Tieck; XII, 22-24, "Erinnerungen an Ludwig Tieck," originally published in the *Ost-Deutsche Post,* Wien, May 4, 1853; 9, 309-14, Hebbel's review of the *Kritische Schriften von Ludwig Tieck* from the *Reichszeitung,* December 23, 1849; and *Briefe,* IV, 295-96. Note also Hebbel's opinion of Tieck, and incidentally of *Vittoria Accorombona* in his reported conversation with Oehlenschläger, December 4, 1842, *Briefe,* II, 143.

19. Kuh, II, 316-21, also *Werke,* X, 177-78.

20. Cf. Köpke, *Ludwig Tieck,* II, 98.

21. For Hebbel's opinion of Webster's play, cf. *Werke,* XII, 160-62 (review of Friedrich Bodenstedt's *Shakespeares Zeitgenossen und ihre Werke,* dating from 1858).

22. Cf. *Hallische Jahrbücher für deutsche Wissenschaft und Kunst,* 1840, pp. 2453-56, 2462-64, 2469-72, 2476-80 (December 23, 24, 25, and 26, 1840), a review signed by A. Wellmann; *Abendzeitung, Blätter für Literatur und bildende Kunst,* 1840, No. 77, pp. 623-24 (September 23, 1840); *Morgenblatt* (Literaturblatt), 1840, No. 113, pp. 449-51 (November 9, 1840).

23. Frankfurt am Main, 1854.

24. He had unquestionably read it by December 4, 1842, *Briefe,* II, 143.

25. *Briefe,* II, 206, letter to Elise Lensing, February 5, 1843, and *Briefe,* II, 357, letter to the same, December 17, 1843.

GYGES UND SEIN RING (*GYGES AND HIS RING*)

CRITICAL COMMENTARY

James L. Hodge (essay date October 1964)

SOURCE: Hodge, James L. "Rhodope: By Any Other Name." *MLN* 79, no. 4 (October 1964): 435-39.

[*In the following essay, Hodge provides an interpretation of* Gyges and His Ring *based on the name of the protagonist of the drama, Rhodope.*]

The question, "What's in a name?" may offer a new insight into the heroine of Friedrich Hebbel's drama, ***Gyges und sein Ring.*** Numerous interpretations of Rhodope—psychological, symbolic and other—have been advanced. Rhodope has been analyzed individually and as an integral part of the drama. She has been said to express the central message of the drama: the modesty of woman. She has been described as passionless and indestructibly virginal. She has been seen as representing the past and tradition, and she has also been seen as timeless, representing neither past, present nor future. Her death has been explained psychologically as a reaction to the dehumanizing execution of Kandaules, and symbolically as a religious and "heavenly" act.

It may be said that Rhodope is, and means, all these things. Textual citations from various parts of the play seem to prove a variety of interpretations. Hebbel himself may have realized, as he wrote the play, that Rhodope was growing into an extremely complex, symbolic figure. However, there is reason to believe that he did not originally consider the queen to be so multi-sided a personality. In fact, her name itself indicates that Hebbel had a very specific symbolic interpretation of the queen in mind when he set out to write his drama. It is more than interesting that the queen is named Rhodope in no other treatment of this story. In Herodotus, Plato, Fontenelle and La Fontaine, the queen is not named at all. In the two most recent French versions, by Gautier and Gide, the queen's name is Nyssia. Even a German reference work of 1937, apparently unaffected by Hebbel's nomenclature, identifies Kandaules' queen as Nyssia, Tudus, Klytra or Gabro.[1] The name "Rhodope" is used nowhere else to identify Kandaules' wife. Why, then, has Hebbel named her thus?

The "Rhodope" who gives significance to Hebbel's heroine and identifies Hebbel's intention is to be found in both French and German lexicons of classical mythology.[2] She is a nymph and a companion to Artemis. In dedicating herself to Artemis, and thus to chastity, she has angered Aphrodite, who causes her to fall in love. Her loss of chastity becomes known to Artemis, who changes her into a spring. The spring, flowing into the grotto in which Rhodope lost her virginity, is used to test the chastity of all who claim to be virgins.

This capsule tale from mythology contains the key to Hebbel's original conception of Rhodope and of her relationships with Kandaules and Gyges. For our purposes, the tale may be divided into four parts: the oath of chastity, the "guiltless" loss of virtue, the revenge or punishment of the virgin, and the "moral." Each of these components or motifs will be seen to have a counterpart in *Gyges und sein Ring*.

Hebbel's Rhodope, although she has not sworn an oath of chasity, is bound just as firmly by her religious convictions to a sacredly, severely monogamous and protected life. Not even her veil is removed before any man except her husband. Although married, she is extremely, even ferociously, modest. That is, she is as "virginal" as a wife can be.

Rhodope the queen thus parallels the mythological Rhodope, and her "eastern" sexual mores parallel the oath of chastity taken by her mythological counterpart. Moreover, the goddesses to whom Hebbel's Rhodope turns, and the order in which she turns to them, offer striking evidence of her similarity to Rhodope the nymph. When Kandaules convinces her at first that she has not been dishonored, Rhodope gratefully puts the "proof" (her missing diamond) into the temple treasure of Aphrodite. The goddess of love is not named, but is indicated by the epithet "Allverknüpferin" (l. 1065)[3] and by reference to the doves sacred to her (l. 1066). Given Rhodope's character, this goddess is probably not the lustful Aphrodite Pandemos, but Aphrodite Genetrix—protectress of marriages.

The goddess to whom Rhodope next appeals is far more conservative in sexual matters than Aphrodite Genetrix. When she is sure of her dishonor, when she has sent Gyges to kill Kandaules and is preparing for her wedding and her death, Rhodope does not prepare before the altar of Aphrodite, but before that of Hestia, who is not merely goddess of the hearth, but has, like Artemis, taken a vow of chastity. Except for Artemis and Athene, Hestia is the only Olympian who has sworn such an oath, and is one of the few over whom Aphrodite has no power. Rhodope's new devotion to such a goddess is so remarkable that Hero is moved to comment upon it:

> Und ist es nicht auch seltsam, dass sie sich
> Anstatt der ewig heitern Aphrodite,
> Die strenge Hestia, vor deren Blicken
> Der grünste Kranz verdorrt, zur Zeugin wählt?
>
> (ll. 1912-1915)

Rhodope has thus turned from a goddess of love and marriage to a goddess of celibate feminine virtue. (It is interesting to note that Hestia's Roman counterpart, Vesta, is always represented veiled.)

It is a short step from this comparison to the next. Aphrodite attacks and destroys the chastity of the nymph, Rhodope. Kandaules does similar violence to the modesty of his queen. In a conversation following the fateful night, when Rhodope only suspects that she has been dishonored, Kandaules seeks to allay her fears and to prove that lie is all a husband should be. During this conversation, he clearly describes the virginal withdrawal and contemplation of his wife, and almost casually opposes the demands of Aphrodite (Pandemos, no doubt) to the chaste seclusion of the queen:

> Dies ist gewiss die Stunde,
> In welcher du, wie du's so lieblich nennst,
> Dich innerlich besiehst! Die will ich nicht
> Entheiligen. Und hätt' auch Aphrodite,
> Holdselig lächelnd diesem frühen Gang,
> Den goldnen Gürtel, den sie nie verschenkt
> Und kaum verleiht, mir für dich zugeworfen:
> Ich käm' ein andermal und reicht' ihn dir!
>
> (II. 975-982)

Unfortunately, Kandaules has already accomplished the work of Aphrodite Pandemos upon his unsuspecting wife. Thus, in the case of both Rhodope the nymph and Rhodope the queen, an outside force—representing the intercourse of the sexes and, therefore, the invasion of the feminine inner soul—has been totally responsible for the fall from grace. Rhodope the nymph and Rhodope the woman are not sinners, but victims. In Hebbel's play Rhodope herself complains that she was defenseless against this act, and even lays the responsibility at the feet of the gods:

> Ihr ew'gen Götter, konnte das geschehn? . . .
> . . . Kein Tapfrer ruft zu Zeus um seinen Blitz!
> Doch dass ihn nicht die Schlange feig beschleiche,
> Wenn er, vom Kampf ermattet, ruhig schlummert,
> Ist euer Werk, denn euch gehört die Nacht!
>
> (l. 907 & ll. 932-935)

The woman seen by Gyges and the nymph blighted by Aphrodite are related, of course, by a spiritual purity rather than by a physical virginity. The nymph is dedicated to absolute chastity, while the queen is dedicated to marital purity. The nymph is dishonored physically, and the queen is dishonored spiritually. In each case, that untouchable portion of the feminine soul which is always held in reserve against a world of brutality and swift innovation has been attacked. A woman, thus violated, is obliged to seek retribution. Before Robert Graves and others began to delve into the sociology behind the Greek myths, the meaning of such episodes as Actaeon being hunted to death by his own hounds after he saw Artemis bathing was taken to be: it is dangerous, if not fatal, to assault the purity of woman. Indeed, when Gyges rebukes both himself and Kandaules, he compares his deed with that of Actaeon (ll. 643-648). Rhodope the wife, like Artemis the maiden, must have vengeance, and she says as much to Lesbia:

> Jetzt rufe ich nach Blut, jetzt ist von mir
> Nur so viel übrig, als die Götter brauchen,
> Um das zu rächen, was ich einmal war!

> (ll. 1197-1199)

It seems peculiar, at first, that Rhodope's actions are directed against herself as well as against her offending husband. When her vengeance has been wrought upon Kandaules and she has married Gyges, she kills herself. As noted earlier, this last action has been explained psychologically as a reaction to the execution of Kandaules, and religiously as a necessary self-immolation. (For a vigorous statement of the latter interpretation, see Detlef Cölln, *Hebbel Jahrbuch* for 1955, pp. 67-84.) When Rhodope the queen is compared to the mythological nymph, it becomes clear that she, too, is a religious sacrifice. That is, she has done all that is in her power to erase the stain on her honor and on her soul, but such a blemish is absolute. It cannot be eradicated completely. Rhodope can no more continue to live as the woman she was than Rhodope the nymph can be purified and received again into Artemis' company. Rhodope the nymph is punished, and Rhodope the queen, impelled by her conscience, punishes herself.

If Gyges cannot understand Rhodope's last act, it is because he lives in a man's world of expediency and relativity. Rhodope's act is obligatory and absolute. The whole conduct of her life has been obligatory and absolute, for she has not lived the life of a woman, but the idealized and spiritualized life of all women. Thus, the "message" Rhodope was originally intended to impart in **Gyges und sein Ring** corresponds to the moral of the mythological tale. As all classical maidens were put to the test of chastity in the spring of Rhodope the nymph, so all married women may now be put to the test of inner purity by comparison with the ideal standard of Rhodope the queen. Rhodope is not a woman, but a grand idea. For this reason, Hebbel named her as he did.

Notes

1. August Friedrich von Pauly, *Paulys Real-Encyclopädie,* eds. Georg Wissowa and Wilhelm Kroll (Stuttgart, 1937), XVII, 1661.

2. *Dictionnaire de la Mythologie Grecque et Romaine,* ed. Pierre Grimal (Paris, 1951), p. 409; *Ausführliches Lexikon der griechischen und rö-*

mischen Mythologie, ed W. H. Roscher (Leipzig, 1909-1915), IV, 115.

3. Citations from *Gyges und sein Ring* are to *Hebbels Werke,* ed. Franz Zinkernagel (Leipzig, 1913), Vol. IV.

DIE NIBELUNGEN (THE NIBELUNGS)

CRITICAL COMMENTARY

Von Patricia Boswell (essay date 1977)

SOURCE: Boswell, Von Patricia. "The Hunt as a Literary Image in Hebbel's *Die Nibelungen.*" *Hebbel-Jahrbuch 1977* (1977): 163-94.

[*In the following essay, Boswell finds Hebbel's linguistic abilities unsuitable for adapting the medieval epic* The Nibelungs, *focusing on the hunting scene as evidence of her theory.*]

> So viel ist gewiß, ich habe nie so viel Arbeit auf ein Werk verwendet, wie auf dieß: ich kann noch nicht fertig werden . . . ich bin ängstlich, wie je in meinem Leben, und prüfe jeden Vers genauer, wie der Geldwechsler einen Ducaten.[1]

These words, written by Hebbel to his publisher as he was engaged in correcting the proofs of **Die Nibelungen,** bear witness to the particular care and attention to detail he expended on the trilogy. Always a very conscious artist in all aspects of his work, it is the language of his plays especially which has drawn much critical interest, and the infinite complexity of their verbal composition is becoming increasingly clear through the smaller and major studies—some of them very recent—which have opened up new insights into the derivation and manipulation of his linguistic material[2]. There has been found plenty to criticize in Hebbel's poetic language, but also much to stimulate and fascinate; its individual quality despite certain derivative elements has not been in doubt. Hebbel himself was very much aware of the importance of learning to identify the unique character of a poet's language as the unavoidable first step towards an appreciation of his work:

> Jeder neue Künstler trägt neue Gedanken in neuer Sprache vor. Die Sprache selbst will gelernt seyn, bevor die Gedanken verstanden werden können.[3]

The language of the **Nibelungen** has been subjected to less critical scrutiny than that of some of Hebbel's other plays, no doubt with good reason, since he had here cast himself in an unexpected and really rather uncharacteristic rôle, that of the interpreter of the work of another[4]:

Ich bin bloß der Dolmetscher eines Höheren und ich will nicht mehr seyn. Aber dieser Höhere, der Dichter unseres unsterblichen Nibelungen-Epos, um das uns alle Völker der Erde beneiden, hat ein Recht, gehört zu werden, und mir ist es vielleicht gelungen, seine Stimme in der engeren und knapperen Form des Dramas, wie in einem Sprachrohr, zu verdichten und zu verstärken.[5]

There are thus two individual languages in Hebbel's sense to be taken into consideration in approaching this trilogy, his own and that of the "higher" poet whose words he was attempting to "translate". And it is precisely in the language that Helmut de Boor in his illuminating comparison between the two finds the greatest discrepancy between the medieval epic and Hebbel's nineteenth-century version:

> So tief sich Hebbel dem Epiker in der Gestaltung des Stoffes verpflichtet fühlte, so wenig hat ihn dessen Sprache angeregt. Selbst wo er sich eng an den Wortlaut des Nibelungenliedes anschließt, überträgt er ihn in seine zugleich analysierende und engagierte Sprache.[6]

In three aspects of Hebbel's language in particular he recognizes its unsuitability for reproducing the spirit of the epic, namely its analytical and reflective quality, its irony and double-entendres, and its characteristic use of imagery and symbolism, the last two especially properties of dramatic rather than epic style.[7] Perhaps Hebbel blundered; his "Recken" are too self-conscious, too given to soul-searching and argumentation, they are also at times too sentimental and at others too deliberately primitive. Nevertheless, in one instance where Hebbel has taken linguistic liberties with a detail from his source it would seem to be genuine poetic intention rather than ineptitude that accounts for his production of these "falsche Töne."[8] The scenes relating to Siegfried's murder whilst out hunting with Hagen and Gunther in the German forest contain both in detail ("Nur den Löwen jag' ich heut'") and in whole scenes obvious divergencies from the spirit—and even the letter—of the original epic.[9] It is relevant for Hebbel's linguistic technique to try to discover why. In passing, it might be recalled that the *Âventiure* of the death of Siegfried was the first that Hebbel ever read of the *Nibelungenlied* in the early days in Hamburg.[10]

It was as a dramatic writer that Hebbel undertook his "translation" of the Nibelungenlied, and, as such, language was of prime importance to him and, he felt, should be the starting-point for any critic:

> Unstreitig ist die Sprache das allerwichtigste Element, wie der Poesie überhaupt, so speciell auch des Dramas, und jede Kritik thäte wohl bei ihr zu beginnen.[11]

Hebbel's understanding of the function of the language in drama has been succinctly expressed:

> As a dramatic writer Hebbel was above all aware of the cumulative effect of words and images and of their

coherence in the work as a whole. For it is through the coherence of the verbal composition of a play that the coherence of its ideas to a considerable degree depends.[12]

His symbolic use of language is one of the most striking features, and one which can be and has been analysed from a number of different perspectives, and yet it can still afford new insights, however slight, into his creative process. For the linguistic texture of the drama is itself a symbol, with at the least a dual purpose, standing as it does as an analogue for both the intellectual world of the dramatist himself and for the environment, both intellectual and physical, of the characters. Through this linguistically created and projected world the dramatist realises his own personality, in the "Fixierung des geistigen Sich-Selbst-Entbindens durch ein körperliches Medium"[13],

> denn nur durch sie und in ihr wird die lange adjectivlose Arbeit des poetischen Geistes, die in einigen Stadien sogar mit dem Geschäft des Denkers, der Thätigkeit des Psychologen in freilich modificierter Form zusammentrifft, zur entschiedenen Dichterthat.[14]

In this same world, and only in this world, his characters have their being. So that, in order to fulfil Hebbel's requirement that "ein Charakter . . . handle und spreche nie über seine Welt hinaus, aber für das, was in seiner Welt möglich ist, finde er die reinste Form und den edelsten Ausdruck, selbst der Bauer,"[15] each individual must express himself in a way which is within the limits and capacity of his own nature, his environment—both physical and linguistic—within his own play, and of the poet's own characteristic range of words and images from which he habitually selects to give poetic and concrete form to his metaphysical speculation. Trivial examples demonstrate this immediately. It ist obvious, for instance, that Hebbel attempts to give to each play a dominant linguistic atmosphere, which usually implies also dominant image-patterns. *Maria Magdalena* is a good example, and one which has aroused much critical interest for this very reason. Images of confinement, water-imagery and biblical language and imagery, for instance, have all been the subject of separate studies.[16] *Judith,* which also has a large component of biblical language in its verbal composition, is perhaps the most striking of the plays in its blending of metaphysical speculation and concrete expression, and in the exploitation of certain imagistic fields, notably that of sleep and dreams which informs and unifies the whole play around the central experience of God.[17] In this play, with its emphasis on excess and destruction, the language is equally violent. This is indicated by the verbs which are characteristic of the play—*vertreiben, vernichten, verzehren, vertilgen, zerstören, zerstampfen, zerschmettern, zertrümmern, zermalmen, entwurzeln, niederhauen, on the* one hand, suggesting cruelty and annihilation, *schaudern, schauern, grauen, grausen,* on the other, indicating fear. For individual images the destructive forces of nature or the destructive—sometimes self-destructive—powers of man are selected:

HOLOFERNES:

Sie . . . flieh'n mich, wie der Hase das Feuer, das ihm den Bart versengen könnte.[18]

JUDITH:

Sein Blick bohrte wie ein Giftpfeil in mich hinein.[19]

Mein Gebet ist dann ein Untertauchen in Gott, es ist nur eine andere Art von Selbstmord, ich springe in den Ewigen hinein, wie Verzweifelnde in ein tiefes Wasser.[20]

EPHRAIM:

Jedes Wort aus seinem Munde ist ein reißendes Thier.[21]

JUDITH:

Ich werde aus mir herausfahren, wie ein Schwert aus der Scheide.[22]

O Hohn, der die Axt an die Wurzeln meiner Menschheit legt.[23]

HOLOFERNES:

Er mag mich im Mörser zerstampfen.[24]

Even a favourite image of Hebbel's, that of the berry or fruit, which recurs throughout his poetical work, both in the lyric and the drama, with purely pleasurable associations, receives an entirely different colouring from the atmosphere of this play, with its combination of unnatural passion and behaviour and violence:

JUDITH:

Meine Schönheit ist die der Tollkirsche; ihr Genuß bringt Wahnsinn und Tod.[25]

In **Herodes und Mariamne,** which has a comparable historical background to that of **Judith,** there is similarity too in the subject-matter and in the conflict between the sexes; but whereas in **Judith** Hebbel expresses violent passions in violent language, there is a sternness and logic in the style of the later play (however false Herodes' reasoning may in fact be) which indicates that the clash between two dominant personalities and strong wills is to an equal extent an intellectual one. It seems fitting, therefore, that metal should be a constant source of imagery; indeed, the imagery in **Herodes und Mariamne** is in general curiously inanimate, reflecting, of course, the fact that Mariamne has been "zum Ding herabgesetzt" by her husband. Appropriately, there is a considerable amount of imagery of buying and selling in the play, which, however, by comparison with Hebbel's other works is generally rather lacking in important image complexes, relying more perhaps on other linguistic devices such as the recurrence of the word "starr" and predominant sentence-structures (for

example, the consistent recourse in argument to parallel construction, amounting in moments of particular emotional stress to triple intensification) to convey the unyielding attitudes which are the source of tragedy in this play.

Such differences in imagistic material and language-pattern as there are between **Judith** and **Herodes und Mariamne** are typical of all Hebbel's dramas, and inevitable, since they are in part a reflection of his changing dramatic style.[26] Nevertheless his attention to detail in this respect is remarkable. Again this can best be demonstrated by trivial examples, since it is these relatively unimportant instances which show his complete professionalism. Each of the male characters characterizes himself, and at the same time evokes the atmosphere of the language of his own play in the way he describes the woman he loves. Holofernes' choice of image by comparison with others is pathetic:

Ist's Einem nicht, so lange man sie anschaut, als ob man ein köstlich Bad nähme?[27]

He shows complete lack of imaginative power beyond the sphere of physical well-being and his own experience. His second attempt is better:

Sie erinnert mich an eine Feuerkugel, die ich einst in dunkler Nacht am Himmel aufsteigen sah.[28]

Even so, he cannot develop his comparison, nor does he seem fully to understand it. In fact, Holofernes' experience is bounded by the limits of physical excitement and an elemental passion for life. Golo, on the other hand, has recourse to analogies with emotional states. His images are marked by continual intensification, and his comparisons are often with fire, flowing water or fever. Each state suggests another, more violent, and this gradual progression is marked by the use of compound adjectives and words which convey anticipation:

O jeder Blick in dieses Angesicht
Ist ein Gewinn, und jedes Wort, entlockt
Dem rührend-süßen Mund, bereichert mich
Und weckt die Ahnung einer Seligkeit,
Fremd und geheim, in meiner tiefsten Brust;
Wie, wenn Musik erklingt, Entzückungen
Durch alle Nerven, leise schwellend, zieh'n.
Und soll der Durst'ge, wenn ein voller Strom
Umfluthend ihn umfaßt, die Lippen feig
Zusammen pressen, daß kein Tropfe ihm,
Durchdringend, kühlt den heißen Herzensbrand?[29]

And yet, however different may be the use they make of them, Holofernes and Golo are both choosing their comparisons from some of the most characteristic image fields in Hebbel's poetic vocabulary; fire in particular is a favourite and well-tapped source in both his poetry and his prose, and it is used in both **Judith** and *Genoveva* extensively with a character peculiar to each play. Mariamne's beauty seems to Herodes to extend beyond the realm of earthly things; nevertheless, he remains firmly based in reality in the way he describes it, and although his images, like those of Golo, build up to a climax, their sequence is an indication of ordered reasoning rather than of emotional association:

> Du bist so schön, daß Jeder, der Dich sieht,
> An die Unsterblichkeit fast glauben muß,
> Mit welchem sich die Pharisäer schmeicheln,
> Weil Keiner faßt, daß je in ihm Dein Bild
> Erlöschen kann; so schön, daß ich mich nicht
> Wundern würde, wenn die Berge plötzlich
> Ein edleres Metall, als Gold und Silber,
> Mir lieferten, um Dich damit zu schmücken.[30]

It is typical of Herodes, the powerful ruler, and in keeping with the stern atmosphere of the play, that he should think of precious metals in connection with Mariamne rather than of the roses and lilies which spring immediately to the minds of the younger, gentler Golo,[31] Albrecht and Gyges. Significantly, Mariamne, on thinking back to the younger days of Herodes' courtship of her, remembers how he said to her in the flower-garden:

> So schön ist keine, daß sie Deine Hand
> Nicht pflücken dürfte![32]

Both these images of Herodes gain added force in the context of the symbolic use made of roses and jewels at Mariamne's banquet. In the flower-image which Albrecht uses to describe Agnes' hair there is a fantastic beauty in keeping with his own youthful imagination und lack of realism; at the same time it marks a climax in the poetic presentation of Agnes within the spiritual dialectics of the play:

> Das ist der Sonnenstrahl, der die Erde niemals berührte,
> er hätte eine Wunderblume erzeugt, vor der sich selbst
> Rosen und Lilien geneigt haben würden, doch er zog es
> vor, sich kosend als schimmerndes Netz um Dein Haupt
> zu legen.[33]

Gyges on the other hand shows an extraordinary sensitivity to sensuous impressions as he muses after seeing Rhodope unveiled:

> Ein Duft
> Liegt in der Luft, so schwer und so betäubend,
> Als hätten alle Blumen sich zugleich
> Geöffnet, um die Menschen zu ersticken,
> Als athmete die Erde selbst sich aus.[34]

Here again, this is a simile which, although of minor significance by comparison with some of the more outstanding images in this play, yet contributes towards the general sense of balance disturbed between man and the universe which is fundamental to *Gyges und sein Ring.* Siegfried too, curiously tongue-tied at this important moment in his life, finds words to declare his love for Kriemhild which have an ironical aptness within the context of *Die Nibelungen* which he could never have suspected:

> Ich kann
> Nicht reden, wie ich mögte, wenn ich Dir
> In's Antlitz sehe, und von meinem Stottern
> Hast Du vorhin wohl schon genug gehabt,
> D'rum frag' ich Dich, wie jeder Jäger fragt,
> Nur, daß ich nicht dabei vom Hut die Federn
> Herunter blase: Jungfrau, willst Du mich?[35]

If flowers were Hebbel's one great love, animals were the other. In his dramas references to animals abound and the group of animal, bird and insect images is perhaps the largest of all. His dramatic world is filled with animals, just as he filled his own real world with them;[36] they may appear as co-actors, or merely companions, or may even fulfil a symbolic rôle as representatives of good and evil.[37] Hebbel's characters share his loves and fears with relation to the animal kingdom, and some of his most compelling images are of the animals he hates, such as Siegfried's picture of treachery as a spider.[38] But not one of the major plays lacks its share of such material, and a comparison of these images alone makes very clear the differences in style and atmosphere between the plays. In *Judith,* for instance, they appear as semi-Biblical references,[39] whereas the animals referred to in *Genoveva* are mostly the bear, wolf, wild boar and deer of the German forest. The most striking of the animal images in *Maria Magdalena* are the comparisons Meister Anton makes with small, common animals or insects.[40] The lions and tigers in the images in *Herodes und Mariamne* are not only suitable reminders that the action of the play lies in the mighty, warlike shadow of Rome, "wo Tiger nöthig sind,"[41] but also of the fights in the arena which Herodes plans to introduce, where men will be pitted against lions and tigers.[42] An interesting example of the way Hebbel adapts the same picture to suit two entirely different plays is when Golo at the end of *Genoveva,* about to blind himself, tells Kaspar:

> Ist das gescheh'n, so führst den Blinden Du
> Ins Innerste des Waldes, reißest ihm
> Die Kleider ab, und bindest nackt und bloß
> Mit Stricken ihn an eine Eiche fest,
> Damit der Eber und der zorn'ge Bär,
> Die Schlange, die von unten sticht, der Aar,
> Der aus der Höhe schießt, sich in sein Fleisch
> Mit Zahn und Kralle theilen.[43]

Herodes, of course, in his famous summary of his position in Act I, Scene 2, of *Herodes und Mariamne,* uses the identical picture, appropriately coloured:

> Ich gleiche
> Dem Mann der Fabel, den der Löwe vorn,
> Der Tiger hinten packte, dem die Geier
> Mit Schnäbeln und mit Klau'n von oben drohten,
> Und der auf einem Schlangenklumpen stand.[44]

This is another trivial but telling instance which shows Hebbel's conscious use of the right word—or animal!—in the right place.

The contrast of light and darkness is an important source of imagery in Hebbel's lyric poems. It recurs perhaps more consistently than any other in his plays, and its usage extends from the isolated word-picture, illuminating a single moment in the experience of an individual character, to its presentation as a concrete symbol in significant stage-setting. Other image-groups illustrate one or more of the various possible types of dramatic usage, but none other embraces so comprehensively the whole range. The imagistic field of light and darkness is by no means new or original; but it is enormously characteristic for Hebbel, right from his early days as a lyric poet, whether he was writing under the influence of Schiller or Schelling. It afforded him his first inklings of poetic awareness,[45] and his Heidelberg experiences of both natural and inorganic phenomena helped him to appropriate it more firmly into his poetic vocabulary, of which it remained a basic ingredient to the end. Certain plays, most notably *Judith* and *Maria Magdalena,* derive much of their characteristic atmosphere from the compelling poetic exploitation of the symbolism of light and darkness. It is one of the basic symbolical dualisms by which Hebbel presents poetically his antithetical view of the world. So by their frequent use of it, his characters are speaking the language of his poetic symbolical world in general. Yet at the same time such images are, in characteristic fashion, tailored to fit the requirements of individual characters and the environment of a particular play. Again a striking comparison can be made between two almost identical images, the one used by Judith and the other by Klara's mother in *Maria Magdalena.* Both these images have been discussed elsewhere to demonstrate how they fit in a quite different way into the dominant verbal and symbolical complexes of their respective plays.[46] In *Maria Magdalena* the imagery of light and darkness is associated, with one important exception, exclusively with Meister Anton, and light acquires symbolic significance as the degree of his spiritual illumination. But for one telling moment Anton's wife takes over this imagery. One of the most successful of Hebbel's word-pictures of light and darkness must surely be her portrayal of death; it is she who (even though she is perhaps the most limited intellectually of all his characters) finds the most personal and telling expression for the spiritual experience afforded by contact with death, since she has come closest to it in her life. This, her first image, gives an immediate and intimate picture of her, and merits close consideration as an extremely effective and characteristic example of Hebbel's use of language. Klara's mother is a quiet ordinary woman whose only aspirations are to be a good housewife and mother. Hebbel could have shown her using a traditional folk-image—Death the Reaper, perhaps, which her husband

uses, or the Angel of Death, with which she would be familiar from church; but instead he selects a picture which indicates her imtimate knowledge of death and her association of it with the pattern of her daily life, which has been so disturbed by illness that she could no longer fulfil her usual tasks and dreaded her isolation in the darkness at the end of the day, rather than welcoming it as rest from labour. The language presents a typical contrast and some favourite words (*verdüstern, finster, schimmern, leuchten*), yet within a sentence structure simple enough for the speaker, and the beautifully balanced antithesis, with all the weight and activity and variety in the first half, throws admirably into relief in the second half the isolation of the individual in moments of intense soul-searching:

> Der Tod ist schrecklicher, als man glaubt, o, er ist bitter: Er verdüstert die Welt, er bläs't all' die Lichter, eins nach dem andern, aus, die so bunt und lustig um uns her schimmern, die freundlichen Augen des Mannes und der Kinder hören zu leuchten auf, und es wird finster allenthalben, aber im Herzen zündet er ein Licht an, da wird's hell, und man sieht viel, sehr viel, was man nicht sehen mag.[47]

This is a fine example of the way Hebbel could adapt a favourite image, that of the cruel, searching light of (self-)knowledge,[48] to suit the requirements of individual character and situation. Other characters choose the same means of expressing sudden revelation, but the picture is different. Judith and Golo, in some ways in a similar situation, and filled with horror at their own feelings, liken their hearts to a hole filled with reptiles, lit up by a bright light,[49] Meister Anton and Gunther, both practical and realistic, select the picture of the light on the table,[50] whereas Alexandra, in happy anticipation of the terrible disclosure she will be able to make to Herodes when Mariamne is dead, promises:

> Vom Schicksal Mariamnens
> Scheid' ich das meinige, und spare mich,
> Wie eine Fackel, für die Zukunft auf![51]

Only one other of Hebbel's dramatic characters, however, uses this basic image in as complex a manner as Klara's mother, namely Judith, who could scarcely be more different from her. In her first appearance on the stage Judith is revealed as a woman in great torment of spirit, afraid of herself and suspecting herself to be abnormal, "ein grauenhaftes, fürchterliches Wesen."[52] The grounds for her misgivings are the strange occurrences of her wedding-night. At first Manasses' desire for darkness was resisted by Judith, who seemed afraid to lose the familiar glow of the candles:

> Wir gingen in die Kammer hinein, . . . mir ward doch wieder schwer und ängstlich, als ich mich mit Manasses allein befand. Drei Lichter brannten, er wollte sie auslöschen; laß, laß, sagte ich bittend; Närrin! sagte er und wollte mich fassen—da ging eins der Lichter

aus, wir bemerkten's kaum; er küßte mich—da erlosch
das zweite. Er schauderte und ich nach ihm, dann lacht'
er und sprach: das dritte lösch' ich selbst; schnell,
schnell, sagte ich, denn es überlief mich kalt; er that's.[53]

But the lights extinguished—two of them by an invisible hand, the third by Manasses after a momentary
shudder of apprehension,—are replaced in the now
chilling darkness by a more revealing, relentless light,
no longer man-made, which shows Judith to Manasses
as if by the clear light of day:

> Der Mond schien hell in die Kammer, ich schlüpfte ins
> Bett, er schien mir gerade ins Gesicht. Manasses rief:
> ich sehe Dich so deutlich, wie am Tage, und kam auf
> mich zu.[54]

The effect of this new revelation of Judith on Manasses
is such that from this moment she becomes a mystery
and a source of horror to herself. The construction of
this picture and of Klara's mother's image is exactly
parallel, only that in *Judith* the symbolism of light and
darkness is fully developed and related to the action
and setting of the play, mirroring thus the inner darkness of Judith's soul and the obscurity of her motives.

Hebbel shows, then, extreme competence and awareness in his choice and manipulation of imagistic material to indicate character, atmosphere and ideological
content in his plays. This holds good in those instances
where he did not have a completely free hand, but was
in some way bound by features of his source. In such
cases he makes use of everything, ignoring no vital
detail, but rather investing it with significance and
rendering it truly meaningful as a symbol of his own
interpretation of the material. Judith's sword, Gyges'
ring, Brunhild's jewelled girdle are such details which
all acquire a new relevance in Hebbel's complex pattern of significant word and sign,[55] though he was the
first to admit that such motifs were not necessarily
indispensable: "Der Gyges ist ohne Ring möglich, die
Nibelungen sind es ohne Hornhaut und Nebelkappe.[56]"
But from whatever components Hebbel creates the
linguistic world of his drama there will exist in it a
similar dualism to that which he noted in the real world
between the general and the particular:

> An der Sprache ist es die wunderbarste Seite, wie der
> allgemeine Geist des Volks, dessen Product sie ist, und
> der individuelle, der sich ihrer zu seinen Einzelzwecken
> bedient, in einander wirken und, sich gegenseitig ergän-
> zend und beschränkend, ein Drittes erzeugen, das
> Beiden gemeinschaftlich angehört . . . Darauf aber ko-
> mmt es an, daß der Geist in der Sprache möglichst
> vollständig zur Erscheinung gelange, daß er hier an der
> Gränze der sich bereits verflüchtigenden materiellen
> Welt den letzten, durchsichtigen Leib erhalte.[57]

The interaction and cross-fertilization of word and image in the language of individual characters within the
general linguistic scope of each play in the end
determines the success with which the ideas are communicated.

In the *Nibelungen* trilogy Hebbel was faced with
specific problems, partly because of the trilogy form
itself. He needed to differentiate the three stages or
spheres of tragic action and characterize each; at the
same time it was essential to reflect the developing plot
and the interconnection and progression of ideas through
the three parts. But since he was regarding himself as
the "Dolmetscher eines Höheren" it was especially
important that he should not introduce any extraneous
imagistic material. For the first and last sections the
material offered him by his source was similar. Brunhild's sphere is distinguished by elemental phenomena—ice and snow, subterranean light,[58] that of Etzel by
fire and blood, apocalyptic visions.[59] That of the Burgundian court has at first sight no obvious characterizing imagistic material. The real action here moves on
a purely human and natural plane, although Siegfried
and Brunhild bring inevitably with them mythological
associations, and Kriemhild when she moves away from
Worms takes on more than purely human proportions.
The relationship with Christianity is important in all
three spheres, and in all it is a continual source of comment, and so could not serve to provide material
exclusive to Gunther's court. Instead Hebbel chose the
hunt, the central episode of *Siegfrieds Tod,* which,
however, like the distinguishing features of Brunhild's
territory and of Etzel's, overlaps into the other two
spheres as well. Hunting is a pastime in Brunhild's
kingdom and in Etzel's, as well as at Worms, but in
both cases there is an implied difference. When Brunhild goes to the hunt the animals and setting are strange:

> Einst kommt der Morgen, wo ich, statt den Bären
> Zu jagen, oder auch die eingefror'ne
> Seeschlange zu erlösen aus der Haft,
> Damit sie den Planeten nicht zerpeitsche,
> Die Burg schon früh' verlasse.[60]

And Hagen is, or pretends to be, surprised that there
should be hunting at Etzel's court at all:

HAGEN:

> Ihr lebt hier still, Herr Dietrich. Wie vertreibt
> Ihr Euch die Zeit?

DIETRICH:

> Durch Jagd und Waffenspiel.

HAGEN:

> Doch! Davon hab' ich heut' nicht viel erblickt.[61]

In the very first words spoken in *Die Nibelungen* it is
made apparent that hunting is on occupation taken for
granted as part of the life of the Burgundian court.
Hagen is amazed and annoyed that the day's hunting
has been cancelled:

> Nun, keine Jagd?

Gunther is ready with the explanation:

> Es ist ja heil'ger Tag!

From the outset the hunting motif is used to show up the insecure foothold Christianity has in the Germanic world, even the antagonism between the two; and this first juxtaposition of hunt and Christian practice recurs and is extended at crucial points later in the trilogy. The opening few speeches of *Der gehörnte Siegfried*[62] have often been commented upon;[63] in them the main linguistic patterns of the trilogy are picked up and the elaborate interweaving of threads is started. The initial antithesis is repeated almost immediately:

HAGEN:

> Geboren ist er längst!
> Das war—laßt seh'n!—Ja, ja, zur Zeit der Flocken!
> Sein Fest verdarb uns eine Bärenhatz.

So that the highest points of the Christian calendar are questioned at the start of the trilogy by the primitive mentality for which hunting and kindred sports are peaks of experience. This is no triviality for Hagen— even at Easter he still remembers that the celebration of Christmas spoilt a bear-baiting. And to the mental outlook which enjoys the hunt to the kill it is difficult to conceive of death as anything but the climax and the end:

> Gekreuzigt ist er auch,
> Gestorben und begraben . . .
> Ist's denn noch nicht aus?

The total irrelevancy for him of the Christian belief in resurrection and salvation is shown in his oblique reference to the Communion and his rejection of it, again through the hunting-image:

> Ich ess' kein Fleisch zur Nacht,
> Das nicht bis Mittag in der Haut noch steckt,
> Auch trink' ich keinen Wein, als aus dem Horn,
> Das ich dem Auerstier erst nehmen muß!

Once more Gunther attempts to bring him back into the observance of Christian ceremony and usage:

> So wirst Du Fische kauen müssen, Freund,
> Am Ostermorgen geh'n wir nicht zur Jagd.

The hunt, which in the old epic was merely the occasion for Siegfried's death (there was no mention of a hunt at the time of his arrival in Worms) is introduced thus at the opening of Hebbel's trilogy and assumes from the start a symbolic function as the ethic of life of Hagen. Hunting is his life, at least when he cannot fight, just as he probably envisages the process of life as similar to that of a hunt, ending ultimately in death.

The next section of this opening scene leads on to Volker's tale and the legend of Siegfried, raising momentarily on the way forewarnings of the events of the night which will end the trilogy and the sequence of the tragic action about to start here:

HAGEN:

> Was ist erlaubt? Ich hör' die Vögel pfeifen,
> Da darf der Mensch sich doch wohl fiedeln lassen?

VOLKER:

> Ich fiedle nicht, so lang' die Sonne scheint,
> Die lust'ge Arbeit spar' ich für die Nacht.
> . . . . .

HAGEN:

> . . . Und fiedelst nur, wenn Du nicht schlagen kannst.

With Hagen's insistence, upon Gunther's request for a tale about heroes and ladies from Volker, that it should be "nur von Lebend'gen", there is a further echo of the ideological antithesis of the opening before the tale of Siegfried begins.

Hebbel presents directly and unequivocally in the opening speeches of his trilogy the opposition between the two ideologies, the pagan Germanic one of Hagen, conceiving of human existence under the aspect of the struggle for survival, and the Christian, in which true life begins where it ends for Hagen. Perhaps the shadow of Schopenhauer is discernible in the background, giving a further dimension to the motif of the hunt. At all events, its symbolic significance having been firmly established at the beginning of *Der gehörnte Siegfried,* no further special use is made of it, nor is any necessary, until its appropriate place in the tragic action in *Siegfrieds Tod,* where it becomes a dramatic image, sustained over several scenes.[64] It is Siegfried himself who first suggests the hunting-party on which he is to find his death:

> Ihr Recken, hört Ihr nicht
> Die Bracken heulen und den jüngsten Jäger
> Sein Hifthorn prüfen? Auf! Zu Pferd! Hinaus![65]

He too, on hearing of the alleged treachery of Lüdegast and Lüdeger, with a natural transition of thought, denounces them as animals to be hunted, in words whose irony is not lost on Hagen, who is quick to think of another application for them:

SIEGRIED:

> Hier gilt's ja keine Fehde, keinen Kampf
> Nach Recht und Brauch, hier gilt es eine Jagd
> Auf böse Thiere! Hagen, lächle nicht!
> Mit Henkerbeilen sollten wir uns waffnen,
> Anstatt mit uns'ren adeligen Klingen,
> Und die sogar erst brauchen, da sie doch
> Von Eisen sind und so dem Schwert verwandt,
> Wenn zu dem Hundefang kein Strick genügt.

HAGEN:

> Wohl wahr!

SIEGFRIED:

> Du spottest meiner, wie es scheint,
> Das fass' ich nicht, Du brennst doch sonst so le-
>   icht![66]

The image is picked up by Hagen and applied to Siegfried when Hagen parts from Kriemhild after having tricked her into disclosing to him her husband's one vulnerable spot:

> Nun ist Dein Held nur noch ein Wild für mich![67]

In the succeeding scenes it is built up in the mouth of Siegfried to be received by Hagen with increasing irony until he himself laconically suggests the hunt:

SIEGFRIED

> Was giebt's?

HAGEN:

> Die Hunde bitten jetzt auf's Neue
> Um Frieden, doch ich ließ die lump'gen Boten
> Vom Hof herunter hetzen, ehe sie
> Noch ausgesprochen hatten.

SIEGFRIED:

> Das war recht!

HAGEN:

> Der König schilt mich zwar, er meint, man könne
> Nicht wissen, was gescheh'n—

SIEGFRIED:

> Nicht wissen! Ha!—
> Ich weiß es, ich! Packt einen Wolf von hinten,
> Da giebt er Ruh' von vorn!

HAGEN:

> Das wird es sein!

SIEGFRIED:

> Was sonst! Es wimmelt ja in ihrem Rücken
> Von wilden Stämmen. Nun, die säen nicht
> Und wollen dennoch ernten.

HAGEN:

> Seht Ihr's nun?

SIEGFRIED:

> Nun werdet Ihr den Wolf nicht schonen wollen,
> Weil er nicht g'rade Zeit hat, sich zu wehren—

HAGEN:

> Gewiß nicht.

SIEGFRIED:

> Stehen wir den Füchsen bei
> Und treiben ihn in's letzte Loch hinein,
> In ihren Magen, mein' ich!

HAGEN:

> Thun wir das,
> Doch scheint's nicht nöthing, daß wir uns erhitzen,
> D'rum rath' ich heut' zur Jagd.[68]

The double-entendres continue through the scene of Siegfried's farewell from Kriemhild:

KRIEMHILD:

> Ihr geht zur Jagd?

SIEGFRIED:

> Ja wohl! Bestell' Dir gleich
> Den Braten.[69]

and in the presence of Hagen:

KRIEMHILD:

> Siegfried!

SIEGFRIED:

> (*wird noch einmal sichtbar*) Was ist?

KRIEMHILD:

> Wenn Du nicht zürnen wolltest—

HAGEN:

> (*folgt Siegfried rasch*) Nun, hast Du Dein Spindel
>   schon?

SIEGFRIED:

> (*zu Kriemhild*) Du hörst,
> Daß sich die Hunde nicht mehr halten lassen![70]

until the scene of the hunt itself. Here Siegfried's enthusiastic, excited comments on his achievements and the pleasures of the chase call forth the comment from Hagen:

>   Nur den Löwen jag' ich heut',
>   Allein, ich traf ihn nicht.

which immediately throws into relief the tragic irony of the situation, especially when the implications of Siegfried's reply:

>   Das glaub' ich wohl,
>   Ich hab' ihn selbst erlegt![71]

are considered. Faithful to the detail of the epic—Siegfried did, however improbably, slay a lion—, the use he makes of it is entirely Hebbel's own. Siegfried, who is referred to in other instances in the trilogy as the lion, indeed slew himself, both through his own tongue[72] and through the "guilt", in Hebbel's sense, of his superhuman strength. The "Doppeldeutigkeit" to which de Boor takes exception is particularly complex here. In the epic events are recounted as they happen; we do not know what form Hagen's revenge will take until it is actually upon us. The false rumours of the treachery of Lüdegast and Lüdeger are invented and circulated; Siegfried offers to ride out on Gunther's behalf; Hagen tricks Siegfried's secret out of Kriemhild; the mission to avenge Gunther on the Danes is called off; and instead, Gunther himself suggests the hunt at the end of Âventiure XV:

> "Nu wir der hereverte ledic worden sîn,
> sô wil ich jagen rîten bern unde swîn
> hin zem Waskenwalde, als ich vil dicke hân."
> daz hete gerâten Hagene, der vil ungetriuwe man.

Siegfried agrees, and the heroes ride off almost immediately, with only a brief delay whilst Siegfried takes his farewell alone from his wife. The hunt itself claims attention in the narrative by the length of the Âventiure which is devoted to the description of it. In Hebbel's version, where there is no place for epic breadth, it has to be given prominence in a manner and using devices proper to the dramatic genre. And so it becomes the striking ironical dramatic image as shown, which serves several functions. By making the initial suggestion of a hunting-party come from Siegfried, and the final invitation from Hagen, Hebbel has linked the two in a sinister chain of word and deed with its own ironic causality, which not only arouses dramatic tension, but can also serve to display character and motive. One almost sees the plan taking full shape in Hagen's clever mind as Siegfried in his naive way rails at the treachery of the Danes and contemptuously derides them as animals to be hunted down. The guileless and impetuous talkativeness to which Hagen took such exception, and which he regards as largely to blame for the need to punish Siegfried, is once more cruelly in evidence as Siegfried, unaware that time is running out on him too, with his own tongue presents his prospective murderer with arguments to justify the deed. Siegfried's openness and hence, despite his impenetrable skin, his defencelessness against Hagen's cunning and single-minded pursuit of his prey could scarcely be more tellingly demonstrated. However inappropriate and anachronistic the modern cynicism in these exchanges may be in this "translation" of the medieval epic, it is dramatically very effective.

The murder of Siegfried then takes place as in the epic. In effect the hunting image is completed with the exchange of words by Hagen and Siegfried on the subject of the lion, and has served its purpose, not to be used again with any great significance[73] until Kriemhild, in her last attempt to obtain justice from Gunther at Et-

zel's court, recalls how Siegfried "ward geschlachtet wie ein wildes Thier."[74] It is sparingly used; introduced in the opening lines of *Der gehörnte Siegfried* and invested with symbolic force; developed and fully integrated into the idea of the trilogy when it appears in its proper place in the tragic action in *Siegfrieds Tod*; and re-stated briefly to trigger off the impulsion of events into the catastrophe in *Kriemhilds Rache*. Without being obtrusive in the verbal texture of the plays the hunting motif is nevertheless at their core, forming a pivot for the tragic action and a centre around which the ideas as expressed in verbal patterns can cohere. The scenes in which Hagen and Siegfried make ready for the hunt illuminate wonderfully their relationship, "den eigentlichen Kern des tragischen Konflikts," and help to show how "sich . . . das ganze Gedicht von diesem Punct aus bis in die fernsten Radien wunderbar lichtet."[75] Their relations are from the start, on Hagen's side at least, uneasy, based half on genuine admiration and half on a sense of personal grievance. Hagen's strong feeling that Siegfried has behaved dishonourably in bathing in the dragon's blood and thereby acquiring for himself an unfair advantage is aggravated by Siegfried's betrayal of their secret into becoming an absolute conviction of a great wrong to be righted, by whatever means are feasible. The episode of the hunt therefore acquires a further aspect as an issue in the discussion of guilt and justice which is central to the plays, and it becomes woven into the verbal complex of Rache and Gericht which starts with Frigga's words immediately after Kriemhild has insulted Brunhild: "Du kannst / Dich rächen, Kind!"[76] Hagen too reacts swiftly. On discovering that Brunhild knows the truth he calls the brothers together on the spot and reaches his verdict without further ado:

HAGEN:

> Nun tretet um mich her und haltet gleich
> Das peinliche Gericht!

GUNTHER:

> Wie redest Du?

HAGEN:

> Fehlt's hier am Grund? Dort steht die Königin
> Und weint die heißen Thränen, welche ihr
> Der Schimpf entpreßt!
> (*zu Brunhild*)
> Du edles Heldenbild,
> Du einz'ges, dem auch ich mich willig beuge:
> Der Mann muß sterben, der Dir das gethan![77]

From this point onwards, whilst the other Burgundians are holding their tortured deliberations, Hagen is concerned solely with the execution of the sentence. By talking too much, no matter how it came about, Siegfried has broken faith; he is now a "Frevler", whom Hagen would clearly have as little compunction in killing as he would an animal in the forest: it is for Gunther to decide:

Er lebt, so lange Du's befiehlst! Und ständ' ich
Im Wald schon hinter ihm, den Speer gezückt,
Du winkst, und statt des Frevlers stürzt ein Thier![78]

But in the end it is Siegfried who pays the price, which is indeed to die like an animal, since he himself had, by his own deeds, rendered any other form of retribution impossible, as Hagen reminds Kriemhild when she charges him with the slaughter of her husband:

Den Recken hätte ich
Gefordert, und mir ist's wohl zuzutrau'n,
Allein er war vom Drachen nicht zu trennen,
Und Drachen schlägt man todt. Warum begab sich
Der stolze Held auch in des Lindwurms Hut![79]

To slay Siegfried in this particular way, then, is for Hagen not "schlachten" but "strafen", the only appropriate form of punishment for one who had by his presumption set himself beyond the reach of the accepted judicial conventions. Hagen's considerations go no further; the implications of Kriemhild's reply: "Und in dem Lindwurm schlug er alle Welt!" are lost on him. But for Hebbel's audience another series of associations has been set up. Hagen has been rightly understood as the Anti-Christ figure of the trilogy;[80] his protests at the beginning of the trilogy that the Easter celebrations have spoilt his hunting have already been noted. And now, in *Siegfrieds Tod,* his hunt for Siegfried is juxtaposed with the picture of Christian martyrdom which the chaplain draws for Ute and her daughter in Act IV, Scene 8, and a possible analogy between Christ and the martyr figure Siegfried is highlighted.[81] Siegfried's murder, and the play itself, are then concluded by the scene in the Cathedral where the chaplain attempts to substitute the Christian concept of forgiveness for the Germanic one of *Rache*. The motif of the hunt is associated thus intimately with Hagen, not only in fact, but also in its symbolic significance, and at the same time it is very deeply involved in the play of ideas of the trilogy.

In describing the murder of Siegfried as Hagen stands before his coffin in the Cathedral Kriemhild relegates his murderer to the animal kingdom and its values:

So standest Du nicht da, als Du ihn schlugst,
Die wölf'schen Augen fest auf ihn geheftet,
Und durch Dein Teufelslächeln den Gedanken
Voraus verkündigend! Von hinten schlichst
Du Dich heran und miedest seinen Blick,
Wie wilde Thiere den des Menschen meiden,
Und spähtest nach dem Fleck, den ich—Du Hund,
Was schwurst Du mir?[82]

Although it is Kriemhild here who uses animal imagery to characterize Hagen, he is the character in the whole trilogy who, appropriately, with Siegfried a good second, most often uses such terminology. Half the images in the trilogy are, in fact, taken from animal life or

the hunt, most of them, with a handful of exceptions, in the mouth of the Burgundians in all three plays. It is indeed a distinguishing feature, intimating their way of life and disposition, which they take with them wherever they go. Thus the language of the whole trilogy is permeated with animal images and images of the hunt, and though Siegfried, for instance, is repeatedly referred to as the lion—Giselher, for example, leading him to woo Kriemhild, compares himself with the child leading the lion—,[83] and Hagen often as the wolf, such designations are by no means constant. Hagen is associated with the huntsman, in the hunt for Siegfried, but also with the stag, hunted by Kriemhild:

Was heucheln wir, Kriemhild?
Wir kennen uns. Doch merke Dir auch dieß:
Gleich auf das erste Meisterstück des Hirsches,
Dem Jäger zu entrinnen, folgt auch das zweite,
Ihn in's Verderben mit hinab zu zieh'n,
Und eins von Beidem glückt uns sicherlich![84]

She is on occasion herself associated with the animal:

Leg' einer Todten
Den Sohn an's Herz und ford're Milch von ihr:
Die heil'ge Quelle der Natur wird eher
In ihrer starren Brust auf's Neue springen,
Als meine Seele aus dem Winterschlaf
Zu wecken war, der nie ein Thier so tief
Bis in das Herz beschlichen hat, wie mich.[85]

but again, too, by Rüdeger, with the huntsman, as he begs to be spared from entering into battle against the Burgundians:

Kriemhild, ich habe Dir den Eid geschworen
Und muß ihn halten, das erklär' ich laut
Für meine Pflicht und mäkle nicht daran.
Wenn Ihr mich dennoch nieder knieen seht,
So denkt des Hirsches, der in höchster Noth
Sich auch noch gegen seinen Jäger wendet,
Und ihm die einz'ge blut'ge Thräne zeigt,
Die er auf dieser Erde weinen darf,
Ob er vielleicht Erbarmen in ihm weckt.[86]

Like Siegfried, who, in Rumolt's words,

unterwegs
Zwei Königssöhne fängt und uns sie schickt,
Als ob es aufgescheuchte Hasen waren,[87]

Brunhild is represented both as the huntsman[88] and, by Hagen, as the hunted:

Brunhild ist jetzt ein angeschoss'nes Wild,
Wer wird es mit dem Pfeil so laufen lassen,
Ein edler Jäger schickt den zweiten nach.[89]

The cumulative effect of these images is twofold. In the first place they suggest that the process of life is like that of the hunt, but a hunt in which today's huntsman may well become tomorrow's prey, in fact a continual sequence of supremacy followed by submission to the new. In the further identification of Siegfried with the dragon which he slew, and from which he then drew his superhuman strength, it is indicated that it is the very strength of the existing order which calls out the forces of destruction against it; when Siegfried is slain, Kriemhild identifies Hagen with the dragon, recalling his own words, and swears similarly to slay him:

> Der grimm'ge Mörder sprach am Sarg
> In bitt'rem Hohn zu mir: Dein Siegfried war
> Vom Drachen nicht zu trennen, und man schlägt
> Die Drachen todt. Das wiederhol' ich jetzt!
> Ich schlag' den Drachen todt und Jeden mit,
> Der sich zu ihm gesellt und ihn beschirmt.[90]

This movement of the image of the hunt among the characters is by no means isolated in the trilogy. It follows the same pattern as other dominant linguistic motifs. In **Die Nibelungen** the emergence of the Christian world from Germanic barbarism and superstition is reflected. The transition in the trilogy from the old Germanic to the Christian ideals is presented as a very gradual one—from the world of Brunhild and Kriemhild to that represented by Dietrich von Bern. It is portrayed symbolically in the gradual disclosure of the significance of the references to the Crucifixion from the opening scene of the trilogy, where we saw Hagen expressing his disgust that the festival of Easter should prevent him from enjoying the pleasures of the chase, right through the three plays until the closing words of **Kriemhilds Rache** as Dietrich von Bern accepts the mantle of the wearied Etzel "im Namen dessen, der am Kreuz erblich". It emerges in the linguistic pattern built up through the three plays on the theme of "Rache" and "Gericht", which links most significantly the closing scenes of **Siegfrieds Tod** and **Kriemhilds Rache,** and in the movement of imagery and symbolism among the characters. Darkness and the colour black are associated first with Brunhild and then, after Siegfried's death, with Kriemhild; jackdaws, crows, ravens, owls, the birds of ill-omen, symbols of an inexorable retribution which befalls those who are guilty of lack of moderation and overweening self-assertion, are connected in turn with Brunhild, Siegfried and Hagen, marking them out as transgressors.[91]

By his symbolic exploitation of the motif of fire, which he found already present in the material of his sources, Hebbel succeeded in indicating with great theatrical immediacy which of the warring forces in the battle "Von Alt und Neu, und wie sie blutig ringen, / Bis Ein's erliegt,"[92] were destined to be overcome and why. The outworn, overpresumptuous codes of behaviour which are to be superseded by the ideals of Christianity are marked by fire, which again moves successively from one victim or sphere of tragic action to the next. Thus Brunhild's protecting wall of flame has a deeper meaning in Hebbel's play than the mere reproduction of the

mythological motive. Great emphasis is laid, too, on the fiery quality of the light in Brunhild's land and she herself is compared with the elements, fire and water.[93] But with the approach of Siegfried the guarding wall of flame is extinguished, and after the death of Siegfried the fire-image, like the imagery of darkness, passes from her to Kriemhild.[94] Etzel too is associated with fire—and blood, in an image which points forward to the battle in his hall,[95] and the death of the Burgundians in the blood and flames provides the climax of the motif, the dramatic purpose of which seems to be to draw attention to the final burst of overflowing life which heralds the extinction of the Burgundians and of their outworn ideals, just as the fire glows up once more brightly before it is extinguished.[96]

But the motif has another function too, not unrelated to this. Fire was the sign of the two great festivals which play an important part in the legends which were Hebbel's sources, Ragnaroke, the defeat of the Gods in Norse legend, synonymous with the end of the world, when the sky would go up in flame and the earth sink into the sea, and the pagan Germanic feast of the solar solstice, celebrated on the eve of the Christian festival of John the Baptist and thus gradually becoming identified with the Christian feast. The Germanic festival signified the prosperity of crops through the purification by fire, hence the "Johannisfeuer" and other fire rituals. This is the celebration to which Kriemhild invites the Burgundians, of which Hagen says in unconscious bitter irony:

> Wir wurden auf das Fest der Sonnenwende
> Geladen, aber nicht zum Jüngsten Tag.[97]

Even before Kriemhild leaves the Burgundian court to marry Etzel her brother Gerenot makes reference to the approach of the feast in words which, like Hagen's, are charged with unintentional double meaning:

> Man spart schon auf das Johannis-Feuer
> Und steckt den Lauch mit Nächstem an den Balken.[98]

Both festivals could thus signify for Hebbel the destruction of old forms and ideals and the birth of new, purer ones.

It is highly revealing that Hebbel should alter the placing of the scene where Dietrich von Bern tells the Markgraf Rüdeger what he learnt at the well of the nixes so that the "Sonnenjahr" to which Dietrich (instead of Rüdeger in the original version) refers no longer relates to the moment of conception of Siegfried and the awakening of Brunhild as his bride, but to the annihilation of the Nibelungs; he tells of a "Sonnenjahr",

> Das über alles menschliche Gedächtniß
> Hinaus in langen Pausen wiederkehrt.

Vom Schöpfungsborn, und wie er kocht und quillt
Und überschäumt in Millionen Blasen,
Wenn das erscheint. Von einem letzten Herbst
Der alle Formen der Natur zerbricht,
Und einem Frühling, welcher bess're bringt.
Von Alt und Neu, und wie sie blutig ringen,
Bis Ein's erliegt.[99]

The "Sonnenjahr" becomes thus identified with the
"Sonnenwende" and with the feast to which the Burgundians are invited, and sets the events which happen
there into a much wider perspective than the personal
revenge of Kriemhild for the murder of her husband.
The plane of the action is the movement of the course
of history, and the guilt of the individuals is incurred by
transgression, not merely against persons, but against
the universal scheme. The collapse of the world of
Brunhild and of that of Kriemhild is related; the reign
of the gods and of the giants is over, but so too is that
of the Germanic ideals of clan-loyalty and revenge. In
the vision of Volker (an invention of Hebbel's), "diese
mystische Grundwurzel des Ganzen,"[100] as he and Hagen
keep their night watch at Etzel's court the blood, fire
and guilt, which characterize the world of Brunhild and
that of Kriemhild, are symbolically concentrated in the
gold of the Nibelungs, lost to the Gods and, by the actions of Hagen, lost to men. This gold is an instrument
of destruction and a symbol of the guilt of Brunhild's
world and of Kriemhild's and is linked verbally and by
implication with the flames of Ragnaroke and the fire
which destroyed the Burgundians; like the jewels in
Hebbel's plays and poems, the Nibelung gold represents
at one time the temptation and the guilt of men:

Und wird es endlich durch den Wechselmord
Auf Erden herrenlos, so schlägt ein Feuer
Daraus hervor mit zügelloser Gluth,
Das alle Meere nicht ersticken können,
Weil es die ganze Welt in Flammen setzen
Und Ragnaroke überdauern soll.[101]

The fire motif, one of the most basic ingredients in
Hebbel's presentation of abstract thought in concrete
symbol in both his poems and his plays, acquires in *Die
Nibelungen* an aspect of finality, embracing as it does
all its associations in his other works—passion, eroti-
cism, spiritual and ethical quality, sacrifice and
martyrdom, destruction and purification—and fusing
into one great image Ragnaroke, *Sonnenfest* and Day of
Judgement. The fire which glows most brightly in the
moment before extinction becomes most convincingly
in Hebbel's last completed great work the ultimate
symbol for the reconciliation of individual and universe
in death.

All the image patterns of the *Nibelungen* trilogy, including that of the hunt, thus tend in the same direction and
towards the same end. They point the movement of
personal guilt as it is incurred successively by one
character after another, and the movement of vengeance,

as each victim in turn becomes the new avenger or the
avenger becomes the new victim, Brunhild-Siegfried-
Hagen; Hagen-Kriemhild-Hildebrant; they point the
movement of power, again a successive one Siegfried-
Etzel-Dietrich. And in so doing they reflect the course
of historical development from one mythology to another.[102] The trilogy which opened on Easter Day ends
with the Day of Judgement. Hagen's oblique references
to the communion wine, the blood of Christ, as he talks
of hunting in the first few speeches of *Der gehörnte
Siegfried,* lead by way of the hunting image[103] and the
many other significant allusions to wine, or bread, or
blood in the course of the three plays to the magnifi-
cently grotesque and profoundly impious sight of the
Burgundians drinking one another's blood in the
holocaust at the end. The wheel of image and symbol
has come full circle, gradually revealing as it turned the
full philosophical meaning of the action as displayed on
the stage. Hebbel uses all the linguistic devices at his
disposal to indicate and underline that this is a time of
ideological crisis, a Weltenwende, though not necessarily the final one. Historically speaking the conflict is
between Germanic heathendom and European Christianity, but it also takes place on another plane. Brunhild
and Siegfried on the one hand, Etzel and Dietrich on
the other, are at least in part mythological figures,
partaking in a sense of universal as well as individual
existence; but Hagen, although he may talk with "Meer-
weiber", remains purely and defiantly human. This is
reflected throughout in his practical, down-to-earth
speech and imagery, and the hunt motif as associated
with him reinforces this impression. Again we are
reminded that the core of the tragedy is a human
relationship, "eine menschliche Tragödie,"[104] which for
Hagen at least remains within human proportions and is
enacted on a human scale. Through the links established
between the hunt as a literary image and the other verbal
patterns of the trilogy, however, this conflict of individuals is shown to be symptomatic of an age of historical
crisis and integrated into the philosophical struggle of
the universe.

The hunt in *Die Nibelungen,* then, provides a small
instance of Hebbel's characteristic use of material.
Given a motif from his source which must be incorporated into his play, he does not feel in any way restricted
by it, nor is it for him a dead prop in his dramatic
creation. On the contrary, he re-forms it, adapts,
develops and uses it inventively so that it serves him in
the characterization of individuals, linguistic environmental presentation and finally to illuminate his intellectual and philosophical world as it is poetically
revealed in all his plays. The hunt thus becomes Hebbel's own genuine imaginative creation. It has been
argued that Hebbel's images are for the reader, not the
listener, and this may well be true.[105] Certainly the careful architectural construction of his plays, where every
piece is deliberately placed and nothing is there by ac-

cident, can only be properly appreciated by the careful reading of the text. The hunt image does not, perhaps, reach the intellectual depth of some of Hebbel's other dramatic images, nevertheless it has a real function in his linguistic creation over and above its place in the legend itself. The following summary of the significance of the image in Hebbel's dramatic composition will also serve to illumine the value of the image of the hunt in *Die Nibelungen*:

> Das Bild wird durch die Sprache der Dichtung erstellt und entzieht sich doch dem dichterischen Wirklichkeitszusammenhang; das einzelne dramatische Symbol schafft die Gesamtsymbolik des Dramas gerade dadurch, daß es sich passiv verhält gegenüber dem aus Aktion hervorgehenden Handlungsverlauf, es treibt die Erregung vorwärts, indem es das Geschehen hemmt. Im Zusammenhang mit dem Nibelungenlied und der eigenen dramatischen Bearbeitung dieses Stoffes sagt Hebbel: "Nie gestatte ich mir, aus der dunklen Region unbestimmter und unbestimmbarer Kräfte, die ich hier vor Augen habe, ein Motiv zu entlehnen, ich beschränke mich darauf, die wunderbaren Lichter und Farben aufzufangen, welche unsere wirklich bestehende Welt in einen neuen Glanz tauchen, ohne sie zu verändern." Das Zeichen schafft also die Struktur des Tragischen nicht, aber es bringt sie zum Ausdruck; im Ganzen des Kunstwerks erhellt es die Funktion seiner Teile, indem es den Zusammenhang zwischen beiden noch einmal eigens signalisiert.[106]

The hunt is not only an integral part of Hebbel's story and source, it is also an integral part of the linguistic pattern of his trilogy. Like his adoption of other details from the epic—the Burgundians quenching their thirst in the blazing hall by drinking the blood of the fallen is a notable example—, the use to which Hebbel puts the slaying of Siegfried whilst hunting shows very clearly the moment where his translation of the medieval epic becomes an interpretation. These episodes are rendered deliberately and extensively "doppeldeutig" by him in his recognition and use of them as symbolic moments, which he then links with each other through verbal inference and association until they present a linguistic and philosophical coherence which is Hebbel's own, and indeed which fulfils his main requirement of the language of the drama, in which it is a matter of "Vergegenwärtigung der Zustände in ihrer organischen Gesammtheit."[107] From the standpoint of the reproduction of the exact spirit of the *Nibelungenlied* Hebbel's language in *Die Nibelungen* is therefore an embarrassing lapse of style; from that of the observer of the development of his dramatic language it may be regarded more positively in the context of his attempt to achieve a successful synthesis of thought and poetic presentation. In its verbal composition *Die Nibelungen* is as characteristic an example of Hebbel's "eigene Sprache" as any other of his plays.

Notes

1. Br. VII, 137.

2. Particularly relevant for this discussion are: Helga Frisch, *Symbolik und Tragik in Hebbels Dramen,* Bonn, 1961; Marie Luise Gansberg, *Zur Sprache in Hebbels Dramen, Hebbel in neuer Sicht,* ed. Helmut Kreuzer, Stuttgart, 1963; Mary Garland, *Hebbel's Prose Tragedies,* Cambridge, 1973.

3. T. IV, 5866.

4. T. IV, 5582, 6286.

5. Br. VII, 31.

6. Helmut de Boor, *Friedrich Hebbel, Die Nibelungen (Dichtung und Wirklichkeit),* Frankfurt/M—Berlin, 1966, p. 70.

7. ibid., pp. 75 f.

8. ibid., p. 78.

9. ibid., p. 76.

10. T. IV, 5555.

11. T. III, 3830 (sketch for *Ueber den Styl des Dramas,* W. XI, 65 ff.).

12. Garland, p. 13. Cf. also Frisch, pp. 24 f.

13. T. II, 1965.

14. W. XI, 66.

15. T. IV, 5328.

16. Mary Garland, op. cit.; Martin Stern, *Das zentrale Symbol in Hebbels "Maria Magdalena",* Hebbel in neuer Sicht, pp. 228-246; J. Fetzer, *Walter Imagery in "Maria Magdalena",* German Quarterly, 43, 4, Nov. 1970, pp. 715-9.

17. Cf. Frisch, pp. 26-44, Garland, pp. 77-89.

18. W. I, 7.

19. W. I, 18.

20. W. I, 19.

21. W. I, 20.

22. W. I, 26.

23. W. I, 61.

24. W. I, 64.

25. w. I, [19.] fft

    W. I, 19. Cf. Garland, pp. 60, 64, 90.

26. Cf. Gansberg, pp. 64 ff.

27. W. I, 50.

28. W. I, 61.

29. W. I, 114.

30. W. II, 220.

31. Cf. W. I, 101, ll. 330 f.; 103, ll. 370 ff.; 110, ll. 532 ff.; 158, ll. 1534 ff.

32. W. II, 325.

33. W. III, 186. Cf. Garland, p. 265.

34. W. III, 268.

35. W. IV, 76.

36. Cf. Heinz Stolte, *Von der liebenden Ehrfurcht. Friedrich Hebbel und die Tiere,* Hebbel-Jahrbuch 1975, pp. 11-37.

37. Cf. Frisch, pp. 97-103.

38. W. IV, 116.

39. W. I, 20.

40. W. II, 25, ll. 11 f.; 18, ll. 12 f.; 28, ll. 13 ff. Also W. II, 40, ll. 10 ff.

41. W. II, 213. Cf. also W. II, 228, ll. 597 ff. and 316, ll. 2359 ff.

42. Cf. W. II, 234-5.

43. W. I, 272 f.

44. W. II, 211.

45. Cf. T. I, 134.

46. Garland, pp. 152 ff. (Klara's mother's image) and pp. 83 ff. (Judith's account of her wedding-night).

47. W. II, 11.

48. Cf. W. I, 190, l. 2066, where Golo speaks of "des Bewußtseins Stral".

49. Cf. Judith, W. 1, 61, ll. 12 ff. and Golo, W. I, 189, ll. 2032 ff.

50. Cf. Meister Anton, W. II, 37, ll. 31 ff. and Gunther, W. IV, 183, ll. 2835 ff.

51. W. II, 339. The same image is used in *Das abgeschiedene Kind an seine Mutter,* W. VI, 294.

52. W. I, 15.

53. W. I, 16 f.

54. W. I, 17.

55. Cf. esp. Frisch, pp. 88-103, *Symbole der tragischen Schuld.*

56. Br. VII, 304, Letter to Sigmund Engländer, 23. 2. 63.

57. W. XI, 66-67.

58. Cf. W. IV, 14, ll. 110 ff., 15, ll. 130 ff., 33, ll. 486 ff., 56, ll. 827 ff. Wolfgang Liepe, *Beiträge zur Literatur- und Geistesgeschichte,* Neumünster, 1963, pp. 273-275 *(Unbekannte und unerkannte Frühprosen Hebbels),* discusses the sources of Hebbel's picture of Brunhild's world.

59. Cf. W. IV, 205, ll. 3280 ff.

60. W. IV, 58.

61. W. IV, 300.

62. W. IV, 11 ff.

63. E.g. Heinz Stolte, *Ein Plädoyer für Hebbels Nibelungen,* Hebbel-Jahrbuch, 1970, pp. 15-16; Garland, pp. 311-13.

64. Siegfrieds Tod, Acts IV and V.

65. W. IV, 114.

66. W. IV, 117.

67. W. IV, 130.

68. W. IV, 136 f.

69. W. IV, 138.

70. W. IV, 140.

71. W. IV, 147.

72. Cf. W. IV, 152, ll. 2425 f. and 153, ll. 2434 ff.

73. There is some unconscious irony in the exchange between Kriemhild and Ute just before the discovery of Siegfried's body: KRIEM.: Sie sind vielleicht / Zurück. UTE: Die Jäger? . . . Sie zogen ja, / So viel ich weiß, nicht für die Küche aus . . . (W. IV, 156 f.).

74. W. IV, 280.

75. Br. VI, 298, Letter to Hettner, 31. 12. 59.

76. W. IV, 109.

77. W. IV, 111.

78. W. IV, 119.

79. W. IV, 171.

80. By Eugen Hollenbach, *Die Hagen-Gestalt bei Hebbel und im Nibelungen-Lied,* Hebbel-Jahrbuch, 1975, pp. 166-7.

81. Cf. Garland, p. 312. The manner of Siegfried's death, however, contrasts sharply with the forgiveness shown by the true Christian martyr. Siegfried curses his murderers, even more strongly than in the epic, so that the analogy is not a true one, even bearing in mind any possible ambiguity in his dying wish for Kriemhild: "Doch besser gehst Du / Zu meinem Vater!" (W. IV, 154.) Perhaps we

have here an example of an impossible situation for Hebbel, where his duty to act as "Dolmetscher" clashes with his philosophical intentions.

82. W. IV, 170.

83. W. IV, 64, ll. 1002 f., cf. also 94, ll. 1485 f.; perhaps 299, ll. 4833 ff.

84. W. IV, 277.

85. W. IV, 192.

86. W. IV, 327.

87. W. IV, 61.

88. W. IV, 58.

89. W. IV, 85.

90. W. IV, 325, Cf. also 297, ll. 4803 ff.; 226, ll. 3616 ff.

91. Cf. Frisch, pp. 97-103; also above, note 37.

92. W. IV, 299.

93. Cf. note 56.

94. W. IV, 284, ll. 4545 f.

95. W. IV, 205 ll. 3280 f.; 223, 3589 f. Cf. also Hagen's reference to himself and the Burgundians, which also points forward with great irony, W. IV, 155, ll. 2468 ff.

96. The image-complex of "Glut" can only be fully understood by reference to Hebbel's poems, where the final burst of intense colour marks the end of the flower's life as in *Sommerbild* (W. VI, 230). It also plays a significant part in *Gyges und sein Ring*.

97. W. IV, 253.

98. W. IV, 193. Cf. also W. IV, 178, ll. 2732 ff.; 244, ll. 3864 ff.; 249, ll. 3976 ff.

99. W. IV, 299.

100. Br. VII, 29, Letter to Dingelstedt, 13. 3. 61.

101. W. IV, 271.

102. Hebbel, though by no means opposed to Christianity, regarded it "nur als ein Symbol neben anderen Symbolen" (Br. VII, 11, Letter to Luck, 21. 1. 61), and wrote at length his views in his letter to Uechtritz, 25. 10. 62: "Das Christentum ist mir, was es war, eine Mythologie neben anderen, und wie ich jetzt . . . leider hinzu fügen muß, nicht einmal die tiefste. Wenn es mir daher gelungen seyn sollte, es in seiner innersten Wesenheit darzustellen, wie Sie mich hoffen lassen, so hat es dazu keiner anderen Kraft bedurft, als derjenigen, die das Valkyrenthum auf Isenland darstellte, welches gleichfalls als gelungen bezeichnet worden ist." (Br. VII, 266).

103. Cf. also Siegfried's reception of Hagen's invitation to the hunt: Sieg.: O Jägerlust! / Ja, wenn man singen könnte! Hag.: Ist Dir recht? Sieg.: Recht? Freund, ich bin so voll von Wuth und Groll, / Daß ich mit einem jeden zanken mögte, / D'rum muß ich Blut seh'n. Hag.: Mußt Du? Nun, ich auch! (W. IV, 138).

104. Cf. T. IV, 5933.

105. By Frisch, pp. 24 f., and Gansberg, p. 73.

106. Frisch, pp. 24 f.

107. W. XI, 72.

Additional coverage of Hebbel's life and career is contained in the following sources published by Gale Group: *Concise Dictionary of World Literary Biography,* **Vol. 2;** *Dictionary of Literary Biography,* **Vol. 129;** *DISCovering Authors Modules*: *Dramatists; European Writers,* **Vol. 6;** *Literature Resource Center; Nineteenth-Century Literature Criticism,* **Vol. 43; and** *Reference Guide to World Literature,* **Eds. 2, 3.**

How to Use This Index

The main references

Calvino, Italo
1923-1985 .... CLC 5, 8, 11, 22, 33, 39,
73; SSC 3, 48

list all author entries in the following Gale Literary Criticism series:

AAL = Asian American Literature
BG = The Beat Generation: A Gale Critical Companion
BLC = Black Literature Criticism
BLCS = Black Literature Criticism Supplement
CLC = Contemporary Literary Criticism
CLR = Children's Literature Review
CMLC = Classical and Medieval Literature Criticism
DC = Drama Criticism
HLC = Hispanic Literature Criticism
HLCS = Hispanic Literature Criticism Supplement
HR = Harlem Renaissance: A Gale Critical Companion
LC = Literature Criticism from 1400 to 1800
NCLC = Nineteenth-Century Literature Criticism
NNAL = Native North American Literature
PC = Poetry Criticism
SSC = Short Story Criticism
TCLC = Twentieth-Century Literary Criticism
WLC = World Literature Criticism, 1500 to the Present
WLCS = World Literature Criticism Supplement

The cross-references

See also CA 85-88, 116; CANR 23, 61;
DAM NOV; DLB 196; EW 13; MTCW 1, 2;
RGSF 2; RGWL 2; SFW 4; SSFS 12

list all author entries in the following Gale biographical and literary sources:

AAYA = Authors & Artists for Young Adults
AFAW = African American Writers
AFW = African Writers
AITN = Authors in the News
AMW = American Writers
AMWR = American Writers Retrospective Supplement
AMWS = American Writers Supplement
ANW = American Nature Writers
AW = Ancient Writers
BEST = Bestsellers
BPFB = Beacham's Encyclopedia of Popular Fiction: Biography and Resources
BRW = British Writers
BRWS = British Writers Supplement
BW = Black Writers
BYA = Beacham's Guide to Literature for Young Adults
CA = Contemporary Authors
CAAS = Contemporary Authors Autobiography Series
CABS = Contemporary Authors Bibliographical Series
CAD = Contemporary American Dramatists
CANR = Contemporary Authors New Revision Series
CAP = Contemporary Authors Permanent Series
CBD = Contemporary British Dramatists
CCA = Contemporary Canadian Authors
CD = Contemporary Dramatists
CDALB = Concise Dictionary of American Literary Biography
CDALBS = Concise Dictionary of American Literary Biography Supplement
CDBLB = Concise Dictionary of British Literary Biography

CMW = St. James Guide to Crime & Mystery Writers
CN = Contemporary Novelists
CP = Contemporary Poets
CPW = Contemporary Popular Writers
CSW = Contemporary Southern Writers
CWD = Contemporary Women Dramatists
CWP = Contemporary Women Poets
CWRI = St. James Guide to Children's Writers
CWW = Contemporary World Writers
DA = DISCovering Authors
DA3 = DISCovering Authors 3.0
DAB = DISCovering Authors: British Edition
DAC = DISCovering Authors: Canadian Edition
DAM = DISCovering Authors: Modules
   DRAM: Dramatists Module; MST: Most-studied Authors Module;
   MULT: Multicultural Authors Module; NOV: Novelists Module;
   POET: Poets Module; POP: Popular Fiction and Genre Authors Module
DFS = Drama for Students
DLB = Dictionary of Literary Biography
DLBD = Dictionary of Literary Biography Documentary Series
DLBY = Dictionary of Literary Biography Yearbook
DNFS = Literature of Developing Nations for Students
EFS = Epics for Students
EXPN = Exploring Novels
EXPP = Exploring Poetry
EXPS = Exploring Short Stories
EW = European Writers
FANT = St. James Guide to Fantasy Writers
FW = Feminist Writers
GFL = Guide to French Literature, Beginnings to 1789, 1798 to the Present
GLL = Gay and Lesbian Literature
HGG = St. James Guide to Horror, Ghost & Gothic Writers
HW = Hispanic Writers
IDFW = International Dictionary of Films and Filmmakers: Writers and Production Artists
IDTP = International Dictionary of Theatre: Playwrights
LAIT = Literature and Its Times
LAW = Latin American Writers
JRDA = Junior DISCovering Authors
MAICYA = Major Authors and Illustrators for Children and Young Adults
MAICYAS = Major Authors and Illustrators for Children and Young Adults Supplement
MAWW = Modern American Women Writers
MJW = Modern Japanese Writers
MTCW = Major 20th-Century Writers
NCFS = Nonfiction Classics for Students
NFS = Novels for Students
PAB = Poets: American and British
PFS = Poetry for Students
RGAL = Reference Guide to American Literature
RGEL = Reference Guide to English Literature
RGSF = Reference Guide to Short Fiction
RGWL = Reference Guide to World Literature
RHW = Twentieth-Century Romance and Historical Writers
SAAS = Something about the Author Autobiography Series
SATA = Something about the Author
SFW = St. James Guide to Science Fiction Writers
SSFS = Short Stories for Students
TCWW = Twentieth-Century Western Writers
WLIT = World Literature and Its Times
WP = World Poets
YABC = Yesterday's Authors of Books for Children
YAW = St. James Guide to Young Adult Writers H

Literary Criticism Series
Cumulative Author Index

Agrippa von Nettesheim, Henry Cornelius
1486-1535 .... **LC 27**

Aguilera Malta, Demetrio
1909-1981 .... **HLCS 1**
See also CA 111; 124; CANR 87; DAM
MULT, NOV; DLB 145; EWL 3; HW 1;
RGWL 3

Agustini, Delmira 1886-1914 .... **HLCS 1**
See also CA 166; HW 1, 2; LAW

Aherne, Owen
See Cassill, R(onald) V(erlin)

Ai 1947- .... **CLC 4, 14, 69**
See also CA 85-88; CAAS 13; CANR 70;
DLB 120; PFS 16

Aickman, Robert (Fordyce)
1914-1981 .... **CLC 57**
See also CA 5-8R; CANR 3, 72, 100; DLB
261; HGG; SUFW 1, 2

Aidoo, (Christina) Ama Ata 1942- ..... **BLCS**
See also AFW; BW 1; CA 101; CANR 62;
CD 5; CDWLB 3; CN 7; CWD; CWP;
DLB 117; DNFS 1, 2; EWL 3; FW; WLIT
2

Aiken, Conrad (Potter) 1889-1973 .... **CLC 1,
3, 5, 10, 52; PC 26; SSC 9**
See also AMW; CA 5-8R; 45-48; CANR 4,
60; CDALB 1929-1941; DAM NOV,
POET; DLB 9, 45, 102; EWL 3; EXPS;
HGG; MTCW 1, 2; RGAL 4; RGSF 2;
SATA 3, 30; SSFS 8; TUS

Aiken, Joan (Delano) 1924- .... **CLC 35**
See also AAYA 1, 25; CA 9-12R, 182;
CAAE 182; CANR 4, 23, 34, 64; CLR 1,
19; DLB 161; FANT; HGG; JRDA; MAI-
CYA 1, 2; MTCW 1; RHW; SAAS 1;
SATA 2, 30, 73; SATA-Essay 109; SUFW
2; WYA; YAW

Ainsworth, William Harrison
1805-1882 .... **NCLC 13**
See also DLB 21; HGG; RGEL 2; SATA
24; SUFW 1

Aitmatov, Chingiz (Torekulovich)
1928- .... **CLC 71**
See Aytmatov, Chingiz
See also CA 103; CANR 38; MTCW 1;
RGSF 2; SATA 56

Akers, Floyd
See Baum, L(yman) Frank

Akhmadulina, Bella Akhatovna
1937- .... **CLC 53; PC 43**
See also CA 65-68; CWP; CWW 2; DAM
POET; EWL 3

Akhmatova, Anna 1888-1966 ..... **CLC 11, 25,
64, 126; PC 2**
See also CA 19-20; 25-28R; CANR 35;
CAP 1; DA3; DAM POET; EW 10; EWL
3; MTCW 1, 2; RGWL 2, 3

Aksakov, Sergei Timofeyvich
1791-1859 .... **NCLC 2**
See also DLB 198

Aksenov, Vassily
See Aksyonov, Vassily (Pavlovich)

Akst, Daniel 1956- .... **CLC 109**
See also CA 161; CANR 110

Aksyonov, Vassily (Pavlovich)
1932- .... **CLC 22, 37, 101**
See also CA 53-56; CANR 12, 48, 77;
CWW 2; EWL 3

Akutagawa Ryunosuke 1892-1927 ... **SSC 44;
TCLC 16**
See also CA 117; 154; DLB 180; EWL 3;
MJW; RGSF 2; RGWL 2, 3

Alabaster, William 1568-1640 .... **LC 90**
See also DLB 132; RGEL 2

Alain 1868-1951 .... **TCLC 41**
See also CA 163; EWL 3; GFL 1789 to the
Present

Alain de Lille c. 1116-c. 1203 .... **CMLC 53**
See also DLB 208

Alain-Fournier .... **TCLC 6**
See Fournier, Henri-Alban
See also DLB 65; EWL 3; GFL 1789 to the
Present; RGWL 2, 3

Al-Amin, Jamil Abdullah 1943- .... **BLC 1**
See also BW 1, 3; CA 112; 125; CANR 82;
DAM MULT

Alanus de Insluis
See Alain de Lille

Alarcon, Pedro Antonio de
1833-1891 .... **NCLC 1**

Alas (y Urena), Leopoldo (Enrique Garcia)
1852-1901 .... **TCLC 29**
See also CA 113; 131; HW 1; RGSF 2

Albee, Edward (Franklin) (III)
1928- .. **CLC 1, 2, 3, 5, 9, 11, 13, 25, 53,
86, 113; DC 11; WLC**
See also AITN 1; AMW; CA 5-8R; CABS
3; CAD; CANR 8, 54, 74; CD 5; CDALB
1941-1968; DA; DA3; DAB; DAC; DAM
DRAM, MST; DFS 2, 3, 8, 10, 13, 14;
DLB 7, 266; EWL 3; INT CANR-8; LAIT
4; LMFS 2; MTCW 1, 2; RGAL 4; TUS

Alberti, Rafael 1902-1999 .... **CLC 7**
See also CA 85-88; 185; CANR 81; DLB
108; EWL 3; HW 2; RGWL 2, 3

Albert the Great 1193(?)-1280 ...... **CMLC 16**
See also DLB 115

Alcala-Galiano, Juan Valera y
See Valera y Alcala-Galiano, Juan

Alcayaga, Lucila Godoy
See Godoy Alcayaga, Lucila

Alcott, Amos Bronson 1799-1888 .... **NCLC 1**
See also DLB 1, 223

Alcott, Louisa May 1832-1888 . **NCLC 6, 58,
83; SSC 27; WLC**
See also AAYA 20; AMWS 1; BPFB 1;
BYA 2; CDALB 1865-1917; CLR 1, 38;
DA; DA3; DAC; DAM MST, NOV;
DLB 1, 42, 79, 223, 239, 242; DLBD 14;
FW; JRDA; LAIT 2; MAICYA 1, 2; NFS
12; RGAL 4; SATA 100; TUS; WCH;
WYA; YABC 1; YAW

Aldanov, M. A.
See Aldanov, Mark (Alexandrovich)

Aldanov, Mark (Alexandrovich)
1886(?)-1957 .... **TCLC 23**
See also CA 118; 181

Aldington, Richard 1892-1962 .... **CLC 49**
See also CA 85-88; CANR 45; DLB 20, 36,
100, 149; LMFS 2; RGEL 2

Aldiss, Brian W(ilson) 1925- . **CLC 5, 14, 40;
SSC 36**
See also AAYA 42; CA 5-8R; CAAE 190;
CAAS 2; CANR 5, 28, 64; CN 7; DAM
NOV; DLB 14, 261, 271; MTCW 1, 2;
SATA 34; SFW 4

Aldrich, Bess Streeter
1881-1954 .... **TCLC 125**
See also CLR 70

Alegria, Claribel 1924- .... **CLC 75; HLCS 1;
PC 26**
See also CA 131; CAAS 15; CANR 66, 94;
CWW 2; DAM MULT; DLB 145; EWL
3; HW 1; MTCW 1

Alegria, Fernando 1918- .... **CLC 57**
See also CA 9-12R; CANR 5, 32, 72; EWL
3; HW 1, 2

Aleichem, Sholom .... **SSC 33; TCLC 1, 35**
See Rabinovitch, Sholem
See also TWA

Aleixandre, Vicente 1898-1984 .... **HLCS 1;
TCLC 113**
See also CANR 81; DLB 108; EWL 3; HW
2; RGWL 2, 3

Aleman, Mateo 1547-1615(?) .... **LC 81**

Alencon, Marguerite d'
See de Navarre, Marguerite

Alepoudelis, Odysseus
See Elytis, Odysseus
See also CWW 2

Aleshkovsky, Joseph 1929-
See Aleshkovsky, Yuz
See also CA 121; 128

Aleshkovsky, Yuz, ... **CLC 44**
See Aleshkovsky, Joseph

Alexander, Lloyd (Chudley) 1924- ... **CLC 35**
See also AAYA 1, 27; BPFB 1; BYA 5, 6,
7, 9, 10, 11; CA 1-4R; CANR 1, 24, 38,
55, 113; CLR 1, 5, 48; CWRI 5; DLB 52;
FANT; JRDA; MAICYA 1, 2; MAICYAS
1; MTCW 1; SAAS 19; SATA 3, 49, 81,
129, 135; SUFW; TUS; WYA; YAW

Alexander, Meena 1951- .... **CLC 121**
See also CA 115; CANR 38, 70; CP 7;
CWP; FW

Alexander, Samuel 1859-1938 .... **TCLC 77**

Alexie, Sherman (Joseph, Jr.)
1966- .... **CLC 96, 154; NNAL**
See also AAYA 28; CA 138; CANR 65, 95;
DA3; DAM MULT; DLB 175, 206, 278;
LATS 1; MTCW 1; NFS 17

al-Farabi 870(?)-950 .... **CMLC 58**
See also DLB 115

Alfau, Felipe 1902-1999 .... **CLC 66**
See also CA 137

Alfieri, Vittorio 1749-1803 .... **NCLC 101**
See also EW 4; RGWL 2, 3

Alfred, Jean Gaston
See Ponge, Francis

Alger, Horatio, Jr. 1832-1899 .... **NCLC 8, 83**
See also CLR 87; DLB 42; LAIT 2; RGAL
4; SATA 16; TUS

Al-Ghazali, Muhammad ibn Muhammad
1058-1111 .... **CMLC 50**
See also DLB 115

Algren, Nelson 1909-1981 ..... **CLC 4, 10, 33;
SSC 33**
See also AMWS 9; BPFB 1; CA 13-16R;
103; CANR 20, 61; CDALB 1941-1968;
DLB 9; DLBY 1981, 1982, 2000; EWL 3;
MTCW 1, 2; RGAL 4; RGSF 2

Ali, Ahmed 1908-1998 .... **CLC 69**
See also CA 25-28R; CANR 15, 34; EWL 3

Ali, Tariq 1943- .... **CLC 173**
See also CA 25-28R; CANR 10, 99

Alighieri, Dante
See Dante

Allan, John B.
See Westlake, Donald E(dwin)

Allan, Sidney
See Hartmann, Sadakichi

Allan, Sydney
See Hartmann, Sadakichi

Allard, Janet .... **CLC 59**

Allen, Edward 1948- .... **CLC 59**

Allen, Fred 1894-1956 .... **TCLC 87**

Allen, Paula Gunn 1939- ..... **CLC 84; NNAL**
See also AMWS 4; CA 112; 143; CANR
63; CWP; DA3; DAM MULT; DLB 175;
FW; MTCW 1; RGAL 4

Allen, Roland
See Ayckbourn, Alan

Allen, Sarah A.
See Hopkins, Pauline Elizabeth

Allen, Sidney H.
See Hartmann, Sadakichi

Allen, Woody 1935- .... **CLC 16, 52**
See also AAYA 10; CA 33-36R; CANR 27,
38, 63; DAM POP; DLB 44; MTCW 1

Allende, Isabel 1942- ... **CLC 39, 57, 97, 170;
HLC 1; WLCS**
See also AAYA 18; CA 125; 130; CANR
51, 74; CDWLB 3; CWW 2; DA3; DAM
MULT, NOV; DLB 145; DNFS 1; EWL

3; FW; HW 1, 2; INT CA-130; LAIT 5; LAWS 1; LMFS 2; MTCW 1, 2; NCFS 1; NFS 6; RGSF 2; RGWL 3; SSFS 11, 16; WLIT 1

Alleyn, Ellen
See Rossetti, Christina (Georgina)

Alleyne, Carla D. .... **CLC 65**

Allingham, Margery (Louise)
1904-1966 .... **CLC 19**
See also CA 5-8R; 25-28R; CANR 4, 58; CMW 4; DLB 77; MSW; MTCW 1, 2

Allingham, William 1824-1889 ...... **NCLC 25**
See also DLB 35; RGEL 2

Allison, Dorothy E. 1949- .... **CLC 78, 153**
See also CA 140; CANR 66, 107; CSW; DA3; FW; MTCW 1; NFS 11; RGAL 4

Alloula, Malek .... **CLC 65**

Allston, Washington 1779-1843 .... **NCLC 2**
See also DLB 1, 235

Almedingen, E. M. .... **CLC 12**
See Almedingen, Martha Edith von
See also SATA 3

Almedingen, Martha Edith von 1898-1971
See Almedingen, E. M.
See also CA 1-4R; CANR 1

Almodovar, Pedro 1949(?)- .... **CLC 114; HLCS 1**
See also CA 133; CANR 72; HW 2

Almqvist, Carl Jonas Love
1793-1866 .... **NCLC 42**

Alonso, Damaso 1898-1990 .... **CLC 14**
See also CA 110; 131; 130; CANR 72; DLB 108; EWL 3; HW 1, 2

Alov
See Gogol, Nikolai (Vasilyevich)

Alta 1942- .... **CLC 19**
See also CA 57-60

Alter, Robert B(ernard) 1935- .... **CLC 34**
See also CA 49-52; CANR 1, 47, 100

Alther, Lisa 1944- .... **CLC 7, 41**
See also BPFB 1; CA 65-68; CAAS 30; CANR 12, 30, 51; CN 7; CSW; GLL 2; MTCW 1

Althusser, L.
See Althusser, Louis

Althusser, Louis 1918-1990 .... **CLC 106**
See also CA 131; 132; CANR 102; DLB 242

Altman, Robert 1925- .... **CLC 16, 116**
See also CA 73-76; CANR 43

Alurista .... **HLCS 1**
See Urista, Alberto H.
See also DLB 82

Alvarez, A(lfred) 1929- .... **CLC 5, 13**
See also CA 1-4R; CANR 3, 33, 63, 101; CN 7; CP 7; DLB 14, 40

Alvarez, Alejandro Rodriguez 1903-1965
See Casona, Alejandro
See also CA 131; 93-96; HW 1

Alvarez, Julia 1950- .... **CLC 93; HLCS 1**
See also AAYA 25; AMWS 7; CA 147; CANR 69, 101; DA3; DLB 282; LATS 1; MTCW 1; NFS 5, 9; SATA 129; WLIT 1

Alvaro, Corrado 1896-1956 .... **TCLC 60**
See also CA 163; DLB 264; EWL 3

Amado, Jorge 1912-2001 ... **CLC 13, 40, 106; HLC 1**
See also CA 77-80; 201; CANR 35, 74; DAM MULT, NOV; DLB 113; EWL 3; HW 2; LAW; LAWS 1; MTCW 1, 2; RGWL 2, 3; TWA; WLIT 1

Ambler, Eric 1909-1998 .... **CLC 4, 6, 9**
See also BRWS 4; CA 9-12R; 171; CANR 7, 38, 74; CMW 4; CN 7; DLB 77; MSW; MTCW 1, 2; TEA

Ambrose, Stephen E(dward)
1936-2002 .... **CLC 145**
See also AAYA 44; CA 1-4R; 209; CANR 3, 43, 57, 83, 105; NCFS 2; SATA 40, 138

Amichai, Yehuda 1924-2000 .. **CLC 9, 22, 57, 116; PC 38**
See also CA 85-88; 189; CANR 46, 60, 99; CWW 2; EWL 3; MTCW 1

Amichai, Yehudah
See Amichai, Yehuda

Amiel, Henri Frederic 1821-1881 .... **NCLC 4**
See also DLB 217

Amis, Kingsley (William)
1922-1995 ...... **CLC 1, 2, 3, 5, 8, 13, 40, 44, 129**
See also AITN 2; BPFB 1; BRWS 2; CA 9-12R; 150; CANR 8, 28, 54; CDBLB 1945-1960; CN 7; CP 7; DA; DA3; DAB; DAC; DAM MST, NOV; DLB 15, 27, 100, 139; DLBY 1996; EWL 3; HGG; INT CANR-8; MTCW 1, 2; RGEL 2; RGSF 2; SFW 4

Amis, Martin (Louis) 1949- .... **CLC 4, 9, 38, 62, 101**
See also BEST 90:3; BRWS 4; CA 65-68; CANR 8, 27, 54, 73, 95; CN 7; DA3; DLB 14, 194; EWL 3; INT CANR-27; MTCW 1

Ammons, A(rchie) R(andolph)
1926-2001 ...... **CLC 2, 3, 5, 8, 9, 25, 57, 108; PC 16**
See also AITN 1; AMWS 7; CA 9-12R; 193; CANR 6, 36, 51, 73, 107; CP 7; CSW; DAM POET; DLB 5, 165; EWL 3; MTCW 1, 2; RGAL 4

Amo, Tauraatua i
See Adams, Henry (Brooks)

Amory, Thomas 1691(?)-1788 .... **LC 48**
See also DLB 39

Anand, Mulk Raj 1905- .... **CLC 23, 93**
See also CA 65-68; CANR 32, 64; CN 7; DAM NOV; EWL 3; MTCW 1, 2; RGSF 2

Anatol
See Schnitzler, Arthur

Anaximander c. 611B.C.-c.
546B.C. .... **CMLC 22**

Anaya, Rudolfo A(lfonso) 1937- ...... **CLC 23, 148; HLC 1**
See also AAYA 20; BYA 13; CA 45-48; CAAS 4; CANR 1, 32, 51; CN 7; DAM MULT, NOV; DLB 82, 206, 278; HW 1; LAIT 4; MTCW 1, 2; NFS 12; RGAL 4; RGSF 2; WLIT 1

Andersen, Hans Christian
1805-1875 .... **NCLC 7, 79; SSC 6, 56; WLC**
See also CLR 6; DA; DA3; DAB; DAC; DAM MST, POP; EW 6; MAICYA 1, 2; RGSF 2; RGWL 2, 3; SATA 100; TWA; WCH; YABC 1

Anderson, C. Farley
See Mencken, H(enry) L(ouis); Nathan, George Jean

Anderson, Jessica (Margaret) Queale
1916- .... **CLC 37**
See also CA 9-12R; CANR 4, 62; CN 7

Anderson, Jon (Victor) 1940- .... **CLC 9**
See also CA 25-28R; CANR 20; DAM POET

Anderson, Lindsay (Gordon)
1923-1994 .... **CLC 20**
See also CA 125; 128; 146; CANR 77

Anderson, Maxwell 1888-1959 .... **TCLC 2**
See also CA 105; 152; DAM DRAM; DFS 16; DLB 7, 228; MTCW 2; RGAL 4

Anderson, Poul (William)
1926-2001 .... **CLC 15**
See also AAYA 5, 34; BPFB 1; BYA 6, 8, 9; CA 1-4R; 181; 199; CAAE 181; CAAS 2; CANR 2, 15, 34, 64, 110; CLR 58; DLB 8; FANT; INT CANR-15; MTCW 1, 2; SATA 90; SATA-Brief 39; SATA-Essay 106; SCFW 2; SFW 4; SUFW 1, 2

Anderson, Robert (Woodruff)
1917- .... **CLC 23**
See also AITN 1; CA 21-24R; CANR 32; DAM DRAM; DLB 7; LAIT 5

Anderson, Roberta Joan
See Mitchell, Joni

Anderson, Sherwood 1876-1941 .. **SSC 1, 46; TCLC 1, 10, 24, 123; WLC**
See also AAYA 30; AMW; BPFB 1; CA 104; 121; CANR 61; CDALB 1917-1929; DA; DA3; DAB; DAC; DAM MST, NOV; DLB 4, 9, 86; DLBD 1; EWL 3; EXPS; GLL 2; MTCW 1, 2; NFS 4; RGAL 4; RGSF 2; SSFS 4, 10, 11; TUS

Andier, Pierre
See Desnos, Robert

Andouard
See Giraudoux, Jean(-Hippolyte)

Andrade, Carlos Drummond de ..... **CLC 18**
See Drummond de Andrade, Carlos
See also EWL 3; RGWL 2, 3

Andrade, Mario de .... **TCLC 43**
See de Andrade, Mario
See also EWL 3; LAW; RGWL 2, 3; WLIT 1

Andreae, Johann V(alentin)
1586-1654 .... **LC 32**
See also DLB 164

Andreas Capellanus fl. c. 1185- .... **CMLC 45**
See also DLB 208

Andreas-Salome, Lou 1861-1937 ... **TCLC 56**
See also CA 178; DLB 66

Andreev, Leonid
See Andreyev, Leonid (Nikolaevich)
See also EWL 3

Andress, Lesley
See Sanders, Lawrence

Andrewes, Lancelot 1555-1626 .... **LC 5**
See also DLB 151, 172

Andrews, Cicily Fairfield
See West, Rebecca

Andrews, Elton V.
See Pohl, Frederik

Andreyev, Leonid (Nikolaevich)
1871-1919 .... **TCLC 3**
See Andreev, Leonid
See also CA 104; 185

Andric, Ivo 1892-1975 .... **CLC 8; SSC 36; TCLC 135**
See also CA 81-84; 57-60; CANR 43, 60; CDWLB 4; DLB 147; EW 11; EWL 3; MTCW 1; RGSF 2; RGWL 2, 3

Androvar
See Prado (Calvo), Pedro

Angelique, Pierre
See Bataille, Georges

Angell, Roger 1920- .... **CLC 26**
See also CA 57-60; CANR 13, 44, 70; DLB 171, 185

Angelou, Maya 1928- ... **BLC 1; CLC 12, 35, 64, 77, 155; PC 32; WLCS**
See also AAYA 7, 20; AMWS 4; BPFB 1; BW 2, 3; BYA 2; CA 65-68; CANR 19, 42, 65, 111; CDALBS; CLR 53; CP 7; CPW; CSW; CWP; DA; DA3; DAB; DAC; DAM MST, MULT, POET, POP; DLB 38; EWL 3; EXPN; EXPP; LAIT 4; MAICYA 2; MAICYAS 1; MAWW; MTCW 1, 2; NCFS 2; NFS 2; PFS 2, 3; RGAL 4; SATA 49, 136; WYA; YAW

Artsybashev, Mikhail (Petrovich)
1878-1927 .... **TCLC 31**
See also CA 170

Arundel, Honor (Morfydd)
1919-1973 .... **CLC 17**
See also CA 21-22; 41-44R; CAP 2; CLR 35; CWRI 5; SATA 4; SATA-Obit 24

Arzner, Dorothy 1900-1979 .... **CLC 98**

Asch, Sholem 1880-1957 .... **TCLC 3**
See also CA 105; EWL 3; GLL 2

Ash, Shalom
See Asch, Sholem

Ashbery, John (Lawrence) 1927- .. **CLC 2, 3, 4, 6, 9, 13, 15, 25, 41, 77, 125; PC 26**
See Berry, Jonas
See also AMWS 3; CA 5-8R; CANR 9, 37, 66, 102; CP 7; DA3; DAM POET; DLB 5, 165; DLBY 1981; EWL 3; INT CANR-9; MTCW 1, 2; PAB; PFS 11; RGAL 4; WP

Ashdown, Clifford
See Freeman, R(ichard) Austin

Ashe, Gordon
See Creasey, John

Ashton-Warner, Sylvia (Constance)
1908-1984 .... **CLC 19**
See also CA 69-72; 112; CANR 29; MTCW 1, 2

Asimov, Isaac 1920-1992 ..... **CLC 1, 3, 9, 19, 26, 76, 92**
See also AAYA 13; BEST 90:2; BPFB 1; BYA 4, 6, 7, 9; CA 1-4R; 137; CANR 2, 19, 36, 60; CLR 12, 79; CMW 4; CPW; DA3; DAM POP; DLB 8; DLBY 1992; INT CANR-19; JRDA; LAIT 5; LMFS 2; MAICYA 1, 2; MTCW 1, 2; RGAL 4; SATA 1, 26, 74; SCFW 2; SFW 4; SSFS 17; TUS; YAW

Askew, Anne 1521(?)-1546 .... **LC 81**
See also DLB 136

Assis, Joaquim Maria Machado de
See Machado de Assis, Joaquim Maria

Astell, Mary 1666-1731 .... **LC 68**
See also DLB 252; FW

Astley, Thea (Beatrice May) 1925- .. **CLC 41**
See also CA 65-68; CANR 11, 43, 78; CN 7; EWL 3

Astley, William 1855-1911
See Warung, Price

Aston, James
See White, T(erence) H(anbury)

Asturias, Miguel Angel 1899-1974 .... **CLC 3, 8, 13; HLC 1**
See also CA 25-28; 49-52; CANR 32; CAP 2; CDWLB 3; DA3; DAM MULT, NOV; DLB 113; EWL 3; HW 1; LAW; LMFS 2; MTCW 1, 2; RGWL 2, 3; WLIT 1

Atares, Carlos Saura
See Saura (Atares), Carlos

Athanasius c. 295-c. 373 .... **CMLC 48**

Atheling, William
See Pound, Ezra (Weston Loomis)

Atheling, William, Jr.
See Blish, James (Benjamin)

Atherton, Gertrude (Franklin Horn)
1857-1948 .... **TCLC 2**
See also CA 104; 155; DLB 9, 78, 186; HGG; RGAL 4; SUFW 1; TCWW 2

Atherton, Lucius
See Masters, Edgar Lee

Atkins, Jack
See Harris, Mark

Atkinson, Kate 1951- .... **CLC 99**
See also CA 166; CANR 101; DLB 267

Attaway, William (Alexander)
1911-1986 .... **BLC 1; CLC 92**
See also BW 2, 3; CA 143; CANR 82; DAM MULT; DLB 76

Atticus
See Fleming, Ian (Lancaster); Wilson, (Thomas) Woodrow

Atwood, Margaret (Eleanor) 1939- ... **CLC 2, 3, 4, 8, 13, 15, 25, 44, 84, 135; PC 8; SSC 2, 46; WLC**
See also AAYA 12, 47; BEST 89:2; BPFB 1; CA 49-52; CANR 3, 24, 33, 59, 95; CN 7; CP 7; CPW; CWP; DA; DA3; DAB; DAC; DAM MST, NOV, POET; DLB 53, 251; EWL 3; EXPN; FW; INT CANR-24; LAIT 5; MTCW 1, 2; NFS 4, 12, 13, 14; PFS 7; RGSF 2; SATA 50; SSFS 3, 13; TWA; YAW

Aubigny, Pierre d'
See Mencken, H(enry) L(ouis)

Aubin, Penelope 1685-1731(?) .... **LC 9**
See also DLB 39

Auchincloss, Louis (Stanton) 1917- .. **CLC 4, 6, 9, 18, 45; SSC 22**
See also AMWS 4; CA 1-4R; CANR 6, 29, 55, 87; CN 7; DAM NOV; DLB 2, 244; DLBY 1980; EWL 3; INT CANR-29; MTCW 1; RGAL 4

Auden, W(ystan) H(ugh) 1907-1973 . **CLC 1, 2, 3, 4, 6, 9, 11, 14, 43, 123; PC 1; WLC**
See also AAYA 18; AMWS 2; BRW 7; BRWR 1; CA 9-12R; 45-48; CANR 5, 61, 105; CDBLB 1914-1945; DA; DA3; DAB; DAC; DAM DRAM, MST, POET; DLB 10, 20; EWL 3; EXPP; MTCW 1, 2; PAB; PFS 1, 3, 4, 10; TUS; WP

Audiberti, Jacques 1900-1965 .... **CLC 38**
See also CA 25-28R; DAM DRAM; EWL 3

Audubon, John James 1785-1851 . **NCLC 47**
See also ANW; DLB 248

Auel, Jean M(arie) 1936- .... **CLC 31, 107**
See also AAYA 7; BEST 90:4; BPFB 1; CA 103; CANR 21, 64, 115; CPW; DA3; DAM POP; INT CANR-21; NFS 11; RHW; SATA 91

Auerbach, Erich 1892-1957 .... **TCLC 43**
See also CA 118; 155; EWL 3

Augier, Emile 1820-1889 .... **NCLC 31**
See also DLB 192; GFL 1789 to the Present

August, John
See De Voto, Bernard (Augustine)

Augustine, St. 354-430 .... **CMLC 6; WLCS**
See also DA; DA3; DAB; DAC; DAM MST; DLB 115; EW 1; RGWL 2, 3

Aunt Belinda
See Braddon, Mary Elizabeth

Aunt Weedy
See Alcott, Louisa May

Aurelius
See Bourne, Randolph S(illiman)

Aurelius, Marcus 121-180 .... **CMLC 45**
See Marcus Aurelius
See also RGWL 2, 3

Aurobindo, Sri
See Ghose, Aurabinda

Aurobindo Ghose
See Ghose, Aurabinda

Austen, Jane 1775-1817 ...... **NCLC 1, 13, 19, 33, 51, 81, 95, 119; WLC**
See also AAYA 19; BRW 4; BRWC 1; BRWR 2; BYA 3; CDBLB 1789-1832; DA; DA3; DAB; DAC; DAM MST, NOV; DLB 116; EXPN; LAIT 2; LATS 1; LMFS 1; NFS 1, 14; TEA; WLIT 3; WYAS 1

Auster, Paul 1947- .... **CLC 47, 131**
See also AMWS 12; CA 69-72; CANR 23, 52, 75; CMW 4; CN 7; DA3; DLB 227; MTCW 1; SUFW 2

Austin, Frank
See Faust, Frederick (Schiller)
See also TCWW 2

Austin, Mary (Hunter) 1868-1934 . **TCLC 25**
See Stairs, Gordon
See also ANW; CA 109; 178; DLB 9, 78, 206, 221, 275; FW; TCWW 2

Averroes 1126-1198 .... **CMLC 7**
See also DLB 115

Avicenna 980-1037 .... **CMLC 16**
See also DLB 115

Avison, Margaret 1918- .... **CLC 2, 4, 97**
See also CA 17-20R; CP 7; DAC; DAM POET; DLB 53; MTCW 1

Axton, David
See Koontz, Dean R(ay)

Ayckbourn, Alan 1939- ...... **CLC 5, 8, 18, 33, 74; DC 13**
See also BRWS 5; CA 21-24R; CANR 31, 59, 118; CBD; CD 5; DAB; DAM DRAM; DFS 7; DLB 13, 245; EWL 3; MTCW 1, 2

Aydy, Catherine
See Tennant, Emma (Christina)

Ayme, Marcel (Andre) 1902-1967 ... **CLC 11; SSC 41**
See also CA 89-92; CANR 67; CLR 25; DLB 72; EW 12; EWL 3; GFL 1789 to the Present; RGSF 2; RGWL 2, 3; SATA 91

Ayrton, Michael 1921-1975 .... **CLC 7**
See also CA 5-8R; 61-64; CANR 9, 21

Aytmatov, Chingiz
See Aitmatov, Chingiz (Torekulovich)
See also EWL 3

Azorin .... **CLC 11**
See Martinez Ruiz, Jose
See also EW 9; EWL 3

Azuela, Mariano 1873-1952 .. **HLC 1; TCLC 3**
See also CA 104; 131; CANR 81; DAM MULT; EWL 3; HW 1, 2; LAW; MTCW 1, 2

Ba, Mariama 1929-1981 .... **BLCS**
See also AFW; BW 2; CA 141; CANR 87; DNFS 2; WLIT 2

Baastad, Babbis Friis
See Friis-Baastad, Babbis Ellinor

Bab
See Gilbert, W(illiam) S(chwenck)

Babbis, Eleanor
See Friis-Baastad, Babbis Ellinor

Babel, Isaac
See Babel, Isaak (Emmanuilovich)
See also EW 11; SSFS 10

Babel, Isaak (Emmanuilovich)
1894-1941(?) .... **SSC 16; TCLC 2, 13**
See Babel, Isaac
See also CA 104; 155; CANR 113; DLB 272; EWL 3; MTCW 1; RGSF 2; RGWL 2, 3; TWA

Babits, Mihaly 1883-1941 .... **TCLC 14**
See also CA 114; CDWLB 4; DLB 215; EWL 3

Babur 1483-1530 .... **LC 18**

Babylas 1898-1962
See Ghelderode, Michel de

Baca, Jimmy Santiago 1952- . **HLC 1; PC 41**
See also CA 131; CANR 81, 90; CP 7; DAM MULT; DLB 122; HW 1, 2

Baca, Jose Santiago
See Baca, Jimmy Santiago

Bacchelli, Riccardo 1891-1985 .... **CLC 19**
See also CA 29-32R; 117; DLB 264; EWL 3

Bach, Richard (David) 1936- .... **CLC 14**
See also AITN 1; BEST 89:2; BPFB 1; BYA 5; CA 9-12R; CANR 18, 93; CPW; DAM NOV, POP; FANT; MTCW 1; SATA 13

Bache, Benjamin Franklin
1769-1798 .... **LC 74**
See also DLB 43

Barnes, William 1801-1886 .... **NCLC 75**
 See also DLB 32
Baroja (y Nessi), Pio 1872-1956 .... **HLC 1;**
 TCLC 8
 See also CA 104; EW 9
Baron, David
 See Pinter, Harold
Baron Corvo
 See Rolfe, Frederick (William Serafino
 Austin Lewis Mary)
Barondess, Sue K(aufman)
 1926-1977 .... **CLC 8**
 See Kaufman, Sue
 See also CA 1-4R; 69-72; CANR 1
Baron de Teive
 See Pessoa, Fernando (Antonio Nogueira)
Baroness Von S.
 See Zangwill, Israel
Barres, (Auguste-)Maurice
 1862-1923 .... **TCLC 47**
 See also CA 164; DLB 123; GFL 1789 to
 the Present
Barreto, Afonso Henrique de Lima
 See Lima Barreto, Afonso Henrique de
Barrett, Andrea 1954- .... **CLC 150**
 See also CA 156; CANR 92
Barrett, Michele .... **CLC 65**
Barrett, (Roger) Syd 1946- .... **CLC 35**
Barrett, William (Christopher)
 1913-1992 .... **CLC 27**
 See also CA 13-16R; 139; CANR 11, 67;
 INT CANR-11
Barrie, J(ames) M(atthew)
 1860-1937 .... **TCLC 2**
 See also BRWS 3; BYA 4, 5; CA 104; 136;
 CANR 77; CDBLB 1890-1914; CLR 16;
 CWRI 5; DA3; DAB; DAM DRAM; DFS
 7; DLB 10, 141, 156; EWL 3; FANT;
 MAICYA 1, 2; MTCW 1; SATA 100;
 SUFW; WCH; WLIT 4; YABC 1
Barrington, Michael
 See Moorcock, Michael (John)
Barrol, Grady
 See Bograd, Larry
Barry, Mike
 See Malzberg, Barry N(athaniel)
Barry, Philip 1896-1949 .... **TCLC 11**
 See also CA 109; 199; DFS 9; DLB 7, 228;
 RGAL 4
Bart, Andre Schwarz
 See Schwarz-Bart, Andre
Barth, John (Simmons) 1930- ... **CLC 1, 2, 3,**
 5, 7, 9, 10, 14, 27, 51, 89; SSC 10
 See also AITN 1, 2; AMW; BPFB 1; CA
 1-4R; CABS 1; CANR 5, 23, 49, 64, 113;
 CN 7; DAM NOV; DLB 2, 227; EWL 3;
 FANT; MTCW 1; RGAL 4; RGSF 2;
 RHW; SSFS 6; TUS
Barthelme, Donald 1931-1989 ... **CLC 1, 2, 3,**
 5, 6, 8, 13, 23, 46, 59, 115; SSC 2, 55
 See also AMWS 4; BPFB 1; CA 21-24R;
 129; CANR 20, 58; DA3; DAM NOV;
 DLB 2, 234; DLBY 1980, 1989; EWL 3;
 FANT; LMFS 2; MTCW 1, 2; RGAL 4;
 RGSF 2; SATA 7; SATA-Obit 62; SSFS
 17
Barthelme, Frederick 1943- ...... **CLC 36, 117**
 See also AMWS 11; CA 114; 122; CANR
 77; CN 7; CSW; DLB 244; DLBY 1985;
 EWL 3; INT CA-122
Barthes, Roland (Gerard)
 1915-1980 .... **CLC 24, 83; TCLC 135**
 See also CA 130; 97-100; CANR 66; EW
 13; EWL 3; GFL 1789 to the Present;
 MTCW 1, 2; TWA
Barzun, Jacques (Martin) 1907- ..... **CLC 51,**
 145
 See also CA 61-64; CANR 22, 95

Bashevis, Isaac
 See Singer, Isaac Bashevis
Bashkirtseff, Marie 1859-1884 .... **NCLC 27**
Basho, Matsuo
 See Matsuo Basho
 See also RGWL 2, 3; WP
Basil of Caesaria c. 330-379 .... **CMLC 35**
Bass, Kingsley B., Jr.
 See Bullins, Ed
Bass, Rick 1958- .... **CLC 79, 143; SSC 60**
 See also ANW; CA 126; CANR 53, 93;
 CSW; DLB 212, 275
Bassani, Giorgio 1916-2000 .... **CLC 9**
 See also CA 65-68; 190; CANR 33; CWW
 2; DLB 128, 177; EWL 3; MTCW 1;
 RGWL 2, 3
Bastian, Ann .... **CLC 70**
Bastos, Augusto (Antonio) Roa
 See Roa Bastos, Augusto (Antonio)
Bataille, Georges 1897-1962 .... **CLC 29**
 See also CA 101; 89-92; EWL 3
Bates, H(erbert) E(rnest)
 1905-1974 .... **CLC 46; SSC 10**
 See also CA 93-96; 45-48; CANR 34; DA3;
 DAB; DAM POP; DLB 162, 191; EWL
 3; EXPS; MTCW 1, 2; RGSF 2; SSFS 7
Bauchart
 See Camus, Albert
Baudelaire, Charles 1821-1867 . **NCLC 6, 29,**
 55; PC 1; SSC 18; WLC
 See also DA; DA3; DAB; DAC; DAM
 MST, POET; DLB 217; EW 7; GFL 1789
 to the Present; LMFS 2; RGWL 2, 3;
 TWA
Baudouin, Marcel
 See Peguy, Charles (Pierre)
Baudouin, Pierre
 See Peguy, Charles (Pierre)
Baudrillard, Jean 1929- .... **CLC 60**
Baum, L(yman) Frank 1856-1919 .. **TCLC 7,**
 132
 See also AAYA 46; CA 108; 133; CLR 15;
 CWRI 5; DLB 22; FANT; JRDA; MAI-
 CYA 1, 2; MTCW 1, 2; NFS 13; RGAL
 4; SATA 18, 100; WCH
Baum, Louis F.
 See Baum, L(yman) Frank
Baumbach, Jonathan 1933- .... **CLC 6, 23**
 See also CA 13-16R; CAAS 5; CANR 12,
 66; CN 7; DLBY 1980; INT CANR-12;
 MTCW 1
Bausch, Richard (Carl) 1945- .... **CLC 51**
 See also AMWS 7; CA 101; CAAS 14;
 CANR 43, 61, 87; CSW; DLB 130
Baxter, Charles (Morley) 1947- . **CLC 45, 78**
 See also CA 57-60; CANR 40, 64, 104;
 CPW; DAM POP; DLB 130; MTCW 2
Baxter, George Owen
 See Faust, Frederick (Schiller)
Baxter, James K(eir) 1926-1972 .... **CLC 14**
 See also CA 77-80; EWL 3
Baxter, John
 See Hunt, E(verette) Howard, (Jr.)
Bayer, Sylvia
 See Glassco, John
Baynton, Barbara 1857-1929 .... **TCLC 57**
 See also DLB 230; RGSF 2
Beagle, Peter S(oyer) 1939- .... **CLC 7, 104**
 See also AAYA 47; BPFB 1; BYA 9, 10;
 CA 9-12R; CANR 4, 51, 73, 110; DA3;
 DLBY 1980; FANT; INT CANR-4;
 MTCW 1; SATA 60, 130; SUFW 1, 2;
 YAW
Bean, Normal
 See Burroughs, Edgar Rice
Beard, Charles A(ustin)
 1874-1948 .... **TCLC 15**
 See also CA 115; 189; DLB 17; SATA 18

Beardsley, Aubrey 1872-1898 .... **NCLC 6**
Beattie, Ann 1947- ..... **CLC 8, 13, 18, 40, 63,**
 146; SSC 11
 See also AMWS 5; BEST 90:2; BPFB 1;
 CA 81-84; CANR 53, 73; CN 7; CPW;
 DA3; DAM NOV, POP; DLB 218, 278;
 DLBY 1982; EWL 3; MTCW 1, 2; RGAL
 4; RGSF 2; SSFS 9; TUS
Beattie, James 1735-1803 .... **NCLC 25**
 See also DLB 109
Beauchamp, Kathleen Mansfield 1888-1923
 See Mansfield, Katherine
 See also CA 104; 134; DA; DA3; DAC;
 DAM MST; MTCW 2; TEA
Beaumarchais, Pierre-Augustin Caron de
 1732-1799 .... **DC 4; LC 61**
 See also DAM DRAM; DFS 14, 16; EW 4;
 GFL Beginnings to 1789; RGWL 2, 3
Beaumont, Francis 1584(?)-1616 .. **DC 6; LC**
 33
 See also BRW 2; CDBLB Before 1660;
 DLB 58; TEA
Beauvoir, Simone (Lucie Ernestine Marie
 Bertrand) de 1908-1986 .... **CLC 1, 2, 4,**
 8, 14, 31, 44, 50, 71, 124; SSC 35;
 WLC
 See also BPFB 1; CA 9-12R; 118; CANR
 28, 61; DA; DA3; DAB; DAC; DAM
 MST, NOV; DLB 72; DLBY 1986; EW
 12; EWL 3; FW; GFL 1789 to the Present;
 LMFS 2; MTCW 1, 2; RGSF 2; RGWL
 2, 3; TWA
Becker, Carl (Lotus) 1873-1945 ..... **TCLC 63**
 See also CA 157; DLB 17
Becker, Jurek 1937-1997 .... **CLC 7, 19**
 See also CA 85-88; 157; CANR 60, 117;
 CWW 2; DLB 75; EWL 3
Becker, Walter 1950- .... **CLC 26**
Beckett, Samuel (Barclay)
 1906-1989 .. **CLC 1, 2, 3, 4, 6, 9, 10, 11,**
 14, 18, 29, 57, 59, 83; SSC 16; WLC
 See also BRWR 1; BRWS 1; CA 5-8R; 130;
 CANR 33, 61; CBD; CDBLB 1945-1960;
 DA; DA3; DAB; DAC; DAM DRAM,
 MST, NOV; DFS 2, 7; DLB 13, 15, 233;
 DLBY 1990; EWL 3; GFL 1789 to the
 Present; LATS 1; LMFS 2; MTCW 1, 2;
 RGSF 2; RGWL 2, 3; SSFS 15; TEA;
 WLIT 4
Beckford, William 1760-1844 .... **NCLC 16**
 See also BRW 3; DLB 39, 213; HGG;
 LMFS 1; SUFW
Beckham, Barry (Earl) 1944- .... **BLC 1**
 See also BW 1; CA 29-32R; CANR 26, 62;
 CN 7; DAM MULT; DLB 33
Beckman, Gunnel 1910- .... **CLC 26**
 See also CA 33-36R; CANR 15, 114; CLR
 25; MAICYA 1, 2; SAAS 9; SATA 6
Becque, Henri 1837-1899 .... **DC 21; NCLC 3**
 See also DLB 192; GFL 1789 to the Present
Becquer, Gustavo Adolfo
 1836-1870 .... **HLCS 1; NCLC 106**
 See also DAM MULT
Beddoes, Thomas Lovell 1803-1849 .. **DC 15;**
 NCLC 3
 See also DLB 96
Bede c. 673-735 .... **CMLC 20**
 See also DLB 146; TEA
Bedford, Denton R. 1907-(?) .... **NNAL**
Bedford, Donald F.
 See Fearing, Kenneth (Flexner)
Beecher, Catharine Esther
 1800-1878 .... **NCLC 30**
 See also DLB 1, 243
Beecher, John 1904-1980 .... **CLC 6**
 See also AITN 1; CA 5-8R; 105; CANR 8
Beer, Johann 1655-1700 .... **LC 5**
 See also DLB 168

Bergelson, David 1884-1952 .... **TCLC 81**
See Bergelson, Dovid
Bergelson, Dovid
See Bergelson, David
See also EWL 3
Berger, Colonel
See Malraux, (Georges-)Andre
Berger, John (Peter) 1926- .... **CLC 2, 19**
See also BRWS 4; CA 81-84; CANR 51,
78, 117; CN 7; DLB 14, 207
Berger, Melvin H. 1927- .... **CLC 12**
See also CA 5-8R; CANR 4; CLR 32;
SAAS 2; SATA 5, 88; SATA-Essay 124
Berger, Thomas (Louis) 1924- .. **CLC 3, 5, 8,
11, 18, 38**
See also BPFB 1; CA 1-4R; CANR 5, 28,
51; CN 7; DAM NOV; DLB 2; DLBY
1980; EWL 3; FANT; INT CANR-28;
MTCW 1, 2; RHW; TCWW 2
Bergman, (Ernst) Ingmar 1918- ...... **CLC 16,
72**
See also CA 81-84; CANR 33, 70; DLB
257; MTCW 2
Bergson, Henri(-Louis) 1859-1941 . **TCLC 32**
See also CA 164; EW 8; EWL 3; GFL 1789
to the Present
Bergstein, Eleanor 1938- .... **CLC 4**
See also CA 53-56; CANR 5
Berkeley, George 1685-1753 .... **LC 65**
See also DLB 31, 101, 252
Berkoff, Steven 1937- .... **CLC 56**
See also CA 104; CANR 72; CBD; CD 5
Berlin, Isaiah 1909-1997 .... **TCLC 105**
See also CA 85-88; 162
Bermant, Chaim (Icyk) 1929-1998 ... **CLC 40**
See also CA 57-60; CANR 6, 31, 57, 105;
CN 7
Bern, Victoria
See Fisher, M(ary) F(rances) K(ennedy)
Bernanos, (Paul Louis) Georges
1888-1948 .... **TCLC 3**
See also CA 104; 130; CANR 94; DLB 72;
EWL 3; GFL 1789 to the Present; RGWL
2, 3
Bernard, April 1956- .... **CLC 59**
See also CA 131
Berne, Victoria
See Fisher, M(ary) F(rances) K(ennedy)
Bernhard, Thomas 1931-1989 ..... **CLC 3, 32,
61; DC 14**
See also CA 85-88; 127; CANR 32, 57; CD-
WLB 2; DLB 85, 124; EWL 3; MTCW 1;
RGWL 2, 3
Bernhardt, Sarah (Henriette Rosine)
1844-1923 .... **TCLC 75**
See also CA 157
Bernstein, Charles 1950- .... **CLC 142**
See also CA 129; CAAS 24; CANR 90; CP
7; DLB 169
Berriault, Gina 1926-1999 .... **CLC 54, 109;
SSC 30**
See also CA 116; 129; 185; CANR 66; DLB
130; SSFS 7,11
Berrigan, Daniel 1921- .... **CLC 4**
See also CA 33-36R; CAAE 187; CAAS 1;
CANR 11, 43, 78; CP 7; DLB 5
Berrigan, Edmund Joseph Michael, Jr.
1934-1983
See Berrigan, Ted
See also CA 61-64; 110; CANR 14, 102
Berrigan, Ted .... **CLC 37**
See Berrigan, Edmund Joseph Michael, Jr.
See also DLB 5, 169; WP
Berry, Charles Edward Anderson 1931-
See Berry, Chuck
See also CA 115
Berry, Chuck .... **CLC 17**
See Berry, Charles Edward Anderson

Berry, Jonas
See Ashbery, John (Lawrence)
See also GLL 1
Berry, Wendell (Erdman) 1934- ... **CLC 4, 6,
8, 27, 46; PC 28**
See also AITN 1; AMWS 10; ANW; CA
73-76; CANR 50, 73, 101; CP 7; CSW;
DAM POET; DLB 5, 6, 234, 275; MTCW
1
Berryman, John 1914-1972 ... **CLC 1, 2, 3, 4,
6, 8, 10, 13, 25, 62**
See also AMW; CA 13-16; 33-36R; CABS
2; CANR 35; CAP 1; CDALB 1941-1968;
DAM POET; DLB 48; EWL 3; MTCW 1,
2; PAB; RGAL 4; WP
Bertolucci, Bernardo 1940- ...... **CLC 16, 157**
See also CA 106
Berton, Pierre (Francis Demarigny)
1920- .... **CLC 104**
See also CA 1-4R; CANR 2, 56; CPW;
DLB 68; SATA 99
Bertrand, Aloysius 1807-1841 .... **NCLC 31**
See Bertrand, Louis oAloysiusc
Bertrand, Louis oAloysiusc
See Bertrand, Aloysius
See also DLB 217
Bertran de Born c. 1140-1215 .... **CMLC 5**
Besant, Annie (Wood) 1847-1933 ..... **TCLC 9**
See also CA 105; 185
Bessie, Alvah 1904-1985 .... **CLC 23**
See also CA 5-8R; 116; CANR 2, 80; DLB
26
Bethlen, T. D.
See Silverberg, Robert
Beti, Mongo .... **BLC 1; CLC 27**
See Biyidi, Alexandre
See also AFW; CANR 79; DAM MULT;
EWL 3; WLIT 2
Betjeman, John 1906-1984 ...... **CLC 2, 6, 10,
34, 43**
See also BRW 7; CA 9-12R; 112; CANR
33, 56; CDBLB 1945-1960; DA3; DAB;
DAM MST, POET; DLB 20; DLBY 1984;
EWL 3; MTCW 1, 2
Bettelheim, Bruno 1903-1990 .... **CLC 79**
See also CA 81-84; 131; CANR 23, 61;
DA3; MTCW 1, 2
Betti, Ugo 1892-1953 .... **TCLC 5**
See also CA 104; 155; EWL 3; RGWL 2, 3
Betts, Doris (Waugh) 1932- ..... **CLC 3, 6, 28;
SSC 45**
See also CA 13-16R; CANR 9, 66, 77; CN
7; CSW; DLB 218; DLBY 1982; INT
CANR-9; RGAL 4
Bevan, Alistair
See Roberts, Keith (John Kingston)
Bey, Pilaff
See Douglas, (George) Norman
Bialik, Chaim Nachman
1873-1934 .... **TCLC 25**
See also CA 170; EWL 3
Bickerstaff, Isaac
See Swift, Jonathan
Bidart, Frank 1939- .... **CLC 33**
See also CA 140; CANR 106; CP 7
Bienek, Horst 1930- .... **CLC 7, 11**
See also CA 73-76; DLB 75
Bierce, Ambrose (Gwinett)
1842-1914(?) ..... **SSC 9; TCLC 1, 7, 44;
WLC**
See also AMW; BYA 11; CA 104; 139;
CANR 78; CDALB 1865-1917; DA;
DA3; DAC; DAM MST; DLB 11, 12, 23,
71, 74, 186; EWL 3; EXPS; HGG; LAIT
2; RGAL 4; RGSF 2; SSFS 9; SUFW 1
Biggers, Earl Derr 1884-1933 .... **TCLC 65**
See also CA 108; 153
Billiken, Bud
See Motley, Willard (Francis)

Billings, Josh
See Shaw, Henry Wheeler
Billington, (Lady) Rachel (Mary)
1942- .... **CLC 43**
See also AITN 2; CA 33-36R; CANR 44;
CN 7
Binchy, Maeve 1940- .... **CLC 153**
See also BEST 90:1; BPFB 1; CA 127; 134;
CANR 50, 96; CN 7; CPW; DA3; DAM
POP; INT CA-134; MTCW 1; RHW
Binyon, T(imothy) J(ohn) 1936- .... **CLC 34**
See also CA 111; CANR 28
Bion 335B.C.-245B.C. .... **CMLC 39**
Bioy Casares, Adolfo 1914-1999 ... **CLC 4, 8,
13, 88; HLC 1; SSC 17**
See Casares, Adolfo Bioy; Miranda, Javier;
Sacastru, Martin
See also CA 29-32R; 177; CANR 19, 43,
66; DAM MULT; DLB 113; EWL 3; HW
1, 2; LAW; MTCW 1, 2
Birch, Allison .... **CLC 65**
Bird, Cordwainer
See Ellison, Harlan (Jay)
Bird, Robert Montgomery
1806-1854 .... **NCLC 1**
See also DLB 202; RGAL 4
Birkerts, Sven 1951- .... **CLC 116**
See also CA 128; 133, 176; CAAE 176;
CAAS 29; INT 133
Birney, (Alfred) Earle 1904-1995 .. **CLC 1, 4,
6, 11**
See also CA 1-4R; CANR 5, 20; CP 7;
DAC; DAM MST, POET; DLB 88;
MTCW 1; PFS 8; RGEL 2
Biruni, al 973-1048(?) .... **CMLC 28**
Bishop, Elizabeth 1911-1979 ..... **CLC 1, 4, 9,
13, 15, 32; PC 3, 34; TCLC 121**
See also AMWR 2; AMWS 1; CA 5-8R;
89-92; CABS 2; CANR 26, 61, 108;
CDALB 1968-1988; DA; DA3; DAC;
DAM MST, POET; DLB 5, 169; EWL 3;
GLL 2; MAWW; MTCW 1, 2; PAB; PFS
6, 12; RGAL 4; SATA-Obit 24; TUS; WP
Bishop, John 1935- .... **CLC 10**
See also CA 105
Bishop, John Peale 1892-1944 ..... **TCLC 103**
See also CA 107; 155; DLB 4, 9, 45; RGAL
4
Bissett, Bill 1939- .... **CLC 18; PC 14**
See also CA 69-72; CAAS 19; CANR 15;
CCA 1; CP 7; DLB 53; MTCW 1
Bissoondath, Neil (Devindra)
1955- .... **CLC 120**
See also CA 136; CN 7; DAC
Bitov, Andrei (Georgievich) 1937- ... **CLC 57**
See also CA 142
Biyidi, Alexandre 1932-
See Beti, Mongo
See also BW 1, 3; CA 114; 124; CANR 81;
DA3; MTCW 1, 2
Bjarme, Brynjolf
See Ibsen, Henrik (Johan)
Bjoernson, Bjoernstjerne (Martinius)
1832-1910 .... **TCLC 7, 37**
See also CA 104
Black, Robert
See Holdstock, Robert P.
Blackburn, Paul 1926-1971 .... **CLC 9, 43**
See also BG 2; CA 81-84; 33-36R; CANR
34; DLB 16; DLBY 1981
Black Elk 1863-1950 .... **NNAL; TCLC 33**
See also CA 144; DAM MULT; MTCW 1;
WP
Black Hawk 1767-1838 .... **NNAL**
Black Hobart
See Sanders, (James) Ed(ward)
Blacklin, Malcolm
See Chambers, Aidan

Bunyan, John 1628-1688 ..... **LC 4, 69; WLC**
See also BRW 2; BYA 5; CDBLB 1660-1789; DA; DAB; DAC; DAM MST; DLB 39; RGEL 2; TEA; WCH; WLIT 3

Buravsky, Alexandr .... **CLC 59**

Burckhardt, Jacob (Christoph) 1818-1897 .... **NCLC 49**
See also EW 6

Burford, Eleanor
See Hibbert, Eleanor Alice Burford

Burgess, Anthony . **CLC 1, 2, 4, 5, 8, 10, 13, 15, 22, 40, 62, 81, 94**
See Wilson, John (Anthony) Burgess
See also AAYA 25; AITN 1; BRWS 1; CD-BLB 1960 to Present; DAB; DLB 14, 194, 261; DLBY 1998; EWL 3; MTCW 1; RGEL 2; RHW; SFW 4; YAW

Burke, Edmund 1729(?)-1797 .... **LC 7, 36; WLC**
See also BRW 3; DA; DA3; DAB; DAC; DAM MST; DLB 104, 252; RGEL 2; TEA

Burke, Kenneth (Duva) 1897-1993 ... **CLC 2, 24**
See also AMW; CA 5-8R; 143; CANR 39, 74; DLB 45, 63; EWL 3; MTCW 1, 2; RGAL 4

Burke, Leda
See Garnett, David

Burke, Ralph
See Silverberg, Robert

Burke, Thomas 1886-1945 .... **TCLC 63**
See also CA 113; 155; CMW 4; DLB 197

Burney, Fanny 1752-1840 .... **NCLC 12, 54, 107**
See also BRWS 3; DLB 39; NFS 16; RGEL 2; TEA

Burney, Frances
See Burney, Fanny

Burns, Robert 1759-1796 ... **LC 3, 29, 40; PC 6; WLC**
See also BRW 3; CDBLB 1789-1832; DA; DA3; DAB; DAC; DAM MST, POET; DLB 109; EXPP; PAB; RGEL 2; TEA; WP

Burns, Tex
See L'Amour, Louis (Dearborn)
See also TCWW 2

Burnshaw, Stanley 1906- .... **CLC 3, 13, 44**
See also CA 9-12R; CP 7; DLB 48; DLBY 1997

Burr, Anne 1937- .... **CLC 6**
See also CA 25-28R

Burroughs, Edgar Rice 1875-1950 . **TCLC 2, 32**
See also AAYA 11; BPFB 1; BYA 4, 9; CA 104; 132; DA3; DAM NOV; DLB 8; FANT; MTCW 1, 2; RGAL 4; SATA 41; SCFW 2; SFW 4; TUS; YAW

Burroughs, William S(eward) 1914-1997 .. **CLC 1, 2, 5, 15, 22, 42, 75, 109; TCLC 121; WLC**
See Lee, William; Lee, Willy
See also AITN 2; AMWS 3; BG 2; BPFB 1; CA 9-12R; 160; CANR 20, 52, 104; CN 7; CPW; DA; DA3; DAB; DAC; DAM MST, NOV, POP; DLB 2, 8, 16, 152, 237; DLBY 1981, 1997; EWL 3; HGG; LMFS 2; MTCW 1, 2; RGAL 4; SFW 4

Burton, Sir Richard F(rancis) 1821-1890 .... **NCLC 42**
See also DLB 55, 166, 184

Burton, Robert 1577-1640 .... **LC 74**
See also DLB 151; RGEL 2

Buruma, Ian 1951- .... **CLC 163**
See also CA 128; CANR 65

Busch, Frederick 1941- ... **CLC 7, 10, 18, 47, 166**
See also CA 33-36R; CAAS 1; CANR 45, 73, 92; CN 7; DLB 6, 218

Bush, Barney (Furman) 1946- .... **NNAL**
See also CA 145

Bush, Ronald 1946- .... **CLC 34**
See also CA 136

Bustos, F(rancisco)
See Borges, Jorge Luis

Bustos Domecq, H(onorio)
See Bioy Casares, Adolfo; Borges, Jorge Luis

Butler, Octavia E(stelle) 1947- .. **BLCS; CLC 38, 121**
See also AAYA 18, 48; AFAW 2; BPFB 1; BW 2, 3; CA 73-76; CANR 12, 24, 38, 73; CLR 65; CPW; DA3; DAM MULT, POP; DLB 33; LATS 1; MTCW 1, 2; NFS 8; SATA 84; SCFW 2; SFW 4; SSFS 6; YAW

Butler, Robert Olen, (Jr.) 1945- ...... **CLC 81, 162**
See also AMWS 12; BPFB 1; CA 112; CANR 66; CSW; DAM POP; DLB 173; INT CA-112; MTCW 1; SSFS 11

Butler, Samuel 1612-1680 .... **LC 16, 43**
See also DLB 101, 126; RGEL 2

Butler, Samuel 1835-1902 .... **TCLC 1, 33; WLC**
See also BRWS 2; CA 143; CDBLB 1890-1914; DA; DA3; DAB; DAC; DAM MST, NOV; DLB 18, 57, 174; RGEL 2; SFW 4; TEA

Butler, Walter C.
See Faust, Frederick (Schiller)

Butor, Michel (Marie Francois) 1926- .... **CLC 1, 3, 8, 11, 15, 161**
See also CA 9-12R; CANR 33, 66; DLB 83; EW 13; EWL 3; GFL 1789 to the Present; MTCW 1, 2

Butts, Mary 1890(?)-1937 .... **TCLC 77**
See also CA 148; DLB 240

Buxton, Ralph
See Silverstein, Alvin; Silverstein, Virginia B(arbara Opshelor)

Buzo, Alexander (John) 1944- .... **CLC 61**
See also CA 97-100; CANR 17, 39, 69; CD 5

Buzzati, Dino 1906-1972 .... **CLC 36**
See also CA 160; 33-36R; DLB 177; RGWL 2, 3; SFW 4

Byars, Betsy (Cromer) 1928- .... **CLC 35**
See also AAYA 19; BYA 3; CA 33-36R, 183; CAAE 183; CANR 18, 36, 57, 102; CLR 1, 16, 72; DLB 52; INT CANR-18; JRDA; MAICYA 1, 2; MAICYAS 1; MTCW 1; SAAS 1; SATA 4, 46, 80; SATA-Essay 108; WYA; YAW

Byatt, A(ntonia) S(usan Drabble) 1936- .... **CLC 19, 65, 136**
See also BPFB 1; BRWS 4; CA 13-16R; CANR 13, 33, 50, 75, 96; DA3; DAM NOV, POP; DLB 14, 194; EWL 3; MTCW 1, 2; RGSF 2; RHW; TEA

Byrne, David 1952- .... **CLC 26**
See also CA 127

Byrne, John Keyes 1926-
See Leonard, Hugh
See also CA 102; CANR 78; INT CA-102

Byron, George Gordon (Noel) 1788-1824 ..... **NCLC 2, 12, 109; PC 16; WLC**
See also BRW 4; CDBLB 1789-1832; DA; DA3; DAB; DAC; DAM MST, POET; DLB 96, 110; EXPP; LMFS 1; PAB; PFS 1, 14; RGEL 2; TEA; WLIT 3; WP

Byron, Robert 1905-1941 .... **TCLC 67**
See also CA 160; DLB 195

C. 3. 3.
See Wilde, Oscar (Fingal O'Flahertie Wills)

Caballero, Fernan 1796-1877 .... **NCLC 10**

Cabell, Branch
See Cabell, James Branch

Cabell, James Branch 1879-1958 .... **TCLC 6**
See also CA 105; 152; DLB 9, 78; FANT; MTCW 1; RGEL 4; SUFW 1

Cabeza de Vaca, Alvar Nunez 1490-1557(?) .... **LC 61**

Cable, George Washington 1844-1925 .... **SSC 4; TCLC 4**
See also CA 104; 155; DLB 12, 74; DLBD 13; RGAL 4; TUS

Cabral de Melo Neto, Joao 1920-1999 .... **CLC 76**
See Melo Neto, Joao Cabral de
See also CA 151; DAM MULT; LAW; LAWS 1

Cabrera Infante, G(uillermo) 1929- . **CLC 5, 25, 45, 120; HLC 1; SSC 39**
See also CA 85-88; CANR 29, 65, 110; CD-WLB 3; DA3; DAM MULT; DLB 113; EWL 3; HW 1, 2; LAW; LAWS 1; MTCW 1, 2; RGSF 2; WLIT 1

Cade, Toni
See Bambara, Toni Cade

Cadmus and Harmonia
See Buchan, John

Caedmon fl. 658-680 .... **CMLC 7**
See also DLB 146

Caeiro, Alberto
See Pessoa, Fernando (Antonio Nogueira)

Caesar, Julius .... **CMLC 47**
See Julius Caesar
See also AW 1; RGWL 2, 3

Cage, John (Milton, Jr.) 1912-1992 . **CLC 41**
See also CA 13-16R; 169; CANR 9, 78; DLB 193; INT CANR-9

Cahan, Abraham 1860-1951 .... **TCLC 71**
See also CA 108; 154; DLB 9, 25, 28; RGAL 4

Cain, G.
See Cabrera Infante, G(uillermo)

Cain, Guillermo
See Cabrera Infante, G(uillermo)

Cain, James M(allahan) 1892-1977 .. **CLC 3, 11, 28**
See also AITN 1; BPFB 1; CA 17-20R; 73-76; CANR 8, 34, 61; CMW 4; DLB 226; EWL 3; MSW; MTCW 1; RGAL 4

Caine, Hall 1853-1931 .... **TCLC 97**
See also RHW

Caine, Mark
See Raphael, Frederic (Michael)

Calasso, Roberto 1941- .... **CLC 81**
See also CA 143; CANR 89

Calderon de la Barca, Pedro 1600-1681 .... **DC 3; HLCS 1; LC 23**
See also EW 2; RGWL 2, 3; TWA

Caldwell, Erskine (Preston) 1903-1987 .... **CLC 1, 8, 14, 50, 60; SSC 19; TCLC 117**
See also AITN 1; AMW; BPFB 1; CA 1-4R; 121; CAAS 1; CANR 2, 33; DA3; DAM NOV; DLB 9, 86; EWL 3; MTCW 1, 2; RGAL 4; RGSF 2; TUS

Caldwell, (Janet Miriam) Taylor (Holland) 1900-1985 .... **CLC 2, 28, 39**
See also BPFB 1; CA 5-8R; 116; CANR 5; DA3; DAM NOV, POP; DLBD 17; RHW

Calhoun, John Caldwell 1782-1850 .... **NCLC 15**
See also DLB 3, 248

Calisher, Hortense 1911- ..... **CLC 2, 4, 8, 38, 134; SSC 15**
See also CA 1-4R; CANR 1, 22, 117; CN 7; DA3; DAM NOV; DLB 2, 218; INT CANR-22; MTCW 1, 2; RGAL 4; RGSF 2

Callaghan, Morley Edward 1903-1990 .... **CLC 3, 14, 41, 65**
See also CA 9-12R; 132; CANR 33, 73; DAC; DAM MST; DLB 68; EWL 3; MTCW 1, 2; RGEL 2; RGSF 2

Callimachus c. 305B.C.-c. 240B.C. .... **CMLC 18**
See also AW 1; DLB 176; RGWL 2, 3

Calvin, Jean
See Calvin, John
See also GFL Beginnings to 1789

Calvin, John 1509-1564 .... **LC 37**
See Calvin, Jean

Calvino, Italo 1923-1985 .... **CLC 5, 8, 11, 22, 33, 39, 73; SSC 3, 48**
See also CA 85-88; 116; CANR 23, 61; DAM NOV; DLB 196; EW 13; EWL 3; MTCW 1, 2; RGSF 2; RGWL 2, 3; SFW 4; SSFS 12

Camara Laye
See Laye, Camara
See also EWL 3

Camden, William 1551-1623 .... **LC 77**
See also DLB 172

Cameron, Carey 1952- .... **CLC 59**
See also CA 135

Cameron, Peter 1959- .... **CLC 44**
See also AMWS 12; CA 125; CANR 50, 117; DLB 234; GLL 2

Camoens, Luis Vaz de 1524(?)-1580
See Camoes, Luis de
See also EW 2

Camoes, Luis de 1524(?)-1580 . **HLCS 1; LC 62; PC 31**
See Camoens, Luis Vaz de
See also RGWL 2, 3

Campana, Dino 1885-1932 .... **TCLC 20**
See also CA 117; DLB 114; EWL 3

Campanella, Tommaso 1568-1639 .... **LC 32**
See also RGWL 2, 3

Campbell, John W(ood, Jr.) 1910-1971 .... **CLC 32**
See also CA 21-22; 29-32R; CANR 34; CAP 2; DLB 8; MTCW 1; SCFW; SFW 4

Campbell, Joseph 1904-1987 .... **CLC 69**
See also AAYA 3; BEST 89:2; CA 1-4R; 124; CANR 3, 28, 61, 107; DA3; MTCW 1, 2

Campbell, Maria 1940- .... **CLC 85; NNAL**
See also CA 102; CANR 54; CCA 1; DAC

Campbell, Paul N. 1923-
See hooks, bell
See also CA 21-24R

Campbell, (John) Ramsey 1946- ..... **CLC 42; SSC 19**
See also CA 57-60; CANR 7, 102; DLB 261; HGG; INT CANR-7; SUFW 1, 2

Campbell, (Ignatius) Roy (Dunnachie) 1901-1957 .... **TCLC 5**
See also AFW; CA 104; 155; DLB 20, 225; EWL 3; MTCW 2; RGEL 2

Campbell, Thomas 1777-1844 .... **NCLC 19**
See also DLB 93, 144; RGEL 2

Campbell, Wilfred .... **TCLC 9**
See Campbell, William

Campbell, William 1858(?)-1918
See Campbell, Wilfred
See also CA 106; DLB 92

Campion, Jane 1954- .... **CLC 95**
See also AAYA 33; CA 138; CANR 87

Campion, Thomas 1567-1620 .... **LC 78**
See also CDBLB Before 1660; DAM POET; DLB 58, 172; RGEL 2

Camus, Albert 1913-1960 ...... **CLC 1, 2, 4, 9, 11, 14, 32, 63, 69, 124; DC 2; SSC 9; WLC**
See also AAYA 36; AFW; BPFB 1; CA 89-92; DA; DA3; DAB; DAC; DAM DRAM, MST, NOV; DLB 72; EW 13; EWL 3; EXPN; EXPS; GFL 1789 to the Present; LATS 1; LMFS 2; MTCW 1, 2; NFS 6, 16; RGSF 2; RGWL 2, 3; SSFS 4; TWA

Canby, Vincent 1924-2000 .... **CLC 13**
See also CA 81-84; 191

Cancale
See Desnos, Robert

Canetti, Elias 1905-1994 .. **CLC 3, 14, 25, 75, 86**
See also CA 21-24R; 146; CANR 23, 61, 79; CDWLB 2; CWW 2; DA3; DLB 85, 124; EW 12; EWL 3; MTCW 1, 2; RGWL 2, 3; TWA

Canfield, Dorothea F.
See Fisher, Dorothy (Frances) Canfield

Canfield, Dorothea Frances
See Fisher, Dorothy (Frances) Canfield

Canfield, Dorothy
See Fisher, Dorothy (Frances) Canfield

Canin, Ethan 1960- .... **CLC 55**
See also CA 131; 135

Cankar, Ivan 1876-1918 .... **TCLC 105**
See also CDWLB 4; DLB 147; EWL 3

Cannon, Curt
See Hunter, Evan

Cao, Lan 1961- .... **CLC 109**
See also CA 165

Cape, Judith
See Page, P(atricia) K(athleen)
See also CCA 1

Capek, Karel 1890-1938 .... **DC 1; SSC 36; TCLC 6, 37; WLC**
See also CA 104; 140; CDWLB 4; DA; DA3; DAB; DAC; DAM DRAM, MST, NOV; DFS 7, 11; DLB 215; EW 10; EWL 3; MTCW 1; RGSF 2; RGWL 2, 3; SCFW 2; SFW 4

Capote, Truman 1924-1984 . **CLC 1, 3, 8, 13, 19, 34, 38, 58; SSC 2, 47; WLC**
See also AMWS 3; BPFB 1; CA 5-8R; 113; CANR 18, 62; CDALB 1941-1968; CPW; DA; DA3; DAB; DAC; DAM MST, NOV, POP; DLB 2, 185, 227; DLBY 1980, 1984; EWL 3; EXPS; GLL 1; LAIT 3; MTCW 1, 2; NCFS 2; RGAL 4; RGSF 2; SATA 91; SSFS 2; TUS

Capra, Frank 1897-1991 .... **CLC 16**
See also CA 61-64; 135

Caputo, Philip 1941- .... **CLC 32**
See also CA 73-76; CANR 40; YAW

Caragiale, Ion Luca 1852-1912 ...... **TCLC 76**
See also CA 157

Card, Orson Scott 1951- .... **CLC 44, 47, 50**
See also AAYA 11, 42; BPFB 1; BYA 5, 8; CA 102; CANR 27, 47, 73, 102, 106; CPW; DA3; DAM POP; FANT; INT CANR-27; MTCW 1, 2; NFS 5; SATA 83, 127; SCFW 2; SFW 4; SUFW 2; YAW

Cardenal, Ernesto 1925- .... **CLC 31, 161; HLC 1; PC 22**
See also CA 49-52; CANR 2, 32, 66; CWW 2; DAM MULT, POET; EWL 3; HW 1, 2; LAWS 1; MTCW 1, 2; RGWL 2, 3

Cardozo, Benjamin N(athan) 1870-1938 .... **TCLC 65**
See also CA 117; 164

Carducci, Giosue (Alessandro Giuseppe) 1835-1907 .... **PC 46; TCLC 32**
See also CA 163; EW 7; RGWL 2, 3

Carew, Thomas 1595(?)-1640 . **LC 13; PC 29**
See also BRW 2; DLB 126; PAB; RGEL 2

Carey, Ernestine Gilbreth 1908- ...... **CLC 17**
See also CA 5-8R; CANR 71; SATA 2

Carey, Peter 1943- .... **CLC 40, 55, 96**
See also CA 123; 127; CANR 53, 76, 117; CN 7; DA3; INT CA-127; MTCW 1, 2; RGSF 2; SATA 94

Carleton, William 1794-1869 .... **NCLC 3**
See also DLB 159; RGEL 2; RGSF 2

Carlisle, Henry (Coffin) 1926- .... **CLC 33**
See also CA 13-16R; CANR 15, 85

Carlsen, Chris
See Holdstock, Robert P.

Carlson, Ron(ald F.) 1947- .... **CLC 54**
See also CA 105; CAAE 189; CANR 27; DLB 244

Carlyle, Thomas 1795-1881 ..... **NCLC 22, 70**
See also BRW 4; CDBLB 1789-1832; DA; DAB; DAC; DAM MST; DLB 55, 144, 254; RGEL 2; TEA

Carman, (William) Bliss 1861-1929 ... **PC 34; TCLC 7**
See also CA 104; 152; DAC; DLB 92; RGEL 2

Carnegie, Dale 1888-1955 .... **TCLC 53**

Carossa, Hans 1878-1956 .... **TCLC 48**
See also CA 170; DLB 66; EWL 3

Carpenter, Don(ald Richard) 1931-1995 .... **CLC 41**
See also CA 45-48; 149; CANR 1, 71

Carpenter, Edward 1844-1929 .... **TCLC 88**
See also CA 163; GLL 1

Carpenter, John (Howard) 1948- ... **CLC 161**
See also AAYA 2; CA 134; SATA 58

Carpenter, Johnny
See Carpenter, John (Howard)

Carpentier (y Valmont), Alejo 1904-1980 . **CLC 8, 11, 38, 110; HLC 1; SSC 35**
See also CA 65-68; 97-100; CANR 11, 70; CDWLB 3; DAM MULT; DLB 113; EWL 3; HW 1, 2; LAW; LMFS 2; RGSF 2; RGWL 2, 3; WLIT 1

Carr, Caleb 1955(?)- .... **CLC 86**
See also CA 147; CANR 73; DA3

Carr, Emily 1871-1945 .... **TCLC 32**
See also CA 159; DLB 68; FW; GLL 2

Carr, John Dickson 1906-1977 .... **CLC 3**
See Fairbairn, Roger
See also CA 49-52; 69-72; CANR 3, 33, 60; CMW 4; MSW; MTCW 1, 2

Carr, Philippa
See Hibbert, Eleanor Alice Burford

Carr, Virginia Spencer 1929- .... **CLC 34**
See also CA 61-64; DLB 111

Carrere, Emmanuel 1957- .... **CLC 89**
See also CA 200

Carrier, Roch 1937- .... **CLC 13, 78**
See also CA 130; CANR 61; CCA 1; DAC; DAM MST; DLB 53; SATA 105

Carroll, James Dennis
See Carroll, Jim

Carroll, James P. 1943(?)- .... **CLC 38**
See also CA 81-84; CANR 73; MTCW 1

Carroll, Jim 1951- .... **CLC 35, 143**
See Carroll, James Dennis
See also AAYA 17; CA 45-48; CANR 42, 115

Carroll, Lewis ... **NCLC 2, 53; PC 18; WLC**
See Dodgson, Charles L(utwidge)
See also AAYA 39; BRW 5; BYA 5, 13; CD-BLB 1832-1890; CLR 2, 18; DLB 18, 163, 178; DLBY 1998; EXPN; EXPP; FANT; JRDA; LAIT 1; NFS 7; PFS 11; RGEL 2; SUFW 1; TEA; WCH

Carroll, Paul Vincent 1900-1968 ...... **CLC 10**
See also CA 9-12R; 25-28R; DLB 10; EWL 3; RGEL 2

Cliff, Michelle 1946- .... **BLCS; CLC 120**
See also BW 2; CA 116; CANR 39, 72; CD-WLB 3; DLB 157; FW; GLL 2

Clifford, Lady Anne 1590-1676 .... **LC 76**
See also DLB 151

Clifton, (Thelma) Lucille 1936- .... **BLC 1; CLC 19, 66, 162; PC 17**
See also AFAW 2; BW 2, 3; CA 49-52; CANR 2, 24, 42, 76, 97; CLR 5; CP 7; CSW; CWP; CWRI 5; DA3; DAM MULT, POET; DLB 5, 41; EXPP; MAICYA 1, 2; MTCW 1, 2; PFS 1, 14; SATA 20, 69, 128; WP

Clinton, Dirk
See Silverberg, Robert

Clough, Arthur Hugh 1819-1861 ... **NCLC 27**
See also BRW 5; DLB 32; RGEL 2

Clutha, Janet Paterson Frame 1924-
See Frame, Janet
See also CA 1-4R; CANR 2, 36, 76; MTCW 1, 2; SATA 119

Clyne, Terence
See Blatty, William Peter

Cobalt, Martin
See Mayne, William (James Carter)

Cobb, Irvin S(hrewsbury)
1876-1944 .... **TCLC 77**
See also CA 175; DLB 11, 25, 86

Cobbett, William 1763-1835 .... **NCLC 49**
See also DLB 43, 107, 158; RGEL 2

Coburn, D(onald) L(ee) 1938- .... **CLC 10**
See also CA 89-92

Cocteau, Jean (Maurice Eugene Clement)
1889-1963 ...... **CLC 1, 8, 15, 16, 43; DC 17; TCLC 119; WLC**
See also CA 25-28; CANR 40; CAP 2; DA; DA3; DAB; DAC; DAM DRAM, MST, NOV; DLB 65, 258; EW 10; EWL 3; GFL 1789 to the Present; MTCW 1, 2; RGWL 2, 3; TWA

Codrescu, Andrei 1946- .... **CLC 46, 121**
See also CA 33-36R; CAAS 19; CANR 13, 34, 53, 76; DA3; DAM POET; MTCW 2

Coe, Max
See Bourne, Randolph S(illiman)

Coe, Tucker
See Westlake, Donald E(dwin)

Coen, Ethan 1958- .... **CLC 108**
See also CA 126; CANR 85

Coen, Joel 1955- .... **CLC 108**
See also CA 126

The Coen Brothers
See Coen, Ethan; Coen, Joel

Coetzee, J(ohn) M(ichael) 1940- ...... **CLC 23, 33, 66, 117, 161, 162**
See also AAYA 37; AFW; BRWS 6; CA 77-80; CANR 41, 54, 74, 114; CN 7; DA3; DAM NOV; DLB 225; EWL 3; LMFS 2; MTCW 1, 2; WLIT 2

Coffey, Brian
See Koontz, Dean R(ay)

Coffin, Robert P(eter) Tristram
1892-1955 .... **TCLC 95**
See also CA 123; 169; DLB 45

Cohan, George M(ichael)
1878-1942 .... **TCLC 60**
See also CA 157; DLB 249; RGAL 4

Cohen, Arthur A(llen) 1928-1986 ...... **CLC 7, 31**
See also CA 1-4R; 120; CANR 1, 17, 42; DLB 28

Cohen, Leonard (Norman) 1934- ...... **CLC 3, 38**
See also CA 21-24R; CANR 14, 69; CN 7; CP 7; DAC; DAM MST; DLB 53; EWL 3; MTCW 1

Cohen, Matt(hew) 1942-1999 .... **CLC 19**
See also CA 61-64; 187; CAAS 18; CANR 40; CN 7; DAC; DLB 53

Cohen-Solal, Annie 19(?)- .... **CLC 50**

Colegate, Isabel 1931- .... **CLC 36**
See also CA 17-20R; CANR 8, 22, 74; CN 7; DLB 14, 231; INT CANR-22; MTCW 1

Coleman, Emmett
See Reed, Ishmael

Coleridge, Hartley 1796-1849 .... **NCLC 90**
See also DLB 96

Coleridge, M. E.
See Coleridge, Mary E(lizabeth)

Coleridge, Mary E(lizabeth)
1861-1907 .... **TCLC 73**
See also CA 116; 166; DLB 19, 98

Coleridge, Samuel Taylor
1772-1834 ...... **NCLC 9, 54, 99, 111; PC 11, 39; WLC**
See also BRW 4; BRWR 2; BYA 4; CD-BLB 1789-1832; DA; DA3; DAB; DAC; DAM MST, POET; DLB 93, 107; EXPP; LATS 1; LMFS 1; PAB; PFS 4, 5; RGEL 2; TEA; WLIT 3; WP

Coleridge, Sara 1802-1852 .... **NCLC 31**
See also DLB 199

Coles, Don 1928- .... **CLC 46**
See also CA 115; CANR 38; CP 7

Coles, Robert (Martin) 1929- .... **CLC 108**
See also CA 45-48; CANR 3, 32, 66, 70; INT CANR-32; SATA 23

Colette, (Sidonie-Gabrielle)
1873-1954 .... **SSC 10; TCLC 1, 5, 16**
See Willy, Colette
See also CA 104; 131; DA3; DAM NOV; DLB 65; EW 9; EWL 3; GFL 1789 to the Present; MTCW 1, 2; RGWL 2, 3; TWA

Collett, (Jacobine) Camilla (Wergeland)
1813-1895 .... **NCLC 22**

Collier, Christopher 1930- .... **CLC 30**
See also AAYA 13; BYA 2; CA 33-36R; CANR 13, 33, 102; JRDA; MAICYA 1, 2; SATA 16, 70; WYA; YAW 1

Collier, James Lincoln 1928- .... **CLC 30**
See also AAYA 13; BYA 2; CA 9-12R; CANR 4, 33, 60, 102; CLR 3; DAM POP; JRDA; MAICYA 1, 2; SAAS 21; SATA 8, 70; WYA; YAW 1

Collier, Jeremy 1650-1726 .... **LC 6**

Collier, John 1901-1980 . **SSC 19; TCLC 127**
See also CA 65-68; 97-100; CANR 10; DLB 77, 255; FANT; SUFW 1

Collier, Mary 1690-1762 .... **LC 86**
See also DLB 95

Collingwood, R(obin) G(eorge)
1889(?)-1943 .... **TCLC 67**
See also CA 117; 155; DLB 262

Collins, Hunt
See Hunter, Evan

Collins, Linda 1931- .... **CLC 44**
See also CA 125

Collins, Tom
See Furphy, Joseph
See also RGEL 2

Collins, (William) Wilkie
1824-1889 .... **NCLC 1, 18, 93**
See also BRWS 6; CDBLB 1832-1890; CMW 4; DLB 18, 70, 159; MSW; RGEL 2; RGSF 2; SUFW 1; WLIT 4

Collins, William 1721-1759 .... **LC 4, 40**
See also BRW 3; DAM POET; DLB 109; RGEL 2

Collodi, Carlo .... **NCLC 54**
See Lorenzini, Carlo
See also CLR 5; WCH

Colman, George
See Glassco, John

Colonna, Vittoria 1492-1547 .... **LC 71**
See also RGWL 2, 3

Colt, Winchester Remington
See Hubbard, L(afayette) Ron(ald)

Colter, Cyrus J. 1910-2002 .... **CLC 58**
See also BW 1; CA 65-68; 205; CANR 10, 66; CN 7; DLB 33

Colton, James
See Hansen, Joseph
See also GLL 1

Colum, Padraic 1881-1972 .... **CLC 28**
See also BYA 4; CA 73-76; 33-36R; CANR 35; CLR 36; CWRI 5; DLB 19; MAICYA 1, 2; MTCW 1; RGEL 2; SATA 15; WCH

Colvin, James
See Moorcock, Michael (John)

Colwin, Laurie (E.) 1944-1992 .... **CLC 5, 13, 23, 84**
See also CA 89-92; 139; CANR 20, 46; DLB 218; DLBY 1980; MTCW 1

Comfort, Alex(ander) 1920-2000 .... **CLC 7**
See also CA 1-4R; 190; CANR 1, 45; CP 7; DAM POP; MTCW 1

Comfort, Montgomery
See Campbell, (John) Ramsey

Compton-Burnett, I(vy)
1892(?)-1969 .... **CLC 1, 3, 10, 15, 34**
See also BRW 7; CA 1-4R; 25-28R; CANR 4; DAM NOV; DLB 36; EWL 3; MTCW 1; RGEL 2

Comstock, Anthony 1844-1915 ...... **TCLC 13**
See also CA 110; 169

Comte, Auguste 1798-1857 .... **NCLC 54**

Conan Doyle, Arthur
See Doyle, Sir Arthur Conan
See also BPFB 1; BYA 4, 5, 11

Conde (Abellan), Carmen
1901-1996 .... **HLCS 1**
See also CA 177; DLB 108; EWL 3; HW 2

Conde, Maryse 1937- ..... **BLCS; CLC 52, 92**
See also BW 2, 3; CA 110; CAAE 190; CANR 30, 53, 76; CWW 2; DAM MULT; EWL 3; MTCW 1

Condillac, Etienne Bonnot de
1714-1780 .... **LC 26**

Condon, Richard (Thomas)
1915-1996 .... **CLC 4, 6, 8, 10, 45, 100**
See also BEST 90:3; BPFB 1; CA 1-4R; 151; CAAS 1; CANR 2, 23; CMW 4; CN 7; DAM NOV; INT CANR-23; MTCW 1, 2

Confucius 551B.C.-479B.C. .... **CMLC 19; WLCS**
See also DA; DA3; DAB; DAC; DAM MST

Congreve, William 1670-1729 ... **DC 2; LC 5, 21; WLC**
See also BRW 2; CDBLB 1660-1789; DA; DAB; DAC; DAM DRAM, MST, POET; DFS 15; DLB 39, 84; RGEL 2; WLIT 3

Conley, Robert J(ackson) 1940- .... **NNAL**
See also CA 41-44R; CANR 15, 34, 45, 96; DAM MULT

Connell, Evan S(helby), Jr. 1924- . **CLC 4, 6, 45**
See also AAYA 7; CA 1-4R; CAAS 2; CANR 2, 39, 76, 97; CN 7; DAM NOV; DLB 2; DLBY 1981; MTCW 1, 2

Connelly, Marc(us Cook) 1890-1980 . **CLC 7**
See also CA 85-88; 102; CANR 30; DFS 12; DLB 7; DLBY 1980; RGAL 4; SATA-Obit 25

Connor, Ralph .... **TCLC 31**
See Gordon, Charles William
See also DLB 92; TCWW 2

Conrad, Joseph 1857-1924 . **SSC 9; TCLC 1, 6, 13, 25, 43, 57; WLC**
See also AAYA 26; BPFB 1; BRW 6; BRWC 1; BRWR 2; BYA 2; CA 104; 131; CANR 60; CDBLB 1890-1914; DA; DA3; DAB; DAC; DAM MST, NOV; DLB 10,

de Andrade, Carlos Drummond
See Drummond de Andrade, Carlos
de Andrade, Mario 1892-1945
See Andrade, Mario de
See also CA 178; HW 2
Deane, Norman
See Creasey, John
Deane, Seamus (Francis) 1940- ...... **CLC 122**
See also CA 118; CANR 42
de Beauvoir, Simone (Lucie Ernestine Marie Bertrand)
See Beauvoir, Simone (Lucie Ernestine Marie Bertrand) de
de Beer, P.
See Bosman, Herman Charles
de Brissac, Malcolm
See Dickinson, Peter (Malcolm)
de Campos, Alvaro
See Pessoa, Fernando (Antonio Nogueira)
de Chardin, Pierre Teilhard
See Teilhard de Chardin, (Marie Joseph) Pierre
Dee, John 1527-1608 .... **LC 20**
See also DLB 136, 213
Deer, Sandra 1940- .... **CLC 45**
See also CA 186
De Ferrari, Gabriella 1941- .... **CLC 65**
See also CA 146
de Filippo, Eduardo 1900-1984 ... **TCLC 127**
See also CA 132; 114; EWL 3; MTCW 1; RGWL 2, 3
Defoe, Daniel 1660(?)-1731 .. **LC 1, 42; WLC**
See also AAYA 27; BRW 3; BRWR 1; BYA 4; CDBLB 1660-1789; CLR 61; DA; DA3; DAB; DAC; DAM MST, NOV; DLB 39, 95, 101; JRDA; LAIT 1; LMFS 1; MAICYA 1, 2; NFS 9, 13; RGEL 2; SATA 22; TEA; WCH; WLIT 3
de Gourmont, Remy(-Marie-Charles)
See Gourmont, Remy(-Marie-Charles) de
de Hartog, Jan 1914-2002 .... **CLC 19**
See also CA 1-4R; 210; CANR 1; DFS 12
de Hostos, E. M.
See Hostos (y Bonilla), Eugenio Maria de
de Hostos, Eugenio M.
See Hostos (y Bonilla), Eugenio Maria de
Deighton, Len .... **CLC 4, 7, 22, 46**
See Deighton, Leonard Cyril
See also AAYA 6; BEST 89:2; BPFB 1; CD-BLB 1960 to Present; CMW 4; CN 7; CPW; DLB 87
Deighton, Leonard Cyril 1929-
See Deighton, Len
See also CA 9-12R; CANR 19, 33, 68; DA3; DAM NOV, POP; MTCW 1, 2
Dekker, Thomas 1572(?)-1632 ..... **DC 12; LC 22**
See also CDBLB Before 1660; DAM DRAM; DLB 62, 172; LMFS 1; RGEL 2
de Laclos, Pierre Ambroise Franois
See Laclos, Pierre Ambroise Francois
Delafield, E. M. .... **TCLC 61**
See Dashwood, Edmee Elizabeth Monica de la Pasture
See also DLB 34; RHW
de la Mare, Walter (John) 1873-1956 . **SSC 14; TCLC 4, 53; WLC**
See also CA 163; CDBLB 1914-1945; CLR 23; CWRI 5; DA3; DAB; DAC; DAM MST, POET; DLB 19, 153, 162, 255, 284; EWL 3; EXPP; HGG; MAICYA 1, 2; MTCW 1; RGEL 2; RGSF 2; SATA 16; SUFW 1; TEA; WCH
de Lamartine, Alphonse (Marie Louis Prat)
See Lamartine, Alphonse (Marie Louis Prat) de
Delaney, Franey
See O'Hara, John (Henry)

Delaney, Shelagh 1939- .... **CLC 29**
See also CA 17-20R, CANR 30, 67; CBD; CD 5; CDBLB 1960 to Present; CWD; DAM DRAM; DFS 7; DLB 13; MTCW 1
Delany, Martin Robison 1812-1885 .... **NCLC 93**
See also DLB 50; RGAL 4
Delany, Mary (Granville Pendarves) 1700-1788 .... **LC 12**
Delany, Samuel R(ay), Jr. 1942- .... **BLC 1; CLC 8, 14, 38, 141**
See also AAYA 24; AFAW 2; BPFB 1; BW 2, 3; CA 81-84; CANR 27, 43, 115, 116; CN 7; DAM MULT; DLB 8, 33; FANT; MTCW 1, 2; RGAL 4; SATA 92; SCFW; SFW 4; SUFW 2
De la Ramee, Marie Louise (Ouida) 1839-1908
See Ouida
See also CA 204; SATA 20
de la Roche, Mazo 1879-1961 .... **CLC 14**
See also CA 85-88; CANR 30; DLB 68; RGEL 2; RHW; SATA 64
De La Salle, Innocent
See Hartmann, Sadakichi
de Laureamont, Comte
See Lautreamont
Delbanco, Nicholas (Franklin) 1942- .... **CLC 6, 13, 167**
See also CA 17-20R; CAAE 189; CAAS 2; CANR 29, 55, 116; DLB 6, 234
del Castillo, Michel 1933- .... **CLC 38**
See also CA 109; CANR 77
Deledda, Grazia (Cosima) 1875(?)-1936 .... **TCLC 23**
See also CA 123; 205; DLB 264; EWL 3; RGWL 2, 3
Deleuze, Gilles 1925-1995 .... **TCLC 116**
Delgado, Abelardo (Lalo) B(arrientos) 1930- .... **HLC 1**
See also CA 131; CAAS 15; CANR 90; DAM MST, MULT; DLB 82; HW 1, 2
Delibes, Miguel .... **CLC 8, 18**
See Delibes Setien, Miguel
See also EWL 3
Delibes Setien, Miguel 1920-
See Delibes, Miguel
See also CA 45-48; CANR 1, 32; HW 1; MTCW 1
DeLillo, Don 1936- ..... **CLC 8, 10, 13, 27, 39, 54, 76, 143**
See also AMWS 6; BEST 89:1; BPFB 1; CA 81-84; CANR 21, 76, 92; CN 7; CPW; DA3; DAM NOV, POP; DLB 6, 173; EWL 3; MTCW 1, 2; RGAL 4; TUS
de Lisser, H. G.
See De Lisser, H(erbert) G(eorge)
See also DLB 117
De Lisser, H(erbert) G(eorge) 1878-1944 .... **TCLC 12**
See de Lisser, H. G.
See also BW 2; CA 109; 152
Deloire, Pierre
See Peguy, Charles (Pierre)
Deloney, Thomas 1543(?)-1600 .... **LC 41**
See also DLB 167; RGEL 2
Deloria, Ella (Cara) 1889-1971(?) ..... **NNAL**
See also CA 152; DAM MULT; DLB 175
Deloria, Vine (Victor), Jr. 1933- ...... **CLC 21, 122; NNAL**
See also CA 53-56; CANR 5, 20, 48, 98; DAM MULT; DLB 175; MTCW 1; SATA 21
del Valle-Inclan, Ramon (Maria)
See Valle-Inclan, Ramon (Maria) del
Del Vecchio, John M(ichael) 1947- .. **CLC 29**
See also CA 110; DLBD 9

de Man, Paul (Adolph Michel) 1919-1983 .... **CLC 55**
See also CA 128; 111; CANR 61; DLB 67; MTCW 1, 2
DeMarinis, Rick 1934- .... **CLC 54**
See also CA 57-60, 184; CAAE 184; CAAS 24; CANR 9, 25, 50; DLB 218
de Maupassant, (Henri Rene Albert) Guy
See Maupassant, (Henri Rene Albert) Guy de
Dembry, R. Emmet
See Murfree, Mary Noailles
Demby, William 1922- .... **BLC 1; CLC 53**
See also BW 1, 3; CA 81-84; CANR 81; DAM MULT; DLB 33
de Menton, Francisco
See Chin, Frank (Chew, Jr.)
Demetrius of Phalerum c. 307B.C.- .... **CMLC 34**
Demijohn, Thom
See Disch, Thomas M(ichael)
De Mille, James 1833-1880 .... **NCLC 123**
See also DLB 99, 251
Deming, Richard 1915-1983
See Queen, Ellery
See also CA 9-12R; CANR 3, 94; SATA 24
Democritus c. 460B.C.-c. 370B.C. . **CMLC 47**
de Montaigne, Michel (Eyquem)
See Montaigne, Michel (Eyquem) de
de Montherlant, Henry (Milon)
See Montherlant, Henry (Milon) de
Demosthenes 384B.C.-322B.C. ...... **CMLC 13**
See also AW 1; DLB 176; RGWL 2, 3
de Musset, (Louis Charles) Alfred
See Musset, (Louis Charles) Alfred de
de Natale, Francine
See Malzberg, Barry N(athaniel)
de Navarre, Marguerite 1492-1549 ..... **LC 61**
See Marguerite d'Angouleme; Marguerite de Navarre
Denby, Edwin (Orr) 1903-1983 .... **CLC 48**
See also CA 138; 110
de Nerval, Gerard
See Nerval, Gerard de
Denham, John 1615-1669 .... **LC 73**
See also DLB 58, 126; RGEL 2
Denis, Julio
See Cortazar, Julio
Denmark, Harrison
See Zelazny, Roger (Joseph)
Dennis, John 1658-1734 .... **LC 11**
See also DLB 101; RGEL 2
Dennis, Nigel (Forbes) 1912-1989 ...... **CLC 8**
See also CA 25-28R; 129; DLB 13, 15, 233; EWL 3; MTCW 1
Dent, Lester 1904(?)-1959 .... **TCLC 72**
See also CA 112; 161; CMW 4; SFW 4
De Palma, Brian (Russell) 1940- ...... **CLC 20**
See also CA 109
De Quincey, Thomas 1785-1859 ..... **NCLC 4, 87**
See also BRW 4; CDBLB 1789-1832; DLB 110, 144; RGEL 2
Deren, Eleanora 1908(?)-1961
See Deren, Maya
See also CA 192; 111
Deren, Maya .... **CLC 16, 102**
See Deren, Eleanora
Derleth, August (William) 1909-1971 .... **CLC 31**
See also BPFB 1; BYA 9, 10; CA 1-4R; 29-32R; CANR 4; CMW 4; DLB 9; DLBD 17; HGG; SATA 5; SUFW 1
Der Nister 1884-1950 .... **TCLC 56**
See Nister, Der
de Routisie, Albert
See Aragon, Louis

Eastman, Charles A(lexander)
1858-1939 .... **NNAL; TCLC 55**
See also CA 179; CANR 91; DAM MULT;
DLB 175; YABC 1

Eaton, Edith Maude 1865-1914 .... **AAL**
See Far, Sui Sin
See also CA 154; DLB 221; FW

Eaton, Winnifred 1875-1954 .... **AAL**
See also DLB 221; RGAL 4

Eberhart, Richard (Ghormley)
1904- .... **CLC 3, 11, 19, 56**
See also AMW; CA 1-4R; CANR 2;
CDALB 1941-1968; CP 7; DAM POET;
DLB 48; MTCW 1; RGAL 4

Eberstadt, Fernanda 1960- .... **CLC 39**
See also CA 136; CANR 69

**Echegaray (y Eizaguirre), Jose (Maria
Waldo)** 1832-1916 .... **HLCS 1; TCLC 4**
See also CA 104; CANR 32; EWL 3; HW
1; MTCW 1

Echeverria, (Jose) Esteban (Antonino)
1805-1851 .... **NCLC 18**
See also LAW

Echo
See Proust, (Valentin-Louis-George-Eugene-
)Marcel

Eckert, Allan W. 1931- .... **CLC 17**
See also AAYA 18; BYA 2; CA 13-16R;
CANR 14, 45; INT CANR-14; MAICYA
2; MAICYAS 1; SAAS 21; SATA 29, 91;
SATA-Brief 27

Eckhart, Meister 1260(?)-1327(?) ... **CMLC 9**
See also DLB 115; LMFS 1

Eckmar, F. R.
See de Hartog, Jan

Eco, Umberto 1932- .... **CLC 28, 60, 142**
See also BEST 90:1; BPFB 1; CA 77-80;
CANR 12, 33, 55, 110; CPW; CWW 2;
DA3; DAM NOV, POP; DLB 196, 242;
EWL 3; MSW; MTCW 1, 2; RGWL 3

Eddison, E(ric) R(ucker)
1882-1945 .... **TCLC 15**
See also CA 109; 156; DLB 255; FANT;
SFW 4; SUFW 1

Eddy, Mary (Ann Morse) Baker
1821-1910 .... **TCLC 71**
See also CA 113; 174

Edel, (Joseph) Leon 1907-1997 .. **CLC 29, 34**
See also CA 1-4R; 161; CANR 1, 22, 112;
DLB 103; INT CANR-22

Eden, Emily 1797-1869 .... **NCLC 10**

Edgar, David 1948- .... **CLC 42**
See also CA 57-60; CANR 12, 61, 112;
CBD; CD 5; DAM DRAM; DFS 15; DLB
13, 233; MTCW 1

Edgerton, Clyde (Carlyle) 1944- ...... **CLC 39**
See also AAYA 17; CA 118; 134; CANR
64; CSW; DLB 278; INT 134; YAW

Edgeworth, Maria 1768-1849 .... **NCLC 1, 51**
See also BRWS 3; DLB 116, 159, 163; FW;
RGEL 2; SATA 21; TEA; WLIT 3

Edmonds, Paul
See Kuttner, Henry

Edmonds, Walter D(umaux)
1903-1998 .... **CLC 35**
See also BYA 2; CA 5-8R; CANR 2; CWRI
5; DLB 9; LAIT 1; MAICYA 1, 2; RHW;
SAAS 4; SATA 1, 27; SATA-Obit 99

Edmondson, Wallace
See Ellison, Harlan (Jay)

Edson, Russell 1935- .... **CLC 13**
See also CA 33-36R; CANR 115; DLB 244;
WP

Edwards, Bronwen Elizabeth
See Rose, Wendy

Edwards, G(erald) B(asil)
1899-1976 .... **CLC 25**
See also CA 201; 110

Edwards, Gus 1939- .... **CLC 43**
See also CA 108; INT 108

Edwards, Jonathan 1703-1758 .... **LC 7, 54**
See also AMW; DA; DAC; DAM MST;
DLB 24, 270; RGAL 4; TUS

Edwards, Sarah Pierpont 1710-1758 .. **LC 87**
See also DLB 200

Efron, Marina Ivanovna Tsvetaeva
See Tsvetaeva (Efron), Marina (Ivanovna)

Egoyan, Atom 1960- .... **CLC 151**
See also CA 157

Ehle, John (Marsden, Jr.) 1925- ...... **CLC 27**
See also CA 9-12R; CSW

Ehrenbourg, Ilya (Grigoryevich)
See Ehrenburg, Ilya (Grigoryevich)

Ehrenburg, Ilya (Grigoryevich)
1891-1967 .... **CLC 18, 34, 62**
See Erenburg, Il'ia Grigor'evich
See also CA 102; 25-28R; EWL 3

Ehrenburg, Ilyo (Grigoryevich)
See Ehrenburg, Ilya (Grigoryevich)

Ehrenreich, Barbara 1941- .... **CLC 110**
See also BEST 90:4; CA 73-76; CANR 16,
37, 62, 117; DLB 246; FW; MTCW 1, 2

Eich, Gunter
See Eich, Gunter
See also RGWL 2, 3

Eich, Gunter 1907-1972 .... **CLC 15**
See Eich, Gunter
See also CA 111; 93-96; DLB 69, 124;
EWL 3

Eichendorff, Joseph 1788-1857 .... **NCLC 8**
See also DLB 90; RGWL 2, 3

Eigner, Larry .... **CLC 9**
See Eigner, Laurence (Joel)
See also CAAS 23; DLB 5; WP

Eigner, Laurence (Joel) 1927-1996
See Eigner, Larry
See also CA 9-12R; 151; CANR 6, 84; CP
7; DLB 193

Einhard c. 770-840 .... **CMLC 50**
See also DLB 148

Einstein, Albert 1879-1955 .... **TCLC 65**
See also CA 121; 133; MTCW 1, 2

Eiseley, Loren
See Eiseley, Loren Corey
See also DLB 275

Eiseley, Loren Corey 1907-1977 .... **CLC 7**
See Eiseley, Loren
See also AAYA 5; ANW; CA 1-4R; 73-76;
CANR 6; DLBD 17

Eisenstadt, Jill 1963- .... **CLC 50**
See also CA 140

Eisenstein, Sergei (Mikhailovich)
1898-1948 .... **TCLC 57**
See also CA 114; 149

Eisner, Simon
See Kornbluth, C(yril) M.

Ekeloef, (Bengt) Gunnar
1907-1968 .... **CLC 27; PC 23**
See Ekelof, (Bengt) Gunnar
See also CA 123; 25-28R; DAM POET

Ekelof, (Bengt) Gunnar 1907-1968
See Ekeloef, (Bengt) Gunnar
See also DLB 259; EW 12; EWL 3

Ekelund, Vilhelm 1880-1949 .... **TCLC 75**
See also CA 189; EWL 3

Ekwensi, C. O. D.
See Ekwensi, Cyprian (Odiatu Duaka)

Ekwensi, Cyprian (Odiatu Duaka)
1921- .... **BLC 1; CLC 4**
See also AFW; BW 2, 3; CA 29-32R;
CANR 18, 42, 74; CDWLB 3; CN 7;
CWRI 5; DAM MULT; DLB 117; EWL
3; MTCW 1, 2; RGEL 2; SATA 66; WLIT
2

Elaine .... **TCLC 18**
See Leverson, Ada Esther

El Crummo
See Crumb, R(obert)

Elder, Lonne III 1931-1996 ..... **BLC 1; DC 8**
See also BW 1, 3; CA 81-84; 152; CAD;
CANR 25; DAM MULT; DLB 7, 38, 44

Eleanor of Aquitaine 1122-1204 ... **CMLC 39**

Elia
See Lamb, Charles

Eliade, Mircea 1907-1986 .... **CLC 19**
See also CA 65-68; 119; CANR 30, 62; CD-
WLB 4; DLB 220; EWL 3; MTCW 1;
RGWL 3; SFW 4

Eliot, A. D.
See Jewett, (Theodora) Sarah Orne

Eliot, Alice
See Jewett, (Theodora) Sarah Orne

Eliot, Dan
See Silverberg, Robert

Eliot, George 1819-1880 ...... **NCLC 4, 13, 23,
41, 49, 89, 118; PC 20; WLC**
See also BRW 5; BRWC 1; BRWR 2; CD-
BLB 1832-1890; CN 7; CPW; DA; DA3;
DAB; DAC; DAM MST, NOV; DLB 21,
35, 55; LATS 1; LMFS 1; NFS 17; RGEL
2; RGSF 2; SSFS 8; TEA; WLIT 3

Eliot, John 1604-1690 .... **LC 5**
See also DLB 24

Eliot, T(homas) S(tearns)
1888-1965 ...... **CLC 1, 2, 3, 6, 9, 10, 13,
15, 24, 34, 41, 55, 57, 113; PC 5, 31;
WLC**
See also AAYA 28; AMW; AMWC 1;
AMWR 1; BRW 7; BRWR 2; CA 5-8R;
25-28R; CANR 41; CDALB 1929-1941;
DA; DA3; DAB; DAC; DAM DRAM,
MST, POET; DFS 4, 13; DLB 7, 10, 45,
63, 245; DLBY 1988; EWL 3; EXPP;
LAIT 3; LATS 1; LMFS 2; MTCW 1, 2;
PAB; PFS 1, 7; RGAL 4; RGEL 2; TUS;
WLIT 4; WP

Elizabeth 1866-1941 .... **TCLC 41**

Elkin, Stanley L(awrence)
1930-1995 .. **CLC 4, 6, 9, 14, 27, 51, 91;
SSC 12**
See also AMWS 6; BPFB 1; CA 9-12R;
148; CANR 8, 46; CN 7; CPW; DAM
NOV, POP; DLB 2, 28, 218, 278; DLBY
1980; EWL 3; INT CANR-8; MTCW 1,
2; RGAL 4

Elledge, Scott .... **CLC 34**

Elliot, Don
See Silverberg, Robert

Elliott, Don
See Silverberg, Robert

Elliott, George P(aul) 1918-1980 .... **CLC 2**
See also CA 1-4R; 97-100; CANR 2; DLB
244

Elliott, Janice 1931-1995 .... **CLC 47**
See also CA 13-16R; CANR 8, 29, 84; CN
7; DLB 14; SATA 119

Elliott, Sumner Locke 1917-1991 ..... **CLC 38**
See also CA 5-8R; 134; CANR 2, 21

Elliott, William
See Bradbury, Ray (Douglas)

Ellis, A. E. .... **CLC 7**

Ellis, Alice Thomas .... **CLC 40**
See Haycraft, Anna (Margaret)
See also DLB 194; MTCW 1

Ellis, Bret Easton 1964- ...... **CLC 39, 71, 117**
See also AAYA 2, 43; CA 118; 123; CANR
51, 74; CN 7; CPW; DA3; DAM POP;
HGG; INT CA-123; MTCW 1; NFS 11

Ellis, (Henry) Havelock
1859-1939 .... **TCLC 14**
See also CA 109; 169; DLB 190

Ellis, Landon
See Ellison, Harlan (Jay)

Ellis, Trey 1962- .... **CLC 55**
See also CA 146; CANR 92

Ford, Jack
See Ford, John
Ford, John 1586-1639 .... **DC 8; LC 68**
See also BRW 2; CDBLB Before 1660;
DA3; DAM DRAM; DFS 7; DLB 58;
IDTP; RGEL 2
Ford, John 1895-1973 .... **CLC 16**
See also CA 187; 45-48
Ford, Richard 1944- .... **CLC 46, 99**
See also AMWS 5; CA 69-72; CANR 11,
47, 86; CN 7; CSW; DLB 227; EWL 3;
MTCW 1; RGAL 4; RGSF 2
Ford, Webster
See Masters, Edgar Lee
Foreman, Richard 1937- .... **CLC 50**
See also CA 65-68; CAD; CANR 32, 63;
CD 5
Forester, C(ecil) S(cott) 1899-1966 ... **CLC 35**
See also CA 73-76; 25-28R; CANR 83;
DLB 191; RGEL 2; RHW; SATA 13
Forez
See Mauriac, Francois (Charles)
Forman, James
See Forman, James D(ouglas)
Forman, James D(ouglas) 1932- .... **CLC 21**
See also AAYA 17; CA 9-12R; CANR 4,
19, 42; JRDA; MAICYA 1, 2; SATA 8,
70; YAW
Forman, Milos 1932- .... **CLC 164**
See also CA 109
Fornes, Maria Irene 1930- . **CLC 39, 61; DC
10; HLCS 1**
See also CA 25-28R; CAD; CANR 28, 81;
CD 5; CWD; DLB 7; HW 1, 2; INT
CANR-28; MTCW 1; RGAL 4
Forrest, Leon (Richard)
1937-1997 .... **BLCS; CLC 4**
See also AFAW 2; BW 2; CA 89-92; 162;
CAAS 7; CANR 25, 52, 87; CN 7; DLB
33
Forster, E(dward) M(organ)
1879-1970 ...... **CLC 1, 2, 3, 4, 9, 10, 13,
15, 22, 45, 77; SSC 27; TCLC 125;
WLC**
See also AAYA 2, 37; BRW 6; BRWR 2;
CA 13-14; 25-28R; CANR 45; CAP 1;
CDBLB 1914-1945; DA; DA3; DAB;
DAC; DAM MST, NOV; DLB 34, 98,
162, 178, 195; DLBD 10; EWL 3; EXPN;
LAIT 3; LMFS 1; MTCW 1, 2; NCFS 1;
NFS 3, 10, 11; RGEL 2; RGSF 2; SATA
57; SUFW 1; TEA; WLIT 4
Forster, John 1812-1876 .... **NCLC 11**
See also DLB 144, 184
Forster, Margaret 1938- .... **CLC 149**
See also CA 133; CANR 62, 115; CN 7;
DLB 155, 271
Forsyth, Frederick 1938- .... **CLC 2, 5, 36**
See also BEST 89:4; CA 85-88; CANR 38,
62, 115; CMW 4; CN 7; CPW; DAM
NOV, POP; DLB 87; MTCW 1, 2
Forten, Charlotte L. 1837-1914 .... **BLC 2;
TCLC 16**
See Grimke, Charlotte L(ottie) Forten
See also DLB 50, 239
Fortinbras
See Grieg, (Johan) Nordahl (Brun)
Foscolo, Ugo 1778-1827 .... **NCLC 8, 97**
See also EW 5
Fosse, Bob .... **CLC 20**
See Fosse, Robert Louis
Fosse, Robert Louis 1927-1987
See Fosse, Bob
See also CA 110; 123
Foster, Hannah Webster
1758-1840 .... **NCLC 99**
See also DLB 37, 200; RGAL 4

Foster, Stephen Collins
1826-1864 .... **NCLC 26**
See also RGAL 4
Foucault, Michel 1926-1984 . **CLC 31, 34, 69**
See also CA 105; 113; CANR 34; DLB 242;
EW 13; EWL 3; GFL 1789 to the Present;
GLL 1; LMFS 2; MTCW 1, 2; TWA
**Fouque, Friedrich (Heinrich Karl) de la
Motte** 1777-1843 .... **NCLC 2**
See also DLB 90; RGWL 2, 3; SUFW 1
Fourier, Charles 1772-1837 .... **NCLC 51**
Fournier, Henri-Alban 1886-1914
See Alain-Fournier
See also CA 104; 179
Fournier, Pierre 1916- .... **CLC 11**
See Gascar, Pierre
See also CA 89-92; CANR 16, 40
Fowles, John (Robert) 1926- . **CLC 1, 2, 3, 4,
6, 9, 10, 15, 33, 87; SSC 33**
See also BPFB 1; BRWS 1; CA 5-8R;
CANR 25, 71, 103; CDBLB 1960 to
Present; CN 7; DA3; DAB; DAC; DAM
MST; DLB 14, 139, 207; EWL 3; HGG;
MTCW 1, 2; RGEL 2; RHW; SATA 22;
TEA; WLIT 4
Fox, Paula 1923- .... **CLC 2, 8, 121**
See also AAYA 3, 37; BYA 3, 8; CA 73-76;
CANR 20, 36, 62, 105; CLR 1, 44; DLB
52; JRDA; MAICYA 1, 2; MTCW 1; NFS
12; SATA 17, 60, 120; WYA; YAW
Fox, William Price (Jr.) 1926- .... **CLC 22**
See also CA 17-20R; CAAS 19; CANR 11;
CSW; DLB 2; DLBY 1981
Foxe, John 1517(?)-1587 .... **LC 14**
See also DLB 132
Frame, Janet .. **CLC 2, 3, 6, 22, 66, 96; SSC
29**
See Clutha, Janet Paterson Frame
See also CN 7; CWP; EWL 3; RGEL 2;
RGSF 2; TWA
France, Anatole .... **TCLC 9**
See Thibault, Jacques Anatole Francois
See also DLB 123; EWL 3; GFL 1789 to
the Present; MTCW 1; RGWL 2, 3;
SUFW 1
Francis, Claude .... **CLC 50**
See also CA 192
Francis, Dick 1920- .... **CLC 2, 22, 42, 102**
See also AAYA 5, 21; BEST 89:3; BPFB 1;
CA 5-8R; CANR 9, 42, 68, 100; CDBLB
1960 to Present; CMW 4; CN 7; DA3;
DAM POP; DLB 87; INT CANR-9;
MSW; MTCW 1, 2
Francis, Robert (Churchill)
1901-1987 .... **CLC 15; PC 34**
See also AMWS 9; CA 1-4R; 123; CANR
1; EXPP; PFS 12
Francis, Lord Jeffrey
See Jeffrey, Francis
See also DLB 107
Frank, Anne(lies Marie)
1929-1945 .... **TCLC 17; WLC**
See also AAYA 12; BYA 1; CA 113; 133;
CANR 68; DA; DA3; DAB; DAC; DAM
MST; LAIT 4; MAICYA 2; MAICYAS 1;
MTCW 1, 2; NCFS 2; SATA 87; SATA-
Brief 42; WYA; YAW
Frank, Bruno 1887-1945 .... **TCLC 81**
See also CA 189; DLB 118; EWL 3
Frank, Elizabeth 1945- .... **CLC 39**
See also CA 121; 126; CANR 78; INT 126
Frankl, Viktor E(mil) 1905-1997 ...... **CLC 93**
See also CA 65-68; 161
Franklin, Benjamin
See Hasek, Jaroslav (Matej Frantisek)

Franklin, Benjamin 1706-1790 .... **LC 25;
WLCS**
See also AMW; CDALB 1640-1865; DA;
DA3; DAB; DAC; DAM MST; DLB 24,
43, 73, 183; LAIT 1; RGAL 4; TUS
**Franklin, (Stella Maria Sarah) Miles
(Lampe)** 1879-1954 .... **TCLC 7**
See also CA 104; 164; DLB 230; FW;
MTCW 2; RGEL 2; TWA
Fraser, Antonia (Pakenham) 1932- . **CLC 32,
107**
See also CA 85-88; CANR 44, 65; CMW;
DLB 276; MTCW 1, 2; SATA-Brief 32
Fraser, George MacDonald 1925- ...... **CLC 7**
See also AAYA 48; CA 45-48, 180; CAAE
180; CANR 2, 48, 74; MTCW 1; RHW
Fraser, Sylvia 1935- .... **CLC 64**
See also CA 45-48; CANR 1, 16, 60; CCA
1
Frayn, Michael 1933- .... **CLC 3, 7, 31, 47**
See also BRWS 7; CA 5-8R; CANR 30, 69,
114; CBD; CD 5; CN 7; DAM DRAM,
NOV; DLB 13, 14, 194, 245; FANT;
MTCW 1, 2; SFW 4
Fraze, Candida (Merrill) 1945- .... **CLC 50**
See also CA 126
Frazer, Andrew
See Marlowe, Stephen
Frazer, J(ames) G(eorge)
1854-1941 .... **TCLC 32**
See also BRWS 3; CA 118
Frazer, Robert Caine
See Creasey, John
Frazer, Sir James George
See Frazer, J(ames) G(eorge)
Frazier, Charles 1950- .... **CLC 109**
See also AAYA 34; CA 161; CSW
Frazier, Ian 1951- .... **CLC 46**
See also CA 130; CANR 54, 93
Frederic, Harold 1856-1898 .... **NCLC 10**
See also AMW; DLB 12, 23; DLBD 13;
RGAL 4
Frederick, John
See Faust, Frederick (Schiller)
See also TCWW 2
Frederick the Great 1712-1786 .... **LC 14**
Fredro, Aleksander 1793-1876 .... **NCLC 8**
Freeling, Nicolas 1927- .... **CLC 38**
See also CA 49-52; CAAS 12; CANR 1,
17, 50, 84; CMW 4; CN 7; DLB 87
Freeman, Douglas Southall
1886-1953 .... **TCLC 11**
See also CA 109; 195; DLB 17; DLBD 17
Freeman, Judith 1946- .... **CLC 55**
See also CA 148; DLB 256
Freeman, Mary E(leanor) Wilkins
1852-1930 .... **SSC 1, 47; TCLC 9**
See also CA 106; 177; DLB 12, 78, 221;
EXPS; FW; HGG; MAWW; RGAL 4;
RGSF 2; SSFS 4, 8; SUFW 1; TUS
Freeman, R(ichard) Austin
1862-1943 .... **TCLC 21**
See also CA 113; CANR 84; CMW 4; DLB
70
French, Albert 1943- .... **CLC 86**
See also BW 3; CA 167
French, Antonia
See Kureishi, Hanif
French, Marilyn 1929- .... **CLC 10, 18, 60**
See also BPFB 1; CA 69-72; CANR 3, 31;
CN 7; CPW; DAM DRAM, NOV, POP;
FW; INT CANR-31; MTCW 1, 2
French, Paul
See Asimov, Isaac
Freneau, Philip Morin 1752-1832 .. **NCLC 1,
111**
See also AMWS 2; DLB 37, 43; RGAL 4

Garcia Lorca, Federico 1898-1936 ...... **DC 2;**
HLC 2; PC 3; TCLC 1, 7, 49; WLC
See Lorca, Federico Garcia
See also AAYA 46; CA 104; 131; CANR
81; DA; DA3; DAB; DAC; DAM DRAM,
MST, MULT, POET; DFS 4, 10; DLB
108; EWL 3; HW 1, 2; LATS 1; MTCW
1, 2; TWA

Garcia Marquez, Gabriel (Jose)
1928- .... **CLC 2, 3, 8, 10, 15, 27, 47, 55,**
68, 170; HLC 1; SSC 8; WLC
See also AAYA 3, 33; BEST 89:1, 90:4;
BPFB 2; BYA 12; CA 33-36R; CANR 10,
28, 50, 75, 82; CDWLB 3; CPW; DA;
DA3; DAB; DAC; DAM MST, MULT,
NOV, POP; DLB 113; DNFS 1, 2; EWL
3; EXPN; EXPS; HW 1, 2; LAIT 2; LATS
1; LAW; LAWS 1; LMFS 2; MTCW 1, 2;
NCFS 3; NFS 1, 5, 10; RGSF 2; RGWL
2, 3; SSFS 1, 6, 16; TWA; WLIT 1

Garcilaso de la Vega, El Inca
1503-1536 .... **HLCS 1**
See also LAW

Gard, Janice
See Latham, Jean Lee

Gard, Roger Martin du
See Martin du Gard, Roger

Gardam, Jane (Mary) 1928- .... **CLC 43**
See also CA 49-52; CANR 2, 18, 33, 54,
106; CLR 12; DLB 14, 161, 231; MAI-
CYA 1, 2; MTCW 1; SAAS 9; SATA 39,
76, 130; SATA-Brief 28; YAW

Gardner, Herb(ert) 1934- .... **CLC 44**
See also CA 149; CAD; CD 5

Gardner, John (Champlin), Jr.
1933-1982 ...... **CLC 2, 3, 5, 7, 8, 10, 18,**
28, 34; SSC 7
See also AAYA 45; AITN 1; AMWS 6;
BPFB 2; CA 65-68; 107; CANR 33, 73;
CDALBS; CPW; DA3; DAM NOV, POP;
DLB 2; DLBY 1982; EWL 3; FANT;
LATS 1; MTCW 1; NFS 3; RGAL 4;
RGSF 2; SATA 40; SATA-Obit 31; SSFS
8

Gardner, John (Edmund) 1926- .... **CLC 30**
See also CA 103; CANR 15, 69; CMW 4;
CPW; DAM POP; MTCW 1

Gardner, Miriam
See Bradley, Marion Zimmer
See also GLL 1

Gardner, Noel
See Kuttner, Henry

Gardons, S. S.
See Snodgrass, W(illiam) D(e Witt)

Garfield, Leon 1921-1996 .... **CLC 12**
See also AAYA 8; BYA 1, 3; CA 17-20R;
152; CANR 38, 41, 78; CLR 21; DLB
161; JRDA; MAICYA 1, 2; MAICYAS 1;
SATA 1, 32, 76; SATA-Obit 90; TEA;
WYA; YAW

Garland, (Hannibal) Hamlin
1860-1940 .... **SSC 18; TCLC 3**
See also CA 104; DLB 12, 71, 78, 186;
RGAL 4; RGSF 2; TCWW 2

Garneau, (Hector de) Saint-Denys
1912-1943 .... **TCLC 13**
See also CA 111; DLB 88

Garner, Alan 1934- .... **CLC 17**
See also AAYA 18; BYA 3, 5; CA 73-76,
178; CAAE 178; CANR 15, 64; CLR 20;
CPW; DAB; DAM POP; DLB 161, 261;
FANT; MAICYA 1, 2; MTCW 1, 2; SATA
18, 69; SATA-Essay 108; SUFW 1, 2;
YAW

Garner, Hugh 1913-1979 .... **CLC 13**
See Warwick, Jarvis
See also CA 69-72; CANR 31; CCA 1; DLB
68

Garnett, David 1892-1981 .... **CLC 3**
See also CA 5-8R; 103; CANR 17, 79; DLB
34; FANT; MTCW 2; RGEL 2; SFW 4;
SUFW 1

Garos, Stephanie
See Katz, Steve

Garrett, George (Palmer) 1929- .. **CLC 3, 11,**
51; SSC 30
See also AMWS 7; BPFB 2; CA 1-4R;
CAAE 202; CAAS 5; CANR 1, 42, 67,
109; CN 7; CP 7; CSW; DLB 2, 5, 130,
152; DLBY 1983

Garrick, David 1717-1779 .... **LC 15**
See also DAM DRAM; DLB 84, 213;
RGEL 2

Garrigue, Jean 1914-1972 .... **CLC 2, 8**
See also CA 5-8R; 37-40R; CANR 20

Garrison, Frederick
See Sinclair, Upton (Beall)

Garro, Elena 1920(?)-1998 .... **HLCS 1**
See also CA 131; 169; CWW 2; DLB 145;
EWL 3; HW 1; LAWS 1; WLIT 1

Garth, Will
See Hamilton, Edmond; Kuttner, Henry

Garvey, Marcus (Moziah, Jr.)
1887-1940 .... **BLC 2; HR 2; TCLC 41**
See also BW 1; CA 120; 124; CANR 79;
DAM MULT

Gary, Romain .... **CLC 25**
See Kacew, Romain
See also DLB 83

Gascar, Pierre .... **CLC 11**
See Fournier, Pierre
See also EWL 3

Gascoyne, David (Emery)
1916-2001 .... **CLC 45**
See also CA 65-68; 200; CANR 10, 28, 54;
CP 7; DLB 20; MTCW 1; RGEL 2

Gaskell, Elizabeth Cleghorn
1810-1865 .... **NCLC 5, 70, 97; SSC 25**
See also BRW 5; CDBLB 1832-1890; DAB;
DAM MST; DLB 21, 144, 159; RGEL 2;
RGSF 2; TEA

Gass, William H(oward) 1924- . **CLC 1, 2, 8,**
11, 15, 39, 132; SSC 12
See also AMWS 6; CA 17-20R; CANR 30,
71, 100; CN 7; DLB 2, 227; EWL 3;
MTCW 1, 2; RGAL 4

Gassendi, Pierre 1592-1655 .... **LC 54**
See also GFL Beginnings to 1789

Gasset, Jose Ortega y
See Ortega y Gasset, Jose

Gates, Henry Louis, Jr. 1950- ... **BLCS; CLC**
65
See also BW 2, 3; CA 109; CANR 25, 53,
75; CSW; DA3; DAM MULT; DLB 67;
EWL 3; MTCW 1; RGAL 4

Gautier, Theophile 1811-1872 .. **NCLC 1, 59;**
PC 18; SSC 20
See also DAM POET; DLB 119; EW 6;
GFL 1789 to the Present; RGWL 2, 3;
SUFW; TWA

Gawsworth, John
See Bates, H(erbert) E(rnest)

Gay, John 1685-1732 .... **LC 49**
See also BRW 3; DAM DRAM; DLB 84,
95; RGEL 2; WLIT 3

Gay, Oliver
See Gogarty, Oliver St. John

Gay, Peter (Jack) 1923- .... **CLC 158**
See also CA 13-16R; CANR 18, 41, 77;
INT CANR-18

Gaye, Marvin (Pentz, Jr.)
1939-1984 .... **CLC 26**
See also CA 195; 112

Gebler, Carlo (Ernest) 1954- .... **CLC 39**
See also CA 119; 133; CANR 96; DLB 271

Gee, Maggie (Mary) 1948- .... **CLC 57**
See also CA 130; CN 7; DLB 207

Gee, Maurice (Gough) 1931- .... **CLC 29**
See also AAYA 42; CA 97-100; CANR 67;
CLR 56; CN 7; CWRI 5; EWL 3; MAI-
CYA 2; RGSF 2; SATA 46, 101

Geiogamah, Hanay 1945- .... **NNAL**
See also CA 153; DAM MULT; DLB 175

Gelbart, Larry (Simon) 1928- .... **CLC 21, 61**
See Gelbart, Larry
See also CA 73-76; CANR 45, 94

Gelbart, Larry 1928-
See Gelbart, Larry (Simon)
See also CAD; CD 5

Gelber, Jack 1932- .... **CLC 1, 6, 14, 79**
See also CA 1-4R; CAD; CANR 2; DLB 7,
228

Gellhorn, Martha (Ellis)
1908-1998 .... **CLC 14, 60**
See also CA 77-80; 164; CANR 44; CN 7;
DLBY 1982, 1998

Genet, Jean 1910-1986 .. **CLC 1, 2, 5, 10, 14,**
44, 46; TCLC 128
See also CA 13-16R; CANR 18; DA3;
DAM DRAM; DFS 10; DLB 72; DLBY
1986; EW 13; EWL 3; GFL 1789 to the
Present; GLL 1; LMFS 2; MTCW 1, 2;
RGWL 2, 3; TWA

Gent, Peter 1942- .... **CLC 29**
See also AITN 1; CA 89-92; DLBY 1982

Gentile, Giovanni 1875-1944 .... **TCLC 96**
See also CA 119

Gentlewoman in New England, A
See Bradstreet, Anne

Gentlewoman in Those Parts, A
See Bradstreet, Anne

Geoffrey of Monmouth c.
1100-1155 .... **CMLC 44**
See also DLB 146; TEA

George, Jean
See George, Jean Craighead

George, Jean Craighead 1919- .... **CLC 35**
See also AAYA 8; BYA 2, 4; CA 5-8R;
CANR 25; CLR 1; 80; DLB 52; JRDA;
MAICYA 1, 2; SATA 2, 68, 124; WYA;
YAW

George, Stefan (Anton) 1868-1933 . **TCLC 2,**
14
See also CA 104; 193; EW 8; EWL 3

Georges, Georges Martin
See Simenon, Georges (Jacques Christian)

Gerhardi, William Alexander
See Gerhardie, William Alexander

Gerhardie, William Alexander
1895-1977 .... **CLC 5**
See also CA 25-28R; 73-76; CANR 18;
DLB 36; RGEL 2

Gerson, Jean 1363-1429 .... **LC 77**
See also DLB 208

Gersonides 1288-1344 .... **CMLC 49**
See also DLB 115

Gerstler, Amy 1956- .... **CLC 70**
See also CA 146; CANR 99

Gertler, T. .... **CLC 34**
See also CA 116; 121

Gertsen, Aleksandr Ivanovich
See Herzen, Aleksandr Ivanovich

Ghalib .... **NCLC 39, 78**
See Ghalib, Asadullah Khan

Ghalib, Asadullah Khan 1797-1869
See Ghalib
See also DAM POET; RGWL 2, 3

Ghelderode, Michel de 1898-1962 ..... **CLC 6,**
11; DC 15
See also CA 85-88; CANR 40, 77; DAM
DRAM; EW 11; EWL 3; TWA

Ghiselin, Brewster 1903-2001 .... **CLC 23**
See also CA 13-16R; CAAS 10; CANR 13;
CP 7

Goebbels, (Paul) Joseph
1897-1945 .... **TCLC 68**
See also CA 115; 148
Goebbels, Joseph Paul
See Goebbels, (Paul) Joseph
Goethe, Johann Wolfgang von
1749-1832 .... **DC 20; NCLC 4, 22, 34, 90; PC 5; SSC 38; WLC**
See also CDWLB 2; DA; DA3; DAB; DAC; DAM DRAM, MST, POET; DLB 94; EW 5; LATS 1; LMFS 1; RGWL 2, 3; TWA
Gogarty, Oliver St. John
1878-1957 .... **TCLC 15**
See also CA 109; 150; DLB 15, 19; RGEL 2
Gogol, Nikolai (Vasilyevich)
1809-1852 .... **DC 1; NCLC 5, 15, 31; SSC 4, 29, 52; WLC**
See also DA; DAB; DAC; DAM DRAM, MST; DFS 12; DLB 198; EW 6; EXPS; RGSF 2; RGWL 2, 3; SSFS 7; TWA
Goines, Donald 1937(?)-1974 ... **BLC 2; CLC 80**
See also AITN 1; BW 1, 3; CA 124; 114; CANR 82; CMW 4; DA3; DAM MULT, POP; DLB 33
Gold, Herbert 1924- ... **CLC 4, 7, 14, 42, 152**
See also CA 9-12R; CANR 17, 45; CN 7; DLB 2; DLBY 1981
Goldbarth, Albert 1948- .... **CLC 5, 38**
See also AMWS 12; CA 53-56; CANR 6, 40; CP 7; DLB 120
Goldberg, Anatol 1910-1982 .... **CLC 34**
See also CA 131; 117
Goldemberg, Isaac 1945- .... **CLC 52**
See also CA 69-72; CAAS 12; CANR 11, 32; EWL 3; HW 1; WLIT 1
Golding, William (Gerald)
1911-1993 ..... **CLC 1, 2, 3, 8, 10, 17, 27, 58, 81; WLC**
See also AAYA 5, 44; BPFB 2; BRWR 1; BRWS 1; BYA 2; CA 5-8R; 141; CANR 13, 33, 54; CDBLB 1945-1960; DA; DA3; DAB; DAC; DAM MST, NOV; DLB 15, 100, 255; EWL 3; EXPN; HGG; LAIT 4; MTCW 1, 2; NFS 2; RGEL 2; RHW; SFW 4; TEA; WLIT 4; YAW
Goldman, Emma 1869-1940 .... **TCLC 13**
See also CA 110; 150; DLB 221; FW; RGAL 4; TUS
Goldman, Francisco 1954- .... **CLC 76**
See also CA 162
Goldman, William (W.) 1931- ...... **CLC 1, 48**
See also BPFB 2; CA 9-12R; CANR 29, 69, 106; CN 7; DLB 44; FANT; IDFW 3, 4
Goldmann, Lucien 1913-1970 .... **CLC 24**
See also CA 25-28; CAP 2
Goldoni, Carlo 1707-1793 .... **LC 4**
See also DAM DRAM; EW 4; RGWL 2, 3
Goldsberry, Steven 1949- .... **CLC 34**
See also CA 131
Goldsmith, Oliver 1730-1774 .... **DC 8; LC 2, 48; WLC**
See also BRW 3; CDBLB 1660-1789; DA; DAB; DAC; DAM DRAM, MST, NOV; POET; DFS 1; DLB 39, 89, 104, 109, 142; IDTP; RGEL 2; SATA 26; TEA; WLIT 3
Goldsmith, Peter
See Priestley, J(ohn) B(oynton)
Gombrowicz, Witold 1904-1969 .... **CLC 4, 7, 11, 49**
See also CA 19-20; 25-28R; CANR 105; CAP 2; CDWLB 4; DAM DRAM; DLB 215; EW 12; EWL 3; RGWL 2, 3; TWA
Gomez de Avellaneda, Gertrudis
1814-1873 .... **NCLC 111**
See also LAW

Gomez de la Serna, Ramon
1888-1963 .... **CLC 9**
See also CA 153; 116; CANR 79; EWL 3; HW 1, 2
Goncharov, Ivan Alexandrovich
1812-1891 .... **NCLC 1, 63**
See also DLB 238; EW 6; RGWL 2, 3
Goncourt, Edmond (Louis Antoine Huot) de
1822-1896 .... **NCLC 7**
See also DLB 123; EW 7; GFL 1789 to the Present; RGWL 2, 3
Goncourt, Jules (Alfred Huot) de
1830-1870 .... **NCLC 7**
See also DLB 123; EW 7; GFL 1789 to the Present; RGWL 2, 3
Gongora (y Argote), Luis de
1561-1627 .... **LC 72**
See also RGWL 2, 3
Gontier, Fernande 19(?)- .... **CLC 50**
Gonzalez Martinez, Enrique
1871-1952 .... **TCLC 72**
See also CA 166; CANR 81; EWL 3; HW 1, 2
Goodison, Lorna 1947- .... **PC 36**
See also CA 142; CANR 88; CP 7; CWP; DLB 157; EWL 3
Goodman, Paul 1911-1972 ..... **CLC 1, 2, 4, 7**
See also CA 19-20; 37-40R; CAD; CANR 34; CAP 2; DLB 130, 246; MTCW 1; RGAL 4
Gordimer, Nadine 1923- ...... **CLC 3, 5, 7, 10, 18, 33, 51, 70, 123, 160, 161; SSC 17; WLCS**
See also AAYA 39; AFW; BRWS 2; CA 5-8R; CANR 3, 28, 56, 88; CN 7; DA; DA3; DAB; DAC; DAM MST, NOV; DLB 225; EWL 3; EXPS; INT CANR-28; LATS 1; MTCW 1, 2; NFS 4; RGEL 2; RGSF 2; SSFS 2, 14; TWA; WLIT 2; YAW
Gordon, Adam Lindsay
1833-1870 .... **NCLC 21**
See also DLB 230
Gordon, Caroline 1895-1981 . **CLC 6, 13, 29, 83; SSC 15**
See also AMW; CA 11-12; 103; CANR 36; CAP 1; DLB 4, 9, 102; DLBD 17; DLBY 1981; EWL 3; MTCW 1, 2; RGAL 4; RGSF 2
Gordon, Charles William 1860-1937
See Connor, Ralph
See also CA 109
Gordon, Mary (Catherine) 1949- .... **CLC 13, 22, 128; SSC 59**
See also AMWS 4; BPFB 2; CA 102; CANR 44, 92; CN 7; DLB 6; DLBY 1981; FW; INT CA-102; MTCW 1
Gordon, N. J.
See Bosman, Herman Charles
Gordon, Sol 1923- .... **CLC 26**
See also CA 53-56; CANR 4; SATA 11
Gordone, Charles 1925-1995 .. **CLC 1, 4; DC 8**
See also BW 1, 3; CA 93-96; 180; 150; CAAE 180; CAD; CANR 55; DAM DRAM; DLB 7; INT 93-96; MTCW 1
Gore, Catherine 1800-1861 .... **NCLC 65**
See also DLB 116; RGEL 2
Gorenko, Anna Andreevna
See Akhmatova, Anna
Gorky, Maxim .... **SSC 28; TCLC 8; WLC**
See Peshkov, Alexei Maximovich
See also DAB; DFS 9; EW 8; EWL 3; MTCW 2; TWA
Goryan, Sirak
See Saroyan, William

Gosse, Edmund (William)
1849-1928 .... **TCLC 28**
See also CA 117; DLB 57, 144, 184; RGEL 2
Gotlieb, Phyllis Fay (Bloom) 1926- .. **CLC 18**
See also CA 13-16R; CANR 7; DLB 88, 251; SFW 4
Gottesman, S. D.
See Kornbluth, C(yril) M.; Pohl, Frederik
Gottfried von Strassburg fl. c.
1170-1215 .... **CMLC 10**
See also CDWLB 2; DLB 138; EW 1; RGWL 2, 3
Gotthelf, Jeremias 1797-1854 .... **NCLC 117**
See also DLB 133; RGWL 2, 3
Gottschalk, Laura Riding
See Jackson, Laura (Riding)
Gould, Lois 1932(?)-2002 .... **CLC 4, 10**
See also CA 77-80; 208; CANR 29; MTCW 1
Gould, Stephen Jay 1941-2002 .... **CLC 163**
See also AAYA 26; BEST 90:2; CA 77-80; 205; CANR 10, 27, 56, 75; CPW; INT CANR-27; MTCW 1, 2
Gourmont, Remy(-Marie-Charles) de
1858-1915 .... **TCLC 17**
See also CA 109; 150; GFL 1789 to the Present; MTCW 2
Govier, Katherine 1948- .... **CLC 51**
See also CA 101; CANR 18, 40; CCA 1
Gower, John c. 1330-1408 .... **LC 76**
See also BRW 1; DLB 146; RGEL 2
Goyen, (Charles) William
1915-1983 .... **CLC 5, 8, 14, 40**
See also AITN 2; CA 5-8R; 110; CANR 6, 71; DLB 2, 218; DLBY 1983; EWL 3; INT CANR-6
Goytisolo, Juan 1931- .... **CLC 5, 10, 23, 133; HLC 1**
See also CA 85-88; CANR 32, 61; CWW 2; DAM MULT; EWL 3; GLL 2; HW 1, 2; MTCW 1, 2
Gozzano, Guido 1883-1916 .... **PC 10**
See also CA 154; DLB 114; EWL 3
Gozzi, (Conte) Carlo 1720-1806 .... **NCLC 23**
Grabbe, Christian Dietrich
1801-1836 .... **NCLC 2**
See also DLB 133; RGWL 2, 3
Grace, Patricia Frances 1937- .... **CLC 56**
See also CA 176; CANR 118; CN 7; EWL 3; RGSF 2
Gracian y Morales, Baltasar
1601-1658 .... **LC 15**
Gracq, Julien .... **CLC 11, 48**
See Poirier, Louis
See also CWW 2; DLB 83; GFL 1789 to the Present
Grade, Chaim 1910-1982 .... **CLC 10**
See also CA 93-96; 107; EWL 3
Graduate of Oxford, A
See Ruskin, John
Grafton, Garth
See Duncan, Sara Jeannette
Grafton, Sue 1940- .... **CLC 163**
See also AAYA 11, 49; BEST 90:3; CA 108; CANR 31, 55, 111; CMW 4; CPW; CSW; DA3; DAM POP; DLB 226; FW; MSW
Graham, John
See Phillips, David Graham
Graham, Jorie 1950- .... **CLC 48, 118**
See also CA 111; CANR 63, 118; CP 7; CWP; DLB 120; EWL 3; PFS 10, 17
Graham, R(obert) B(ontine) Cunninghame
See Cunninghame Graham, Robert (Gallnigad) Bontine
See also DLB 98, 135, 174; RGEL 2; RGSF 2
Graham, Robert
See Haldeman, Joe (William)

Graham, Tom
See Lewis, (Harry) Sinclair

Graham, W(illiam) S(idney)
1918-1986 .... **CLC 29**
See also BRWS 7; CA 73-76; 118; DLB 20;
RGEL 2

Graham, Winston (Mawdsley)
1910- .... **CLC 23**
See also CA 49-52; CANR 2, 22, 45, 66;
CMW 4; CN 7; DLB 77; RHW

Grahame, Kenneth 1859-1932 ...... **TCLC 64, 136**
See also BYA 5; CA 108; 136; CANR 80;
CLR 5; CWRI 5; DA3; DAB; DLB 34,
141, 178; FANT; MAICYA 1, 2; MTCW
2; RGEL 2; SATA 100; TEA; WCH;
YABC 1

Granger, Darius John
See Marlowe, Stephen

Granin, Daniil .... **CLC 59**

Granovsky, Timofei Nikolaevich
1813-1855 .... **NCLC 75**
See also DLB 198

Grant, Skeeter
See Spiegelman, Art

Granville-Barker, Harley
1877-1946 .... **TCLC 2**
See Barker, Harley Granville
See also CA 104; 204; DAM DRAM;
RGEL 2

Granzotto, Gianni
See Granzotto, Giovanni Battista

Granzotto, Giovanni Battista
1914-1985 .... **CLC 70**
See also CA 166

Grass, Guenter (Wilhelm) 1927- ... **CLC 1, 2, 4, 6, 11, 15, 22, 32, 49, 88; WLC**
See also BPFB 2; CA 13-16R; CANR 20,
75, 93; CDWLB 2; DA; DA3; DAB;
DAC; DAM MST, NOV; DLB 75, 124;
EW 13; EWL 3; MTCW 1, 2; RGWL 2,
3; TWA

Gratton, Thomas
See Hulme, T(homas) E(rnest)

Grau, Shirley Ann 1929- .... **CLC 4, 9, 146; SSC 15**
See also CA 89-92; CANR 22, 69; CN 7;
CSW; DLB 2, 218; INT CA-89-92;
CANR-22; MTCW 1

Gravel, Fern
See Hall, James Norman

Graver, Elizabeth 1964- .... **CLC 70**
See also CA 135; CANR 71

Graves, Richard Perceval
1895-1985 .... **CLC 44**
See also CA 65-68; CANR 9, 26, 51

Graves, Robert (von Ranke)
1895-1985 .. **CLC 1, 2, 6, 11, 39, 44, 45; PC 6**
See also BPFB 2; BRW 7; BYA 4; CA 5-8R;
117; CANR 5, 36; CDBLB 1914-1945;
DA3; DAB; DAC; DAM MST, POET;
DLB 20, 100, 191; DLBD 18; DLBY
1985; EWL 3; LATS 1; MTCW 1, 2;
NCFS 2; RGEL 2; RHW; SATA 45; TEA

Graves, Valerie
See Bradley, Marion Zimmer

Gray, Alasdair (James) 1934- .... **CLC 41**
See also CA 126; CANR 47, 69, 106; CN
7; DLB 194, 261; HGG; INT CA-126;
MTCW 1, 2; RGSF 2; SUFW 2

Gray, Amlin 1946- .... **CLC 29**
See also CA 138

Gray, Francine du Plessix 1930- ..... **CLC 22, 153**
See also BEST 90:3; CA 61-64; CAAS 2;
CANR 11, 33, 75, 81; DAM NOV; INT
CANR-11; MTCW 1, 2

Gray, John (Henry) 1866-1934 ...... **TCLC 19**
See also CA 119; 162; RGEL 2

Gray, Simon (James Holliday)
1936- .... **CLC 9, 14, 36**
See also AITN 1; CA 21-24R; CAAS 3;
CANR 32, 69; CD 5; DLB 13; EWL 3;
MTCW 1; RGEL 2

Gray, Spalding 1941- ..... **CLC 49, 112; DC 7**
See also CA 128; CAD; CANR 74; CD 5;
CPW; DAM POP; MTCW 2

Gray, Thomas 1716-1771 .... **LC 4, 40; PC 2; WLC**
See also BRW 3; CDBLB 1660-1789; DA;
DA3; DAB; DAC; DAM MST; DLB 109;
EXPP; PAB; PFS 9; RGEL 2; TEA; WP

Grayson, David
See Baker, Ray Stannard

Grayson, Richard (A.) 1951- .... **CLC 38**
See also CA 85-88; CAAE 210; CANR 14,
31, 57; DLB 234

Greeley, Andrew M(oran) 1928- ...... **CLC 28**
See also BPFB 2; CA 5-8R; CAAS 7;
CANR 7, 43, 69, 104; CMW 4; CPW;
DA3; DAM POP; MTCW 1, 2

Green, Anna Katharine
1846-1935 .... **TCLC 63**
See also CA 112; 159; CMW 4; DLB 202,
221; MSW

Green, Brian
See Card, Orson Scott

Green, Hannah
See Greenberg, Joanne (Goldenberg)

Green, Hannah 1927(?)-1996 .... **CLC 3**
See also CA 73-76; CANR 59, 93; NFS 10

Green, Henry .... **CLC 2, 13, 97**
See Yorke, Henry Vincent
See also BRWS 2; CA 175; DLB 15; EWL
3; RGEL 2

Green, Julian (Hartridge) 1900-1998
See Green, Julien
See also CA 21-24R; 169; CANR 33, 87;
DLB 4, 72; MTCW 1

Green, Julien .... **CLC 3, 11, 77**
See Green, Julian (Hartridge)
See also EWL 3; GFL 1789 to the Present;
MTCW 2

Green, Paul (Eliot) 1894-1981 .... **CLC 25**
See also AITN 1; CA 5-8R; 103; CANR 3;
DAM DRAM; DLB 7, 9, 249; DLBY
1981; RGAL 4

Greenaway, Peter 1942- .... **CLC 159**
See also CA 127

Greenberg, Ivan 1908-1973
See Rahv, Philip
See also CA 85-88

Greenberg, Joanne (Goldenberg)
1932- .... **CLC 7, 30**
See also AAYA 12; CA 5-8R; CANR 14,
32, 69; CN 7; SATA 25; YAW

Greenberg, Richard 1959(?)- .... **CLC 57**
See also CA 138; CAD; CD 5

Greenblatt, Stephen J(ay) 1943- ...... **CLC 70**
See also CA 49-52; CANR 115

Greene, Bette 1934- .... **CLC 30**
See also AAYA 7; BYA 3; CA 53-56; CANR
4; CLR 2; CWRI 5; JRDA; LAIT 4; MAI-
CYA 1, 2; NFS 10; SAAS 16; SATA 8,
102; WYA; YAW

Greene, Gael .... **CLC 8**
See also CA 13-16R; CANR 10

Greene, Graham (Henry)
1904-1991 .... **CLC 1, 3, 6, 9, 14, 18, 27, 37, 70, 72, 125; SSC 29; WLC**
See also AITN 2; BPFB 2; BRWR 2; BRWS
1; BYA 3; CA 13-16R; 133; CANR 35,
61; CBD; CDBLB 1945-1960; CMW 4;
DA; DA3; DAB; DAC; DAM MST, NOV;

DLB 13, 15, 77, 100, 162, 201, 204;
DLBY 1991; EWL 3; MSW; MTCW 1, 2;
NFS 16; RGEL 2; SATA 20; SSFS 14;
TEA; WLIT 4

Greene, Robert 1558-1592 .... **LC 41**
See also BRWS 8; DLB 62, 167; IDTP;
RGEL 2; TEA

Greer, Germaine 1939- .... **CLC 131**
See also AITN 1; CA 81-84; CANR 33, 70,
115; FW; MTCW 1, 2

Greer, Richard
See Silverberg, Robert

Gregor, Arthur 1923- .... **CLC 9**
See also CA 25-28R; CAAS 10; CANR 11;
CP 7; SATA 36

Gregor, Lee
See Pohl, Frederik

Gregory, Lady Isabella Augusta (Persse)
1852-1932 .... **TCLC 1**
See also BRW 6; CA 104; 184; DLB 10;
IDTP; RGEL 2

Gregory, J. Dennis
See Williams, John A(lfred)

Grekova, I. .... **CLC 59**

Grendon, Stephen
See Derleth, August (William)

Grenville, Kate 1950- .... **CLC 61**
See also CA 118; CANR 53, 93

Grenville, Pelham
See Wodehouse, P(elham) G(renville)

Greve, Felix Paul (Berthold Friedrich)
1879-1948
See Grove, Frederick Philip
See also CA 104; 141, 175; CANR 79;
DAC; DAM MST

Greville, Fulke 1554-1628 .... **LC 79**
See also DLB 62, 172; RGEL 2

Grey, Zane 1872-1939 .... **TCLC 6**
See also BPFB 2; CA 104; 132; DA3; DAM
POP; DLB 9, 212; MTCW 1, 2; RGAL 4;
TCWW 2; TUS

Grieg, (Johan) Nordahl (Brun)
1902-1943 .... **TCLC 10**
See also CA 107; 189; EWL 3

Grieve, C(hristopher) M(urray)
1892-1978 .... **CLC 11, 19**
See MacDiarmid, Hugh; Pteleon
See also CA 5-8R; 85-88; CANR 33, 107;
DAM POET; MTCW 1; RGEL 2

Griffin, Gerald 1803-1840 .... **NCLC 7**
See also DLB 159; RGEL 2

Griffin, John Howard 1920-1980 ..... **CLC 68**
See also AITN 1; CA 1-4R; 101; CANR 2

Griffin, Peter 1942- .... **CLC 39**
See also CA 136

Griffith, D(avid Lewelyn) W(ark)
1875(?)-1948 .... **TCLC 68**
See also CA 119; 150; CANR 80

Griffith, Lawrence
See Griffith, D(avid Lewelyn) W(ark)

Griffiths, Trevor 1935- .... **CLC 13, 52**
See also CA 97-100; CANR 45; CBD; CD
5; DLB 13, 245

Griggs, Sutton (Elbert)
1872-1930 .... **TCLC 77**
See also CA 123; 186; DLB 50

Grigson, Geoffrey (Edward Harvey)
1905-1985 .... **CLC 7, 39**
See also CA 25-28R; 118; CANR 20, 33;
DLB 27; MTCW 1, 2

Grile, Dod
See Bierce, Ambrose (Gwinett)

Grillparzer, Franz 1791-1872 .... **DC 14; NCLC 1, 102; SSC 37**
See also CDWLB 2; DLB 133; EW 5;
RGWL 2, 3; TWA

Grimble, Reverend Charles James
See Eliot, T(homas) S(tearns)

Haggard, H(enry) Rider
1856-1925 .... **TCLC 11**
See also BRWS 3; BYA 4, 5; CA 108; 148;
CANR 112; DLB 70, 156, 174, 178;
FANT; LMFS 1; MTCW 2; RGEL 2;
RHW; SATA 16; SCFW; SFW 4; SUFW
1; WLIT 4

Hagiosy, L.
See Larbaud, Valery (Nicolas)

Hagiwara, Sakutaro 1886-1942 .... **PC 18;**
TCLC 60
See Hagiwara Sakutaro
See also CA 154; RGWL 3

Hagiwara Sakutaro
See Hagiwara, Sakutaro
See also EWL 3

Haig, Fenil
See Ford, Ford Madox

Haig-Brown, Roderick (Langmere)
1908-1976 .... **CLC 21**
See also CA 5-8R; 69-72; CANR 4, 38, 83;
CLR 31; CWRI 5; DLB 88; MAICYA 1,
2; SATA 12

Haight, Rip
See Carpenter, John (Howard)

Hailey, Arthur 1920- .... **CLC 5**
See also AITN 2; BEST 90:3; BPFB 2; CA
1-4R; CANR 2, 36, 75; CCA 1; CN 7;
CPW; DAM NOV, POP; DLB 88; DLBY
1982; MTCW 1, 2

Hailey, Elizabeth Forsythe 1938- ..... **CLC 40**
See also CA 93-96; CAAE 188; CAAS 1;
CANR 15, 48; INT CANR-15

Haines, John (Meade) 1924- .... **CLC 58**
See also AMWS 12; CA 17-20R; CANR
13, 34; CSW; DLB 5, 212

Hakluyt, Richard 1552-1616 .... **LC 31**
See also DLB 136; RGEL 2

Haldeman, Joe (William) 1943- .... **CLC 61**
See Graham, Robert
See also AAYA 38; CA 53-56, 179; CAAE
179; CAAS 25; CANR 6, 70, 72; DLB 8;
INT CANR-6; SCFW 2; SFW 4

Hale, Janet Campbell 1947- .... **NNAL**
See also CA 49-52; CANR 45, 75; DAM
MULT; DLB 175; MTCW 2

Hale, Sarah Josepha (Buell)
1788-1879 .... **NCLC 75**
See also DLB 1, 42, 73, 243

Halevy, Elie 1870-1937 .... **TCLC 104**

Haley, Alex(ander Murray Palmer)
1921-1992 .... **BLC 2; CLC 8, 12, 76**
See also AAYA 26; BPFB 2; BW 2, 3; CA
77-80; 136; CANR 61; CDALBS; CPW;
CSW; DA; DA3; DAB; DAC; DAM MST,
MULT, POP; DLB 38; LAIT 5; MTCW
1, 2; NFS 9

Haliburton, Thomas Chandler
1796-1865 .... **NCLC 15**
See also DLB 11, 99; RGEL 2; RGSF 2

Hall, Donald (Andrew, Jr.) 1928- ...... **CLC 1,**
13, 37, 59, 151
See also CA 5-8R; CAAS 7; CANR 2, 44,
64, 106; CP 7; DAM POET; DLB 5;
MTCW 1; RGAL 4; SATA 23, 97

Hall, Frederic Sauser
See Sauser-Hall, Frederic

Hall, James
See Kuttner, Henry

Hall, James Norman 1887-1951 ..... **TCLC 23**
See also CA 123; 173; LAIT 1; RHW 1;
SATA 21

Hall, (Marguerite) Radclyffe
1880-1943 .... **TCLC 12**
See also BRWS 6; CA 110; 150; CANR 83;
DLB 191; MTCW 2; RGEL 2; RHW

Hall, Rodney 1935- .... **CLC 51**
See also CA 109; CANR 69; CN 7; CP 7

Hallam, Arthur Henry
1811-1833 .... **NCLC 110**
See also DLB 32

Halleck, Fitz-Greene 1790-1867 .... **NCLC 47**
See also DLB 3, 250; RGAL 4

Halliday, Michael
See Creasey, John

Halpern, Daniel 1945- .... **CLC 14**
See also CA 33-36R; CANR 93; CP 7

Hamburger, Michael (Peter Leopold)
1924- .... **CLC 5, 14**
See also CA 5-8R; CAAE 196; CAAS 4;
CANR 2, 47; CP 7; DLB 27

Hamill, Pete 1935- .... **CLC 10**
See also CA 25-28R; CANR 18, 71

Hamilton, Alexander
1755(?)-1804 .... **NCLC 49**
See also DLB 37

Hamilton, Clive
See Lewis, C(live) S(taples)

Hamilton, Edmond 1904-1977 .... **CLC 1**
See also CA 1-4R; CANR 3, 84; DLB 8;
SATA 118; SFW 4

Hamilton, Eugene (Jacob) Lee
See Lee-Hamilton, Eugene (Jacob)

Hamilton, Franklin
See Silverberg, Robert

Hamilton, Gail
See Corcoran, Barbara (Asenath)

Hamilton, Mollie
See Kaye, M(ary) M(argaret)

Hamilton, (Anthony Walter) Patrick
1904-1962 .... **CLC 51**
See also CA 176; 113; DLB 10, 191

Hamilton, Virginia (Esther)
1936-2002 .... **CLC 26**
See also AAYA 2, 21; BW 2, 3; BYA 1, 2,
8; CA 25-28R; 206; CANR 20, 37, 73;
CLR 1, 11, 40; DAM MULT; DLB 33,
52; DLBY 01; INT CANR-20; JRDA;
LAIT 5; MAICYA 1, 2; MAICYAS 1;
MTCW 1, 2; SATA 4, 56, 79, 123; SATA-
Obit 132; WYA; YAW

Hammett, (Samuel) Dashiell
1894-1961 .... **CLC 3, 5, 10, 19, 47; SSC**
17
See also AITN 1; AMWS 4; BPFB 2; CA
81-84; CANR 42; CDALB 1929-1941;
CMW 4; DA3; DLB 226; DLBD 6; DLBY
1996; EWL 3; LAIT 3; MSW; MTCW 1,
2; RGAL 4; RGSF 2; TUS

Hammon, Jupiter 1720(?)-1800(?) .... **BLC 2;**
NCLC 5; PC 16
See also DAM MULT, POET; DLB 31, 50

Hammond, Keith
See Kuttner, Henry

Hamner, Earl (Henry), Jr. 1923- ...... **CLC 12**
See also AITN 2; CA 73-76; DLB 6

Hampton, Christopher (James)
1946- .... **CLC 4**
See also CA 25-28R; CD 5; DLB 13;
MTCW 1

Hamsun, Knut .... **TCLC 2, 14, 49**
See Pedersen, Knut
See also EW 8; EWL 3; RGWL 2, 3

Handke, Peter 1942- .... **CLC 5, 8, 10, 15, 38,**
134; DC 17
See also CA 77-80; CANR 33, 75, 104;
CWW 2; DAM DRAM, NOV; DLB 85,
124; EWL 3; MTCW 1, 2; TWA

Handy, W(illiam) C(hristopher)
1873-1958 .... **TCLC 97**
See also BW 3; CA 121; 167

Hanley, James 1901-1985 ..... **CLC 3, 5, 8, 13**
See also CA 73-76; 117; CANR 36; CBD;
DLB 191; EWL 3; MTCW 1; RGEL 2

Hannah, Barry 1942- .... **CLC 23, 38, 90**
See also BPFB 2; CA 108; 110; CANR 43,
68, 113; CN 7; CSW; DLB 6, 234; INT
CA-110; MTCW 1; RGSF 2

Hannon, Ezra
See Hunter, Evan

Hansberry, Lorraine (Vivian)
1930-1965 ... **BLC 2; CLC 17, 62; DC 2**
See also AAYA 25; AFAW 1, 2; AMWS 4;
BW 1, 3; CA 109; 25-28R; CABS 3;
CAD; CANR 58; CDALB 1941-1968;
CWD; DA; DA3; DAB; DAC; DAM
DRAM, MST, MULT; DFS 2; DLB 7, 38;
EWL 3; FW; LAIT 4; MTCW 1, 2; RGAL
4; TUS

Hansen, Joseph 1923- .... **CLC 38**
See Brock, Rose; Colton, James
See also BPFB 2; CA 29-32R; CAAS 17;
CANR 16, 44, 66; CMW 4; DLB 226;
GLL 1; INT CANR-16

Hansen, Martin A(lfred)
1909-1955 .... **TCLC 32**
See also CA 167; DLB 214; EWL 3

Hansen and Philipson eds. .... **CLC 65**

Hanson, Kenneth O(stlin) 1922- .... **CLC 13**
See also CA 53-56; CANR 7

Hardwick, Elizabeth (Bruce) 1916- . **CLC 13**
See also AMWS 3; CA 5-8R; CANR 3, 32,
70, 100; CN 7; CSW; DA3; DAM NOV;
DLB 6; MAWW; MTCW 1, 2

Hardy, Thomas 1840-1928 .... **PC 8; SSC 2,**
60; TCLC 4, 10, 18, 32, 48, 53, 72;
WLC
See also BRW 6; BRWC 1; BRWR 1; CA
104; 123; CDBLB 1890-1914; DA; DA3;
DAB; DAC; DAM MST, NOV, POET;
DLB 18, 19, 135, 284; EWL 3; EXPN;
EXPP; LAIT 2; MTCW 1, 2; NFS 3, 11,
15; PFS 3, 4; RGEL 2; RGSF 2; TEA;
WLIT 4

Hare, David 1947- .... **CLC 29, 58, 136**
See also BRWS 4; CA 97-100; CANR 39,
91; CBD; CD 5; DFS 4, 7, 16; DLB 13;
MTCW 1; TEA

Harewood, John
See Van Druten, John (William)

Harford, Henry
See Hudson, W(illiam) H(enry)

Hargrave, Leonie
See Disch, Thomas M(ichael)

Harjo, Joy 1951- .... **CLC 83; NNAL; PC 27**
See also AMWS 12; CA 114; CANR 35,
67, 91; CP 7; CWP; DAM MULT; DLB
120, 175; EWL 3; MTCW 2; PFS 15;
RGAL 4

Harlan, Louis R(udolph) 1922- .... **CLC 34**
See also CA 21-24R; CANR 25, 55, 80

Harling, Robert 1951(?)- .... **CLC 53**
See also CA 147

Harmon, William (Ruth) 1938- .... **CLC 38**
See also CA 33-36R; CANR 14, 32, 35;
SATA 65

Harper, F. E. W.
See Harper, Frances Ellen Watkins

Harper, Frances E. W.
See Harper, Frances Ellen Watkins

Harper, Frances E. Watkins
See Harper, Frances Ellen Watkins

Harper, Frances Ellen
See Harper, Frances Ellen Watkins

Harper, Frances Ellen Watkins
1825-1911 ..... **BLC 2; PC 21; TCLC 14**
See also AFAW 1, 2; BW 1, 3; CA 111; 125;
CANR 79; DAM MULT, POET; DLB 50,
221; MAWW; RGAL 4

Harper, Michael S(teven) 1938- ... **CLC 7, 22**
See also AFAW 2; BW 1; CA 33-36R;
CANR 24, 108; CP 7; DLB 41; RGAL 4

Hoffman, William M(oses) 1939- ..... **CLC 40**
    See Hoffman, William M.
    See also CA 57-60; CANR 11, 71
Hoffmann, E(rnst) T(heodor) A(madeus)
    1776-1822 .... **NCLC 2; SSC 13**
    See also CDWLB 2; DLB 90; EW 5; RGSF
    2; RGWL 2, 3; SATA 27; SUFW 1; WCH
Hofmann, Gert 1931- .... **CLC 54**
    See also CA 128; EWL 3
Hofmannsthal, Hugo von 1874-1929 ... **DC 4;**
    TCLC 11
    See also CA 106; 153; CDWLB 2; DAM
    DRAM; DFS 17; DLB 81, 118; EW 9;
    EWL 3; RGWL 2, 3
Hogan, Linda 1947- ..... **CLC 73; NNAL; PC**
    35
    See also AMWS 4; ANW; BYA 12; CA 120;
    CANR 45, 73; CWP; DAM MULT; DLB
    175; SATA 132; TCWW 2
Hogarth, Charles
    See Creasey, John
Hogarth, Emmett
    See Polonsky, Abraham (Lincoln)
Hogg, James 1770-1835 .... **NCLC 4, 109**
    See also DLB 93, 116, 159; HGG; RGEL 2;
    SUFW 1
Holbach, Paul Henri Thiry Baron
    1723-1789 .... **LC 14**
Holberg, Ludvig 1684-1754 .... **LC 6**
    See also RGWL 2, 3
Holcroft, Thomas 1745-1809 .... **NCLC 85**
    See also DLB 39, 89, 158; RGEL 2
Holden, Ursula 1921- .... **CLC 18**
    See also CA 101; CAAS 8; CANR 22
Holderlin, (Johann Christian) Friedrich
    1770-1843 .... **NCLC 16; PC 4**
    See also CDWLB 2; DLB 90; EW 5; RGWL
    2, 3
Holdstock, Robert
    See Holdstock, Robert P.
Holdstock, Robert P. 1948- .... **CLC 39**
    See also CA 131; CANR 81; DLB 261;
    FANT; HGG; SFW 4; SUFW 2
Holinshed, Raphael fl. 1580- .... **LC 69**
    See also DLB 167; RGEL 2
Holland, Isabelle (Christian)
    1920-2002 .... **CLC 21**
    See also AAYA 11; CA 21-24R; 205;
    CAAE 181; CANR 10, 25, 47; CLR 57;
    CWRI 5; JRDA; LAIT 4; MAICYA 1, 2;
    SATA 8, 70; SATA-Essay 103; SATA-Obit
    132; WYA
Holland, Marcus
    See Caldwell, (Janet Miriam) Taylor
    (Holland)
Hollander, John 1929- .... **CLC 2, 5, 8, 14**
    See also CA 1-4R; CANR 1, 52; CP 7; DLB
    5; SATA 13
Hollander, Paul
    See Silverberg, Robert
Holleran, Andrew 1943(?)- .... **CLC 38**
    See Garber, Eric
    See also CA 144; GLL 1
Holley, Marietta 1836(?)-1926 .... **TCLC 99**
    See also CA 118; DLB 11
Hollinghurst, Alan 1954- .... **CLC 55, 91**
    See also CA 114; CN 7; DLB 207; GLL 1
Hollis, Jim
    See Summers, Hollis (Spurgeon, Jr.)
Holly, Buddy 1936-1959 .... **TCLC 65**
Holmes, Gordon
    See Shiel, M(atthew) P(hipps)
Holmes, John
    See Souster, (Holmes) Raymond
Holmes, John Clellon 1926-1988 ...... **CLC 56**
    See also BG 2; CA 9-12R; 125; CANR 4;
    DLB 16, 237

Holmes, Oliver Wendell, Jr.
    1841-1935 .... **TCLC 77**
    See also CA 114; 186
Holmes, Oliver Wendell
    1809-1894 .... **NCLC 14, 81**
    See also AMWS 1; CDALB 1640-1865;
    DLB 1, 189, 235; EXPP; RGAL 4; SATA
    34
Holmes, Raymond
    See Souster, (Holmes) Raymond
Holt, Victoria
    See Hibbert, Eleanor Alice Burford
    See also BPFB 2
Holub, Miroslav 1923-1998 .... **CLC 4**
    See also CA 21-24R; 169; CANR 10; CD-
    WLB 4; CWW 2; DLB 232; EWL 3;
    RGWL 3
Holz, Detlev
    See Benjamin, Walter
Homer c. 8th cent. B.C.- .... **CMLC 1, 16; PC**
    23; WLCS
    See also AW 1; CDWLB 1; DA; DA3;
    DAB; DAC; DAM MST, POET; DLB
    176; EFS 1; LAIT 1; LMFS 1; RGWL 2,
    3; TWA; WP
Hongo, Garrett Kaoru 1951- .... **PC 23**
    See also CA 133; CAAS 22; CP 7; DLB
    120; EWL 3; EXPP; RGAL 4
Honig, Edwin 1919- .... **CLC 33**
    See also CA 5-8R; CAAS 8; CANR 4, 45;
    CP 7; DLB 5
Hood, Hugh (John Blagdon) 1928- . **CLC 15,**
    28; SSC 42
    See also CA 49-52; CAAS 17; CANR 1,
    33, 87; CN 7; DLB 53; RGSF 2
Hood, Thomas 1799-1845 .... **NCLC 16**
    See also BRW 4; DLB 96; RGEL 2
Hooker, (Peter) Jeremy 1941- .... **CLC 43**
    See also CA 77-80; CANR 22; CP 7; DLB
    40
hooks, bell .... **CLC 94**
    See Watkins, Gloria Jean
    See also DLB 246
Hope, A(lec) D(erwent) 1907-2000 .... **CLC 3,**
    51
    See also BRWS 7; CA 21-24R; 188; CANR
    33, 74; EWL 3; MTCW 1, 2; PFS 8;
    RGEL 2
Hope, Anthony 1863-1933 .... **TCLC 83**
    See also CA 157; DLB 153, 156; RGEL 2;
    RHW
Hope, Brian
    See Creasey, John
Hope, Christopher (David Tully)
    1944- .... **CLC 52**
    See also AFW; CA 106; CANR 47, 101;
    CN 7; DLB 225; SATA 62
Hopkins, Gerard Manley
    1844-1889 .... **NCLC 17; PC 15; WLC**
    See also BRW 5; BRWR 2; CDBLB 1890-
    1914; DA; DA3; DAB; DAC; DAM MST,
    POET; DLB 35, 57; EXPP; PAB; RGEL
    2; TEA; WP
Hopkins, John (Richard) 1931-1998 .. **CLC 4**
    See also CA 85-88; 169; CBD; CD 5
Hopkins, Pauline Elizabeth
    1859-1930 .... **BLC 2; TCLC 28**
    See also AFAW 2; BW 2, 3; CA 141; CANR
    82; DAM MULT; DLB 50
Hopkinson, Francis 1737-1791 .... **LC 25**
    See also DLB 31; RGAL 4
Hopley-Woolrich, Cornell George 1903-1968
    See Woolrich, Cornell
    See also CA 13-14; CANR 58; CAP 1;
    CMW 4; DLB 226; MTCW 2
Horace 65B.C.-8B.C. .... **CMLC 39; PC 46**
    See also AW 2; CDWLB 1; DLB 211;
    RGWL 2, 3

Horatio
    See Proust, (Valentin-Louis-George-Eugene-
)Marcel
Horgan, Paul (George Vincent
    O'Shaughnessy) 1903-1995 .. **CLC 9, 53**
    See also BPFB 2; CA 13-16R; 147; CANR
    9, 35; DAM NOV; DLB 102, 212; DLBY
    1985; INT CANR-9; MTCW 1, 2; SATA
    13; SATA-Obit 84; TCWW 2
Horkheimer, Max 1895-1973 .... **TCLC 132**
    See also CA 41-44R
Horn, Peter
    See Kuttner, Henry
Horne, Frank (Smith) 1899-1974 .... **HR 2**
    See also BW 1; CA 125; 53-56; DLB 51;
    WP
Hornem, Horace Esq.
    See Byron, George Gordon (Noel)
Horney, Karen (Clementine Theodore
    Danielsen) 1885-1952 .... **TCLC 71**
    See also CA 114; 165; DLB 246; FW
Hornung, E(rnest) W(illiam)
    1866-1921 .... **TCLC 59**
    See also CA 108; 160; CMW 4; DLB 70
Horovitz, Israel (Arthur) 1939- .... **CLC 56**
    See also CA 33-36R; CAD; CANR 46, 59;
    CD 5; DAM DRAM; DLB 7
Horton, George Moses
    1797(?)-1883(?) .... **NCLC 87**
    See also DLB 50
Horvath, odon von 1901-1938
    See von Horvath, Odon
    See also EWL 3
Horvath, Oedoen von -1938
    See von Horvath, Odon
Horwitz, Julius 1920-1986 .... **CLC 14**
    See also CA 9-12R; 119; CANR 12
Hospital, Janette Turner 1942- .... **CLC 42,**
    145
    See also CA 108; CANR 48; CN 7; DLBY
    2002; RGSF 2
Hostos, E. M. de
    See Hostos (y Bonilla), Eugenio Maria de
Hostos, Eugenio M. de
    See Hostos (y Bonilla), Eugenio Maria de
Hostos, Eugenio Maria
    See Hostos (y Bonilla), Eugenio Maria de
Hostos (y Bonilla), Eugenio Maria de
    1839-1903 .... **TCLC 24**
    See also CA 123; 131; HW 1
Houdini
    See Lovecraft, H(oward) P(hillips)
Hougan, Carolyn 1943- .... **CLC 34**
    See also CA 139
Household, Geoffrey (Edward West)
    1900-1988 .... **CLC 11**
    See also CA 77-80; 126; CANR 58; CMW
    4; DLB 87; SATA 14; SATA-Obit 59
Housman, A(lfred) E(dward)
    1859-1936 .... **PC 2, 43; TCLC 1, 10;**
    WLCS
    See also BRW 6; CA 104; 125; DA; DA3;
    DAB; DAC; DAM MST, POET; DLB 19,
    284; EWL 3; EXPP; MTCW 1, 2; PAB;
    PFS 4, 7; RGEL 2; TEA; WP
Housman, Laurence 1865-1959 .... **TCLC 7**
    See also CA 106; 155; DLB 10; FANT;
    RGEL 2; SATA 25
Houston, Jeanne (Toyo) Wakatsuki
    1934- .... **AAL**
    See also AAYA 49; CA 103; CAAS 16;
    CANR 29; LAIT 4; SATA 78
Howard, Elizabeth Jane 1923- ..... **CLC 7, 29**
    See also CA 5-8R; CANR 8, 62; CN 7
Howard, Maureen 1930- .... **CLC 5, 14, 46,**
    151
    See also CA 53-56; CANR 31, 75; CN 7;
    DLBY 1983; INT CANR-31; MTCW 1, 2

Howard, Richard 1929- .... **CLC 7, 10, 47**
　　See also AITN 1; CA 85-88; CANR 25, 80;
　　CP 7; DLB 5; INT CANR-25
Howard, Robert E(rvin)
　　1906-1936 .... **TCLC 8**
　　See also BPFB 2; BYA 5; CA 105; 157;
　　FANT; SUFW 1
Howard, Warren F.
　　See Pohl, Frederik
Howe, Fanny (Quincy) 1940- .... **CLC 47**
　　See also CA 117; CAAE 187; CAAS 27;
　　CANR 70, 116; CP 7; CWP; SATA-Brief
　　52
Howe, Irving 1920-1993 .... **CLC 85**
　　See also AMWS 6; CA 9-12R; 141; CANR
　　21, 50; DLB 67; EWL 3; MTCW 1, 2
Howe, Julia Ward 1819-1910 .... **TCLC 21**
　　See also CA 117; 191; DLB 1, 189, 235;
　　FW
Howe, Susan 1937- .... **CLC 72, 152**
　　See also AMWS 4; CA 160; CP 7; CWP;
　　DLB 120; FW; RGAL 4
Howe, Tina 1937- .... **CLC 48**
　　See also CA 109; CAD; CD 5; CWD
Howell, James 1594(?)-1666 .... **LC 13**
　　See also DLB 151
Howells, W. D.
　　See Howells, William Dean
Howells, William D.
　　See Howells, William Dean
Howells, William Dean 1837-1920 ... **SSC 36;**
　　TCLC 7, 17, 41
　　See also AMW; CA 104; 134; CDALB
　　1865-1917; DLB 12, 64, 74, 79, 189;
　　LMFS 1; MTCW 2; RGAL 4; TUS
Howes, Barbara 1914-1996 .... **CLC 15**
　　See also CA 9-12R; 151; CAAS 3; CANR
　　53; CP 7; SATA 5
Hrabal, Bohumil 1914-1997 .... **CLC 13, 67**
　　See also CA 106; 156; CAAS 12; CANR
　　57; CWW 2; DLB 232; EWL 3; RGSF 2
Hrotsvit of Gandersheim c. 935-c.
　　1000 .... **CMLC 29**
　　See also DLB 148
Hsi, Chu 1130-1200 .... **CMLC 42**
Hsun, Lu
　　See Lu Hsun
Hubbard, L(afayette) Ron(ald)
　　1911-1986 .... **CLC 43**
　　See also CA 77-80; 118; CANR 52; CPW;
　　DA3; DAM POP; FANT; MTCW 2; SFW
　　4
Huch, Ricarda (Octavia)
　　1864-1947 .... **TCLC 13**
　　See also CA 111; 189; DLB 66; EWL 3
Huddle, David 1942- .... **CLC 49**
　　See also CA 57-60; CAAS 20; CANR 89;
　　DLB 130
Hudson, Jeffrey
　　See Crichton, (John) Michael
Hudson, W(illiam) H(enry)
　　1841-1922 .... **TCLC 29**
　　See also CA 115; 190; DLB 98, 153, 174;
　　RGEL 2; SATA 35
Hueffer, Ford Madox
　　See Ford, Ford Madox
Hughart, Barry 1934- .... **CLC 39**
　　See also CA 137; FANT; SFW 4; SUFW 2
Hughes, Colin
　　See Creasey, John
Hughes, David (John) 1930- .... **CLC 48**
　　See also CA 116; 129; CN 7; DLB 14
Hughes, Edward James
　　See Hughes, Ted
　　See also DA3; DAM MST, POET

Hughes, (James Mercer) Langston
　　1902-1967 ..... **BLC 2; CLC 1, 5, 10, 15,**
　　35, 44, 108; DC 3; HR 2; PC 1; SSC 6;
　　WLC
　　See also AAYA 12; AFAW 1, 2; AMWR 1;
　　AMWS 1; BW 1, 3; CA 1-4R; 25-28R;
　　CANR 1, 34, 82; CDALB 1929-1941;
　　CLR 17; DA; DA3; DAB; DAC; DAM
　　DRAM, MST, MULT, POET; DFS 6;
　　DLB 4, 7, 48, 51, 86, 228; EWL 3; EXPP;
　　EXPS; JRDA; LAIT 3; LMFS 2; MAI-
　　CYA 1, 2; MTCW 1, 2; PAB; PFS 1, 3, 6,
　　10, 15; RGAL 4; RGSF 2; SATA 4, 33;
　　SSFS 4, 7; TUS; WCH; WP; YAW
Hughes, Richard (Arthur Warren)
　　1900-1976 .... **CLC 1, 11**
　　See also CA 5-8R; 65-68; CANR 4; DAM
　　NOV; DLB 15, 161; EWL 3; MTCW 1;
　　RGEL 2; SATA 8; SATA-Obit 25
Hughes, Ted 1930-1998 . **CLC 2, 4, 9, 14, 37,**
　　119; PC 7
　　See Hughes, Edward James
　　See also BRWR 2; BRWS 1; CA 1-4R; 171;
　　CANR 1, 33, 66, 108; CLR 3; CP 7;
　　DAB; DAC; DLB 40, 161; EWL 3; EXPP;
　　MAICYA 1, 2; MTCW 1, 2; PAB; PFS 4;
　　RGEL 2; SATA 49; SATA-Brief 27;
　　SATA-Obit 107; TEA; YAW
Hugo, Richard
　　See Huch, Ricarda (Octavia)
Hugo, Richard F(ranklin)
　　1923-1982 .... **CLC 6, 18, 32**
　　See also AMWS 6; CA 49-52; 108; CANR
　　3; DAM POET; DLB 5, 206; EWL 3; PFS
　　17; RGAL 4
Hugo, Victor (Marie) 1802-1885 .... **NCLC 3,**
　　10, 21; WLC
　　See also AAYA 28; DA; DA3; DAB; DAC;
　　DAM DRAM, MST, NOV, POET; DLB
　　119, 192, 217; EFS 2; EW 6; EXPN; GFL
　　1789 to the Present; LAIT 1, 2; NFS 5;
　　RGWL 2, 3; SATA 47; TWA
Huidobro, Vicente
　　See Huidobro Fernandez, Vicente Garcia
　　See also EWL 3; LAW
Huidobro Fernandez, Vicente Garcia
　　1893-1948 .... **TCLC 31**
　　See Huidobro, Vicente
　　See also CA 131; HW 1
Hulme, Keri 1947- .... **CLC 39, 130**
　　See also CA 125; CANR 69; CN 7; CP 7;
　　CWP; EWL 3; FW; INT 125
Hulme, T(homas) E(rnest)
　　1883-1917 .... **TCLC 21**
　　See also BRWS 6; CA 117; 203; DLB 19
Hume, David 1711-1776 .... **LC 7, 56**
　　See also BRWS 3; DLB 104, 252; LMFS 1;
　　TEA
Humphrey, William 1924-1997 .... **CLC 45**
　　See also AMWS 9; CA 77-80; 160; CANR
　　68; CN 7; CSW; DLB 6, 212, 234, 278;
　　TCWW 2
Humphreys, Emyr Owen 1919- .... **CLC 47**
　　See also CA 5-8R; CANR 3, 24; CN 7;
　　DLB 15
Humphreys, Josephine 1945- ..... **CLC 34, 57**
　　See also CA 121; 127; CANR 97; CSW;
　　INT 127
Huneker, James Gibbons
　　1860-1921 .... **TCLC 65**
　　See also CA 193; DLB 71; RGAL 4
Hungerford, Hesba Fay
　　See Brinsmead, H(esba) F(ay)
Hungerford, Pixie
　　See Brinsmead, H(esba) F(ay)
Hunt, E(verette) Howard, (Jr.)
　　1918- .... **CLC 3**
　　See also AITN 1; CA 45-48; CANR 2, 47,
　　103; CMW 4

Hunt, Francesca
　　See Holland, Isabelle (Christian)
Hunt, Howard
　　See Hunt, E(verette) Howard, (Jr.)
Hunt, Kyle
　　See Creasey, John
Hunt, (James Henry) Leigh
　　1784-1859 .... **NCLC 1, 70**
　　See also DAM POET; DLB 96, 110, 144;
　　RGEL 2; TEA
Hunt, Marsha 1946- .... **CLC 70**
　　See also BW 2, 3; CA 143; CANR 79
Hunt, Violet 1866(?)-1942 .... **TCLC 53**
　　See also CA 184; DLB 162, 197
Hunter, E. Waldo
　　See Sturgeon, Theodore (Hamilton)
Hunter, Evan 1926- .... **CLC 11, 31**
　　See McBain, Ed
　　See also AAYA 39; BPFB 2; CA 5-8R;
　　CANR 5, 38, 62, 97; CMW 4; CN 7;
　　CPW; DAM POP; DLBY 1982; INT
　　CANR-5; MSW; MTCW 1; SATA 25;
　　SFW 4
Hunter, Kristin 1931-
　　See Lattany, Kristin (Elaine Eggleston)
　　Hunter
Hunter, Mary
　　See Austin, Mary (Hunter)
Hunter, Mollie 1922- .... **CLC 21**
　　See McIlwraith, Maureen Mollie Hunter
　　See also AAYA 13; BYA 6; CANR 37, 78;
　　CLR 25; DLB 161; JRDA; MAICYA 1,
　　2; SAAS 7; SATA 54, 106, 139; WYA;
　　YAW
Hunter, Robert (?)-1734 .... **LC 7**
Hurston, Zora Neale 1891-1960 .... **BLC 2;**
　　CLC 7, 30, 61; DC 12; HR 2; SSC 4;
　　TCLC 121, 131; WLCS
　　See also AAYA 15; AFAW 1, 2; AMWS 6;
　　BW 1, 3; BYA 12; CA 85-88; CANR 61;
　　CDALBS; DA; DA3; DAC; DAM MST,
　　MULT, NOV; DFS 6; DLB 51, 86; EWL
　　3; EXPN; EXPS; FW; LAIT 3; LATS 1;
　　LMFS 2; MAWW; MTCW 1, 2; NFS 3;
　　RGAL 4; RGSF 2; SSFS 1, 6, 11; TUS;
　　YAW
Husserl, E. G.
　　See Husserl, Edmund (Gustav Albrecht)
Husserl, Edmund (Gustav Albrecht)
　　1859-1938 .... **TCLC 100**
　　See also CA 116; 133
Huston, John (Marcellus)
　　1906-1987 .... **CLC 20**
　　See also CA 73-76; 123; CANR 34; DLB
　　26
Hustvedt, Siri 1955- .... **CLC 76**
　　See also CA 137
Hutten, Ulrich von 1488-1523 .... **LC 16**
　　See also DLB 179
Huxley, Aldous (Leonard)
　　1894-1963 .... **CLC 1, 3, 4, 5, 8, 11, 18,**
　　35, 79; SSC 39; WLC
　　See also AAYA 11; BPFB 2; BRW 7; CA
　　85-88; CANR 44, 99; CDBLB 1914-1945;
　　DA; DA3; DAB; DAC; DAM MST, NOV;
　　DLB 36, 100, 162, 195, 255; EWL 3;
　　EXPN; LAIT 5; LMFS 2; MTCW 1, 2;
　　NFS 6; RGEL 2; SATA 63; SCFW 2;
　　SFW 4; TEA; YAW
Huxley, T(homas) H(enry)
　　1825-1895 .... **NCLC 67**
　　See also DLB 57; TEA
Huysmans, Joris-Karl 1848-1907 ... **TCLC 7,**
　　69
　　See also CA 104; 165; DLB 123; EW 7;
　　GFL 1789 to the Present; LMFS 2; RGWL
　　2, 3

Hwang, David Henry 1957- .. **CLC 55; DC 4**
See also CA 127; 132; CAD; CANR 76; CD 5; DA3; DAM DRAM; DFS 11; DLB 212, 228; INT CA-132; MTCW 2; RGAL 4

Hyde, Anthony 1946- .... **CLC 42**
See Chase, Nicholas
See also CA 136; CCA 1

Hyde, Margaret O(ldroyd) 1917- ..... **CLC 21**
See also CA 1-4R; CANR 1, 36; CLR 23; JRDA; MAICYA 1, 2; SAAS 8; SATA 1, 42, 76, 139

Hynes, James 1956(?)- .... **CLC 65**
See also CA 164; CANR 105

Hypatia c. 370-415 .... **CMLC 35**

Ian, Janis 1951- .... **CLC 21**
See also CA 105; 187

Ibanez, Vicente Blasco
See Blasco Ibanez, Vicente

Ibarbourou, Juana de 1895-1979 ..... **HLCS 2**
See also HW 1; LAW

Ibarguengoitia, Jorge 1928-1983 ...... **CLC 37**
See also CA 124; 113; EWL 3; HW 1

Ibn Battuta, Abu Abdalla
1304-1368(?) .... **CMLC 57**
See also WLIT 2

Ibsen, Henrik (Johan) 1828-1906 .... **DC 2; TCLC 2, 8, 16, 37, 52; WLC**
See also AAYA 46; CA 104; 141; DA; DA3; DAB; DAC; DAM DRAM, MST; DFS 1, 6, 8, 10, 11, 15, 16; EW 7; LAIT 2; LATS 1; RGWL 2, 3

Ibuse, Masuji 1898-1993 .... **CLC 22**
See Ibuse Masuji
See also CA 127; 141; MJW; RGWL 3

Ibuse Masuji
See Ibuse, Masuji
See also DLB 180; EWL 3

Ichikawa, Kon 1915- .... **CLC 20**
See also CA 121

Ichiyo, Higuchi 1872-1896 .... **NCLC 49**
See also MJW

Idle, Eric 1943-2000 .... **CLC 21**
See Monty Python
See also CA 116; CANR 35, 91

Ignatow, David 1914-1997 .... **CLC 4, 7, 14, 40; PC 34**
See also CA 9-12R; 162; CAAS 3; CANR 31, 57, 96; CP 7; DLB 5; EWL 3

Ignotus
See Strachey, (Giles) Lytton

Ihimaera, Witi 1944- .... **CLC 46**
See also CA 77-80; CN 7; RGSF 2

Ilf, Ilya .... **TCLC 21**
See Fainzilberg, Ilya Arnoldovich
See also EWL 3

Illyes, Gyula 1902-1983 .... **PC 16**
See also CA 114; 109; CDWLB 4; DLB 215; EWL 3; RGWL 2, 3

Immermann, Karl (Lebrecht)
1796-1840 .... **NCLC 4, 49**
See also DLB 133

Ince, Thomas H. 1882-1924 .... **TCLC 89**
See also IDFW 3, 4

Inchbald, Elizabeth 1753-1821 ...... **NCLC 62**
See also DLB 39, 89; RGEL 2

Inclan, Ramon (Maria) del Valle
See Valle-Inclan, Ramon (Maria) del

Infante, G(uillermo) Cabrera
See Cabrera Infante, G(uillermo)

Ingalls, Rachel (Holmes) 1940- .... **CLC 42**
See also CA 123; 127

Ingamells, Reginald Charles
See Ingamells, Rex

Ingamells, Rex 1913-1955 .... **TCLC 35**
See also CA 167; DLB 260

Inge, William (Motter) 1913-1973 ..... **CLC 1, 8, 19**
See also CA 9-12R; CDALB 1941-1968; DA3; DAM DRAM; DFS 1, 3, 5, 8; DLB 7, 249; EWL 3; MTCW 1, 2; RGAL 4; TUS

Ingelow, Jean 1820-1897 .... **NCLC 39, 107**
See also DLB 35, 163; FANT; SATA 33

Ingram, Willis J.
See Harris, Mark

Innaurato, Albert (F.) 1948(?)- ... **CLC 21, 60**
See also CA 115; 122; CAD; CANR 78; CD 5; INT CA-122

Innes, Michael
See Stewart, J(ohn) I(nnes) M(ackintosh)
See also DLB 276; MSW

Innis, Harold Adams 1894-1952 .... **TCLC 77**
See also CA 181; DLB 88

Insluis, Alanus de
See Alain de Lille

Iola
See Wells-Barnett, Ida B(ell)

Ionesco, Eugene 1912-1994 ... **CLC 1, 4, 6, 9, 11, 15, 41, 86; DC 12; WLC**
See also CA 9-12R; 144; CANR 55; CWW 2; DA; DA3; DAB; DAC; DAM DRAM, MST; DFS 4, 9; EW 13; EWL 3; GFL 1789 to the Present; LMFS 2; MTCW 1, 2; RGWL 2, 3; SATA 7; SATA-Obit 79; TWA

Iqbal, Muhammad 1877-1938 .... **TCLC 28**
See also EWL 3

Ireland, Patrick
See O'Doherty, Brian

Irenaeus St. 130- .... **CMLC 42**

Irigaray, Luce 1930- .... **CLC 164**
See also CA 154; FW

Iron, Ralph
See Schreiner, Olive (Emilie Albertina)

Irving, John (Winslow) 1942- ... **CLC 13, 23, 38, 112, 175**
See also AAYA 8; AMWS 6; BEST 89:3; BPFB 2; CA 25-28R; CANR 28, 73, 112; CN 7; CPW; DA3; DAM NOV, POP; DLB 6, 278; DLBY 1982; EWL 3; MTCW 1, 2; NFS 12, 14; RGAL 4; TUS

Irving, Washington 1783-1859 . **NCLC 2, 19, 95; SSC 2, 37; WLC**
See also AMW; CDALB 1640-1865; DA; DA3; DAB; DAC; DAM MST; DLB 3, 11, 30, 59, 73, 74, 183, 186, 250, 254; EXPS; LAIT 1; RGAL 4; RGSF 2; SSFS 1, 8, 16; SUFW 1; TUS; WCH; YABC 2

Irwin, P. K.
See Page, P(atricia) K(athleen)

Isaacs, Jorge Ricardo 1837-1895 ... **NCLC 70**
See also LAW

Isaacs, Susan 1943- .... **CLC 32**
See also BEST 89:1; BPFB 2; CA 89-92; CANR 20, 41, 65, 112; CPW; DA3; DAM POP; INT CANR-20; MTCW 1, 2

Isherwood, Christopher (William Bradshaw)
1904-1986 .... **CLC 1, 9, 11, 14, 44; SSC 56**
See also BRW 7; CA 13-16R; 117; CANR 35, 97; DA3; DAM DRAM, NOV; DLB 15, 195; DLBY 1986; EWL 3; IDTP; MTCW 1, 2; RGAL 4; RGEL 2; TUS; WLIT 4

Ishiguro, Kazuo 1954- .. **CLC 27, 56, 59, 110**
See also BEST 90:2; BPFB 2; BRWS 4; CA 120; CANR 49, 95; CN 7; DA3; DAM NOV; DLB 194; EWL 3; MTCW 1, 2; NFS 13; WLIT 4

Ishikawa, Hakuhin
See Ishikawa, Takuboku

Ishikawa, Takuboku 1886(?)-1912 ..... **PC 10; TCLC 15**
See Ishikawa Takuboku
See also CA 113; 153; DAM POET

Iskander, Fazil (Abdulovich) 1929- .. **CLC 47**
See also CA 102; EWL 3

Isler, Alan (David) 1934- .... **CLC 91**
See also CA 156; CANR 105

Ivan IV 1530-1584 .... **LC 17**

Ivanov, Vyacheslav Ivanovich
1866-1949 .... **TCLC 33**
See also CA 122; EWL 3

Ivask, Ivar Vidrik 1927-1992 .... **CLC 14**
See also CA 37-40R; 139; CANR 24

Ives, Morgan
See Bradley, Marion Zimmer
See also GLL 1

Izumi Shikibu c. 973-c. 1034 .... **CMLC 33**

J. R. S.
See Gogarty, Oliver St. John

Jabran, Kahlil
See Gibran, Kahlil

Jabran, Khalil
See Gibran, Kahlil

Jackson, Daniel
See Wingrove, David (John)

Jackson, Helen Hunt 1830-1885 .... **NCLC 90**
See also DLB 42, 47, 186, 189; RGAL 4

Jackson, Jesse 1908-1983 .... **CLC 12**
See also BW 1; CA 25-28R; 109; CANR 27; CLR 28; CWRI 5; MAICYA 1, 2; SATA 2, 29; SATA-Obit 48

Jackson, Laura (Riding) 1901-1991 .... **PC 44**
See Riding, Laura
See also CA 65-68; 135; CANR 28, 89; DLB 48

Jackson, Sam
See Trumbo, Dalton

Jackson, Sara
See Wingrove, David (John)

Jackson, Shirley 1919-1965 . **CLC 11, 60, 87; SSC 9, 39; WLC**
See also AAYA 9; AMWS 9; BPFB 2; CA 1-4R; 25-28R; CANR 4, 52; CDALB 1941-1968; DA; DA3; DAC; DAM MST; DLB 6, 234; EXPS; HGG; LAIT 4; MTCW 2; RGAL 4; RGSF 2; SATA 2; SSFS 1; SUFW 1, 2

Jacob, (Cyprien-)Max 1876-1944 .... **TCLC 6**
See also CA 104; 193; DLB 258; EWL 3; GFL 1789 to the Present; GLL 2; RGWL 2, 3

Jacobs, Harriet A(nn)
1813(?)-1897 .... **NCLC 67**
See also AFAW 1, 2; DLB 239; FW; LAIT 2; RGAL 4

Jacobs, Jim 1942- .... **CLC 12**
See also CA 97-100; INT 97-100

Jacobs, W(illiam) W(ymark)
1863-1943 .... **TCLC 22**
See also CA 121; 167; DLB 135; EXPS; HGG; RGEL 2; RGSF 2; SSFS 2; SUFW

Jacobsen, Jens Peter 1847-1885 .... **NCLC 34**

Jacobsen, Josephine 1908- .... **CLC 48, 102**
See also CA 33-36R; CAAS 18; CANR 23, 48; CCA 1; CP 7; DLB 244

Jacobson, Dan 1929- .... **CLC 4, 14**
See also AFW; CA 1-4R; CANR 2, 25, 66; CN 7; DLB 14, 207, 225; EWL 3; MTCW 1; RGSF 2

Jacqueline
See Carpentier (y Valmont), Alejo

Jagger, Mick 1944- .... **CLC 17**

Jahiz, al- c. 780-c. 869 .... **CMLC 25**

Jakes, John (William) 1932- .... **CLC 29**
See also AAYA 32; BEST 89:4; BPFB 2; CA 57-60; CANR 10, 43, 66, 111; CPW; CSW; DA3; DAM NOV, POP; DLB 278;

DLBY 1983; FANT; INT CANR-10; MTCW 1, 2; RHW; SATA 62; SFW 4; TCWW 2

James I 1394-1437 .... **LC 20**
See also RGEL 2

James, Andrew
See Kirkup, James

James, C(yril) L(ionel) R(obert)
1901-1989 .... **BLCS; CLC 33**
See also BW 2; CA 117; 125; 128; CANR 62; DLB 125; MTCW 1

James, Daniel (Lewis) 1911-1988
See Santiago, Danny
See also CA 174; 125

James, Dynely
See Mayne, William (James Carter)

James, Henry Sr. 1811-1882 .... **NCLC 53**

James, Henry 1843-1916 .... **SSC 8, 32, 47; TCLC 2, 11, 24, 40, 47, 64; WLC**
See also AMW; AMWC 1; AMWR 1; BPFB 2; BRW 6; CA 104; 132; CDALB 1865-1917; DA; DA3; DAB; DAC; DAM MST, NOV; DLB 12, 71, 74, 189; DLBD 13; EWL 3; EXPS; HGG; LAIT 2; MTCW 1, 2; NFS 12, 16; RGAL 4; RGEL 2; RGSF 2; SSFS 9; SUFW 1; TUS

James, M. R.
See James, Montague (Rhodes)
See also DLB 156, 201

James, Montague (Rhodes)
1862-1936 .... **SSC 16; TCLC 6**
See James, M. R.
See also CA 104; 203; HGG; RGEL 2; RGSF 2; SUFW 1

James, P. D. .... **CLC 18, 46, 122**
See White, Phyllis Dorothy James
See also BEST 90:2; BPFB 2; BRWS 4; CDBLB 1960 to Present; DLB 87, 276; DLBD 17; MSW

James, Philip
See Moorcock, Michael (John)

James, Samuel
See Stephens, James

James, Seumas
See Stephens, James

James, Stephen
See Stephens, James

James, William 1842-1910 .... **TCLC 15, 32**
See also AMW; CA 109; 193; DLB 270, 284; RGAL 4

Jameson, Anna 1794-1860 .... **NCLC 43**
See also DLB 99, 166

Jameson, Fredric (R.) 1934- .... **CLC 142**
See also CA 196; DLB 67; LMFS 2

Jami, Nur al-Din 'Abd al-Rahman
1414-1492 .... **LC 9**

Jammes, Francis 1868-1938 .... **TCLC 75**
See also CA 198; EWL 3; GFL 1789 to the Present

Jandl, Ernst 1925-2000 .... **CLC 34**
See also CA 200; EWL 3

Janowitz, Tama 1957- .... **CLC 43, 145**
See also CA 106; CANR 52, 89; CN 7; CPW; DAM POP

Japrisot, Sebastien 1931- .... **CLC 90**
See Rossi, Jean Baptiste
See also CMW 4

Jarrell, Randall 1914-1965 .... **CLC 1, 2, 6, 9, 13, 49; PC 41**
See also AMW; BYA 5; CA 5-8R; 25-28R; CABS 2; CANR 6, 34; CDALB 1941-1968; CLR 6; CWRI 5; DAM POET; DLB 48, 52; EWL 3; EXPP; MAICYA 1, 2; MTCW 1, 2; PAB; PFS 2; RGAL 4; SATA 7

Jarry, Alfred 1873-1907 .... **SSC 20; TCLC 2, 14**
See also CA 104; 153; DA3; DAM DRAM; DFS 8; DLB 192, 258; EW 9; EWL 3; GFL 1789 to the Present; RGWL 2, 3; TWA

Jarvis, E. K.
See Ellison, Harlan (Jay)

Jawien, Andrzej
See John Paul II, Pope

Jaynes, Roderick
See Coen, Ethan

Jeake, Samuel, Jr.
See Aiken, Conrad (Potter)

Jean Paul 1763-1825 .... **NCLC 7**

Jefferies, (John) Richard
1848-1887 .... **NCLC 47**
See also DLB 98, 141; RGEL 2; SATA 16; SFW 4

Jeffers, (John) Robinson 1887-1962 .. **CLC 2, 3, 11, 15, 54; PC 17; WLC**
See also AMWS 2; CA 85-88; CANR 35; CDALB 1917-1929; DA; DAC; DAM MST, POET; DLB 45, 212; EWL 3; MTCW 1, 2; PAB; PFS 3, 4; RGAL 4

Jefferson, Janet
See Mencken, H(enry) L(ouis)

Jefferson, Thomas 1743-1826 . **NCLC 11, 103**
See also ANW; CDALB 1640-1865; DA3; DLB 31, 183; LAIT 1; RGAL 4

Jeffrey, Francis 1773-1850 .... **NCLC 33**
See Francis, Lord Jeffrey

Jelakowitch, Ivan
See Heijermans, Herman

Jelinek, Elfriede 1946- .... **CLC 169**
See also CA 154; DLB 85; FW

Jellicoe, (Patricia) Ann 1927- .... **CLC 27**
See also CA 85-88; CBD; CD 5; CWD; CWRI 5; DLB 13, 233; FW

Jemyma
See Holley, Marietta

Jen, Gish .... **CLC 70**
See Jen, Lillian

Jen, Lillian 1956(?)-
See Jen, Gish
See also CA 135; CANR 89

Jenkins, (John) Robin 1912- .... **CLC 52**
See also CA 1-4R; CANR 1; CN 7; DLB 14, 271

Jennings, Elizabeth (Joan)
1926-2001 .... **CLC 5, 14, 131**
See also BRWS 5; CA 61-64; 200; CAAS 5; CANR 8, 39, 66; CP 7; CWP; DLB 27; EWL 3; MTCW 1; SATA 66

Jennings, Waylon 1937- .... **CLC 21**

Jensen, Johannes V(ilhelm)
1873-1950 .... **TCLC 41**
See also CA 170; DLB 214; EWL 3; RGWL 3

Jensen, Laura (Linnea) 1948- .... **CLC 37**
See also CA 103

Jerome, Saint 345-420 .... **CMLC 30**
See also RGWL 3

Jerome, Jerome K(lapka)
1859-1927 .... **TCLC 23**
See also CA 119; 177; DLB 10, 34, 135; RGEL 2

Jerrold, Douglas William
1803-1857 .... **NCLC 2**
See also DLB 158, 159; RGEL 2

Jewett, (Theodora) Sarah Orne
1849-1909 .... **SSC 6, 44; TCLC 1, 22**
See also AMW; AMWR 2; CA 108; 127; CANR 71; DLB 12, 74, 221; EXPS; FW; MAWW; NFS 15; RGAL 4; RGSF 2; SATA 15; SSFS 4

Jewsbury, Geraldine (Endsor)
1812-1880 .... **NCLC 22**
See also DLB 21

Jhabvala, Ruth Prawer 1927- . **CLC 4, 8, 29, 94, 138**
See also BRWS 5; CA 1-4R; CANR 2, 29, 51, 74, 91; CN 7; DAB; DAM NOV; DLB 139, 194; EWL 3; IDFW 3, 4; INT CANR-29; MTCW 1, 2; RGSF 2; RGWL 2; RHW; TEA

Jibran, Kahlil
See Gibran, Kahlil

Jibran, Khalil
See Gibran, Kahlil

Jiles, Paulette 1943- .... **CLC 13, 58**
See also CA 101; CANR 70; CWP

Jimenez (Mantecon), Juan Ramon
1881-1958 .... **HLC 1; PC 7; TCLC 4**
See also CA 104; 131; CANR 74; DAM MULT, POET; DLB 134; EW 9; EWL 3; HW 1; MTCW 1, 2; RGWL 2, 3

Jimenez, Ramon
See Jimenez (Mantecon), Juan Ramon

Jimenez Mantecon, Juan
See Jimenez (Mantecon), Juan Ramon

Jin, Ha .... **CLC 109**
See Jin, Xuefei
See also CA 152; DLB 244; SSFS 17

Jin, Xuefei 1956-
See Jin, Ha
See also CANR 91

Joel, Billy .... **CLC 26**
See Joel, William Martin

Joel, William Martin 1949-
See Joel, Billy
See also CA 108

John, Saint 107th cent. -100 .... **CMLC 27**

John of the Cross, St. 1542-1591 .... **LC 18**
See also RGWL 2, 3

John Paul II, Pope 1920- .... **CLC 128**
See also CA 106; 133

Johnson, B(ryan) S(tanley William)
1933-1973 .... **CLC 6, 9**
See also CA 9-12R; 53-56; CANR 9; DLB 14, 40; EWL 3; RGEL 2

Johnson, Benjamin F., of Boone
See Riley, James Whitcomb

Johnson, Charles (Richard) 1948- .... **BLC 2; CLC 7, 51, 65, 163**
See also AFAW 2; AMWS 6; BW 2, 3; CA 116; CAAS 18; CANR 42, 66, 82; CN 7; DAM MULT; DLB 33, 278; MTCW 2; RGAL 4; SSFS 16

Johnson, Charles S(urgeon)
1893-1956 .... **HR 3**
See also BW 1, 3; CA 125; CANR 82; DLB 51, 91

Johnson, Denis 1949- . **CLC 52, 160; SSC 56**
See also CA 117; 121; CANR 71, 99; CN 7; DLB 120

Johnson, Diane 1934- .... **CLC 5, 13, 48**
See also BPFB 2; CA 41-44R; CANR 17, 40, 62, 95; CN 7; DLBY 1980; INT CANR-17; MTCW 1

Johnson, E. Pauline 1861-1913 .... **NNAL**
See also CA 150; DAC; DAM MULT; DLB 92, 175

Johnson, Eyvind (Olof Verner)
1900-1976 .... **CLC 14**
See also CA 73-76; 69-72; CANR 34, 101; DLB 259; EW 12; EWL 3

Johnson, Fenton 1888-1958 .... **BLC 2**
See also BW 1; CA 118; 124; DAM MULT; DLB 45, 50

Johnson, Georgia Douglas (Camp)
1880-1966 .... **HR 3**
See also BW 1; CA 125; DLB 51, 249; WP

Johnson, Helene 1907-1995 .... **HR 3**
See also CA 181; DLB 51; WP

Johnson, J. R.
See James, C(yril) L(ionel) R(obert)

Kafka, Franz 1883-1924 ... **SSC 5, 29, 35, 60; TCLC 2, 6, 13, 29, 47, 53, 112; WLC**
See also AAYA 31; BPFB 2; CA 105; 126; CDWLB 2; DA; DA3; DAB; DAC; DAM MST, NOV; DLB 81; EW 9; EWL 3; EXPS; LATS 1; LMFS 2; MTCW 1, 2; NFS 7; RGSF 2; RGWL 2, 3; SFW 4; SSFS 3, 7, 12; TWA

Kahanovitsch, Pinkhes
See Der Nister

Kahn, Roger 1927- .... **CLC 30**
See also CA 25-28R; CANR 44, 69; DLB 171; SATA 37

Kain, Saul
See Sassoon, Siegfried (Lorraine)

Kaiser, Georg 1878-1945 .... **TCLC 9**
See also CA 106; 190; CDWLB 2; DLB 124; EWL 3; LMFS 2; RGWL 2, 3

Kaledin, Sergei .... **CLC 59**

Kaletski, Alexander 1946- .... **CLC 39**
See also CA 118; 143

Kalidasa fl. c. 400-455 .... **CMLC 9; PC 22**
See also RGWL 2, 3

Kallman, Chester (Simon)
1921-1975 .... **CLC 2**
See also CA 45-48; 53-56; CANR 3

Kaminsky, Melvin 1926-
See Brooks, Mel
See also CA 65-68; CANR 16

Kaminsky, Stuart M(elvin) 1934- ..... **CLC 59**
See also CA 73-76; CANR 29, 53, 89; CMW 4

Kandinsky, Wassily 1866-1944 .... **TCLC 92**
See also CA 118; 155

Kane, Francis
See Robbins, Harold

Kane, Henry 1918-
See Queen, Ellery
See also CA 156; CMW 4

Kane, Paul
See Simon, Paul (Frederick)

Kanin, Garson 1912-1999 .... **CLC 22**
See also AITN 1; CA 5-8R; 177; CAD; CANR 7, 78; DLB 7; IDFW 3, 4

Kaniuk, Yoram 1930- .... **CLC 19**
See also CA 134

Kant, Immanuel 1724-1804 ..... **NCLC 27, 67**
See also DLB 94

Kantor, MacKinlay 1904-1977 .... **CLC 7**
See also CA 61-64; 73-76; CANR 60, 63; DLB 9, 102; MTCW 2; RHW; TCWW 2

Kanze Motokiyo
See Zeami

Kaplan, David Michael 1946- .... **CLC 50**
See also CA 187

Kaplan, James 1951- .... **CLC 59**
See also CA 135

Karadzic, Vuk Stefanovic
1787-1864 .... **NCLC 115**
See also CDWLB 4; DLB 147

Karageorge, Michael
See Anderson, Poul (William)

Karamzin, Nikolai Mikhailovich
1766-1826 .... **NCLC 3**
See also DLB 150; RGSF 2

Karapanou, Margarita 1946- .... **CLC 13**
See also CA 101

Karinthy, Frigyes 1887-1938 .... **TCLC 47**
See also CA 170; DLB 215; EWL 3

Karl, Frederick R(obert) 1927- .... **CLC 34**
See also CA 5-8R; CANR 3, 44

Kastel, Warren
See Silverberg, Robert

Kataev, Evgeny Petrovich 1903-1942
See Petrov, Evgeny
See also CA 120

Kataphusin
See Ruskin, John

Katz, Steve 1935- .... **CLC 47**
See also CA 25-28R; CAAS 14, 64; CANR 12; CN 7; DLBY 1983

Kauffman, Janet 1945- .... **CLC 42**
See also CA 117; CANR 43, 84; DLB 218; DLBY 1986

Kaufman, Bob (Garnell) 1925-1986 . **CLC 49**
See also BG 3; BW 1; CA 41-44R; 118; CANR 22; DLB 16, 41

Kaufman, George S. 1889-1961 ...... **CLC 38; DC 17**
See also CA 108; 93-96; DAM DRAM; DFS 1, 10; DLB 7; INT CA-108; MTCW 2; RGAL 4; TUS

Kaufman, Sue .... **CLC 3, 8**
See Barondess, Sue K(aufman)

Kavafis, Konstantinos Petrou 1863-1933
See Cavafy, C(onstantine) P(eter)
See also CA 104

Kavan, Anna 1901-1968 .... **CLC 5, 13, 82**
See also BRWS 7; CA 5-8R; CANR 6, 57; DLB 255; MTCW 1; RGEL 2; SFW 4

Kavanagh, Dan
See Barnes, Julian (Patrick)

Kavanagh, Julie 1952- .... **CLC 119**
See also CA 163

Kavanagh, Patrick (Joseph)
1904-1967 .... **CLC 22; PC 33**
See also BRWS 7; CA 123; 25-28R; DLB 15, 20; EWL 3; MTCW 1; RGEL 2

Kawabata, Yasunari 1899-1972 ..... **CLC 2, 5, 9, 18, 107; SSC 17**
See Kawabata Yasunari
See also CA 93-96; 33-36R; CANR 88; DAM MULT; MJW; MTCW 2; RGSF 2; RGWL 2, 3

Kawabata Yasunari
See Kawabata, Yasunari
See also DLB 180; EWL 3

Kaye, M(ary) M(argaret) 1909- .... **CLC 28**
See also CA 89-92; CANR 24, 60, 102; MTCW 1, 2; RHW; SATA 62

Kaye, Mollie
See Kaye, M(ary) M(argaret)

Kaye-Smith, Sheila 1887-1956 .... **TCLC 20**
See also CA 118; 203; DLB 36

Kaymor, Patrice Maguilene
See Senghor, Leopold Sedar

Kazakov, Yuri Pavlovich 1927-1982 . **SSC 43**
See Kazakov, Yury
See also CA 5-8R; CANR 36; MTCW 1; RGSF 2

Kazakov, Yury
See Kazakov, Yuri Pavlovich
See also EWL 3

Kazan, Elia 1909- .... **CLC 6, 16, 63**
See also CA 21-24R; CANR 32, 78

Kazantzakis, Nikos 1883(?)-1957 .... **TCLC 2, 5, 33**
See also BPFB 2; CA 105; 132; DA3; EW 9; EWL 3; MTCW 1, 2; RGWL 2, 3

Kazin, Alfred 1915-1998 ..... **CLC 34, 38, 119**
See also AMWS 8; CA 1-4R; CAAS 7; CANR 1, 45, 79; DLB 67; EWL 3

Keane, Mary Nesta (Skrine) 1904-1996
See Keane, Molly
See also CA 108; 114; 151; CN 7; RHW

Keane, Molly .... **CLC 31**
See Keane, Mary Nesta (Skrine)
See also INT 114

Keates, Jonathan 1946(?)- .... **CLC 34**
See also CA 163

Keaton, Buster 1895-1966 .... **CLC 20**
See also CA 194

Keats, John 1795-1821 ...... **NCLC 8, 73, 121; PC 1; WLC**
See also BRW 4; BRWR 1; CDBLB 1789-1832; DA; DA3; DAB; DAC; DAM MST, POET; DLB 96, 110; EXPP; LMFS 1; PAB; PFS 1, 2, 3, 9, 16; RGEL 2; TEA; WLIT 3; WP

Keble, John 1792-1866 .... **NCLC 87**
See also DLB 32, 55; RGEL 2

Keene, Donald 1922- .... **CLC 34**
See also CA 1-4R; CANR 5

Keillor, Garrison .... **CLC 40, 115**
See Keillor, Gary (Edward)
See also AAYA 2; BEST 89:3; BPFB 2; DLBY 1987; EWL 3; SATA 58; TUS

Keillor, Gary (Edward) 1942-
See Keillor, Garrison
See also CA 111; 117; CANR 36, 59; CPW; DA3; DAM POP; MTCW 1, 2

Keith, Carlos
See Lewton, Val

Keith, Michael
See Hubbard, L(afayette) Ron(ald)

Keller, Gottfried 1819-1890 .... **NCLC 2; SSC 26**
See also CDWLB 2; DLB 129; EW; RGSF 2; RGWL 2, 3

Keller, Nora Okja 1965- .... **CLC 109**
See also CA 187

Kellerman, Jonathan 1949- .... **CLC 44**
See also AAYA 35; BEST 90:1; CA 106; CANR 29, 51; CMW 4; CPW; DA3; DAM POP; INT CANR-29

Kelley, William Melvin 1937- .... **CLC 22**
See also BW 1; CA 77-80; CANR 27, 83; CN 7; DLB 33; EWL 3

Kellogg, Marjorie 1922- .... **CLC 2**
See also CA 81-84

Kellow, Kathleen
See Hibbert, Eleanor Alice Burford

Kelly, M(ilton) T(errence) 1947- ...... **CLC 55**
See also CA 97-100; CAAS 22; CANR 19, 43, 84; CN 7

Kelly, Robert 1935- .... **SSC 50**
See also CA 17-20R; CAAS 19; CANR 47; CP 7; DLB 5, 130, 165

Kelman, James 1946- .... **CLC 58, 86**
See also BRWS 5; CA 148; CANR 85; CN 7; DLB 194; RGSF 2; WLIT 4

Kemal, Yashar 1923- .... **CLC 14, 29**
See also CA 89-92; CANR 44; CWW 2

Kemble, Fanny 1809-1893 .... **NCLC 18**
See also DLB 32

Kemelman, Harry 1908-1996 .... **CLC 2**
See also AITN 1; BPFB 2; CA 9-12R; 155; CANR 6, 71; CMW 4; DLB 28

Kempe, Margery 1373(?)-1440(?) ... **LC 6, 56**
See also DLB 146; RGEL 2

Kempis, Thomas a 1380-1471 .... **LC 11**

Kendall, Henry 1839-1882 .... **NCLC 12**
See also DLB 230

Keneally, Thomas (Michael) 1935- ... **CLC 5, 8, 10, 14, 19, 27, 43, 117**
See also BRWS 4; CA 85-88; CANR 10, 50, 74; CN 7; CPW; DA3; DAM NOV; EWL 3; MTCW 1, 2; NFS 17; RGEL 2; RHW

Kennedy, Adrienne (Lita) 1931- .... **BLC 2; CLC 66; DC 5**
See also AFAW 2; BW 2, 3; CA 103; CAAS 20; CABS 3; CANR 26, 53, 82; CD 5; DAM MULT; DFS 9; DLB 38; FW

Kennedy, John Pendleton
1795-1870 .... **NCLC 2**
See also DLB 3, 248, 254; RGAL 4

Landor, Walter Savage
1775-1864 .... **NCLC 14**
See also BRW 4; DLB 93, 107; RGEL 2
Landwirth, Heinz 1927-
See Lind, Jakov
See also CA 9-12R; CANR 7
Lane, Patrick 1939- .... **CLC 25**
See also CA 97-100; CANR 54; CP 7; DAM
POET; DLB 53; INT 97-100
Lang, Andrew 1844-1912 .... **TCLC 16**
See also CA 114; 137; CANR 85; DLB 98,
141, 184; FANT; MAICYA 1, 2; RGEL 2;
SATA 16; WCH
Lang, Fritz 1890-1976 .... **CLC 20, 103**
See also CA 77-80; 69-72; CANR 30
Lange, John
See Crichton, (John) Michael
Langer, Elinor 1939- .... **CLC 34**
See also CA 121
Langland, William 1332(?)-1400(?) ..... **LC 19**
See also BRW 1; DA; DAB; DAC; DAM
MST, POET; DLB 146; RGEL 2; TEA;
WLIT 3
Langstaff, Launcelot
See Irving, Washington
Lanier, Sidney 1842-1881 .... **NCLC 6, 118**
See also AMWS 1; DAM POET; DLB 64;
DLBD 13; EXPP; MAICYA 1; PFS 14;
RGAL 4; SATA 18
Lanyer, Aemilia 1569-1645 ...... **LC 10, 30, 83**
See also DLB 121
Lao-Tzu
See Lao Tzu
Lao Tzu c. 6th cent. B.C.-3rd cent.
B.C. .... **CMLC 7**
Lapine, James (Elliot) 1949- .... **CLC 39**
See also CA 123; 130; CANR 54; INT 130
Larbaud, Valery (Nicolas)
1881-1957 .... **TCLC 9**
See also CA 106; 152; EWL 3; GFL 1789
to the Present
Lardner, Ring
See Lardner, Ring(gold) W(ilmer)
See also BPFB 2; CDALB 1917-1929; DLB
11, 25, 86, 171; DLBD 16; RGAL 4;
RGSF 2
Lardner, Ring W., Jr.
See Lardner, Ring(gold) W(ilmer)
Lardner, Ring(gold) W(ilmer)
1885-1933 .... **SSC 32; TCLC 2, 14**
See Lardner, Ring
See also AMW; CA 104; 131; MTCW 1, 2;
TUS
Laredo, Betty
See Codrescu, Andrei
Larkin, Maia
See Wojciechowska, Maia (Teresa)
Larkin, Philip (Arthur) 1922-1985 ... **CLC 3,**
5, 8, 9, 13, 18, 33, 39, 64; PC 21
See also BRWS 1; CA 5-8R; 117; CANR
24, 62; CDBLB 1960 to Present; DA3;
DAB; DAM MST, POET; DLB 27; EWL
3; MTCW 1, 2; PFS 3, 4, 12; RGEL 2
La Roche, Sophie von
1730-1807 .... **NCLC 121**
See also DLB 94
Larra (y Sanchez de Castro), Mariano Jose
de 1809-1837 .... **NCLC 17**
Larsen, Eric 1941- .... **CLC 55**
See also CA 132
Larsen, Nella 1893(?)-1963 .... **BLC 2; CLC**
37; HR 3
See also AFAW 1, 2; BW 1; CA 125; CANR
83; DAM MULT; DLB 51; FW; LATS 1;
LMFS 2
Larson, Charles R(aymond) 1938- ... **CLC 31**
See also CA 53-56; CANR 4
Larson, Jonathan 1961-1996 .... **CLC 99**
See also AAYA 28; CA 156

Las Casas, Bartolome de
1474-1566 .... **HLCS; LC 31**
See Casas, Bartolome de las
See also LAW
Lasch, Christopher 1932-1994 .... **CLC 102**
See also CA 73-76; 144; CANR 25, 118;
DLB 246; MTCW 1, 2
Lasker-Schueler, Else 1869-1945 ... **TCLC 57**
See Lasker-Schuler, Else
See also CA 183; DLB 66, 124
Lasker-Schuler, Else
See Lasker-Schueler, Else
See also EWL 3
Laski, Harold J(oseph) 1893-1950 . **TCLC 79**
See also CA 188
Latham, Jean Lee 1902-1995 .... **CLC 12**
See also AITN 1; BYA 1; CA 5-8R; CANR
7, 84; CLR 50; MAICYA 1, 2; SATA 2,
68; YAW
Latham, Mavis
See Clark, Mavis Thorpe
Lathen, Emma .... **CLC 2**
See Hennissart, Martha; Latsis, Mary J(ane)
See also BPFB 2; CMW 4
Lathrop, Francis
See Leiber, Fritz (Reuter, Jr.)
Latsis, Mary J(ane) 1927(?)-1997
See Lathen, Emma
See also CA 85-88; 162; CMW 4
Lattany, Kristin
See Lattany, Kristin (Elaine Eggleston)
Hunter
Lattany, Kristin (Elaine Eggleston) Hunter
1931- .... **CLC 35**
See also AITN 1; BW 1; BYA 3; CA 13-
16R; CANR 13, 108; CLR 3; CN 7; DLB
33; INT CANR-13; MAICYA 1, 2; SAAS
10; SATA 12, 132; YAW
Lattimore, Richmond (Alexander)
1906-1984 .... **CLC 3**
See also CA 1-4R; 112; CANR 1
Laughlin, James 1914-1997 .... **CLC 49**
See also CA 21-24R; 162; CAAS 22; CANR
9, 47; CP 7; DLB 48; DLBY 1996, 1997
Laurence, (Jean) Margaret (Wemyss)
1926-1987 . **CLC 3, 6, 13, 50, 62; SSC 7**
See also BYA 13; CA 5-8R; 121; CANR
33; DAC; DAM MST; DLB 53; EWL 3;
FW; MTCW 1, 2; NFS 11; RGEL 2;
RGSF 2; SATA-Obit 50; TCWW 2
Laurent, Antoine 1952- .... **CLC 50**
Lauscher, Hermann
See Hesse, Hermann
Lautreamont 1846-1870 .. **NCLC 12; SSC 14**
See Lautreamont, Isidore Lucien Ducasse
See also GFL 1789 to the Present; RGWL
2, 3
Lautreamont, Isidore Lucien Ducasse
See Lautreamont
See also DLB 217
Laverty, Donald
See Blish, James (Benjamin)
Lavin, Mary 1912-1996 . **CLC 4, 18, 99; SSC**
4
See also CA 9-12R; 151; CANR 33; CN 7;
DLB 15; FW; MTCW 1; RGEL 2; RGSF
2
Lavond, Paul Dennis
See Kornbluth, C(yril) M.; Pohl, Frederik
Lawler, Raymond Evenor 1922- .... **CLC 58**
See also CA 103; CD 5; RGEL 2
Lawrence, D(avid) H(erbert Richards)
1885-1930 ... **SSC 4, 19; TCLC 2, 9, 16,**
33, 48, 61, 93; WLC
See Chambers, Jessie
See also BPFB 2; BRW 7; BRWR 2; CA
104; 121; CDBLB 1914-1945; DA; DA3;
DAB; DAC; DAM MST, NOV, POET;

DLB 10, 19, 36, 98, 162, 195; EWL 3;
EXPP; EXPS; LAIT 2, 3; MTCW 1, 2;
PFS 6; RGEL 2; RGSF 2; SSFS 2, 6;
TEA; WLIT 4; WP
Lawrence, T(homas) E(dward)
1888-1935 .... **TCLC 18**
See Dale, Colin
See also BRWS 2; CA 115; 167; DLB 195
Lawrence of Arabia
See Lawrence, T(homas) E(dward)
Lawson, Henry (Archibald Hertzberg)
1867-1922 .... **SSC 18; TCLC 27**
See also CA 120; 181; DLB 230; RGEL 2;
RGSF 2
Lawton, Dennis
See Faust, Frederick (Schiller)
Laxness, Halldor .... **CLC 25**
See Gudjonsson, Halldor Kiljan
See also EW 12; EWL 3; RGWL 2, 3
Layamon fl. c. 1200- .... **CMLC 10**
See Layamon
See also RGEL 2
Laye, Camara 1928-1980 ..... **BLC 2; CLC 4,**
38
See Camara Laye
See also AFW; BW 1; CA 85-88; 97-100;
CANR 25; DAM MULT; MTCW 1, 2;
WLIT 2
Layton, Irving (Peter) 1912- .... **CLC 2, 15,**
164
See also CA 1-4R; CANR 2, 33, 43, 66; CP
7; DAC; DAM MST, POET; DLB 88;
EWL 3; MTCW 1, 2; PFS 12; RGEL 2
Lazarus, Emma 1849-1887 ...... **NCLC 8, 109**
Lazarus, Felix
See Cable, George Washington
Lazarus, Henry
See Slavitt, David R(ytman)
Lea, Joan
See Neufeld, John (Arthur)
Leacock, Stephen (Butler)
1869-1944 .... **SSC 39; TCLC 2**
See also CA 104; 141; CANR 80; DAC;
DAM MST; DLB 92; EWL 3; MTCW 2;
RGEL 2; RGSF 2
Lead, Jane Ward 1623-1704 .... **LC 72**
See also DLB 131
Leapor, Mary 1722-1746 .... **LC 80**
See also DLB 109
Lear, Edward 1812-1888 .... **NCLC 3**
See also AAYA 48; BRW 5; CLR 1, 75;
DLB 32, 163, 166; MAICYA 1, 2; RGEL
2; SATA 18, 100; WCH; WP
Lear, Norman (Milton) 1922- .... **CLC 12**
See also CA 73-76
Leautaud, Paul 1872-1956 .... **TCLC 83**
See also CA 203; DLB 65; GFL 1789 to the
Present
Leavis, F(rank) R(aymond)
1895-1978 .... **CLC 24**
See also BRW 7; CA 21-24R; 77-80; CANR
44; DLB 242; EWL 3; MTCW 1, 2;
RGEL 2
Leavitt, David 1961- .... **CLC 34**
See also CA 116; 122; CANR 50, 62, 101;
CPW; DA3; DAM POP; DLB 130; GLL
1; INT 122; MTCW 2
Leblanc, Maurice (Marie Emile)
1864-1941 .... **TCLC 49**
See also CA 110; CMW 4
Lebowitz, Fran(ces Ann) 1951(?)- ... **CLC 11,**
36
See also CA 81-84; CANR 14, 60, 70; INT
CANR-14; MTCW 1
Lebrecht, Peter
See Tieck, (Johann) Ludwig

Manning, Olivia 1915-1980 .... **CLC 5, 19**
    See also CA 5-8R; 101; CANR 29; EWL 3;
    FW; MTCW 1; RGEL 2
Mano, D. Keith 1942- .... **CLC 2, 10**
    See also CA 25-28R; CAAS 6; CANR 26,
    57; DLB 6
Mansfield, Katherine . **SSC 9, 23, 38; TCLC
    2, 8, 39; WLC**
    See Beauchamp, Kathleen Mansfield
    See also BPFB 2; BRW 7; DAB; DLB 162;
    EWL 3; EXPS; FW; GLL 1; RGEL 2;
    RGSF 2; SSFS 2, 8, 10, 11
Manso, Peter 1940- .... **CLC 39**
    See also CA 29-32R; CANR 44
Mantecon, Juan Jimenez
    See Jimenez (Mantecon), Juan Ramon
Mantel, Hilary (Mary) 1952- .... **CLC 144**
    See also CA 125; CANR 54, 101; CN 7;
    DLB 271; RHW
Manton, Peter
    See Creasey, John
Man Without a Spleen, A
    See Chekhov, Anton (Pavlovich)
Manzoni, Alessandro 1785-1873 ... **NCLC 29,
    98**
    See also EW 5; RGWL 2, 3; TWA
Map, Walter 1140-1209 .... **CMLC 32**
Mapu, Abraham (ben Jekutiel)
    1808-1867 .... **NCLC 18**
Mara, Sally
    See Queneau, Raymond
Maracle, Lee 1950- .... **NNAL**
    See also CA 149
Marat, Jean Paul 1743-1793 .... **LC 10**
Marcel, Gabriel Honore 1889-1973 . **CLC 15**
    See also CA 102; 45-48; EWL 3; MTCW 1,
    2
March, William 1893-1954 .... **TCLC 96**
Marchbanks, Samuel
    See Davies, (William) Robertson
    See also CCA 1
Marchi, Giacomo
    See Bassani, Giorgio
Marcus Aurelius
    See Aurelius, Marcus
    See also AW 2
Marguerite
    See de Navarre, Marguerite
Marguerite d'Angouleme
    See de Navarre, Marguerite
    See also GFL Beginnings to 1789
Marguerite de Navarre
    See de Navarre, Marguerite
    See also RGWL 2, 3
Margulies, Donald 1954- .... **CLC 76**
    See also CA 200; DFS 13; DLB 228
Marie de France c. 12th cent. - ..... **CMLC 8;
    PC 22**
    See also DLB 208; FW; RGWL 2, 3
Marie de l'Incarnation 1599-1672 ...... **LC 10**
Marier, Captain Victor
    See Griffith, D(avid Lewelyn) W(ark)
Mariner, Scott
    See Pohl, Frederik
Marinetti, Filippo Tommaso
    1876-1944 .... **TCLC 10**
    See also CA 107; DLB 114, 264; EW 9;
    EWL 3
Marivaux, Pierre Carlet de Chamblain de
    1688-1763 .... **DC 7; LC 4**
    See also GFL Beginnings to 1789; RGWL
    2, 3; TWA
Markandaya, Kamala .... **CLC 8, 38**
    See Taylor, Kamala (Purnaiya)
    See also BYA 13; CN 7; EWL 3
Markfield, Wallace 1926-2002 .... **CLC 8**
    See also CA 69-72; 208; CAAS 3; CN 7;
    DLB 2, 28; DLBY 2002

Markham, Edwin 1852-1940 .... **TCLC 47**
    See also CA 160; DLB 54, 186; RGAL 4
Markham, Robert
    See Amis, Kingsley (William)
Markoosie .... **NNAL**
    See Markoosie, Patsauq
    See also CLR 23; DAM MULT
Marks, J
    See Highwater, Jamake (Mamake)
Marks, J.
    See Highwater, Jamake (Mamake)
Marks-Highwater, J
    See Highwater, Jamake (Mamake)
Marks-Highwater, J.
    See Highwater, Jamake (Mamake)
Markson, David M(errill) 1927- .... **CLC 67**
    See also CA 49-52; CANR 1, 91; CN 7
Marlatt, Daphne (Buckle) 1942- .... **CLC 168**
    See also CA 25-28R; CANR 17, 39; CN 7;
    CP 7; CWP; DLB 60; FW
Marley, Bob .... **CLC 17**
    See Marley, Robert Nesta
Marley, Robert Nesta 1945-1981
    See Marley, Bob
    See also CA 107; 103
Marlowe, Christopher 1564-1593 . **DC 1; LC
    22, 47; WLC**
    See also BRW 1; BRWR 1; CDBLB Before
    1660; DA; DA3; DAB; DAC; DAM
    DRAM, MST; DFS 1, 5, 13; DLB 62;
    EXPP; LMFS 1; RGEL 2; TEA; WLIT 3
Marlowe, Stephen 1928- .... **CLC 70**
    See Queen, Ellery
    See also CA 13-16R; CANR 6, 55; CMW
    4; SFW 1
Marmion, Shakerley 1603-1639 .... **LC 89**
    See also DLB 58; RGEL 2
Marmontel, Jean-Francois 1723-1799 .. **LC 2**
Maron, Monika 1941- .... **CLC 165**
    See also CA 201
Marquand, John P(hillips)
    1893-1960 .... **CLC 2, 10**
    See also AMW; BPFB 2; CA 85-88; CANR
    73; CMW 4; DLB 9, 102; EWL 3; MTCW
    2; RGAL 4
Marques, Rene 1919-1979 .. **CLC 96; HLC 2**
    See also CA 97-100; 85-88; CANR 78;
    DAM MULT; DLB 113; EWL 3; HW 1,
    2; LAW; RGSF 2
Marquez, Gabriel (Jose) Garcia
    See Garcia Marquez, Gabriel (Jose)
Marquis, Don(ald Robert Perry)
    1878-1937 .... **TCLC 7**
    See also CA 104; 166; DLB 11, 25; RGAL
    4
Marquis de Sade
    See Sade, Donatien Alphonse Francois
Marric, J. J.
    See Creasey, John
    See also MSW
Marryat, Frederick 1792-1848 .... **NCLC 3**
    See also DLB 21, 163; RGEL 2; WCH
Marsden, James
    See Creasey, John
Marsh, Edward 1872-1953 .... **TCLC 99**
Marsh, (Edith) Ngaio 1899-1982 .. **CLC 7, 53**
    See also CA 9-12R; CANR 6, 58; CMW 4;
    CPW; DAM POP; DLB 77; MSW;
    MTCW 1, 2; RGEL 2; TEA
Marshall, Garry 1934- .... **CLC 17**
    See also AAYA 3; CA 111; SATA 60
Marshall, Paule 1929- .. **BLC 3; CLC 27, 72;
    SSC 3**
    See also AFAW 1, 2; AMWS 11; BPFB 2;
    BW 2, 3; CA 77-80; CANR 25, 73; CN 7;
    DA3; DAM MULT; DLB 33, 157, 227;
    EWL 3; LATS 1; MTCW 1, 2; RGAL 4;
    SSFS 15

Marshallik
    See Zangwill, Israel
Marsten, Richard
    See Hunter, Evan
Marston, John 1576-1634 .... **LC 33**
    See also BRW 2; DAM DRAM; DLB 58,
    172; RGEL 2
Martha, Henry
    See Harris, Mark
Marti (y Perez), Jose (Julian)
    1853-1895 .... **HLC 2; NCLC 63**
    See also DAM MULT; HW 2; LAW; RGWL
    2, 3; WLIT 1
Martial c. 40-c. 104 .... **CMLC 35; PC 10**
    See also AW 2; CDWLB 1; DLB 211;
    RGWL 2, 3
Martin, Ken
    See Hubbard, L(afayette) Ron(ald)
Martin, Richard
    See Creasey, John
Martin, Steve 1945- .... **CLC 30**
    See also CA 97-100; CANR 30, 100;
    MTCW 1
Martin, Valerie 1948- .... **CLC 89**
    See also BEST 90:2; CA 85-88; CANR 49,
    89
Martin, Violet Florence 1862-1915 .. **SSC 56;
    TCLC 51**
Martin, Webber
    See Silverberg, Robert
Martindale, Patrick Victor
    See White, Patrick (Victor Martindale)
Martin du Gard, Roger
    1881-1958 .... **TCLC 24**
    See also CA 118; CANR 94; DLB 65; EWL
    3; GFL 1789 to the Present; RGWL 2, 3
Martineau, Harriet 1802-1876 .... **NCLC 26**
    See also DLB 21, 55, 159, 163, 166, 190;
    FW; RGEL 2; YABC 2
Martines, Julia
    See O'Faolain, Julia
Martinez, Enrique Gonzalez
    See Gonzalez Martinez, Enrique
Martinez, Jacinto Benavente y
    See Benavente (y Martinez), Jacinto
Martinez de la Rosa, Francisco de Paula
    1787-1862 .... **NCLC 102**
    See also TWA
Martinez Ruiz, Jose 1873-1967
    See Azorin; Ruiz, Jose Martinez
    See also CA 93-96; HW 1
Martinez Sierra, Gregorio
    1881-1947 .... **TCLC 6**
    See also CA 115; EWL 3
Martinez Sierra, Maria (de la O'LeJarraga)
    1874-1974 .... **TCLC 6**
    See also CA 115; EWL 3
Martinsen, Martin
    See Follett, Ken(neth Martin)
Martinson, Harry (Edmund)
    1904-1978 .... **CLC 14**
    See also CA 77-80; CANR 34; DLB 259;
    EWL 3
Martyn, Edward 1859-1923 .... **TCLC 131**
    See also CA 179; DLB 10; RGEL 2
Marut, Ret
    See Traven, B.
Marut, Robert
    See Traven, B.
Marvell, Andrew 1621-1678 .... **LC 4, 43; PC
    10; WLC**
    See also BRW 2; BRWR 2; CDBLB 1660-
    1789; DA; DAB; DAC; DAM MST,
    POET; DLB 131; EXPP; PFS 5; RGEL 2;
    TEA; WP
Marx, Karl (Heinrich)
    1818-1883 .... **NCLC 17, 114**
    See also DLB 129; LATS 1; TWA

McCorkle, Jill (Collins) 1958- .... **CLC 51**
  See also CA 121; CANR 113; CSW; DLB 234; DLBY 1987

McCourt, Frank 1930- .... **CLC 109**
  See also AMWS 12; CA 157; CANR 97; NCFS 1

McCourt, James 1941- .... **CLC 5**
  See also CA 57-60; CANR 98

McCourt, Malachy 1931- .... **CLC 119**
  See also SATA 126

McCoy, Horace (Stanley)
  1897-1955 .... **TCLC 28**
  See also CA 108; 155; CMW 4; DLB 9

McCrae, John 1872-1918 .... **TCLC 12**
  See also CA 109; DLB 92; PFS 5

McCreigh, James
  See Pohl, Frederik

McCullers, (Lula) Carson (Smith)
  1917-1967 .... **CLC 1, 4, 10, 12, 48, 100; SSC 9, 24; WLC**
  See also AAYA 21; AMW; BPFB 2; CA 5-8R; 25-28R; CANR 18; CDALB 1941-1968; DA; DA3; DAB; DAC; DAM MST, NOV; DFS 5; DLB 2, 7, 173, 228; EWL 3; EXPS; FW; GLL 1; LAIT 3, 4; MAWW; MTCW 1, 2; NFS 6, 13; RGAL 4; RGSF 2; SATA 27; SSFS 5; TUS; YAW

McCulloch, John Tyler
  See Burroughs, Edgar Rice

McCullough, Colleen 1938(?)- .. **CLC 27, 107**
  See also AAYA 36; BPFB 2; CA 81-84; CANR 17, 46, 67, 98; CPW; DA3; DAM NOV, POP; MTCW 1, 2; RHW

McCunn, Ruthanne Lum 1946- .... **AAL**
  See also CA 119; CANR 43, 96; LAIT 2; SATA 63

McDermott, Alice 1953- .... **CLC 90**
  See also CA 109; CANR 40, 90

McElroy, Joseph 1930- .... **CLC 5, 47**
  See also CA 17-20R; CN 7

McEwan, Ian (Russell) 1948- .... **CLC 13, 66, 169**
  See also BEST 90:4; BRWS 4; CA 61-64; CANR 14, 41, 69, 87; CN 7; DAM NOV; DLB 14, 194; HGG; MTCW 1, 2; RGSF 2; SUFW 2; TEA

McFadden, David 1940- .... **CLC 48**
  See also CA 104; CP 7; DLB 60; INT 104

McFarland, Dennis 1950- .... **CLC 65**
  See also CA 165; CANR 110

McGahern, John 1934- ... **CLC 5, 9, 48, 156; SSC 17**
  See also CA 17-20R; CANR 29, 68, 113; CN 7; DLB 14, 231; MTCW 1

McGinley, Patrick (Anthony) 1937- . **CLC 41**
  See also CA 120; 127; CANR 56; INT 127

McGinley, Phyllis 1905-1978 .... **CLC 14**
  See also CA 9-12R; 77-80; CANR 19; CWRI 5; DLB 11, 48; PFS 9, 13; SATA 2, 44; SATA-Obit 24

McGinniss, Joe 1942- .... **CLC 32**
  See also AITN 2; BEST 89:2; CA 25-28R; CANR 26, 70; CPW; DLB 185; INT CANR-26

McGivern, Maureen Daly
  See Daly, Maureen

McGrath, Patrick 1950- .... **CLC 55**
  See also CA 136; CANR 65; CN 7; DLB 231; HGG; SUFW 2

McGrath, Thomas (Matthew)
  1916-1990 .... **CLC 28, 59**
  See also AMWS 10; CA 9-12R; 132; CANR 6, 33, 95; DAM POET; MTCW 1; SATA 41; SATA-Obit 66

McGuane, Thomas (Francis III)
  1939- .... **CLC 3, 7, 18, 45, 127**
  See also AITN 2; BPFB 2; CA 49-52; CANR 5, 24, 49, 94; CN 7; DLB 2, 212; DLBY 1980; EWL 3; INT CANR-24; MTCW 1; TCWW 2

McGuckian, Medbh 1950- .... **CLC 48, 174; PC 27**
  See also BRWS 5; CA 143; CP 7; CWP; DAM POET; DLB 40

McHale, Tom 1942(?)-1982 .... **CLC 3, 5**
  See also AITN 1; CA 77-80; 106

McIlvanney, William 1936- .... **CLC 42**
  See also CA 25-28R; CANR 61; CMW 4; DLB 14, 207

McIlwraith, Maureen Mollie Hunter
  See Hunter, Mollie
  See also SATA 2

McInerney, Jay 1955- .... **CLC 34, 112**
  See also AAYA 18; BPFB 2; CA 116; 123; CANR 45, 68, 116; CN 7; CPW; DA3; DAM POP; INT 123; MTCW 2

McIntyre, Vonda N(eel) 1948- .... **CLC 18**
  See also CA 81-84; CANR 17, 34, 69; MTCW 1; SFW 4; YAW

McKay, Claude .... **BLC 3; HR 3; PC 2; TCLC 7, 41; WLC**
  See McKay, Festus Claudius
  See also AFAW 1, 2; AMWS 10; DAB; DLB 4, 45, 51, 117; EWL 3; EXPP; GLL 2; LAIT 3; LMFS 2; PAB; PFS 4; RGAL 4; WP

McKay, Festus Claudius 1889-1948
  See McKay, Claude
  See also BW 1, 3; CA 104; 124; CANR 73; DA; DAC; DAM MST, MULT, NOV, POET; MTCW 1, 2; TUS

McKuen, Rod 1933- .... **CLC 1, 3**
  See also AITN 1; CA 41-44R; CANR 40

McLoughlin, R. B.
  See Mencken, H(enry) L(ouis)

McLuhan, (Herbert) Marshall
  1911-1980 .... **CLC 37, 83**
  See also CA 9-12R; 102; CANR 12, 34, 61; DLB 88; INT CANR-12; MTCW 1, 2

McManus, Declan Patrick Aloysius
  See Costello, Elvis

McMillan, Terry (L.) 1951- . **BLCS; CLC 50, 61, 112**
  See also AAYA 21; BPFB 2; BW 2, 3; CA 140; CANR 60, 104; CPW; DA3; DAM MULT, NOV, POP; MTCW 2; RGAL 4; YAW

McMurtry, Larry (Jeff) 1936- .. **CLC 2, 3, 7, 11, 27, 44, 127**
  See also AAYA 15; AITN 2; AMWS 5; BEST 89:2; BPFB 2; CA 5-8R; CANR 19, 43, 64, 103; CDALB 1968-1988; CN 7; CPW; CSW; DA3; DAM NOV, POP; DLB 2, 143, 256; DLBY 1980, 1987; EWL 3; MTCW 1, 2; RGAL 4; TCWW 2

McNally, T. M. 1961- .... **CLC 82**

McNally, Terrence 1939- .... **CLC 4, 7, 41, 91**
  See also CA 45-48; CAD; CANR 2, 56, 116; CD 5; DA3; DAM DRAM; DFS 16; DLB 7, 249; EWL 3; GLL 1; MTCW 2

McNamer, Deirdre 1950- .... **CLC 70**

McNeal, Tom .... **CLC 119**

McNeile, Herman Cyril 1888-1937
  See Sapper
  See also CA 184; CMW 4; DLB 77

McNickle, (William) D'Arcy
  1904-1977 .... **CLC 89; NNAL**
  See also CA 9-12R; 85-88; CANR 5, 45; DAM MULT; DLB 175, 212; RGAL 4; SATA-Obit 22

McPhee, John (Angus) 1931- .... **CLC 36**
  See also AMWS 3; ANW; BEST 90:1; CA 65-68; CANR 20, 46, 64, 69; CPW; DLB 185, 275; MTCW 1, 2; TUS

McPherson, James Alan 1943- . **BLCS; CLC 19, 77**
  See also BW 1, 3; CA 25-28R; CAAS 17; CANR 24, 74; CN 7; CSW; DLB 38, 244; EWL 3; MTCW 1, 2; RGAL 4; RGSF 2

McPherson, William (Alexander)
  1933- .... **CLC 34**
  See also CA 69-72; CANR 28; INT CANR-28

McTaggart, J. McT. Ellis
  See McTaggart, John McTaggart Ellis

McTaggart, John McTaggart Ellis
  1866-1925 .... **TCLC 105**
  See also CA 120; DLB 262

Mead, George Herbert 1863-1931 . **TCLC 89**
  See also CA 212; DLB 270

Mead, Margaret 1901-1978 .... **CLC 37**
  See also AITN 1; CA 1-4R; 81-84; CANR 4; DA3; FW; MTCW 1, 2; SATA-Obit 20

Meaker, Marijane (Agnes) 1927-
  See Kerr, M. E.
  See also CA 107; CANR 37, 63; INT 107; JRDA; MAICYA 1, 2; MAICYAS 1; MTCW 1; SATA 20, 61, 99; SATA-Essay 111; YAW

Medoff, Mark (Howard) 1940- .... **CLC 6, 23**
  See also AITN 1; CA 53-56; CAD; CANR 5; CD 5; DAM DRAM; DFS 4; DLB 7; INT CANR-5

Medvedev, P. N.
  See Bakhtin, Mikhail Mikhailovich

Meged, Aharon
  See Megged, Aharon

Meged, Aron
  See Megged, Aharon

Megged, Aharon 1920- .... **CLC 9**
  See also CA 49-52; CAAS 13; CANR 1; EWL 3

Mehta, Ved (Parkash) 1934- .... **CLC 37**
  See also CA 1-4R; CAAE 212; CANR 2, 23, 69; MTCW 1

Melanchthon, Philipp 1497-1560 .... **LC 90**
  See also DLB 179

Melanter
  See Blackmore, R(ichard) D(oddridge)

Meleager c. 140B.C.-c. 70B.C. ...... **CMLC 53**

Melies, Georges 1861-1938 .... **TCLC 81**

Melikow, Loris
  See Hofmannsthal, Hugo von

Melmoth, Sebastian
  See Wilde, Oscar (Fingal O'Flahertie Wills)

Melo Neto, Joao Cabral de
  See Cabral de Melo Neto, Joao
  See also EWL 3

Meltzer, Milton 1915- .... **CLC 26**
  See also AAYA 8, 45; BYA 2, 6; CA 13-16R; CANR 38, 92, 107; CLR 13; DLB 61; JRDA; MAICYA 1, 2; SAAS 1; SATA 1, 50, 80, 128; SATA-Essay 124; WYA; YAW

Melville, Herman 1819-1891 ..... **NCLC 3, 12, 29, 45, 49, 91, 93, 123; SSC 1, 17, 46; WLC**
  See also AAYA 25; AMW; AMWR 1; CDALB 1640-1865; DA; DA3; DAB; DAC; DAM MST, NOV; DLB 3, 74, 250, 254; EXPN; EXPS; LAIT 1, 2; NFS 7, 9; RGAL 4; RGSF 2; SATA 59; SSFS 3; TUS

Members, Mark
  See Powell, Anthony (Dymoke)

Milosz, Czeslaw 1911- ...... **CLC 5, 11, 22, 31, 56, 82; PC 8; WLCS**
See also CA 81-84; CANR 23, 51, 91; CD-WLB 4; CWW 2; DA3; DAM MST, POET; DLB 215; EW 13; EWL 3; MTCW 1, 2; PFS 16; RGWL 2, 3

Milton, John 1608-1674 ..... **LC 9, 43; PC 19, 29; WLC**
See also BRW 2; BRWR 2; CDBLB 1660-1789; DA; DA3; DAB; DAC; DAM MST, POET; DLB 131, 151, 281; EFS 1; EXPP; LAIT 1; PAB; PFS 3, 17; RGEL 2; TEA; WLIT 3; WP

Min, Anchee 1957- .... **CLC 86**
See also CA 146; CANR 94

Minehaha, Cornelius
See Wedekind, (Benjamin) Frank(lin)

Miner, Valerie 1947- .... **CLC 40**
See also CA 97-100; CANR 59; FW; GLL 2

Minimo, Duca
See D'Annunzio, Gabriele

Minot, Susan 1956- .... **CLC 44, 159**
See also AMWS 6; CA 134; CANR 118; CN 7

Minus, Ed 1938- .... **CLC 39**
See also CA 185

Mirabai 1498(?)-1550(?) .... **PC 48**

Miranda, Javier
See Bioy Casares, Adolfo
See also CWW 2

Mirbeau, Octave 1848-1917 .... **TCLC 55**
See also DLB 123, 192; GFL 1789 to the Present

Mirikitani, Janice 1942- .... **AAL**
See also CA 211; RGAL 4

Miro (Ferrer), Gabriel (Francisco Victor) 1879-1930 .... **TCLC 5**
See also CA 104; 185; EWL 3

Misharin, Alexandr .... **CLC 59**

Mishima, Yukio ... **CLC 2, 4, 6, 9, 27; DC 1; SSC 4**
See Hiraoka, Kimitake
See also BPFB 2; GLL 1; MJW; MTCW 2; RGSF 2; RGWL 2, 3; SSFS 5, 12

Mistral, Frederic 1830-1914 .... **TCLC 51**
See also CA 122; GFL 1789 to the Present

Mistral, Gabriela
See Godoy Alcayaga, Lucila
See also DNFS 1; EWL 3; LAW; RGWL 2, 3; WP

Mistry, Rohinton 1952- .... **CLC 71**
See also CA 141; CANR 86, 114; CCA 1; CN 7; DAC; SSFS 6

Mitchell, Clyde
See Ellison, Harlan (Jay)

Mitchell, Emerson Blackhorse Barney 1945- .... **NNAL**
See also CA 45-48

Mitchell, James Leslie 1901-1935
See Gibbon, Lewis Grassic
See also CA 104; 188; DLB 15

Mitchell, Joni 1943- .... **CLC 12**
See also CA 112; CCA 1

Mitchell, Joseph (Quincy) 1908-1996 .... **CLC 98**
See also CA 77-80; 152; CANR 69; CN 7; CSW; DLB 185; DLBY 1996

Mitchell, Margaret (Munnerlyn) 1900-1949 .... **TCLC 11**
See also AAYA 23; BPFB 2; BYA 1; CA 109; 125; CANR 55, 94; CDALBS; DA3; DAM NOV, POP; DLB 9; LAIT 2; MTCW 1, 2; NFS 9; RGAL 4; RHW; TUS; WYAS 1; YAW

Mitchell, Peggy
See Mitchell, Margaret (Munnerlyn)

Mitchell, S(ilas) Weir 1829-1914 .... **TCLC 36**
See also CA 165; DLB 202; RGAL 4

Mitchell, W(illiam) O(rmond) 1914-1998 .... **CLC 25**
See also CA 77-80; 165; CANR 15, 43; CN 7; DAC; DAM MST; DLB 88

Mitchell, William 1879-1936 .... **TCLC 81**

Mitford, Mary Russell 1787-1855 ... **NCLC 4**
See also DLB 110, 116; RGEL 2

Mitford, Nancy 1904-1973 .... **CLC 44**
See also CA 9-12R; DLB 191; RGEL 2

Miyamoto, (Chujo) Yuriko 1899-1951 .... **TCLC 37**
See Miyamoto Yuriko
See also CA 170, 174

Miyamoto Yuriko
See Miyamoto, (Chujo) Yuriko
See also DLB 180

Miyazawa, Kenji 1896-1933 .... **TCLC 76**
See Miyazawa Kenji
See also CA 157; RGWL 3

Miyazawa Kenji
See Miyazawa, Kenji
See also EWL 3

Mizoguchi, Kenji 1898-1956 .... **TCLC 72**
See also CA 167

Mo, Timothy (Peter) 1950(?)- ... **CLC 46, 134**
See also CA 117; CN 7; DLB 194; MTCW 1; WLIT 4

Modarressi, Taghi (M.) 1931-1997 ... **CLC 44**
See also CA 121; 134; INT 134

Modiano, Patrick (Jean) 1945- .... **CLC 18**
See also CA 85-88; CANR 17, 40, 115; CWW 2; DLB 83; EWL 3

Mofolo, Thomas (Mokopu) 1875(?)-1948 .... **BLC 3; TCLC 22**
See also AFW; CA 121; 153; CANR 83; DAM MULT; DLB 225; EWL 3; MTCW 2; WLIT 2

Mohr, Nicholasa 1938- .... **CLC 12; HLC 2**
See also AAYA 8, 46; CA 49-52; CANR 1, 32, 64; CLR 22; DAM MULT; DLB 145; HW 1, 2; JRDA; LAIT 5; MAICYA 2; MAICYAS 1; RGAL 4; SAAS 8; SATA 8, 97; SATA-Essay 113; WYA; YAW

Moi, Toril 1953- .... **CLC 172**
See also CA 154; CANR 102; FW

Mojtabai, A(nn) G(race) 1938- ..... **CLC 5, 9, 15, 29**
See also CA 85-88; CANR 88

Moliere 1622-1673 ..... **DC 13; LC 10, 28, 64; WLC**
See also DA; DA3; DAB; DAC; DAM DRAM, MST; DFS 13; DLB 268; EW 3; GFL Beginnings to 1789; LATS 1; RGWL 2, 3; TWA

Molin, Charles
See Mayne, William (James Carter)

Molnar, Ferenc 1878-1952 .... **TCLC 20**
See also CA 109; 153; CANR 83; CDWLB 4; DAM DRAM; DLB 215; EWL 3; RGWL 2, 3

Momaday, N(avarre) Scott 1934- ...... **CLC 2, 19, 85, 95, 160; NNAL; PC 25; WLCS**
See also AAYA 11; AMWS 4; ANW; BPFB 2; CA 25-28R; CANR 14, 34, 68; CDALBS; CN 7; CPW; DA; DA3; DAB; DAC; DAM MST, MULT, NOV, POP; DLB 143, 175, 256; EWL 3; EXPP; INT CANR-14; LAIT 4; LATS 1; MTCW 1, 2; NFS 10; PFS 2, 11; RGAL 4; SATA 48; SATA-Brief 30; WP; YAW

Monette, Paul 1945-1995 .... **CLC 82**
See also AMWS 10; CA 139; 147; CN 7; GLL 1

Monroe, Harriet 1860-1936 .... **TCLC 12**
See also CA 109; 204; DLB 54, 91

Monroe, Lyle
See Heinlein, Robert A(nson)

Montagu, Elizabeth 1720-1800 .... **NCLC 7, 117**
See also FW

Montagu, Mary (Pierrepont) Wortley 1689-1762 .... **LC 9, 57; PC 16**
See also DLB 95, 101; RGEL 2

Montagu, W. H.
See Coleridge, Samuel Taylor

Montague, John (Patrick) 1929- ..... **CLC 13, 46**
See also CA 9-12R; CANR 9, 69; CP 7; DLB 40; EWL 3; MTCW 1; PFS 12; RGEL 2

Montaigne, Michel (Eyquem) de 1533-1592 .... **LC 8; WLC**
See also DA; DAB; DAC; DAM MST; EW 2; GFL Beginnings to 1789; LMFS 1; RGWL 2, 3; TWA

Montale, Eugenio 1896-1981 ... **CLC 7, 9, 18; PC 13**
See also CA 17-20R; 104; CANR 30; DLB 114; EW 11; EWL 3; MTCW 1; RGWL 2, 3; TWA

Montesquieu, Charles-Louis de Secondat 1689-1755 .... **LC 7, 69**
See also EW 3; GFL Beginnings to 1789; TWA

Montessori, Maria 1870-1952 ...... **TCLC 103**
See also CA 115; 147

Montgomery, (Robert) Bruce 1921(?)-1978
See Crispin, Edmund
See also CA 179; 104; CMW 4

Montgomery, L(ucy) M(aud) 1874-1942 .... **TCLC 51**
See also AAYA 12; BYA 1; CA 108; 137; CLR 8; DA3; DAC; DAM MST; DLB 92; DLBD 14; JRDA; MAICYA 1, 2; MTCW 2; RGEL 2; SATA 100; TWA; WCH; WYA; YABC 1

Montgomery, Marion H., Jr. 1925- .... **CLC 7**
See also AITN 1; CA 1-4R; CANR 3, 48; CSW; DLB 6

Montgomery, Max
See Davenport, Guy (Mattison, Jr.)

Montherlant, Henry (Milon) de 1896-1972 .... **CLC 8, 19**
See also CA 85-88; 37-40R; DAM DRAM; DLB 72; EW 11; EWL 3; GFL 1789 to the Present; MTCW 1

Monty Python
See Chapman, Graham; Cleese, John (Marwood); Gilliam, Terry (Vance); Idle, Eric; Jones, Terence Graham Parry; Palin, Michael (Edward)
See also AAYA 7

Moodie, Susanna (Strickland) 1803-1885 .... **NCLC 14, 113**
See also DLB 99

Moody, Hiram (F. III) 1961-
See Moody, Rick
See also CA 138; CANR 64, 112

Moody, Minerva
See Alcott, Louisa May

Moody, Rick .... **CLC 147**
See Moody, Hiram (F. III)

Moody, William Vaughan 1869-1910 .... **TCLC 105**
See also CA 110; 178; DLB 7, 54; RGAL 4

Mooney, Edward 1951-
See Mooney, Ted
See also CA 130

Mooney, Ted .... **CLC 25**
See Mooney, Edward

Moorcock, Michael (John) 1939- ...... **CLC 5, 27, 58**
See Bradbury, Edward P.
See also AAYA 26; CA 45-48; CAAS 5; CANR 2, 17, 38, 64; CN 7; DLB 14, 231, 261; FANT; MTCW 1, 2; SATA 93; SCFW 2; SFW 4; SUFW 1, 2

Northrup, B. A.
  See Hubbard, L(afayette) Ron(ald)
North Staffs
  See Hulme, T(homas) E(rnest)
Northup, Solomon 1808-1863 ...... **NCLC 105**
Norton, Alice Mary
  See Norton, Andre
  See also MAICYA 1; SATA 1, 43
Norton, Andre 1912- .... **CLC 12**
  See Norton, Alice Mary
  See also AAYA 14; BPFB 2; BYA 4, 10,
    12; CA 1-4R; CANR 68; CLR 50; DLB
    8, 52; JRDA; MAICYA 2; MTCW 1;
    SATA 91; SUFW 1, 2; YAW
Norton, Caroline 1808-1877 .... **NCLC 47**
  See also DLB 21, 159, 199
Norway, Nevil Shute 1899-1960
  See Shute, Nevil
  See also CA 102; 93-96; CANR 85; MTCW
    2
Norwid, Cyprian Kamil
  1821-1883 .... **NCLC 17**
  See also RGWL 3
Nosille, Nabrah
  See Ellison, Harlan (Jay)
Nossack, Hans Erich 1901-1978 .... **CLC 6**
  See also CA 93-96; 85-88; DLB 69; EWL 3
Nostradamus 1503-1566 .... **LC 27**
Nosu, Chuji
  See Ozu, Yasujiro
Notenburg, Eleanora (Genrikhovna) von
  See Guro, Elena
Nova, Craig 1945- .... **CLC 7, 31**
  See also CA 45-48; CANR 2, 53
Novak, Joseph
  See Kosinski, Jerzy (Nikodem)
Novalis 1772-1801 .... **NCLC 13**
  See also CDWLB 2; DLB 90; EW 5; RGWL
    2, 3
Novick, Peter 1934- .... **CLC 164**
  See also CA 188
Novis, Emile
  See Weil, Simone (Adolphine)
Nowlan, Alden (Albert) 1933-1983 ... **CLC 15**
  See also CA 9-12R; CANR 5; DAC; DAM
    MST; DLB 53; PFS 12
Noyes, Alfred 1880-1958 ...... **PC 27; TCLC 7**
  See also CA 104; 188; DLB 20; EXPP;
    FANT; PFS 4; RGEL 2
Nugent, Richard Bruce 1906(?)-1987 ... **HR 3**
  See also BW 1; CA 125; DLB 51; GLL 2
Nunn, Kem .... **CLC 34**
  See also CA 159
Nwapa, Flora (Nwanzuruaha)
  1931-1993 .... **BLCS; CLC 133**
  See also BW 2; CA 143; CANR 83; CD-
    WLB 3; CWRI 5; DLB 125; EWL 3;
    WLIT 2
Nye, Robert 1939- .... **CLC 13, 42**
  See also CA 33-36R; CANR 29, 67, 107;
    CN 7; CP 7; CWRI 5; DAM NOV; DLB
    14, 271; FANT; HGG; MTCW 1; RHW;
    SATA 6
Nyro, Laura 1947-1997 .... **CLC 17**
  See also CA 194
Oates, Joyce Carol 1938- .. **CLC 1, 2, 3, 6, 9,
    11, 15, 19, 33, 52, 108, 134; SSC 6;
    WLC**
  See also AAYA 15; AITN 1; AMWS 2;
    BEST 89:2; BPFB 2; BYA 11; CA 5-8R;
    CANR 25, 45, 74, 113, 113; CDALB
    1968-1988; CN 7; CP 7; CPW; CWP; DA;
    DA3; DAB; DAC; DAM MST, NOV,
    POP; DLB 2, 5, 130; DLBY 1981; EWL
    3; EXPS; FW; HGG; INT CANR-25;
    LAIT 4; MAWW; MTCW 1, 2; NFS 8;
    RGAL 4; RGSF 2; SSFS 17; SUFW 2;
    TUS

O'Brian, E. G.
  See Clarke, Arthur C(harles)
O'Brian, Patrick 1914-2000 .... **CLC 152**
  See also CA 144; 187; CANR 74; CPW;
    MTCW 2; RHW
O'Brien, Darcy 1939-1998 .... **CLC 11**
  See also CA 21-24R; 167; CANR 8, 59
O'Brien, Edna 1936- ..... **CLC 3, 5, 8, 13, 36,
    65, 116; SSC 10**
  See also BRWS 5; CA 1-4R; CANR 6, 41,
    65, 102; CDBLB 1960 to Present; CN 7;
    DA3; DAM NOV; DLB 14, 231; EWL 3;
    FW; MTCW 1, 2; RGSF 2; WLIT 4
O'Brien, Fitz-James 1828-1862 ..... **NCLC 21**
  See also DLB 74; RGAL 4; SUFW
O'Brien, Flann .... **CLC 1, 4, 5, 7, 10, 47**
  See O Nuallain, Brian
  See also BRWS 2; DLB 231; EWL 3;
    RGEL 2
O'Brien, Richard 1942- .... **CLC 17**
  See also CA 124
O'Brien, (William) Tim(othy) 1946- . **CLC 7,
    19, 40, 103**
  See also AAYA 16; AMWS 5; CA 85-88;
    CANR 40, 58; CDALBS; CN 7; CPW;
    DA3; DAM POP; DLB 152; DLBD 9;
    DLBY 1980; MTCW 2; RGAL 4; SSFS
    5, 15
Obstfelder, Sigbjoern 1866-1900 .... **TCLC 23**
  See also CA 123
O'Casey, Sean 1880-1964 .... **CLC 1, 5, 9, 11,
    15, 88; DC 12; WLCS**
  See also BRW 7; CA 89-92; CANR 62;
    CBD; CDBLB 1914-1945; DA3; DAB;
    DAC; DAM DRAM, MST; DLB 10;
    EWL 3; MTCW 1, 2; RGEL 2; TEA;
    WLIT 4
O'Cathasaigh, Sean
  See O'Casey, Sean
Occom, Samson 1723-1792 .... **LC 60; NNAL**
  See also DLB 175
Ochs, Phil(ip David) 1940-1976 .... **CLC 17**
  See also CA 185; 65-68
O'Connor, Edwin (Greene)
  1918-1968 .... **CLC 14**
  See also CA 93-96; 25-28R
O'Connor, (Mary) Flannery
  1925-1964 .... **CLC 1, 2, 3, 6, 10, 13, 15,
    21, 66, 104; SSC 1, 23, 61; TCLC 132;
    WLC**
  See also AAYA 7; AMW; AMWR 2; BPFB
    3; CA 1-4R; CANR 3, 41; CDALB 1941-
    1968; DA; DA3; DAB; DAC; DAM MST,
    NOV; DLB 2, 152; DLBD 12; DLBY
    1980; EWL 3; EXPS; LAIT 5; MAWW;
    MTCW 1, 2; NFS 3; RGAL 4; RGSF 2;
    SSFS 2, 7, 10; TUS
O'Connor, Frank .... **CLC 23; SSC 5**
  See O'Donovan, Michael Francis
  See also DLB 162; EWL 3; RGSF 2; SSFS
    5
O'Dell, Scott 1898-1989 .... **CLC 30**
  See also AAYA 3, 44; BPFB 3; BYA 1, 2,
    3, 5; CA 61-64; 129; CANR 12, 30, 112;
    CLR 1, 16; DLB 52; JRDA; MAICYA 1,
    2; SATA 12, 60, 134; WYA; YAW
Odets, Clifford 1906-1963 ..... **CLC 2, 28, 98;
    DC 6**
  See also AMWS 2; CA 85-88; CAD; CANR
    62; DAM DRAM; DFS 17; DLB 7, 26;
    EWL 3; MTCW 1, 2; RGAL 4; TUS
O'Doherty, Brian 1928- .... **CLC 76**
  See also CA 105; CANR 108
O'Donnell, K. M.
  See Malzberg, Barry N(athaniel)
O'Donnell, Lawrence
  See Kuttner, Henry

O'Donovan, Michael Francis
  1903-1966 .... **CLC 14**
  See O'Connor, Frank
  See also CA 93-96; CANR 84
Oe, Kenzaburo 1935- .. **CLC 10, 36, 86; SSC
    20**
  See Oe Kenzaburo
  See also CA 97-100; CANR 36, 50, 74;
    CWW 2; DA3; DAM NOV; DLB 182;
    DLBY 1994; EWL 3; LATS 1; MJW;
    MTCW 1, 2; RGSF 2; RGWL 2, 3
Oe Kenzaburo
  See Oe, Kenzaburo
  See also EWL 3
O'Faolain, Julia 1932- .... **CLC 6, 19, 47, 108**
  See also CA 81-84; CAAS 2; CANR 12,
    61; CN 7; DLB 14, 231; FW; MTCW 1;
    RHW
O'Faolain, Sean 1900-1991 ...... **CLC 1, 7, 14,
    32, 70; SSC 13**
  See also CA 61-64; 134; CANR 12, 66;
    DLB 15, 162; MTCW 1, 2; RGEL 2;
    RGSF 2
O'Flaherty, Liam 1896-1984 .... **CLC 5, 34;
    SSC 6**
  See also CA 101; 113; CANR 35; DLB 36,
    162; DLBY 1984; MTCW 1, 2; RGEL 2;
    RGSF 2; SSFS 5
Ogai
  See Mori Ogai
  See also MJW
Ogilvy, Gavin
  See Barrie, J(ames) M(atthew)
O'Grady, Standish (James)
  1846-1928 .... **TCLC 5**
  See also CA 104; 157
O'Grady, Timothy 1951- .... **CLC 59**
  See also CA 138
O'Hara, Frank 1926-1966 .... **CLC 2, 5, 13,
    78; PC 45**
  See also CA 9-12R; 25-28R; CANR 33;
    DA3; DAM POET; DLB 5, 16, 193; EWL
    3; MTCW 1, 2; PFS 8; 12; RGAL 4; WP
O'Hara, John (Henry) 1905-1970 . **CLC 1, 2,
    3, 6, 11, 42; SSC 15**
  See also AMW; BPFB 3; CA 5-8R; 25-28R;
    CANR 31, 60; CDALB 1929-1941; DAM
    NOV; DLB 9, 86; DLBD 2; EWL 3;
    MTCW 1, 2; NFS 11; RGAL 4; RGSF 2
O Hehir, Diana 1922- .... **CLC 41**
  See also CA 93-96
Ohiyesa
  See Eastman, Charles A(lexander)
Okada, John 1923-1971 .... **AAL**
  See also BYA 14; CA 212
Okigbo, Christopher (Ifenayichukwu)
  1932-1967 .... **BLC 3; CLC 25, 84; PC 7**
  See also AFW; BW 1, 3; CA 77-80; CANR
    74; CDWLB 3; DAM MULT, POET; DLB
    125; EWL 3; MTCW 1, 2; RGEL 2
Okri, Ben 1959- .... **CLC 87**
  See also AFW; BRWS 5; BW 2, 3; CA 130;
    138; CANR 65; CN 7; DLB 157, 231;
    EWL 3; INT CA-138; MTCW 2; RGSF
    2; WLIT 2
Olds, Sharon 1942- .. **CLC 32, 39, 85; PC 22**
  See also AMWS 10; CA 101; CANR 18,
    41, 66, 98; CP 7; CPW; CWP; DAM
    POET; DLB 120; MTCW 2; PFS 17
Oldstyle, Jonathan
  See Irving, Washington
Olesha, Iurii
  See Olesha, Yuri (Karlovich)
  See also RGWL 2
Olesha, Iurii Karlovich
  See Olesha, Yuri (Karlovich)
  See also DLB 272

Pavic, Milorad 1929- .... **CLC 60**
See also CA 136; CDWLB 4; CWW 2; DLB
181; EWL 3; RGWL 3

Pavlov, Ivan Petrovich 1849-1936 . **TCLC 91**
See also CA 118; 180

Payne, Alan
See Jakes, John (William)

Paz, Gil
See Lugones, Leopoldo

Paz, Octavio 1914-1998 . **CLC 3, 4, 6, 10, 19,
51, 65, 119; HLC 2; PC 1, 48; WLC**
See also CA 73-76; 165; CANR 32, 65, 104;
CWW 2; DA; DA3; DAB; DAC; DAM
MST, MULT, POET; DLBY 1990, 1998;
DNFS 1; EWL 3; HW 1, 2; LAW; LAWS
1; MTCW 1, 2; RGWL 2, 3; SSFS 13;
TWA; WLIT 1

p'Bitek, Okot 1931-1982 ..... **BLC 3; CLC 96**
See also AFW; BW 2, 3; CA 124; 107;
CANR 82; DAM MULT; DLB 125; EWL
3; MTCW 1, 2; RGEL 2; WLIT 2

Peacock, Molly 1947- .... **CLC 60**
See also CA 103; CAAS 21; CANR 52, 84;
CP 7; CWP; DLB 120, 282

Peacock, Thomas Love
1785-1866 .... **NCLC 22**
See also BRW 4; DLB 96, 116; RGEL 2;
RGSF 2

Peake, Mervyn 1911-1968 .... **CLC 7, 54**
See also CA 5-8R; 25-28R; CANR 3; DLB
15, 160, 255; FANT; MTCW 1; RGEL 2;
SATA 23; SFW 4

Pearce, Philippa
See Christie, Philippa
See also CA 5-8R; CANR 4, 109; CWRI 5;
FANT; MAICYA 2

Pearl, Eric
See Elman, Richard (Martin)

Pearson, T(homas) R(eid) 1956- .... **CLC 39**
See also CA 120; 130; CANR 97; CSW;
INT 130

Peck, Dale 1967- .... **CLC 81**
See also CA 146; CANR 72; GLL 2

Peck, John (Frederick) 1941- .... **CLC 3**
See also CA 49-52; CANR 3, 100; CP 7

Peck, Richard (Wayne) 1934- .... **CLC 21**
See also AAYA 1, 24; BYA 1, 6, 8, 11; CA
85-88; CANR 19, 38; CLR 15; INT
CANR-19; JRDA; MAICYA 1, 2; SAAS
2; SATA 18, 55, 97; SATA-Essay 110;
WYA; YAW

Peck, Robert Newton 1928- .... **CLC 17**
See also AAYA 3, 43; BYA 1, 6; CA 81-84,
182; CAAE 182; CANR 31, 63; CLR 45;
DA; DAC; DAM MST; JRDA; LAIT 3;
MAICYA 1, 2; SAAS 1; SATA 21, 62,
111; SATA-Essay 108; WYA; YAW

Peckinpah, (David) Sam(uel)
1925-1984 .... **CLC 20**
See also CA 109; 114; CANR 82

Pedersen, Knut 1859-1952
See Hamsun, Knut
See also CA 104; 119; CANR 63; MTCW
1, 2

Peeslake, Gaffer
See Durrell, Lawrence (George)

Peguy, Charles (Pierre)
1873-1914 .... **TCLC 10**
See also CA 107; 193; DLB 258; EWL 3;
GFL 1789 to the Present

Peirce, Charles Sanders
1839-1914 .... **TCLC 81**
See also CA 194; DLB 270

Pellicer, Carlos 1900(?)-1977 .... **HLCS 2**
See also CA 153; 69-72; EWL 3; HW 1

Pena, Ramon del Valle y
See Valle-Inclan, Ramon (Maria) del

Pendennis, Arthur Esquir
See Thackeray, William Makepeace

Penn, William 1644-1718 .... **LC 25**
See also DLB 24

PEPECE
See Prado (Calvo), Pedro

Pepys, Samuel 1633-1703 ... **LC 11, 58; WLC**
See also BRW 2; CDBLB 1660-1789; DA;
DA3; DAB; DAC; DAM MST; DLB 101,
213; NCFS 4; RGEL 2; TEA; WLIT 3

Percy, Thomas 1729-1811 .... **NCLC 95**
See also DLB 104

Percy, Walker 1916-1990 .... **CLC 2, 3, 6, 8,
14, 18, 47, 65**
See also AMWS 3; BPFB 3; CA 1-4R; 131;
CANR 1, 23, 64; CPW; CSW; DA3;
DAM NOV, POP; DLB 2; DLBY 1980,
1990; EWL 3; MTCW 1, 2; RGAL 4;
TUS

Percy, William Alexander
1885-1942 .... **TCLC 84**
See also CA 163; MTCW 2

Perec, Georges 1936-1982 .... **CLC 56, 116**
See also CA 141; DLB 83; EWL 3; GFL
1789 to the Present; RGWL 3

**Pereda (y Sanchez de Porrua), Jose Maria
de** 1833-1906 .... **TCLC 16**
See also CA 117

Pereda y Porrua, Jose Maria de
See Pereda (y Sanchez de Porrua), Jose
Maria de

Peregoy, George Weems
See Mencken, H(enry) L(ouis)

Perelman, S(idney) J(oseph)
1904-1979 .. **CLC 3, 5, 9, 15, 23, 44, 49;
SSC 32**
See also AITN 1, 2; BPFB 3; CA 73-76;
89-92; CANR 18; DAM DRAM; DLB 11,
44; MTCW 1, 2; RGAL 4

Peret, Benjamin 1899-1959 .... **PC 33; TCLC
20**
See also CA 117; 186; GFL 1789 to the
Present

Peretz, Isaac Leib 1851(?)-1915
See Peretz, Isaac Loeb
See also CA 201

Peretz, Isaac Loeb 1851(?)-1915 ...... **SSC 26;
TCLC 16**
See Peretz, Isaac Leib
See also CA 109

Peretz, Yitzkhok Leibush
See Peretz, Isaac Loeb

Perez Galdos, Benito 1843-1920 ..... **HLCS 2;
TCLC 27**
See Galdos, Benito Perez
See also CA 125; 153; EWL 3; HW 1;
RGWL 2, 3

Peri Rossi, Cristina 1941- .. **CLC 156; HLCS
2**
See also CA 131; CANR 59, 81; DLB 145;
EWL 3; HW 1, 2

Perlata
See Peret, Benjamin

Perloff, Marjorie G(abrielle)
1931- .... **CLC 137**
See also CA 57-60; CANR 7, 22, 49, 104

Perrault, Charles 1628-1703 ... **DC 12; LC 2,
56**
See also BYA 4; CLR 79; DLB 268; GFL
Beginnings to 1789; MAICYA 1, 2;
RGWL 2, 3; SATA 25; WCH

Perry, Anne 1938- .... **CLC 126**
See also CA 101; CANR 22, 50, 84; CMW
4; CN 7; CPW; DLB 276

Perry, Brighton
See Sherwood, Robert E(mmet)

Perse, St.-John
See Leger, (Marie-Rene Auguste) Alexis
Saint-Leger

Perse, Saint-John
See Leger, (Marie-Rene Auguste) Alexis
Saint-Leger
See also DLB 258; RGWL 3

Perutz, Leo(pold) 1882-1957 .... **TCLC 60**
See also CA 147; DLB 81

Peseenz, Tulio F.
See Lopez y Fuentes, Gregorio

Pesetsky, Bette 1932- .... **CLC 28**
See also CA 133; DLB 130

Peshkov, Alexei Maximovich 1868-1936
See Gorky, Maxim
See also CA 105; 141; CANR 83; DA;
DAC; DAM DRAM, MST, NOV; MTCW
2

Pessoa, Fernando (Antonio Nogueira)
1898-1935 ..... **HLC 2; PC 20; TCLC 27**
See also CA 125; 183; DAM MULT; EW
10; EWL 3; RGWL 2, 3; WP

Peterkin, Julia Mood 1880-1961 ...... **CLC 31**
See also CA 102; DLB 9

Peters, Joan K(aren) 1945- .... **CLC 39**
See also CA 158; CANR 109

Peters, Robert L(ouis) 1924- .... **CLC 7**
See also CA 13-16R; CAAS 8; CP 7; DLB
105

Petofi, Sandor 1823-1849 .... **NCLC 21**
See also RGWL 2, 3

Petrakis, Harry Mark 1923- .... **CLC 3**
See also CA 9-12R; CANR 4, 30, 85; CN 7

Petrarch 1304-1374 .... **CMLC 20; PC 8**
See also DA3; DAM POET; EW 2; LMFS
1; RGWL 2. 3

Petronius c. 20-66 .... **CMLC 34**
See also AW 2; CDWLB 1; DLB 211;
RGWL 2, 3

Petrov, Evgeny .... **TCLC 21**
See Kataev, Evgeny Petrovich

Petry, Ann (Lane) 1908-1997 .. **CLC 1, 7, 18;
TCLC 112**
See also AFAW 1, 2; BPFB 3; BW 1, 3;
BYA 2; CA 5-8R; 157; CAAS 6; CANR
4, 46; CLR 12; CN 7; DLB 76; EWL 3;
JRDA; LAIT 1; MAICYA 1, 2; MAIC-
YAS 1; MTCW 1; RGAL 4; SATA 5;
SATA-Obit 94; TUS

Petursson, Halligrimur 1614-1674 .... **LC 8**

Peychinovich
See Vazov, Ivan (Minchov)

Phaedrus c. 15B.C.-c. 50 .... **CMLC 25**
See also DLB 211

Phelps (Ward), Elizabeth Stuart
See Phelps, Elizabeth Stuart
See also FW

Phelps, Elizabeth Stuart
1844-1911 .... **TCLC 113**
See Phelps (Ward), Elizabeth Stuart
See also DLB 74

Philips, Katherine 1632-1664 . **LC 30; PC 40**
See also DLB 131; RGEL 2

Philipson, Morris H. 1926- .... **CLC 53**
See also CA 1-4R; CANR 4

Phillips, Caryl 1958- .... **BLCS; CLC 96**
See also BRWS 5; BW 2; CA 141; CANR
63, 104; CBD; CD 5; CN 7; DA3; DAM
MULT; DLB 157; EWL 3; MTCW 2;
WLIT 4

Phillips, David Graham
1867-1911 .... **TCLC 44**
See also CA 108; 176; DLB 9, 12; RGAL 4

Phillips, Jack
See Sandburg, Carl (August)

Phillips, Jayne Anne 1952- .... **CLC 15, 33,
139; SSC 16**
See also BPFB 3; CA 101; CANR 24, 50,
96; CN 7; CSW; DLBY 1980; INT
CANR-24; MTCW 1, 2; RGAL 4; RGSF
2; SSFS 4

Phillips, Richard
 See Dick, Philip K(indred)
Phillips, Robert (Schaeffer) 1938- .... **CLC 28**
 See also CA 17-20R; CAAS 13; CANR 8;
 DLB 105
Phillips, Ward
 See Lovecraft, H(oward) P(hillips)
Piccolo, Lucio 1901-1969 .... **CLC 13**
 See also CA 97-100; DLB 114; EWL 3
Pickthall, Marjorie L(owry) C(hristie)
 1883-1922 .... **TCLC 21**
 See also CA 107; DLB 92
Pico della Mirandola, Giovanni
 1463-1494 .... **LC 15**
 See also LMFS 1
Piercy, Marge 1936- .... **CLC 3, 6, 14, 18, 27,**
 62, 128; PC 29
 See also BPFB 3; CA 21-24R; CAAE 187;
 CAAS 1; CANR 13, 43, 66, 111; CN 7;
 CP 7; CWP; DLB 120, 227; EXPP; FW;
 MTCW 1, 2; PFS 9; SFW 4
Piers, Robert
 See Anthony, Piers
Pieyre de Mandiargues, Andre 1909-1991
 See Mandiargues, Andre Pieyre de
 See also CA 103; 136; CANR 22, 82; EWL
 3; GFL 1789 to the Present
Pilnyak, Boris 1894-1938 . **SSC 48; TCLC 23**
 See Vogau, Boris Andreyevich
 See also EWL 3
Pinchback, Eugene
 See Toomer, Jean
Pincherle, Alberto 1907-1990 ...... **CLC 11, 18**
 See Moravia, Alberto
 See also CA 25-28R; 132; CANR 33, 63;
 DAM NOV; MTCW 1
Pinckney, Darryl 1953- .... **CLC 76**
 See also BW 2, 3; CA 143; CANR 79
Pindar 518(?)B.C.-438(?)B.C. .... **CMLC 12;**
 PC 19
 See also AW 1; CDWLB 1; DLB 176;
 RGWL 2
Pineda, Cecile 1942- .... **CLC 39**
 See also CA 118; DLB 209
Pinero, Arthur Wing 1855-1934 .... **TCLC 32**
 See also CA 110; 153; DAM DRAM; DLB
 10; RGEL 2
Pinero, Miguel (Antonio Gomez)
 1946-1988 .... **CLC 4, 55**
 See also CA 61-64; 125; CAD; CANR 29,
 90; DLB 266; HW 1
Pinget, Robert 1919-1997 .... **CLC 7, 13, 37**
 See also CA 85-88; 160; CWW 2; DLB 83;
 EWL 3; GFL 1789 to the Present
Pink Floyd
 See Barrett, (Roger) Syd; Gilmour, David;
 Mason, Nick; Waters, Roger; Wright, Rick
Pinkney, Edward 1802-1828 .... **NCLC 31**
 See also DLB 248
Pinkwater, Daniel
 See Pinkwater, Daniel Manus
Pinkwater, Daniel Manus 1941- .... **CLC 35**
 See also AAYA 1, 46; BYA 9; CA 29-32R;
 CANR 12, 38, 89; CLR 4; CSW; FANT;
 JRDA; MAICYA 1, 2; SAAS 3; SATA 8,
 46, 76, 114; SFW 4; YAW
Pinkwater, Manus
 See Pinkwater, Daniel Manus
Pinsky, Robert 1940- .... **CLC 9, 19, 38, 94,**
 121; PC 27
 See also AMWS 6; CA 29-32R; CAAS 4;
 CANR 58, 97; CP 7; DA3; DAM POET;
 DLBY 1982, 1998; MTCW 2; RGAL 4
Pinta, Harold
 See Pinter, Harold

Pinter, Harold 1930- .. **CLC 1, 3, 6, 9, 11, 15,**
 27, 58, 73; DC 15; WLC
 See also BRWR 1; BRWS 1; CA 5-8R;
 CANR 33, 65, 112; CBD; CD 5; CDBLB
 1960 to Present; DA; DA3; DAB; DAC;
 DAM DRAM, MST; DFS 3, 5, 7, 14;
 DLB 13; EWL 3; IDFW 3, 4; LMFS 2;
 MTCW 1, 2; RGEL 2; TEA
Piozzi, Hester Lynch (Thrale)
 1741-1821 .... **NCLC 57**
 See also DLB 104, 142
Pirandello, Luigi 1867-1936 .. **DC 5; SSC 22;**
 TCLC 4, 29; WLC
 See also CA 104; 153; CANR 103; DA;
 DA3; DAB; DAC; DAM DRAM, MST;
 DFS 4, 9; DLB 264; EW 8; EWL 3;
 MTCW 2; RGSF 2; RGWL 2, 3
Pirsig, Robert M(aynard) 1928- ... **CLC 4, 6,**
 73
 See also CA 53-56; CANR 42, 74; CPW 1;
 DA3; DAM POP; MTCW 1, 2; SATA 39
Pisarev, Dmitrii Ivanovich
 See Pisarev, Dmitry Ivanovich
 See also DLB 277
Pisarev, Dmitry Ivanovich
 1840-1868 .... **NCLC 25**
 See Pisarev, Dmitrii Ivanovich
Pix, Mary (Griffith) 1666-1709 .... **LC 8**
 See also DLB 80
Pixerecourt, (Rene Charles) Guilbert de
 1773-1844 .... **NCLC 39**
 See also DLB 192; GFL 1789 to the Present
Plaatje, Sol(omon) T(shekisho)
 1878-1932 .... **BLCS; TCLC 73**
 See also BW 2, 3; CA 141; CANR 79; DLB
 125, 225
Plaidy, Jean
 See Hibbert, Eleanor Alice Burford
Planche, James Robinson
 1796-1880 .... **NCLC 42**
 See also RGEL 2
Plant, Robert 1948- .... **CLC 12**
Plante, David (Robert) 1940- . **CLC 7, 23, 38**
 See also CA 37-40R; CANR 12, 36, 58, 82;
 CN 7; DAM NOV; DLBY 1983; INT
 CANR-12; MTCW 1
Plath, Sylvia 1932-1963 ..... **CLC 1, 2, 3, 5, 9,**
 11, 14, 17, 50, 51, 62, 111; PC 1, 37;
 WLC
 See also AAYA 13; AMWR 2; AMWS 1;
 BPFB 3; CA 19-20; CANR 34, 101; CAP
 2; CDALB 1941-1968; DA; DA3; DAB;
 DAC; DAM MST, POET; DLB 5, 6, 152;
 EWL 3; EXPN; EXPP; FW; LAIT 4;
 MAWW; MTCW 1, 2; NFS 1; PAB; PFS
 1, 15; RGAL 4; SATA 96; TUS; WP;
 YAW
Plato c. 428B.C.-347B.C. ... **CMLC 8; WLCS**
 See also AW 1; CDWLB 1; DA; DA3;
 DAB; DAC; DAM MST; DLB 176; LAIT
 1; LATS 1; RGWL 2, 3
Platonov, Andrei
 See Klimentov, Andrei Platonovich
Platonov, Andrei Platonovich
 See Klimentov, Andrei Platonovich
 See also DLB 272
Platonov, Andrey Platonovich
 See Klimentov, Andrei Platonovich
 See also EWL 3
Platt, Kin 1911- .... **CLC 26**
 See also AAYA 11; CA 17-20R; CANR 11;
 JRDA; SAAS 17; SATA 21, 86; WYA
Plautus c. 254B.C.-c. 184B.C. ...... **CMLC 24;**
 DC 6
 See also AW 1; CDWLB 1; DLB 211;
 RGWL 2, 3
Plick et Plock
 See Simenon, Georges (Jacques Christian)

Plieksans, Janis
 See Rainis, Janis
Plimpton, George (Ames) 1927- .... **CLC 36**
 See also AITN 1; CA 21-24R; CANR 32,
 70, 103; DLB 185, 241; MTCW 1, 2;
 SATA 10
Pliny the Elder c. 23-79 .... **CMLC 23**
 See also DLB 211
Plomer, William Charles Franklin
 1903-1973 .... **CLC 4, 8**
 See also AFW; CA 21-22; CANR 34; CAP
 2; DLB 20, 162, 191, 225; EWL 3;
 MTCW 1; RGEL 2; RGSF 2; SATA 24
Plotinus 204-270 .... **CMLC 46**
 See also CDWLB 1; DLB 176
Plowman, Piers
 See Kavanagh, Patrick (Joseph)
Plum, J.
 See Wodehouse, P(elham) G(renville)
Plumly, Stanley (Ross) 1939- .... **CLC 33**
 See also CA 108; 110; CANR 97; CP 7;
 DLB 5, 193; INT 110
Plumpe, Friedrich Wilhelm
 1888-1931 .... **TCLC 53**
 See also CA 112
Po Chu-i 772-846 .... **CMLC 24**
Poe, Edgar Allan 1809-1849 ..... **NCLC 1, 16,**
 55, 78, 94, 97, 117; PC 1; SSC 1, 22,
 34, 35, 54; WLC
 See also AAYA 14; AMW; AMWC 1;
 AMWR 2; BPFB 3; BYA 5, 11; CDALB
 1640-1865; CMW 4; DA; DA3; DAB;
 DAC; DAM MST, POET; DLB 3, 59, 73,
 74, 248, 254; EXPP; EXPS; HGG; LAIT
 2; LATS 1; LMFS 1; MSW; PAB; PFS 1,
 3, 9; RGAL 4; RGSF 2; SATA 23; SCFW
 2; SFW 4; SSFS 2, 4, 7, 8, 16; SUFW;
 TUS; WP; WYA
Poet of Titchfield Street, The
 See Pound, Ezra (Weston Loomis)
Pohl, Frederik 1919- .... **CLC 18; SSC 25**
 See also AAYA 24; CA 61-64; CAAE 188;
 CAAS 1; CANR 11, 37, 81; CN 7; DLB
 8; INT CANR-11; MTCW 1, 2; SATA 24;
 SCFW 2; SFW 4
Poirier, Louis 1910-
 See Gracq, Julien
 See also CA 122; 126; CWW 2
Poitier, Sidney 1927- .... **CLC 26**
 See also BW 1; CA 117; CANR 94
Pokagon, Simon 1830-1899 .... **NNAL**
 See also DAM MULT
Polanski, Roman 1933- .... **CLC 16**
 See also CA 77-80
Poliakoff, Stephen 1952- .... **CLC 38**
 See also CA 106; CANR 116; CBD; CD 5;
 DLB 13
Police, The
 See Copeland, Stewart (Armstrong); Sum-
 mers, Andrew James; Sumner, Gordon
 Matthew
Polidori, John William 1795-1821 . **NCLC 51**
 See also DLB 116; HGG
Pollitt, Katha 1949- .... **CLC 28, 122**
 See also CA 120; 122; CANR 66, 108;
 MTCW 1, 2
Pollock, (Mary) Sharon 1936- .... **CLC 50**
 See also CA 141; CD 5; CWD; DAC; DAM
 DRAM, MST; DFS 3; DLB 60; FW
Pollock, Sharon 1936- .... **DC 20**
Polo, Marco 1254-1324 .... **CMLC 15**
Polonsky, Abraham (Lincoln)
 1910-1999 .... **CLC 92**
 See also CA 104; 187; DLB 26; INT 104
Polybius c. 200B.C.-c. 118B.C. ...... **CMLC 17**
 See also AW 1; DLB 176; RGWL 2, 3
Pomerance, Bernard 1940- .... **CLC 13**
 See also CA 101; CAD; CANR 49; CD 5;
 DAM DRAM; DFS 9; LAIT 2

Proust,
    (Valentin-Louis-George-Eugene-)Marcel
    1871-1922 .... **TCLC 7, 13, 33; WLC**
    See also BPFB 3; CA 104; 120; CANR 110;
    DA; DA3; DAB; DAC; DAM MST, NOV;
    DLB 65; EW 8; EWL 3; GFL 1789 to the
    Present; MTCW 1, 2; RGWL 2, 3; TWA
Prowler, Harley
    See Masters, Edgar Lee
Prus, Boleslaw 1845-1912 .... **TCLC 48**
    See also RGWL 2, 3
Pryor, Richard (Franklin Lenox Thomas)
    1940- .... **CLC 26**
    See also CA 122; 152
Przybyszewski, Stanislaw
    1868-1927 .... **TCLC 36**
    See also CA 160; DLB 66; EWL 3
Pteleon
    See Grieve, C(hristopher) M(urray)
    See also DAM POET
Puckett, Lute
    See Masters, Edgar Lee
Puig, Manuel 1932-1990 .... **CLC 3, 5, 10, 28,**
    65, 133; HLC 2
    See also BPFB 3; CA 45-48; CANR 2, 32,
    63; CDWLB 3; DA3; DAM MULT; DLB
    113; DNFS 1; EWL 3; GLL 1; HW 1, 2;
    LAW; MTCW 1, 2; RGWL 2, 3; TWA;
    WLIT 1
Pulitzer, Joseph 1847-1911 .... **TCLC 76**
    See also CA 114; DLB 23
Purchas, Samuel 1577(?)-1626 .... **LC 70**
    See also DLB 151
Purdy, A(lfred) W(ellington)
    1918-2000 .... **CLC 3, 6, 14, 50**
    See also CA 81-84; 189; CAAS 17; CANR
    42, 66; CP 7; DAC; DAM MST, POET;
    DLB 88; PFS 5; RGEL 2
Purdy, James (Amos) 1923- .... **CLC 2, 4, 10,**
    28, 52
    See also AMWS 7; CA 33-36R; CAAS 1;
    CANR 19, 51; CN 7; DLB 2, 218; EWL
    3; INT CANR-19; MTCW 1; RGAL 4
Pure, Simon
    See Swinnerton, Frank Arthur
Pushkin, Aleksandr Sergeevich
    See Pushkin, Alexander (Sergeyevich)
    See also DLB 205
Pushkin, Alexander (Sergeyevich)
    1799-1837 .... **NCLC 3, 27, 83; PC 10;**
    SSC 27, 55; WLC
    See Pushkin, Aleksandr Sergeevich
    See also DA; DA3; DAB; DAC; DAM
    DRAM, MST, POET; EW 5; EXPS; RGSF
    2; RGWL 2, 3; SATA 61; SSFS 9; TWA
P'u Sung-ling 1640-1715 .... **LC 49; SSC 31**
Putnam, Arthur Lee
    See Alger, Horatio, Jr.
Puzo, Mario 1920-1999 .... **CLC 1, 2, 6, 36,**
    107
    See also BPFB 3; CA 65-68; 185; CANR 4,
    42, 65, 99; CN 7; CPW; DA3; DAM
    NOV, POP; DLB 6; MTCW 1, 2; NFS 16;
    RGAL 4
Pygge, Edward
    See Barnes, Julian (Patrick)
Pyle, Ernest Taylor 1900-1945
    See Pyle, Ernie
    See also CA 115; 160
Pyle, Ernie .... **TCLC 75**
    See Pyle, Ernest Taylor
    See also DLB 29; MTCW 2
Pyle, Howard 1853-1911 .... **TCLC 81**
    See also BYA 2, 4; CA 109; 137; CLR 22;
    DLB 42, 188; DLBD 13; LAIT 1; MAI-
    CYA 1, 2; SATA 16, 100; WCH; YAW

Pym, Barbara (Mary Crampton)
    1913-1980 .... **CLC 13, 19, 37, 111**
    See also BPFB 3; BRWS 2; CA 13-14; 97-
    100; CANR 13, 34; CAP 1; DLB 14, 207;
    DLBY 1987; EWL 3; MTCW 1, 2; RGEL
    2; TEA
Pynchon, Thomas (Ruggles, Jr.)
    1937- ...... **CLC 2, 3, 6, 9, 11, 18, 33, 62,**
    72, 123; SSC 14; WLC
    See also AMWS 2; BEST 90:2; BPFB 3;
    CA 17-20R; CANR 22, 46, 73; CN 7;
    CPW 1; DA; DA3; DAB; DAC; DAM
    MST, NOV, POP; DLB 2, 173; EWL 3;
    MTCW 1, 2; RGAL 4; SFW 4; TUS
Pythagoras c. 582B.C.-c. 507B.C. . **CMLC 22**
    See also DLB 176
Q
    See Quiller-Couch, Sir Arthur (Thomas)
Qian, Chongzhu
    See Ch'ien, Chung-shu
Qian Zhongshu
    See Ch'ien, Chung-shu
Qroll
    See Dagerman, Stig (Halvard)
Quarrington, Paul (Lewis) 1953- ..... **CLC 65**
    See also CA 129; CANR 62, 95
Quasimodo, Salvatore 1901-1968 .... **CLC 10;**
    PC 47
    See also CA 13-16; 25-28R; CAP 1; DLB
    114; EW 12; EWL 3; MTCW 1; RGWL
    2, 3
Quatermass, Martin
    See Carpenter, John (Howard)
Quay, Stephen 1947- .... **CLC 95**
    See also CA 189
Quay, Timothy 1947- .... **CLC 95**
    See also CA 189
Queen, Ellery .... **CLC 3, 11**
    See Dannay, Frederic; Davidson, Avram
    (James); Deming, Richard; Fairman, Paul
    W.; Flora, Fletcher; Hoch, Edward
    D(entinger); Kane, Henry; Lee, Manfred
    B(ennington); Marlowe, Stephen; Powell,
    (Oval) Talmage; Sheldon, Walter J(ames);
    Sturgeon, Theodore (Hamilton); Tracy,
    Don(ald Fiske); Vance, John Holbrook
    See also BPFB 3; CMW 4; MSW; RGAL 4
Queen, Ellery, Jr.
    See Dannay, Frederic; Lee, Manfred
    B(ennington)
Queneau, Raymond 1903-1976 ..... **CLC 2, 5,**
    10, 42
    See also CA 77-80; 69-72; CANR 32; DLB
    72, 258; EW 12; EWL 3; GFL 1789 to
    the Present; MTCW 1, 2; RGWL 2, 3
Quevedo, Francisco de 1580-1645 .... **LC 23**
Quiller-Couch, Sir Arthur (Thomas)
    1863-1944 .... **TCLC 53**
    See also CA 118; 166; DLB 135, 153, 190;
    HGG; RGEL 2; SUFW 1
Quin, Ann (Marie) 1936-1973 .... **CLC 6**
    See also CA 9-12R; 45-48; DLB 14, 231
Quincey, Thomas de
    See De Quincey, Thomas
Quinn, Martin
    See Smith, Martin Cruz
Quinn, Peter 1947- .... **CLC 91**
    See also CA 197
Quinn, Simon
    See Smith, Martin Cruz
Quintana, Leroy V. 1944- ...... **HLC 2; PC 36**
    See also CA 131; CANR 65; DAM MULT;
    DLB 82; HW 1, 2
Quiroga, Horacio (Sylvestre)
    1878-1937 .... **HLC 2; TCLC 20**
    See also CA 117; 131; DAM MULT; EWL
    3; HW 1; LAW; MTCW 1; RGSF 2;
    WLIT 1

Quoirez, Francoise 1935- .... **CLC 9**
    See Sagan, Francoise
    See also CA 49-52; CANR 6, 39, 73; CWW
    2; MTCW 1, 2; TWA
Raabe, Wilhelm (Karl) 1831-1910 . **TCLC 45**
    See also CA 167; DLB 129
Rabe, David (William) 1940- .. **CLC 4, 8, 33;**
    DC 16
    See also CA 85-88; CABS 3; CAD; CANR
    59; CD 5; DAM DRAM; DFS 3, 8, 13;
    DLB 7, 228; EWL 3
Rabelais, Francois 1494-1553 .... **LC 5, 60;**
    WLC
    See also DA; DAB; DAC; DAM MST; EW
    2; GFL Beginnings to 1789; LMFS 1;
    RGWL 2, 3; TWA
Rabinovitch, Sholem 1859-1916
    See Aleichem, Sholom
    See also CA 104
Rabinyan, Dorit 1972- .... **CLC 119**
    See also CA 170
Rachilde
    See Vallette, Marguerite Eymery; Vallette,
    Marguerite Eymery
    See also EWL 3
Racine, Jean 1639-1699 .... **LC 28**
    See also DA3; DAB; DAM MST; DLB 268;
    EW 3; GFL Beginnings to 1789; LMFS
    1; RGWL 2, 3; TWA
Radcliffe, Ann (Ward) 1764-1823 ... **NCLC 6,**
    55, 106
    See also DLB 39, 178; HGG; LMFS 1;
    RGEL 2; SUFW; WLIT 3
Radclyffe-Hall, Marguerite
    See Hall, (Marguerite) Radclyffe
Radiguet, Raymond 1903-1923 ...... **TCLC 29**
    See also CA 162; DLB 65; EWL 3; GFL
    1789 to the Present; RGWL 2, 3
Radnoti, Miklos 1909-1944 .... **TCLC 16**
    See also CA 118; 212; CDWLB 4; DLB
    215; EWL 3; RGWL 2, 3
Rado, James 1939- .... **CLC 17**
    See also CA 105
Radvanyi, Netty 1900-1983
    See Seghers, Anna
    See also CA 85-88; 110; CANR 82
Rae, Ben
    See Griffiths, Trevor
Raeburn, John (Hay) 1941- .... **CLC 34**
    See also CA 57-60
Ragni, Gerome 1942-1991 .... **CLC 17**
    See also CA 105; 134
Rahv, Philip .... **CLC 24**
    See Greenberg, Ivan
    See also DLB 137
Raimund, Ferdinand Jakob
    1790-1836 .... **NCLC 69**
    See also DLB 90
Raine, Craig (Anthony) 1944- .. **CLC 32, 103**
    See also CA 108; CANR 29, 51, 103; CP 7;
    DLB 40; PFS 7
Raine, Kathleen (Jessie) 1908- ..... **CLC 7, 45**
    See also CA 85-88; CANR 46, 109; CP 7;
    DLB 20; EWL 3; MTCW 1; RGEL 2
Rainis, Janis 1865-1929 .... **TCLC 29**
    See also CA 170; CDWLB 4; DLB 220;
    EWL 3
Rakosi, Carl .... **CLC 47**
    See Rawley, Callman
    See also CAAS 5; CP 7; DLB 193
Ralegh, Sir Walter
    See Raleigh, Sir Walter
    See also BRW 1; RGEL 2; WP
Raleigh, Richard
    See Lovecraft, H(oward) P(hillips)

Roberts, Michele (Brigitte) 1949- ..... **CLC 48**
See also CA 115; CANR 58; CN 7; DLB 231; FW

Robertson, Ellis
See Ellison, Harlan (Jay); Silverberg, Robert

Robertson, Thomas William
1829-1871 .... **NCLC 35**
See Robertson, Tom
See also DAM DRAM

Robertson, Tom
See Robertson, Thomas William
See also RGEL 2

Robeson, Kenneth
See Dent, Lester

Robinson, Edwin Arlington
1869-1935 .... **PC 1, 35; TCLC 5, 101**
See also AMW; CA 104; 133; CDALB 1865-1917; DA; DAC; DAM MST, POET; DLB 54; EWL 3; EXPP; MTCW 1, 2; PAB; PFS 4; RGAL 4; WP

Robinson, Henry Crabb
1775-1867 .... **NCLC 15**
See also DLB 107

Robinson, Jill 1936- .... **CLC 10**
See also CA 102; INT 102

Robinson, Kim Stanley 1952- .... **CLC 34**
See also AAYA 26; CA 126; CANR 113; CN 7; SATA 109; SCFW 2; SFW 4

Robinson, Lloyd
See Silverberg, Robert

Robinson, Marilynne 1944- .... **CLC 25**
See also CA 116; CANR 80; CN 7; DLB 206

Robinson, Smokey .... **CLC 21**
See Robinson, William, Jr.

Robinson, William, Jr. 1940-
See Robinson, Smokey
See also CA 116

Robison, Mary 1949- .... **CLC 42, 98**
See also CA 113; 116; CANR 87; CN 7; DLB 130; INT 116; RGSF 2

Rochester
See Wilmot, John
See also RGEL 2

Rod, Edouard 1857-1910 .... **TCLC 52**

Roddenberry, Eugene Wesley 1921-1991
See Roddenberry, Gene
See also CA 110; 135; CANR 37; SATA 45; SATA-Obit 69

Roddenberry, Gene .... **CLC 17**
See Roddenberry, Eugene Wesley
See also AAYA 5; SATA-Obit 69

Rodgers, Mary 1931- .... **CLC 12**
See also BYA 5; CA 49-52; CANR 8, 55, 90; CLR 20; CWRI 5; INT CANR-8; JRDA; MAICYA 1, 2; SATA 8, 130

Rodgers, W(illiam) R(obert)
1909-1969 .... **CLC 7**
See also CA 85-88; DLB 20; RGEL 2

Rodman, Eric
See Silverberg, Robert

Rodman, Howard 1920(?)-1985 .... **CLC 65**
See also CA 118

Rodman, Maia
See Wojciechowska, Maia (Teresa)

Rodo, Jose Enrique 1871(?)-1917 .... **HLCS 2**
See also CA 178; EWL 3; HW 2; LAW

Rodolph, Utto
See Ouologuem, Yambo

Rodriguez, Claudio 1934-1999 .... **CLC 10**
See also CA 188; DLB 134

Rodriguez, Richard 1944- .... **CLC 155; HLC 2**
See also CA 110; CANR 66, 116; DAM MULT; DLB 82, 256; HW 1, 2; LAIT 5; NCFS 3; WLIT 1

Roelvaag, O(le) E(dvart) 1876-1931
See Rolvaag, O(le) E(dvart)
See also CA 117; 171

Roethke, Theodore (Huebner)
1908-1963 .... **CLC 1, 3, 8, 11, 19, 46, 101; PC 15**
See also AMW; CA 81-84; CABS 2; CDALB 1941-1968; DA3; DAM POET; DLB 5, 206; EWL 3; EXPP; MTCW 1, 2; PAB; PFS 3; RGAL 4; WP

Rogers, Carl R(ansom)
1902-1987 .... **TCLC 125**
See also CA 1-4R; 121; CANR 1, 18; MTCW 1

Rogers, Samuel 1763-1855 .... **NCLC 69**
See also DLB 93; RGEL 2

Rogers, Thomas Hunton 1927- .... **CLC 57**
See also CA 89-92; INT 89-92

Rogers, Will(iam Penn Adair)
1879-1935 .... **NNAL; TCLC 8, 71**
See also CA 105; 144; DA3; DAM MULT; DLB 11; MTCW 2

Rogin, Gilbert 1929- .... **CLC 18**
See also CA 65-68; CANR 15

Rohan, Koda
See Koda Shigeyuki

Rohlfs, Anna Katharine Green
See Green, Anna Katharine

Rohmer, Eric .... **CLC 16**
See Scherer, Jean-Marie Maurice

Rohmer, Sax .... **TCLC 28**
See Ward, Arthur Henry Sarsfield
See also DLB 70; MSW; SUFW

Roiphe, Anne (Richardson) 1935- .. **CLC 3, 9**
See also CA 89-92; CANR 45, 73; DLBY 1980; INT 89-92

Rojas, Fernando de 1475-1541 .... **HLCS 1; LC 23**
See also RGWL 2, 3

Rojas, Gonzalo 1917- .... **HLCS 2**
See also CA 178; HW 2; LAWS 1

Rolfe, Frederick (William Serafino Austin Lewis Mary) 1860-1913 .... **TCLC 12**
See Corvo, Baron
See also CA 107; 210; DLB 34, 156; RGEL 2

Rolland, Romain 1866-1944 .... **TCLC 23**
See also CA 118; 197; DLB 65, 284; EWL 3; GFL 1789 to the Present; RGWL 2, 3

Rolle, Richard c. 1300-c. 1349 .... **CMLC 21**
See also DLB 146; LMFS 1; RGEL 2

Rolvaag, O(le) E(dvart) .... **TCLC 17**
See Roelvaag, O(le) E(dvart)
See also DLB 9, 212; NFS 5; RGAL 4

Romain Arnaud, Saint
See Aragon, Louis

Romains, Jules 1885-1972 .... **CLC 7**
See also CA 85-88; CANR 34; DLB 65; EWL 3; GFL 1789 to the Present; MTCW 1

Romero, Jose Ruben 1890-1952 .... **TCLC 14**
See also CA 114; 131; EWL 3; HW 1; LAW

Ronsard, Pierre de 1524-1585 . **LC 6, 54; PC 11**
See also EW 2; GFL Beginnings to 1789; RGWL 2, 3; TWA

Rooke, Leon 1934- .... **CLC 25, 34**
See also CA 25-28R; CANR 23, 53; CCA 1; CPW; DAM POP

Roosevelt, Franklin Delano
1882-1945 .... **TCLC 93**
See also CA 116; 173; LAIT 3

Roosevelt, Theodore 1858-1919 ..... **TCLC 69**
See also CA 115; 170; DLB 47, 186, 275

Roper, William 1498-1578 .... **LC 10**

Roquelaure, A. N.
See Rice, Anne

Rosa, Joao Guimaraes 1908-1967 ... **CLC 23; HLCS 1**
See also CA 89-92; DLB 113; EWL 3; WLIT 1

Rose, Wendy 1948- . **CLC 85; NNAL; PC 13**
See also CA 53-56; CANR 5, 51; CWP; DAM MULT; DLB 175; PFS 13; RGAL 4; SATA 12

Rosen, R. D.
See Rosen, Richard (Dean)

Rosen, Richard (Dean) 1949- .... **CLC 39**
See also CA 77-80; CANR 62; CMW 4; INT CANR-30

Rosenberg, Isaac 1890-1918 .... **TCLC 12**
See also BRW 6; CA 107; 188; DLB 20, 216; EWL 3; PAB; RGEL 2

Rosenblatt, Joe .... **CLC 15**
See Rosenblatt, Joseph

Rosenblatt, Joseph 1933-
See Rosenblatt, Joe
See also CA 89-92; CP 7; INT 89-92

Rosenfeld, Samuel
See Tzara, Tristan

Rosenstock, Sami
See Tzara, Tristan

Rosenstock, Samuel
See Tzara, Tristan

Rosenthal, M(acha) L(ouis)
1917-1996 .... **CLC 28**
See also CA 1-4R; 152; CAAS 6; CANR 4, 51; CP 7; DLB 5; SATA 59

Ross, Barnaby
See Dannay, Frederic

Ross, Bernard L.
See Follett, Ken(neth Martin)

Ross, J. H.
See Lawrence, T(homas) E(dward)

Ross, John Hume
See Lawrence, T(homas) E(dward)

Ross, Martin 1862-1915
See Martin, Violet Florence
See also DLB 135; GLL 2; RGEL 2; RGSF 2

Ross, (James) Sinclair 1908-1996 ... **CLC 13; SSC 24**
See also CA 73-76; CANR 81; CN 7; DAC; DAM MST; DLB 88; RGEL 2; RGSF 2; TCWW 2

Rossetti, Christina (Georgina)
1830-1894 .... **NCLC 2, 50, 66; PC 7; WLC**
See also BRW 5; BYA 4; DA; DA3; DAB; DAC; DAM MST, POET; DLB 35, 163, 240; EXPP; LATS 1; MAICYA 1, 2; PFS 10, 14; RGEL 2; SATA 20; TEA; WCH

Rossetti, Dante Gabriel 1828-1882 . **NCLC 4, 77; PC 44; WLC**
See also BRW 5; CDBLB 1832-1890; DA; DAB; DAC; DAM MST, POET; DLB 35; EXPP; RGEL 2; TEA

Rossi, Cristina Peri
See Peri Rossi, Cristina

Rossi, Jean Baptiste 1931-
See Japrisot, Sebastien
See also CA 201

Rossner, Judith (Perelman) 1935- . **CLC 6, 9, 29**
See also AITN 2; BEST 90:3; BPFB 3; CA 17-20R; CANR 18, 51, 73; CN 7; DLB 6; INT CANR-18; MTCW 1, 2

Rostand, Edmond (Eugene Alexis)
1868-1918 .... **DC 10; TCLC 6, 37**
See also CA 104; 126; DA; DA3; DAB; DAC; DAM DRAM, MST; DFS 1; DLB 192; LAIT 1; MTCW 1; RGWL 2, 3; TWA

Roth, Henry 1906-1995 ..... **CLC 2, 6, 11, 104**
See also AMWS 9; CA 11-12; 149; CANR 38, 63; CAP 1; CN 7; DA3; DLB 28; EWL 3; MTCW 1, 2; RGAL 4

Roth, (Moses) Joseph 1894-1939 ... **TCLC 33**
See also CA 160; DLB 85; EWL 3; RGWL 2, 3

Saunders, Caleb
See Heinlein, Robert A(nson)

Saura (Atares), Carlos 1932-1998 .... **CLC 20**
See also CA 114; 131; CANR 79; HW 1

Sauser, Frederic Louis
See Sauser-Hall, Frederic

Sauser-Hall, Frederic 1887-1961 ...... **CLC 18**
See Cendrars, Blaise
See also CA 102; 93-96; CANR 36, 62;
MTCW 1

Saussure, Ferdinand de
1857-1913 .... **TCLC 49**
See also DLB 242

Savage, Catharine
See Brosman, Catharine Savage

Savage, Thomas 1915- .... **CLC 40**
See also CA 126; 132; CAAS 15; CN 7;
INT 132; TCWW 2

Savan, Glenn (?)- .... **CLC 50**

Sax, Robert
See Johnson, Robert

Saxo Grammaticus c. 1150-c.
1222 .... **CMLC 58**

Saxton, Robert
See Johnson, Robert

Sayers, Dorothy L(eigh)
1893-1957 .... **TCLC 2, 15**
See also BPFB 3; BRWS 3; CA 104; 119;
CANR 60; CDBLB 1914-1945; CMW 4;
DAM POP; DLB 10, 36, 77, 100; MSW;
MTCW 1, 2; RGEL 2; SSFS 12; TEA

Sayers, Valerie 1952- .... **CLC 50, 122**
See also CA 134; CANR 61; CSW

Sayles, John (Thomas) 1950- . **CLC 7, 10, 14**
See also CA 57-60; CANR 41, 84; DLB 44

Scammell, Michael 1935- .... **CLC 34**
See also CA 156

Scannell, Vernon 1922- .... **CLC 49**
See also CA 5-8R; CANR 8, 24, 57; CP 7;
CWRI 5; DLB 27; SATA 59

Scarlett, Susan
See Streatfeild, (Mary) Noel

Scarron 1847-1910
See Mikszath, Kalman

Schaeffer, Susan Fromberg 1941- ..... **CLC 6,**
11, 22
See also CA 49-52; CANR 18, 65; CN 7;
DLB 28; MTCW 1, 2; SATA 22

Schama, Simon (Michael) 1945- ..... **CLC 150**
See also BEST 89:4; CA 105; CANR 39,
91

Schary, Jill
See Robinson, Jill

Schell, Jonathan 1943- .... **CLC 35**
See also CA 73-76; CANR 12, 117

Schelling, Friedrich Wilhelm Joseph von
1775-1854 .... **NCLC 30**
See also DLB 90

Scherer, Jean-Marie Maurice 1920-
See Rohmer, Eric
See also CA 110

Schevill, James (Erwin) 1920- .... **CLC 7**
See also CA 5-8R; CAAS 12; CAD; CD 5

Schiller, Friedrich von 1759-1805 ...... **DC 12;**
NCLC 39, 69
See also CDWLB 2; DAM DRAM; DLB
94; EW 5; RGWL 2, 3; TWA

Schisgal, Murray (Joseph) 1926- .... **CLC 6**
See also CA 21-24R; CAD; CANR 48, 86;
CD 5

Schlee, Ann 1934- .... **CLC 35**
See also CA 101; CANR 29, 88; SATA 44;
SATA-Brief 36

Schlegel, August Wilhelm von
1767-1845 .... **NCLC 15**
See also DLB 94; RGWL 2, 3

Schlegel, Friedrich 1772-1829 .... **NCLC 45**
See also DLB 90; EW 5; RGWL 2, 3; TWA

Schlegel, Johann Elias (von)
1719(?)-1749 .... **LC 5**

Schleiermacher, Friedrich
1768-1834 .... **NCLC 107**
See also DLB 90

Schlesinger, Arthur M(eier), Jr.
1917- .... **CLC 84**
See also AITN 1; CA 1-4R; CANR 1, 28,
58, 105; DLB 17; INT CANR-28; MTCW
1, 2; SATA 61

Schlink, Bernhard 1944- .... **CLC 174**
See also CA 163; CANR 116

Schmidt, Arno (Otto) 1914-1979 ...... **CLC 56**
See also CA 128; 109; DLB 69; EWL 3

Schmitz, Aron Hector 1861-1928
See Svevo, Italo
See also CA 104; 122; MTCW 1

Schnackenberg, Gjertrud (Cecelia)
1953- .... **CLC 40; PC 45**
See also CA 116; CANR 100; CP 7; CWP;
DLB 120, 282; PFS 13

Schneider, Leonard Alfred 1925-1966
See Bruce, Lenny
See also CA 89-92

Schnitzler, Arthur 1862-1931 ..... **DC 17; SSC**
15, 61; TCLC 4
See also CA 104; CDWLB 2; DLB 81, 118;
EW 8; EWL 3; RGSF 2; RGWL 2, 3

Schoenberg, Arnold Franz Walter
1874-1951 .... **TCLC 75**
See also CA 109; 188

Schonberg, Arnold
See Schoenberg, Arnold Franz Walter

Schopenhauer, Arthur 1788-1860 .. **NCLC 51**
See also DLB 90; EW 5

Schor, Sandra (M.) 1932(?)-1990 ..... **CLC 65**
See also CA 132

Schorer, Mark 1908-1977 .... **CLC 9**
See also CA 5-8R; 73-76; CANR 7; DLB
103

Schrader, Paul (Joseph) 1946- .... **CLC 26**
See also CA 37-40R; CANR 41; DLB 44

Schreber, Daniel 1842-1911 .... **TCLC 123**

Schreiner, Olive (Emilie Albertina)
1855-1920 .... **TCLC 9**
See also AFW; BRWS 2; CA 105; 154;
DLB 18, 156, 190, 225; EWL 3; FW;
RGEL 2; TWA; WLIT 2

Schulberg, Budd (Wilson) 1914- .. **CLC 7, 48**
See also BPFB 3; CA 25-28R; CANR 19,
87; CN 7; DLB 6, 26, 28; DLBY 1981,
2001

Schulman, Arnold
See Trumbo, Dalton

Schulz, Bruno 1892-1942 .. **SSC 13; TCLC 5,**
51
See also CA 115; 123; CANR 86; CDWLB
4; DLB 215; EWL 3; MTCW 2; RGSF 2;
RGWL 2, 3

Schulz, Charles M(onroe)
1922-2000 .... **CLC 12**
See also AAYA 39; CA 9-12R; 187; CANR
6; INT CANR-6; SATA 10; SATA-Obit
118

Schumacher, E(rnst) F(riedrich)
1911-1977 .... **CLC 80**
See also CA 81-84; 73-76; CANR 34, 85

Schuyler, George Samuel 1895-1977 .... **HR 3**
See also BW 2; CA 81-84; 73-76; CANR
42; DLB 29, 51

Schuyler, James Marcus 1923-1991 .. **CLC 5,**
23
See also CA 101; 134; DAM POET; DLB
5, 169; EWL 3; INT 101; WP

Schwartz, Delmore (David)
1913-1966 ... **CLC 2, 4, 10, 45, 87; PC 8**
See also AMWS 2; CA 17-18; 25-28R;
CANR 35; CAP 2; DLB 28, 48; EWL 3;
MTCW 1, 2; PAB; RGAL 4; TUS

Schwartz, Ernst
See Ozu, Yasujiro

Schwartz, John Burnham 1965- .... **CLC 59**
See also CA 132; CANR 116

Schwartz, Lynne Sharon 1939- .... **CLC 31**
See also CA 103; CANR 44, 89; DLB 218;
MTCW 2

Schwartz, Muriel A.
See Eliot, T(homas) S(tearns)

Schwarz-Bart, Andre 1928- .... **CLC 2, 4**
See also CA 89-92; DLB 299

Schwarz-Bart, Simone 1938- . **BLCS; CLC 7**
See also BW 2; CA 97-100; CANR 117;
EWL 3

Schwerner, Armand 1927-1999 .... **PC 42**
See also CA 9-12R; 179; CANR 50, 85; CP
7; DLB 165

Schwitters, Kurt (Hermann Edward Karl
Julius) 1887-1948 .... **TCLC 95**
See also CA 158

Schwob, Marcel (Mayer Andre)
1867-1905 .... **TCLC 20**
See also CA 117; 168; DLB 123; GFL 1789
to the Present

Sciascia, Leonardo 1921-1989 .. **CLC 8, 9, 41**
See also CA 85-88; 130; CANR 35; DLB
177; EWL 3; MTCW 1; RGWL 2, 3

Scoppettone, Sandra 1936- .... **CLC 26**
See Early, Jack
See also AAYA 11; BYA 8; CA 5-8R;
CANR 41, 73; GLL 1; MAICYA 2; MAI-
CYAS 1; SATA 9, 92; WYA; YAW

Scorsese, Martin 1942- .... **CLC 20, 89**
See also AAYA 38; CA 110; 114; CANR
46, 85

Scotland, Jay
See Jakes, John (William)

Scott, Duncan Campbell
1862-1947 .... **TCLC 6**
See also CA 104; 153; DAC; DLB 92;
RGEL 2

Scott, Evelyn 1893-1963 .... **CLC 43**
See also CA 104; 112; CANR 64; DLB 9,
48; RHW

Scott, F(rancis) R(eginald)
1899-1985 .... **CLC 22**
See also CA 101; 114; CANR 87; DLB 88;
INT CA-101; RGEL 2

Scott, Frank
See Scott, F(rancis) R(eginald)

Scott, Joan .... **CLC 65**

Scott, Joanna 1960- .... **CLC 50**
See also CA 126; CANR 53, 92

Scott, Paul (Mark) 1920-1978 ...... **CLC 9, 60**
See also BRWS 1; CA 81-84; 77-80; CANR
33; DLB 14, 207; EWL 3; MTCW 1;
RGEL 2; RHW

Scott, Sarah 1723-1795 .... **LC 44**
See also DLB 39

Scott, Sir Walter 1771-1832 .... **NCLC 15, 69,**
110; PC 13; SSC 32; WLC
See also AAYA 22; BRW 4; BYA 2; CD-
BLB 1789-1832; DA; DAB; DAC; DAM
MST, NOV, POET; DLB 93, 107, 116,
144, 159; HGG; LAIT 1; RGEL 2; RGSF
2; SSFS 10; SUFW 1; TEA; WLIT 3;
YABC 2

Scribe, (Augustin) Eugene 1791-1861 . **DC 5;**
NCLC 16
See also DAM DRAM; DLB 192; GFL
1789 to the Present; RGWL 2, 3

Scrum, R.
See Crumb, R(obert)

Scudery, Georges de 1601-1667 .... **LC 75**
See also GFL Beginnings to 1789

Scudery, Madeleine de 1607-1701 .. **LC 2, 58**
See also DLB 268; GFL Beginnings to 1789

Scum
See Crumb, R(obert)

Scumbag, Little Bobby
See Crumb, R(obert)

Seabrook, John
See Hubbard, L(afayette) Ron(ald)

Sealy, I(rwin) Allan 1951- .... **CLC 55**
See also CA 136; CN 7

Search, Alexander
See Pessoa, Fernando (Antonio Nogueira)

Sebastian, Lee
See Silverberg, Robert

Sebastian Owl
See Thompson, Hunter S(tockton)

Sebestyen, Igen
See Sebestyen, Ouida

Sebestyen, Ouida 1924- .... **CLC 30**
See also AAYA 8; BYA 7; CA 107; CANR
40, 114; CLR 17; JRDA; MAICYA 1, 2;
SAAS 10; SATA 39, 140; WYA; YAW

Secundus, H. Scriblerus
See Fielding, Henry

Sedges, John
See Buck, Pearl S(ydenstricker)

Sedgwick, Catharine Maria
1789-1867 .... **NCLC 19, 98**
See also DLB 1, 74, 183, 239, 243, 254;
RGAL 4

Seelye, John (Douglas) 1931- .... **CLC 7**
See also CA 97-100; CANR 70; INT 97-
100; TCWW 2

Seferiades, Giorgos Stylianou 1900-1971
See Seferis, George
See also CA 5-8R; 33-36R; CANR 5, 36;
MTCW 1

Seferis, George .... **CLC 5, 11**
See Seferiades, Giorgos Stylianou
See also EW 12; EWL 3; RGWL 2, 3

Segal, Erich (Wolf) 1937- .... **CLC 3, 10**
See also BEST 89:1; CA 25-28R;
CANR 20, 36, 65, 113; CPW; DAM POP;
DLBY 1986; INT CANR-20; MTCW 1

Seger, Bob 1945- .... **CLC 35**

Seghers, Anna .... **CLC 7**
See Radvanyi, Netty
See also CDWLB 2; DLB 69; EWL 3

Seidel, Frederick (Lewis) 1936- .... **CLC 18**
See also CA 13-16R; CANR 8, 99; CP 7;
DLBY 1984

Seifert, Jaroslav 1901-1986 . **CLC 34, 44, 93;
PC 47**
See also CA 127; CDWLB 4; DLB 215;
EWL 3; MTCW 1, 2

Sei Shonagon c. 966-1017(?) .... **CMLC 6**

Sejour, Victor 1817-1874 .... **DC 10**
See also DLB 50

Sejour Marcou et Ferrand, Juan Victor
See Sejour, Victor

Selby, Hubert, Jr. 1928- .... **CLC 1, 2, 4, 8;
SSC 20**
See also CA 13-16R; CANR 33, 85; CN 7;
DLB 2, 227

Selzer, Richard 1928- .... **CLC 74**
See also CA 65-68; CANR 14, 106

Sembene, Ousmane
See Ousmane, Sembene
See also AFW; CWW 2; EWL 3; WLIT 2

Senancour, Etienne Pivert de
1770-1846 .... **NCLC 16**
See also DLB 119; GFL 1789 to the Present

Sender, Ramon (Jose) 1902-1982 ...... **CLC 8;
HLC 2; TCLC 136**
See also CA 5-8R; 105; CANR 8; DAM
MULT; EWL 3; HW 1; MTCW 1; RGWL
2, 3

Seneca, Lucius Annaeus c. 4B.C.-c.
65 .... **CMLC 6; DC 5**
See also AW 2; CDWLB 1; DAM DRAM;
DLB 211; RGWL 2, 3; TWA

Senghor, Leopold Sedar 1906-2001 ... **BLC 3;
CLC 54, 130; PC 25**
See also AFW; BW 2; CA 116; 125; 203;
CANR 47, 74; DAM MULT, POET;
DNFS 2; EWL 3; GFL 1789 to the
Present; MTCW 1, 2; TWA

Senna, Danzy 1970- .... **CLC 119**
See also CA 169

Serling, (Edward) Rod(man)
1924-1975 .... **CLC 30**
See also AAYA 14; AITN 1; CA 162; 57-
60; DLB 26; SFW 4

Serna, Ramon Gomez de la
See Gomez de la Serna, Ramon

Serpieres
See Guillevic, (Eugene)

Service, Robert
See Service, Robert W(illiam)
See also BYA 4; DAB; DLB 92

Service, Robert W(illiam)
1874(?)-1958 .... **TCLC 15; WLC**
See Service, Robert
See also CA 115; 140; CANR 84; DA;
DAC; DAM MST, POET; PFS 10; RGEL
2; SATA 20

Seth, Vikram 1952- .... **CLC 43, 90**
See also CA 121; 127; CANR 50, 74; CN
7; CP 7; DA3; DAM MULT; DLB 120,
271, 282; EWL 3; INT 127; MTCW 2

Seton, Cynthia Propper 1926-1982 .. **CLC 27**
See also CA 5-8R; 108; CANR 7

Seton, Ernest (Evan) Thompson
1860-1946 .... **TCLC 31**
See also ANW; BYA 3; CA 109; 204; CLR
59; DLB 92; DLBD 13; JRDA; SATA 18

Seton-Thompson, Ernest
See Seton, Ernest (Evan) Thompson

Settle, Mary Lee 1918- .... **CLC 19, 61**
See also BPFB 3; CA 89-92; CAAS 1;
CANR 44, 87; CN 7; CSW; DLB 6; INT
89-92

Seuphor, Michel
See Arp, Jean

Sevigne, Marie (de Rabutin-Chantal)
1626-1696 .... **LC 11**
See Sevigne, Marie de Rabutin Chantal
See also GFL Beginnings to 1789; TWA

Sevigne, Marie de Rabutin Chantal
See Sevigne, Marie (de Rabutin-Chantal)
See also DLB 268

Sewall, Samuel 1652-1730 .... **LC 38**
See also DLB 24; RGAL 4

Sexton, Anne (Harvey) 1928-1974 ..... **CLC 2,
4, 6, 8, 10, 15, 53, 123; PC 2; WLC**
See also AMWS 2; CA 1-4R; 53-56; CABS
2; CANR 3, 36; CDALB 1941-1968; DA;
DA3; DAB; DAC; DAM MST, POET;
DLB 5, 169; EWL 3; EXPP; FW;
MAWW; MTCW 1, 2; PAB; PFS 4, 14;
RGAL 4; SATA 10; TUS

Shaara, Jeff 1952- .... **CLC 119**
See also CA 163; CANR 109

Shaara, Michael (Joseph, Jr.)
1929-1988 .... **CLC 15**
See also AITN 1; BPFB 3; CA 102; 125;
CANR 52, 85; DAM POP; DLBY 1983

Shackleton, C. C.
See Aldiss, Brian W(ilson)

Shacochis, Bob .... **CLC 39**
See Shacochis, Robert G.

Shacochis, Robert G. 1951-
See Shacochis, Bob
See also CA 119; 124; CANR 100; INT 124

Shaffer, Anthony (Joshua)
1926-2001 .... **CLC 19**
See also CA 110; 116; 200; CBD; CD 5;
DAM DRAM; DFS 13; DLB 13

Shaffer, Peter (Levin) 1926- .. **CLC 5, 14, 18,
37, 60; DC 7**
See also BRWS 1; CA 25-28R; CANR 25,
47, 74, 118; CBD; CD 5; CDBLB 1960 to
Present; DA3; DAB; DAM DRAM, MST;
DFS 5, 13; DLB 13, 233; EWL 3; MTCW
1, 2; RGEL 2; TEA

Shakespeare, William 1564-1616 .... **WLC**
See also AAYA 35; BRW 1; CDBLB Before
1660; DA; DA3; DAB; DAC; DAM
DRAM, MST, POET; DLB 62, 172, 263;
EXPP; LAIT 1; LATS 1; LMFS 1; PAB;
PFS 1, 2, 3, 4, 5, 8, 9; RGEL 2; TEA;
WLIT 3; WP; WS; WYA

Shakey, Bernard
See Young, Neil

Shalamov, Varlam (Tikhonovich)
1907(?)-1982 .... **CLC 18**
See also CA 129; 105; RGSF 2

Shamlu, Ahmad 1925-2000 .... **CLC 10**
See also CWW 2

Shammas, Anton 1951- .... **CLC 55**
See also CA 199

Shandling, Arline
See Berriault, Gina

Shange, Ntozake 1948- ... **BLC 3; CLC 8, 25,
38, 74, 126; DC 3**
See also AAYA 9; AFAW 1, 2; BW 2; CA
85-88; CABS 3; CAD; CANR 27, 48, 74;
CD 5; CP 7; CWD; CWP; DA3; DAM
DRAM, MULT; DFS 2, 11; DLB 38, 249;
FW; LAIT 5; MTCW 1, 2; NFS 11;
RGAL 4; YAW

Shanley, John Patrick 1950- .... **CLC 75**
See also CA 128; 133; CAD; CANR 83;
CD 5

Shapcott, Thomas W(illiam) 1935- .. **CLC 38**
See also CA 69-72; CANR 49, 83, 103; CP
7

Shapiro, Jane 1942- .... **CLC 76**
See also CA 196

Shapiro, Karl (Jay) 1913-2000 ...... **CLC 4, 8,
15, 53; PC 25**
See also AMWS 2; CA 1-4R; 188; CAAS
6; CANR 1, 36, 66; CP 7; DLB 48; EWL
3; EXPP; MTCW 1, 2; PFS 3; RGAL 4

Sharp, William 1855-1905 .... **TCLC 39**
See Macleod, Fiona
See also CA 160; DLB 156; RGEL 2

Sharpe, Thomas Ridley 1928-
See Sharpe, Tom
See also CA 114; 122; CANR 85; INT CA-
122

Sharpe, Tom .... **CLC 36**
See Sharpe, Thomas Ridley
See also CN 7; DLB 14, 231

Shatrov, Mikhail .... **CLC 59**

Shaw, Bernard
See Shaw, George Bernard
See also DLB 190

Shaw, G. Bernard
See Shaw, George Bernard

Shaw, George Bernard 1856-1950 .. **TCLC 3,
9, 21, 45; WLC**
See Shaw, Bernard
See also BRW 6; BRWC 1; BRWR 2; CA
104; 128; CDBLB 1914-1945; DA; DA3;
DAB; DAC; DAM DRAM, MST; DFS 1,
3, 6, 11; DLB 10, 57; EWL 3; LAIT 3;
LATS 1; MTCW 1, 2; RGEL 2; TEA;
WLIT 4

Shaw, Henry Wheeler 1818-1885 .. **NCLC 15**
See also DLB 11; RGAL 4

Shaw, Irwin 1913-1984 .... **CLC 7, 23, 34**
See also AITN 1; BPFB 3; CA 13-16R; 112;
CANR 21; CDALB 1941-1968; CPW;
DAM DRAM, POP; DLB 6, 102; DLBY
1984; MTCW 1, 21

Shaw, Robert 1927-1978 .... **CLC 5**
See also AITN 1; CA 1-4R; 81-84; CANR 4; DLB 13, 14

Shaw, T. E.
See Lawrence, T(homas) E(dward)

Shawn, Wallace 1943- .... **CLC 41**
See also CA 112; CAD; CD 5; DLB 266

Shchedrin, N.
See Saltykov, Mikhail Evgrafovich

Shea, Lisa 1953- .... **CLC 86**
See also CA 147

Sheed, Wilfrid (John Joseph) 1930- . **CLC 2, 4, 10, 53**
See also CA 65-68; CANR 30, 66; CN 7; DLB 6; MTCW 1, 2

Sheehy, Gail 1937- .... **CLC 171**
See also CA 49-52; CANR 1, 33, 55, 92; CPW; MTCW 1

Sheldon, Alice Hastings Bradley
1915(?)-1987
See Tiptree, James, Jr.
See also CA 108; 122; CANR 34; INT 108; MTCW 1

Sheldon, John
See Bloch, Robert (Albert)

Sheldon, Walter J(ames) 1917-1996
See Queen, Ellery
See also AITN 1; CA 25-28R; CANR 10

Shelley, Mary Wollstonecraft (Godwin)
1797-1851 ...... **NCLC 14, 59, 103; WLC**
See also AAYA 20; BPFB 3; BRW 3; BRWS 3; BYA 5; CDBLB 1789-1832; DA; DA3; DAB; DAC; DAM MST, NOV; DLB 110, 116, 159, 178; EXPN; HGG; LAIT 1; LMFS 1, 2; NFS 1; RGEL 2; SATA 29; SCFW; SFW 4; TEA; WLIT 3

Shelley, Percy Bysshe 1792-1822 .. **NCLC 18, 93; PC 14; WLC**
See also BRW 4; BRWR 1; CDBLB 1789-1832; DA; DA3; DAB; DAC; DAM MST, POET; DLB 96, 110, 158; EXPP; LMFS 1; PAB; PFS 2; RGEL 2; TEA; WLIT 3; WP

Shepard, Jim 1956- .... **CLC 36**
See also CA 137; CANR 59, 104; SATA 90

Shepard, Lucius 1947- .... **CLC 34**
See also CA 128; 141; CANR 81; HGG; SCFW 2; SFW 4; SUFW 2

Shepard, Sam 1943- .... **CLC 4, 6, 17, 34, 41, 44, 169; DC 5**
See also AAYA 1; AMWS 3; CA 69-72; CABS 3; CAD; CANR 22; CD 5; DA3; DAM DRAM; DFS 3, 6, 7, 14; DLB 7, 212; EWL 3; IDFW 3, 4; MTCW 1, 2; RGAL 4

Shepherd, Michael
See Ludlum, Robert

Sherburne, Zoa (Lillian Morin)
1912-1995 .... **CLC 30**
See also AAYA 13; CA 1-4R; 176; CANR 3, 37; MAICYA 1, 2; SAAS 18; SATA 3; YAW

Sheridan, Frances 1724-1766 .... **LC 7**
See also DLB 39, 84

Sheridan, Richard Brinsley
1751-1816 .... **DC 1; NCLC 5, 91; WLC**
See also BRW 3; CDBLB 1660-1789; DA; DAB; DAC; DAM DRAM, MST; DFS 15; DLB 89; WLIT 3

Sherman, Jonathan Marc .... **CLC 55**

Sherman, Martin 1941(?)- .... **CLC 19**
See also CA 116; 123; CAD; CANR 86; CD 5; DLB 228; GLL 1; IDTP

Sherwin, Judith Johnson
See Johnson, Judith (Emlyn)
See also CANR 85; CP 7; CWP

Sherwood, Frances 1940- .... **CLC 81**
See also CA 146

Sherwood, Robert E(mmet)
1896-1955 .... **TCLC 3**
See also CA 104; 153; CANR 86; DAM DRAM; DFS 11, 15, 17; DLB 7, 26, 249; IDFW 3, 4; RGAL 4

Shestov, Lev 1866-1938 .... **TCLC 56**

Shevchenko, Taras 1814-1861 .... **NCLC 54**

Shiel, M(atthew) P(hipps)
1865-1947 .... **TCLC 8**
See Holmes, Gordon
See also CA 106; 160; DLB 153; HGG; MTCW 2; SFW 4; SUFW

Shields, Carol 1935- .... **CLC 91, 113**
See also AMWS 7; CA 81-84; CANR 51, 74, 98; CCA 1; CN 7; CPW; DA3; DAC; MTCW 2

Shields, David 1956- .... **CLC 97**
See also CA 124; CANR 48, 99, 112

Shiga, Naoya 1883-1971 ..... **CLC 33; SSC 23**
See Shiga Naoya
See also CA 101; 33-36R; MJW; RGWL 3

Shiga Naoya
See Shiga, Naoya
See also DLB 180; EWL 3; RGWL 3

Shilts, Randy 1951-1994 .... **CLC 85**
See also AAYA 19; CA 115; 127; 144; CANR 45; DA3; GLL 1; INT 127; MTCW 2

Shimazaki, Haruki 1872-1943
See Shimazaki Toson
See also CA 105; 134; CANR 84; RGWL 3

Shimazaki Toson .... **TCLC 5**
See Shimazaki, Haruki
See also DLB 180; EWL 3

Sholokhov, Mikhail (Aleksandrovich)
1905-1984 .... **CLC 7, 15**
See also CA 101; 112; DLB 272; EWL 3; MTCW 1, 2; RGWL 2, 3; SATA-Obit 36

Shone, Patric
See Hanley, James

Showalter, Elaine 1941- .... **CLC 169**
See also CA 57-60; CANR 58, 106; DLB 67; FW; GLL 2

Shreve, Susan Richards 1939- .... **CLC 23**
See also CA 49-52; CAAS 5; CANR 5, 38, 69, 100; MAICYA 1, 2; SATA 46, 95; SATA-Brief 41

Shue, Larry 1946-1985 .... **CLC 52**
See also CA 145; 117; DAM DRAM; DFS 7

Shu-Jen, Chou 1881-1936
See Lu Hsun
See also CA 104

Shulman, Alix Kates 1932- .... **CLC 2, 10**
See also CA 29-32R; CANR 43; FW; SATA 7

Shusaku, Endo
See Endo, Shusaku

Shuster, Joe 1914-1992 .... **CLC 21**

Shute, Nevil .... **CLC 30**
See Norway, Nevil Shute
See also BPFB 3; DLB 255; NFS 9; RHW; SFW 4

Shuttle, Penelope (Diane) 1947- .... **CLC 7**
See also CA 93-96; CANR 39, 84, 92, 108; CP 7; CWP; DLB 14, 40

Sidhwa, Bapsy (N.) 1938- .... **CLC 168**
See also CA 108; CANR 25, 57; CN 7; FW

Sidney, Mary 1561-1621 .... **LC 19, 39**
See Sidney Herbert, Mary

Sidney, Sir Philip 1554-1586 . **LC 19, 39; PC 32**
See also BRW 1; BRWR 2; CDBLB Before 1660; DA; DA3; DAB; DAC; DAM MST, POET; DLB 167; EXPP; PAB; RGEL 2; TEA; WP

Sidney Herbert, Mary
See Sidney, Mary
See also DLB 167

Siegel, Jerome 1914-1996 .... **CLC 21**
See also CA 116; 169; 151

Siegel, Jerry
See Siegel, Jerome

Sienkiewicz, Henryk (Adam Alexander Pius)
1846-1916 .... **TCLC 3**
See also CA 104; 134; CANR 84; EWL 3; RGSF 2; RGWL 2, 3

Sierra, Gregorio Martinez
See Martinez Sierra, Gregorio

Sierra, Maria (de la O'LeJarraga) Martinez
See Martinez Sierra, Maria (de la O'LeJarraga)

Sigal, Clancy 1926- .... **CLC 7**
See also CA 1-4R; CANR 85; CN 7

Sigourney, Lydia H.
See Sigourney, Lydia Howard (Huntley)
See also DLB 73, 183

Sigourney, Lydia Howard (Huntley)
1791-1865 .... **NCLC 21, 87**
See Sigourney, Lydia H.; Sigourney, Lydia Huntley
See also DLB 1

Sigourney, Lydia Huntley
See Sigourney, Lydia Howard (Huntley)
See also DLB 42, 239, 243

Siguenza y Gongora, Carlos de
1645-1700 .... **HLCS 2; LC 8**
See also LAW

Sigurjonsson, Johann 1880-1919 ... **TCLC 27**
See also CA 170; EWL 3

Sikelianos, Angelos 1884-1951 .... **PC 29; TCLC 39**
See also EWL 3; RGWL 2, 3

Silkin, Jon 1930-1997 .... **CLC 2, 6, 43**
See also CA 5-8R; CAAS 5; CANR 89; CP 7; DLB 27

Silko, Leslie (Marmon) 1948- .... **CLC 23, 74, 114; NNAL; SSC 37; WLCS**
See also AAYA 14; AMWS 4; ANW; BYA 12; CA 115; 122; CANR 45, 65, 118; CN 7; CP 7; CPW 1; CWP; DA; DA3; DAC; DAM MST, MULT, POP; DLB 143, 175, 256, 275; EWL 3; EXPP; EXPS; LAIT 4; MTCW 2; NFS 4; PFS 9, 16; RGAL 4; RGSF 2; SSFS 4, 8, 10, 11

Sillanpaa, Frans Eemil 1888-1964 ... **CLC 19**
See also CA 129; 93-96; EWL 3; MTCW 1

Sillitoe, Alan 1928- .. **CLC 1, 3, 6, 10, 19, 57, 148**
See also AITN 1; BRWS 5; CA 9-12R; CAAE 191; CAAS 2; CANR 8, 26, 55; CDBLB 1960 to Present; CN 7; DLB 14, 139; EWL 3; MTCW 1, 2; RGEL 2; RGSF 2; SATA 61

Silone, Ignazio 1900-1978 .... **CLC 4**
See also CA 25-28; 81-84; CANR 34; CAP 2; DLB 264; EW 12; EWL 3; MTCW 1; RGSF 2; RGWL 2, 3

Silone, Ignazione
See Silone, Ignazio

Silva, Jose Asuncion
See da Silva, Antonio Jose
See also LAW

Silver, Joan Micklin 1935- .... **CLC 20**
See also CA 114; 121; INT 121

Silver, Nicholas
See Faust, Frederick (Schiller)
See also TCWW 2

Silverberg, Robert 1935- .... **CLC 7, 140**
See also AAYA 24; BPFB 3; BYA 7, 9; CA 1-4R; 186; CAAE 186; CAAS 3; CANR 1, 20, 36, 85; CLR 59; CN 7; CPW; DAM POP; DLB 8; INT CANR-20; MAICYA 1, 2; MTCW 1, 2; SATA 13, 91; SATA-Essay 104; SCFW 2; SFW 4; SUFW 2

Silverstein, Alvin 1933- .... **CLC 17**
See also CA 49-52; CANR 2; CLR 25; JRDA; MAICYA 1, 2; SATA 8, 69, 124

Smith, Iain Crichton 1928-1998 .... **CLC 64**
See also CA 21-24R; 171; CN 7; CP 7; DLB 40, 139; RGSF 2
Smith, John 1580(?)-1631 .... **LC 9**
See also DLB 24, 30; TUS
Smith, Johnston
See Crane, Stephen (Townley)
Smith, Joseph, Jr. 1805-1844 .... **NCLC 53**
Smith, Lee 1944- .... **CLC 25, 73**
See also CA 114; 119; CANR 46, 118; CSW; DLB 143; DLBY 1983; EWL 3; INT CA-119; RGAL 4
Smith, Martin
See Smith, Martin Cruz
Smith, Martin Cruz 1942- .. **CLC 25; NNAL**
See also BEST 89:4; BPFB 3; CA 85-88; CANR 6, 23, 43, 65; CMW 4; CPW; DAM MULT, POP; HGG; INT CANR-23; MTCW 2; RGAL 4
Smith, Patti 1946- .... **CLC 12**
See also CA 93-96; CANR 63
Smith, Pauline (Urmson)
1882-1959 .... **TCLC 25**
See also DLB 225; EWL 3
Smith, Rosamond
See Oates, Joyce Carol
Smith, Sheila Kaye
See Kaye-Smith, Sheila
Smith, Stevie .... **CLC 3, 8, 25, 44; PC 12**
See Smith, Florence Margaret
See also BRWS 2; DLB 20; EWL 3; MTCW 2; PAB; PFS 3; RGEL 2
Smith, Wilbur (Addison) 1933- .... **CLC 33**
See also CA 13-16R; CANR 7, 46, 66; CPW; MTCW 1, 2
Smith, William Jay 1918- .... **CLC 6**
See also CA 5-8R; CANR 44, 106; CP 7; CSW; CWRI 5; DLB 5; MAICYA 1, 2; SAAS 22; SATA 2, 68
Smith, Woodrow Wilson
See Kuttner, Henry
Smith, Zadie 1976- .... **CLC 158**
See also CA 193
Smolenskin, Peretz 1842-1885 .... **NCLC 30**
Smollett, Tobias (George) 1721-1771 ... **LC 2, 46**
See also BRW 3; CDBLB 1660-1789; DLB 39, 104; RGEL 2; TEA
Snodgrass, W(illiam) D(e Witt)
1926- .... **CLC 2, 6, 10, 18, 68**
See also AMWS 6; CA 1-4R; CANR 6, 36, 65, 85; CP 7; DAM POET; DLB 5; MTCW 1, 2; RGAL 4
Snorri Sturluson 1179-1241 .... **CMLC 56**
See also RGWL 2, 3
Snow, C(harles) P(ercy) 1905-1980 ... **CLC 1, 4, 6, 9, 13, 19**
See also BRW 7; CA 5-8R; 101; CANR 28; CDBLB 1945-1960; DAM NOV; DLB 15, 77; DLBD 17; EWL 3; MTCW 1, 2; RGEL 2; TEA
Snow, Frances Compton
See Adams, Henry (Brooks)
Snyder, Gary (Sherman) 1930- . **CLC 1, 2, 5, 9, 32, 120; PC 21**
See also AMWS 8; ANW; BG 3; CA 17-20R; CANR 30, 60; CP 7; DAM POET; DLB 5, 16, 165, 212, 237, 275; EWL 3; MTCW 2; PFS 9; RGAL 4; WP
Snyder, Zilpha Keatley 1927- .... **CLC 17**
See also AAYA 15; BYA 1; CA 9-12R; CANR 38; CLR 31; JRDA; MAICYA 1, 2; SAAS 2; SATA 1, 28, 75, 110; SATA-Essay 112; YAW
Soares, Bernardo
See Pessoa, Fernando (Antonio Nogueira)
Sobh, A.
See Shamlu, Ahmad

Sobol, Joshua 1939- .... **CLC 60**
See Sobol, Yehoshua
See also CA 200; CWW 2
Sobol, Yehoshua 1939-
See Sobol, Joshua
See also CWW 2
Socrates 470B.C.-399B.C. .... **CMLC 27**
Soderberg, Hjalmar 1869-1941 ...... **TCLC 39**
See also DLB 259; EWL 3; RGSF 2
Soderbergh, Steven 1963- .... **CLC 154**
See also AAYA 43
Sodergran, Edith (Irene) 1892-1923
See Soedergran, Edith (Irene)
See also CA 202; DLB 259; EW 11; EWL 3; RGWL 2, 3
Soedergran, Edith (Irene)
1892-1923 .... **TCLC 31**
See Sodergran, Edith (Irene)
Softly, Edgar
See Lovecraft, H(oward) P(hillips)
Softly, Edward
See Lovecraft, H(oward) P(hillips)
Sokolov, Alexander V(sevolodovich) 1943-
See Sokolov, Sasha
See also CA 73-76
Sokolov, Raymond 1941- .... **CLC 7**
See also CA 85-88
Sokolov, Sasha .... **CLC 59**
See Sokolov, Alexander V(sevolodovich)
See also CWW 2; EWL 3; RGWL 2, 3
Sokolov, Sasha .... **CLC 59**
Solo, Jay
See Ellison, Harlan (Jay)
Sologub, Fyodor .... **TCLC 9**
See Teternikov, Fyodor Kuzmich
See also EWL 3
Solomons, Ikey Esquir
See Thackeray, William Makepeace
Solomos, Dionysios 1798-1857 .... **NCLC 15**
Solwoska, Mara
See French, Marilyn
Solzhenitsyn, Aleksandr I(sayevich)
1918- .. **CLC 1, 2, 4, 7, 9, 10, 18, 26, 34, 78, 134; SSC 32; WLC**
See Solzhenitsyn, Aleksandr Isaevich
See also AAYA 49; AITN 1; BPFB 3; CA 69-72; CANR 40, 65, 116; DA; DA3; DAB; DAC; DAM MST, NOV; EW 13; EXPS; LAIT 4; MTCW 1, 2; NFS 6; RGSF 2; RGWL 2, 3; SSFS 9; TWA
Solzhenitsyn, Aleksandr Isaevich
See Solzhenitsyn, Aleksandr I(sayevich)
See also EWL 3
Somers, Jane
See Lessing, Doris (May)
Somerville, Edith Oenone
1858-1949 .... **SSC 56; TCLC 51**
See also CA 196; DLB 135; RGEL 2; RGSF 2
Somerville & Ross
See Martin, Violet Florence; Somerville, Edith Oenone
Sommer, Scott 1951- .... **CLC 25**
See also CA 106
Sondheim, Stephen (Joshua) 1930- . **CLC 30, 39, 147**
See also AAYA 11; CA 103; CANR 47, 67; DAM DRAM; LAIT 4
Sone, Monica 1919- .... **AAL**
Song, Cathy 1955- .... **AAL; PC 21**
See also CA 154; CANR 118; CWP; DLB 169; EXPP; FW; PFS 5
Sontag, Susan 1933- .... **CLC 1, 2, 10, 13, 31, 105**
See also AMWS 3; CA 17-20R; CANR 25, 51, 74, 97; CN 7; CPW; DA3; DAM POP; DLB 2, 67; EWL 3; MAWW; MTCW 1, 2; RGAL 4; RHW; SSFS 10

Sophocles 496(?)B.C.-406(?)B.C. .... **CMLC 2, 47, 51; DC 1; WLCS**
See also AW 1; CDWLB 1; DA; DA3; DAB; DAC; DAM DRAM, MST; DFS 1, 4, 8; DLB 176; LAIT 1; LATS 1; LMFS 1; RGWL 2, 3; TWA
Sordello 1189-1269 .... **CMLC 15**
Sorel, Georges 1847-1922 .... **TCLC 91**
See also CA 118; 188
Sorel, Julia
See Drexler, Rosalyn
Sorokin, Vladimir .... **CLC 59**
Sorrentino, Gilbert 1929- .. **CLC 3, 7, 14, 22, 40**
See also CA 77-80; CANR 14, 33, 115; CN 7; CP 7; DLB 5, 173; DLBY 1980; INT CANR-14
Soseki
See Natsume, Soseki
See also MJW
Soto, Gary 1952- ... **CLC 32, 80; HLC 2; PC 28**
See also AAYA 10, 37; BYA 11; CA 119; 125; CANR 50, 74, 107; CLR 38; CP 7; DAM MULT; DLB 82; EWL 3; EXPP; HW 1, 2; INT CA-125; JRDA; MAICYA 2; MAICYAS 1; MTCW 2; PFS 7; RGAL 4; SATA 80, 120; WYA; YAW
Soupault, Philippe 1897-1990 .... **CLC 68**
See also CA 116; 147; 131; EWL 3; GFL 1789 to the Present; LMFS 2
Souster, (Holmes) Raymond 1921- .... **CLC 5, 14**
See also CA 13-16R; CAAS 14; CANR 13, 29, 53; CP 7; DA3; DAC; DAM POET; DLB 88; RGEL 2; SATA 63
Southern, Terry 1924(?)-1995 .... **CLC 7**
See also AMWS 11; BPFB 3; CA 1-4R; 150; CANR 1, 55, 107; CN 7; DLB 2; IDFW 3, 4
Southey, Robert 1774-1843 .... **NCLC 8, 97**
See also BRW 4; DLB 93, 107, 142; RGEL 2; SATA 54
Southworth, Emma Dorothy Eliza Nevitte
1819-1899 .... **NCLC 26**
See also DLB 239
Souza, Ernest
See Scott, Evelyn
Soyinka, Wole 1934- .. **BLC 3; CLC 3, 5, 14, 36, 44; DC 2; WLC**
See also AFW; BW 2, 3; CA 13-16R; CANR 27, 39, 82; CD 5; CDWLB 3; CN 7; CP 7; DA; DA3; DAB; DAC; DAM DRAM, MST, MULT; DFS 10; DLB 125; EWL 3; MTCW 1, 2; RGEL 2; TWA; WLIT 2
Spackman, W(illiam) M(ode)
1905-1990 .... **CLC 46**
See also CA 81-84; 132
Spacks, Barry (Bernard) 1931- .... **CLC 14**
See also CA 154; CANR 33, 109; CP 7; DLB 105
Spanidou, Irini 1946- .... **CLC 44**
See also CA 185
Spark, Muriel (Sarah) 1918- ..... **CLC 2, 3, 5, 8, 13, 18, 40, 94; SSC 10**
See also BRWS 1; CA 5-8R; CANR 12, 36, 76, 89; CDBLB 1945-1960; CN 7; CP 7; DA3; DAB; DAC; DAM MST, NOV; DLB 15, 139; EWL 3; FW; INT CANR-12; LAIT 4; MTCW 1, 2; RGEL 2; TEA; WLIT 4; YAW
Spaulding, Douglas
See Bradbury, Ray (Douglas)
Spaulding, Leonard
See Bradbury, Ray (Douglas)
Spelman, Elizabeth .... **CLC 65**
Spence, J. A. D.
See Eliot, T(homas) S(tearns)

Tartt, Donna 1964(?)- .... **CLC 76**
   See also CA 142
Tasso, Torquato 1544-1595 .... **LC 5**
   See also EFS 2; EW 2; RGWL 2, 3
Tate, (John Orley) Allen 1899-1979 .. **CLC 2, 4, 6, 9, 11, 14, 24**
   See also AMW; CA 5-8R; 85-88; CANR 32, 108; DLB 4, 45, 63; DLBD 17; EWL 3; MTCW 1, 2; RGAL 4; RHW
Tate, Ellalice
   See Hibbert, Eleanor Alice Burford
Tate, James (Vincent) 1943- ..... **CLC 2, 6, 25**
   See also CA 21-24R; CANR 29, 57, 114; CP 7; DLB 5, 169; EWL 3; PFS 10, 15; RGAL 4; WP
Tauler, Johannes c. 1300-1361 ...... **CMLC 37**
   See also DLB 179; LMFS 1
Tavel, Ronald 1940- .... **CLC 6**
   See also CA 21-24R; CAD; CANR 33; CD 5
Taviani, Paolo 1931- .... **CLC 70**
   See also CA 153
Taylor, Bayard 1825-1878 .... **NCLC 89**
   See also DLB 3, 189, 250, 254; RGAL 4
Taylor, C(ecil) P(hilip) 1929-1981 .... **CLC 27**
   See also CA 25-28R; 105; CANR 47; CBD
Taylor, Edward 1642(?)-1729 .... **LC 11**
   See also AMW; DA; DAB; DAC; DAM MST, POET; DLB 24; EXPP; RGAL 4; TUS
Taylor, Eleanor Ross 1920- .... **CLC 5**
   See also CA 81-84; CANR 70
Taylor, Elizabeth 1932-1975 ..... **CLC 2, 4, 29**
   See also CA 13-16R; CANR 9, 70; DLB 139; MTCW 1; RGEL 2; SATA 13
Taylor, Frederick Winslow 1856-1915 .... **TCLC 76**
   See also CA 188
Taylor, Henry (Splawn) 1942- .... **CLC 44**
   See also CA 33-36R; CAAS 7; CANR 31; CP 7; DLB 5; PFS 10
Taylor, Kamala (Purnaiya) 1924-
   See Markandaya, Kamala
   See also CA 77-80; NFS 13
Taylor, Mildred D(elois) 1943- .... **CLC 21**
   See also AAYA 10, 47; BW 1; BYA 3, 8; CA 85-88; CANR 25, 115; CLR 9, 59; CSW; DLB 52; JRDA; LAIT 3; MAICYA 1, 2; SAAS 5; SATA 135; WYA; YAW
Taylor, Peter (Hillsman) 1917-1994 .. **CLC 1, 4, 18, 37, 44, 50, 71; SSC 10**
   See also AMWS 5; BPFB 3; CA 13-16R; 147; CANR 9, 50; CSW; DLB 218, 278; DLBY 1981, 1994; EWL 3; EXPS; INT CANR-9; MTCW 1, 2; RGSF 2; SSFS 9; TUS
Taylor, Robert Lewis 1912-1998 .... **CLC 14**
   See also CA 1-4R; 170; CANR 3, 64; SATA 10
Tchekhov, Anton
   See Chekhov, Anton (Pavlovich)
Tchicaya, Gerald Felix 1931-1988 .. **CLC 101**
   See Tchicaya U Tam'si
   See also CA 129; 125; CANR 81
Tchicaya U Tam'si
   See Tchicaya, Gerald Felix
   See also EWL 3
Teasdale, Sara 1884-1933 .... **PC 31; TCLC 4**
   See also CA 104; 163; DLB 45; GLL 1; PFS 14; RGAL 4; SATA 32; TUS
Tecumseh 1768-1813 .... **NNAL**
   See also DAM MULT
Tegner, Esaias 1782-1846 .... **NCLC 2**
Teilhard de Chardin, (Marie Joseph) Pierre 1881-1955 .... **TCLC 9**
   See also CA 105; 210; GFL 1789 to the Present
Temple, Ann
   See Mortimer, Penelope (Ruth)

Tennant, Emma (Christina) 1937- .. **CLC 13, 52**
   See also CA 65-68; CAAS 9; CANR 10, 38, 59, 88; CN 7; DLB 14; EWL 3; SFW 4
Tenneshaw, S. M.
   See Silverberg, Robert
Tenney, Tabitha Gilman 1762-1837 .... **NCLC 122**
   See also DLB 37, 200
Tennyson, Alfred 1809-1892 ... **NCLC 30, 65, 115; PC 6; WLC**
   See also BRW 4; CDBLB 1832-1890; DA; DA3; DAB; DAC; DAM MST, POET; DLB 32; EXPP; PAB; PFS 1, 2, 4, 11, 15; RGEL 2; TEA; WLIT 4; WP
Teran, Lisa St. Aubin de .... **CLC 36**
   See St. Aubin de Teran, Lisa
Terence c. 184B.C.-c. 159B.C. ...... **CMLC 14; DC 7**
   See also AW 1; CDWLB 1; DLB 211; RGWL 2, 3; TWA
Teresa de Jesus, St. 1515-1582 .... **LC 18**
Terkel, Louis 1912-
   See Terkel, Studs
   See also CA 57-60; CANR 18, 45, 67; DA3; MTCW 1, 2
Terkel, Studs .... **CLC 38**
   See Terkel, Louis
   See also AAYA 32; AITN 1; MTCW 2; TUS
Terry, C. V.
   See Slaughter, Frank G(ill)
Terry, Megan 1932- .... **CLC 19; DC 13**
   See also CA 77-80; CABS 3; CAD; CANR 43; CD 5; CWD; DLB 7, 249; GLL 2
Tertullian c. 155-c. 245 .... **CMLC 29**
Tertz, Abram
   See Sinyavsky, Andrei (Donatevich)
   See also CWW 2; RGSF 2
Tesich, Steve 1943(?)-1996 .... **CLC 40, 69**
   See also CA 105; 152; CAD; DLBY 1983
Tesla, Nikola 1856-1943 .... **TCLC 88**
Teternikov, Fyodor Kuzmich 1863-1927
   See Sologub, Fyodor
   See also CA 104
Tevis, Walter 1928-1984 .... **CLC 42**
   See also CA 113; SFW 4
Tey, Josephine .... **TCLC 14**
   See Mackintosh, Elizabeth
   See also DLB 77; MSW
Thackeray, William Makepeace 1811-1863 .... **NCLC 5, 14, 22, 43; WLC**
   See also BRW 5; CDBLB 1832-1890; DA; DA3; DAB; DAC; DAM MST, NOV; DLB 21, 55, 159, 163; NFS 13; RGEL 2; SATA 23; TEA; WLIT 3
Thakura, Ravindranatha
   See Tagore, Rabindranath
Thames, C. H.
   See Marlowe, Stephen
Tharoor, Shashi 1956- .... **CLC 70**
   See also CA 141; CANR 91; CN 7
Thelwell, Michael Miles 1939- .... **CLC 22**
   See also BW 2; CA 101
Theobald, Lewis, Jr.
   See Lovecraft, H(oward) P(hillips)
Theocritus c. 310B.C.- .... **CMLC 45**
   See also AW 1; DLB 176; RGWL 2, 3
Theodorescu, Ion N. 1880-1967
   See Arghezi, Tudor
   See also CA 116
Theriault, Yves 1915-1983 .... **CLC 79**
   See also CA 102; CCA 1; DAC; DAM MST; DLB 88; EWL 3
Theroux, Alexander (Louis) 1939- .... **CLC 2, 25**
   See also CA 85-88; CANR 20, 63; CN 7

Theroux, Paul (Edward) 1941- ..... **CLC 5, 8, 11, 15, 28, 46**
   See also AAYA 28; AMWS 8; BEST 89:4; BPFB 3; CA 33-36R; CANR 20, 45, 74; CDALBS; CN 7; CPW 1; DA3; DAM POP; DLB 2, 218; EWL 3; HGG; MTCW 1, 2; RGAL 4; SATA 44, 109; TUS
Thesen, Sharon 1946- .... **CLC 56**
   See also CA 163; CP 7; CWP
Thespis fl. 6th cent. B.C.- .... **CMLC 51**
   See also LMFS 1
Thevenin, Denis
   See Duhamel, Georges
Thibault, Jacques Anatole Francois 1844-1924
   See France, Anatole
   See also CA 106; 127; DA3; DAM NOV; MTCW 1, 2; TWA
Thiele, Colin (Milton) 1920- .... **CLC 17**
   See also CA 29-32R; CANR 12, 28, 53, 105; CLR 27; MAICYA 1, 2; SAAS 2; SATA 14, 72, 125; YAW
Thistlethwaite, Bel
   See Wetherald, Agnes Ethelwyn
Thomas, Audrey (Callahan) 1935- .... **CLC 7, 13, 37, 107; SSC 20**
   See also AITN 2; CA 21-24R; CAAS 19; CANR 36, 58; CN 7; DLB 60; MTCW 1; RGSF 2
Thomas, Augustus 1857-1934 .... **TCLC 97**
Thomas, D(onald) M(ichael) 1935- . **CLC 13, 22, 31, 132**
   See also BPFB 3; BRWS 4; CA 61-64; CAAS 11; CANR 17, 45, 75; CDBLB 1960 to Present; CN 7; CP 7; DA3; DLB 40, 207; HGG; INT CANR-17; MTCW 1, 2; SFW 4
Thomas, Dylan (Marlais) 1914-1953 ... **PC 2; SSC 3, 44; TCLC 1, 8, 45, 105; WLC**
   See also AAYA 45; BRWS 1; CA 104; 120; CANR 65; CDBLB 1945-1960; DA; DA3; DAB; DAC; DAM DRAM, MST, POET; DLB 13, 20, 139; EWL 3; EXPP; LAIT 3; MTCW 1, 2; PAB; PFS 1, 3, 8; RGEL 2; RGSF 2; SATA 60; TEA; WLIT 4; WP
Thomas, (Philip) Edward 1878-1917 .... **TCLC 10**
   See also BRW 6; BRWS 3; CA 106; 153; DAM POET; DLB 19, 98, 156, 216; EWL 3; PAB; RGEL 2
Thomas, Joyce Carol 1938- .... **CLC 35**
   See also AAYA 12; BW 2, 3; CA 113; 116; CANR 48, 114; CLR 19; DLB 33; INT CA-116; JRDA; MAICYA 1, 2; MTCW 1, 2; SAAS 7; SATA 40, 78, 123, 137; WYA; YAW
Thomas, Lewis 1913-1993 .... **CLC 35**
   See also ANW; CA 85-88; 143; CANR 38, 60; DLB 275; MTCW 1, 2
Thomas, M. Carey 1857-1935 .... **TCLC 89**
   See also FW
Thomas, Paul
   See Mann, (Paul) Thomas
Thomas, Piri 1928- .... **CLC 17; HLCS 2**
   See also CA 73-76; HW 1
Thomas, R(onald) S(tuart) 1913-2000 .... **CLC 6, 13, 48**
   See also CA 89-92; 189; CAAS 4; CANR 30; CDBLB 1960 to Present; CP 7; DAB; DAM POET; DLB 27; EWL 3; MTCW 1; RGEL 2
Thomas, Ross (Elmore) 1926-1995 .. **CLC 39**
   See also CA 33-36R; 150; CANR 22, 63; CMW 4
Thompson, Francis (Joseph) 1859-1907 .... **TCLC 4**
   See also BRW 5; CA 104; 189; CDBLB 1890-1914; DLB 19; RGEL 2; TEA
Thompson, Francis Clegg
   See Mencken, H(enry) L(ouis)

Wilhelm, Kate .... **CLC 7**
See Wilhelm, Katie (Gertrude)
See also AAYA 20; CAAS 5; DLB 8; INT
CANR-17; SCFW 2

Wilhelm, Katie (Gertrude) 1928-
See Wilhelm, Kate
See also CA 37-40R; CANR 17, 36, 60, 94;
MTCW 1; SFW 4

Wilkins, Mary
See Freeman, Mary E(leanor) Wilkins

Willard, Nancy 1936- .... **CLC 7, 37**
See also BYA 5; CA 89-92; CANR 10, 39,
68, 107; CLR 5; CWP; CWRI 5; DLB 5,
52; FANT; MAICYA 1, 2; MTCW 1;
SATA 37, 71, 127; SATA-Brief 30; SUFW
2

William of Malmesbury c. 1090B.C.-c.
1140B.C. .... **CMLC 57**

William of Ockham 1290-1349 ..... **CMLC 32**

Williams, Ben Ames 1889-1953 ..... **TCLC 89**
See also CA 183; DLB 102

Williams, C(harles) K(enneth)
1936- .... **CLC 33, 56, 148**
See also CA 37-40R; CAAS 26; CANR 57,
106; CP 7; DAM POET; DLB 5

Williams, Charles
See Collier, James Lincoln

Williams, Charles (Walter Stansby)
1886-1945 .... **TCLC 1, 11**
See also CA 104; 163; DLB 100, 153, 255;
FANT; RGEL 2; SUFW 1

Williams, Ella Gwendolen Rees
See Rhys, Jean

Williams, (George) Emlyn
1905-1987 .... **CLC 15**
See also CA 104; 123; CANR 36; DAM
DRAM; DLB 10, 77; IDTP; MTCW 1

Williams, Hank 1923-1953 .... **TCLC 81**
See Williams, Hiram King

Williams, Hiram Hank
See Williams, Hank

Williams, Hiram King
See Williams, Hank
See also CA 188

Williams, Hugo 1942- .... **CLC 42**
See also CA 17-20R; CANR 45; CP 7; DLB
40

Williams, J. Walker
See Wodehouse, P(elham) G(renville)

Williams, John A(lfred) 1925- . **BLC 3; CLC**
5, 13
See also AFAW 2; BW 2, 3; CA 53-56;
CAAE 195; CAAS 3; CANR 6, 26, 51,
118; CN 7; CSW; DAM MULT; DLB 2,
33; EWL 3; INT CANR-6; RGAL 4; SFW
4

Williams, Jonathan (Chamberlain)
1929- .... **CLC 13**
See also CA 9-12R; CAAS 12; CANR 8,
108; CP 7; DLB 5

Williams, Joy 1944- .... **CLC 31**
See also CA 41-44R; CANR 22, 48, 97

Williams, Norman 1952- .... **CLC 39**
See also CA 118

Williams, Sherley Anne 1944-1999 ... **BLC 3;**
CLC 89
See also AFAW 2; BW 2, 3; CA 73-76; 185;
CANR 25, 82; DAM MULT, POET; DLB
41; INT CANR-25; SATA 78; SATA-Obit
116

Williams, Shirley
See Williams, Sherley Anne

Williams, Tennessee 1911-1983 . **CLC 1, 2, 5,**
7, 8, 11, 15, 19, 30, 39, 45, 71, 111; DC
4; WLC
See also AAYA 31; AITN 1, 2; AMW;
AMWC 1; CA 5-8R; 108; CABS 3; CAD;
CANR 31; CDALB 1941-1968; DA;

DA3; DAB; DAC; DAM DRAM, MST;
DFS 17; DLB 7; DLBD 4; DLBY 1983;
EWL 3; GLL 1; LAIT 4; LATS 1; MTCW
1, 2; RGAL 4; TUS

Williams, Thomas (Alonzo)
1926-1990 .... **CLC 14**
See also CA 1-4R; 132; CANR 2

Williams, William C.
See Williams, William Carlos

Williams, William Carlos
1883-1963 .... **CLC 1, 2, 5, 9, 13, 22, 42,**
67; PC 7; SSC 31
See also AAYA 46; AMW; AMWR 1; CA
89-92; CANR 34; CDALB 1917-1929;
DA; DA3; DAB; DAC; DAM MST,
POET; DLB 4, 16, 54, 86; EWL 3; EXPP;
MTCW 1, 2; NCFS 4; PAB; PFS 1, 6, 11;
RGAL 4; RGSF 2; TUS; WP

Williamson, David (Keith) 1942- ..... **CLC 56**
See also CA 103; CANR 41; CD 5

Williamson, Ellen Douglas 1905-1984
See Douglas, Ellen
See also CA 17-20R; 114; CANR 39

Williamson, Jack .... **CLC 29**
See Williamson, John Stewart
See also CAAS 8; DLB 8; SCFW 2

Williamson, John Stewart 1908-
See Williamson, Jack
See also CA 17-20R; CANR 23, 70; SFW 4

Willie, Frederick
See Lovecraft, H(oward) P(hillips)

Willingham, Calder (Baynard, Jr.)
1922-1995 .... **CLC 5, 51**
See also CA 5-8R; 147; CANR 3; CSW;
DLB 2, 44; IDFW 3, 4; MTCW 1

Willis, Charles
See Clarke, Arthur C(harles)

Willy
See Colette, (Sidonie-Gabrielle)

Willy, Colette
See Colette, (Sidonie-Gabrielle)
See also GLL 1

Wilmot, John 1647-1680 .... **LC 75**
See Rochester
See also BRW 2; DLB 131; PAB

Wilson, A(ndrew) N(orman) 1950- .. **CLC 33**
See also BRWS 6; CA 112; 122; CN 7;
DLB 14, 155, 194; MTCW 2

Wilson, Angus (Frank Johnstone)
1913-1991 . **CLC 2, 3, 5, 25, 34; SSC 21**
See also BRWS 1; CA 5-8R; 134; CANR
21; DLB 15, 139, 155; EWL 3; MTCW 1,
2; RGEL 2; RGSF 2

Wilson, August 1945- ... **BLC 3; CLC 39, 50,**
63, 118; DC 2; WLCS
See also AAYA 16; AFAW 2; AMWS 8; BW
2, 3; CA 115; 122; CAD; CANR 42, 54,
76; CD 5; DA; DA3; DAB; DAC; DAM
DRAM, MST, MULT; DFS 3, 7, 15, 17;
DLB 228; EWL 3; LAIT 4; LATS 1;
MTCW 1, 2; RGAL 4

Wilson, Brian 1942- .... **CLC 12**

Wilson, Colin 1931- .... **CLC 3, 14**
See also CA 1-4R; CAAS 5; CANR 1, 22,
33, 77; CMW 4; CN 7; DLB 14, 194;
HGG; MTCW 1; SFW 4

Wilson, Dirk
See Pohl, Frederik

Wilson, Edmund 1895-1972 .. **CLC 1, 2, 3, 8,**
24
See also AMW; CA 1-4R; 37-40R; CANR
1, 46, 110; DLB 63; EWL 3; MTCW 1, 2;
RGAL 4; TUS

Wilson, Ethel Davis (Bryant)
1888(?)-1980 .... **CLC 13**
See also CA 102; DAC; DAM POET; DLB
68; MTCW 1; RGEL 2

Wilson, Harriet
See Wilson, Harriet E. Adams
See also DLB 239

Wilson, Harriet E.
See Wilson, Harriet E. Adams
See also DLB 243

Wilson, Harriet E. Adams
1827(?)-1863(?) .... **BLC 3; NCLC 78**
See Wilson, Harriet; Wilson, Harriet E.
See also DAM MULT; DLB 50

Wilson, John 1785-1854 .... **NCLC 5**

Wilson, John (Anthony) Burgess 1917-1993
See Burgess, Anthony
See also CA 1-4R; 143; CANR 2, 46; DA3;
DAC; DAM NOV; MTCW 1, 2; NFS 15;
TEA

Wilson, Lanford 1937- ... **CLC 7, 14, 36; DC**
19
See also CA 17-20R; CABS 3; CAD; CANR
45, 96; CD 5; DAM DRAM; DFS 4, 9,
12, 16; DLB 7; EWL 3; TUS

Wilson, Robert M. 1944- .... **CLC 7, 9**
See also CA 49-52; CAD; CANR 2, 41; CD
5; MTCW 1

Wilson, Robert McLiam 1964- .... **CLC 59**
See also CA 132; DLB 267

Wilson, Sloan 1920- .... **CLC 32**
See also CA 1-4R; CANR 1, 44; CN 7

Wilson, Snoo 1948- .... **CLC 33**
See also CA 69-72; CBD; CD 5

Wilson, William S(mith) 1932- .... **CLC 49**
See also CA 81-84

Wilson, (Thomas) Woodrow
1856-1924 .... **TCLC 79**
See also CA 166; DLB 47

Wilson and Warnke eds. .... **CLC 65**

Winchilsea, Anne (Kingsmill) Finch
1661-1720
See Finch, Anne
See also RGEL 2

Windham, Basil
See Wodehouse, P(elham) G(renville)

Wingrove, David (John) 1954- .... **CLC 68**
See also CA 133; SFW 4

Winnemucca, Sarah 1844-1891 .... **NCLC 79;**
NNAL
See also DAM MULT; DLB 175; RGAL 4

Winstanley, Gerrard 1609-1676 .... **LC 52**

Wintergreen, Jane
See Duncan, Sara Jeannette

Winters, Janet Lewis .... **CLC 41**
See Lewis, Janet
See also DLBY 1987

Winters, (Arthur) Yvor 1900-1968 .... **CLC 4,**
8, 32
See also AMWS 2; CA 11-12; 25-28R; CAP
1; DLB 48; EWL 3; MTCW 1; RGAL 4

Winterson, Jeanette 1959- .... **CLC 64, 158**
See also BRWS 4; CA 136; CANR 58, 116;
CN 7; CPW; DA3; DAM POP; DLB 207,
261; FANT; FW; GLL 1; MTCW 2; RHW

Winthrop, John 1588-1649 .... **LC 31**
See also DLB 24, 30

Wirth, Louis 1897-1952 .... **TCLC 92**
See also CA 210

Wiseman, Frederick 1930- .... **CLC 20**
See also CA 159

Wister, Owen 1860-1938 .... **TCLC 21**
See also BPFB 3; CA 108; 162; DLB 9, 78,
186; RGAL 4; SATA 62; TCWW 2

Witkacy
See Witkiewicz, Stanislaw Ignacy

Witkiewicz, Stanislaw Ignacy
1885-1939 .... **TCLC 8**
See also CA 105; 162; CDWLB 4; DLB
215; EW 10; EWL 3; RGWL 2, 3; SFW 4

Wittgenstein, Ludwig (Josef Johann)
1889-1951 .... **TCLC 59**
See also CA 113; 164; DLB 262; MTCW 2

Literary Criticism Series
Cumulative Topic Index

This index lists all topic entries in Gale's *Classical and Medieval Literature Criticism* (CMLC), *Contemporary Literary Criticism* (CLC), *Drama Criticism* (DC), *Literature Criticism from 1400 to 1800* (LC), *Nineteenth-Century Literature Criticism* (NCLC), *Short Story Criticism* (SSC), and *Twentieth-Century Literary Criticism* (TCLC). The index also lists topic entries in the Gale Critical Companion Collection, which includes the following publications: *The Beat Generation* (BG), and *Harlem Renaissance* (HR).

Topic Index

DC Cumulative Nationality Index

ALGERIAN
Camus, Albert **2**

AMERICAN
Albee, Edward (Franklin III) **11**
Baldwin, James (Arthur) **1**
Baraka, Amiri **6**
Brown, William Wells **1**
Bullins, Ed **6**
Chase, Mary (Coyle) **1**
Childress, Alice **4**
Chin, Frank (Chew Jr.) **7**
Elder, Lonne III **8**
Fornés, Mariá Irene **10**
Fuller, Charles (H. Jr.) **1**
Glaspell, Susan **10**
Gordone, Charles **8**
Gray, Spalding **7**
Guare, John **20**
Hansberry, Lorraine (Vivian) **2**
Hellman, Lillian (Florence) **1**
Henley, Beth **6, 14**
Hughes, (James) Langston **3**
Hurston, Zora Neale **12**
Hwang, David Henry **4**
Kaufman, George S. **17**
Kennedy, Adrienne (Lita) **5**
Kramer, Larry **8**
Kushner, Tony **10**
Mamet, David (Alan) **4**
Mann, Emily **7**
Miller, Arthur **1**
Norman, Marsha **8**
Odets, Clifford **6**
O'Neill, Eugene **20**
Rabe, David (William) **16**
Shange, Ntozake **3**
Shepard, Sam **5**
Sheridan, Richard Brinsley **1**
Simon, (Marvin) Neil **14**
Stein, Gertrude **19**
Terry, Megan **13**
Valdez, Luis (Miguel) **10**
Vogel, Paula **19**
Wasserstein, Wendy **4**
Wilder, Thornton (Niven) **1**
Williams, Tennessee **4**
Wilson, August **2**
Wilson, Lanford **19**
Zindel, Paul **5**

AUSTRIAN
Bernhard, Thomas **14**
Grillparzer, Franz **14**
Handke, Peter **17**

Hofmannsthal, Hugo von **4**
Schnitzler, Arthur **17**

BARBADIAN
Kennedy, Adrienne (Lita) **5**

BELGIAN
Ghelderode, Michel de **15**

CANADIAN
Pollock, Sharon **20**

CUBAN
Fornés, Mariá Irene **10**

CZECH
Chapek, Karel **1**
Havel, Václav **6**

DUTCH
Bernhard, Thomas **14**

ENGLISH
Ayckbourn, Alan **13**
Beaumont, Francis **6**
Beddoes, Thomas Lovell **15**
Behn, Aphra **4**
Chapman, George **19**
Churchill, Caryl **5**
Congreve, William **2**
Dekker, Thomas **12**
Dryden, John **3**
Fletcher, John **6**
Ford, John **8**
Jonson, Ben(jamin) **4**
Kyd, Thomas **3**
Lyly, John **7**
Marlowe, Christopher **1**
Middleton, Thomas **5**
Orton, Joe **3**
Pinter, Harold **15**
Rattigan, Terence (Mervyn) **18**
Shaffer, Peter (Levin) **7**
Stoppard, Tom **6**
Webster, John **2**

FRENCH
Anouilh, Jean (Marie Lucien Pierre) **8, 21**
Artaud, Antonin (Marie Joseph) **14**
Beaumarchais, Pierre-Augustin Caron de **4**
Becque, Henri **21**
Camus, Albert **2**
Cocteau, Jean **17**
Corneille, Pierre **21**
Dumas, Alexandre (fils) **1**
Ionesco, Eugène **12**
Marivaux, Pierre Carlet de Chamblain de **7**

Molière **13**
Perrault, Charles **12**
Rostand, Edmond (Eugene Alexis) **10**
Sartre, Jean-Paul **3**
Scribe, (Augustin) Eugène **5**

GERMAN
Brecht, (Eugen) Bertolt (Friedrich) **3**
Goethe, Johann Wolfgang von **20**
Hebbel, Friedrich **21**
Schiller, Friedrich von **12**

GREEK
Aeschylus **8**
Aristophanes **2**
Euripides **4**
Menander **3**
Sophocles **1**

IRISH
Friel, Brian **8**
Goldsmith, Oliver **8**
Joyce, James (Augustine Aloysius) **16**
O'Casey, Sean **12**
Sheridan, Richard Brinsley **1**
Synge, (Edmund) J(ohn) M(illington) **2**
Wilde, Oscar **17**

ITALIAN
Fo, Dario **10**
Machiavelli, Niccolò **16**
Pirandello, Luigi **5**
Plautus **6**

JAPANESE
Zeami **7**

NIGERIAN
Clark Bekedermo, J(ohnson) P(epper) **5**
Soyinka, Wole **2**

NORWEGIAN
Ibsen, Henrik (Johan) **2**

ROMAN
Plautus **6**
Seneca, Lucius Annaeus **5**
Terence **7**

ROMANIAN
Ionesco, Eugène **12**

RUSSIAN
Chekhov, Anton (Pavlovich) **9**
Gogol, Nikolai (Vasilyevich) **1**
Turgenev, Ivan (Sergeevich) **7**

SOUTH AFRICAN

Fugard, (Harold) Athol **3**

SPANISH

Buero Vallejo, Antonio **18**
Calderón de la Barca, Pedro **3**

García Lorca, Federico **2**
Molina, Tirso de **13**

ST. LUCIAN

Walcott, Derek (Alton) **7**

SWEDISH

Strindberg, (Johan) August **18**

DC Cumulative Title Index, Vols. 1-21

Title Index

ISBN 0-7876-6811-7

90000

9 780787 668112